ENCYCLOPEDIA OF

Humor Studies

Editorial Board

ENCYCLOPEDIA OF

Humor Studies

Editor

Salvatore Attardo

Texas A&M University–Commerce

2

SAGE reference

Los Angeles | London | New Delhi
Singapore | Washington DC

SAGE

Los Angeles | London | New Delhi
Singapore | Washington DC

FOR INFORMATION:

SAGE Publications, Inc.
2455 Teller Road
Thousand Oaks, California 91320
E-mail: order@sagepub.com

SAGE Publications Ltd.
1 Oliver's Yard
55 City Road
London, EC1Y 1SP
United Kingdom

SAGE Publications India Pvt. Ltd.
B 1/I 1 Mohan Cooperative Industrial Area
Mathura Road, New Delhi 110 044
India

SAGE Publications Asia-Pacific Pte. Ltd.
3 Church Street
#10-04 Samsung Hub
Singapore 049483

Acquisitions Editor: Jim Brace-Thompson
Developmental Editors: Diana E. Axelsen, Shirin Parsavand
Production Editor: Tracy Buyan
Reference Systems Manager: Leticia Gutierrez
Reference Systems Coordinators: Anna Villaseñor, Laura Notton
Copy Editors: Diane DiMura, Colleen Brennan
Typesetter: Hurix Systems (P) Ltd.
Proofreaders: Lawrence W. Baker, Kristin Bergstad
Indexer: Virgil Diodato
Cover Designer: Scott Van Atta
Marketing Manager: Carmel Schrire

Printed in the United States of America.

Library of Congress Cataloging-in-Publication Data

Encyclopedia of humor studies / editor, Salvatore Attardo, Texas A&M University.

volumes cm
Includes bibliographical references and index.

ISBN 978-1-4129-9909-0 (hardcover)

1. Laughter–Encyclopedias. 2. Wit and humor–Encyclopedias. I. Attardo, Salvatore, 1962- editor of compilation.

BF575.L3E53 2014
809.7–dc23 2013036046

SUSTAINABLE FORESTRY INITIATIVE
Certified Chain of Custody
Promoting Sustainable Forestry
www.sfiprogram.org
SFI-01268
SFI label applies to the text stock

14 15 16 17 18 10 9 8 7 6 5 4 3 2 1

Contents

List of Entries

Reader's Guide

Anthropology, Folklore, and Ethnicity

Animal-Related Humor
Anthropology
Anti-Proverb
Blason Populaire
Carnival and Festival
College Humor
Dialect Humor
Ethnic Jokes
Ethnicity and Humor
Feast of Fools
Folklore
Fools
Foolstowns
Hoax and Prank
Insult and Invective
Jewish Humor
Joke Cycles
Joking Relationship
National and Ethnic Differences
Philogelos
Practical Jokes
Race, Representations of
Rituals of Laughter
Social Network
Stereotypes
Targets of Humor
Trickster
Urban Legends
Verbal Dueling
Xeroxlore

Antiquity

Ancient Egypt, Humor in
Ancient Greek Comedy
Ancient Roman Comedy
Aristophanes
Aristotelian Theory of Humor
Assyrian and Babylonian Humor
Greek Visual Humor
Jest, Jestbooks, and Jesters
Menander
Mime
Philogelos
Platonic Theory of Humor
Plautus
Roman Visual Humor
Sanskrit Humor
Satyr Play

Components of Humor

Ambiguity
Bisociation
Cognitive Aspects
Complexity
Creativity
Humor Content Versus Structure
Humor Mindset
Humorous Stimuli, Characteristics of
Incongruity and Resolution
Maxim
Mechanisms of Humor
Misdirection
Nonsense
Play and Humor
Punch Line
Reframing
Sense of Humor, Components of
Targets of Humor

Culture

Anthropology
Carnival and Festival
Cross-Cultural Humor
Culture
Education, Humor in
Fools
Foolstowns

Gallows Humor
High-Context Humor
Humorous Names
Intercultural Humor
Jewish Humor
Obscenity
Puppets
Race, Representations of
Ritual Clowns
Rituals of Inversion
Scatology
Sick Humor
Sports
Stereotypes
Verbal Dueling
Xiangsheng
Xiangsheng, History of

Entertainment Industry

Audience
Audiovisual Translation
Clowns
Comic Books
Comic Frame
Comic Strips
Internet Humor
Journalism
Magazines and Newspapers, U.S.
Magazines and Newspapers Outside the United States
Mockumentary
Monty Python
Movie Humor Types
Movies
Music
Music Hall
Puppets
Satire News
Sitcoms
Spoofing

History

Ancient Egypt, Humor in
Arabic Culture, Humor in
Assyrian and Babylonian Humor
Biblical Humor
Buddhism
Christianity
Confucianism
Fabliau
Feast of Fools
Forest of Laughter and Traditional Chinese Jestbooks
Greek Visual Humor
History of Humor: Classical and Traditional China
History of Humor: Early Modern Europe
History of Humor: Medieval Europe
History of Humor: Modern and Contemporary China
History of Humor: Modern and Contemporary Europe
History of Humor: Modern Japan
History of Humor: 19th-Century Europe
History of Humor: Premodern Japan
History of Humor: Renaissance Europe
History of Humor: U.S. Frontier
History of Humor: U.S. Modern and Contemporary
Huaji-ists, The
Islam
Jest, Jestbooks, and Jesters
Magazines and Newspapers, U.S.
Magazines and Newspapers Outside the United States
Masks
Medieval Visual Humor
Menander
Mock Epic
Molière
Philogelos
Plautus
Rabelais, François
Sanskrit Humor
Satire
Shakespearean Comedy
Sitcoms
Sketch Comedy Shows
Slapstick
Stand-Up Comedy
Tall Tale
Tragicomedy
Travesty
Xiangsheng, History of

Humor Theory

Aristotelian Theory of Humor
Arousal Theory (Berlyne)
Benign Violation Theory
Bergson's Theory of the Comic
Bisociation
Evolutionary Explanations of Humor
Framing Theory
Freudian/Psychoanalytic Theory

Linguistics

Literature and Major Literary Figures

Postmodern Irony
Puns
Rabelais, François
Rakugo
Rhetoric and Rhetorical Devices
Satire
Satyr Play
Schwank
Science, Science Fiction, and Humor
Senryū
Shakespearean Comedy
Share
Simple Form
South American Literature, Humor in
Tall Tale
Tragicomedy
Travesty
Trickster
Witz

Mathematics, Computer Science, and the Internet

Computational Humor
E'gao: Culture of Internet Spoofing in China
Humor, Computer-Generated
Internet Humor
Mathematical Humor
Mathematics and Humor

National, Ethnic, and Regional Humor

Africa
Akan Humor
Igbo Humor
South African Humor

Americas
American Indian Cultures, Humor in
History of Humor: U.S. Frontier
History of Humor: U.S. Modern and Contemporary
South American Literature, Humor in

Asia
Buddhism
Confucianism
E'gao: Culture of Internet Spoofing in China
Forest of Laughter and Traditional Chinese Jestbooks
History of Humor: Classical and Traditional China
History of Humor: Modern and Contemporary China
History of Humor: Modern Japan
History of Humor: Premodern Japan
Huaji-ists, The
Islam
Kyōgen
Rakugo
Senryū
Share
Southeast Asia, Cartooning in
Taoism
Xiangsheng
Xiangsheng, History of
Xiehouyu

Europe
Ancient Greek Comedy
Ancient Roman Comedy
Byzantine Humor
Commedia dell'Arte
Fabliau
Greek Visual Humor
History of Humor: Early Modern Europe
History of Humor: Medieval Europe
History of Humor: Modern and Contemporary Europe
History of Humor: 19th-Century Europe
Lazzi
Medieval Visual Humor
Pointe
Satyr Play
Schwank
Witz

Middle East
Ancient Egypt, Humor in
Arabic Culture, Humor in
Assyrian and Babylonian Humor
Byzantine Humor
Islam

Performing Arts

Ancient Greek Comedy
Ancient Roman Comedy
Burlesque
Carnivalesque
Clowns
Comedy
Comedy Ensembles
Comic Opera
Commedia dell'Arte
Farce

Philosophy and Religion

Physiology and Biology

Politics

Professions

Business World

Education

Law

Psychology

Clinical and Counseling Psychology

Visual Humor

K

KYŌGEN

Of the extant comedy genres on the Japanese stage, *Kyōgen,* which is written with characters meaning "mad words," is generally considered the oldest, although *Manzai* may be older. *Kyōgen* is the humorous twin genre of the stately *Nō* and is performed on the same stage, providing the comic relief between *Nō* plays. A full *Nō* program consists of three *Nō* plays interspersed with two *Kyōgen* plays, forming a full day's performance. Such full-day performances are no longer common. This entry discusses the elements of *Kyōgen*, its history, and types of professional *Kyōgen* performance.

The word *kyōgen* was used by the monk Dōgen in a pejorative sense in the 9th century and also by Fujiwara Teika in his diary (1188 CE). It is believed the term was first used about stage art during the mid-14th century. Zeami, the theorist of *Nō*, used it in his *Shūdōsho* (early 15th century), along with the earlier name for *Kyōgen* (*Okashi* or *Wokashi*, meaning "funny").

Both the serious *Nō* and the humorous *Kyōgen* derive from *Sarugaku*, a comedic mimic genre of early times. Zeami and his father Kan'ami, talented *Nō* actors, obtained the Shōgun's patronage for their art, so that *Nō* and *Kyōgen* became theater for the upper classes and a Shōgunate drawing-room art. During the Edo period, however, rich merchants could also learn *Nō* singing, so it was by no means an exclusively aristocratic or *samurai* pursuit.

By the 20th century, *Nō* and *Kyōgen* had declined, but with government subvention they were revived and preserved as national treasures in the second half of the 20th century. Whereas both are arts that have been handed down within training schools whose members were men, in the second half of the 20th century women were learning and performing both arts.

Until the 20th century, *Kyōgen* was more exclusively an oral tradition than was *Nō*. *Nō* is in literary Japanese, convoluted poetic language, chanted

This somewhat grotesque *Kyōgen* mask of Oto (a version of the more popular character Okami) emphasizes one squinting and one staring eye to comic effect.

Source: Far Eastern Collection, Victoria and Albert Museum, London.

at an exaggeratedly slow speed, often muffled by a mask and so not comprehensible to the untrained ear. *Kyōgen* scripts are close to the ordinary spoken language of the Muromachi period (ca. 15th or 16th century) and thus as comprehensible to native speakers of Japanese as Elizabethan conversation might be to native English speakers. For a *Nō* performance, part of the audience may pore over the script, but it is possible to sit back, relax, and enjoy a *Kyōgen* play.

Many *Nō* playwrights are known, and scripts were probably written down before being performed. *Kyōgen* playwrights are not known, and scripts have very obviously developed as improvisations. *Kyōgen* actors are still taught orally, although written scripts have existed since the publication of *Kyōgenki* (Records of *Kyōgen*) in 1660.

Kyōgen mask of the character Buaku. The faintly comical demon mask of Buaku is the *Kyōgen* version of the *Nō* theater mask of Beshimi. Both the characterization and stylized carving of this mask reflect the original prototype. The mask is carved from a single piece of cypress, with the features in high relief. The surface has been treated with a layer of gofun that has been painted a deep flesh color. The folds of flesh around the eyes, cheeks, brow, and mouth have been accentuated by the creases painted in a deep red color with additional highlights in black ink. Black ink, applied in firm yet sensitive lines, has also been used for the hair, eyebrows, mustache, and whiskers. The eyeballs have had gold leaf applied, with the edges emphasized by lines of ink accentuated by red painted rims. This follows the *Nō* theater tradition of coloring the eyes of a demon red and gold.

Source: Far Eastern Collection, Victoria and Albert Museum, London.

Kyōgen is popularly identified with the stock character Tarō Kaja, the wily servant who, with his accomplice, Jirō Kaja, plays tricks on, cheats, and cozens his master, the country gentleman. Tarō Kaja is a name almost universally known in Japan, even to people who have never seen *Kyōgen,* partly because the trickster character is popular the world over and partly because he and Jirō Kaja are the only *Kyōgen* characters with names, almost all others being identified only by their roles, "The Daimyō" (Baron), "The Son-in-Law," "The Priest," "The Woman," and so on.

Mime is highly developed in *Kyōgen.* The most complex *Kyōgen* mime is probably in the play *Kirokuda,* in which the lead actor is driving a team of horses over a mountain pass in winter and everything possible goes wrong. The actor rates his performance on how many horses the audience sees him driving. In professional *Kyōgen,* masks are used occasionally for outlandish characters such as demons, gods, foreigners, and women. They are generally grotesque and tend to be rather jolly caricatures of *Nō* masks.

There are three types of professional *Kyōgen* performance. The first—no doubt the oldest—is *Sambasō* or *Fùryū*, the ceremonial, religious, auspicious dance form related to the *Okina* of *Nō*.

The second type of play is the *ai-Kyōgen*, in which the *Kyōgen* actor takes part in a *Nō* play (usually between the two acts), telling the story of the play in slightly simpler language. A much more complex form of *ai-Kyōgen* occurs in the *Nō* play, *Adachigahara*, in which some traveling Buddhist priests are given shelter for the night by an old woman who goes out to collect firewood, warning that they must not look into her room. Being guests and gentleman, the priests naturally comply, but the *Kyōgen* actor playing their servant is under no such obligation. In an amusing mime, he checks that the priests are asleep and tries to creep out of the room. Twice he is caught and scolded, but the third time he *rolls* out of the room and manages to look into the old woman's chamber. He is horrified by what he sees there, as she is a demon and her familiars are in the room. Returning to her true form, she is subdued by the Buddhist priests' prayers. This is one of the few cases of comedy in the normally unmixedly serious *Nō*.

The third kind of *Kyōgen* is the stand-alone comic play that forms the comic relief between two *Nō* plays. These plays are usually for two or three actors, but there are a few for one actor and some for ten actors or more. They may include song and

The *Kyōgen* mask of Ebisu, one of the Seven Gods of Good Fortune. The features are extremely expressive, with the smiling deity creasing his face in laughter. The face is fuller than other examples of masks of this character. The eyes are comma-shaped, with laugh lines reaching toward the ears. The nose is full, with wide, flaring nostrils. The mouth is fully open, revealing the upper set of deeply carved teeth. The cheeks are full and express the jolly nature of the god. The ears are long and pendulous (although traditionally Ebisu is deaf). There are two paper-covered textile pads fixed to the top interior of the mask so that the eyeholes are angled downward. This enabled the performer to see better and at the same time make the mask more comfortable to wear. It is likely that, with the mask in this unusual position, the performer would be able to see through the noseholes rather than through the eyeholes.

Source: Far Eastern Collection, Victoria and Albert Museum, London.

dance, especially in drinking scenes, and song and dance may be integral to the plot. The hilariously funny *Yobigoe* (Calling Voices), for example, is a play about a serf who has not been turning up for compulsory work on his master's farm. The master and another serf believe he is feigning absence and go to his house to trick him into revealing that he is there. They know he can never resist a rhythm, so they sing and dance outside the house until, overcome with the music, the serf unwittingly joins in the song, dances out of the house, and is chased off the stage by a master intent on revenge, leaving the audience in stitches.

Plots like this are true farce-plots, designed to indulge a moment's comic rebellion against the established way of things but then to safely restore order. *Kyōgen* plays tend to be amusing rather than hilarious, dealing as they do with family and household ructions, discombobulated priests, persistently pestiferous owls, and dancing mushrooms.

Marguerite Wells

See also Comedy; Comedy Ensembles; Comic World; Farce; Genres and Styles of Comedy; History of Humor: Modern Japan; History of Humor: Premodern Japan; Improv Comedy; *Lazzi*; Masks; Mime; Rituals of Inversion; Slapstick; Stereotypes; Targets of Humor

Further Readings

Brandon, J. R. (Ed.). (1997). Nō *and* Kyōgen *in the contemporary world*. Honolulu: University of Hawai'i Press.

Brazell, K. (Ed.). (1998). *Traditional Japanese theater: An anthology of plays*. Ithaca, NY: Cornell University Press.

Davis, J. M., & Wells, M. A. (2006). *Kyōgen* as comic relief: Farce and satire in the Japanese classical theatre. In J. M. Davis (Ed.), *Understanding humor in Japan* (pp. 127–153). Detroit, MI: Wayne State University Press.

Kenny, D. (1989). *The* Kyōgen *book: An anthology of Japanese classical comedies*. Tokyo: Japan Times.

Kenny, D. (1999). *A* Kyōgen *companion*. Tokyo, Japan: National Noh Theatre.

Koyama Hiroshi. (1961). *Kyōgen shū*. In *Nihon Koten Bungaku Taikei* [Outline of classical Japanese literature] (Vols. 42 & 43). Tokyo, Japan: Iwanami Shoten.

Morley, C. A. (1993). *The mountain priest plays of* Kyōgen: *Translations with commentary*. Ithaca, NY: Cornell University, East Asia Program.

Sasano Ken. (1943). *Nō Kyōgen* (3 vols.). Tokyo, Japan: Iwanami Bunko, Iwanami Shoten.

L

Lampoon

Lampoon is a virulent attack on a person, institution, or society in prose, verse, or graphic caricature. It is a sharp and funny (or not funny) satire that is malicious and severe. The origin of *lampoon* is from the French word *lampon* or *lampons* "let us drink" and the verb *lamper* means "to booze," which suggests excess. The word is attested in 17th-century French. However, it dates back to as early as the 3rd century BCE when Aristophanes lampooned Euripides in *Frogs* and Socrates in *Clouds.* The form was popular in English literature during the Restoration and the 18th century when writers such as John Dryden, John Wilkes, Alexander Pope, and Samuel Butler lampooned particular aspects of their times. One of the notable examples of the form can be seen in the poem "Absalom and Achitophel," written by Dryden, who lampooned Thomas Shadwell (here Og) with these lines (Cuddon, 1999, p. 449):

> Now stop your noses, Readers, all and some,
> For here's a tun of Midnight work to come,
> Og from a Treason Tavern rowling home.
> Round as a Globe and Liquored ev'ry chink,
> Goodly and Great he Sayls behind his Link.
> With all this Bulk there's nothing lost in Og,
> For ev'ry inch that is not Fool is Rogue:
> A Monstrous mass of foul corrupted matter,
> As all the Devils had spew'd to make the batter.
> When wine has given him courage to Blaspheme,
> He curses God, but God before curst him;
> And if man cou'd have reason, none has more,
> That made his Paunch so rich and him so poor.

Examples of lampoons appearing in 17th- and 18th-century English literature include Jonathan Swift's *A Modest Proposal,* which lampoons then-influential William Petty; Francis Beaumont's *The Knight of the Burning Pestle,* lampooning the pretensions of the middle class; and Samuel Butler's *Hudibras,* a long lampoon in which the Puritans were likened to a hunchback monster and the Commonwealth was satirized.

Apart from these, the lampoons of Alexander Pope are also notable. His *The Rape of the Lock* lampoons 18th-century society as a whole, and *Epistle to Dr. Arbuthnot* is a direct attack on John Hervey. He also lampoons bad writers and their dull-witted verses in *The Dunciad.* His *An Essay on Man* was lampooned by John Wilkes's *An Essay on Woman.*

The Harvard Lampoon

The Harvard Lampoon is a humor publication founded by undergraduate students at Harvard University in Cambridge, Massachusetts, in 1876. Published since that date, it has become the longest continually published humor magazine. Apart from its magazines, *The Harvard Lampoon* also produces parodies of famous books (the J. R. R. Tolkien parody *Bored of the Rings* is the best known book published by *The Harvard Lampoon*) and national magazines.

The Harvard Lampoon's success was more prominent with the publication of *Bored of the Rings* in 1969, and this success and attention led to the publication of a new humor magazine: the *National Lampoon*. *The Harvard Lampoon* also produced some other books such as *Nightlight*, a parody of *Twilight* in 2009, and *The Hunger Pains*, parody of *The Hunger Games* in 2012. There are five issues published by the *Lampoon* annually, and since 2006 it has been releasing the content of the magazines on its website, which contains some pieces from the magazine and web-only content.

National Lampoon

National Lampoon first appeared in print in 1970 as a spinoff from *The Harvard Lampoon* and was published monthly through 1998. It became one of the most important humor magazines in the United States and had its heyday between 1971 and 1975 when it had a significant effect on American humor. *National Lampoon* took the form of a feature magazine and it included articles and issued parodies on cultural artifacts in the United States. The magazine led to the development and production of other print products, films, radio, and live theater. What made *National Lampoon* successful was its parodies, which formed the most important part of the magazine. Issues of the magazine also included texts, cartoons, and comic strips. At the front of each magazine, an editor prepared his or her page, which was always in the form of a parody. The magazine lost its glory in the late 1980s and never regained its old popularity again, and it stopped publishing in 1998.

Metin Özdemir

See also Humor Group; Magazines and Newspapers, U.S.

Further Readings

Cuddon, J. (1999). *The Penguin dictionary of literary terms and literary theory*. London, UK: Penguin Books.

Karp, J. (2006). *A futile and stupid gesture: How Doug Kenney and* National Lampoon *changed comedy forever*. Chicago, IL: Chicago Review Press.

Kuiper, K. (2012). *Prose literary terms and concepts*. New York, NY: Britannica Educational Publishing.

Naughton, J., Snyders, T., & Rubin, S. (2004). National Lampoon*'s big book of true facts*. New York, NY: Rugged Land.

Rubin, S., Crespo, S., & Brown, M. (2004). National Lampoon*'s big book of love*. New York, NY: Rugged Land.

Simmons, M. (1994). *If you don't buy this book, we'll kill this dog! Life, laughs, love, and death at the* National Lampoon. New York, NY: Barricade Books.

Zwicker, S. (1998). *The Cambridge companion to English literature, 1650–1740*. Cambridge, UK: Cambridge University Press.

Websites

The Harvard Lampoon: http://harvardlampoon.com

Laugh, Laughter, Laughing

Humor and laughter are often associated. They occur together so often, in fact, that there is a natural tendency to regard them as manifestations of a single phenomenon. Their association, however, is far from complete. It is quite possible to experience humor without laughing and, conversely, laughter often occurs in situations that are devoid of humor. Described here are the ways laughter is produced, the ways different laughs can differ, the ways laughter can be superimposed on speaking, and relations between laughter, smiling, and breathing. Attention is then given to the question of why people laugh, both in the presence of humor and in its absence. There is mention of the role of laughter during conversations. Finally there is the question of whether nonhuman animals also laugh.

How Laughter Is Produced

Laughter consists of sudden, spasmodic expulsions of air from the lungs, typically with greater force than is found during normal breathing or speaking. These exhalation pulses are usually followed by a single, more prolonged inhalation that replenishes the lost air. The sound wave shown in Figure 1 illustrates 12 exhalation pulses followed by a single inhalation.

These laugh pulses pass from the lungs into the larynx, where in many cases they set the vocal folds to vibrating, producing a buzzing sound known as voicing. In speech, voicing distinguishes, for example, a Z (voiced) from an S (voiceless). Voiced laugh pulses are more audible than voiceless pulses, communicating laughter more effectively to others. The vocal folds can vibrate at a wide range of different

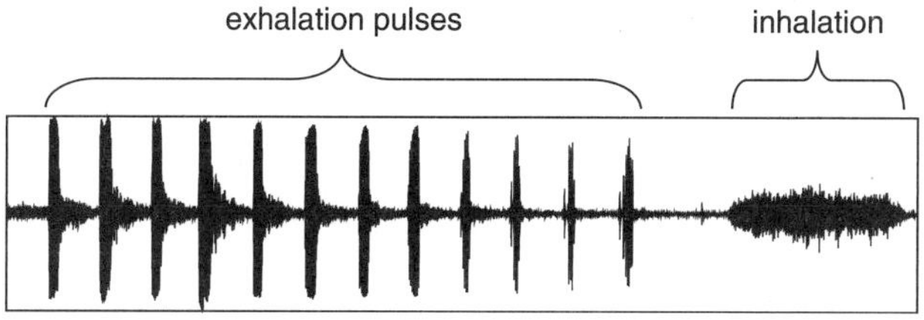

Figure 1 Basic Components of a Laugh

Source: Wallace Chafe.

frequencies, allowing sequences of laugh pulses to show rising or falling pitch contours. The pulses shown in this illustration began at a frequency of 516 hertz and descended to 157 hertz, but rising frequencies are also observed. Laugh pulses pass from the larynx into the mouth, where their sound is further modified by configurations of the tongue and lips. The tongue most often occupies a relaxed position and most laugh pulses resemble the sound of the first vowel in a casual pronunciation of potato. Sounds like "ho ho ho" or "hee hee hee" are not typical.

Varieties of Laughter

Laugh pulses vary in number, timing, and intensity. The number of pulses can vary from one to many, although there are seldom more than about a dozen. Laughs show a typical rate of slightly under five pulses per second, but sometimes there is an acceleration or deceleration. Although the pulses are typically voiced, voiceless laughs are by no means rare. Some laughs are produced in the falsetto range. A particularly distinctive sound is produced by laugh pulses during which air is inhaled rather than exhaled. Most laughs allow the expelled air to pass relatively freely through the mouth, but sometimes the lips are closed so that air can pass only through the nose, resulting in a laugh with an M-like sound. Some people exhibit their own distinctive laugh patterns that others can easily identify.

Laughing While Speaking

People often laugh while they are speaking. Because speaking and laughing both begin with air from the lungs that passes through the larynx and exits through the mouth, these two competing uses of the same vocal channel must be combined in some way. Sometimes the two activities are separated, with segments of speech alternating with bursts of laughter. Sometimes speech is superimposed on the laugh pulses, either with one spoken syllable per pulse or with a more complex intermingling of the two. Particularly interesting is the introduction of tremolo: rapid oscillations imposed on a single exhalation to yield a machine-gun-like sound. Tremolo is relatively common when laughter is superimposed on speaking, but it has not been observed elsewhere.

Laughter and Breathing

Laughter forcefully removes air from the lungs, but the lost air is replenished by the subsequent inhalation. This interference with normal breathing affects the cardiovascular system, elevating the heart rate to a degree roughly proportional to the duration and intensity of the laugh. Nevertheless, although both speaking and laughing interfere with breathing, neither produces a drop in blood-oxygen level, suggesting that the human body has evolved to retain stability in spite of the respiratory disturbances produced by speech and laughter.

Laughter and Smiling

It is difficult to laugh naturally without smiling at the same time. Smiling expresses the euphoria associated with humor and communicates that feeling to others, establishing an attitude of friendliness. If the feeling fails to rise to the level of audible laughter, smiling may be its only observable manifestation.

Why We Laugh

The physical properties of laughter sketched in the previous section are relatively easy to record and measure, but the question of why people behave in this special way remains open to varied speculations. The question is closely related to speculations on the nature of humor, but the laughter-humor relation cannot provide a complete answer because laughter also occurs without humor. The search must thus extend to factors underlying laughter that are shared with both humor and nonhumor.

One suggestion, put forward by Jo-Anne Bachorowski and her colleagues, is that a laugh aims at eliciting some sort of emotional response in those who hear it. The special sound of laughter captures the attention of listeners while simultaneously it arouses an emotion. Variations in the sound of laughter signal the gender and other identifying features of the laughter but are correlated as well with the social context of the laugh. One study found a positive emotional response to voiced laughs but a negative response to voiceless laughs. It was suggested that laughers use the variable acoustic features of their laughs to shape the particular emotional responses they want their listeners to experience.

The studies just mentioned were conducted in a laboratory environment, but another investigator, Robert Provine, recorded over a thousand instances of spontaneous laughter in shopping malls and a university student union. He noted the gender of the person who was speaking prior to the laugh and the gender of the listener, and whether it was the speaker or the listener who laughed. He also noted what the speaker said to elicit the laugh. In a separate study, he approached people with a recorder in hand, told them he was studying laughter, and simply asked them to laugh, a request he found would usually elicit genuine laughter.

Provine discovered that speakers laughed more often than listeners did, showing that laughter is not just a reaction to things said by others but more often an accompaniment to one's own speech. He also found women laughing more often than men, whereas men did more to provoke laughter. He found, too, that laughter occurred more often in social situations than in solitary environments. Significantly, he found that things said just prior to a laugh were often not humorous. He concluded that laughter functions to solidify friendships and bring people together. He went further to speculate on the place of laughter in human evolution, noting that the evolution of bipedality gave humans (as compared with chimpanzees, for example) a freedom of breath control that set the stage for both speech and laughter. He saw tickling, impossible to inflict on oneself, as an ancient stimulus for laughter that discriminated the self from the nonself in a manner distinctive to humans.

Wallace Chafe has suggested that laughter is the expression of an emotion he called the feeling of nonseriousness. Much of what we experience in daily life can be added to what we know of the real world, but when we recognize that an experience cannot be accepted in a serious way, it elicits the feeling in question. This feeling acts as a safety valve that keeps us from taking seriously experiences for which seriousness would be counterproductive. We are hindered from responding physically by spasmodic expulsions of air from our lungs that interfere with breathing and make it difficult to perform physical tasks. (Try doing pushups while laughing.) At the same time, we are psychologically distracted from serious thought by an accompanying euphoria. We are thus momentarily incapable of either doing serious things or thinking serious thoughts. Chafe saw humor as nothing more than a collection of ways that have been invented to elicit this feeling because of its highly pleasurable nature.

Laughing Without Humor

The feeling of nonseriousness also serves usefully to mitigate unpleasantness, as can be observed in the many instances where laughter occurs without humor. In fact, this feeling could not have evolved as a response to humor if it were not already in place as a response to experiences of other kinds. Chafe found a variety of nonhumorous experiences eliciting laughter, including the use of profanity, talk of something disgusting or depressing, uncertainty about a choice of words, interrupting another person's talk, self-deprecation, regret, bereavement, embarrassment, criticism, and talking of subjects that are abnormal, anomalous, surprising, or awkward.

Other Triggers for Laughter

Is laughter sometimes elicited by experiences other than the feeling of nonseriousness? There is of course nitrous oxide, the so-called laughing gas, and there is a pathological event known as a gelastic seizure, an uncontrollable and unmotivated burst of laughter. More commonly experienced, however, is tickling, during which laughter is elicited by someone stroking a sensitive area of someone else's body. The laughter mitigates what would otherwise be an unpleasant attack on one's body that one would seek to avoid.

Laughter in Conversations

While much depends on the people involved and the topic under discussion, laughter can be a frequent element of ordinary conversations. As an overt and contagious response to conversational joking, punning, sarcasm, or irony, laughter can heighten the social functioning of a nonserious attitude. Laughter contributes to conversations as an overt manifestation of the feeling of nonseriousness, whether it is triggered by humor or by experiences whose disagreeableness or abnormality it serves to mitigate. The ability to manipulate that feeling in conversational interaction appears to be a frequently manifested human trait.

Do Other Animals Laugh?

The question of whether laughter is restricted to humans or whether other animals also laugh is controversial. It is true that chimpanzees and other primates emit a panting sound that sounds a bit like laughing. However, each noisy exhalation is immediately followed by an equally noisy inhalation, a pattern quite different from the sequence of exhalations followed by a single inhalation that is characteristic of human laughter.

Jaak Panksepp and Jeff Burgdorf discovered that stroking rats in sensitive areas caused them to emit a chirping sound well above the range of human hearing. The rats evidently enjoyed the experience, and their chirping communicated their pleasure to other rats. There is a temptation to equate this experience with human tickling. The chirping, however, is physiologically unlike human laughter, and the rats appeared to enjoy the stroking with none of the unpleasantness associated with tickling, thus leaving room for doubt that rats actually laugh in the same way or for the same reasons that humans do.

Wallace Chafe

See also Laughter, Psychology of; Laughter and Smiling, Physiology of; Reactions to Humor, Non-Laughter; Reception of Humor; Rituals of Laughter; Tickling

Further Readings

Bachorowski, J.-A., Smoski, M. J., & Owren, M. J. (2001). The acoustic features of human laughter. *Journal of the Acoustical Society of America, 110,* 1581–1597.

Chafe, W. (2007). *The importance of not being earnest: The feeling behind laughter and humor*. Amsterdam, Netherlands: John Benjamins.

Norrick, N. R. (2009). *Conversational joking: Humor in everyday talk*. Bloomington: Indiana University Press.

Provine, R. R. (2000). *Laughter: A scientific investigation.* New York, NY: Viking.

Ruch, W., & Ekman, P. (2001). The expressive pattern of laughter. In A. W. Kaszniak (Ed.), *Emotion, qualia, and consciousness* (pp. 426–443). Tokyo, Japan: World Scientific.

Laughter, Psychology of

Laughter is a human universal, a vocal signal so closely linked to humor that the two are considered almost interchangeable. However, although often triggered by mirth, laughter also occurs in a variety of other circumstances, and it is increasingly investigated in its own right. This entry reviews resulting findings, focusing on laughter biology, acoustics, and function. It concludes that these sounds have likely long been central in human social communication.

Laughter Biology

Several kinds of evidence show that laughter has deep biological roots, including that humankind's closest relatives, the great apes, all make positively toned calls during tickling and play. Although different-sounding than human laughter, tickle-induced vocalizations in young chimpanzees, bonobos, gorillas, and orangutans are acoustically related both across these species and to human versions. The acoustic similarities and differences involved indicate a common origin in an ape ancestor living 12 million to 16 million years ago. Laughter production is furthermore innate—not only in these apes, but in humans as well. Human infants begin to laugh just a few months after birth, even in cases of congenital deafness. While never experiencing the sounds directly, deaf individuals laugh throughout their lives, making the same sounds as hearing laughers.

The brain circuitry involved has been revealed by *pathological laughter,* a syndrome that can include uncontrollable fits of genuine-sounding but emotionless laughter occurring entirely "on its own." Taken together, the various findings show that human laughter has two biologically distinguishable forms. One is emotion triggered and *spontaneous,* involving subcortical, limbic circuits that humans share with apes and other mammals. The other is cortically controlled, *volitional* laughter that vocalizers learn to produce and that simulates spontaneous versions. Volitional laughter is used in many social situations, such as when laughing politely at unfunny jokes or being purposefully friendly. This form is uniquely human and can be difficult to distinguish from emotion-triggered sounds.

The Sounds of Laughter

Studies of laughter acoustics reveal differences from typical conceptions. For example, although often described as "hah-hah-hah," "hee-hee-hee," or perhaps "hoo-hoo-hoo" sounds, spontaneous laughter rarely includes these vowel qualities. Instead, neutral "uh" sounds are the most frequent, produced without the tongue movement needed to create more distinct vowels. These individual *bursts* are about 100 milliseconds long and grouped into *bouts*. Yet laughter sounds are also quite variable (see Figure 1). Some bursts involve regular vocal fold vibration, or *voicing*, whereas others are breathy and based on noisy, *unvoiced* airflow. Laughter can also commonly include wheezy, laryngeal whistles and click-like pulses. Each can be made either with the mouth open or closed, in the latter case shifting airflow through the nose to create muted or snort-like sounds. When the mouth is open, some bursts show an "h"-like onset, whereas others do not. Marked variation is also evident in features such as the number of bursts per bout and pitch and amplitude patterning. Although every laugher can thus produce a diversity of sounds, some researchers nonetheless propose that each also probably has an individually distinctive, "signature" version.

Laughter Function

Historically, laughter has been considered to provide tension release and health benefits. The latter idea became particularly popular following Norman Cousins's 1979 account of using humor and laughter to combat a debilitating illness. However, subsequent scientific studies have not shown a convincing effect of laughing on health. Although found to increase pain tolerance, human laughter is unlikely to have evolved to its present form for that reason.

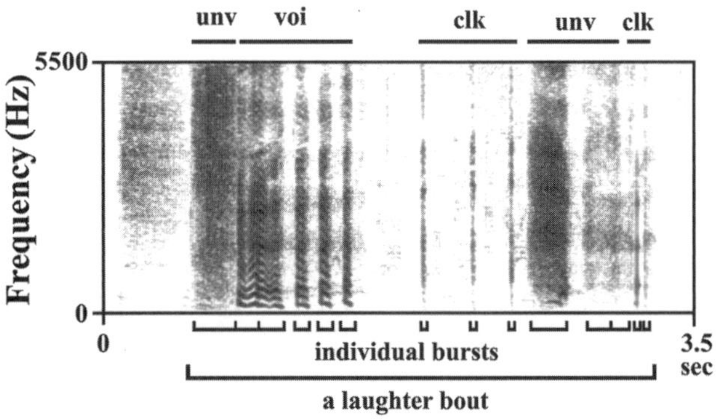

Figure 1 Spectrogram of Spontaneous Male Laughter, Illustrating Sound Types and Acoustic Variability Typifying Spontaneous Laughter

Source: Michael J. Owren.

Notes: Spectrographic representation shows the distribution of sound energy over frequency (vertical axis) and time (horizontal axis) with amount of energy occurring at any point shown by the darkness of shading (produced with a 22.05-kHz sampling rate and 0.03-sec., Gaussian analysis window). The laughter bout is preceded by a noisy, preparatory inhalation, followed by a similarly noisy, unvoiced burst (unv), several vowel-like voiced bursts (voi), three click-like pulses (clk), three more unvoiced bursts, and two final clicks.

Laughter more likely concerns communication occurring in a wide range of social settings but rarely in solitary individuals. In that vein, it is often considered language-like, with distinctive sounding variants that "stand for" and convey different nuances of vocalizer emotion. These states may be positive (e.g., joy, mirth, contentedness, sexual attraction), negative (e.g., nervousness, embarrassment, fear, disdain), or not so clear-cut (e.g., self-deprecation, subservience, surprise). Unfortunately, this argument is hard to test, if only because it is very difficult to get samples of truly spontaneous laughter from vocalizers known to be experiencing various emotions. In addition, given that mirth alone is associated with a wide variety of laughter sounds, it may not be the case that different emotions and contexts can each trigger specific and unique laugh types.

An alternative explanation is that laughter did not evolve to stand for vocalizer states but rather as a means of inducing positive emotion and liking in listeners. For example, spontaneous laughter is known to be "contagious," triggering smiling and laughter in others. It is also widely considered to a key ingredient in social bonding. Although triggered by diverse states and circumstances, laughter is nonetheless likely most common in positive situations. If so, individuals interacting repeatedly with companions they like and enjoy can be expected to form associations between the laughter being heard from these friends and their own positive emotions at the time.

Laughter thereby becomes a vehicle for fostering and maintaining social relationships, while also allowing vocalizers facing more challenging circumstances to potentially use these sounds to induce positive responses, liking, and goodwill in others. Such situations would include facing the kinds of circumstances that cause embarrassment, nervousness, or outright fear, or simply being in a subservient social role. Inducing positive emotion in listeners under such conditions can encourage supportive action from a companion or favorable treatment by a superior. This interpretation is consistent with laughter evolving to become more broadly used in humans than in apes, as well as becoming more regularly voiced. Voicing is known to increase vocal distinctiveness, thereby creating an effective vehicle of potential associative learning.

Therein, too, may lie the close connection between spontaneous laughter and the capacity for humor. If the adaptive value of spontaneous laughter lies in its power to induce positive emotion and liking in others, the goal of the humorist is much the same. Success for the latter is shown by an audience's genuine, positive laughter, with this ancient vocal system arguably setting the evolutionary stage for eventual emergence of humor as a deliberate and powerful strategy of creating enjoyment and encouraging social bonding.

Michael J. Owren

See also Brain, Neuropsychology of Humor; Gelotophobia; Health Benefits of Humor, Physical; Health Benefits of Humor, Psychological; Laughter and Smiling, Physiology of; Mirth; Smiling and Laughter: Expressive Patterns

Further Readings

Gervais, M., & Wilson, D. S. (2005). The evolution and functions of laughter and humor: A synthetic approach. *Quarterly Journal of Theoretical Biology, 80,* 395–430.

Owren, M. J., & Amoss, R. T. (in press). Spontaneous human laughter. In M. Tugade, M. Shiota, & L. Kirby (Eds.), *Handbook of positive emotions.* New York, NY: Guilford Press.

Provine, R. R. (2000). *Laughter: A scientific investigation.* New York, NY: Viking.

Wild, B., Rodden, F. A., Grodd, W., & Ruch, W. (2003). Neural correlates of laughter and humour. *Brain, 126,* 2121–2138.

Laughter and Smiling, Physiology of

Smiling and laughter are affective displays. This means they are transitory and most often triggered by some kind of stimulus related to interpersonal communication. In this way acute physiological changes induced by smiling and laughter differ from more enduring bodily effects of sense of humor. A distinction is made between assumptions about physiological processes based on direct observations of expressive behavior and measurements of covert musculoskeletal, respiratory, autonomic, and immunologic, as well as brain, processes related to mirthful laughter.

Inferences Based on Expressive Displays

The pioneering French physiologist Guillaume Duchenne was a contemporary of Charles Darwin and provided him with ideas about facial muscles involved in smiling and other affective displays, as reported in one of Darwin's classic works, *The Expression of the Emotions in Man and Animals,* published in 1872. Thus, chapter 8, titled "Joy, High Spirits, Love, Tender Feelings, Devotion," described affective states that could elicit a genuine smile, and criteria were given for the distinction of what later became known as the Duchenne smile. The distinction between a false and genuine expression of joy is due primarily to the contraction of the orbicular muscles (pars lateralis) of the lower eyelids not being sufficiently contracted in the former. Marked contraction is accompanied by the drawing of the upper lip caused by contraction of the great zygomatic muscle of the chin. In pronounced laughter, the corrugator muscle between the eyebrows also will be contracted, causing slightly lowered eyebrows and wrinkles to appear between them.

A somewhat paradoxical effect on tear secretion was noted already by Darwin, who pointed out the secretion of tears both during intense laughter and bitter crying. The secretion of tears is due to activation of the parasympathetic branch of the autonomic nervous system that generally triggers during anabolic (energy-preserving) processes. These autonomic changes, therefore, may not be specific to smiling and mirthful laughter. However, there appears to be a continuum of intensity in these physiological changes from the mild to the broad smile and, further, to the gentle laugh and, finally, to excessive laughter. The most obvious difference is that in smiling, no reiterated sound is uttered.

Assumptions of profound respiratory changes are also based on direct observations of smiling and laughter. A prolonged expiratory movement in smiling was pointed out by Darwin, and this movement increases with the more intense smiling with no vocal expression even in the intense smile. Laughter, in contrast, is produced by rhythmic oscillation of the diaphragm and the intercostal muscles attached to the ribs in combination with the tensing of the glottis muscles that compose the vocal apparatus of the larynx.

Covert Physiological Changes During Smiling and Laughter

The assumptions about which facial muscles are involved in smiling and laughter have been confirmed by electromyographic laboratory studies with the use of surface electrodes sensitive to the electric nerve stimulation to contract specific muscles under the surface of the skin.

Respiratory and Cardiovascular Systems

Respiratory movements have been recorded during smiling and laughter by instruments that are sensitive to changes in trunk circumference due to contractions of the diaphragm (abdominal) and intercostal (chest) muscles. Illustrations of such changes in mirthful laughter can be found in several scientific reports. The expiratory movement in smiling and laughter has been confirmed, and operational criteria to distinguish between smiling and laughter have been defined. The occurrence of oscillatory trunk muscle movements at the end of the expiratory phase is the criterion that distinguishes laughter from smiling even when there may be suppression of audible laughter. The magnitude and number of these trunk circumference changes can be calculated precisely with current technology. Some studies have tested the curative effect of forced laughter on various chronic lung diseases, under the assumption that forced laughter might improve alveolar membrane gas (oxygen, carbon dioxide) transport, but the results so far have not been encouraging.

The cardiovascular system is immediately and transitorily activated in all kinds of affective displays. The magnitude of activation during smiling and laughter has proven to be intimately associated with the magnitude and duration of respiratory changes. These cardiorespiratory interactions were illustrated in a 1987 study by Sven Svebak. Evidence was provided for heart rate to increase substantially and immediately at the onset of mirthful laughter. These increases could be more than 50 beats per minute over the few seconds of laughter duration. Deactivation followed immediately afterward, often ending at heart rates below that of the onset. In this way, laughter appears to trigger a sympathetic (catabolic) activation of the cardiac muscle, with a simultaneous hemodynamic increase of systolic blood pressure, and a marked vagal rebound of deactivation typically follows at the end of vigorous laughter. The vagal nerve is the most important autonomic nerve involved in anabolic processes.

Immune System

Speculations have flourished about effects of smiling and laughter on the immune system. One area of research that has attracted research funding is the effect of mirthful laughter, which activates the sympathetic nervous system. Exposure to stressors can cause immediate changes in the immune system, such as an increase of CD8+ T-cells and an increase in the number and toxicity of natural killer cells. In addition, one may infer from the oscillatory movements of the trunk during laughter that lymphatic circulation is increased. In contrast to the cardiovascular system, the lymphatic vascular system has no pump to ensure circulation and, instead, is dependent on pressure changes due to all kinds of physical activity, including mirthful laughter. Some of these studies addressed the moderating effect of sense of humor on the relation between exposure to stressors as well as the effect of comedy on people with a high versus low sense of humor. Results from these few studies have been somewhat encouraging although equivocal, as pointed out by Rod Martin. So far, it may be justified to conclude that studies of effects of a friendly sense of humor on bodily health, including longevity, have provided stronger support than those studying the transitory effects of smiling and laughter.

Brain Processes

Several studies have supported that more left frontal brain activation is present during the increasingly intense experience of positive emotions and that right frontal activation is present in the experience of negative emotions. These asymmetrical patterns have been observed during exposure to positive versus negative film clips, respectively. Also, greater relative left frontal baseline activation has predicted more positive affect in response to films eliciting positive affect, whereas the opposite baseline activation has predicted more negative affect to films eliciting negative affect. These brain differences in affective bias relate to a broad distinction between positive versus negative affect.

One example of positive affect is expressed in the Duchenne (genuine) smile. It is likely that less than half of the population can voluntarily produce the contractions involved in a Duchenne smile. It appears to activate the left frontal and anterior temporal lobes, relative to activation in these areas of the right hemisphere. These responses may be activated also when voluntarily making the Duchenne smile and have given support to the idea of "grin and bear it" as an antidote to adversity. There is some evidence that heart rate decreases more in subjects instructed to smile, and in particular for those with Duchenne smiles, when performing stressful tasks, and after recovery from the stressful activities. More research is needed to explore the health effects of these ways of coping. Affective display typically is transitory and may have trivial effects on physical health in the long run, whereas the processing of a friendly sense of humor is a more enduring approach to everyday life and may be of greater importance to physical health.

Studies of brain processes following exposure to jokes have revealed consistent increase of P300 (an event-related potential component, which refers to the measured brain response as a result of attention allocated to the processing of a specific event) following the punch line, disregarding level of funniness, thus suggesting increase of nonspecific attention. However, immediately following the P300 positivity, a negative wave has been reported with higher amplitude in response to the funnier jokes. One series of experiments addressed hemispheric asymmetry during appreciation of humor. Results suggested that the right hemisphere is better coordinated with activity of the left following humor appreciation. This effect appears to be a result of the cognitive processing of humor rather than respiratory changes during laughter.

Magnetic resonance and other studies of brain activity during affective display have provided support to the idea that certain brain areas are more likely than others to be activated. These areas are known to be active during the organization of affective displays in general, and they include the left hemisphere basal ganglia, right hemisphere putamen, the insular cortex, thalamus, lower occipital gyri, and the cauda nuclei. The cognitive processes and the related organization of affective responses in humor appreciation are so complex that they are not confined to only a few areas of the brain.

Some types of brain damage can have serious effects on the ability to appreciate humor. Epilepsy of the temporal lobes has been associated with reduced sexual drive, increase of social aggression, extremism, and no sense of humor. Seizures or stroke in the temporobasal regions may be accompanied by mirthful gelastic seizures (facial expressions that mimic mirth). Another type of brain damage is due to infarction of the upper section of the corticospinal tract. Moderate cases of such thrombosis may result in pseudobulbar paresis and related dysphagia as well as the loss of a volitional affective control. Some of these patients may display unmotivated crying as well as fits of laughter. This concludes the review of covert physiological changes associated with laughter and smiling. Together with the overt, expressive displays reviewed in the first part of the entry, they constitute the physiological correlates of laughter and smiling.

Sven Svebak

See also Laugh, Laughter, Laughing; Laughter, Psychology of; Smiling and Laughter: Expressive Patterns

Further Readings

Ekman, P., & Davidson, R. J. (1993). Voluntary smiling changes regional brain activity. *Psychological Science, 4,* 342–345.

Kraft, T. L., & Pressman, S. D. (2012). Grin and bear it: The influence of manipulated facial expression on the stress response. *Psychological Science, 23,* 1372–1378.

Martin, R. A. (2007). *The psychology of humor: An integrative approach.* New York, NY: Elsevier Academic Press.

Svebak, S. (1982). The effect of mirthfulness upon amount of discordant right-left occipital EEG alpha. *Motivation and Emotion, 6,* 133–147.

Svebak, S. (1987). Humor og helse: Et perspektiv på mestring av stress [Humor and health: A perspective on coping with stress]. *Tidsskrift for Norsk Psykologforening, 24,* 355–361.

Svebak, S., Romundstad, S., & Holmen, J. (2010). A seven-year prospective study of sense of humor and mortality in an adult county population: The HUNT-2 study. *International Journal of Psychiatry in Medicine, 40,* 125–146.

Lazzi

Of debatable origin, the words *lazzi* (plural) and *lazzo* (singular) define the transferable comic routines inserted into *commedia dell'arte* plots and are now also used to refer to any actor's stage "business" teased out of a plot. *Lazzo* is generally accepted as deriving from *l'azzo* or *l'azione,* meaning "action" or activity on stage, although some authorities also apply it to verbal pyrotechnics, "a jest, a witticism, or a metaphor, in words or actions" (Perrucci, 1699/2008, p. 192).

Through numerous historical records, the titles of many hundred *commedia lazzi* are known, although only about 250 have any descriptive details. The records cover situations, scenarios, and sketchy plots, but without dialogue, although clearly in performance, text was improvised around most of them. The *arte* (guild or profession) in *commedia dell'arte* is often interpreted as "craft" or "skill" and associated with "the craft of improvisation" (its full name in 16th-century Italy was *commedia dell'arte all improvviso*). Although *commedia* text was developed through improvisation, debate remains on what percentage was invented during performance; the requirements of *lazzi* suggest a great deal of familiarity with both plot and key sentences.

Commedia's *lazzi* are invariably comic, their purpose being to divert and entertain, even amaze with physical skill. They often used topical satire to appeal to the widest audience; their comic scenarios involved familiar situations, usually ones in the public eye, and involved easily recognizable character traits. Many echo long-established elements of Roman comedies, for example, Plautine satire of types, class/status, and cunning survival skills, together with laughable human qualities such as greed, envy, and weakness in the face of temptation. Such elements have been numerously identified in Shakespeare's plays and in the plays of many others.

Traditional *lazzi* situations require considerable physicality and depend on acrobatic skills, using symbolic or exaggerated props such as the huge enema-syringe illustrated in Pierre Louis Duchartre's *The Italian Comedy* (1924/1966, p. 336) from the Corsini manuscript of 1610. Often elaborate and involving several performers, most *lazzi* would have been learned by all (usually 10) members of the company. As in any comic routine, spontaneity prevails in improvising amusement, although with pre-agreed cues, both verbal and physical, signaling start, transition, or end of the *lazzo*. One can presume that as long as an audience's laughter continued, the *lazzo* was further explored.

There is no complete list of *lazzi* from *commedia*'s most popular period, 1550–1750, although some 300 to 400 appear to have been commonly used, and the same *lazzi* titles are often found in records of various companies. Mel Gordon (1983) categorized 250 traditional *lazzi* under 12 headings (12 to 19 in each): Acrobatic and Mimic *Lazzi* (e.g. *Lazzi* of the Ladder, of the Statue); Comic Violence/Sadistic Behavior (floggings, beatings, tooth extraction, circumcision); Food *Lazzi* (from the famous "fly eating" of the stock characters Arlecchino and Truffaldino, to complete feasts, as in Carlo Goldoni's later plays); Stage Properties (where action necessitates specific props); Sexual/Scatological (*Lazzi* of the Enema, chamber pots, "erecting" swords); Social/Class Rebellion (for plots that commonly delighted audiences by taking the side of the underdog); Stupidity/Inappropriate Behavior (ignorance, memory lapses); Transformation (essentially major changes of character brought about by a new and often contradictory emotion, mocking the inconsistency of human nature); Word Play (puns, dialects, malapropisms, insults); Trickery (basic to all *lazzi*, but here Gordon groups the more elaborate deceptions); Illogical *Lazzi* (where the comedy departs totally from plot and arises from absurdities and pure silliness). There is another category that illuminates the actor-audience relationship, as many *lazzi* played with the double reality of stage and life: breaking illusions, objectifying character/actions, and developing comedy through topical interchange with audience members.

The actor Domenico Biancolelli (1636–1686) recorded his own mimed *lazzi* for playing Arlecchino/Harlequin in the late 17th century:

> I arrive on the stage; there I find Trivelin [a famous clown] stretched on the ground. I think him dead and try to drag him to his feet; then I let my wooden sword fall down. He takes it and hits me on the buttocks. I turn round without speaking, and he gives me a kick on the back so that I tumble down. Up I get again; I seize and carry him; I lean him against the wings on the right-side of the stage. I look round at the footlights, and meanwhile he gets up and leans against the left-hand side-wings. This *Lazzi* is repeated two or three times. (Nicholls, 1931, p. 221)

Arlecchino's wooden sword or stick (*batocio* or *batocchio*) developed the ability to produce a loud slapping noise, and its frequent use gave the name *slapstick* to cartoon-like exaggerated violence and thus to an entire comic genre as used by Charlie Chaplin, Buster Keaton, the Keystone Cops, and others.

A close non-Western relative to *lazzi* stock situations, routines, and characters is found in the *Kyōgen* plays of Japanese *Nō* theater, similarly exploiting physical and verbal tropes of status (servant-master), basic needs (food, warmth, sex), and frailties (temptation, greed, ambition) combined with farce plots. Chinese *Xiqu* (Chinese "opera") also allows its clown characters considerable improvised liberties, usually in physical comedy. In Southern and Southeast Asia, narrative episodes in popular theater are constantly interrupted with comic *lazzi* (e.g., in Yakshagana, the musical theater of Karnataka, India, a long, wordless, comic sequence of Sita, the wife of the god-like Rama, dressing while feeling that she is being watched by her "invisible" husband—much to the audience's delight). Although both of the ancient Sanskrit play cycles, *Ramayana* and *Mahabharata,* lack a definitive form, they consist of variants that are embroidered anew in every performance, sometimes according to preplanned needs of sponsors and drawing on *lazzi*-like stock routines. Spontaneous comedy, elaborating something purely for the audience's enjoyment, seems to be a shared feature of theater worldwide.

Improvisation from basic situations, comic ideas, and characters is commonly found in both traditional performing arts and contemporary comedy. Topical references and familiar stock characters and themes became common features interspersed and juxtaposed into the plot proper, as seen in Goldoni's comedy *Il servitore di due padroni* (The Servant of Two Masters, 1743). Although Samuel Beckett allowed no improvisation in his plays, sections of *Waiting for Godot* (1953) exactly parallel *commedia*'s verbal *lazzi.* Many modern stand-up comedians and street mimes extend the category of absurd and illogical *lazzi* to dispense with plot altogether, playing only with subject and, like jazz players with a melody, surrounding it with verbal *lazzi,* now called gags.

With increased use of *commedia* techniques now part of modern actor training, the word *lazzi* is now commonly appropriated by actors and directors to refer to any section of a plot that consists primarily of elaboration.

Aubrey Mellor

See also Absurdist Humor; *Commedia dell'Arte*; Farce; Gag; Goldoni, Carlo; Improv Comedy; *Kyōgen*; Mime; Plautus; Practical Jokes; Sanskrit Humor; Slapstick

Further Readings

Capozza, N. (1985). *Tutti i lazzi della commedia dell'arte: Un catalogo ragionato del patrimonio dei comici* [All the *lazzi* of the *commedia dell'arte*: A complete catalog of the patrimony of the comedians]. Rome, Italy: Dino Audino.

Duchartre, P. L. (1966). *The Italian comedy: The improvisation, scenarios, lives, portraits, and masks of the illustrious characters of the* commedia dell'arte (R. T. Weaver, Trans.). New York, NY: Dover. (Original work published 1924)

Gordon, M. (1983). Lazzi: *The comic routines of the* commedia dell'arte. New York, NY: Performing Arts Journal Publications.

Nicholls, A. (1931). *Masks mimes and miracles: Studies in the popular theatre.* London, UK: Harrap.

Oreglia, G. (1968). *The commedia dell'arte* (L. F. Edwards, Trans.). London, UK: Methuen.

Perrucci, A. (2008). *A treatise on acting, from memory and by improvisation/Dell'arte rappresentativa, premeditata ed all'improvviso* (F. Cotticelli, A. Goodrich Heck, & T. F. Heck, Trans. & Eds.). Lanham, MD: Scarecrow Press. (Original work published 1699)

Legal Education

Legal education encompasses the teaching and study of law, whether taught in formal scholastic settings, conducted as part of continuing legal education programs, or exhibited in other environments where there is a teacher-student relationship between parties.

In legal education, where material is often dry and complex, humor can be an extremely valuable tool to help an instructor or educator solidify a point or an idea. To articulate an important concept or idea with a humorous perspective means that a speaker can help capture the audience's attention.

Although such a connection may not be instantly intuitive, there tends to be a strong crossover between humor and the study of law, given the type of intelligence and skills each requires. This entry discusses the overlap between humor and the law, the benefits of using humor in education, and how teaching improvisational skills can be particularly useful in legal education.

An Analysis of Humor and Law

Many people are familiar with at least a few jokes about lawyers. The nature of the profession tends to lend itself to a humorous perspective, whether because of the frustrations people sometimes endure in their interactions with lawyers, the breadth of the field, or popular culture depictions of law and the legal system.

Numerous lawyers and law school graduates have gone on to have significant careers in humor and comedy. The late Greg Giraldo, a comedian and panelist on the network television program *Last Comic Standing*, practiced law before he began performing in the nightclubs of New York City. An alumnus of Harvard Law School, Justin Shanes left his law firm career after 2 years and became a monologue writer for the television program *Late Night With Jimmy Fallon*. Comedian Demetri Martin dropped out of New York University School of Law at the end of his second year to pursue his comedic passions, which have led him to his own television program as well as several movie scripts and acting opportunities.

It might be appropriate that there is so much overlap between the legal profession and the desire to write and perform comedy. Lawyers typically have better-than-average writing skills, as do comedic writers. Law school students typically hone their logic skills, and a main facet of humor relies on the ability to note the inconsistencies and illogicality of everyday life.

Humor in Education

Many studies confirm that humor can be an extremely effective teaching tool. Humor can engage an audience and help the audience retain the material presented. If a respected leader makes a joke or shows a funny clip to illustrate a concept, that person is likely to be more positively received than had he or she not connected to the audience using humor.

Educators use humor as a tool to help establish rapport and build trust, while creating a memorable experience for the students. However, it is less common for teachers to use humor as a teaching mechanism within law. This may be because of the sometimes difficult subject matter, or because some legal subjects, such as a wrongful death scenario, simply do not seem appropriate as a joking matter.

It's extremely common for law school instructors to use the Socratic method of teaching. The Socratic method is a question-and-answer format in which the instructor poses a question or scenario to a student and then continues to ask a series of questions in order to lead to a single point. Although sometimes such a method can lead to instances of humor, it is not an inherently humorous teaching method. Perhaps it is this insistence on such a formal teaching style that makes it more difficult for educators to incorporate humor into the study of the law.

Law and the Art of Improvisation

Improvisation is a comedic skill that people can hone to become more spontaneous, quick-witted, and outgoing. Many people who fear public speaking are able to overcome such fears after taking a series of improvisational courses, which often put the speaker at the center of attention. Improvisation can also assist with team-building skills, as the improvisational practices teach people to support one another.

Courses in improvisation can help teach important legal skills such as team building, public speaking, logical reasoning, pattern finding, and creative thinking. Such skills may be tremendously important to lawyers, and using improv as a basis for teaching such real-life skills can be tremendously valuable.

Legal educators who are interested in using improvisation can look at a breadth of resources, such as groups that specialize in corporate and workplace improvisation tactics. These organizations typically can help students learn a variety of skills that can be applied to the legal profession.

Conclusion

When used correctly and appropriately, humor is an excellent teaching tool for people in legal education and the legal profession. Humor helps break up the monotony of subject matter that may be otherwise dry and therefore helps people retain information for longer periods of time, thereby enhancing the effectiveness of the tool.

People who are interested in using humor as a teaching tool may wish to experiment to find out which methods work best. Visual humor can be an effective storytelling device, and improvisational humor can be an effective mechanism to help build trust and rapport. Using these tools, a legal educator can create a lesson plan that is engaging and perhaps also interactive, which creates a strong foundation from which one can learn.

Whitney Meers

See also Education, Humor in; Legal Restriction and Protection of Humor; Persuasion and Humor; Supreme Court

Further Readings

Ewick, P., & Silbey, S. S. (2007). No laughing matter: Humor and contradictions in stories of law. *DePaul Law Review, 50*, 559–573.

Lubet, S., & Hankinson, T. (2006). In Facetiis Veritas: How improvisational comedy can help trial lawyers get some chops. *Texas Review of Entertainment and Sports Law, 7*, 1–14.

Meers, W. (2009). The funny thing about mediation: A rationale for the use of humor in mediation. *Cardozo Journal of Conflict Resolution, 10*, 657–686. Retrieved July 31, 2012, from http://cojcr.org/vol10no2/657-686.pdf

Novick, J. (n.d.). *What is improv for lawyers?* Retrieved July 31, 2012, from http://www.improvforlawyers.com/public_html_improvforlawyers.com/What_is_Improv_for_Lawyers.html

Legal Restriction and Protection of Humor

Legal rules do not sort neatly into a discrete category officially recognized as "legal regulation of humor." Indeed, legal restrictions and protections touching humorous expression are as diverse and wide-ranging as humor itself. Nonetheless, one may begin to understand how law and humor intersect by dividing laws into two categories: those that protect humor and those that directly or indirectly restrict its expression.

Legal Protections of Humor

The First Amendment

The most prominent law that *protects* humor is the First Amendment of the U.S. Constitution, which governs the individual right to freedom of expression in the United States. As interpreted by the U.S. Supreme Court as well as other courts in the United States, the First Amendment prohibits the government from restricting both verbal and nonverbal expression. Accordingly, the First Amendment protects humor communicated through words as well as through pictures or expressive conduct.

U.S. courts hold the First Amendment on a high pedestal, sometimes describing it is as the Constitution's most important individual right. Legal thinkers argue that the First Amendment guards the operation of U.S. democracy and acts as a handmaiden to ensure that citizens enjoy other individual liberties guaranteed in the Constitution. Despite its extraordinary status, the First Amendment is not absolute, and courts may therefore find some humor outside the ambit of First Amendment protection. For example, humor that poses a clear and imminent threat to public safety is not protected under the First Amendment. Thus, if the distribution of a religiously provocative cartoon is likely to ignite a riot, a court might find that the cartoon can be censored. Likewise, the First Amendment does not prevent the government from implementing reasonable time, place, and manner restrictions on humorous expressions. This means, for example, that the government may prohibit the reading of jokes from a high-volume sound truck driving in a residential neighborhood in the middle of the night. To be valid, however, such regulation must usually be "content neutral." To enjoy the status of a time, place, and manner restriction, the regulation must be motivated by policies unrelated to the content of the jokes.

The line separating constitutionally protected and constitutionally unprotected humor is often difficult to draw. Certain trends in cases, however, provide some guidance in making this distinction. Where humor implicates political ideas or debate about a matter of public concern, the humor is more likely to enjoy First Amendment protection. This result flows from the importance of the First Amendment to ensuring a functioning democracy and a robust marketplace of ideas. By contrast, humor that is indecent or obscene is unlikely to enjoy First Amendment protection. One humorous genre found particularly deserving of constitutional protection is the political cartoon. As stated by the U.S. Supreme Court in *Hustler v. Falwell*, 485 U.S. 46, 54–55 (1988), "the appeal of the political cartoon or caricature is often based on exploitation of unfortunate physical traits or politically embarrassing events . . . From the viewpoint of history it is clear that our political discourse would have been considerably poorer without them."

Although U.S. constitutional law cases evince themes and trends that can help one identify which types of humorous expression will enjoy constitutional protections, matters become more uncertain when the expression is published on the Internet. The Internet lacks the geographical boundaries that usually limit the scope of a nation's laws. Thus, a comical communication may be uploaded onto the Internet in the United States but accessed in another country. Although the communication may enjoy First Amendment protection in the United States, it may be subject to censure or punishment under the laws of other nations. Indeed, the United States currently tends to have the strictest and most speech protection laws of all the nations of the world. Cases have occurred where U.S. entities have uploaded legally protected content in the United States and have encountered prosecution and other legal problems in other countries. Accordingly, before producing and uploading potentially objectionable content on the Internet, a prudent humorist might therefore consider the possible status of the communication under the laws of other nations where others may access the communication.

Intellectual Property Protection

An altogether different but important form of legal protection for humor comes in the form of intellectual property laws. Intellectual property traditionally includes patents, trademarks, and copyright. Although patentable inventions may be capable of communicating humor, it is copyright and trademark laws that prove most relevant to humor protection.

The U.S. copyright statute protects all expressions once they are fixed in a tangible medium. Thus, the author of a humorous work is protected against "theft" or infringement of her rights in her work as soon as the work is recorded in a concrete way. This would include audio or visual recordings as well as books that provide a record of the humorous work. Significantly, jokes that are uttered orally, but are not recorded, are not eligible for copyright protection. This limitation is particularly significant for stand-up comedians, who often do not create a tangible record of their stock in trade. Nonetheless, scholars have documented that stand-up comedians have developed their own robust social norms that serve to compensate for the deficiencies in formal legal protection for their creative work.

Trademark law developed initially to prevent producers from passing off products created and marketed by others as if the products were their own. Trademark law now also protects consumers, who rely on trademarks to ensure that products possess a certain quality. Producers of humorous products (such as book publishers or movie production companies) may thus use trademarks to promote a product and to suggest to consumers that the product possesses a certain level of quality—comedic or otherwise.

Another important way in which trademark law intersects with humor concerns those who develop parodies of trademarks. Trademark holders often do not hesitate to sue producers of such parodies, claiming infringement or dilution of the mark. Where the court determines that the parodist should avoid liability, the court effectively protects the creative humorous expression. For the most part, however, the trademark laws act in this context as a restriction on the parodist—a set of standards that the parodist must navigate in order to stay out of trouble. The next section on restrictions on humor addresses these standards.

Legal Restrictions of Humor

Laws restrict humor both directly and indirectly. Direct regulations can restrain the humorist before humor is expressed or impose criminal punishment after communication has been expressed, thereby raising the stakes of compliance so that many may simply stifle their inclination to make an objectionable joke, particularly if they are communicating in a public forum. An example of a prior restraint that may implicate humor is the U.S. Federal Communication Commission's attempt to prevent broadcast of fleeting expletives (and to impose heavy fines on media outlets that fail to "bleep out" an expletive during a broadcast). Outside the United States, courts and regulatory authorities directly ban or enjoin humorous communications such as songs or advertisements with relative frequency. Injunctions against speech are rare in the United States and are unlikely to implicate humor because the law limits these injunctions to grave matters such as the stealth movement of troops during wartime. There are, however, several U.S. criminal laws that directly punish humor, such as statutes criminalizing threats to the life of the president of the United States (even when stated in jest) and statutes criminalizing jokes about blowing up a plane or an airport.

Indirect regulation usually comes in the form of a civil lawsuit for alleged injuries received from a joke or other humorous communication. In such suits, a private person sues another for damages allegedly received from a legal harm done. Where a court finds liability and imposes damages, this verdict sends a message both to the party who must pay damages and to others who may be tempted to make similar jokes. Thus, the damage verdict has an indirect regulatory effect—indeed a potentially chilling effect—on future jokes. Four common legal theories for these private civil lawsuits that affect humor are related to trademark violations, contract, employment discrimination, and defamation.

Trademark Violations

Trademark infringement cases are designed to protect against harm both to consumers who are misled into buying a product they did not expect and to trademark owners who are deprived of sales. Key to the infringement claim is consumer confusion: Courts look to the "likelihood of confusion" between the trademark-protected product and the challenged product or communication in evaluating whether civil liability is merited. A question significant from a humor perspective arises when the alleged infringer argues that the claimed infringement is actually a parody of the trademark-protected product.

In resolving disputes about allegedly infringing parodies, trademark courts tend to invoke a concept known well among humor scholars: incongruity. In so doing, the courts do not explicitly invoke the wisdom of humor theorists but instead rely on trademark law's "likelihood of confusion" test, which—it turns out—dovetails with the concept of incongruity. If the infringed product is consistent with the qualities or purposes of the trademark-protected product, then one might describe the products as congruent and a consumer may confuse the two. By contrast, a consumer is not likely to be confused if the connection between the trademark-protected product and the allegedly infringing product is unexpected, outlandish, or implausible. In such a situation, the court will reject the trademark infringement claim, leaving the parodist free to create the parody and even to profit from it. The result is for courts to insulate parodists from infringement liability when their parodies embody a significant degree of incongruous humor.

Another type of trademark theory of liability—trademark dilution—does not tend to implicate incongruity theory as vividly as the infringement cases. The theory of trademark dilution holds that just because a parody does not mislead a consumer into believing a trademark holder would ridicule its own mark, the trademark owner might still be harmed by a lessening of the commercial attraction and appeal of the mark. This harm can result because the consumer starts to associate the mark with a diverse set of sources or with something offensive or distasteful. Not surprisingly, then, trademark dilution cases tend to find liability where the parodist indulges topics often associated with release humor: excrement, sex, violence, death, and the like. Nonetheless, the protection of parody appears as an important value in many trademark dilution cases, so that the cases sometimes do reflect a tendency to protect incongruity humor.

Contract

Questions relating to humor arise most often in contract cases confronting whether the parties to the suit created a legally enforceable contract. In such a situation, one party files a breach of contract suit, and the other party defends by arguing that she did not intend to create a legally enforceable obligation but instead was merely making a joke. Sometimes the "joke" or "contract" was uttered during a state of intoxication or in the course of an advertisement. In evaluating such contract claims and humor defenses, courts ask whether the parties' words and actions manifested an objective intent to be legally bound. Where the parties' words and actions reflect strong incongruities, courts are less likely to find the intent to enter an enforceable agreement. Such incongruities therefore lay the groundwork for a court embracing the defendant's defense that she was simply trying to be funny. Where the court embraces this defense, the court is, in effect, protecting the joke from contract liability.

Employment Discrimination

As interpreted by courts, state and federal employment discrimination statutes allow individuals to sue their employers for a form of employment discrimination known as hostile work environment harassment. To make out this claim, a plaintiff must establish that speech or conduct within the workplace is "severe or pervasive" enough to create a hostile work environment based on race, religion, sex, national origin, age, disability, or veteran status. In some jurisdictions, the harassment may also concern sexual orientation, political affiliation, citizenship status, marital status, or personal appearance.

Often the pattern of harassment includes communications made in the form of jokes. In such circumstances, courts must evaluate whether the communications were sufficiently lighthearted to constitute simply an attempt at humor or whether they are sufficiently malicious or disparaging as to change the conditions of employment for the target of the humor. Courts tend to find liability where the jokes ridicule the target or showcase salacious subjects. The more puns, wit, or incongruity there are in the jokes, the more likely that the defendant will prevail in defeating the plaintiff's employment discrimination claim.

Defamation

Defamation is a tort theory designed to protect an individual's interest in preserving personal reputation. Defamation is one of several dignitary harms, or harms resulting from certain legally recognized indignities, that can be asserted by a plaintiff asking a court to impose damages for hurtful jokes. Other dignitary harms that often involve joking include intentional infliction of emotional distress and invasion of privacy. Defamation, however, is by far the most common theory used to remedy jokes that allegedly inflict harm.

A defamatory statement is generally defined as one that "tends so to harm the reputation of another as to lower him in the estimation of the community or to deter third persons from associating or dealing with him" (Restatement [Second] of Torts § 559 [1977]). In the United States, a defamation plaintiff must show that the defamatory statement was false. This creates a problem for defamation actions based on jokes because humor does not fit neatly into the paradigm of truth and falsity. Humor is by definition not "serious" and thus not verifiable. Yet it also provides a vehicle for delivering a truthful message. As the adage goes: "Many a truth is said in jest."

One mechanism that courts use to distinguish defamatory humor from humor that is protected from defamation liability is the distinction between fact and opinion. Both defamation and First Amendment law maintain that liability can arise only when the defendant asserts untrue statements of facts, not when the defendant asserts opinion. In applying this fact/opinion dichotomy in the context of humor, courts ask whether humor contains material that a reasonable reader could interpret as suggesting actual facts. This approach is problematic because courts encounter substantial difficulty charting the differences between fact and opinion. Moreover, further complications arise because humor is particularly artful in concealing the possible factual content of its message. It is interesting that courts often deal with these difficulties by resorting to a form of incongruity analysis in determining whether the assertions in a joke are sufficiently distinct from factual assertions as to cast the joke as a mere expression of opinion, protected from liability.

Conclusion

Legal protections and restrictions of humor are ad hoc and not the result of an integrated system of laws. Nonetheless, certain patterns of regulation emerge from the statutes and court cases that touch humor. Perhaps the most notable pattern is the tendency of legal rules to privilege humor that reflects incongruity and to suppress and restrict humor that disparages others or concerns topics associated with release humor, such as sex, excrement, violence, and death. These patterns are especially remarkable since courts seem to have unwittingly made their way to the same distinctions and insights reflected in years of research by humor scholars on the theories of incongruity, superiority, and release humor.

Laura E. Little

See also Legal Education; Supreme Court

Further Readings

Ewick, P., & Silbey, S. (2008). No laughing matter: Humor and contradiction in stories of law, *DePaul Law Review, 50,* 559–573.

Little, L. (2009). Regulating funny: Humor and the law. *Cornell Law Review, 95,* 1235–1292.

Little, L. (2011). Just a joke: Defamatory humor and incongruity's promise. *Southern California Interdisciplinary Law Journal, 21,* 93–163.

Oliar, D., & Sprigman, C. (2008). There's no free laugh (anymore): The emergence of intellectual property norms and the transformation of stand-up comedy. *Virginia Law Review, 94,* 1787–1867.

Restatement (Second) of Torts. (1977). Philadelphia, PA: American Law Institute.

Volokh, E. (1997). What speech does "hostile work environment" harassment restrict? *Georgetown Law Journal, 85,* 627–648.

Limericks

The origin of the term *limerick,* as applied to a particular form of humorous verse, cannot be established with any certainty. The theory most commonly proposed reputes it to be derived from a custom at convivial parties whereby each member sang an improvised nonsense verse, followed by a chorus containing the words "Will you come up to Limerick?" (*Oxford English Dictionary*). Both the *Encyclopaedia Britannica* and *Brewer's Dictionary of Phrase and Fable* mention the same supposed derivation, as well as the theory that the chorus in question was originally that of an 18th-century Irish soldiers' song. *Brewer's* correctly adds that there is no evidence that this is the case, and in fact there is nothing in the chorus supposedly sung in Limerick that fits either the meter or the pattern of the limerick verse form. It is probably safest to say that the origin of the term (while presumably connected in some way to the Irish town and county of Limerick) is unknown.

The true limerick form consists of five lines of anapaests (feet consisting of two unstressed syllables followed by one stressed) rhyming *aabba,* with two feet in the third and fourth lines (typically indented in written form) and three in the others. The earliest recorded examples are in *The History of Sixteen Wonderful Old Women,* published in London by John Harris in 1821. The following year *Anecdotes and Adventures of Fifteen Gentlemen* appeared, by an unknown author (possibly R. S. Sharpe). It included:

There was a sick man of Tobago
Liv'd long on rice-gruel and sago.
But at last, to his bliss,
The physician said this—
"To a roast leg of mutton you may go."

This book was apparently drawn to the attention of Edward Lear in 1831 while he was staying with friends, and he immediately saw this as an ideal form in which to exploit his gift for comic invention. The outcome was Lear's first collection of limericks, although he did not use that term: *A Book of Nonsense* was published in 1846 and attributed by him to "Derry down Derry":

There was an Old Derry down Derry
Who loved to see little folks merry;
So he made them a Book
And with laughter they shook
At the fun of that Derry down Derry.

The reference to "little folks" indicates that the work was written for children.

Several more volumes of Lear's "nonsense verse" followed, the limericks often having as their subject an "Old Man" or "Old Person," with an occasional variant such as "Young Lady" or "Young Person":

There was a Young Person of Crete
Whose toilette was far from complete:
She dressed in a sack
Spickle-speckled with black,
That ombliferous Person of Crete.

Although many of Lear's limericks come across today as somewhat lacking in creativity (especially as their last line so closely approximates their first, save perhaps for the insertion of a fantastic invented word such as *ombliferous*), the verse form became extremely popular toward the turn of the 19th century, with limerick competitions often being held by magazines and business houses. By then, a major difference from Lear's limericks was that the last line, instead of being a near-repeat of the first, had in effect become the "punch line," with a brand new and unexpected word providing the final rhyme.

Subject Matter

"Intellectual" Limericks

Although the limerick form has been used over the years to treat a wide variety of subjects, two areas in particular—very different from each other—have been favored by its composers. The first area is that of amusing philosophical, literary, or theological commentary. The most celebrated example of this subgenre is undoubtedly Monsignor Ronald Knox's commentary on the "immaterialism" expounded by the Irish bishop George Berkeley (1685–1753), who, in opposition to the materialism propounded by Thomas Hobbes, taught that things did not exist in themselves but only as perceived by the mind (the doctrine known as *esse est percipi,* "to exist is to be perceived"). Knox wrote,

There once was a man who said: "God
Must think it exceedingly odd
If he finds that this tree
Continues to be
When there's no-one about in the quad."

which prompted the following riposte by an anonymous author (claimed, rather improbably, by some writers to be Bertrand Russell):

Dear Sir, Your astonishment's odd;
I am always about in the quad.
And that's why this tree
Will continue to be
Since observed by, Yours faithfully, God.

A further subset of this intellectual type of limerick relies for its effect on the peculiarities of English spelling and its sometimes tenuous relationship to pronunciation, and depends on the reader's deriving a feeling of intellectual superiority from the esoteric knowledge required in order to understand it. It was for some years a specialty of the magazine *Punch* and of Oxford and Cambridge university dons. An example follows:

There was an old priest of Dún Laoghaire
Who stood on his head for the Kaoghaire.
When people asked why,
He explained it all by
The latest liturgical thaoghaire.

(The name of the town Dún Laoghaire in Ireland is pronounced "Dunleary," which is here rhymed with "Kyrie" and "theory.")

A further example is the following:

There was a young curate of Salisbury
Whose manners were Halisbury-Scalisbury.
He wandered round Hampshire
Without any pampshire
Till the Vicar compelled him to Walisbury.

To understand this limerick, it is necessary to be aware that the old Latin name for Salisbury in England (still used in some ecclesiastical contexts) is *Sarum* and that the traditional abbreviation of the county of Hampshire is *Hants*.

Ribald and Obscene Limericks

A much more popular subject area than that of intellectual wordplay is the realm of the salacious. One of the most frequently quoted of limericks (the work of an anonymous writer) runs as follows:

The limerick packs laughs anatomical
Into space that is quite economical,
But the good ones I've seen
So seldom are clean,
And the clean ones so seldom are comical.

Although the validity of this observation is open to question, the popularity of what are sometimes referred to as "dirty limericks" is undeniable and is attested by the considerable number of anthologies that have been devoted to this subgenre. The earliest such collections date from the later 1800s, but the two most important anthologies appeared in the 20th century, these being *Some Limericks* (1928), a frequently reprinted compilation by the Scottish novelist and antiquarian Norman Douglas, and *The Limerick,* a massive work of over 500 pages whose authorship/editorship is not acknowledged but was later revealed to be that of the American cultural critic and folklorist Gershon (originally George Alexander) Legman, famous for his analysis of sexual humor, *The Rationale of the Dirty Joke* (1968). Both anthologies have frequently been plagiarized, a notable example being *Count Palmiro Vicarion's Book of Limericks,* put together by the English poet and poetic translator Christopher Logue and published in Paris by Olympia Press in 1953 (no English press was prepared to risk prosecution by daring to publish such material at the time).

Some of the limericks found in these collections are mildly amusing, an example being,

There was a plump girl from Bryn Mawr
Who committed a dreadful faux pas;
She loosened a stay
On her décolleté
Thus exposing her je ne sais quoi.

Of a similar nature are a number of moderately salacious limericks involving real people:

There once was a girl from Pretoria
Who had sex with Sir Gerald du Maurier,
Jack Hylton, Jack Payne,
Then Sir Gerald again,
And the band of the Waldorf Astoria.

The comic effect of this limerick is increased when one is aware that the three persons named were British show-business personalities of the 1930s: Jack Hylton and Jack Payne were well-known bandleaders, and Sir Gerald du Maurier was an actor and theater manager.

Other limericks quoted in the bawdier anthologies appear to be aimed mainly, or even exclusively, at shocking the reader:

There was a young lady of Devon
Who was raped in the vestry by seven
High Anglican priests
—The lascivious beasts—
Of such is the Kingdom of Heaven.

As to the particular attractiveness of the limerick form for the expression of such vulgar and obscene material, one can only speculate that it has to do with the pleasure of transgression, of the violation of taboo—the sort of pleasure that a small boy may derive from saying a "naughty word" and which, in the case of adults, may be derived from telling or hearing a "dirty joke." In the case of the limerick, the transgression is encapsulated in a pithy and memorable form—the "space that is quite economical," as the limerick quoted earlier puts it. Because the mention of religion in the context of obscenity serves to heighten the sense of transgression (as earlier), it is not surprising that a considerable number of ribald or obscene limericks have a religious setting:

There was a young lady named Alice
Who peed in a Catholic chalice.
The Padre agreed
'Twas done out of need,
And not out of Protestant malice.

No further examples will be given here, but the reader is left to imagine the possibilities offered by a first line such as "The jolly old Bishop of Buckingham. . . ."

This analysis certainly accords with the observation that, although many limericks (both clean and dirty) are by unknown hands, those historical authors whose identity is known are, almost without exception, men—exclusively so in the case of bawdy or obscene works. A related observation is that when women appear in bawdy limericks, it is often as victims or villains—certainly in a manner that would be regarded by feminists (among others) as sexist.

Limericks in Other Languages

The limerick seems a quintessentially Anglo-Saxon phenomenon, a reliable signal of humor in English. Attempts have been made to explain this by reference to the peculiarly malleable nature of the English language. For instance, in the line *The limerick packs laughs anatomical* the word *limerick* needs to be pronounced *lim'rick* if the line is to scan correctly—a possibility not available in more rigidly structured languages. There is no doubt some truth in this argument. A number of other (European) languages also tend to have their own favored verse forms, which make use of a simple rhyming scheme to convey humorous or ironic intent (e.g., the Russian *chastuska,* the Spanish *quintilla*), forms which are in each case better suited than the limerick form to the cadences of that language.

This is not to say, however, that other (particularly European) languages are incapable of being turned to the limerick form. A frequently quoted example is the French,

Il était un homme de Madère
Qui a frappé le nez à son père.
On demanda: 'Pourquoi?'
Il répondit: 'Ma foi!
Vous n'avez pas connu mon père!'

It should be noted, however, that this limerick is the work of the French-born but English-raised George du Maurier (the son of Sir Gerald mentioned earlier), who helpfully provided a translation:

A young man from Madeira arose
And punched his progenitor's nose;
When the people asked, 'Why?'
He responded, 'My eye!
You don't know the old man, I suppose.'

George du Maurier wrote a number of such limericks, another example being the following:

Il était un gendarme à Nanteuil
Qui n'avait qu'une dent et qu'un œil,
Mais cet œil solitaire
Était plein de mystère,
Cette dent, d'importance et d'orgueil.

[Translation: There was a gendarme in Nanteuil, who had only one tooth and one eye. But that lone eye was full of mystery, while the tooth was full of pride and self-importance.]

In fact a good many of the limericks written in other languages are essentially virtuoso pieces by native speakers of English. There are exceptions, however, and indeed there was something of a craze for the limerick form in Germany during the 1990s. The following example—a "limerick of co-ordinated orthography," no less—appeared in a German newspaper in 1994:

Ein Spanier mit Namen Rodriguez,
Der kaufte ein Pferd und bestiguez.
Doch war dieser Gaul
Selbst zum Fressen zu faul;
Nur der Pferdehändler verschwiguez.

Here, the last words of lines two and three would normally be written *bestieg es* and *verschwieg es.* The limerick is clever rather than amusing, an approximate translation being: "A Spaniard by the name of Rodriguez bought a horse and mounted it. But this nag was too worthless even to be turned into horsemeat—though the horse-dealer kept that a secret."

Common Characteristics

Attempts have been made to propose a general theory that would account for the peculiar charm exerted by the limerick, whatever its subject. One theory is that the first line introduces the main character, the second describes the character's action, the third and fourth (their brevity intensifying the suspense) develop or explain the action, and the fifth reveals its *dénouement* in a startling manner. While instructive as far as it goes, this explanation applies chiefly if not solely to those limericks beginning "There was a . . . /Who . . ." (or one of the many variants of this formula). Other writers, noting that many limericks have a first line ending in a place-name (usually the protagonist's place of origin), refer to the suspense leading up to the clever rhyme on the town's name in the final line.

Neither of these theories is applicable to all limericks. Clearly there is something inherent in the very *form* of the limerick—in the jogging rhythm and arrangement of the lines—that appeals to our innate sense of humor. It is difficult to imagine a "serious" limerick, given that even those written on intellectual topics treat them in a humorous way.

This account does not propose any general theory applicable to all limericks, but it does note that—in the case of "non-Lear" limericks at least—the lead-up to the all-important last line, with its deftly surprising play on the rhyme with lines 1 and 2, has certain affinities with the classical symphony or concerto. In the case of the musical work, an opening statement of the theme or themes (perhaps *allegro* or *maestoso*) may be followed by a movement marked *adagio* or *andante* (or better still *adagietto*), to come to a climax in an *allegro vivace* or *con brio* that brings the work to a dazzling conclusion. Such a progression is deeply satisfying—in the sense of an expectation aroused, wittily elaborated on, and then triumphantly answered—corresponding perhaps to a deep-seated pattern within the human psyche.

Subverting Expectations

So familiar has the limerick form become that some writers have enjoyed toying with the expectations of readers:

A bather whose clothing was strewed
By breezes that left her quite nude
Saw a man come along
And, unless I am wrong,
You expected this line to be lewd.

In another example, the point of the limerick is the assumption that the reader or listener, on hearing the words ending the first and third lines, will be anticipating that the corresponding rhymes will be of an obscene nature:

There was a young lady named Tuck
Who had the most terrible luck.
She went out on a punt
And fell off the front
And was bit on the leg by a duck.

An extreme form of the subversion of expectations is sometimes referred to as an "anti-limerick." For example, Edward Lear wrote:

There was an old man in a tree,
Who was horribly bored by a bee.
When they said, "Does it buzz?"
He replied, "Yes, it does.
It's a regular brute of a bee."

An anti-limerick version, attributed variously to W. S. Gilbert and George Bernard Shaw, runs as follows:

There was an old man of St. Bees,
Who was stung in the arm by a wasp.
When asked, "Does it hurt?"
He replied, "No, it doesn't;
I'm so glad that it wasn't a hornet."

Of many further examples of the subversion of expectations, one of the best known is the following:

There was a young man from Japan
Whose limericks never would scan.
When they asked him, "Why?"
He replied with a sigh:
"It's because I always try to fit as many words
into the last line as I possibly can."

An opposite approach is taken in the following example:

A limerick fan from Australia
Regarded his work as a failure.
His verses were fine
Until the fourth line. . . .

And the even more extreme

There once was a man from Peru
Whose limericks stopped at line two.

Whereas the ribald or obscene limerick is certainly the single most common type in terms of subject matter, it cannot be claimed as the sole natural form of expression of the limerick genre, nor even as the most amusing. That the limerick has come so far in the past 200 years testifies to its enduring attraction for all lovers of whimsy and nonsense, especially those who are fascinated by the skillful arrangement of words.

Kenneth R. Dutton

See also Absurdist Humor; Children's Humor Stages; College Humor; Gender Roles in Humor; Nonsense; Obscenity; Poetry; Punch Line; Puns; *Share*; *Xiehouyu*

Further Readings

Baring-Gould, W. S. (1968). *The lure of the limerick: An uninhibited history.* London, UK: Panther.

Cohen, J. M. (Ed.). (1952). *The Penguin book of comic and curious verse.* Harmondsworth, UK: Penguin.

Legman, G. (Ed.). (1976). *The limerick.* London, UK: Panther.

Lehmann, J. (1977). *Edward Lear and his world.* London, UK: Thames & Hudson.

Reed, H. L. (1925). *The complete limerick book.* New York, NY: G. P. Putnam's Sons.

Linguistic Theories of Humor

Linguistic theories of humor are theoretical models of humor that take into account only verbal or written text. The purpose of linguistic theories of humor is to analyze jokes based on information that is stated in the text, without taking into account outside factors, such as how well a joke is delivered or what kind of audience would find it humorous. As such, these theories deal with humor competence rather than with humor performance. This entry outlines a family of linguistic theories that attempt to describe generic humorous texts but are typically applied to short jokes.

Although humor is largely recognized as a multidisciplinary field, linguistic theories of humor are based predominantly on linguistic analysis and comparison. As such, the family of linguistic theories takes into account morphology (the study of word parts and parts of speech), phonology (the study of language sounds, with their variants, or allophones, and more important word-distinguishing invariants, or phonemes), syntax (the study of how a sentence is structured), semantics (the study of word, or lexical, and sentence, or compositional, meaning), and pragmatics (the study of individualized and contextual semantics).

Jokes typically vary in length, topic, and description. The goal of a linguistic theory of humor is to determine whether any given text can be humorous (based on its text only) or to compare any two or more humorous texts. It is possible to restrict the application of a theory to a particular topic or a genre of text, but the theory itself does not have to be modified for such applications. As with any generalized theory, linguistic theories of humor describe the phenomena at a very coarse grain, and thus it is possible to add finer grain mechanisms to enrich the analysis for humor subgenres (one-liners, puns, etc.).

Script-Based Semantic Theory of Humor

The script-based semantic theory of humor is arguably the first and oldest linguistic theory of humor. According to the theory, any joke-carrying text is compatible, fully or in part, with two different scripts that overlap and oppose. To simplify the matter, if a text activates two different situations that a person is aware of, and some kind of oppositeness between these situations is found, the text satisfies the linguistic criteria to be a joke.

In more formal terms, a script is a sequence of events that are associated with the constituent word meanings and evoked by specific words. Any script can also be considered as a cognitive structure that represents a person's knowledge of a small part of the world.

The scripts can be linguistic, general knowledge, restricted, or individual. Linguistic scripts are known to any "average," "standard" native speaker (adult, reasonably educated, mainstream culture, etc.). General knowledge scripts, such as crossing the street or going to a store, are known to a large number of people and are not affected by their use of language. Restricted knowledge scripts are known to a smaller number of people and are not affected by their use of language.

According to Victor Raskin, who developed the theory, intentional verbal humor is based on ambiguity that is created deliberately. However, ambiguity by itself is not enough for humor: The scripts must not only be opposed, they must be so unexpectedly. This means that if one expects both scripts to appear, the text will not be found humorous. Some other examples of oppositeness are *good/*

bad, real/unreal, money/no money, life/death, and so forth.

There may be more than one pair of scripts associated with any joke. For example, in "A man walks into a bar. Ouch," there are at least two associated scripts. The first one describes entering a bar. It is evoked by the words *man, walk in* (in the sense of entering), and *bar* (in the sense of a drinking establishment). The second one describes hitting something. It is evoked by the words *man, walk in* (in the sense of stumbling on), *bar* (in the sense of a long and round piece of wood or metal), and *ouch.* The overlap is obvious: words, some in different senses, are shared by both scripts. The oppositeness between the two scripts is *expected pleasure* versus *pain.* These two scripts are not the only ones that might be associated with the joke. Other activations may result from "man walking into a bar" being the setup of another joke; and, unexpectedly, being a punch line, triggered by the word *ouch.*

Just like scripts in jokes may be of different grain size (activate very small or very large cognitive structures), script oppositeness can vary too. Typically it is agreed that oppositeness in a pair of scripts can be treated as antonyms: situational, contextual, or local. These general-type antonyms are rarely found in text, but they are easily identified by any native speaker who reads a joke.

General Theory of Verbal Humor

The general theory of verbal humor, proposed by Raskin and Salvatore Attardo in 1991, enriches the script-based semantic theory of humor by adding five knowledge resources to script-based text description. These five knowledge resources are *logical mechanism*, *situation*, *target*, *narrative strategy*, and *language of the joke*. It should be noted that although the theory relies on the linguistic toolset, it is informed by other disciplines that study phenomena described by the resources.

Each of the knowledge resources has its purpose: *Logical mechanism* accounts for the way in which the two scripts in the joke are brought together, the pseudological reasoning in a text. *Situation* accounts for the textual materials evoked by the scripts of the joke that are not necessarily funny. *Target* is a stereotypical individual or group from whom humorous behavior is expected. *Narrative strategy* describes the rhetorical structure of the text, such as the riddle, 1-2-3 structure, question and answer, or other. Finally, *language* is the actual lexical, syntactic, and phonological choices at the linguistic level that instantiate all the other choices.

The general theory of verbal humor provides an ability to describe any joke in terms of its six knowledge resources, with a possible omission of a target, which is optional. Such a description enables joke comparison, which becomes part of the scope of humor analysis. The theory predicts that the similarity of jokes is based on the number of similar knowledge resources: A pair of jokes that has three identical knowledge resources is more similar than a pair of jokes that has only two. A similarity of jokes with an equal number of identical knowledge resources is rated according to where the said resources are in the knowledge resource hierarchy. Such a hypothesis was based on the notion of top-down gradual restriction of the resources: The higher level resource may dictate the choice of that on a lower level. The hypothesis was generally confirmed in a 1993 experiment by Willibald Ruch, Attardo, and Raskin. The only exception was found to be the logical mechanism, which continues to be the most controversial of the six resources.

Ontological Semantic Theory of Humor

The description and analysis of the previous two theories rely on the native speaker's knowledge and interpretation of a joke. The latest incarnation of the script-based theories attempts to formalize such knowledge and remove human bias from such interpretations.

The early idea behind the script-based family of theories was that it would only be fully formalized when the semantic component of language processing could be automated or formalized. With the development of semantic technologies for text understanding, such formalization becomes possible. The goal of the ontological semantic theory of humor is to put the previous version of the script-based humor theories on a firm semantic basis. As such, it does not add any new resources to the humor toolkit but instead formalizes the use of the existing one.

Ontological semantic theory of humor is based on ontological semantics technology—a theory, methodology, and implementation of text interpretation by a machine. As such, it contains a generic model of the world that is shared by most native speakers and lexical definitions of various meanings of words. What it means for a script-based humor theory is that the scripts of the jokes that are evoked by the specific words can now be uniformly accessed and represented. It also means that the size (or grain size) of a script becomes explicit, together with all information that it contains.

The question of computational overlap and oppositeness can be formalized according to the tools of ontological semantic technology. It also means that the falsification of the theory can be taken one step further and becomes not a matter of opinions but a matter of formal logical reasoning.

The scripts are not the only knowledge resources that can be represented in the ontological semantic theory of humor. With the exception of logical mechanism, which requires additional handling respective to regular text processing, all other resources can be compared for their similarity. Because of the mathematically driven nature of the semantic description, the similarity of a more generic description will be lower than a similarity of a less generic description. For example, the similarity between jokes in which the targets are Polish American and Irish, respectively, is likely to be greater than jokes in which the targets are human and animal, respectively (provided that all other knowledge resources are the same). This is so because both members of the first pair of targets are human, and therefore they diverge in the graph at a lower, finer grain level than the second pair.

The ontological semantic theory of humor was not meant as a replacement of its predecessors but rather as a next-level formalization of them. As such, it should not be used for informal analysis of humorous texts in general and jokes in particular. Its significance lies in the fact that script-based semantic theory of humor was premised on the development of a computational system providing the semantic interpretation of text. Such a system was not available at the time, and its development currently renders the approach more realistic.

Julia M. Taylor

See also Humor Theories; Jokes; Linguistics; Punch Line; Puns

Further Readings

Attardo, S. (1994). *Linguistic theories of humor.* Berlin, Germany: Mouton de Gruyter.

Attardo, S. (2008). Semantics and pragmatics of humor. *Language and Linguistics Compass, 2*(6), 1203–1215.

Attardo, S., & Raskin, V. (1991). Script theory revis(it)ed: Joke similarity and joke representation model. *HUMOR: International Journal of Humor Research, 4*(3–4), 293–347.

Raskin, V. (1985). *Semantic mechanisms of humor.* Dordrecht, Netherlands: Reidel.

Raskin, V., Hempelmann, C. F., & Taylor, J. M. (2009) How to understand and assess a theory: The evolution of the SSTH into the GTVH and now into the OSTH, *Journal of Literary Theory, 3*(2), 285–312.

Ruch, W., Attardo, S., & Raskin, V. (1993). Toward an empirical verification of the general theory of verbal humor. *HUMOR: International Journal of Humor Research, 6*(2), 123–136.

Linguistics

Linguistics is a well-established academic discipline with a vast area of research and multiple applications. Linguistics has also been a leading contributor to the multidisciplinary area of humor research because humor is very often verbal. This entry discusses some pertinent elements of linguistics and their contributions to the study of humor.

Linguistics as an Academic Discipline

Linguistics is an academic discipline that studies language as a universal human faculty. Linguistics, in its various aspects, spans the humanities, social sciences, hard sciences, engineering, and technology because all these groups of disciplines use language and depend on certain aspects of it, in one way or another.

Linguistics is also one of the most ancient areas of research. The first grammatical description of a language, namely, Sanskrit, an ancient language of India, was written in verse by Panini several millennia ago. Historically and individually, people become aware of linguistic facts when they encounter a foreign language for the first time. Panini wanted to describe Sanskrit, the language of the Hindu sacred texts, as it was giving way to colloquial dialects that later developed into Hindi, Urdu, and several other languages of modern India.

Language is viewed by contemporary linguists as a complex dynamic structure of interrelated elements governed by a large number of intricate rules that are internalized in the minds of the native speakers, who use these rules without necessarily being aware of them or being able to formulate them correctly. Since Noam Chomsky's "revolution" in linguistics in the late 1950s to mid-1960s, linguistics has also been seen as a principal contributor to cognitive science, and its goal is to explicate these rules, some of which are universal (i.e., the same for all natural languages) and others language-specific. These rules also afford greater access to the study of the human mind than most other cognitive disciplines. Humor also offers a window to the mind, with or without language.

Language is essentially a mechanism for constructing a complexly organized set of pairings between sounds and meanings. Whatever we say normally has a sound (a sign, for the hearing impaired) and conveys a meaning. The sound is studied by the linguistic subdiscipline of phonology, a theoretical expression of the empirical findings by phonetics, assisted by acoustics. The meaning is studied by semantics, accompanied by pragmatics: the former studies meaning more generally while pragmatics customizes and contextualizes it.

Mediating the pairings is the complex edifice of syntax, the study of sentential structure, that is, how the words of a language are assembled by native speakers into sentences. Syntax depends on morphology, the study of the structure of words and, especially, their membership in parts of speech that defines their behavior in sentences, so that nouns are typically subjects and objects, verbs predicates, adjectives attributes, and so on.

Syntax also interfaces with semantics, the study of meaning at the other end of the pairings, because the words of a sentence contribute their meanings to that of the sentence in the order imposed by the syntactic structure. If semantics is in charge of the general and generic meaning of words and sentences, pragmatics customizes and contextualizes it, thus adding another level of complexity to language structure by reflecting individual, group, and situational differences of usage. The latter is particularly attuned to the social aspects of language use.

Linguistics of Humor

Linguistics has become a major disciplinary contributor to the multidisciplinary field of humor research, catching up with and perhaps overtaking psychology in this role. Characteristically, it has achieved this role as a result of expanded linguistic expertise applied to humor research. Before the late 1970s, the term *linguistic humor* was reserved for simple puns, and no linguistic knowledge was used in their treatment. This formerly limited view is easy to explain: In spite of its ancient origins and the essential role of language in human society, linguistics remains largely unknown to all but a small army of researchers. It is not generally studied in high school, and precious little of it trickles down into English or foreign language classes. It is not at all uncommon for highly educated people in other academic disciplines and outside of academia to ignore almost entirely the huge purview of linguistics and the accumulation of technical information about language. It is a plausible guess, then, that the only reason puns became associated with linguistics is that they are usually untranslatable from language to language. In fact, there are some interlanguage jokes playing up this non-translatability as illustrated by the so-called false friends, cognate words whose meanings have diverged in different languages: for instance, an old joke about a diplomatic conflict because an English diplomat mistook his French colleague's declaring himself to be *deçu* (disappointed, from Fr. *decevoir*) for a charge of being deceived (from Engl. *deceive*), that is, lied to by the English.

Verbal jokes can be based on virtually any level of language structure, namely, sound, word, or sentence. At the level of *sound*, phonetically rather than phonologically, various deviations from the normative pronunciation may serve as a basis for imputed or real accents associated, often falsely, with joke targets. These targets may range from socioeconomic minorities, including recent immigrants, to pompous British aristocracy. Enriched with certain prosodic, intonational features, these pronunciations may claim similarity to, say, Yiddish, Black, or gay speech mannerisms. Certain sound distortions may confuse words for a comic effect. Some similar-sounding words may be used in deliberately imperfect punning. Many jokes about George W. Bush, such as his purported pronunciation of *nuclear* as *nukelar,* ridiculed him as uneducated. Dave Letterman, himself a native of Indiana, used to make fun of the Hoosier pronunciation of *special* as *spatial.*

The brief dialogue, "*But you love me!*"—"*-ed,*" is more readily understood as funny when read and probably not funny at all to the first interlocutor, just informed of a romantic break-up. The past tense suffix *-ed* was used similarly—and possibly, originally—in a Harold Pinter absurdist play, which probably suggests a marginal, avant-garde usage. It is one of the clear cases of using *morphology* for potentially humorous effect. Another example would be to add the feminine gender suffix to create non-existent words like *boss-ess,* probably for a misogynistic effect. Bush, again, was ridiculed for lumping prefixes *mis-* and *under-* in his infamous complaint about being "misunderestimated."

Syntactic ambiguity, exhaustively explored by Dallin D. Oaks Jr., can be exploited for humor, as in "Visiting professors can be boring."—"So, don't visit them!" The intended meaning of the first cue is, most likely, about professors who are visiting rather than being visited, and the hearer is, again most likely, choosing the marginal but structurally possible interpretation on purpose in order to create, probably in jest, a hostile situational, or spontaneous, joke. Thus, current humor research depends heavily on just about any linguistic subdiscipline but especially heavily and often intricately so on semantics and pragmatics.

Victor Raskin

See also Ambiguity; Dialect Humor; Jokes; Linguistic Theories of Humor; Maxim; Puns; Semantics; Social Interaction; Speech Play

Further Readings

Attardo, S. (1994). *Linguistic theories of humor.* Berlin, Germany: Mouton de Gruyter.

Hempelmann, C. F. (2003). *Paronomasic puns: Target recoverability towards automatic generation* (Unpublished doctoral dissertation). Purdue University, West Lafayette, IN.

Oaks, D. D. (2010). *Structural ambiguity in English* (Vols. 1 & 2). London, UK: Continuum.

Pepicello, W. J., & Weisberg, R. W. (1983). Linguistics and humor. In P. E. McGhee & J. H. Goldstein (Eds.), *Handbook of humor research* (Vols. 1, pp. 59–83). New York, NY: Springer.

Raskin, V. (1985). *Semantic mechanisms of humor.* Dordrecht, Netherlands: Reidel.

Raskin, V. (Ed.). (2008). *The primer of humor research.* Berlin, Germany: Mouton de Gruyter.

Literature

Whatever language it is written in, literature is a reflection of cultural preoccupations and thus is a useful way of studying humor across languages, cultures, and time periods. Even the oldest recorded works—whether performance texts, poems, or prose narratives—display a range of types of humor, from farcical foolery to more serious satire and witty debate. This suggests that humor has formed an essential part of literature from the beginning and that those aspects of human life we call comic or humorous—whether experienced by oneself or by others—are as important to the literary approach as are the nonhumorous.

In fact, the development of some literary genres—dramatic comedy, for example, and especially the novel, a relatively late arrival on the literary scene—was accompanied by an evolving awareness of, and discussion about, the nature of humor and the comic. Thus, in ancient Athens, where tragedy and comedy first took formal shape, humor was the subject of philosophical and aesthetic speculation. While joking and the craft of comedy form a self-conscious theme in Aristophanes's play *Frogs* (404 BCE), Aristotle's *Poetics* (ca. 335 BCE) is the first known book to examine systematically laughter and the comic in literature. Although the section dedicated to dramatic comedy has not survived, its structural outline is probably recorded in the 10th-century manuscript the *Tractatus Coislinianus* (from the library of Henri-Charles du Cambout, Duc de Coislin, and published in 1839). This may have formed a pupil's notes of an Aristotelian lecture on comedy complementing the writings on tragedy and the epic found in the *Poetics*. Similarly, in the period in which the novel was emerging as a new genre, European men of letters were actively canvassing the notion that a sense of humor might be a desirable civilizing trait.

Comedy is a performative humorous genre, intended to be watched as well as read for enjoyment. It is not always of literary merit, as is recognized by the traditional distinction between "high comedy" (verbal comedy with literary aspirations) and "low comedy" (more visual, dependent on practical joking and stock characterization). Drama amounts to words in action, and most comic texts intended for performance will combine both registers, the high and the low. Because literary texts (the focus of this entry) are intended more for reading than for enactment or recitation, their humor is chiefly mediated by verbal techniques. Despite this, literary humor must involve the reader in visualizing the scenes and characters described in words, so that words are also accompanied by mental images.

Comic Characterization

Whether literary humor is dramatic or narrative, at its heart lies humor derived from the creation and doings of individual comic characters: These are its most memorable creations—a long line of larger-than-life but seemingly real people striding down the ages. Some are warmly funny, some grotesquely nightmarish, but all are memorable. They include masterpieces of comic genius such as Moliere's Tartuffe, Miguel de Cervantes's Don Quijote, William Shakespeare's Falstaff, Laurence Sterne's Tristram Shandy, Wu Cheng'en's Monkey, Anton Chekhov's Uncle Vanya, Jane Austen's Mrs. Bennett, Oscar Wilde's Lady Bracknell, and Alfred Jarry's Ubu the King. In studying literary humor, then, the usual theories of verbal humor, incongruity, and superiority prove inadequate: Such lively creations defy one-dimensional frameworks. Analysis of comedy of character requires some of the traditional tools of literary and genre studies—even when dealing with flat stereotypes and especially when fully rounded, psychologically valid personalities are concerned.

Early Literary Humor

Comic scenes are found in the world's first known literary texts. The *Epic of Gilgamesh* is probably the oldest surviving written narrative, inscribed on 12 clay tablets from ancient Sumeria in approximately 2000 BCE. As described by Barbara Babcock (1978, pp. 14–15), it includes a comic role reversal for the Goddess Ishtar who becomes a humanly spiteful, jealous female when spurned by the hero, Gilgamesh. The Bible itself possesses a tragedy that becomes a comedy—the book of Job, which concludes with Job being promised 140 happy years and the words "Behold, happy is the man whom God correcteth" (5:17, *King James Version*). Homer's *The Odyssey* has been described as poetic high comedy for its structure and individual scenes of sulking heroes and their tricksy behavior. Indeed, many works of classical Greco-Roman literature embraced the funny and the ridiculous, along with heroic characters and deeds. Verbal humor such as riddles and wordplay form a vital part of traditions such as Old Norse and Anglo-Saxon sagas, and they also feature in the records of early Chinese emperors whose jesting court wits used puns (*huaji*) to entertain but also advise their semi-divine rulers. As scholars such as Erich Auerbach and Northrop Frye have pointed out, these early literary records suggest that our forefathers around the world recognized and embraced what was humorous as an essential part of the human condition.

One highly influential early form was Menippean satire, named after the Greek poet Menippus, whose idiomatic diatribes are now lost. Roman satiric poets Varro (116–27 BCE) and Lucian (ca. 120–180 CE) wrote in this idiom, mixing prose and poetry and establishing the preeminent mode of surviving classical prose narratives. Influencing writers as varied as Petronius and Appian, followed in the Renaissance by Rabelais, Cervantes, and their successors, Menippean satire's flexible, often comically anarchic form points forward to the rise of the most important form for literary humor, the novel.

Other literary forms celebrating humor include narrative poetry—essentially storytelling in verse. Early European vernacular examples include Pierre de Saint-Cloud's *Roman de Renart* (ca. 1170, drawing on an earlier Latin comic poem). This author wrote tales of trickery and cunning among a group of anthropomorphic animals to satirize the clergy and aristocracy. Geoffrey Chaucer's *Canterbury Tales* (ca. 1380–1400), a series of comic and often ribald tales recounted by a group of would-be pilgrims, is one of the earliest and most enduring literary works printed in English. Prose narrative was also important and in this area Italian man of letters Boccaccio (1313–1375) was exceptionally influential. In his book *Decameron* (ca. 1349–1352), he created amusing themes and tropes that would appear in many other forms—drama, poetry, and novels—over the following centuries. Medieval prose humor also bequeathed later writers a rich stock of entertaining stories such as the French *fabliaux* and German *Schwänke* (amusing tales). Adopting the veneer of a moral message helped ensure that such amusements survived when writing was a rare skill and written records were costly objects.

Humor and the Evolution of the Novel

The development of printing increased the circulation of all kinds of literary works, encouraging the rise of longer, character-based and increasingly self-conscious prose narratives—important for the development of the novel. The European Renaissance brought a renewal of interest in Menippean texts like Petronius's *Satyricon* (late 1st century CE) and Apuleuis's *The Golden Ass* (late 2nd century CE). These influenced the development of prose genres such as the picaresque, in which a typically roguish and lower class protagonist meets with a series of (usually humorous) adventures set in a grittily realistic satirical narrative world. Usually dated from the anonymous novella *Lazarillo de Tormes* (1554), picaresque was popular in 16th-century Spain before spreading across Europe. It was an important comic milestone in the development of the novel. Its episodic, often plotless structure embraced humor that was frequently cruel and was supplanted at the beginning of the 18th century by developments in narrative technique and more sympathetic types of humor. The genre influenced many later humorous works, including Paul Scarron's *Roman Comique* (Comic Novel, 1651–1657), Henry Fielding's *Tom Jones* (1749), Denis Diderot's *Jacques the Fatalist and His Master* (1778–1796), and Mark Twain's *Adventures of Huckleberry Finn* (1884).

Also drawing on the Menippean tradition, the five books of François Rabelais's *Gargantua and Pantagruel* cycle (1532–1552) recount the adventures of a family of grotesque giants, using a large range of comic devices to explore the shift in worldview from medieval scholasticism to Renaissance humanism. This latter perspective informs the view of laughter in *Gargantua's* preface ("It is better to write about laughter than tears / For laughter is particular to man"), using a quotation from Aristotle to highlight the role of laughter in humanist thought. Addressed "To the reader" (whom Rabelais goes on, jokingly, to insult), this preface also flags the humorous potential of literary self-consciousness, where a text breaks the narrative illusion by knowingly flaunting its status as fiction and/or as a printed book. Narrative self-consciousness, a comic device used since antiquity, became significant in the developing economy of writers and readers (and, by extension, narrators and characters) that characterized the evolution of the novel.

More carefully structured than Rabelais's work but also incorporating elements of picaresque humor, Cervantes's *Don Quijote* (1605–1615) is regarded as an archetype for later self-conscious novels. Its hero takes the chivalric romances with which he obsessed as a template for interacting with reality, and many of the characters in the second part of the novel (published 10 years after the first part—after several unauthorized continuations) encounter Don Quijote both as a figure belonging to their narrative world and as a character belonging to other narratives (by Cervantes or his imitators) they have read. This existential incongruity is mirrored by Cervantes's constant play with narrative framing, such as shifting mid-scene from an anonymous third-person narrator to what is presented as a (potentially biased and unreliable) translation from an Arabic manuscript found by chance in a marketplace (Part 1, Chapters 8–9). Don Quijote's best known antics, such as tilting at the windmills he mistakes for giants, mark him out as an object of ridicule, but the multiple embedded incongruities in Cervantes's narrative also provide a rich source of less aggressive, more conceptual, even whimsical humor that focuses attention on the relationship among text, character, and reader. These experiments in narrative self-consciousness resonate with the shifting use of the English term *humor* from its earlier, medical sense of an involuntary imbalance of bodily fluids to the developing early modern sense of an affected, often comic, eccentricity (exemplified in the "humor comedies" of Cervantes's near-contemporary Ben Jonson, such as *Every Man in His Humour,* 1598). While cruel and aggressive laughter did not disappear from humorous literature, the rise of the self-conscious novel shows how evolutions in literary form reflect conceptual developments about humor itself.

At least in Western Europe, the main traditions of humorous literature in the 17th and 18th centuries tend to reflect the divide between proponents of what are now termed *superiority theories* (e.g., Thomas Hobbes, 1588–1679) and *incongruity theories* (e.g., the Third Earl of Shaftesbury, 1671–1713). The former, mainly satirical, tradition includes works of both poetry and prose, often emulating classical literary forms. Mock epic poetry remained popular, such as Paul Scarron's *Virgile Travesti* (1648–1653, parodying Virgil's *Aeneid*), Samuel Butler's *Hudibras* (1663–1684), and Alexander Pope's *The Rape of the Lock* (1712–1717). The Quarrel of the Ancients and Moderns—a debate over classicism in art and literature in both France and England at the turn of the 18th century—provided Jonathan Swift with the theme for his 1704 prose satire, *The Battle of the Books.* Another strand of prose satire, seen in works like Swift's *Gulliver's Travels* (1729), Cyrano de Bergerac's *Other Worlds: The Comical History of the States and Empires of the Moon and Sun* (1657–1662), and Voltaire's *Micromégas* (1752), uses the trope of fantastical worlds as a means to satirize contemporary society. Better remembered today as a philosopher than a satirist, Voltaire also influenced the 18th- and 19th-century tradition of the *conte philosophique* (philosophical tale) with works like *Candide* (1759), whose picaresque plot and sarcastic tone lampoon contemporary Leibnizian optimism as well as politics and religion.

Overlapping with this satirical tradition, a slightly later strand of humorous literature drew on the emerging formal conventions of the novel and came to be associated with a gentler understanding of humor based on incongruity and self-conscious eccentricity. Works like Henry Fielding's *Shamela* (1741) and *Joseph Andrews* (1742) parodied—but also incorporated—the epistolary form and sentimental subject matter of Samuel Richardson's popular novel *Pamela* (1740). Transposing Cervantes's parody of chivalric romance literature onto a contemporary literary economy, this technique allowed Fielding and his contemporaries to combine the self-conscious narrative incongruities of *Don Quijote* with interest in psychological realism. Characters like the scheming, distinctly unchaste Shamela do not undergo the moral development associated with the later *Bildungsroman* but are more often celebrated for their human eccentricities than targeted as objects of satire. Fielding extends these humorous characterizations outward by playing on the implied existential divide between (fictional) narrators and characters and (real) authors and readers. His preface to *Tom Jones* (1749) states, "An Author ought to consider himself, not as a gentleman . . . but rather as one who keeps a public Ordinary [eating house], to which all persons are welcome for their money."

The novel form encouraged this self-conscious technique, which was taken to even greater extremes in Laurence Sterne's *Life and Opinions of Tristram Shandy, Gentleman* (1759–1768), whose narrator frequently breaks off to address, and sometimes comically abuse, his implied reader. His supposed attempt at an unabridged autobiography is soon overtaken by narrative digressions and typographical games, which allow this narrator to associate both himself and his eccentric family with the joyful philosophy of "Shandyism," self-consciously invoking both Rabelais's grotesque "Pantagruelism" and Sancho Panza's desire for a "kingdom of hearty laughing subjects" in Cervantes's *Don Quijote* (Vol. 4, Chapter 32). *Tristram Shandy* thus represents a milestone in the development of the self-conscious novel during the 18th century as well as one in the evolving understanding of humor.

Eclipse and Return of the Self-Conscious Novel

Cervantes and Sterne influenced German Romantic philosophers, including Jean Paul Richter, whose *School of Aesthetics* (1804) set out a recognizably modern theory of humor (as opposed to laughter or ridicule) at the turn of the 19th century. In France, Sterne's sentimental humor was echoed in shorter works by writers like Xavier de Maistre (1763–1852) and Alphonse Karr (1808–1890). Across Europe, writers like Heinrich Heine (1797–1856) and Nicolai Gogol (1809–1852) combined humorous writing with romantic sensibility. Gogol's use of grotesque imagery in works like *The Nose* (1836)—in which a bureaucrat's nose leaves his face and takes on a life of its own—influenced many 20th-century surrealists.

As Robert Alter has noted (1975, Chapter 4), the humorous, self-conscious novel was largely eclipsed during the 19th century by a focus on narrative realism. Self-conscious humor nevertheless remained a localized feature of many full-length novels, such as Gustave Flaubert's *Madame Bovary* (1857, which borrows several elements from *Don Quijote*) and Charles Dickens's *Great Expectations* (1861, whose eccentric characters Wemmick and his Aged Parent resemble Uncle Toby and Corporal Trim from *Tristram Shandy*). But at least in Western Europe, the main focus of literary humor moved away from the novel and toward other genres. One was nonsense poetry, exemplified in the work of Edward Lear (1812–1888); another was children's literature, such as the *Alice* books of Lewis Carroll (1832–1898). Both continued the tradition of essentially gentle, reflexive humor but in a different way: Lear's made-up words and phrases shift the narrative incongruities of the self-conscious novel onto language itself, while Carroll (the mathematician Charles Dodgson) exploited the humorous potential of the logical inversions and absurdities that govern his writings. They formed an important model for whimsical, Anglophile French *humoristes* of the late 19th century such as Alphonse Allais (1854–1905) and Tristan Bernard (1866–1947), who are mainly known for witticisms, short stories, and press articles. Oscar Wilde (1854–1900) is likewise remembered for his witty epigrams as well as his stage plays (such as *The Importance of Being Earnest*, 1895) and short stories, which combined wittiness with memorably comic characterization. His only novel (*The Picture of Dorian Gray*, 1890) is essentially serious in tone despite its provocative subject matter.

An important exception is George Meredith's influential novel *The Egoist* (1879), consciously exemplifying his theoretical views about humor published in *An Essay on Comedy and the Uses of the Comic Spirit* (1877). The novel's subtitle is "A Comedy in Narrative," and its characters both interact as in drama and speak via the narrator to the audience as they cross-examine—and deceive—themselves. Self-awareness and the ability to laugh at oneself are held up as essential for a fully rounded human being, reflecting Meredith's understanding—like that of Shaftesbury nearly two centuries before him—that the comic is a means of criticizing society and an individual in order to civilize both.

From Humor to Irony and Beyond

The advent of 20th-century modernism marked a return to self-conscious literary humor as a key point in artistic experimentation. Influenced by turn-of-the-century writers such as Alfred Jarry (1873–1907) and Guillaume Apollinaire (1880–1918), writers of Dadaist, futurist, and surrealist persuasions used humor among other shock techniques to destabilize literary conventions. Luigi Pirandello's 1921 play *Six Characters in Search of an Author* presents the metatheatrical joke of a group of characters discussing the need for them to find a role to play. Pirandello's work also bridges from the tradition of Cervantes and Sterne to later humorous metafictional novels such as André Gide's *Les faux-monnayeurs* (The Counterfeiters, 1925), Flann O'Brien's *At Swim-Two-Birds* (1939), and Raymond Queneau's *Le vol d'Icare* (The Flight of Icarus, 1968). High modernist works like James Joyce's *Ulysses* (1922) combine self-conscious narrative techniques with a mixture of highly intellectual and often ribald humor that recalls the tradition of Rabelais and Menippean satire.

The effects of World War I inspired a short-lived tradition of acerbic satire in Weimar Germany and a turn toward absurdist humor in central and eastern Europe that was taken up in Paris after World War II by dramatists such as Samuel Beckett, Eugène Ionesco, Arthur Adamov, and Jean Genet in what is now known as thc *theater of the absurd*. Here, humor is combined with other destabilizing techniques to explore the demise of existential certainties—among them the very notion of a gentle, civilizing understanding of humor, which proved both vulnerable to, and a potential weapon against, the so-called postmodern death of affect. Beckett's experimental novel *How It Is* (1961) mentions a "deterioration of the sense of humor fewer tears too," wryly commenting on the apparent demise of both humor and tears while simultaneously engaging in a form of self-conscious metahumor. Some postwar movements, such as the French OuLiPo (Workshop for Potential Literature), responded to these concerns by retreating into formalist experimentation: Queneau's *Exercices de Style* (Exercises in Style, 1947), for example, repeats a single anecdote in 99 different literary styles. A more typical response was to focus on irony and self-detachment as do postmodern novels like Thomas Pynchon's *The Crying of Lot 49* (1966) and Don DeLillo's *White Noise* (1985). But in the novel—unlike the theater, where characters literally stride the stage, interact directly with the audience and impose their own personal empathetic bond—the shift in humorous tone was often a highly self-conscious one—a form of intellectualized irony without real laughter.

Thus in the West, the history of literary humor reflects evolving understanding of the nature and social codes of humor, while continuing traditions hark back to the earliest written comic narrative and poetic forms. Eastern literary canons including the Chinese and the Japanese also boast works of great literary humor. Recent scholarship by Weihe Xu has demonstrated how one of the greatest, the 18th-century novel *Honglou meng* (Romance of the Red Chamber, or Story of the Stone, by Cao Xueqin and Gao E) displays complex self-examination via humor on the part of its heroine, Xue Baochai. This long predates the advent of the modern concept of humor (Ch. *youmo*), promulgated by the literati Lin Yutang (1895–1976) and Qian Zhongshu (1910–1998) in 1930s Shanghai. Such anachronisms suggest that these traditions await full contextualization in terms of their own histories of the concepts of humor and laughter.

Will Noonan and Jessica Milner Davis

See also Absurdist Humor; Aristophanes; Aristotelian Theory of Humor; Boccaccio, Giovanni; Cervantes, Miguel de; Fabliau; Genres and Styles of Comedy; History of Humor: Classical and Traditional China; History of Humor: Early Modern Europe; History of Humor: Medieval Europe; History of Humor: Modern and Contemporary China; History of Humor: Modern and Contemporary Europe; History of Humor: Modern Japan; History of Humor: 19th-Century Europe; History of Humor: Premodern Japan; History of Humor: Renaissance Europe;

History of Humor: U.S. Frontier; History of Humor: U.S. Modern and Contemporary; *Huaji*-ists, The; Incongruity and Resolution; Inversion, Topsy-Turvy; Irony; Limericks; Molière; Nonsense; Parody; Pastiche; Pirandello, Luigi; Poetry; Postmodern Irony; Rabelais, François; Satire; Schwank; Science, Science Fiction, and Humor; Stereotypes; Tall Tale; Travesty; Trickster; Verbal Humor

Further Readings

Alter, R. (1975). *Partial magic: The novel as a self-conscious genre.* Berkeley: University of California Press.

Auerbach, E. (2003). *Mimesis: The representation of reality in western literature* (W. Trask, Trans.; 50th anniversary ed.). Princeton, NJ: Princeton University Press.

Babcock, B. A. (Ed.). (1978). *The reversible world: Symbolic inversion in art and society.* Ithaca, NY: Cornell University Press.

Blanchard, W. S. (1995). *Scholars' bedlam: Menippean satire in the Renaissance.* Lewisburg, PA: Bucknell University Press.

Clark, T. (2003). *A case for irony in* Beowulf, *with particular reference to its epithets.* Bern, Switzerland: Peter Lang.

Cornwell, N. (2006). *The absurd in literature.* Manchester, UK: Manchester University Press.

Frye, N. (1957). *Anatomy of criticism; four essays.* Princeton, NJ: Princeton University Press.

Hart, W. M. (1943). *High comedy in* The Odyssey. Berkeley: University of California Press.

Janko, R. (1984). *Aristotle on comedy: Towards a reconstruction of poetics II.* London, UK: Duckworth.

Meredith, G. (1927). *An essay on comedy and the uses of the comic spirit.* London, UK: Constable.

Pirandello, L. (1974). *On humor* (A. Illiano & D. P. Testa, Trans.). Chapel Hill: University of North Carolina Press.

Sangsue, D. (1987). *Le récit excentrique: Gautier, De Maistre, Nerval, Nodier* [Eccentric narratives: Gautier, De Maistre, Nerval, Nodier]. Paris, France: Corti.

Tigges, W. (1988). *Anatomy of literary nonsense.* Amsterdam, Netherlands: Rodopi.

Walls, A. (Ed.). (1891). *The book of Job.* New York, NY: Hunt & Haton. Retrieved from http://archive.org/stream/oldestdramainwor00wall#page/n3/mode/2up

Watt, I. (1957). *The rise of the novel.* London, UK: Chatto & Windus.

Xu, W. (2011). How humour humanizes a Confucian paragon: The case of Xue Baochai in *Honglou meng.* In J. Chey & J. Milner Davis (Eds.), *Humour in Chinese life and letters: Traditional and classical approaches* (pp. 139–167). Hong Kong: Hong Kong University Press.

Low Comedy

The term *low comedy* is usually paired with the term *high comedy*. Both are general categories usually applied to stage comedy and are performed by actors using either a full or partial script. Like high comedy, low comedy describes both the material (characters, actions, and dialogue) included and its performance style. However, it can also be used figuratively to describe real-life events or concepts that seem broadly to share that spirit or flavor of comedy, as when a comic novel or painting includes scenes of low comedy, such as the vignettes of pratfalls and mishaps included in Pieter Bruegel the Elder's *Netherlandish Proverbs* (1559) or the well-known footage in *Modern Times* (1936) of a hapless Charlie Chaplin being slowly spun through the massive cogs of an industrial machine.

The 2002 online version of the *Oxford English Dictionary* links low comedy to farce, defining it as "comedy in which the subject and treatment border upon farce," but in theatrical usage it refers more precisely to episodes or characters that raise cheap laughter requiring little skill on the part of the performer, who usually relies on the simple breaking of taboos, gratuitous references to what Mikhail Bakhtin (1968)—or at least his translator—delicately termed the *material bodily lower stratum* (meaning digestive, sexual, and excretory functions), slapstick as in pratfalls, and physical humiliations such as on-stage beatings. Low comedy can thus occur within a farce, but a farce may be high or low, depending on how cleverly wrought it is.

As it has an ancient heritage, the term *slapstick* deserves particular attention. The slap-stick is a stage prop traditionally used by clowns to produce the appearance and sound of hitting someone while not actually causing them bodily harm. In the Renaissance *commedia dell'arte*, it is the special prop for the masked character called Arlecchino (ancestor to the modern Harlequin, but minus the tearfulness associated with that mask). Usually from Bergamo in northern Italy, a town famous for its commercial to-and-fro, Arlecchino was a cunning, agile, and speedy servant, who, like a cat, successfully twisted his way out of trouble. His slapstick was made from two thin strips of wood that could be held as one, but, being separated at the handle by a short length of leather, could also be smartly slapped together to produce the appropriate cracking noise. Thus slapstick comedy refers specifically to low comedy that includes physical beatings.

Even in 5th century BCE Athens, the distinction between high and low in comedy was familiar to Aristophanes; for example, in the Prologue to *The Wasps,* the slave Xanthias says:

Don't expect anything profound,
Or any slapstick à la Megara.
And we got no slaves to dish out baskets
Of free nuts—or the old ham scene
Of Heracles cheated of his dinner;
. . . . Our little story
Has meat in it and a meaning not
Too far above your heads, but more
Worth your attention than low comedy.
(Aristophanes, 1970, Vol. 1, p. 171)

Not surprisingly, the play proceeds to serve up much knockabout fun.

Despite their antique origins, the distinction between low and high in comedy seems only to have been explicitly recognized in the early 17th century, when dramatists aspired to and discussed the suitability of classical models. Thus the Greek New Comedy of Menander was considered "higher" than the farcical burlesque of Aristophanic Old Comedy, George Puttenham in his *Arte of English Poesie* (1589) describing New Comedy as "more ciuill and pleasant a great deale" than "This bitter poeme called the old Comedy" (1.14.25). Aristophanes's trenchant satire and juxtaposition of low comedy with high has discomfited many a critic.

In fact literary criticism still largely reflects the attitudes of John Dryden, outlined in a lengthy preface to his (successful) play *An Evening's Love, or, The Mock Astrologer* (1668) and which explained why it pained him to pen such low comedy:

> Low comedy especially requires, on the writer's part, much of conversation with the vulgar, and much of ill nature in the observation of their follies . . . my disgust of low comedy proceeds not so much from my judgment as from my temper; which is the reason why I so seldom write it; and that when I succeed in it, (I mean so far as to please the audience) yet I am nothing satisfied with what I have done; but am often vexed to hear the people laugh, and clap, as they perpetually do, where intended them no jest; while they let pass the better things, without taking notice of them.

Indeed, Samuel Pepys, an avid theatergoer by no means averse to farce and low comedy, dismissed this play as "very smutty" (McAfee, 1916, p. 148). Borrowing much from one of Molière's early plays, *Le dépit amoureux* (The Love-Tiff, 1656), it is decidedly livelier than other Dryden pieces, all of which he wrote after the Restoration of Charles II for the newly reopened London playhouses.

Just as high comedy is no guarantee of theatrical excellence, so low comedy is not necessarily synonymous with poor performance or theatrical ineptitude. George Bernard Shaw observed in one of his London theater reviews for the 1890s, "After the exasperatingly bad acting one constantly sees at the theatres where high comedy and 'drama' prevail, it is a relief to see even simple work creditably done" (*The Saturday Review,* April 27, 1895). Clearly a skilled low comedian can be highly esteemed by professionals and audiences alike, and although Shaw was no proponent of low comedy and farce (indeed he attempted to "humanize" farce by writing his own, although to uncertain effect), he knew good stagecraft when he saw it. Moreover, the idea that low comedy and high should never combine is disproved in the theater by the work of such geniuses as Molière, William Shakespeare, and Anton Chekhov (not to mention the absurdists) and in fiction by François Rabelais, Lawrence Sterne (1713–1768), Charles Dickens, George Meredith (1828–1909), James Joyce (1882–1941), Céline (Louis Ferdinand Destouches, 1894–1961), Günter Grass (b. 1927), and many others.

Jessica Milner Davis

See also Absurdist Humor; Ancient Greek Comedy; Aristophanes; Carnivalesque; *Commedia dell'Arte*; Farce; Genres and Styles of Comedy; High Comedy; Molière; Obscenity; Rabelais, François; Satire; Shakespearean Comedy; Slapstick

Further Readings

Aristophanes. (1970). *Plays of Aristophanes* (P. Dickinson, Trans., 2 vols.). London, UK: Oxford University Press.

Bakhtin, M. M. (1968). *Rabelais and his world* (H. Iswolsky, Trans.). Cambridge: MIT Press.

Charney, M. (Ed.). (2005). *Comedy: A geographical and historical guide* (2 vols.). Westport, CT: Praeger.

McAfee, H. (Ed.). (1916). *Pepys on the restoration stage.* New Haven, CT: Yale University Press.

Websites

John Dryden's "Prologue to an Evening's Love" read by Paul Scofield: http://www.dailymotion.com/video/xhcza7_john-dryden-prologue-to-an-evening-s-love_creatio

M

Magazines and Newspapers, U.S.

U.S. humor magazines have tracked American political and cultural history since 1765, when *The (Philadelphia) Bee*, which lasted for three issues, scourged the colonial governor of Pennsylvania. Federal, Civil War, industrial, jazz age, wartime/postwar, and contemporary periods of humor magazines can be differentiated in literary style, topical matter, and, notably, in graphics and visual formatting. The orientation toward social satire, economic critique, and cultural and literary burlesque has been consistent. As of 2013, the humor magazine as a physical artifact is in decline, although *MAD* magazine continues its half-century-plus run, but online avatars seem vibrant enough to sustain accompanying print versions, including *The Onion* and *Humor Times*. This entry explores the various styles of humor periodicals throughout U.S. history and examines their future outlook.

Federal Era

The Augustan style of Juvenalian satire dominated comic political commentary through the 1820s. The period around 1807 to 1815 was particularly rich in political and social satire, as suggested by the names of various offerings: *The Corrector* (1804, with another in 1814), *The Thistle* (1807), *The Fool* (1807), *The Scourge* (1810 in Boston; 1811 in Baltimore), and many more. A comic literary culture was begun as well, most notably with writers Washington Irving and James Kirke Paulding's *Salmagundi* and George Helmbold's *The (Philadelphia) Tickler,* both starting in 1807. Irving and Paulding were highly successful in mild social satire; Helmbold was decried by one of newspaper publisher Isaiah Thomas's correspondents as being libelous and salacious, although there is not much scandal in its social observations that seems objectionable, as in the doggerel,

I am a merchant bold,
On South Wharves is my store.
Hard times like these, for honest folks,
None can too much deplore.
With tongue as smooth as oil,
Each day untruths I tell.
Look sharp for fools to take them in.
Charge twice for mackerel. (*The [Philadelphia] Tickler*, 1811)

Herald of Glory and Adopted Citizen's Journal in the second—and possibly last—issue of its first volume on August 13, 1834, edited by Tar Feathers, & Co., took as its motto "I take the responsibility" for attacking "hog tories, Antimasons, and Irishtocrats" of its home city, Boston. Humor throughout the era maintained its role as a social and political force.

The transition to a national journalistic style appears in the 1830s, notably with writer Seba Smith's character Jack Downing, who introduced the cracker-barrel voice and skeptical pragmatism of the backwoods to national politics by way of his satiric letters roasting the legislature in the state capitol in the Portland (Maine) *Daily Courier*. Editor B. P. Shillaber's (Boston) *Carpet-Bag* (1851–1853) was another notable advance in style and content broadened to include literary interests and urban scenes. Shillaber's periodical holds the distinction of publishing "first" works by humorists Artemus Ward, John Phoenix, and a young man, Samuel Clemens, who would make his mark under the pseudonym Mark Twain. Their writing blended literary fancy and irony with pragmatic political humor and vulgar dialect. Add a dash of reportorial burlesque and it is easy to trace the lineage to Twain's legislative reporting in 1863 for the Virginia City (Nevada) *Territorial Enterprise.* National sources as diverse as editor William T. Porter's *The Spirit of the Times*, editor Lewis Gaylord Clarke's *Knickerbocker Magazine*, and *The New Orleans Picayune,* all products of the 1830s that lasted for a couple of decades, captured and printed the roughhouse frontier stories that would later be identified as the native American humor of the old Southwest. During the same era, author Joseph C. Neal more-or-less single-handedly invented the vulgar urban type in Philadelphia "Charcoal" sketches, published in various magazines. Other long-lived humor magazines such as *Yankee Notions* (1852) and publisher Frank Leslie's *Budget of Fun* (1858) blended various forms of cartoons and short jokes that still characterize the genre, mirroring London's *Punch*, but with brief anecdotes and jokes, along with letters from fictional correspondents, suited to an American audience that "runs as it reads."

Civil War Era

The Civil War and its aftermath brought forth a new generation of comic newspapers and periodicals addressing an increasingly literate readership ready to track internationalism, spreading economic and political corruption, and the industrialization of America's Manifest Destiny. *Vanity Fair* (1859–1863), first edited under Charles G. Leland and then under Artemus Ward, burlesqued politics, religious communities, and national politics, mixing literary comedians, New England and female humorists, and other political and social comedians, with some throwbacks to the Downing era of regional politics and local issues, and others looking forward to the aggressive politics of the coming age of the great comic illustrated magazines. Without being overly literary, *Vanity Fair* elevated literary expectations for humor, but it also suffered by being too neutral for a society polarized by the conflict between the North and the South. By the 1870s, a vast number of newspapers devoted pages to humor generated by "locals" and the updated "exchange system," which circulated comic columnists nationally. The phrase *Phunny Phellows*, title of a comic journal lasting from 1859 to 1876, characterized many of these lesser comedians, suggesting both their tendency toward literary humor and their overuse of cacography, which Ward used cleverly to create social and historical satire, but which became a national plague of pointless puns and silly distractions after Josh Billings's columns and "Almanacks" in the 1860s and 1870s. By the end of the century, some of these writers had risen to permanence as American literary institutions. Twain vaulted from the *Virginia City Territorial Enterprise* to San Francisco's *Alta California* and then to New York's *Galaxy* as a columnist before reaching the pinnacle of *The Atlantic Monthly* in 1875. In 1881, Ambrose Bierce began creating his unique aphorisms—later titled *The Devil's Dictionary*—in the *San Francisco Wasp*, and Bill Nye founded the Laramie, Wyoming, *Boomerang,* also the name of his fictional mule, and rode his folksy small-town style to national prominence.

Industrial Age

Puck (1877–1917), *LIFE* (1883–1936), and *Judge* (1881–1937) formed the great triumvirate of pictorial comic magazines that dominated the period between the Civil War and World War I. The latter two maintained a readership to World War II. Joseph Keppler's brilliantly graphic satiric political cartoons in *Puck* were complemented by writer H. C. Bunner's wit and literary awareness, and the age of chromolithography provided brilliant colors. Always hostile to the monopolies and political corruption, several of *Puck*'s cartoonists represent the best political caricature America has produced, with the exception of Thomas Nast, whose cartoons undermined New York's Tammany Hall, the most powerful and corrupt political machine of its time. *Judge* took a more conservative position, even directly serving the Republican Party from 1885 through 1909. James Montgomery Flagg's illustrations represented another transition to a softer, slightly sexier art, and Norman Anthony as editor in the 1920s brought it to its most sophisticated literary form. Its centrist conservatism and hackneyed whimsy lost its appeal in the Great Depression. *LIFE* (1883–1936), published by John Ames Mitchell, diverged from the others in improving its black-and-white photo engraving and favoring its English model *Punch*. Its creators derived their

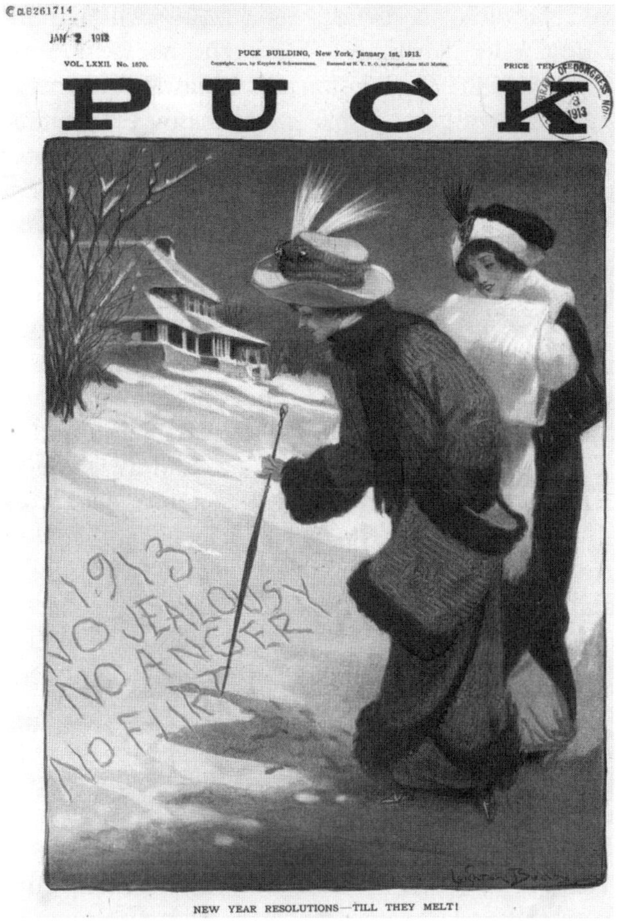

"New Year resolutions—till they melt!" *Puck* magazine, January 1, 1913. Illustration shows two young women stopping in the snow so that one of them can write her New Year's resolutions in the snow, "1913 No Jealousy No Anger No Flirt..."; it is unclear whether she is flirting or having second thoughts.

Source: Illustration by Leighton Budd. Library of Congress Prints and Photographs Division, Washington, DC, Reproduction Number LC-DIG-ppmsca-27906.

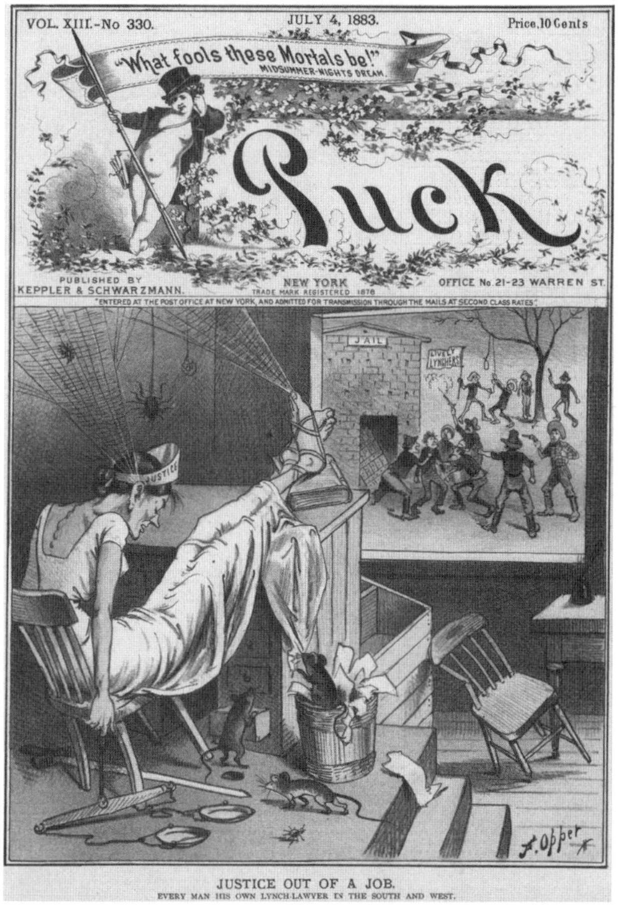

"Justice out of a Job," *Puck* magazine, July 4, 1883. Illustration shows Justice as an old woman, asleep at a desk, with cobwebs, spiders, and mice taking over the courtroom. Outside a window, an armed group of vigilantes have broken down the door to a jail and removed a man whom they are about to hang from a nearby tree; one man carries a flag that states "Lively Lynchers."

Source: Illustration by Fredrick Burr Opper. Library of Congress Prints and Photographs Division, Washington, DC, Reproduction Number LC-DIG-ppmsca-28402.

experience from the *Harvard Lampoon,* where *LIFE* editor Edward S. Martin had honed his sense of comic copy. The great age of college humor magazines lay ahead in the jazz age. Graphic artist Charles Dana Gibson, an unlikely novice still in his teens, was recruited in 1886; his images would form the characteristic visual identity of the era. Also notable was the creation of *LIFE*'s Fresh Air Fund to bring the children of New York's inner city to Connecticut farms for summer vacations. Humor and social purpose blended in this era to an unprecedented extent, and Mark Twain's *The Innocents Abroad, Life on the Mississippi*, most of his short stories, and chapters of *Adventures of Huckleberry Finn* and *A Connecticut Yankee* appeared in periodicals before publication in hard cover. Cartoons depicting the plight of Blacks and Chinese immigrants were found in major magazines, including *Harper's*, but without enough power to transform those scandalous shortcomings into a program of national reform.

Jazz Age

The era of literary "little magazines"—magazines that were smaller in size than their forerunners and more tightly focused on an intellectual or selected readership—was foreshadowed by little magazines of humor that sprung from various regions beginning before the turn of the 20th century. *Sagebrush Philosophy* (1904–1910), edited by Bill Barlow, is representative with its motto: "Consider the mummy, he ain't had no fun in 4,000 years." The "apostle of sunshine," however, was printed on "prickly pear papyrus," with a shotgun, cracker-barrel skepticism that joyfully excoriated social nonsense, blue-stocking restraint, and hypocrisy. *The American Mercury*, created by H. L. Mencken in 1924, broadened Barlow's good-natured skepticism into the verbal pyrotechnics that gave him the authoritative voice and cultural scope to skewer the American "booboisie" and the wide swath of American, really Southern, culture representing "the Sahara of the Bozarts." Mencken brought his journal to major national status, so vitriolic in advocacy of higher culture that it left its imprint on American attitudes for decades. Grimmer and less joyful were the progressive socialist *Art Young Quarterly* (1922) and, somewhat later, *Americana* (1932), which blazed warnings of Hitler's evil when many others indulged in mild, usually mindless, anti-Semitism.

Another example of a regional magazine was *Hot Dog: Regular Fellows Monthly* (1922–1927), from Cleveland and later New York City, which was quite sexy and more virulently anti-Semitic, reveling in the "tough-guy" humor of its period. Other regional humor offerings abounded. World War I even produced a variety of "trench" humor magazines published by American troops in Europe, a phenomenon that returned in World War II, but with a wider ranging sexual content and a much heavier emphasis on commercial sources on the home front, which had a vastly different mindset. Bill Mauldin's cartoons for *Yank*, fresh though they were, and important as they remain in showing the attitude of the lower class American GI, suggested more of the earlier and less frivolously sexy war humor.

Gibson's girls and James Montgomery Flagg's drawings might or might not be antecedents of the pinup girls of George Petty and Alberto Vargas or the busty pinup girls of Jefferson Machamer, Russell Patterson, and Bill Ward, but at some point the theme of sex and sexual humor entered the stream of American humor periodicals. Sam H. Clark originated *Jim Jam Jems* in 1912 as a mid-Western journal of opinion, but was misperceived, he felt, as the licentious bad boy of the 1910s and the 1920s. Clark appeared not to be interested in humor magazines for the money—as he didn't even accept advertising revenue for a long time, and up until 1922 he didn't even take subscriptions—but his heavy sarcasm on social issues was a goad to antagonize a do-gooder like John S. Sumner of the New York Society for the Suppression of Vice. In 1922, Sumner succeeded in getting sellers of periodicals containing sexual humor arrested; these arrests were later reversed in court hearings in which Clark testified. Clark was a far cry from Captain Billy Fawcett who edited *Captain Billy's Whiz-Bang*, which flourished from 1919 to 1936 and perhaps longer in an attenuated version by Fawcett's son. *Whiz-Bang* carried plenty of jokes featuring double entendres, but there were even more frankly sexual jokes, chatter, and pinups of jazz-age models in stockings and underwear. Circulation reached close to half a million in 1923; America's sexuality and sexual mores were emerging in new ways. Clark did not approve, but Fawcett bought *Jim Jam Jems* after Clark's death and re-made it into his own style anyhow. Fawcett's ex-wife challenged him with *The Calgary Eye Opener*, which had originated as a Canadian little magazine like the other regional offerings around 1902. The world of humor magazines had changed.

Wartime and Postwar Eras

The age of sexuality in humor fully opened after World War I. Titles such as *French Humor* and *French Follies* telegraphed their humor; likewise, *The Flapper, Co-ed Campus Quarterly, Paris Nights, Broadway Breeze*, and others abounded. Both on and off campus, the 1920s roared into the 1930s. Some upscale magazines like *College Humor* (1934) offered distinguished artwork and higher level engagement, but *Reel Screen Fun, Screen Humor*, and *Film Fun* kept to a more sexy brand. They would be followed in turn by tabloid-sized photo-cheesecake-humor magazines like *Gags, TNT, WIT, Titters*, and *Tit-bits,* which were, in their turn, superseded in the 1950s and 1960s by digest-sized sleazecake, a sexier version of cheesecake, much of it from the Humorama firm, which went for sexy nudity interspersed with comic captions and witty sayings of models whose assets were more visible in photographs than was verbal humor. *Hustler Humor, Sex to Sexty*, and their grossly sexual counterparts would make them seem modest and constrained by comparison, but not for another decade.

The New Yorker, whose annual February cover of Eustace Tilley eyeing a butterfly through his monocle is often taken as the first harbinger of spring, may be hard to think of as a regional magazine, but so it proclaimed itself in staking out its territory as the

Algonquin Hotel's Round Table, disavowing the old lady from Dubuque as a target reader. Writer-critic Dorothy Parker's wit, writer Christopher Morley's clever reversals of domesticity, and the selection of cartoons, along with copy editing by Harold Ross made *The New Yorker* peerless. Contributors such as E. B. White, S. J. Perelman, Peter Arno, and others whose names continue to be familiar years after their deaths raised the level of diction, sentence construction, underplayed wit, and sheer intellectual power, which allowed the magazine to sustain itself, although with various reinventions, up to the present.

Norman Anthony created another type of humor magazine with *Ballyhoo* in 1931, an unlikely year to start a commercial venture (because of the Great Depression), but his purposefully rag-tag construction and egregiously colorful visual presentation, coupled with a don't-care verbal humor and burlesque advertising was just what the era demanded. It had as many imitators in the early 1930s as *MAD* had in the 1950s, and for much the same reason. The breezy skepticism and the shrewd panning of cultural pretension, linked to irreverence toward the rich, the formal, and the mundane, was all its readership dreamed of, juvenile though their tastes seemed to critics. A close look at one of the theme figures of *Ballyhoo* suggests *MAD*'s mascot Alfred E. Newman, so the "What, Me Worry?" iconoclasm of *MAD* had an earlier precedent. *Ballyhoo* remained a massive cultural presence for almost a decade, but World War II needed war-oriented humor. *MAD* in the early 1950s thus had an open field. Even Congress was concerned at the further erosion of the morals of American youth in the 1950s by *MAD*, but without much effect on humor magazines. Censors did not have great success because of the irrelevance of their attempts to the real underlying human issues of the era. *MAD*'s imitators called themselves *Sick, Crazy, Cracked, Frenzy*, and other equally indicative names. In the late 1950s and 1960s, even more biting iconoclasm was produced by *The Realist*, founded and edited by Paul Krasner, which featured a cartoon of Uncle Sam lying across Vietnam in missionary position as its iconic comment on the United States' entry into the conflict in Southeast Asia.

Contemporary Era

Contemporary attempts to found serious humor magazines have failed. *Spy*, closely allied to the magic of the Kennedy name, could not sustain itself. *MAD* and *National Lampoon* seem to be the only titles to have retained national prominence over a long period of time. Begun in 1970, *National Lampoon*'s run was sustained through 1998 by the exploitation of sex, politics, and violence in varied forms of parody and satire: One cover threatened that if we didn't buy this magazine, they would shoot the dog on the cover. Tasteless humor became their mode, bleeding over into films like *National Lampoon's Animal House* (1978; John Landis, director) and other ventures. Yet, the history of humor magazines may have come full circle, as politics, now, as in the earliest period, seems to remain a driving force.

Future Outlook

The death of the American humor magazine may be greatly exaggerated, even if the old standbys are gone, with the exception of *MAD*. Drugstore shelves were once populated by cartoon magazines by Charlton Press. Now, niche-comedy humor magazines cover dogs, nursing, health, hot-rods, cycles, and you-name-it, but they have been as transient as their precursors, which may be the nature of humor magazine life cycles generally. Online, however, *The Onion* and *Humor Times* flourish, both dedicated to ethical and political humor that is smart and demanding. Both are sufficiently robust to sustain paper publications. A number of lesser offerings exist. Otherwise, a scattered universe of zines proliferates, seemingly without limits, an interesting genre as uncharitable to American cultural norms as it is irregular in form, format, and venue. Where consumers of published periodical humor go from here is anybody's guess. The book was declared dead as a medium with the arrival of microforms; the theater and the movies were supposed cadavers in the 1970s, but neither genre has died, and the life of the humor magazines, even if the physical medium alters, is likely to continue as long as they serve a cultural need in an information-driven world.

David E. E. Sloane

See also Cartoons; History of Humor: U.S. Modern and Contemporary; Journalism

Further Readings

Blair, W. (1960). *Native American humor.* San Francisco, CA: Chandler. (Original work published 1937)

Ellenbogen, G. C. (1985). *The directory of humor magazines and humor organizations in America (and Canada)*. New York, NY: Wry-Bred Press.
Mott, F. L. (1930–1968). *History of American magazines* (5 vols.). Cambridge, MA: Harvard University Press.
Peterson, T. (1956). *Magazines in the twentieth century.* Urbana: University of Illinois Press.
Sloane, D. E. E. (Ed.). (1987). *American humor magazines and comic periodicals.* Westport, CT: Greenwood Press.

Magazines and Newspapers Outside the United States

This entry provides a list of primarily humorous magazines that appear or have appeared outside of the United States. The purpose is to balance the treatment of the topic of magazines in the United States, where significant research on the subject exists. Conversely, there is no comprehensive treatment of European or Asian magazines, with the notable exception of John Lent's work on cartooning and visual humor, which overlaps significantly with the study of magazines but cannot replace it. A few trends emerge even from this small and unrepresentative sample: the influence of *Punch*, which has been felt worldwide and has led to the creation of many local humorous magazines, and the emergence of political humor magazines at the beginning of the 20th century; the tendency of humor magazines under repressive regimes to last for a very short time and close as a result of censorship; and the emergence of the "fake news" genre, along the lines of *The Onion*, in recent times.

Academia Cațavencu

Academia Cațavencu is a satirical magazine founded in 1991 in Romania. Before publishing this magazine, the editorial team had edited the satirical magazines *Cațavencu Incomod* and *Cațavencu Internațional*. *Academia Cațavencu* is known as an advocate of press freedom and opposes manipulation through mass media.

The Arousal

The Arousal was a Pakistani anarchist newsletter, which started publication in 1988. *The Arousal* was distributed in Karachi and Lahore. It acquired notoriety for its humor and satirical attacks on politicians and religious parties. After harassment by the authorities, the magazine folded in 1991.

Bayan Yanı

Bayan Yanı, translated as "the seat next to the woman," is a humor magazine founded in 2011 in Turkey. The magazine is the only female-oriented one in the country and contains jokes, cartoons, and humorous articles about the oppression women in Turkish society face.

Il Becco Giallo

Il Becco Giallo (The Yellow Beak) was a satirical magazine known for its anti-Fascist content and was one of the most important satirical magazines in Italy in the 1920s. Founded in 1924, it was forced to close in 1926 by the Fascist regime.

Bezbozhnik

Bezbozhnik (Atheist) was a monthly Soviet satirical magazine published between 1922 and 1941. The magazine ridiculed all kinds of religion and published articles and cartoons depicting religion as a superstition. However, later the magazine started to publish political articles. The invasion of the Soviet Union by Nazi Germany in 1941 caused the magazine to cease its publication.

Bilete de Papagal

Bilete de Papagal (Parrot Notes) was a satirical publication in Romania that was founded in 1928 and published intermittently between 1928 and 1945.

The Cane Toad Times

The Cane Toad Times was an Australian satirical humor magazine that appeared between 1977 and 1990, based in Brisbane, Queensland. The magazine contained countercultural philosophy, irreverent journalism, cartoons, satirical articles, and caricatures. The magazine took a role of political opposition.

Charlie Hebdo

Charlie Hebdo is a weekly French satire and humor newspaper that includes cartoons, reports, and jokes. The magazine is known for its anti-religious stance and mocks the extreme right perspective. The magazine was founded in 1969 after the controversial satirical magazine *Hara-Kiri* was closed down. *Charlie Hebdo* folded in 1981, but it was revived in 1992.

Chayan

Chayan is a satirical magazine in Russia. It has been published in Tatar since 1923. In 1956, it started publishing in Russian. During the Soviet era, the magazine cooperated closely with *Mushtum* from Uzbekistan.

The Clinic

The Clinic is a weekly satirical publication that has been in operation since 1998 in Chile. It contains a wide range of cultural affairs, jokes, and investigative work and mocks most politicians but is generally leftist.

Dikobraz

Dikobraz is a weekly satirical magazine published in Czechoslovakia and Czech Republic between 1945 and 1995. The magazine had a motto saying "with a smile everything is easier." Although the magazine was revived in 2004, it closed down again in 2005.

Diyojen

Diyojen was the first humor magazine of Turkey and was published between 1869 and 1873. After being published in French and Armenian, the magazine started publishing in Turkish and introduced the first examples of Turkish humor to its readers. It had 183 issues, and in 1873 it was closed down because of its political writings.

Dodgem Logic

Dodgem Logic is a bimonthly British humor and entertainment magazine that started publishing in December 2009. It includes comics, short stories, poetry, articles and reviews, and art work. Its editor, Alan Moore, describes it as a publication that brings "the subterranean vitality and color of the last century's underground press into the present day."

al Domari

al Domari (The Lamplighter) was among the early independent publications in Syria since the beginning of the Baath Party rule in 1963. *al Domari* was published by a well-known Syrian political cartoonist, Ali Farzat. The newspaper issued political satire and its style was inherited from the French weekly *Le Canard enchaîné* (The Chained Duck). The paper started its circulation in February 2001 and sold its entire run of 50,000 copies in less than 4 hours. However, *al Domari* closed down in 2003 due to lack of funds and steady government censorship.

Dou

Dou, which started publishing in 2008, means "funny" or "tease" in Chinese. It is a general humor magazine that is put together by several famous Chinese humorists such as Sun Rui and Lin Changzhi.

Faking News

Faking News is an Indian website that was launched in 2008. It publishes fake news reports that satirize and spoof topics and events familiar to the Indian audience and has both English and Hindi editions.

Feral Tribune

Feral Tribune was a weekly satirical magazine in Croatia. Founded in 1993, the magazine announced itself as a "weekly magazine for Croatian anarchists, protesters and heretics." Its circulation decreased in the 2000s, and it closed in 2008.

Fun

Fun was an English weekly Victorian magazine, founded in 1861 and published until 1901. Its radical politics were in competition with the more conservative *Punch* magazine. The magazine contained parody and satirical verse, political and literary criticism, articles on sports, and full- or double-page cartoons, often on political topics.

Gırgır

Gırgır was a Turkish humor magazine published from 1972 to 1993. The magazine was known for its sharp satirical cartoons about politicians active at that time. It also became one of the best-selling humor magazines in Europe with a circulation of 450,000 in the 1970s. However, after key staff members such as Oğuz Aral left the magazine and it was taken over by another publishing group, the magazine lost its popularity and folded in 1993.

Grönköpings Veckoblad

Grönköpings Veckoblad is a monthly Swedish satirical magazine that has been published since 1902. The title, translated "*Grönköpings* Weekly," refers to a fictional Swedish town.

El Gugeton

El Gugeton was a Ladino-language satirical journal launched in 1908. Ladino is a Judeo-Spanish language, spoken by some Sephardic Jewish communities. *El Gugeton*, edited by Elia Carmona, was the second longest running Ladino publication in Istanbul, closing in 1931.

Hara-Kiri

Hara Kiri was a notorious satirical French magazine published in the 1960s. The subtitle of the magazine *Journal bête et méchant* means "stupid and evil magazine." The highly controversial magazine was known for criticizing public officials and policies and was temporarily banned by the French government.

Hoy!

Hoy! was a Filipino humor magazine. Because it was founded shortly after the People Power Revolution in May 1986, most of its contents satirized the times. The magazine was similar to the American humor magazine *MAD* in terms of its size and number of pages. However, the magazine was short-lived, with only a few issues appearing. *Lipang Kalabaw* and *Telembang* were other magazines that also published only a few issues in Indonesia.

HUMOR

HUMOR was an Argentinean humor magazine published between 1978 and 1997. It was considered as a satirical current event magazine of its time. During the Falklands War in 1982, the magazine had a prominent impact on Argentinean media and people.

The Japan Punch

The Japan Punch was named after the British magazine *Punch,* and it aimed to inform the foreign community in Yokohama of Japan's politics and society. The magazine contained cartoons on all 10 pages. *The Japan Punch* made use of Japanese techniques: It was printed by woodblock on Japanese paper (*washi*) and stitched in Japanese style. In 1965, after the magazine had gained popularity, it was published on a monthly basis. The magazine had an important impact on Japanese comic art. It was active between 1862 and 1887.

Joe

Joe magazine was published between 1973 and 1979 in Kenya. At its widest distribution it reached 30,000 copies. The magazine was named after an everyman character that founder Hilary Ng'weno and artist Terry Hirst had created for an earlier publication. The magazine published joke contests, comic strips and cartoons, feature columns, and one short story in every issue.

Journal of Irreproducible Results

The *Journal of Irreproducible Results* is a bimonthly humor magazine founded in 1955 in Israel. The *Journal of Irreproducible Results* contains a wide range of humor types from parodies and burlesques to satires. The *Journal of Irreproducible Results* is generally about science and it appeals to scientists. The magazine features a mix of jokes, science cartoons, and funny research reports.

El Jueves

El Jueves is a Spanish weekly satirical magazine that started publishing in 1977. The magazine contains political, social, and economic affairs and comic strips. It was inspired by *Charlie Hebdo* and *Hara Kiri* in the political thaw that followed the abrogation of the Francoist censorship laws.

Kayhan Caricature

Kayhan Caricature is a humor magazine founded in 1992 in Iran. It became Iran's first humor publication to specialize in cartoon and caricature. This made the magazine famous, and it became popular among cartoonists in Iran. The magazine also helped found the Tehran International Cartoon Biennial.

El Koshary Today

Founded in 2009, *El Koshary Today* is an Egyptian online website (www.elkoshary.com) that uses fake headlines and stories to satirize current events, similar to the U.S. website *The Onion.* According to the *El Koshary* website, its philosophy "is to use sarcasm and imagination to raise awareness of some of the serious (and not so serious) issues plaguing our nation. It is not intended to relay any factual information or credible circumstances, though where possible readers will find news links to the actual issues being satirized herein."

Krokodil

Krokodil was the premier satirical magazine of the Soviet Union. It started publishing in 1922 and got its name from Fyodor Dostoyevsky's story, "The Crocodile." Unlike the short-lived satirical magazines *Zanoza* and *Prozhektor*, *Krokodil* continued until 1991. The magazine lampooned political figures and ridiculed the countries that opposed the Soviet system. Similar magazines were found in all the Soviet republics, such as *Pepper* in Ukrainian Soviet Socialist Republic; *Hedgehog* in Belarusian Soviet Socialist Republic, Azerbaijani Soviet Socialist Republic, and Tajik Soviet Socialist Republic and Armenian Soviet Socialist Republic; *Bumblebee* in Kazakh Soviet Socialist Republic; *Scorpion* in Tatar Autonomous Soviet Socialist Republic; and *Crocodile* in Georgian Soviet Socialist Republic.

Le Canard enchaîné

Le Canard enchaîné was founded in 1915 as a humorous alternative to news that was censored by the French government. Today, it sells about 500,000 copies weekly and is known for scoops and satirical reports on French governmental and business leaders. A source of investigative journalism in France, its exposés of French governmental and business leaders have led to resignations by cabinet ministers.

Leman

Leman is a quintessential left-wing humor magazine published weekly in Turkey. After *Limon,* another humor magazine in Turkey, was closed down, *Leman* was founded in 1991 by the same cartoonists. *Leman* is important in Turkey because the magazine has become a role model for other humor magazines in Turkey such as *Penguen* and *Uykusuz.*

Lemon People

Lemon People was a *hentai Manga* (erotic Japanese comics featuring bizarre sexual desires and acts) magazine published in Japan from February 1982 to November 1998. The stories in the magazine often involved humor and parody. Other magazines in the country such as *Manga Burikko* and *Manga Hot Milk* used *Lemon People*'s style. However, these magazines were not as successful as *Lemon People.*

Il Male

Il Male (Evil), published between 1978 and 1982, was one of the most successful satirical magazines in Italy. It was fiercely anti-establishment and was often pulled off newsstands by the police for violating anti-defamation laws. Its best known prank was publishing fake newspaper front pages, such as one in which a fake edition of *Corriere dello Sport* (the premier sports newspaper at the time) announced that the 1978 World Cup, in which Italy lost out to the Netherlands, had been canceled and a new final would be played.

Marko Paşa

Marko Paşa was a weekly satire and humor magazine published between 1946 and 1947 in Turkey. The magazine experienced continuous censorship from the authorities at that time due to its sarcastic style. Despite the oppression, the magazine was popular, with a circulation of 60,000 to 70,000.

Melbourne Punch

Melbourne Punch was an Australian humor magazine published between 1855 and 1925. It was the most successful of colonial magazines that took the London *Punch* as a model.

Molla Nasreddin

Molla Nasreddin was an Azerbaijani satirical periodical published between 1906 and 1930 in Azeri and in Russian. The magazine was popular all over the Muslim world, from Morocco to Iran. *Molla Nasreddin* was named after 13th-century "mullah" Nasreddin, famous in the Islamic world for his wisdom and comical stories. The magazine satirized corruption, inequality, and religion, thus drawing significant hostility from religious conservatives. The magazine is credited with starting Iranian cartooning.

Mshana

Mshana was an entertainment magazine based in Cape Town, South Africa, founded in 2007. It contained comics and entertaining articles.

Mushtum

Mushtum (Fist) is an Uzbek satire and humor magazine that began publication in 1923. It was temporarily suspended because of World War II. During the Soviet era, *Mushtum* cooperated with the humorous magazines *Perets'* (Ukraine), *Vozhyk* (Belarus), *Chayan* (the Tatar Republic), and *Macaw* (Kazakhstan). It resumed publication in 1951.

Nebelspalter

The *Nebelspalter*, translated as "fog-smasher," is a satirical magazine in Switzerland. It was established in 1875 as an "illustrated humorous political weekly' and is still published today, although it has been published monthly since 1996. *Nebelspalter* is now the oldest satirical magazine in the world, after the closing of *Punch*.

Noseweek

Noseweek is a South African monthly humor and investigative magazine founded in 1993. According to its website, the magazine features "irreverent, independent, inside information" about economics, politics, and society in the country.

The Nugget

With the slogan "Bahrain's 1st humor magazine!" *The Nugget* is an English-language general humor magazine based in Bahrain. The magazine, founded in 2012, aims to satirize common aspects of social and popular culture and present topics in a humorous perspective. The nature of the topics is broad in order to reach worldwide readers of all ages.

Pancada

Pandaca was a humor magazine published in Brazil from 1979 to the mid-1980s. It is the reworking of *Cracked* magazine in the United States, a magazine that was a knock-off of *MAD* magazine. The content was translated from *Cracked* magazine and adapted to Brazilian society. Although most of the content was transferred from the original American magazine, some of it was created by local artists.

Penguen

Penguen is a weekly humor magazine published in both Turkey and North Cyprus. It was founded by a group of cartoonists and writers who left *Leman* magazine in 2002. The magazine lampoons political figures and publishes cartoons and articles about the social and political problems in Turkey.

Perets'

Perets' (Pepper) is a Ukrainian satirical newspaper that was founded in 1922 and is still published today. Its current editor in chief and Ukrainian comic writer Mykhailo Prudnyk, won the Aleko international competition for humorous short stories in 2013. In an interview in the Kiev newspaper *The Day*, Prudnyk noted that the newspaper continues its humorous political commentary, commenting that "the task of satire and humor is not only to make fun of things, but also to help. Perhaps, those, at the high ranks of power, should not be angry at journalists but rather say: 'Thank you for helping us to see the problem!'" (Oliinyk, 2013).

The Phoenix

The Phoenix is a best-selling political and current affairs magazine in Ireland. It has been published on a regular basis, usually every 2 weeks, since 1983, with a larger annual issue each December. The magazine includes a news column, "Affairs of the Nation," that deals with political scandals; a financial column, "Moneybags"; a section "Craic and Codology," which includes satirical coverage of events outside Dublin; and features on arts and entertainment. Its cover features a photo montage of ironic and humorous comments of notable people on current events.

Pikker

Pikker was an Estonian satirical and humor magazine that was active between 1943 and 2001, albeit not continuously. It published caricatures, humor, satire, and anecdotes.

Private Eye

Private Eye is a British magazine. It started publishing in 1961, and it been called a "thorn in the side" of the British establishment because of its sharp satirical bent.

Punch

Punch, also known as the *London Charivari*, was a British weekly humor and satire magazine that was published from July 17, 1841, to April 8, 1992. It was relaunched on September 6, 1996, and continued until May 28, 2002. It published the works of great comic poets and writers and introduced the term *cartoon* as it used today in the 1850s. Its irreverent political and social cartoons were known for the detailed pictures of 19th- and 20th-century life.

Random Magazine

Random Magazine is a humor magazine in India. It appeared first in 2008 and has a circulation of 50,000 copies. The magazine contains satire and parody on current affairs and famous people in India.

Satyricón

Satyricón was a satirical humor magazine that was published from 1972 to 1974 in Buenos Aires, Argentina. *Satyricón* had a very aggressive satirical humor. Government forces shut it down in 1974 because of its attacks on Isabel Perón, who succeeded her husband, Juan Perón, as president after his death in 1974.

Shabkhand

Shabkhand (Night Laugh) was one of the most prominent satirical publications published in Pakistan during the Taliban era. However, it published only a few issues. Although the magazine contained satire, cartoons and verse comprised most of its content.

Shankar's Weekly

Shankar's Weekly, India's *Punch*, was founded in 1948 by Kesava Shankara Pillai, a well-known political cartoonist. *Shankar's Weekly* was fully devoted to cartoons and humorous articles. It was closed in 1975 during the "emergency" in which Prime Minister Indira Gandhi suspended democratic rule.

Shudaung

Shudaung, literally translated as "viewpoint journal," was a humor journal founded by left-wing Burmese politician and journalist Thakin Lwin in Burma in 1969. He was its editor until it closed down in 1971.

Svikmøllen

Svikmøllen is an annual Danish satirical magazine in Denmark. It started publishing in 1915 and contains articles and cartoons that satirize the events and affairs in the past year.

TelQuel

TelQuel is a French Moroccan satirical magazine. Since it started publication in 2001, it has been known for its opposition to Islamic ideology in Morocco. For this reason, the magazine has been continuously subjected to pressure from the government. The magazine also started another satirical magazine, named *Nichane,* in Moroccan Arabic. However, it closed down in 2010 as a consequence of governmental pressure.

Titanic

Titanic is a monthly German satirical magazine based in Frankfurt. It was founded in 1979 by a group of editors and contributors from the satirical magazine *Pardon*.

Tofigh

Tofigh was a weekly satirical newspaper published in Iran. "Truth is bitter, so we say it sweetly" was the motto of the newspaper. It started publishing in 1923 as a literary periodical; then it changed its style to humor by adding cartoons to its content. *Tofigh* faced oppression from the government and was suspended several times due to its criticism of the government. *Tofigh* mirrored the hopes and desires of low- and middle-class people in Iran. It closed down in 1971.

Unmad

Unmad, meaning "mad (or insane)," is a monthly satire magazine in Bangladesh. It was launched in 1978, and it had a style similar to *MAD* magazine.

Uykusuz

Uykusuz is a weekly humor magazine published in both Turkey and North Cyprus. It is similar to *Penguen* magazine in that it publishes articles and cartoons related to social, political, and economic problems in Turkey. It was founded in 2007 and has become one of the best-selling magazines in Turkey.

The Vacuum

The Vacuum is a free, monthly newspaper published in Belfast, Northern Ireland. Each issue is themed and contains a wide range of content, including satire and commentary about the city and larger cultural issues. Founded in 2003, the paper is distributed in public places such as bars and cafes and by mail.

Vikingen

Vikingen is a former Norwegian satirical magazine published from 1862 to 1932. After a short time, the magazine became an important source of humor, satire, and public debate.

Wanita and *Gila-Gila*

Wanita (Woman) and *Gila-Gila* (Mad) attract large numbers of readers in Malaysia. However, *Gila-Gila*, which has been around for 20 years, has become the leader due to "an increase in the number and quality of cartoons and humorous articles especially for female readers" (Lent, 2001, p. 187). *Wanita* and *Gila-Gila* discuss a wide collection of cultural, social, and political issues in Malay language. Additionally, both magazines deal with traditional and modernist Islamic matters. Yet, *Gila-Gila* pays more attention to controversial issues than does *Wanita*.

Viz

Viz is a British adult humor magazine launched in 1979. It publishes a number of contemporary comic strips and includes a tabloid newspaper with satirical articles and letters. Its content has at times led to controversy; the magazine was reprimanded by the United Nations for publishing a comic strip titled "The Thieving Gypsy Bastards," and it was questioned by Scotland Yard's anti-terrorist branch after it ran a "top tip" advising readers to call the airport with a bomb threat if they were late for a flight.

Zanbel-e-Gham

Zanbel-e-Gham was the only satirical magazine published in Afghanistan during the Taliban regime. It was launched in 1997 by Osman Akram and a friend; Akram photocopied the magazine on a hidden photocopier and smuggled copies to readers. The magazine not only defied Taliban edicts but made fun of them. Now published openly, *Zanbel-e-Gham* continues to print cartoons critical of political and religious leaders. Today, it is supported in part by the Afghan Media and Culture Center, which works to establish a free press in Afghanistan.

Ziligurti

Ziligurti, founded in 2005, is an independent Turkish-language monthly humor magazine in North Cyprus. It tackles political issues and daily life.

Metin Özdemir

See also Caricature; Cartoons; Comic Strips; Magazines and Newspapers, U.S.; Satire

Further Readings

Allen, T. (2002, December). The word is freedom. *National Geographic Magazine*. Washington, DC: National Geographic Society. Retrieved from http://ngm.nationalgeographic.com/ngm/0212/aina/online_extra.html

Attardo, S. (1992, April). The naked bunch: Italian satire in the 1980s. *The World and I*, pp. 671–679.

Douglas, A., & Douglas, F. (1994). *Arab comic strips: Politics of an emerging mass culture*. Bloomington: Indiana University Press.

Eduardo, R. (2012). Entre a comicidade, o senso comum e a disidência. A revista *Humor* como espaço controversial (1978–1980) [Between comedy, common sense, and dissent: The magazine *Humor* as controversial space]. *Antiteses, 5*(9), 77–97.

Faridullah, B. (2005). Satire in modern Afghanistan. *Comparative Studies of Asia, Africa and the Middle East, 25*(2), 465–479.

Fontes Garnica, I., & Menéndez, M. A. (2004). *El parlamento de papel: Las revistas españolas en la transición democrática* [The paper parliament: Spanish magazines in the democratic transition]. Madrid, Spain: Asociación de la Prensa de Madrid.

Fredericksen, B. F. (1991). *Joe*, the sweetest reading in Africa: Documentation and discussion of a popular magazine in Kenya. *African Languages and Cultures, 4*(2), 135–155.

Keller, C. (Ed.). (2011). *Slavs and Tatars presents: Molla Nasreddin: The magazine that would've, could've, should've*. Zurich, Switzerland: JRP-Ringier. Retrieved from http://www.slavsandtatars.com/works.php?id=72

Lent, J. (1996). *Comic art in Africa, Asia, Australia, and Latin America: A comprehensive, international bibliography*. Westport, CT: Greenwood Press.

Lent, J. (2001). *Illustrating Asia: Comics, humour magazines, and picture books*. Honolulu: University of Hawai'i Press.

Lent, J. (2009). *Cartooning in Africa*. Cresskill, NJ: Hampton Press.

Oliinyk, V. (2013, June 19). Pepper satire. *The Day Newspaper*, Kiev, Ukraine.

Press, C. (1981). *The political cartoon*. Rutherford, NJ: Fairleigh Dickinson University Press.

Simmons, S. (1993). War, revolution and the transformation of the German humor magazine, 1914–1927. *Art Journal, 52*(1), 46–54.

Yücebaş, H. (2004). *Türk Mizahçıları*. İstanbul, Turkey: L&M Yayınları.

Websites

Faking News: http://www.fakingnews.firstpost.com

Management

When considering the relationship between humor and management, several questions may arise: Is humor a management tool? How may humor be utilized by managers? How may humor assist managers in getting their work done and in achieving their various objectives? This entry addresses these questions by briefly outlining some of the various functions of humor as a management tool. After having outlined some of the positive functions of humor as a management tool, the entry also briefly discusses "another" side of humor, namely, as a means of coercion and control. Differences in the use of humor across workplaces are also mentioned.

Humor as a Management Tool

Although the link between humor and management is not immediately obvious, humor may indeed be used as a tool to assist and enhance the practice of management. In particular, humor may perform valuable functions to support a wide diversity of management activities, including those that are both interpersonally as well as transactionally oriented. Interpersonal functions include, for example, enhancing teamwork and creating a positive working atmosphere, motivating staff and increasing their productivity, as well as minimizing status differences. Transactionally oriented behaviors refer to more immediately task-oriented activities, such as getting things done and communicating negative messages (such as criticism, rejection, or disagreement). Each of these functions of humor as a management tool is discussed briefly in this section.

Enhancing Team Work and Creating a Positive Working Atmosphere

Perhaps one of the best known functions of humor is to create solidarity and a positive and often friendly atmosphere. This effect of humor is particularly important in a workplace context where humor may be used to create and maintain friendly social relationships between colleagues, as well as between managers and their team members. These positive effects of humor, in turn, may contribute toward enhancing teamwork and establishing a positive working atmosphere where members feel included, valued, and appreciated. The process of creating a positive working atmosphere is often described more widely in terms of contributing to the creation (and maintenance) of a particular workplace or corporate culture that characterizes a specific workplace or company. There is some evidence that the kinds of humor used by those in management positions tend to have an impact on the culture of a particular workplace, for example, whether its members value collaboration, inclusiveness, and mutual support or whether they encourage individualistic behavior and competitiveness. For example, frequent teasing, jocular abuse, and short witty comments with which people may try to outwit each other tend to be characteristic of more individualistic and highly competitive workplaces. Through their repeated use of these specific types of humor, managers (and, to a lesser extent, other team members) contribute to constructing and reinforcing the norms (and culture) of their specific workplace.

These processes of enhancing teamwork and creating a positive atmosphere or culture of a particular workplace may also have positive effects on a team's cohesion and performance, which in turn may contribute to increasing that team's high productivity.

Motivating Staff and Increasing Their Productivity

One of the main aims of managers is to motivate their staff with the ultimate goal of increasing their productivity. The link between staff motivation and productivity has long been established, and there is some evidence that suggests that people who are happy work more productively. Humor is an excellent tool to achieve this, not only by creating a positive, friendly, and generally supportive workplace atmosphere but also by establishing and maintaining friendly collegial relationships among staff. Several research studies have described some of the positive effects of humor on staff motivation, creativity, and productivity, in particular through increasing employees' overall job satisfaction. Some of the functions of humor that contribute to achieving this include relieving tensions and dealing with stress, stimulating people's intellectual activity and preventing boredom and fatigue, boosting morale, facilitating teamwork, sparking discussions, and encouraging lateral thinking.

Minimizing Status Differences

Although minimizing status differences may not be one of the activities typically associated with management, downplaying power differentials may actually have several positive effects for the relationship between managers and their team members.

For example, it may create a positive atmosphere and enhance team spirit by downplaying the special status and more powerful role of the manager within a team. This may be achieved, for example, by drawing on self-denigrating humor, which may be used by those in higher positions to make fun of themselves and to portray themselves in a favorable light, namely, as someone who knows about his or her mistakes and laughs about them. An example that illustrates these functions quite nicely is the following quote by the director of the board of an information technology company who, in an interaction with one of her subordinates, humorously referred to herself as a "technical klutz," thereby drawing attention to her reputation as being technically ignorant and incompetent. Although clearly being tongue-in-cheek, humorous remarks like this contribute to minimizing status differences, thereby making managers more approachable, and they also contribute to creating a friendly workplace atmosphere.

Getting Things Done

In addition to these interpersonal functions of humor that primarily aim at establishing and maintaining friendly interpersonal relationships, humor may also be used as a tool to "do power" and to get things done. These functions of humor are particularly useful for the performance of a range of transactionally and outcome-oriented managerial tasks. In particular, humor may be used to assist managers in achieving their transactional aims, such as making sure people do their work. The following brief example illustrates how this may be accomplished.

> *Context*: Manager (Beth) to administrative assistant (Marion) who is chatting to a secretary.
> *Beth*: Okay Marion I'm afraid serious affairs of state will have to wait. We have some trivial issues needing our attention [all laugh]. (Holmes & Stubbe, 2003, p. 116)

By humorously describing the chat between Marion and the secretary as "serious affairs of state" and referring to the work-related tasks that need to be done as "trivial issues," the manager, Beth, performs a range of management activities. More specifically, she reminds her subordinate, Marion, that it is about time she gets back to work. Although the main function of this brief humorous exchange is to get things done and to inform subordinates to get on with their work, the humor also contributes to creating and reinforcing the friendly and collegial relationship between Beth and her subordinates. Thus, rather than telling them more directly to get back to work, by using humor Beth makes this potentially threatening message more palatable for her subordinates while still achieving her transactional aims.

Communicating Negative Messages

As this short example has shown, humor is also an effective tool to communicate negative messages, such as criticisms and disagreements, in relatively nonthreatening ways. This function of humor is particularly useful in a workplace context, as it may facilitate the potentially threatening and often unpleasant tasks of managers to communicate a negative message to their team members, for example, that their promotion has been rejected. Using humor in these contexts makes the rejection or criticism more palatable and thus easier to accept for those who are receiving the rejection or criticism. However, these positive functions of humor to tone down or mitigate the potential threat of a negative message do not apply to all types of humor to the same extent. More specifically, the threat of a negative message may actually be enhanced when specific, that is, more challenging, types of humor are used. For example, a rejection that is accompanied by sarcasm and teasing may actually be perceived as more threatening than the same message communicated without any humor.

Humor as a Double-Edged Sword

In addition to these positive functions that humor may perform as a management tool, it is important not to forget that humor is a double-edged sword that may also be used as means of coercion and control. For example, not only is humor a vehicle to establish and reinforce collegial relationships and to create a positive working atmosphere but also it may be used to exert power and to assert authority—especially in a workplace context. In this function, humor may be used, for example, to bring people back into line and to silence critical voices. Using humor in these functions, then, disguises the otherwise relatively overt display and exercise of power that such activities involve.

However, humor may be used not only by those in powerful positions as a means to exercise and display their power but also by subordinates as a contestive strategy that allows them to challenge existing power relations and institutional practices and norms. For example, humor can help mask the subversive nature of negative or challenging messages for subordinates toward their superiors, thus providing an acceptable vehicle for communicating subversive attitudes.

Humor Across Workplaces

Humor is not a homogenous category; there are numerous types of humor. The specific types of humor that are considered to be most appropriate or effective—for example, to perform various management activities—vary across workplaces. Hence, whereas communication in one workplace may be characterized by frequent teasing, sarcasm, jocular abuse, and other potentially challenging types of humor, these types of humor in another workplace may be perceived as inappropriate and perhaps even offensive and rude. Thus, although the various functions of humor as a management tool outlined earlier may potentially apply to any workplace, it is important to remember that the specific ways in which these functions are achieved and the diverse kinds of humor that may be used to achieve them may differ considerably across workplaces.

Clearly, humor is a valuable management tool that has the potential to assist people in performing a wide range of different management activities, as it may facilitate the achievement of interpersonal as well as transactional aims. However, the specific types of humor that are most appropriate to achieve these various functions and the specific ways in which they are most productively used vary considerably across workplaces. Nevertheless, the various benefits of humor to perform a wide variety of interpersonal and transactional functions—sometimes even simultaneously—make humor a valuable management tool.

Stephanie Schnurr

See also Humor and Relational Maintenance; Humor Styles; Workplace Control; Workplace Humor; Workplace Productivity; Workplace Resistance

Further Readings

Collinson, D. (2002). Managing humour. *Journal of Management Studies, 39*(3), 269–288.

Consalvo, C. (1989). Humor in management: No laughing matter. *Humor, 2*(3), 285–297.

Holmes, J. (2002). Politeness, power and provocation: How humour functions in the workplace. *Discourse Studies, 2*(2), 159–185.

Holmes, J., & Stubbe, M. (2003). *Power and politeness in the workplace: A sociolinguistic analysis of talk at work.* London, UK: Longman.

Schnurr, S. (2009). *Leadership discourse at work: Interactions of humour, gender and workplace culture.* Basingstoke, UK: Palgrave Macmillan.

Marriage and Couples

Choosing a marriage partner or significant other means potentially committing yourself to a very long-term relationship. Mistakes in choosing can be costly on many different levels. When people are asked about the qualities they most desire in a marriage partner or significant other, among the most commonly identified qualities is "a sense of humor." No doubt one reason humor is so desirable in a partner is that someone who makes you laugh can be pleasant to be around and make you feel good. When shared humor is part of early interactions with someone new, expectations for a positive relationship rise. Beyond that, many people see a good sense of humor as a reliable indicator of other desirable qualities in a partner. People with an above average sense of humor are assumed to be more extroverted, more agreeable, and less neurotic. Generally, a good sense of humor also is believed to be associated with a variety of socially desirable qualities (e.g., friendly, interesting, creative), but not with less desirable qualities (e.g., cold, mean). Thus, a good sense of humor seems to signal that a person will have many attractive, stable qualities and be a reliable source of positive experiences. This entry discusses how humor is related to partner selection, how partners use humor within a relationship, and how relationships are affected by positive humor and negative humor.

Gender Differences in Humor Preferences in Partners

Men and women both value humor, but what a good sense of humor means may vary according to one's gender, especially in the context of partner selection. An evolutionary perspective suggests that men must display a desirable sense of humor to convince women to choose them as a mate. Dominant and confident men tell more jokes, so, for women, humor expression and creation in potential mates may serve as indicators of potential success in resource acquisition. In situations where men are trying to attract women, they are quite likely to engage in "competitive" humor, trying to be the funniest person in the room in order to demonstrate their potential superior mating fitness. Thus, for men, the production of humor is more important than it is for women. Women, on the other hand, must be the evaluators, judging and responding to humor. So, whereas women prefer men who can make them laugh, men are less influenced by differences in humor production among women. In fact, men prefer women who appear to appreciate and respond to their attempts at humor, regardless of how funny the woman may be in her own right. Even within established couples, wives are found to laugh more than their husbands, and husbands are seen as producing more humor.

Do Partners Share Humor Preferences?

It turns out that opposites do not usually attract; most people seek partners who share similar interests and attitudes. This preference for similarity extends to humor. In fact, merely laughing at someone's joke can make you seem more attractive to that person than finding agreement on a multitude of attitudinal issues. In dating couples, higher levels of agreement about what is funny predict greater attraction and an enhanced desire for continuing the relationship. Among married couples, there also appears to be similarity in judgments of what is funny and in attitudes toward the appropriate use of humor. Happy couples appreciate the same types of humor and use humor in similar ways.

Does Humor Matter in Relationship Success?

Over 90% of married couples surveyed said that humor plays an important role in their relationship success. Among long-term married couples, being able to laugh together was one of the top perceived reasons for the continued success of their relationship. In fact, the presence of humor in a relationship leads to higher levels of positive affect, which often leads to positive global evaluations. Used effectively, humor can increase closeness, facilitate communication, deflect or defuse conflict, and allow for criticisms to be delivered in a more positive manner (e.g., friendly teasing). When discussing issues with potential for creating conflict, couples have been found to use humor at least once a minute. When positive humor is used, conflicts are less likely to escalate and partners feel more satisfied. In divorced and distressed couples, positive humor and an appreciation of a partner's humor are less evident.

Humor is a shared experience, so its impact depends heavily on how it is received. When couples are asked to describe both their own humor style and their partner's style, it is the perception of humor style that predicts satisfaction more strongly than the partners' self-reported style. So it is not what you think about your humor style that affects your partner; rather it is how your efforts at humor are perceived by your partner that matters most. Once again, there are some potentially important gender differences in how humor affects relationship satisfaction. Although everyone benefits from a good joke, the effects of humor on relationship satisfaction are often more evident in women than in men, a finding consistent with the notion that men are expected to be the primary humor initiators in a relationship.

A Caveat: Good and Bad Humor in Relationships

Humor can be expressed in many ways, and not all uses of humor are positive. Only recently has adequate attention been paid to the important differences between humor used well and humor used poorly. Although the distinction has always been evident, too often humor was globally viewed as a positive. In reality, humor can be used positively when sharing common experiences, reducing tension, and coping with potential stressors, but humor also can be used aggressively to belittle or demean others or their ideas. It is interesting that when people are asked a global question about their partner's sense of humor and then are asked to describe their partner's humor style (do they use humor positively or negatively), only the positive uses of humor predict a good sense of humor. Negative uses of humor are not even seen as part of what most people understand to be a truly "good" sense of humor. When a partner's perceived uses of positive and negative humor are separately considered, the clear pattern is that positive humor facilitates interactions and enhances relationship satisfaction, while negative humor can escalate conflict, produce tension, and reduce satisfaction. Even negative humor used outside the context of a relationship can end up having harmful effects on the relationship. People in a relationship with someone who frequently uses aggressive humor report being more embarrassed by their partner. In relationships, having a good sense about how and when you use humor is critical. Trying to be funny at inappropriate moments and attacking others with humor are behaviors that can do serious harm to close relationships, even if the one being attacked is not the relationship partner.

Arnie Cann and Adam T. Cann

See also Evolutionary Explanations of Humor; Gender and Humor, Psychological Aspects of; Humor and Relational Maintenance; Positive Psychology; Psychology; Reception of Humor; Sexuality

Further Readings

Barelds, D. P. H., & Barelds-Dijkstra, P. (2010). Humor in intimate relationships: Ties among sense of humor, similarity in humor and relationship quality. *HUMOR: International Journal of Humor Research, 23,* 447–465.

Bippus, A. P., Young, S. L., & Dunbar, N. E. (2011). Humor in conflict discussions: Comparing partners' perceptions. *HUMOR: International Journal of Humor Research, 24,* 287–303.

Cann, A., & Calhoun, L. G. (2001). Perceived personality associations with differences in sense of humor: Stereotypes of hypothetical others with high and low senses of humor. *HUMOR: International Journal of Humor Research, 14,* 117–130.

Cann, A., Calhoun, L. G., & Banks, J. S. (1997). On the role of humor appreciation in interpersonal attraction: It's no joking matter. *HUMOR: International Journal of Humor Research, 10,* 77–89.

Cann, A., Zapata, C. L., & Davis, H. B. (2011). Humor style and relationship satisfaction in dating couples: Perceived versus self-reported humor styles as predictors of satisfaction. *HUMOR: International Journal of Humor Research, 24,* 1–20.

Priest, R. F., & Thein, M. T. (2003). Humor appreciation in marriage: Spousal similarity, assortative mating, and disaffection. *HUMOR: International Journal of Humor Research, 16,* 63–78.

Masks

Masks are any transformational adornment of the face, including everything from makeup to elaborate head coverings. Masks are often worn in combination with appropriate costuming. They derive from the human capacity for pretense, deception, and play. Cross-culturally, masks are closely associated with festival, ritual, and theater, including, but not limited to, comedy.

The term *masking* can also refer, figuratively, to playing any role, whether on a stage or in everyday life. The term *social masking* is used to refer to the disjunction between public and private face. "All the world's a stage," wrote William Shakespeare in *As You Like It* (2.7.139), and many other writers from Erasmus of Rotterdam to 20th-century sociologist Erving Goffman have similarly noted the similarities between the experience of day-to-day living and the practice of wearing a mask and acting a role. Understanding this model of the human being as someone who puts on a "face" to interact with others is foundational for understanding how we construct identities. The humor in masking, both literal and figurative, may come from the discrepancy between the person and the mask he or she is wearing, from the predictability of the role prescribed by the mask, or from the surge of energy that is released when one escapes from civic roles and fulfills one's inner dreams. This entry discusses both literal and figurative masking.

Masks in Ritual and Festival Contexts

Traditional occasions for masking are generally at points of transition in the calendar or the life cycle—that is, when the seasons change or individuals reach certain rites of passage. Masking is associated with initiation rituals or funerary rites in cultures across the world. Even in serious rituals, however, masked figures indulge in playful and humorous expression—masked Native American ritual clowns, for example, play outrageous tricks on spectators but are respected as powerful ritual beings.

In the West, the most familiar masking traditions are associated with the pre-Lenten festivals variously known as Carnival, Mardi Gras, or Fasnacht. More than just disguise, Carnival masks function as forms of play and adornment; much creative energy goes into making and decorating them. The Carnival masks of Venice and the *vejigantes* masks of Ponce in Puerto Rico have achieved particular recognition for their artistic elaboration.

In Louisiana, Cajun Mardi Gras runs are quite different from the better known Mardi Gras spectacles and parades in New Orleans. The rural Mardi Gras "runners" wear masks while touring through local communities and engaging in playful inversions. The runners ask for permission to enter the yard and there wreak playful havoc, enacting roles of trickster, beggar, thief, wildman, and outlaw. The runners are masked and costumed. Masks are often handmade by the runners themselves or by recognized mask makers in the community, and they are designed to thoroughly disguise the identity of the maskers. Householders will try to guess their identity. Maskers engage in clowning, trickery, and artful begging and are rewarded with gifts of food and money, which go into a communal gumbo feast at the end of the day.

Another widespread masking custom is *mumming*, also known as *janneying* or *guysing*. Various mumming traditions in Europe and the European diaspora occur annually throughout the winter season. Masked mummers make the rounds of local homes, where they may perform traditional plays involving stock characters, speeches, and songs, and performers are rewarded with gifts of food and drink, and sometimes cash. In some traditions, mummers are expected to discipline and terrorize children—to the amusement of the adults. In addition to the disguise offered by their costumes and masks, mummers traditionally also disguise their speech, for example, with ingressive speech (speaking while breathing in).

Masks are often accompanied by related full-body costumes, which leads to such other present-day instances of masking as the masked ball, the fancy dress party, and Halloween trick-or-treating. Mask-costume combinations are used as satirical commentary to tame fears in cartoonish or elaborately aestheticized form. Another contemporary manifestation of the masked actor-dancer is the costumed athletic team mascot who helps amuse the fans at sporting events.

Masks in Theater and Comedy

Not only are masks and masking found in both serious and humorous literary works, but, in addition, masking has played a more continuous role within the comedic tradition. Western theater derives from the masked dramas played by ancient Greek and later Roman actors, giving us the emblem of all drama, the combined masks of laughing and weeping. The male actors in Greek tragedy and comedy wore masks to represent the different characters they played, distinguishing them from members of the chorus, and these masks signified their gender, societal position, and age, denoting, for example, the hierarchical difference between the noble King Oedipus and the shepherd who found him as a child. In the *phylax* comedies of southern Italy (4th century BCE), masks denoted bearded old men or balding slaves, often parodying their tragic counterparts with their snub noses, chubby cheeks, and hideous gaping mouths. By the time of Greek New Comedy (mid-3rd century BCE), masks had evolved

Olympic mascots often represent an animal native to the hosting country. Miga, a mascot of the 2010 Winter Olympics in Vancouver, British Columbia, is a sea bear who lives in the ocean with her family pod. According to First Nations legend, the sea bear is a killer whale at sea that becomes a Kermode or spirit bear on land. The spirit bear is a black bear born with white or cream-colored fur, the result of a genetic anomaly.

Source: Chase N./Wikimedia Commons.

Theater mask representing the type of the First Slave of New Comedy. Pentelic marble, 2nd century BCE.

Source: National Archaeological Museum, Athens, Greece/ Wikimedia Commons.

to denote stock character types, such as the ardent young lover, the cunning slave, the grumpy old man, and the beautiful courtesan. Early animal choruses (mid-6th century BCE), precursors to Athenian comedy, showcased performers dressed in animal costumes and masks. Such festal choruses of humans dressed as animals suggested a close relationship between humans and animals. The masks and costumes worn in satyr plays, a type of tragicomedy with bawdy and scatological elements, hinted even more at man's bestial nature; they depicted the satyrs with curly hair, large pointed ears, white horse's tails, and sometimes the legs of a goat.

Roman theater, likewise, followed the tradition of masked acting, as evident in the comedies of Plautus and Terence, portraying with absurd facial distortions the various city types and family members involved in domestic squabbles. The Romans also incorporated masks in their pantomimes, a type of performance spectacle that combined gymnastics, dance, and storytelling derived from folk traditions.

Masks used to denote human attributes have proved a lasting sign system, in part because the mask predicts the character's formulaic responses, and audiences delight in seeing their expectations fulfilled. Medieval audiences, well-versed in the medieval Church's didactic morality plays, knew what to expect from characters dressed allegorically as human vices or virtues. Personified vices wore ugly, monstrous-looking masks with bestial facial hair or bottle-noses to suggest the corruption of mankind's soul. Witnessed by a predominantly illiterate audience, these disguises helped to crystallize abstract iniquities such as Covetousness, Hypocrisy, Malicious Judgment, or Infidelity. Devils in morality plays wore grotesque black masks, outfitted to emit fire and smoke from their mouths; such masked figures, while eliciting laughter, would also inspire theological terror due to their concrete representation of sin.

From the 16th through the 18th centuries CE, the Italian *commedia dell'arte* continued the tradition of using masks to help represent stock comic characters, and masks are still used in similar fashion in folk and traditional theater traditions worldwide, such as Japanese *Nō* theater.

Similar satirical masking reappears in the 20th century, most evident in theater of the absurd and black comedy. Just as the masking in morality plays illustrated moral defects, these literal masks showing physiognomic deformity or animal traits indicate humanity's spiritual emptiness. The most famous example is Alfred Jarry's creation of King Ubu (*Ubu Roi*, 1896), a greedy, grotesquely infantile man, whose pear-shaped head sported an elephant trunk, signifying his essential animal nature. Masking to identify a particular kind of moral imbalance continued throughout the 20th century when avant-garde playwrights such as Jean Cocteau, Elmer Rice, and Carl Hauptmann used deformed human heads or animal masks for satirical purposes. In J. B. Priestly's expressionist play *Johnson Over Jordon* (1939), a panderer becomes a vulture, a boxer a gorilla, and a lecher a wolf through the use of masks. Later in the century, Jean-Claude van Itallie placed two actors with over-sized heads in *Motel: A Masque for Three Dolls* (1965), the crudely designed facial features of their masks symbolizing their savagery as they destroy a hotel room and murder the motel-keeper. In these instances, the satiric mask isolates negative traits through facial deformities. More playful masking appears in Broadway musicals, such as the vivid puppetry and masks that portrayed the African creatures in Disney's *The Lion King* (1997), proving that masking still entertains audiences today.

Social Masking and Identity

Masks are first and foremost tools in duplicity and trickery, from the mischief of the Mardi Gras runners to outright dishonesty. By hiding one's true self, one can deceive others, as evidenced by the wily Callimaco who disguises himself as a street ruffian as part of an elaborate plot to sleep with another man's wife in Niccolò Machiavelli's comedy *La mandragola* (The Mandrake Root, 1520). While masked, a person can control his opponent by the element of shock or surprise, a feat most readily seen by present-day television comedian Stephen Colbert, who, by adopting the figurative mask of a conservative political pundit, easily manipulates the guests on his show *The Colbert Report*. In other words, the mask denotes the dividing line between the performed or public role and the private self.

Social masking, which involves a figurative rather than literal mask, is a theatrical metaphor to describe how humans perform roles in order to protect their private selves. In the theater or in film, much comic humor derives from highlighting the duality between the public appearance of a person and the real self underneath. Dramatic tension arises as the person tries to deceive others (or even himself) with a false identity, and the laughter and humor associated with situational comedy erupts when the real self is exposed. Social masking becomes the topic of satire in Molière's *Le bourgeois gentilhomme* (The Bourgeois Gentleman, 1670). The lead character, Monsieur Jourdain, is a social climber. Wishing to don the mask of a nobleman through self-cultivation, he invites to his home instructors in fencing, dancing, music, and philosophy in order to attain the outward mannerisms and erudition he associates with nobility. The more he attempts to transform his outward self, the more pathetic his true self appears; his self-improvement strategy makes him an object of comic ridicule.

In contrast to the hypocrite whose serious public mask belies his own ridiculous nature, the Fool is a character who wears a mask of folly in order to dispense wisdom, or the truth. His mask deceives people into lowering their own defenses; while they assume the Fool to be naive or ignorant, they are taken unawares when he utters wisdom. The professional fool or jester who entertained the courts in the 15th and 16th centuries wore a hood or hat with bells and a motley or patched coat, but earlier depictions envisioned him as a half-human, half-animal figure, with animal legs, hooves, and ears on a grotesquely painted face. Because court fools had the license to speak bluntly, they could be audacious in their statements and they used humor to speak the truth and question the status quo. One example of such a fool is the character of Bottom in Shakespeare's *A Midsummer Night's Dream* who spends most of the play sporting the mask of a donkey head; however, once he has been magically transformed into an ass, he utters words of wisdom highly applicable to the play's theme of misguided romance: "Reason and love keep little company together nowadays" (3.1.145–146). These words, coming from the comic mask of an ass, remind us of the irrational nature of love and the perspicacity of folly.

The trajectory from fool to clown is difficult to trace because of the numerous permutations the fool has undergone, from court jester to folkloric figure to the masked *commedia dell'arte* player, Arlecchino. The modern-day circus clown originated from the French Arlequin, or Harlequin, the silent clown who first painted his face white. Today circus clowns add a half-mask or red nose to their faces and make distorted facial expressions to elicit laughter, transforming their natural faces into expressive, emotional masks.

A more controversial form of theatrical masking is blackface, in which performers blacken their faces with burned cork or greasepaint to enact comic caricatures of stereotyped Black people. This form of racial mimicry is especially associated with American minstrel shows featuring White performers in blackface. Later, Black performers also adopted blackface. Although minstrel shows are no longer popular, blackface masking is still a part of folk performance, such as in some rural Mardi Gras traditions.

Irish poet and playwright Oscar Wilde once wrote: "Man is least himself when he talks in his own person. Give him a mask and he will tell you the truth" (1913, p. 185). Masks, both literal and figurative, liberate those who wear them and give them license to explore possibilities and take personal risks while their true identities remain hidden. Sometimes, dramatizing the "real self" beneath the social mask reveals the hypocrisy, whereas at other times the animal-like or disfigured mask denounces the deformed behavior of humankind. As much as masking disguises and conceals, it also reveals much about human nature. The physical masks we wear at Halloween or Mardi Gras parties remind us of our role as divided beings, performing roles before each other and witnessing ourselves as actors. This division permits us to laugh at ourselves, as the mask creates a doubleness to existence that allows us to step back from life, detach ourselves from life's dilemmas, and laugh at the pathos of the human situation.

Miriam M. Chirico

See also Ancient Greek Comedy; Ancient Roman Comedy; Aristophanes; Carnival and Festival; Comedy; *Commedia dell'Arte*; Folklore; Fools; Greek Visual Humor; History of Humor: Medieval Europe; Improv Comedy; *Lazzi*; Mime; Plautus; Ritual Clowns; Roman Visual Humor; Satyr Play; Stereotypes

Further Readings

Aching, G. (2002). *Masking and power: Carnival and popular culture in the Caribbean.* Minneapolis: University of Minnesota Press.

Billington, S. (1984). *A social history of the fool.* Sussex, UK: Harvester Press.

Fava, A. (2007). *The comic mask in the* commedia dell'arte: *Actor training, improvisation, and the poetics of survival.* Chicago, IL: Northwestern University Press.

Glasgow, R. D. V. (1995). *Madness, masks, and laughter: An essay on comedy.* Madison, NJ: Fairleigh Dickinson University Press.

Glassie, H. (1975). *All silver and no brass: An Irish Christmas mumming*. Bloomington: Indiana University Press.

Halpert, H. (1990). *Christmas mumming in Newfoundland*. Toronto, Ontario, Canada: University of Toronto Press.

Harris Smith, S. (1984). *Masks in modern drama*. Berkeley: University of California Press.

Hart, M. L. (2010). *The art of ancient Greek theater*. Los Angeles, CA: J. Paul Getty Museum.

Lindahl, C., & Ware, C. (1997). *Cajun Mardi Gras masks*. Jackson: University Press of Mississippi.

Nunley, J. W., & McCarty, C. (1999). *Masks: Faces of culture*. New York, NY: Abrams in association with the Saint Louis Art Museum.

Tseëlon, E. (Ed.). (2001). *Masquerade and identities: Essays on gender, sexuality, and marginality*. London, UK: Routledge.

Twycross, M., & Carpenter, S. (2002). *Masks and masking in medieval and early Tudor England*. Aldershot, UK: Ashgate.

Wilde, O. (1913). The critic as artist. In *Intentions*. London, UK: Methuen. Retrieved from http://www.ucc.ie/celt/online/E800003-007

Wilde, O. (1968). *The artist as critic: Critical writings of Oscar Wilde* (R. Ellmann, Ed.). New York, NY: Random House.

Mathematical Humor

Mathematics has served as a source of humor in two broad ways: (1) by using humor within mathematics, to either parody a concept or lambast a persona, and (2) by using mathematics within humor as a means of furthering the plot of a joke or story. This entry examines each of these ways of using mathematics as a servant of humor.

Humor Within Mathematics

The history of making jokes using mathematics is a long and complex one going back at least to the fanciful but historically real character of Meton, the mathematician, in Aristophanes's classic Greek comedy, *Birds*. Mathematics has been humorously mocked and parodied (mostly by non-mathematicians) in every era with, perhaps, the gentlest example being contained on a postcard sent by the famous 19th-century mathematician, Leonard Euler, to announce the birth of his first child. It read, simply:

$$1 + 1 = 3.$$

Other famous classic examples are found in the writings of Lewis Carroll (Rev. Charles Dodgson) and Jonathan Swift. Most of the text of Carroll's *Alice in Wonderland* is a subtle mocking of the concepts of Victorian mathematics, and the unredacted collection of Swift's *Gulliver's Travels* contains the story of the island of Laputa, inhabited by very logical but harebrained mathematicians.

It is surprising that, given the large quantity of material, no collection of purely mathematical humor seems to exist before the 20th century (although there are many puzzle books containing sporadic humor). Short story collections, such as Clifton Fadiman's *Fantasia Mathematica* (1958) and *The Mathematical Magpie* (1962), proliferated in the early to middle part of the century, but the first serious collection of math jokes in book form seems to be Friedrich Wille's *Humor in der Mathematik* (Humor in Mathematics, 1984), with the first English collection being Desmond Machale's *Comic Sections* from 1985. With the rise of the Internet, several modern sites continue to update and contribute their own collections.

Other venues have also seen their share of math-mocking, most especially in cartoons. Sidney Harris in *American Scientist*, Nick Kim of the website Nearing Zero, and Randall Monroe, the creator of the comic strip *xkcd*, have contributed an extensive collection of cartoons mocking many aspects of mathematics and the mathematician's life.

Mathematicians have even more devious ways than laymen of punishing themselves with humor. Almost every field of mathematics has a corpus of jokes that either plays on concepts within that field or mocks the terminology. Specialist humor can be found in such areas as real analysis, differential geometry, set theoretic geometry, affine geometry, measure theory, number theory, algebra (both simple and advanced), topology, linear algebra, Fourier series, numerical analysis, probability, combinatorics, statistics, logic, computer science, applied mathematics, harmonic analysis, and set theory.

A single example will suffice to illustrate how specialists tease each other with humor. The following example (somewhat abridged) is provided by Robert Smith: Several mathematicians are asked, "How do you put an elephant in a refrigerator?"

Real Analyst:

Let $\varepsilon > 0$. $\forall \varepsilon \exists \delta > 0$ such that $\lim_{n \to 0} \left(\frac{elephant}{2^n} \right) = 0$.

Since $\left(\frac{1}{2}\right)^n < \left(\frac{1}{n^2}\right)$, for $n \geq 5$, by comparison, we know that $\sum_{n \to 0}\left(\frac{elephant}{2^n}\right)$ converges, identically at elephant. As such, cut the elephant into two pieces. Put one-half inside the fridge, then repeat as $n \to \infty$

Differential Geometer: Differentiate it and put into the refrigerator. Then integrate it in the refrigerator.

Set Theoretic Geometer: Apply the Banach-Tarsky theorem to form a refrigerator with more volume.

Algebraist: Show that parts of it can be put into the refrigerator. Then show that the refrigerator is closed under addition.

Topologist: The elephant is compact, so it can be put into a finite collection of refrigerators. That's usually good enough.

Geometer: Create an axiomatic system in which "an elephant can be placed in a refrigerator" is an axiom.

Complex Analyst: Put the refrigerator at the origin and the elephant outside the unit circle. Then get the image under inversion.

Probabilist: Keep trying to push it in in random ways and eventually it will fit.

Combinatorist: Discretize the elephant, partition it, and find a suitable rearrangement.

Statistician: Put its tail in the refrigerator as a sample, and say, "done!"

Logician: I know it's possible, I just can't do it.

Category Theorist: Isn't this just a special case of Yoneda's lemma?

Experimental Mathematician: I think it'd be much more interesting to get the refrigerator inside the elephant.

The general character traits of many mathematicians as well as those of specific individuals have served as fodder for humor. For instance, one need only think "statistician" to see the humor in the following:

> Three statisticians went duck hunting. A duck flew out and the first statistician took a shot, the shot went a foot too high. The second statistician took his shot and the shot went a foot too low. The third statistician said, "We got it!"

The abstruseness of mathematicians is set in even more relief when mathematicians are compared with other, more practical, scientists. This has given rise to a whole class of jokes that starts, "A mathematician, a physicist, and a [chemist, engineer, etc.] . . ." For example:

> An engineer, a physicist, and a mathematician are staying in a hotel. The engineer wakes up and smells smoke. He goes out into the hallway and sees a fire, so he fills a trash can from his room with water and douses the fire. He goes back to bed. Later, the physicist wakes up and smells smoke. He opens his door and sees a fire in the hallway. He walks down the hall to a fire hose and after calculating the flame velocity, distance, water pressure, trajectory, etc., extinguishes the fire with the minimum amount of water and energy needed. Later, the mathematician wakes up and smells smoke. He goes to the hall, sees the fire and then the fire hose. He thinks for a moment and then exclaims, "Ah, a solution exists!" and then goes back to bed.

Humor has also been used as an aid in the teaching of mathematics. The American Council of Mathematics Teachers has provided books of math jokes suitable for use in early classroom instruction.

Mathematics Within Humor

Mathematics has also supplied subsidiary material for several types of humorous venues. Matt Groening, the creator of *The Simpsons* television cartoon series, has made the smart-aleck (but not book smart) protagonist, Bart Simpson, speak advanced mathematics at times, while Ken Keeler (who has a PhD in mathematics) created a new math theorem especially for use in the cartoon series, *Futurama*.

The Harvard-trained-mathematician-turned-satirist Tom Lehrer has created several songs that parody math, most notably, the songs, "Lobachevsky" (named for mathematician Nikolai Lobachevsky) and "New Math."

The android, Data, from the television series, *Star Trek: The Next Generation*, explored the concept of humor in the episode, "The Outrageous Okona." In questioning the computer, he finds:

> *Data:* Of all performers available, who is considered funniest?
> *Computer:* Twenty-third-century Stan Orega specialized in jokes about quantum mathematics. . . .

In most jokes, the punch line exposes two different interpretations of the joke text (called scripts). A normal human brain is poor at multitasking, so the processing of more than two joke scripts at one time produces both processing lags and network fatigue. Because jokes using quantum mathematics take place in an infinite-dimensional Hilbert space, the punch line exposes an infinite number of scripts at once. If these sorts of jokes existed, they would be "too funny to be funny."

Finally, several journals, such as the *Annals of Improbable Research* and the *Journal of Irreproducible Results* are repositories of truly awful, hysterically funny, but occasionally brilliant mathematics.

Donald Casadonte

See also Aristophanes; Mathematics and Humor

Further Readings

Fadiman, C. (Ed.). (1958). *Fantasia mathematica.* New York, NY: Simon & Schuster.

MacHale, D. (1990). *Comic sections.* Dublin, Ireland: Boole Press.

Smith, R. (2010, November 21). A joke. *Symb01ics Ideas.* Retrieved April 18, 2013, from http://symbo1ics.com/blog/?p=389

Vinik, A., Silvey, L., & Hughes, B. (Eds.). (1978). *Mathematics and humor.* Reston, VA: National Council of Teachers of Mathematics.

Wille, F. (1982). *Humor in der Mathematik* [Humor in mathematics]. Göttingen, Germany: Vandenhoeck & Ruprecht.

Mathematics and Humor

Mathematics has served both as a means to analyze the processes involved in humor and as a source of humor. This entry examines the first of these uses.

Descriptive Mathematics

The use of mathematical methods specifically in an attempt to understand the elements of humor is of relatively recent origin and still in its infancy. Perhaps first mention should be given to the mathematician, George Birkhoff, who, in his 1933 book, *Aesthetic Measure,* derived a method whose purpose was "within each class of aesthetic objects, to define the order O and the complexity C so that their ratio M = O/C yields the aesthetic measure of any object in the class." Birkhoff applied his method to measure the aesthetic "goodness" of objects as diverse as geometric designs, poetry, and musical harmony. His method was intended to provide a measure of the aesthetic goodness of any type of art, including prose and humor. Birkhoff did not apply his method to humor, per se, but clearly intended it to be applicable.

The first direct use of mathematics to analyze the processes of humor was made by John Allen Paulos, in two books: *Mathematics and Humor* and *I Think, Therefore I Laugh.* In *Mathematics and Humor,* Paulos related humor to the problem of self-reference in logic (briefly touching on the paradoxes of Bertrand Russell, Alfred Tarski, and Kurt Gödel), arguing that, in some cases, self-reference gives rise to either two different discourse levels or two different interpretations of the linguistic material within a joke. The idea of the splitting of a joke into two competing interpretations was not new with Paulos, but in Chapter 5 of *Mathematics and Humor* he used techniques of René Thom's catastrophe theory, specifically, the cusp catastrophe, in an attempt to provide a diagrammatic representation of the process of humor. The cusp catastrophe (one of seven classes of catastrophes), whose equation is

$$V = x^4 + ax^2 + bx,$$

creates a fold in parameter space (V is the potential surface, and a, b are control variables) so that the first interpretation of the joke lies on the bottom part of the fold and the second interpretation lies on the upper part with continual jumping back and forth between the two interpretations as the control variable, b, cycles between two values ($a < 0$).

As an illustration of the process of humor, this method has great explanatory power, but Paulos never defines in any explicit way exactly what the variables a and b stand for or how they should be measured. This is one basis for Martin Gardner's scathing review of Paulos's catastrophe theory model in his book, *Science: Good, Bad and Bogus.*

In the linguistic analysis of humor, graph theory, set theory, and lattice theory applications have been developed by Christian F. Hempelmann, Salvatore Attardo, and Victor Raskin, among others, to model important relationships between elements of the two competing interpretations of material within a joke, called *scripts* by Raskin. Each script, A and A' of the joke, contains a set of script elements (objects and actions within the script). Hempelmann and Attardo showed that some set elements are common between the two script sets (forming a script overlap

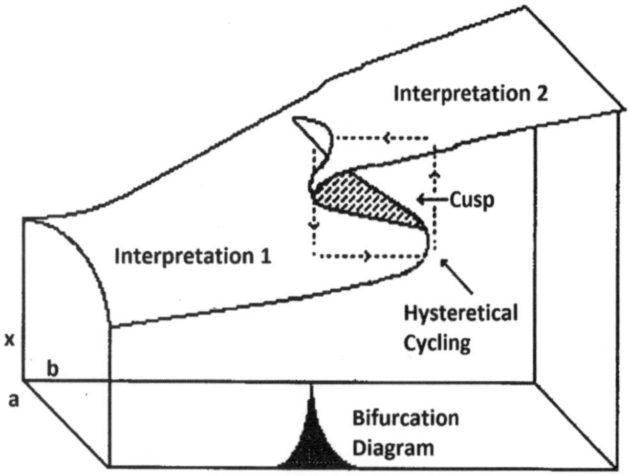

Figure 1 Cusp Catastrophe Model of Humor (after Paulos)

Source: Donald Casadonte.

Notes: In hysteretical cycling, the path forward and the path backward are different. There is a sudden transition forward from interpretation 1 to interpretation 2 at the fold in the figure, but the transition back occurs only after the curve spends some time in interpretation 1 (this is called the hysteresis lag). Thermostats are hysteretically controlled. If the thermostat is set at 72 degrees, then it instantaneously shuts off at 72 degrees, but it doesn't automatically switch back on an instant after it shuts off when the temperature drops below 72 degrees. Hysteresis says that the thermostat must spend some time in the off state before it turns back on, even if the temperature drops below 72 degrees.

set) and some are opposed (forming a script opposition set)—in set theory terms:

$$A \cap A' = \text{Overlap Set and } \overline{A \cap A'} = \text{Opposition Set.}$$

Using material from the opposition sets of a wide variety of jokes, they were able to isolate several classes of set opposition types (which they call *logical mechanisms*) that exist between scripts in any joke and form the basis for resolving the incongruity between the scripts. In the computer applications of this set-theoretic approach, the linguistic classification of word meanings using slot-filler techniques gives rise, naturally, to relational graphs. Raskin, in seeking a deeper method of representing the semantic relationships between objects and actions within a joke text, developed and used a general classification scheme called *ontological semantics*. The classification of elements within a joke using ontological semantics forms a relational lattice. The exact mechanism of lattice dynamics in humor is a matter under investigation.

Igor Krishtafovich claims to have found a formula for the "effectiveness" of humor (HE). His formula,

$$HE = PI \times C/T + BM,$$

where PI = personal involvement, C = complexity of a joke (higher = better—cf. Birkhoff, earlier), T = time to solve the joke (longer = poorer), and BM = background mood (livelier = better), is an interesting heuristic, but, as in the case with Paulos's cusp catastrophe model and several other descriptive equations by other authors, none of the variables is well defined or easy to measure.

Semi-Quantitative Mathematics

Use of quantifiable rather than descriptive mathematics has also been made to model certain individual aspects of humor. Donald Casadonte used a modified Van der Pol oscillator equation,

$$\begin{aligned} x' &= \varepsilon x(1 - y^2) - [y(1 - rgy)/(1 + jy^2)] + s \\ &\quad + k\cos(\omega z + \phi) \\ y' &= x \\ z' &= p, \end{aligned}$$

to create a semi-quantitative model of the pressure variations in respiration that arise in laughter that compare quite closely with empirically measured pressure changes made both by the expanding diaphragm and inside of the trachea during laughter. By varying the parameters r, g, s, k, ω, and φ, even ape-like vocalizations could be modeled.

Shiva Sundaram and Shrikanth Narayanan modeled vocal-tract sound generation in human-like laughter by comparing the larynx with a damped, forced sinusoidal oscillator of the type

$$M\, d^2x/dt^2 = -kx - b\, dx/dt,$$

whose solution is

$$x(t) = Ae^{-bt/2m}e^{-j(\mathrm{sqrt}(k/m))t}.$$

Casadonte's equation reduces to this as a limiting case ($y \rightarrow 0$).

They were able to create a program with adjustable variables k, m, and b that allowed for the creation of near-human acoustic laughter.

Several researchers have used fast Fourier transform (FFT) methods to study the acoustical properties of laughter. Robert R. Provine, Jo-Anne Bachorowski and Michael J. Owren, Hartmut Rothgänger, Casadonte, and many others have, independently, measured the frequency spectra for laughter-like vocalizations using FFT computations of the recorded waveforms. Erich S. Luschei and colleagues have used mathematics to analyze the electromyographic signals generated in laughter, finding values close to those determined acoustically.

Donald Casadonte

See also Computational Humor; Humor, Computer-Generated; Laugh, Laughter, Laughing; Mathematical Humor

Further Readings

Attardo, S., Hempelmann, C. F., & Di Maio, S. (2002). Script oppositions and logical mechanisms: Modeling incongruities and their resolutions. *HUMOR: International Journal of Humor Research, 15*(1), 3–46.

Bachorowski, J.-A., Smoski, M. J., & Owren, M. J. (2001). The acoustic features of human laughter. *Journal of the Acoustic Society of America, 110,* 1581–1597.

Birkhoff, G. D. (1933). *Aesthetic measure.* Cambridge, MA: Harvard University Press.

Casadonte, D. (2003). A note on the neuro-mathematics of laughter. *HUMOR: International Journal of Humor Research, 16*(2), 133–156.

Gardner, M. (1989). *Science: Good, bad, and bogus.* New York, NY: Prometheus Books.

Krishtafovich, I. (2006). *Humor theory: Formula for laughter.* Parker, CO: Outskirts Press.

Luschei, E. S., Ramig, L. O., Finnegan, E. M., Bakker, K. K., & Smith, M. E. (2006). Patterns of laryngeal electromyography and the activity of the respiratory system during spontaneous laughter. *Journal of Neurophysiology, 96*(1), 442–450.

Paulos, J. A. (1980). *Mathematics and humor.* Chicago, IL: University of Chicago Press.

Paulos, J. A. (2000). *I think, therefore I laugh.* New York, NY: Columbia University Press.

Provine, R. R. (1996). Laughter. *American Scientist, 84*(1), 38–47.

Rothgänger, H., Hauser, G., Cappellini, A. C., & Guidotti, A. (1998). Analysis of laughter and speech sounds in Italian and German students, *Naturwissenschaften, 85,* 394–402.

Sundaram, S., & Narayanan, S. (2007). Automatic acoustic synthesis of human-like laughter. *Journal of the Acoustical Society of America, 121*(1), 527–523.

Maxim

In everyday language, the word *maxim* refers to a rule of conduct adopted by an individual to get on in life (e.g., "Trust your crazy ideas!"), or it is used as a synonym for aphorism, a general truth expressed in a laconic form (e.g., François de La Rochefoucauld's maxims). Theoretically, in the seminal framework developed by the philosopher Herbert Paul Grice (1913–1988), maxims are understood to be basic assumptions of rational conversation mutually shared by the participants. Grice subsumes his maxims under a cooperative principle ("Make your conversational contribution such as is required") and four categories borrowed from Immanuel Kant. They are cornerstones of bona fide communication, and, thus, their opposites might be regarded as containing the recipe for humorous conversation.

Grice's work has attracted enormous interest. Relativists have questioned the universality of the maxims, reductionists have tried to reformulate and eliminate them, whereas expansionists have introduced further maxims to capture various aspects of language use. Humor theorists have discovered their explanatory power and offer ways the Gricean framework can tackle or can be accommodated to humorous material such as jokes. This entry discusses how Grice's maxims and a subsequent list of politeness maxims postulated by linguistics professor Geoffrey N. Leech account for some humor.

Maxims of Cooperation and Politeness

Despite the widespread criticism of his model, most textbooks and studies that discuss Grice's maxims use the original version that Grice developed and ignore the maxims that others added later.

Quantity

Make your contribution as informative as is required.

Do not make your contribution more informative than is required.

Quality

Do not say what you believe to be false.

Do not say that for which you lack adequate evidence.

Relation/Relevance

Be relevant.

Manner

Be perspicuous:

- Avoid obscurity of expression.
- Avoid ambiguity.

- Be brief.
- Be orderly. (Grice, 1975)

A set of politeness maxims that account for a broader range of humor phenomena was postulated by Leech:

Tact

Minimize cost to *other.*

Maximize benefit to *other.*

Generosity

Minimize benefit to *self.*

Maximize cost to *self.*

Approbation

Minimize dispraise of *other.*

Maximize praise of *other.*

Modesty

Minimize praise of *self.*

Maximize dispraise of *self.*

Agreement

Minimize disagreement between *self* and *other.*

Maximize agreement between *self* and *other.*

Sympathy

Minimize antipathy between *self* and *other.*

Maximize sympathy between *self* and *other.* (Leech, 1983)

Everyone occasionally behaves in ways that are inconsistent with (fail to fulfill, violate, infringe) one or more of these maxims. Grice describes four types of such instances: (1) unostentatious violation (e.g., misleading), (2) opting out (when the speaker indicates that he or she cannot obey the maxims for some reasons), (3) clashing (when the speaker is unable to fulfill a maxim without violating another), and (4) flouting (when a patent violation of a maxim urges the hearer to discover an implicit meaning conveyed by the speaker). Hyperbole and irony flout the first quality maxim, according to Grice.

Leech argues that the relationships between illocutionary goals and social goals can be competitive, convivial, collaborative, or conflictive. These four situations are parallel to the possible relationships between Grice's and Leech's maxims. Conflictive situations are greatly sensitive to humor. Clashes between Gricean and Leechian maxims may be humorous.

People sometimes fail to follow the maxims unintentionally. Non-native speakers, for example, may not always be aware of the different meanings and the socially adequate use of words they employ. Helen Spencer-Oatey recalls a case when she, in her early 50s, helped a foreign student of low proficiency in English find his way across London. On reaching the train, the young man tried to express his gratitude by saying, "Thank you very much. You are a very kind old lady," a quite paradoxical "compliment" (according to the approbation maxims) to which she reacted, understandably, with mixed emotions. Public notices posted to inform an international audience are common sources of ambiguity, such as the following advertisement for donkey rides somewhere outside the English-speaking countries: "Would you like to ride on your own *ass?*" Ambiguous statements accidentally made by politicians quickly become widely known via traditional media and Internet folklore.

By contrast, banterers, ironists, jokers, comedians, sitcom writers, and the like consciously infringe on the tacit assumptions of conversation, at least within the boundaries of their genre.

Humorous Infringements of the Maxims in Different Genres

There has been a debate about whether humorous texts intrinsically violate, pretend to violate, or flout one or more of the maxims, and at which level this takes place: that of the author/narrator or that of the character who is speaking in the story. Moreover, the length of the violation has been called into question, with Andrew Goatly's claim that the violation in humor is very short.

Either way, a great number of jokes (if not all of them) deliberately infringe on a maxim when arriving at their punch line. For example, the stock boy violates the relevance maxim in the following joke:

> A lady was picking through the frozen turkeys at the grocery store, but couldn't find one big enough for her family. She asked a stock boy, "Do these turkeys get any bigger?" The stock boy replied, "No, ma'am, they're dead."

Genres such as sitcom and stand-up comedy abound with maxim violations. What normally would count as rough and inappropriate in daily exchanges may be usual from satirical sitcom heroes such as Al Bundy of *Married . . . With Children*. Dialogues in the internationally popular *Friends* are also saturated with humorous infringements of both the Gricean and the Leechian maxims.

Attila L. Nemesi

See also Comedy; Exaggeration; Irony; Jokes; Punch Line; Sitcoms

Further Readings

Attardo, S. (1993). Violation of conversational maxims and cooperation: The case of jokes. *Journal of Pragmatics, 19*(6), 537–558.

Attardo, S. (1994). *Linguistic theories of humor.* Berlin, Germany: Mouton de Gruyter.

Farghal, M. (2006). Accidental humor in international public notices displayed in English. *Journal of Intercultural Communication, 12*. Retrieved from http://www.immi.se/intercultural/nr12/farghal.htm

Goatly, A. (2012). *Meaning and humour.* Cambridge, UK: Cambridge University Press.

Grice, H. P. (1975). Logic and conversation. In P. Cole & J. L. Morgan (Eds.), *Syntax and semantics: Vol. 3. Speech acts* (pp. 41–58). New York, NY: Academic Press.

Leech, G. N. (1983). *Principles of pragmatics.* London, UK: Longman.

Nemesi, A. L. (2012). Two masters of playing with conversational maxims. In A. T. Litovkina et al. (Eds.), *Hungarian humour* (pp. 13–30). Cracow, Poland: Tertium.

Raskin, V. (1985). *Semantic mechanisms of humor.* Dordrecht, Netherlands: Reidel.

Spencer-Oatey, H. (2007). Theories of identity and the analysis of face. *Journal of Pragmatics, 39*(4), 639–656.

Mechanisms of Humor

Mechanisms of humor are specific semantic constellations used in humorous stimuli intended to achieve what many theories call the resolution of incongruity. These mechanisms are conceptualized as textual structures of a symbolic stimulus that are paralleled by cognitive structures on the part of the consumer of that stimulus. They motivate the incongruous parts of the text so that two opposing scripts can overlap. This motivation of the overlap, or masking of the contrast, is done in a logical manner that is ultimately flawed, or paralogical, which is crucial to the humorousness of the stimulus. This entry discusses theories of how these mechanisms of humor function.

An early discussion of the general concept of a mechanism of wit—humorous but also nonhumorous—by Maciej Kazimierz Sarbiewski does not yet focus on the flawed manner of the reasoning but mentions it in terms of a conclusion of the incongruity in humor that is merely apparent, not logical. Although Sigmund Freud's heterogeneous list of "techniques of humor"—largely types of wordplay—has not proven useful in humor research, in the context of the general reasoning mechanism under discussion here, he spoke of a "sense in nonsense," inspiring Norman Maier's slightly more developed notion of a "limited sense" that holds true only temporarily.

It was not until the groundbreaking 1948 study by Elie Aubouin that this aspect of humor was discussed in real detail. His central concept in the context of mechanisms of humor is the "justification" for two incongruous senses, which leads to "acceptance" of their simultaneous validity by the hearer. This necessarily requires false logic, because a valid logic would eliminate one of the senses. But for humor, the two "irreconcilable aspects" have to be allowed to exist in parallel. Accordingly, Aubouin assumed that the mechanisms never lead to full resolution in favor of one sense but that a text is most humorous when the "justification" is close to being perfect by almost discarding one sense. Aubouin considers this justification as an error in reasoning on the part of the consumer of a humorous text. But it has since been understood to be commonly triggered by a pseudological mechanism built into the text for the sake of the simultaneous acceptance of both its irreconcilable readings. A mechanism of humor can therefore have a static symbolic component in text or images and a dynamic, cognitive, reasoning component.

In contemporary research, Elliott Oring, citing James Beattie, has outlined in several places what slightly earlier Avner Ziv called *local logic* and Giovannantonio Forabosco termed *congruent incongruity*. Oring's term is *appropriate incongruity,* and among the mechanisms responsible for the appropriateness of the incongruity are double meaning, vacuous reversal, and contrastive iteration. Oring adds that for any such technique to be successful, it must not be transparent for a given hearer, but enough of an intellectual challenge, which, for example, two senses connected in a pun often are not. In this context, several studies suggest that the complexity of the false reasoning correlates with perceived funniness in terms of a person's general preference for, or inclination to, processing complex stimuli. Similarly, children seem to be progressing through various stages of humor competence, and consequently preference, in relation to their general cognitive development.

The main explication of the general "logical mechanism" of humor, using that term and its acronym, LM, was begun with the general theory of verbal humor and has since then been pursued within this paradigm. Figure-ground reversal was identified early as a mechanism used in humor, for example, turning a house around a lightbulb rather than the other way around. This makes clear that these mechanisms aren't exclusive to humor but are merely used there. This type of reversal can be found outside of humor, as are the other mechanisms from the first inventory: chiasmus, analogy, false priming, and juxtaposition. Later inventories became much more expansive but not exhaustive, were derived from humor beyond canned jokes, and include two general classes of faultiness in logical mechanisms: (1) logic that is in principle false, like the assumption underlying the mechanism in puns, namely, that the sound of a word is related to the meaning of the word; and (2) logic that could be correct but is applied in a wrong, or at least defeasible, way. Correct reasoning can fail, for example, when it is based on wrong premises. Other supercategories of mechanisms of humor could be postulated at a similarly abstract level, for example, metahumor based on playing with the expectation of a mechanism or absurd types of humor based on the denial of any such mechanism. In general, mechanisms of humor can be analyzed at varying levels of abstraction, depending on the research issue at hand.

Attempts at formally capturing logical mechanisms quickly advanced past set theory, which defines rules for sets or collections of objects, and derived more adequacy from graph theory, which can show multiple, labeled connections between conceptual units. Initial research based on the overall formalization of humor theory in computational linguistics, in particular in terms of the ontological semantic theory of humor, is under way and should yield further results in the near future. But because these mechanisms of humor are intended to be barely detectable in their faultiness—which makes them hard to pin down and unpack—their overall nature and even their existence continue to be debated.

Christian F. Hempelmann

See also Cognitive Aspects; Development of Humor; Incongruity and Resolution; Linguistic Theories of Humor

Further Readings

Attardo, S., Hempelmann, C. F., & Di Maio, S. (2002). Script oppositions and logical mechanisms: Modeling incongruities and their resolutions. *HUMOR: International Journal of Humor Research, 15*(1), 3–46.

Attardo, S., & Raskin, V. (1991). Script theory revis(it)ed: Joke similarity and joke representation model. *HUMOR: International Journal of Humor Research, 4*(3/4), 293–347.

Aubouin, E. (1948). *Technique et psychologie du comique* [Technique and psychology of humor]. Marseille, France: OFEP.

Hempelmann, C. F. (2004). Script opposition and logical mechanism in punning. *HUMOR: International Journal of Humor Research, 17*(4), 381–392.

Hempelmann, C. F. (2012). Formal humor logic beyond second-most plausible reasoning. *Artificial Intelligence of Humor. Papers from the 2012 AAAI Fall Symposium. Technical Report FS-12–02* (pp. 14–17). Palo Alto, CA: AAAI Press.

Hempelmann, C. F., & Attardo, S. (2011). Resolutions and their incongruities: Further thoughts on logical mechanisms. *HUMOR: International Journal of Humor Research, 24*(2), 125–149.

Maier, N. R. (1932). A gestalt theory of humour. *British Journal of Psychology. General Section, 23*(1), 69–74.

Oring, E. (1992). Appropriate incongruity. In *Jokes and their relations* (pp. 1–15). Lexington: University Press of Kentucky.

Oring, E. (2003). Appropriate incongruity redux. In *Engaging Humor* (pp. 1–12). Champaign: University of Illinois Press.

Sarbiewski, M. K. (1963). De acuto et arguto sive Seneca et Martialis [Concerning sharp and witty style, or Seneca and Martial]. In S. Skimina (Ed. & Trans.), *Wiklady poetyki (praecepta poetica)* [Poetic precepts] (pp. 1–41). Wroclaw/Krakow, Poland: Polska Akademia Nauk. (Original work published 1619/1623)

Medieval Visual Humor

Because the visual arts were largely in the service of the Christian Church during the Middle Ages in Western Europe, levity may be unexpected. However, medieval artists participated in the long history of witty, clever, even overtly humorous imagery. Although no two examples are identical, certain categories of medieval mischief may be noted.

Clever in Context

The humor of an image may depend on its location—if placed in different surroundings, the joke would be lost. The meaning of these visual puns is readily understood and equally accessible to everyone, no matter one's origin, language, or level of education. The viewer needs only to look in order to appreciate the artist's ingenuity. For example, King Charles IV of Bohemia, accompanied by his wife and courtiers, addresses his subjects from the balcony on the south transept facade of the Marienkirche in Mühlhausen. Although carved of stone (ca.1370–1380), these figures look and act as if alive. Similarly, on the street facade of the palace built by Jacques Coeur in Bourges (1443–1451) are life-size, highly realistic figures of the owner and his wife, Macée de Léodepart, looking out of second-story windows, as if trying to engage the people who pass by in conversation. Today, even without their original paint, the level of realism remains so high it seems certain that visual trickery was intended (see Palace of Jacques Coeur images).

Other figures observe the observer, seemingly watching our every move. Stone people stand in the crenellations on the west facade of Exeter Cathedral (dated 1346–1375), quietly observing everyone who comes to church. Similarly, visitors to the Sicilian cathedral of Palermo who enter the south porch (constructed 1426–1430) may find their attendance is monitored by the sculpted nobles and clergy standing in the loggia arches, noting all that transpires in the piazza below.

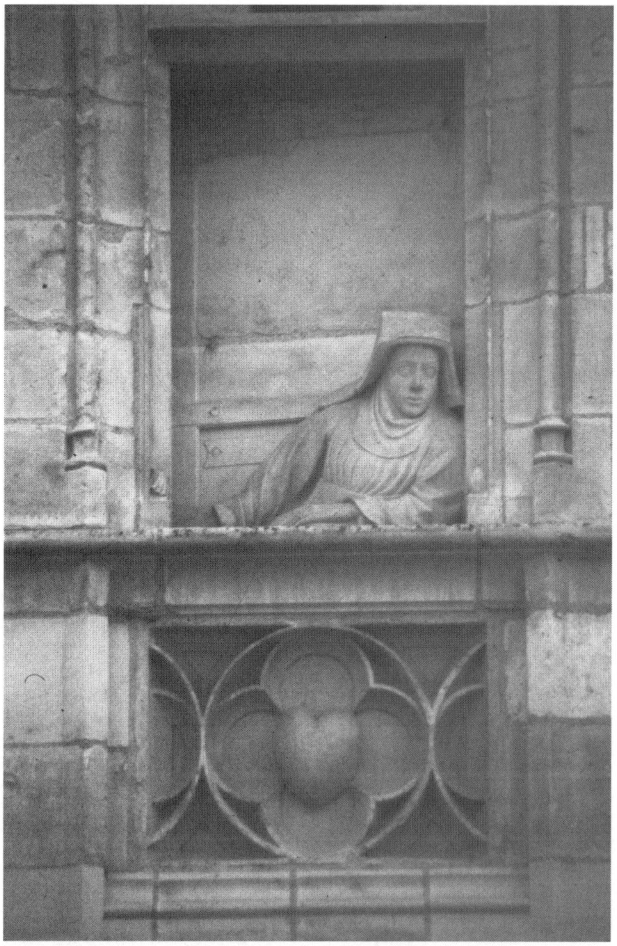

Palace of Jacques Coeur, Bourges, France, street facade, 1443–1451. Extremely realistic stone sculptures, originally painted, of Jacques Coeur and his wife, Macée de Léodepart, leaning out of false windows and attempting to engage people who pass by on the street in conversation.

Source: Janetta Rebold Benton.

Climbing on Buildings

A witty interaction between sculpture and architecture is achieved by stone or wood figures that appear to scale buildings. At the cathedral of Notre-Dame in Embrun, France, halfway up a slender column on the north porch, one diminutive column-climber uses his arms and legs to cling to the column while another sticks his head out between two columns. These figures, tiny and barely noticeable, may seem out of context in a religious setting, but the man imprisoned here in stone is said to be the chapter provost/rector who underpaid the workers. They had their revenge with these caricatures, believed to be the work of an Italian sculptor.

Many highly realistic stone people, dressed in the costumes current in the carver's day (ca. 1500), appear to have scaled the walls and now straddle the flying buttresses of the cathedral of Saint John (*Sint-Janskathedraal*) in 's-Hertogenbosch, the Netherlands. They may regret the results of their efforts to attain so lofty a location, for at the top of each buttress a fierce open-mouthed gargoyle blocks their path of ascent and lunges threateningly toward them, causing them to recoil in fear.

Eating the Architecture

A curious interaction between sculpture and architecture is seen in carved heads, more often monstrous than human, that appear to consume parts of medieval buildings—column capitals and bases, beams, tracery, and ribs. Columns, in particular, were the preferred cuisine. On the upper left arch of the facade of the church of Saint-Nicolas in Civray, France, in place of a traditional column capital is a creature with large eyes and many pointed teeth who dines with gusto on the column below. At the Cathedral of Santa María de la Regla in León, Spain, human heads carved on capitals in the 13th- to 14th-century cloister open their mouths wide to consume the columns that support them (see Cathedral of Santa María de la Regla image). In the Gothic portion of Southwell Minster in England, capitals carved in the form of monstrous heads have pairs of slender colonnettes in their mouths, as if sucking on straws!

Alternatively, rather than the top of the column, the bottom may provide nourishment. In the 12th-century cloister beside the cathedral of Monreale, Sicily, the molding on several column bases is being eaten by little monsters that open their mouths wide like boa constrictors.

Cathedral of Santa María de la Regla, León, Spain, cloister, 13th to 14th century. The usual capitals are replaced by heads that consume the columns below.

Source: Janetta Rebold Benton.

Ceiling beams also were on the medieval monsters' menu. In the Hôtel-Dieu in Beaune, France, in the Great Hall of the Poor (opened in 1452), brightly painted dragon heads chew the ends of the ceiling beams. Thought to be the work of Flemish or Burgundian sculptors, some of these beam-biters wear clothing akin to monks' habits, whereas others are caricatures of human heads. Pairs of dragon heads have been gnawing the ends of wood beams in the cathedral of Saint-Lazare in Autun, France, up in the shadows of the north aisle, since the early 16th century.

At the little church of Barfreston, England, built in the last quarter of the 12th century, the circular east window attracts no unusual attention—until the fantastic animal heads biting the ends of the radiating tracery bars are noticed. The motif of a sculpted monster eating the architecture was cleverly used to mask an error during construction of the retrochoir of Wells Cathedral in England (ca.1320). On either side of the processional way, three ribs were started but then found to be superfluous. Rather than removing the ribs, at the end of each was placed a dragon head that appears to be eating the unwanted rib with the gastronomic gusto of a gourmand, a clever sculptor turning an error into amusement.

Modifying the Architecture

Sculpture might be used to enhance the appearance of a structure. A highly realistic example is seen in the cloister beside the Utrecht cathedral. The bishop had remarked that one of the delicate arches filled with curving tracery that borders the cloister looked "rather unstable." Jacob van den Borgh, the master builder, devised a permanent solution in 1396 by reinforcing the tracery of this arch with a carefully carved, extremely realistic, stone rope.

A variation on the usual cylindrical column shaft is the "knotted column" in which two or four small columns appear to be tied together by another column looped around them, as if to reinforce them. This was especially popular in Romanesque Italy, where the four columns flanking the south transept porch of Modena Cathedral and seemingly tied together by a flexible fifth column are the work of Master Wiligelmo. Knotted columns are seen on the facade of San Michele in Foro in Lucca, the loops emphasized by inlay. In such examples, by giving a sculptural form to an architectural support, medieval masons and sculptors blur the customary division between architecture and sculpture.

Among the various clever ways in which columns were treated on medieval buildings, an especially amusing example is found on the Romanesque basilica of Santa Maria Maggiore in Tuscania, built between the end of the 11th and first half of the 12th century. A row of nine small columns form a dwarf loggia on the facade. The penultimate column on the right side is wider in diameter than the other eight. Rather than chipping away at this column to make it conform to the narrower diameter of the others, the sculptor provided it with a corset, implying that the corset can simply be laced tighter, to diminish this column's dimensions, thereby making it as slender and svelte as its neighbors. (See Church of Santa Maria Maggiore image.)

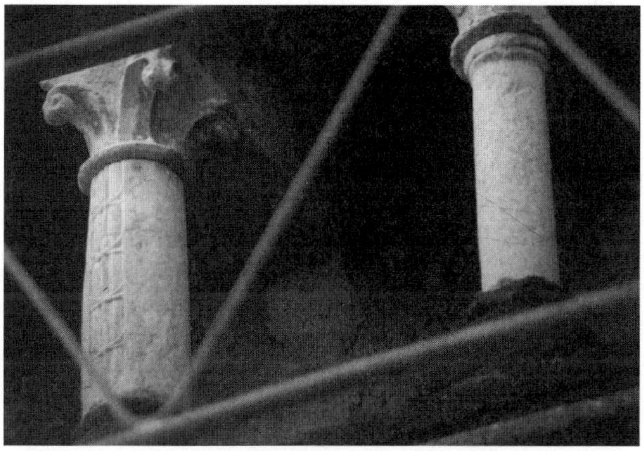

Church of Santa Maria Maggiore in Tuscania (Latium, Province of Viterbo, Italy), facade loggia, 12th to 13th century. The widest column wears a corset, as if aspiring to be as thin as its neighboring columns.

Source: Janetta Rebold Benton.

Supporting Roles

Sculpted figures frequently appear to hold up or reinforce medieval buildings. A sculptor literally lent a helping hand at the cathedral of Le Puy-en-Velay in France where, on the back porch, an engaged column ends abruptly midway down the wall—contrary to structural logic, this column is not supported from the ground below. But the visitor need not worry about its stability, for a sense of security is provided by an 11th- to 12th-century hand (albeit carved of stone) holding up the bottom of the column. Theologically, this is interpreted as the hand of God the Creator supporting the dome of Heaven represented by the vault above. The hand is not prominently located—the visitor must peer under the column to discover it. Because the visual puns in medieval art are unlikely to be obvious, they have largely gone unnoticed and unappreciated by recent visitors.

Elsewhere, more than merely a hand was needed; complete figures sculpted of stone or wood serve as structural supports on medieval buildings, appearing to hold up columns, arches, lintels, brackets, and corbels, and are usually posed as if working hard to keep the building from collapsing. An extremely subtle example is the tiny man who supports an arch on the back porch of the cathedral of Le Puy. At first glance one sees three miniature piers, but inquisitive eyes discover the center one is actually a miniature atlas—seated, hands on knees, head bent under the weight he bears.

The compressed body of the Le Puy figure contrasts with that of an extremely slender figure on the facade trumeau of the church of Saint-Pierre in Beaulieu-sur-Dordogne, France, who strains to support the capital with his hands and his shoulders, causing him to bow his head under the weight. This ethereal immaterial figure requires the assistance of a smaller man standing on the shoulders of yet another on the side of the trumeau.

Seated men hold up columns on the north porch of the cathedral of Notre-Dame at Embrun. Given the difficulty of the task, their evident exertion is understandable. The impression created is that real people, who expected to hold up the columns momentarily while the porch was being constructed, were never relieved of their task, instead abandoned to become frozen in stone. Inside this building, a group effort is required by small, nearly nude figures, each in a different pose, struggling to prevent an engaged capital from collapsing and crushing them.

The support of an arch requires a great many figures on the south transept portal of Saint-Pierre in Aulnay-de-Saintonge, France. The complex iconography carved in relief on the voussoirs (the wedge-shaped stones that make up the arch) is readily visible, but only by looking directly up under the archivolts will the numerous little people who have struggled for centuries to keep this structure standing be discovered.

In addition to stone figures that assist in supporting buildings, wood figures support misericords. In spite of the fact that misericords are located inside churches, close to the altar, and intended for use only by the clergy, the great majority of subjects carved on them are secular. Given the function of misericords as seats, the theme of the supporting figure was a natural match. A late-15th-century misericord in the abbey church of La Trinité in Vendôme, France, is carved with an image of a man who stretches his arms wide—the distance between his hands seemingly indicating the girth of the clergyman to whom this seat was assigned.

Loyal Employees

Certain tasks were part of the daily routine of medieval life. For example, the bell of the church of Saint-Hilaire in Foussais-Payré must be rung regularly. Inside, in the left corner of the facade wall, a half-length helpful stone man pulls a stone rope, as if to ring the bell above him. Similarly, in the cloister of Sainte-Foy in Conques, France, construction continues uninterrupted as miniature monks work as masons to construct a column capital in the form of a tiny tower.

In fact, some sculpted figures actually performed very useful tasks. The guards atop the two massive crenelated cylindrical towers of the medieval gateway of Monk's Bar are always ready to defend the city of York—because they are carved of stone. With missiles in hand, these stalwart sentries threaten to stone unwelcome visitors, perpetually protecting the city with complete reliability. Late in the day, when the shadows diminish our visual acuity, an unsuspecting assailant might hesitate before attempting entry through this gate.

Moralizing Messages

The art of the Middle Ages is filled with advice and warnings, the messages made more memorable by the ingenuity of their presentation; wit and humor were used intentionally as effective didactic devices. Images and ethics have long been allies, pictorial preaching being particularly appropriate because of the widespread illiteracy among the medieval audience. Parables, edifying tales, proverbs, and sayings well known to the residents of medieval Western Europe were frequently depicted. One of the best examples of visual narrative ever created is seen on the doors made for Bishop Bernward in the years 1011 to 1015, originally installed at St. Michael's Church in Hildesheim, Germany (subsequently moved to St. Mary's Cathedral in Hildesheim). In the story of Genesis told in cast relief on these bronze doors, Adam and Eve are shown to do the *one thing* they have been told not to do in the Garden of Eden—eat the forbidden fruit from the Tree of Knowledge. God points the accusatory finger at Adam. Having eaten from the Tree of Knowledge and therefore now aware of his nudity, Adam covers himself with one hand and points to Eve with the other, passing the blame to her. Eve, in turn, covers herself with one hand and points to the serpent with the other, as if claiming "the devil made me do it." No one takes responsibility for his or her own actions. That this scene will ever be depicted with greater narrative clarity, or more astute understanding of human nature, seems unlikely.

In medieval art, retribution for sin was shown to be swift, severe, and sometimes amusing. For example, on the Stonyhurst Chasuble, also referred to as the Saint Dunstan high mass vestment, embroidered circa 1470, is depicted Saint Dunstan, archbishop of Canterbury (960–988) and patron saint of English goldsmiths, jewelers, and locksmiths. While working in his shop, he receives a visit from the devil. When the devil mocks him, Dunstan uses his goldsmith tongs to pinch the devil on one of his noses.

A more permanent punishment is suffered by another devil, known as the Lincoln imp. Only about 12 inches high, once brightly painted, he has sat in a spandrel in the Angel Choir of Lincoln Cathedral in England since the 13th century. When the devil sent his imps out to play, one caused a nuisance at this cathedral by attempting to trip the bishop, knock down the dean, and pester the vergers and choir. When the imp began to break the windows, to the angels' request that he cease, he retorted, "Stop me if you can!" And they did—by turning him to stone.

A consequence of thievery is depicted at Wells Cathedral on four capitals of a 13th-century pillar in the south transept. On the first capital, the thief steals the grapes. On the second, the farmer is told of the theft. On the third, the thief is caught carrying the incriminating grapes. And on the fourth, the farmer hits the thief on the head with a pitchfork and the grapes are lost!

The Church's position on transgressions was succinctly summarized as the Seven Deadly Sins. Lust (*Luxuria*) and Greed (*Avaritia*) were, according to the medieval clergy, the major failings of the populace, whereas Lust and Gluttony (*Gula*) were, according to the populace, the primary flaws of the clergy. The remaining four Deadly Sins are Pride (*Superbia*), Wrath (*Ira*), Envy (*Invidia*), and Sloth (*Acedia*).

The sin of Greed is the subject of a misericord in the parish church of Saint Laurence in Ludlow, England, carved in the first half of the 15th century. A barmaid, a specific resident of Ludlow, was known to give short measure. The sculptor shows what happened when she died. Hoisted over the shoulder of a demon the Devil has sent to fetch her, she still clutches the fraudulent tankard in her hand—a *tot* measure used for liquids, specifically for alcoholic beverages. On the right supporter she is pitched head first into the Mouth of Hell. Given broader meaning, this was a warning to greedy merchants who asked too high a price for their goods or charged the customer for a larger quantity of goods than was actually delivered.

The sin of Pride and its manifestations as Vanity is the subject of another of the misericords in Saint Laurence in Ludlow, which mocks a woman wearing the horned headdress, a style popular at the time. Those who wear this style are not shown to be beautiful; instead, extremes in fashion are paired with physical ugliness.

Pride of a different sort is scorned in the story of the master builder of the cathedral of Saint John in 's-Hertogenbosch, where a permanent public record of his behavior is carved in stone on the north side of this cathedral for all to see. The builder had become rich, as indicated by his large purse, and, believing that the pot of peas his wife prepared for his meal was beneath him, arrogantly threw it down. His mournful expression as he gestures to the spilt peas indicates his remorse.

When represented by medieval artists, the sin of Gluttony was more likely to involve excessive consumption of alcoholic beverages rather than of solid food. On a facade corbel of the church of Saint-Hilaire in Foussais-Payré, a man is shown to have bypassed the cup and is drinking directly from the barrel, which he grasps with both hands. Carved on the church of Notre-Dame in L'Épine, France, built 1405–1527, an excited man holds a pitcher in one hand and a cup in the other. That he has already had too much to drink is suggested by the head of a fool below, identified by his cap and ass's ears. And, because he is a gargoyle, the result of his overconsumption becomes clear when it rains and he performs his function as a water spout.

Anger and conflict within the Church is shown on a capital in the cloister of the cathedral of Le Puy-en-Velay, which depicts a tonsured abbot and an abbess both tugging on a crozier, a symbol of the Church. Because the crozier is always held with the crook curving outward, in order to draw souls to God, this must be the abbot's crozier that the abbess now grasps. Does the abbot fear the abbess will take control? Is this a competition between monastery and convent? Is this the age-old battle of the sexes? Such an image may be viewed as having a broadly applicable meaning while simultaneously alluding to local events and specific individuals.

Those who gossip or slander, connected with the sin of Envy, are punished in various ways in medieval art. Emphatically clear in meaning is the 16th-century misericord of a woman with a lock on her mouth, carved on a stall now in the church of Saint-Maurille in Les-Ponts-de-Cé, France.

A compendium of the Deadly Sins and their punishment in Hell is offered by the depiction of the Last Judgment carved on the 12th-century tympanum of the church of Sainte-Foy in Conques. Medieval art sought to mold public behavior through visual intimidation; it was said that if love of God would not deter people from sin, perhaps fear of Hell would be more effective. In Hell, people suffer punishments appropriate to their transgressions. Greatly enhancing the impact of this sermon in stone, the individual sins are represented by specific people living in Conques at the time. Pride is represented by a neighbor of the abbey who coveted its wealth and, in fact, died from a fall from his horse, as shown here. Lust is depicted by an adulterous couple, partly naked, tied together. Lying idle under Satan's feet is Sloth, a sluggard enveloped by the flames of Hell and approached by a frog, a medieval symbol of sin. Greed is represented by the miser with a sack of coins around his neck—he hangs by its cord. Envy is shown to be a slanderer whose tongue is torn out by a devil. And Gluttony is represented by a poacher who hunted in the abbey's woods, now tied to a pole and cooked over an open fire by a retaliatory rabbit-chef (see Church of Saint-Foi image).

Church of Saint-Foi (Foy), Conques, France, tympanum, detail of Last Judgement, 12th century. A poacher is tied to a pole and roasted on a spit like a rabbit—by a rabbit.

Source: Janetta Rebold Benton.

Whether one's final destination would be Heaven or Hell was decided—according to medieval art and literature—by weighing one's soul, which was shown literally to hang in the balance. On the tympanum at Sainte-Foy the balance beam scale is shown, the devil cheating by pushing down on his basket with one finger. But neither the devil nor the angel is honest when the souls are weighed on the tympanum of the cathedral of Saint-Lazare in Autun, France (dated ca.1130–1145), for the devil hangs on the balance beam while the angel pulls down on his basket. (See Cathedral of Saint-Lazare image.)

Among the many depictions of the Seven Deadly Sins in medieval art, the message is especially emphatic in a painting by the Netherlandish artist Hieronymus Bosch on a table top (ca.1475), now in the Museo del Prado, Madrid. Anger is shown by a domestic dispute. Pride is represented by a woman in fancy attire admiring herself in a mirror held by a demon—who sports a similar headdress. Lust is displayed by lovers inside a tent. Sloth sleeps, his eyes closed to the offer of a rosary. Food is the sole interest of Gluttony. Avarice is portrayed by a judge who listens to one person while taking a bribe from another. Envy is represented by a dog that has two bones, yet wants another held just out of reach, and by a man laboring under the burden he carries on his back, envious of the man who does not work.

Animals as Vehicles for Satire

Through the use of animal imagery, medieval artists simultaneously made their messages more memorable and introduced an element of humor, thereby making it possible to say things likely to provoke a negative reaction if illustrated with human figures. A subtle use of animal imagery to make a political statement is found on the south porch of the duomo of Verona. As is common in northern Italy, lions are used as supports. But here a small dog bites the lion from behind. The lion is the symbol of Venice; the dog represents Verona, biting Venice on the butt. The Republic of Venice acquired the smaller city of Verona as a possession in 1405 (see Cathedral of Santa Maria Matricolare image).

Cathedral of Saint-Lazare, Autun, France, tympanum, detail of Last Judgement, 12th century. When the souls are weighed, both the devil and the angel cheat as they compete for this soul.

Source: Janetta Rebold Benton.

Although commonly kept as pets, monkeys were given negative connotations in art and literature, their ability to "ape" human behavior making them natural subjects for the *inversus mundi* (world upside down) theme favored during the Middle Ages. For

Cathedral of Santa Maria Matricolare, Verona, Italy, south porch. The dog, representing Verona, bites the lion, symbol of Venice, which had taken control of the smaller city.

Source: Janetta Rebold Benton.

example, on the outside of a painted enamel beaker, probably created in the southern Lowlands (ca.1425–1450), now in the Cloisters in New York City, a multitude of monkey-thieves relieve a sleeping peddler of his wares. On the inside, in contrast, the monkeys mock the aristocracy by aping their fondness for stag hunting, the favored pastime of the upper class. Monkeys and apes appear with notable frequency in medieval art, especially in the margins of manuscripts, where animal humor was common.

The fox was often depicted wearing religious garb and preaching from the pulpit to a congregation of geese—with the intention of savoring, rather than saving, them. The subject derives from tales ascribed to the storyteller Aesop (ca. 600 BCE), popular during the Middle Ages in the stories of Reynard the Fox and his son Reynardine. The tale is told also by Chaucer in his *Nun's Priest's Tale*. This satire targets the itinerant preachers, who were criticized by the clergy as rapacious hypocrites who misled their innocent parishioners. The clergy were criticized in turn by the wandering friars as corrupt and wealthy. A fox in a monk's habit, preaching to geese, some already in his cowl, while another fox bites a goose's neck as a lucky goose flies away, is exquisitely painted in enamel and gilded on a silver spoon, a Flemish work of the second quarter of the 15th century, perhaps circa 1430, now in the Museum of Fine Arts, Boston, Massachusetts. Ultimately the geese seek to hang the fox. In literature he gets a reprieve at the last moment, but medieval artists were less forgiving: On the facade of San Zeno in Verona, two roosters strut as they carry the captured fox, now tied to a pole and hanging upside down, for all to see.

Bosch's painting of the *Garden of Delights* (dated ca. 1505–1510), now in the Museo del Prado, Madrid, includes an outstanding example of satirical animal imagery. In the lower right corner of this iconographically complex triptych is a pig dressed as a mother superior. She gives a dying man—as indicated by his nudity—an embrace he resists while a demonic creature offers him a quill and inkwell to sign a document. Bosch uses humor to criticize the Church for pressuring dying people into signing over their possessions to the Church.

Bad Behavior

Just as earthy humor is a characteristic of medieval literature, some significant evasions of propriety appear in medieval art. Thus four naked males who appear to urinate form a fountain in the middle of a public square in Lacaune, France. Said to publicize the desirable qualities of the local water by showing its diuretic effect, this fountain is known, without subtlety, as the *pissaires*. The project for the fountain is believed to date circa 1399.

The great many gargoyles on Romanesque and Gothic churches spew water in other ways. While the vast majority of these gutter spouts issue rain water from their mouths, several gargoyles carved in the form of nude men employ a different orifice, their full effect apparent when it rains. Not the slightest hint of restraint is shown by the gargoyle on the south side of 12th-century Autun cathedral, buttocks thrust out, as he glances over his shoulder at the visitor. The same is true of the exhibitionist gargoyle with an equally protruding posterior on the south side of 15th-century Freiburg Minster in Germany (see Freiburg Minster image).

Another man displays his derriere on the side of the late-15th-century House of Adam in Angers, France. Nothing is hidden as he boldly glances over his shoulder at the viewer. Has this immodest medieval man been caught literally with his pants down, fleeing from a bedroom window?

A man, carved and polychromed on a corbel, has displayed his buttocks since 1494 on the exterior of a building originally owned by the cloth-cutters' guild (now the Hotel Kaiserworth), in Goslar, Germany. Wearing only a hat, this caricature turns his back to the viewer and defecates gold coins! Known as *Dukatenkakker* (Goldshitter), he may depict the German saying, "Money doesn't fall out of my ass"—as one might wish. The image of a man defecating coins appears elsewhere, including in the

Freiburg Minster, Freiburg im Breisgau, Germany. This stone gargoyle is carved in the form of a man with his buttocks thrust outward, looking over shoulder. Because a gargoyle functions as a gutter spout, imagine the effect during a rainstorm.

Source: Janetta Rebold Benton.

painting by Bosch of the *Garden of Delights*, mentioned earlier, where the Miser, condemned to Hell, defecates gold coins into a sewer, a commentary on the true value of money and material possessions.

Earthy humor is found even inside the church. If one imagines the 16th-century misericord in the church of Saint-Pierre in Saumur, France, that is carved with the figure of a man, nose upward (which Michael Camille calls "sniffing the bottom"), with someone sitting here, it is difficult for even the most inventive art historian or theologian to find redeeming religious symbolism here.

He Who Laughs Last, Laughs Best

Thomas Bekynton (d. 1465), bishop of Bath and Wells, had his tomb constructed in the choir south aisle of Wells Cathedral with a cadaver below and an effigy in ecclesiastical vestments above. Unlike other medieval effigies, however, Bekynton's *smiles*—and rightly so. A good bishop who actively improved the cathedral and city of Wells, Bekynton was known for his happy disposition. But he faced disappointment when his request to have his jester buried near him was refused by the dean and chapter. Yet Bekynton and his jester had the last laugh, for Bekynton had a stone figurine (approximately 6 inches high) of his jester placed on the corner of his tomb, closer to the altar than his own effigy, which will continue to smile for eternity.

Janetta Rebold Benton

See also Animal-Related Humor; Art and Visual Humor; Biblical Humor; Christianity; Rituals of Inversion; Satire

Further Readings

Benton, J. R. (1997). *Holy terrors: Gargoyles on medieval buildings*. New York, NY: Abbeville Press.

Benton, J. R. (1992). *Medieval menagerie: Animals in the art of the Middle Ages*. New York, NY: Abbeville Press.

Benton, J. R. (2004). *Medieval mischief: Wit and humour in the art of the Middle Ages*. Thrupp, UK: History Press.

Block, E. C. (2003). *Corpus of medieval misericords in France XIII-XVI century*. Turnhout, Belgium: Brepols.

Camille, M. (1992). *Image on the edge: The margins of medieval art*. Cambridge, MA: Harvard University Press.

Grössinger, C. (1997). *The world upside down: English misericords*. London, UK: Harvey Miller.

Grössinger, C. (2002). *Humour and folly in secular and profane prints of northern Europe 1430–1540*. London, UK: Harvey Miller.

Kenaan-Kedar, N. (1995). *Marginal sculpture in medieval France: Towards the deciphering of an enigmatic pictorial language*. Aldershot, UK: Scolar Press.

Mellinkoff, R. (1993). *Outcasts: Signs of otherness in northern European art of the late Middle Ages* (2 vols.). Berkeley: University of California Press.

Randall, L. M. C. (1966). *Images in the margins of gothic manuscripts*. Berkeley: University of California Press.

Remnant, G. L. (1998). *A catalogue of misericords in Great Britain*. Oxford, UK: Oxford University Press.

Menander

Menander (342/341–291/290 BCE) is the only writer of New Comedy by whom any substantial work survives. He first competed at the theatrical festivals in Athens in 321 and wrote 108 plays. One of them (*The Bad-Tempered Man*) survives complete, and there are substantial fragments of six more comedies, together with shorter fragments and more than 900 citations of words, lines, or short passages quoted by later ancient writers.

Menander was less popular in his lifetime than his contemporary Philemon (he won only eight victories at the festivals), but in the 3rd century BCE he rapidly became the most celebrated comic playwright in Greece. The Roman comedies of Plautus and Terence drew heavily on Menander for plots, situations, and characters, and he was highly regarded by Hellenistic scholars, being lavishly

Relief with Menander and New Comedy Masks (Roman, 40–60 CE), part of the Getty Villa collection in Los Angeles. The masks show three of his canonical New Comedy characters: youth, false maiden, and old man.

Source: Wikimedia Commons.

praised by Aristophanes of Byzantium (he is said to have asked: "Menander and life, which of you imitated which?"). But Menander fell into disfavor in the Byzantine era, and his plays were not copied into the medieval manuscript tradition, unlike the Old Comedy of Aristophanes. We are dependent for first-hand knowledge of Menander on his popularity in Egypt during the Hellenistic and Roman periods; Egyptian papyri are the source of the surviving play and fragments.

Menander lived in an Athens that was subservient to rulers installed by its Macedonian conquerors; as a consequence, unlike Aristophanes, he only rarely referred to contemporary political issues; almost never made jokes that would only be appreciated by one Athenian audience in one particular year; and never (as far as we know) introduced caricatures of real individuals from the audience.

Menander's plays contain very few laugh-out-loud jokes. Humor is principally derived from misunderstandings and intrigue, and from the foibles of mankind—for example, a cantankerous father in *The Bad-Tempered Man,* or an over-jealous lover, who wrongly accuses his mistress of cheating on him and cuts off her hair, in *The Shorn Girl*; toward the end of these plays, both of these characters are forced to recognize their past wrongdoing and make amends. A typical Menander plot, constantly creating new surprises through misunderstandings, is seen at its best in *The Girl From Samos,* in which Moschion, the adopted son of the wealthy Athenian Demeas, has impregnated his neighbor's daughter Plangon at a festival. Demeas has been overseas, and his Samian mistress Chrysis has been raising Plangon's baby as if it were her own. Demeas sees Chrysis nursing the baby, draws the obvious but wrong conclusion, and throws her out of his house. Then he overhears servants' gossip that the child is Moschion's—which is of course correct but only reinforces his anger against Chrysis and Moschion. All is not resolved until the fifth act, when Moschion—after an initial outburst of obstinacy against his father for wrongfully accusing him—is married to Plangon.

Moralizing on the human condition is frequent, as when in *The Bad-Tempered Man* the farmer Gorgias rebukes the rich playboy Sostratos for despising the poor and committing wrong simply because he is rich enough to do so. Fortunately Sostratos is able to convince this hotheaded critic that his intentions toward the girl he is pursuing (who is actually Gorgias's half-sister) are honorable.

The physical crudity that is characteristic of Aristophanes is almost entirely absent from Menander. But in the surviving fragment of *The Girl From Perinthos,* the slave Daos, who has angered his master by scheming and has taken refuge at an altar, is surrounded by brushwood and about to be forced to leave divine sanctity by being literally smoked out. He shits himself in fear. Similar high-action scenes, often involving preparation for a sacrifice to the gods and/or a feast, occur frequently in the surviving work. For all the gentleness of his verbal comedy, Menander is a writer with a keen eye for theatrical effects, and he exploits the conventions and resources of his theater fully.

Because it was not anchored like Old Comedy (500–404 BCE) to topicality in a particular place and time, Menander's style of drama provided an attractive export industry; traveling companies toured his and other New Comedies (321–143 BCE) from Athens to throughout the Greek-speaking world. This kind of comedy possesses the lasting capacity to appeal to a wide audience, as it gently mocks universal features of human nature. Even though the social customs and laws of contemporary Athens are often central to Menander's plots, these elements could be modified by subsequent playwrights to suit their own social context. Menander's comedies were therefore adapted for Roman conditions by the two leading writers of Latin comedy, Plautus and Terence, and these Roman comedies carried the influence of Menander through to the Renaissance.

The early comedies of William Shakespeare and the work of Molière are both heavily dependent on conventions, stock characters, and plot devices that originate with Menander. To a certain extent the same is true of much more recent comic playwrights such as Oscar Wilde, Joe Orton, and Alan Ayckbourne, and indeed the American television sitcom may plausibly be regarded as a (somewhat debased) contemporary descendant of the Menandrian tradition.

Michael Ewans

See also Ancient Greek Comedy; Aristophanes; Comedy

Further Readings

Arnott, W. G. (1975). *Menander, Plautus, Terence.* Oxford, UK: Clarendon Press.

Goldberg, S. M. (1980). *The making of Menander's comedy.* Berkeley: University of California Press.

Hunter, R. L. (1985). *The New Comedy of Greece and Rome.* Cambridge, UK: Cambridge University Press.

Menander. (1987). *Plays and fragments* (N. Miller, Trans.). Harmondsworth, UK: Penguin.

Menander. (2001). *The plays and fragments* (M. Balme, Trans.). Oxford, UK: Oxford University Press.

METAPHOR

The focus of this entry is on a subset of verbal metaphors, those that happen to be humorous. As such, discussion of metaphors in and of themselves is presented only marginally and as relevant to the subject. It is common to use the terms *source* and *target* of a metaphor. In the metaphor "an argument is war," the source domain is the conceptual domain from which the "comparison" is drawn (war), whereas the target is the concept being metaphorized (argument). So in the example "Mary won that argument," "winning" is drawn from the source conceptual domain of war (wars can be won or lost), whereas the target of the metaphor is "argument." This entry discusses some explanations for why metaphors can be humorous.

Most accounts of humorous metaphors (including works by Ivan Fónagy, Maureen Morrissey, Howard Pollio, and Marta Dynel), rely on variants of the distance theory. This essentially consists of postulating a threshold of semantic distance beyond which the linkage between the source and target domains in the metaphor becomes stretched (i.e., too distant) and is therefore perceived as humorous. The most obvious problem for the distance theory is that no precise (or even approximate) quantification of the threshold exists.

A related distinction, introduced by Reuven Tsur and Howard Pollio, is between metaphors that have an emphasis on the incongruous aspects of the source and target concepts and those that background the differences between source and target and focus on the similarities between them. Tsur speaks of "split" and "integrated" focus metaphors, while Pollio speaks of emphasizing the "line" between source and target or "fusing" it. Metaphors that emphasize the incongruity of speaking of a target concept in terms of a source tend to be perceived as humorous, whereas those that downplay the incongruity are perceived as figurative or poetic. The problem with these approaches is that they do not answer the basic question of what makes a metaphor emphasize the incongruous aspects or, conversely, downplay them.

Elliott Oring has proposed a different approach to humorous metaphors, which relies on ideas commonly used in humor theory, that is, incongruity and resolution. According to Oring, metaphors seek to find appropriateness in an incongruous connection between two frames or contextual cues leading to the interpretation of a message, but they are not humorous because the appropriateness they find is "genuine" (i.e., legitimate), whereas riddles and jokes find "spurious" appropriateness in the connection of two frames. Humor always involves incongruities that are not fully resolved. Metaphors, conversely, fully resolve the incongruity of the mapping between domains.

Oring's explanation combines semantic and pragmatic factors. The incongruity of the mapping deals with semantics, or the rules of word meanings, whereas the attempt to find appropriateness deals with pragmatics, or the relation between language and its context. It is obvious that it could be recast in blending terms, that is, as a mental space consisting of a blend of features from two other mental spaces, a leading approach to metaphors, without any loss of analytical power. It differs from the distance approach in that the distance between domains is not a factor relevant to the humorous effect, whereas the processing of the blend/metaphor is assumed to be the crucial factor. A further difference between Oring's approach and the distance theories is that

Oring's is a dynamic theory, based on the inferential process of finding appropriateness in (i.e., resolving the incongruity of) the comparison of two different domains. The distance theories are based on a priori metrics, or on vague and undefined terms such as *emphasis* or *focus* on the incongruity or congruity of the comparison. Moreover, Oring's approach has the further advantage of being fully integrated, even terminologically, with humor theory. It should be also noted that Oring's account is not necessarily antagonistic to the distance theory, which could possibly be integrated in his account.

An approach that recasts Oring's theory in blending terms is presented in Salvatore Attardo's work, which examines a corpus of humorous metaphors collected on the Internet. Attardo finds that the folk usage of the term *humorous metaphor* is in fact an umbrella term covering a fairly disparate set of phenomena. These include metaphors that describe inherently funny referents: "As independent as a hog on ice"; un-metaphors: "The red brick wall was the color of a brick red Crayola crayon" (mapping one domain on itself); mixed metaphors: "They jumped on the bandwagon going nowhere" (unrelated, sequentially added metaphors); and overdone metaphors: "It hurt the way your tongue hurts after you accidentally staple it to the wall," which violate primary metaphors. Primary metaphors are basic and very general connections, such as "good is up." Moreover, Attardo found that many folk categorizations of humorous metaphors also include simple puns that are not metaphors at all.

The literalization of metaphors, mentioned by Elena Semino, Andrew Goatly, and Marta Dynel, is another well-known process whereby metaphors may become humorous. Semino also notes that "target triggered" metaphors are often humorous. Jeffery Mio and Arthur Graesser offer a different perspective, noting that disparaging metaphors (i.e., comparison of a high-status subject to a low-status subject) are perceived as more humorous. This shows strong support for the disparagement theory of humor and would mean that the incongruity aspect of the metaphor would be backgrounded in the perception of humor.

Finally, there exists some research on humorous visual metaphors, which is not examined here, and on ironical similes by Tony Veale and Yanfen Hao. Veale and Hao find that a remarkably large number (20%) of similes of the "as Adjective as Noun or Noun Phrase" ("as red as a ruby") structure, retrieved through Google searches, are ironical. Also, Veale finds that a marker (the word *about*) often co-occurs with humorous similes.

Overall, the analysis of humorous metaphors is still in its infancy. It will develop best if it heeds Jeffery Mio's (2009) conclusion that "although metaphors can be humorous, this is not the primary task of this rhetorical device" (p. 182).

Salvatore Attardo

See also Exaggeration; Incongruity and Resolution; Verbal Humor

Further Readings

Attardo, S. (2007, July). *Humorous metaphors.* Paper presented at the 10th International Cognitive Linguistics Conference, Krakow, Poland.

Attardo, S. (in press). Humorous metaphors. In G. Brône, K. Feyaerts, & T. Veale (Eds.), *Cognitive linguistics meets humor research: Current trends and new developments.* Berlin, Germany: Mouton de Gruyter.

Dynel, M. (2009). Metaphor is a birthday cake: Metaphor as the source of humour. *Metaphoric.de, 17,* 27–48.

Fónagy, I. (1982). He is only joking (joke, metaphor and language development). In F. Keifer (Ed.), *Hungarian linguistics* (pp. 31–108). Amsterdam, Netherlands: John Benjamins.

Goatly, A. (2012). *Meaning and humour.* Cambridge, UK: Cambridge University Press.

Grady, J. E., Oakley, T., & Coulson, S. (1999). Blending and metaphor. In R. Gibbs & G. Steen (Eds.), *Metaphor in cognitive linguistics* (pp. 101–124). Philadelphia, PA: John Benjamins.

Krikmann, A. (2009). On the similarity and distinguishability of humour and figurative speech. *Trames, 13*(1), 14–40.

Mio, J. S. (2009). Metaphor, humor, and psychological androgyny. *Metaphor and Symbol, 24*(3), 174–183.

Mio, J. S., & Graesser, A. C. (1991). Humor, language, and metaphor. *Metaphor and Symbol, 6*(2), 87–102.

Morrissey, M. M. (1989). Script theory for the analysis of humorous metaphors. In S. F. D. Hughes & V. Raskin (Eds.), *WHIMSY VII. Proceedings of the 1988 WHIM conference held April 1–4, 1988 at Purdue University* (pp. 124–125). West Lafayette, IN: International Society for Humor Studies.

Oring, E. (2003). *Engaging humor.* Urbana: University of Illinois Press.

Pollio, H. R. (1996). Boundaries in humor and metaphor. In J. S. Mio & A. N. Katz (Eds.), *Metaphor: Implications and applications* (pp. 231–253). Mahwah, NJ: Lawrence Erlbaum Associates.

Semino, E. (2008). *Metaphor in discourse.* Cambridge, UK: Cambridge University Press.
Tsur, R. (1992). *What makes sound patterns expressive: The poetic mode of speech-perception.* Durham, NC: Duke University Press.
Tsur, R. (2003). *On the shore of nothingness: Space, rhythm, and semantic structure in religious poetry and its mystic-secular counterpart: A study in cognitive poetics.* Exeter, UK: Imprint Academic.
Veale, T. (2013). Humorous similes. *HUMOR: International Journal of Humor Research, 26*(1), 3–22.
Veale, T., & Hao, Y. (2007). Learning to understand figurative language: From similes to metaphors to irony. In D. S. McNamara & J. G. Trafton (Eds.), *Proceedings of the 29th Annual Cognitive Science Society* (pp. 683–688). Austin, TX: Cognitive Science Society.
Veale, T., & Hao, Y. (2008). A context-sensitive framework for lexical ontologies. *Knowledge Engineering Review, 23*(1), 101–115.

Mime

Mime is the art of communicating without words and is used internationally to express ideas across language barriers both professionally in the theater and in personal behavior. In theater, the words *mime* and *pantomime* are often used to define the same thing, although the English pantomime is a distinct theater genre (properly shortened to "panto"). Deriving from the Greek word *mimos* (a mimic or imitator), mime is both verb and noun, thus both the act of miming and a practitioner of the art (although mimes use the word for the mimic act itself and use *pantomime* for sketches, scenes, or plays using mime).

Mime demands complete control of muscular isolation, focusing on communicative bodily and facial expression. Although some of the art is naturalistic, most involves exaggeration and stylization; for instance, miming walking on the spot or ascending/descending stairs differs greatly from the real actions, yet communicates very clearly. The imaginative participation of the audience is an essential part of mime, as in a game of charades, where the audience is continually guessing what the mime's gestures mean. Consequently its associated humor springs in part from the delight of recognition, flattering the viewer's cognitive skills. The act of mimicry seems inherently to carry the seeds of comedy, a joke shared privately between the mimes and their audience. This entry discusses the elements that make up the tradition of mime and how it has evolved in various cultures.

Early Miming

The tradition of mime predates formal theater and is found in all cultures. Mime was used extensively in performance by Greeks (the name of the masked Greek dancer Pantomimus is thought to be the origin of *pantomime*). Earliest records make little distinction between a mime and an actor, who was at once singer, dancer, and mime; but the word was more commonly used for a range of comic expression than for the more formal style of tragedy that stressed presentational, rhetorical, and vocal performance. Both tragic and comic mimes used masks (Latin *larvae*), but the built-up shoes (Latin *cothurni*), which created stature for tragedians and limited actors' physical expression, were less used by comedic mimes, who evidently were primarily dancers and acrobats. The comedies of Aristophanes and Menander, Plautus, and Terence clearly require physicality in both bodily and facial expression. They satirically mock human desires, ambition, and folly, differing little from modern comedy, which also usually requires considerable physicality. Distorted features and exaggerated props were clearly used in comic ways, especially the huge phalli notoriously used in Aristophanes's *Lysistrata* (411 BCE) and evidenced in vase and wall paintings (indeed re-creating their extreme political and scatological license has not been possible until very recent times). Such physical expression is at the heart of mime, with or without words; however, the mimic emphasis on human physical expression tended toward the comic while the abstract tended toward dance. The concept of the physical entrapment of a soul in flesh lies at the heart of all comedy.

Mimic elements from Greek theater carried over into Roman and later medieval theaters, and many have speculated that itinerant street entertainers long preceded Greek theater proper. One can confidently say that mime, dance, and storytelling preexisted the earliest forms of entertainment in all cultures. In the polyglot world of the Roman theater audience, mime was taken to crude extremes, leading the Christian Church to associate the form with the pagan and demonic, although because of its attractions, it was never truly absent from the streets of most towns. Along with clowning, acrobatics, and comedy itself, mime became a crucial element of the *commedia dell'arte* and the even older folk plays such as English mummers' plays and Dutch *Abele Spelen;* no doubt it was part of the skills of a court jester, and gestural language is part of all "foolery," even for puppets. The lasting impact of mimes and mimicry is evidenced in the work of William Shakespeare (the "dumb show" in *Hamlet* being the most famous example), Lope de Vega, and Molière. Always popular from the 15th- to the mid-19th century, groups of such "strolling players" offered short satirical sketches on makeshift stages, incorporating vulgarity, grotesquery, and farce. Crossing many national boundaries and languages as they did, mime must surely have been the principal element in their performances.

The Italian groups that traversed Europe were known as *funambuli* (literally, "rope dancers") and they used both mime and language, creating hundreds of stock characters, and using masks, makeup, props, and costumes. The central *commedia* role of Arlecchino was particularly bound up with mime, using gestural language and highly articulated physical skills—his famous comic routine (*lazzi*) of catching and swallowing a fly was totally mimed.

The *funambuli* influenced most of Europe, with the English transforming Pulcinella into Mr. Punch and developing a unique form of pantomime. But the most significant new developments occurred in France: Arlecchino was romanticized into the internationally recognized Harlequin and Pedrolino transformed into Pierrot. In the first half of the 19th century, Jean Gaspard Deburau developed this role, adding melancholy to his clown Pierrot and retrieving from the street performers of medieval France the tradition of the "white face" (*enfariné*) to neutralize identity, emphasizing mouth, eyes, and eyebrows. While such French pantomime characters developed their own visual and performance style, diluting satire, developing romance, and extending music, stock comic routines (with ladders, lanterns, buckets, etc.) retained *commedia* traditions.

The routines from *commedia, jongleurs,* masquerades, and Harlequinades diverged into vaudeville, variety, and circus and even influenced early silent-film comedy. Mime is evident in the comedies of Charlie Chaplin, Buster Keaton, Laurel and Hardy, and many others, including Clara Bow. And correspondingly, several elements from the silent screen (e.g., the Keystone Cops) are standard for many modern mimes. Often called low comedy because of its preoccupation with bodily functions and desires, such physical comedy always requires considerable skill and warrants respect. Visual gags are more

Lindsay Kemp, a British actor, mime artist, dancer, choreographer, and teacher. He studied with Marcel Marceau and taught David Bowie.

Source: Allan Warren/Wikimedia Commons.

instantly understood by audiences of mixed artistic sophistication, and this fact has always guided physical comedy in its outreach. The eye-catching appeal of physical extremis is as much a part of farce as it is of a Jackie Chan Kung Fu movie or of comic routines in all plays, films, and musicals. One modern example is Kevin Kline's extraordinary mime sequence in the 1978 musical, *On the Twentieth Century.*

Silent actors, like silent-movie comedians, are in fact mimes. W. C. Fields was a pantomime silent comic and juggler before his screen career; some, such as Chaplin and Rowan Atkinson (a.k.a. Mr. Bean), use their entire body and grotesque facial grimaces. Others, such as Buster Keaton, developed blank-face comedy, which, like the *Nō* mask, allows the audience to imagine the thoughts that are not being expressed on the face, with increased humorous effect. Such deadpan humor is admired by practitioners as a more subtle art form than facial "clowning" (face-pulling).

Despite its skill and popularity, physical performance was kept off the "legit" stage for many centuries and made secondary to actors who gave voice to the wealth of more literary drama. Its influence nevertheless underlies most theater: On the 19th-century stage, for example, rhetorical gestures had to grow to reach the back row of seating capacity of more than 3,500. Accompanied by music, this heightened physical style of both acting and play gained the name *melodrama*, known for its exaggerated and melodramatic style of plot and acting. Such gestural language survives today in realms as widely disparate as French mimes and classical ballet, where it is often seen as romantic or parodying romance. Street mimes can be found performing or "busking" around the world.

Miming in Asia

Although mime prioritizes communication, and therefore reflects life, it can also deal with abstraction and distillation of emotion. In classical forms such as rhetorical gesture and classical ballet, a formal sign language has evolved that links to ritual, dance, and Asian forms of mime. The Sanskrit treatise on the performing arts, the *Natya Shastra,* attributed to Bharata Muni (between 200 BCE and 200 CE), refers to silent performance as *mukhabinaya.* This remains common in India theater, as does clowning and the use of stock comic characters. The famous southwest Indian Kathakali dance form has sung narration, but its silent performers are thoroughly trained in mime, much of which involves the imitation of animals and highly expressive body and facial gestures. The north Indian Kathak, evolved from Persian storytelling, now uses less mime, and the southeastern Bharata Natyam, evolved from the court mime with poses and gestures from Hindu religious sculpture, has now completely abstracted its expressive aspects so that, like much of Kathakali, original meaning has often been lost with the gestures retained only for aesthetic reasons.

As in ancient and medieval time in the West, the actor in Asia is always also a dancer, and in Asian performance, physical expression is often valued more highly than vocal. Because Asian performance usually involves traditional or time-honored narratives, mime remains an essential element in all Asian performance, assisting the storyteller with illustration. For Cambodia's Khmer theater and its close relative, Thailand's Khon and Lakhon, drama is often indivisible from dance. Mime is similarly used in all Malay, Indonesian, and Philippines traditional dance theater. Comedy is also a valued part of all Southeast Asian cultures, essential to character and storytelling: all have their clowns and comics, with accompanying mime elements.

Through Mei Lan Fang (1894–1961), the great Chinese *Dan* actor (female portrayer), the influence of *Xiqu* (Chinese "opera") on Western theater is now well known. The term *opera* is questioned by scholars and discounts the fact that *Xiqu* is essentially physical theater, still popular largely because of its battle scenes, acrobatics, mime, and comedy. One of the world's most famous mime sequences is China's "Ferryman and the Maiden," from *Qiu Jiang* (Autumn River), where a boat journey around river bends and dangerous rapids is exquisitely communicated by two actors on a bare stage. *Xiqu* shares many elements with the more visually spectacular *Kabuki* theater of Japan, deriving from *ka* (music), *bu* (dance), and *ki* (skill or performance). Both forms contain a lot of physical mime in battle and combat scenes (like many Shakespeare plays); both involve elaborate facial makeup on a white rice base and often use limited props such as a fan to serve as another object. Both put comedy sequences side-by-side with tragedy and explore class systems, enjoying comedy in the form of rebellious servants as much as dullard army generals. Another feature in common is frequent mime sequences in imagined darkness (Japanese *dammari*, literally "silent," but in *Kabuki* also a pantomime fight in the dark). These parallel *commedia*'s *lazzi* of Nightfall and are triggered usually by the dropping of a candle or lantern, with imaginary darkness descending on stage in which characters circle each other blindly, skillfully almost bumping into each other, swinging swords, and ducking or groping for some precious object. British playwright Peter Shaffer (b. 1926) used such a "reversed lighting" technique in his play *Black Comedy* (1965), which is played entirely as if in blackout. Because audiences are the only ones privy to "seeing in the dark," the actors' mime skills make this one of comedy's most universally loved sequences.

Masks and masked features, deadpan, blank-faced characters that magnify physicality and/or encourage audience's imagination are also commonly used in Asian theater. Examples include narrators such as Japan's "sit-down comedy," *Rakugo,* where only the fan or a folded piece of cloth is used to assist the narrator in miming anything and everything. *Nō* theater goes further and deliberately masks all emotions, even on unmasked actors, while the leading character (the *Shite*) wears the mask of his or her role group (gods, warriors, maidens, mad people, and demons). While *Nō* sometimes uses surprisingly communicative mime (e.g., the pouring of wine or water using a fan), the best known *Nō* mime is also the international gesture for weeping: with palm curved slightly upward, one hand is slowly raised to the face. Apart from having their own plays known as *Kyōgen,* comic actors are frequent in *Nō* , usually in small character parts where mime rather than extended dialogue is important, for example, the ferryman in *Sumidagawa* (The Sumida River), a classical *Nō* play by Motomasa (1401?–1432). *Kyōgen* alternate with *Nō* plays as comic relief in a full program, echoing the Greek concept of a world well-balanced when presented in both comic and tragic forms.

The purity of Japanese *Nō* technique greatly influenced many modern mimes, including Jacques Copeau (1879–1949) and Jacques Lecoq (1921–1999), and the *Kabuki onnagata* (female role) was copied by Lindsay Kemp (b. 1938) in his androgynous mime and transformed to comic decadence. *Butoh* dance uses extreme physical expression, born of the ashes of Hiroshima; similar to Jerzy Grotowski's (1933–1999) work arising from the turmoil of World War II, it has developed into a silent aesthetic, common now in contemporary physical theater.

Modern mime, fully embraced by the United States, was first analyzed and legitimized in France and is usually understood as a European art form. In 1921 Jacques Copeau founded L'École du Vieux-Colombier (named for the eponymous theater in Paris) and for 3 years he, with Étienne Decroux, Jean-Louis Barrault, Jean Dasate, and others, explored concepts of physical theater, mask, and mime. Decroux and Barrault developed a form now known as corporeal mime, which emphasizes the body rather than facial expression; their most famous student was Marcel Marceau (1923–2007) with his company La Nouvelle Compagnie de Mimodrame, whose "Pip" became the epitome of the white-faced mime, exploring its limitations until Marceau's death. Jacques Lecoq was a student of Jean Daste and returned to the *commedia* to develop methods now known as "Mime for the Actor." This training evolved various strands with both neutral masks and character masks, clowning, and latterly the revival of the concept of the Fool and its Italian counterpart, the Buffone. The more grotesque clown, or Buffone, was taken further in French theater and training and acclaimed in the work of Italian Nobel laureate, Dario Fo (b. 1926).

From Decroux's work developed French classical mime, which uses classical ballet positions, posture, and grace, as well as tights and dance pumps. Whereas dance defies gravity, mime is earthbound, often struggling with obstructive natural forces such as gravity and wind, creating strong comic effects. It uses economy and essence (evidently influenced by Japanese *Nō*) and features slow-motion, statues, machine-like movements, and patterns, and its comedy can be easily analyzed using Henri Bergson's principles of mechanical patterning in comedy (*Le rire,* 1900). In this tradition, the Swiss group Mummenschanz, founded in 1972, remains internationally popular; it uses Lecoq technique together with masks and props, introducing the surreal into mime. In recent years, Philippe Genty (b. 1938) has surrounded the mime with huge visual and magical effects, and mime's scientific study of the human body and gestural language has reentered the world of dance, influencing innovative American companies such as Momix (founded 1980) and Pilobolus (1971).

Miming Today

There are now many mime groups, understood as physical theater companies, often hugely influential, particularly in the United States. "Purer" forms, like Marceau mime, are found now mainly in amateur or children's shows (in 2012, some 49 mimes advertised their availability in New York City alone). However, mime and its disciplines and principles are commonly part of actor, dancer, and circus training worldwide, an essential training for the physical actor, together with clowning, Asian martial arts, and Western combat. Mime schools and teachers are in demand internationally, especially the core skills that start—as in Kathakali training—with muscular isolation exercises and the essential principles of physics.

Festivals of mime are held today in many countries. Mimos, an international mime festival held in Périgueux, France, since 1983, includes mime, clowning, circus, dance (e.g., hip-hop), puppetry, plastic arts, and music. All are nonverbal and range across ages and cultures, with shows including exhibitions, discussions, and films or videos. The annual London International Mime Festival is Britain's longest established international theater season, founded in 1977 by producer Joseph Seelig and mime/clown Nola Rae, inspired by Cologne's Gaukler Festival and Amsterdam's Festival of Fools.

Jean and Brigitte Soubeyran. Jean (1921–2000) was a French-trained mime, who had an extensive career primarily in Germany, where he married Brigitte. He performed for the Marcel Marceau ensemble and wrote a book on pantomime, titled *The Silent Language*.

Source: Ronald (Inge Worringen, Cologne)/Wikimedia Commons.

Helen Lannaghan joined in 1987 and national and international collaborations have been common, again spanning the entire spectrum of wordless performance including "live art" (performance art), physical theater, new circus, puppetry, and "object theater." Artists who have participated define the field, including Jacques Lecoq, Bolek Polivka (b. 1949), Philippe Genty, Lindsay Kemp, Annie Fratellini (1932–1997), Jérôme Deschamps (b. 1947), Marcel Marceau, and the new generation such as La Ribot, Compagnie 111, Josef Nadj, Licedei, Simon McBurney's Complicité, Phelim McDermot's Improbable Theatre, and leading new circus ensembles. Both Seelig and Lannaghan have been honored by the French government. The longevity and adaptability of mime as a communication form suggests it will forever remain part of the performer's art, whether humorous or serious.

Aubrey Mellor

See also Aristophanes; Bergson's Theory of the Comic; Burlesque; Carnival and Festival; Clowns; Comedy Ensembles; Comic Versus Tragic Worldviews; *Commedia dell'Arte*; Exaggeration; Farce; Feast of Fools; Fools; Greek Visual Humor; Improv Comedy; Jests, Jestbooks, and Jesters; *Lazzi*; Low Comedy; Masks; Medieval Visual Humor; Menander; Music Hall; Musical Comedy; Plautus; Play and Humor; Puppets; Race, Representation of; *Rakugo*; Ritual Clowns; Roman Visual Humor; Shakespearean Comedy; Slapstick; Stereotypes

Further Readings

Bergson, H. (2005). *Laughter: An essay on the meaning of the comic* (C. Brereton & F. Rothwell, Trans.). Mineola, NY: Dover. (Original work published 1900)

Decroux, E., & Leabhart, T. (2009). *The Decroux sourcebook* (T. Leabhart & F. Chamberlain, Trans.). London, UK: Routledge.

Dorcy, J. (Ed.). (1961). *The mime* (R. Speller Jr. & P. de Fontnouvelle, Trans.). New York, NY: Robert Speller & Sons.

Lecoq, J. (2006). *The theatre of movement and gesture* (D. Bradbury, Trans.). New York, NY: Routledge.

Lecoq, J. (2009). *The moving body.* London, UK: Bloomsbury.

Lust, A. B. (2003). *From the Greek mimes to Marcel Marceau and beyond: Mimes, actors, Pierrots and clowns: A chronicle of the many visages of mime in the theatre.* Lanham, MD: Scarecrow Press.

Nicoll, A. (1963). *Masks, mimes and miracles.* New York, NY: Cooper Square.

Mirth

Mirth refers to the unique positive emotion associated with humor. Alternative terms sometimes used in the research literature to refer to this emotion are *amusement, exhilaration,* and *humor appreciation.* Many theories of humor focus particularly on its cognitive aspects, but it is also important to recognize that humor is fundamentally an emotional phenomenon. Just as other emotions (e.g., joy, anger, fear) occur in response to specific types of cognitive appraisals of the environment, the emotion of mirth is evoked by a particular set of cognitive appraisals that we commonly refer to as humor. This entry discusses the elements that characterize mirth, the physiological responses associated with mirth, how mirth is displayed, and the possible motivational functions of mirth.

In addition to humor, the emotion of mirth may be elicited by other stimuli, such as nitrous oxide (N_2O, or laughing gas), rough-and-tumble childhood play, and playful tickling. An individual's threshold for experiencing mirth at any given time can also be raised or lowered by factors such as the social context (e.g., the presence of other laughing people), one's current mood state (cheerful vs. depressed), health status, level of fatigue, or ingestion of alcohol or psychoactive drugs. There are also more enduring individual differences in the tendency to experience mirth, which are associated with personality traits such as extraversion and one's overall sense of humor.

Mirth is closely related to other positive emotions such as joy or happiness, but it also has some qualitatively distinct experiential elements, including suddenness of onset, perception of funniness, feeling of playfulness, and sense of diminishment of the seriousness or importance of things. Like other emotions, mirth can range in intensity, from the mild feelings of amusement evoked by a simple pun, to intense paroxysms of hilarity accompanied by rollicking laughter. Also like other emotions, mirth has physiological, expressive, and motivational aspects, in addition to the experiential component.

Physiological Aspects

Mirth is associated with increased heart rate, skin conductance, blood pressure, skin temperature, and muscle tension. These bodily changes result from activation of the sympathetic-adrenal-medullary (SAM) system, the well-known fight-or-flight response under the control of the hypothalamus, and are mediated by increased production of catecholamines (epinephrine and norepinephrine) in the adrenal glands. In addition to SAM activation, extended periods of mirth can be associated with activation of the hypothalamic-pituitary-adrenocortical system, the classic stress response involving increased cortisol production in the adrenal cortex.

It may seem strange that the positive emotion associated with humor, which is thought to be beneficial for health, is accompanied by the same pattern of physiological arousal as are stress-related negative emotions such as anxiety and anger, which have been associated with adverse health outcomes. However, it is important to note that stress-related illnesses tend to result from chronic activation and inadequate recovery from sympathetic arousal, whereas mirth is associated with phasic, short-term arousal increases that are less likely to have adverse consequences. It is also likely that these emotions have important differences at the neurological level, including the biochemical molecules (e.g., neuropeptides, neurotransmitters) that are produced in the brain, which in turn may have different effects on health.

Brain imaging studies reveal that the perception of humor produces activation of the mesolimbic reward network, a well-known dopamine-based system involving structures in the limbic region of the brain, including the nucleus accumbens, anterior thalamus, hypothalamus, and amygdala. The more humorous a stimulus is perceived to be, the more strongly this system of the brain is activated. In addition to humor, this system has been shown to underlie a variety of pleasurable, emotionally rewarding activities, including listening to enjoyable music, playing video games, being sexually aroused, and ingesting certain mood-altering drugs. Thus, at the neurological level, the emotion of mirth appears to be based on this dopaminergic reward network.

Emotion Expression

Most emotions (e.g., fear, anger, surprise) are associated with distinctive patterns of facial expression or bodily gestures that comprise largely innate, species-specific signals for communicating one's affective state to other individuals. In the case of mirth, these expressive displays take the form of smiling and laughter. The more intense the level of mirth is, the stronger the expressive display will be. At low levels of intensity, mirth is expressed by a faint smile, which turns into chuckling and laughter as the emotional intensity increases. At very high intensity, it is expressed by loud guffaws, often accompanied by a reddening of the face as well as bodily movements such as throwing back the head, rocking the body, and slapping one's thighs. In addition to communicating to others that one is experiencing mirth, these vigorous expressive displays seem to serve the purpose of inducing mirth and increasing emotional arousal in others. This would explain why laughter is so contagious.

Motivational Aspects

Emotions typically have motivational functions. For example, fear motivates the individual to escape a threatening situation. Although the motivational functions of mirth are less obvious, researchers have suggested that they have to do with the enhancement of cognitive functioning and social cohesiveness. According to the "broaden-and-build" model, positive emotions such as mirth serve to broaden the scope of the individual's attention, allowing for more creative problem solving and improved physical, intellectual, and social resources for dealing with life's challenges. Research has shown that when people experience mirth and other similar positive emotions, they tend to have increased cognitive flexibility, judgment, and memory, leading to more creativity and better problem solving. They also have increased levels of social responsibility, concern for others, and social behaviors such as helpfulness and generosity.

Rod A. Martin

See also Appreciation of Humor; Brain, Neuropsychology of Humor; Positive Psychology; Psychology; Smiling and Laughter: Expressive Patterns

Further Readings

Frederickson, B. L. (2006). The broaden-and-build theory of positive emotions. In M. Csikszentmihalyi & I. S. Csikszentmihalyi (Eds.), *A life worth living: Contributions to positive psychology* (pp. 85–103). New York, NY: Oxford University Press.

Martin, R. A. (2007). *The psychology of humor: An integrative approach*. Burlington, MA: Elsevier Academic Press.

Panksepp, J. (2000). The riddle of laughter: Neural and psychoevolutionary underpinnings of joy. *Current Directions in Psychological Science, 9*, 183–186.

Ruch, W. (1993). Exhilaration and humor. In M. Lewis & J. M. Haviland (Eds.), *Handbook of emotions* (pp. 605–616). New York, NY: Guilford Press.

MISDIRECTION

Misdirection is a broad term that applies to techniques of information presentation that implicitly encourage the audience to adopt one interpretation of what is being presented, despite the fact that another interpretation is not only possible but will later become more obvious. This is relevant to humor (such as jokes) in which expectations are established only to be violated later. This entry discusses how misdirection can lead an audience away from an interpretation that subsequently is revealed to be central to the humorous effect.

The notion of misdirection fits within a particular account of humor, often discussed with reference to humor presented in language. Humor can occur in ordinary life when a person misperceives or misunderstands a situation, perhaps making unconscious predictions, then realizes what the true circumstances are, and that the initial predictions are not borne out. This pattern of events is adopted in many specially constructed cultural artifacts, such as jokes, in order to achieve humor. Some scholars even propose that this is the essential mechanism for all jokes, not merely for a large subset of jokes.

The initial portion of such a joke (usually known as the *setup*) establishes (in the mind of the audience) certain ideas about the situation being described. These initial ideas may trigger some expectations on the part of the audience. The joke then has a final short portion, usually known as the *punch line* (or sometimes simply *punch*), which causes the audience to revise the ideas established by the setup and perhaps discard some expectations. This means that the setup must be compatible with two different interpretations, either through vagueness (i.e., the information leaves certain details unspecified) or through ambiguity (i.e., the information has two or more clearly distinct meanings). Moreover, for the joke to work, one of these possible interpretations must be more "obvious," in the sense that the audience is most likely to be aware of that interpretation and not to be conscious of the other interpretation. If the audience does become aware, during the presentation of the setup, of the interpretation evoked by the punch line, then the joke will probably fail to work, as there will be no corrected misunderstanding, no violated expectations, and no surprise.

Although this device (misinterpretation followed by sudden revision) can be used in any medium (visual, tactile, verbal, etc.), it crucially depends on information being released gradually to the audience over some period of time, for example, by the joke being delivered in language. Where a humorous artifact does not have this sequential presentation (e.g., a single-frame cartoon, where the reader's eye is free to explore the areas of the picture in any order), it is harder to control the order of presentation of information.

Misdirection is part of the technique for crafting these misinterpretation-based jokes. The setup of a joke must be constructed in such a way that both possible interpretations are available in principle, but also so that the interpretation associated with the punch line is unlikely to be noticed during the setup. To this end, the joke creator must express the setup appropriately, so as to guide (misdirect) the audience toward the required interpretation. In language, this can involve careful choice of vocabulary and other discourse elements.

Sometimes, little work is required, since the second interpretation is unusual in some way, so that the audience is likely to behave as required without additional stage management. An audience will usually interpret a narrative using assumptions about "normal" or "default" courses of events, unconsciously filling in details that have not been expressed explicitly. That is, notions of social or cultural normality may confer "obviousness" on a particular interpretation with little or no special work (misdirection) by the joke creator. Consider this example joke:

> While driving on a motorway, an old man answers his phone, to hear his anxious wife. "Dearest," she says, "the radio news just said that there's a car going the wrong way on the motorway. Please be careful." "Jeez," he replies, "It's not just one car. It's hundreds of them!"

Here, the setup suppresses some facts within the fictional world that are crucial to the humorous interpretation of the punch line, but this requires little specialized work, because the default understanding of "driving on a motorway" is "driving on a motorway in the correct lane."

An example where more contrivance is needed is this joke:

> A pair of suburban couples who had known each other for quite some time talked it over and decided to do a little conjugal swapping. The trade was made the following evening, and the newly arranged couples retired to their respective houses. After about an hour of bedroom bliss, one of the wives propped herself up on her elbow, looked at her new partner and said "Well, I wonder how the boys are getting along." (Yamaguchi, 1988, p. 332)

The main misdirection is in the choice "conjugal swapping" rather than the more common "wife-swapping," along with the vague phrases "the trade was made," and "newly arranged couples." None of these terms is ambiguous in a linguistic sense, but all are carefully vague or underspecified.

The term *misdirection* is more familiar in the realm of stage conjuring, where a performer may "misdirect" the audience in the course of a magic trick. There are both similarities and differences between the two usages. A conjuror uses misdirection so that the audience will not be aware of some action or situation *even after the trick has been completed.* A joke-teller uses misdirection as a *temporary* measure, to ensure that the audience does not notice a particular interpretation until the moment when the joke-teller wants this interpretation to become evident.

Graeme Ritchie

See also Ambiguity; Bisociation; Incongruity and Resolution; Jokes; Punch Line

Further Readings

Dolitsky, M. (1992). Aspects of the unsaid in humor. *HUMOR: International Journal of Humor Research, 5*(1/2), 33–43.

Ritchie, G. (2004). *The linguistic analysis of jokes.* London, UK: Routledge.

Yamaguchi, H. (1988). How to pull strings with words: Deceptive violations in the garden-path joke. *Journal of Pragmatics, 12,* 323–337.

Mock Epic

Mock epic is a poetic genre that originated in a parodic or allusive dependence on the epic genre but eventually developed its own identity and its own dynamism. Its heyday was the 18th century, when rationalism banished the marvelous from poetry but allowed it to survive in humorous and satirical form.

The ancestry of mock epic is diverse. In ancient times, the Homeric epics were parodied in the *Batrachomyomachia* (Battle of the Frogs and Mice), once ascribed to Homer but probably dating from the 5th century BCE, in which a war among tiny creatures is described in the comically inflated language that later came to be called mock-heroic. Such grandiose language was similarly applied to a trivial topic by Alessandro Tassoni (1565–1635) in his *La secchia rapita* (The Stolen Bucket, 1622). Mock epic derived a fund of narrative material from Italian romance epic, especially from the humorous narrative of love, war, and enchantments in *Orlando furioso* (Orlando Enraged, 1532) by Ludovico Ariosto (1474–1533). It drew also from the genre of travesty, in which the action of a serious literary work is retold in comic, vulgar, and often anachronistic language: A famous example is the travesty of Virgil's *Aeneid* by Paul Scarron (1610–1660).

Full-blown mock epic emerges in the Enlightenment era. While Alexander Pope (1688–1744) wrote mock heroic on a trivial subject in *The Rape of the Lock* (1712–1717), his *Dunciad* (1728–1743) is mock epic in parodying epic—the epic suffix *-iad* announces a satire on dunces, or inferior writers and scholars—in a twofold movement. The many allusions to Virgil and John Milton not only serve to debase Pope's targets, such as the playwright Colley Cibber and the scholarly editor Richard Bentley, but also to give them a playful, even endearing liveliness, and, with the "awful Aristarch" Bentley, a paradoxical dignity. Parody liberates Pope's imagination so that scatology, as when the dunces compete in urinating, coexists with grandeur, seen most famously in the closing invocation of the apocalyptic extinction of true learning by the goddess Dulness. Mock epic thus transcends mere parody and creates a space for unrestrained imaginative play.

The mock epic *La pucelle* (The Maid, 1755) by Voltaire (1694–1778) retells the story of Joan of Arc as a satire on the Church and on superstitious belief in marvels and miracles. It includes a comic combat between the patron saints of France and England; a visit to hell, which is full of clerics; and the machinations of a lecherous archbishop. Joan's greatest miracle is said to be that she preserved her virginity for a whole year. But when she willingly surrenders to her lover Dunois, Voltaire celebrates a love that is both physical and tender, in contrast to the brutal rapes carried out by Joan's English antagonists. Again, the license of mock epic permits an unexpected range of emotions.

Among the many witty novels, essays, and poems of Christoph Martin Wieland (1733–1813), sometimes called the German Voltaire, his mock epics *Idris und Zenide* (1767) and *Oberon* (1780) stand out; the latter was translated into English by U.S. president John Quincy Adams. The unfinished *Idris*, set in a sensuous fairyland, gently mocks the Platonism of its hero, who in search of an unattainable ideal love overlooks the physical possibilities at hand. *Oberon*, a rewriting of the medieval romance of Huon of Bordeaux, compromises more with the prudery of Wieland's public. Its hero, one of Charlemagne's paladins, is given the task of challenging the Caliph of Baghdad and bringing back his daughter and four of his teeth. In this absurd mission, he is helped by the fairy Oberon, on condition that Huon and Amanda (as the Caliph's daughter is christened) must abstain from sex before marriage. They fail and must do penance by captivity in Tunis, where Huon resists the assaults of the lustful Sultaness, and the two lovers, about to be burned at the stake, are finally saved by a relenting Oberon.

Not only does Wieland, like Voltaire, explore the scope and limits of sexual liberation, but he also foregrounds another theme of mock epic, the relations of East and West. Homer opposed the Greeks to the Asiatic Trojans; Ariosto's romance epic centers on Charlemagne's war against the Saracens; modern mock epic reflects Europe's uneasy relations with the Islamic world by adapting these models with many tropes of what, since the publication of Edward Said's book *Orientalism* in 1978, we call Orientalism.

Love and Orientalism are prominent in *Don Juan* (1818–1824) by George Gordon, commonly known as Lord Byron (1788–1824). Although Byron declared "My poem's epic," its humorous, digressive style, and Byron's admission of indebtedness to Ariosto and Voltaire, place it in the mock-epic tradition. The legendary womanizer Don Juan is here a passive character whose affairs are often with older women, the exception being his idyll with the Greek girl Haidée. Sold into slavery by Haidée's angry father, Juan (like Huon) defies a sultaness but later becomes the lover of Catherine the Great of Russia. His sojourns in Turkey and Russia permit explorations in cultural relativism: Byron suggests that the confinement of Turkish women is no worse than the prudish hypocrisy that governs Englishwomen's conduct. Unlike most Orientalists, Byron uses the East to question the moral standards of the West and to cast doubt in general on "thy great joys, civilization!"

In the 19th century, mock-epic poetry fades away, but Heinrich Heine (1798–1856) presented a last masterpiece in his poem *Atta Troll* (1847). Atta Troll, a dancing bear who breaks his chains and escapes, is a political figure, whose bombastic speeches convey Heine's unease about both nationalism and communism. The narrator undertakes an arduous journey to shoot this enemy of humanity, and his many episodic adventures include a vision of the Wild Hunt, a strange assembly including Charlemagne, William Shakespeare, Johann Wolfgang von Goethe, and three goddesses, all embodying the pagan sensuality that has been suppressed by modern Christian Europe.

During its heyday, mock epic outgrew its origins in parody and used the license of humorous writing to explore searchingly the relations between men and women, and between West and East. In drawing on myth, romance, and fairy tale, it preserved their imaginative power in a period officially dominated by rationality and the reality principle.

Ritchie Robertson

See also Burlesque; Parody; Pastiche; Subversive Humor; Travesty

Further Readings

Robertson, R. (2009). *Mock-epic poetry from Pope to Heine*. Oxford, UK: Oxford University Press.

Terry, R. (2005). *Mock-heroic from Butler to Cowper*. Aldershot, UK: Ashgate.

Mockumentary

A mockumentary (or mocumentary or mock-documentary) is popularly understood to be a fictional audiovisual text, such as a feature film or television program, that looks and sounds like a documentary. These texts feature fictional characters and events that appear to have been "captured" on location and through interviews by a documentary film crew. The term *mockumentary* was first widely used to describe the fake rockumentary *This Is Spinal Tap* (1984; Rob Reiner, director), and is often assumed by commentators to refer only to similarly parodic or satiric material. Because of the range of material that now falls under this label, however, it is more useful to consider mockumentary as a *discourse* that is characterized by the *appropriation* of codes and conventions from the full continuum of nonfiction and fact-fiction forms. A mockumentary might borrow from the codes and conventions of documentary, fact-fiction texts such as nature documentary, the wide variety of television factual-based formats such as reality game shows and docusoaps, or from traditional nonfiction forms including newsreels, news bulletins, and current affairs programs.

Mockumentary has been applied toward a variety of ends; from being used as a gimmick or novelty style (e.g., single episodes of the popular television programs *M*A*S *H** [1976], *ER* [1997], *X-Files* [2000], and *The West Wing* [2009]) through to dramatic productions that might appear to be a documentary investigation of a political assassination (*Death of a President* [2006; Gabriel Range, director]), the video diary of a high school massacre (*Zero Days* [2003; Ben Coccio, director]), or the home movie of an alien invasion (*Cloverfield* [2008; Matt Reeves, director]). Mockumentary is not limited to cinematic or televisual productions; an early example of mockumentary is the infamous 1939 radio version of *War of the Worlds* developed by Orson Welles's theatrical troupe that transformed H. G. Wells's science fiction classic into an apparent breaking news bulletin.

Mockumentary as Playful and Reflexive

Mockumentary discourse is important because it embodies a playful and less reverential approach toward nonfiction media than was the case for the early decades of the 20th century (the time when documentary became codified as a genre). Most crucially, mockumentary demonstrates the ease with which nonfiction can be faked, which offers an immediate challenge to audiences' expectations toward these forms, and potentially has broader implications for the extent to which audiences remain willing to put their trust in documentary, news, and other nonfiction media.

Some mockumentaries, such as the Belgian black comedy *C'est arrivé près de chez vous* (Man Bites Dog, 1992; Rémy Belvaux, André Bonzel, and Benoît Poelvoorde, directors) about a documentary crew following a serial killer, are less playful than explicitly antagonistic toward the variety of assumptions and expectations associated with documentary practices. Such examples of mockumentary are deliberately *reflexive* toward the nonfiction form that they appropriate. As used here, reflexivity involves a foregrounding of how and why a text has been put together. In a documentary, these moments might inadvertently appear when a cameraperson is caught reflected in a mirror, a boom mike floats into frame, or gaps appear in the authority of the voice-over narration. Mockumentaries, in general, are reflexive toward the production practices, textual strategies, and range of audience expectations and interpretations that characterize documentary and reality-based media, precisely because they encourage their audiences to consider how *constructed* these kinds of media are.

Flagging Fictionality

Given their playfulness toward nonfiction codes and conventions, a key aspect of any mockumentary is the degree to which it flags to its audience that it is fictional. Some mockumentary texts, such as *This Is Spinal Tap*, are intended to be immediately recognized by viewers as fake; their pleasure derives from the ways in which they might reference ideas from popular culture, play with typical or iconic scenes from documentary culture, or simply present the more conventional aspects of their narrative. Other mockumentaries leave it up to viewers to make up their minds whether what they are viewing is real or not. A key example here is *The Blair Witch Project* (1999; Daniel Myrick and Eduardo Sánchez, directors), a horror film about three missing student filmmakers that was convincingly promoted as a real documentary. It is no coincidence that *The Blair Witch Project* relied on online marketing for its impact—the production of mockumentary has flourished within the more playful spaces of online video, where it can be more difficult to discern whether or not a text is fictional.

The Naturalization of Mockumentary Discourse

Parodic and satiric mockumentaries have proliferated since the 1990s, and their recent popularity within film and television has some key implications for the future of mockumentary discourse. First, it has become much harder to fool most audiences by either using mockumentary to perpetrate a hoax or engaging with unwitting participants in faux documentary style, as Sasha Baron Cohen achieved for key scenes within *Borat: Cultural Learnings of America for Make Benefit Glorious Nation of Kazakhstan* (2006; Larry Charles, director). Second, mockumentaries are increasingly being explored as simply another style of storytelling across a range of genres and media forms. The UK and U.S. versions of the television series *The Office* are exemplars of "mockusoaps," series that appropriate the conventions of docusoaps. They suggest the manner in which television producers have become increasingly confident of using mockumentary discourse to revitalize and reorient sitcom conventions. These series employ innovative ways of constructing television comedy (just as film producers have used mockumentary to develop inventive approaches toward cinematic science fiction and horror). Using a *verité* aesthetic within a sitcom has broadened the ways in which comedic situations can be developed and has allowed, in some cases, a meshing with a more improvisational style of comedic performance that has long been a feature of mockumentary film (*This Is Spinal Tap* is an early exemplar of this production technique).

Because of these developments, mockumentary has lost much of its subversive or reflexive stance toward documentary and related forms. As a more naturalized storytelling style within contemporary film and television media, mockumentary's playful appropriation of nonfiction aesthetics both draws on and sits comfortably with the full range of texts that mediate reality.

Craig Hight

See also Hoax and Prank; Improv Comedy; Parody; Satire; Spoofing; Subversive Humor

Further Readings

de Siefe, E. (2007). *This is Spinal Tap*. London, UK: Wallflower Press.

Hight, C. (2010). *Television mockumentary: Reflexivity, satire and a call to play*. Manchester, UK: Manchester University Press.

Higley, S. L., & Weinstock, J. A. (Eds.). (2004). *Nothing that is: Millennial cinema and the Blair Witch controversies*. Detroit, MI: Wayne State University Press.

Juhasz, A., & Lerner, J. (Eds.). (2006). *F is for phony: Fake documentary and truth's undoing*. Minneapolis: University of Minnesota Press.

Roscoe, J., & Hight, C. (2001). *Faking it: Mock documentary and the subversion of factuality*. Manchester, UK: Manchester University Press.

Torchin, L. (2008). Cultural learnings of Borat make for benefit of glorious study of documentary. *Film & History*, *38*(1), 53–63.

Walters, B. (2005). *The office*. London, UK: British Film Institute.

MOLIÈRE

Molière, born Jean-Baptiste Poquelin in 1622, bears the unchallenged mantle of France's greatest comic dramatist. Supported by a wealthy bourgeois family, he was educated in a Parisian Jesuit college that introduced him both to classical literature (Terence and Plautus strongly influenced certain plays) and, doubtless, to acting. Shunning the family trade of tapestry weaving, and the law, which he studied in Orléans, he formed in his early 20s the Illustre Théâtre, a company whose success was soon quashed by debts that remained unresolved for decades and even caused his imprisonment. On release, he led his troupe to the provinces where he toured long and widely, also gaining important noble patrons, before returning to Paris in 1658.

His own plays figured frequently in their established repertoire, many deriving from the standard traditions of farce and *commedia dell'arte*, and several no doubt lost: He only began publishing his work in 1660. However, in *L'étourdi* (The Giddy-Pate) and *Le dépit amoureux* (The Love-Tiff), he had already set the pattern of five-act comedies composed in alexandrines, later applied in various major works that helped cement his fame. One also notes the plot structure generally favored during his career whereby, prior to wedlock, pairs of young lovers overcome difficulties mounted by parental opposition. Meanwhile, doctors and pedants form stock butts for ridicule, while considerable comic energy derives from the clown Mascarille, whose cynicism, misfortunes, and counter-morality help undercut the love-plot.

Once reinstalled in the capital, Molière quickly acquired both royal patronage and a permanent site for his company, while success and notoriety followed rapidly on his landmark comedy *Les précieuses ridicules* (The Affected Ladies), a brief satire in prose of salon society and its pseudo-intellectuals that would help springboard a much later masterpiece, *Les femmes savantes* (The Learned Ladies). Otherwise, given Louis XIV's predilection for theater, it is unsurprising that Molière should receive royal commissions for court performance, sometimes at embarrassingly short notice, but the resultant so-called *comédies-ballets* combined theater, music, and dance to a spectacular degree. He continued to compose briefer farces such as *Sganarelle,* which was in fact the work produced most often during his lifetime, whereas the two plays *L'école des maris* (The School for Husbands) and *L'école des femmes* (The School for Wives) exploit his standard themes of young love frustrated by parental power, although now treated with a psychological depth that has encouraged long-standing critical attention.

In the discussions following the success of the latter play in particular, Molière claimed, in a deliberate flout of 17th-century critical consensus, that comedy was a more problematic genre than tragedy. However, still greater controversy followed his *Tartuffe,* a satire on religious hypocrisy, and *Dom Juan,* a spectacular but highly ambiguous treatment of the career and death of the womanizing anti-hero Don Juan. The former work, judged impious, was banned for some years, and the author never presented the latter following its first run, yet modern directors have often chosen them in preference to the remainder of Molière's works. Meanwhile, the playwright never lost royal favor, enjoying, by the mid-1660s, both wealth and fame.

Nevertheless, and despite illnesses that possibly sharpened his anti-medical lampoons, his output continued in a variety of works, including *Le misanthrope,* a fascinating if morally disturbing treatment of social alienation; *Amphitryon,* whose subject derived from classical mythology; *Monsieur de Pourceaugnac,* an anti-provincial satire; and *Le bourgeois gentilhomme* (The Bourgeois Gentleman), a *comédie-ballet* mocking the nouveaux riches. Alternatively, in plays like *Georges Dandin* and *Le médecin malgré lui* (The Doctor in Spite of Himself), he resorted to stock themes of marital disharmony and the professional dishonesty of doctors.

Comedies such as *L'avare* (The Miser) or his final work, *Le malade imaginaire* (The Imaginary Invalid), propound a favored pattern whereby monomaniac fathers (miserly in the first play, hypochondriac in the second) threaten to destroy the younger generation's happiness by pursuing their own obsession: Harpagon (the *avare*) has chosen a (for him) financially advantageous match for his daughter, while Argan (the *malade imaginaire*) seeks to wed his child to an idiotic young doctor. Naturally the youngsters win out, although sometimes via contrivances so artificial as to amount to self-parody, and one notes an additional intriguing feature whereby, even though family harmony is restored, the protagonists' obsessions ultimately remain intact.

This pattern, although not universal among Molière heroes, helps question the socially corrective force of humor that several of his prefaces propound in order to refute charges of immorality. Actors and directors in fact remain free to exploit the comical glamour of protagonists like his Dom Juan, if not Monsieur Jourdain, his ignorant would-be gentleman, or even Tartuffe, his outrageous and libidinous religious hypocrite; meanwhile, valet characters such as Mascarille, Sganarelle, and Scapin provide a carnivalesque inversion of responsible values that one indulges at one's leisure. One notes, accordingly, that those figures seeking to instill moderation and reason in his comic heroes rarely, if ever, achieve their

A colored engraving from the early 19th century titled "Thénard, rôle de Sganarelle dans Le médecin malgré lui" (Thénard, in the role of Sganarelle in The Doctor in Spite of Himself). Below the image is a quote from the play: "(Embrassant sa bouteille) Ah! ma petite friponne, que je t'aime, mon petit bouchon!" [(Hugging his bottle) Ah, my little rogue, how I love you, my little cork!]. Molière's comedy was first performed in 1666.

Source: Harry R. Beard Collection, given by Isobel Beard, in the Theatre and Performance Collection, Victoria and Albert Museum; © Victoria and Albert Museum, London.

aim, Molière remaining supremely committed to theatrical performance and experiment rather than the development of a philosophy.

Even the pretentious females of *Les précieuses ridicules* have enjoyed positive readings, particularly among feminists, while a character such as Agnès, ingénue heroine of *L'école des femmes*, reveals an ambiguity sufficient to permit manifold interpretations: Arnolphe, her controlling guardian, has sealed her from society while grooming her for marriage with himself, but her naïveté need not mask a demanding libido that Horace, her successful suitor, might one day have trouble satisfying. Meanwhile, a particular and related poignancy lies in Molière's own marriage in 1662 to Armande Béjart, an actress greatly his junior and whose alleged infidelities reflect Arnolphe's anxious fears of cuckoldry.

A scarcity of documents renders biographical interpretations of Molière problematic, and rightly so, since his theater's vitality depends on the exploitation of comic types rather than authorial self-examination. Nonetheless, it is strikingly ironic that as a sick man, he should die in 1673 just after performing as Argan in one of his supreme attacks on charlatanry in the medical profession.

John Parkin

See also Comedy; *Commedia dell'Arte*; Plautus; Tragicomedy

Further Readings

Bray, R. (1954). *Molière homme de théâtre* [Molière, theater man]. Paris: Mercure de France.

Moore, W. G. (1962). *Molière, a new criticism.* Oxford, UK: Oxford University Press.

Scott, V. (2000). *Molière: A theatrical life.* Cambridge, UK: Cambridge University Press.

Monty Python

Monty Python's Flying Circus was one of the most influential and acclaimed comedy shows in British television history. Broadcast in four series from 1969 to 1974, it mixed absurdist humor, parody, satire, and surreal animation in a free-flowing style that largely dispensed with the standard comedy sketch format. This innovative blend of the intellectual and the silly quickly developed a cult following in Britain and then internationally. The members of *Monty Python* were John Cleese, Graham Chapman, Eric Idle, Michael Palin, and Terry Jones (all Oxford or Cambridge University graduates) and the American-born animator Terry Gilliam. The success of the television series prompted books, records, stage shows, and five feature-length films, two of which—*Monty Python and the Holy Grail* (1974) and *Monty Python's Life of Brian* (1979)—are recognized comedy classics. The group formally stopped working together after the film *Monty Python's Meaning of Life* (1983), but they retain a huge following and a deserved reputation for transforming modern television comedy. In the *Oxford English Dictionary, Pythonesque* is defined as signifying absurd, surreal humor.

Before forming as a group, different Pythons wrote material for and performed in important satirical television shows such as *That Was the Week That Was* (1962–1963) and *The Frost Report* (1966–1967). Cleese and Chapman starred in *At Last the 1948 Show* (1967). Idle, Palin, and Jones produced an imaginative children's comedy show, *Do Not Adjust Your Set* (1967–1969), where Gilliam joined them, contributing technically simple but marvelously inventive cut-up animations that mixed arresting images with a grotesque comic sense. Cleese had been offered a comedy television series by the BBC and suggested collaboration to Palin, a move that brought the six members together. The nonsensical name *Monty Python's Flying Circus* was preferred to alternatives, including *Owl Stretching Time.* With Gilliam's stream-of-consciousness titles playing over John Philip Sousa's "The Liberty Bell" march, *Monty Python's Flying Circus* was first broadcast on BBC television in October 1969. The combination of satirical and surrealist comedy drew on verbal and visual influences, including the anarchic genius of Spike Milligan (the creator of the revered *Goon Show,* an absurdist radio program of the 1950s) and the cerebral comedy of the *Beyond the Fringe* group (Peter Cook, Dudley Moore, Jonathan Miller, and Alan Bennett). The Pythons added their brand of visual and verbal silliness, pieces such as "Cheese Shop," "Dead Parrot," "Spanish Inquisition," "Lumberjack Song," and the "Ministry of Silly Walks" marking high points in British television comedy. Not everything worked, but collectively the profusion of imaginative flashes linked by Gilliam's animation kept viewers entranced. The show parodied television conventions and formats such as game shows, interviews, news broadcasts, documentaries, and pretentious cultural programs. It ventured regularly into the absurd ("Flying Sheep"), the pseudo-intellectual ("Summarise Proust Competition"), the silly ("Spam," in which the main item on a café menu is Spam, a brand of spiced ham served from a can), and the grotesque (a cartoon figure decapitates himself while shaving). *Monty Python*'s self-mocking catchphrase, "And now for something completely different," captures its subversive approach. The strong performing talents of the group added substantially to the show's scope and quality, with the gifted Carol Cleveland appearing regularly in straight female roles. Cleese felt that the group had started to repeat itself by the third series and did not participate in the final fourth series, usually recognized as a falling away from the early high standards.

Before the television show ended in 1974, the Pythons had branched into books, records, stage shows, and films, the first film being *And Now for Something Completely Different* (1971). This compilation of popular sketches helped establish an international fan base. *Monty Python and the Holy Grail* (1974), directed by Gilliam and Jones, proved a substantial critical and popular success, linking hilarious sketches via a loose narrative based on the Grail myth. The film lampooned film conventions, opening with faux–Ingmar Bergman credits, acknowledging that its sets sometimes were models, and including a parody of a Hollywood song-and-dance number. It was financed in part by rock groups Led Zeppelin and Pink Floyd, fans of the show. Jones directed the more ambitious and coherent *Monty Python's Life of Brian* (1979), which satirized unthinking political and religious zealots through the story of Brian, a figure mistaken for the long-awaited Messiah. The religious content caused the original producers to pull out just before shooting, and the film was financed by another Python fan, Beatle George Harrison. On release, it initially proved highly controversial for those who misread it as an attack on Christ. It is now recognized as among the best and most successful British comedies ever made, but Palin has declared that in the current climate of religious sensitivity it would not be made. Idle performed its superb closing song, "Always Look on the Bright Side of Life," at the 2012 London Olympics. *Monty Python's Meaning of Life* was a partially successful attempt to connect a sketch format to a larger theme. Its best moments—as when the morbidly obese Mr. Creosote explodes, his innards spraying over others at a restaurant, or the musical number "Every Sperm Is Sacred," which mocks religious opposition to birth control—confirmed the Python capacity to amuse and shock, sometimes simultaneously. This was the last major project involving all of the Pythons, as Chapman died in 1989.

From the early 1970s, individual members of the group had begun successful careers in writing, stage, television, and film. Notable examples on television include Cleese's *Fawlty Towers* (1975–1979), Palin and Jones's *Ripping Yarns* (1977–1979), and Palin's travel series. Films such as *A Fish Called Wanda* (cowritten by and starring Cleese) as well as Gilliam's *Brazil* (1985) and *Twelve Monkeys* (1995) displayed the creative versatility that underpinned Python projects. The immense commercial and critical success of the Tony award–winning musical comedy *Spamalot* (2005–), written by Idle and based on *The Holy Grail* film, testifies to the quality of the original material and the group's enduring esteem. Although *Monty Python*'s unique blend of surrealism, absurdity, and satire made imitation by other groups impossible, it opened up comedic possibilities that are still being used. The continuing international popularity of reruns of the television shows and the films ensures *Monty Python*'s place in British film and television history.

Peter Marks

See also Absurdist Humor; Aristophanes; Parody; Satire; Sketch Comedy Shows; Verbal Humor

Further Readings

Chapman, G., Cleese, J., Gilliam, T., Idle, E., Jones, T., Palin, M., & McCabe, B. (2003). *The Pythons: Autobiography by the Pythons.* London, UK: Orion.

Palin, M. (2008). *Diaries 1969–1979: The Python years.* London, UK: Weidenfeld & Nicolson.

Wilmut, R. (1980). *From fringe to flying circus: Celebrating a unique generation of comedy 1960–1980.* London, UK: Methuen.

Movie Humor Types

From its slapstick beginnings, honed in music halls and vaudeville circuits, film comedy would proliferate into numerous subgenres. At least 10 dominant, albeit overlapping, categories would evolve to elicit peculiar kinds of laughing experiences: slapstick, parody, character comedy, comedy of manners, romantic/screwball comedy, musical comedy, farce (animal comedy), satire/black comedy, hybrids, and mockumentary. This entry discusses each of these types of film comedy and gives some examples of them.

The earliest form of film comedy emerged as slapstick (from the theatrical device of two flat slabs of wood used by actors to make a loud noise when striking another), a rough and tumble form of visual horseplay. Director Mack Sennett mastered the pratfalls of the Keystone Cops and careening automobiles with panache. Slapstick would explode into hilarious anarchy with the Marx Brothers (in their 1933 film *Duck Soup*) and shorts and features with Stan Laurel and Oliver Hardy. Later physical slapstick comedies such as *The Pink Panther* (1963), *Home Alone* (1990), and *Toy Story* (1995) would combine slapstick and character comedy. Often the genre showcased riffing, as in *Tampopo* (1985), a richly comic film about noodles.

Closely aligned to the slapstick came film parodies, satirizing other films or genres. In the silent era, the cross-eyed Ben Turpin mocked the romanticism of Rudolph Valentino in *The Shriek of Araby* (1923). Beginning in 1948, Bud Abbott and Lou Costello took on the horror film genre with their silly encounters with Frankenstein, the Invisible Man, and the Mummy. More modern parodies would be the province of Mel Brooks upending the conventions of the horror genre (*Young Frankenstein,* 1974) and westerns (*Blazing Saddles,* 1974), with literary sophistication appearing in the Monty Python parody of medieval romances in *Monty Python and the Holy Grail* (1975). Chuck Jones would sacrifice high culture with *What's Opera, Doc?* (1957) while Italian animator Bruno Bozzetto would spoof Disney's *Fantasia* (1940) with his hilarious *Allegro Non Troppo* (1976).

Out of the wild physical playground of slapstick evolved several notable comedians, whose personality distinguished their unique styles. In contrast to the falling and pie throwing of the Sennett studio, character comedy developed around distinct natural talents, the baggy pants and derby and cane of Charlie Chaplin's tramp (*The Gold Rush*, 1925), the stone-faced stoic of Buster Keaton (*Steamboat Bill, Jr.,* 1928), the All American boy-next-door "glasses" character of Harold Lloyd (*Safety Last!* 1923), and the infantile Harry Langdon (*Tramp, Tramp, Tramp,* 1926). The work of Keaton and Lloyd led as well to the thrill comedies of the 1920s, wild rapid adventures in which speed propelled the stories into lively entertainments. The picaro existed as a stranger in a strange land, even if the land were the beach in summer as in Jacques Tati's *Mr. Hulot's Holiday* (1953). Jerry Lewis augmented his wacky persona into the dual roles in *The Nutty Professor* (1963).

Sound technology joined wit and wordplay to polish a comedy of manners, in which dialogue showcased witty repartee. Grounded in an Oscar Wilde tradition of sparkling wit, early sound comedies like *Dinner at Eight* (1933) would keep audiences attuned to epigrammatic dialogue regarding social class pretentions. Writer/director Preston Sturges, who perfected the genre with his *Sullivan's Travels* (1941) and *The Lady Eve* (1941), quipped, "There's something to be said for making people laugh."

The ancient New Comedy of Rome, which involved boy meets girl, boy loses girl, boy gets girl back, set the stage for cinematic romantic comedies, those in which women and men matched wits and fell in and out of love. These films, which included a special subgenre of "screwball comedies," enlivened the Depression years of the 1930s. In comedies of remarriage, couples would bicker until they rejoined in the final reel. *It Happened One Night* (1934) and *Philadelphia Story* (1940) illustrated the essence of the screwball comedies, while certain directors would creatively extend the tradition (Billy Wilder's *Some Like It Hot* [1959], Woody Allen's *Annie Hall* [1977], and Rob Reiner's *When Harry Met Sally* [1989]).

The advent of sound also enabled musical comedies to premiere and delight audiences. René Clair's elaborate musical constructions, Busby Berkeley's all-dancing and all-singing extravaganzas, and Eddie Cantor's wild, chauvinistic romps paved the way for classics like Gene Kelly's *Singin' in the Rain* (1952), and *Mary Poppins,* produced by Walt Disney (1964). Popular films such as *Sister Act* (1992) and the teen Disney franchise *High School Musical,* which included TV movies in 2006 and 2007 and a big-screen film in 2008, achieved box office success.

In the old tradition of vulgar laughter, farce or animal comedy combined slapstick with outrageous jokes, eventually leading to gross-out comedies (*There's Something About Mary,* 1998; *The Hangover,* 2009) with body liquids from vomit to semen covering the screens. Spectators cringed while they laughed.

In contrast to parody, which lampoons a particular genre or work, satire ridiculed social, political, or cultural institutions or individuals. Stanley Kubrick's masterly nightmarish comedy *Dr. Strangelove, Or: How I Learned to Stop Worrying and Love the Bomb* (1964) played with the absurdity of the nuclear arms race and an impending doomsday. Director Robert Townsend targeted the film industry's exploitation of African Americans in *Hollywood Shuffle* (1987). André Breton coined the term *humour noir,* or black comedy, to describe the cynical, gallows laughter associated with suffering, death, and cultural taboos. *Harold and Maude* (1971) followed a suicidal youth romancing an elderly woman. The comically squalid British *Withnail and I* (1986) portrays the outrageous fortunes of two unemployed actors.

Hybrid comedies blended comedy with other genres, such as action films (*Beverly Hills Cop* [1984], *A Bug's Life* [1998], *Who Framed Roger Rabbit?* [1988]), soap opera (*Tootsie,* 1982), horror (*Ghostbusters* [1984], *Scary Movie* [2000], *Shaun of the Dead* [2004]), and historical adventure (*The Princess Bride* [1987]). Each plays on the codes and conventions and offers esoteric pleasures for informed viewers. One gets the jokes when one knows the traditions.

Finally, the mockumentary genre applies parody to the documentary tradition, creating some of the most brilliantly improvised satires: Rob Reiner's *This is Spinal Tap* (1984) and Christopher Guest's *Waiting for Guffman* (1996) expose the vanity and venality of the music and theatrical worlds, while the daring *Borat* (2006) starring Sacha Baron Cohen subverted American and "Kazakh" cultural practices.

Film comedy continues to evolve, particularly in its juxtaposition with other movie forms, finding new ways to break into a thousand more pieces of laughter.

Terry Lindvall

See also Comedy; Farce; Mockumentary; Monty Python; Movies; Slapstick

Further Readings

Cavell, S. (1984). *Pursuits of happiness: The Hollywood comedy of remarriage.* Boston, MA: Harvard University Press.

Dale, A. (2002). *Comedy is a man in trouble: Slapstick in American movies.* Minneapolis: University of Minnesota Press.

Gehring, W. (2002). *Romantic vs. screwball comedy: Charting the difference.* Lanham, MD: Scarecrow Press.

Harvey, J. (1998). *Romantic comedy in Hollywood: From Lubitsch to Sturges.* New York, NY: DaCapo Press.

Jenkins, H. (1992). *What made pistachio nuts? Early sound comedy and the vaudeville aesthetic.* New York, NY: Columbia University Press.

Johnson, K. (1999). *The first 28 years of Monty Python.* New York, NY: St. Martin's Press.

Karnick, K. B., & Jenkins, H. (Eds.). (1994). *Classical Hollywood comedy.* London, UK: Routledge.

King, B., & Paulus, T. (Eds.). (2010). *Slapstick comedy.* London, UK: Routledge.

Mast, G. (1979). *The comic mind: Comedy and the movies.* Chicago, IL: University of Chicago Press.
Miller, C. (2012). *Too bold for the box office: The mockumentary from big screen to small.* Lanham, MD: Scarecrow Press.

Movies

Movies that incorporate humorous elements in an attempt to evoke laughter from an audience comprise the genre of film comedy. Such movies often borrow comedic conventions and gags and add novel twists to adapt the same goal for mediated audiences. The genre of film comedy has persisted since one of Thomas Edison's assistants, Fred Ott, sneezed for the camera in 1891 and provided the first comic action for the fledging art. This entry explores the genre of film comedy from the silent film era to the 21st century.

Silent Laughter

In 1895, the Lumière brothers of France devised a gag film with their *L'arroseur arrosé* (The Gardener; Louis Lumière, director), in which a mischievous boy bends the hose of a gardener who ends up getting squirted when he looks into it. However, the boy gets his comeuppance when he is caught and spanked. In the late 19th century and early 20th century, the more fantastic filmmaker and former magician Georges Méliès played a light-hearted devil in his trick films. One of Méliès's actors, André Deed, revived the Pierrot stock figure from *commedia dell'arte* in his Italian clown named Cretinetti.

After working with dramatic filmmaker D. W. Griffith, Mack Sennett ran off to California in 1913 to produce his own brand of slapstick, crowded with his grotesques, the Keystone Cops, who were fat, skinny, cross-eyed, short, and stubby, and could perform pratfalls and summersaults. Speed, abuse of the body, and destruction of property constituted the major themes of Sennett productions, with stars like the agile Fatty Arbuckle and Mabel Normand. Adding to the fun, Sennett introduced the Sennett Bathing Beauties in 1915, garnering front-page pictures in the newspaper with his bevy of beauties dressed in bathing suits. In this comic mode of presentation, gags dominated, with narrative assuming a secondary, or nonexistent, role.

Out of Sennett's fun factory came the quintessential clown of the century, Charlie Chaplin, whose underdog roguish character, the Little Tramp, introduced in the 1914 film *Kid Auto Races at Venice* (Henry Lehrman, director), triumphed over the vicissitudes of the American experience. Inspired by dapper French comedian Max Linder and his own Karno Music Hall roots, Chaplin was easily exported throughout the growing film world. The impact of the Little Tramp spanned continents, with his popularity establishing him as one of the first global celebrities.

Other comic characters imitated and paralleled the rise of Chaplin. The thrill comedies of Harold Lloyd, the intellectual, kinetic, and deadpan comedy of Buster Keaton, and the bathetic humor of Harry Langdon kept American audiences laughing in the 1920s. Movies like *The Gold Rush* (1925; Charlie Chaplin, director), *Safety Last* (1923; Fred C. Newmeyer and Sam Taylor, directors), *Sherlock Jr.* (1924; Buster Keaton and Roscoe Arbuckle, directors), and *The Strong Man* (1926; Frank Capra, director) sold tickets to jazz age audiences.

The legion of film comics was joined by animated characters that jumped around, imitating the great comedians. In 1919, brothers Max and Dave Fleischer drew Koko the Clown and began the animated series *Out of the Ink Well,* and Otto Messmer provided the comic antics of Felix the Cat through surreal metamorphoses.

Stepping out of the Ziegfeld Follies, vaudeville and burlesque amusements of the early 20th century, numerous entertainers hit the silver screen with diverse comic talents: W. C. Fields juggling and muttering sotto voce, Will Rogers lassoing and philosophizing, the Marx Brothers exploding with anarchy and comic chaos, and Mae West gyrating and insinuating all matter of risqué material.

The Sound of Laughter

The innovation of sound technology through Warner Bros. Studios in the late 1920s opened up new modes of film comedy for the entire industry. Sound ushered in a spate of musical comedies, with Eddie Cantor, for instance, singing and dancing, and director-producer Busby Berkeley choreographing complex numbers while using the quick comic patter of female characters to accelerate his comedy and simultaneously make pointed social commentary on the Great Depression.

In France, visionary director René Clair applied Dadaesque sensibilities to his silent films (*Paris qui dort* [The Crazy Ray], 1924) and his wildly innovative early sound films like *Le Million* (1931). In Great Britain, music hall performers like Gracie Fields, the befuddled Will Hay, and buck-toothed ukulele-playing George Formby showcased plenty of pluck and wit and a bit of slapstick.

Sound also inaugurated a zoo of talking animated animals, with the Disney Brothers Studios premiering Mickey and Minnie Mouse in *Steamboat Willie* (Ub Iwerks and Walt Disney, directors) in 1928, an homage to Buster Keaton's *Steamboat Bill, Jr.* In the 1930s, the Fleischer brothers shaped other Paramount cartoon stars with a gartered Betty Boop and a pipe-smoking Popeye the Sailor Man, and Warner Bros. Studios began redefining cartoon comedy with wise-cracking rascals like Bugs Bunny and Daffy Duck.

Hal Roach Studios made the transition from the silent *Our Gang* series with multiethnic rascals into sound with *Our Gang* characters Spanky and Alfalfa and with character actors like Charlie Chase in *The Pip From Pittsburg* (1931; James Parrott, director). The studio's silent shorts with Stan Laurel and Oliver Hardy extended into sound shorts and features, combining pantomime (tie-twaddle and eye-blinks), pet phrases ("well, here's another fine mess you've gotten me into"), reciprocal violence, and escalating tit-for-tat in the classic *Big Business* (1929; Leo McCarey and James W. Horne, directors) and *The Music Box* (1932; James Parrott, director).

Historian Wes Gehring distinguished the comic styles of two 20th-century Roman Catholic directors: Frank Capra and Leo McCarey. The former developed a populist style featuring a "Cracker-Barrel Yankee" who was gainfully employed, politically active, providing a paternal or grandfatherly figure, and serving as somewhat of a rural, homespun philosopher spouting country wisdom. Such American archetypes included the real Will Rogers and the fictional Mr. Deeds and Mr. Smith. The latter mischievously propagated the figure of the anti-hero, essentially an incompetent, urban male with lots of leisure time. McCarey was typically frustrated with women and domestic problems, being a bit of an infantile figure himself, such as can be found in his team of Laurel and Hardy. Writers from *The New Yorker,* such as Robert Benchley who turned into a film star, exemplified such domestic bumblers. Droll writers from the Algonquin Round Table in New York City arrived to write for the screen, such as the quaintly humorous Robert Benchley (*Sex Life of a Polyp* [1928; Thomas Chalmers, director]), who taught Americans *How to Sleep* (1935; Nick Grinde, director).

Anarchic figures, such as the cantankerous clown/juggler misanthrope W. C. Fields and the motley comedy team of the Marx Brothers, crashed onto the screen in the 1920s and 1930s. The Marx Brothers subverted social discourse and language with malapropisms, misunderstandings, absurd and loose logic, indecorous discourse, extended clichés, and chutzpah, perfecting comic transgressions of verbal communication and social propriety. Groucho's grease-painted moustache, stooped walk with baggy pants and cigar, and glib, wise-cracking non sequiturs confused the usually unflappable Margaret Dumont, the straight woman in several Marx Brothers' films. Chico's ethnic dialect games mangled the English language. Harpo's silent character, yet equipped with whistle, taxi-cab horn, and scissors, responded literally to his conspirators and used props from his magic coat to improvise with impunity. His leg gag shtick and mirroring of Groucho in *Duck Soup* (1933; Leo McCarey, director) remain pinnacles of the art of pantomime. On the female side, an edgy, tongue-in-cheek Mae West tested the limits of movie censorship.

However, although these wilder comics were not among Quigley Publishing's annual Top Ten Money Makers poll, other comic and dramatic stars commanded the highest profits. Such figures as Marie Dressler, Will Rogers, Shirley Temple, Mickey Rooney, Bing Crosby, and Bob Hope were major earners for the studios, and theatergoers derived great pleasure from watching them perform.

Comic directors and actors immigrated to the United States during the early sound era, infusing Hollywood with continental sensibilities. German director Ernst Lubitsch captured French insouciance with *The Love Parade* (1929), a light-hearted operetta drafting French actor-singer Maurice Chevalier to charm the world. He then got actress Greta Garbo to laugh in *Ninotchka* (1939) and satirized Adolf Hitler through the comic timing of Jack Benny in the daring *To Be or Not to Be* (1942). On the verge of World War II, Marcel Carne's dark comedy *Drôle de drame* (Bizarre, Bizzare, 1937) dealt with lurid crimes and a psychopath who kills butchers. Following the end of the war, Carne released a dramatic story of a white clown in France, *Children of Paradise* (1946), which contained the bittersweet sorrow and laughter of an occupied people.

Romance found gender equality in the screwball comedies of the 1930s. Beginning with multiple

Academy Award–winning *It Happened One Night* (1934; Frank Capra, director), the genre lasted throughout the Depression. Capra's movie took Americans across their country showcasing motels, hitchhiking, and donut dunking. The subgenre celebrated rituals of marriage and remarriage, in which women and men matched wits through scintillating verbal fireworks and physical slapstick. Critic Andrew Sarris called these screwball comedies—films like *My Man Godfrey* (1936; Gregory La Cava, director), *Bringing up Baby* (1938; Howard Hawks, director), *Theodora Goes Wild* (1936; Richard Boleslawski, director), and *Nothing Sacred* (1937; William A. Wellman, director)—"sex comedies without sex." Marriage comedy was wedded with the detective novels of Dashiell Hammett to bring forth the charming martini-laden Thin Man series. Screwball comediennes descended into femme fatales as seen in director Howard Hawks's funny version of the fairy tale Snow White, *Ball of Fire* (1941), starring Barbara Stanwyck, and slipped into film noir like *Double Indemnity* (1944; Billy Wilder, director).

Capra's populist comedies such as *Mr. Deeds Goes to Town* (1936) populated the Depression years and were supplanted during the World War II by religious comedies, such as McCarey's *Going My Way* (1944), and a species of fantasy film Peter Valenti called *film blanc*, giving hope during such grim times, such as director Alexander Hall's *Here Comes Mr. Jordan* (1941) and Capra's *It's a Wonderful Life* (1947).

A 1940 promotional picture for the film *His Girl Friday* with Cary Grant, Rosalind Russell, and Ralph Bellamy.

Source: Wikimedia Commons.

In the shadow of the Marx Brothers, the Ritz Brothers and the Three Stooges, composed of Moe, Larry, and Curly in various manifestations, revived physical slapstick and inanity to attract male audiences. During World War II, comedians Bud Abbott and Lou Costello performed in *Naughty Nineties* (1945; Jean Yarbrough, director), their now-classic comedy routine in which they tried to figure out "Who's on First?" World geography expanded with the global treks of entertainers Bob Hope and Bing Crosby following Paramount Studio's "roads" in *Road to Singapore* (1940; Victor Schertzinger, director), *Road to Zanzibar* (1941; Victor Schertzinger, director), *Road to Morocco* (1942; David Butler, director), *Road to Utopia* (1946; Hal Walker, director), *Road to Rio* (1947; Norman McLeod, director), *Road to Bali* (1952; Hal Walker, director), and *Road to Hong Kong* (1962; Norman Panama, director), with songs, their signature patty-cake routine, and costar Dorothy Lamour in a sarong. A tipsy suave Dean Martin and infantile Jerry Lewis teamed up as crooner and pubescent sidekick in popular film comedies such as *My Friend Irma* (1949; George Marshall, director) and *Hollywood or Bust* (1956; Frank Tashlin, director).

Bob Hope (and Bugs Bunny and, later, Woody Allen) inaugurated a style of comedy that Steve Seidman labeled "comedian comedy," one in which the celebrity entertainer occasionally breaks the fourth wall of the film narrative. Thus, Hope would step out of his character to address the spectators directly, advising them it was a good time to go buy popcorn in the lobby because Crosby was about to sing. This direct, even Brechtian, address engaged viewers in fresh, interactive ways.

In the United States, after World War II, a domestic mode of comedy appeared along with the baby boom, such as the comedies on gender relations starring Katharine Hepburn and Spencer Tracy, with *Adam's Rib* (1949; George Cukor, director) comically signifying the tensions in marital arrangements. So, too, cinema in which the story structure opened up comic possibilities emerged, such as with entertainer Danny Kaye in *The Inspector General* (1949; Henry Koster, director) or *The Court Jester* (1955; Melvin Frank and Norman Panama, directors).

After working with screenwriter Charles Brackett on *Ninotchka* and *Ball of Fire*, Billy Wilder directed the satirical *Sunset Boulevard* (1950) and the transvestite comedy *Some Like It Hot* (1959). In contrast to tame comedies like *Pillow Talk* (1959; Michael

Gordon, director) and *Francis the Talking Mule* (1950; Arthur Lubin, director), Wilder's provocative films were previews of the 1960s, when film comedy showcased funny women, such as Judy Holliday, Doris Day, Lucille Ball, and Marilyn Monroe.

The advent of television necessitated film to become more daring and spectacular. Director Frank Tashlin challenged the small medium in 1957 with *Will Success Spoil Rock Hunter?* in which his star, Tony Randall, addresses the movie audience: "Ladies and gentlemen, this break in our motion picture is made out of respect for the TV fans in our audience, who are accustomed to constant interruptions in their programs for messages from sponsors. We want all you TV fans to feel at home, and not forget the thrill you get, watching television on your big, 21-inch screens." Tashlin also directed films with Bob Hope and Jerry Lewis and titillating ones such as *The Girl Can't Help It* (1956) with actress Jane Mansfield.

A World of Laughter

From postwar comedies in Europe to the present productions, a bevy of great comics and directors reflected national identities. Neopolitan comic actor Totò ruled Italian comedy as the prince of laughter until the baroque and extravagant comedies of director Federico Fellini appeared; Fellini's comedies were an amalgam of dreams, satire, autobiography, and circus life on film, overflowing with giants and dwarfs and monstrous women. The tradition of *commedia all'italiana* (comedy in the Italian style) offered sardonic glimpses into marriage and infidelity in *Divorce Italian Style* (1961; Pietro Germi, director). European comedy darkened into satire. Director Luis Buñuel's sardonic and surreal *Discreet Charm of the Bourgeoisie* (1972) mocks modern society (with a group of upper middle-class diners futilely trying to have a meal). Near the end of the 20th century, Roberto Benigni wrote, directed, and starred in the Academy Award–winning *La vita è bella* (*Life Is Beautiful*, 1998), in which comedy interrupted the horrors of a Nazi concentration camp.

In France, actor Fernandel's rubbery face delighted audiences in *L'auberge rouge* (The Red Inn, 1951; Claude Autant-Lara, director) and *The Little World of Don Camillo* (1952, Julien Duvivier, director). However, perhaps the greatest picaro character was writer-director-actor Jacques Tati, whose long shots and almost silent films, such as *Les vacances de Monsieur Hulot* (Mr. Hulot's Holiday, 1953), charmed spectators with endearing scenes of life. Playing the unluckiest man in the world in director Francis Veber's *La chèvre* (Knock on Wood [lit. The Goat], 1981), underdog klutz Pierre Richard is teamed with a tough guy detective played by Gerard Depardieu to hunt down a kidnapped young lady, also accident prone, putting the French style of farce to fresh use.

Juxtaposed cultures offered comic incongruities, as in director Jamie Uys's 1984 surprise hit, *The Gods Must Be Crazy*. Like the Australian fish-out-of-water tale, *Crocodile Dundee* (1986; Peter Faiman, director) starring Paul Hogan, French comedy traversed not only geography but also time with medieval time travelers stumbling into modern France in director Jean-Marie Poire's *Les visiteurs* (The Visitors, 1993).

The sweet sorrows of poignant human comedy, as found with Nino Manfredi as the hapless Italian immigrant in Switzerland in *Bread and Chocolate* (1974; Franco Brusati, director) and the lonely hearts linguists of *Italian for Beginners* (2002; Lone Scherfig, director), opened the charms of continental laughter. French comedy had turned quirky with troglodyte frogmen and cannibalism forming the underbelly of society in a bizarre dystopian comedy from writer-directors Jean-Pierre Jeunet and Marc Caro, *Delicatessen* (1992). Director Jeunet's sweetly surreal *Amélie* (2001) brought charity and sentiment into comedy. In 2011, French director Michel Hazanavicius's homage to silent film, *The Artist*, revived both visual and sound gags in a sophisticated production.

The Ealing Studios featured comedies starring Alec Guinness and directed by Alexander Mackendrick (*The Man in the White Suit* [1951], *The Ladykillers* [1955]) and eccentric character films like *Whiskey Galore* (1949). Droll dry British humor carried into director Bill Forsyth's whimsical *Local Hero* (1983). Director Gerald Thomas's low-budget *Carry On* series (1958–1992) showcased the talents of an ensemble group, with British postcard naughty humor, exemplified by the comedy troupe Monty Python's signature phrase "wink, wink, nudge, nudge," suggesting sexual tomfoolery—all precursors of Monty Python's outlandish genre-busters *Monty Python and the Holy Grail* (1975; Terry Gilliam and Terry Jones, directors) and *Life of Brian* (1979; Terry Jones, director). The wacky Monty Python humor extended into cross-genre hybrids like *Shaun of the Dead* (2004: Edgar Wright, director).

After British import Peter Sellers starred as bumbling Inspector Clouseau in director Blake Edwards's phenomenally successful *Pink Panther* series, he took on triple roles in director Stanley Kubrick's black comedy *Dr. Strangelove* (1964), with the specter of an impending nuclear holocaust looming. The British continued their madcap ways with Richard Lester directing *A Hard Day's Night* (1964), starring the British band The Beatles, and Tony Richardson directing an earthy, lusty adaptation of Henry Fielding's story of foundling *Tom Jones* (1963) and an adaptation of Evelyn Waugh's funereal satire *The Loved One* (1965). Walt Disney Productions celebrated the musical comedy with the jolly holiday of the magical British nanny *Mary Poppins* (1964; Robert Stevenson, director), adding the song "A Spoonful of Sugar" and actors Julie Andrews and Dick van Dyke to the cinema. The swan song of classic slapstick, *It's a Mad, Mad, Mad World* (1963; Stanley Kramer, director), featured Terry Thomas, Jonathan Winters, and a cast of crazies.

Satirical Laughter

The 1960s also sparked the hegemony of popular celebrity culture in the musical in *Bye, Bye Birdie* (1963; George Sidney, director) and fomenting teenage troubles amid divorce and other problems, as evinced in Walt Disney Production's *The Parent Trap* (1961; David Swift, director) and director Hal Ashby's *Harold and Maude* (1971). Movies had to announce they were comedies, as in *A Funny Thing Happened on the Way to the Forum* (1966; Richard Lester, director) and *Funny Girl* (1968; William Wyler, director).

Times were changing, and so were the comedies. With the demise of the morality guidelines known as the Motion Picture Production Code, or Hays Code, in 1968, the industry spawned a host of more daring comedies. Social and political satire splashed onto the screens. The Vietnam War also darkened the way Americans laughed, moving from the silly to the cynical, from the lighthearted to protests. While *What's Up, Doc?* (1972) celebrated director Peter Bogdanovich's homage to classic screwball comedy, a counterculture ambiguity marked director Paul Mazurky's *Bob & Carol & Ted & Alice* (1969), director Mike Nichols's *The Graduate* (1967), and director Robert Altman's subversive *M*A*S*H** (1972).

Sid Caesar's live television *Your Show of Shows* (1950–1954) incubated fresh young comic writers who would shape the film comedies of the late 1960s and beyond, bringing Jewish sensibilities and shticks to the big screen. Neil Simon's *The Odd Couple* (1968; Gene Saks, director), Mel Brooks's *The Producers* (1968; Mel Brooks, director), and Woody Allen's *Bananas* (1971; Woody Allen, director) inaugurated an era of comic *auteurs*, filmmaking authors who put their personal signatures onto films. Simon explored relationship problems in *The Goodbye Girl* (1977; Herbert Ross, director), and writer-director Allen confessed his male anxieties and sexual obsessions, constructing an alternative life on the screen: literate, self-reflexive and starring his various girlfriends—Diane Keaton in *Love and Death* (1975) and *Annie Hall* (1977), Mia Farrow in *Hannah and Her Sisters* (1986). In films he wrote and directed, Brooks kept to his template of parodying various genres: westerns in *Blazing Saddles* (1974) and horror in *Young Frankenstein* (1974). Joining Brooks's parodic style was the outlandish producer-director team of Jim Abrahams, David Zucker, and Jerry Zucker, whose *Airplane!* (1980) and *Naked Gun* series (1988, 1991, 1994) revived deadpan humor through the likes of a literalist actor Leslie Nielsen. So, too, writer-actor Mike Myers's *Austen Powers* (1997; Jay Roach, director) spoofed the James Bond spy films, overflowing with inane sexual innuendo and tomfoolery.

The late-night television show *Saturday Night Live* (1975–present) propelled its own alumni into film comedy. National Lampoon's *Animal House* (1978; John Landis, director) brought not only a revival of slapstick and the infantile but also resuscitated the medieval practice of carnival as Mikhail Bakhtin described it, full of topsy-turvy and grotesque celebration. Its cafeteria food fights and sexual shenanigans eventually lead to gross-out comedies by the end of the century. Comedies from *Saturday Night Live* alumni (e.g., *Caddyshack* [1980; Harold Ramis, director]; *Stripes* [1981; Ivan Reitman, director]) expanded the goofy into an art form. Key to their success was screenwriter Harold Ramis, who shaped modern comedies that surprised and slimed spectators (*Ghostbusters* [1986; Ivan Reitman, director]) and raised philosophical and theological questions (*Groundhog Day* [1993; Harold Ramis, director]).

Some comedies featured male characters who had a Peter Pan complex (i.e., who do not want to grow up), such as those played by Dudley Moore in *10* (1979; Blake Edwards, director) or *Arthur* (1981; Steve Gordon, director). Others placed actors in drag to learn gender equality—for example, *Tootsie* (1982; Sydney Pollack, director) and *Mrs. Doubtfire* (1993; Chris Columbus, director). Director Hal Ashby's *Being There* (1979) gently explored the theme of a video culture through Peter Sellers's stellar performance as Chauncey [the] Gardiner. Men just did not grow up, as testified by *Three Men and a Baby* (1987; Leonard Nimoy, director) to *Wedding Crashers* (2005; David Dobkin, director), *Talledega Nights* (2006; Adam McKay, director), and *The Hangover* (2009; Todd Phillips, director).

Other literate, sophisticated comedies sprouted up with *As Good as It Gets* (1997; James L. Brooks, director), Tom Stoppard and Marc Norman's scripted *Shakespeare in Love* (1998; John Madden, director), and *Election* (1999; Alexander Payne, director); while romantic comedies were revised with a new morality (*Moonstruck* [1987; Norman Jewison, director], *When Harry Met Sally* [1989; Rob Reiner, director]) and a legion of wedding movies was planned, from *Four Weddings and a Funeral* (1994; Mike Newell, director), *Runaway Bride* (1999; Garry Marshall, director), *27 Dresses* (2008; Anne Fletcher, director), *My Big Fat Greek Wedding* (2002; Joel Zwick, director), and so on. The classic juxtaposition of an individual in an alien society continued to prosper, with *Sister Act* (1992; Emile Ardolino, director) starring actress-comedian Whoopi Goldberg; *Legally Blonde* (2001; Robert Luketic, director), featuring actress Reese Witherspoon; and *Napoleon Dynamite* (2004; Jared Hess, director), often with the transformation or triumph of an underdog character.

In the late 20th century, ethnic actors, such as Richard Pryor, Eddie Murphy, and Jackie Chan, crossed over into stardom. In 2001, king of Hong Kong comedy, Stephen Chow, inserted heart into nonsense action with *Shaolin Soccer*, a film that he wrote, directed, and starred in.

Top box office animated comedies not only came out of Walt Disney Pictures (e.g., *Aladdin,* 1992; Ron Clements and John Musker, directors; featuring actor-comedian Robin Williams as the Genie), but hilarious franchises developed from Dreamworks Animation (director Andrew Adamson's ogre series *Shrek,* 2001–2010) and Pixar (director John Lasseter's *Toy Story* [1995] and *A Bug's Life* [1998]). The appeal to all ages also emerged from the energetic works of director Robert Zemeckis's *Back to the Future* (1985) and *Who Framed Roger Rabbit* (1988) as well as the peculiarly fun productions from Tim Burton such as *Pee Wee's Big Adventure* (1985) and *Dark Shadows* (2012). Certain films caught the public with kid humor, often situated around Christmas time, such as *Home Alone* (1990; Chris Columbus, director), *A Christmas Story* (1983; Bob Clark, director), and *Elf* (2003; Jon Favreau, director) with actor-comedian Will Ferrell playing Elf. The unflappably cool persona of actor-comedian Bill Murray ranged from *Scrooged* (1988; Richard Donner, director) to *What About Bob?* (1991; Frank Oz, director).

Talented directors at the end of the 20th century emerged to raise the intellectual quality of film comedy. Paul Masurksy's nervous comedies, full of angst and uncertainty, tapped into cultural malaise, while Tom Shadyac ventured forth with comedies starring actor-comedian Jim Carey, soaring with *Bruce Almighty* (2003). The versatile Coen Brothers showcased an exuberant style with *Raising Arizona* (1987) and *O Brother, Where Art Thou?* (2000).

These intelligent and richly textured comedies contrasted sharply with the gross-out and transgressive humor of writer-directors Bobby and Peter Farrelly. Their funny but prickly *There's Something About Mary* (1998) generated laughter from dog abuse, fishhooks in the mouth, mental retardation, and semen hair goo. Vulgar comedy grinned forth with actors like Adam Sandler (*The Wedding Singer* [1998; Frank Coraci, director]) and Ben Stiller (*Meet the Parents* [2000; Jay Roach, director]). Producer Judd Apatow's outrageous comedies for the juvenile market like *Superbad* (2007; Greg Mottola, director) and *Knocked Up* (2007; Judd Apatow, director) wedded sentiment with filth to surprisingly affirm chastity, integrity, and pro-life values. Boundaries have nevertheless been pushed to new limits, in which brutal slapstick was now applied to horses, dogs, and cows in *Animal House* (1978; John Landis, director), *A Fish Called Wanda* (1988; Charles Crichton, director), and *There's Something About Mary* (1998; Bobby Farrelly and Peter Farrelly, directors).

Comedies don't die. They are often recycled and refurbished for each generation. With all his flatulence, satire, and gender politics, Greek comic playwright Aristophanes could be writing film comedy screenplays today.

Terry Lindvall

See also Comedy; Comedy Ensembles; Monty Python; Movie Humor Types; Satire; Sitcoms; Sketch Comedy Shows

Further Readings

Bakhtin, M. M. (1984). *Rabelais and his world* (H. Iswolsky, Trans.). Bloomington: Indiana University Press.

Cavell, S. (1981). *Pursuits of happiness: The Hollywood comedy of remarriage*. Cambridge, MA: Harvard University Press.

de Seife, E. (2012). *Tashlinesque: The Hollywood comedies of Frank Tashlin*. Middletown, CT: Wesleyan University Press.

Gehring, W. D. (1986). *Screwball comedy: A genre of madcap romance*. Westport, CT: Praeger.

Horton, A., & Rapf, J. E. (Eds.). (2012). *A companion to film comedy*. Oxford, UK: Wiley-Blackwell.

Karnick, K. B., & Jenkins, H. (Eds.). (1995). *Classical Hollywood comedy*. New York, NY: Routledge.

Kerr, W. (1975). *The silent clowns*. New York, NY: Knopf.

Mast, G. (1979). *The comic mind: Comedy and the movies*. Chicago, IL: University of Chicago Press.

Sarris, A. (1978). The sex comedy without sex. *American Film, 3*(5), 8–15.

Seidman, S. (1981). *Comedian comedy: A tradition in Hollywood film*. Ann Arbor, MI: UMI Research Press.

Tueth, M. V. (2012). *Reeling with laughter: American film comedies—From anarchy to mockumentary*. Lanham, MD: Scarecrow Press.

Valenti, P. (1978). The "film blanc": Suggestions for a variety of fantasy, 1940–1945. *Journal of Popular Film, 6*(4), 294–304.

Multidimensional Sense of Humor Scale

See Factor Analysis of Humor Items

Music

Music is a culturally conditioned means of communication through sound. Although music is often vocal, a chief distinction between nonvocal music and language is that music without a text is primarily connotative rather than denotative in nature. Instrumental music's meaning is therefore often more elusive than that of language, and interpretations of a given musical expression may be widely divergent even among informed listeners within a culture. The complex and imprecise meaning of music, and its connection to the emotions and physical expression, perhaps explain its traditional importance in all human cultures.

Because music is a significant means of communication like language, musicians and composers are able to convey humor through musical gesture and structure. Music of most traditions relies heavily on pattern recognition and the establishment of expectation. By fulfilling or thwarting expectations, a musician or composer is able to generate an emotional or logical response in a culturally informed listener. Through use of an element of surprise, music is able to convey humor in much the same way as a joke conveys humor, provided that a playful context can be inferred from cues internal or external to the music.

Music in some cultures is closely tied to art forms such as theater and dance, which have evolved into distinct traditions in Europe. Whether alone or paired with physical gesture or language, music is associated with ceremony and ritual in all cultures, and in its ceremonial role it is employed for the purpose of instilling a communal mood or emotion. Use of humor may be appropriate in ceremonial music of a celebratory nature, but more often humor is encountered in music that functions as entertainment or narrative. Signifiers of musical humor may be used to establish or reinforce an overall playful mood, or humorous music may be used selectively to underscore moments of comic relief in tragic narratives.

Comedians and comic actors such as Jack Benny, Adam Sandler, Victor Borge, and Harpo Marx are renowned for using music in their comedy, but the focus of this entry is on humor in music. This entry discusses the ways in which music can connote or denote the target of humor, reviews methods of establishing play mode, examines various types of humorous incongruity in music, and concludes with some examples of types of musical humor.

Establishing the Target or Subject of Musical Humor

By far the most prevalent means of establishing the target or subject of musical humor is through the use of text. Examples of vocal music with humorous lyrics include songs by Frank Zappa, They Might Be Giants, and Tenacious D. While vocal music establishes the target of the musical humor in the lyrics, the titles of humorous instrumental works may identify the subject matter, without necessarily implying the humorous nature of the music itself, as in Camille Saint-Saëns's *Le carnaval des animaux* (The Carnival of the Animals). In this work, the humor is apparent from the play mode established by the use of musical signs.

However, nontextual extra-musical features of a musical work or performance may also play a role. Theatrical elements such as facial expressions, gestures, staging, wardrobe, or makeup may be employed to suggest the subject of the humor in a piece of music. In Robert Erickson's *General Speech*, for example, the costume required of the trombone soloist is suggestive of General Douglas MacArthur. In parodies of popular musicians, comedians often borrow and exaggerate the musicians' gestures or vocal idiosyncrasies.

Explicitly referencing or quoting other musical works or sounds is another common and effective way to clarify the subject of the humorous passage. For example, in the fourth movement of his Concerto for Orchestra, Béla Bartók quotes and ridicules a theme from Dmitri Shostakovich's Symphony no. 7. In song parodies that mock the original singer, the appropriation of the preexisting music is usually sufficient to identify the target of the humor, even if the new lyrics do not explicitly do so (e.g., "Weird" Al Yankovic's song "Perform This Way"). More generally, parodies may reference musical style or genre, such as The Lonely Island's parody of rap music, "I'm on a Boat," or the heavy metal parodies of Spinal Tap.

Lastly, humor may be purely musical or self-referential in nature. By playing with the rules of musical grammar, composers and musicians can engage in the musical equivalent of wordplay without the use of language. The subject of the humor is the musical tradition itself, and either the tradition or the listener can be considered the object. In this sense, musical humor can be compared to the concept of the "meta-joke." This type of musical humor relies largely on incongruity (see next section for examples).

Establishing Play Mode

In his influential 1956 book *Emotion and Meaning in Music*, Leonard Meyer proposed that music's emotional effect results from fulfillment or frustration of expectations. Because resolution and lack of resolution are key indicators of meaning in music, regardless of affect, incongruity in music can be inferred as intentionally humorous only when other contextual cues in or around the music imply a "play mode."

The most widespread method of establishing play mode in music is through the use of text. Humorous popular songs may have comic titles (e.g., "If I Said You Had a Beautiful Body [Would You Hold It Against Me]" by the Bellamy Brothers), nonsense lyrics ("Witch Doctor" by David Seville), or amusing narratives ("Just a Friend" by Biz Markie). A nonvocal example from the classical literature is W. A. Mozart's *Ein musikalischer Spass* (A Musical Joke), which could be interpreted as the work of a second-rate composer if not for the intentionality implied by the title. Likewise, the aforementioned theatrical elements (costume, making faces, etc.) can clearly convey a sense of play, enabling any incongruous elements in the music to be heard as comedic.

Music that shares sonic qualities with vocal expressions of joy can generally be understood to convey a more playful quality than music that aurally resembles vocal expressions of sadness or anger. Music that is high in register, more light than heavy (*staccato* instead of *legato*), and animated rather than lethargic tends to be more appropriate for communicating humor. However, the opposite extremes can be humorous if exaggerated. Occasionally, music directly mimics human laughter (e.g., in "Mein Herr Marquis" from Johann Strauss's *Die Fledermaus*).

Instruments that are associated with humor in Western culture are typically very low or very high: tuba, bassoon, xylophone, and piccolo. The exaggerated gesture of a trombone slide may also be considered humorous. Toy instruments can very effectively project a playful quality, as in the *Toy* Symphony, believed to be the work of Leopold Mozart. Noises with humorous extra-musical connotations, such as that of a slide whistle, or noises that resemble laughter or bodily functions (the "whoopee cushion" or trombone "raspberry," for example) also indicate levity; moreover, they function as incongruities in Western classical music. An instrument such as the theremin can evoke humor perhaps due to its eerie combination of human and mechanical qualities. In Javanese gamelan, use of the *ciblon* drum, and lively interlocking playing of *saron* or *bonang*, may lend a humorous quality to the music. Timbral associations are not always preserved across cultures; for example, the sound of sleigh bells is associated with Christmas and good cheer in North America, whereas it is associated with funerals in Korea.

A standard harmonic and melodic device used in Western music to establish a comedic mood is the major mode; the minor mode is reserved typically for negative emotional implications. The existence of this kind of valence cue (positive vs. negative) is crucial, because the high register and fast delivery of vocal expressions of joy can resemble those of anger and fear. The ideas presented in early music theoretical treatises on musical affect (*Affektenlehre*) suggest that the major-minor mode distinction has a long history. Some theorists even associated keys with specific emotions, particularly before the rise of equal temperament; the aesthetician Christian Schubart, for example, wrote "Noisy shouts of joy, laughing pleasure and not yet complete, full delight lies in E Major" (Steblin, 2002, p. 117).

The major-minor mode distinction is not universal, however. In Indian classical music, a wider variety of modes (*ragas*) and intonation systems are used, and emotional associations are not clear-cut. Nevertheless, some theorists in this tradition have ascribed emotions such as "playfulness" to particular scale degrees and intervals. The tuning systems of Javanese gamelan also defy comparison to Western scales and can vary significantly from one set of instruments to another. As these structural conventions accrue meaning through association with cultural practices, their significance tends to override that of psychophysical considerations.

A distinction must be made between use of "play mode" and use of humor, as music in play mode can convey a comic mood without necessarily including moments of comedy. Gustav Holst's "Jupiter, Bringer of Jollity" from his orchestral suite *The Planets,* for example, draws on a playful and joyful musical idiom but does not contain clear examples of comedy. Also, music that is intended to be humorous is not necessarily perceived as such. In addition to being culturally specific in a broad sense, musical humor can rely on a very specific understanding of musical style and grammar; for example, even the most informed of present-day classical music listeners are likely to miss most of the jokes in Mozart's *Ein musikalischer Spass*. Concert music is sometimes not heard as humorous because of the inhibition against laughter in the concert hall; music in the classical tradition is sometimes referred to in the writings of Theodor Adorno and others as "serious music." Conversely, unintentional humor, in the absence of play mode, is evident in the performances of sincere but unskilled musicians and composers. The collected recordings of amateur soprano Florence Foster Jenkins offer an excellent example of unintentional humor.

Methods of Incongruity and Defying Expectation

As in other forms of humor, incongruity is a significant aspect of humorous music. The significance and meaning of the incongruity in music usually requires an understanding of the musical culture and practice, but uninformed listeners may be able to detect shifts in music that are particularly sudden or extreme. Like slapstick, the purest musical humor can sometimes be appreciated across cultural lines. For example, because of the prevalence of rhythmic pattern and meter in the music of all cultures, the unexpected timing of musical events can evoke humor that may be understood by listeners outside of the practice; as in joke-telling, timing plays an important role in musical humor. Patterns constructed using other musical parameters can also be broken to convey humor: Tempo, register, dynamic, timbre, harmony, and melodic contour can all be manipulated in unexpected ways. Sudden shifts from one tuning system to another in Javanese gamelan (*molakmalik*) may be perceived as humorous. A famous example in the classical repertoire can be found in the second movement of Joseph Haydn's Symphony no. 94 (the *Surprise* Symphony; see Figure 1). The quiet and childishly simple main theme is presented by the string instruments in a major mode and with a light articulation. At the end of the second statement of the theme, the final note is played by the full orchestra at different octave levels, at a fortissimo. The sudden change in dynamic level, timbre, and register, coupled with the unexpected timing of the auditory shift, is made funnier by the quiet and lyrical passage that follows, seemingly unaffected by the exaggerated interruption. Another type of pattern disruption can occur if change is expected but not provided, as in the first movement of the *Toot Suite* by P. D. Q. Bach (Peter Schickele).

Each of the preceding examples also relies, in part, on an understanding of the syntax of European classical music, and incongruity that is perceptual in nature is often stylistically incongruous as well. In the Haydn example, the humor is enhanced by comprehension of the typical phrase model and of the customary consistency applied to musical parameters throughout the duration of a phrase. In the Schickele example, the joke is enhanced by an understanding

Figure 1 F. J. Haydn, Symphony no. 94 (*Surprise* Symphony), Mvt. II, mm. 1–16

Note: The major mode, light articulation, and simple melody of this movement establish a playful mood, and the surprising fortissimo chord functions as the joke.

of aspects of Baroque style, specifically the "correct" applications of phrase length, cover tones, harmonic rhythm, and consonance and dissonance. Any passage perceived as stylistically "incorrect" can be interpreted as humorous, provided that play mode has been established or suggested. In addition, certain elements of the vocabulary of Western classical music, such as tendency tones and dominant seventh chords, have such strong tendencies toward resolution that they are ripe for humor. In the orchestral introduction to the famous comic aria "La donna è mobile" (The Woman Is Fickle) from Giuseppi Verdi's opera *Rigoletto,* the sudden silence that interrupts the melody is made more awkward and humorous by the failure of the dominant chord to resolve at the expected time. Unexpected events in music in a serious tone, however, may instead be associated with negative emotions such as fear or anger.

Sudden changes of style, as in Charles Ives's short piano work *Bad Resolutions and Good WAN!* can also be perceived as humorous, particularly if the two styles are highly incongruous. The Beatles' pastiche "Happiness Is a Warm Gun" uses shifts in style to humorous effect. The simultaneous referencing of two or more seemingly incompatible styles or genres functions similarly (e.g., heavy metal music arranged for children's chorus). Musical humor of this type is ironic in the sense that *what* is being conveyed is undermined by *how* it is being conveyed. More generally, humor can result when the meanings of any two aspects of a musical excerpt are in apparent conflict. For example, the second movement of Dmitri Shostakovich's Symphony no. 5 employs an accompanimental and metric pattern that suggests a waltz, but its timbral, harmonic, and melodic material are at times harsh and unexpected. Because the waltz reference conveys elegance and grace and regularity, but other aspects of the music suggest awkwardness and disjointedness, the work has a dark and grotesque humor. Because of the cultural complexity of musical connotation, ironic tension can easily be constructed in this manner across various parameters.

Similarly incongruous interactions can result between texts and music, in what may be called "lyrical dissonance." Humorous texts are made funnier when paired with serious music (as in the Looney Tunes opera parodies), and serious texts can seem humorous with the addition of light-hearted music (as in the Ramones' "The KKK Took My Baby Away"). Even combinations of neutral texts and music can be humorous, provided that the incongruity is pronounced (e.g., a mundane list of items sung in an operatic style).

Theatricality has been discussed as a method of establishing play mode, but it may also create incongruity in a work. An inherent incongruity is presented in works that break the rules of performance practice, as for instance when a performer in a concert work plays an instrument in an unconventional fashion, moves in a choreographed manner, or makes faces. Unconventional use of nonmusical material in an otherwise musical work can also seem humorous, as in Leroy Anderson's *The Typewriter.*

Along any parameter, music with stylized or exaggerated qualities can be considered humorous. In the "Galop" from Act I of Dmitri Shostakovich's opera *The Nose,* humor is evoked by the very fast tempo paired with extremes in register and exaggerated flourishes. The Haydn *Surprise* Symphony is an example of musical humor that is partly a result of its exaggerated quality. Another example from the works of Haydn occurs during the serene and lyrical second movement of his Symphony no. 93, in which a loud low bassoon note punctuates a thinly scored quiet treble passage for strings and winds. Although the pitch and register are appropriate, the inappropriateness of the biting timbre and *forte* dynamic level can be compared to that of a crass bodily function. Similarly, the music of cartoons is often wildly exaggerated, to parallel the one-dimensionality of characters and bizarre shifts in plot. Highly exaggerated music in a mock serious style can be understood as grotesquely humorous; the pompous and banal march theme from the first movement of Shostakovich's Symphony no. 7, which Bartók misconstrued to be a sincere musical statement, may be considered an example of satirical exaggeration.

Further Examples of Nontext Musical Humor

Humor is commonplace enough in instrumental music that the names of many works in the standard repertoire reference the comic: Ludwig van Beethoven's "Bagatelles," Robert Schumann and Antonín Dvořák's "Humoreskes," Niccolò Paganini and Johannes Brahms's "Caprices" and "Capriccios," and Richard Strauss's "Burleske" are all prominent examples. The scherzo (meaning "joke" in Italian) is well represented in the literature by both stand-alone works (e.g., those of Frédéric Chopin) and by movements in a great many symphonies and other multimovement works of the romantic era. The humor in these and other classical works is often subtle, and it relies on manipulation of the listener's expectation. A brief analysis of a passage from the first movement of Haydn's Piano Sonata in D Major (Hob. XVI:37) suffices to demonstrate the kind of musical "wit" that pervades comic music, for which Haydn is particularly famous.

The passage (see Figure 2), in A major, contains a series of unexpected harmonic shifts in m. 29–31: first a minor tonic chord, then a suddenly loud Neapolitan chord. But the humorousness lies chiefly in the sudden pause at the end of m. 31—it is the first lengthy pause in the work—and the dissonant fortissimo fully diminished seventh chord that follows. One's anticipation is enhanced by the sudden silence, and Haydn surprises the listener with the dissonant seventh chord, which acts as an unexpected extension of the predominant area before the cadence. The storminess of the dissonant chord then proves to be a passing tantrum, as it tumbles into a typical and proper-sounding cadence in the next two bars; the humor in the way the dissonance is resolved arises in part from what Immanuel Kant referred to as the "sudden transformation of a strained expectation into nothing" (Kant, 2007, p. 133). Moreover, humor is experienced through logically reconciling the expected outcome (the cadence) and the punch line (the unexpected measure).

Several additional categories of nonvocal musical humor deserve special attention: "romantic irony" and absurdity. Although various types of irony are clearly applicable to vocal music, Friedrich Schlegel's interpretation of "romantic irony," in which an author draws attention to the artifice and mechanisms of the narrative structure, is particularly relevant to humor in instrumental music. Musical passages that serve to destroy the mood established by the preceding material may be perceived in this light. In the last movement of Haydn's String Quartet, op. 33, no. 2, called "The Joke," the final passage features a series of long pauses that undermine a listener's ability to identify the end of the piece. Then, in an ironic twist, Haydn concludes the piece with the same two measures that began the movement. The irony is lost on listeners who have not listened carefully and on those who are unaware of the oddness

Figure 2 F. J. Haydn, Piano Sonata in D Major (Hob. XVI:37), Mvt. I, mm. 28–35

Note: A more subtle example of Haydn's musical "wit."

of this compositional conceit. Although the "joke" is in keeping with the mood of the rest of the movement, it also draws attention away from the aesthetic experience and toward the composer "behind the scenes." Passages that sound mechanical, especially those that appear broken, stuck, overly repetitive, or stylized, may also serve to deliberately shatter the illusion of artlessness and may be used for humorous effect; examples abound in the works of Beethoven.

Absurdity—akin to infinite or "existential irony"—can be either humorous or serious. Perhaps the best known absurdist work of concert music is John Cage's *4'33"*, during which no sound is intentionally created by the performer for 4 minutes and 33 seconds. A truly ironic work in that it is both utterly silent and purports to be music, *4'33"* is readily experienced as humorous but can also be understood as a philosophical statement, as an incitement to deeper listening, or as a mental exercise in the style of a koan. Cage's other experiments with aleatory musical composition also deliberately challenged basic assumptions about the definition of music, particularly with regard to intentionality and originality. Erik Satie, composer of piano works with such bizarre and ironic titles as *Embryons desséchés* ("Desiccated Embryos") and *Trois morceaux en forme de poire* ("Three Pieces in the Shape of a Pear"), added an inscription to his work *Vexations* that implies that it be repeated 840 times. Mauricio Kagel's self-referential "anti-opera" *Staatstheater* requires singers to dance and dancers to sing; his work *Exotica* requires musicians to perform on instruments other than their own.

Carl Schimmel

See also Cognitive Aspects; Comic Versus Tragic Worldviews; Exaggeration; Incongruity and Resolution; Musical Comedy; Parody; Pattern Recognition; Variety Shows

Further Readings

Arias, E. A. (2001). *Comedy in music: A historical bibliographical resource guide.* Westport, CT: Greenwood Press.

Bonds, M. E. (1991). Haydn, Laurence Sterne, and the origins of musical irony. *Journal of the American Musicological Society, 44*(1), 57–91.

Casablancas, B. (2000). *El humor en la música: Broma, paradia e ironía: Un ensayo* [Humor in music: Joke, parody, and irony: An essay]. Kassel, Germany: Reichenberger.

Dalmonte, R. (1995). Towards a semiology of humour in music. *International Review of the Aesthetics and Sociology of Music, 26*(2), 167–187.

Kant, I. (2007). *Critique of judgement* (J. H. Bernard, Trans.). New York, NY: Cosimo Classics.

Kidd, J. C. (1976). Wit and humor in tonal syntax. *Current Musicology, 21,* 70–82.

Levy, J. M. (1992). "Something mechanical encrusted upon the living": A source of musical wit and humor. In W. J. Allanbrook, J. M. Levy, & W. P. Mahrt (Eds.),

Convention in eighteenth- and nineteenth-century music: Essays in honor of Leonard G. Ratner (pp. 225–256). Stuyvesant, NY: Pendragon Press.

London, J. (2002). A Cohenian approach to musical expression. *Journal of Aesthetics and Art Criticism, 60*(2), 182–185.

Lowry, L. R. (1974). *Humor in instrumental music: A discussion of musical affect, psychological concepts of humor and identification of musical humor* (Unpublished doctoral dissertation). Ohio State University, Columbus.

Meyer, L. B. (1956). *Emotion and meaning in music.* Chicago, IL: University of Chicago Press.

Russell, T. A. (1985–1986). "Über das Komische in der Musik": The Schütze-Stein controversy. *Journal of Musicology, 4*(1), 70–90.

Sheinberg, E. (2000). *Irony, satire, parody, and the grotesque in the music of Shostakovich: A theory of musical incongruities.* Aldershot, UK: Ashgate.

Steblin, R. (2002). *A history of key characteristics in the 18th and early 19th centuries.* Rochester, NY: University of Rochester Press.

Sutton, R. A. (1997). Humor, mischief, and aesthetics in Javanese gamelan music. *Journal of Musicology, 15*(3), 390–415.

Wheelock, G. A. (1992). *Haydn's "ingenious jesting with art": Contexts of musical wit and humor.* New York, NY: Schirmer.

Music Hall

The term *music hall* denotes both a historic industry and its distinctive form of humor. A prototype modern show business incorporating a wide range of entertainments, the British music hall grew from the early Victorian pub with a working-class clientele into a nationwide network of grandiose purpose-built halls with a mass audience, paralleling the development of American vaudeville. In its early 1900s heyday, music hall aspired to more respectable status as variety, although the original label endured. Following its abrupt decline after World War I as a result of competition from radio and film, the industry enjoyed a renewed boom in the 1930s in synergy with the new media. Although the business side was killed off by television in the 1950s, its style of humor and comic performance lived on. Summarily characterized as crudely but unabashedly "vulgar" or "low," music hall was a diverse, complex, and slippery discursive mode, much of its impact derived from its interactive live form. This entry discusses the songs performed in music halls, the interaction between the performers and the audience, the major types of performers, and the role of music halls in British society.

An 1894 color lithograph poster advertising the Eldorado Music Hall in Paris, France, featuring a leaping woman holding a tambourine and a clown playing the banjo.

Source: Prints, Drawings, and Paintings Collection, Victoria and Albert Museum; © Victoria and Albert Museum, London.

The Music Hall Comic Song

The prime vehicle of humor in the Victorian halls was the comic song. Major themes combined elements of the traditional, folk, and carnivalesque with a naturalistic reading of everyday life to produce an anecdotal comic realism that spoke to the shared experience of an economically and socially subaltern working class. Food and drink were foregrounded as essentials of a precarious material existence invoked in carnivalesque visions of plenty: "May his beef and beer increase each year, And his wages never go down." Beef and beer were the material and symbolic props of an Englishman's historic birthright and superiority over other nationalities. Drink, the essential fuel of the authentic good time, stimulated heroic yet comically befuddling feats of consumption. "When I take a drink on a Saturday night," sings a self-proclaimed "common or working man," "Glasgow belongs to me!" "But there's something the matter with Glasgow, 'cos it's going round and round."

Food, drink, and sex were comically triangulated in the body, the major site of pleasure and unease, whose appetites and afflictions were fundamentals of the comic repertoire. Food metaphors provided phallic equivalents in cucumbers, "my old hambone," or the magic unguent ensuring a husband's sexual fulfillment: "Put a bit of treacle on my pudding Mary Ann." Food similes invoked the grotesque carnivalesque body, both fascinating and repellent. "I went to a christening, the baby looked a treat, It was pink and purple like a lot of sausage meat." Cheese, like sausage, was inherently funny. Invariably smelly, it was a simulacrum of the fart, the original rude noise, a source of corporeal treachery and embarrassment. Scatology—"toilet" or "lavatory" humor—was a frequent entry in the list of themes registered by contemporaries, confirmation for some of a national fixation. Deformities were other targets of "jocular cruelty" in an alleged pathology of insult and humiliation. Mass Observation, a social survey of the 1930s, reported ill health as the leading subject of jokes, for which music hall with its bodily preoccupations was a prime platform.

Romance, courtship, and marriage were other comic staples, also in frequent jeopardy. Flirtatious adventures turned into misadventures with women as deceivers, an ancient trope modernized in the anonymous milieu of the big city, which was also the site for conning the greenhorn, laughed at as the victim's folly rather than a moral or criminal offense. Working-class marriage was a comic calamity of henpecked husbands and domineering wives with mothers-in-law as classic spoilers. Lodgers, numerous and intrusive, brought the temptations of adultery to underloved wives, although husbands were the more frequent cheats. Both sexes were more liable to stray at the seaside, the liminal site of social and sexual freedoms and the proletarian good time. In or out of marriage, sex was robustly lascivious rather than erotic or sensual, often rather daunting. A young woman serving admiring males in a city cigar shop "has a novel scale of charge," one song went. "For instance an Havanna Smoke would cost you one and four, But if Milly bit the end off she would charge a shilling more." In the entrenched misogynist culture of the halls, women were at best a mixed blessing: "They ease life's shocks, they mend our socks but can't they spend the money."

Parody was the principal genre and technique of humorous articulation. Parody, as form of comic imitation, worked through hyperbole or bathos, sending up or putting down, often in ironic or equivocal tandem. Common targets included overblown patriotism and sentimentality. Absurdity collapsed fantasy in "The Man Who Broke the Eggs at Monte Carlo," a parody of "The Man Who Broke the Bank at Monte Carlo," sung on the same bill as the star who launched the original bank busting hit. "Hardly a song succeeds," said a music publisher in the 1890s, "that is not instantly the subject of fifty parodies." As in much else, parody was spiced up by innuendo, the art of the sexually suggestive, often in the form of the double entendre, a persistent element in music hall humor.

Artist, Audience, and Artifact: Music Hall Interaction

The humor gained its fullest expression in performance, ideally the dynamic integration of artist, audience, and artifact. Songs were interspersed with "patter" or the "spoken," an interpolated commentary offering cues for gags and improvisation in exchanges with the audience, replicating the back-and-forth vernacular of the street and marketplace. Typical song form included a chorus, taken up by the audience in ritual antiphony with the performer, often generating a catchphrase— "Does your mother know you're out?"— an infectious shorthand repeated incessantly in the wider world. Nods, winks, and gesticulations, plus various forms of stage business, accented the words and music of the comic text, informing innumerable popular imitations.

Such signals activated and celebrated a collective "knowingness," the implicit understanding of how the world really works among a street-smart underclass joyously adept at deciphering its codes and debunking its orthodoxies. "(If You Want to Know the Time, Ask a) Policeman" was a hit song invoking the visitor's cozy image of the helpful London bobby while signaling his corrupt propensity for drinking out of hours. The knowing crowd translated sexual innuendos for themselves in a gleeful conspiracy against moral reformers who attacked music hall for obscenity but were unable to provide explicit evidence. Wordplay—puns, riddles, euphemisms—was a ubiquitous feature of the halls, a knowing mockery of official knowledge and high culture that flattered the literacy of its audience.

Music Hall Performers

Performers played an extensive range of comic routines and personas. Most predictable and formulaic was the "red-nosed" comedian, heir to the traditional clown in his latter-day motley of battered top hat and distressed dress suit, red nosed through drink, coarsely suggestive and physical in humor. The newer "turn" on the halls from the 1860s was the comic actor appearing "in character," personalizing a particular social type in specific dress and manner. As Champagne Charlie, the star George Leybourne played the swell, a lordly man-about-town of resplendent dress and "magnificent cheek," exulting in the finest of potables and the adoration of the ladies. In this combined parody and celebration of the aristocratic rogue male, Leybourne exploited the tensions of a class-bound society, offering a role model for aspirant young swells in the audience while making fun of their own maladroit reach for gentility. Dan Leno, billed as "The Funniest Man on Earth," played the classic little man whom life kicks around, the bumpkin loser of folk humor brought up to date in tragic-comic cameos of lowly workers. In Leno's surreal and alarming world, inanimate objects were endowed with a disturbing life of their own, and a laughable minor blemish in the song "My Wife's Pimple" turns out to be a tumor. Another great favorite, Marie Lloyd, played the naughty but faux innocent young woman for whom "Every Little Movement (Has a Meaning All Its Own)." Of an amorous adventure on a train, she claimed, with her trademark semaphore wink, "She'd never had her ticket punched before." "Our Marie" was a cockney, London's fiercely independent proletarian tribe whose wry wit came wrapped in a local dialect that baffled authority. The stage cockney was the most prominent of roles in an otherwise minor genre exploiting the comic potential of regional and ethnic difference.

Cover of sheet music featuring George Leybourne as "Champagne Charlie"

Source: Illustration by Alfred Concanen; image courtesy of the Victoria and Albert Museum; © Victoria and Albert Museum, London.

Although it retained much of its classic music hall style, comic form and performance changed considerably in the interwar years with the industry's rebranding as variety and the impact of the new media. The larger scale and theatricalized design of variety houses, together with stricter audience controls and the managerial prohibition of "direct address" from the stage, limited free exchange between artist and audience. The popularity of early film in its silent phase gave a new salience to sight gags and physical humor, stimulating a revival of slapstick on stage, while the legitimization of the sketch popularized dramatic interludes prefiguring the sitcom. Radio variety privileged the verbal, foregrounding patter over sight and song, the faster pace and timing reflecting the growing influence of American styles, reinforced by the dominance of American cinema. The "cross talk" double act, an earlier import of the minstrel show, became a new staple, minus the blackface. By the 1930s, British comedians were plundering shortwave radio broadcasts from the United States for jokes.

Both change and continuity were exemplified in star comedian Max Miller, "The Cheeky Chappie." Miller was the professional funny man rather than the comic character actor, a cockney delivering a string of quick-fire jokes in transatlantic stand-up mode. His persona was that of the marauding commercial traveler and modern trickster, his dress combining the urbane and contemporary with the gaudy attire of the circus clown. Max overcame the inhibitions of greater scale and threat of censorship to engage his audience in a direct but confidential manner, recruiting them into a ready fraternity of the knowing. In classic style, sexual inferences were left for the audience to complete as he remonstrated in mock indignation at their dirty minds. The genius of Max Miller and his like, pronounced George Orwell (2000), was "entirely masculine," adding "a good male comedian can give the impression of something irredeemable, and yet innocent, like a sparrow" (p. 162). This was the "honest vulgarity" that the profession defended against its critics, resisting the charge that performances were obscene, camp, or effeminate. As always, Miller worked the borderline. "Is this Cockfosters?" asks one man inquiring of another regarding station stops on a crowded London tube train. "No," comes the reply, "My name's Robinson."

With its leading performers featured on film, radio, and recordings, music hall as variety reached a wider, more socially mixed audience, less the product of its original working-class base. George Formby retained his northern working-class accent while becoming a national idol from wide exposure across the media. Playing the underestimated little man as victor rather than casualty, Formby was the lower middle-class individualist as much as working-class pal. His hit song "With My Little Stick of Blackpool Rock," its priapic candy successfully deployed at the most popular of seaside resorts, maintained the tradition of low humor in a continuing vein of comic realism, even as his persona moved marginally but significantly upmarket. Irrepressibly cheerful—"Turned out nice again" was his tag line—Formby was an antidote to the travails of economic depression and World War II. Humor was championed as an essential component of the national character. As one newspaper put it: "We crack jests where our continental neighbors would be cracking skulls."

Conclusion

Functioning as "survival humor" for its original working-class constituency, music hall in the classic phase did much to allay the typical anxieties of its audiences while reasserting their right to life's pleasures. As such, it affirmed membership in a particular way of life and a worldly competence in its negotiations. If music hall humor displayed no formal political challenge or radical social edge, it maintained an instrumental derision of petty authority, corrective morality, and social pretension that preserved a vital sense of license and independence. With the extension of the audience for variety, its comic discourse of conceit, parody, and knowing innuendo became a second language for all classes enjoying release from the constraints of British respectability and repression.

Peter Bailey

See also Parody; Sexuality; Variety Shows

Further Readings

Bailey, P. (1998). *Popular culture and performance in the Victorian city.* Cambridge, UK: Cambridge University Press.

Bratton, J. S. (1986). *Music hall: Performance and style.* Philadelphia, PA: Open University Press.

Medhurst, A. (2007). *A national joke: Popular comedy and English cultural identities.* London, UK: Routledge.

Orwell, G. (2000). *My country right or left: 1940–1943* (S. Orwell & I. Angus, Eds.). Boston, MA: Godine.

Wilmut, R. (1958). *Kindly leave the stage! The story of variety 1919–1960.* London, UK: Methuen.

Musical Comedy

Musical comedy is a theatrical entertainment that emerged in the 1890s and flourished through the 1940s. Musical comedies contain alternating passages of dialogue and song in a variety of styles, but the music is always light in character and simple in construction, in other words non-operatic, allowing for performance by singers without classical vocal training. The plots tend to be set in present-day (at the time of the plots' writing) New York City and are predominantly light vehicles for star performers. Stars' onstage personas, comedy routines, and song and dance acts, often derived from vaudeville, are loosely interwoven with insignificant and frivolous narratives. Musical comedy is therefore more diversionary entertainment than serious drama. Although it faded in popularity in the mid-20th century, its theatrical style and techniques influenced the more serious musical play that became the dominant form of popular musical theater in the 1940s, and, to a lesser degree, the musical comedy continues to influence popular theater today.

Origins

London producer George Edwardes introduced the term *musical comedy* in 1893 to distinguish *A Gaiety Girl* from shows with complex plots and music. Edwardes brought *A Gaiety Girl* to New York City in 1894 and, after its success, proceeded to export similar shows in the following years. To claim that musical comedy originated solely in London, however, would be to overlook important developments in America, where shows resembling the form had appeared intermittently since *The Black Crook* (1866) and some vaudeville performers were extending their acts into longer shows. In the 1870s Edward Harrigan and Tony Hart developed their comic Irish immigrant routine, which was influenced by blackface minstrelsy's stereotypes and racial jokes and became a mainstay on the vaudeville circuit. They introduced a song in 1873 that was soon expanded into a short skit, then a 40-minute "play" in 1878, and finally a full-length play with musical numbers, called *The Mulligan Guard Ball,* in 1879. Joe Weber and Lew Fields similarly expanded their Dutch act of Mike and Meyer, and after the duo separated in 1904, Fields worked some of their routines and his immigrant character into musical comedies such as *It Happened in Nordland* (1904). American musical comedy was therefore both an import from England and an outgrowth of the American popular theater.

The first two works by George M. Cohan, *Little Johnny Jones* (1904) and *George Washington, Jr.* (1906), exemplify early musical comedy. They are comprised of simple plots, and their music is dominated by the march and influenced by the then-popular style of ragtime; these traits are evident in Cohan's hit songs "The Yankee Doodle Boy" and "Give My Regards to Broadway." This theatrical style thrived until the New York premiere of Franz Lehár's Viennese operetta *The Merry Widow* in 1907, two years after its European debut. For the next decade, musical comedy was overshadowed by operettas with classical singing, waltzes and marches, and richly developed plots taking place in historical and exotic settings.

The Peak of Musical Comedy

Author Guy Bolton, lyricist P. G. Wodehouse, and composer Jerome Kern helped to revitalize musical comedy during World War I, writing a series of shows referred to as the Princess Musicals (*Very Good Eddie,* 1915; *Oh, Boy!* 1917; *Leave It to Jane,* 1917; *Oh, Lady! Lady!!* 1918), named after the Princess Theater where most of them were performed. Perhaps their greatest innovation was Kern's embrace of the foxtrot, which ballroom dancers like Vernon and Irene Castle were popularizing in the 1910s. Initially the only music to which dancers could foxtrot were blues songs, which replaced the triple meter of the waltz and the fast duple meter of the march with a moderately paced meter of four beats. Kern's foxtrots such as "Till the Clouds Roll By" (from *Oh, Boy!*) were not in the style of the blues but were love songs that took advantage of the expressive potential of this meter and tempo. By the early 1920s, the foxtrot love song was established as the definitive song style of musical comedy, initiating the theater's alignment with ballroom dance music that would continue through the 1960s.

In the 1920s, George Gershwin introduced the snappy rhythms and extended harmonies of jazz in musical comedies such as *Lady Be Good* (1924). Shows in this decade were often "Cinderella stories" in which young working-class women married wealthy men. Marilyn Miller made a career starring as such leading ladies, first in variety acts and then shows such as *Sally* (1920). *Whoopee!* (1928) perhaps stands above all as a star vehicle; its minimal plot allowed Eddie Cantor to perform his famous vaudeville shticks: improvising in blackface and interpolating popular songs. Alongside these shows, however, were musical comedies that began to absorb elements of operetta. Most notable is *Show Boat* (1927), which contains the waltz "You Are Love" and the foxtrot "Can't Help Lovin' Dat Man" and does not possess a light plot about romance in New York City but rather is a serious drama about racism in Mississippi in the 1880s and Chicago in the 1890s and concludes in 1927, the year it was premiered.

After the stock market crash in 1929, most composers and writers explored the cheaper-to-produce and potentially more lucrative Hollywood film, but a few writers drew audiences to Broadway with innovative productions. Cole Porter's shows adopted a more serious tone through satire. *The New Yorkers* (1930) took on the relationship between the New York police, prostitutes, and murderers; *Anything Goes* (1934) poked fun at the current obsession with "public enemies"; and *Jubilee* (1935) lambasted Franklin Roosevelt and the New Deal. After early Broadway successes in the 1920s and in Hollywood in the early 1930s, composer-lyricist team Richard Rodgers and Lorenz Hart returned to Broadway in 1935, where their shows similarly became more serious. Their *Pal Joey* (1940), for example, became the first musical comedy whose leading male was an antihero who ends up as lonely as he is when the show begins.

The slightly more serious tone of these shows paralleled an increasing seriousness of form and a desire to create works that might withstand the test of time. The most successful shows of this type are two written by playwrights George S. Kaufman and Morrie Ryskind with lyrics by Ira Gershwin and music by his brother George Gershwin: *Strike Up The Band* (1927, revised 1930) and *Of Thee I Sing* (1931). These shows satirized international politics; Republicans, Democrats, and socialists; all branches of the U.S. government; the military; the electorate; and American businesses. *Of Thee I Sing* became the first musical comedy to win the Pulitzer Prize for Drama in 1932; the committee's belief that it was classifiable as a play demonstrates the extent to which these shows presaged the musical plays that flourished in the following decade.

The Musical Play

Oklahoma! (1943), the product of a new partnership between Rodgers and librettist Oscar Hammerstein 2nd, officially ushered in the age of the musical play. In their collaborations, Rodgers and Hammerstein replace the frivolity of earlier musical comedy with serious plays intended to challenge audiences. *South Pacific* (1949) and *The King and I* (1951), for example, address racism and promote human rights and tolerance. However, important elements of the musical comedy remain. First, traditional escapist fare is often included in "show-within-a-show" scenes. In *South Pacific,* for example, Nellie Forbush entertains troops by singing "Honey Bun," a light, syncopated number that has little bearing on the drama. Occasionally the collaborators did not use such devices to integrate traditional musical comedy elements, such as in the dance sequence in *Carousel,* "June Is Bustin' Out All Over" (1945), in which the ensemble unrealistically dances in celebration of spring. Musical plays also continue musical comedy's preference for ballroom styles, observed in the abundance of foxtrots of which *Oklahoma!*'s "People Will Say We're in Love" and *South Pacific*'s "My Girl Back Home" serve as famous examples. Finally, many of Rodgers and Hammerstein's comic characters are descendants of vaudeville's ethnic types. *Oklahoma!*'s Ali Hakim and *South Pacific*'s Bloody Mary are ethnic outsiders who often humorously fail to understand American customs and etiquette.

With the popularity of such serious shows, the designation *musical comedy* fell into desuetude in the 1940s, giving way to *musical play* or just *musical.* Another common label was *integrated musical,* because, unlike the loosely stitched together musical comedy, song and dance were said to work together to propel the drama, despite occasional shortcomings. Such works by writers and composers other than Rodgers and Hammerstein include *Street Scene* (1947), *Brigadoon* (1947), *My Fair Lady* (1956), *West Side Story* (1957), and *Camelot* (1960). While these works tend to dominate histories of the American musical theater, some composers continued to work with others to produce more traditional musical comedies, although they were not labeled as such. Much of the music by Irving Berlin in *Annie Get Your Gun* (1946), Cole Porter in *Kiss Me, Kate* (1948), Frank Loesser in *Guys and Dolls* (1950) and *How to Succeed in Business Without Really Trying* (1961), Jule Styne in *Gypsy* (1959), and Jerry Herman in *Hello, Dolly!* (1964), for example, is geared more toward entertaining audiences than deepening character and moving the drama forward.

After the Golden Age

The golden age of the American musical is considered to have begun with the popularity of the musical play in 1943, after the height of musical comedy, and extends through the 1960s. At this point the conventions of the musical largely ceded to disparate theatrical approaches and styles, including the emphasis on visual spectacle, the preference for musical styles not found in the ballroom (rock, R&B, hip-hop, and others), and the fragmentation of plots into non-linear vignettes. Although limited, at

Fred Astaire in the famous ceiling dance "You're All the World to Me" from the musical comedy *Royal Wedding* (1951)

Source: Wikimedia Commons.

best, to fleeting moments within otherwise modern shows, musical comedy conventions persist. *Follies* (1971) and *Chicago* (1975) use older song styles to develop older characters and to establish setting in the 1920s, respectively. The camp classic *The Rocky Horror Show* (1973; adapted for film as *The Rocky Horror Picture Show* in 1975) embraces the frivolity and artificiality of the musical comedy style, as do recent escapist musical farces produced by Mel Brooks, such as *The Producers* (2001) and *Young Frankenstein* (2007). The latter contains a scene in which an actor breaks character and jokes with the audience, harking back to such scenes in pre–golden age musical comedies and destroying the illusion of realism central to serious musical plays. Furthermore, musical comedy song styles are often employed for expressive purposes, as their long associations with the theater allow them to connote a sense of theatricality and, therefore, artificiality. The jazzy foxtrot style of "A Summer in Ohio" from *The Last Five Years* (2001), for example, illustrates the sarcastic nature of the song's lyrics. "King Herod's Song" from *Jesus Christ Superstar* (1971) and "Wonderful" from *Wicked* (2003), moreover, use the showy style of ragtime to characterize King Herod and the Wizard as disingenuous tricksters. In these ways and with the ongoing interest in revivals of classic musicals, the importance of the musical comedy endures.

Christopher Lynch

See also Burlesque; Comic Opera; Ethnic Jokes; Ethnicity and Humor; Music; Pastiche; Political Humor; Presidential Humor; Race, Representation of; Satire; Stereotypes; Variety Shows

Further Readings

Bordman, G. (1982). *American musical comedy from* Adonis *to* Dreamgirls. New York, NY: Oxford University Press.

Bordman, G., & Norton, R. (2011). *American musical theatre: A chronicle* (4th ed.). New York, NY: Oxford University Press.

Grant, M. N. (2004). *The rise and fall of the Broadway musical.* Boston, MA: Northeastern University Press.

Kirle, B. (2005). *Unfinished show business: Broadway musicals as works-in-process.* Carbondale: Southern Illinois University Press.

Stempel, L. (2010). *Showtime: A history of the Broadway musical.* New York, NY: Norton.

N

National and Ethnic Differences

This entry outlines differences in the status, content, and form of humor of groups defined by their nationality or ethnicity. It also presents perceptions about the humor styles of some national or ethnic groups known for their particular sense of humor, for example, British humor, Jewish humor.

People produce, communicate, and react to humor in different ways. Even though researchers have maintained that personal differences in the use and appreciation of humor outweigh national and ethnic differences, the observations about group differences have a long history. Recent studies about the effects of globalization describe the intertextuality of humor that translates across borders with greater ease than ever—though carrying an inherent incomprehension that accompanies the dissemination of humor to different audiences with various tastes in humor, as explained in the last section of this entry.

National and ethnic differences within the universal phenomenon of humor should be explained in the light of the sociocultural background of particular ethnic groups. To start with, the social value of humor differs among nations. In Europe and North America, humor has been highly valued as a character trait. East Asian countries (e.g., China), however, regard having a sense of humor as a much less important personality characteristic.

Differences arise from the social salience of topics for a particular group of joke-tellers and the social order or the position of the group joked about. For instance, one can find many jokes about drinking and fist fighting in Irish jokelore, whereas these jokes tend not to be found in Jewish humor. Christie Davies's models about target choice in ethnic jokes about stupidity explain the prevalence of certain butts and subjects over others through dichotomies created by center versus periphery, monopoly versus competition, and mind over matter in these cultures.

Forms of humor are also culture- and language-bound, which is why different genres emerge in different cultural contexts. For example, the tall tale of the "new continents" of North America and Australia is often connected to the spaciousness of the land and pioneering attitude of the settlers. Similarly, Japanese subtle puns, *Dajare,* differ from the Western loud and boisterous humor as they aim to give insight into the surrounding reality while avoiding impolite bursts of laughter.

Examples of Particular Types of National and Ethnic Humor

Some countries, groups, or nations are popularly recognized as possessing a particular sense of humor.

African American Humor

African American humor developed in the background for at least a century before becoming widely accepted in the 1950s. The dynamics of African

American comic performances rely on the vigorous African and North American folk tradition, intertwined with the Black experience in the New World ranging from slavery to segregation. Nowadays, it is considered as having become part of the mainstream comedy culture in the United States, especially in stand-up.

British Humor

British humor has been shaped by freedom from invasion and the relative stability of the society as a whole. It ridicules mundane reality by satirically revealing the absurdity of everyday life, relying largely on puns and intellectual humor. Sexual humor is found to be prominent, consisting of innuendo and the delight one gets from breaking taboos. In addition, much of British humor, even today, stems from class differences.

Chinese Humor

Chinese humor, for centuries, had been modest and unnoticeable. Because of prevailing traditional Confucianist attitudes, engaging in humor was sometimes considered a disgrace. From the 1970s onward, new types of humor, influenced by the Western world, have evolved; these include *cold humor,* a variation of black humor known in the West (harsh and bitter); *jerk humor,* which is widely popular among young people (self-deprecating and bragging); and *nonsense humor,* characterized by malicious wit and sarcasm.

Jewish Humor

Jewish humor has been affected by the fact that the Jews have had a long history of marginalization and persecution, which, combined with the traditional multilingualism of Jewish families and appreciation for learning endless logical argumentation (*pilpul*) makes up a specific style of humor. It favors wordplay, irony, and satire, and is anti-authoritarian in all ways, also mocking religious authorities. As it is so well permeated into other societies, Jewish humor varies widely; for example, the self-disparagement aspect of Jewish humor, also said to be the central misunderstanding of Jewish jokelore, is questioned in the studies that deal with Israeli humor alone.

Russian Humor

Russian humor is centered on the *anekdot* (joke, often with a political connotation) that fed on the prolific raw material of the absurdities in the totalitarian Soviet Union. It reached its heyday during the so-called Khrushchev's Thaw and Brezhnev's Stagnation from the 1960s onward. The rapid decline of the genre in the 1990s was brought along by the collapse of its main subject, the totalitarian regime, along with an availability of different channels for discussing politics or expressing humor; lighter modes of irony and nostalgia replaced the sharp satire of the Soviet joke.

Effects of Globalization on National and Ethnic Humor

In recent decades, national and ethnic differences in humor production and evaluation have been eroding as cultural borders become more ephemeral, partly due to the global reach of the media. The Internet has blurred the differences in the content and form of humor, making jokes shorter, more visual, and less dependent on language—English has become the dominant language for humor circulation. This does not mean, however, that national and ethnic differences have been erased altogether. On the contrary, in some cases there has been a turn to stressing local history of, and taste for, humor. The publication of cartoons depicting the prophet Muhammad in a Danish newspaper in 2005 caused international conflict and pointed to an evolving set of dilemmas that accompanies the globalization of humor. The cartoons were published with the intent of spurring discussion, but other conflicts have occurred simply because of the conflicting humor tastes of a large and anonymous global audience. The source of a possible cultural misunderstanding becomes marked when a text that is intended to be amusing reaches an audience that regards it as blasphemous or threatening, and when differences in the appreciation and acceptance of topics, targets, and circumstances for humor persist or are strengthened.

Liisi Laineste

See also American Indian Cultures, Humor in; Arabic Culture, Humor in; Cross-Cultural Humor; Ethnic Jokes; Ethnicity and Humor; Internet Humor; Jewish Humor

Further Readings

Davies, C. (2011). *Jokes and targets.* Bloomington: Indiana University Press.

Ziv, A. (1988). *National styles of humor.* New York, NY: Greenwood Press.

Native American Cultures, Humor in

See American Indian Cultures, Humor in

Nonsense

Nonsense applies to a wide range of meaningless ways of expression, from incomprehensible sentences to perfectly formed linguistic texts that block interpretation. Nonsense expressions easily become humorous ones, as humans often obtain pleasure from linguistic play and are ready to look for alternative paths to produce meaning. Nonsense has been experienced as a form of freedom, especially as a means to free thinking from the conventional bindings of logic and language. Complementarily, it has turned out to be a felicitous cognitive tool to venture off into the unknown, to explore unfamiliar regions of mind. In a historical sense, nonsense has to be considered as a literary genre, attaining particular interest during the Victorian period of English literature; its value as witty wordplay has equally to be taken into account, as well as its role in humorous utterances, in connection with the findings about humor appreciation; lastly, its implications with related categories like play or paradox merit are also to be mentioned.

Literary nonsense was already present in the oldest forms of European verse like those of Occitan troubadours or the early French ludic poems called *fatrasies,* and also in German *Lügendichtung* (lie-poetry), mainly related to *impossibilia* (impossible things), like hens capturing hawks or flying millstones. Nonsense verse was an influential practice during medieval times as a form of humorous play, one that exploited the frailty of linguistic devices. In the *Divina commedia* (Divine Comedy), Dante also explored incomprehensible language in his depiction of Nemrod (Inferno, XXI), a giant speaking a language of its own. But it was in the Renaissance that nonsense attained the status of a humanistic discussion, with Erasmus of Rotterdam's *Praise of Folly* (1509), a literate and funny defense of foolishness. François Rabelais also cultivated the genre, as did the popular Italian poet Domenico di Giovanni, alias Il Burchiello, who wrote sonnets of desolate and comical nonsense, like his famous quatrain: *Nominativi fritti, e mappamondi, / E l'arca di Noè fra duo colonne / Cantavan tutti "Kyrieleisonne" / Per la'nfluenza de 'taglier mal tondi*, which translates as "Fried nominatives and global maps / And Noah's Ark between two columns / Were all singing Kyrie Eleison / Under the influence of badly rounded trenchers" (Zaccarello, 2004, p. 10).

During the Enlightenment, nonsense practices grew, and authors like Jonathan Swift, Lawrence Sterne, and Georg C. Lichtenberg made use of them for different purposes. In the Victorian period of English literature, two main writers of nonsense emerged: Edward Lear (1812–1888) and Lewis Carroll (1832–1898). Lear composed nonsense prose and verse that have amused English-speaking children for decades. His famous limericks (although he did not use the word *limericks*), short five-line nonsense cyclic compositions, show both the caprices of rhyme and the pleasure of futile play: "There was a young lady of Sweden, / Who went by the slow train to Weedon, / When they cried, "Weedon Station!" / She made no observation, / But she thought she should go back to Sweden" (Jackson, 1947, p. 52). As these verses make no sense whatsoever, readers are only required to enjoy the poetic play, which constitutes a challenge of its own. Lear gathered his limericks in *The Book of Nonsense* (1846), invented characters as the Quangle-Wangle or the Jumbies, and wrote the celebrated nonsense poem *The Owl and the Pussycat* (1867), among other fanciful productions. G. K. Chesterton called him a complete citizen in the world of unreason.

Lewis Carroll has obtained worldwide renown with *Alice's Adventures in Wonderland* (1865) and *Through the Looking Glass* (1871), the two intriguing stories about Alice that defy standard logic and linguistic conventions. In the first, a series of adventures that Alice finds odd and counterintuitive, Carroll presents characters like the March Hare, the Cheshire Cat, and the Queen of Hearts or situations like the Mad Tea Party that build and sustain a world of their own, with their proper rules of logic and their linguistic principles. Nonsense is constructed through dialogues and bizarre explanations, sometimes implying phonetic, morphologic, or syntactic twists of language, like in the interrogation of Alice at the trial in the last chapter:

> "What do you know about this business?" The King said to Alice.
> "Nothing," said Alice.
> "Nothing *whatever?*" persisted the King.
> "Nothing whatever," said Alice.

> "That's very important," the King said, turning to the jury. They were just beginning to write this down on their slates, when the White Rabbit interrupted: "*Un*important, your Majesty means, of course," he said, in a very respectful tone, but frowning and making faces at him as he spoke. "*Un*important, of course, I meant," the King hastily said, and went on to himself in an undertone "important—unimportant—unimportant—important" as if he were trying which word sounded best. (Gardner, 1965, p. 155)

In the second *Alice,* the plot follows the plan of a chess match, with the action being developed in an enormous chessboard, under looking-glass principles, that is, inverted time and cause-and-effect relationships with regard to our conventional world. A methodical subversion of logic pervades every dialogue. But Carroll's most inventive creation is probably the *Jabberwocky,* followed by Humpty-Dumpty's decoding of it. The *Jabberwocky* looks like perfect English but defies any exegesis, as all the vocabulary is a pure creation. Despite this, Humpty-Dumpty affords an interpretation, so pretentious as to be hilarious. This famous nonsense poem has been translated countless times in many different languages in a literary *tour de force,* reminding us that meaningless linguistic artifices, in their poetic and creative use, lie at the origins of play and fun.

Carroll still produced a complete nonsense narrative poem, *The Hunting of the Snark* (1876), the feverish search for a queer and impossible animal that allegedly was slow in understanding jokes and usually looked *grave* at a pun. Here not only the name of *Snark* is part of the poetical game, but its very appearance makes it mutate (into a Boojum) and suddenly vanish. Paradoxes and contradictions invade the verses, and the whole enterprise, with the Snark as a symbol, turns out humorous in its futility, showing the purposeless, playful, and somehow intriguing task of building nonsense, which, by all means, requires a good and skilled linguistic work.

Witty wordplay is the base for all linguistic work producing nonsense, through a collection of well-known rhetorical devices, like semantic changes, lexical distortions, or figurative uses. Wordplay mainly frees an expression from its predictable contextual matrix and, consequently, its reduction to mere phonetic elements is one of the possibilities. Carrollian-like *portmanteau* terms (i.e., lexical coinages that pack two words in one, such as *chaosmos* or *narraction*) are also among the most enjoyable linguistic creations; they lie at the current origin of wordplay, complementary to puns, and then must be registered in the long tradition of verbal wit, which extends so productively along the 20th-century literature, from European avant-gardes to Joyce's *Finnegans Wake* (1939). Nonsense wordplay goes back to games of early childhood and to nursery rhymes as a source of pleasure and fantasy.

Partial or total nonsense is an ordinary component in jokes and humor in general. As a joke or a humorous utterance usually has to combine different cognitive frames (i.e., cognitive marks or reference), some degree of incongruity must be expected. When the degree of incongruity impedes a logical resolution, we usually qualify the joke or the humorous utterance as nonsensical. The blocking of logical resolution is a question of degree, depending on accessible properties of the implied cognitive frames. Nonsense jokes frequently adopt the structure of a riddle. The next exchange allows an acceptable degree of logical resolution (as the supposed action is actually possible, but unusual): "Should a person stir his coffee with his right hand of his left hand? Neither. He should use a spoon." But the standard nonsense riddle-like joke could be like the following (where the degree of logical resolution is only residual): "Why did the elephant stand on the marshmallow? Because he didn't want to fall into the hot chocolate." Here no particular connections arise between question and answer, beyond the general principle of doing something to avoid something else, or the fact that elephants do not particularly flee from hot chocolate. We also can find riddle-like jokes that explicitly distort their inner logical structure, like the next one: "What's the difference between the sparrow? No difference whatsoever. Both halves are identical, especially the left one." Here complexity increases as nonsense moves up through contradictions, blocking interpretation at every step. This is how degrees of incongruity work in producing humorous nonsense. And we could still move one step forward in nonsense practices, suggesting a riddle without a standard solution, like the Mad Tea Party riddle in the first *Alice,* "Why is a raven like a writing desk?" a pure invention that contravenes pragmatic expectancies, as it was created as a question without any answer.

Research about humor appreciation by Willibald Ruch and his team has highlighted how nonsense humor is valued compared with near-to-resolution humor (called usually incongruity-resolution humor), at the other end of the spectrum. Using humor tests to assess ratings of funniness and aversiveness of jokes and cartoons, Ruch's findings showed that nonsense humor was positively correlated with openness to experience, nonconformism, and youth. Conservative attitudes, self-control, need for order, and older age were instead positively correlated with incongruity-resolution humor, that which allows an acceptable degree of logical explanation. A positive appraisal of complexity, fantasy, and abstract forms of art were clearly related to appreciation of nonsense humor.

Although its overt component consists of verbal play, nonsense is also possible on a non-linguistic basis, as the way traced by the 20th-century literature and, particularly, the theater of the absurd have shown. Authors such as Eugène Ionesco, Samuel Beckett, Harold Pinter, and Václav Havel built plays containing absurd dialogues that frequently dive into humor. More on the facetious side, the Marx Brothers built dialogues that combined wordplay and a particular sense of logical subversion and the absurd. As Wim Tigges puts it, absurd literature deepens our uncertainties about reality. One interesting question is whether the uncertainties created by absurd and nonsense humor somehow lead to new, alternative, or more complex interpretations. Indeed, a certain agreement can be found about the complementary question that only human expressions are able to produce nonsense, this being a particular property of human communication.

Humor contains nonsense, to a certain degree, but not all nonsense is humorous. A certain amount of play on interpretation is needed for a nonsense utterance to become a humorous one. In nonsense, the logic that sustains interpretation collapses. Related to nonsense is paradox, where logic apparently fulfills its own requirements. Play on paradoxes often shows its comic side too, as in Jaroslav Hasek's *The Fateful Adventures of the Good Soldier Švejk During the World War* (1923) or in Joseph Heller's *Catch-22* (1961). These narrow relationships between categories help explain why we move so easily from one into another. So, nonsense can fruitfully be used to teach philosophy, as in Zen koans (study dialogues in Zen practices), which freely exploit quasi-comical or paradoxical utterances, like the famous initiation question, "What is the sound of one hand clapping?" Nonsense dialogues in Zen koans records and collections are used to gain insight and to approach alternative and original forms of understanding that defy standard reason.

Amadeu Viana

See also Absurdist Humor; Limericks; Puns; Riddle; 3 WD Humor Test

Further Readings

Chesterton, G. K. (1916). A defence of nonsense. In E. Rhys (Ed.), *A century of English essays* (pp. 446–450). London, UK: Dent.

Gardner, M. (Ed.). (1965). *The annotated Alice.* Harmondsworth, UK: Penguin.

Jackson, H. (Ed.). (1947). *The complete nonsense of Edward Lear.* London, UK: Faber & Faber.

Lecercle, J.-J. (1994). *Philosophy of nonsense.* London, UK: Routledge.

Malcolm, N. (1997). *The origins of English nonsense.* London, UK: Harper.

Ruch, W. (Ed.). (1998). *The sense of humor.* Berlin, Germany: Mouton de Gruyter.

Stewart, S. (1978). *Nonsense.* Baltimore, MD: Johns Hopkins University Press.

Tarantino, E. (Ed.). (2009). *Nonsense and other senses.* Newcastle upon Tyne, UK: Cambridge Scholars Publishing.

Tigges, W. (1988). *An anatomy of literary nonsense.* Amsterdam, Netherlands: Rodopi.

Zaccarello, M. (Ed.). (2004). *I sonetti del Burchiello* [The sonnets of Burchiello]. Torino, Italy: Einaudi.

O

Obscenity

This entry describes the nature of humorous obscenity and outlines the recent history of obscenity in popular culture, including the backlash to it, particularly in the United States. Etymologically, obscenity can be derived from the Latin *obscenus,* meaning "from or with filth," or from *obscaena,* meaning "off stage." Thus, obscenity has to do with what is deemed not fit to be seen or talked about. Its phenomenological core is feelings of revulsion associated with the breaking of norms about what is morally prohibited. Consequently, there is large social and cultural variation in what is deemed to be obscene, because what is taboo in one group or culture may not be in another. Nevertheless, topics like body parts and functions, bodily deformity, death, ethnicity, mental illness, politics, and religion are often found to have strong moral force in many societies and cultures and therefore are closely associated with obscenity. Also central to obscenity is sexuality, which can be combined with many of these other topics to produce strong feelings of revulsion. It is no exaggeration to say that the most common source domain of obscenity is sex and the body. This helps explain the ready connection between humor and obscenity, as a great deal of humor circulating in everyday life has sexual themes.

The production of humor from obscenities can have both visual- and language-based components. A good example of the former is the 2005 "Bloody Mary" episode of the animated sitcom *South Park,* which featured a statue of the Virgin Mary bleeding out of its anus. This image attracted vociferous protest, particularly from Catholic groups, but attempts to ban the episode were only partly successful. The protestors' claims that the episode was obscene and/or blasphemous only created more viewer attention. Similarly, the 1979 Monty Python film *Life of Brian* was banned in some places for blasphemy and for mocking Christianity, but the bans created so much attention that they served as free advertising. In Sweden, *Life of Brian* was marketed as "the film so funny that it was banned in Norway."

The fact that sex is often treated highly seriously makes it a ready candidate for the incongruity device frequently at the heart of humor. The graphic visual depiction of sexual acts in pornography seems deadly serious in its focus on body parts and their sexual connection, but it is not difficult to make a gestalt switch and see the awkward thrashings of people copulating as hugely comical. The spasms and release of orgasm can resemble the whole body in laughter, making a connection between humor and sex easy to make. Philosophers have grasped this idea to argue that breaking moral prohibitions can lead to both thrill and repulsion, with a judgment of obscenity occurring where there is an excessively depersonalized portrayal or perception of human sexuality. Even the language we use to talk about sexuality partakes of this dynamic tension. Alongside the proper vocabulary of sex and the body (including euphemisms) is a vast array of improper words (or dysphemisms) that can be judged obscene, depending on the context in which they are used.

Just like the comical aspect to sex, language-based obscenities have a strong element of release. Much humor employs obscene words partly because of the simple pleasure of breaking taboos, of saying something you are not supposed to. The use of obscenities in joking discourse can also act as emotional intensifiers, helping to encourage laughter, which therefore may partly overcome feelings of revulsion about the breaking of taboos.

To be offended by obscenity in humorous talk is to refuse an invitation to engage in like-minded informal discourse. The offended party effectively refuses the proffered self and role of the one who introduced the obscenities. This refusal itself can be humorous, causing the person who finds obscenities distasteful to become the target of verbal aggression, another very common source and technique of humor. Thus, obscenities are powerful, in both positive and negative ways.

It is through experiences with obscenities that children learn that anything that is forbidden is powerful. This power can lead to reproach and sanction, but it can also be intimately connected with laughter. At some stage in early life, infants will discover that their use of various swearwords can make adults laugh. The infant may not know this, but the laughter is because of a basic incongruity: The child is swearing but does not know what it means to swear, let alone the meaning of the words used. There is a whole genre of jokes based around children's inappropriate knowledge of obscene words, as when a little boy sees his mother in the shower, and asks, "What's that?" with the embarrassed mother replying, "Oh, that's where God hit me with an axe," to which the little boy says, "Got you right in the cunt, eh?"

Obscenity is often associated with humor in performances by stand-up comedians and in music hall and burlesque performances. At one time, comic performers made indirect references to sexual practices, often by means of double entendre. Sexual puns can be highly creative and skilled constructions, with the advantage of not being directly obscene because they are based on homonyms of the actual words taken to be obscene.

A watershed moment in stand-up comedy occurred with the routines of Lenny Bruce (1925–1966) in the 1950s and early 1960s. The previously common mother-in-law jokes of many male comedians seemed distinctly insipid when Bruce performed his routines. His performances were a kind of jazz style free association during which he talked about sex, among other things, with no self-censorship. Bruce was first arrested on an obscenity charge in 1961 for using the words *cocksucker* and *come* (in the sense of orgasm). He was acquitted, but his subsequent performances were monitored, leading to a successful conviction on another obscenity charge in 1964. Today, Bruce's routines would be relatively tame. For example, the 2006 film *The Aristocrats* featured dozens of comedians telling their variation of a well-known joke involving a family-based stage show, the challenge being to make it filthier than any other.

Bruce opened the door for many comedians to work up routines that used obscenities to refer to sexual acts. The best known comedian to follow Bruce's lead was George Carlin (1937–2008). His routine on the "seven words you can never say on television" (actually performed as a radio monologue in 1972) was another watershed moment in the history of obscenity. He thought these forbidden words were *shit, piss, fuck, cunt, cocksucker, motherfucker,* and *tits*. Court action brought by the Federal Communications Commission over the broadcast of Carlin's list of dirty words helped establish legal precedent over their use in broadcast media, but this judgment did not diminish Carlin's basic comedic logic of finding out where the authorities drew the line, then stepping over it. The use of obscenity has become far more common in radio and television since that time, due in part to the pioneering efforts of Bruce and Carlin.

Compared to the frequency of obscenities on television and radio in the United States, obscenities are far more common in film, probably because fewer film producers are dependent on advertising interests. The means of censoring obscenity have declined further still with the birth and subsequent pervasiveness of the Internet. Research on swearing on the Internet suggests that it is very frequent and generally used more by males than females, although this difference is fast disappearing.

Contemporary stand-up comedians still use obscenities to indicate intimacy, informality, and accessibility, particularly in the bar or nightclub atmosphere where much comedy is performed. However, given widespread knowledge of extant stand-up comedy routines, and an arguably greater prevalence of swearing in everyday life, the desire for novelty may have changed how routines with sexual content are performed. On one hand, the self-respecting road comic tries to invent original material, but on the other hand, there is no such thing as an original joke; accordingly, comedians need to display caution and subtlety in their use of obscenity, lest they be regarded as hack comedians. Fortunately, changes in society may provide the conditions for inventive manipulations of tried and true comedic routines, with obscenities functioning primarily as emotional intensifiers. For example, race, religion, and disability may be providing new topics for humor construction in some countries. These topics are not obscene in themselves, but the constant boundary-pushing of humor will undoubtedly result in connection with sexual topics, thus raising new questions about the acceptable limits of humor.

Mike Lloyd

See also Burlesque; Insult and Invective; Scatology; Sexuality; Stand-Up Comedy

Further Readings

Davis, M. S. (1983). *Smut: Erotic reality/obscene ideology.* Chicago, IL: University of Chicago Press.

Kieran, M. (2002). On obscenity: The thrill and repulsion of the morally prohibited. *Philosophy and Phenomenological Research, 64*(1), 31–55.

Legman, G. (1978). Dysphemism and insults. In *No laughing matter: Rationale of the dirty joke* (Second series, pp. 766–803). Frogmore, UK: Granada.

Lloyd, M. (2011). Miss Grimshaw and the white elephant: Categorization in a risqué humor competition. *Humor, 24*(1), 63–86.

Robson, J. (2006). *Humour, obscenity and Aristophanes.* Tübingen, Germany: Gunter Narr Verlag.

Seizer, S. (2011). On the uses of obscenity in live stand-up comedy. *Anthropological Quarterly,* 84(1), 209–234.

Thelwall, M. (2008). Fk yea I swear: Cursing and gender in a corpus of MySpace pages. *Corpora, 3*(1), 83–107.

Wajnryb, R. (2005). *Expletive deleted.* New York: Free Press.

Ontological Semantic Theory of Humor

See Linguistic Theories of Humor

OSTH

See Linguistic Theories of Humor

P

Paradox

The most basic type of paradox is a dramatic rhetorical device that offers an unorthodox insight because of using a single word with different or contradictory meanings. On a very simple level, if John is walking through the door of a room, it can be said that "John is in the room," or that "John is not in the room," or that "John is partly in the room and partly not in the room." That John can be considered to be in the room or not in the room is a paradox, because these statements can be seen as true but are contradictory.

Some scholars view paradox as a superficial and trivial rhetorical device, comparable to a pun. However, others view paradox as being on almost the same level as the four master tropes: metaphor, metonymy, synecdoche, and irony. Sometimes a paradox results from a major paradigm shift in the history of ideas, as when particular words take on expanded meanings. A simplified example is the word *man.* Its most basic meaning or earliest meaning may have been *man* in contrast to *animal,* that is, *human* compared to *beast.* But then it took on the meaning of *man* in contrast to *woman,* followed by the word acquiring the additional connotations of bravery, noble behavior, or whatever "strong" qualities the speaker admires.

Paradoxes can also be approached philosophically. Willard Van Orman Quine divided resolvable paradoxes into two kinds: veridical paradoxes, which lead to a true conclusion, and falsidical paradoxes, which lead to a false conclusion. Frederic's "birthday paradox" in Gilbert and Sullivan's *The Pirates of Penzance* is that he has had only five birthdays, yet he is 21 years old. The explanation is that he was born on "leap day," February 29, and the paradoxical statement is based on whether a birthday is a particular number on a calendar or the celebration of one more year (365 and one-fourth days) of life. Because the conclusion is true, given the premises, Quine considers this a veridical paradox.

In contrast, the "grandfather paradox" is said to show the absurdity of time travel; if you could travel back in time, then you could kill your grandfather before your father was conceived. But this isn't possible, because if you did so, you would not exist. Therefore, you can't travel back in time; because the conclusion is false, this is a falsidical paradox.

A third class of paradoxes is antinomy, which cannot be resolved through rational evidence. For example, with the old explanation that the world is sitting on the back of a giant turtle, the obvious question is, "But what is that turtle sitting on?" The reason people smile when they answer, "It's turtles all the way down," is that they recognize the paradox as an antinomy.

There is another, nonphilosophical, sense of paradox, which is based on the wording, the verbiage, as when a statement treats two different senses of a word as though they have the same meaning. In his essay, "The Crack-Up," F. Scott Fitzgerald said, "The test of a first-rate intelligence is the ability to hold two opposed ideas in the mind at the same time, and still retain the ability to function." One of the reasons that young children have so much fun with riddles, especially knock-knock jokes, is that these jokes encourage children to take their first steps toward developing the ability to hold opposing ideas. Some of the jokes they find so funny are "accidental" puns, meaning they are based on words that sound the same but have totally different meanings simply as an accident in the language, because English speakers have adopted and adapted words from so many different languages, as with the titles of Fred Gwynne's children's picture books, including *The King Who Rained, A Chocolate Moose for Dinner,* and *A Little Pigeon Toad.* But children also love the puns in Peggy Parish's *Amelia Bedelia* books, in which the jokes are mostly based on the dual meanings of words that are semantically related to each other. Amelia Bedelia is a house maid who constantly misunderstands the directions from her employers. When they tell her to "stamp the envelopes," she puts them on the ground and stamps on them with her feet, and when they tell her to "draw the drapes" she gets out pencil and paper and draws a picture of the drapes. Whereas adults take the double meanings in so-called dead metaphors for granted, children may give them more thought. For example, consider this riddle:

Question: Why did the Little Moron throw the clock out the window?
Answer: He wanted to see time fly.

Allison Lurie, an author and critic, has explained that this riddle might give children a mental image of a clock flying through the air because they may have wanted to destroy their own clock when their mother told them it was bedtime or time to turn the TV off. An adult equivalent to children's riddles is the way that adults are amused by the paradoxical implications of oxymorons such as *jumbo shrimp* and *tough love.* The contradictions exist because the adjectives (*jumbo* and *tough*) are being used to describe characteristics that might seem the opposite of their modifiers.

Words that refer to important phenomena such as life, love, and truth are likely to have developed a number of extended meanings. An example of such multiple meanings is Marshall McLuhan's comment, "The vital question today is not whether there will be life after death, but whether there was life before death." In one sense, McLuhan was using *life* to mean "existence," while in another sense he was using *life* to mean something like "fulfillment."

Paradoxes are harder to process when supposed opposites are being demonstrated as when in John Milton's *Paradise Lost,* the narrator says that the fires of hell emit "no light, but darkness visible." A more amusing paradoxical statement was made by Michel de Montaigne when he used nonmatching senses of *high* and *bottom* to create what might be labeled a "non-parallel" comparison: "Sits he on ever so high a throne, a man still sits on his bottom."

Don Lee Fred Nilsen and Alleen Pace Nilsen

See also Irony

Further Readings

Fitzgerald, F. S. (1936). The crack-up. *Esquire.* http://www.esquire.com/features/the-crack-up

Gans, E. (1997). *Signs of paradox, irony, resentment, and other mimetic structures.* Stanford, CA: Stanford University Press.

Hofstadter, D. R. (1980). *Godel, Escher, and Bach: An eternal golden braid.* New York, NY: Vintage Books.

Quine, W. V. O. (1976). *The ways of paradox, and other essays.* Cambridge, MA: Harvard University Press.

Shershow, S. C. (1986). *Laughing matters: The paradox of comedy.* Amherst: University of Massachusetts Press.

Parody

Parody is a term used since ancient Greece to denote the comic reworking of other serious, heroic, or epic works. This entry provides a historical perspective of the various definitions and uses of parody in the arts.

Derived from the noun for *ode* and prefix *para* (meaning "near to" and "opposite"), the word *parodia* was applied early on to mock-heroic epics such as the *Batrachomyomachia* or *Battle of the Frogs and Mice*, in which the eponymous creatures are given roles accorded human heroes in the Homeric epics. Such mock-heroic epics (see also Aristotle's *Poetics* from the 4th century BCE on Hegemon of Thasos, a near contemporary of Aristophanes) have also been described as travesties, following Lalli's *Eneide travestita* (Virgil's *Aeneid* travestied) of circa 1634.

The word *travesty* in fact translates from the Italian *travestire,* meaning "to disguise" or "reclothe," and has been used as an alternative to the terms *parody* and *mock-heroic epic.* Some critics have nonetheless tried to distinguish parody and travesty as high and low burlesque. These writers argue that parody as high burlesque imitates the form of the original while replacing its content with a more trivial subject matter, which is thereby elevated to a higher status, whereas travesty as low burlesque changes the manner of the original in an overall more mocking or familiar way. Both form and content of the original are, however, imitated and reworked for comic effect in ancient parody as well as in post-Renaissance travesty, and for a variety of purposes.

Modern Italian dictionary translations for the English word *travesty* give *parodia* as the Italian equivalent for that term. In the early 20th century, the word *spoof* transferred from a game of bluff to examples of parody. Whereas the mock-heroic epic can be described as a genre, parody may best be understood as a technique used for the comic reworking of other genres rather than as a distinct genre in itself. Devices used by the parodist to obtain a comic effect include ironic or satiric juxtaposition, transference, or, more generally, subtraction and addition.

The term *paratragodein* (or *paratragoedia*) was also used by the ancient Greeks to describe parody in drama, one notable example of which is *The Frogs* by Aristophanes (ca. 450–ca. 388 BCE), in which the tragedians Aeschylus and Euripides vie for supremacy over each other and parody is used to mock both. Here, parody is also used in ironic metafictional ways (the dramatists represented on stage are unaware that parody is being used by Aristophanes to both mock their styles and to create a new type of comedy from their works) and to satirize the audience of other, less complex forms of comedy. Ancient Greek use of the term *parody* was also extended to cover works in prose or speech (see Quintilian's 1st century CE *Institutio Oratoria* on *parodia* and *parode*).

The use of parody as a comic but also metafictional device for the creation of new, more sophisticated fictional works of comedy is one that was developed most notably in the early 17th century by Miguel de Cervantes Saavedra (1547–1616) in his *Don Quijote* (1630). In this work, books of chivalry are satirized and made part of a more complex metafictional work when the heroic dreams of their all too avid reader Don Quijote are revealed as delusions by his family and servant Sancho Panza as well as by the narrator. The "hero" of Cervantes's work is also shown to be yet another fictional character by the appearance of readers of volume 1 as characters in volume 2, who recognize and praise Don Quijote for his adventures.

Novelists and dramatists inspired by Cervantes have included Henry Fielding in his novel *Joseph Andrews* of 1742 and Charlotte Lennox in her *The Female Quixote* of 1752, a work read by Jane Austen, whose *Northanger Abbey* of 1818 parodies the gothic novels popular in her time. William Shakespeare's use of the comic play-within-the-play in his *Midsummer Night's Dream* of 1595–1600 is yet another example of how parody may be used by the sophisticated parodist to both mock and satirize the unwitting parodist or incompetent author and create another, ironic and more complex, mirror to the fictional work within which it is placed.

The term *parody* has been used in music to refer to the transfer of sacred music to a secular text and vice versa. In recent decades it has been extended even further to describe parody in the pictorial arts, including film and other such visual media. Examples of pictorial parody can be found, moreover, in ancient art, as well as in that of the Renaissance and after. Pictorial parody has also been used in caricature for satiric purposes, as in the reworking of popular paintings for contemporary political and social comment by John Leech (1817–1864) for *Punch* or by Peter Brookes (b. 1943) for the *The Times*.

Parody may also be used for an overriding creative, meta-artistic purpose, by means of which the works of earlier artists are reworked within a new art work, and with new media, as in the paintings of Roy Lichtenstein (1923–1997). Here the "interpictorial" reuse of older works can be seen as both an homage to and a development of the work of the imitated artist. In such works, pastiche (traditionally a noncomic imitation and compilation of older works within another artistic or architectural piece) may also be used and brought closer to parody with its ironic, "double-coded" juxtapositions of old and new content and form, or parody may be used as an additional device to pastiche to add a comic or ironic element to the application of the latter.

With regard to the attitude of the parodist in deriving humor from the reworking of older, more serious works, this can usually only be defined with reference to the specific work in which parody is used and may not necessarily involve mockery of the original as in a lampoon. Because the older work forms part of the parody, and contributes to its reception, the relationship of the parodist to that work may often be ambivalent and complex rather than dismissive or one-dimensional.

Margaret A. Rose

See also Ancient Greek Comedy; Aristophanes; Art and Visual Humor; Burlesque; Caricature; Cervantes, Miguel de; Hoax and Prank; Irony; Lampoon; Pastiche; Satire; Shakespearean Comedy; Travesty

Further Readings

Rose, M. A. (1993). *Parody: Ancient, modern, and post-modern.* Cambridge, UK: Cambridge University Press.

Rose, M. A. (2011). *Pictorial irony, parody, and pastiche: Comic interpictoriality in the arts of the 19th and 20th centuries.* Bielefeld, Germany: Aisthesis.

Pastiche

Pastiche is a French word that began to be used regularly in English in the 1880s and 1890s. In 18th-century France, it meant a work of art imitating another author's style. The French word was derived from the Italian *pasticcio,* meaning (from late Latin antiquity) a kind of mixed pastry, then indicating a musical form made up of various parts imitated from other composers. The English "pastiche" still shows these two influences: the "musical medley" meaning and more generally the idea of a "hodgepodge" or incongruous mixture derived directly from the Italian term, whereas the *Oxford English Dictionary* definition of pastiche as "an artistic work in a style that imitates that of another work, artist, or period" comes from French. It must be noted right away that pastiche is not necessarily humorous. For example, pastiche as a way of learning good writing by imitating great authors, as teachers in 19th-century French schools made their pupils practice doing, was a very serious matter. The same is true of some artistic instances of pastiche, depending on the conditions of their reception. For example, the cover illustration on Richard Dyer's *Pastiche* prompts the reader to interpret the 2002 film *Far From Heaven,* starring Julianne Moore in a story that takes place in the 1950s, as a pastiche. In fact the film makes a very touching drama. However, discussing *Far From Heaven* in 2003, Peter Bradshaw, critic for *The Guardian* newspaper, described how everybody had been enjoying the first 5 minutes of the film, which struck Bradshaw as a rather detailed "Hi-honey-I'm-home" 1950s skit, at the previous year's Venice Film Festival, before recounting how the giggling disappeared to be replaced by an absolute approval of every aspect of its elaboration. The "first giggling" effect and its link with the comic dimension of pastiche is discussed later.

Elements of Definition

It is complex to define what pastiche is and how to distinguish it from other forms usually associated with it. Attempting to distinguish parody from related forms such as pastiche, Margaret Rose reviews different definitions of "pastiche" in English, underlining their negative critical connotations, due to the derivative aspect in art of imitation as opposed to originality. An example is Russell Sturgis's (1902) definition, which is general enough to extend to other art forms: "A work of art produced in deliberate imitation of another or several others, as of the works of a master taken together" (vol. 3, p. 73). This is close to Dyer's (2007) "pastiche is a kind of imitation that you are meant to know is an imitation" (p. 1). However, the latter insists on the spectator's or reader's point of view, whereas the former focuses on the author's intention. Accordingly, the definition of humorous pastiche proposed here can refer either to an entire work or to parts of that work: a deliberate imitation of a style or genre, with an amusing effect.

Differentiating Pastiche From Parody

Pastiche is very close to parody and is regularly confused with it in the public mind because of the complex and mixed nature of all parodic works, which are humorous remakes of linguistic or artistic performances, according to Margaret Rose. In most practical cases, the two words are used interchangeably about any work that humorously rewrites a recognizable source or style. The French novelist Marcel Proust spoke alternatively of "pastiche" and *parodie* about his own imitations of 19th-century novelists; in Italian, Umberto Eco (b. 1932) does the same about his *Diario minimo* (Misreadings). Similarly, in Mikhail Bakhtin's polyphonic theory of enunciation, pastiche and parody are effectively the same thing: the presence or imitation of another discourse in one's own speech.

Clear landmarks for differentiating pastiche from parody are nevertheless given by French critic Gérard Genette (1982/1997), who attempts to distinguish various categories of "hypertextuality," the word he proposed for "any relationship uniting a text B (which I shall call hypertext) to an earlier text A

(I shall, of course, call it the hypotext), upon which it is grafted in a manner that is not that of commentary" (p. 5). This structuralist approach is not devoid of humor itself, and Genette was aware that it could be unsatisfactory for the analysis of "general parody," but it is a useful basis for defining pastiche. Setting aside the subtleties of Genette's six hypertextual categories (he admits they are bound to dissolve when applied to any complex work), two kinds of "relations" between texts emerge: transformation and imitation. In fact these are the principal differences between parody and pastiche. Parody is predominantly a transformative technique (Linda Hutcheon [2000] terms it "repetition with critical distance, which marks difference rather than similarity" [p. 6]). Pastiche, however, is an imitative technique, characterized by marking similarities rather than differences.

A good illustration of this distinction is provided by Martin Rowson's graphic novel (cartoon) version (1996) of Laurence Sterne's early novel, *Tristram Shandy* (1759–1767). Adapting Sterne's own playful rewriting of various books, the cartoonist uses parody and pastiche as two clearly different forms. His "plates" illustrating the story of Slawkenbergius (adapting Book IV of *Tristram Shandy,* a tale about a long-nosed traveler) are respectful parodies of well-known pictures—successively Albrecht Dürer's *Knight, Death and the Devil* (1513), William Hogarth's *Southwark Fair* (1733/1734), and Aubrey Beardsley's *The Eyes of Herod* (1894)—whose comic meaning relies on slight changes of content arising from the story being told. This is parody. Later on, to access the transposed version of Book V, when "some dangerous nerd" has downloaded the entire text of *Tristram Shandy,* the "reader" inside Rowson's graphic novel has to hack into this digitalized text to "find out what happens next." But this operation sets off a huge "bug," which generates alternative versions of Sterne's story, each in the style of a 20th-century novelist or literary movement and each illustrated with a caricature of the author and a pastiched speech bubble. Martin Amis, Raymond Chandler's Philip Marlowe, South American magical realism, D. H. Lawrence, and T. S. Eliot are all imitated. Although each stylized story-bit still contains elements linking it with *Tristram Shandy* (e.g., characters' names), its comic effect derives from pastiche as it relies on its resemblance to its "hypotext" rather than on transformation of content or context.

Pastiche and Caricature in the Past

In the 17th and 18th centuries, pastiche of the mock-heroic variety was more highly regarded than caricature (also called burlesque travesty), because its principle was to preserve the dignity of the noble genre and high style being imitated, even though applied to a trifling incident. The canonical example of such a heroicomical poem is Alexander Pope's *The Rape of the Lock* (1712).

Another noted exponent was novelist Henry Fielding, whose writing included what he called "burlesque in diction" (preface to *Joseph Andrews,* 1742) purely for entertainment, for example in heroic descriptions of battles involving dogs or drunkards. Nowadays this would be called "mock-heroic pastiche" and its mainly imitative principle bears out Fielding's conception of the novel as a "comic epic in prose." However, Fielding condemned *caricatura* and its exaggerated satiric deformation as contradicting his aim of drawing comic characters from nature.

During periods of intense renewal of forms and genres such as occurred during the romantic period (late 18th and early 19th centuries), pastiche was a very useful, hence widespread, form of writing. Paul Aaron demonstrates how the French romantics used pastiche to explore all kinds of ironic or eccentric forms to condemn ancient literary forms and compromise new ones. For the authors of the revolutionary generation that discovered the notion of personal originality in art, criticizing outworn classical forms by imitating them was a way of experimenting with what a century later was theorized by the Russian formalists as the "laying bare" of mechanical devices.

Pastiche and Satire

Besides parody, satire is commonly associated with pastiche. Although the imitation in pastiche must be recognizable (or else it could not be identified as pastiche), satirical exaggeration of the model's typical traits may tend toward caricature. Then, satire is aimed at the hypotext itself, whose "saturation" (Gérard Genette's term) with these traits is mocked by copying and exhibiting them to the reader. The difference between pastiche and caricature here is a matter of degree: Pastiche is more neutral and less satirical in purpose. In the Rowson example given earlier, Martin Amis is pastiched: His stylistic habits are playfully summed up in one speech bubble. But on the next page, T. S. Eliot is the object of a caricature: His style is ridiculed into being nothing more than meaningless mumbles. Rowson publicly declared his irritation with Eliot and also adapted *The Waste Land* as a satirical graphic transposition. In *Far From Heaven*, the film mentioned earlier, the critic's first five minutes of "giggles" result from the same mechanism: At first sight, Todd Haynes's reconstruction of a 1950s aesthetic passes for a caricature of past narrative forms saturated with easily recognizable traits. But then, Dyer points out, the story reveals the re-creation to be meaningful and touching—a serious pastiche.

Is Pastiche "Blank Parody"?

The relative neutrality of pastiche, compared with both parody (in the transforming relationship) and caricature (in the imitative relationship), led postmodernist scholar Frederic Jameson to regard pastiche as "blank parody." Showing how the concept of a norm in postmodern art and literature is replaced by "private styles and mannerisms," Jameson pessimistically regards pastiche as similarly replacing value-laden parody. He calls it "blank parody, a statue with blind eyeballs" (1991, p. 17). It may, he concedes, involve some humor, being "at the least compatible with addiction—with a whole historically original consumers' appetite for a world transformed into sheer images of itself and for pseudoevents." In other words, postmodern pastiche is an empty form because it is the perpetual reflection of a self-centered consumer society that has lost its sense of history.

Nevertheless, today pastiche often remains one of the conditions for a satiric parody to be fully effective, serving as the background against which the parody takes place. For instance, when the Reduced Shakespeare Company (the name parodies the Royal Shakespeare Company) gave an abridged version of *Titus Andronicus* in the form of a culinary TV program, that type of show was pastiched without any evident critical intent, while Shakespeare's play was very funnily parodied. Satire here was not aimed at cooking programs but at the accumulation of violent deaths in the Bard's first tragedy. The parodic RSC imitated a popular form to remind their public joyfully about Shakespearian (or Jacobean) aesthetics of cruelty. In this case, pastiche actually helps maintain historical and cultural heritage.

Playful rather than satirical tone underlying humorous pastiche is also exemplified by American Bill Watterson's comic strip *Calvin and Hobbes* (1985–1995). Here the reader is invited to share the viewpoint of a little boy named Calvin (after John Calvin, 16th-century French Reformation theologian and paired with a stuffed tiger named after Thomas Hobbes, 17th-century English political philosopher). When Calvin's mother tries to make him eat his dinner, for example, what we see through the boy's eyes is a monstrous alien from science fiction comics or TV shows. This is graphical pastiche, and its humorous effect relies on reusing visual codes associated with another genre (sci-fi) to depict a small boy's fantasies. Through pastiched images that are part of each generation's common cultural background, the adult reader is put back in touch with his or her own former childlike imaginings. The young reader may also recognize his or her own fantasies and perhaps, by identifying the imitation as such, may apprehend them differently with humorous distance (distancing) and a knowing amusement.

Humorous Pastiche as Imitation

Because pastiche is based on the imitative principle, a final question is whether imitation itself provokes laughter or smiling, independent of the transformations common to pastiche and parody. Gérard Genette believed it did and French philosopher Henri Bergson saw laughter as generally arising from "something mechanical encrusted upon the living." He cited imitation as one instance of this "law" of the comic: "Gestures, at which we never dreamt of laughing, become laughable when imitated by another individual. . . . To imitate any one is to bring out the element of automatism he has allowed to creep into his person" (Bergson, 1900/2008, p. 22). Moreover, for Bergson, this was "the very essence of the ludicrous": a "deflection of life towards the mechanical" that he believed was the real cause of laughter.

Yen-Mai Tran-Gervat

See also Bergson's Theory of the Comic; Burlesque; Caricature; Cartoons; Comic Books; Comic Strips; Exaggeration; Genres and Styles of Comedy; History of Humor: Early Modern Europe; History of Humor: Modern and Contemporary Europe; History of Humor: 19th-Century Europe; Lampoon; Mock Epic; Parody; Satire; Spoofing; Travesty

Further Readings

Aaron, P. (2008). *Histoire du pastiche: Le pastiche littéraire français de la Renaissance à nos jours* [History of pastiche: Literary French pastiche from the Renaissance to our times]. Paris: Presses Universitaires de France.

Bergson, H. (2008). *Laughter: An essay on the meaning of the comic* (C. Brereton & F. Roswell, Trans.). Rockville, MD: Arc Manor. (Original work published 1900)

Bradshaw, P. (2003, March 7). *Far From Heaven* [Critique]. *The Guardian.* Retrieved from http://www.guardian.co.uk/culture/2003/mar/07/artsfeatures2

Dyer, R. (2007). *Pastiche: Knowing imitation.* London, UK: Taylor & Francis.

Eco, U. (1993). *Misreadings* (W. Weaver, Trans.). San Diego, CA: Harcourt Brace. (Original work published 1963)

Genette, G. (1997). *Palimpsests: Literature in the second degree* (C. Newman & C. Doubinski, Trans.). Lincoln: University of Nebraska Press. (Original work published 1982)

Hutcheon, L. (2000). *A theory of parody: The teachings of twentieth-century art forms.* Urbana: University of Illinois Press.

Jameson, F. (1991). *Postmodernism, or, The cultural logic of late capitalism.* Durham, NC: Duke University Press.

Rose, M. (1993). *Parody: Ancient, modern, postmodern.* Cambridge, UK: Cambridge University Press.

Rowson, M. (1996). *The life and opinions of Tristram Shandy, gentleman.* London, UK: Picador.

Sturgis, R. (1902). *Dictionary of architecture and building* (Vol. 3). London, UK: Macmillan.

Pattern Recognition

Pattern recognition in psychology is the identification of a pattern in a stimulus. In humor studies, it is the name of an evolutionary theory arguing that humor is an advanced form of a data-processing faculty whose influence has played a vital role in the expansion of the human race's cognitive abilities. First proposed by British author Alastair Clarke in 2008, it suggests that the enjoyment of being amused encourages an individual to identify certain relationships between novel bits of information. This entry provides a brief overview of the theory's ideas and its implications.

Basic Principles

Disagreeing with alternative ideas proposing that the perception of incongruity constitutes the foundation for humor, pattern recognition theory contends that the recognition of patterns has enabled the human race to develop an intellect that is unparalleled in its plasticity and adaptability, later stimulating the expression of this capacity for nongenetic self-modification in the form of advanced culture. Emphasizing the positive usefulness of humorous perceptions, it was released as one of two contrasting evolutionary theories, with the other, information normalization theory, intentionally reversing its arguments to suggest that humor exists not to identify novel insights but to motivate the avoidance of potential pitfalls in poor-quality data. Pattern recognition is therefore distinctly opposed to the interpretation of humor as a corrective mechanism and makes much of the utility of patterns in human cultural development.

Types of Pattern

According to the schematic mechanism of humor presented by pattern recognition theory, there are two main types of pattern that are central to the process of cultural and intellectual adaptability. The first, known as *patterns of fidelity*, are recognized by the brain when multiple units are compared for their similarity, thereby producing a pattern of repetition in those shared qualities. For example, if two individuals are judged to exhibit a similarity of appearance, the individuals constitute multiple units and their physical resemblance provides a point of duplication or a "context" for their comparison. The second, *patterns of magnitude*, are recognized when a single unit is repeated in multiple contexts. For example, the same person may be relocated to a previously unexpected environment, providing an element of duplication within a framework of shifting conditions. Various names are given to a number of different subtypes of pattern (such as *opposition*, *translation*, *completion*, *qualitative recontextualization*, and *scale*), but the definitions of these terms are not essential for a rudimentary understanding of the theory provided the data being identified conform to these basic stipulations of unit and context interaction.

Surprise

To complete the model, pattern recognition theory insists on the presence of novelty in humorous perceptions. The apprehension of repetitive designs, such as may appear in wallpaper or other graphic illustrations, provides an intuitively identifiable pattern but would usually fail to do so in a surprising or novel fashion. Perceptions of this type would not therefore meet the necessary conditions that pattern recognition theory proposes for humor, whereas the unexpected duplication of a unit in stimuli such as mimicry or caricature may do so.

Claims

Pattern recognition theory claims universality regarding its application, maintaining that it can be used to explain any instance of humor regardless of its nature or level of complexity. It also emphasizes that patterns only exist as facets of perception while the brain attempts to order and interpret external stimuli rather than as reflections of objective reality. By suggesting that a substructure of patterns beneath the content of the stimulus forms the basis of humor but insisting that their perception is highly individualized, the theory denies the possibility of intrinsic funniness within any stimulus or genre of humor. As a consequence, any subject matter may be found amusing provided the individual's subjective assessment allows the conditions of novel pattern recognition to be met. However, cultural influences will inevitably affect the tendency and ability to select and recognize patterns and will also lead to varying degrees of surprise at their apprehension, as will the individual's repeated exposure to the stimulus. Humor is therefore an abstract, cognitive process encouraging the recognition of novel patterns of potential value to the specific individual assessing the information with which he or she is confronted.

Sense of Humor Failure

Pattern recognition theory agrees with the general consensus that the activity and expression of humor is bound to fail at times for good reasons, but states that this process of curtailment has less to do with the faculty of humor per se and more to do with the necessity of curbing any emotional high, regardless of its cause, during potentially dangerous situations. This brake on the system is referred to as "the futility of dying happy" and is presented alongside the altruistic impulse as one of two significant but subjective restrictions on humor's response mechanism.

Evolution

On an evolutionary basis, pattern recognition theory proposes that humor exists to identify that which is positive and useful in information rather than that which is incorrect, and emphasizes its role in the formation of human intellect, the proliferation of culture, and the ultimate success of the species. Patterns of fidelity are considered to relate to the benefits of various social superstructures such as calendrical routines and linguistic communication, whereas patterns of magnitude are correlated with the progress of technological improvement. Although the theory does not deny that other species are capable of many of the cognitive feats it identifies as examples of the human race's ingenuity, it argues that humor has facilitated their unprecedented expansion in human beings. Its evolution is therefore suggested to have occurred only in *Homo sapiens*, appearing as a faculty somewhere between the advent of anatomically modern humans approximately 200,000 years ago and the cultural watershed of the Upper Paleolithic 160,000 years later.

Alastair Clarke

See also Cognitive Aspects; Creativity; Evolutionary Explanations of Humor; Incongruity and Resolution

Further Readings

Clarke, A. (2010). *The faculty of adaptability: Humour's contribution to human ingenuity*. Cumbria, UK: Pyrrhic House.

Clarke, A. (2012). *The attractive error: Humour's role in the war against infected memes*. Cumbria, UK: Pyrrhic House.

Pedagogy

Pedagogy is the art and science of education and teaching. It is a term that can also be used as a reference to certain instructional strategies or approaches. This entry discusses the research on the use of humor in teaching and its effects on students and teachers, with a focus on the most effective ways for teachers to use humor.

A number of studies have shown positive benefits in using humor as a teaching supplement or tool. The pedagogical use of humor has been shown to have both psychological and physiological effects on learners. Psychologically, humor has been shown to reduce anxiety, decrease stress, enhance self-esteem, and increase self-motivation. Each of these effects can be beneficial in the learning process by creating a more positive social and emotional environment in which defenses are lessened and students are better able to focus and attend to the information. Physiologically, laughter has been shown to improve respiration and circulation, lower pulse rate, decrease blood pressure, oxygenate blood, and release endorphins. Such effects can improve attention and lessen stresses that might adversely impact learning.

There is a growing body of research relating the use of humor with positive effects on teaching and learning. Student surveys reveal that effective use of humor in the classroom can increase their interest in learning and provide a means to engage in more divergent thinking. Humor was reported to make the learning experience more enjoyable and accessible. Additionally, humor in pedagogical settings has been shown to increase the retention of material presented in the classroom as compared with the presentation of the same material offered in a less engaging format. Further, studies have found that instructors who use appropriate and targeted humor in courses enjoy an increase in participant attendance.

A review of teaching evaluations showed that college students tend to strongly favor teachers who possess a good sense of humor and rate these instructors with higher evaluative scores. When asked to describe the positive attributes of good teachers, college students frequently mentioned "a sense of humor." When students and faculty members were asked to rate teachers based on their written teaching philosophies, the teachers who were ranked the highest revealed their approach to instruction emphasized a positive sense of humor both in and outside of the classroom. Humor can serve as a bridge between educators and students by demonstrating a shared understanding.

Using Humor With Caution

Humor can be complicated because it can be highly personal, subjective, and contextual. Research has demonstrated that there are a number of important caveats when using humor in the classroom. Like other senses that we possess, each person has his or her own "sense of funny"—what one person may perceive as amusing, another might find to be less so, or even offensive. The pedagogical use of humor must be carefully considered. Such humor must be appropriate to the audience and targeted to the topic. It must be clearly placed within the context of the learning experience. The objective of the pedagogical use of humor is to communicate a connection. The goal is to enhance the learning process and, thus, humor must ensure mutual respect of all parties. Ill-conceived attempts at pedagogical uses of humor can elicit unintended consequences or create the very barriers that we seek to avoid. The use of poor or unrelated humor, practical jokes (that occur at another's expense), excessive sarcasm, or material that defames or discriminates is not appropriate.

Not Mere Joke-Telling

Mere joke-telling is not likely an appropriate pedagogical use of humor. For humor to be most effective in an academic setting, it must be specific, targeted, and appropriate to the subject matter. Other than for general icebreaking, offering a litany of unrelated jokes has not been related to positive pedagogical effects. It is not the humor, per se, that has the greatest impact; it is the effective use of well-planned, contextual humor that is key. One study revealed that an excessive use of humor by instructors did not have the desired positive effect; learning was not enhanced by merely trying to interject humor at every opportunity. The goal is not to offer pure comic relief, but to present the material in a manner that helps others better understand the point.

Proper Pedagogical Humor

Proper use of humor in pedagogical settings has a number of characteristics. It is often helpful to focus on positive humor and create a climate of reciprocal humor in which students can feel free to offer a lighthearted reply. This also speaks to the importance of consistency in using humor. It can become confusing for students if an instructor engages in appropriate humor to enhance the class one day but becomes dull and seemingly disinterested the next. Students would be unsure as to the appropriate tone of the class. This can create the very barriers to effective communication that we seek to avoid with the application of humor as a teaching tool.

It is important that the humor be relevant to the content, context, and situation. The proper use of humor for pedagogical purposes is usually brief so as not to create confusion by having people get lost in the joke or story. It is also important to use humor in a style that is comfortable for the teacher or instructor. Awkward insertions of humor for the sake of inclusion within the presentation can have detrimental effects. Effective uses of humor in the classroom are often enthusiastically delivered and may appear to be spontaneous. Such apparent spontaneity can be deceiving, however, as the best use of humor is often well-prepared and carefully thought out. Some have suggested that teachers and instructors could benefit from the use of a humor journal to track what worked and what did not as they prepare for future presentations. This allows for a more reflective approach in determining what humorous elements might best fit the content.

Less Is Usually More

Humor can be hard to sustain and, fortunately, that is not the intention in the classroom. The instructor is not there to do an "act"; the goal is to effectively use humor to help others learn something of value. Drawn-out stories or complicated joke-telling may have the opposite effect. The desired impact is found in helping others to see a point or better understand a concept through the effective use of humor, not to be a comedian. In fact, studies have shown that brief, spur-of-the-moment applications of humor that specifically relate to the class discussion can be among the most beneficial uses in pedagogical settings. Such an application of humor can demonstrate the attentiveness of the instructor and display currency with the topic. In contrast, other research has found that simply adding increased humor elements to the content of a class was not effective. In one study, highly rated instructors were found to use humor much more judiciously and sparingly than other faculty who received only average teaching evaluations.

Using Funny Material

Some of the best uses of humor in pedagogical applications involve using humorous cartoons, videos, and stories to illustrate a point. Again, the essence of this strategy is the appropriate use of a humorous element that works to help others better understand an important issue or topic. Educators who may not personally possess a comfortable sense of humor may still enhance the classroom environment by using outside sources. Humorous video clips from situation comedies, game shows, reality TV, and so forth, can be used in the learning environment. The inclusion of well-targeted cartoons or a humorous Top 10 List, for example, has been shown to produce a positive pedagogical effect, resulting in a more relaxed classroom atmosphere and increased student interest and retention of material. Some research has suggested a sequence for including humorous material into the classroom. According to this approach, the instructor would first start by explaining the content or information without humor. This would then be followed by a humorous demonstration, visual, or activity. Finally, the information and how it relates to the humorous example would be explored and discussed.

Humor Effects for the Instructor

The benefits of using humor in pedagogical settings are not restricted to the student. Studies have shown that using humor in the classroom can make teaching more fun and enjoyable. Achieving excellence in teaching requires creativity and challenges one to present information in a way that can be more successful for the student. Such a challenge helps instructors to be more engaged and involved. Those who thoroughly know the content of *what* is being taught can find stimulation and enjoyment as they seek to discover new ways of presenting the information. Researchers have found that instructors who regularly use well-targeted humor report that it can relieve their own stress and tension, resulting in a more conducive environment for both the teacher and the students.

Randy Garner

See also Education, Humor in; Teachers' Evaluations, Effect of Humor Use in Classroom on; Testing and Evaluation

Further Readings

Garner, R. (2005, Winter). Humor, analogy, and metaphor: H.A.M. it up in teaching. *Radical Pedagogy, 6*(2). Retrieved August 27, 2013, from http://www.radicalpedagogy.org/radicalpedagogy8/Humor,_Analogy,_and_Metaphor__H.A.M._it_up_in_Teaching.html

Garner, R. (2006). Humor in pedagogy: How ha-ha can lead to aha! *College Teaching, 57*(1), 177–180.

Glenn, R. (2002). Brain research: Practical applications for the classroom. *Teaching for Excellence, 21*(5), 1–2.

Hill, D. (1988). *Humor in the classroom: A handbook for teachers*. Springfield, IL: Charles C Thomas.

Personality, Humor and

Humor is often thought of as being a personal characteristic of an individual. Thus, some individuals have a "good sense of humor," whereas others do not. This personality approach to humor assumes that humor is a relatively stable attribute within the individual and that it is expressed across numerous events and situations. Over the years, personality psychologists have expended considerable energy investigating what "sense of humor" actually consists of and then determining how to best measure this construct. This has led to the development of a number of different measures of sense of humor, ranging from actual behavioral tests (e.g., construct a funny monologue on a given topic, engage in a creative humorous task) to a wide variety of self-report measures (e.g., rate oneself on the ability to appreciate humor, express humor, tell jokes, or use humor to cope). This entry explores sense of humor as a personality construct, including its various aspects and its relation to other personality constructs, and examines relevant research.

Documenting the Various Aspects of Sense of Humor

Psychological work in this domain, which can be traced back at least 50 years, was focused on documenting individual differences in humor appreciation for cartoons, jokes, and other humorous stimuli. In addition to examining differences between individuals in their funniness and enjoyment ratings for this type of material, this work also considered how these humor appreciation ratings were related to other aspects of personality. Typical findings indicated that more extroverted people tended to show higher funniness ratings for jokes and cartoons, whereas more authoritarian people had a greater appreciation for humor that could be resolved (e.g., jokes) than for nonsense humor.

This early work on humor appreciation provided initial empirical support for the proposal that humor could be usefully conceptualized as a personality construct. It failed, however, to consider that there are many other aspects of sense of humor that are *not* captured by funniness ratings. Humor appreciation focuses almost exclusively on one's ability to comprehend and enjoy "canned" humor (i.e., jokes, cartoons, comedy routines). As such, it virtually ignores many other important aspects of sense of humor, such as creating or engaging in humorous banter in social settings and interpersonal relationships or using humor to cope effectively with stressful life events.

This issue was dealt with by the next generation of humor personality theorists, as they developed various self-report measures that captured several of these additional aspects of sense of humor. One of the earliest of these measures, the Sense of Humor Questionnaire, emerged in the mid-1970s and helped promote the view that sense of humor should be thought of as a multifaceted construct that functions in a very broad social and intrapersonal context. Thus, one of the subscales on this measure assessed "meta-message sensitivity," or the cognitive ability to shift to a nonserious playful perspective on the world; a second subscale assessed attitudes toward humorous situations and people; and a third assessed mirth or laughter for a wide range of situations. The first two subscales have shown acceptable (i.e., reliable and valid) psychometrics, with both evolving into much shorter versions that are still in use today. However, in recognition of psychometric problems with the third subscale, other humor researchers have developed a more reliable measure for assessing mirth and laughter, namely, the Situational Humor Response Questionnaire (SHRQ). This scale focuses on one specific aspect of sense of humor: the frequency of emotional expression of smiling and laughter in typical situations that a person might encounter. This laughter scale and a brief self-report Coping Humor Scale (e.g., "I can usually find something to laugh or joke about, even in trying situations") have been employed successfully for many years to examine how individuals use their sense of humor to deal effectively with stressful life experiences and how these two personality aspects of sense of humor may relate to increased physical and psychological well-being. In particular, those displaying greater laughter or mirth, as well as those using more coping humor, typically show a stress-moderator effect for these two aspects of humor, as they have much lower depression levels after encountering negative life events that those with low levels of mirth or coping humor.

Over the next 20 years or so (to the turn of the 21st century), a number of additional personality-based measures of sense of humor were developed. The increasing recognition of the multifaceted nature of this personality construct resulted in the Multidimensional Sense of Humor Scale, with separate self-report assessments of coping humor, humor appreciation, humor production, creative ability, social humor, and playfulness. This playful aspect of sense of humor has also been captured by the State-Trait Cheerfulness Inventory, which suggested that those with a good sense of humor are more temperamentally cheerful and maintain a nonserious attitude toward life.

This strong psychological tradition of describing and measuring different personality aspects of sense of humor has continued into the 21st century. One recent approach, for example, stems from a positive psychology perspective, with its description and measurement of 24 positive character strengths that individuals may possess, including humor, love, and kindness. This work has shown that a greater sense of humor (when defined as liking to joke, laugh, and bring smiles to others) can enhance life satisfaction and contribute to one's psychological well-being. This singular focus on social humor, however, falls prey to the same limitation raised over 40 years ago in the context of work on humor appreciation; namely, it ignores other potentially important personality aspects of humor. This issue remains relevant, given that contemporary personality approaches to sense of humor have clearly documented very different relationships between individual aspects of sense of humor and other personality constructs.

Sense of Humor in Relation to Other Personality Characteristics

In addition to describing the various aspects of sense of humor, personality investigators have begun to explore how these aspects relate to other personal attributes an individual may possess. One robust and consistent pattern is that many of the aspects of sense of humor are linked to greater extraversion. Thus, individuals who display increased laughter, greater humor appreciation, and heightened coping humor (including self-enhancing humor) are also more outgoing and gregarious, with a stronger social focus. Furthermore, these individuals approach life with a more adaptive orientation, as they are more joyful and optimistic and have greater self-esteem and more positive affect. These personal characteristics then lead them to seek out and engage in a wider range of positive life experiences.

It is important to note, however, that not all aspects of sense of humor display the same pattern of associations with these personality constructs. In this regard, one prominent personality-based model has identified four different humor styles: self-enhancing, self-defeating, aggressive, and affiliative. Self-enhancing humor reduces personal stress by using a humorous perspective when dealing with adverse life situations. This style is closely aligned with coping humor and shows the same strong positive relationship with psychological well-being. In particular, those with higher levels of self-enhancing humor have lower levels of depression and anxiety and higher levels of intimacy, self-esteem, social support, and relationship satisfaction.

In marked contrast, those with higher levels of self-defeating humor (the characteristic use of humor to excessively put down one's self in order to gain approval from others) show precisely the opposite pattern: They exhibit higher depression and anxiety, along with lower self-esteem, reduced intimacy, and poorer social support. Furthermore, those with high levels of aggressive humor (a maladaptive style) generally report higher levels of hostility and lower relationship satisfaction, whereas those high on affiliative humor show modest increases in positive relationships and well-being.

Taken together, the previously described pattern clearly points to instances in which the different aspects of sense of humor can have either positive or negative implications for the individual (or others). In doing so, this work highlights the need for contemporary personality approaches to sense of humor to consider more complex models that acknowledge multiple aspects of sense of humor, not all of which are beneficial. In particular, maladaptive aspects, such as self-defeating humor, show how detrimental humor can be, as these individuals are also characterized by increased levels of neuroticism, negative affect, poor interpersonal relationships, and reduced social skills.

Further Investigations of Sense of Humor as a Personality Construct

Over the past decade there has been a virtual explosion of research on personality aspects of humor. Some of this work has examined how sense of humor may impact physical health and well-being. As one illustration, as part of a large public health survey in Norway, a recent epidemiological study assessed the cognitive, social, and affective components of sense of humor in more than 52,000 adults. These individuals were then followed prospectively for 7 years. Of special note is that individuals scoring higher on this sense of humor measure had significantly lower mortality rates until the age of 65 years. Similar findings have been reported for other studies involving patient samples (end-stage renal disease, cancer), with a greater sense of humor improving quality of life while ill, and sometimes increasing longevity. Very little is yet known, however, about whether any of the maladaptive aspects of humor (e.g., self-defeating humor) have a long-term detrimental impact on physical health and longevity.

As described earlier, other research has examined how sense of humor may relate to psychological well-being and quality of life. Many of these personality-based studies have found significant links, with certain aspects of sense of humor (e.g., self-enhancing) contributing to enhanced psychological well-being and other aspects (e.g., self-defeating) leading to a decrement in quality of life and well-being. It is only recently, however, that the proposed mechanisms underlying these relationships have been examined in more detail. It has been suggested that adaptive humor fosters a change of perspective and emotional distancing from stressful life events, thus minimizing negative affect. In addition, however, the use of adaptive humor can also increase the expression of mirth and positive affect. This positive enhancement effect then provides a broader foundation for searching out additional positive experiences that can also contribute to the richness in one's life.

A large portion of the recent psychological work on humor and personality has been guided by the humor styles model, as this contemporary personality-based approach provides a robust theoretical and empirical foundation for considering other issues surrounding both adaptive and maladaptive humor styles. Some of this research, for example, has addressed the perennial nature versus nurture distinction for traits, with the adaptive humor styles (i.e., self-enhancing and affiliative) showing stronger genetic influences and the maladaptive styles (i.e., self-defeating and aggressive) showing stronger environmental contributions. Other work has shown that the ability to more accurately perceive emotions (one aspect of emotional intelligence), along with other important social skills and competencies such as the ability to strike up a conversation, are much more evident in those individuals displaying higher levels of adaptive humor. Finally, a very recent line of research has examined the impact of using the different humor styles in brief social interactions. Not unexpectedly, the use of aggressive humor had the most detrimental effects on recipients' willingness to remain engaged in a social interaction or seek out further meetings with the individual using that maladaptive humor style. It is interesting that the style of humor used also had an impact on how recipients (who were exposed to that humor) felt about themselves, with adaptive humor leading to more positive and less negative self-evaluations than maladaptive humor.

Nicholas A. Kuiper

See also Depression; Health Benefits of Humor, Psychological; Humor Styles

Further Readings

Cann, A., Zapata, C. L., & Davis, H. (2011). Humor style and relationship satisfaction in dating couples: Perceived versus self-reported humor styles as predictors of satisfaction. *HUMOR: International Journal of Humor Research, 24,* 1–20.

Ibarra-Rovillard, M. S., & Kuiper, N. A. (2011). The effects of humor and depression labels on reactions to social comments. *Scandinavian Journal of Psychology, 52,* 448–456.

Jovanovic, V. (2011). Do humor styles matter in the relationship between personality and subjective well-being? *Scandinavian Journal of Psychology, 52,* 502–507.

Martin, R. (2007). *The psychology of humor: An integrative approach*. New York, NY: Academic Press.

Svebak, S. (2010). The Sense of Humor Questionnaire: Conceptualization and review of 40 years of findings in empirical research. *Europe's Journal of Psychology, 6*(3), 288–310.

Persuasion and Humor

The study of humor and persuasion focuses on how the amusement felt in response to a message influences the attitudes and behaviors of its audience. This overview addresses the use and effects of humor in advertising and other persuasion contexts, articulating the extent of humor's persuasive power, the conditions under which it tends to be effective, the psychological mechanisms that may explain its effects, and more recent contexts of humor and persuasion inquiry.

Humor's Persuasive Influence in Advertising

The use of humor as a persuasive tool in advertising has evolved over the past 100 years, gaining greater favor more recently because of multiple factors, including the more frequent use of emotional appeals generally, changing technologies of message delivery, and the changing tone and content of entertainment media. As such, there has been increasing attention in the academic literature to humor's persuasive effects.

Several early reviews of the humor in advertising literature concluded that no consistent evidence existed to support its persuasive effect. However, a recent meta-analysis, or statistically based review, of the literature supported the following conclusions: First, humor increases attention to advertisements and produces positive affect. Second, despite these effects, humor does not meaningfully impact the positive or negative thoughts audiences have during ad exposure nor does it enhance liking of the message source, as previously thought. Indeed, not only does it not enhance source liking, humor can actually detract from the source's credibility or the audience's views of the source's expertise and trustworthiness. Third, and especially important, humor associates with increases in ad liking, brand liking, and purchase intention—all of which are direct measures of persuasive influence. However, there is no consistent evidence that humor impacts ad recall or purchase behavior, the ultimate goal of commercial advertisements. Thus, humor has the potential to enhance psychological states associated with persuasion—attitudes and intentions specifically—although the lack of behavioral effects suggests tempered enthusiasm for its persuasive benefit.

Conditions of Humor's Persuasive Effect

As with the study of emotions and persuasion generally, a key question is less about whether humor has effect but rather under what conditions it does. Couched largely within the context of cognitive response theories of persuasion, which assume that thoughts during message processing predict persuasive outcomes, studies have identified individual and message variables that moderate humor's influence, including prior attitude, involvement level, need for cognition, argument strength, and source reactions. Research results suggest that humor is effective primarily if one is predisposed to like a product or if one is not motivated to process a message carefully, in which case humor's persuasive impact is likely to be short-lived, according to cognitive response theorizing. In sum, the advertising literature supports humor's capacity to persuade, but its effects are likely more modest than many assume them to be.

Psychological Mechanisms Underlying the Persuasive Effect of Humor

To the extent humor has persuasive influence, scholars have investigated the routes through which these effects emerge, specifically focusing on whether they are affectively or cognitively based. Affect-based arguments suggest humor influences attitudes through the positive feelings evoked. Cognitive-based arguments focus on how humor influences the thoughts generated about the message. In fact, meta-analytic research indicates that although the affective model explains the collection of humor effects quite well, there is strong support for a combined affective-cognitive model. Specifically, evidence suggests that the positive affect generated by humorous advertisements directs cognitive effort to both reduce motivation to counterargue message claims and maintain the positive emotional state. Additionally, the cognitive demands of processing humor itself further detracts from an audience's ability to counterargue claims, thus setting the stage for influence, albeit likely short-lived.

Newer Directions of Humor and Persuasion Research

Recently, the study of humor and persuasion has extended beyond marketing contexts to other domains, specifically political and health communication, which has led to newer theorizing about the extent and process of humor's persuasive influence. This line of inquiry was largely motivated by the emergence of highly popular political satire programs, like *The Daily Show With Jon Stewart,* that have attracted millions of viewers to their humorous and potentially persuasive social commentary. Although empirical findings regarding the persuasive influence of such programming are limited, these and other more novel message forms (e.g., viral videos) have led to a greater appreciation for humor's value in the current media environment. Specifically, scholars have begun to emphasize the critical advantage humor has in attracting attention to persuasive messages, an essential step in the persuasion process. If humor helps garner attention to messages beyond what serious messages might, as is the case in political entertainment, for example, humorous messages enjoy an inherent and substantial persuasive advantage over other message styles. Further, humorous messages are more likely to be socially shared than nonhumorous ones, thus increasing their potential exposure and influence.

Entertainment-based humor and persuasion contexts have also generated new insights into the process and timing of persuasive influence. Specifically, growing evidence supports the idea that humor may generate "sleeper effects," or persuasive effects that emerge after some time from message exposure has passed. To explain this effect, the discounting cue hypothesis has been proposed, suggesting that humor may not have immediate persuasive effect because although audiences attend closely to humorous messages for enjoyment, they discount them as jokes not intended to persuade, thus minimizing the immediate effect of message content on their attitudes. However, given humor generated close message attention and processing, message content is stored cognitively such that it can exert influence on attitudes over time. Of particular interest, this hypothesis suggests humor has the potential for more long-lived persuasive influence than previous models have allowed.

As the potential advantages of humor use have been explored in serious contexts, like health promotion, there is increasing acknowledgment that it can also be counterproductive by appearing to trivialize important issues. Thus, as with all humor and persuasion contexts, the type of humor employed and its integration with message content become particularly important issues to consider as scholars continue to specify the conditions under which humor exerts persuasive influence.

Robin L. Nabi

See also Advertising, Effectiveness of Humor in; Cognitive Aspects; Political Humor; Rhetoric and Rhetorical Devices; Satire News

Further Readings

Eisend, M. (2009). A meta-analysis of humor in advertising. *Journal of the Academy of Marketing Science, 37,* 191–203.

Eisend, M. (2011). How humor in advertising works: A meta-analytic test of alternative models. *Marketing Letters, 22,* 115–132.

Nabi, R. L., Moyer-Guse, E., & Byrne, S. (2007). All joking aside: A serious investigation into the persuasive effect of funny social issue messages. *Communication Monographs, 74,* 29–54.

Weinberger, M. G., & Gulas, C. S. (1992). The impact of humor in advertising: A review. *Journal of Advertising, 21,* 35–59.

Philogelos

Philogelos (The Laughter-Lover) is the only surviving jokebook from antiquity written in ancient Greek. Other traces include the Roman author Fulgentius (5th/6th centuries CE), who mentions *liber facetiarum* (a jokebook) written by Tacitus, but the book's existence is most likely to be fabricated by Fulgentius himself, as was noted by Barry Baldwin. Some scholars see a possible predecessor for the *Philogelos* in a jokebook that may have been produced by a "Group of Sixty," whose members lived in Athens in the time of Demosthenes and Philip the Macedonian. The title of this jokebook is attested in manuscript tradition and its authorship is sometimes ascribed to Hierocles and Philagrius, a grammatician, but whether these were the actual writers is unknown. Nothing else is known about the identities of Hierocles and Philagrius, despite hypotheses by scholars such as Baldwin and Andreas Thierfelder.

Hierocles has been identified as the famous 5th-century Neoplatonist philosopher by that name, but this seems to be a misconception by the *Philogelos*'s 17th-century editor. A grammarian called Philagrius is also virtually unknown (although a sophist Philagrius is mentioned in *Lives of the Sophists* by Philostratus). The Byzantine lexicon *Suda* credits a mime writer, Philistion, with the authorship of the *Philogelos,* describing it as the book that is aimed at or brought to the *koureus*, as suggested by Baldwin. This was interpreted as information that such jokes were common at the barber's (which is what *koureus* may mean) or as a corrupt version of the toponym Kurium. The word *koureus* also was emended, unconvincingly, to Hierocles. A 12th-century scholar, John Tzetzes, mistakenly writes about a book *by* Philogelos, thus confusing author and title. It is thus impossible to tell with absolute certainty who invented the jokes in the *Philogelos* (but wouldn't this be equally true for most jokes throughout the centuries?), although it is plausible that Hierocles and Philagrius were indeed the compilers.

Dating and Origins

Because there is no external information regarding the composition date, scholars have tried to extrapolate the date from internal evidence, although this did not prove completely successful. It is now believed the collection was put together sometime between the 4th and 5th centuries CE. Yet that says nothing about the original date or dates of the jokes themselves, which may have been rearranged linguistically to suit later audiences. Language and cultural realities of various periods (classical times and the imperial period) coexist in *Philogelos.* A later date is suggested by a number of Latinisms and some expressions that are latecomers to the Greek language (such as *kyrios/kyrie,* a later generic form of address, "Mister!"). As Baldwin pointed out, the language is usually a simplified Greek. Some jokes point to specific historical occasions, which can be dated as pre–4th century; for instance, joke number 62 alludes to the games organized in 248 by the Emperor Philip the Arab, and joke number 76 refers to the Serapeum in Alexandria, destroyed in 391. The birthplace and time of the *Philogelos* are simply impossible to ascertain. Some of the jokes also appear in other sources, for example, in Plutarch (nos. 263, 264) and Cicero (no. 193).

Nature of the Collection

The collection consists of 265 jokes (a number of them repeated) arranged according to the characters that are ridiculed. The protagonist of nearly half of them (nos. 1–103) is the *scholastikos*, sometimes translated as "professor" and, perhaps more convincingly, as "egghead" by Baldwin. Then follow the jokes that could be termed "ethnic," since they mock the inhabitants of cities such as Abdera (nos. 110–127), Sidon (nos. 128–139), and Kyme (nos. 154–182). Whereas the reputation for stupidity of citizens of Abdera and Kyme is well attested in other sources, it is not quite clear why the Sidonians earned a place in this collection. There are also jests about doctors (a popular and recurring theme in ancient literature) and people with bad breath, some of them bordering on disgusting (e.g., no. 231: "A man with bad breath decided to kill himself, so he covered his face and was asphyxiated").

In many cases the humor of the joke does not require any knowledge of antiquity to be understood and appreciated. For example, "When buying some windows, a man from Kyme asked if they faced south" (no. 165) is intelligible even if a reader is ignorant of the proverbial stupidity of the citizens of Kyme. In fact, only a limited number of jokes either need a very specialized commentary or are completely incomprehensible. As some scholars have noted, the collected jokes do not contain any moral messages but are based on principles such as absurdity and wordplay. Possibly this explains the longevity of the collection, which in recent years has been celebrated by the media as a direct inspiration for the jokes of Monty Python.

Modern Versions

The first modern translation of the *Philogelos* was into Latin (the *editio princeps* of 1605), followed by German (1618, 1747, 1789, etc.), French, and Modern Greek (both prepared in 1812 by Adamantios Korais, a founder of Modern Greek literature). Twenty-eight jokes, heavily bowdlerized, appeared in English translation in an anonymous article (most likely authored by Samuel Johnson) published in *The Gentleman's Magazine* in 1741 and titled "The Pedants, or Jests of Hierocles."

Przemysław Marciniak

See also Absurdist Humor; Ancient Greek Comedy; Ancient Roman Comedy; Ethnic Jokes; Foolstowns; *Forest of Laughter* and Traditional Chinese Jestbooks; Jest, Jestbooks, and Jesters; Jokes; National and Ethnic Differences; Nonsense; Stereotypes; Targets of Humor; Translation; Verbal Humor

Further Readings

Andreassi, M. (2004). *Le facezie del* Philogelos: *Barzellette antiche e umorismo moderno* [The witty remarks of the *Philogelos*: Antique jokes and modern humor]. Lecce, Italy: Pensa Multimedia Editore.

Baldwin, B. (Ed. & Trans.). (1983). *The* Philogelos *or Laughter-lover*. Amsterdam, Netherlands: Gieben.

Baldwin, B. (1989). John Tzetzes and the *Philogelos*. In B. Baldwin, *Roman and Byzantine papers* (pp. 329–331). Amsterdam, Netherlands: Gieben.

Baldwin, B. (1989). The *Philogelos:* An ancient jokebook. In B. Baldwin, *Roman and Byzantine papers* (pp. 624–637). Amsterdam, Netherlands: Gieben.

Fornaro, S. (2013). Philogelos. *Brill's New Pauly.* Retrieved from http://www.paulyonline.brill.nl/entries/brill-s-new-pauly/philogelos-e920910

Thierfelder, A. (Ed.). (1968). Philogelos: *Der Lachfreund* [*Philogelos:* The friend of laughter]. Munich, Germany: Heimeran.

Philosophy of Humor

The philosophy of anything is both descriptive and evaluative, examining what it is and how it fits into human life. The philosophy of art, for example, considers possible definitions of art and explores the value of art. This entry examines three traditional accounts of humor and its place in human life: the superiority, relief, and incongruity theories. Because the word *humor* did not have its current meaning associated with funniness until the 18th century, in searching for earlier ideas about humor, researchers look for other key words, such as *laughter* and *comedy*.

The Superiority Theory

In Western thought, the earliest documents that describe and evaluate humor were written by Plato in the 4th century BCE. They present laughter and comedy in a predominantly negative light as based on scorn for the people being laughed at. Plato's thinking here seems to have been influenced by Aristophanes's mockery of Plato's teacher, Socrates, in his comedy *The Clouds*. Plato also objected to the way laughing people lose control of their bodies and their mental processes. With that loss of control, he says, our violent urges often emerge and people get hurt. Understanding laughter in this way, Plato saw it as mostly harmful. In the ideal state, he said, comedy should be tightly censored and no one should be allowed to make fun of citizens, leaders, or the gods.

Plato's student Aristotle agreed that laughter puts people down, but he saw some value to wittiness in conversation. Both Plato's and Aristotle's accounts of humor are considered versions of what is now called the superiority theory. In that account, humorous amusement is the enjoyment of feeling superior to other people, or to a former state of ourselves. A classic proponent of the superiority theory was Thomas Hobbes, who said that the feeling expressed in laughter is sudden glory. Like Plato, Hobbes saw laughter as antisocial and often cruel. René Descartes, a contemporary of Hobbes, offered a more complex explanation of laughter as accompanying three of the six basic emotions—(mild) hatred, wonder, love, desire, joy, and sadness—but he gave most of his attention to laughter as an expression of scorn and ridicule.

From the time of Plato to the 18th century, the superiority theory was the dominant way of understanding humor, and so most thinkers who wrote about laughter and comedy evaluated them negatively. Many early Christian thinkers condemned laughter for the same reasons Plato did, as being malicious, involving a loss of control, and leading to violence. They got this idea not only from Greek philosophy but from the Bible, in which there is a strong connection between laughter and aggression. The only way God is represented as laughing in the Bible is with scorn and hostility. The Christian institution that most emphasized self-control—the monastery—had harsh criticisms of laughter, and penalties for monks who laughed during rituals. Similarly, 17th-century Puritans condemned laughter as incompatible with Christian sobriety, and when they took control of England under Oliver Cromwell, they outlawed comedy.

A century after Hobbes and Descartes, Francis Hutcheson wrote a critique of the superiority theory. Feeling superior to other people, he said, is neither necessary nor sufficient for laughter. We may laugh at clever wordplay, for instance, without feeling superior to anyone, and we may feel superior to beggars in the street without laughing at them. To such counterexamples to the superiority theory, we could add more. In the silent movies of a century ago, comic characters like Charlie Chaplin often got laughs by displaying surprising acrobatic skills that the audience lacked. If people in the audience compared themselves at all to Chaplin as they laughed, they did not come out superior. Another counterexample to the superiority theory is our laughter at our current selves, not just earlier stages of ourselves, as, for example, when we look for our glasses for 5 minutes, only to find them on our head.

The Relief Theory

In the 18th century, two new accounts of laughter began to compete with the superiority theory. They are now called the relief theory and the incongruity theory. In neither account are feelings of superiority even mentioned. The relief theory says that laughter functions in the nervous system much as a pressure-relief valve works in a steam boiler—it releases pent-up energy that is not necessary for anything. According to a simple version by Herbert Spencer, nervous energy naturally leads to bodily movement. When we are angry, our nervous energy produces small aggressive movements such as clenching our fists. When we are frightened, we make small movements of self-protection or escape. When those emotions get strong enough, we may hit someone or run away. According to Spencer, laughter also releases nervous energy, but the muscular movements in laughter are not the early stages of larger actions such as attacking or fleeing. The movements of laughter are merely a release of nervous energy.

The nervous energy relieved through laughter, Spencer said, is associated with emotions that are found to be unnecessary. If we are riding a bicycle, for example, and think we are going to fall but then regain safety, our laughter is the release of our pent-up fear. John Dewey had a similar explanation of laughter as the sudden relaxation of stress.

The best known version of the relief theory is that of Sigmund Freud, the father of psychoanalysis. Freud analyzes three laughter situations. He called them "*der Witz*" (often translated "jokes" or "joking"), "the comic," and "humor." The laughter in all three is a release of nervous energy that has become unnecessary. In *der Witz*, the superfluous energy was summoned to repress feelings; in the comic, it is energy summoned to think; and in humor, it is the energy of feeling emotions.

In *der Witz*, Freud says, we express emotions that we ordinarily repress, and the psychic energy released by laughing is energy that would have repressed these emotions. The most commonly repressed emotions, according to Freud, are sexual desire and hostility, so most jokes and witty remarks are sexual, aggressive, or both. In telling such a joke, we bypass our internal censor and give vent to our real feelings, so the psychic energy normally used to do the repressing becomes superfluous and is vented in laughter.

Freud's second laughter situation, the comic, also involves a release of energy summoned but then found unnecessary, but here it is energy for thinking. Freud assumes here that we expend a large amount of energy to understand something large and a small amount of energy to understand something small. Suppose that we are watching the clumsy actions of a circus clown. As we watch him stumble through actions that we would execute smoothly, our mental representation of those clumsy movements calls for more energy than the energy we would expend to mentally represent our own smooth movements in performing the same task. So, Freud says, we "save" the energy we might have spent on understanding the clown's movements, and we vent that surplus energy by laughing.

Freud calls his third laughter situation humor and analyzes it in the way Spencer analyzed laughter in general. We summon nervous energy to feel some emotion, but then we realize that that emotion is inappropriate. So the energy is laughed away. That would explain our laughter as we regain our safety on the bicycle.

Of the three traditional theories of humor, the relief theory has found the least acceptance. Today almost no scholar explains laughter or humor as a release of pent-up nervous energy. Some funny things and situations may evoke emotions, but many do not. If I see a cloud that looks like an elephant, for example, I may laugh without releasing any unnecessary built-up emotional energy. Even when funny stimuli evoke emotions, few thinkers today defend the claims of Spencer and Freud that the laughter is a release of energy summoned to feel or to repress those emotions. The hydraulic model of the nervous system on which the relief theory is based seems outdated.

The Incongruity Theory

Whereas the relief theory did not pose much of a challenge to the superiority theory, the other account of humor that arose in the 18th century, the incongruity theory, did. In this account, the cause of laughter is the perception of something incongruous—something that violates our mental patterns and expectations. In ancient times, Aristotle and Cicero hinted at this idea, although neither developed it. Aristotle said that one way for a speaker to get a laugh from an audience is to create an expectation and then violate it. Cicero said that in jokes we often expect one thing but something else is said. This explanation of joking is similar to that of stand-up comedians today, who speak of the setup and the punch line. The setup is the beginning of the joke that creates the expectation. The punch line is the ending that violates that expectation.

In the 18th and 19th centuries, a number of philosophers worked out versions of the incongruity theory, including James Beattie, Immanuel Kant, Arthur Schopenhauer, and Søren Kierkegaard. In the 20th century, the incongruity theory became the dominant account of laughter and humor in both philosophy and psychology.

The most famous early version of the incongruity theory is that of Kant, who described laughter as an emotion caused by the sudden transformation of an expectation into nothing. The end of a joke, for example, requires listeners to shift to an absurd second meaning for a word or phrase. That frustrates the desire to understand, Kant said, and is not gratifying to the mind, but the jostling of ideas causes a physical jostling of our internal organs that feels good. As a joke evokes, shifts, and then dissipates our thoughts, we do not learn anything or understand anything better, Kant thinks, and so he finds nothing of intellectual worth in jokes or humor generally.

A later version of the incongruity theory, by Schopenhauer, granted it more philosophical significance. For him the incongruity, the lack of fit, in humor is between our sense perceptions of things and our abstract rational knowledge of those same things. Our sense perception is of unique individual things with many properties. But as we subsume our sense perceptions under abstract concepts, we pick out just one or two properties of any individual thing. In doing so, we lump quite different things under a single concept, as when we call both a Chihuahua and a St. Bernard dogs. Humorous amusement occurs, according to Schopenhauer, when we suddenly notice the incongruity, the lack of fit, between a concept and a perception that are supposedly of the same thing.

Creating jokes requires intellectual skill, Schopenhauer says, especially the ability to think of an abstract idea under which very different things can be subsumed. So he gives humor more credit than Kant gave it, just as Aristotle gave it more credit than Plato did. Schopenhauer also finds in humor an intellectual pleasure that Kant denied. Where perceptions clash with abstract thoughts, he says, what is perceived is bound to be right. Perception is the original kind of human knowledge; it is automatic and immediately gratifying. Abstract thought, on the other hand, is secondary knowledge and requires exertion. When the two clash in humor, it is gratifying to have perception validated and abstract thought discredited.

Like Schopenhauer and unlike Kant, Kierkegaard thought of humor as philosophically significant. He locates the essence of humor in a discrepancy between what is expected and what is experienced, although he calls it contradiction rather than incongruity. The violation of expectations is the essence not only of the comic, he says, but of the tragic. In both, some experience contradicts our expectations. The difference is that in the tragic mode, we despair of a way out, whereas in the comic mode, we figure a way out.

In these and later versions of the incongruity theory, the core meaning of *incongruity* is that some thing or some event we perceive or think about violates our mental patterns and expectations. Beyond that core, different thinkers add different details. In psychology, for example, theorists such as Thomas Schultz and Jerry Suls claim that what we enjoy in humor is not incongruity per se, but the *resolution* of incongruity. With children over the age of 6 years, Schultz says, it is not enough to present them with something incongruous in order to amuse them. Something in the humor must fit the apparently anomalous element into some conceptual schema. That is precisely what "getting" a joke is. Schultz is even unwilling to call unresolvable incongruity humor—he calls it nonsense. The examples cited by those who insist on the resolution of incongruity are typically jokes in which a word or phrase has a second meaning that emerges in the punch line. Consider the children's riddle:

Why can't you starve in the desert?
Because of the sand which is there.

Initially, the hearer of this joke is confronted with the incongruity of an absurd explanation: You can't starve in a place that has sand. But then the hearer notices that "sand which is there" sounds like "sandwiches there." That awareness resolves the incongruity and allows the answer to make sense in a certain way: In a place that has sandwiches, you won't starve.

Although this incongruity-resolution theory of humor sounds plausible with many jokes, it does not seem to apply to most nonverbal humor, in which we simply notice something odd and take pleasure in that oddity. Consider the "Nun Bun," a pastry found in a coffee shop in Nashville, Tennessee, in 1996 that resembled Mother Teresa of Calcutta. To find this incongruity funny, it does not seem necessary to resolve it. What, indeed, would resolve it, other than a story about a baker shaping the dough so that it would come out of the oven looking like Mother Teresa? What seems funny here is the odd coincidence itself, not an explanation of that coincidence. And even where humor involves the resolution of incongruity, the pleasure in amusement seems quite different from the pleasure of solving a puzzle.

As philosophers and psychologists carried on debates like this in the late 20th century, one flaw in several older versions of the incongruity theory became obvious. Older theories often said or implied that all that is necessary for humor is the *perception* of incongruity. But, however necessary the perception of incongruity might be for humor, it is clearly not sufficient. When our mental patterns and expectations are violated, we may feel fear, disgust, or anger rather than amusement. To learn that a loved one has unexpectedly died in a plane crash, for example, is incongruous but not funny. One way to correct this flaw is to say that humorous amusement is not just any response to incongruity; it is the *enjoyment* of incongruity. In fear, disgust, and anger, we are upset by the incongruity; in humor, the incongruity delights us.

That refinement helps, but it still seems not specific enough, because there are other ways of enjoying incongruity besides humorous amusement. Indeed, there are at least five aesthetic categories beyond the comic based on enjoying incongruity. In the grotesque, the macabre, the horrible, the bizarre, and the fantastic, our mental patterns and expectations are violated, and we enjoy that violation, but there need be no humorous amusement.

Although there is still no version of the incongruity theory that satisfies everyone, the general approach of the theory seems better able to account for laughter and humor than either the excessively narrow superiority theory or the scientifically obsolete relief theory.

Humor as Mental Play

At the beginning, we noted that when the superiority theory was the only widely accepted understanding of humor, philosophers' evaluations of humor were generally negative. Even though over the past two centuries the incongruity theory has made humor look less objectionable than the superiority theory did, the published opinions of philosophers about humor have not improved much. Part of that continued bad reputation comes from the way the incongruity theory makes humor look irrational. As Kant suggested in his comment that laughter cannot gratify our minds but only our bodies, it seems perverse to enjoy the violation of our mental patterns and expectations. If humor is to be evaluated positively, it seems that we need some explanation of how our higher mental functions can operate in a way that is different from ordinary theoretical and practical reasoning but is beneficial rather than harmful. One way to do that is to analyze humor as a kind of mental play and to explain the benefits of such play. This approach was sketched by Aristotle and by Thomas Aquinas, who spoke of joking as a kind of play and saw this play as relaxation from serious mental exertion. The person who amuses others in conversation, they said, has the virtue of *eutrapelia*, mentally "turning well." Contemporary philosophers such as John Morreall and psychologists have begun to explore the value of such nonserious mental activity, linking humor with stress reduction, friendship, creative thinking, and medical benefits such as the boosting of the immune system. As the reputation of humor improves in the future, we will undoubtedly find more benefits of the playful enjoyment of incongruity.

John Morreall

See also Aesthetics; Christianity; Health Benefits of Humor, Physical; Health Benefits of Humor, Psychological; Humor Theories

Further Readings

Freud, S. (1974). *Jokes and their relation to the unconscious*. New York, NY: Penguin.
Monro, D. H. (1951). *Argument of laughter*. Melbourne, Australia: Melbourne University Press.
Morreall, J. (Ed.). (1987). *The philosophy of laughter and humor*. Albany: State University of New York Press.
Morreall, J. (2009). *Comic relief: A comprehensive philosophy of humor*. Oxford, UK: Wiley-Blackwell.
Schultz, T. (1976). A cognitive-developmental analysis of humor. In T. Chapman & H. Foot (Eds.), *Humor and laughter: Theory, research and applications* (pp. 12–13). New York, NY: Wiley.
Suls, J. (1972). A two-stage model for the appreciation of jokes and cartoons: An information-processing analysis. In J. Goldstein & P. McGhee (Eds.), *The psychology of humor* (pp. 81–99). New York, NY: Academic Press.

Phonological Jokes

The term *phonological joke* describes a type of humor that uses the words or phonemes of one's own language to imitate or parody the sounds of another language. The term originates with Pawel Adrjan and Javier Muñoz-Basols, who characterize phonological jokes as tending to follow a structure characterized by the following:

- A question-answer format, where the prompt makes reference to a particular language or culture
- A punch line composed of a sequence of sounds that attempt to imitate the foreign language mentioned in the question

Let us consider the following example:

How do you say, "I stepped in excrement" in Chinese?
Dung on Mai Shu [Dung on my shoe]

The joke provides a "translation" for the expression "I stepped in excrement" by using monosyllabic English words that imitate the Chinese language. Despite appearing to be genuine Chinese to an English speaker, the answer only has meaning in the language of the joke: English. The Anglophone listener readily recognizes that the expression "Dung on Mai Shu" is a parody of the monosyllabic and tonal features of Chinese but corresponds phonologically to the English words "dung on my shoe."

In the joke's written form, the spelling of two words is modified to create an additional effect of a transcription of Chinese into the Latin alphabet: *My* has been modified to *Mai* and *shoe* to *Shu*.

This signals to the reader that a Chinese-sounding pronunciation of the phrase would be appropriate to capture its humorous intent. Characteristically, when producing a phonological joke, the joke-teller often focuses on verbal aspects of performance, such as adopting a specific accent or intonation. The verbal quality of these jokes thus encapsulates a series of communicative and phonological strategies during their enunciation.

A phonological joke is typically created using formulaic introductions consisting of an interrogative that follows one of these patterns: What do you call X in Y? How do you say X in Y? or What is the name of X from country Z? In using them, the joke-teller seeks to surprise the audience by translating the sequence presented in the question, a task that in many cases appears impossible to accomplish because of the linguistic sequence per se or its meaning, or because the audience knows that the joke-teller does not speak the language chosen. In some cases, phonological jokes can also be found as part of a longer humorous narrative or in the form of stand-alone proper nouns that appear to belong to a particular culture or relate to a specific language. An example can be found in scene 12 of Monty Python's film *Life of Brian* (1979), where a character makes reference to the Latin-sounding names "Naughtius Maximus," "Sillius Soddus," and "Biggus Dickus."

Through interviews with native speakers of various languages, Muñoz-Basols has collected and analyzed samples of phonological jokes in 30 languages, confirming the widespread nature of this phenomenon. Few other studies or publications have explicitly addressed this type of humor. It is mentioned by Gilda Rosa Arguedas Cortés, who describes the structure of phonological jokes generally and provides some examples in Spanish. Mohammad El-Yasin makes reference to this type of humor in a general discussion about the translatability of jokes between Arabic and English. Emil A. Draitser, quoting Abraham Roback's *Dictionary of International Slurs*, also mentions Russian as an example of where this type of humorous sequence can be found, whereby Russian children use words that bear a resemblance to Japanese names and are often scatological.

In addition to harnessing the phonological aspects of language for humorous purposes, phonological jokes also take advantage of the morphology of words. Prefixes, suffixes, and other morphemes (meaningful language units), in many instances, can play a role in the syntactic and the semantic structure of the joke, as in the following example in Polish:

Jak się nazywa najszybszy rosyjski biegacz?
Naskrutow

Translation:

What's the name of the fastest Russian runner?
Shortcutov

This example establishes a parody of features easily identifiable for a Polish speaker as characteristic of the Russian language. The answer to the question about the name of the fastest Russian runner, *Naskrutow*, is a combination of the preposition *na* and the noun *skrót* ("abbreviation" or "shortcut"), which together give the expression *Na skróty*, meaning "through a shortcut." The ending *-ow*, which does not contain any semantic value in Polish, is only added to make the expression create a phonological effect of a Russian name.

In phonological jokes, sounds carry an encoded cultural message and are used deliberately and purposefully as the sine qua non of the joke, as in the following example in Spanish in which onomatopoeia is used:

¿Cómo se dice testigo de Jehová en chino?
¡Ding, dong!

Translation:

What do you call a Jehovah's Witness in Chinese?
Ding, dong!

Here a religious group, Jehovah's Witnesses, is represented in parody form by an onomatopoeic phrase, which at the same time intends to be an imitation of the Chinese language. The punch line in this joke has to do with the way people of this faith are stereotyped as proselytizing by going from house to house.

Phonological jokes are separate from the notion of punning, because the words used to create this type of humor need not have more than one interpretation, whereas in a pun multiple meanings can often be found. Most phonological jokes do not fall under the notion of ethnic humor either, in the sense that their humorous intent does not need to be driven by portraying stereotypical traits of another cultural group. This is demonstrated by the first two examples in this entry, where humor is derived primarily from phonological patterns that contribute to the representation of foreignness, that is, imitating a foreign language or a particular community of speakers based on how it is perceived to sound, rather than any specific ethnic or cultural connotations or judgments. In many cases, phonological jokes constitute a mere play on sounds and are created and told by children.

Phonological jokes are based on culturally bound perceptions developed from the particular standpoint of our own well-developed language systems, influenced by actual and historical language contact between cultures or by exposure to the sounds of other languages through foreign foods, brand names, the mass media, and so forth. They produce a humorous effect by displaying a shared perception, contrasting cultures, and employing a range of phonological and morphological strategies to imitate what a particular foreign language and its community of speakers sound like.

Javier Muñoz-Basols

See also Children's Humor Research; Ethnicity and Humor; Humorous Names; Jokes; Monty Python; Verbal Humor

Further Readings

Adrjan, P., & Muñoz-Basols, J. (2003). The sound of humor: Linguistic and semantic constraints in the translation of phonological jokes. *SKY: Journal of Linguistics, 16,* 239–246.

Arguedas Cortés, G. R. (1996). Análisis lingüístico de chistes del tipo "¿Cómo se dice 99 en chino? Cachi chen" [A linguistic analysis of jokes following the pattern "How do you say 99 in Chinese? Almost one hundred"]. *Revista de filología y lingüística, 22*(1), 129–140.

Draitser, E. A. (1998). *Taking penguins to the movies: Ethnic humor in Russia.* Detroit, MI: Wayne State University Press.

El-Yasin, M. (1997). The translatability of Arabic jokes into English. *Meta, 52*(4), 671–676.

Muñoz-Basols, J. (2012). *The sound of humor: Translation, culture and phonological jokes.* Unpublished doctoral dissertation, Universitat Pompeu Fabra, Barcelona, Spain.

Muñoz-Basols, J., Adrjan, P., & David, M. (2013). Phonological humor as perception and representation of foreignness. In L. Ruiz Gurillo & B. Alvarado Ortega (Eds.), *Irony and humor: From pragmatics to discourse* (pp. 159–188). Amsterdam, Netherlands: John Benjamins.

Roback, A. (1944). *A dictionary of international slurs (ethnophaulisms).* Cambridge, MA: Sci-Art.

Pirandello, Luigi

Luigi Pirandello (1867–1936), winner of the Nobel Prize for literature in 1934, wrote an influential essay, *On Humor,* in 1908. The essay consists of a collection of his lessons at the Istituto Superiore di Magistero in Rome. His first six chapters are a history of humor examined in literary, psychological, and philosophical authors—some quoted, others, such as Henri Bergson and Sigmund Freud, not even acknowledged. The second, more original part develops Pirandello's own personal conception of humor, which, however, owes much to German, French, and Italian thinkers, such as Freud, Bergson, Theodor Lipps, Charles Baudelaire, Alfred Binet, Alberto Cantoni, and Giovanni Marchesini. Although he was born and grew up in Sicily and displayed some typical Sicilian traits (mistrust of others, strong sense of possession, jealousy), his academic education took place first at the university of Rome and then of Bonn, where he became acquainted with modern philosophical thought. Pirandello dedicated *On Humor* to the deceased Mattia Pascal, librarian. The reference was to the protagonist of his novel *The Late Mattia Pascal* (1904), the first humorist in Pirandello's production. By the time he wrote *On Humor,* Pirandello was already well known for his novels and short stories but had not yet written his more popular plays, which brought him international fame.

If we are looking for a precise definition of humor in Pirandello we will be disappointed. He only wrote the essay to secure his job at the Magistero. Like Friedrich Nietzsche, he did not believe in concepts, definitions—labels that falsify a phenomenon by fixing it into an abstraction. Life, in fact, for Pirandello, is flux, movement, change. Thus humor is not a literary or rhetorical choice but an existential one. It is born in the age of the crisis of reason, where all absolute beliefs and axioms have collapsed and where, therefore, there is no more space for systematic thought. Accordingly, Georg Wilhelm Friedrich Hegel's idealism and Benedetto Croce's version of idealist thought, which were extremely influential in Italy, were Pirandello's targets. This was also the age of Freud, who recognized the power of the irrational in human life, and its many victories over reason.

If we substitute humor for the comic, Pirandello agreed with Bergson that the spirit of humor cannot be imprisoned within a definition but must be regarded as a living thing. He thus writes that his essay simply wants to explain the process that takes place in the so-called humorist writers. He distinguishes humor from irony—a rhetorical figure of speech that implies contradiction between what we say and what we want others to understand from what we have said. Humor, instead, is born out of an ontological contradiction: the contradiction between life, which is unstoppable flux, and the forms (concepts, ideals, systems) in which we fix it in order to make sense out of its chaos. But those concepts, ideas, systems, are abstractions that kill life, leaving us with a series of useless corpses. Whereas the traditional artist composes a character or a story in an orderly and harmonious manner, the humorist deconstructs them and exposes their hidden contradictions and incoherence. For Pirandello, therefore, modern writers cannot be anything but humorists. They must dismantle humanity's illusory constructions, the masks everyone creates, and bring out their other faces, their contradictory aspects. In his essay, Pirandello calls Copernicus the first humorist because Copernicus dismantled the proud image man had created of the universe, removing him from the center where he had placed himself for centuries.

After distinguishing humor from irony, Pirandello distinguishes it from the comic, which he calls the "perception of the opposite," or the initial awareness of incongruity. He gives the now famous example of the old lady who makes herself up to appear much younger. Our first reaction on such a sight is laughter. We realize that the old lady is the contrary of what a respectable old lady should be. Yet, if we do not stop at this level and instead let our reflection intervene, we may become aware that the poor lady might not have liked at all to make herself up as a young woman, but she did it in the desperate hope to keep alive the interest of her younger husband. At this point we can no longer laugh, or at least our laughter would be tempered by pity, and the "perception of the opposite" changes into the "feeling of the opposite." We feel compassion. Humor is this feeling of the opposite.

In Pirandello's large artistic production (plays, novels, essays, poems, and hundreds of short stories), there are many humorist characters, or *raisonneurs*. Their function is unmasking the other characters who live with the illusion that the way they appear to the world is the way they actually are. In Pirandello's play *It Is So (If You Think So)*, Lamberto Laudisi is the humorist philosopher who spends his time proving to a curious, gossiping crowd that the way we see ourselves is different from the way others see us. Henry IV, in the homonymous play, is a perfect example of imprisonment in a mask. He wants, in fact, to continue to live within the mask of the emperor Henry IV and in order to do this, he constructs his immutable reality outside time, blotting out the flux of life. Thus he is condemned never to return to the present. In Pirandello's novel *One, No One and One Hundred Thousand,* Vitangelo Moscarda, unable to recognize himself in all the masks or images that his wife and the town people have made of him, proceeds to destroy them one by one in the frustrated hope to get to his real self. The conclusion is its total annihilation.

Pirandello's concept of humor has mirrored and in part shaped Italian culture up to the present. This can be seen clearly in the cinematic production of directors such as Federico Fellini, Mario Monicelli, Dino Risi, and Nanni Moretti, to mention only a few, in the film genre called *commedia all'italiana* (comedy Italian style). Moreover and perhaps more important, its influence is felt in the importance Italians give appearances, in their need to impress others through the way they dress or speak—their anxiety to cover up their cultural and historical insecurities under attractive masks.

Daniela Bini

See also Bergson's Theory of the Comic; Freudian/Psychoanalytic Theory; History of Humor: Modern and Contemporary Europe; Irony; Literature

Further Readings

Bini, D. (1991). Pirandello's philosophy and philosophers. In J. L. DiGaetani (Ed.), *A companion to Pirandello studies* (pp. 17–46). Westport, CT: Greenwood Press.

Casella, P. (2008). *L'umorismo* and female portraits: Between theory and fiction. *PSA: Journal of Pirandello Society of America, 21,* 31–43.

Dashwood, J. (Ed.). (1996). *Luigi Pirandello: The theater of paradox.* New York, NY: Edwin Mellen Press.

Gieri, M. (1995). *Contemporary Italian filmmaking: Strategies of subversion: Pirandello, Fellini, Scola, and the directors of the new generation.* Toronto, Ontario, Canada: University of Toronto Press.

Marcus, M. (2000). "Me lo dici Babbo che gioco è?" The serious humor of *La vita è bella. Italica, 77*(2), 153–170.

Mariani, U. (2008). The ethical essence of "umorismo." *PSA: Journal of the Pirandello Society of America, 21,* 31–43.
Pirandello, L. (1974). *On humor* (A. Illiano & D. P. Testa, Trans.). Chapel Hill: University of North Carolina Press.
Pirandello, L. (1987). *The late Mattia Pascal* (W. Weaver, Trans.). Hygiene, CO: Eridanos Press.
Pirandello, L. (1990). *One, no one and one hundred thousand* (W. Weaver, Trans.). Boston, MA: Eridanos Press.
Syrimis, M. (2008). From Nestoroff to Garbo: Pirandellian humour in its cinematic vernacular. *Quaderni d'italianistica, 29*(2), 9–52.
Syrimis, M. (2008). The humoristic lens on Pirandello's *Si gira. PSA: Journal of the Pirandello Society of America, 21,* 45–63.

Platonic Theory of Humor

Greek philosopher Plato is the first scholar known to have taken a theoretical interest in humor. However, this interest was motivated not by a concern with humor as such but with its place in intellectual and public life. This motivation must be kept in mind to better understand Plato's views on humor itself.

Plato was critical of humor in the performing arts, arguing that it encouraged unfounded attitudes in audiences (*The Republic*, Book 10). For example, Plato criticized the comic playwright Aristophanes (*Apology*, 18d, 19c) for satirizing Plato's mentor, Socrates. In Plato's view, this caricature of Socrates misinformed the attitudes of Athenians toward the real man. This caricature contributed to Socrates's later conviction on trumped-up charges of impiety, for which Socrates was then executed.

In general, Plato deplored the comedic stereotype of philosophers as conceptual speculators laughably detached from reality. He notes the story of the philosopher Thales, who fell into a ditch while walking outdoors to observe the stars (*Theatetus*, 174a–175b). A Thracian slave woman laughed at the great philosopher for his farcical tumble. The stereotype of the clumsy wise man was sometimes brought out in public debates to ridicule philosophers, as a kind of illogical, ad hominem response to rational, philosophical arguments. In brief, Plato saw such humor as a regrettable source of unreason.

In spite of these points, Plato's view of humor was not entirely negative. He argues, for example, that it is acceptable for philosophers to be amused at the intellectual failings of those who ridicule them. For example, people who claim to know what justice is frequently turn out to be hopelessly confused when their ideas are closely examined (*Theatetus*, 175c–175d). In contrast to the clumsy wiseman stereotype, then, it is such pseudo-intellectuals who are truly ridiculous for their farcical tumbles into confusion when fundamental concepts are debated.

Not coincidently, Plato's view of humor is colored by his admiration for Socrates. In his writings, Plato depicts Socrates as a man who was amused at the confusion that he found in people who engaged him in discourse. This amusement evidently annoyed many who debated with Socrates. However, Plato is careful to portray Socrates as someone who did not indulge in ridicule. Indeed, Socrates laughs only once, and only slightly, in the entire Platonic corpus (*Phaedo*, 115c–115e).

Plato's theorizing about humor can be understood as a way of making sense of these negative and positive aspects of humor. First, Plato treats the *feelings* that people experience when they laugh at something. Plato states that ridiculous things evoke a mixture of opposed feelings: the pain of malice felt toward the object of ridicule as well as the pleasure of laughing at that object (*Philebus*, 47c–47d). In this respect, Plato's account of humor anticipates the modern ambivalence theory. It also jibes with his view of humor as irrational, since Plato regards such mixtures of feelings as destructive of reason.

Second, Plato treats the *conceptual* side of humor. Plato notes that humor tends to involve a juxtaposition of incompatible ideas or representations. For example, incompetent musicians might set masculine lyrics to feminine tunes, resulting in ludicrous music (*Laws*, 2.669b–2.670c). Here, Plato anticipates the modern incongruity theory of humor, on which humor comprises a juxtaposition of conceptually incongruous things. This observation also reveals a positive aspect of humor as a means of flagging confused ideas.

Beyond the basic psychology of humor, Plato was concerned about its deployment in the arts and philosophy. As noted earlier, poets and speakers deployed ridicule as an easy means of attack. This tactic is embodied by the advice of rhetorician Gorgias that it is good to confound your opponents' seriousness with playfulness and their playfulness with seriousness (Aristotle, *Rhetoric,* 1419b7). In other words, in a debate, being humorous is an effective means of opposing someone who is being serious. Perhaps it is this view of humor as a weapon that Plato has in mind when he says that humor involves a kind of triumph over someone who is the butt of ridicule (*Philebus,* 49b). Here, Plato anticipated the modern superiority theory and the aggression theory of humor.

Of course, the example of Socrates suggests that humor is not merely a source of put-downs. The salutary use of humor is embodied in what may have been an aphorism in Plato's time, that "sometimes playfulness is a relief from seriousness" (*Philebus,* 30e). Socrates uses this expression to characterize a discussion in which he has been obliged to provide a circuitous explanation of an idea that he probably thought was straightforward. Here, *playfulness* refers to the childlike enjoyment of games, fun, or amusements that accompany and facilitate learning. Playful humor involves not knocking people down as opponents but cajoling them along into being receptive to new ideas, a practice appropriate for a philosopher. In this respect, Plato anticipated modern ideas about humor and well-being, although his focus is on *intellectual* well-being.

Although Plato did not theorize at length about humor, he did have a nuanced understanding of the subject. In many ways, his ideas about humor anticipate modern theories. However, Plato's ideas are best understood in their original context, that is, in his concern for the role of humor in intellectual and public life. This concern is one that remains valid for scholars of humor today.

Cameron Shelley

See also Ancient Greek Comedy; Humor Theories; Linguistic Theories of Humor; Philosophy of Humor; Psychology

Further Readings

Attardo, S. (1994). *Linguistic theories of humor.* Berlin, Germany: Mouton de Gruyter.

Keith-Spiegel, P. (1972). Early conceptions of humor: Varieties and issues. In J. H. Goldstein & P. E. McGhee (Eds.), *The psychology of humor: Theoretical perspectives and empirical issues.* New York, NY: Academic Press.

Morreall, J. (1983). *Taking laughter seriously.* Albany: State University of New York Press.

Piddington, R. (1963). *The psychology of laughter: A study in social adaptation.* New York, NY: Gamut Press.

Robinson, V. (1983). Humor and health. In P. E. McGhee & J. H. Goldstein (Eds.), *Handbook of humor research* (Vol. 2). New York, NY: Springer Verlag.

Shelley, C. (2003). Plato on the psychology of humor. *HUMOR: International Journal of Humor Research, 16*(4), 351–367.

Plautus

As is generally the case for Roman comedy, humor in the work of Plautus (d. 184 BCE) is generated by the theatrical spectacle, innovative treatment of the stereotypical plots and characters inherited from Greek New Comedy, opportunities for metacomedy, and the tensions inhering in the Roman family. Plautine verbal humor, however, stands out in the Roman tradition for its exuberance. This entry focuses on some of the characteristic marks of Plautine verbal fanfare.

Neologisms

Plautus is extraordinarily creative in comic word formations, especially significant names. Whereas Greek New Comedy employed stock names for its characters, Plautus, preferring Greek to Latin roots, amped up his source plays' character names, as was proved by the 1968 papyrus discovery of a section of Menander's *Double Deceiver,* Plautus's source play for *Two Bacchises.* In the Plautine adaptation, the stereotypically named slave Syrus becomes Chrysalus (Greek for "golden one"), a transformation that allows for various bilingual puns (e.g., "This golden [Latin *aurarium*] matter is my concern" (spoken by Chrysalus at 229) and this metacomic declaration: "I don't care for those . . . Syruses who rob their masters of small change" (649–650). Soldiers' names are especially creative, for example, Polymachaeroplagides ("son of many dagger blows," *Pseudolus,* 988), Bumbomachides-Clytomestoridysarchides ("son of roaring noise fighter-son of famous advisor ruling badly," *Miles Gloriosus,* 14); so, too, prostitutes' names, for example, Gymnasium ("nude exercise facility," *Casket Comedy*), Palaestra ("wrestling school," *Rope*). A fictitious wealthy man is improbably named *Thensaurochrysonicochrysides* ("golden son of treasures of gold," *Captives,* 285). Other types of neologisms can be found on almost any page of Plautus, including purely Latin ones such as *dentifrangibula* ("tooth-crackers" = "fists," *Two Bacchises,* 596), *Suauisauiatio* ("Erotikissia," a comic deity, *Two Bacchises,* 116), and portmanteau coinages such as *lumbifragium* ("prickwreck," based on *naufragium,* "shipwreck," *Amphitryon,* 454). These examples collectively show that audience members in Rome were assumed to know some Greek, ranging from the demotic (there is low-level code-switching at *Pseudolus,* 481–488) to extensive knowledge of Greek language, literature, and culture.

Wordplay

Instances of wordplay in the work of Plautus include many examples of parechesis (echoing of etymologically distinct words), for example, *Epidicus,* 119: "I'd prefer friends of that sort to be overwhelmed in a furnace (*forno*) rather than in the forum (*foro*)" (i.e., "burned rather than bankrupt") and mondegreens, for example, *Truculentus,* 262: Astaphium "Such anger (*eiram*)! Put a plug in it!" Truclentus "What's that about plugging [the verb *comprimere,* "control," can have a sexual sense]? You want me to bang her [he mishears *eram,* "mistress," for *eiram*]?" Puns requiring some knowledge of Greek are pervasive and range from simple hybrids such as Epidamnus, a real place that is dubbed "Loserville" (construed as the Greek preposition *epi* "for" + Latin *damnum* "financial loss," *Menaechami,* 263–264]. The name of the clever prostitute in *Truculentus,* Phronesium, perhaps recalled both the Greek word for "wisdom" (*phronesis*) and a diminutive of Phryne, a notorious courtesan of 4th-century Athens.

Typological Jokes

Several types of jokes are often found in Plautus's work. These include refrains (jokes turning on the repetition of words), for examples at *Rudens* 1212, the slave Trachalio responds to the commands of Daemones with the word *licet* ("okay") 13 times until, while departing, he gives Daemones an order. Daemones then expostulates to the audience: "OKAY! (*licet*) / And I hope Hercules renders him *un-okay* (*infelicet*) for all his *okay-itude* [imparting a new meaning to *licentia* ("lack of control"), 1224–1226]. Also common are parapraxes ("Freudian slips," often combined with epanorthosis ("correction," i.e., "I meant to say . . ."), for example, the aged lover Lysidamus's slipups at *Casina,* 365–367, 672–674, 701–703, wherein he reveals his plot to sleep with the 16-year-old girl whom he has arranged for his farm manager to marry. There are also *para prosdokian* (jokes ending in unexpected twists), for example, *Truclulentus,* 887: "Oh, I do love that soldier more than I do myself—while I get what I want from him" (spoken by the mercenary prostitute). There are legal jokes (i.e., jokes turning on technical points of Roman law); for example, as Mercury bullies the slave (Sosia) he impersonates in *Amphitryon,* he asks "Who owns you?" to which the overwhelmed Sosia responds, "You do. Your fists have claimed me by right of occupation" (375) [a reference to *usucapio* ("squatter's right")]. There are mythological jokes (dissonant comparisons between mythic and comic figures), as when at *Two Bacchises* 925 the triumphant slave Chrysalus declares himself both Odysseus, master planner in the Trojan war (940), and Agamemnon, the Greeks' commander-in-chief (947). Finally, there are jokes of identification, or those proposing incongruous equivalencies between persons and/or things), for example, *Epidicus,* 188–189: "I'll turn myself into a leech and suck the blood / Of those renowned pillars of the senate."

Engaging Contemporary Rome

But there is more than verbal fireworks in Plautus, whose comedies betray an anarchic and carnivalesque spirit. Recent scholarship has demonstrated that Plautus was more engaged with contemporary politics and society than has been assumed. For example, Plautus's heyday corresponds with a period of enormous cultural transformation brought about by unprecedented military expansionism, in which Roman generals aggressively competed for public acclaim and the right to celebrate a triumph, the ultimate achievement in elite culture. Roman comedy inherited the stock figure of the braggart soldier, but characters such as the egotistical Pyrgopolynices in *Miles Gloriosus* must have resonated with Roman audiences as grotesque parodies of celebrity-seeking aristocratic generals. And when Plautine clever slaves appropriate the language and ideology of military conquest to celebrate their successful ruses, sometimes even claiming, as Pseudolus (581), that their victory is owed to the valor of their ancestors (Roman slaves by a legal fiction had no parents), it is hard not to see satire. Chrysalus in *Two Bacchises* declares his campaign of trickery against his master a complete success (1069–1071), but demurs from celebrating a Roman-style triumph: "Don't be surprised, spectators, / That I'm not holding a triumph: I don't care for that, they're too common" (1072–1073). Plautus's satirical engagement with contemporary society can be much more subtle, and much scholarly work remains to be done in this area. So, too, the fact that the humor of several Plautine plays rests on ontological confusions brought about by the presence of doubles is surely significant in a period marked by cultural revolution and the formation of identity.

David M. Christenson

See also Ancient Greek Comedy; Ancient Roman Comedy; Comedy; Farce; Genres and Styles of Comedy; History of Humor: Renaissance Europe; Humorous Names; Inversion, Topsy-Turvy; Low Comedy; Masks; Menander; Puns; Rhetoric and Rhetorical Devices; Roman Visual Humor; Stereotypes; Verbal Humor

Further Readings

Fontaine, M. (2010). *Funny words in Plautine comedy.* Oxford, UK: Oxford University Press.

Leigh, M. (2005). *Comedy and the rise of Rome.* Oxford, UK: Oxford University Press.

McCarthy, K. (2000). *Slaves, masters, and the art of authority in Plautine comedy.* Princeton, NJ: Princeton University Press.

Moore, T. (1998). *The theater of Plautus.* Austin: University of Texas Press.

Slater, N. (2000). *Plautus in performance.* London, UK: Routledge.

Play and Humor

Play is difficult to define, as it has multiple meanings. It can be useful to think of it as a spirit that encompasses theatrical presentation as improvisation, motion, and an ethos of action. "It is a mood, an activity, an eruption, of liberty," Richard Schechner (2002, p. 79) explains. But it is also paradoxical. Sometimes, play takes the shape of a formal commercial or competitive activity one participates in or enjoys; examples include a tennis match at the U.S. Open or an off-Broadway show. In its less formal incarnations, play can involve a pick-up soccer game in the park, or occur at social gatherings, in playgrounds, sidewalks, or streets. Yet, from time to time, it departs from the mundane, and through the use of subversive humor, expands into a status quo–threatening endeavor. After describing several conceptualizations of play, this entry examines the role of play and subversive humor in social movements and discusses other advantages of play.

Conceptualizations

Although there are countless ways to conceptualize the term *play*, it is useful to begin with Johan Huizinga's 1938 work *Homo Ludens: A Study of the Play Element in Culture*. His definition encompasses many of the threads already discussed:

> Summing up the formal characteristics of play we might call it a free activity standing quite consciously outside the ordinary life as being "not serious," but at the same time absorbing the player intensely and utterly. It is an activity connected with no material interest, and no profit can be gained by it. It proceeds within its own proper boundaries of time and space according to fixed rules and in an orderly manner. It promises the formation of social groupings which tend to surround themselves with secrecy and to stress their difference from the common world by disguise or other means. (Huizinga, 1938/1950, p. 13)

Huizinga goes on to suggest it is accompanied by a "feeling of tension, joy and consciousness that it is different from ordinary life" (p. 28).

There are many forms of play. For Huizinga, play is anything but serious: It is a space for joy. For Schechner, play involves doing something that is not exactly "real." It is looser; it is "double edged, ambiguous, moving in several directions simultaneously" (Schechner, 2002, p. 79). The *Oxford English Dictionary* lists pages and pages of definitions and meanings for play as both a noun and a verb. As a verb, it is used to describe the state of being "busily engaged," to "leap for joy, rejoice." It involves "living being[s]" that "move about swiftly with a lively, irregular, or capricious motion, spring, sly, or dart to and fro, gambol, frisk, or flutter." As a noun, play is understood as an "active bodily exercise, brisk and vigorous action of the body or limbs in fencing, dancing, or leaping." It can be thought of as "an action, activity, operation, working, esp[ecially] with rapid movement or change, or variety."

The verb *to play* is the operative function for expressions related to games. The multiple meanings of *play* help reimagine what is real, argues sociologist Peter Nardi. The term's uses encompass dramatic gestures, street theatrics, subversive forms of humor, and various other modes of communication and meaning creation. Play is best understood along a continuum from its meanings as a noun (a performance/means of communication) toward those as a verb (as a liberatory, sometimes subversive, form of action; a resource for group support).

In this respect then, play is considered in the context of social movement activity encompassing a range of affects and outcomes, including experimentation, social eros, liberation, and healthy exchange. It can be both affective and instructive.

Play and Social Movements

Play can also be thought of as a theatrical presentation. This performative spirit may support social movements in countless ways. Play and performance borrow from the clowning tradition of radical ridicule to minimize the legitimacy of political opponents. Although some forms of political performance may not feel inherently playful, the struggle to create a space for this performance has to do with creating a space for play. In this sense, notions of serious play function as cornerstones of a struggle for public space and pluralistic democratic engagement.

Many protests, from the 1960s to the new millennium, include some form of subversive humor, play, or carnival. For Barbara Ehrenreich, such forms of "collective joy" are essential components of social movement practice. "People must find, in their movement, the immediate joy of solidarity, if only because, in the face of overwhelming state or corporate power, solidarity is their sole source of strength" (Ehrenreich, 2007, p. 259). Most organizers recognize that such activities offer a useful complement to an ongoing organizing campaign. They add a little flavor to a sometimes bland stew of movement tactics. Without them, such efforts tend to lose steam or people's attention. Still, some remain critical of mixing play and activism. Yet, increasingly, activists and scholars take issue with this line of logic. Despite the contention that such activities are counterproductive, movements continue to put the right to party on the table as a part of a larger process of social change; the logic being that humor and pleasure disrupt monotony while disarming systems of power. They are also a lot of fun.

Examples abound. Bogad talks about how the Dutch Provos illegally distributed blank leaflets as they declared, "Write Your Own Manifestos" in 1966. Queer youth formed a Rockette kick-line and sang, "We are the Stonewall Girls," as they thwarted riot cops during the Stonewall Riots of June 1969. Members of ACT UP (AIDS Coalition to Unleash Power) taunted white-gloved police officers with the jeer, "Your gloves don't match your shoes, we'll see you in the news!" as they were arrested at the Food and Drug Administration in 1988 while fighting for access to lifesaving AIDS drugs.

Anarchists catapulted teddy bears over a fence mocking tear gas–wielding police during the Free Trade of the Americas actions of April 2001 in Quebec, Canada. Anti-war protesters performed the hokey-pokey amid riots and Red Alerts in New York City during the largest anti-war protest in world history on February 15, 2003. Salsa tunes emanated through the air as nearly one million people converged in downtown Los Angeles for an immigrant rights rally in the spring of 2006. These are just a few examples from many. In recent years, the streets of cities around the world have been filled with any number of examples of theatrical protest. In a nutshell, people are playing. Joyous humor is a singular part of this effort.

Elements of fun, improvisation, and subversive wit are cornerstones of such moments. With different meanings for differing situations, *play* is a simple term for drag, ACT UP zaps, pranks, the use of food and mariachi bands in the Latino community, dance dramaturgy, culture jamming, the carnival, and other creative community-building activities. It is the exhilarating feeling of pleasure, the joy of building a more emancipatory, caring world.

Much of the contemporary ludic spirit of movement practices date back to Dada, surrealism, situationism, ACT UP, and the global justice movement. Countless groups and movements have explored the relation among humor, play, fantasy, and possibility, tying a sense of the practice to their own contexts.

Building on the legacies of civil rights activists who danced in the face of Jim Crow–era social controls, this tradition begins with the ludic campaigns of the Yippies, who made use of the prank as a means of political protest, in contrast with the street actions of the Young Lords. From here, it traces the work of ACT UP, which made arts, design, and a defense of pleasure cornerstones of its struggle against oblivion. By the 1990s, do-it-yourself (DIY) agitational groups sought to break down the lines between art and life and introduce play and pleasure, creativity and fantasy into activism (Duncombe, 2007; Jordan, 1998). With events such as Critical Mass, festive bicyclists created protests as amoeba-like bike cavalcades. In New York City, community garden activists created their own Central Park within the rubble of neighborhood vacant lots, and DJs transformed bland streets into spaces for dance, protest, and community building. For many in movements, play is seen as an appropriate response to the lunacy of wars stretching from World War I to Vietnam to the recent involvement with Iraq.

Some of these campaigns make use of play as a prefigurative approach that seeks to create a community in an image of the world in which activists hope to live. Others use creativity to achieve policy victories. What links these questions and gestures is a recognition of the multiple possibilities of the free activity understood as play.

Henry Bial (2004) said that "play may involve an erosion or inversion of social status" (p. 115) such as with the Trinidad Carnival, Boxing Day, or other role reversal holidays. For this reason, authorities often seek to close spaces where improvised play takes place. Recent events resulting in police crackdowns include Critical Mass bike rides and permitted immigrant rights marches populated by women and children. In recent years, even traditionally spontaneous gatherings, such as the transcendent New Orleans funeral marches, drum circles, and dance parties, have been controlled and even outlawed. To the extent that such play spaces invert social hierarchies, they take on a subversive dimension. Over and over again, play supports a subversive use of public space.

Other Advantages of Play

At its core, play offers us a space to experiment within a space in between material and imaginary spaces, offering a space for transition between the two. Children and adults alike create, mold, and engage with the limits of what is real and what is make-believe. This is a space that is not real but is utterly engaging, as Huizinga reminds us. Children grow through this activity. They learn from play experiments; problem solving and active imagination become part of an engaged mind. As the surrealists have long suggested, play is a space to walk on the edge between reality and possibility, within a space between work and leisure; it is a fantastical space. Yet, it is harder for adults to really play.

Supporters of play suggest there is nothing wrong with people occasionally just enjoying themselves or acting like children (Shepard, 2011). The nonpurposeful aspects of play are many, especially for children, but also for adults. Here, we find a space for activities that extend beyond the means of necessity to another way of living, being, creating, and experimenting with living. Play helps open new ways of looking at the world. It is a free activity, involving hands, stories, moving back and forth between reality and fantasy, experiment, and frivolity. Without this space for refreshing and engaging creative energies, many find it difficult to cope with the harder tasks of life (Wenner, 2009). Batteries recharged, actors are ready to re-engage. Play inspires innovation in any number of ways. It also inspires laughter, which is useful in and of itself. From here, bodies and minds become just a little bit more free, if even for a moment in time.

Benjamin Shepard

See also Carnival and Festival; Carnivalesque; Comic World; Feast of Fools; Inversion, Topsy-Turvy; Political Humor; Subversive Humor

Further Readings

Bial, H. (2004). *The performance studies reader.* New York, NY: Routledge.

Bogad, L. M. (2005). *Electoral guerrilla theatre: Radical ridicule and social movements.* New York, NY: Routledge.

Duncombe, S. (2007). *Dream: Re-imagining progressive politics in an age of fantasy.* New York, NY: New Press.

Ehrenreich, B. (2007). *Dancing in the streets: A history of collective joy.* New York, NY: Metropolitan Books.

Huizinga, J. (1950). *Homo ludens: A study of the play element in culture.* Boston, MA: Beacon Press. (Original work published 1938)

Jordan, J. (1998). The art of necessity: The subversive imagination of anti-road protest and Reclaim the Streets. In G. McKay (Ed.), *DIY culture: Party and protest in nineties Britain* (pp. 129–151). London, UK: Verso.

Nardi, P. (2006). Sociology at play, or truth in the pleasant disguise of illusion. *Sociological Perspectives, 49*(3), 285–295.

Sanders, B. (1996). *Sudden glory: Laughter as subversive history.* Boston, MA: Beacon Press.

Schechner, R. (2002). *Performance studies: An introduction.* New York, NY: Routledge.

Shepard, B. (2011). *Play, creativity and social movements.* New York, NY: Routledge.

Wenner, M. (2009, January 28). The serious need for play. *Scientific American.* Retrieved from http://www.sciam.com/article.cfm?id=the-serious-need-for-play

Poetry

The connection between humor and poetry is a long and storied one. Notwithstanding the common assumption that poetry is largely an expression of personal angst, today there are thousands of practicing poets producing poems that, while exploring such age-old topics as love and death, do so with comic techniques ranging from sly wit to pie-in-the-face slapstick.

Yet, as transcripts of oral performances from preliterate peoples show, poets from every culture have used humor since the first days of human history, and every period since then has seen rich expression that is, at the same time, both poetic and humorous. In fact, the earliest instances of humor in human culture may have more to do with tribal cohesion than anything else.

Humor in poetry is as old as the earliest poems themselves. In *Beowulf,* for example, one character praises another but qualifies his praise by pointing out that the fellow is the biggest hero in *that* place on *that* day; as critics have observed, this is a little like saying "She was the most beautiful woman on *that* bar stool on *that* night."

Then again, poetry and humor are a natural fit for each other. A similarity between poems and jokes is that people appreciate them on a level that is difficult, or perhaps impossible, to fake. When everyone but you appreciates a poem or understands a joke, you can't claim that it is subjective or doesn't make sense, since you are the only one having difficulty.

So jokes and poems both assume that some assembly is required; fresh from the box, each is incomplete, and each requires the listener or reader to supply material necessary to the product's performance. But jokes and poems share more than a basic structure. They share common themes, for example; humorists, too, write primarily about love, death, religion, politics, and sex. Yet the most important similarity between jokes and poems is that both create connections: between text and audience ("That's a good one!"), artist and audience ("Have any more like that?"), one audience member and another ("Wait'll you hear this!").

Not everyone thinks there is a place for humor in poetry. In recent years, the Poetry Foundation has awarded the Mark Twain Poetry Award of $25,000, which recognizes a poet's contributions to humor in American poetry. In the foundation's language, "The Award is given in the belief that humorous poetry can also be seriously good poetry and in the hope that American poetry will in time produce its own Mark Twain." This seems like an idea hardly anyone would object to, but a number of poets went on record with their distrust. The foundation's officers "seem to be aiming low," in the words of J. D. McClatchy, a poet and editor of the *Yale Review*. "They want their initiatives to be popular and populist." Yet some of the greatest authors are "low," "popular and populist"; William Shakespeare, Mark Twain, Charles Dickens, and Walt Whitman didn't go to college and never took a writing workshop of the kind taken and taught by the prominent American poet and his ilk. Perhaps not coincidentally, theirs is some of the most laughter-filled work as well.

Friedrich Nietzsche described a witticism as an "epitaph on the death of a feeling," and therein lies both the truth of and the problem with humor. Take the problem first: If a joke is just a bandage on a bruised psyche, then humor is trivial, because it masks what's really important. No wonder funny people can't be trusted if they're covering something up. But if a joke can lead to a feeling, especially a serious one, then what could be more significant?

As an illustration, consider one of the largest categories of jokes, those on marriage. The number and variety of jokes on the wedded state suggest just how seriously marriage is taken in our culture. A classic example is Henny Youngman's "Take my wife—please!" This joke is not going to work unless the audience gets the hostility at its base, but it will also flop if the audience doesn't see the affection there as well; no man would make a joke like this about a wife he didn't love, and no wife would permit it unless she loved him, too.

Yet the statement "I adore my wife" has as much entertainment value as "I hate the shrew." To work, both ideas have to come together in a single phrase. When two people stand before a duly appointed official and say "I do," they are entering half-consciously into a complex and mutually agreed-upon surrendering of much of their individual freedom so they can enjoy a higher kind obtainable only through an often heady, sometimes infuriating (or the other way around) union that has emotional, psychological, intellectual, religious, historical, legal, and financial dimensions.

And all that in four little words. How does Henny Youngman do it? German theorist Wolfgang Iser said that all great texts have a "fundamental asymmetry," by which he means the writer deliberately leaves gaps for the reader to fill. The same is true for a joke: no one listening to Henny Youngman says, "Oh, I get it: the verb 'take' means both 'consider' as well as 'relieve someone of,' and therefore Henny is inviting me to both think about his wife and also help him get rid of her. A double meaning! What do you know."

Like jokes, poems, too, create connections. But are both equally cerebral? Yes: humor and brains have been associated throughout history. Where both humor and poetry fail is in the realm of the literal minded; perhaps this is what the Duchess of Orléans meant when she noted approvingly of Gottfried Wilhelm von Leibniz that "it is so rare for an intellectual to dress properly, not to smell, and to understand jokes." By the same token, humor is antithetical to snobbery and self-centeredness. The French novelist Marc Levy says that "humor and ego fight to occupy the same place in the brain." A poem about how smart one is is egotistical; a funny poem is generous.

This has been the case throughout literary history. Geoffrey Chaucer is uproarious (consider the ribald "The Miller's Tale," for example) as is Shakespeare, Jonathan Swift, Lord Byron, Robert Browning, and Emily Dickinson. In an interview in *The Paris Review*, in which he argued that much of modern poetry lacks humor, former U.S. poet laureate Billy Collins said,

> The romantic poets drove sex and humor out of poetry. If you look before 1798 you find plenty of sex and humor. Just look at "The Rape of the Lock," or Chaucer, for that matter. They don't call Shakespeare's comedies *comedies* for nothing. But [William] Wordsworth and [Samuel Taylor] Coleridge drove those two things out of poetry—humor was consigned to the subcategory of light verse.

Collins's work shows the effectiveness of humor used in contrast with bleakness. "The Lanyard," for example, gains comedic power with its imagining of a rueful conversation between a mother who has done everything for the son who can only repay her with a handmade trinket.

> Here are thousands of meals, she said,
> and here is clothing and a good education.
> And here is your lanyard, I replied,
> which I made with a little help from a counselor.
> Here is a breathing body and a beating heart,
> strong legs, bones and teeth,
> and two clear eyes to read the world, she whispered,
> and here, I said, is the lanyard I made at camp.
> (Collins, 2005, pp. 45–46)

With his use of humor, Billy Collins has reinvented the American poem. The short lyric that most poets write today, the one that dramatizes the relation between the self and the world, begins with Ralph Waldo Emerson, although it was perfected by Emily Dickinson and even reached a kind of peak with her, a zenith that most poets cannot touch, even now. So what lyric poets have done ever since is renovate that basic structure. For example, William Carlos Williams and Elizabeth Bishop update the form by substituting deceptively plain speech for the ornate language that we associate with poetry. And certainly the confessional poets, such as Robert Lowell and Sylvia Plath, sensationalized lyric poetry by using it to air their alcoholic excesses, sexual misbehavior, and so on.

But whereas the poets named so far show us a picture of the self, Billy Collins shows us a mirror. Nor is he the only one. "Poets who would appear to have the greatest claim on sorrow are often the funniest," Barbara Hamby and David Kirby (2010) write in the introduction to *Seriously Funny: Poems About Love, Death, Religion, Art, Politics, Sex, and Everything Else:*

> Take Lucia Perillo, who was diagnosed with multiple sclerosis in the 1980s. Yet her poem "Fubar" (the title is an acronym for an expression perhaps best rendered as "[fouled] up beyond all repair") is incontestably radiant. "Fubar" appears to be addressed to a friend who is paraplegic, and Perillo starts by wagging her finger at those who haven't earned the same right to sympathy, such as the woman mourning her dead cat ("sorry, but pet death barely puts the needle in the red zone"). (p. xiv)

"But come on," says Perillo in the poem's last lines of the poem, "the sun is rising, I'll put a bandage on my head, / and we'll be like those guys at the end of the movie— / you take this crutch made from a stick. . . . / And looky, looky here at me: I'm playing the piccolo."

According to Hamby and Kirby (2010), "If the humor in Perillo's poems and others like them glow often with a starry sheen, that is because there is a black sky behind it" (p. xiv).

As Twain wrote in *Following the Equator*, "The secret source of humor is not joy but sorrow; there is no humor in Heaven." Lorca talked about how great poems, even funny poems, have *duende*, or the shadow of death. The poet Lawrence Raab once wrote that he liked work that is both serious and funny when "its essential seriousness emerges from its humor, rather than the humor being a kind of overlay or a set of asides" (personal communication, May 7, 2008).

In addition to the poets already named in this entry, others such as George Bilgere, Charlotte Boulay, Matthew Dickman, Denise Duhamel, Amy Gerstler, Mark Halliday, Terrance Hayes, and James Tate are continuing the tradition of poetry that is both serious and funny, a tradition that goes back to the earliest poems ever composed.

David Kirby

See also Doggerel; Epigram; Fabliau; Humor, Forms of; Humor Content Versus Structure; Lampoon; Literature; Mock Epic; Nonsense; Parody; Pastiche; Speech Play

Further Readings

Collins, B. (2001). The art of poetry no. 83. Interview with George Plimpton. *Paris Review.* Retrieved from http://www.theparisreview.org/interviews/482/the-art-of-poetry-no-83-billy-collins

Collins, B. (2005). The lanyard. In *The trouble with poetry* (pp. 45–46). New York, NY: Random House.

Duhamel, D., & Attardo, S. (Eds.). (2009). Humor in contemporary poetry [Special issue]. *HUMOR: International Journal of Humor Research, 22*(3).

Hamby, B., & Kirby, D. (2010). *Seriously funny: Poems about love, death, religion, art, politics, sex, and everything else.* Athens: University of Georgia Press.

Iser, W. (1978). *The art of reading.* Baltimore, MD: Johns Hopkins University Press.

Nemerov, H. (1978). Poetry and meaning. In *Figures of thought.* Boston, MA: Godine.

Perillo, L. (2005). Fubar. In *Luck is luck* (pp. 51–52). New York, NY: Random House.

Rothenberg, J. (Ed.). (1985). *Technicians of the sacred: A range of poetries from Africa, America, Asia, Europe and Oceania* (2nd ed.). Berkeley: University of California Press.

POINTE

The term *pointe,* defined by the *Oxford-Duden German Dictionary* as a "punch line, conceit or [plot] twist," refers in French and German to the witty effect of funny, surprising, and ingenious twists. Prototypically, *pointes* can be found at the end of short literary narrative texts, such as jokes, anecdotes, and epigrams.

For the sake of a terminological overview, it is useful to differentiate between (1) the use of *pointe* in normative treatises of the 17th and 18th centuries that give advice on how to write literary texts, and (2) its descriptive use in research (in particular in German), where the term has a meaning similar to that of "punch line."

History

Etymologically, *pointe* is something acute or pointed, and during the Renaissance it appears as a literary term in French literature as a translation of the Latin *acutus* (acumen). However, the most pertinent treatises on the *pointe,* which were written at that time in Spain and Italy, used different words to refer to witty, surprising, so-called ingenious literary effects (Spanish *agudezza, concepto*; Italian *acutezza, argutia, argutezza, concetto*). These treatises were particularly interested in the means used to impress an audience with surprising stylistic artistry, so-called conceits (although *concetti* and *conceptos* were not confined to metaphors). In Spain, Baltasar Gracián (1648) presented the *concepto* as a way of producing new and surprising ideas. In Italy, Emanuele Tesauro (1654) praised the *accutezze* for the intellectual delight of combining "far-fetched" concepts. This poetic interest in the *pointe* coincided with a general fondness for antithetical style. For instance, John Donne contrasted burning fire with water in his epigram on "Hero and Leander," two mythical lovers who drowned in the Hellespont: "Both rob'd of aire we both lye on the ground / Both whom one fire had burnt, one water drowned."

The term *pointe* itself is connected to French classicists' criticism of the excessive use of rhetoric and ingenious style in literature in the 18th century. Charles Batteux (1754), for instance, stressed that the *pointe* should only be used in epigrams, if it is based on a similarity of ideas and not only of words. Samuel Johnson (1779) criticized the "metaphysical poets" for their "far-fetched" and "false conceits." Nevertheless, the *pointe* continued to be a serious subject of inquiry in relation to epigrams throughout the 18th century. In Germany, the poet and philologist Gotthold Ephraim Lessing (1777) adopted the word *pointe* into German, in order to describe the bipartite structure of epigrams consisting of an "expectation" (*Erwartung*) and a resolution (*Aufschluß*) that triggers the *pointe* through a witty but not artificial ending.

The *Pointe* in Modern Research

Modern research on the *pointe* differs from poetical treatises in that it is less concerned with the issue of how and when poets should use this literary device. Rather, toward the end of the 19th century, it starts to systematically explore the aesthetic effect of the *pointe* and to analyze the objects that trigger such an effect. Emil Kraepelin, one of the founding fathers of empirical psychology, understood the *pointe* as an effect created by an "intellectual contrast." Theodor Lipps, on the other hand, understood *pointes* in terms of overcoming a psychological inhibition, which influenced Freud's book on *Jokes and Their Relation to the Unconscious* (1905/1960).

Today, research in literature, psychology, and linguistics has mostly focused on jokes and rarely takes into account the historical background of the *pointe* in the poetics of the Renaissance and classicism. In academic usage, the *pointe* is mostly considered to be a necessary condition of a joke, and the term refers either to the final words in a text, which cause the striking effect of a *pointe*, or to the event of understanding a *pointe*. Its functioning may be distinguished from other forms of humor by its combination of incongruity and incongruity resolution (whereas humor does not necessarily require an incongruity resolution). As a consequence, a *pointe* requires a basic narrative sequence of setup and surprising resolution. Such a sequence may elicit certain expectations, which are subsequently disappointed in an incongruous unexpected ending, as can be observed in garden-path jokes. (An example is this: "Bush has a short one, Gorbachev has a long one, Madonna rarely uses hers, and the Pope doesn't use his. What is it? Answer: a last name.")

Or an open, or even incongruous, exposition may be followed by an unexpected solution. This can be observed in the 1999 film *The Sixth Sense* by M. Night Shyamalan, where the protagonist's behavior surprisingly turns out to be motivated by paranormal phenomena.

Ralph Müller

See also Anecdote, Comic; Aphorism; Epigram; Incongruity and Resolution; Jokes; Punch Line; *Witz*

Further Readings

Batteux, C. (1809). *Principes de la littérature* [Principles of literature] (New ed.). Avignon, France: Chambeau.

Blanco, M. (1992). *Les rhétoriques de la pointe: Baltasar Gracián et le conceptisme en Europe* [The rhetoric of the conceit: Baltasar Gracián and the theory of the conceit in Europe]. Paris, France: Librairie Honoré Champion.

Freud, S. (1960). Jokes and their relation to the unconscious. In J. Starchey, A. Freud, A. Strachey, & A. Tyson (Eds.), *The standard edition of the complete psychological works of Sigmund Freud* (Vol. 8). London, UK: Hogarth Press. (Original work published 1905)

Gracián, B. (1969). *Agudeza y arte de ingenio* [Wit and the art of ingenuity]. Madrid, Spain: Castalia.

Johnson, S. (2006). Cowley. In R. Lonsdale (Ed.), *The lives of the most eminent English poets; with critical observations on their works* (Vol. 1, pp. 193–234). Oxford, UK: Clarendon.

Kraepelin, E. (1885). Zur Psychologie des Komischen [On the psychology of humor]. In W. Wundt (Ed.), *Philosophische Studien* (Vol. 2, pp. 128–193, 327–369). Leipzig, Germany: Engelmann.

Lessing, G. E. (1973). Zerstreute Anmerkungen über das Epigramm und einiger der vornehmsten Epigrammisten [Scattered notes on the epigram and some of the finest epigram writers]. In H. G. Göpfert & J. Schönert (Eds.), *Werke* (Vol. 5). Darmstadt, Germany: Wissenschaftliche Buchgesellschaft.

Lipps, T. (1898). *Komik und Humor: Eine psychologisch-ästhetische Untersuchung* [The comic and humor: A psychological-aesthetic study]. Leipzig, Germany: Voss.

Müller, R. (2003). The *Pointe* in German research. *HUMOR: International Journal of Humor Research, 16*(2), 225–242.

Ruthven, K. K. (1969). *The conceit*. London, UK: Methuen.

Tesauro, E. (1968). *Il cannocchiale aristotelico* [The Aristotelian telescope]. Bad Homburg, Germany: Gehlen.

Wenzel, P. (1989). *Von der Struktur des Witzes zum Witz der Struktur: Untersuchungen zur Pointierung in Witz und Kurzgeschichte* [From the structure of the joke to the joke of the structure: Studies on the pointedness in jokes and short stories]. Heidelberg, Germany: Winter.

Politeness

Politeness is a set of strategies that can be used for face-saving in social interactions. Erving Goffman (1955/2003) described *face* as "the social value a person effectively claims for himself" (p. 7), and Penelope Brown and Stephen Levinson used the term in defining their theory of politeness. According to Brown and Levinson, there are two types of politeness, namely, positive and negative. Positive politeness comes from the need to be acknowledged, liked, and valued and the need to have a positive public image. Negative politeness can be said to derive from the rebellious side, the need to announce one's relative independence from social conventions. Humor is one way to adhere to politeness. This entry discusses the intersections between humor and politeness.

Brown and Levinson list humor among the strategies of positive politeness. Janet Holmes explores the issue further and lists four ways in which humor can express positive and negative politeness. Positive politeness can be expressed via humor (1) by addressing the hearer's positive face needs through shared norms and common ground, and (2) by protecting the speaker's positive face needs through expressing self-deprecatory sentiments. Negative politeness can be achieved through humor (3) by attenuating the threat to the hearer's negative face (e.g., decreasing the commanding tone in a directive), and (4) by attenuating the threat to the hearer's positive face, such as cushioning a criticism.

Many a truth is said in jest, as the saying goes, and figuratively speaking, speakers (or writers) may be more likely to speak their mind when they hide their (or their addressee's) "face" behind the mask of humor. According to Anat Zajdman, face-threatening acts can be implemented in joking in on-record (being bald about it), redressed (threat minimized), and off-record (indirect face-threatening act usually by violating a maxim) modes. However, she claims face-threatening acts do not need to be avoided in an act of joking, as jokes can serve negative politeness strategies as much as positive ones and "breed respect." As such, "joking is considered as a feature characterizing the language of the group in power, [whereas] polite language is attributed to the weaker group" (Zajdman, 1995, p. 328). Humor helps shape power relationships, and as Janet Holmes and Meredith Marra point out, although it is usually a means of positive politeness, it may not be as positive when used by people in different levels of power and status.

Politeness also plays an important role in responses to failed humor. Failing at humor is a highly face-threatening act for the speaker, as humor is part of constructing one's identity in social circumstances, and it is up to the person on the receiving end of the joke whether to save the joke-teller's face. Nancy Bell states that humor can fail as a result of the text of the joke or the way it is delivered, and she found that when the hearers in her corpus did not appreciate a joke, they chose to criticize the joke rather than the person who has told it in order to comply with politeness. Bell (2009b) also found that hearers sometimes respond to failed humor with "polite laughter and comments that seem designed to help the teller save face after his or her failed attempt to amuse" (p. 1832).

When an attempt at humor fails, both the speaker and the hearer's faces are threatened. As Neal Norrick points out in his discussion of the reception of the performance of jokes, the hearer may not appreciate the humor and not laugh out of mirth, but she or he wants to make sure that it is not due to incomprehension, so the humorous attempt has to be somehow acknowledged. In a study on the impolite responses to failed humor between persons in intimate relationships, Bell discovered that hearers may choose to be aggressive in their responses and implement negative impoliteness strategies such as making the other uncomfortable, remaining silent, ignoring, using taboo words, and so forth. She concludes that face claims of the hearer constitute one of the main aggressive responses to failed humor.

The last major intersection of politeness and humor is the production of irony. Shelly Dews and colleagues found that speakers prefer irony to literal language for a number of reasons: to be funny, to attenuate an insult, to maintain their relationship with the hearer, and to prove that they can control their emotions. According to Shelly Dews and Ellis Winner's tinge hypothesis, hearers process the literal meaning of an ironic statement in accordance with its intended meaning, which affects the hearer's interpretation. In other words, if irony is used to communicate negative meaning like a criticism (e.g., "awesome movie!" to mean the movie is bad), politeness is violated less. If speakers use negative words, on the other hand, they are considered less polite even if they are paying a compliment. Jacqueline Matthews and colleagues tested the tinge hypothesis, but their findings did not support it on the grounds that people refrained from offering ironic criticisms as well as literal ones when saying nothing was an option. Although their findings suggest that people use verbal irony to be humorous and not to be polite, Matthews and colleagues point out that the scenarios they used in their study always depicted intimates, and therefore their study may reveal different results if strangers rather than close friends or partners are used in the scenarios.

Hilal Ergül

See also Culture; Failed Humor; Gender Roles in Humor; Irony

Further Readings

Bell, N. D. (2009a). Impolite responses to failed humor. In D. Chiaro & N. Norrick (Eds.), *Humor in interaction* (pp. 143–164). Amsterdam, Netherlands: John Benjamins.

Bell, N. D. (2009b). Responses to failed humor. *Journal of Pragmatics, 41*(9), 1825–1836.

Brown, P., & Levinson, S. C. (1987). *Politeness.* Cambridge, UK: Cambridge University Press.

Dews, S., Kaplan, J., & Winner, E. (1995). Why not say it directly? The social functions of irony. *Discourse Processes, 19*(3), 347–367.

Dews, S., & Winner, E. (1995). Muting the meaning: A social function of irony. *Metaphor and Symbol, 10*(1), 3–19.

Goffman, E. (2003). On face-work: An analysis of ritual elements in social interaction. *Reflections, 4*(3), 7–13. (Original work published 1955 in *Psychiatry: Journal for the Study of Interpersonal Processes, 18*(3), 213–231.

Holmes, J. (2000). Politeness, power and provocation: How humour functions in the workplace. *Discourse Studies, 2*(2), 159–185.

Holmes, J., & Schnurr, S. (2005). Politeness, humor and gender in the workplace: Negotiating norms and identifying contestation. *Journal of Politeness Research, 1*(1), 121–149.

Lakoff, R. (1973). The logic of politeness; or, minding your p's and q's. In C. Corum, T. C. Smith-Stark, & A. Weiser (Eds.), *Papers from the ninth regional meeting of the Chicago Linguistic Society* (pp. 292–305). Chicago, IL: Chicago Linguistic Society.

Matthews, J. K., Hancock, J. T., & Dunham, P. J. (2006). The roles of politeness and humor in the asymmetry of affect in verbal irony. *Discourse Processes, 41*(1), 3–24.

Norrick, N. R. (2003). Issues in conversational joking. *Journal of Pragmatics, 35*(9), 1333–1359.

Zajdman, A. (1995). Humorous face-threatening acts: Humor as strategy. *Journal of Pragmatics, 23*(3), 325–339.

Political Humor

A wide range of social phenomena fall under the umbrella of political humor. *Politics* refers broadly to social behaviors related to the governing bodies of a nation or comparable entity. Political humor, then, encompasses humor directed at or derived from politics, policies, political parties, institutions, and individuals involved in the political process, as well as humor used by politicians themselves.

Humor About Politics and Politicians

Humor directed at politics and politicians may be seen as a means by which constituents figuratively undermine the ruling powers. Such humor may address the suppression of personal and political freedoms, as has been noted in contemporary Asian political humor, or highlight the contrast between politicians' public promises and the reality of their actions, which has been fodder for observers of American election campaigns.

Political humor can take myriad forms, including joke, pun, riddle, song, parable, and satire. In turn, it can perform numerous functions, including exposing incompetence or immorality, defusing aggression or encouraging cooperation, critiquing ideology, or promoting common ground.

One of the earliest jokes can be traced to an ancient Egyptian one about pharaohs: A hieroglyph dated to 2600 BCE has been translated as "How do you entertain a bored pharaoh? You sail a boatload of young women dressed only in fishing nets down the Nile and urge the pharaoh to go catch a fish." Another 3,500-year-old example from a tablet found in southern Mesopotamia included a riddle about a governor.

The ancient Greeks provided more extensive examples of early political humor. Aristophanes's *Lysistrata* (411 BCE) is a commonly cited seminal work of political satire, in which women attempt to influence the politics of the Peloponnesian War through sexual deprivation. Aristotle, Plato, and Cicero all offered explanations and critiques of the use of humor as a rhetorical strategy in the public realm. Satire, the mocking of human flaws on the personal and societal level, has been a mainstay of political humor from Aristophanes, Obayd-e Zakani's fable "Mouse and Cat" to Jonathan Swift's "A Modest Proposal," through Britain's *Punch* magazine (1841–2002) up to today's *The Daily Show* and *The Colbert Report* and various websites. Since the 1800s, political cartoons in newspapers have enjoyed widespread popularity across the globe, including in Japan, the United States, and the United Kingdom.

Humor aimed at politicians has several typical targets. Vice and moral weakness is a common topic; Romans emperors, including Constantine, were subjected to ridicule for their public drunkenness. More recently, U.S. President Bill Clinton's affair with

"A Thanksgiving Truce," a cartoon that appeared in the November 22, 1905, issue of *Puck* magazine.

Source: Cartoon by J. S. Pughe. Library of Congress Prints and Photographs Division, Washington, DC, Reproduction Number LC-DIG-ppmsca-26010.

White House intern Monica Lewinsky and Italian Prime Minister Silvio Berlusconi's sex-inspired "bunga bunga" parties were the subject of mockery.

Politicians' intellectual prowess is another common target for humor. George W. Bush's intelligence was regarded as suspect by many comedians. One joke compared his State of the Union address to Groundhog Day: "It is an ironic juxtaposition of events: one involves a meaningless ritual in which we look to a creature of little intelligence for prognostication, while the other involves a groundhog."

Appearance or gestures as fodder for humor is a particularly popular domain for cartoonists. A *Harper's Weekly* cartoon from 1908 showed the hefty William Howard Taft, U.S. president, in a tight-fitting outfit reminiscent of former president Theodore Roosevelt's Rough Rider uniform, with Uncle Sam saying, "Bill, you'd look so much better in your own clothes." Representations of Richard Nixon routinely emphasized his nose and often portrayed him with his arms raised in the double "V for victory" stance. British Prime Minister Margaret Thatcher's hairstyle, Prime Minister of Japan Junichiro Koizumi's long gray mane of hair, and Cuban President Fidel Castro's beard and cigar were invariably caricatured.

Political humor may be aimed at an institution or the vagaries of political life rather than a specific figure. For example, a Japanese verse from a prominent newspaper wryly noted the high turnover among officials in the early 1990s with "The Japanese live long, but life as a prime minister is short." Sir Cyril Smith referred to the UK's House of Commons as "the longest running farce in the West End." American humorist Mark Twain was famously quoted as quipping, "Suppose you were an idiot. And suppose you were a member of Congress. But I repeat myself." Given their lack of a specific target and distinctive criticism, jokes of this sort are often co-opted across political target, contexts, and borders.

Humor is a common strategy for pushing the boundaries of political expression in repressive societies. Silvio Berlusconi's government blocked a political satire form the state-owned television show. One version of a North Korean joke reported by defectors from the country reveals the political tensions inherent in daily life for its citizens:

> A man in North Korea goes fishing and lands a fish. Returning home, he excitedly asks his wife, "Shall we eat fried fish today?" She replies, "We have no cooking oil!" "Shall we stew it, then?" "We have no pot!" "Shall we grill it?" "We have no firewood!" Frustrated, the man returns to the river and throws the fish back in the water. The fish, happy to have escaped, sticks its head above water and shouts: "Long live Kim Jong Il!"

"The Last Blow," a drawing of a female symbol of Democracy punching German soldiers, labeled "Militarism," who are lying on a pile of skulls as a house burns in the background.

Source: Cartoon by C. D. Gibson, published in *LIFE* magazine, August 29, 1918, p. 749. Library of Congress Prints and Photographs Division, Washington, DC, Reproduction Number LC-DIG-ppmsca-33518.

Governments may view such humor as subversive and therefore police outlets for it. Singapore's newspapers have rejected editorial cartoons about local politics, and political jokes continue to be grounds for arrest in China. However, the ambiguity of humor may be advantageous to fledgling political expression, as it allows criticisms to be broached while retaining the plausible cover of levity and goodwill.

Humor From Politicians

Humor from political figures likewise takes many forms and achieves various purposes. Among American politicians, President Ronald Reagan has received perhaps the most attention for his use of one-liners and their argued effect on his popularity. One of his most famous jokes was spoken during a debate with Walter Mondale, in which he was questioned about his ability to function as president at his advanced age. He replied, "I want you to know that I will not make age an issue in this campaign. I am not going to exploit, for political purposes, my opponent's youth and inexperience." This is one of many age-related jokes that Reagan used to effectively embrace and defuse the issue of age through humor, a topic of concern for many voters.

Self-deprecating humor, in particular, has the ability to balance the confidence, privilege, and egotism required to run for political office and has been found to garner more positive reactions from audiences than humor targeting a political opponent. A frequent ploy has been for politicians to portray themselves as somehow subservient to their wives, such as U.S. President John F. Kennedy's comment that he was simply the man who accompanied Jacqueline Kennedy to Paris and British Prime Minister Winston Churchill's claim that his most brilliant achievement was his ability to be able to persuade his wife to marry him. Such humor may endear candidates to the electorate, enhancing their popularity and influence.

Politicians' humor does not enjoy unanimously positive results. In 2009, the mayor of Los Alamitos, California, resigned after criticism of an e-mail he circulated showing the Barack Obama White House lawn planted with watermelons, which was widely regarded as a reflecting a racist stereotype. Chilean President Sebastián Piñera was criticized in 2011 for a sexist joke comparing politicians and women. A Japanese minister resigned after receiving criticism for an irreverent remark about radiation poisoning after his country's tsunami and resulting nuclear crisis of 2011. Criticism of such would-be humorists is often grounded in the perception that they display a lack of judgment and cultural sensitivity that is necessary for effective leadership.

Research

A small body of research has taken an empirical or experimental approach to studying the effects of political humor. Given the current dependence of many young Americans on late night comedy programs such as *The Daily Show* and *The Colbert Report* for news, examining how such shows target humor and affect their audiences may facilitate understanding of the impact of contemporary political humor. In total, these shows may focus more often on ad hominem attacks rather than ideological issues, but some scholars have argued that these shows tend to showcase policy issues more so than traditional late night comedy formats such as *The Tonight Show* or *The David Letterman Show*. Humor directed at female politicians on U.S. television has tended to focus disproportionately on appearance and gendered issues. For example, David Letterman said of the 2008 Republican vice presidential candidate, "I like that Sarah Palin. She looks like the weekend anchor on Channel 9. She looks like the hygienist who makes you feel guilty about not flossing. She looks like the relieved mom in a Tide commercial."

Some research has begun to explore the individual qualities associated with viewers' affinity for and reactions to political humor, including age, political knowledge, and the effect of political humor consumption on political interest and participation. Research has produced apparently contradictory findings that consumption of political humor on television may lead viewers to perceive themselves as politically knowledgeable; in contrast, the humor on such shows is associated with cynicism toward the political process and decreased argument scrutiny. Although a significant body of literature has documented politicians' performance of humor and speculated as to its impact on key initiatives and elections, less scholarship has directly assessed the effect of politicians' humor on voters' attitudes or behaviors.

Amy M. Bippus

See also Journalism; Presidential Humor; Satire News

Further Readings

Baumgartner, J. C., & Morris, J. S. (Eds.). (2007). *Laughing matters: Humor and American politics in the media age.* New York, NY: Routledge.

Gardner, G. C. (1994). *Campaign comedy: Political humor from Clinton to Kennedy.* Detroit, MI: Wayne State University Press.

Schulz, C. E. (1977). *Political humor: From Aristophanes to Sam Ervin.* Cranbury, NJ: Associated University Presses.

Stewart, P. A. (2012). *Debatable humor: Laughing matters on the 2008 presidential primary campaign.* Lanham, MD: Rowman & Littlefield.

Tsakona, V., & Popa, D. E. (2011). *Studies in political humour: In between political critique and public entertainment.* Amsterdam, Netherlands: John Benjamins.

Positive Psychology

Positive psychology is a field of study that focuses on emotions, traits, and institutions that enable people to function at their best and lead happy and fulfilling lives. This approach came to prominence in 1998, when Martin Seligman served as president of the American Psychological Association and called for a new direction in psychological research. He noted that much of the focus of psychology had been on pathology and problems in living, neglecting the study of human strengths and flourishing.

The roots of positive psychology can be traced to ancient philosophers and religious thinkers who sought to define a good life, virtuous character, and authentic happiness. In the 1960s and 1970s, humanistic psychologists such as Abraham Maslow and Carl Rogers also emphasized the importance of studying human potential, authenticity, and self-actualization. Positive psychology may be viewed as a revival of these humanistic emphases, along with more rigorous research methodologies.

With its emphasis on positive emotion, health, and social cohesion, the psychological study of humor seems to fit naturally within the field of positive psychology. In particular, links between humor and positive psychology have been made in two topic areas that are primary interests of positive psychologists: positive emotions and character strengths. This entry discusses these two topic areas and the limitations of positive psychology in addressing humor.

Humor and Positive Emotion

Positive psychology has shifted the focus of emotion research from the traditional emphasis on negative emotions (e.g., depression, anxiety, anger) to include positive emotions such as joy, gratitude, and love. Barbara Fredrickson's broaden-and-build theory has emerged as the leading model of positive emotion and has stimulated a good deal of research. According to this theory, positive emotions "broaden" the individual's thought-action repertoire in the short term, producing more flexible thinking and openness to a wider array of thoughts, activities, and relationships. This in turn leads to "building" more enduring long-term personal resources (e.g., social support, resilience, skills, knowledge), which contributes to enhanced health, survival, and resilience.

This theoretical framework seems to apply well to mirth, the positive emotion associated with humor (often called *amusement* in the positive psychology literature). The cognitive social play of humor is based on shifting perspectives and flexibility of thought, while the laughter accompanying mirth signals openness to friendly interactions with other people, which may in turn lead to more creative thinking and enhanced social bonds. Indeed, a considerable amount of experimental research has shown that exposure to comedy (as well as other elicitors of positive emotions) leads to increases in creativity, memory, problem solving, altruism, and prosocial behavior.

Humor as a Character Strength

Researchers in positive psychology have identified 24 character strengths (one of which is humor), which in turn are classified into six core virtues that have been valued across cultures since ancient times. These strengths and virtues are viewed as important contributors to a life of fulfillment and satisfaction. The six virtues are *wisdom* (including such strengths as creativity and love of learning); *courage* (e.g., authenticity, perseverance); *humanity* (e.g., love, kindness); *justice* (e.g., fairness, leadership); *temperance* (e.g., forgiveness, self-regulation); and *transcendence* (e.g., gratitude, religiousness, humor). The Values in Action Inventory of Strengths (VIA-IS) is a 240-item questionnaire designed to measure each of these character strengths.

Humor (conceived as a trait-like variable) is one of the 24 strengths included in this classification, and a 10-item humor scale is included in the VIA-IS. Research using this measure has found that humor is one of the character strengths most highly related to subjective well-being, confirming its importance in positive psychology. Although humor is categorized within the virtue of transcendence, research indicates that it could equally belong with all six of the virtues, and particularly humanity and wisdom. Thus, there is still some question about where humor fits into the classification of character strengths and virtues.

Limitations

Although there seem to be clear overlaps between humor and positive psychology, there has been a surprising neglect of humor in much of the positive psychology literature. Humor even fails to appear at all in the indexes of several of the leading texts and reference works in the field. This may be due in part to the multifaceted nature of humor, which makes it difficult to define as a purely salutary construct. When they do talk about humor, positive psychologists tend to use a narrower definition of the concept than do most humor researchers. In positive psychology, *humor* is used in the traditional philosophical sense to refer only to benign amusement at the incongruities of life, the ability to see the funny side of adverse situations, and avoiding taking oneself too seriously. In most humor research, in contrast, the word is used as a broader umbrella term to refer to all phenomena of the funny, including sarcasm and satire as well as irony and whimsy. Not all forms of humor, in this broader sense, are likely to be considered virtuous or conducive to a life of fulfillment and well-being. Indeed, research on the virtuousness of humor indicates that items taken from numerous widely used humor measures span the gamut from virtue to vice. Studies on associations between humor styles and well-being also suggest that psychological well-being has as much to do with the avoidance of certain deleterious styles of humor as the presence of beneficial styles. Thus, although there is an overlap between humor research and positive psychology that merits further exploration, there is not a perfect fit between the two.

Rod A. Martin

See also Health Benefits of Humor, Psychological; Mirth; Psychology; Sense of Humor, Components of

Further Readings

Beerman, U., & Ruch, W. (2009). How virtuous is humor? What we can learn from current instruments. *Journal of Positive Psychology*, *4*, 528–539.

Fredrickson, B. L. (2006). The broaden-and-build theory of positive emotions. In M. Csikszentmihalyi & I. S. Csikszentmihalyi (Eds.), *A life worth living: Contributions to positive psychology* (pp. 85–103). New York, NY: Oxford University Press.

Lopez, S. J., & Snyder, C. R. (Eds.). (2009). *Oxford handbook of positive psychology*. New York, NY: Oxford University Press.

Peterson, C., & Seligman, M. E. P. (2004). *Character strengths and virtues: A handbook and classification.* Washington, DC: American Psychological Association.

Postmodern Irony

Irony is the central mode of consciousness of postmodernism and one of the main forms of expression of postmodernist literature. It marks the postmodern attitude of disenchantment toward the totalizing narratives that legitimate Western culture (history, philosophy, religion, science, etc.) and is also one of the main strategies used by postmodernist fiction to retain the ability to represent the world while raising awareness of art's own status as cultural artifice and potential instrument of power. Modernism had already used the dissecting power of laughter as a means to expose both the conformism of bourgeois society and art's own ideological limitations. Modernist works such as James Joyce's *Ulysses* and Carlo Emilio Gadda's *That Awful Mess on Via Merulana* use parodic dialogism and linguistic polyphony as a way to subvert the tendency toward unity and closure of the conventional realist plot, which, ultimately, makes artistic discourse into an instrument to perpetuate the dominant ideology. Nonetheless, modernist texts often reduce the ambiguity of parodic discourse by placing the artists above the culture they seek to criticize; the past as referent is overcome through the creation of an experimental metalanguage that either restores the belief in the redemptive force of the artistic aura or attests to art's ultimate inability to add meaning to the world. Overcoming this nihilist attitude toward the past, postmodernist works embrace the ambiguity of irony and use parodic dialogism as a way to criticize culture from within the language of tradition, without imposing alternative metaphysical viewpoints. As Umberto Eco argues in his "Postscript to *The Name of the Rose*," destroying the past can lead art to reach the point of incommunicability, as happened to some avant-garde movements. Instead of following this route, postmodernism repeats tradition with ironic difference; it uses old forms in order to expose and rescue them from the monolithic viewpoints that inform them and reactivate their ability to promote critical awareness. Conventional narrative plots, such as the Victorian novel in John Fowles's *The French Lieutenant's Woman*, are used as strategies to rescue readers from their passive reception of cultural messages and make them conscious of the ideological constructs that influence their understanding of the world. Aware of their own implication in the legitimization of ideology, postmodernist authors, or "integrated" intellectuals as Eco has defined them, use the language of power, and the mechanisms of power production used by the culture industry, against themselves. Their ironic use of cultural conventions and artistic forms that appeal to a wide readership aims at turning literature from a potential mode of control to a freedom-inducing act.

Marxist critics such as Fredric Jameson have been skeptical about the political engagement of postmodernist parody. They have interpreted the duplicity of postmodernist irony and its ambiguous attitude toward tradition as symptoms of a lack of depth and a commitment to anarchy that makes postmodernist texts complicit with the ideology of late capitalist society. In their view, postmodernist irony is a form of blank parody, a cannibalization of old styles that is not inspired by a genuine historicism and ultimately turns cultural tradition into a set of dusty spectacles deprived of any value and unable to add meaning to the present. According to this view, unlike modernist irony, whose formal experimentation provided a utopia of liberation, postmodernist irony does not offer a way out of the cultural impasse; its ambiguity is a form of institutionalization, a way to surrender to fragmentation and the power mechanisms of global capitalism.

Rescuing postmodernism from the accusation of relativism, critics such as Linda Hutcheon and, more recently, Amy Elias have highlighted the ethical intent of the postmodernist revival of tradition. Hutcheon argues that the political commitment of postmodernist fiction, or "historiographic metafiction" as she defines it, lays in its attempt to engage in a critical dialogue with culture whose ultimate goal is to denaturalize the contrived notions of reality and history that readers assume as unmediated, natural truths. Hence, parodic arbitrariness is not a form of relativism but, rather, an ethical project that consists in the simultaneous revisitation and critique of the totalitarian narratives that shaped the public imaginary. Ultimately, postmodernist irony is informed by a reader-oriented ethics: It fosters the development of a critical attitude toward reality instead of imposing metaphysical values fashioned by art in a top-down way. Building on Hutcheon's argument, while emphasizing the continuity between postmodernist novels and old forms of historical fiction, Elias has defined the "metahistorical romance" as the historical narrative par excellence of the postmodernist age. Postmodernist fiction, Elias contends, adapts the 19th-century historical romance to the changed understanding of history that characterizes contemporary historiography, namely, to today's rejection of the totalizing concept of history—the linear notion of history as progress deriving from Enlightenment rationalism—that legitimized Western colonialism and nationalism and is also responsible for the traumas of the World Wars. The postmodernist ironic attitude toward the past reflects history's own emancipation from cultural master narratives. Thus, postmodernist parody goes beyond the mere academic joke and is inspired by the ethical desire to make sense of the past while avoiding the dominant viewpoints of masters, despots, and colonizers.

In philosophy, together with the French poststructuralists, who were the first to elaborate a theory of postmodernism, and the American pragmatists, the Italian philosophers of "weak thought" have been among the main supporters of postmodernism. "Weak thought" is inspired by the same type of antifoundational hermeneutics that informs the thought of philosophers such as Jean-François Lyotard and Richard Rorty. Nonetheless, it refuses to abandon rationalism even in the absence of strong foundations, thus adding a dimension of nuance to discussions about contemporary philosophy, which provides an important argument against the Marxist accusations of relativism and loss of historical sense. As Gianni Vattimo contends, inspired by Friedrich Nietzsche's and Martin Heidegger's theories on the destabilization of ontology, postmodernists do not intend to overcome tradition but, rather, to weaken the past in order to liberate history from the dogma of metaphysical interpretations. Thus, the postmodernist ironic recollection of the past does not entail an entirely nihilistic attitude toward history and the cognitive value of tradition; instead, it denotes an attitude of *pietas*, or devoted attention, toward the cultural monuments left to us in legacy. Postmodernism reaffirms that the present is grounded in history and that, although devoid of metaphysical value, the past can still offer criteria of reasonability and fragments of meaning that can help communities to orient themselves in a life devoid of, but also emancipated by, strong values. This is evident in postmodernist literature, where, as critic Alan Wilde has argued, "suspensive irony," which marks the acceptance of the multiplicity of contingency, is often complemented by "generative irony," namely, the search for temporary meanings that make precarious sense of the world. In other words, as Wilde argues, postmodernists deny the heroism of the modernist enterprise and its quest for alternative metaphysical values but nevertheless attempt a partial recovery of humanism and strive to find, within the realm of ordinary life, possibilities of momentary meaning.

Eco's novel *The Name of the Rose* offers both an important reflection on postmodernism and a striking example of postmodernist double coding. With its dense intertextuality, Eco's novel parodies a number of monological genres, from the theological argument to the detective novel, while also "replenishing" their ability to convey meaning. Upon finding the main culprit and motive for the abbey's crimes, the novel's protagonist, William of Baskerville, claims that his overtly rational mind—he is a postmodern Sherlock Holmes, as his name suggests—has mistakenly led him to untangle a plan that does not exist. The task of the modern thinker, as William ultimately understands, is to "make truth laugh," instead of replacing old metaphysical truths, such as that of the divine *logos*, with newer myths such as that of the ordering mind. Nonetheless, when reminded that "by imagining an erroneous order" he "still found something," William also understands that the mind cannot do away with old structuring systems altogether, that one must appreciate their usefulness while coming to terms with the necessity to undermine closure: "The order that our mind imagines is like a net, or like a ladder, built to attain something. But afterward you must throw the ladder away, because you discover that, even if it was useful, it was meaningless" (Eco, 1984b, p. 492). As Eco's novel suggests, postmodernists believe that the past can still add meaning to the present even though, ultimately, it must be deprived of any dogmatic value.

Like their modernist forerunners, postmodernist artists consider the intellectual as an ironist whose ethical task is to provide a critical insight into culture. Yet, unlike the modernists, postmodernist ironists do not have an "apocalyptic" attitude toward culture; they do not dismiss familiar conventions to create a metalanguage that reasserts art's authority over reality. Thus, although in *The Name of the Rose* Eco acknowledges the important influence of an author such as Jorge Luis Borges, whose use of parody and intertexuality anticipated the postmodernist way of operating, he also casts the Argentinean author into the villain Jorge of Burgos, the blind and erudite librarian who forbids Aristotle's book on laughter from causing the collapse of the medieval system of belief. The metaphysical *logos* that Jorge of Burgos attempts to protect is the symbol of any totalizing narrative, including that of Borges's modernism, whose authority is undermined by the double coding of postmodernist parody. Modernists considered formal experimentation as the measure of their ethical commitment toward reality. Their ironic stance toward culture produced a self-reflexive language that can make it difficult for the average reader to come out of the intertextual labyrinth and establish a connection, even though a precarious one, between text and world. Instead, mixing the highbrow with the lowbrow, combining intertextuality with enjoyable plots, the postmodernist writer constructs fictional worlds that foster "worldly" connections, narrations that allow many different types of readers to negotiate some kind of meaning and witness a transformative experience that will impact their understanding of the world. Many modernist works lack the democratic quality and the type of social solidarity that are the quintessential characteristics of postmodernist irony, an irony whose ethical program, as Rorty argues, consists in facilitating the reader's spontaneous identification with the oppressed instead of imposing from above the acceptance of metaphysical universals such as liberty, equality, and dignity. Nonetheless, it can be argued that this project of social solidarity "constructed out of little pieces" is fully realized only in those postmodernist works where parody poses an overt challenge to power relations in addition to subverting the type of metaphysical thought that generates them. The social engagement of postmodernist irony comes to the fore particularly in works that are located at the intersection of the postmodern and the postcolonial, such as Salman Rushdie's *Midnight's Children*. Here, parody creates a disjunctive narration where history is told neither from the viewpoint of the oppressor nor merely from that of a disenfranchised minority, but is constructed, rather, as a hybrid text of cultural in-betweenness that promotes the awareness of shared differences or, as Homi Bhabha (1994/2004) argues, of the "otherness of the people-as-one" (p. 215).

Loredana Di Martino

See also History of Humor: Modern and Contemporary Europe; Irony

Further Readings

Barth, J. (1984). *The Friday book: Essays and other nonfiction*. New York, NY: Putnam.

Bhabha, H. (2004). *The location of culture*. New York, NY: Routledge. (Original work published 1994)

Di Martino, L. (2011). From Pirandello's humor to Eco's Double coding: Ethics and irony in modernist and postmodernist Italian fiction. *MLN* (Italian Issue), *126*(1), 137–156.

Eco, U. (1984a). The frames of comic "freedom." In T. A. Sebeok (Ed.), *Carnival!* (pp. 1–9). Berlin, Germany: Mouton de Gruyter.

Eco, U. (1984b). *The name of the rose* (W. Weaver, Trans.). New York, NY: Harcourt.

Eco, U. (1984c). Postscript to *The Name of the Rose*. In W. Weaver (Trans.), *The name of the rose* (pp. 505–535). New York, NY: Harcourt.

Eco, U. (1986). *Travels in hyperreality* (W. Weaver, Trans.). New York, NY: Harcourt.

Eco, U. (1994). *Apocalypse postponed* (R. Lumley, Ed.). Bloomington: Indiana University Press.

Elias, A. (2001). *Sublime desire: History and post-1960s fiction*. Baltimore, MD: Johns Hopkins University Press.

Hutcheon, L. (1985). *A theory of parody: The teachings of twentieth-century art forms*. New York, NY: Methuen.

Hutcheon, L. (1988). *A poetics of postmodernism: History, theory, fiction*. New York, NY: Routledge.

Hutcheon, L. (1992). The power of postmodern irony. In B. Rutland (Ed.), *Genre, trope and gender: Essays by Northrop Frye, Linda Hutcheon and Shirley Neuman*. Ottawa, ON, Canada: Carleton University Press.

Hutcheon, L. (1994). *Irony's edge: The theory and politics of irony*. New York, NY: Routledge.

Jameson, F. (1991). *Postmodernism or, the cultural logic of late capitalism*. Durham, NC: Duke University Press.

Rorty, R. (1989). *Contingency, irony and solidarity*. Cambridge, UK: Cambridge University Press.

Rose, M. A. (1993). *Parody: Ancient, modern and post-modern*. Cambridge, UK: Cambridge University Press.

Vattimo, G. (1988). *The end of modernity: Nihilism and hermeneutics in postmodern culture* (J. R. Snyder, Trans.). Baltimore, MD: Johns Hopkins University Press.

Vattimo, G., & Rovatti, P. A. (Eds.). (1983). *II pensiero debole* [Weak thought]. Milano, Italy: Feltrinelli.

Vattimo, G., & Rovatti, P. A. (Eds.). (2013). *Weak thought* (P. Carravetta, Trans.). Albany: State University of New York Press.

Wilde, A. (1981). *Horizons of assent: Modernism, postmodernism, and the ironic imagination*. Baltimore, MD: Johns Hopkins University Press.

Practical Jokes

A practical joke or prank is a play activity in which one party (called *the trickster* or *tricksters*) arranges things so that another party (*the target* or *targets*) is led to have a false idea about what is currently going on. The targets of practical jokes may also be called *dupes*, *butts*, or *victims*. When practical jokes are played on large groups of people in public settings, they are often called *hoaxes*.

Practical jokes may be divided into several types. *Put-ons* or *leg-pulls* are intended to fool the targets only momentarily. *Booby traps* trick the targets into treating an adulterated part of their environment as if it were untouched, often causing them mess and inconvenience. Physical humor may be part of the enjoyment in this type of practical joke. *Fool's errands* go further by encouraging targets to act on their erroneous beliefs; as they do so, their error is revealed for the amusement of a hidden audience. Any situation in which individuals have differential knowledge may become fodder for the practical joker. A tall tale, for example, may be enacted as a practical joke on the greenhorn, leading to such traditional amusements as the snipe hunt (a futile search for a fictitious snipe).

Theories about metacommunication help to explain the operation of practical jokes. Both play and joking are accompanied by metacommunicative signals that tell participants that what is going on is not serious. In Erving Goffman's extension of the theory of metacommunication, practical jokes are a type of benign fabrication in which these signals of play are hidden from the targets. The incongruity between the targets' and tricksters' framing of the same strip of activity is an important source of the humor of this genre.

Practical jokes are "practical" in the sense that they are enacted rather than being told. They are miniature plays in which the central characters—the targets—are ideally unaware that they have been contained in a strip of framed activity. In this state, they are the unwitting objects of close attention by an audience consisting of the jokers and others. Many verbal jokes have targets, but the targets of practical jokes are live people. Many, but not all, practical joke targets eventually find out that they have been made fools of, at which time they must decide whether or not to treat their discomfiture in the same way that the jokers and their audiences do—as just a joke. In this respect, practical jokes resemble teasing and jocular insults. The remainder of this entry focuses on acceptable occasions for practical jokes and the impact practical jokes can have on social bonds.

Practical Joke Occasions

Certain calendar occasions—notably April Fools' Day (April 1), Halloween (October 31), and Bonfire Night (November 5)—are widely recognized as conferring license to play practical jokes, and each occasion has its own recognized style of appropriate practical joking. Halloween pranks are generally played by groups of young people on older people, especially householders, and are intended to cause the targets inconvenience and irritation. Pranksters keep their identities secret to avoid retribution because they do not necessarily expect their targets to be amused.

In contrast, on April Fools' Day, practical jokes involve all age groups. Targets may be family members, friends, colleagues, or even strangers. Children have license to play jokes on their elders, including teachers. Because April Fools' Day jokes are rarely anonymous, they offer opportunities for reciprocity, sometimes leading to sequences of reciprocal jokes that extend from one year to the next. Beginning in the 20th century, journalists in radio, television, and the Internet have made a practice of taking advantage of this date to perpetrate elaborate spoofs and hoaxes on their audiences.

Rites of passage—especially weddings, initiations, birthdays, and funeral wakes—are associated with traditional practical jokes. Popular wedding pranks include booby trapping the newlyweds' car so as to make it temporarily unusable, or setting booby traps in the couple's house, especially the kitchen and bedroom. In occupational groups, neophytes may be sent to fetch such fictitious items as a check stretcher or a bucket of steam. Both wedding pranks and initiation pranks function as a form of hazing, in which the reactions of targets help determine whether they achieve full social inclusion.

Practical Jokes and Relationships

The patterns of practical joking—who may play a joke on whom and who joins in the communal laughter at the discomfiture of the dupe—align with salient boundaries between social groups.

The most common context for practical joking is between friends and relatives. In these settings, targets may get even with jokers by playing jokes on them in turn, sometimes leading to extended sequences of reciprocal practical jokes. Such sequences are often found between people who enjoy a *joking relationship,* and such patterns of esoteric or in-group joking serve to build solidarity between participants. In these cases, it is the relationship that gives each person the license to joke with the other, and the shared laughter enhances the bonds between them.

In contrast, exoteric practical jokes rarely offer opportunity for reciprocity. When targets are left unaware of their victimization or when they are unable to join in the laughter, at their expense, practical jokes have an exclusionary and boundary-heightening effect. In occupational settings, anonymous practical jokes on superiors enhance solidarity within other ranks; an individual trickster may represent the feelings of the group and provide a playful outlet for resentment. Initiation pranks can be either inclusive or exclusive, depending, in part, on how targets react to being fooled.

When exoteric practical joke traditions occur between salient groups rather than individuals, they accentuate the differences between groups. Hoaxes, which occur in public between groups of people, arise from and display perceived relationships between groups. College students are known for large-scale public pranks that are not always intended to fool people but instead rely on secrecy and surprise to astonish outsiders. The "hacks" created by generations of MIT students are one example. Such public pranks operate as displays of group identity and group boundaries.

Moira Marsh

See also Fools; Jokes; Joking Relationship; Puns; Spoofing; Tall Tale; Teasing

Further Readings

Basso, K. H. (1979). *Portraits of "the Whiteman": Linguistic play and cultural symbols among the western Apache*. Cambridge, UK; New York, NY: Cambridge University Press.

Bauman, R. (1986). We was always pullin' jokes: The management of point of view. In *Story, performance, and event: Contextual studies of oral narrative* (pp. 33–53). New York, NY: Cambridge University Press.

Dundes, A. (1989). April fool and April fish: Towards a theory of ritual pranks. In *Folklore matters* (pp. 98–109). Knoxville: University of Tennessee Press.

Goffman, E. (1974). *Frame analysis: An essay on the organization of experience*. New York, NY: Harper & Row.

Smith, M. (2009). Arbiters of truth at play: Media April Fools' Day hoaxes. *Folklore, 120*, 274–290.

Smith, M. (2009). Humor, unlaughter, and boundary maintenance. *Journal of American Folklore, 122*(484), 148–171.

Steinberg, N. (1992). *If at all possible, involve a cow: The book of college pranks*. New York, NY: St. Martin's Press.

Tallman, R. (1974). A generic approach to the practical joke. *Southern Folklore Quarterly, 38*(4), 259–274.

PREJUDICE, HUMOR AND

Disparagement humor (e.g., racist or sexist humor) is humor that denigrates, belittles, or maligns an individual or social group. Humor theorists have argued that such humor fosters the expression of prejudice—a negative attitude toward a social group or a person perceived to be a member of that group. Empirical research on the relationship between disparagement humor and prejudice has been guided by two different conceptualizations of disparagement humor: disparagement humor as a "producer" of prejudice, and disparagement humor as a "releaser" of prejudice.

Disparagement Humor as a Producer of Prejudice

Theoretical Overview

Humor theorists guided by the conceptualization of disparagement humor as a producer of prejudice have suggested that disparagement humor has negative consequences at both the individual or psychological level and at the macro-sociological level. At the individual level, disparagement humor is thought to create and reinforce prejudice and negative stereotypes of the targeted group.

By reinforcing negative stereotypes and prejudice at the individual level, disparagement humor is thought to maintain cultural or societal prejudice at the macro-sociological level. Theorists have proposed that racist humor depicted on television, for instance, reinforces stereotypes and prejudice among racist people, and thus functions to perpetuate a racist society. Furthermore, disparagement humor functions as a means of social control, allowing members of the dominant group in society to maintain their privileged position. Sexist humor, for instance, perpetuates power imbalances between men and women.

Empirical Evidence

Consistent with the theoretical positions described in the previous paragraphs, *reciting* disparagement humor can have a negative effect on the humorist's attitudes and stereotypes of the targeted group. Researchers have shown that when people agree to recite jokes about lawyers and other social groups, their attitudes toward those groups become more negative. Daryl Bem's self-perception theory and Leon Festinger's cognitive dissonance theory can account for these findings. According to self-perception theory, the negative remarks people make about a social group can inform them of their attitude toward the group and thus lead them to report more negative attitudes and stereotypes. From the framework of cognitive dissonance theory, people's negative remarks can be inconsistent with their attitudes and thus create cognitive dissonance. Participants might change their attitudes and stereotypes to become more consistent with their negative remarks in order to reduce cognitive dissonance. According to either explanation, the negative consequences of reciting disparagement humor do not implicate any unique effects of humor as a medium of communication apart from the disparaging content.

The effects of *exposure* to disparagement humor are less consistent with the position that disparagement humor produces prejudice. James Olson, Gregory Maio, and Karen Hobden exposed participants to either disparagement humor targeting men, disparagement humor targeting lawyers, neutral humor, nonhumorous disparagement of men, or nonhumorous disparagement of lawyers. They then measured the content and accessibility of stereotypes about, and attitudes toward, the men and lawyers. Across the three experiments, they performed a total of 83 analyses, and only one revealed a significant effect of exposure to disparagement humor relative to exposure to neutral humor or nonhumorous disparagement. Exposure to disparagement humor simply did not affect the content or accessibility of stereotypes about, and attitudes toward, the targeted groups relative to nonhumorous disparagement or neutral humor.

Likewise, other research has shown that exposure to sexist humor does not affect the evaluative content of men's stereotypes about women relative to nonhumorous disparagement or neutral humor. Collectively, then, existing empirical research provides no evidence that exposure to disparagement humor uniquely affects stable, internal knowledge structures, such as stereotypes about, and attitudes toward, the targeted group.

Disparagement Humor as a Releaser of Prejudice

Theoretical Overview

Thomas E. Ford and Mark A. Ferguson's prejudiced norm theory describes the process by which exposure to disparagement humor fosters the outward expression or "release" of prejudice. The theory is grounded in research on the way prejudiced people manage the conflict between their negative attitude toward a social group and external nonprejudiced norms of appropriate conduct. Highly prejudiced people tend to respond to targets of prejudice in accordance with prevailing social norms. They suppress prejudice when the norms in a given context dictate restraint; they express prejudice when the prevailing norms communicate approval to do so. Events that socially sanction or justify the expression of prejudice are known as "releasers" of prejudice. Releasers allow people to express prejudice without fearing social reprisals.

Prejudiced norm theory proposes that disparagement humor (e.g., a sexist or racist joke) trivializes or makes light of expressions of prejudice against the targeted group and, in so doing, communicates an implicit message or normative standard that in this context prejudice can be treated in a playful, noncritical manner. In contrast, nonhumorous disparagement does not activate such a conversational rule of levity. On exposure to nonhumorous disparagement, the recipient essentially brings to bear the usual critical reactions to such sentiments prescribed by nonprejudiced norms of conduct. In fact, it is possible that nonhumorous disparagement makes the usual nonprejudiced norms more salient.

The recipient's response to disparagement humor contributes to whether or not he or she will define the context as one in which discrimination need not be considered critically. If the recipient approves of disparagement humor—that is, accepts it as "only a joke"—he or she tacitly assents to a shared understanding (a social norm) that it is acceptable in this context to make light of discrimination. People essentially negotiate an agreement to suspend the typical, serious norms for responding to such sentiments. In the context of disparagement humor, then, discrimination against the targeted group may seem less inappropriate.

The recipient, however, could object to the disparagement humor and challenge (reject) the normative standard implied by the humor. The recipient's opposition to disparagement humor prevents the emergence of a shared local norm of tolerance of discrimination against the targeted group. Consequently, the recipient should be less likely to tacitly define the context as one in which discrimination need not be considered critically. As a result, the usual nonprejudiced standards of conduct would not be displaced by the disparagement humor, and instances of discrimination would still be perceived in accordance with those norms.

Highly prejudiced people are especially likely to accept disparagement humor and interpret it in a lighthearted manner. Consequently, on exposure to disparagement humor, people high in prejudice are especially likely to perceive and assent to an emergent prejudiced norm in the immediate social context and use that norm to guide their own responses toward members of the targeted group.

Empirical Evidence

Research has shown that exposure to disparagement humor affects people's perceptions of discrimination and their willingness to engage in subtle forms of discrimination. For instance, men who are exposed to sexist jokes report greater acceptance of rape myths and violence against women, but only when they accept the jokes—that is, interpret them in a nonserious, lighthearted manner. Also, to the extent that men are sexist, they perceive a norm of tolerance of sexism in the immediate context on exposure to sexist jokes but *not* on exposure to nonsexist jokes or nonhumorous sexist statements.

Furthermore, on exposure to sexist humor, men higher in sexism use the implicit prejudiced norm to guide their own reactions to a sexist event. In one study, for instance, sexist men expressed greater tolerance of sexist remarks that a manager had made to a new female employee when they had first read sexist jokes than when they had read nonsexist jokes or nonhumorous sexist statements. This effect was due to the perception of normative tolerance of sexism in the immediate context.

Other research has demonstrated that on exposure to disparagement humor, prejudiced people are more willing to engage in discriminatory behavior. For instance, on exposure to sexist comedy skits, men higher in sexism have been found to discriminate against women by allocating greater funding cuts to a women's organization on their college campus. In a similar study, people higher in prejudice against gays discriminated against a gay student organization more on exposure to anti-gay jokes than on exposure to neutral jokes.

Conclusion

A review of the theoretical and empirical literature reveals that disparagement humor is not simply benign amusement. It expands the bounds of socially appropriate behavior, creating social conditions in which discrimination can be more easily rationalized as not inappropriate. Accordingly, disparagement humor promotes the behavioral release of prejudice against its target.

Thomas E. Ford

See also Humor Mindset; Psychology; Stereotypes

Further Readings

Bem, D. J. (1972). Self-perception theory. In L. Berkowitz (Ed.), *Advances in experimental social psychology* (Vol. 6, pp. 1–62). San Diego, CA: Academic Press.

Festinger, L. (1957). *A theory of cognitive dissonance.* Stanford, CA: Stanford University Press.

Ford, T. E., Boxer, C., Armstrong, J., & Edel, J. (2008). More than "just a joke": The prejudice-releasing function of sexist humor. *Personality and Social Psychology Bulletin*, *34*(2), 159–170. doi:10.1177/0146167207310022

Ford, T. E., & Ferguson, M. (2004). Social consequences of disparagement humor: A prejudiced norm theory. *Personality and Social Psychology Review*, *8*, 79–94. doi:10.1207/S15327957PSPR0801_4

Maio, G. R., Olson, J. M., & Bush, J. (1997). Telling jokes that disparage social groups: Effects on the joke-teller's stereotypes. *Journal of Applied Social Psychology*, *27*, 1986–2000.

Olson, J. M., Maio, G. R., & Hobden, K. L. (1999). The (null) effects of exposure to disparagement humor on stereotypes and attitudes. *HUMOR: International Journal of Humor Research*, *12*, 195–219.

Romero-Sánchez, M., Durán, M., Carretero-Dios, H., Megias, J. L., & Moya, M. (2010). Exposure to sexist humor and rape proclivity: The moderator effect of aversiveness ratings. *Journal of Interpersonal Violence*, *25*(12), 2339–2350. doi:10.1177/0886260509354884

Ryan, K., & Kanjorski, J. (1998). The enjoyment of sexist humor, rape attitudes, and relationship aggression in college students. *Sex Roles*, *38*, 743–756. doi:10.1023/A:1018868913615

Presidential Humor

Presidential humor refers to either the use of humor by presidents and presidential candidates or humorous images, texts, or expressions that mock, ridicule, or satirize presidents and presidential candidates. Presidential humor is a subset of political humor. Since its inception, the U.S. presidency has served as an important target and scapegoat for comedians, editorialists, and satirists. From Thomas Nast's 19th-century political cartoons in *Harper's Weekly*, to Will Rogers's 1928 mock campaign for presidency in *LIFE*, to Stephen Colbert's formation of a "Super PAC" on *The Colbert Report* during the 2012 presidential campaign, and in myriad other examples, humor has been central to how candidates run for office and how commentators criticize political leaders. According to the framework developed by David L. Paletz in his 1990 article "Political Humor and Authority: From Support to Subversion," political humor, including presidential humor, can range from being supportive to being subversive. Supportive presidential humor is relatively innocuous and friendly to the dominant political order, incumbent individuals, and prevailing institutions. Subversive presidential humor challenges the norms and values of status quo political power and institutions.

Humor Used by Presidents and Presidential Candidates

The first type of presidential humor is the rhetorical use of humor by presidents and presidential candidates. The United States has a long history of presidents employing humor, and humor use by presidents has increased in the 20th century with the rise of television. Presidents including John F. Kennedy, Ronald Reagan, and Bill Clinton were recognized for their quick wit and their ability to use humor. For instance, in the 1980 campaign, Ronald Reagan humorously attacked incumbent President Jimmy Carter's description of the economic downturn as a "recession" and not a "depression," when Reagan quipped, "If the President wants a definition, I'll give him one. Recession is when your neighbor loses his job, depression is when you lose yours, and recovery will be when Jimmy Carter loses his." Humor is also used by presidential candidates. Vice presidential and presidential candidate Bob Dole was known for his deadpan humor and published *Great Presidential Wit*, a book of jokes told by presidents, in which Dole ranks the presidents according to their humor level.

Humor is an effective rhetorical tool for presidential candidates to build their image by making themselves more accessible to the public or to make their opponents less attractive. It can be used to soften attacks or to relax a hostile audience. A candidate who is able to elicit laughter through a humorous comment, often at the expense of the opposition candidate, has built a common bond with the audience. Humor can increase a candidate's likeability, and humor often produces a halo effect on voter evaluations of a candidate's honesty, warmth, attractiveness, sincerity, honesty, and believability. Presidents may use humor to ingratiate themselves with audiences, and humor can also make a presidential address more entertaining. In the cases of Presidents Kennedy and Reagan, "playful" humor was a central element of their charismatic leadership style and has contributed to their enduring personal legacies. Humor can also make a point or argument such as when a president leads the public through a comical anecdote. Abraham Lincoln, perhaps the best known presidential storyteller, was adept at using humorous, folksy anecdotes to draw moral conclusions and support his point of view. Last, humor can deflect criticism by using a joke to brush aside or minimize a critique or question. In the 1980 debates, for example, Reagan brushed aside Carter's lengthy critique with his now famous one-liner, "There you go again."

A subtype of this rhetorical use of humor is self-deprecating humor. Presidents and presidential candidates frequently use self-deprecating humor to build identification and perceived commonality with the public. Self-deprecating humor allows candidates to address and respond to their personal flaws and can actually build a president's perceived credibility because only confident leaders with high prestige could afford to poke fun at themselves. For example, when Ronald Reagan's age was raised as an issue in the 1984 presidential debates, Reagan responded with a joke that acknowledged and rebutted this critique, saying, "I will not make age an issue of this campaign. I am not going to exploit, for political purposes, my opponent's youth and inexperience." This classic retort allowed Reagan to reframe and energize his candidacy and inoculate himself against future age-related critiques.

Humor Used to Mock, Ridicule, or Satirize Presidents and Presidential Candidates

The second dominant form of presidential humor is the use of humorous images, texts, or expressions that mock, ridicule, or satirize presidents or presidential candidates. The lampooning of presidents is important because research shows a strong relationship between humorous media portrayals of candidates and how the public perceives them, with a corresponding influence on voters' likelihood to vote for or against candidates. Bob Hope, a versatile performer who could act, dance, sing, and deliver a joke, began his career on vaudeville stages before moving to Broadway, radio, film, and television. Hope's brand of presidential humor would singe, but not burn, as he joked about the state of the nation and its leaders. Hope did at times cross the ever-changing line of good taste, and he received an inordinate amount of criticism in his career. For instance, Hope's 1949 satirical radio sketch portraying President Harry Truman and First Lady Bess Truman as hosts of a breakfast radio show caused a national uproar about the appropriateness of ridiculing the president and his family.

Other comedians such as Art Buchwald, Mark Russell, Bill Maher, Dennis Miller, and Lewis Black made careers lambasting and teasing U.S. presidents. Beginning in the 1950s, a new generation of comedians, labeled "sick comics" by the press of the time, created presidential satire that was experimental, biting, and irreverent. These comedians, such as Lenny Bruce, Mort Sahl, Dick Gregory, George Carlin, and Bill Hicks, used hard-edged satire to critique what they saw as the hollow rhetoric and crass structure of the dominant political culture.

A ubiquitous form of presidential humor is parody, in which a humorist exaggerates and magnifies some aspect of a person or event. Parodies include impersonations of presidents wherein an impersonator distorts or exaggerates some aspect of the political figure for comic effect. Illustrator David Levine used heavy shadow and expressive lines to draw enduring caricatures of presidents in his cartoons. Most commentators, including President Gerald Ford himself, agreed that Chevy Chase's "bumbling fool" impersonation of Ford on *Saturday Night Live* hurt the president in public opinion polls. *Saturday Night Live* became well known for its vivid caricatures of presidents, including Dana Carvey's aristocratic George H. W. Bush, Darrell Hammond's insatiable Bill Clinton, and Will Ferrell's buffoonish George W. Bush.

One subtype of presidential parody, the political cartoon, has a long history in U.S. politics and emerged out of the fine art tradition in Europe. Early presidential humor focused on newspaper editorial cartoons, with cartoonists employing caricature to lampoon and ridicule politicians. Scholars date the first U.S. political cartoon to Benjamin Franklin's 1747 drawing of "The Waggoner and Hercules" in the pamphlet *Plain Truth*. Franklin used the illustration of Aesop's fable along with the caption "Non Votis" ("God helps those who help themselves") to persuade Pennsylvanians to fight for pacifist Quakers. Franklin's later cartoon depicting a severed snake and captioned "Join or Die" was used to unite the American colonies during the French and Indian War and the American Revolution in 1776. Political cartoons matured over the next century and were again popularized in the second half of the 19th century when influential cartoonists such as Thomas Nast, Joseph Keppler, and Walt McDougall used their drawings to spread reform and critique entrenched politicians. In the second half of the 20th century, cartoonist Herb Block used his position at *The Washington Post* to lambast presidents from Franklin D. Roosevelt to George W. Bush, with his attacks on Richard Nixon during the Watergate scandal playing a pivotal role in defining the public image of Nixon. Other important editorial cartoonists during the 20th century include Paul Conrad, Pat Oliphant, Jeff MacNelly, Garry Trudeau, and Jules Feiffer.

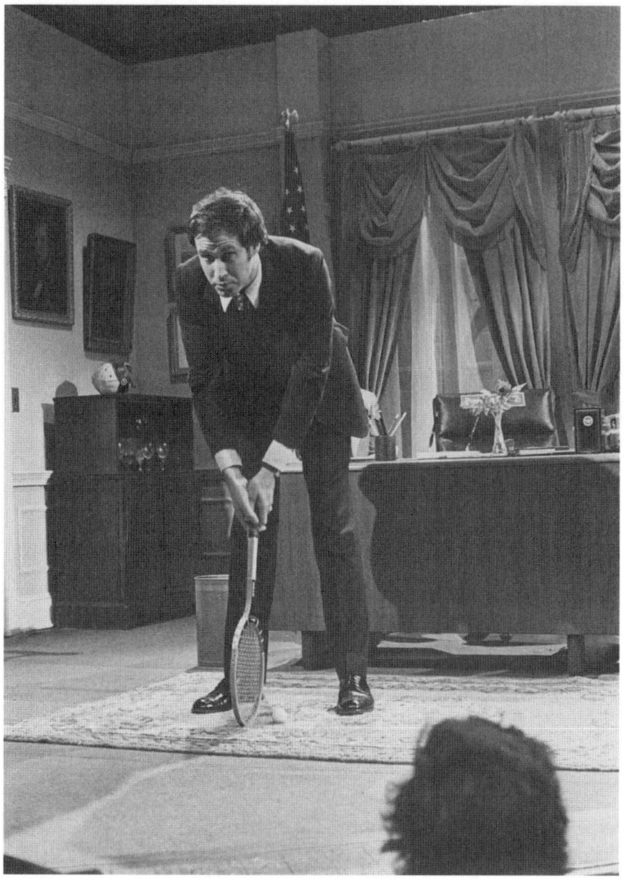

A *Saturday Night Live* skit with Chevy Chase as President Gerald Ford during "An Oval Office" skit on April 17, 1976

Source: NBCU Photo Bank via Getty Images.

The rise of television and new media led to a golden age of presidential mockery, and the presidents in the second half of the 20th century provided considerable material to televised comedians. In the 1960s, television programs such as *Laugh-In*, *The Smothers Brothers Comedy Hour*, and *That Was the Week That Was* brought presidential humor to baby boomers entering adolescence and adulthood. More

Woodcut with Benjamin Franklin's warning to the British colonies in America, "Join or Die," exhorting them to unite against the French and the Natives, shows a segmented snake, "S.C., N.C., V., M., R., N.J., N.Y., [and] N.E." Illustration in the *Philadelphia Gazette*, May 9, 1754.

Source: Cartoon by Benjamin Franklin. Library of Congress Prints and Photographs Division, Washington, DC, Reproduction Number LC-USZC4-5315.

than any other post–World War II president, Nixon made an easy target for these televised comedians, who had an hour or more of television time to fill each week. Leading this charge was Johnny Carson, who once joked, "Whenever anyone in the White House tells a lie, Nixon gets a royalty." *The Tonight Show Starring Johnny Carson* established the modern format of a late-night talk show, which began with a monologue of one-liners, often poking fun at presidents. Subsequent late night hosts, such as Jay Leno and David Letterman, used this format to ridicule and tease presidents for their personal and political shortcomings from Bill Clinton's impeachment to George W. Bush's verbal gaffes.

Satirists Jon Stewart and Stephen Colbert perfected "fake news" on *The Daily Show* and *The Colbert Report*, respectively, at the turn of the century. Stewart's coverage of the 2000 and 2004 election propelled *The Daily Show* to high ratings and critical admiration. Colbert, a former correspondent for *The Daily Show*, satirizes conservative, personality-driven political talk programs and also frequently critiques the political process. Colbert made headlines by testifying in character as his right-wing alter ego before a House of Representative committee in 2010 and by hammering President Bush, who was seated only a few feet away, in character at the 2006 White House Correspondents' Association Dinner.

As broadband Internet access spread in the 1990s and 2000s, the style of presidential humor institutionalized on radio, television, and print migrated online. One can now easily access the full spectrum of presidential jokes, humorous videos, political cartoons, satire, and more on the Internet. Founded by Gregg and Evan Spiridellis, JibJab.com's 2004 video of presidential candidates George W. Bush and John Kerry singing an updated version of Woody Guthrie's "This Land Is Your Land" set a high standard for online cartoon parody of presidential elections. The satirical newspaper and website *The Onion* (and the corresponding satirical web video broadcast *The Onion News Network*) has caricaturized presidents with headlines such as "Clinton Vetoes 'Stab Clinton' Bill," "Bush Actually President, Nation Suddenly Realizes," and "Shirtless Biden Washes Trans Am in White House Driveway."

Dan Schill

See also Caricature; Internet Humor; Political Humor; Satire; Satire News

Further Readings

Alisky, M. (1990). White House wit: Presidential humor to sustain policies, from Lincoln to Reagan. *Presidential Studies Quarterly, 20*, 373–382.

Baumgartner, J. D., & Morris, J. S. (Eds.). (2008). *Laughing matters: Humor and American politics in the media age*. New York, NY: Routledge.

Gardner, G. (1988). *The mocking of the president: A history or campaign humor from Ike to Ronnie.* Detroit, MI: Wayne State University Press.

Meyer, J. (1990). Ronald Reagan and humor: A politician's velvet weapon. *Communication Studies, 41*, 76–88.

Nitz, M., Cypher, A., Reichert, T., & Mueller, J. E. (2003). Candidates as comedy: Political presidential humor on late-night television shows. In L. L Kaid, J. C. Tedesco, D. G. Bystrom, & M. S. McKinney (Eds.), *The millennium election: Communication in the 2000 campaign* (pp. 165–175). New York, NY: Rowman & Littlefield.

Paletz, D. L. (1990). Political humor and authority: From support to subversion. *International political science review, 11*, 483–493.

Sloane, A. A. (2001). *Humor in the White House: The wit of five American Presidents*. Jefferson, NC: McFarland.

Smith, C., & Voth, B. (2002). The role of humor in political argument: How "strategery" and "lockboxes" changed a political campaign. *Argumentation and Advocacy, 39,* 110–129.

Stewart, P. A. (2011). The influence of self- and other-deprecatory humor on presidential candidate evaluation during the 2008 U.S. election. *Social Science Information, 50*(2), 201–222.

Psychiatric Disorders

A substantial amount of research has been done to understand the relationship between psychiatric disorders and humorous phenomena such as sense of humor and humor appreciation. There are two research questions that are of particular interest:

1. How do cognitive and affective impairments associated with various psychiatric disorders affect emotional and cognitive processes or subprocesses associated with humor appreciation or the sense of humor in general?
2. How do sense of humor and humor appreciation (or the lack thereof) influence the development or maintenance of psychiatric disorders?

This entry focuses on a select number of well-researched and more common psychiatric disorders, including depression, anxiety (focusing mainly on social anxiety), and schizophrenia. In addition, this entry summarizes findings on humor in autism spectrum disorder (ASD; disorders in this group are classified as developmental disorders). ASD is particularly interesting in relation to humor, because it is the only group of disorders in which humorlessness is claimed to be an essential characteristic.

Depression

Results from several studies investigating the relationship between sense of humor and depression suggest that individuals with depression score lower on multiple humor scales and enjoy humorous material to a lesser extent than do healthy controls. Perhaps due to their predominant negative mood, individuals with depression are less susceptible to positive humorous stimuli and less motivated to engage in humorous activities. Additionally, research has suggested that individuals with depression experience a negative processing bias, which, due to a decrease in the ability to interpret events or experiences as positive, may exacerbate this aversion to humor.

The impact of depression on the experience of humor is not only related to the mood and emotional components of depression but to the cognitive components as well. The decreased ability to mentalize (i.e., to attribute mental states to other people and to take perspective; also known as having a *theory of mind*) as well as lower executive functioning (inhibition, set shifting, working memory, and verbal fluency) in individuals with depression can negatively affect humor processing.

Anxiety

A majority of the studies that examine anxiety and humor have focused on the effect humor has in reducing anxiety. The results of these studies suggest that humor is only effective in individuals with low to moderate levels of anxiety, whereas in individuals with high levels of anxiety, humor may actually have detrimental effects. Additionally, other studies focused on sense of humor in people with high levels of anxiety and suggest a negative relationship between the two variables. It should be noted that a negative relationship is only seen in specific types of humor (e.g., coping humor).

Recently, numerous studies have been conducted to better understand the phenomenon of *gelotophobia*, or the fear of being laughed at. Individuals with gelotophobia find it hard to perceive even positive humor as something of value and find aggressive, negative types of humor particularly distressing.

It is plausible that socially anxious individuals find situational or incidental humor distressing, especially if it is unclear whether people are laughing with them (i.e., teasing them in a benevolent way) or at them (i.e., making fun of them in a malevolent way). This is in line with the general finding that ambiguous social situations may induce stress in individuals with social phobia. A recent study examined responses to different types of cartoons (i.e., visual puns, semantic cartoons, and theory of mind cartoons) in individuals with either high or low levels of social anxiety. Participants with high levels of social anxiety had difficulties appreciating cartoons based on theory of mind, which often play with false mental states of others. They perceived jokes about other people's mental states as negative and threatening, perhaps due to a negative interpretation bias. These findings suggest that social cognition, and the correct interpretation of other people's mental states in particular, plays an important role in humor processing and may be disrupted in individuals with social anxiety.

Schizophrenia

Past research examining the relationship between schizophrenia and humor have repeatedly demonstrated that individuals with schizophrenia are less able to understand and appreciate humorous material than are individuals without schizophrenia. Results from an extensive study assessing humor skills and various affective and cognitive skills suggest that the deficit in humor appreciation in schizophrenia may be attributed to impairments in basic neurocognitive domains, such as selective and sustained attention, as well as phonological word fluency. The disruption of normal humor processing in individuals with schizophrenia may also be related to their difficulty in mentalizing. As in depression and ASD, difficulties in attributing mental states to others (theory of mind) negatively impact humor processing.

In addition to diminished humor appreciation, excessive or pathological forms of laughter are observed in some individuals with schizophrenia. This pattern may also be seen in some individuals experiencing a manic phase and who become euphoric in response to simple positive stimuli, often finding humor in everything. In contrast to other pathological forms of laughter (e.g., gelastic seizures), these excessive outbursts of laughter are likely manic episodes in which overreactions to any (non)sentimental stimulus can occur.

Autism Spectrum Disorders

Humorlessness is an essential characteristic in Asperger's syndrome, which is characterized as a high-functioning autism spectrum disorder (ASD). Hans Asperger, who first described the disorder, stated that ASD subjects do not comprehend jokes, are unable to be cheerful in a relaxed manner, and are unable to understand the world in a peaceful way— all of which can be seen as a foundation for a good sense of humor.

Several studies have examined the relationship between ASD and humor. When focusing on appreciation of humorous material, results have suggested that individuals with ASD have a decreased ability to understand and enjoy humor, particularly if the humorous material plays with false mental states of others (i.e., theory of mind jokes). However, individuals with ASD do understand simpler forms of humor, such as wordplays, visual puns, and slapstick. These results suggest that the basic cognitive processes that underlie humor (e.g., incongruity and resolution) are not impacted in ASD; however, characteristic deficits in social cognition (e.g., cognitive empathy, theory of mind) observed in individuals with ASD may inhibit their ability to appreciate certain (social) forms of humor. In addition, social-communicative functions of emotions seem to be interrupted, as suggested in a recent study whose results demonstrated that in response to humorous stimuli, individuals with ASD display incoherence between experienced positive emotions associated with humor and the expression of it (laughter).

In addition to deficits in social-communicative functions, one recent study has suggested that individuals with ASD typically exhibit high seriousness and low cheerfulness. This lack of playfulness, an important characteristic for engagement in humorous activities or indulgence in positive emotions of a joke, may hinder individuals with ASD from actively engaging in humor. Relatedly, it has been suggested that individuals with ASD prefer incongruity-resolution humor to nonsense humor. Perhaps due to their serious nature, individuals with ASD find the absurdity of nonsense humor to be less funny than do individuals without ASD.

A third component that may influence humor processing in individuals with ASD is their detail-oriented processing style. It has been shown that individuals with ASD often focus on details that are not relevant to the comprehension of the joke. This attention to irrelevant details may lead individuals with ASD to interpret humorous stimuli in a way that differs from the one intended by the author of a cartoon, for example.

Humor and the Development of Mental Disorders

Having a good sense of humor is often viewed as a protective factor against developing psychiatric disorders. Humor is positively associated with intimacy, emotional stability, social skills, and social support—all of which have been linked to positive psychosocial functioning. Additionally, research has suggested that sense of humor, especially in more positive styles of humor (e.g., affiliative, self-enhancing) may serve a stress-moderating function. Further, the cognitive shift produced by humor (similar to the process of problem solving or perspective change) may function as a means to establish distance between an individual and a negative situation, which can help to effectively regulate emotions. Finally, positive emotions that are associated with humor have been shown to have the ability to "undo" negative emotions. However, humor is not an effective means in every disorder. One study showed that humor served as moderator of stress for depressive symptomatology but not anxiety.

Conclusion

Studies examining humor in psychiatric disorders have elucidated the affective and cognitive components that are essential in understanding and appreciating humor. Both cognitive executive functioning (e.g., verbal fluency, set shifting) and the ability to mentalize dramatically impact the ability to understand and appreciate humor. Emotional components, such as mood states and traits, which affect the susceptibility to humor, and negative processing bias, which impacts humor appreciation, are also of great importance. This brief overview demonstrates the complexity involved in the humor processes that enable positive humor experiences and responses, and how humor can be affected in several disorders because of cognitive or affective subcomponents that are disrupted.

Andrea C. Samson

See also Brain, Neuropsychology of Humor; Cognitive Aspects; Gelotophobia; Humor Styles; Incongruity and Resolution; Mirth

Further Readings

Bozikas, V., Kosmidis, M., Giannakou, M., Anezoulaki, D., Patrikis, P., Fokas, K., & Karavatos, A. (2007). Humor appreciation deficits in schizophrenia: The relevance of basic neurocognitive functioning. *Journal of Nervous and Mental Disease, 194,* 325–331.

Martin, R. A. (2007). Humor and mental health. In R. A. Martin (Ed.), *The psychology of humor: An integrative approach* (pp. 269–308). London, UK: Academic Press.

Samson, A. C. (2013). Humor(lessness) elucidated—Sense of humor in individuals with autism spectrum disorders: Review and introduction. *HUMOR: International Journal of Humor Research, 26*(3), 391–409.

Samson, A. C., Lackner, H. K., Weiss, E. M., & Papousek, I. (2012). Perception of other people's mental states affects humor in social anxiety. *Journal of Behavior Therapy and Experimental Psychiatry, 43,* 625–631.

Ueckermann, J., Channon, S., Lehmkämper, C., Abdel-Hamid, M., Vollmoeller, W., & Daum, I. (2008). Executive function, mentalizing and humor in major depression. *Journal of the International Neuropsychological Society, 14,* 55–62.

Psychological Distance

When Mark Twain said, "Humor is tragedy plus time," he intuitively understood how distance from an aversive event can facilitate humor. Mel Brooks also acknowledged the role of distance when he famously quipped, "Tragedy is when I cut my finger. Comedy is when you walk into an open sewer and die." Indeed, experiencing something as close or far away—what scientists call psychological distance—is an important factor in humor appreciation. This entry discusses how distance helps or harms humor and offers a theoretical account of its role in humor appreciation.

Sometimes Distance Helps Humor

In some cases, psychological distance makes things funnier. This is especially true for highly aversive events. There are four ways that something can seem close or far away, and each can help transform tragedy into comedy: temporal distance, social distance, spatial or physical distance, and hypothetical distance.

Temporal distance (e.g., a year is more distant than a day): War stories, like getting lost in the woods or getting hit by a car, are not funny at the time, but are often amusing years later. Similarly, jokes often fail if attempted too soon after a tragedy, but Academy Award–winning movies like *Life Is Beautiful* and *Inglorious Bastards* illustrate that even Nazi genocide can be funny if enough time has passed.

Social distance (e.g., a stranger is more distant than a friend): Disparaging jokes are more amusing to people who are not the target of the joke (e.g., sexist jokes are funnier to men). Similarly, disgusting, painful, and upsetting behaviors are funnier when they afflict someone else. For example, laboratory subjects who watched a film clip of a woman eating feces are more amused when they take the perspective of an outside observer rather than the woman's perspective.

Spatial or physical distance (e.g., a mile is more distant than a foot): It is easier to joke about disasters that happen on the other side of the globe than about disasters in one's backyard. Similarly, highly disturbing photographs are more amusing to laboratory participants when the photographs were presented from a distant visual perspective.

Hypothetical distance (e.g., an imagined event is more distant than a real event): Cartoons, like *South Park* and *Looney Tunes,* demonstrate how extreme violence and biting satire is often funny when it is not real. Similarly, laboratory subjects find highly disturbing photographs funnier when the images have ostensibly been altered, or Photoshopped, than when the photos are believed to be real.

Sometimes Distance Hurts Humor

Although less intuitive, there are cases in which closeness appears to facilitate perceptions of humor, as exemplified in popular expressions like "you had to be there" and "it's funny because it's true." It is interesting that most of the examples in which distance reduces humor involve events that are far less aversive than the examples discussed in the previous section. For example, speaking in an unusual accent might prompt laughter at the time, but later recounting how the accent was used may be less funny.

Recent research illustrates that although tragedies are more humorous when temporally, socially, hypothetically, or spatially distant, mild mishaps are more humorous when psychologically close. For example, a Facebook post about accidentally donating $2,000 is funnier when the person losing the money is a stranger rather than a friend, but a milder mishap, a post about accidentally donating $50, is funnier when the person losing the money is a friend rather than a stranger. And whereas a tragedy such as being hit by a car is funnier if it happened 5 years ago than if it happened yesterday, a mild mishap such as stumbling on a curb is funnier if it happened yesterday than if it happened 5 years ago.

Sometimes Distance Hurts, Then Helps, and Then Hurts Humor

To complicate matters further, even though a tragedy can become humorous with distance, too much distance may inhibit humor appreciation. Although people often quip "too soon" in response to a joke about a tragedy immediately after the tragedy, that same joke can be deemed "too late" at a distant point in time. For example, following the untimely demise of a celebrity, a string of jokes may be immediately disseminated, but the telling and retelling of the jokes typically fade with time (e.g., people rarely joke about Michael Jackson's death now). These occurrences suggest that the effect of distance is dynamic, with three categories: a "too close" category when something seems disturbing or offensive, a "just right" category when something seems funny, and a "too far" category when something seems boring.

Why Does Distance Influence Perceptions of Humor?

Humor theories generally have a difficult time explaining why distance sometimes helps and sometimes hurts humor. One theory offers a plausible explanation for the different effects that distance has on humor perception. It does so by taking into account the way that psychological distance helps reduce the threat of aversive events. The benign violation theory, which proposes that humor occurs when something that seems wrong, threatening, or unsettling (i.e., a violation) also seems okay or acceptable (i.e., benign), suggests that either too much or too little threat can inhibit humor perception. Some threat is necessary in order to perceive a violation, but too much threat may make it difficult to perceive a violation as benign.

This theory explains why distance typically makes tragedies more humorous: Distance reduces the threat associated with a severe tragedy, making it easier to see the violation as benign. It also explains why distance typically makes mishaps less humorous: Distance completely eliminates the threat in a mild mishap, making it difficult to perceive a violation.

Finally, the benign violation theory explains why joking about a tragic event can change from "too soon," to "just right," to "too late." At first there is too much threat associated with the event to find jokes about it benign. However, increasing distance reduces threat, initially making it easier to perceive the violations as benign but later making it difficult to perceive any violation at all.

Overall, the benign violation theory and research findings on the role of psychological distance on humor appreciation illustrate how there is a sweet spot in comedy. It is important to get the right mix between how bad something is and how distant it is in order to make people laugh.

A. Peter McGraw, Lawrence E. Williams, and Caleb Warren

See also Appreciation of Humor; Benign Violation Theory; Humor Theories

Further Readings

Hemenover, S. H., & Schimmack, U. (2007). That's disgusting! . . . , but very amusing: Mixed feelings of amusement and disgust. *Cognition and Emotion, 21,* 1102–1113.

McGraw, A. P., & Warren, C. (2010). Benign violations: Making immoral behavior funny. *Psychological Science, 21,* 1141–1149.

McGraw, A. P., Warren, C., Williams, L., & Leonard, B., (2012). Too close for comfort, or too far to care? Finding humor in distant tragedies and close mishaps. *Psychological Science, 25,* 1215–1223.

Veatch, T. C. (1998). A theory of humor. *HUMOR: International Journal of Humor Research, 11,* 161–215.

Wolff, H. A., Smith, C. E., & Murray, H. A. (1934). The psychology of humor. *Journal of Abnormal and Social Psychology, 28,* 341–365.

Psychology

Often defined as the scientific study of human behavior, psychology is a very broad discipline with a number of subfields. Psychologists employ quantitative experimental and correlational research methods to study thinking, feeling, and social behavior. Psychologists have always played a leading role in academic humor research. Many interesting questions about humor may be addressed by each of the subdisciplines of psychology, including cognitive (e.g., What are the mental processes involved in "getting a joke"?), social (e.g., What role does humor play in interpersonal relationships?), biological (e.g., What parts of the brain are involved in the enjoyment of humor?), personality (e.g., How does a sense of humor correlate with other personality traits?), developmental (e.g., What do children find funny at different stages of development?), and clinical (e.g., Does a sense of humor contribute to better mental health?).

Cognitive Psychology

Cognitive psychology focuses on the study of mental processes involved in thinking, feeling, and behaving. Much of the research on cognitive processes in humor comprehension has been based on incongruity theories, which suggest that humor involves the bringing together of two normally incompatible ideas, concepts, or situations in a surprising or unexpected manner. Psychologists have employed a number of research methods to investigate these theories. In some studies, ordinary jokes were modified to manipulate the degree of incongruity and resolution that they contain, and researchers then observed the effects of these manipulations on funniness ratings given by participants. Other researchers have used more artificial types of stimuli to quantify incongruity in terms of the discrepancy between items, such as the semantic distance between pairs of words, or weight differences in a weight judgment paradigm. More recently, researchers have used semantic priming techniques to explore schema activation during the processing of humorous materials. This research has generally supported the importance of incongruity in humor, although more study is needed to fully understand the cognitive processes involved.

In addition, researchers in psycholinguistics, a subfield of cognitive psychology, have investigated humorous uses of everyday language, such as irony and sarcasm. They have sought to understand, for example, how people recognize that these sorts of speech are intended to be interpreted as humor rather than to be taken literally. Studies indicate that this is a complex process, requiring the hearer to combine information from the social context as well as linguistic factors to arrive at an interpretation of the intended meaning.

Researchers have also studied the ways humor may influence other cognitive processes. Experiments have provided considerable evidence that exposure to humor produces an increase in creativity, cognitive flexibility, and problem solving, and the findings suggest that these effects are due to the increased positive emotion associated with humor rather than to cognitive factors. Other research has shown positive effects of humor on memory, largely due to the increased attention and rehearsal given to humorous material.

Social Psychology

Social psychology is concerned with the study of how people influence one another's thoughts, feelings, and behaviors. One topic of investigation has been the various purposes for which people use humor in their everyday social interactions. Because humorous messages are inherently ambiguous, they can often be used to communicate messages indirectly in a way that allows both the speaker and the listener to save face. For example, playful teasing can be used to convey mild criticism in a socially acceptable manner. Humor can also be used to enhance group identity and cohesiveness, to enforce social norms, and to establish status.

Social psychologists are also interested in the role of humor in social perception and interpersonal attraction. A number of studies have shown that people tend to be attracted to others who are perceived to have a sense of humor. When asked to rate the most desirable characteristics of a potential friend, dating partner, or spouse, both men and women rate a sense of humor as one of the most desirable traits. Experiments have demonstrated that engaging in humorous activities and laughing together makes people feel closer and more attracted to one another.

Other research has examined the role of humor in intimate relationships. Married couples who are more satisfied with their relationship are more likely to engage in humorous interactions together, saying funny things and laughing together, even when they are having an argument. However, different styles of humor can have different effects on relationships. If humor is used to make fun of a partner or to make light of problems and avoid discussing conflicts, it can be detrimental to the relationship.

Another topic of interest to social psychologists is social attitudes and prejudice, and a considerable amount of research has investigated humor in this regard. Jokes are often based on stereotypes about particular groups of people based on their race, gender, religion, or sexual orientation. Research has shown that people who enjoy these types of jokes are more likely to have prejudiced attitudes toward the targeted groups. Experimental studies have revealed that, after being exposed to sexist jokes, as compared to equally sexist but nonhumorous statements, people who already have negative attitudes toward women are more likely to be tolerant of discriminatory behavior toward them. The humorous nature of jokes seems to cause people to have a less critical mindset toward the sexist attitudes being conveyed and to perceive discrimination as being more socially acceptable.

Other topics of interest to social psychologists include the role of humor in persuasion and gender differences in humor.

Biological Psychology

Like all psychological phenomena, humor is based on complex biological processes taking place in the brain and nervous system. Psychologists taking a biological approach have made use of numerous methods for investigating humor-related biological phenomena. Electrophysiological studies have examined humor-related changes in autonomic nervous system activity, such as heart rate, blood pressure, and skin conductance. To investigate the brain areas involved in humor, researchers have made use of electroencephalograph (EEG) techniques, in which the electrical activity of the brain is measured by means of electrodes attached to the scalp. By examining various deficits in humor comprehension and appreciation in individuals who have experienced damage to particular parts of the brain as a result of accidents or strokes, researchers have been able to piece together clues about which areas of the brain are involved in humor. Recent advances in neuroimaging techniques such as functional magnetic resonance imaging (fMRI) and positron emission tomography (PET) have enabled researchers to investigate in greater detail the areas of the brain that underlie the perception, comprehension, and enjoyment of humor.

Taken together, this research suggests that numerous regions of the brain are involved in humor. The perception of humor involves many parts of the cerebral cortex that are important for visual, auditory, and linguistic processing. An area at the junction of the left temporal and occipital lobes seems to be particularly important for the perception of humorous incongruity. Another area of the left frontal lobe appears to be involved in the perception of coherence or resolution of incongruity. Once humor has been perceived, the dopamine-based reward network in the limbic system of the brain is activated, underlying the pleasurable feelings of mirth. This induction of positive emotion in turn activates brain areas involved in emotion expression (smiling and laughter) and physiological arousal.

Other humor-related topics of relevance to biological psychology include the physiology of laughter, laughter and smiling in other animals, and the evolutionary origins of humor and laughter.

Personality Psychology

Personality psychology has to do with the measurement and study of habitual individual differences in thinking, feeling, and behaving. Sense of humor is one such personality trait or individual difference variable that has long been of interest to psychologists.

Prior to the 1980s, the most popular approach to measuring individual differences in humor was the use of humor appreciation tests. In these measures, participants are asked to rate the funniness of a series of jokes, cartoons, and other humorous materials, which are clustered into various categories either on a theoretical basis or by means of factor analysis. In this approach, sense of humor is defined in terms of the degree to which the individual enjoys particular types or categories of humor. Factor analytic research by Willibald Ruch and colleagues has revealed that humor appreciation is influenced more by the structure of humorous stimuli (the degree to which incongruity is resolved in the joke) than by the content (e.g., sexual themes). Correlational studies have demonstrated associations between individual differences in humor appreciation and personality traits such as conservatism, tough-mindedness, extraversion, sensation-seeking, and openness to experience.

In recent decades, studies of humor appreciation have largely given way to research employing self-report measures of various aspects of sense of humor. Numerous measures have been devised to assess such aspects as sensitivity to humor, enjoyment of humor, tendency to laugh and smile, and use of humor to cope with stress. The State-Trait Cheerfulness Inventory (STCI) assesses three dimensions that are thought to form the temperamental basis of a sense of humor: cheerfulness, seriousness, and bad mood. The Humor Styles Questionnaire (HSQ) assesses four different styles of humor, two of which are considered to be potentially beneficial for psychological well-being and interpersonal relationships (affiliative and self-enhancing) and two that are potentially detrimental (aggressive and self-defeating). The Humorous Behavior Q-Sort Deck (HBQD) is a Q-sort technique for characterizing individuals' everyday humor-related behaviors. Numerous studies have employed these measures to explore associations with other personality traits such as the Big Five (extraversion, neuroticism, conscientiousness, agreeableness, and openness), coping styles, social skills, attachment, relationship satisfaction, and measures of psychological well-being (e.g., self-esteem, optimism, depression).

To investigate individual differences in the ability to create humor, psychologists have employed various humor creation tests, in which participants are asked to generate humorous responses such as funny captions for cartoons, which are then rated for funniness. Researchers have also explored pathological dimensions of humor, particularly gelotophobia, which is the fear of being laughed at. Studies reveal that individuals who are high on this trait tend to associate laughter with fear and shame and have an aversive response to most forms of humor.

Overall, research using these various measures indicates that the sense of humor is not a unitary construct. Instead, it comprises a number of traits (e.g., cheerfulness, nonserious attitude, humor appreciation, humor creation ability, humor styles) that are not necessarily highly correlated with one another.

Developmental Psychology

Developmental psychology is the study of behavioral, cognitive, social, and affective development over the life span. With regard to humor, researchers have investigated the development of smiling and laughter; comprehension, enjoyment, and production of humor; and individual differences in sense of humor. Infants typically begin to smile in response to other people when they are about 1 month of age, and laughter first appears around 4 months of age in the context of playful social interaction. During the first 2 years, babies tend to laugh in response to incongruous tactile, auditory, and visual stimuli such as funny animal sounds, peek-a-boo, and playful chasing games. With the development of language, humor takes on more complex cognitive forms involving verbal and conceptual incongruity.

Paul McGhee conducted extensive early research on the development of humor during childhood, focusing particularly on cognitive aspects. He proposed a four-stage theory of humor development that parallels Jean Piaget's cognitive stages. According to this model, humor is derived from make-believe play, in which children playfully assimilate objects and actions into cognitive schemas to which they do not normally apply (e.g., pretending a banana is a telephone). As cognitive capacities develop, humor expands into the playful manipulation of language, making use of linguistic ambiguities in phonology, morphology, semantics, and syntax.

Developmental researchers have also investigated the development of children's comprehension of irony and sarcasm. These studies indicate that children do not begin to understand the intended meaning of ironic statements until about age 6 years. This comprehension ability appears to depend on the development of a theory of mind, or the ability to infer a speaker's beliefs or intentions. Appreciation of the humorous nature of irony takes even longer to acquire, beginning around 8 or 9 years of age.

Several studies involving pairs of identical and fraternal twins have been conducted to determine the contribution of genetic versus shared and unshared environmental factors to the development of humor-related traits. This research indicates that genetics and environment have different contributions, depending on the way a sense of humor is conceptualized and measured. When humor is defined in terms of the appreciation of particular types of humorous stimuli, genetic influences have been found to be negligible; most of the variance in humor appreciation can be attributed to both shared and unshared environmental effects. When humor is defined in terms of positive emotionality and the tendency to laugh frequently, genetic factors play a more significant role, although both shared and unshared environmental influences are also important. Finally, a sizable genetic contribution, as well as unshared environmental influences, is found with self-report measures of sense of humor and humor styles.

Researchers have suggested two contrasting hypotheses about the role of the family environment to explain why some children develop a stronger sense of humor than others. According to the modeling/reinforcement model, a strong sense of humor develops in the context of a family in which the parents model and positively reinforce humorous interactions and enjoyment. In contrast, the stress and coping hypothesis suggests that children develop a sense of humor as a way of coping with distress, conflict, and anxiety in an uncongenial family environment. There is some research evidence in support of both these hypotheses, suggesting that there may be different routes to the development of a particularly strong sense of humor.

Clinical Psychology

Clinical psychology has to do with the study, assessment, and treatment of psychological disorders, as well as the study and promotion of factors contributing to positive mental health. In recent decades, a good deal of psychological humor research has focused on the role of humor in emotional well-being and coping with stress. Experimental laboratory studies have demonstrated that exposure to humorous stimuli, such as comedy videos, produces increased positive moods and decreased negative moods, and counteracts the effects of experimentally induced depressed moods. Correlational studies using various self-report measures of sense of humor have generally found positive correlations with measures of well-being (such as self-esteem, optimism, positive moods, and life satisfaction) and negative correlations with measures of depression, anxiety, and other negative moods. Research using the HSQ indicates that certain styles of humor (affiliative and self-enhancing) may be particularly beneficial for psychological well-being, whereas other styles (aggressive and self-defeating) may be detrimental. However, most of this research has been correlational, limiting the ability to draw conclusions about the direction of causality.

Other research has investigated humor as a stress-buffering variable. Researchers have hypothesized that humor, because it inherently involves incongruity and multiple interpretations, provides a way for individuals to shift perspective on a stressful situation, reappraising it from a new and less threatening point of view. As a consequence of this reappraisal, the situation becomes less stressful and more manageable. Experiments using laboratory stressors, such as videos depicting gruesome accidents, have confirmed that the use of humor to cope with these sorts of stressors results in lower levels of self-reported emotional distress as well as reductions in the physiological effects of stress, such as heart rate and skin conductance. Several correlational studies have also reported reduced associations between life stressors and mood disturbance among individuals with higher scores on measures of sense of humor.

The view of humor as a healthy coping strategy and a means of enhancing psychological well-being has led a number of clinical psychologists and psychotherapists to recommend its use in therapy and counseling. It has been suggested that humor may be an important therapeutic tool for establishing rapport between the therapist and patient, helping patients gain insight and alternative perspectives on their problems, reducing emotional distress, and helping to modify dysfunctional behavior. However, other therapists have noted that the use of humor in therapy is not without risk, as it may be perceived by patients as a way of making fun of their problems. Unfortunately, there is currently very little research on beneficial and detrimental uses of humor in therapy, although there is some evidence of effectiveness of humor-based desensitization interventions in the treatment of phobias. Recently researchers have also begun to investigate whether it is possible to improve individuals' sense of humor through a systematic training program and the degree to which this is associated with improvements in psychological well-being. This is an important area for future research.

Rod A. Martin

See also Appreciation of Humor; Brain, Neuropsychology of Humor; Comprehension of Humor; Development of Humor; Health Benefits of Humor, Psychological; Humor Styles; Laughter, Psychology of; Marriage and Couples; Personality, Humor and; Persuasion and Humor; Positive Psychology; Prejudice, Humor and; Psychotherapy, Humor in; Test Measurements of Humor

Further Readings

Ford, T. E., & Ferguson, M. A. (2004). Social consequences of disparagement humor: A prejudiced norm theory. *Personality and Social Psychology Review*, *8*, 79–94.

Kuiper, N. A., Grimshaw, M., Leite, C., & Kirsh, G. (2004). Humor is not always the best medicine: Specific components of sense of humor and psychological well-being. *HUMOR: International Journal of Humor Research*, *17*, 135–168.

Lefcourt, H. M. (2001). *Humor: The psychology of living buoyantly*. New York, NY: Kluwer Academic.

Martin, R. A. (2007). *The psychology of humor: An integrative approach*. Burlington, MA: Elsevier Academic Press.

Martin, R. A., Puhlik-Doris, P., Larsen, G., Gray, J., & Weir, K. (2003). Individual differences in uses of humor and their relation to psychological well-being: Development of the Humor Styles Questionnaire. *Journal of Research in Personality*, *37*, 48–75.

McGhee, P. E. (1979). *Humor: Its origins and development*. New York, NY: Freeman.

Ruch, W. (Ed.). (2007). *The sense of humor: Explorations of a personality characteristic*. Berlin, Germany: Mouton de Gruyter.

Ruch, W. (2008). Psychology of humor. In V. Raskin (Ed.), *The primer of humor research* (pp. 17–100). Berlin, Germany: Mouton de Gruyter.

Ruch, W., Kohler, G., & Van Thriel, C. (1996). Assessing the "humorous temperament": Construction of the facet and standard trait forms of the State-Trait-Cheerfulness Inventory—STCI. *HUMOR: International Journal of Humor Research*, *9*, 303–339.

Psychotherapy, Humor in

Although humor and laughter typically occur together, humor, a complex cognitive stimulus, and laughter, a fairly stereotypical physiological response, can have differing potential consequences in psychotherapy. The ability for a psychotherapy client to experience humor in a context that has previously been highly troublesome and associated with intense negative emotion can, in itself, constitute a significant beneficial shift in cognitive perspective. Humor can also implicitly model that there is more than one way to construe one's experience. Mutually enjoyed laughter, at a minimum, conveys feelings of positive connection between therapist and client in psychotherapy. Arguably, laughter may physiologically relieve excessive negative emotional arousal and can enable clients to feel more at ease in discomforting situations in therapy, but empirical support for this latter claim is lacking. This entry discusses the use of humor in psychotherapy, the benefits of its use, and research on the outcomes.

Humor can occur spontaneously in psychotherapy, introduced by either therapist or client, or it can be deliberately implemented by a therapist to accomplish a particular goal. When humor arises spontaneously, as with most things, there are potential advantages and disadvantages. On the advantageous side, the ability to share humor may reflect or contribute to rapport and a comfortable, trusting therapeutic relationship. Shared understanding and mutual enjoyment of humor implicitly demonstrate a significant level of empathy between two people, therapists and clients included. However, there is always some risk that therapeutic humor, offered with good intentions, may not only fail to be enjoyed by the listener but may be actively misunderstood and found to be offensive. There also exists the possibility that some instances of therapeutic humor may not arise from therapeutic motives. For example, spontaneous therapeutic humor may sometimes reflect a client's motivation to avoid discomforting or more threatening material that needs to be addressed, or a therapist may act on a need to be seen as entertaining and witty when a focus on the client should take precedence. Further, given the powerful impact of immediate reinforcement, for either therapist or client, the anticipation of the immediate reinforcing consequences of laughter from another can sometimes lead one to joke, when other therapeutic goals should have a higher priority.

Humor as Clinical Assessment

It has been argued that particularly for children, who may lack the verbal ability to fully report their own therapeutic concerns, asking for the child's favorite joke (not necessarily the most recent joke heard) can often be revealing of salient underlying issues or conflicts. The favorite joke is, in effect, treated as a projective technique. Although some empirical support exists for this claim, the practice has never been very widely used on any regular basis.

Deliberate Humor

There are a variety of reasons why a therapist may choose to introduce humor into therapy. These include the following:

Insight

Because humor involves an element of surprise, and the emergence of a different perspective at a punch line, humor can sometimes trigger insight or simply vividly represent an insightful lesson from therapy. As a hypothetical example, a Gary Larson cartoon shows a clown in full costume and makeup, standing in a gun shop staring into a display case full of pistols, and thinking to himself, "Laugh at me, will they?" One could not more vividly depict the irony that we often unknowingly and unconsciously create and contribute to problem situations with which we consciously struggle. As in this example, sometimes a reference to commercial or publicly available humor can provide such insight or exemplify it.

Optimism

In a more general sense, the acceptance and mild encouragement of humor in psychotherapy can embody a point emphasized by Sigmund Freud. Freud argued that humor was one of the most liberating and mature defense mechanisms. He claimed that by engaging in humor in response to difficult experiences, one asserts his or her ability to prevail in the face of hardship. Unlike in less mature defense mechanisms (e.g., denial) the stressor is acknowledged and owned, but the person refuses to be overcome by the challenge. Freud's statement was not specifically targeted to humor in psychotherapy; nonetheless, many in psychotherapy experience life in negative ways, and some limited modeling and reinforcement of humor by a therapist can gently encourage greater optimism in facing adversity while still realistically acknowledging the difficulties and challenges present.

Positive Affect

There currently exists an extensive literature showing that positive affect leads to a broadening of one's thought-action repertoire, or openness to a wider range of thoughts and activities, as opposed to the constricting effect of negative affect, which is likely to be salient for psychotherapy clients. Further, positive affect can help people build personal resources, such as social support and resilience. Given that psychotherapy is a context in which clients bring up and process troublesome unresolved issues, the inclusion of humor, as one prominent form of positive affect, could foster both broadening the thought-action repertoire and building personal resources.

Spontaneous Humor

The most typical instance of humor in psychotherapy consists of either therapist or client responding spontaneously to the situational experience without plan or deliberate intention. Even though unplanned, such humor may still serve a variety of therapeutic purposes. The issues about which a client may experience informative insights are highly diverse, but there are many therapeutic goals for which spontaneous humor may serve fairly predictable functions. Sharing appropriate humor can foster rapport and enhance the therapeutic alliance. Sometimes, a humorous perspective may simply make painful material more bearable. Because humor typically involves shifting perspectives, it may also implicitly model flexible thinking and the ability to entertain multiple perspectives regarding clinical concerns. This can be valuable because habitual pessimistic tunnel vision can constitute a substantial barrier to therapeutic improvement. In a survey of psychotherapists reporting on instances of humor from their own personal psychotherapy, multiple instances of each of the following therapeutic functions of humor were reported and identified as helpful, and single examples of each are presented.

Irony to Foster Insight

Sometimes a lighthearted expression of the opposite, or at least some variation, of what is literally intended by the therapist can result in benign provocation and serve as a reminder to the client of a troublesome tendency. For example, a therapist referred to his unassertive client as a "nice guy" on a few occasions in which the client described some troublesome exchange with others. The client was reminded that indeed, he was perhaps being too nice in many contexts, to his distinct disadvantage.

Self-Disclosure Fostering Normalization

Lighthearted self-disclosure by a therapist can sometimes serve to normalize a client's concerns. In one reported example, a client came in for a session, sat down, and said, "I feel stupid sitting here." The therapist responded that sometimes he felt stupid sitting in his own chair as well. The client found the reaction "humorous and real" and felt reassured that even experts did not always have to have all the answers.

Exaggeration of a Client Tendency

This sort of response can sometimes provide a different perspective and desensitize a client's over concern. A client expressed obsessive concern about an aggressive thought that was recurring, and the therapist noted that such thoughts were perfectly normal and that she would "like to pull their eyeballs out and stomp on them." The client found this "hilarious" and was relieved. Humorous exaggeration of others' responses can also sometimes be informative, as clients' social inhibitions are often maintained by exaggerated expectations about negative responses from others. Realization that relevant others would never react as extremely as a therapist's playful depiction in role play can facilitate insight regarding a client's exaggerated assumptions about how others may respond.

The few instances of inappropriate therapist humor volunteered by psychotherapist survey respondents featured aggressive humor or humor with sexual content. Although not literally prohibited, given the emotional connotations of aggressive humor or sexual concerns, therapists need to be particularly sensitive to the possible negative consequences of either of these types of humor.

Humor-Based Therapies

Various authors have argued for therapy approaches in which humor is regarded as the basic therapeutic ingredient. As one example, Frank Farrelly developed provocative therapy, which was originally advanced as an approach for use with schizophrenic clients but later generalized to other problems. The humor engaged in was typically provocative, as implied in the name, and the hypothesis was that in coping with the humor, and making sense of it, the client would become more capable in general. A second therapeutic approach based on humor is Walter O'Connell's Natural High Therapy, in which humor is regarded as a crucial facilitator of self-actualization, or fulfilling one's potential.

Outcome Research

Although there has long been interest among psychotherapists in uses of humor in psychotherapy, there has been very little controlled outcome research on the topic. Systematic desensitization is a behavioral approach for reducing irrational fear. It consists of developing a hierarchy of fear-relevant scenes in collaboration with the client and then having the client imagine the scenes while remaining deeply relaxed. In a relatively rare controlled study of humor in therapy, it has been shown that humor presented in hierarchy scenes in the context of systematic desensitization can be equally as effective as traditional desensitization in reducing irrational fear. This finding emerged in the absence of training in relaxation, even though relaxation was originally regarded as a necessary ingredient to countercondition the fear response.

In observational studies of spontaneous occurrences of humor in psychotherapy, therapy sessions including humor have typically not been found to be associated with more constructive responses by clients than sessions in which there was no humor. This negative finding is qualified by the fact that there are many other possible beneficial effects of humor that have not been assessed in this type of research.

Conclusion

The idea that humor can have therapeutic consequences is substantiated by a wealth of case studies but very minimal formal research. The claim that humor, per se, is therapeutic is unfounded and does not allow for the many ways in which humor is experienced and created or for the variety of circumstances in which it may occur. Humor is a highly diverse and complex topic. Humor research has only begun to identify relatively positive versus negative forms of humor, and even as these are identified, the specific context can often make a great difference in how humor is experienced and perceived. As attempts to integrate humor into psychotherapy continue, psychotherapists must continue to be vigilant regarding not only therapeutic consequences of humor but potential deleterious consequences as well.

W. Larry Ventis

See also Defense Mechanism; Freudian/Psychoanalytic Theory; Positive Psychology; Psychology

Further Readings

Fredrickson, B. L. (2001). The role of positive emotions in positive psychology. *American Psychologist, 56*(3), 218–226.

Fry, W. F., & Salameh, W. (1987). *Handbook of humor and psychotherapy: Advances in the clinical use of humor.* Sarasota, FL: Professional Resource Exchange.
Kuhlman, T. L. (1984). *Humor and psychotherapy.* Homewood, IL: Dow Jones–Irwin Dorsey Professional Books.
Martin, R. A. (2007). *The psychology of humor: An integrative approach.* Burlington, MA: Elsevier Academic Press.
Salameh, W., & Fry, W. F. (1993). *Advances in humor and psychotherapy.* Sarasota, FL: Professional Resource Exchange.
Ventis, W. L., & Friedman, F. (2011, July). *Psychotherapists' experience of humor in their own psychotherapy.* Paper presented at the International Society for Humor Studies Conference, Boston, MA.
Ventis, W. L., Higbee, G., & Murdock, S. A. (2001). Using humor in systematic desensitization to reduce fear. *Journal of General Psychology, 128*(2), 241–253.

Punch Line

The term *punch line* refers to an important part of the joke, often following the joke setup, that produces an unexpected twist in the narrative, resulting in humor. It is possible, in a one-liner, for the punch line to constitute the whole joke, in which case the setup is implied. The punch line is typically the very last part of a joke, but in rare cases, parts of the setup follow it.

A punch line can be looked at as the highest point of tension toward the end of the joke. Once such an assumption is made, a joke can be looked at in terms of "pulses," in Robert Hetzron's terminology, and the punch lines can be described in terms of the pulses or episodes of the joke, as stated by Salvatore Attardo. A straight-line, one-pulse joke would linearly build up the expectation of something and then drop such expectation at the very end, which is where the punch line lies.

Jokes can also contain two pulses, with two corresponding punch lines. An example of such a joke is the "good news–bad news" type, where two characteristics of the same event contrast each other, yet each of them is funny. The following joke adds a macabre twist:

> A Neanderthal leader tells his tribe, "Folks, I have good news and bad news." "What's the bad news?" ask the tribesmen. "We have very little food saved for the winter. We'll have to eat shit." "So, what's the good news?" "We have an enormous amount of shit."
>
> A doctor calls his patient and says, "Fred, I have very bad news and much worse news. The bad news is that you have a terminal inoperable cancer and 24 hours to live." "That's awful," says the patient. "What can be worse than this?" "Oh, I forgot to call you yesterday."

The latter joke, besides the two obvious pulses, both funny (the first one is so because such a phone call cannot be for real: A terminal patient is given months or even years to live, never 24 hours), is also a play on the usual good news–bad news joke. Robert Hetzron describes a somewhat less frequent subtype with two pulses:

> The Parisian Little Moritz is asked in school: "How many deciliters are there in a liter of milk?" He replies: "One deciliter of milk and nine deciliters of water." In France, this is a good joke; in Hungary, this is good milk.

The joke has a punch line (the first pulse) and a commentary afterward (the second pulse) that turns out to be funnier than the punch line. According to Attardo, longer texts can be described in similar terms, and the separate funny utterances would be referred to as "jab lines."

There are other jokes where a punch line is the last answer to a repeating question and, thus, it could be viewed as occurring in parts throughout the text. A typical example of such jokes is any joke involving three characters. The repetition of the question and various answers contribute to the funniness of the last one given. It is possible, of course, for the answers to the questions to be funny in their own right, such as in the following joke:

> What happens when two men and one woman of each nationality, Russian, French, and English, find themselves on three uninhabited islands? The Russian woman falls in love with one man, marries the other, and all three are miserable. The French woman marries one, takes the other as a lover, and all three are blissfully happy. The English go each to their corner of the island because there is nobody to introduce them.

The punch lines can work through different devices that can be thought of as the "logical mechanisms" of a joke. If one considers the expectation buildup in the setup, the punch line can deliberately defeat that for a humorous effect. Notable among those are jokes with a pseudo-punch line, where a question is answered literally and tautologically rather than for real, as in the following two canonical jokes:

"Do you have the time?" "Yes."

"Why did the chicken cross the road?" "To get to the other side."

Robert Hetzron has described a more specific subtype of punch lines as having a relative or an absolute interpretation of the setup, when the opposite was expected. The next two jokes illustrate an absolute expectation replaced by a relative one and expected relative used as absolute:

Upon seeing a funeral procession: "Who died?" "I believe the one in the hearse."

A man approached a policeman walking his beat in the street: "Could you tell me please; where is the other side of the street?" The policeman points to it over there. The man says: "It can't be there, they told me it was over here."

A punch line can be shorter or longer than the other part of the joke. In some cases, the punch line is the only explicitly stated component of a joke. Regardless of the length of the punch line relative to the setup, much of the information in the joke is implied and is readily understood by the audience without being stated. It is, therefore, hard to approximate a typical best length for a punch line. What can be stated with relative certainty is that in most cases, based on analyses by Attardo and colleagues, the punch line is the final part of the joke and the setup does not normally continue after it—and perhaps should not.

Julia M. Taylor

See also Jokes; Linguistic Theories of Humor; Mechanisms of Humor; Puns

Further Readings

Attardo, S. (2001). *Humorous texts: A semantic and pragmatic analysis*. Berlin, Germany: Mouton de Gruyter.

Attardo, S., Attardo, D. H., Baltes, P., & Petray, M. J. (1994). The linear organization of jokes: Analysis of two thousand texts. *HUMOR: International Journal of Humor Research, 7*(1), 27–54.

Hetzron, R. (1991). On the structure of punchlines. *HUMOR: International Journal of Humor Research, 4*(1), 61–108.

Tsakona, W. (2003). Jab lines in narrative jokes. *HUMOR: International Journal of Humor Research, 16*(3), 315–329.

Puns

A pun is a type of joke in which one sound sequence (e.g., a word) has two meanings, and this similarity in sound creates a relationship for the two meanings from which humor is derived. Puns are one of the most prominent types of humorous text and are thought to be both typical as well as comparatively simple—if not simple-minded. For these reasons puns are the manifestation of humor most extensively studied by researchers in disciplines such as linguistics who are interested in humor stimuli and their processing. This entry focuses on the general mechanism of puns and discusses the various classifications of puns as identified in the literature.

General Distinctions

Puns are not simpler in principle than other instances of humorous stimuli, they are merely very condensed. In puns, the textual items that carry the mechanisms that make a text potentially humorous are relatively few: often just one punning word, a similar or identical target word (which may or may not be present), and two meanings that are spuriously appropriate in light of the joke's setup. Consider the following pun:

What did the fish say when it swam
into the wall?
Damn.

In this example, the punch line "Dam(n)" is appropriate in two of its meanings: a structure walling in water in which fish swim can be a dam, and, given its painful accident, a fish might exclaim "damn" (never mind that fish don't swear, or speak at all, because for the sake of jokes such inconsistencies are ignored). This pun is phonetically "perfect," in that both meanings share the exact same sounds, but they can be distinguished by the presence or absence of the final *n* as a spelling difference. In other words, this pun is homophonic (identically sounding) but not homographic (identically written), which is one of the various classifications of puns found in the literature. Most of the classifications are based on superficial differences that are easily identified by the methods of various disciplines, but they don't reflect fundamentally different mechanisms of puns.

Cicero is one of the earliest persons to distinguish puns from other types of jokes. He saw puns as being not just about the meaning, or the concepts the words stand for, but also about the words themselves, their manifestation in sounds or the letters that represent those sounds. As with all symbols, the physical manifestations of words are related to an underlying meaning. This relationship is, in principle, arbitrary, with no logical, inherent, natural reason to assign a certain sound sequence to a certain meaning. This arbitrariness can be illustrated by the fact that different languages have chosen completely different sound sequences for the same meanings. Notable exceptions are onomatopoeic words that refer to objects or events that are associated with a certain sound. These words often imitate the sound emitted by the object or occurring in the event, such as animal calls ("meow"), or the sound of one object being emitted from another object ("bang"). In onomatopoeia there is a (partially) motivated relation between the sound of a word and the meaning of the word, which is imitated by the sound of the word.

In Plato's dialogue named after that character, Kratylos defends the notion that a motivated, natural relationship between sound and meaning that exists in onomatopoeia exists for all words in general. It is this "cratylistic" assumption for all words (clearly a false assumption in the light of the earlier discussion on arbitrariness) that plays the key role of bringing two incongruous meanings into a spurious conjunction in puns. That two separate, but possibly historically related, meanings can become manifest in identical (or at least very similar) sound sequences provides a necessary mechanism for a text to be humorous.

The cratylistic fallacy underlying the humorousness of puns is accepted in other realms of language use as well, where the assumption of a motivated relationship between the sounds or letters of a word and what the word stands for gives the sounds or letters the power of what they stand for. Thus, saying the name of a supernatural entity may invoke the power of that entity, for example, a deity or a dead person, leading to strong taboos about the usage of such names. This logic also lends power to many poetic devices and surfaces in folk etymology.

If the sound similarity is the only overlap of the two meanings, the pun is forced, which has led to the low status puns have as a type of joke for many people.

Knock, knock.
Who's there?
Orange.
Orange who?
Orange you glad I didn't say apple?

In this example of knock-knock puns, which are associated with children's humor and often considered to be weak jokes, there is no other motivation for speaking about oranges than the sound similarity between *orange* and *aren't*. If, on the other hand, the setup were to create parallel contexts to justify the presence of the two meanings, as in the "damn" pun, the joke would be stronger, that is, potentially funnier. Without justification beyond the sound similarity, there is only wordplay, a weak pun, lacking the contextual ambiguity that is often found in other jokes. Cicero observed that cratylism alone is a weak basis for humor and needs to be accompanied by meaning overlap.

Perfect and Imperfect Puns

One of the many distinctions of pun types is the difference between perfect and imperfect ones. A perfect pun is a pun in which the two meanings surface in the same sound sequence, or word; whereas an imperfect, but otherwise possibly just as humorous, pun is one in which the sound sequences, or words, are similar, but not identical. This is also called paronymy. As in the following example, usually only one of the words (i.e., the pun) is part of the joke text, while the other (the pun's target word) is implied by the context and sound similarity:

Schnapps: a ginlike beverage that bites.

Here, the punning word, "schnapps," is actually part of the setup and its targeted second meaning, "snaps," is revealed through the punch line "bites" and is not identical to the punning word in the text in either pronunciation or spelling.

Not only is the sound similarity in imperfect puns used to create the spurious meaning overlap, but it is also used to identify, or recover, the target word of the pun in the text. Only a limited degree of difference is possible between a pun and its target for the target to still be recognizable from the pun. If the sound difference passes a certain threshold, the target can no longer be recovered from the pun and the cratylistic assumption of its relation to the pun also breaks down. Recent research has tried, with partial success, to establish this threshold in terms of complex acoustic models, including claims for universality of types of phonetic mechanisms (e.g., substitutions vs. insertions) and overall number of sound differences across languages and language families. The main problem for such research is that sound overlap in imperfect puns is both a semantic factor for the humorousness of the pun, which is particularly hard to measure quantitatively, as well as an acoustic factor for the recovery of the target.

The problem is further complicated by the fact that other contextual factors assist in the recovery of the target when it is not similar to the pun, like the idiomaticity of a phrase. In *unctions speak louder than words*, "actions" is sufficiently similar in sound to "unctions" to be potentially funny, but its recovery is certainly aided by the underlying proverb. Thus, the threshold of sound similarity between a pun and its target can be lowered when other factors help the target recovery.

Paradigmatic and Syntagmatic Puns

Sometimes a distinction is made between paradigmatic puns like the schnapps example, where the pun and target surface in only one word in the text, and syntagmatic puns, where the word is repeated in its two meanings (*traductio* or *antanaclasis*) or the similar pun and target of imperfect puns both occur (*adnominatio*). This distinction seems to have little bearing outside of classic rhetorical guides, like most of the distinctions from which pun taxonomies are derived.

Homophones and Homographs

Taxonomies that identify when the relationship between a pun and its target no longer holds, in both sounds and their written representations, are not particularly relevant from a scientific point of view, as they do not relate to the underlying mechanism of puns that is responsible for their humorousness, but still receive much attention in research on puns. As mentioned, another type of distinction among puns is related to the degree to which a pun and its target sound and look the same: Homophones sound identical but can be written differently (e.g., *loo* and *Lou*), whereas homographs are written identically but may be pronounced differently.

Homographs are a subclass of puns for which, unusually, the way they are written, not the sound sequence, is the primary symbolic manifestation. In these eye puns, or orthographic puns, the way two meanings are written is similar or identical, but the pronunciation can be different. A joke using "lead" both in the sense of the verb and the metal would constitute an example in English. Eye puns are common in writing systems that are more independent from their function to indicate pronunciation, such as Japanese and Mandarin, where the sounds of a pun and its target can even be completely different, but the ideographic symbol is (almost) the same.

Additional Distinctions

Further distinctions among puns are made according to the way they are embedded into the joke text and context, like the distinction of syntagmatic and paradigmatic puns mentioned earlier. These include malapropisms ("as headstrong as an allegory [alligator] on the Nile") and spoonerisms ("three cheers for our queer old dean [dear old queen]!"). Further classifications are based on the fact that puns can cross word lines and span several of them ("When is a door not a door? When it is a jar [ajar]"), and the same incongruence in meaning can be carried across several puns, which is a common strand in conversational punning.

Another issue frequently discussed is the historical relation of the two senses in a pun in terms of homonymy and polysemy. Two (or more) senses of perfect homographic or homophonic puns can be etymologically related because historically they derive from the same meaning, as in the rodent "mouse" and the computer "mouse." Here the device meaning was derived from the rodent meaning because of the size and shape similarity and the resemblance of the cord of a computer mouse to the tail of the rodent mouse. There are many ways in which the senses of a word can be related, and words with related senses are called polysemous. Yet, in contrast to the rather recent coining of the computer term, humans are rarely consciously aware that a relation between the senses of a word is historical, but when asked about it, almost always claim that it is so.

When senses of a word are not related, this constitutes homonymy, as in "ear" standing for the body part as well as the grain-bearing tip of a cereal plant. The two senses derive from different roots but happen to coincide in present-day English. The difference in the Indo-European roots they derive from can be shown in their ancient Greek manifestations as *ous* (body part) and *akros* (pointed [tip of cereal]). Nevertheless, when asked, most people will generate a plausible relationship between homonymous senses by claiming an overlap in meaning that can be explained etymologically; that is, they indulge in folk etymology and claim that senses, such as those of *ear*, are polysemous. The question of the influence of polysemy on the funniness of puns is an open issue, and researchers have argued that an etymological relationship between the senses can either strengthen the pun as an additional overlap or make it too obvious and thus weaken it.

Visual Puns

Although language is considered their main habitat, puns do not exist only in spoken or written language. A physical manifestation of a symbol may also have two meanings that can be used for the central incongruity required by humor. Visual puns, which have been seen as early as in classical vase painting, refer to an element of a drawing, painting, or photo that can simultaneously represent two objects in a humorous incongruous relationship. To achieve this, there must be a certain level of abstraction in the representation of the two objects in the pun so that the visual symbol can stand for both. For example, for a drop shape to also represent a candle flame, not much more than the outline needs to be drawn, but for both meanings to be recovered, both must explicitly be reinforced by the context. The reason for this difference between verbal and more restricted visual punning is that visual symbols are generally not arbitrary but iconic; that is, they resemble that for which they stand. Verbal symbols, on the other hand, are generally arbitrary in that they are associated with but don't resemble what they stand for. The verbal symbol, or word, *house* does not look, sound, smell, or feel like a house. But a visual symbol, like a drawing of a house, will to some degree look like a house and can less easily look like, say, a football. Thus, iconic visual symbols are less free to pun than arbitrary verbal ones.

Christian F. Hempelmann

See also Jokes; Punch Line

Further Readings

Attardo, S. (1994). *Linguistic theories of humor.* Berlin, Germany: Mouton de Gruyter.

Guidi, A. (2012). Are pun mechanisms universal? A comparative analysis across language families. *HUMOR: International Journal of Humor Research, 25*(3), 339–336.

Hausmann, F. J. (1974). *Studien zu einer Linguistik des Wortspiels* [Studies on the linguistics of wordplay]. Tübingen, Germany: Niemeyer.

Hempelmann, C. F. (2004). Script oppositeness and logical mechanism in punning. *HUMOR: International Journal of Humor Research, 17*(4), 381–392.

Hempelmann, C. F., & Samson, A. C. (2007). Visual puns and verbal puns: Descriptive analogy or false analogy? In D. Popa & S. Attardo (Eds.), *New approaches to the linguistics of humor* (pp. 180–196). Galati, Romania: Editura Academica.

Sobkowiak, W. (1991). *Metaphonology of English paronomasic puns.* Frankfurt, Germany: Peter Lang.

Puppets

As inanimate objects, puppets resemble, move like, and talk like the humans they imitate, parody, or mock. This interplay of similarity and difference, along with conventional and not so conventional aspects of puppets, causes audiences to laugh at them. Puppetry involves people looking at and reframing themselves and their social lives in a comical mode. This entry describes traditional and contemporary puppets and discusses the role of puppetry in culture.

Traditional and Contemporary Puppets

Puppets are classified as either traditional or contemporary (modern), a distinction that is only partially

Shadow puppets are cut-out figures that are held between a source of light and a translucent screen or scrim. The cut-out shapes of the puppets sometimes include translucent color or other types of detailing. Shown here are Javanese shadow puppets (*wayang kulit*). In 2003, UNESCO recognized wayang kulit as a Masterpiece of Oral and Intangible Heritage of Humanity.

Source: Sentausa/Wikimedia Commons.

useful. Traditional puppets are puppets that have been in communities for many generations, sometimes for hundreds of years, whereas modern puppets are recent creations. Several types of puppets are widespread around the world. These include glove puppets (England, France), shadow puppets (China, Greece, India, Indonesia, Malaysia, Turkey), rod or string puppets (Belgium, Italian mainland, Japan, Sicily), story scrolls (India), masks (Bali), water puppets (Vietnam), and even humans themselves imitating puppets (Indonesia). The word *marionette* is used to refer to both string puppets and puppets in general. A well-defined line between traditional puppets and contemporary puppets does not exist. Both are found in the same forms and express the same kinds of humor. And all forms of puppetry, even if invented yesterday, draw on many features and techniques that have always been characteristic of puppets.

Traditional puppetry still exists in many places, and contemporary puppetry is present in all major population centers. Puppetry is practiced in Palermo in Sicily, as well as other places in Italy; Brussels and Liege in Belgium; Amiens, Charleville-Mézières, and Lyon in France; in Central and Eastern Europe, especially in Prague in the Czech Republic and Moscow in Russia; in Egypt and Greece; in many Asian countries, including Cambodia, China, India, Japan, China, Vietnam, and Taiwan; in Africa; in New York City and other cities in the United States; and in northeastern Brazil and other places in Latin America. In these places, puppets are performed both in public places, often as part of festivals and rituals, and in museums, schools, and libraries.

One of 35 marionettes from the Tiller-Clowes Family Marionette Company, one of the last Victorian marionette troupes in England. Shown here is Clown, the character who developed from the Italian *commedia dell'arte*. In Great Britain, traveling marionette shows were a popular form of entertainment for adults in the 19th century.

Source: Theatre and Performance Collection, Victoria and Albert Museum; © Victoria and Albert Museum, London.

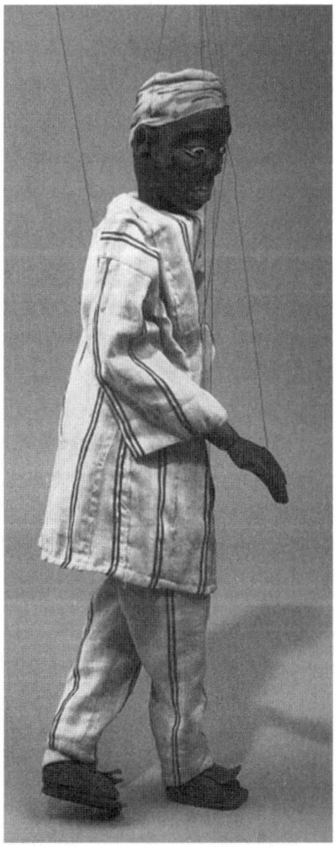

String puppet from the Tropenmuseum in Amsterdam, the Netherlands.

Source: Tropenmuseum of the Royal Tropical Institute (KIT)/Wikimedia Commons.

Puppetry as Popular Culture

Puppetry is an expression of popular and folk culture. It is intended for audiences of adults as well as children and is a form of communication and entertainment and an aesthetic creation. The dominant feature of puppetry is humor. Puppets become animate through the (usually hidden) activities of the puppeteers, who make them perform—walk, talk, sing, dance, burp, fart, and laugh. This disparity and intersection between the animate and the inanimate, the human and the nonhuman, is at the heart of the humor of puppets. Ironically because they are not human, puppets usually can do more and get away with more than can humans.

Play, humor, and comedy in puppetry are significant for a number of reasons. Puppets celebrate the dynamism and diversity of popular culture—linguistically, culturally, socially, and individually—in contrast to official, elite, and standardizing high culture, to which puppets are a comic counterpoint and which they often debase. Puppets constantly and dangerously test the boundaries of the licit and the illicit, the permitted and the forbidden. They parody customs, proper social behavior, rules of etiquette and politeness, and even themselves, and usually make fun of the source text they interpret.

Puppets are both a reflection of, and a commentary on, the society and culture in which they are performed. An extremely vibrant, rich, and complex form of popular culture, they involve both social and individual creativity and expression. In addition, they constitute an escape from, commentary on, and source of inspiration for high and elite forms of cultural expression. Whatever else puppets are and do, they are funny. These often small objects behave like humans and animals, engage in physical buffoonery and slapstick, use all kinds of wordplay, stereotype, exaggerate, and degrade human behavior, break ordinary rules of etiquette, and comment on, poke fun at, and trick other puppets and members of the audience.

Traditional puppet performances are playful, comic re-creations of old, sometimes ancient stories and often insert contemporary humorous episodes and interludes. This is precisely the case of the Sicilian and Belgian performances of the Charlemagne stories and the song of Roland and the Balinese and Javanese performances of Indian epics, such as the Ramayana and the Mahabharata. The mingling of the ancient and the modern, the traditional and the contemporary, are great sources of humor.

The satirical parody of social rules and social boundaries characteristic of puppetry constitutes a subversion of social structure and especially a comic attack on the hegemonic role of the dominating class. Puppets provide a social critique and a letting off of steam. In complex societies, puppets draw on stratified class structures to express different humorous messages.

The nature of puppet humor changes over time as the role of the puppet theater changes, from a popular to a middle-class phenomenon, from the fairground to the museum, the library, and the public school. Puppetry, like other forms of humor, is used in both verbal and physical therapy. Puppetry continues to be an exuberant and vital form of popular culture.

Dina Sherzer and Joel Sherzer

See also Caricature; Culture; Folklore; Parody; Slapstick; Sociology

Further Readings

And, M. (1987). Karagöz: *Turkish shadow theatre.* Istanbul, Turkey: Dost.

Baird, B. (1965). *The art of the puppet.* New York, NY: Macmillan.

Gerity, L. E. (1999). *Creativity and the dissociative patient: Puppets, narrative, and art in the treatment of survivors of childhood trauma.* London, UK: Jessica Kingsley.

Gross, J. (2001). *Speaking in other voices: An ethnography of Walloon puppet theaters.* Amsterdam, Netherlands: John Benjamins Press.

Herbert, M. (2002). *Voices of the puppet masters: The* wayang golek *theater of Indonesia.* Honolulu: University of Hawai'i Press.

Hironaga, S. (1976). *The Bunraku handbook.* Tokyo, Japan: Maison des Arts.

Hobart, A. (1987). *Dancing shadows of Bali: Theater and myth.* London, UK: KPI.

Jairazbhoy, N. A. (2007). *Kathputli: The world of Rajasthani puppeteers.* Ahmedabad, India: Rainbow.

Keeler, W. (1987). *Javanese shadow plays: Javanese selves.* Princeton, NJ: Princeton University Press.

Malkin, M. R. (1977). *Traditional and folk puppets of the world.* New York, NY: Barnes.

McCormick, J. (2010). *The Italian puppet theater: A history.* Jefferson, NC: McFarland.

Obraztsov, S. (1954). *Puppets and the puppet theatre.* London, UK: Society for Cultural Relations With the USSR.

Osnes, B. (2010). *The shadow puppet theatre of Malaysia: A study of* wayang kulit *with performance scripts and puppet designs*. Jefferson, NC: McFarland.

Pasqualino, A. (1981). *Sicilian puppets*. Palermo, Italy: Association for the Preservation of Popular Traditions.

Scott, A. C. (1963). *The puppet theatre of Japan*. Rutland, VT: Tuttle.

Sherzer, D., & Sherzer, J. (Eds.). (1987). *Humor and comedy in puppetry: Celebration in popular culture*. Bowling Green, OH: Bowling Green State University Popular Press.

Simmen, R. (1975). *The world of puppets*. London, UK: Elsevier Phaidon.

Singer, N. F. (1992). *Burmese puppets*. Singapore: Oxford University Press.

Speaight, G. (1990). *The history of the English puppet theatre* (2nd ed.). Carbondale: Southern Illinois University Press.

Stalberg, R. H. (1984). *China's puppets*. San Francisco, CA: China Books.

Zurbuchen, M. (1987). *The shadow theater of Bali: Explorations in language and text*. Princeton, NJ: Princeton University Press.

R

Rabelais, François

François Rabelais, often acknowledged as France's, if not Europe's, greatest comic genius produced four volumes of mock-epic narrative over a period of 20 years, commencing with *Pantagruel* (1532), continued by its prequel *Gargantua* (1534/1535), the so-called *Third Book* of Pantagruel's adventures (1546) and then a *Fourth Book* of the same, published in possibly incomplete form in 1552 shortly before his death. It is astonishing that he began his literary career so late (the earliest estimated date of birth is 1483), but his erudition reveals a profound awareness of contemporary intellectual trends, surely acquired during his many years of monastic study, while his provincial upbringing in the predominantly rural area of the Loire Valley clearly afforded him an acquaintance and sympathy with a peasant way of life reflected in his presentation of rustic folklore, vocabulary, and attitudes.

In many ways, this sometimes unstable combination of popular and learned patterns creates his works' greatest fascination. In terms of comic writing, he extends richly the satiric traditions generated by European humanists via their often exaggerated satires of their great enemy, medieval scholasticism. Here his acknowledged mentor is Desiderius Erasmus, whom he seems to have hero-worshipped and whose witty dialogues, titled the *Colloquies* and written exclusively in Latin, inspire several of Rabelais's most memorable comic episodes. He differs from Erasmus in his use of vernacular French, but, more important for humor, in his unashamed scatology and his cultivation of the morally irresponsible and anarchic comedy developed by many predecessors, but which sits parallel to the erudite and spiritual messages he simultaneously conveys.

Thus his heroes, the father-and-son Gargantua and Pantagruel, while promoting humanist principles via their education, and enhancing the spirit of Christian evangelism in their piety (like Erasmus, Rabelais clearly opposed the Lutheran Reformation), involve themselves in riotous adventures alongside thoroughly disreputable characters whom, unlike, say, Prince Hal to Falstaff, they never denounce or abandon. Thus, Rabelais counters the epic pattern of birth-education-fulfillment of the hero with one of drinking, overindulgence, sex, and reckless violence, counterposing his heroes to two particular anti-heroes, namely, the rumbustious Friar John, lieutenant to Gargantua, and, regarding Pantagruel, the scapegrace Panurge, whom, despite his fornication, criminality, obsessions, and, in due course, abject cowardice, Pantagruel loves throughout his life.

So the epic models of the first two volumes are fulfilled in predictable victories achieved by the heroes who defend their homeland against aggressors in the tradition of the medieval *chanson de geste*, while their brave deeds stand against a whole series of alternative episodes that place them in comic question. This much had already been done by Rabelais's late medieval and early Renaissance forebears, but when he dosed that combination with the Erasmian spirit of critical satire whereby, for instance, he lampooned the warlike politics of contemporary European monarchs such as Francis I and especially the Emperor Charles V, he achieved a literary amalgam of inexhaustible richness.

Having achieved notable success with *Pantagruel*, which enjoyed many editions, Rabelais adapted the same epic paradigm to *Gargantua*, an obvious improvement that climaxes in a more interesting and in some ways credible war for which the hero is prepared by a far fuller education where the anti-medieval attitudes of the Renaissance are made glaringly and farcically apparent. Thereafter, however, rather than adding a further generation to the giants' genealogy, following an interval of some 12 years, Rabelais produced in some ways his most interesting book, *Le tiers livre* (The Third Book). This proto-novel describes the problems encountered by the neurotic Panurge, still Pantagruel's sidekick, but now preoccupied by a desire to marry coupled with a dread of cuckoldry, which fate he had no doubt visited previously on many an unwitting husband. His lord Pantagruel, fully sympathetic to his dilemma, gives him clear and sensible advice whereby, if his mind is made up, he should be wed and face the consequences. When his friend proves unwilling to comply, however, Pantagruel recommends a series of oracles, none of whom he holds to be fully reliable, since the future is in God's hands, but who might yet prove useful. Thereupon Rabelais exploits this pattern as a series of comic vignettes that, again, deliver important humanist lessons, often satirically presented, alongside a now less prominent but still discernible spirit of popular humor.

As no source of advice satisfies Panurge, he and his companions decide ultimately to visit the land of the Holy Bottle, source of ultimate truth, but only reachable after a long journey, which therefore provides the stuff of Rabelais's *Le quart livre* (The Fourth Book), published incomplete in 1548 and then more fully in 1552. Here Panurge's role is less central, although he can still generate enormous comic power when he does dominate the scene. Otherwise Rabelais downgrades the purpose of the journey in order to offer his readers a series of comically portrayed landings and encounters that occur en route to their ultimate goal, where in fact, and for whatever reason, they never arrive.

Although the basic narrative structure is now the quest paradigm rather than epic war, Rabelais maintains and enhances his scholarly agenda by exploiting classical sources such as the satirist Lucian, while also drawing, and rather more than in *Le tiers livre*, on folklore and folktales. Some find the humor and mood of this volume more somber, given the virtual collapse of the Erasmian movement in the face of the Calvinist Reformation and the incipient Counter-Reformation. In this connection, Rabelais conducts biting satires of the Council of Trent while also responding vigorously to Calvin and what he calls the Genevan impostors, and the disharmony within Christendom is clearly reflected in various episodes on the journey. Even so, and despite certain traces of despondency, some of his greatest comic writing does emerge within it, for instance, during the storm sequence where Panurge collapses into abject terror and does nothing to help, while Frère Jean berates him for idleness and Pantagruel struggles to save the ship. Of course they survive, supported by the grace of God, and indeed by the demands of the genre Rabelais has chosen.

What is genuinely fascinating, moreover, is the unresolved nature of Rabelais's work. Just as the reader is left to imagine the conclusion to the Pantagruelists' journey, so he is free to suggest for himself how a hero of such spiritual grandeur as the mature Pantagruel is prepared to endure and indulge his disreputable antithesis, namely, the eternally maddening but infuriatingly lovable Panurge.

John Parkin

See also Anecdote, Comic; Carnivalesque; Cervantes, Miguel de; History of Humor: Renaissance Europe; Humorous Names; Inversion, Topsy-Turvy; Parody; Satire; Scatology; Targets of Humor

Further Readings

Bakhtin, M. M. (1968). *Rabelais and his world.* Cambridge: MIT Press.
Huchon, M. (2011). *Rabelais.* Paris, France: Gallimard.
Screech, M. A. (1979). *Rabelais.* London, UK: Duckworth.

Race, Representations of

Over time, representations of race have played a significant role in the production of humor in the United States. Writers of different backgrounds ranging from Bret Harte and Mark Twain to Zora Neale Hurston and Langston Hughes have drawn on race representations to create humor in their work, but over time, visual media have had a greater audience among the American public than have written media. This entry focuses on past and present humorous portrayals of various racial groups in America on stage, in silent films, in television, and in motion pictures. Humorous representations of race have both influenced and been influenced by attitudes related to political, social, and economic circumstances. Because African Americans, who have been the most frequently portrayed minority racial group, exemplify this relationship between context and the production of humor, this entry devotes considerable time to discussion of African Americans in a social and historic context. This entry also discusses portrayals of Native Americans, Hispanics, Asians, and Whites. Whereas most portrayals of racial groups brought before the public have originated in the White mainstream, the entry shows that groups such as African Americans have offered sometimes contrasting and self-empowering humorous images of themselves.

Stereotypes

Discussion of humorous constructions of race necessarily calls for attention to the concept of stereotype. The set of beliefs comprising an ideology forms the basis for a stereotype that develops within a group with regard to an outside group. The ideology promotes a perception that all members of the outside group are alike in sharing a non-normative characteristic or set of characteristics that sets them apart as different from the group making the assessment. The targeted characteristics of a stereotyped group may be related to a range of human domains, such as physical features, behavior, or attitudes. Humorous representations exaggerate in foregrounding those characteristics.

Stereotypes in humor can be useful as a shorthand method of helping to convey complex issues and ideas, particularly in relation to social identity. For example, stereotyping is a useful tool for quick delineation of character types in stand-up comedy, where performers have limited time in which to construct characters necessary for the progression of a joke or narrative. A stereotype can not only help establish an instantly recognizable type but also influence audience expectations surrounding the attitudes and behavior of a character. The incongruity that is an outcome of exaggerating a stereotype may itself be a source of humor.

Stereotyping may be innocuous, amounting to good-natured teasing. The danger of stereotyping is that it often combines with prejudice, where ideological thinking allows individuals to take their own group as a normative, positive point of reference and form a negative image of another group based on comparison of the two groups. In forming a negative stereotype, the group making the assessment casts the outside group as either possessing characteristics that the assessing group spurns, or lacking characteristics that the assessing group possesses and considers natural and desirable. Negative stereotyping may serve the function of castigating and demeaning a social group as inferior and undesirable.

Comic Portrayals of Whites

Whites are often viewed as unmarked and normative, but Whites in America have never been a social monolith. By the early 1800s, humorous representations of certain regional groups of Whites had become staples in comic stage performances. White rural types were the frequent butt of jokes; the backwoodsman and the Yankee were also popular comic figures. In the early days of the 20th century, attention shifted to the newly arriving Southern and East European immigrants. Anglo Americans, who had become established as a group comfortable with the technological advances of the industrial revolution, developed ideologies and stereotypes that lent legitimacy to showing great hostility toward the new immigrants. This played out in intense discrimination and humor that maligned the less sophisticated new arrivals by highlighting perceived traits of ignorance, laziness, and lack of sophistication.

To combat the stereotyping and discrimination, since there were no racial differences between Southern and Eastern Europeans and Anglo Americans, the new immigrants and their children gradually relinquished their old country customs and began to assimilate into the emerging White culture. In 1908, the term *melting pot* came into use as a metaphor to describe the process by which immigrants would gradually become assimilated into the dominant American culture and society. The various groups of Whites eventually coalesced into a single overarching group constituting the dominant White majority. Public expression of humor that ridiculed most White ethnic groups became increasingly less frequent.

Creators of comic White characters in silent films and early radio shows increasingly called on stereotypes that downplayed ethnicity and focused on social class. For example, in silent films, Charlie Chaplin created humor that championed the working class. Notable among early comic television representations of the White working class is Jackie Gleason's *The Honeymooners*. Beginning in the 1950s, a plethora of sitcoms focusing on the middle class became popular. These include *Father Knows Best*, *The Dick Van Dyke Show*, *The Brady Bunch*, and a host of other shows. In *I Love Lucy*, Lucille Ball provided a humorous exaggeration of the trope of the White woman, which casts White women as naive, innocent, pure, and totally dependent on men. Many other sitcoms cast middle-class White women in similar roles. Sitcoms such as *The Mary Tyler Moore Show* and *That Girl* portrayed wholesome and angelic single, middle-class White women attempting to escape the strictures of subordination to men that society placed on them.

Demonstrating the potential for multidimensionality in portrayals of Whites, *The Beverly Hillbillies* portrayed a stereotype of a White family from Appalachia. The sitcom shows the prominent role language can play in constructing comic characters meant to represent social groups. In the past, isolation caused by the remoteness of the mountainous Appalachian area led to linguistic and cultural differences that set Appalachians apart from mainstream Whites. Characters in *The Beverly Hillbillies* drew on the stereotypes that the metalinguistic awareness of audiences elicited when they heard linguistic features that index traits that they were likely to stereotypically associate with people from Appalachia. The characters exaggerated in their use of these features. An example is *a-prefixing*, where speakers append *a-* to the front of a progressive activity verb, as in *John went a-hunting*. In constructing his comic persona, a member of the Appalachian underclass, the stand-up comedian Larry the Cable Guy draws on a-prefixing and other features such as the grammatical construction *might could*, in *I might could help next week*.

Comic Portrayals of African Americans

As early as the 18th century, African American comic characters occasionally appeared on the American stage. An example is in the 1764 play *The Disappointment, or the Force of Credulity*. The major figure in this play was a wealthy African American with a White mistress. The African American role was comic, yet lacked the racial disparagement that came later.

Onstage comic portrayals of African Americans changed dramatically in the 1800s with the advent of minstrelsy, which soon became the most popular form of stage comedy in the United States. Minstrelsy came to the fore at a time of social, political, and economic turmoil. Increasing numbers of free African Americans were competing with Whites for jobs in a difficult economy. The abolitionist movement was gaining power, in opposition to those who wanted a continuation of slavery.

Originally, performers in minstrelsy were exclusively White men. Covering their faces with burned cork, they built comic portrayals of African Americans that cast them as childlike, shiftless, and irresponsible. The image of African Americans that these minstrels promoted as happily enslaved and incapable of managing their own lives served the function of supporting an ideology of racism and encouraging the continuation of slavery. The White performers generally had little knowledge of African Americans or of the plantation life that provided the background for the characters they portrayed. Rather, they built their performances on hearsay, exaggeration, and misconceptions about African Americans.

Research has shown that most of the songs the White minstrels performed, such as "Jump Jim Crow," "Possum up a Gum Tree," and "My Long Tail Blue," were of European origin. But the language they delivered the songs in was the effect of their stereotyped perception of African American English. The White minstrels performed their songs in a way that mimicked and ridiculed African American speech and style.

In the mid-1800s, free African Americans entered the field of minstrelsy, also covering their skin with burned cork for performances. Several individuals, such as Billy Kersands and Bob Height, became almost as successful as Whites performing in blackface. With racial stereotypes and audience expectations already in place from the earlier minstrels, African American blackface minstrel performers were forced to enact the negative images that previous minstrels had promoted. Like their White counterparts, most African American minstrel performers had never experienced plantation life. Still,

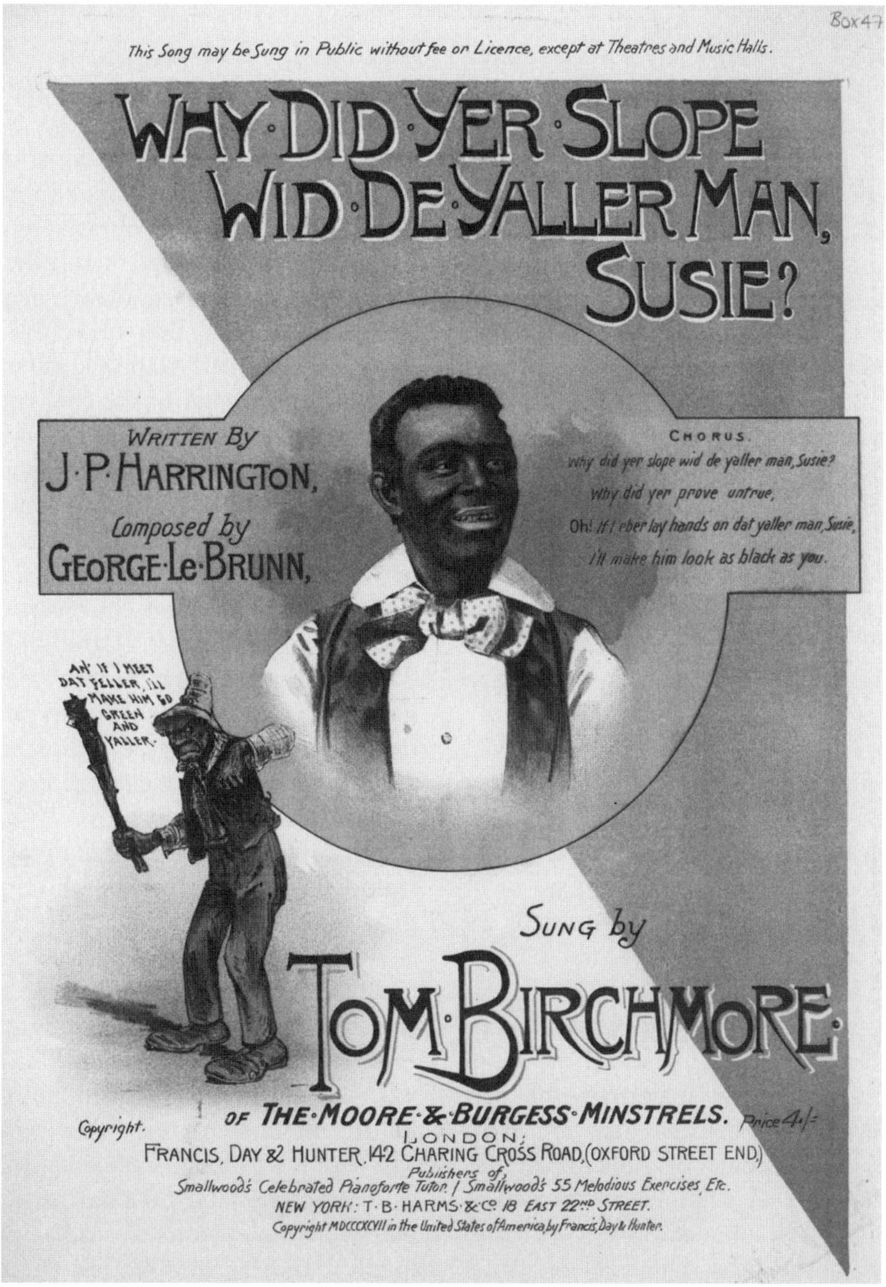

Cover of the sheet music for "Why Did Yer Slope Wid De Yaller Man, Susie?" by John P. Harrington (lyrics) and George Le Brunn (music) and sung by Tom Birchmore of the Moore & Burgess Minstrels.

Source: Theater and Performance Collection, Victoria and Albert Museum; © Victoria and Albert Museum, London.

many non–African Americans viewing the shows saw the performances as authentic representations of African American plantation life, in which the African American performers engaged in their normal childlike, irresponsible behaviors and expressed their natural tendencies to sing, dance, be funny, and, without inhibition, express their primitive passions.

The African American minstrels were ostensibly enacting African American life. But according to Jacquelyn Rahman, who has researched African American language and humor, African American humor has been traditionally grounded in an esteem-enhancing self-perception that contributed to the psychological survival of the group. Rahman states that through the use of counterlanguage and code whose meaning was only available to insiders, African Americans have historically used language to convey meanings that were unavailable to outsiders. Mel Watkins, who has researched African American comedy, states that African American minstrel performers used minstrelsy to critique racism and hypocrisy; in performing in blackface, they were actually mimicking Whites in their imitation of the speech and behavior of African Americans.

Minstrelsy declined in popularity and nearly died after the end of Reconstruction in 1877, although isolated White performers such as Al Jolson continued the genre into the mid-1900s. What replaced minstrel shows in popularity were variety shows and silent films, where, again, Whites in blackface portrayed African Americans. Minstrel portrayals influenced representations of African Americans in media for years to come. Stereotypes that had developed during the minstrel era persisted, with stock characters such as coon, sambo, and mammy emerging to appear in sometimes subtle forms well into the future. Still, African American minstrelsy provided a vehicle for the development of the first professional African American musical and comic entertainers.

Comic representations of African Americans by Whites continued into the early days of radio (1920–1930). Language became particularly important in radio because it was the only tool actors had for constructing character and conveying social meaning. Radio actors did their work by making use of their stereotyped perceptions of African American grammar, phonology, and lexicon. For audience understanding, they relied on the metalinguistic awareness of audiences that made connections between the stereotyped speech of the radio characters and traits the comedians were attempting to convey.

Amos 'n' Andy, a radio program that debuted in the 1920s, featured the White creators of the show, Freeman Gosden and Charles Correll, portraying African American characters. The characters projected stereotypical traits that had been popularized by blackface minstrelsy, but the show was groundbreaking in presenting the characters as grappling with everyday life problems in ways that transcended race. *Amos 'n' Andy* was one of the few early situation comedies that featured African Americans in roles other than that of servant. One of the main characters of the show was a struggling business owner.

Because of its national popularity, the program lasted for several decades. In 1951, Gosden and Correll unsuccessfully transferred *Amos 'n' Andy* to television. African American civil rights groups were offended by the depictions, charging that they reinforced stereotypes. An example they cited was Sapphire, a shrill and abrasively overbearing wife character whose name entered the slang lexicon as a term denoting an aggressive hen-pecking African American woman. Denouncement from civil rights groups contributed to the demise of the show.

With the coming of the civil rights movement in the 1950s, African Americans became more visible in all forms of media. Stereotypes persisted, but with protests from the African American community, the tone of films featuring African Americans became less blatantly stereotypical and exaggerated. African American actors themselves, such as Esther Rolle and John Amos, stars in the 1970s sitcom *Good Times*, protested what they perceived as racist content of the sitcoms in which they performed. Moving toward the present, the mainstream has increasingly presented positive comic portrayals of African Americans.

African Americans have always had their own brand of self-empowering humor that reflected their cultural past and their experiences in America. African American self-representation often contrasted markedly with portrayals originating outside the community. For example, during and after slavery, African Americans engaged in *toasting*, a genre where a member of the community told an epic tale before an audience of other African Americans. The story was filled with coded language, as well as exaggerated and fictional accounts of the storyteller's heroic exploits and adventures, which often involved outsmarting Whites.

In the 20th century, as the social condition of African Americans changed, humorous self-representation of African Americans also began to change. African Americans developed a new identity and offered more direct social commentary. Jackie "Moms" Mabley exemplifies this. Performing from the vaudeville era into the 1970s, Mabley remains one of the few African American women to attain success in comedy. To combat the extreme sexism and harassment she encountered as a young woman, Mabley adopted the persona of an outspoken old woman that she modeled after her grandmother, a former slave. In the character of a community elder, Mabley was able to pioneer in producing socially conscious humor that highlights the hypocrisy of racism. An example of her work follows.

> I was on my way down to Miami... I mean "*They*"-ami. I was ridin' along..., goin' through one of them little towns in South Carolina. Pass through a red light. One of them big cops come runnin' over to me, say, "Hey woman, don't you know you went through a red light." I say, "Yeah, I know I went through a red light." "Well, what did you do that for?" I said 'Cause I seen all you white folks goin' on the green light... I thought the red light was for us!" (Watkins, 1999, p. 392)

In the late 1960s, Richard Pryor introduced a new style of stand-up comedy. Pryor told long narratives in which he portrayed the streetwise, earthy dignity and survival skills of characters of the African American underclass. Like Mabley, Pryor provided social commentary on the hypocrisies and incongruences that characterize racist thinking. Pryor's work continues to influence stand-up comedians; a plethora of African American comedians followed his style, demonstrated by the highly successful 2000 film *The Original Kings of Comedy*. This movie compiled footage from a 2000 road show that featured comedians Steve Harvey, D. L. Hughley, Cedric the Entertainer, and Bernie Mack. *The Queens of Comedy*, a female comedy tour film released in 2001, was a spinoff that featured Adele Givens, Laura Hayes, Sommore, and Mo'Nique.

In the 1980s, Bill Cosby, who had been a mentor of Pryor, combined his performance experience with knowledge gained while earning a PhD in education when he created and starred in *The Cosby Show*. This sitcom featured an educated upper middle–income African American couple raising five children. A number of sitcoms presenting positive portrayals of African Americans followed, so as of 2012, there have been numerous popular venues featuring positive portrayals of African Americans.

Comic Media Portrayals of Other Races

The popularity of African American comic venues in the media helped open the door for mainstream acceptance of comedians of other groups. Until the 1960s, virtually all comic media portrayals of Hispanics, East and South Asians, and Native Americans were grounded in negative stereotypes. There were great cultural differences among these racial groups, but there is a thread of similarity in their comic representations. The stereotypes for each group were based on perceived characteristics that differed from characteristics valued in the mainstream and that were considered inferior. As with African Americans, stereotypes of these groups were grounded in social and political issues that existed before the groups began to be represented in the media. Where characters from these groups appeared in humorous venues, they were cast in such roles as Indian chief with feathered headdress, karate-chopping Asian male, Mexican bandito, and passionate Latina. For instance, the Frito Bandito was a character who helped to sell corn chips, while a scantily clad and heavily accented singing female banana named Chiquita appeared in advertisements for bananas.

Twenty-first-century humorous representations of racial groups differ markedly from those of earlier years. In contemporary American society, sensitivities are such that purposeful racial derogation is generally taboo; a range of sitcoms and stand-up comedians present portrayals of members of various races. Bobby Lee, a Korean physician turned comedian, is well known for his work in the *MADtv* sketch comedy show, where he has played a number of Asian characters.

In stand-up, comedians have begun to present their own images of their groups. Charlie Hill, Howie Miller, and Thomas King are Native American stand-up comedians who sometimes employ stereotypes in order to challenge false beliefs that remain embedded in American society. Where East Asians were once portrayed as buffoons, contemporary East Asian comedians present a number of perspectives. In the persona of a socially conscious Asian American woman, Margaret Cho presents stand-up comedy that is empowering to Asians and to women.

Russell Peters, of South Asian ancestry, has gained international acclaim for his stand-up work that often lays bare the hypocrisy of racism. Similarly, Aziz Ansari, Rajiv Satyal, and Hari Kondabolu, all of South Asian ancestry, present socially conscious humor.

Inspired by earlier work by African American comedians, *The Original Kings of Latin Comedy* was a 2002 film depicting a road show that highlighted facets of Mexican culture. The show featured the comedians George Lopez, Cheech Marin, Joey Medina, Alex Reymundo, and Paul Rodriguez. In the 1970s and 1980s, Cheech and Chong, a

Hispanic comedy team, were popular yet controversial because of their perceived portrayal of Hispanics as participating in drug culture. Because of the subversive nature of much of comedy, the work of comedians of many racial groups has been controversial within their respective communities.

Jacquelyn Rahman

See also Ethnic Jokes; Ethnicity and Humor; Prejudice, Humor and; Sitcoms; Stand-Up Comedy; Stereotypes

Further Readings

Cowan, W. T. (2001). Plantation comic modes. *HUMOR: International Journal of Humor Research, 14,* 1–24.

Downing, J., & Husband, C. (2005). *Representing race: Racism, ethnicities and media.* Thousand Oaks, CA: Sage.

Fought, C. (2006). *Language and ethnicity.* New York, NY: Cambridge University Press.

Lippi-Green, R. (1997). *English with an accent: Language, ideology, and discrimination in the United States.* New York, NY: Routledge.

Rahman, J. (2007). An ay for an ah: Language of survival in African American comedy. *American Speech, 82*(1), 65–96.

Rahman, J. (2012). The N word: Its history and use in the African American community. *Journal of English Linguistics, 40*(2), 137–171.

Raskin, V. (1985). *Semantic mechanisms of humor.* Hingham, MA: Reidel.

Raskin, V. (1999). Laughing at and laughing with: The linguistics of humor and humor in literature. In R. S. Wheeler (Ed.), *The workings of language: From prescriptions to perspectives* (pp. 201–209). Westport, CT: Praeger.

Watkins, M. (1999). *On the real side: A history of African American comedy.* Chicago, IL: Lawrence Hill Books.

Wilson, C. C., II, Gutierrez, F., & Chao, L. M. (2003). *Racism, sexism, and the media* (3rd ed.). Thousand Oaks, CA: Sage.

Rakugo

Rakugo, which is written with characters meaning "falling words," is the Japanese art of the professional teller of funny stories. It is a direct descendant of the ancient art of the village storyteller, the teller of tales, and the jester employed by large households in the Middle Ages. In Japan in the 1790s, it moved into the theaters and its material today is largely a modernized version of the funny stories of the Edo period (1603–1868 CE).

Rakugo performers wear kimono and sit, kneeling on a cushion. In this sense they might be called sit-down stand-up comedians. They use no props except those that a gentleman of the Edo period might have had about him—a fan, a pipe, a handkerchief, and a tobacco pouch—although these days, pipe and pouch are not so evident. The fan, however, is used with consummate skill as a pair of chopsticks, a sake cup, a rice bowl, a teacup, or as any other object that may appear in the story, including a fan.

The mime and characterization of the *Rakugo* performer rival and perhaps outclass those of the *Kyōgen* or Japanese farce actor in subtlety and delicacy. This skill is necessary, as the *Rakugo* performer appears alone on the stage and, while seated throughout, plays the parts of all the characters in the story. There may be as many as a half dozen roles in one story—men, women, old, young, children, of both high and low status. Each character is marvelously delineated by the performer in face, voice, gesture, and bodily poise. A *Rakugo* piece is thus a short play (normally a half hour long), consisting of at least one dialogue plus narration, all parts being performed by a single actor. As an example, in July 1988 at the Minami-za theater in Kyoto, Katsura Shijaku performed *Jagansō* (Snake-Grass). A man goes to visit a neighbor and finds him grilling rice cakes that have been left over from a wedding. The visitor helps himself to a cutting from a strange plant. It comes from the mountains where lives an enormous snake that eats monkeys and rabbits and sometimes also hunters and hikers. After eating a human being, the snake feels unwell, so it eats some

A *Rakugo* performance at the Sanma Festival in Meguro, a ward in Tokyo, Japan, on September 14, 2008.

Source: vera46/Wikimedia Commons.

of the snake grass, which dissolves the human being in its stomach, and then it feels better.

The performer tells how, uninvited, the visitor starts scoffing the rice cakes and how his host, annoyed at his bad manners, bets that he cannot eat them all. After tossing them on his nose and catching them in his mouth (all of course in mime), he manages to eat all but one and returns home, humiliated at having lost the bet and at being reproved for bad manners, but also in agony from the lump in his stomach. He collapses on the bed, moaning that he only wishes that there were some way of getting rid of it. An idea comes to him! He eats some of the snake grass. Then the neighbor comes round to find out if the man is all right, and he and the man's wife come into the bedroom to check.

Now, because the snake grass dissolves the human being in the snake's stomach (here the audience begins to laugh), when they open the door, all they find on the bed is a lump of rice cakes.

Stories like this are old but have modern touches. The snake eats hikers, for example, from when hiking began in Japan in the Meiji era (1868–1912 CE). The tales themselves are substantially unchanged but there is an introduction called a *makura* (pillow), which is a piece of patter individual to the performer. For example, in the same program, another performer, Katsura Kitchō, said in his own *makura* that it was most unseasonable to tell a story about stew in summer, as he was about to do, but he had been *told* to perform *Fugu-nabe* (Blowfish Stew). The audience laughed. Second, he continued, talking about stew in summer might evoke memories of winter and make the audience feel cool. The audience laughed again because this is a twist on the conventional wisdom that talking about ice in summer makes people feel cool—but about stew in summer?

Japanese writers emphasize that a *Rakugo* tale has an *ochi* (a fall or a drop), which equates to the English punch line or unexpected twist in the tale. In English it would hardly be worth mentioning that a funny story has a punch line, but the Japanese humorous tradition specializes in puns and related linguistic humor (called *share*, pronounced "sharray"), so it is in contrast with this highly wrought language that the punch line is pointed out as characteristic of *Rakugo*.

The punch line in *Rakugo*, the *ochi*, used to also be called a *sage* (pronounced "sar-gay," meaning "letdown"). *Otoshi-banashi*, one of the former names of *Rakugo*, means "dropped stories," and *rakugo* itself (as noted earlier) means "falling words." The fact that all four terms have the common meaning of dropping or falling seems to suggest that the story lets the audience down with a thump, confirming the element of surprise as an important factor in its humor.

After *Rakugo* found its way into the formal theater, the center of the genre moved from Osaka to Edo (Tokyo) and back again at different times. With the new Meiji era that began in 1868, new audiences came to Tokyo and adaptations from European literature began to be included in the repertoire, along with a certain amount of nonsense humor and "gags." In Japanese the word *gyagu* refers to what are known in English as sight gags—very short visual jokes, such as hitting people, throwing buckets of water over them, tearing clothing, breaking things, or spewing water or smoke. As different branches of *Rakugo* modernized in different ways, the genre divided into "classic" and "modern" *Rakugo*. Performers had their own trademarks, and new stories were written for the new industrial age.

Rakugo underwent difficult times during World War II, but in the postwar era it flourished on radio and television and subsequently on audiotape, video, CD, DVD, and the Internet. University *Rakugo* clubs have been important in giving younger generations performance experience in the genre.

By the end of the 19th century there was one Australian *Rakugo* performer working in Japan (Henry Black), and by the end of the 20th century, *Rakugo* could be heard, occasionally, performed in English. Performers now travel extensively and the genre is known across the world.

Marguerite Wells

See also Anecdote, Comic; Gag; History of Humor: Premodern Japan; History of Humor: Modern Japan; Improv Comedy; Incongruity and Resolution; Jest, Jestbooks, and Jesters; *Kyōgen*; *Lazzi*; Mime; *Share*; Verbal Humor

Further Readings

Brau, L. (2008). Rakugo: *Performing comedy and cultural heritage in contemporary Tokyo*. Lanham, MD: Lexington Books.

McArthur, I. (2013). *A biography of Henry Black: On stage in Meiji Japan*. Clayton, Australia: Monash University Press.

Morioka, H., & Miyoko, S. (1990). Rakugo*: The popular narrative art of Japan*. Cambridge, MA: Council on East Asian Studies & Harvard University Press.

Ōshima, K. (2006). *Rakugo* and humor in Japanese interpersonal communication. In J. Milner Davis (Ed.), *Understanding humor in Japan* (pp. 99–110). Detroit, MI: Wayne State University Press.

Reactions to Humor, Non-Laughter

Laughter is commonly thought to accompany humor, and despite the insistence of humor scholars that this is not always so, this idea continues to appear, not only in everyday talk about the topic but in scholarly research as well. Of course, laughter does often occur as a response to humor, and the link between the two has intuitive appeal, yet investigations of responses to humor in interaction demonstrate that the range of responses is much broader than simply laughter. Understanding the variety of responses and the conditions under which they tend to occur is important for the formulation of audience-based theories of humor, as well as for understanding how humor is negotiated in interaction. This entry begins with a description of the different types of non-laughter responses to humor that have been catalogued and the functions that such responses can fulfill in conversation. Then, the relationship between different types of humor and different types of non-laughter responses is examined.

Laughter in response to a humorous utterance may not necessarily indicate audience appreciation, and a lack of laughter need not signal a lack of appreciation. In fact, it is worth noting that laughter is, in fact, a regularly occurring response to humor that hearers did not find amusing. Through non-laughter responses, hearers of the humor can communicate a variety of subtle messages regarding their stance toward the humor. For instance, they can express degrees of appreciation or amusement, or the extent to which they agree or disagree with any message implied by the humor. One option that need not include laughter, but that often demonstrates support for a preceding attempt at humor, is when an interlocutor responds by contributing more humor. Thus, rather than laughing at an individual's teasing of another individual, a third participant may instead opt to join in the teasing or to share a humorous anecdote. A special case of this type of behavior, called mode adoption, occurs when an interlocutor joins in by using the same type of humor. Mode adoption may signal appreciation of humor, but this is not necessarily the case. For instance, in the case of joke-capping sessions where interlocutors tell one canned joke after another, this type of response may not always signal appreciation of the previous joke, as participants attempt to out-do each other.

Repetition of a humorous utterance or part of it (e.g., a punch line) is another possible response to humor that need not be accompanied by laughter. Repetition of another's words is recognized as a resource for building cohesion and showing supportive collaboration in conversation, in general, and can function in this way when one interlocutor repeats something humorous. The role of prosody in communicating stance is important. With varying intonation, repetition may range from enthusiastic and appreciative to disappointed or even scornful. Thus, many non-laughter responses implicitly evaluate a joke. A verbalization may also act as an explicit evaluation of the humor (e.g., "That's funny/not funny" or "I like that!"), although this may be more common as a response to failed humor than to humor that was enjoyed.

Sometimes an attempt at humor may meet with no discernible response, and in this case, the context is crucial in determining the meaning of the silence. On one hand, a complete lack of response may be unintentional—the hearer simply may not be attending to the utterance. On the other hand, the hearer may deliberately be ignoring the humor, intending to communicate a lack of appreciation of, or perhaps offense at, the joke. Intonation, again, can play an important role in helping a speaker determine whether a change of subject following his or her joke should be interpreted as a sign of an unappreciative recipient or merely a distracted conversational partner. Finally, sometimes humor is used as a response to another utterance, rather than an initiation, and in these cases no response is usually necessary. Instead, the conversation continues because the humor itself was merely an interjection or a way of lending support to the topic at hand.

Finally, although nonverbal responses to humor have not received extensive attention from researchers, they, too, play an important part in communicating a hearer's recognition of and personal reaction to an attempt at humor. Smiles, suppressed smiles, nodding, and clapping may also express appreciation. If performed in a sarcastic manner, though, they would function in the opposite way. Other ways of expressing disapproval or lack of appreciation include eye rolls, frowning, sighing, or dismissive hand gestures. Any of these actions may be combined with another and with a wide variety of verbal responses to communicate precise and subtle reactions. Again, however, less is known about the presence and distribution of these nonverbal reactions, as few studies of humor have involved videotaping of interaction (or, if they have, an analysis of responses was not the focus).

Although scant, the research on responses to humor suggests that certain types of humor tend to elicit specific types of non-laughter responses. Mode adoption, for instance, appears to be rare as a reaction to irony but may be more frequent as a response to puns and canned jokes, which often seem to elicit competitive sequences, in which participants attempt to out-do each other. Similarly, joint fictionalization, in which an imaginary scenario is constructed, is often responded to through elaboration by other conversational participants, who add details and information to further the humorous fantasy.

Aggressive forms of humor that contain a negative, if playful, message seem more likely to receive a serious response than do other forms of humor. The reaction to teasing, for instance, is quite frequently a denial of the content of the tease. Irony tends to receive the same treatment, with the hearer responding in a serious manner to the literal or implied meaning of the ironical statement. Jocular abuse is another aggressive form of humor, similar to teasing. It, too, has been found to most often be ignored, or responded to seriously, through denial, retaliation, or correction of the content.

Self-deprecating humor is also likely to be responded to seriously, particularly when it is presented in a conversation in which a speaker is describing personal tribulations. Some speakers, for example, might attempt to make light of their troubles by directing humor at themselves. In such contexts, commiseration and other forms of sympathetic support, rather than laughter, appear more often as a response. Self-deprecating humor also often works to inoculate the speaker against teasing that may ensue following, for example, a clumsy action. In this context, laughter may not be an appropriate response.

The systematic, sociolinguistic investigation of non-laughter responses to humor remains a neglected area in humor studies. Basic questions regarding the types of responses that occur, as well as who tends to use what types of responses and under what conditions, remain. Very little—and in some cases no—work has been done to examine the ways that response types vary according to age, race, class, gender, or social relationship. In addition, laughter may often accompany the types of responses outlined here, yet the blending of laughter and non-laughter responses has also received little attention.

Nancy Bell

See also Appreciation of Humor; Audience; Comprehension of Humor; Failed Humor; Reception of Humor

Further Readings

Attardo, S. (2001). Humor and irony in interaction: From mode adoption to failure of detection. In L. Anolli, R. Ciceri, & G. Riva (Eds.), *Say not to say: New perspectives on miscommunication* (pp. 166–185). Amsterdam, Netherlands: IOS Press.

Drew, P. (1987). Po-faced receipts of teases. *Linguistics, 25*(1), 219–253.

Eisterhold, J., Attardo, S., & Boxer, D. (2006). Reactions to irony in discourse: Evidence for the least disruption principle. *Journal of Pragmatics, 38*(8), 1239–1256.

Hay, J. (1994). Jocular abuse patterns in mixed-group interaction. *Wellington Working Papers in Linguistics, 6*, 26–55.

Hay, J. (2001). The pragmatics of humor support. *HUMOR: International Journal of Humor Studies, 14*(1), 55–82.

Reception of Humor

The reception of humor can theoretically range from very negative to neutral to very positive. Different dimensions have been identified that may extend from neutral to positive (e.g., funniness), from neutral to negative (e.g., aversion), or in both directions from the neutral pole (e.g., affiliation [positive] vs. aggression [negative]). Most psychological theories assume that some degree of surprise is part of the reception of humor. The reception of humor leading to overt reactions can in turn have an effect on the person generating it, should he or she be present at the time of reception and not removed, such as authors of written or drawn humor are.

Although they are hard to quantify, notions of cognitive complexity have been related to humor comprehension or failure to comprehend. Researchers assume different degrees of appreciation to be related to the amount of effort involved in humor reception. One assumption is that cognitive complexity of the stimulus needs to be just at the right level for the cognitive ability of the recipient for humor reception to be as positive as possible. Furthermore, different themes in humor (e.g., sexual or gallows humor) lead to different types of reception for different people. Theories that focus on the influence of the personality of the recipient are almost exclusively psychological—in particular, personality psychology—and usually refer to the character trait "sense of humor" as the central concept. Sense of humor is a construct related to gender, age, and ethnicity, often gauged by which language recipients speak natively. Personality-centered theories de-emphasize or ignore more contextual factors but sometimes take into account stimulus properties, as well as contrast personality trait factors such as mood. Theories that focus on stimulus properties are usually linguistic, but cognitive psychology and cognitive science also work on that aspect of humor perception. Finally, theories that are intended for the investigation of the conversational interaction in which humor reception occurs are informed by the fields of linguistic pragmatics, sociolinguistics, sociology, and social psychology. Additional fields that can illuminate the reception of humor are literary studies and aesthetics.

The reception of humor begins with the realization on the part of the recipient that a stimulus with intended or unintended humor has been received. This can occur through overt triggers, for example, informing the recipient that a joke is about to be told or stating on the cover of a cartoon collection that it contains humor. More commonly in conversational humor, there is no trigger preceding the stimulus, and often a punch line itself is the trigger that lets the recipient reevaluate preceding text as part of a humorous stimulus. Not uncommonly, no trigger is included at all—for example, in unintentional humor. But inferential triggers are also common in intentional humor and are rarely an obstacle to humor reception.

An important distinction for the analysis of the reception of humor is that between humorousness and funniness, as claimed by Amy Carrell and Salvatore Attardo. A recipient may have the competence to identify a stimulus as potentially humorous but, because of some other factor, not appreciate the stimulus and ascribe funniness to it. If recipients not only identify a humorous stimulus but also can and want to appreciate its funniness, they do so to varying degrees. Thus, the reception of humor is influenced by, and may fail for, a large variety of reasons.

Failed humor (i.e., a reaction to a humorous stimulus that does not indicate appreciation or understanding of the stimulus) has proven a fruitful area of study within discourse analysis but surprisingly far less within aesthetics or literary studies. Studies show that humor may fail at any level of the linguistic communication, from the hearing and decoding of the acoustic stimuli (e.g., if the hearer cannot hear properly the stimulus), all the way up to pragmatics and discourse (e.g., if the speaker does not realize that a given topic is taboo for humor).

Christian F. Hempelmann

See also Aesthetics; Appreciation of Humor; Incongruity and Resolution; Literature; Reactions to Humor, Non-Laughter; Sense of Humor, Components of

Further Readings

Attardo, S. (1997). The semantic foundations of cognitive theories of humor. *HUMOR: International Journal of Humor Research*, *10*(4), 395–420.

Attardo, S. (2008). Semantics and pragmatics of humor. *Language and Linguistics Compass*, *2*(6), 1203–1215.

Carrell, A. (1997). Joke competence and humor competence. *HUMOR: International Journal of Humor Research*, *10*(2), 173–185.

Giora, R. (2002, April). Optimal innovation and pleasure. In O. Stock, C. Strapparva, & A. Nijholt (Eds.), *Proceedings of the April Fools' Day Workshop on Computational Humour* (pp. 11–28). Trento, Italy: ITC-irst.

Martin, R. (2007). *The psychology of humor*. Burlington, MA: Academic Press.

Ruch, W. (1998). *Sense of humor: Explorations of a personality characteristic*. Berlin, Germany: Mouton de Gruyter.

Suls, J. M. (1972). A two-stage model for the appreciation of jokes and cartoons: An information-processing analysis. In J. H. Goldstein & P. E. McGhee (Eds.), *The psychology of humor: Theoretical perspectives and empirical issues* (pp. 81–100). New York, NY: Academic Press.

Ziv, A. (1984). *Personality and sense of humor*. New York, NY: Springer.

Reframing

Reframing is a term that signifies a shift in perspective or understanding of a situation. When a person experiences a situation, whether in real time or narrative, the characteristics of that situation engender a world of interrelated assumptions and expectations, mostly unconscious, for that person. This world of assumptions and expectations is the "frame" of the situation, which can comprise several interlocking frames. Terms that are synonymous with *frame* include *scheme* and *script*. When one refers to a perspective shift as "reframing," one is hearkening to the fact that a new set of assumptions and expectations, differing from those that were initially present before the reframing, has been applied to the situation. Humorous reframing occurs when the shift in perspective or understanding is experienced as humorous (per Attardo's perlocutionary definition of humor as a text whose purpose is to produce the perception of humor).

Humorous Reframing in Psychotherapy

Humorous reframing has long been a technique for change in the practice of psychotherapy, although it has not always been referred to by this label. In his logotherapy, Viktor Frankl frequently used the method of "paradoxical intention," in which he would encourage his clients to reframe their symptoms (e.g., profuse sweating, stuttering, compulsive washing, insomnia) from distressing events to be avoided to events that are desired and pursued. In other words, Frankl advised his patients to stop trying to avoid neurotic symptoms and instead pursue them as fully as possible. Frankl cited many cases in which this kind of reframing brought about fast relief of debilitating symptoms, and he argues that a humorous attitude about one's symptoms, even ridiculing them, is an important part of the success of the method of paradoxical intention.

Another well-known figure in the history of psychotherapy, Albert Ellis, used humorous reframing as a central part of his rational emotive therapy (RET), which is the precursor to the now-dominant cognitive behavioral therapy (CBT). Ellis argued that what makes one depressed, anxious, or otherwise miserable are one's "irrational beliefs." To alleviate one's psychological symptoms, one must alter the irrational frame through which one views the world. He argued that one of the most effective means by which this reframing can be accomplished is humor. Ellis called the process through which one changes the irrational frame(s) through which one experiences the world, "disputing." Ellis is famous for using hilarious and irreverent methods to dispute his patients' irrational frames, including requiring clients to sing "rational humorous songs" that ridicule and belittle the irrational beliefs (i.e., frames) of clients. These songs had such titles as "Whine, Whine, Whine," "Maybe I'll Move My Ass," and "I Am Just a Love Slob!" He made a significant impact with this and other methods for helping clients reframe distressing experiences, an impact that clients reportedly felt in their clinical work with him and an impact that is still felt in the field of psychotherapy.

Besides Frankl and Ellis, many other pioneers in psychotherapy, including Alfred Adler and Milton Erickson, have advocated for humor's effectiveness in helping clients reframe their symptoms and distress. Humor has increasingly been appreciated as an agent for change in psychotherapy, and many books and collections have been dedicated to its use. A common theme in writings on humor in psychotherapy is that humor is a potent tool to help clients reframe their perspective and adopt new ways of experiencing and relating.

Theoretical Understandings of the Action of Humorous Reframing

Many aspects of humor make it a potent agent for change of perspective, or reframing. First, humor is pleasant, attractive, and compelling. People seek to enjoy humor with others and wish to be a part of humor and laughter when it occurs around them. Humor has the power to draw people in and pull them through an initial frame into a new perspective.

In addition, the pleasure experienced in humor reinforces the pursuit of humor and, in a parallel manner, the pursuit of reframing; hence, humor can substantially motivate a client to alter his or her maladaptive frames. When humor is shared with others, one experiences a tacit, pre-reflective sense that those other(s) went through a progression of frames in the humor perception similar to one's own and found the stimuli humorous for reasons similar to one's own. In other words, one sees others as aligned with oneself in the final "reframed" perspective attained through humor. Shared humor can hence contribute to making the reframed perspective an enduring one because one presumes that the humor perceptions are shared and endorsed by others.

Something that also plays a role in humor's efficacy to reframe one's perspective is that humor often diminishes or trivializes the initial frame, prior to the shift involved in humor perception. Because the original perspective is put down, made irrelevant, or ridiculed, the latter frame or perspective feels more encompassing and insightful in comparison to the initial frame.

Finally, humor essentially involves a shift. Theories of humor universally recognize a shift between perspectives as a central ingredient, whether the theory is Thomas Hobbes's "sudden glory" theory or incongruity theory. This widespread recognition suggests that in its essence, humor involves the juxtaposition of incompatible yet overlapping scripts (or frames). If humor inextricably involves patching together two substantially different perspectives, then it makes sense that humor is a natural means for cognitive reframing.

Joshua Gregson

See also Psychology

Further Readings

Attardo, S. (2002). Semiotics and pragmatics of humor communication. *BABEL: Aspectos de Filoloxia Inglesa e Alemana, 11,* 25–66.

Buckman, E. S. (1994). Humor as a communication facilitator in couples' therapy. In E. S. Buckman (Ed.), *The handbook of humor: Clinical applications in psychotherapy* (pp. 75–90). Malabar, FL: Krieger.

Ellis, A. (1987). The use of rational humorous songs in psychotherapy. In W. Fry & W. Salameh (Eds.), *Handbook of humor and psychotherapy: Advances in the clinical use of humor.* Sarasota, FL: Professional Resource Exchange.

Frankl, V. (1984). *Man's search for meaning.* New York, NY: Washington Square Press.

Fry, W. F., Jr., & Salameh, W. A. (Eds.). (1987). *Handbook of humor and psychotherapy: Advances in the clinical use of humor.* Sarasota, FL: Professional Resource Exchange.

Fry, W. F., Jr., & Salameh, W. A. (Eds.). (1993). *Advances in humor and psychotherapy.* Sarasota, FL: Professional Resource Press.

Fry, W. F., Jr., & Salameh, W. A. (Eds.). (2001). *Humor and wellness in clinical intervention.* Westport, CT: Praeger.

Kuhlman, T. L. (1984). *Humor and psychotherapy.* Homewood, IL: Dow Jones-Irwin.

Martin, R. (2007). *The psychology of humor: An integrative approach.* Burlington, MA: Elsevier Academic Press.

Minsky, M. (1975). A framework for representing knowledge. In P. Winston (Ed.), *The psychology of computer vision* (pp. 99–128). New York, NY: McGraw-Hill.

Morreall, J. (Ed.). (1987). *The philosophy of laughter and humor.* Albany: State University of New York Press.

Mosak, H. H. (1987). *Ha ha and aha: The role of humor in psychotherapy.* Muncie, IN: Accelerated Development.

Mosak, H. H., & Maniacci, M. (1993). An "Alderian" approach to humor and psychotherapy. In W. F. Fry Jr. & W. A. Salameh (Eds.), *Advances in humor and psychotherapy* (pp. 1–18). Sarasota, FL: Professional Resource Press.

O'Hanlon, B., & Beadle, S. (1999). *A guide to possibility land: Fifty-one methods for doing brief, respectful therapy.* New York, NY: Norton.

Strean, H. (1994). *The use of humor in psychotherapy.* Northvale, NJ: Jason Aronson.

Relationships, Nonromantic

Several humor theorists have taught us that humor is fundamentally a social experience. For one, we laugh much more when we are surrounded by other people than when we are alone. Indeed, laughter is contagious, and it has even been proven to work as a form of therapy for people who are depressed or just feel sad. Jokes are meant to be shared with others, and comedians know that when the audience is not being amused, the humor is probably not very funny. Above all, humor can greatly reduce the tension among people and enable individuals who are different from each other to get along and even live together in harmony.

In his famous essay titled *In Praise of Folly*, Desiderius Erasmus (1509/1941) eloquently captures the social value of humor and silliness. Written in 1509, this essay is a long speech made by the goddess Folly on her own behalf in which she argues that it is foolishness rather than reason that makes possible everything we value most in life:

> In sum, no society, no union in life, could be either pleasant or lasting without me [Folly]. A people does not for long tolerate its prince, or a master tolerate his servant, a handmaiden her mistress, a teacher his student, a friend his friend, a wife her husband, a landlord his tenant, a partner his partner, or a boarder his fellow boarder, except as they mutually or by turns are mistaken, on occasion flatter, on occasion wisely wink, and otherwise soothe themselves with the sweetness of folly. (p. 28)

Erasmus's point is that to have harmonious relationships with our colleagues, family members, or friends, we need to be able to overlook some of their blemishes and laugh when they make mistakes. It is folly and our sense of humor, no less than reason, that enable us to live together with others, form close relationships with them, and tolerate their shortcomings. In short, when used appropriately, humor can even enhance intimacy in friendships and other close relationships.

The fact that humor can enhance the quality of our relationships with significant others suggests that it may have a role to play in building intimacy among friends and companions. Intimacy, in this context, should not be confused with sexual encounters, although it is obvious that many intimate relationships include the physical aspect. Rather, an intimate relationship is one that we value for its own sake as opposed to one in which two people use each other or one that is relatively insignificant to us.

Based on this understanding of intimacy, the question is this: How can humor enhance intimacy in friendships and other close relationships? First, it seems obvious that humor and laughter can increase the pleasure of friendships. Noel Carroll (2002) notes that "laughter among friends is a pleasure, and one of the pleasures of friendship is the opportunity to share laughter" (p. 205). Humor enables us to get beyond the tense moments that we experience in our relationships and move to a more comfortable place. Because humor can increase pleasure among friends, it seems reasonable to conclude that it can also lead two people to become more intimate in the sense of feeling that their relationship is getting closer and becoming more meaningful.

In contrast, when a friendship between two persons deteriorates, the earlier pleasure they enjoyed of sharing a joke or just laughing together often begins to dissipate as well. In such cases, one person's sense of humor no longer amuses the other and may even annoy or offend him or her. Summing up this point, John Morreall (1983) writes:

> When two people are quarreling, one of the first things they stop doing together is laughing; they refuse to laugh at each other's attempts at humor, and refuse to laugh together at something incongruous happening to them. As soon as they begin to laugh once more, we know that the end of the quarrel is at hand. (p. 115)

Second, humor and laughter can strengthen intimacy by exposing our identities and making us vulnerable in the face of others. As Carroll (2002) puts it, "Laughter reveals something about who we are—our beliefs, attitudes, and emotions—and, for that reason, we are often only willing to be so open about our sensibilities around friends" (p. 205). Carroll's point is that because laughter exposes our personal whims and quirks, we tend to laugh in the company of our friends rather than strangers. Yet precisely because humor and laughter often leave us more exposed and vulnerable, they can lead us to become more intimate with our friends. That is, intimacy with our significant others can be forged when we use humor to take risks and disclose our deepest feelings and beliefs.

Last, humor can enhance intimacy in relationships by prompting people to view things from a different perspective and see something in a new light. Our sense of humor and the capacity to laugh at ourselves involves a willingness to consider ourselves silly or foolish; it implies an openness to evaluate some of our habitual ways of thinking or acting in light of the perspectives of our significant others whose viewpoints and preferences may be very different from our own. Ralph Waldo Emerson argued correctly that friends do not always agree with each other and that ideally they should challenge each other's point of view. The point is that by espousing the perspectives of our friends and close relations, we demonstrate that we care about their feelings and beliefs and are open to becoming more intimate with them.

Mordechai Gordon

See also Marriage and Couples

Further Readings

Carroll, N. (2002). Art and friendship. *Philosophy and Literature*, 26(1), 199–206.

Emerson, R. W. (1876). Friendship. In *Emerson, essays: First and second series* (pp. 183–206). New York, NY: Houghton Mifflin.

Erasmus, D. (1941). *In praise of folly* (H. H. Hudson, Trans.). Princeton, NJ: Princeton University Press. (Original work written 1509)

Morreall, J. (1983). *Taking laughter seriously*. Albany: State University of New York.

Morreall, J. (2009). *Comic relief: A comprehensive philosophy of humor*. Oxford, UK: Wiley-Blackwell.

Release Theories of Humor

Release theory focuses on the psychological and physical processes of tension build-up in people and the release of this tension by humor. According to John Morreall, humor is best understood as a release process in which laughter operates like a safety valve in a steam pipe, releasing built-up nervous energy. Herbert Spencer had a simple version of the theory in which a laughter stimulus evokes emotions but then shows them to be inappropriate. This entry begins with a review of Sigmund Freud's analysis of humor, which focuses on the way in which humor can help release built-up psychological energy. The entry then examines humor as a potential source of liberation from psychological constraints, as suggested by M. M. Bakhtin and Harvey Mindess. It then deals with the importance of the social context within which humor occurs, as analyzed by Mary Douglas, and the healing potential of humor, as described by William Fry. The entry concludes with a look at Morreall's theory of humor as cognitive play.

Freud can be considered the father of the psychoanalytic approach to humor, which argues, in essence, that humor is based on masked aggression, frequently involving human sexuality, and that this humor offers us gratifications we all desire. According to Morreall, Freud found three laughter situations: jokes, the comic, and humor. In jokes, laughter generates a release of psychic energy normally used to repress emotions such as hatred and sexual desire. The psychic energy "saved" in the comic is energy that can be used for thinking; and the energy "saved" in humor is the energy of feeling emotions that are suddenly rendered unnecessary.

As Freud explained in *Jokes and Their Relation to the Unconscious,* what jokes do is make possible our satisfying an instinct, whether a hostile or a lustful one, in the face of an obstacle that tries to prevent this satisfaction. By satisfying an instinct and overcoming obstacles, humor generates a sense of freedom and power. There are many other gratifications that humor provides, and Freud and his followers, such as Martin Grotjahn, have explicated a number of them. Implicit in Freud's analysis is the idea that humor has therapeutic value and releases us, temporarily, from inhibitions. Freud's book also has some wonderful Jewish jokes in it.

Many other writers and scholars have offered variations on release theory that are worth considering. One of the most important and influential scholars who wrote about humor was the Russian literary theorist M. M. Bakhtin, who argued that in the Middle Ages, humor functioned as an important release mechanism and a kind of safety valve. As he writes in his classic study *Rabelais and His World*:

> As opposed to laughter, medieval seriousness was infused with elements of fear, weakness, humility, submission, falsehood, hypocrisy, or on the other hand with violence, intimidation, threats, prohibitions. As a spokesman of power, seriousness terrorized, demanded and forbade.... Distrust of the serious tone and confidence in the truth of laughter had a spontaneous, elemental character. It was understood that fear never lurks behind laughter . . . and that hypocrisy and lies never laugh but wear a serious mask. Laughter created no dogmas and could not become authoritarian; it did not convey fear but a feeling of strength. It was linked with the procreating act, with birth, renewal, fertility, abundance. Laughter was also related to food and drink and the people's earthly immortality, and finally it was related to the future of things to come and was to clear the way for them. (Bakhtin, 1984, pp. 94–95)

For Bakhtin, laughter functioned as a liberating force; this is a theme that is found in the writings of many release theorists of humor, although they may not identify themselves as such. Bakhtin (1984) is explicit on the function of humor as a life-enhancing force:

> Laughter liberates not only from external censorship but first of all from the great interior censor; it liberates from the fear that has developed in man during thousands of years: fear of the sacred, of prohibitions, of power. It unveils the material bodily principle in its true meaning. (p. 94)

Bakhtin argued that humor is connected to the life force, to bodily functions, and to a desire for freedom from restraint.

The British social anthropologist Mary Douglas offers an insight into the relation between jokes and societies. Jokes, she suggests, provide a kind of relaxation of consciousness in favor of the unconscious, allowing them to function as liberating agents. Jokes are conventionally defined as short narratives with punch lines that generate mirthful laughter. Douglas explains that jokes are tied to the social structure in which they are found. As she writes in *Implicit Meanings: Essays in Anthropology* (1975),

> I confess that I find Freud's definition of the joke highly satisfactory. The joke is an image of the relaxation of conscious control in favor of the subconscious. . . . The joke merely affords opportunity for realizing that an accepted pattern has no necessity. Its excitement lies in the suggestion

> that any particular ordering of experience may be arbitrary and subjective. It is frivolous in that it produces no real alternative, only an exhilarating sense of freedom from form in general. (p. 96)

For Douglas, jokes always relate to the social situations in which they are found and involve a dominant pattern of relations being challenged by a different one—the one expressed in the joke. A joke is seen and allowed when it offers a symbolic pattern of a social pattern occurring at the same time. According to Douglas (1975), "if there is no joke in the social structure, no other joking can occur" (p. 98). The exhilarating "freedom from form" in Douglas's analysis refers to the liberating nature of jokes, and we can suggest that humor in general has this function.

William Fry, a psychiatrist who has written extensively on humor, has discussed the physiological benefits of mirthful laughter. As he explained in an address to the American Orthopsychiatric Association in Washington, D.C., in April 1979, laughter has a number of scientifically demonstrable impacts on our bodies. As he explains,

> Muscles are activated; heart rate is increased; respiration is amplified, with increase in oxygen exchange—all similar to the desirable effects of athletic exercise. Stress is antagonized by humor in both its mental or emotional aspects and its physical aspect. Emotional tension, contributing to stress, is lowered through the cathartic effects of humor. Mirthful laughter is followed by state of compensatory physical relations, diminishing physical tension.

It is this diminution of tension and stress from humor that ties his work to release theorists. Fry has made numerous other contributions dealing with the relation of humor and health, and a considerable number of other scholars have done so as well.

Many scholars suggest that humor helps people in a number of different ways. That is, humor has a healing and liberating effect on people—both the teller of jokes and those listening to them. The notion of release of masked aggression may have negative connotations, but we can also see release in a positive light as enhancing our psychological and physical well-being. This point is elaborated by Harvey Mindess, a clinical psychologist, in his book *Laughter and Liberation*. The first part of the book deals with how laughter frees us from what Mindess describes as "inner obstacles," while the second part investigates the relationship that exists between humor and creativity. Humor helps "liberate" us from various obsessions because humor involves surprise, which frees us from the demands of our superegos and "the chains of our perceptual, conventional, logical, linguistic and moral systems" (Mindess, 1971/2011, p. 28).

For Mindess, one of humor's most important powers is its ability to free us from the bonds of conformity and to enable us to violate, at times, the codes that shape our behavior. It is humor, he argues, that provides a kind of elasticity and support for nonconformist moments in our daily lives. As he writes, "if we acquire . . . the frame of mind in which humor flourishes—the individual, iconoclastic outlook—we have set ourselves on the a [sic] springboard to freedom" (Mindess, 1971/2011, p. 41).

Morreall presents a variation on release theory in which he suggests that humor is a form of cognitive play. We must recognize, he suggests, that humor is not serious, that it is social in nature, and that it is a form of play. Elements in his theory can be found in the four basic theories of humor: superiority theory, incongruity theory, psychoanalytic theory, and what we might call cognitive and communication theory. The notion that humor is a kind of play is found in the cognitive and communication theory, as elaborated by William Fry Jr., described earlier, and the writings of Gregory Bateson, with whom Fry collaborated. There are numerous books that deal with the release theory of humor, and it remains a subject of both controversy and interest among humor scholars.

Arthur Asa Berger

See also Carnivalesque; Freudian/Psychoanalytic Theories

Further Readings

Bakhtin, M. M. (1984). *Rabelais and his world* (H. Iswolsky, Trans.). Bloomington: Indiana University Press.

Bateson, G. (1972). *Steps to an ecology of mind.* New York, NY: Ballantine.

Berger, A. A. (1993). *An anatomy of humor.* New Brunswick, NJ: Transaction.

Berger, A. A. (1995). *Blind men and elephants: Perspectives on humor.* New Brunswick, NJ: Transaction.

Douglas, M. (1975). Jokes. In *Implicit meanings: Essays in anthropology.* London, UK: Routledge & Kegan Paul.

Freud, S. (1963). *Jokes and their relation to the unconscious* (J. Strachey, Ed. & Trans.). New York, NY: Norton.

Fry, W. (1963). *Sweet madness: A study of humor*. Palo Alto, CA: Pacific Books.

Fry, W. (1979). *Using humor to save lives* [Address given at the annual convention of the American Orthopsychiatric Association in Washington, DC]. Retrieved from http://www.humor.ch/inernsthaft/fry2.htm

Mindess, H. (2011). *Laughter and liberation*. Los Angeles, CA: Nash. (Original work published 1971)

Morreall, J. (2009). *Comic relief: A comprehensive philosophy of humor*. Malden, MA: Wiley.

Morreall, J. (2009). Humor as cognitive play. *Journal of Literary Theory, 3*(2), 241–260.

Religion

Religion and humor have holistic tendencies. Religion's ideal is to have an impact on many if not all aspects of human life, especially those that are important for the self. Humor intends to play with all domains of human activity and life in general, and it is stronger when it plays with important human concerns. In this entry, the complex relations between religion and humor are described. These include how religion sees humor, how humor works within religion, and how humor uses religion as a target. Finally, recent psychological studies have shed some light on the complex links between (a) religion or individual differences in religiosity and (b) humor or individual differences in sense of humor.

Religion's Attitudes on Humor

Religious attitudes toward humor vary greatly across religions and cultures, as well as across different historical periods within the same culture or religion. This can be concluded from historical, anthropological, sociological, and religious studies. Interesting differences seem to exist, for instance, between monotheistic religions and other religions, between Western and Eastern cultures, and between traditional and contemporary Christianity. Globally, the latter poles of each of the difference pairs mentioned above are perceived to be more tolerant of, and open to, humor and laughter, and to place a higher value on them or some of their aspects. The former poles are perceived to be more suspicious of some or many aspects of humor, and especially laughter, that could be qualified as immoral or contrary to spiritual ideals.

The variation in religious attitudes toward humor and laughter seems to follow variations in the way culture, and consequently religion, considers—values or devalues—body and bodily expressions, eroticism and sexuality, and emotions and their expression. It also seems to parallel the differences between (a) unstructured and fragmented religious beliefs, practices, and divinities and (b) structured and integrative religions disposing of personal, moralizing, and exclusivist Gods. (Note that, intriguingly, the latter religions have historically succeeded over others.)

Contemporary theological and philosophical thinking within religions that have historically been suspicious of humor and laughter (typically, but not only, Christianity) finds today several spiritual qualities within them. Both religion and humor constitute ways of transcending the self, searching for alternative meanings of things, and questioning the "superficial" everyday reality. Humor can contribute to self-criticism, reflexivity, creative doubt, intellectual and spiritual maturity, and wisdom. It also has a psychological strengthening value, thus contributing to joy and well-being, which today are valued within modern religious and nonreligious spiritualities. In some new religious movements and expressions (including fundamentalist ones), similar to some Eastern religions and ancient Greek religion, one can also find ritualized expressions of humor and practice of "spiritual," even "holy laughter."

Such positive attitudes remain, though at the margin of the global expression of religiousness across cultures, societies, and historical periods. Indeed, even today, the majority of world believers within established religions (more than 70% of the world population) belong to religions that have expressed, or still express, ambivalence, serious concerns about, and criticism of, several aspects of the comic, or at least prudent tolerance rather than enthusiastic endorsement. This is the case typically of Christianity and Islam, but, to some extent, also Buddhism and Hinduism. Partial suspicion of humor does not constitute an exception across religions, but rather the rule.

Cross-cultural psychological research suggests that, beyond important cultural variability, human psychological functioning also presents some universals. This is also the case with the psychology of humor (some universal psychological characteristics, predictors, and consequences) as well as with the psychology of religion (characteristics, predictors, and consequences). If one combines this kind of empirical psychological knowledge with religious and philosophical considerations of humor marked by prudence and suspicion, an almost fundamental distrust, if not partial incompatibility, between humor and religion emerges.

Humor entails a play on meaning, openness to the possibility of a meaningless world, introduction of disorder, and the transgression of societal norms. It implies surprise, loss of control, openness to novelty and ambiguity, and disengagement with regard to truth, morality, and affection. Religion, on the other hand, despite sharing with humor a willingness for an alternative perception of reality, emphasizes the meaningfulness of the world, order and structure in life and closure in cognition, need for control, discomfort with ambiguity and novelty, as well as engagement with regard to truth, morality, and interpersonal relations. Note that the historical religious mistrust of immoderate laughter was justified because such laughter was perceived as constituting a failure of the ideal of self-mastery. Consequently, the religious condemnation of many kinds of humor as immoral (i.e., sexual, sick, earthy, aggressive, and disparaging of others) eliminates most of humor's essential components.

In fact, from a rigid moralistic perspective, humor threatens and possibly violates all five major foundations of morality across cultures: care (disparaging and hostile humor), fairness/reciprocity (humor betrays truth and the common rules of human communication), loyalty, respect for authority (rebellious humor), and purity/divinity (disgusting, sexual, and blasphemous humor).

Humor *in* Religion

Although religions have often been suspicious of humor and have condemned excessive laughter, they are also expressions of human activity and creativity. Consequently, humor is present in various manifestations of religious creativity and in people's and key religious figures' spiritual lives. Humor within religion thus plays the same psychological, sociological, and anthropological functions that it plays in the lives of individuals and groups in general. However, given the specifications of the religious context, religious humor is characterized by several particularities that are worthy of being noted.

First, humor exists at the margins of core religious activities and expressions. One can find humor in decorative artistic expressions, for instance, at the margins of illustrations in medieval religious manuscripts, at very secondary places in religious architecture and religious iconography, or in the margins of religious sermons. The main goal of religious art is to transmit normative religious teachings and to provide spiritual opportunities for the experience of the sublime and the emotion of awe when in contact with a transcendent reality. These are not the primary goals of humor, although humor may be helpful here by offering some rest and reprieve when individuals are engaged in religious and spiritual life. (This was, indeed, what caused 13th-century philosopher and theologian Thomas Aquinas to perceive moderate humor and laughter to be legitimate, seeing as how the latter allowed for some relaxation in the middle of the spiritual fight.)

Second, an intriguing question is what kind of humor, if any, exists in key religious figures' lives and writings, especially in the lives of the founders of the dominant world religions and in major foundational religious texts such as the Bible or the Qur'an. For centuries, main religious texts and figures have been perceived in a highly idealized manner, as sources of ultimate meaning, moral behavior, and spiritual modeling. More recently, scholars in religious studies, especially those in biblical studies, but also historians and other social scientists, have started to detect humor in religious texts and historical figures, or at least to reinterpret some elements as possibly suggesting the presence of humor. Also, anthologies of the humor of saints and important religious figures (e.g., modern popes) have begun to be published.

The investigation of humor in Christianity, compared with other religions, has been intense. A strong emphasis has been placed on the study of humor in the Bible (Old and New Testaments), with particular attention to Jesus's humor. An inspection of this work confirms that humor is marginal in these texts—this is not surprising, given the very nature of the Bible compared with other kinds of literature—but also that two kinds of humor are predominant. The first is didactic, pedagogical humor that aims to underline spiritual teachings and norms of religious beliefs and behavior. When criticizing various beliefs and behaviors as morally and religiously inappropriate, biblical humor is usually ironic. Moral irony is in fact the predominant type of humor in the major religious texts, and hyperbole is often used to accentuate the effect. The second major kind of biblical humor is social, allowing for social inclusion into the normative religious in-group and exclusion of various out-groups, that is, other religions, nonbelievers, or other ethnic groups. This is especially the case in the Old Testament where God often shows humor that disparages his enemies. Apart from moralizing humor and irony and disparaging out-group humor, it is hard to find in key religious texts and figures—at least as far as the major world religions of today are concerned—the typical kinds, topics, and targets of humor that have made humans laugh heartily for thousands of years (i.e., absurd, sexual, scatological, morbid, and aggressive/insulting humor).

One can also find, in a very marginal manner, religious burlesque-like expressions, be it through exceptional rituals (e.g., carnival feasts, often connected to the Easter calendar) or exceptional religious figures who, against the conventional social order, endorsed a particularly joyful, clownish, or foolish and rebellious way of life such as the saint Philippe Neri in Catholicism or the Fools for Christ in the Orthodox Church.

Third, religious humor also exists through a substantial corpus of religious jokes that have been orally transmitted among people for years and have only recently been increasingly codified through published volumes. There is also humor in religious cartoons, or in political cartoons that heavily rely on religious themes, often during religious holidays. Of course, many everyday jokes may include some religious elements. However, strictly speaking, religious jokes are those whose religious elements (e.g., "the minister, the priest, and the rabbi") cannot be replaced by other, secular equivalent elements (e.g., "the German, the French, and the Jew") and whose understanding presupposes some minimal knowledge of the religious culture; otherwise, they would just not be funny. Recent analyses of hundreds of these jokes from Christian contexts suggest that religious jokes often play on the typical religious and spiritual oppositions of sacred/profane, moral/sinful, life/death, spiritual-eternal/worldly-material, and divine/human and are most often targeted at religious professionals (clergy and monks) and, to some extent, religious practitioners, rather than the divine itself. In one of these studies that compared church puns with secular puns in the United States, the authors found, based on typical criteria from humor theory, that the church puns were not plainly humorous, possibly because these churches may still tend to avoid humor.

Biblical themes (in particular, Adam and Eve's story, and Saint Peter's gatekeeper role in heaven), as well as stereotypes of other religious denominations or specific religious subgroups (e.g., jokes on Catholics and Protestants or Catholic jokes on Jesuits) rather than other religions, are two dominant sources of religious Christian humor. Note that a core characteristic of religious humor is to reinforce norms rather than to question or demolish them, or to question some religious practices in the name of higher spiritual ideals.

Interreligious humor (i.e., humor on and between religious groups) can be intimately related to interethnic humor. Humor on Jews often combines religious and ethnic/cultural sources and components. Also, typical jokes making fun of canny versus stupid groups usually apply to ethnic groups that have historically been, respectively, predominantly Protestant versus Catholic. Max Weber's sociological theory of the Protestant ethic of capitalism seems thus to translate into jokes about excessively competitive, individualistic, and achievement-oriented and financial gain–oriented Protestants.

Humor *on* Religion

Laughing at religion, often but not necessarily from an outsider's perspective, has also been pervasive possibly since the very existence of humor and religion. Religion has historically been (a) an important societal source of power and force of establishment and maintenance of social hierarchies; (b) a major provider of ideas, norms, and practices aimed to control sexuality; and (c) one of the rare ideological systems that encompasses into one integrative set the beliefs, emotions, behaviors, and groups that allow humans to deal with deep existential needs and ultimate concerns. For all of these reasons, religion, together with secular authorities of political, moral, and ideological power, has been a main target of humor. Humor is indeed uncomfortable with totalizing systems, ideas, and feelings; or better, humor is nourished by these systems, in that it needs to criticize them.

The history of satire on religion has followed the cultural history of the interplay between powerful religions, individual religious doubting, and social anti-religious sentiment. It has also paralleled the history of the conflict between protection of the sacred from profanation and defense of individuals' right to express their ideas, including those for or against religion. Overall, it seems that there are three major types of religious satire. One type focuses on ironic criticism of religious professionals (e.g., the many sexual jokes on clergy and monks) and norms and practices of religious institutions and religious devotees. This type may be aggressive at moments of high anti-religious and anti-clerical hostility (such as the wave of anti-religious cartoons following the

French Revolution). However, religious satire is also present among sympathizers who question current religious elements possibly in the name of higher spiritual or moral values (e.g., the humor on religion in *The Simpsons*). The third type, more radical in content, but yet today more discrete in extent and form, criticizes or ridicules the divine itself. This type of humor is typically perceived as blasphemy by believers.

The argumentation often used in the humorous, ironic, or sarcastic criticism of religion is of the same nature as the three major sources of religious doubting and apostasy. Among doubters or atheists, several religious aspects, or even the very central elements of religious faith, are criticized for being morally unacceptable (some religious norms may be in conflict with universal moral values), intellectually irrational (religious beliefs are, by definition, unverifiable and may appear implausible), or socially irrelevant (religious practices often present some discrepancy with an evolving society). The alternative contemporary form of humor on religion is a soft one, not strictly anti-religious: It mocks religious themes and symbols not because the target is religion per se, but because religious parody is an efficient strategy for memorizing the advertisement of secular products.

Recently, in secularized Western countries, emphasis has been placed on the subtle distinction between (a) religious ideas and sacred figures and symbols that should no longer be legally protected, thus being possible subjects of ridicule, and (b) religious individuals and groups who should not be targets of prejudice for their beliefs, practices, and affiliation. Therefore, in most of these societies there is no longer a law against blasphemy, whereas this is still the case in traditional and collectivistic countries. At the same time, in the former societies, clearer and stronger legal protection has been put in place against interreligious and interconvictional (between believers and nonbelievers) prejudice, compared with the latter countries.

However, the strong connection between religion and ethnicity/culture, and thus between interreligious and interethnic prejudice, has made extremely difficult the effort to distinguish, in some cases, between (a) satire of religious ideas and symbols, (b) interreligious prejudice, and (c) interethnic prejudice. The Danish "Muhammad cartoons affair" in the mid-2000s and other, subsequent anti-Islam satiric expressions in the West are typical examples. In fact, two symmetric suspicions exist in the public domain. On one hand, anti-Muslim satire may use freedom of (anti-)religious expression to propagate ethnic prejudice. On the other hand, violent protestations by Muslim individuals and communities may use the banishment of religious and ethnic prejudice as a way to legitimize their unwillingness to allow Islam to be criticized by others, especially outsiders.

Psychological Studies

A series of recent psychological studies has investigated the complex links between religion and humor. More precisely, these studies investigated three kinds of questions. The first is whether religiosity (i.e., individual differences on how religious or nonreligious a person is) or specific forms of religiosity (e.g., orthodox and fundamentalist versus open-minded faith) indicates any specifics on a person's sense of humor: global sense of humor, use of humor as a coping mechanism, humor creation, and appreciation of humor in general or specific humor styles in particular. The second question is whether religious stimulation (i.e., activation of religious ideas, symbols, and emotional experiences) has any impact on humor. The third question is whether the experience of humor and amusement has any influence on a person's attitudes toward religion and spirituality.

When focusing on self-evaluations, it appears that religious people do not tend to perceive themselves as having a low sense of humor. If anything, self-reported spirituality is often accompanied by positive attitudes toward humor and its appreciation as a virtue. However, when the emphasis on the questionnaire is not on humor or religion per se (either of which could accentuate some social desirability), religious people and those who use religion to cope with stress and adversity actually report low use of humor as a means to cope (i.e., as a way to face stress and adversity). More important, when the evaluations come from others (e.g., spouses), it appears that religious people tend to be perceived by their spouses as generally using less humor, and using less negative (i.e., hostile and earthy) humor in particular.

When it comes to alternative measures of humor, such as the appreciation of jokes provided to participants or the spontaneous creation of humor in the laboratory, the existing studies show first that religious people tend not to spontaneously create humor when they are requested to provide their written responses in hypothetical situations inducing stress. They also tend to not find funny the jokes that reflect sick humor (i.e., those that are morbid, disgusting, and disparaging of people with disabilities), and orthodox religious people dislike incongruity in humor, be it resolved or not. On the contrary, being relativistic and ready to question one's own attitudes toward religion predicts an appreciation of nonsense, absurd jokes, and high levels of spontaneous creation of humor in response to hypothetical daily hassles.

In another laboratory study, exposure to a video clip presenting various religious ideas, images, and feelings led to the inhibition of participants' tendency to spontaneously use humor as a way to cope with hypothetical daily hassles. In yet another study, implicit activation ("priming") of religious ideas decreased participants', especially religious practitioners', ratings of the funniness of cartoons provided in the study.

Examining the opposite causal direction (i.e., from humor to religion), a series of laboratory studies investigated the consequences of inducing different positive emotions on participants' attitudes toward religion and spirituality. Positive emotions such as awe, elevation, and admiration, also called self-transcendent emotions, but not humor-related amusement (all emotions were induced either through video clips or through recall of personal experiences) increased participants' positive attitudes toward spirituality and related feelings and behavioral intentions.

In these psychological studies, the conflict, or at least, discomfort, between humor and religion was thus consistently attested through self-reports, peer reports, and behavioral measures of appreciation and creation of humor. The effect is clearer when it comes to morally questionable forms of humor, but it sometimes extends to the social, common form of humor as well as to its common use as a coping mechanism. Not surprisingly, therefore, in another study measuring stereotypes (what group A thinks about group B) and meta-stereotypes (what group A believes group B thinks about group A) between believers and nonbelievers, it turned out that the two groups share the perception of high versus low humor as being associated with, respectively, nonbelievers and believers.

These series of psychological studies were mainly carried out in Western, relatively secularized countries (Belgium, New Zealand, and the United States) with a Christian, often Catholic, background. It is of great interest to examine in future research whether these results generalize to other religions and non-Western cultural contexts. The possibility is not excluded that in some other religious groups, especially those where religion in not used primarily as a way to gain self-control, humor usage may be, on average, higher than among people of Catholic or, more generally, Christian traditions. However, as some universality in the psychological characteristics of humor as well as in the psychological characteristics of religion exists, it is reasonable to suspect that the studies described in this entry reflect something deeper, and possibly universal, regarding inherent discrepancies between religion and humor. Both religion and humor are a means for reframing and transcending everyday life experience. However, humor does so by diminishing things seen to be important in the visible reality, whereas religion does so by idealizing the importance of things that are part of an invisible reality.

In conclusion, religion and humor are neither good friends nor eternal enemies. Their ties are reminiscent of the ambivalent relations developed by competitive neighbors who have been constrained to live together.

Vassilis Saroglou

See also Biblical Humor; Buddhism; Christianity; Clergy; Confucianism; Islam; Judaism; Taoism

Further Readings

Baconski, T. (1996). *Le rire des pères: Essai sur le rire dans la patristique grecque* [The laughter of the fathers: Essay on laughter in Greek patristics]. Paris, France: Desclée de Brouwer.

Davies, C. (1992). The Protestant ethic and the comic spirit of capitalism. *The British Journal of Sociology, 43,* 421–442.

Feltmate, D. S. (2010). *Springfield's sacred canopy: Religion and humour in* The Simpsons. Doctoral dissertation. Retrieved from http://uwspace.uwaterloo.ca/handle/10012/5628

Geybels, H., & Van Herck, W. (Eds.). (2011). *Humor and religion: Challenges and ambiguities*. London, UK: Continuum.

Gilhus, I. S. (1997). *Laughing gods, weeping virgins: Laughter in the history of religion*. London, UK: Routledge.

Hempelmann, C. F. (2003). "99 nuns giggle, 1 nun gasps": The not-all-that-Christian natural class of Christian jokes. *HUMOR: International Journal of Humor Research, 16,* 1–31.

Morreall, J. (1999). *Comedy, tragedy, and religion*. Albany: State University of New York Press.

Saroglou, V. (2002). Religion and sense of humor: An a priori incompatibility? Theoretical considerations from a psychological perspective. *HUMOR: International Journal of Humor Research, 15,* 191–214.

Saroglou, V., & Anciaux, L. (2004). Liking sick humor: Coping styles and religion as predictors. *HUMOR: International Journal of Humor Research, 17,* 257–277.

Websites

Center for Psychology of Religion: http://www.uclouvain.be/en-331357

Resolution

See Incongruity and Resolution

Reversal Theory

Reversal theory is a general psychological theory of motivation, emotion, and personality that has generated much research since the 1970s and continues to be applied in such areas as sport coaching and management consultancy. As a general theory, it shows how humor fits into a broad pattern of motivations and emotions rather than being an ad hoc theory of humor alone. Reversal theory posits that humor will result from three features of experience—playful arousal, cognitive synergy, and identity diminishment—all of which are seen to be essential ingredients. If any one of these is missing, something other than humor will be experienced. Thus, according to reversal theory, humor elicited by jokes, cartoons, wit, parody, slapstick, sarcasm, caricature, and farce occurs through one common underlying process.

Playful Arousal

The observer must be in a playful state of mind, which is another way of saying that he or she must experience the world through a "protective frame," feeling safe from danger or serious consequences. According to reversal theory, any arousal, including that which derives from a comic stimulus, will be felt as a form of pleasant excitement in this state. However, if there is a reversal to the opposite serious state, then the very same arousal will be experienced instead as unpleasant anxiety, and the material seen as threatening, offensive, or embarrassing. In other words, the pleasantness/unpleasantness of the arousal is inverted as one reverses between the playful and the serious state. The trick of humor is to remain within the protective frame when presented with arousing material. The higher the arousal is under these conditions, the funnier the situation will seem to be—hence, the frequent use of sexual, violent, racist, religious, personal, and other arousing content. Such content must not, however, destroy the protective frame. Surprise also helps to raise arousal, and cognitive synergies can themselves be arousing, especially when they are surprising. Also, a social context in which other people are laughing helps both to maintain the protective frame ("if others are laughing, it must be OK") and to increase arousal.

Cognitive Synergy

To be humorous, a communication must assign mutually exclusive qualities or meanings to some identity (person, object, statement, etc.). This kind of incongruity is referred to in reversal theory as cognitive synergy because it produces an effect that cannot be achieved by either quality alone. The identity apparently escapes from logic, and more specifically from Aristotle's law of identity, which says that an identity cannot simultaneously be both A and not-A. For example, a person cannot be both an adult (A) and a child (not-A) at the same time. But a child dressed up as an adult can indeed be funny because she is perceived as having qualities of both adult and child. Likewise, the identity in humor may be a statement: Thus, a compliment that turns out to be an insult can be funny. A sarcastic statement is one that has an ostensible and a real meaning. In slapstick, a man who is treated like an object can be comic, because man and object are mutually exclusive categories.

The enjoyment of the humor is said in reversal theory to be felt at the moment of greatest awareness of incongruity rather than afterward, as it is according to some other theories. Communications that do not contain cognitive synergy, such as scientific papers or legal contracts, cannot be funny (unless by mistake). Synergies may become complex: for example, a child pretending to be a scarecrow pretending to be a human pretending to be aggressive. In fact, research shows that the more cognitive work that has to be done to disentangle the synergy, the funnier it will be.

Identity Diminishment

Third, the effect of the cognitive synergy must be to downgrade the identity concerned. There must be diminishment. Thus, recognizing the child as being "only" a child rather than the woman she pretends to be, diminishes the identity. If there is no diminishment, then we have whimsy, or perhaps a pun or a riddle. If there is enhancement rather than diminishment, then we may have art. (Art also makes use of its own kinds of synergies, such as metaphor and ambiguity.)

There are two ways in which diminishment can be achieved. The first is disclosure. This means that the first meaning applied to a situation is supplanted by a second, diminishing, meaning, which discloses that the first meaning was false. But both meanings continue to resonate, so that taken as a whole we have a cognitive synergy. The following simple one-liner joke can serve as an example: "Change is inevitable, except from vending machines." Here *change* has two meanings. But the second meaning only becomes apparent from the second half of the statement and discloses that the first meaning was false. If the identity is the word *change*, then it is diminished from a broad philosophical concept to a mere coin. The second form of diminishment is distortion. This usually comes in the form of exaggeration that highlights a weakness and makes it more apparent. For example, a caricaturist will exaggerate some facial characteristic: The resulting synergy both is and isn't a representation of the person and, in any case, diminishes that person.

Michael Apter and Mitzi Desselles

See also Humor Mindset; Humor Theories; Jokes; Play and Humor; Psychology

Further Readings

Apter, M. J. (1982). Humour and reversal theory. In M. J. Apter, *The experience of motivation: The theory of psychological reversals* (pp. 177–195). London, UK: Academic Press.

Apter, M. J., & Smith, K. C. P. (1977). Humour and the theory of psychological reversals. In A. Chapman & H. Foot (Eds.), *It's a funny thing, humour* (pp. 95–100). Oxford, UK: Pergamon Press.

Coulson, A. S. (2001). Cognitive synergy. In M. J. Apter (Ed.), *Motivational styles in everyday life: A guide to reversal theory* (pp. 229–248). Washington, DC: American Psychological Association.

Wyer, R. S., Jr., & Collins, J. E. (1992). A theory of humor elicitation. *Psychological Review, 99*, 663–688.

Rhetoric and Rhetorical Devices

Rhetorical devices primarily describe aspects of style in persuasive texts and are commonly referred to as "figures of speech," although they extend beyond syntactic and semantic figures in explaining three related phenomena in humorous texts. First, they reveal various uses of topoi, or commonplace tools for the invention or systematic discovery of persuasive arguments. Second, they explain how various comedic devices—such as simile, metaphor, hyperbole, paradox, oxymoron, and personification—support the construction and delivery of these arguments. Third, they justify how humorous arguments can be understood as appeals to *logos* (logic or reason) by revealing how successful humor relies on shared perspectives between author, audience, and worldview.

Topoi

The first comprehensive organization of rhetorical devices occurs in the anonymously authored *Rhetorica ad Herennium* (Rhetoric to Herennius), although rhetorical devices have been named and discussed as early as Plato's *Ion* (Dialogue) and more extensively in Book III of Aristotle's *Rhetoric*. Book IV of the four-part *Rhetorica ad Herennium* contains a catalogue of levels and qualities of style, arranged so that the orator could achieve—through what James J. Murphy has called the "judicious use of figures"—*dignitas* (distinction) in grand, middle, and plain styles.

Following this catalogue are 45 "figures of speech" (including 10 tropes or "special" figures of speech) and 19 "figures of thought." Of the 45 figures of speech, several have historically been relevant in analyzing the communicability of humor, including *repetitio*, the anaphoric repetition of a word or phrase at the beginning of successive sentences; *contentio*, the use of antithesis, or contrasting ideas organized in parallel phrases; *sententia,* the use of maxims; *occultatio*, or paralipsis, drawing attention to a characteristic by seeming to pass over it; *circumitio*, or periphrasis, describing something according to what it is not, and more specifically, substituting a descriptive word for a proper name; *superlatio*, or hyperbole; and *permutatio*, or allegory.

As did its antecedent and succedent treatises, the *Rhetorica ad Herennium* most likely organized its figures according to how they enabled orators to fulfill the common logical operations of addition, omission (or subtraction), substitution, and transposition (or transferring). For example, several devices were regularly discussed in Book II of Marcus Tullius Cicero's *De oratore* (On the Orator), a dialogue composed circa 55 BCE but set in 91 BCE as a disagreement among characters about the qualities and talents comprising the ideal orator. In the dialogue, the character named "Caesar" admires such acts of omission and substitution for their ability "to turn the force of a word to quite another sense than that in which other people take it" (2.62.254) and for eliciting surprise rather than laughter. These logical operations were formalized as categories of thought in Marcus Quintilian's *Institutio oratoria* (The Institutes of Oratory) in 95 CE, which significantly aligned rhetorical devices with invention strategies, or strategies concerned with the discovery of what makes certain arguments possible.

Comedic Devices

Like rhetorical devices, comedic devices evolve in number and classification as they become contemporized. As tropes, figures, and schemes that elicit laughter, comedic devices have historically revealed developments in how specific figures become linked to the delivery of arguments they helped to invent. Quintilian's division of over 200 devices is more extensive than Cicero's, occupying much of Books IV, IIX, and IX in his *Institutio oratoria*, and differentiating between "figures," which involved changes in the syntactic structure of an utterance for its emphasis or ornamentation, and "tropes," which involved substitutions of some words for others so as to transform their meaning (e.g., metaphor, synecdoche, metonymy). Book VI also includes a long treatment on laughter, describing the role of wit and humor in preparing the judge to receive an appeal. Whereas Cicero's comedic devices often promoted distraction or conciliation among witnesses, Quintilian's comedic devices were intended to redirect the good will of the judges in ethically challenging cases. However, both *De oratore* and the *Institutio oratoria* suggest eliciting comedic responses in certain parts of the speech, while arousing more passionate responses—such as anger, hatred, jealousy, pity—elsewhere in the speech, separating the responses so as to better dispel the judges' pity and redirect their attention toward a consideration of justice.

Katherine Geffcken has noted Cicero's appreciation for humor's extra-logical functions—that is, its capacity to exert control in an argument when logic cannot succeed. In this sense, comedic devices are better formed when they avoid arousing excessive emotion, appealing instead to the audience's sense of recognition. She cites the 56 BCE *Pro Caelio* (In Defense of Caeilius) as a principal example, in which each character in Cicero's speech represents a comic figure that breaks established social codes through antithesis, feigned apology, or double entendre. These are strategies that Quintilian would later cite as exemplary passages in Book VI of his *Institutio oratoria* because they simultaneously reinforced and drew attention away from the judges' notions of Caeilius's character in order to redirect their attention to the character of Caeilius's accuser.

Most of what Cicero and Quintilian indicated as devices for humor or laughter was addressed less enthusiastically in the *ars praedicandi* (art of preaching), one of three arts that comprised a rhetorical curriculum throughout the Middle Ages and was published in a variety of forms. In this curriculum, humorous devices were often discussed according to their (un)suitability for the various realms of pulpit and polis. Yet they occur again in Henry Peacham's 1577 *Garden of Eloquence*, this time as a division of 184 figures into sets of vernacular "tropes" and "schemes," catalogued according to how their grammatical and rhetorical forms could embellish words, organize sentences, or amplify ideas, respectively. For Peacham, the effectiveness of such schemes was in the writer's avoidance of excess or exaggeration, and in their strategic use.

Appeals to *Logos*

Whereas rhetorical devices have historically explained ways of achieving *dignitas* in oratory and literacy, more recent theories of rhetorical agency have repositioned them to better explain how humor relies on shared perspectives between author, audience, and worldview to be successful. An early example of this tendency can be found in *The New Rhetoric* of Chaim Perelman and Lucie Olbrechts-Tyteca. Olbrechts-Tyteca's 1974 work is predicated on the idea that humor helps the realization of the argumentation.

Cheryl Geisler observed that 21st-century theories of agency seem to be as concerned with ways of reflection as they are with the resources and means to act. In the study of rhetorical devices, this reflection may occur as a revelation of fallacies in the rhetor's or audience's logic, or as a demonstration of how the roles of victim, subject, target, and vehicle can become blurred in humorous texts. For example, John Poulakos has argued that Cicero's comedic devices in *De oratore* and *Pro Caelio* make good examples of what Greek philosophers called *dissoi logoi*—literally, an argumentative strategy that functioned according to the use of "different words"—because they demand a cognizance of both sides of a particular controversy or, in the case of *De oratore*, of the competing worldviews that must be accommodated to attain the ideal orator.

Twenty-first–century perspectives on rhetorical devices are characterized by efforts to redefine "strategies" as what Sean Zwagerman calls humor's "strategic uses"—broad and interdependent speech situations that deconstruct persuasive logics, rather than disparate figures of speech. This deconstructionist sentiment is echoed in what J. L. Austin has called "whole chains of discourse" and in what Kenneth Burke has called "dramatism," that is, using language, a symbolic system, to achieve intercooperation among symbol-using beings. It is also echoed in M. Jimmie Killingsworth's redefinition of tropes such as metaphor, metonymy, synecdoche, and irony according to the relationships they reveal between writer(s), audience(s), and shared worldview(s). For example, metaphor requires a kind of identification of the audience(s) with something powerful and often physical; metonymy requires a kind of association with something contiguous; synecdoche enables the representation of a whole through one of its parts; and irony closes the interpretive distance between the writer and one set of audiences, while increasing that distance for another set. For Killingsworth and modern-day theorists, tropes and other rhetorical "figures" can function at the level of whole discourses as well as individual phrases, making their classification somewhat fraught.

Tarez Samra Graban

See also Ancient Roman Comedy; Audience; Incongruity and Resolution; Irony; Misdirection; Satire

Further Readings

Anonymous. (1954). *Rhetorica ad Herennium* [Rhetoric to Herennius] (H. Caplan, Trans.). Cambridge, MA: Harvard University Press.

Burke, K. B. (1969). *A rhetoric of motives*. Berkeley: University of California Press.

Burton, G. O. (2007). The four categories of change. *Silva Rhetoricae*. Retrieved April 1, 2012, from http://rhetoric.byu.edu/Four Changes/Four Changes.htm

Cicero. (1970). *De oratore* [On the orator] (J. S. Watson Trans.). Carbondale: Southern Illinois University Press.

Frank, D. A., & Bolduc, M. K. (2011). Lucie Olbrechts-Tyteca's new rhetoric. In J. T. Gage (Ed.), *The promise of reason: Studies in the new rhetoric* (pp. 55–79). Carbondale: Southern Illinois University Press.

Geffcken, K. A. (1995). *Comedy in the* Pro Caelio. Wauconda, IL: Bolchazy-Carducci.

Geisler, C. (2004). How ought we to understand the concept of rhetorical agency? Report from the ARS. *Rhetoric Society Quarterly, 34*(3), 9–17.

Killingsworth, M. J. (2005). Appeal through tropes. In *Appeals in modern rhetoric: An ordinary-language approach* (pp. 121–135). Carbondale: Southern Illinois University Press.

Murphy, J. J. (1974). *Rhetoric in the Middle Ages: A history of rhetorical theory from Saint Augustine to the Renaissance*. Berkeley: University of California Press.

Olbrechts-Tyteca, L. (1974). *Le comique du discours* [The humor of discourse]. Brussels, Belgium: Université de Bruxelles.

Peacham, H. (1977). *The garden of eloquence*. Delmar, NY: Scholars' Facsimiles and Reprints. (Original work published 1577)

Poulakos, J. (1993). Terms for sophistical rhetoric. In T. Poulakos (Ed.), *Rethinking the history of rhetoric: Multidisciplinary essays on the rhetorical tradition* (pp. 53–74). Boulder, CO: Westview.

Quinn, A., & Rathbun, L. (1996). Figures of speech. In T. Enos (Ed.), *Encyclopedia of rhetoric and composition: Communication from ancient times to the information age* (pp. 269–271). New York, NY: Garland.

Quintilian. (1922). *Institutio oratoria* [Institutes of oratory] (H. E. Butler, Trans.). Cambridge, MA: Loeb/Harvard University Press.

Richards, J. (2008). *Rhetoric*. London, UK: Routledge.

Zwagerman, S. (2010). *Wit's end: Women's humor as rhetorical and performative strategy*. Pittsburgh, PA: University of Pittsburgh Press.

Riddle

Riddle is a term commonly used to describe humorous texts in a question-and-answer format that exploit conceptual or linguistic ambiguity. In folklore research, the term denotes a traditional genre of verbal art, while in literature it implies a literary trope. In linguistics and humor research, riddling is often considered a discourse type establishing a link between two scripts. It is assumed that riddling is an aspect of the oral and/or literary traditions of all cultures, and can be traced back to the ancient civilizations of India and Greece. Etymologically, the word *riddle* comes from the Old English *raedels* or *raedelse*, meaning "counsel, opinion, conjecture." This entry defines *riddle*, presents a brief overview of traditional and contemporary riddle forms (with special attention to the devices of ambiguity and humor), and touches on the significance of riddles in the development of children's sense of humor.

Definition and Forms

A riddle is composed of two parts: a question (or image) and an answer connected by a cognitive link, based on a metaphor, lexical or grammatical ambiguity, or some other "block element" making the riddle more difficult to solve. A riddling occasion presumes at least two participants: a riddler posing a question and a riddlee who is challenged to find the question's answer. This means riddling is always competitive, and the relationship between the two parties is hierarchic: The riddler (to whom the answer is known) is in a superior position, until the riddlee correctly comes to the solution.

In traditional societies, riddles are part of the verbal art of adults and play an important role in rites of passage such as initiation ceremonies, courtship, weddings, and wakes. However, many individuals may organize riddle contests or engage in leisure-time riddling. The function of riddles is complex, but inevitably they provide amusement and fulfill the cognitive function of reaffirming the common values in a community.

Traditional riddles are usually fix-phrased, involving formulated or archaic language. Objects, characters, and topics included in the riddle text are drawn from an environment familiar to both the riddler and riddlee. *True riddles* are descriptive texts that, as Archer Taylor states, compare an object to an entirely different object (e.g., in the riddle, "Thirty white horses on a red hill. Now they dance, now they prance, now they stand still." The solution is "teeth").

Following true riddles, the most significant riddle subgenres are *joking questions,* wherein puns shift the frame of reference; *wisdom questions,* requiring specific knowledge; *neck riddles,* based on odd, personal experience presented in a narrative frame of saving one's life; and *parody riddles,* intended to confuse the riddlee by using and frustrating conventional riddle patterns. Visual and literary riddles also have a long and continuing history.

Classic riddles attached to the traditional, rural lifestyle have now reached the state of static folklore or become children's lore. Riddling, as a type of discourse, is still widely used, especially by young adults. Contemporary riddle forms exploit the question-and-answer format as a base for wordplay and improvisation. Punning riddles or *conundrum*s mainly involve linguistic triggers, coupling similarity of form with difference in meaning (e.g., "What is black and white and red all over?" "A newspaper"). A *droodle* is a visual form of conundrum. It is a simple drawing claimed to represent an unexpectedly complex situation (e.g., a horizontal line described as an old lady dragging a goat, yet only the rope can be seen).

Riddle jokes, on the other hand, are more firmly connected to context. They usually come in waves, comment on current events in a humorous form, and follow a formulaic construction. In these riddles, the question sets up the punch line, usually provided by the riddler; riddle jokes are basically jokes presented in the form of a riddle. Most riddle jokes are topical, reflecting up-to-date, local or global news, usually of a tragic nature. They comment on accidents and catastrophes, politics, and the situation of ethnic minorities and are popular as long as they are topical. They are a way of speaking the unspeakable and questioning contemporary values and norms.

Riddling in the Development of Children's Sense of Humor

A number of studies have shown that riddling plays an important part in the early development of a child's sense of humor (roughly between the ages of 4 and 8 years). Initially, riddles are simply questions with arbitrary answers, but children quickly become capable of understanding and following the rules related to riddling as a form of social interaction (being a riddler means possessing [limited] authority, and laughter should follow when a riddle or joke is delivered). At around the age of 6 years, (lexical) ambiguity is incorporated into simple descriptive routines. By the age of 8 years, riddles of all sorts are performed properly and enjoyed, even if the child cannot explain why they are funny.

Riddles take objects from a familiar environment and combine them in an unexpected way, following basic rules that children gradually acquire. It is a form of verbal play involving the language and culture they are growing up in. Therefore, this process plays an important part not only in the development of linguistic and cognitive skills but also in the course of socialization.

Katalin Vargha

See also Ambiguity; Children's Humor Stages; Joke Cycles; Puns; Speech Play; Verbal Humor

Further Readings

Bergen, D. (2009). Gifted children's humor preferences, sense of humor, and comprehension of riddles. *HUMOR: International Journal of Humor Research, 4,* 419–436.

Cook, E. (2006). *Enigmas and riddles in literature.* Cambridge, UK: Cambridge University Press.

Kaivola-Bregenhøj, A. (2001). *Riddles: Perspectives on the use, function and change in a folklore genre.* Helsinki: Finnish Literature Society.

McDowell, J. (1979). *Children's riddling.* Bloomington: Indiana University Press.

Nørgaard, N. (Ed.). (2010). *The language of riddles, humor and literature. Six essays by John M. Dienhart.* Odense: University Press of Southern Denmark.

Taylor, A. (1951). *English riddles from oral tradition.* Berkeley: University of California Press.

Ritual Clowns

Ritual clowns reverse and challenge accepted norms in their specific societies through theatrics. Performing in ritual contexts in small-scale premodern societies (as well in some modern ones), ritual clowns perform their theatrics in costumes and masks. These premodern ritual contexts resemble festivals in modern societies in that the events intertwine the sacred and the secular, the serious and the humorous.

Arguing that the ritual clown is rooted in premodern religion, William Mitchell notes that the ritual clown is tied to a powerful magical world. However, as modern religions and scientific views of the world circulated around the globe, they collided with ancient beliefs, marginalizing the ritual clown in the process and separating sacred domains from secular, and ritual from humor.

Indigenous practices continue to integrate the serious and the comic, enacting fundamental social and cultural concepts such as gender roles, sexual practices, political relations, and kinship rules. This integration was described by Roy Sieber and Roslyn Walker (1987) for African societies: "Much of what we consider social, political, or cultural and thereby secular is considered religious in African thought" (p. 21). This view of the world as interrelated phenomena permits the ritual enactment of reversals that affirm the social order in some instances and criticize it in others. Through the performance of hyperbole, taboos, and buffoonery, ritual clowns juxtapose the social and natural order with violations of it. They are licensed to perform parody and satire directed at authorities, the opposite sex, tourists, and outsiders, but also to call attention to deviant or excessive behavior within the community. This entry describes the special powers attributed ritual clowns, provides examples of ritual clowns in social context, and examines the contradictions presented by ritual clowns.

Special Powers

One key to the ritual clown's license resides in the special powers he or she is believed to possess. While clowns' profane behavior elicits laughter from their audience, they may also possess esoteric knowledge and expertise through which they accrue respect. Some clowns are credited with having mystical or supernatural powers, others with being endowed with healing abilities, and some with possessing extraordinary physical skills. Through this duality—the hidden power of the supernatural or superhuman and the public power of performance—clowns embody a human paradox.

Clowns in Social Contexts

Ritual clowns may dress as the opposite sex or in rags or in unique local variations, but they are universally recognizable by their license to reveal clandestine behaviors, violate taboos, and burlesque cherished values or authority figures. The targets of their performances range from the culturally profound to the contemporary specific. This section provides several examples of ritual clowning in various social contexts and societies throughout the world.

The role of ritual clowns is nowhere more complex than among Native American cultures. North American Indian groups characteristically have a clown or a "contrary" figure. Most documented, however, are the clown societies of the Pueblo Indians of the southwestern United States, the Hopi and Zuni in particular. Among the latter are two clown societies, the *Koyemci* and the *Newekwe,* who enact representations of sexual behavior and make jokes on taboo topics. Although the Koyemci elicit humor from the audience, they are nevertheless feared for their supernatural powers. The Newekwe, who are painted in black and white bands, enact burlesques of missionaries, tourists, teachers, and Navajos. Significantly, they are also a medicine society.

In a Mayan village in the Yucatan of Mexico, a ritual clown is the star of a full-scale community parody—a saint's procession in which a large pig is substituted for a saint. A clown dressed in tattered clothing and faking drunkenness leads the procession and performs poetic recitations about illicit sexual episodes and about tensions between villagers and the state.

The Mende women of Sierra Leone perform a women's masquerade featuring the *ndoli jowei*, a powerful female leader costumed in a carved wooden helmet mask and black palm leaf. Two other women maskers, the *gonde* and the *samawa*, perform parody and satire. The *gonde* is "a clown-like figure who overturns all the conventions proper to *ndoli jowei*. She can also be frightening when she shakes a bundle of switches at wrongdoers. The *samawa* satirizes males, some of whom have violated the women's conventions and suffer disease as a result" (Phillips, 1995, p. 90).

Parody and burlesque are equally significant in the Melanesian societies of Papua New Guinea, where women frequently perform the role of ritual clown. Among the Lusi-Kaliai people, clowning occurs in rituals such as weddings and rites for first-born children. Performing as transvestites (women dressed as men), they parody the male behavior of warriors, village leaders, drunks, and outsiders. In his comments on clowning in the Pacific, Mitchell (1992) observes that clowning "creates mayhem by dismantling cognitive coherence and continuity" and consequently serves as social criticism (p. 19).

In the United States, clowns have a crucial role in the rodeo, a ritual drama of cattle culture. They, too, are licensed to mention sexual behavior and to jumble categories and violate taboos in the jokes performed in the rodeo arena. With a painted face and tattered clothes and a large red nose, the rodeo clown appears drunk or stupid while his trained animal seems much smarter than he is, reversing the relationship between the cowboy and horses and cattle. In bull-riding events, after the bull has bucked the cowboy off, the clown must distract the bull away from the cowboy on the ground. Although he appears very foolish, the clown enacts a heroic but dangerous role, producing much respect from the bull riders. Like other ritual clowns, he embodies a dual role, combining humor and apparent foolishness with danger and heroism.

Contradictions

Embedded in specific social contexts, ritual clowns open a fissure in the societal edifice with their nonsense, revealing cultural ambiguities and social frailties, overturning conventions through reversals, and enacting tensions and taboos, some shrouded in secrecy and others on display in public life. While flirting with danger, challenging political or religious authority, and affirming or reversing social practices, clowns perform critical commentary. Juxtaposing categories, transgressing boundaries, and jumbling fundamentals, the clown transforms as she or he entertains. Whether introducing alternative perspectives or affirming conventional practices, the clown stretches the imagination with foolishness, yet embodies the powers of the supernatural and the capacities of the superhuman. These contradictions combine to create the performing paradox known as the ritual clown.

Beverly J. Stoeltje

See also Anthropology; Carnival and Festival; Clowns; Clowns in Medical Settings; Fools; Feast of Fools; Rituals of Inversion; Rituals of Laughter; Slapstick

Further Readings

Hieb, L. (1972). Meaning and mismeaning: Toward an understanding of the ritual clown. In A. Ortiz (Ed.), *New perspectives on the Pueblos* (pp. 163–195). Albuquerque: University of New Mexico Press.

Loewe, R. (2010). *Maya or Mestizo? Nationalism, modernity, and its discontents.* Toronto, Ontario, Canada: University of Toronto Press.

Mitchell, W. E. (Ed.). (1992). *Clowning as critical practice.* Pittsburgh, PA: University of Pittsburgh Press.

Phillips, R. B. (1995). *Representing woman: Sande masquerades of the Mende of Sierra Leone.* Los Angeles: UCLA Fowler Museum of Cultural History.

Sieber, R., & Walker, R. A. (1987). *African art in the cycle of life.* Washington, DC: Smithsonian Institution Press.

Stoeltje, B. J. (1985). The rodeo clown and the semiotics of metaphor. *Journal of Folklore Research, 22*(2/3), 155–177.

Stoeltje, B. J. (1992). Festival. In R. Bauman (Ed.), *Folklore, cultural performances, and popular entertainments* (pp. 261–271). New York, NY: Oxford University Press.

Towsen, J. H. (1976). *Clowns.* New York, NY: Hawthorn Books.

Rituals of Inversion

Rituals of inversion, also known as rituals of reversal, occur when a ritual or special event provides a frame that gives license for people to violate everyday cultural norms and social codes. The modifier *ritual* suggests that these violations are in some sense considered temporary, playful, or restricted to a special time and/or place. It is these constraints and frames that provide license for behavior that would incur social sanctions outside of the ritual setting. Ritual inversions are frequently humorous and often include satire and mockery—expressions intended to elicit a humorous reaction from a given segment of a population by recourse to making fun of another at the other's expense. This entry considers some common occasions for rituals of inversion before examining the ritual inversion commonly found in festival, with both historical and contemporary examples.

Rituals of inversion are either the special province of certain ritual specialists, such as clowns, or confined to specific special occasions, especially rites of passage and annual calendar customs or festivals. In many cultures, ritual clowns have license to mock and play tricks on others and to engage in scatological play. On special occasions such as rites of passage or certain calendar customs, almost anyone has the license to violate or invert everyday norms. For example, during the rite of passage known as "Crossing the Line," sailors who are crossing the Equator for the first time are subjected to a rite of passage by their shipmates—a ritual that involves cross-dressing, rough play, and ordinary sailors in costume temporarily "taking over" the ship from the officers. Another rite of passage sometimes marked by rituals of inversion is the wedding anniversary. In rural communities in the Great Plains, communities celebrate the wedding anniversaries of couples in their midst with mock weddings—parodies of weddings that involve cross-dressing and good-natured mockery of the couple being honored.

April Fools' Day is widely recognized as a day when anyone may play practical jokes on others, including targets that it would normally be inappropriate to joke with. Children may play jokes on parents and teachers, and journalists may temporarily abandon the strictures of their profession to publish hoax stories in newspapers, on websites, or in television and radio programs. At other times, the agents of ritual inversion belong to a counterculture positioned in opposition to a mainstream institution.

Scholars have frequently noted that Carnival and other traditional festivals are sites for institutionalized disorder, for rituals of reversal that counter and deny the established order. In early modern Europe, festivals included political satire, dressing in costumes, cross-dressing, drunkenness, and intense sexual activity, as well as weddings and mock weddings. Also in medieval and early modern Europe, the Feast of Fools was another site for multiple forms of symbolic inversion, including cross-dressing, masking as animals, wafting foul-smelling incense, and electing burlesque bishops, popes, and patriarchs. The thrust of these burlesque forms was mockery of serious ritual and of the dominant social order behind it.

Although the Feast of Fools did include rituals of inversion, Max Harris has recently argued that they were not designed as mockery but instead were offered within a Christian context as thanksgiving for the incarnation of Christ. The role reversals exemplified God's work at putting down the proud and exalting the humble. Thus, in Harris's reconstruction, the Feast of Fools is best understood as a sanctified rather than sacrilegious event.

An example of contemporary rituals of inversion is found in Burning Man Festival, an annual art and alternative cultural event that takes place in the desert outside Reno, Nevada, in connection with Labor Day weekend. Burning Man may be interpreted as a counterculture. Countercultures are those groups that situate themselves in ways that draw on themes of conflict with the dominant values of a given group or society. Countercultural protest may take the form of direct opposition to dominant values, opposition also to power structures, or a combination of these. Burning Man Festival may be interpreted as the expression of a countercultural movement that sets itself in opposition to modernity by way of, according to J. Milton Yinger's (1984) typology, "the search for ecstasy and mystical insight" (p. 94).

One way to understand how rituals of inversion work is the temporary autonomous zone (TAZ) theory described by Hakim Bey. As the name implies, the TAZ describes a fleeting fixture in space and time where the individual can claim autonomy over the self and complete freedom in opposition to authority structures, a freedom that provides opportunities for the individual to create new expressions of the self and society. As such, the TAZ provides a context for the nonviolent alteration of existing structures and serves as a radical tactic of opposition to the mainstream.

With these thoughts in mind, the connection can be made between Burning Man as a festive counterculture and a ritual expression of acts of social inversion. As previously noted, Burning Man can be understood as a counterculture situated in opposition to aspects of modernity, especially consumer culture. Individuals come to the festival to carve out their own place in space and time (the TAZ), which includes social inversion as well as acts of creativity, including the production of various forms of art, the naming of various living areas within the broader temporary community of the festival, seminars presented during the event, the taking of temporary names unique to the festival event, forms of clothing, gender bending, and many other things. Whatever the form of opposition, each inverts the structures it opposes in mainstream culture, or the "default world" in the nomenclature of "Burners." Burning Man activities include costuming, cross-dressing, sexual activity, weddings, and mock weddings—the same activities known to have occurred during carnival and festival in early modern Europe. An argument could be made that Burning Man Festival represents a contemporary expression of festival that parallels the historical events, particularly the Feast of Fools. Burning Man Festival provides an interesting contemporary case study of rituals of inversion in opposition to a mainstream social group that helps deepen our understanding of the many facets of humor.

John W. Morehead

See also Burlesque; Carnival and Festival; Clowns; Feast of Fools; Hoax and Prank; Inversion, Topsy-Turvy; Practical Jokes; Ritual Clowns

Further Readings

Babcock, B. A. (1978). *The reversible world: Symbolic inversion in art and society*. Ithaca, NY: Cornell University Press.

Bakhtin, M. (1984). *Rabelais and his world*. Bloomington: Indiana University Press.

Bey, H. (2003). *TAZ: The temporary autonomous zone, ontological anarchy, poetic terrorism* (2nd ed.). Brooklyn, NY: Autonomedia.

Bronner, S. J. (2006). *Crossing the line: Violence, play, and drama in naval equator traditions*. Amsterdam, Netherlands: Amsterdam University Press.

Burke, P. (1990). *Popular culture in early modern Europe* (Rev. ed.). Aldershot, UK: Ashgate.

Duvignaud, J. (1976). Festivals: A sociological approach. *Cultures, 3*(1), 13–25.

Harris, M. (2003). *Carnival and other Christian festivals: Folk theology and folk performance*. Austin: University of Texas Press.

Harris, M. (2011). *Sacred folly: A new history of the Feast of Fools*. Ithaca, NY: Cornell University Press.

Manning, F. E. (1983). Cosmos and chaos: Celebration in the modern world. In F. E. Manning (Ed.), *The celebration of society: Perspectives on contemporary cultural performance*. Bowling Green, OH: Bowling Green University Press.

Morehead, J. W. (2011). *Burning Man Festival: A life enhancing, post-Christendom, "middle way."* Saarbrücken, Germany: Lambert Academic.

Pieper, J. (1999). *In tune with the world: A theory of festivity*. South Bend, IN: St. Augustine's Press.

Smith, M. (2009). Arbiters of truth at play: Media April Fools' Day hoaxes. *Folklore, 120*(3), 274–290.

Taft, M. (1997). Men in women's clothes: Theatrical transvestites on the Canadian prairie. In P. Greenhill & D. Tye (Eds.), *Undisciplined women: Tradition and culture in Canada* (pp. 131–138). Montreal, QC, Canada: McGill-Queen's University Press.

Yinger, J. M. (1984). *Countercultures: The promise and peril of a world turned upside down*. New York, NY: Free Press.

Rituals of Laughter

Rituals of laughter are traditional rites in which laughter is deliberately performed for religious purposes. They are often connected to folk festivals, as in Japan, which has seven major traditional festivals that feature formal, ritual performances of laughter. This entry explains the religious significance of these rituals, describes two examples, and compares them with other annual calendar traditions around the world also closely associated with laughter.

Japanese laughter rituals are embedded in the Shinto myths of Japanese folk religion and in the social organization of the community where each festival takes place. Japanese people traditionally believed in two kinds of gods: those bringing happiness and those bringing misfortune and disaster. Ritual performances of laughter (*warai*) are dedicated to pleasing and entertaining the gods so that they listen to the people's prayers. Human laughter at such rituals is a symbolic expression of divine pleasure, invoking a positive response from the gods to those who laugh and also lightening the hearts and mood of the laughers themselves.

The seven surviving regional laughter rituals in Japan differ in their details, but all are organized by local community associations (*ko*). They do not employ jokes or banter to stimulate laughter, but they create a festive and indulgent spirit, including eating and drinking. Despite obscure and ancient origins, they continue to be popular today, attracting media coverage and many visitors.

Warai-Ko

The laughter ritual *Warai-ko* in Hofu City, Yamaguchi Prefecture, has been held annually since 1199 and today takes place on the first Sunday in December. The Warai-ko association, also founded in 1199, has 21 hereditary members, each of whom hosts the ritual in their house once every 21 years. Seated in fixed order before a Shinto priest and altar, participants enjoy special food and drink and then take turns in laughing on command either individually or in pairs. One member acts as judge, evaluating the quality of the laughs. At the climax of the rite, everyone present—both Warai-ko members and Shinto priest—laughs the last big laugh together. The ritual must include three kinds of symbolic laughter, each with a specific purpose: (1) to celebrate and give thanks for the year's good harvest, (2) to pray for next year's good harvest, and (3) to purge worries accumulated during the year.

Mountain Goddess Festival

The Mountain Goddess festival (*Yama-no-kami Matsuri*), also called the Stonefish Festival (*Okoze*), has been held since 1856 in Owase, Mie Prefecture. According to the folk origin narrative of the district, the area was divided between seafarers and foresters. When the mountain goddess and the sea goddess encountered each other on the beach, they began boasting about the number of their followers. The sea goddess summoned the sea-bream, flat fish, and mackerel, while the mountain goddess summoned the fox, badger, and bear, resulting in a tie. Then the stonefish emerged from the sea, giving his goddess one more follower to win the contest. Since then, the mountain goddess has always hated the stonefish.

At the festival, two people each carry a stonefish before the mountain goddess's shrine. Allowing the fish to "peep out" from their robes, the bearers show them to the goddess and burst into laughter along with all the participants. The purpose of this ritual laughter is to entertain the goddess by saying the stonefish is incomparably uglier than herself — so ugly it doesn't even count as a member of the fish class. This big, loud laugh ridiculing the fish pleases the goddess, who will then descend to the fields in the spring to protect agricultural activities.

Laughter and Annual Festivals

Other countries both east and west also highlight humor and laughter in annual festivals. In Nepal, *Gaijatra*, the Hindu festival of holy cows, is held in memory of the recently deceased. Because cows are thought to convey the souls of the dead to heaven, the festival features a parade of cows, and people dressed as cows. Gaijatra is intended to show laughter's power to relieve earthly cares, and it is closely related to the Nepalese tradition of social and political satire. It is said to have begun when one of the Malla kings of Kathmandu lost his son to illness and sought to cheer up his bereaved queen with parades of people in funny costumes, exhibitions of drawings, and exchanges of jokes, all of which helped her laugh and accept the harsh realities of life. Since the 19th century, Gaijatra has included topical satire of social and political issues, permitted only during the festival.

The annual European tradition of Carnival satire provides an evident parallel, but jokes and humorous performances are significant parts of annual ritual events in many other cultures, including Native American cultures with their ritual clowning. In the West, the first of April is widely recognized as conveying license for people to play jokes on each other. Similarly, the folk customs of trick-or-treating at Halloween (October 31) and house visits on Bonfire Night (November 5) often include trickery.

Although the laughter rituals of Japan differ from other occasions of festive humor in formally emphasizing the physical role of laughter, they serve a similar function. Whether ritualized or not, the sharing of laughter and enjoyment changes mood and attitude to life while reinforcing communal beliefs about the universe. Formal performances of laughter reveal much about the symbolic and practical effects of festive communal humor and laughter.

Goh Abe

See also Carnival and Festival; Feast of Fools; Folklore; History of Humor: Premodern Japan; Laugh,

Laughter, Laughing; Psychotherapy, Humor in; Religion

Further Readings

Abe, G. (2003). A ritual performance of laughter in southern Japan. In J. Milner Davis (Ed.), *Understanding humor in Japan* (pp. 37–49). Detroit, MI: Wayne State University Press.

Abe, G. (2010). Japanese ritual performance of laughter. *Society, 47*(1), 31–34.

Gerbert, E. (2011). Laughing priests in the Atsuta Shrine Festival. In H. Geybels & W. van Herck (Eds.), *Humour and religion: Challenges and ambiguities* (pp. 54–65). London, UK: Continuum.

Gilhus, I. S. (1997). *Laughing god, weeping virgins: Laughter in the history of religion*. London, UK: Routledge.

Panday, R. K. (2000). *Nepalese humor*. Kathmandu, Nepal: Muskan Prakshan.

Roman Visual Humor

Visual humor is culture-specific, making it difficult for outsiders to a culture to understand it. The more context we have for a visual representation, the better chance we have of understanding its humor. We can understand the context surrounding a visual representation by analyzing the building where it came from, by considering the circumstances of viewing it, by questioning the meanings of the image itself, and by comparing it with nonhumorous images of the same type. But the most useful question about context is how a humorous Roman image indexes Roman attitudes about the practices of everyday life.

To frame humor in terms of social dynamics, sociologists have stressed the distinction between intra-group humor, where members of a particular social class or group can poke fun at each other, and inter-group humor, the kind that pits one social class against another. We find good examples of both types of humor in Roman visual culture.

Intra-Group Humor

Typical of intra-group humor is a series of four captioned scenes painted on the walls of an ancient tavern at Pompeii (see Figure 1). The in-group in the Tavern of Salvius consists of the non-elites who frequented taverns rather than entertaining at home, as the elites invariably did. They were people with no access to the upper classes; they were slaves, former slaves, the freeborn working poor, and foreigners. There are two ways to create social humor in this situation: either to mock the elite who aren't there or to poke fun at members of your own group.

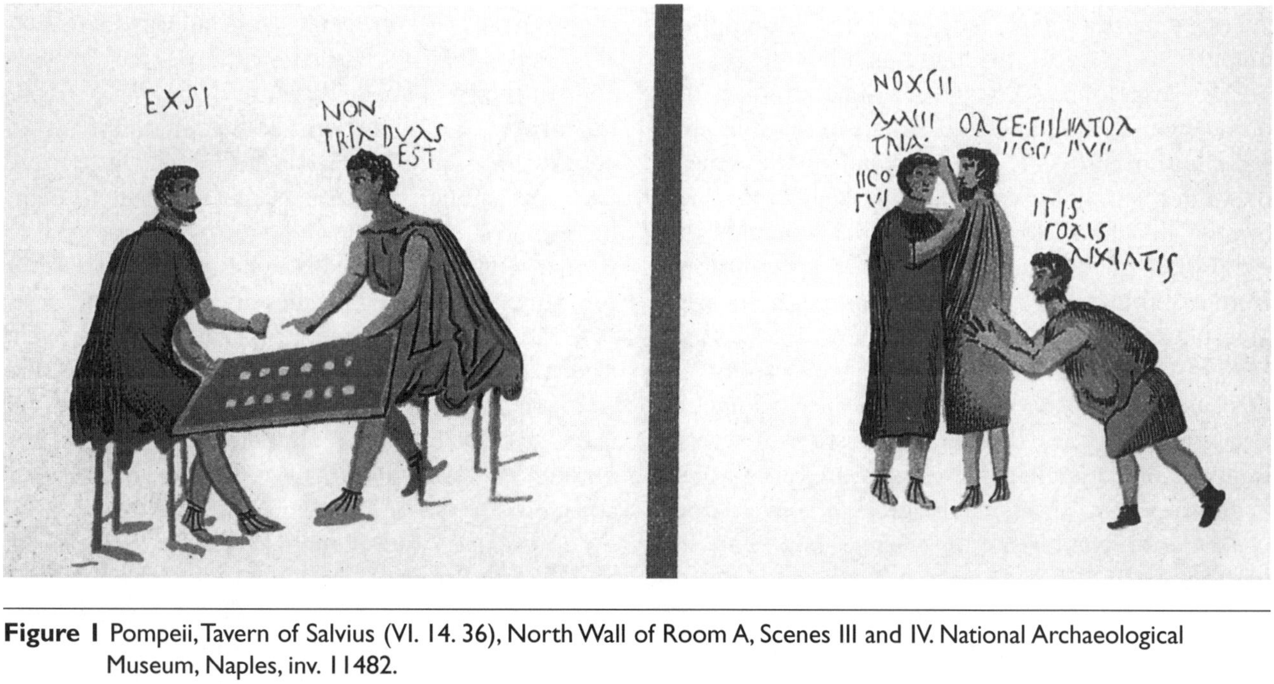

Figure 1 Pompeii, Tavern of Salvius (VI. 14. 36), North Wall of Room A, Scenes III and IV. National Archaeological Museum, Naples, inv. 11482.

Source: Drawing by the author, after E. Presuhn, 1882.

For example, scenes III and IV form a two-frame narrative where two men get into trouble over gambling. In scene III they are playing dice. The man on the left holds the dice-cup in his right hand and says: "I won." His companion asserts: "It's not three; it's two." This disagreement turns ugly in the following scene, where the two men, now standing, come to blows. The man on the left grabs his dice-partner, who holds a fist up to his face. They exchange insults. The man on the left says: "You no-name. It was three for me. I was the winner." The other responds: "Look here, cocksucker. I was the winner." The innkeeper wants none of this. He tells them: "Go outside and fight it out."

What's telling about these vignettes is that their humor addresses anxieties of the in-group. The class of people who frequented the tavern might have worried about getting thrown out for arguing. And the pictures, like modern cartoons, depend on a viewer's ability to read to get the joke. The act of looking, reading, and laughing empowers the viewer—and that's where the laugh is. It's a laugh of relief as the viewer thinks: "That could've been me!"

Images meant for private viewing among a different in-group, consisting of upper class Pompeians, remind us that all social classes embraced intra-group visual humor. The target of a series of frescoes belonging to an elite house is the Emperor Augustus himself and his dynastic propaganda. Augustus enlisted the poet Virgil to write the *Aeneid* in order to make the Trojan prince Aeneas into Augustus's ancestor. Aeneas flees Troy, wanders about, then prepares the stage for the founding of Rome.

The target of this Pompeian visual parody is the quintessential monument to Augustus's claims: his great Forum in Rome. In it, Augustus made Aeneas the centerpiece of the courtyard displaying the members of his clan, the *gens Iulia,* and Romulus the centerpiece of the courtyard opposite it, celebrating Roman military and civic heroes. Although the original statues have disappeared, reproductions of them abound. But there's also an outrageous spoof on this ideologically loaded pair of the fleeing Aeneas and the triumphant Romulus, consisting of several fragments of a painted frieze, excavated in a house at Pompeii; they present our great heroes as dog-headed apes, complete with tails and long phalluses (see Figure 2).

Why would a Pompeian householder commission such an irreverent parody? It is clear some citizens resented Roman rule in general and Augustus in particular. Pompeii was an independent town that sided with the anti-Sullan forces in the civil war of 89–82 BCE. Sulla punished the town by reducing it to a colony, confiscating elite lands, and planting new, pro-Roman colonists, who took over rule. Under Augustus, there was an expectation that everyone pay homage to the emperor's official propaganda.

Figure 2 Pompeii, Masseria di Cuomo, Frieze of Aeneas the Ape, 20 × 24 cm. National Archaeological Museum, Naples, inv. 9089.

Source: Photo by Michael Larvey.

It is possible to reconstruct the original appearance of these fragments because of the many parallels for such friezes in rooms painted in the Augustan period (see Figure 3). The owner of this little frieze harbored enough anti-Augustan sentiment to commission this dual spoof on Augustus's blatant use of Roman myth to bolster his dynasty. He or she happily laughed at these parodies and knew that guests invited into the room would laugh at them as well. The Aeneas-Romulus paintings constitute a second example of humor generated for the group or social class that consumes it. It's the joke that circulates among the knowing in-group, not suitable for consumption beyond the strict social limits of that group because of its potential to make its members look like bad citizens.

To employ the terms of sociology, because the intra-group situation applies to humor initiated in and consumed by the "in-group," humor can control group behavior, intensify group identity, or control conflict within the group. Situated within a private house at Pompeii, the paintings serve to intensify group identity among viewers who, like the owner, were elite, or at least moneyed, individuals.

Inter-Group Humor

Parallel to these examples of intra-group humor, we find many varieties of inter-group, or "them versus us," humor in Roman visual culture. The most outrageous are representations where the differences are not between the upper and lower classes but between Romans and what postcolonial theory would call the "Other." In ancient Roman visual culture, this kind of them versus us humor runs the gamut from mockery of non-Romans (barbarians, Egyptians) to laughter at deformed persons. A special case is the so-called pygmy, a visual representation that "others" Egypt by setting the actions of the foolhardy, incontinent pygmy on the Nile in order to make the pygmy opposite in every way from the ideals of body type and behavior for proper Romans (see Figure 4). By the late 1st century BCE, after Romans had finally subjugated Egypt, the noble Black African (*Aethiops*) becomes a hyperphallic, incontinent clown. Throughout the 1st century CE, visual representations increasingly feature the pygmy rather than the *Aethiops*. This is not the ethnic pygmy, unknown to the Romans, but rather a clown type representing individuals afflicted with dwarfism, including large heads, small limbs, exaggerated penises, and protruding buttocks. Found especially in garden paintings and tombs, these pygmies function as comic fertility symbols, copulating and defecating in the Nile landscape, or they engage in foolhardy hunting exploits against wild animals—negative examples of the Roman valor (*virtus*) in battle.

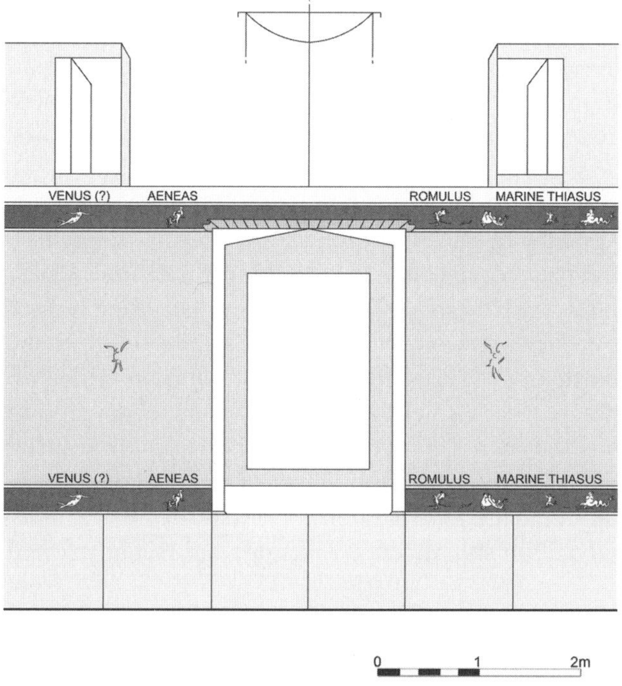

Figure 3 Frieze of Aeneas and Romulus, Hypothetical Reconstruction

Source: Drawing by Onur Öztürk.

In contrast to these "othering" scenarios featuring seemingly ubiquitous pygmy follies, the groups set in opposition in the paintings decorating the Tavern of the Seven Sages at Ostia are ordinary men, who appear seated on a common latrine bench at the bottom of the walls, and the Sages, seated on philosophers' stools above (see Figure 5).

When we read the captions above both the Sages and the seated men, the conflict that is the basis of the humor becomes clear. A Greek label announces

Figure 4 Pompeii, House of the Doctor (VIII. 5. 24), Pluteus of Peristyle G, West Side, North Part, Pygmies at Outdoor Banquet. National Archaeological Museum, Naples, inv. 113196.

Source: Photo by Michael Larvey.

Solon of Athens, but the line of Latin above him says: "To shit well Solon stroked his belly." Above Thales of Miletus we read: "Thales advised those who shit hard to really work at it." We learn that "Cunning Chilon (of Sparta) taught how to fart without making noise."

As for the five men below, they must be sitting and defecating, to judge from the words written above their heads in Latin. The first man on the back wall says, "I'm hurrying up"; he may be responding to the man next to him who says: "Shake yourself about so that you'll go sooner." Another man says: "Friend, the adage escapes you. Shit well and force the doctors to fellate you." A more colloquial translation might be: "Hey buddy—don't you know the saying? If you shit well—to hell with the doctors—you don't need them."

The humor here sets up a battle between intellectuals and ordinary men, inter-group humor, where one group (the non-elite tavern-goers) mocks the upper classes represented by the Sages. A useful tool for understanding the reversals in the visual humor is Mikhail Bakhtin's concept of the carnivalesque, or the world-turned-upside-down. Among the many reversals enacted in the painting is what Bakhtin calls the reversal of upper and lower material bodily strata. The upper register of the walls, with the Seven Sages, stands for the head: intellect, reasoning, the face. For ordinary persons, the Sages represent the values of elites and their sophisticated systems of philosophy, rhetoric, and religion. In contrast, the bottommost register represents what Bakhtin calls the lower material body, specifically the belly, genitals, and anus.

Sexual Humor

The many humorous visual representations of debased sexual practices are particularly useful for understanding Roman attitudes toward sexuality. The recently discovered vignettes in the Suburban Baths at Pompeii derive their humor from the representation of taboo sex acts such as cunnilungus (performed by both men and women), fellatio, threesomes (see Figure 6), foursomes, and a lesbian encounter. In each of these representations, the artist invokes a different taboo, such as that of the unclean mouth or the rule against citizen males being penetrated. For a Roman viewer who sees these debased acts, the only proper response is laughter.

A less complex, mass-produced sexual humor appears in the mold-made medallions applied to the terracotta vessels produced in the Rhone Valley of Roman France. Many of them get their humor by showing women getting the upper hand in the battle of the sexes: for instance, a woman taking up her partner's shield and sword, even while caption has the man saying, "Look out!"—and we see that he has lost his erection. Most of the medallions rely on language to drive home the joke. A nearly intact medallion still attached to its pot and recently found

Figure 5 Ostia, Tavern of the Seven Sages (III. 10. 2–3), Room 5, View of South and West Walls, Sages and Sitting Men.

Source: Photo by Michael Larvey.

Figure 6 Pompeii, Suburban Baths, Dressing Room 7. Scene VI, a Threesome of a Man Being Penetrated by Another Man Penetrating a Woman.

Source: Photo by Michael Larvey.

Figure 7 Lyons, Male-Female Couple on a Boat With Caption NAVIGIUM VENERIS, Applied Medallion on Vase, Terra-Cotta, Diam. 6½ in. Gallo-Roman Museum, Lyons, inv. CEL 76451.

Source: Drawing by Armand Desbat.

in Lyons shows a man steering a riverboat while penetrating his female partner (see Figure 7). The caption says "The Steersmanship of Venus" or more colloquially "On Course for Sex." The pun on his skills as navigator in both senses is funny even to us moderns.

Roman visual humor, because it targets all the practices of everyday life, from emperor worship to defecation, provides uncannily close views of how various communities formed their attitudes toward these practices. Humor reveals acculturation, but no single theoretical framework explains Roman humor.

The eye that recognizes humor is, like the ear that hears the joke, a socially conditioned one. To look and laugh is to announce your position within a complex social matrix. Humor can target anyone and anything—whether it's the overbearing ego of an individual in your own group or the emperor himself. More than most visual forms, humor allows us to understand the cultural horizons of ancient Romans.

John R. Clarke

See also Ancient Roman Comedy; Art and Visual Humor; Carnivalesque; Ethnic Jokes; Gender Roles in Humor; Inversion, Topsy-Turvy; Obscenity; Parody; Prejudice, Humor and; Reversal Theory; Rituals of Inversion; Satire; Sociology

Further Readings

Bakhtin, M. (1984). *Rabelais and his world* (H. Iswolsky, Trans.). Bloomington: Indiana University Press.

Clarke, J. R. (2007). *Looking at laughter: Humor, power, and transgression in Roman visual culture, 100 B.C.–A.D. 250*. Berkeley: University of California Press.

Martineau, W. H. (1972). A model of the social functions of humor. In J. H. Goldstein & P. E. McGhee (Eds.), *The psychology of humor* (pp. 101–125). New York, NY: Academic Press.

Romantic Comedy

See Comedy; Genres and Styles of Comedy; Tragicomedy

S

Sanskrit Humor

Humor was defined and established as a literary sentiment (*rasa*) by Indian aestheticians two millennia ago. The comic sentiment (*hasya rasa*) was codified along with eight other sentiments, including love, heroism, and tragedy. Literature transformed universal emotions into refined aesthetic sentiments.

The comic sentiment mocks the serious ones and arises out of their failure. So, for example, when a beautiful woman, the heroine of a love story, rejects the affections not of a handsome hero, but of an obese drunkard, a parody of love creates a humorous response. As the amorous sentiment falls apart, the comic manifests. In one farce from the 11th century, a general leaves his command in the middle of battle, fleeing on the horse of the king himself, in order to rendezvous with a ravishing consort. When such a stock character of heroic stories misses the battle for the sake of a prostitute, the failure of the heroic sentiment gives rise to the comic.

The ways in which people react to humor were also elucidated by the aestheticians: In his 16th-century work *Rasatarangani* (River of Rasa), the poet Bhanu Datta describes the various types of laughter displayed in theatrical plays. Members of the upper class smile and snicker at something humorous. Middle-class characters laugh loudly and show their teeth. Lastly, characters of the lowest class let out bellowing guffaws with tears streaming down their faces. The aestheticians represented each sentiment by a different color and associated each with a unique deity. The color representing comedy was white—for when someone laughs we see the whiteness of their teeth. For a play dominated by the comic sentiment, a white flag or curtain would be shown so the audience knew what to expect. The associated patron deities are the *pramathas*, a gang of divine pranksters. This entry discusses several types of humor found in literary texts written or performed in Sanskrit, the classical language of India.

The Farce

The classical Sanskrit *prahasana* was a satirical farce aimed at exposing the hypocrisy of authority figures. As always in literary satire, the justification is the claim that it intends to heal society's ills by exposing the pretenses of the venerable. The ability to laugh at those characters protects us from the power invested in them.

Religious Figures Mocked

These farces were classified into two types according to the characters in each. The first category involves Indian religious figures such as Brahmin priests, ascetics, yogis, and Jain and Buddhist monks. For a society defined and in a sense ruled by figures of religious authority, satire was particularly humorous when directed at hypocrisy in the guise of piety.

In King Mahendravarmana's 7th-century *Mattavilasa* (Drunken Sports), a Buddhist monk, speculating as to whether or not the Buddha, founder of his religion, really did forbid monks wine and women, entertains the notion that the Buddha would never have done such a thing. Known for his compassion, he would not have wanted to deprive us of fun.

Instead, the monk reasons, it must have been those puritanical, jealous elders who composed such rules in an effort to deprive young men of the joys in life.

The 9th-century comedy *Agamadambara* (Much Ado About Religion) by Bhatta Jayanta showcases, among other representatives of various Indian religious sects, the hypocrisy of naked Jain monks. These ascetics are so extreme in their austerities that they shed their clothes and pluck out all their hairs one by one in order to show their detachment from the body and all worldly things. However, religious does not mean righteous. A servant, sent to summon an elder of the local Jain order, stumbles upon a squabble between an ascetic and a nun. When the nun angrily exits, the servant disguises himself as a woman in order to trick the hypocritical ascetic. Although the lusty Jain monk is distraught over the nun's departure, he quickly forgets his sorrow when he sees the disguised servant. The holy man advances eagerly on the boy (supposing he is a woman) and when he reaches down the boy's pants and gets a hold of his genitals, his disappointment, folly, and hypocrisy arouse the audience's laughter.

Another butt of laughter is a Brahmin in the 12th-century *Hasyacudamani* (The Crest-Jewel of Laughter) by Vatsaraja, supposedly knowledgeable in astrology and soothsaying. When an acolyte asks him his method of fooling people out of their money, the elder is offended by such a forward remark and smacks his student. Despite this, he proceeds to explain that the best way to profit from being an astrologer is to make your prognostications esoteric and confusing.

Secular Authority Figures Mocked

The second class of Sanskrit *prahasana* goes beyond religious figures to expose other supposedly respectable and upstanding people in secular society. Doctors, soldiers, bureaucrats, astrologers, professors, and other esteemed and honored figures are all revealed as pretenders lacking in their supposed skills.

Among the sundry characters in the 11th-century *Latakamelaka* (Gathering of Rogues) by Skankhadhara Kaviraja is the quack doctor, a stock figure in Sanskrit satire (as around the world). He is renowned for furthering the cause of Death and indeed, when he steps onstage, he boasts that diseases are nourished by his care. He claims sick people have no need of Death when he is present since he will certainly hasten their departure. When a bawd's daughter (also a prostitute) chokes on a fish-bone, the doctor prescribes a remedy so utterly idiotic that it actually makes the girl laugh so hard at his incompetence that the fishbone flies out of her throat. The quack uses this as a demonstration of his expertise, but the audience is well aware it is her laughter that saved her. Laughter, not doctors, evidently has the greatest potential to cure and rescue us from the abuses of dubious authority figures.

Sanskrit is the language of priests, philosophers, gods, and sophisticated, learned people: Thus, using it to portray vulgar debaucheries creates a comic incongruity between the sacred language and what it expresses. Full of dirty humor, the obscenities of Sanskrit comedy are all the funnier when spoken in a sanctimonious manner. In the 12th-century *Hasyarnava* (The Ocean of Laughter), a doctor is called to cure an old woman both because her vagina has lost its lubricative facility and because she has cataracts. A male prostitute laughs the quack offstage when he prescribes driving a fiery stake into the woman's pupils—although the doctor points out that logically if someone has no eyes, they cannot have cataracts. Laughter drives such hypocrites off the stage that is our own world even today.

Literary texts in which the heroic sentiment is dominant are characterized by strong, powerful, and brave men. The humor of heroism's failure gives rise to the comic sentiment. Thus, military leaders in the *prahasanas* are depicted as cowardly and grossly ill qualified. The military commander in *The Ocean of Laughter* makes his stage entrance boasting to the king that he has just killed a bee. This warrior is so terrified of blood that he faints when he sees women wearing red makeup.

Prostitute figures in Sanskrit satires act as foils to falsely righteous men. No one expects them to be moral and their beauty typically exposes the desire of many a holy man. More often than not, the prostitute has a procuress mother who inevitably ends up in a love triangle with her low-class daughter and a man of high station, creating more humor.

The Comic Monologue

The prostitute is also a stock figure in the comic Sanskrit monologues known as *bhanas*. These were one-man, single-act shows in which the performer plays walking through a bustling city from the rising of the sun to the rising of the moon. He is always a *vita*, a parasite down on his luck, and, according the *Kama Sutra*, usually married but well respected in the red-light district. One *bhana* begins with the *vita* leaving his house because for the whole rainy season he has been tortured by a horrible sound—his wife's nagging voice.

Unlike the falsely righteous characters of the *prahasanas* who live concealed by pretenses, the *vitas*, prostitutes, and bawds of the *bhanas* flaunt their depravity. To the audiences, it was absurdly funny that someone should be so brazen and upfront about their unsavory behavior and degenerate nature and they laughed at the characters' audacity.

Since the *bhanas* were a kind of stand-up comedy, much of the humor was physical. The *vita* would walk around the stage, using body movement and physical gesture to make his audience imagine what he was doing. As he paraded in mime through non-existent streets, he would engage in mock conversations with passers-by. Calling out their names, he would then speak in an aside to himself in order to inform the audience with whom he was about to converse, making jokes about his subject.

Frequently in these imaginary exchanges, the *vita* himself would laugh aloud and, when he did not want his unreal conversation partner to hear, he would turn his head, block his mouth with his hand, and sarcastically utter a humorous aside to the watching crowd. In one *bhana*, the parasite comes across a squabble between two men from rival religious sects. The surviving text shows him relating what they are saying to one another, presumably jumping back and forth as he about-faces on stage to replicate their bickering.

The *vita* also possessed a flair for comic vulgarity. In the *Dhurtavita Samavada* (Loads of the Shady Vita), he flamboyantly sings the praises of female buttocks. Hyperbole intensifies the humor when he proclaims a posterior heavy enough to weigh its owner down to the point where she can barely walk.

In the *Ubhayabhisarika* (Both Girls Stepping Out), the *vita* runs into a young prostitute dismayed over having just had sex with an ugly, old, trade caravan owner. The *vita* chuckles and tells her there is nothing to worry about and, on the contrary, she should congratulate herself, since having sex with a nasty old man is undoubtedly more satisfying than engaging in intercourse with a gorgeous young man—the former is sure to pay much better.

In the same *bhana*, the *vita* spots a transvestite and refers to this incongruous figure as one of the "third sex." In order to avoid the cross-dresser seeing him, he crosses the street while hiding his face, but the transvestite recognizes him and calls him over. Trapped, the *vita* congratulates him (or her) as the most desirable of courtesans, for three reasons: "she" has no breasts to get in the way during lovemaking, "she" does not have to take a few days off each month for her period, and, best of all, "she" cannot get pregnant.

In the *Padmaprabhritaka* (Before Bearing Beauty, attributed to King Shudraka), when the *vita* spots another *vita* who has grown old, he cannot resist making fun of him. He laughs at the older one's preposterous appearance, complete with grey hair dyed black and individually plucked facial hairs to give the appearance of a smooth, unshaven youth. The old man's vanity and failed attempts to look young arouse laughter.

Poetry and Satirical Prose

Sanskrit humor was not limited to the stage. The *hasya rasa* also informed poetry and humorous satirical narrative, as the following examples show.

Kshemendra's 11th-century *Samaya Matrika* (The Courtesan's Keeper) opens with the prostitute protagonist distraught over her grandmother's death at the hands of a quack doctor. Filled with desire for the courtesan, the doctor had given her his own draught for staying young. Mistakenly thinking it was medicine for herself, the girl's grandmother drank it and just as in the modern-day cartoon image of the crook seeing dollar signs over everyone's heads, she began to see a world in which everything seemed made of gold and exhausted herself.

The bawd protagonist of *The Courtesan's Keeper* relates a time when she was incredibly tired from lovemaking all day. To avoid more intercourse, she lied and told her innocent young customer that her body was in pain. As dawn broke, she felt rather guilty at having cheated the boy and convinced him that if he put his penis in her vagina her pain might subside: Sure enough, she told him, it does. The naive boy however burst into tears, exclaiming that a similar pain had killed his mother and if he had known his penis possessed such healing power when placed in a vagina, he could have saved her.

Prostitutes and their patrons are mocked in just the same fashion as in the *bhanas*, with the humor springing from the totally cavalier attitude of both toward debauchery. The women constantly change their clothes so their newest patron cannot see whatever unsavory token the previous customer has left behind. If a moneyless man manages to make it past the guardian bawd, all the women in the room fall suddenly ill and are unable to entertain the intruder. The same types of characters as are found in the *prahasanas* displaying false pretenses are customers, including a general, a temple manager, and city officials. One bawd even adds *vitas* to this list, forbidding them to enter her brothel since on the night depicted, she is entertaining only so-called men of merit.

Kshemendra's *Narma Mala* (Garland of Mirth) is an acerbic critique of bureaucracy. He describes government officials squandering their money, overly willing to condemn others, displaying empty pomp and circumstance, all to construct an importance that cloaks their essential uselessness. The highest ranking official in this text is in fact a wealthy fat slob married to a gorgeous trophy wife. While he showers this young woman with gifts, she is busy with illicit adulterous affairs. Such cuckolds are also stock figures in Sanskrit comic literature.

Besides their comic characters, these narratives are rich in verbal humor. *Garland of Mirth* compares a woman's pubic mound to Mount Meru, a holy place of pilgrimage, creating humor from the incongruous juxtaposition of very sacred and very profane. Other figures of speech such as hyperbole and paronomasia are commonly and wittily used to enhance the humor of Sanskrit poetic description.

The Fool

When the amorous or heroic sentiment dominates, the *hasya rasa* often provides comic relief, often through another standard figure in Sanskrit drama, the fool, or *vidushaka*. He is a fat gluttonous brahmin who typically thinks of nothing but eating and like the pot-bellied, elephant-headed god Ganesha, is particularly fond of sweets. While the serious characters yearn for romance, revenge, and glory, the *vidushaka* wants only one thing—more food. Thus in the *Abhijñānashākuntala* (Recognition of Shakuntala) by Kalidasa, composed in the first half of the 1st millennium CE and regarded as one of the great Sanskrit love stories, the hero, a king, recites powerful love poetry while his *vidushaka* whines for more food. The effect is very funny but also serves to strengthen the sublime and amorous sentiment by juxtaposing it to the base and comic.

As a rite of passage, Brahmin boys are given a sacred thread that they must wear for life, a symbol of their ritual purity as well as their prominence in society. Nevertheless, in Shudraka's *Mricchakatika* (The Little Clay Cart), the hero of the play yanks the *vidushaka's* precious thread in order to make him sit down beside him and stop chasing pigeons. In Kalidasa's 4th-century *Malavikagnimitram* (Fiery Female Friend), the thread is even used as a tourniquet to block the flow of blood from a pretend snakebite. Once again, humor is created by the incongruity between the sacred and the profane. The *vidushaka* has a fool's appearance, conventionally bald with two locks of hair hanging down on either side of his head, red eyes, and most often a hunchback. Emphasizing his absurd appearance and incongruous nature, his makeup is a motley of colors, with his beard dyed green or yellow. As a bumbling idiot despite his Brahmin status, the *vidushaka* speaks a vernacular language rather than Sanskrit.

Conclusion

The comic conventions established by Sanskrit humor have had a widespread influence upon vernacular literature as well as popular comedy and film in contemporary India. Traditional *prahasanas* and *bhanas* as well as more serious plays featuring the *vidushaka* continue to be performed. Thus, the theories established by aestheticians millennia ago continue to influence modern Indian literature, theater, and film.

Samuel Grimes

See also Aesthetics; Burlesque; Carnival and Festival; Clergy; Comic Relief; Exaggeration; Farce; Fools; Genres and Styles of Comedy; Inversion, Topsy-Turvy; Low Comedy; Marriage and Couples; Obscenity; Philosophy of Humor; Rhetoric and Rhetorical Devices; Satire; Scatology; Stereotypes; Targets of Humor; Tragicomedy; Verbal Humor

Further Readings

Bhanudatta, B. (2009). *Bouquet of rasa and river of rasa* (S. Pollock, Trans.). New York, NY: New York University Press.

Bhat, G. (1959). *The Vidusaka*. Ahmedabad, India: New Order Book.

Bhatta, J. (2005). *Much ado about religion* (C. Dezső, Trans.). New York, NY: New York University Press.

Ghosh, M. (Trans.). (1975). *Glimpses of sexual life in Nanda-Maurya India: Translation of the Caturbhani together with a critical edition of text*. Calcutta, India: Manisha Granthalaya.

Goswami, B. (Trans.). (1998). *Sanskrit prahasanas: Sanskrit text, English translation, and annotations*. Kolkata: Sanskrit Pustak Bhandar.

Haksar, A. N. D. (Trans.). (2008). *The courtesan's keeper: A satire from ancient Kashmir: Translation of Kshemendra's Samayamātāka from the original Sanskrit.* New Delhi, India: Rupa & Co.

Haksar, A. N. D. (Trans.). (2011). *Three satires from ancient Kashmir.* New Delhi, India: Penguin Books.

Schwartz, S. L. (2004). *Rasa: Performing the divine in India.* New York, NY: Columbia University Press.

Siegel, L. (1987). *Laughing matters: Comic tradition in India.* Chicago, IL: University of Chicago Press.

Sarcasm

See Irony

Satire

Satire is now popularly regarded as a mode of mass media entertainment: humor or comedy with social content. The established academic view is that satire is a literary genre. As such, satire is largely a creation of modern university disciplinary demarcation dating from the 19th century; the notion of literature as a distinct type of canonical imaginative writing has been expanded from the more venerable field of poetics. The best historical evidence for satire being a genre comes from the Juvenalian tradition of critical poetry—but this is largely innocent of humorous intent. Conversely, the wit and humor typical of Menippean satire persistently upsets the expectations of coherence on which conceptions of genre rely. A corrective to modern expectations is found in N. Bailey's *Etymological Dictionary* of 1735, which defined *satire* as either a form of poetry, or any sharp rebuke. Even the association of satire with humor is contingent and has traditionally been secondary to claimed moral purpose. Considering the diversity of phenomena that have been taken as satiric, any single definition may be unsatisfactory—and indeed any cohesive history of satire (beyond a narrative of semantic adaptation) illusory. This entry discusses changes in the meaning of satire, as well as its purposes and targets.

The word itself indicates the difficulties involved: Satire is a metaphorical derivation from the Latin *satira,* a medley or stew. Quintilian (35–ca. 100 CE) claimed that satire was a Roman invention, but he seems to have had in mind poetry in Latin hexameters and may have been reacting against a Hellenistic cultural hegemony to which Romans were sensitive. One meaning of satire remained a designation for a form of poetry, most specifically associated with the Roman poets Juvenal (ca. 60–130 CE) and Horace (65–8 BCE) and this became a lively if sporadic tradition of adaptive emulation that survived beyond Alexander Pope (1688–1744). Other understandings however, would extend the range of satire to include Greek verse and especially the Attic Old Comedy of Aristophanes (ca. 450–ca. 385 BCE). During the Renaissance, philological interest in the origins of the word *satire* was tied to an endeavor to establish a proper meaning. This was never really achieved, but Isaac Casaubon (1559–1614) argued persuasively that the origins did indeed lie in Latin rather than in the Greek satyr plays that accompanied Attic tragedy.

Nevertheless, there remained some conceptual plausibility to belief in an ultimately Greek origin for satire, not least because the Roman satiric poet Varro (116–27 BCE) wrote in the idiom of the 3rd-century BCE Greek poet Menippus, whose diatribes are now lost. The name Menippus was used in the satires of Lucian (ca. 120–180 CE) by which time satire could be prose or—true to its metaphorical origins—a medley of prose and poetry. Lucian's work is central to the unbroken and self-conscious tradition of humorous satire running from the Renaissance to the 19th century.

Purpose of Satire

From classical antiquity into the early modern Western world, the provocation of laughter had the critical purpose of exposing moral, social, and intellectual failings. It was thus an important topic in rhetorical theory, and over time such justifications for corrective laughter have become synonymous with satire. The reception and sustained authority of Aristotle's *Poetics* reinforced this association, although neither in the *Poetics* nor the *Rhetoric* did Aristotle (384–322 BCE) discuss satire. The first dealt extensively with comedy, the second with the means of persuasion, including the provocation of laughter. Translations of *The Poetics,* however, were apt to conflate comedy and Roman satire, while the strongly ethical dimension both of poetry and the proper functions of practical reasoning remained in place. From the 16th century onward, Aristotle's works could be, and were, taken directly or indirectly as foundational texts for the moral end or purpose of satire.

There are, however, three aspects to be distinguished in this supposedly informing purpose for the use of humor. First is the attempt to expose in order to reform; the second is the affirmation of the values implicit in the process of making someone a laughingstock. Satire is by no means always subversive or challenging and these aspects of satiric intent are often communicated more easily in visual form. William Hogarth (1697–1764), for example, turned to satiric painting and his image of a gin-sodden mother indifferent to her child (Beer Street and Gin Lane, 1751) negatively affirms the established virtues of sobriety and parental responsibility. The third aspect lies in the need to punish or to persecute, for which humor needs to be at its most destructive. This also is likely to offer either reassurance, or even the satisfactions of vengeance, to the righteous.

The location, as it were, of much satire at the junction of rhetoric and moral philosophy also helps explain the prominence of rhetorical tropes such as irony and sarcasm in what is easily recognized as satiric literature. Many nowadays take "humorous means to a moral end" as actually defining satire. It certainly captures a good deal, but still requires us to overlook the early-modern distinction between satire and humorous satire: It makes awkward, for example, the conventional designation of George Orwell's 1949 dark novel *1984* as satire.

Historically, justifications for satirical writing have been predominantly ethical rather than ludic. Adopting the persona of the satirist—as for example both Pope and Jonathan Swift (1667–1745) did—was to assume a moral, even a philosophical position asserted to be at odds with prevailing evils. This claim on a moral office or responsibility amounted to an extension of the traditional legitimating function of the poet as philosopher and teacher. Concomitantly, satirists have frequently laid claim to the virtues of courage and outspokenness—Lucian's own advertised virtue of *parrhesia* (straight-speaking) was defended as necessary in a corrupt environment. The fact that, from antiquity, the satirist could be presented as a distinct persona serving a moral office helped stretch the range of satire beyond any specific genre. Satire could be whatever the satirist wrote, with as little or as much use of instrumental humor as seemed required. Conversely, those hostile to satirists largely ignored or dismissed any wit or humor, concentrating instead on satirists as irresponsible and cruel.

Satire can largely be seen as humor in the service of some ethical end; but this understanding does not exhaust the scope of the notion. First, because there has been no overall restriction as to the form satire might take, it might be found in work that is not principally satiric. Thus, the novels of Jane Austen (1774–1817) and Charles Dickens (1812–1870), the tragedies of William Shakespeare (1564–1616) and Ben Jonson (1572–1637), and the paintings of Honoré Daumier (1808–1879) all have in different degrees a satiric edge. If *1984* is satiric, so too might be Pablo Picasso's *Guernica* (1937). The satiric permeates the world of film and is common in all forms of the mass media. The range of satire is probably best grasped by considering the term adjectivally.

Second, between societies and subgroups within them, there are marked differences over time in what counts as humorous and also there are varying patterns of social and even politically enforced taboo concerning the legitimate subjects of humor. The 19th-century writer William Hone (1780–1842) was tried for blasphemy because he had used a biblical parody for satiric effect. As Margaret Rose argues (1979), he was acquitted partly on the grounds that the Bible had been the means and not a target of his parodic satire. But this distinction between means and ends can be uncertain. The reception of the Monty Python film *Life of Brian* (1979) was clouded by confusion as to whether Christianity was itself being satirized. Many would insist that satire making any reference to religion is unacceptable: That is certainly the case in some countries now under Islamic law. Yet during the Middle Ages, religion and its putative corruption was a principal focus of much satire, and piety could easily generate anti-clerical critique. When Christianity fractured into hostile confessions with the Reformation, the satire of opposing denominations became standard fare to be found across a range of religious writings, from theology to ecclesiological polemic.

Some societies and political groups have had little toleration for the satire of leaders or have allowed it only under limited circumstances. The genuine or feigned fears of retribution have sometimes stimulated satirists to adopt modes of protective indirection, such as the satiric allegory *Absalom and Achitophel* (1681) by John Dryden (1631–1700), or Orwell's *Animal Farm* (1945). Nowadays, satires touching (though not necessarily targeting) children and the disabled, or different minority, cultural, or racial groupings, can also stimulate discomfort or hostility. Further, there are different degrees of acceptance for the vehicles conveying satirical intent. The sexually explicit humor of Aristophanes has usually been subject to censorship or euphemistic translation. Scatological humor, quite conventional between the 16th and 18th centuries as a medium for satiric wit and denigration, fell from favor and went into relative disuse during the 19th century.

General Satire Versus Personal Satire

The need for satirists to tread carefully has led to a distinction between general satire directed at broad moral failings such as hypocrisy and greed, and personal satire designed to isolate and shame specific people or groups. This, however, does less to establish any stable typology of satire than to stir up arguments about what sort of rhetorical strategy is likely to be most effective, and thus to emphasize the instrumental uses of humor. Desiderius Erasmus (1466–1536) considered direct personal attack counterproductive, but thought generality might include the satirist as the butt of humor and encourage a greater degree of moral self-awareness. Conversely, Pope held that generality allowed people to see themselves as immune from critique by laughing only at others: For him, satire, to be effective, had to offend its intended victims.

Satire as found in contemporary mass media is particularly subject to low offense thresholds and usually needs to be sensitive to effective libel and slander laws, among other less structured forms of retaliation. To remain popular entertainment, it must either reinforce rather than criticize mainstream conceptions of propriety or have a particularly clear focus on a specific audience. Particularly because of pressures to be ethically safe rather than confronting, subversive, or courageous, contemporary emphasis has shifted to making people laugh.

Moreover, different societies and their subsets have adhered to differing standards of what counts as morally proper. Consequently, satire expressing generally unacceptable standards—such as that produced in the Third Reich during World War II—can be delegitimated as mere propaganda. One man's satiric chastisement is another's slanderous imputation and humor is likely to be appreciated only where the satire is liked. This drift toward the de facto restriction of satire to that which conforms to acceptable moral standards has been an important factor in specifying its nature. Despite this, it is naive to take at face value the satirist's conventional self-promotional positioning, which is that satire is on the side of the angels, subversive of oppression, and fights for freedom and decency, requiring the courage to say what might be offensive. Satire is too diverse and flexible a phenomenon to be seen as existing in a fixed relationship to any ideological group or social structure. Consequently it is not to be seen as necessarily either radical or conservative (a dichotomy that would anyway have made little sense before the 19th century). Its value to those feeling oppressed is well known, but its persuasive potential has also long been recognized by political elites. In England, for example, Queen Anne's principal minister from 1710 to 1712, Robert Harley, was himself a member of the satirical Scriblerus group; in 1984, British Prime Minister Margaret Thatcher cowrote and took part in a short *Yes, Prime Minister* sketch, performed when the popular television series was given an award.

Modern understandings often make political and social failings central to satire and can even build such preoccupations into attempted definition. Yet Lucian's satires were overwhelmingly directed to those of the intellectual world. Their focus was on religious gullibility, superstition, philosophy, and rhetoric. Thus satire could be an idiom of philosophizing, as it is in the writings of Thomas Hobbes (1588–1679) and less formally in those of Thomas More (1478–1535). This point is easily obscured by seeing satire exclusively as a literary genre and not also an intermittent part of the history of philosophy. It is instructive to note that at the end of the 18th century, T. J. Mathias's much reprinted *The Pursuits of Literature* regarded most of the written output of a culture as constituting its literature, took the philosopher to be a satirist and regarded philosophy as enjoyable precisely because it can make us laugh.

Conal Condren

See also Aggressive and Harmless Humor; Ancient Greek Comedy; Aristophanes; Audience; Burlesque; Caricature; Failed Humor; Genres and Styles of Comedy; History of Humor: Early Modern Europe; History of Humor: Renaissance Europe; Insult and Invective; Lampoon; Legal Restriction and Protection of Humor; Literature; Obscenity; Parody; Personality, Humor and Conversation; Persuasion and Humor; Philosophy of Humor; Political Humor; Reception of Humor; Scatology; Subversive Humor; Targets of Humor; Verbal Humor

Further Readings

Condren, C. (2011). *Hobbes, the Scriblerians and the history of philosophy*. London, UK: Pickering & Chatto.

Elliott, R. C. (1960). *The power of satire: Magic, ritual and art.* Princeton, NJ: Princeton University Press.
Frye, N. (1957). *The anatomy of criticism.* Princeton, NJ: Princeton University Press.
Griffin, D. (1994). *Satire: A critical reintroduction.* Louisville: Kentucky University Press.
Rose, M. (1979). *Parody//Meta-fiction.* London, UK: Croom Helm.
Rosenheim, E. W. (1963). *Swift and the satirist's art.* Chicago, IL: University of Chicago Press.
Sutherland, J. (1962). *English satire.* Cambridge, UK: Cambridge University Press.
Weinbrot, H. D. (2005). *Menippean satire reconsidered: From antiquity to the eighteenth century.* Baltimore, MD: Johns Hopkins University Press.

Satire News

Satire news is a type of political media content that combines elements of both entertainment and public affairs. Satire has been defined as pregeneric in that all forms of satire reflect existing genres. Two genres that have been used for satirical purposes are the nightly television news broadcast (e.g., *The Daily Show With Jon Stewart, Saturday Night Live*'s "Weekend Update") and news commentary and punditry programming (*The Colbert Report*). In addition to embracing television-based genres, satire news can reflect the basic formatting of other media outlets such as the daily newspaper (*The Onion*). Researchers have argued that content of this kind is used as a vehicle to present the human folly of politics as well as the inherent weaknesses of the news industry. This entry discusses research done on satire news, its effects, and possible directions for future research.

Various strains of empirical research have begun to investigate the audience for news satire, the information it contains, and its potential effects. Viewers of television news satire tend to be heavy news consumers, politically knowledgeable, young, male, and liberal, though partisans on both sides may interpret news satire to align with their beliefs. Content analyses have found that *The Daily Show* contains roughly the same amount of substantive political information as network news broadcasts and a large percentage of its content is policy coverage. Viewing news satire has been shown to produce negative views of politics. However, viewership is also linked to increased attention to political issues, campaign news, political debates, and science news. Satire news viewing predicts interpersonal political discussion and numerous types of political participation.

Paralleling the empirical study of satire news is critical, culturally based research on this type of media content. Much of this work focuses on providing political and popular culture context for the rise of this type of discourse. In addition, satire news is discussed in relation to our changing media environment. Research based in these epistemological traditions has focused on both the entertainment and journalism components of this concept. For example, it has been argued that the rise of various forms of satire news (e.g., *The Daily Show, The Colbert Report*) is a reflection of a postmodern media environment. As it has become increasingly difficult to maintain strict professional boundaries of expertise in a postmodern era, it is natural for various forms of traditional news to begin looking more like entertainment programming and for different types of entertainment-driven content to look more like news. This metamorphosis of political media content has led scholars to raise several normative concerns, such as that satire news in a cynical vein encourages cynicism in viewers, as well as to note specific democratic advantages this material may afford a citizenry by questioning the dominant version of events found in the news media.

The difficulty in studying satire news is that it comes in many different forms, and that some forms have received much more research attention than others. The knowledge generated to date about the influence of satire news on a citizenry is seemingly disparate, making it difficult to link individual pieces of satire news research together to form a coherent whole. Much research on political satire still treats humor as a monolithic entity, and only recently have researchers started to look at the differential effects of unique types of satire (e.g., Juvenalian vs. Horatian). We do know that various types of satire news have the potential to generate influence (direct or indirect) that spans the hierarchy of effects from salience to knowledge to attitudes to behaviors.

The phases of scientific inquiry include description, prediction, and explanation. The study of news satire is a very young area of research that has focused primarily on the first two phases, descriptions and predictions. The third area, explanation, is only now emerging. The small number of studies that have referenced theories of effects have discussed dual process models of persuasion, media dependency theory, or media priming, but no theories specific to satire or satire news have yet been developed.

An area where theoretical progress is sorely needed is in distinguishing various elements within satirical messages. With rare exception, both the types of satirical news and the components of satirical news have remained largely undifferentiated. In addition, research on satire in the mass media needs to incorporate existing scholarship from areas as diverse as literature, media effects, and humor processing in order to use a range of knowledge to develop robust theories with strong explanatory power.

R. Lance Holbert and John M. Tchernev

See also History of Humor: U.S. Modern and Contemporary; Journalism; Political Humor; Postmodern Irony; Satire; Spoofing

Further Readings

Amarasingam, A. (2011). *The Stewart/Colbert effect: Essays on the real impacts of fake news.* Jefferson, NC: McFarland.

Baumgartner, J., & Morris, J. S. (2008). *Laughing matters: Humor and American politics in the media age.* New York, NY: Routledge.

Baym, G. (2010). *From Cronkite to Colbert: The evolution of broadcast news.* Boulder, CO: Paradigm.

Day, A. (2011). *Satire and dissent: Interventions in contemporary political debate.* Bloomington: Indiana University Press.

Gray, J., Jones, J. P., & Thompson, E. (2009). *Satire TV: Politics and comedy in the post-network era.* New York, NY: New York University Press.

Hart, R. P., & Hartelius, J. (2007). The political sins of Jon Stewart. *Critical Studies in Media Communication, 24,* 263–272.

Hmielowski, J. D., Holbert, R., & Lee, J. (2011). Predicting the consumption of political TV satire: Affinity for political humor, *The Daily Show,* and *The Colbert Report. Communication Monographs, 78,* 96–114.

Holbert, R. L. (2005). A typology for the study of entertainment television and politics. *American Behavioral Scientist, 49,* 436–453.

Holbert, R. L., & Young, D. G. (2013). Exploring relations between political entertainment media and traditional political communication information outlets: A research agenda. In E. Scharrer (Ed.), *The international encyclopedia of media studies* (Vol. V, pp. 484–504). West Sussex, UK: Wiley-Blackwell.

Jones, J. (2010). *Entertaining politics: Satiric television and political engagement* (2nd ed.). Lanham, MD: Rowman & Littlefield.

Van Zoonen, L. (2005). *Entertaining the citizen: When politics and popular culture converge.* Lanham, MD: Rowman & Littlefield.

Young, D. G. (in press). Theories and effects of political humor: Discounting cues, gateways, and the impact of incongruities. In K. Kenski & K. H. Jamieson (Eds.), *Handbook of political communication theories.* Oxford, UK: Oxford University Press.

Satyr Play

A satyr play, also called a satyr-drama, was a drama performed at the Festival of Dionysus in Athens from very early in the 5th century BCE. As part of the festival, a drama competition was held, and each competing tragic dramatist had to provide three tragedies and one satyr-drama as entry into the competition. The satyr-dramas provided a light and humorous conclusion to the day's entertainment after the set of three tragedies and were often based on a story from the same group of myths. They were normally much shorter than Greek tragedies.

It is probable that each competing dramatist had to provide both tragedies and a satyr-drama from the first competition (in 501 BCE) onward; tragedy and satyr-drama go naturally together since they are both direct developments of the celebration of Dionysus. In myth, in iconography, and in cult, Dionysus's followers include satyrs as well as his human worshippers, bacchantes. We know from vase paintings that the satyr chorus members wore a bearded, slightly balding mask, with pointed ears and a snub nose; they were naked except for a furry loincloth, from which a phallus protruded at the front and a horse-like tail from the rear. They invariably accompanied their father, Silenus; his features were similar, and he wore a body suit of white hair. In the surviving play and fragments, the satyrs have a consistent character: They were amoral hedonists (especially in the pursuit of sex and wine), boastful but cowardly.

Apart from small fragments, we possess one complete satyr-drama (Euripides's *Cyclops*), about one hundred lines each from Aeschylus's *Fishermen* and *Ambassadors to the Isthmian Games,* and the first four hundred lines of Sophocles's *Trackers.* These ribald, sometimes obscene dramas use techniques that we would associate with farce and burlesque to tell stories, based on Dionysiac ritual, in which the sacred band of satyric worshippers of Dionysus, played by the chorus, comes into conflict with other, more normal gods and goddesses, heroes and heroines—who have to survive their mockery, abuse, deception, and (if female) the threat of sexual harassment. Typically, the satyrs find themselves temporarily freed from the service of Dionysus, either voluntarily (*Ambassadors*) or under compulsion (*Cyclops*, where as the play opens, they are the Cyclops's prisoners); it is not clear from the fragment of *Trackers* why Silenus and his sons are free to enter Apollo's service to try to find his cows. Their natural curiosity is stimulated by an encounter with some marvelous new discovery—Danaë and her baby son Perseus washed ashore in a chest in *Fishermen*; Hephaestus's "new toys" in *Ambassadors*; and Hermes's strange invention, the lyre, whose sound drives them crazy in *Trackers*. In *Fishermen* and *Trackers*, the satyrs are confronted by a woman or nymph who emerges miraculously from under the sea or the earth (Danaë in *Fishermen*, Cyllene in *Trackers*). In both these dramas, and in the lost *Amymone* by Aeschylus, they harass or threaten to harass this female; a god rescues her from them. In *Fishermen*, they find themselves temporarily caring for a heroic male infant (Perseus); it is possible that in the lost second half of *Trackers*, they similarly nurtured the boy Hermes.

All of this is grounded in aspects of Dionysiac ritual; the surviving play and the fragments all take a fairly straightforward story from myth—in *Trackers*, the story of the invention of the lyre from the Homeric *Hymn to Hermes*; and in *Cyclops* a famous episode from the *Odyssey* (Book IX)—and inject the satyrs into it, creating situations where their farcical, burlesque, and amoral behavior clashes with the more elevated world of gods, goddesses, and heroes. These latter characters try to speak the language of tragedy; Danaë in *Fishermen*, Odysseus in *Cyclops*, Cyllene and above all Apollo in *Trackers* attempt a heroic tone. However, their role as characters in a satyr-drama soon punctures their rhetoric, and their speech descends into bathos. Danaë becomes a sulky teenager, Odysseus turns coward, Cyllene abuses the satyrs like a fishwife, and Apollo's noble rage and grief soon become mere petulance.

It has been hard for many modern critics, nurtured on a firm division between high and low culture, to imagine the inclusive, wide-ranging tastes of the Athenian theater, where poets had to satisfy at once the demands of peasant and philosopher, craftsman and priest. It is no surprise, therefore, to find that *Cyclops* is among Euripides's least admired surviving dramas (though the English poet Percy Bysshe Shelley knew better) and that Sophocles's *Trackers* was regarded even by one of the archaeologists who discovered it as "slight enough."

The surviving fragments of two satyr-dramas by Aeschylus provide strong support for the ancient view that he was the best writer of satyr-drama. They reveal the same mastery of dramatic form and space that is evident in his surviving tragedies, allied with a light and racy, but also crisp and incisive, poetic style that seems to encapsulate the essence of the genre.

Like Athenian tragedy, satyr-drama was written to be theatrically effective. A powerful scene like that beginning at line 92 in *Trackers*, where groups of satyrs hunt, lying doglike on the ground to look at the tracks and search for Apollo's cattle, then retreat in fear as they hear the terrifying new sound of the lyre from the cave, was designed for open-air performance before a vast, diverse audience. Thus, when reading a satyr-drama, making an effort to imagine the text in performance may elicit more meaning.

Michael Ewans

See also Ancient Greek Comedy; Aristophanes; Burlesque; Farce; Greek Visual Humor; Genres and Styles of Comedy; Masks; Menander; Monty Python; Obscenity; Political Humor; Satire; Scatology; Stereotypes; Subversive Humor; Travesty

Further Readings

Aeschylus. (1996). *Fishermen and ambassadors to the Isthmian games; fragments in Aeschylus: Suppliants and other dramas* (M. Ewans, Ed. & Trans.). London, UK: Dent.

Euripides. (1956). Cyclops (W. Arrowsmith, Trans.). In D. Grene & R. Lattimore (Eds.), *Euripides II: The Cyclops and Heracles, Iphigenia in Tauris, Helen.* Chicago, IL: University of Chicago Press.

Harrison, G. W. M. (Ed.). (2005). *Satyr drama: Tragedy at play.* Swansea, UK. Classical Press of Wales.

Seaford, R. (Ed.). (1984). *Euripides: Cyclops.* Oxford, UK: Oxford University Press.

Sophocles. (2000). Trackers. In M. Ewans (Ed.), *Three dramas of old age: Elektra, Philoktetes, Oidipous at Kolonos—wirh Trackers and other selected fragments.* London, UK: Dent.

Scatology

Scatology is a biological term for the study of excrement and excretion, but it is also used in folkloristic studies to refer to speech, rituals, narratives, pranks, and songs with or about feces, urine, excretion, and anally produced emissions such as flatulence. It is in this cultural sense that scatology commonly relates to humor. A scatological analysis typically interprets the symbolism and function of feces in these expressions by referring to social and psychological attitudes toward the material. Central to this analysis is the idea that excrement and excretion are taboo subjects related to the body, usually kept private and hence comparable to other risqué topics in humor such as sexuality. In humor studies, different theories have been proposed for what renders this serious, private matter the stuff of laughter and the various ways that perceptions of excrement and excretion fit into cultural systems and worldview.

An early universalistic perspective on scatology came from evolutionary anthropology in which changes in public rites related to feces were viewed as signs of progress through stages of savagery, barbarism, and civilization. John G. Bourke in *Scatalogic Rites of All Nations* (1891/1994) proposed that primitive cultures invested excretions of feces and urine with mystical properties because they externalized human substance. Theories of cultural evolution posit that modern customs involving feces are "survivals" of past beliefs that have lost their original religious meanings. Sigmund Freud, the father of psychoanalysis, commented that Bourke's work showed that excremental and sexual instincts are not distinct from each other. The pleasure and "narcissistic esteem" children derive from excretion in an anal stage of development (usually from age 18 months to 3 years) persist into normal adult lives, but society represses these feelings, forcing people to keep them secret and feel shame and disgust at feces. In psychoanalytic theory, a cognitive need arises to project conflicts about the enjoyment of excretion and one location for this projection is in humor.

Freud's theory connecting excretion to psychosexual development has been applied to various forms of scatological humor. For instance, scholars have analyzed (1) the ubiquity of fecal play among children, (2) the framing of jokes and cartoons with excretory themes as *dirty*, (3) the characterization of human organizing and hoarding as signs of constipatory "anal retention" subject to humorous comment, (4) humorous inscriptions on institutional bathroom walls, and (5) the symbolism of flatulence in humor related to the embarrassment or aggressiveness of fecal odor. Related to digital culture, Simon Bronner has interpreted humor about the similarity of "sitting at a computer" to the position of excretion on a toilet as a sign of subversive play of workers in office situations.

Particularly influential in these different queries have been the post-Freudian humor studies of folklorist Alan Dundes, who observed that not only are children proud of their defecations, but they also make use of them in asserting themselves against adults or authority figures. For example, Dundes interpreted a frequently collected joke told among Navy personnel concerning a fecal "kush" being thrown overboard (the punch line refers to the sound of a "kush" in the water) as a subversive act in defiance of strict, that is paternal, military discipline. Dundes also considered cross-cultural differences in attitudes toward the taboo of feces such as in his explanation of German humor about feces in a cultural personality preoccupied with cleanliness and order.

Bathroom graffiti, which Dundes labeled *latrinalia*, is a prime context for scatological humor. Dundes suggested a behavioral correlation of humorous inscriptions on bathroom stalls to fecal smearing that protests institutional control of natural urges. College students away from home, he contended, in the safe confines of the stall exhibit their repressed desires to play with feces. Some scholars have interpreted more social than projective functions in the creation of humorous "shithouse" poetry, and argued that the communications in women's bathrooms differ from those in men's.

Gershon Legman categorized jokes about dirtiness relating to buttocks, toilets, farting, babies' diapers, underwear, and anal sex under the heading of the sexualization of scatology. He took the controversial position that scatological jokes purposely shock and essentially harm the listener (a verbal equivalent of "pissing on" or "shitting on" the "butt of the joke") under the shallow pretext of recounting a fictional hygienic incident. He hypothesized that those listeners who laugh in answer to such an assault are those most affected by social repression. Challenges to this view have been made with alternative structural and sociological explanations that the humor of defecation arises out of the "appropriate incongruity" between the private behavior of excretion and the public nature of the joke.

Simon J. Bronner

See also Folklore; Graffiti; Xeroxlore

Further Readings

Allen, V. (2007). *On farting: Language and laughter in the Middle Ages*. New York, NY: Palgrave Macmillan.

Blank, T. J. (2010). Cheeky behavior: The meaning and function of "Fartlore" in childhood and adolescence. *Children's Folklore Review, 32*, 61–86.

Bourke, J. G. (1994). *The portable scatalog: Excerpts from scatalogic rites of all nations* (L. P. Kaplan, Ed.). New York, NY: William Morrow. (Original work published 1891)

Bronner, S. J. (2011). *Explaining traditions: Folk behavior in modern culture*. Lexington: University Press of Kentucky.

Bronner, S. J. (2012). *Campus traditions: Folklore from the old-time college to the modern mega-university*. Jackson: University Press of Mississippi.

Dawson, J. (1999). *Who cut the cheese? A cultural history of the fart*. Berkeley, CA: Ten Speed Press.

Dundes, A. (1989). *Life is like a chicken coop ladder: A study of German national character through folklore*. Detroit, MI: Wayne State University Press.

Dundes, A. (2007). *The meaning of folklore: The analytical essays of Alan Dundes* (S. J. Bronner, Ed.). Logan: Utah State University Press.

Dundes, A., & Pagter, C. R. (1978). *Work hard and you shall be rewarded: Urban folklore from the paperwork empire*. Bloomington: Indiana University Press.

Legman, G. (1968). *Rationale of the dirty joke: An analysis of sexual humor* (Second series). New York, NY: Breaking Point.

Mechling, J. (2001). *On my honor: Boy Scouts and the making of American youth*. Chicago, IL: University of Chicago Press.

Praeger, D. (2007). *Poop culture: How America is shaped by its grossest national product*. Los Angeles, CA: Feral House.

Schwank

Schwank is a German term, now also used internationally, which originally meant a practical joke. Presently it denotes a rather short humorous narrative, song, or play depicting a comical action. As opposed to the even shorter joke, it is more epic; and the point is not at the end but within the story. On occasions, there may be two or even three punch lines. There is, however, not always a strict borderline between schwank and joke. In the three volumes of *The Types of International Folktales*, schwanks are listed under the heading "Jokes and Anecdotes." The present entry analyzes structure and style as well as the historical development of schwank and gives a summary of its predominant themes and motifs.

There has been discussion as to whether schwank is a real genre or just a possibility within any genre of folk poetry. In fact, practically all types of folktales can be converted into schwanks by adding a humorous element. In reality, there are many mixed forms, such as schwank legends and schwank fairy tales. Disclaiming that schwank is a genre and does not have stable structural or stylistic criteria, however, disregards the creative qualities of comicality. These materialize in its subject matter rather than its literary form or composition. It is the comical action that is in the center of the genre. In addition, schwank presents its contents straight, disregarding formal principles that other genres have to take into account. And, like the joke, it neglects all taboos, which made it widely unprintable during Victorian times. Thus, schwank can be justly regarded as a genre in its own right.

Schwank in the oral and also in the older literary tradition proffers a simple, straightforward style. It outlines persons and actions with few and concise descriptions. This is also the reason why in the secondary literature there are fewer treatments concerning the structure of schwank as opposed to fairy tales, which have a much more complicated form. As in other genres, the schwank plot is divided into opening situation, crisis, and solution. The more modern literary tradition, however, tends to lengthen the subject matter by adding new elements or by elaborating the story. The characteristic situation of a schwank is a contest between two parties, one of which wins the fight. The winner need not be the good one in a moral sense. He may be just somebody who is cleverer and employs a more effective ruse, but nevertheless carries the sympathy of the listeners or readers. Moral standards are thus frequently disregarded. Ruses are the crux of the matter. Pure entertainment rather than propagation of ethic principles or other didactic intentions are the aim of the genre. Notwithstanding these facts, on occasion a moral may be found at the end of a text—or perhaps with a wink during a recitation—to justify, for instance, a grossly sexual tale as suitable for print or rendering.

Hermann Bausinger has analyzed the structure of schwank, based on older interpretations. According to Bausinger, there exist three types of action, similar to the course of a sport contest:

Type 1: *Ausgleichstyp Revanche* (equalization by revenge)—The loser of a first action takes revenge and this time gets the better of his opponent.

Type 2: *Ausgleichstyp Übermut* (equalization because of arrogance)—The winner of the first action gets into high spirits, becomes inattentive, and therefore loses.

Type 3: *Steigerungstyp Revanche* (intensification by revenge)—The loser of the first action is beaten again.

Examples of the above types describe more than one action. Less frequent types with a single action are called *shrink types*. The punch lines are not final points but merely mark a change or reinforcement of the former situation, after which the tale carries on. The comic elements focus on action rather than on language.

The protagonists of a schwank can be anyone, ranging from low-class people to those at the top of social hierarchies. They are not real individuals but mere stereotypes. Some groups of persons appear more frequently than others. One such group is clergymen. They can be cunning and get the better of their opponents. But the majority of schwanks depict them as victims—the reason being that the fall from an elevated position is especially effective. An unmasked adulterous Catholic priest provides a much better point than just a nondescript person violating ethical standards. This also holds true for other characters in top positions, for instance nobility, teachers, city managers, among others. Such plots may employ social criticism. Schwank outlines a cheerful counterworld.

Other characteristic schwank protagonists are fictive persons: jokers like the oriental Nasreddin Hodja or the German Till Eulenspiegel. The "dumb" tradition is represented by likewise fictive groups as the old Greek Abderites or the Wise Men of Gotham and their equivalents in other cultures. Conflicts are the basis for schwanks about men and women, landlords or farmers and their farm hands, and rulers and their subjects, to name only a few possible opponents. Tall tales as narratives or on postcards are also part of the schwank tradition, often ascribed to particular tellers like, for instance, the North American Paul Bunyan or the German Baron Münchhausen. As compared to other folktale genres, schwanks have a closer affinity to reality. Yet schwanks do not directly reflect reality but diversify it according to the rules of the genre or according to the intentions of the narrators. More so than any other genre except the joke, schwank is the place for direct sexual and fecal themes.

The history of schwank reaches far back into history, and it is assumed to be present in all cultures worldwide. Some see the genre related to archetypes as defined by the psychoanalyst Carl Gustav Jung. Well researched is the schwank history of oriental, (old) Egyptian, Sanskrit, Greek, Jewish, and European traditions. Printed sources in Europe exist since the Middle Ages, cumulated in collections like the British jestbooks, the French *fabliaux oder*, and the German *Schwankbücher*. Whether the printed texts have influenced the oral tradition or vice versa is an unsolved question. In the present day, schwanks are well represented among oral traditions, for instance as "contemporary legends," many of which are actually schwanks and not legends.

Rainer Wehse

See also Cross-Cultural Humor; Humor Group; Targets of Humor

Further Readings

Bausinger, H. (2007). Schwank. In R. W. Brednich (Ed.), *Enzyklopädie des Märchens. Handwörterbuch zur historischen und vergleichenden Erzählforschung* [Encyclopedia of fairy tales: Handbook of historical and comparative folk narrative research] (Vol. 12, pp. 318–332). Berlin, Germany: Walter de Gruyter.

Masterson, J. R. (1943). *Tall tales of Arkansas*. Boston, MA: Chapman & Grimes.

Wehse, R. (1979). *Schwanklied und Flugblatt in Grossbritannien* [Schwank songs on broadsides in Great Britain]. Frankfurt, Germany: Peter Lang.

Science, Science Fiction, and Humor

It is easy to categorize science as a quintessentially serious activity, but humor offers an unexpectedly useful framework for reflecting on the scientific method and discourse and for charting the role of science in wider society. Just as humor has become a fruitful and increasingly respectable field for both hard and social sciences, science and science fiction illustrate the nexus between humor, creativity, and discovery developed in Arthur Koestler's 1964 theory of bisociation. Far beyond the jokes used by teachers and researchers to lighten the presentation of dense information, humor offers a standpoint from which to scrutinize the assumptions of rationalist logic and to approach new problems and paradigms in creative ways. The annual Ig Nobel prize, awarded by the *Annals of Improbable Research* for "research that makes people laugh and then think," is widely respected by serious researchers, while pseudoscience, satire, and hoax have characterized the so-called postmodern science wars. Like the dystopian humor characteristic of many science-fiction narratives, these examples help chart the fault lines between scientific and humanistic thought.

Early Science and Science Fiction

While science fiction as a recognizable genre is often categorized as a 20th-century phenomenon, humorous writing on scientific themes dates back at least to Aristophanes's *Clouds* (produced 423 BCE), whose attack on the pretensions of Sophism includes hoisting the philosopher Socrates up in a basket to better observe the sun. A more obvious predecessor to modern science fiction conventions is Lucian's prose satire *The True History* (2nd century CE), which describes a voyage to the moon including an interplanetary war fought by armies of outlandish extraterrestrials. However, Lucian's parody of traveler's tales is more fantasy—a genre still frequently conflated with science fiction—than science proper. Space and time travel recur as themes in early modern works like Cyrano de Bergerac's *Other Worlds: The Comical History of the States and Empires of the Moon and Sun* (1657–1662) and Voltaire's *Micromégas* (1752): Both works use the still-common trope of external worlds to satirize the shortcomings of earthbound society. In contrast to the serious tone of much 20th-century science fiction, humor and satire represent a key ingredient of these earlier narratives.

Utopias feature prominently both in otherworldly tales and in the Renaissance humanist tradition that influenced modern scientific method, although utopian humor is often ambiguous. The methodology for scientific inquiry outlined in Francis Bacon's utopian *New Atlantis* (1624–1627) is lampooned in Jonathan Swift's *Gulliver's Travels* (1726), in the form of a flying island populated by scientists incapable of developing useful applications for their knowledge. While Swift's example exemplifies a long tradition of satire directed against science, it also suggests a link between humor understood as a social corrective, and its potential for reinforcing the skeptical, self-reflexive impulse of good scientific practice.

Humor and Science in Popular Culture

The developing relationship between science and popular culture is reflected in various strands of 19th- and early-20th-century science fiction. Often described as the earliest true science fiction story, Mary Shelley's *Frankenstein; or The Modern Prometheus* (1818) properly belongs to the gothic horror tradition, though a rich vein of grotesque humor is evident in later derivative works such as Mel Brooks and Gene Wilder's film *Young Frankenstein* (1974). The works of Jules Verne (1828–1905) revolve around futuristic extrapolations of contemporary technology, tending more toward adventure than humor. H. G. Wells's *The Time Machine* (1895), which sets the development of time travel against a backdrop of social degeneration, and *The War of the Worlds* (1898), a deadpan account of a Martian invasion, show a greater tendency toward imaginative, sometimes comically unrealistic, plotlines, as well as moralistic satire. *The War of the Worlds* has inspired several humorous derivatives, ranging from Orson Welles's famous radio broadcast (1938), which reportedly caused mass panic, to Jeff Wayne's highly camp musical adaptation (1978).

Influenced by the tradition of Wells as well as contemporary popular science writing, Alfred Jarry (1873–1907) postulated a "science of imaginary solutions," dubbed *pataphysics*, in his 1911 novel *Exploits and Opinions of Doctor Faustroll, Pataphysician*. Pataphysics is interested less in generalities than in exceptions and in contradictions between frames of reference, and Jarry's eccentric writing provides a unique reflection on the ferment of scientific thought at the turn of the 20th century. His key principle of "equivalence" curiously anticipates subsequent discoveries including relativity and quantum mechanics, as well as the debates between science and postmodern philosophy exemplified by the 1996 "Sokal hoax," in which editors of a cultural studies journal published an article by New York University physics professor Alan Sokal without realizing it was a parody. While pataphysics claims to be entirely serious, it arguably develops a logic resembling that of humor into a mode of (pseudo-)scientific enquiry.

Modern Science Fiction

The establishment of science fiction as a mainstream genre over the course of the 20th century—in novels and short stories, but also magazine serials, comics, and on radio, film, and television—has also given rise to a large number of subgenres. "Soft" science fiction, exploring the social consequences of new situations or worlds, is perhaps closest to the tradition of Swift and Voltaire; like works by these predecessors, its humor tends toward the dystopian, often revolving around the fate of individuals thwarted by the consequences of scientific progress. "Soft" authors noted for their humorous output include Philip K. Dick (1928–1982) and Ray Bradbury (1920–2012).

Despite the potential for humor latent in all fantastical situations, much if not most modern science fiction is essentially serious. From the 1940s onward, "comic" science fiction began to emerge as a distinct subgenre that frequently parodied the unrealistic conventions of the genre as a whole. Archetypal examples of this tradition include the "short" short stories of Fredric Brown (1906–1972), who uses humor to drive plotlines often only a page or two in length, and the prolific Robert Sheckley (1928–2005). The rise of epic-scale "space opera" and of film as a widespread medium for science fiction gave further impetus to this subgenre. The *Star Wars* and *Star Trek* franchises are parodied in Mel Brooks's film *Spaceballs* (1987) as well as numerous popular culture references. And in an amusing rejoinder to the recurring tropes of space travel, anthropocentrism, and planetary apocalypse, Douglas Adams's five-part "trilogy" *Hitchhiker's Guide to the Galaxy* (1979–1992) opens with destruction of the Earth in order to make way for an intergalactic bypass.

Will Noonan

See also Aristophanes; Bisociation; Comic Versus Tragic Worldviews; History of Humor: Early Modern Europe; History of Humor: Modern and Contemporary Europe; History of Humor: U.S. Modern and Contemporary; Hoax and Prank; Irony; Mock Epic; Parody; Pastiche; Postmodern Irony; Satire; Subversive Humor; Tall Tale; Urban Legends

Further Readings

Abrahams, M. (2002). *The Ig Nobel prizes: The annals of improbable research.* London, UK: Orion.

Adams, D. (2009). *Hitchhiker's guide to the galaxy: Part one in the trilogy of five.* London, UK: Pan.

Aristophanes. (1998). *Clouds.Wasps.Peace* (J. Henderson, Ed. & Trans.). Cambridge, MA: Harvard University Press.

Asimov, I., & Jeppson, J. O. (Eds.). (1982). *Laughing space: Funny science fiction* [Anthology]. Boston, MA: Houghton Mifflin.

Barron, N. (Ed.). (2004). *Anatomy of wonder: A critical guide to science fiction* (5th ed.). Westport, CT: Greenwood.

Bergerac, C. de. (1976). *Other worlds: The comical history of the states and empires of the moon and sun* (G. Strachan, Ed. & Trans.). London, UK: New English Library.

Garrott-Wejkswora, L. (2009). Comedic science fiction and fantasy. In R. A. Reid (Ed.), *Women in science fiction and fantasy* (Vol. 2., pp. 72–74). Westport, CT: Greenwood.

Hugill, A. (2012). *A useless guide to pataphysics.* Cambridge: MIT Press.

Jarry, A. (1996). *Exploits and opinions of Doctor Faustroll, pataphysician* (S. W. Taylor, Ed. & Trans.). Cambridge, MA: Exact Change.

Kimmel, D. (2007). A funny thing happened on the way to the future. *Internet Review of Science Fiction, 4*(3). Retrieved from http://www.irosf.com/q/zine/article/10369

Koestler, A. (1964). *The act of creation.* London, UK: Hutchinson.

Langford, D. (2005). Humor. In G. Westfahl (Ed.), *The Greenwood encyclopedia of science fiction and fantasy: Themes, works, and wonders* (pp. 401–404). Westport, CT: Greenwood.

Lucian of Samosata. (n.d.). *The true history.* Lucian of Samosata project. Retrieved February 20, 2013, from http://lucianofsamosata.info/TheTrueHistory.html

Swift, J. (2009). *Gulliver's travels and a modest proposal.* London, UK: Capuchin Classics. (Original work published 1726)

Voltaire. (2002). *Micromégas and other short fictions* (H. Mason, Ed., & T. Cuffe, Trans.). London, UK: Penguin.

Walsh, L. (2006). *Sins against science: The scientific media hoaxes of Poe, Twain, and others.* Albany: State University of New York Press.

Wells, H. G. (1895–1898/1999). *The time machine and the war of the worlds.* London, UK: Millennium.

Websites

Improbable Research, publisher of the magazine the *Annals of Improbable Research* and the organization behind the Ig Nobel Prizes: http://www.improbable.com

Screwball Comedy

See Movies

Script Opposition

See Linguistic Theories of Humor

Script-Based Semantic Theory of Humor

See Linguistic Theories of Humor

Second Language Acquisition

This entry brings together the topics of humor and second language acquisition, focusing mainly on issues concerning adult and adolescent language learners, as the situation of child language learners, who are still developing both humor and linguistic competence, is too complex to address here. The term *second language acquisition* can be understood as encompassing all additional language learning, rather than simply a second language. It includes language learning that is undertaken in a classroom, as well as that which takes place naturalistically, without instruction. Both the use and understanding of humor represent a formidable linguistic and cultural challenge to language learners, yet it is crucial that they meet this challenge, given the important role humor plays in human interaction. This entry begins with a discussion of two topics directly related to the acquisition of a second language, focusing first on whether language learning may be facilitated if taught via the mode of humorous communication, and second, on what knowledge a learner may need to acquire about second language humor and how this knowledge might be taught. Finally, because social interaction is an important factor in language development, issues relating to learner experiences using and understanding second language humor are discussed.

Language teachers have long incorporated humor into the classroom in the belief that it facilitates learning, if only by increasing student interest and motivation. Research to confirm this has been lacking; however, since the late 1990s, applied linguists began taking an interest in this topic, often examining it under the rubric of "language play," which frequently, although not always, entails humor. These scholars theorized that language play may be an important—perhaps even necessary—component of language acquisition, allowing learners to experiment with new voices and new ways of expressing themselves. Such experimentation is thought to destabilize the learner's system, preventing what is known as *fossilization*, or the cessation of change and development in the second language. In addition, they proposed that playing with and in a new language may work to draw learners' attention to form meaning relationships within the language being studied. Noticing the way that the language is used is also important for facilitating development. A body of empirical research investigating these propositions is growing, and with it, evidence that humor can facilitate second language acquisition is beginning to mount. However, the majority of the work so far has been qualitative and descriptive and has mainly served to outline the various functions that humor and language play may have for learners, rather than to provide evidence for learning. Still, a few studies have attempted to examine within a controlled, quantitative paradigm whether encountering a new language within a humorous context makes it more memorable. The consensus of these studies, thus far, is positive.

Although probably less common than pedagogy that incorporates humor for the purposes of language acquisition, some language instructors do attempt to teach students about the linguistic and cultural norms of humor use by native speakers of the language they are learning. Until recently, most of this work had to be undertaken based merely on the intuitions that teachers or textbook writers had regarding native uses of humor. This is far from ideal, as intuitions about language use are notoriously poor, yet it is only recently that textbook writers have begun relying on research reports of sociolinguistic behaviors in compiling textbooks. Another problem is the lack of such systematic, sociolinguistic research with respect to humor. While the forms and functions of humor in some languages, such as English and Japanese, are developing a substantial body of research from which course developers may draw, for many other languages such work is scant or nonexistent. However, teachers may remedy this by undertaking, along with their students, investigations of humor use in the language they are studying. Students might be asked, for instance, to observe interactions (either live or via various forms of media, including the Internet, film, books, and television) and analyze for themselves such things as how humor is contextualized, who uses what type of humor with whom, and how different types of humor are responded to. Studies of this type of instruction with regard to other linguistic behaviors like giving and responding to compliments show that it is effective in improving learners' awareness of and performance in these types of interactions. As of this writing, however, no such research exists concerning the effectiveness of a humor curriculum.

Humor can be particularly difficult for learners to navigate in social interaction. Reports from language learners who have had frustrating or even humiliating experiences with second language humor abound. Learners' attempts at humor are often corrected as errors, suggesting that their native speaker interlocutors do not expect them to be able to construct humor, and, in some cases, may even see their attempts as a type of linguistic infringement. Despite this, some research demonstrates that native speakers make accommodations for language learners with respect to humor, for instance by avoiding certain types of humor or by ignoring learner attempts at humor that might be seen as rude. Such accommodations, however, can also have the effect of marginalizing learners, by assuming they are unable to engage in this type of discourse. On the other hand, there are also reports of learners who enjoy playing with their new language and who feel liberated by their ability to use humor in it. In the classroom, student-initiated humor has generally been dismissed as off-task behavior by both teachers and scholars. Some research, however, suggests that humor can play an important role in helping learners negotiate the language classroom. Students have been shown to use humor to cope with difficult learning tasks, to challenge classroom norms, and to construct particular identities for themselves.

Nancy Bell

See also Cross-Cultural Humor; Development of Humor; Education, Humor in; Pedagogy; Translation

Further Readings

Bell, N. (2011). Humor scholarship and TESOL: Applying findings and establishing a research agenda. *TESOL Quarterly, 45*(1), 134–159.

Bell, N. (2012). Comparing playful and non-playful incidental attention to form. *Language Learning, 62*(1), 236–265.

Cook, G. (2000). *Language play, language learning.* Oxford, UK: Oxford University Press.

Davies, C. E. (2003). How English-learners joke with native speakers: An interactional sociolinguistic perspective on humor as collaborative discourse across cultures. *Journal of Pragmatics, 35*, 1361–1385.

Tocalli-Beller, A., & Swain, M. (2007). Riddles and puns in the ESL classroom: Adults talk to learn. In A. Mackey (Ed.), *Conversational interaction in second language acquisition: Empirical studies* (pp. 143–167). Oxford, UK: Oxford University Press.

Semantic Script Theory of Humor

See Linguistic Theories of Humor

Semantics

Semantics designates the study of meaning in various academic disciplines and for various purposes. This entry deals with linguistic semantics and its usage in verbal humor.

Linguistic Semantics

Semantics is one of the main subdisciplines of linguistics. Linguistic semantics, or semantics of natural language, is also one of the several distinct disciplines that carry this name; the others are parts of philosophy, mathematical logic, and semiotics. All the *semantics* differ from each other in all the components of a theory, namely in their purview, premises, body, goals, falsifiability, and justification and evaluation.

The purview of linguistic semantics includes all the meaningful elements of natural language, from the morpheme—a meaningful part of a word, such as prefixes, roots, suffices, and infixes—to the word, then the phrase, and finally the sentence. The meaning of the word, lexical semantics, and that of the sentence, compositional or sentential semantics, are the main responsibilities of the semantics of natural language.

The premises include the seemingly obvious association of every word in a language with one or more elements of reality (or their mental images), such as objects, events, attributes, or relations between or among those elements. In other words, the premise states that each word in a language has a meaning or several meanings, as in the case of *polysemy*, that is, words having several senses, as most words of most languages do. Clear indeed as this premise may be to lay persons who have to learn new words of their own or foreign languages by memorizing the pairing between the sound (or spelling) of the new word with its meaning(s), Austrian British philosopher Ludwig Wittgenstein (1953), however, and the whole British school of thought called "ordinary language philosophy" denied this premise, thus adding the urgency to making the premise explicit. This premise may be referred to as *essentialist*.

Another premise is *compositionality*. It assumes that, in the common case, a language unit, consisting of two or more smaller meaningful units, has a meaning that includes the component meanings. Simplistically, it is the sum of those meanings; in reality, it is a function depending on how these smaller units are arranged within a larger one. British American philosopher of language H. Paul Grice (1975), the founder of linguistic pragmatics, denied that it was the case, citing various contextual violations and exceptions. But those may occur only with a rule in place, and the compositional premise is that rule.

The third premise is so ingrained in the very core of human communication and, hence, language as its main tool, that it is hardly ever explicated. It may be referred to as the *shorthand* premise. Language underdetermines reality by stating a very small part of any situation and letting the hearers reconstruct the whole picture on the basis of their shared commonsense knowledge. This premise of constantly having to extend an explicit into a much larger implicit narrative is so "natural" to human users of language that numerous recall experiments of a few decades ago confirmed the virtual impossibility of recalling identically for several witnesses of a dialog a week later what had been actually said verbatim. Rather, the witnesses would recall various possible parts of the situation, and it was always the same situation. This "aura" around an explicitly stated sentence is the mysterious "context" that scholars bring up both to indicate the different interpretations of a sentence and the impossibility of full description. The ubiquity of shorthand has been brought home painfully in computational semantics because the computer is unable to expand a sentence referring to a situation into the whole picture. But much more important here is that the shorthand premise explains how the same sentence or even the whole text may evoke two different whole pictures that linguistic theories of humor call *scripts*.

The body of a semantic theory contains statements about multiple pairings of sounds and (sets of) meanings, in lexical semantics, and how they all mesh together in sentences, in compositional semantics. Various semantic theories chart this territory differently: Until 1963, there had been no theories of compositional semantics, just loose talk about the meaning of the sentence, assuming quite a few of undefined premises; the so-called formal semantics of the last couple of decades cannot reach most of lexical semantics—because it attempts to apply first-order predicate logic to everything in language that it can manage.

There are, in the body of semantic theory, some statements that are almost universally shared among various approaches. One such statement, in lexical semantics, postulates that the meaning of a word, once considered an elementary and indivisible unit, itself is an aggregate of semantic features, many of which recur within many lexical meanings. Thus, the meaning of the English word *man* in its nonsexist meaning that stands for "human," that is both men and women, can be analyzed as the combination of the features of physical object, animate, human, male, and adult. Not all features are created equal, so *human* implies physical object and animate.

The original dream of reducing all the lexical meanings to a handful of binary features was defeated by the fact that many specific lexical meanings require the introduction of a new feature, and they accumulate in numbers and lose their explanatory power. It is one thing for a feature to be applicable to a large class of meanings, dividing it in half, such as the male or female gender for the class of all animates, and it is totally different for the "never-married" feature that defines *bachelor*, the archaic *spinster* and the phrasal *old maid* and is not applicable to any other (hundreds of thousands) meanings. Contrary to the stereotype of their enforced and usually defeated chastity vows in jokes, *monk* and *nun* are semantically defined by their membership in cloistered religious communities, not by the never-married feature, especially since some of them might have been married before taking their vows.

In spite of the "lost dream" about the "handful" of features, they are still used in various semantic approaches. Recently, more and more scholars are coming to a realization that something very much like those features—and many more, but still within hundreds, that is, three to four orders of magnitude fewer than the meanings they should represent—can be organized to connect concepts in an ontology, a language-independent conceptual hierarchy, in terms of which all the senses of all lexical entries in any specific language can be defined. As shown in the next section, ontology-based semantics makes the early promise of the first full-fledged linguistic theory of humor a reality.

Another important statement in the body of semantic theory, this time in compositional semantics, is that the exact way the meanings of the words contributed to the meaning of the sentence in which they are used is defined by the syntactic structure of the sentence. It has always been known, taught, and learned that the sentence "The mother loves the daughter" and the sentence "The daughter loves the mother" have different meanings because the nouns trade the subject and object positions. Nevertheless, it had been not until the 1963 publication by Jerald J. Katz and Jerry A. Fodor—Massachusetts Institute of Technology (MIT) linguist and psychologist, respectively, and both early adherents of the MIT most prominent linguist Noam Chomsky's new paradigm in linguistic theory—of the first ever semantic theory that the syntactic foundation of semantics became explicit and obvious.

Starting with a syntactic tree of a sentence and proceeding bottom up, they demonstrated the various types of phrases, such as an adjective modifying a noun in a noun phrase, a verb taking in an appropriate object, and for each type of phrase, defined a rule of combining the lexical entries for the words. The rules ranged in simplicity from mere concatenation, that is, listing the lexical entries' components together to check whether an adjective sense is compatible with the noun sense or verb's with object's. Katz and Fodor were criticized for many flaws in their theory but not for using the syntactic tree as an input for calculating the meaning of the sentence in a well-defined syntax-dependent way.

The goals of semantic theory are, of course, to represent the meaning of each sentence the way a native speaker understands. For the falsifiability criterion, a sentence must be found that the theory cannot explain in a way that is compatible with human interpretation and cannot be corrected to do so. Justification and evaluation are provided by human raters or, in the case of computer implementation, by the results of an application. Evaluation can also be achieved by comparing the theory to its competitors, if any. An important application of linguistic semantics is to the field of humor research.

Semantics of Humor

Verbal humor cannot be perceived, let alone appreciated, without understanding the joke-carrying text. A text cannot be understood without knowing the meanings of the words in it and of the ways they are combined together. In other words, verbal humor is nearly impossible without the full mastery of the semantics of the language, that is, without utilizing the semantic competence that a native or near-native speaker must possess (much of which is actually universal). It is interesting to note a strand of research in computational humor that claims the ability to recognize jokes without understanding any text. It is indeed possible to do with a degree of precision that is not much higher than random, but, in any case, the features that the ingenious statistics of machine learning recognize are external to humor and rather similar to recognizing a play in a foreign language because each paragraph begins with a short string followed by a colon (whose cue it is), followed by a cue of often considerable length (the cue itself). The comparison is a bit on the harsh side but the degree of understanding the text is indeed commensurable.

It has been argued that humor competence is an add-on to that competence because language is used in humor differently than in ordinary, casual language in a number of ways. In casual language, the speaker tries, mostly unconsciously, to be unambiguous to avoid misunderstanding; in humor, ambiguity is often deliberate. In "serious" communication, the speaker is committed to the factual truth of what is said—not so in humor. In humor, surprisingly many jokes follow a few popular patterns, whereas non-humorous texts are less patterned.

One of the most popular patterns in humor is the pun. In the simplest form, the pun is formed by a word that has two different senses, and the joke is phrased in such a way as to send the hearers toward one sense and then abruptly switch them to a different sense in the punch line. In English, due to its spelling system, the switch may occur over words that are pronounced the same way but spelled differently. Christian Hempelmann's 2003 doctoral dissertation explored imperfect puns, where the deliberately confused words are close in pronunciation rather than being identical. Many humor consumers find puns too obvious and jokes that are based on them cheap:

They are often called the "groaners." Consider the following example:

> Did you hear about the guy whose whole *left* side was cut off?
> He's all right now.

Puns do switch the text from one situation to a different one: from left-right sides to being correct in the example above. This is pretty much universal in jokes, as per the dominant family of linguistic theories of humor. This is how humor takes full advantage of the shorthand usage of language that underdetermines reality.

Crafting a joke, one has to make sure that the first situation, or script, that the hearers conjure up as the whole picture is easily compatible with its text, and so when the punch line hits and switches the hearers to the alternative script, the compatibility remains. Thus, replacing "whole left side" with "left limbs" in the first sentence to make it less unrealistic will destroy the joke, making "all" incompatible with the first script.

The first full-fledged and fully defined theory of humor is semantic. The script-based semantic theory of humor (SSTH) postulated that the joke-potential nature of a text could be established in the course of normal semantic interpretation. It talked about joke potential rather than simply a joke in full recognition that whether a text will be perceived as a joke depends on a number of circumstances including the quality and especially timing as well as the readiness and willingness of the audience to treat this semantic material as funny, which is impossible in the case of taboos, prejudices, or mere unfamiliarity with the culture, professional domain, or the target personalities.

SSTH was scrupulously honest about the nature of its claim that a text has a joke potential if it is fully or partially compatible with two distinct and opposing scripts. It made the claim contingent on the availability of the full semantic interpretation for each text, and none was yet in place at the time. Nevertheless, most humor researchers were so impressed with the first complete theory of humor that they largely ignored the disclaimer, especially if they were not linguists, let alone semanticists. The main results were that, innocent of professional semantic analysis, humor scholars tended to metaphorize the essential notion of script to talk about the script of Emily Dickenson's poetry and the scripts of life (in both cases, the subject of the real-world dissertations successfully defended at the time). In fact, scripts were set up as just a simple sequence of events corresponding to entering a restaurant, morning routines, filling up a car, going to a store. The more complex an intended script, the harder it would be for the author or teller of a joke to guide the hearers through the reasonably easy task of reconstructing the intended whole picture. A complex whole picture would contain too many forks or choices—and quite simply too many events or sentences to go through. And it is known, if not really explored, that the amount of mental effort required of an audience should be just right: The users reject obvious puns as too easy, but most reject a sophisticated joke, such as

> What's the difference between the sparrow?
> No difference whatsoever: The two sides of the sparrow are perfectly identical, especially the left one.

Absurd jokes take some acculturation, but this one requires that the users perform a near-record number of transitions from one link to another, trying to get the joke. At a very coarse and simplistic level, first, they must overcome the surprise of the missing second item necessary for comparison with a sparrow in order to answer the question about any difference that the comparison may produce. Then, in a bold, unusual, and creative mental move, they must imagine cutting the sparrow in half vertically so as to acquire the two items from one. Then, an answer is attempted—yet, it is counterfactual: The two halves may be mirror reflections of each other, which means still nonidentical, especially not so in terms of the invisible internal organs the two halves contain. In principle, the joke could end there, with the opposition of the real script of a sparrow being a single item and the unreal one of making into two halves. But a secondary absurd joke is developed by reversing the identity statement that does require two items back into one by coining the ridiculous notion of "especially identical" for just one of the two halves. Most users refuse to work this hard, and the joke fails to elicit amusement.

The semantic resources and methodologies that were not available at the time SSTH emerged have been since developed, and there is enough explanatory power in semantics to represent, formalize, and even compute the entire line of reasoning in the previous paragraph. This makes the consecutive script-based guises of the linguistic theories of humor a reality rather than the promise it originally was.

As semantics expands in its explanatory and descriptive power, it covers the increasingly complex territory of inference and reasoning that quite a few semanticists, constrained by the limitations of the so-called formal semantics that imposes a limited purview on itself, have relegated to an amorphous notion of context and to the informal discipline of pragmatics. Ultimately, as the context is as completely formalized as necessary for representing and explaining the semantics of every joke, pragmatics may retreat more and more into the realm of individual distinctions, different senses of humor. Recent research outlines ways of eventually semanticalizing that as well.

Victor Raskin

See also Incongruity and Resolution; Jokes; Linguistic Theories of Humor; Maxim; Puns

Further Readings

Attardo, S. (1994). *Linguistic theories of humor*. Berlin, Germany: Mouton de Gruyter.

Chomsky, N. (1965). *Aspects of the theory of syntax*. Cambridge: MIT Press.

Grice, H. P. (1975). Logic and conversation. In P. Cole & J. L. Morgan (Eds.), *Syntax and semantics: Vol. 3. Speech acts* (pp. 41–58). New York, NY: Academic Press.

Hempelmann, C. F. (2003). *Paronomasic puns: Target recoverability towards automatic generation*. Doctoral dissertation. Retrieved from http://search.proquest.com/docview/305319467

Katz, J. J., & Fodor, J. A. (1963). The structure of a semantic theory. *Language, 39*(4), 170–210.

Nirenburg, S., & Raskin, V. (2004). *Ontological semantics*. Cambridge: MIT Press.

Raskin, V. (1985). *Semantic mechanisms of humor*. Dordrecht, Netherlands: D. Reidel.

Raskin, V., Hempelman, C. F., & Taylor, J. M. (2009). How to understand and assess a theory: The evolution of the SSTH into the GTVH and now into the OSTH. *Journal of Literary Theory, 3*(2), 285–312.

Strapparava, C., Stock, O., & Mihalcea, R. (2011). Computational humour. In P. Petta, C. Pelachaud, & R. Cowie (Eds.), *Emotion-oriented systems: The Humaine handbook, cognitive technologies* (Chapter 6.4). Berlin, Germany: Springer.

Wittgenstein, L. (1953). *Philosophical investigations*. Oxford, UK: Blackwell.

Senryū

Senryū and *Haiku* are related Japanese poetic genres. Although whimsy, even humor, were original elements of *Haiku*, by the last decades of the 20th century, *Haiku* had become well known outside Japan as a serious form of poetry that can also be written in English and other languages. Its genius is to capture, in a poem consisting of three lines of 5–7–5 syllables, a moment frozen in time. The classic and widely known *Haiku* poem is one by Matsuo Bashō (1644–1694; translations by Marguerite Wells unless otherwise stated):

Furu ike ya (5)	Ah, an old pond
Kawazu tobikomu (7)	A frog jumps in
Mizu no oto (5)	The sound of water

Senryū developed out of *Renga*, an ancient verse-capping game where players were given a verse and had to add another three lines to the original. In 1757, for the first time, the winning verses from a competition were printed in broadsheet form and the poems took off as an independent verse form, becoming wildly popular. Thus, the appearance of *Senryū* can be dated exactly; and although *Senryū* and *Haiku* have the same 5–7–5 verse structure and *Senryū* appeared 2½ centuries later than *Haiku*, *Senryū* clearly did not develop from *Haiku*. Rather, both developed from the same ancient *Renga* poetic tradition. This entry discusses the genre and give some examples from both the Edo period and the modern period.

From its inception, *Senryū* has been associated with competitions in which ordinary people could participate and record their perceptions of a perverse world. It is written with characters meaning *river willow,* and is named after Karai Senryū (1718–1790), who edited a competition anthology, *Yanagidaru* (A Barrel of Willow) that appeared regularly from 1765 until 1838, long after his death.

Senryū are often referred to as satirical (two of R. H. Blyth's well-known collected English translations of *Senryū* include "satirical" in their titles). But wry observations of the foibles of people or society, or even sarcasm or bitterness, do not by themselves constitute satire. Asō Jirō's book, *What Is Senryū?* (1955), which sets out the rules of the genre, begins, "There are people who say *senryū* is satire but that is not so." While it is possible to find satirical *Senryū*, in general they are humorous social comment. They are aphorisms that scan as poetry.

Edo Period *Senryū*

The first *Yanagidaru* anthology was published in Edo in 1765, about 8 years after the first *Senryū* broadsheet. The examples below are from Okada Hajime's *Senryū: Ehon Yanagidaru* (*Senryū: Yanagidaru* Picture Book), which accompanies its poems with reprints of woodblock prints by Yashima Gotake from the school of the great woodblock artist Hokusai (1760–1849).

Omoshiroku	Amusingly
Kasa o toraruru	Robbed of his umbrella
Tsumuji kaze	In a whirlwind (Okada: 76)

Since umbrellas came late to Europe, this poem may predate a theme now universal in farce. Here, the desperate clutching and clinging of the umbrella owner is left to the imagination.

Hayarikaze	The flu's going round
Mitsui no mise ni	In the Mitsui shop
Shō hantoshi	Nearly half a year (Okada: 80)

Even at this early point in its history, the Mitsui kimono shop (owned by the later Mitsui *zaibatsu* family, and now the huge Mitsukoshi Department Store) has so many staff living in its dormitory that if one apprentice catches the flu, someone will be coughing for nearly 6 months afterward.

Nyōbō o	A bloke who fears
Kowagaru yatsu wa	His wife
Kane ga deki	Makes money (Okada: 164)

Why? Because he doesn't spend it on women, drink, or gambling and doesn't dare waste it in any other way either.

Some poems extracted fun from the Kabuki theater:

Gakuyaban	The prop man
Iwa o mushitte	Peels a rock
Hana o kami	To blow his nose (Okada: 274)

The on-stage rock is made of a bamboo frame with paper pasted over it: handy in need.

Edo no uma	The horse from Edo
Inaka shibai de	In the country play
Hito to nari	Turns into a human (Okada: 276)

A country actor appears on the city stage as a horse, and comes home to stardom, playing a human being.

Ikigawari	Coming to life
Shinigawari	Coming to death
Heta yakusha	A bad actor (Okada: 276)

Killed in a previous scene, the hack actor is not a specialist but doubles his roles and so comes back to life to fight in a later scene.

There is also social protest. One poem notes that in a filthy slum there is one white wall—naturally it is the pawnbroker's, who prospers on the poverty around him.

Gomigomi no	In the midst of the garbage
Naka no shirakabe	The white wall
Shichiya nari	Is the pawnbroker's (Okada: 30)

An early *Senryū* even gives humorous voice to a wry comment that is, however, no plea for gender equity or "women's liberation":

Nobori ni mo	Even on the banner
Shita ni natteru	The lower one
Haha no mon	Is the mother's crest (Okada: 30)

On the banner beside the typical Japanese carp streamers that fly over the house for Boys' Day, the family crests are displayed: Of course, the mother's crest is below the father's crest.

Bawdy *Senryū*

From time immemorial, bawdy humor has been part of Japanese performance genres, including dance. When in the 18th-century *Senryū* found a place as comment written in elegant calligraphy on woodblock printed *Ukiyoe* ("pictures of the floating world" that lay outside society and included the theater), some of these were also erotic. For example, in *Fūryū jūniki no eiga* (Manners in the Blossoming of Flowers in the Twelve Seasons) by Isoda Koryūsai (fl. 1764–1784), a husband and wife are pictured engaging in anal intercourse. The poem that graces this picture evokes the man's fantasy of being a fisherman, triumphant over his catch. The poem reads (Kuriyama and Fister [Trans]: 15)

Hito ami ni	Captured by
Sukui agete ya	A single swoop of the net:
Kurage tori	Trawling for jellyfish

The movement of penetration is envisioned here as the swoop of the fisherman's net, targeting the softness of a jellyfish (a delicacy in Japanese cuisine). While "jellyfish" refers to the woman's buttocks, it is written with the characters for "sea" and "moon," thus adding another erotic seascape reference. Meanwhile the word "net" evokes both fishing and the mosquito net that surrounds the marital bedding. Here verbal humor allies itself with visual art to achieve an elegantly comic effect about what in other cultures might be "unmentionable."

Twentieth-Century *Senryū*

By the end of the Pacific War, the whole Japanese nation was living on two thirds of the calories needed to support body weight, and strange foods were appearing:

Resutoran	Restaurants
Hen na namae no	Are making dishes
Meshi ga deki	With strange names
	(Takasaki: 14)

Senryū also noted that a lot of official orders were being issued:

Mimi ni me ni	My ears and eyes
Sekkyō ōku	With so many sermons
Tsukaretari	Are tired (Takasaki: 142)

And the war dead were deified: Was the next lady one saw yet another war widow, her husband now a god?

Ano kata mo	I turn
Kami no tsuma ka to	Is that lady
Furikaeri	Another wife of a god?
	(Takasaki: 218)

On March 20, 1995, the Aum Shinrikyō cult made its sarin gas attacks on five Tokyo subway trains, killing 13 people, injuring 54, and affecting perhaps thousands more. Some of the *Senryū* written in response to this homegrown terrorism and published in two major newspapers were collected by Richard A. Gardner in a 2002 article for *Asian Folklore Studies.* The public shock was so great that open season for satire against Aum might have been expected, and indeed, as Gardner's selection shows, satire did appear:

Meisō no	In his meditations
Naka ni nakatta	He did not see
Taiho geki	The arrest drama (Gardner: 57)

Terebi wa	The TV
Shaberisugi. Keisatsu	Talks too much. The police
Damarisugi	Don't talk enough
	(Gardner: 54)

Ichi nimen	Page one and two,
Ōmu sanmen	Aum; page three
Sumi sōri	In a corner, the Prime Minister
	(Gardner [Trans]: 50)

Ichioku ga	There was a time
Sennō sareta	When they brainwashed
Toki mo ari	One hundred million
	(Gardner: 51)

Brainwashing was one of the techniques that Aum used and *ichioku* (a hundred million) is an epithet meaning the whole Japanese population.

Overwhelmingly, however, the jokes were rueful reflections on how people's behavior changed as a result:

Chikatetsu ni	Summoning courage
Yūki o dashite	I will try
Notte miru	Taking the subway
	(Gardner: 48)

Chikatetsu no	Subway stairs:
Kaidan kaketara	Rush up them
Mina tsurare	And everyone follows
	(Gardner: 45)

Chikatetsu de	A phone call comes:
Buji ni tsuita	Arrived safely
Denwa kuru	On the subway (Gardner: 47)

The attacks came just before cherry blossom season. Cherry blossoms are the ancient Buddhist symbol of the evanescence of life, and also the symbol of the warrior falling in battle, so in the following *Senryū*, the mention of flowers blooming and falling is a many-layered allusion, quite apart from the reflection that life goes on.

Konna toshi	Even in a year like this
Demo hana wa saki	Cherries bloom
Hana wa chiru	Cherries fall (Gardner: 52)

One can read *Senryū* merely for pleasure in their humor; one can also see them as a record of social mores and comment down the ages, pithily and vividly conveying insight into Japanese culture and history as experienced by ordinary people.

Marguerite Wells

See also Aphorism; Genres and Styles of Comedy; History of Humor: Modern Japan; History of Humor: Premodern Japan; Irony; Poetry; Puns; Satire; *Share*; Verbal Humor

Further Readings

Asō Jirō. (1955). *Senryū to wa nani ka: Senryū no tsukurikata to ajiwaikata* [What is *senryū*? How to make and appreciate *senryū*]. Tokyo, Japan: Shibundō, Gakusei Kyōyō Shinsho.

Blyth, R. H. (1949). *Senryu: Japanese satirical verses.* Tokyo, Japan: Hokuseido Press.

Blyth, R. H. (1960). *Japanese life and character in Senryu.* Tokyo, Japan: Hokuseido Press.

Blyth, R. H. (1960). *Oriental humour.* Tokyo, Japan: Hokuseido Press.

Blyth, R. H. (1961). *Edo satirical verse anthologies.* Tokyo, Japan: Hokuseido Press.

Gardner, R. A. (2002). The blessing of living in a country where there are *Senryū!*: Humor in the response to Aum Shinrikyō. *Asian Folklore Studies, 61*(1), 35–75.

Horton, H. M. (2001). Laughs to banish sleep: Selections from Seisuishō (1623) by Anrakuan Sakuden. In J. Solt (Ed.), *An episodic Festschrift for Howard Hibbett* (Vol. 6). Hollywood, CA: Highmoonoon.

Kobayashi, M. (2006). *Senryū*: Japan's short comic poetry. In J. Milner Davis (Ed.), *Understanding humor in Japan* (pp. 153–177). Detroit, MI: Wayne State University Press.

Isoda Koryūsai. (2004). *Fūryū jūniki no eiga* [Manners in the blossoming of flowers in the twelve seasons]. In Hayakawa Kita (Ed.), Kuriyama, & P. Fister (Trans.). *Nichibunken shozō: Kinse enbon shiryō shūsei III* (Vol. 1, Isoda Koryūsai). Kyoto, Japan: Kokusai Nihon Bunka Kenkyū Sentaa.

Okada Hajime. (1969). *Senryū: Ehon Yanagidaru* [*Senryū* picture book: A barrel of *Senryū*]. Tokyo, Japan: Hōga Shoten.

Rabson, S. (Trans.). (2003). Edo Senryū on waka and women. In J. Solt (Ed.), *An episodic Festschrift for Howard Hibbett* (Vol. 12). Hollywood, CA: Highmoonoon.

Solt, J. (2000–2010). *An episodic Festschrift for Howard Hibbett* (26 vols.). Hollywood, CA: Highmoonoon.

Takasaki Ryūji. (1991). *Senryū ni miru senjika no sesō: Kyōkasho ni kakarenakatta sensō II* [Signs of the times—the war and aftermath as seen in *senryū*: The war not recorded in the textbooks, Part II]. Tokyo, Japan: Nashi no Ki Sha.

Ueda, M. (1999). *Light verse from the floating world: An anthology of premodern Japanese Senryu.* New York, NY: Columbia University Press.

Sense of Humor, Components of

Sense of humor is a personality concept that is used to describe, predict, and eventually explain humor-related differences among people. Individuals may be high or low in sense of humor and we assume some stability of this trait. Likewise, it has all the other qualities of personality traits, such as being a hypothetical construct (i.e., not directly observable but inferred via indicators), consisting of individual differences (rather than being of a dichotomous nature), and usually being assessed via psychometrically sound instruments. There are at least three variants of sense of humor in the literature, namely (1) as an everyday expression or folk concept, (2) a scientific concept of narrow nature, or (3) a scientific concept of a broader scope. Importantly, as discussed in this entry, these variants differ in what is subsumed under them.

Core Ingredients

The expression "sense of humor" as it is used in quotidian conversations is typically a very positive one and it represents a socially desirable personal asset. Its meaning was shaped by the rise of humanism and it acquired additional connotations further on. By the end of the 17th century, people became weary of put-down witticisms and it was argued that people should not be laughed at because of peculiarities since they were not responsible for them. As Wolfgang Schmidt-Hidding (1963) explains, at first *good humor*, later *humor*, was the term for humanitarian, tolerant, and benevolent forms of laughter. At this time *good humor* also came to mean the sovereign attitude of exposing oneself to adversity, such as a "test of ridicule." This may have been the origin of the notion of "sense of humor," although this expression was not yet in use. While sense of humor was a positive trait from then on, it experienced further shifts into a philosophical attitude, a worldview, or a defense mechanism. This is a meaning that still prevails in everyday conversations but it lacks precision. Also, until about 1980, there were no attempts to measure it scientifically; that is, it remained a prescientific folk-concept. Willibald Ruch proposed to measure two components of humor aiming at the good, namely benevolent and corrective humor (as measured by a short instrument—the BENCOR).

Various authors in this tradition such as Franz-Josef Hehl, Ruch, and Philipp Lersch proposed core ingredients of the sense of humor. These are typically short formulae that should explain the nature of sense of humor. In this category, there are ingredients like not taking oneself too seriously, being able to laugh at oneself, being able to distance from one's problems, to see the light side of things, to display a smiling attitude toward life and its imperfections, having an understanding of the incongruities of existence, or a cheerful composed frame of mind amidst the adversities and insufficiencies of life. It is not known whether these identified core ingredients are homogeneous (i.e., are indicative of the same trait) and which of these might be more central than others, as there is no research utilizing these ingredients and subjecting them to factor analysis. These definitions clearly entail a virtuous view of humor and see it as a highly developed human trait. At the same time, they are vague and more metaphorical, which might impair the likelihood of being measured successfully. It is apparent, however, that sense of humor is carefully distinguished from sense of fun, sense of wit, sense of ridicule, sense of comic, or others. In other words, the understanding of *humor* is in opposition to the understanding of wit, satire, ridicule, and not an umbrella term for all kinds of the funny.

Components of the Sense of Humor as Unitary Concept

While none of the contemporary approaches to sense of humor emphasize the virtuous or humanitarian aspect of humor, several authors broke down sense of humor into components, albeit in different ways. In 1974, Sven Svebak postulated that the sense of humor has three components, namely what he called metamessage sensitivity, personal liking of humor, and emotional expressiveness. While these components are ordered sequentially to reflect the sequence of taking up a humorous message, liking it, and expressing amusement and laughter, Paul McGhee sees the components structurally different and ordered in terms of difficulty. In his multifaceted concept of sense of humor, six other facets represent more genuine humor skills and humor behavior and relate to individual differences in the fields of enjoyment of humor, laughter, verbal humor, finding humor in everyday life, laughing at yourself, and humor under stress. The homogeneity of these facets has been supported empirically in the findings of Willibald Ruch and Amy Carrell. The concept by McGhee also has a further structural element, namely the bipolar dimension of playfulness versus seriousness. For McGhee, humor is a form of play, namely play with ideas. Without a playful frame of mind, one may see the same event as interesting, puzzling, annoying, frightening, but not as funny. While some people might be good at spotting the incongruities, absurdities, and ironies of life, only the mentally playful will find humor in them while those with a serious attitude or frame of mind will not treat them humorously. Therefore, playfulness is seen as the foundation of the sense of humor.

Here, sense of humor is still meant to be something beneficial and positive, but it does not have the virtuous connotation. These conceptualizations of humor see it as a good antidote to stress, as McGhee does, or as a variable describing individual differences in the enjoyment of humor as inherent in life like Svebak does. None of these includes critical forms of humor, such as satire, sarcasm, or ridicule. Thus, these components relate to humor as a positive personality trait.

Components of the Sense of Humor as a Comprehensive Multidimensional Trait

In the prior treatments of sense of humor, the positive or even virtuous elements of humor were emphasized and kept strictly separate from more destructive forms. However, as *humor* is contemporarily used as an umbrella term for everything that is funny (including "aggressive" humor), it has also been suggested that sense of humor needs to strip off its exclusively positive connotations. If one were to use *sense of humor* as an umbrella term for all dispositions to humor behavior and experience, it must also incorporate dispositions to mockery, ridicule, or scatological humor. In this approach, *sense of humor* is a neutral descriptive term referring to all components of humor, be they negative, neutral, or positive. Clearly, elements like the degree to which individuals comprehend and appreciate jokes, cartoons, and other humorous materials, their memory for jokes or funny events, the amount they laugh and are easily amused, their ability to create humorous comments or perceptions, the tendency to tell funny stories and amuse other people, the degree to which people actively seek out sources that make them laugh, and their tendency to use humor as a coping mechanism are not subsumed under sense of humor in the narrow sense, as they are either neutral or slightly positive (but not virtuous). Likewise, one can add the tendency to make funny remarks on people's apparent weaknesses or the habit of spoiling fun by not telling jokes appropriately as components of sense of humor in a broader sense (i.e., one not restricted to the good). Such approaches are occasionally labeled "styles of humor" to avoid a conflict with the positive connotation of sense of humor.

Alternatively, one could call them trait humor as a multidimensional concept. It has been argued that if one wants to use *humor* as a neutral umbrella term for all types of funny then *sense of humor* should also be treated as a neutral term. Components of humor (more precisely, everyday humorous conduct) of a less positive meaning are socially cold humor, boorish humor, inept humor, mean-spirited humor, or earthy humor as identified by Kenneth Craik, Martin Lampert, and Arvalea Nelson (1996). In this domain, dimensions of humor appreciation and humor creation are also added. A comprehensive approach to this third understanding of humor does not yet exist and it will most likely be based on a representative sampling of humor behaviors, thoughts, and feelings subjected to factor analysis to derive descriptive components.

Conclusion

There is disagreement on how to define sense of humor. It is not even entirely clear how and when one should use this expression. Nevertheless, there have been speculations what the core of sense of humor is, what components are best used to break the scientific concept down to measurable elements, and even to use it as a broad term like *intelligence* or *emotion* to incorporate negative, neutral, and positive components. Like for any personality trait, it is important to define the substance of sense of humor via facets or components. It remains one of the foremost goals of humor research to fill this gap in the literature. As the virtuousness aspect of humor received attention again recently, one will need to see whether the empirical research findings with the BENCOR supports the utility (i.e., incremental validity) of this component of sense of humor.

Willibald Ruch

See also Cheerfulness, Seriousness, and Humor; Factor Analysis of Humor Items; Factor Analysis of Humor Scales; Humor Styles; Humor Styles Measurement; Test Measurements of Humor

Further Readings

Craik, K. H., Lampert, M. D., & Nelson, A. J. (1996). Sense of humor and styles of everyday humorous conduct. *HUMOR: International Journal of Humor Research, 9*, 273–302. doi: 10.1515/humr.1996.9.3-4.273

Hehl, F.-J., & Ruch, W. (1985). The location of sense of humor within comprehensive personality spaces: An exploratory study. *Personality and Individual Differences, 6*(6), 703–715. doi: 10.1016/0191-8869(85)90081-9

Lersch, P. (1962). *Aufbau der Person* [Structure of personality]. München, Germany: Barth.

McGhee, P. E. (1999). *Health, healing, and the amuse system: Humor as survival training*. Dubuque, IA: Kendall/Hunt.

Ruch, W. (1996). Measurement approaches to the sense of humor: Introduction and overview. *HUMOR: International Journal of Humor Research, 9*, 239–250. doi: 10.1515/humr.1996.9.3-4.239

Ruch, W. (Ed.). (1998). *The sense of humor: Explorations of a personality characteristic*. Berlin, Germany: Mouton de Gruyter.

Ruch, W. (2008). The psychology of humor. In V. Raskin (Ed.), *A primer of humor* (pp. 17–100). Berlin, Germany: Mouton de Gruyter.

Ruch, W. (2013, July 3). *Humor in transgressions: Benevolent and corrective humor.* Keynote speech presented at the 25th International Society for Humor Studies Conference, Williamsburg, VA.

Ruch, W., & Carrell, A. (1998). Trait cheerfulness and the sense of humor. *Personality and Individual Differences, 24*, 551–558. doi: 10.1016/S0191-8869(97)00221-3

Schmidt-Hidding, W. (1963). *Europäische Schlüsselwörter. Band I: Humor und Witz* [European key terms. Volume I: Humor and wit]. Munich, Germany: Huber.

Svebak, S. (1974). Revised questionnaire on the sense of humor. *Scandinavian Journal of Psychology, 15*, 328–331. doi: 10.1111/j.1467-9450.1974.tb00597.x

Sexuality

The connections between sexuality and humor are myriad and can be interpreted in several ways. This entry focuses on two of the most common relationships between humor and sexuality: the use and appreciation of sexual humor and the role humor plays in increasing one's sexual desirability as a mate. The entry also discusses individual and sex differences as they pertain to both topics.

Sexual Humor

Sexual humor is a type of humor intended to elicit laughter through references to sex or sexual activities. Sexual humor can come in many forms, such as jokes, cartoons, or physical humor, and it is not meant to increase the sexual libido of the appreciator or the producer of humor. The sexual nature of the humor can be either explicit or implied. For example, the following joke does not include any direct reference to sex, but the sexual nature of the joke is clear:

> "Is the doctor at home?" the patient asked in his bronchial whisper.
> "No," the doctor's young and pretty wife whispered in reply. "Come right in."

There are many individual differences in the use and enjoyment of sexual humor. Some people find such humor offensive and not funny, while others enjoy telling and hearing sexual jokes. Studies have found that sexual humor is appreciated more by people who exhibit a high sexual drive, have more positive attitudes toward sexuality, have greater sexual experiences, and generally enjoy sex more.

When comparing men and women, men tend to create and enjoy sexual humor more than women, especially when it is explicit. Many sexual jokes and cartoons target women and depict them in a disparaging way; thus, it is not surprising that women may not like them. When the target of the humor is men, or the humor is not sexist, women seem to enjoy sexual humor as much as men. Also, women in all-female groups are more likely to tell sexual jokes or share humorous sexual anecdotes, compared to mixed groups, and their level of enjoyment of such humor is equal to men's.

Enhancing Desirability as a Mate With Humor

People with a good sense of humor are considered to have many other desired attributes, such as being friendly and social, intelligent, warm, and confident. It is not surprising, then, that sense of humor is considered a valuable and attractive trait for a mate. In fact, a good sense of humor consistently ranks as one of the most desirable traits when looking for a mate and is especially valued by women (men usually value physical attractiveness the most). For example, studies conducted on dating sites show that women seek a mate with a sense of humor twice as much as men do, and men who use humor in their ads are more likely to find a date. However, men tend to exaggerate their ability to produce high-quality humor. Most men think of themselves as having above average humor production ability, a statistical impossibility.

Certain types of humor seem to be more attractive than others. For example, self-deprecating humor is highly valued, especially when it comes from a high-status individual, maybe because it makes that person more approachable and vulnerable. Also, less aggressive and less sexual types of humor are much more appreciated by women, especially in the early stages of courtship. These types of humor are often seen as being offensive and deter women from continuing to pursue a relationship. Thus, using sense of humor to attract mates should be done intelligently, which includes the ability to tell appropriate jokes to the right person and at the right time.

It has been suggested that the different ways men and women use and appreciate humor during the mating game result from different evolutionary life histories. Females in most mammalian species bear the heavier costs of reproduction, such as pregnancy and child rearing, while having shorter reproduction spans. Thus, females must be more careful when choosing a mate because the consequences of selecting the wrong mate could be dire. As a result, females tend to be choosier when selecting mates, while males fight with other males for female attention, trying to out-compete them and signal their mate quality. If humor is a good signal for mate quality, then we should expect men to try to impress women with their sense of humor, while women should be good evaluators of humor.

Recent studies find support for the different ways men and women process, produce, and appreciate humor in light of these evolutionary differences. On average, men score higher than women on humor creativity tasks, and those who have a good sense of humor enjoy better mating success—start having sex earlier, have a higher number of sexual partners, and have more sex in general—compared to the less funny individuals. Also, when men and women indicate that they are interested in a mate with a sense of humor, they often mean different things. Women want someone that will make them laugh, while men are interested in someone that will laugh at their humor. Indeed, studies show that women tend to laugh more and especially in response to male speakers or when men are around.

Gil Greengross

See also Appreciation of Humor; Evolutionary Explanations of Humor; Gender and Humor, Psychological Aspects of; Gender Roles in Humor; Marriage and Couples

Further Readings

Bressler, E., & Balshine, S. (2006). The influence of humor on desirability. *Evolution and Human Behavior, 27,* 29–39.

Greengross, G., & Miller, G. F. (2011). Humor ability reveals intelligence, predicts mating success, and is higher in males. *Intelligence, 39*, 188–192.

Lampert, M. D., & Ervin-Tripp, S. M. (1998). Exploring paradigms: The study of gender and sense of humor near the end of the 20th century. In W. Ruch (Ed.), *The sense of humor: Explorations of a personality characteristic* (pp. 231–270). Berlin, Germany: Walter de Gruyter.

Ruch, W., & Hehl, F. (1988). Attitudes to sex, sexual behaviour and enjoyment of humour. *Personality and Individual Differences*, 9(6), 983–994.

Shakespearean Comedy

To speak of "Shakespearean comedy" is to speak of more than just the 12 plays of William Shakespeare that resolve temporary problems more or less happily into social, family, or marital union, as comedy usually does. In any account of Shakespearean comedy, it is also important to consider the humorous elements throughout his work, for example in the histories of *Henry IV* (Parts I and II, 1596–1598) and *Henry V* (1599) and in his most famous tragedies, *Hamlet* (1600), *Othello* (1603), *Lear* (1605), and *Macbeth* (1606), where humorous characters and situations provide comic relief from the intense tragic action unfolding all around. Alongside the 12 well-recognized comedies, Shakespeare's first editors, John Heminges and Henry Condell, who put together the First Folio (1623), also included in their list of his comedies two late plays, *The Winter's Tale* (1609) and *The Tempest* (1610), which are commonly regarded as "romances," along with two others, *Pericles* (1607) and *Cymbeline* (1610). The fact that Heminges and Condell included those two romances indicates just how much Shakespeare's handling of romance draws on the convention of comedy that the plot denouement should dissolve a play's conflicts and tensions. Such categorizing also indicates just how much that particular plot arrangement was thought to define comedy. "Comedy" in Shakespeare's cultural world, which was so greatly influenced by Aristotle, was, once again, very much defined by both plot construction and humor.

Shakespeare's comic plots and preferred forms of humor draw especially on the Roman writers of comedy, Plautus and Terrence, and the Italian tradition of *commedia dell'arte* but develop a distinct style of their own that goes well beyond straight farce and verbal wit. Particularly important sources are Plautus's plays *Mostellaria, Menaechmi,* and, to a lesser extent, *Amphitruo,* and *Rudens*. Shakespeare takes from such plays and the *commedia dell'arte* the comic elements of trickery, disguise, confusion, master-slave tension, checked desire, tokens such as rings that bring recognition and plot resolution, and stereotypical comic characters such as the *senex* (old man) who locks up his daughter to prevent young men from getting at her and the *miles gloriosus* (braggart soldier) whose unbounded pride usually ends with a good comeuppance. Some of these are the elements of pure farce. Shakespeare takes them and gives them a decidedly romantic cast, both in the sense that he embeds characters with farcical roots in plots driven by the quest for marital consummation of romantic love and also in the sense that his comic plots often tilt toward the genre of romance in their semitragic endings and supernatural interventions. For that reason, Shakespearean comedy often feels quite distinct from the highly satirical cast of the comedies of his contemporary Ben Jonson (1572–1637). The romantic shape of Shakespearean comedy also involves a significant role for the "witty woman," who, in many plays, is instrumental in bringing about the necessary resolution to the plot's complications.

Critics have also pointed out that the materiality of the Roman stage had an influence on its comedy and thus on the comedy of Shakespeare and his contemporaries. For example, the doors onto the *proscaenium* (stage) were often used to represent oppositions between competing moralities, families, or urban spaces. Shakespeare's oppositions of place, such as Athens and the wood in *A Midsummer Night's Dream*—perhaps draw on this aspect of Roman comedy.

Shakespearean comedy mixes a variety of high and low comic elements, many of which had roots in Roman comedy and its Greek forebears, Aristophanes and Menander. Low comedy includes such elements as farce, the stage jig, and clownish fools; high comedy elements include the learned imitation of the classics, controlled verbal displays of wit, and explorations of upper class manners. Low comedy provides comic relief in Shakespeare's tragedies and some of the key elements of comedies such as *A Midsummer Night's Dream* and *The Merry Wives of Windsor.* Yet, while Shakespeare's comedies never quite aim for the flavor of French High Comedy or Italian *commedia erudita,* plays like *Love's Labour's Lost* and *Much Ado About Nothing* exemplify the comedy of manners and verbal wit. In this respect, Shakespeare's middle ground between high and low forms of comedy has more similarities with the "mixed genre" *comedias de ingenio* and *comedias de ruido* of Spanish Golden Age drama.

Adapting Roman Models for Elizabethan Tastes

The first four comedies Shakespeare wrote at the beginning of his more than 20-year career were *The Two Gentlemen of Verona, The Taming of the Shrew, The Comedy of Errors,* and *Love's Labour's Lost* (ca. 1590–1594). Each of them may be characterized as experiments in adapting Roman models for Elizabethan tastes and interests. Each of those four plays experiments with characteristics that will become more common in later Shakespearean comedy. *The Two Gentlemen of Verona* is perhaps the earliest instance of Shakespeare's interest in romantic comedy, incorporating multiple pairings and stereotypical names for the play's "heroes"—Valentine and Proteus (Latin, "changer"). Such names epitomize the play's interest in both the courtly love conventions of Petrarchan discourse and the volatility of erotic desire, respectively. The "foolishness" of love drives much of the humor of Proteus and Valentine's servants, Lance and Speed. At its height, the play's tension revolves around the faithful lover Valentine forgiving his friend Proteus for betrayal and an attempted rape of the former's beloved, Silvia, by offering Silvia to him! For such reasons critics have often felt that both *Two Gentlemen* and *The Taming of the Shrew* were Shakespearean warm-ups. *Taming* picks up the names and characters of the servants Tranio and Grumio out of Plautus's *Mostellaria,* as well as the farce stereotypes of the *senex* and shrew. Shakespeare's characters Baptista and his daughter Kate develop those stereotypes. *Taming* also develops the farce elements of emotionally unselfconscious characters and preposterous slapstick violence, especially toward Kate who is subdued by Petruccio, a suitor. Kate, the young marriageable "shrew," is never beaten but Petruccio's violation of her well-being and agency is so extreme it all too easily remains farcical and unthreatening. Shakespeare, however, complicates the farce elements by putting the play action within another play. The comic gulling of Christopher Sly, which frames the drama of Petruccio and Kate, makes Shakespeare's audience look through one further lens at the gender politics accompanying romantic love in marriage.

The Comedy of Errors is a well-rounded extension of Plautus's *Menaechmi*—replete with the farce elements of doubled-up twins, mistaken identities, locked-door gags, and violence removed from deep suffering. Yet the play develops the assertiveness of *Taming*'s Kate into the commanding presence of Adriana, the frustrated wife of the philandering Antipholus (of Ephesus). Adriana's character partly evinces the stereotype of the complaining shrew but shatters it with intense lines about the pathos of female suffering that evoke an audience's empathy by focusing on a poignant feeling. Consider the following example, in which Adriana, speaking of her own suffering, upbraids her sister for failing to commiserate with her, arguing that since she is not married and has never felt Adriana's burden, her sister cannot empathize: "A wretched soul, bruised with adversity, / We bid be quiet when we hear it cry. / But were we burdened with like weight of pain, / As much or more we should ourselves complain" (2.1.34–37). Despite all, this is a romantic comedy that ends not only in multiple marriages but also in the emotionally satisfying family resolutions that Shakespeare would return to time and time again. Dromio of Syracuse's punning jest about arrested clock-time (4.2.52–62) also points to Shakespeare's tendency, in many of the comedies that follow *The Comedy of Errors,* to position the main action in forests or other detemporalized spaces, outside the rigid constraints of clock-time on human freedom and happiness.

Love's Labour's Lost experiments with other Plautine elements than those of farce that have been described. Much of Roman comedy was written in long metrical lines for chanting and would have been staged with musical accompaniment. Shakespeare takes the pleasures of language and sound to his own heights in *Love's Labour's Lost,* filling it with a humor driven largely by battles of wit between its romantic protagonists, comic deflations of overreaching linguistic play by the braggart soldier Armado, and the peevish pedantry of Holofernes in contact with characters such as Constable Dull and the "natural" (rustic) fool Costard. Shakespeare's *miles gloriosus* here, Armado, is not simply brought down a peg. He repents of his deceit and self-importance (5.2.718–720) and self-consciously promises to be a committed husband to Jaquenetta, whom he has got pregnant (5.2.872–873). This takes him well beyond the comic stereotype of the braggart.

Shakespeare's Comic Art Reaches Maturity

Shakespeare's next six comedies take him into the new century and the full maturation of his comic art. They include some of his most famous: *A Midsummer Night's Dream* (1595), *The Merchant of Venice* (1596), *The Merry Wives of Windsor* (1597), *Much Ado About Nothing* (1598), *As You Like It* (1599), and *Twelfth Night, or What You Will* (1601).

Both *A Midsummer Night's Dream* and *The Merchant of Venice* are romantic comedies set in the formal contexts of public and courtly life. Their plots are driven by the need to escape from the "civilized" demands of deference to authority and financial obligation. Their forms of low comedy humor mix poignantly with darker undercurrents. The humor in *A Midsummer Night's Dream* is largely focused through the observing eyes of the naughty fairy spirit Puck, or Robin Goodfellow. Puck delights in slapstick and pratfalls (2.1.42–57). At various points, Shakespeare aligns the audience with Puck and his comic delight in the "foolishness" that romantic love brings to otherwise dignified human beings. Through his eyes the audience is encouraged to view the extreme threats of violence in acts 3 and 4 as merely farcical (3.2.110–121). Yet the height of the discord in act 3 sees the two male lovers ready to club each other to death, the female lovers ready to scratch each other's eyes out, and the Queen of immortal fairies brought into bestial copulation with a donkey. *The Merchant of Venice,* too, combines the low comedy of Launcelot's stand-up and Gratiano's vulgar jokes about women's "rings" with an incredibly poignant extension of a comic stereotype, the avaricious Jew, Shylock. Again, like the braggart Armado in *Love's Labour's Lost,* and even more so, Shylock is not just ridiculed as an unseemly stereotype. Shakespeare takes us deep into the ideological conflict that Shylock faces and which marginalizes him, evoking both our empathy toward his plight at the same time as our disapproval of his vindictive behavior. Fascinatingly, both *A Midsummer Night's Dream* and *The Merchant of Venice* quash the darker undertones of their third and fourth acts in fifth acts that sweep away the problems by improbable forms of intervention and an unsettling return to the farce of buffoonish acting and vulgar punning, respectively. In the case of *Dream,* the intervention comes from magical love juice and apparently benevolent fairies. In that of *Merchant,* it is the intervention of the brilliant Portia dressed up as a young male lawyer suddenly endowed with sufficient legal credentials to convince the Duke and the court of (her) being a wise and "learned" judge. For the young male lawyers of the Inns of Court in Shakespeare's audience, the whole scenario is meant to sound unlikely. With such interventions, Shakespeare reminds us of the thin veil that stands between comic resolution and the tragedies of life.

Vince Cardinale as Puck in the Pacific Repertory Theatre production of Shakespeare's *A Midsummer Night's Dream,* at the Carmel Shakespeare Festival, September 2000.

Source: Wikimedia Commons/Pacific Repertory Theatre.

Just as in *Dream,* the romantic comedy *As You Like It* compounds the comedy of thwarted sexual desire with familial discord. Urban discontent again finds recourse in the green world of a forest. *As You Like It*'s forest of Arden has its own inverted court, drawing on the myths of Robin Hood, where loyalty and justice reign with a strong tinge of melancholy, ironically, given the greenwood's removal from the city. Once again, the plot reaffirms the bonds of marriage and family via the intervention of one of the lovers, the witty and wise young woman Rosalind.

Shakespeare's famous comedies *Much Ado About Nothing* (1598) and *Twelfth Night, or What You Will* (1601) take us into a form of romantic comedy that has become a modern staple, as familiar from Jane Austen as it is from Hollywood film. The lovers end up together but only after internal struggles that have more to do with character and feeling than with the interferences of authority figures. With *Much Ado,* Shakespeare approaches the kind of high comedy of manners later popularized by the French playwright Molière. A "battle of the sexes" humor is present in the buffoonish war of wit between the eventual lovers Benedick and Beatrice. Shakespeare takes the eavesdropping scenes in Plautus's *Miles Gloriosus* and uses them not for the exposure of vice but for the development of the romantic plot. While the two lovers are eavesdropping, their friends trick them into thinking that each is really in love with the other, while only pretending to be hostile. Of course, this just ignites the erotic fervor underlying their war of wit. These moments enact the play's concern with the performance of certain states of mind and the emotional shifts involved in love.

In *Twelfth Night,* Shakespeare revisits the comic confusions of cross-gendered twins. Yet he darkens the plot resolution with an episode involving the character of Malvolio, the countess Olivia's steward. Malvolio's name in Italian means "I dislike" and hints also at "ill will." He is a stereotypical killjoy. While Malvolio is roundly mocked for his dampening spirit, the extreme trickery put upon him by Sir Toby, Olivia's drunken kinsman, is so severe it casts a shadow over the joyful family reunions and marriages the play ends with.

A similar ambivalence pervades the endings of the late comedies that are often dubbed "problem plays"—*Measure for Measure* (1603) and *All's Well That Ends Well* (1606)—and also the endings of the later "romances" such as *The Tempest* (1610). The denouements of these plays resolve most of the romantic and familial conflicts but not without significant struggles and lingering unhappiness for some characters. In *All's Well* Bertram, the young count of Rossillion, is far from pleased by his enforced marriage to Helena at the king's behest. We legitimately ask whether Helena can really be confident that marriage will be a happy one. Since *All's Well* is Shakespeare's last clearly identifiable comedy, it is reasonable to think that the title forms an ironic comment on the enforced closure implicit in comedy's representation of the world. The lingering discomfort is also reflected in the "tragicomic" romances. Caliban, for instance, the pitiful "deformed slave" who inhabits the island of Prospero in *The Tempest,* remains utterly dispossessed while the other characters are reunited. In *Cymbeline* (1610), the strained relationships are smoothed out but the emotional baggage of betrayal and confusion lingers.

Comic Relief in Tragedy

In Shakespeare's four great tragedies—*Hamlet* (1600), *Othello* (1603), *King Lear* (1605), and *Macbeth* (1606)—humor is used for comic relief. Hamlet makes bawdy jests to Ophelia (3.2.121–131) in the middle of the intense moment in which Hamlet seeks to "catch the conscience of the king" (2.2.603), while in the first scene of act 5, the gravediggers' gallows humor flows seamlessly into Hamlet's morbid reflection on mortality. The tragedy in *Othello* is punctuated with comic scenes of the gulling of Roderigo. *Lear*'s Fool attempts to alleviate the king's suffering with little success. The comic doorknocking in act 2 scene 2 of *Macbeth* immediately follows the eponymous hero's murder of the hapless king and his harrowing expression of guilt.

Fools and fool figures, too, are a major aspect of Shakespearean comedy. Foolish clown figures turn up in all the genres Shakespeare wrote in and function both to generate humor and to express unsettling criticism. Shakespeare experiments with a range of fool figures familiar in European literary culture. For instance, the character of Bottom from *A Midsummer Night's Dream* exemplifies the figure of the natural fool or rustic, who is unable to stand up to the taunts of wittier characters and is regularly made the butt of others' jokes. Feste, from *Twelfth Night,* on the other hand, provides an example of the learned fool whose very wit holds a mirror up to the vices and shortcomings of the society around him. To that extent, he largely reflects the wise fool figure that Erasmus developed in *The Praise of Folly.*

One of Shakespeare's most fascinating fools is the figure of Falstaff, who makes an appearance in the two *Henry IV* plays and in the comedy *The Merry Wives of Windsor.* The Falstaff of *Merry Wives* combines two shades of the fool. He is a lecherous "Lord of Misrule," who gathers around him the disreputable characters that enhance the play's bawdy farce, and cares not a jot for the sanctity of social institutions such as marriage. At the same time, he brings together the braggart soldier and vice figure of medieval morality plays. In the

Henry IV plays, Shakespeare retains Falstaff's low comedy credentials but also makes him parody the wise fool. Shakespeare makes him stand up on the battlefield and brazenly deconstruct the value of honor for which people are dying all around him. In *Henry IV Part 1* (5.1.127–140), to the young Prince Hal's statement to Falstaff that "thou owest God a death," he replies,

> 'Tis not due yet. I would be loath to pay him before his day . . . Well, 'tis no matter. Honor pricks me on. Yea, but how if honor prick me off when I come on? How then? Can honor set to a leg? no. Or an arm? no. Or take away the grief of a wound? no. Honor hath no skill in surgery, then? No. What is honor? A word. What is in that word "honor"? What is that "honor"? Air. A trim reckoning! Who hath it? He that died o' Wednesday. Doth he feel it? no. Doth he hear it? No . . . Therefore I'll none of it. Honor is a mere scutcheon. And so ends my catechism.

This is partly a jest designed to make us laugh at Falstaff's unseemly cowardice, but, in being that, it is also a veiled and careful critical unsettling of contemporary preoccupations with honor. When Shakespeare offers a critical voice on the world around him, it is often put in the mouth of fools and buried in the layers of both conservative and less conservative humor.

Daniel Derrin

See also Ancient Roman Comedy; Boccaccio, Giovanni; Carnivalesque; Cervantes, Miguel de; Clowns; Comedy; Comic Relief; Comic Versus Tragic Worldviews; Comic World; *Commedia dell'Arte*; Farce; Folklore; Fools; Genres and Styles of Comedy; Goldoni, Carlo; High Comedy; History of Humor: Renaissance Europe; Inversion, Topsy-Turvy; Irony; Jest, Jestbooks, and Jesters; Low Comedy; Menander; National and Ethnic Differences; Nonsense; Parody; Play and Humor; Plautus; Satire; Spoofing; Tragicomedy; Verbal Humor

Further Readings

Doran, M. (1964). *Endeavors of art: A study of form in Elizabethan drama*. Madison: University of Wisconsin Press.

Gay, P. (2008). *The Cambridge introduction to Shakespeare's comedies*. Cambridge, UK: Cambridge University Press.

Miola, R. (1994). *Shakespeare and classical comedy: The influence of Plautus and Terence*. Oxford, UK: Oxford University Press.

Ornstein, R. (1986). *Shakespeare's comedies: From Roman farce to romantic mystery*. Newark: University of Delaware Press.

Ryan, L. (2009) *Shakespeare's comedies*. Basingstoke, UK: Palgrave Macmillan.

Share

Share, pronounced as two syllables, *sha-re* (*shar-ray*), is the general Japanese term for linguistic humor, wordplay, wit, elegance of diction. The most common meaning of the word is "decoration." *Oshare* (with an honorific *o-*) means anything from dressed up, to elegance, or dandyism and foppery. *Share* therefore means elegance of speech or writing: thus anything from a simple pun to a tissue of poetic rhetorical flourishes. Today when Japanese people talk about *Share* meaning wordplay, puns of some kind are generally indicated. This entry discusses *Share* in Japan in both modern and traditional times.

The Japanese language is peculiarly well suited to puns but not at all to rhyme. Like the Polynesian languages, Japanese has a small number of phonemes and a consonant-vowel-consonant-vowel structure (CVCV), with only five vowel sounds (the five pure vowels). There are thus, in the written language, only six ways in which any word may end—in one of the five vowels or in the letter *n*—so rhyme occurs all the time and is neither noticed nor used as *Share*. Because there are huge numbers of possible syllables in European languages (e.g., English can produce thousands of different syllables), finding a rhyme is clever; but in Japanese, with fewer than a hundred possible syllables, it is not. Thus other forms of literary elegance developed in Japanese.

Because of the small number of possible syllables, the same ones need to be used over and over, creating huge numbers of homophones. Lecturing in Australia during the 1970s, dramatist Hisashi Inoue (1934–2012) pointed out that the prime minister of Japan can be delivering a perfectly serious speech and make a horrendous string of puns. These will not be noticed because the situation is defined as inappropriate for punning.

Chinese characters were imported into Japan in the 6th century CE. Their Chinese readings were Japanized and Japanese readings attributed to them. Almost all characters therefore have at least two readings and many have more. Vocabulary and characters were borrowed from several different Chinese dialects, depending on which area of

China was culturally dominant at the time. Thus the hundreds of different syllables and the various ways they were pronounced in different dialects of Chinese all had to be squeezed into the 90 or so syllables of Japanese, multiplying again the number of homophones. The standard Kenkyusha dictionary, for example, lists 22 words read as *kanshō,* ranging in meaning from spikenard (a rare plant), a chime, and a government office, to meddling and sentiment. These homophones can be unambiguously distinguished by being written in Chinese characters, but if spelled out in the hiragana or katakana syllabaries also used in Japanese, they may become ambiguous and "punny."

Some Modern Japanese Puns

Kotoba asobi uta (*Wordplay Songs* or *Wordplay Poems*) by eminent poet Shuntarō Tanikawa (b. 1931) provides many accessible and charming modern examples of wordplay. One is a poem that plays on the pun IRUKA 海豚; いるか (dolphin) and IRU KA 居るか; いるか (Are you there?). Its first line is

Iruka iruka?

This can mean

Are you there, dolphins? ***or***
Dolphins, are you there? ***or maybe even***
Dolphins, dolphins ***or***
Are you there, are you there?

Two words in one line of poetry thus give four possible meanings. The second line has only two possible meanings:

Inaika iruka?
Are you not there, dolphins? ***or***
Are you not there or are you there?

Dajare (Gratuitous Pun)

The word for pun most commonly used in daily speech is the denigrating term *Dajare,* which means "packhorse-share" and refers generally to a gratuitous pun or a "bad pun." Someone who has made a pun in normal Japanese conversation (this does not happen often) may excuse it, marking it retrospectively as a joke by saying, "I like *Dajare.*"

An example of a gratuitous pun is the name of a hotel in Nara, one of the ancient capital cities of Japan. In 2011, the hotel was called "Cotton 100%." This is written in Japanese as 古っ都ん１００%、This is read "Ko-t-to-N 100%," and means "100% cotton," but is written with characters meaning "Old-t-Capital-N 100%." In Japan, where summer is humid and cotton clothes are known to absorb perspiration, Cotton 100% implies good quality. In accordance with the spirit of the *Dajare,* the writing system has been somewhat tortured to produce this joke so that we get three meanings: old capital, Cotton 100%, and the implication of good quality. Since there is no link of meaning between old capital and cotton, it is not only tortured, but a gratuitous pun.

Goro awase (Mnemonic pun)

The most common, indeed, virtually universal, use of punning in modern Japanese is the use of the first syllable of numbers as a mnemonic.

Because Japanese uses a counting system derived from Chinese (*ichi-ni-san* 1, 2, 3) along with the native counting system (*hitotsu-futatsu-mittsu* 1, 2, 3), many different syllables can be used to represent numbers to assist memory. To simplify them, these include

1	2	3	4	5	6	7	8	9
i	ni	mi	shi	go	ro	na	ya	ku

One story recounted by Hisashi Inoue concerns a doctor who changed his telephone number because his patients were remembering it by its string of numbers 37564:

3 - 7 - 5 - 6 - 4
Mi - na - go - ro - shi

which means "massacre."

If the unfortunate Dr. Massacre had lived in Nagoya, he might have been better pleased with this phone number:

4 - 7 - 7 - 1 – 7 - 5 - 8 - 4
Shi - na - **na** - i Na - go - ya - shi

Although nonsensical, it would be instantly and permanently remembered because it would mean: "Do not die Nagoya City."

Traditional *Share*

Wordplay in Japan developed long ago to a sophisticated level. For example, in the *Nō* play *Motomezuka* (14th to 15th centuries), traditional Japanese scholarship identifies "as many as twelve poetic allusions, fourteen pivot words, six related words, two Chinese verses and one preface appropriated from the Japanese classic traditions, all in the space of two or three pages" (Terasaki, 2002). Thus 40% of the above linguistic embellishments are puns. A modern reader would study and appreciate these through an edition where the traditional scholars' analyses are given on each page below the text, in the same way that editions of the works of Geoffrey Chaucer and other medieval European writers may be annotated to make them understandable to readers of modern European languages.

The Japanese humorous tradition specializes in puns of various kinds and much of the humorous literature of the Edo period (1603–1868) interweaves puns with other linguistic humor and wordplay that may or may not be intended to be funny. Together they are a way of embellishing diction and allowing a rich world of allusion despite the severe constraints of even a poem only a few syllables long.

This linguistic wit is most effective and reaches its greatest heights of complexity in the written form. The author has a choice of scripts to make meanings explicit or ambiguous as desired, and readers can untangle and savor the humor at their own pace so that very great complications are possible, particularly in comic poetry in the forms known as *Kyōka* and *Senryū.*

Traditional Kinds of Japanese Pun

Fashion has affected wordplay as well as things like clothing. As in the other arts, there has in the past been a tendency for schools (or at least groups) to form, with followers apprenticing themselves to a master to learn a particular kind of *Share.*

Partly because of this tradition of individuals' taking ownership of various genres and devices, there seems to be no single generic term for *pun* in Japanese. *Share* itself means wordplay, the bulk of which are puns of one sort or another; but there are also particular words for many different kinds of pun. *Nihongo no share* (Japanese Wordplay), by Suzuki Tōzō, devotes chapters to many kinds of wordplay. Somewhat dauntingly, these include: *Shūku, Kyōgen* (a kind of joke, not the theatrical genre), *Rikō, Kosegoto, Kasuri, Kuchiai, Mojiri, Goro, Shiritori, Jiguchi, Sharekotoba, Herazuguchi,* and *Murimondō.* There is room here for only a brief look at two types of pun.

Kakekotoba (Pivot Words)

A *kakekotoba* or pivot word is an ancient device, which, at its most sophisticated, is a complex use of a pun to form what Lewis Carroll (author of *Alice in Wonderland,* 1865) might have called a portmanteau sentence. Ideally, instead of collapsing two *words* into one (a portmanteau word such as Carroll's *slithy* = *slimy* + *lithe*), the sentence pivots on a pun, which collapses two *sentences* into one. It thus jumps, via the punning pivot word, from halfway through one sentence to halfway through the second sentence. This gives two sentences for the price of one, allowing great density of allusion.

The following example of a pivot word comes from the *Nō* play, *Matsukaze* (Wind in the Pines):

Tachiwakare	We part
Inaba no yama no	But as soon as I hear
Mine ni ouru	That on the peak of Mount Inaba
***MATSU** to shi kikaba*	You PINE for me, A WAITING PINE TREE
Ima kaerikomu	I shall return

The pun in the fourth line of the verse relies on its rendering in hiragana. The pivot word is *matsu*:

まつとしきかば

Matsu 松 means "a pine tree" and *matsu* 待つ means "to wait." When they are spelled out in hiragana however, they are both written まつ and therefore become ambiguous. The pun on pining and pine tree is Terasaki Etsuko's, but pining as an implication of waiting in Japanese is legitimate poetic license. What took four words to capture in English (TO PINE, WAITING and PINE TREE), is elegantly expressed in Japanese with the one word (*matsu*), which results in the poem pivoting from an image of a lone pine to an image of a lone woman waiting (Terasaki, 2002, 35; Marguerite Wells, Trans.).

Kuchiai and Jiguchi

Kuchiai are a kind of extended pun where a whole sentence (or part of one) parallels—although it is not homophonous with—a more familiar phrase. It is a parody on a pun and the word means something like "Mouth-fit," the implication perhaps being that one needs to get one's tongue around the puns, fitting one's mouth to the unfamiliar new words that take so familiar a form. This name comes from the area near Osaka, whereas in the Edo area (Tokyo), it was called *Jiguchi.* Many literary genres of the Edo period (particularly *Kibyōshi*) exploited *Share* and punning.

A simple example quoted by Ono (1999, p. 37) is a *Kuchiai* by Saitō Gesshin (1804–1878) on the Japanese proverb that means the same as the English "pearls before swine":

Neko ni koban Gold coins to a cat

The *Kuchiai* is

Neko ni goban A Go board to a cat

A Go board (used in the ancient Chinese game of Go) would be as much use to a cat as a chessboard.

Modern *Kuchiai* from Japanese television were recorded by Heiyō Nagashima (2007, p. 75). One is an advertisement featuring Nobunaga Oda (1543–1582), the warlord who unified Japan. Exhorting customers to place all their insurance policies with the one company, Nobunaga says

Hoken tōitsu ja. Unify our insurance!

This is a *Kuchiai* on Nobunaga's real historical policy:

Nippon tōitsu ja. Unify Japan!

There are cases of *Kuchiai* used in English, for example by Lewis Carroll (1865). In an extended series of them, the Mock Turtle questions Alice about the subjects that she took at school. His own curriculum at the bottom of the sea included

Reeling and Writhing, Ambition, Distraction, Uglification and Derision
(instead of Reading and Writing, Addition, Subtraction, Multiplication and Division)
Mystery, Ancient and Modern with Seaography
(instead of History, Ancient and Modern with Geography)
Drawling, Stretching and Fainting in Coils,
(instead of Drawing, Sketching and Painting in Oils)
Classics: Laughing and Grief
(instead of Classics: Latin and Greek)

Conclusion

In English, all the different devices outlined above would be called puns. Despite the difficulty of translating Japanese puns, it has been done, as is exemplified by the English translation of the classic, *Tōkaidōchū Hizakurige* by Jippensha Ikku (1960). Other translations (Shiba, 2003) are offered as part of a Festschrift for Howard Hibbett, scholar in Japanese literature. An accessible Japanese collection of modern puns is Tanikawa (1982), which is in hiragana and easy to read, although the *Share* are challenging.

Marguerite Wells

See also Absurdist Humor; Ambiguity; Anti-Proverb; Epigram; History of Humor: Modern Japan; History of Humor: Premodern Japan; Jokes; *Kyōgen*; *Pointe*; Puns; *Senryū*; Translation; Verbal Humor; *Witz*; *Xiehouyu*

Further Readings

Carroll, L. (1865), *Alice's adventures in wonderland.* London, UK: D. Appleton.

Cohn, J. (Trans.). (2003). In the soup, hand-made: The thousand sliced arms of the Bodhisattva of Mercy by Shiba Zenkō. In J. Solt (Ed.), *An episodic Festschrift for Howard Hibbett* (Vol. 14). Hollywood, CA: Highmoonoon.

Jippensha Ikku. (1960). *Hizakurige, or Shanks's mare* (T. Satchell, Trans.). Tokyo, Japan: Charles E. Tuttle.

Kern, A. L. (2006). *Manga from the floating world: Comicbook culture and the Kibyôshi of Edo Japan.* Boston, MA: Harvard University Asia Center.

Nagashima, H. (2007). *Sha-re:* A widely accepted form of Japanese wordplay. In J. Milner Davis (Ed.), *Understanding humor in Japan* (pp. 75–84). Detroit, MI: Wayne State University Press.

Ono Mitsuyasu. (1999). *Kotoba asobi no bungakushi* [A literary history of wordplay]. Tokyo, Japan: Shintensha Sensho 11.

Suzuki Tōzō. (1979). *Nihongo no share* [Japanese wordplay]. Tokyo, Japan: Kōdansha Gakujutsu Bunko.

Tanikawa Shuntarō. (1982). *Kotoba asobi uta* [Wordplay songs]. Tokyo, Japan: Fukuinkan.

Terasaki, E. (2002). *Figures of desire: Wordplay, spirit possession, fantasy, madness and mourning in Japanese Noh plays.* Ann Arbor: Center for Japanese Studies, University of Michigan.

Wells, M. (1997). *Japanese humour.* London, UK: Macmillan.

Wells, M. (2010). Translating humour for performance: Two hard cases from Inoue Hisashi's play, *Yabuhara Kengyō.* In D. Chiaro (Ed.), *Translation and humour* (pp. 134–157). London, UK: Continuum.

Sick Humor

Sick humor can be described as humor that breaks social conventions as to what it is appropriate to joke about. The *New Oxford Dictionary of English* defines sick humor as "having something unpleasant such as death, illness or misfortune as its subject and dealing with it in an offensive way." Likewise, Harvey Mindess, Carolyn Miller, Joy Turek, Amanda Bender, and Suzanne Corbin (1985) see sick humor as being about death, disease, deformity, and the handicapped. These definitions complement each other but also need to be completed by including jokes about the human tendency toward cruelty. Sick humor is often perceived as "tasteless," macabre, or morbid. Research literature doesn't draw a clear distinction between sick humor and black humor. The *New Oxford Dictionary of English*'s definition of *black humor* is "presenting tragic or harrowing situations in comic terms," which suggests intersections between sick and black humor as well as gallows humor. Black and even more so, sick humor, have the potential of being offensive, sometimes intentionally so.

Examples for sick humor reported in research literature are cruel jokes such as the "Shut up and keep digging" joke cycle (e.g., "But mother I don't want to go to China." "Shut up and keep digging."; "Mommy, I want a new dog." "Shut up, we haven't finished eating this one yet." [Sutton-Smith, 1960, pp. 15, 17]), but also jokes about handicaps; disasters such as the Chile mining accident in 2010 or the September 11, 2001, terror attacks; the death of celebrities; Holocaust jokes; and pranks at wakes (e.g., making corpses move); or so-called graveyard humor. While gallows humor generally refers to actual threats and great dangers, sick jokes exist both about fictional situations and events that actually have taken place. Typically, jokes about cruelties or disasters present themselves as joke cycles with a certain pattern. For example, in "Dead Baby" jokes (e.g., "What's red and white, red and white, pink, pink, pink?—Baby in a blender" [Dundes, 1987, p. 8]), the incongruity arises from a symbol of innocence (a baby) that comes to a gruesome death. The NASA joke cycle uses an actual event: the explosion of the space shuttle *Challenger* in 1986 that was broadcast live over television and witnessed by many people. This cycle usually starts with the same joke: "What does NASA stand for?—Need another seven astronauts" (Oring, 1987, p. 280).

Historical Development

Early documentation of sick jokes can already be found in the oldest Greek collection of jokes, the *Philogelos* (10th century CE). Another example of sick humor is Jonathan Swift's satirical essay "A Modest Proposal" from 1729. Swift proposes that the Irish should fight famine and poverty by eating their own children at the age of 1, when they are most tasty. Thus they would be able to save money not only on food as they have their food resource at home, but also on "maintenance" costs for the children after the first year. Other predecessors to sick humor cycles date back to the English poet J. H. C. "Harry" Graham in the 1890s, who published popular collections of rhymed verses playing with macabre topics:

> Billy, in one of his nice new sashes,
> Fell in the fire and was burnt to ashes;
> Now, although the room grows chilly,
> I haven't the heart to poke poor Billy. (Quoted in Dundes, 1979, p. 146)

Graham's rhymes might have inspired "Little Willie" humor cycles, which came up in the 1930s and usually involved a little boy who, for example, kills other family members and either gets no more than a raised finger or is even admired for what he is able to achieve at the tender age of 6. Sick jokes of the modern kind first appeared in the 1940s (e.g., the little moron jokes). Jokes about disasters only emerged when television started broadcasting news about disasters directly into people's living rooms. By superimposing feelings of involvement onto an actually uninvolved audience, says Christie Davies in 2011, an absurd incongruity evolves that leads to the sick jokes. The Internet makes it possible to distribute this kind of joke very quickly.

Appreciation of and Motivation for Sick Humor

Psychologists have looked at personality or other variables that might predict the appreciation of sick jokes or humorous behaviors related to sick humor. In these studies, appreciation of and behavior related to sick humor are usually measured either by rating the funniness of sets of sick jokes or by questionnaire measures. Men have usually been found to appreciate sick humor to a higher degree than women. People who appreciate sick humor tend to be more liberal; more rebellious; less emotionally responsive toward other people's situations, both positive and negative (e.g., fictional or real tragedies); and less religious and spiritual. However, they seem to be more likely to engage in a coping style that involves venting and the expression of their own emotions in public, whether socially appropriate or not. Persons liking earthy and sick humor also seem to be less conformist and less agreeable. Sick jokes are, however, not a homogeneous group and appreciation for different kinds of jokes may differ.

There are diverse views on the motivations for and psychological functions of sick jokes. While many scholars and researchers refer to the use of sick humor as a means of coping with the subject that is joked about, to speak the unspeakable, to show *Schadenfreude*, or to deal with a somewhat disturbed mind (e.g., a hidden wish to kill), other researchers state that a joke in and of itself cannot have any implication as to its morality or motivation. These scholars emphasize that what makes the crucial difference to interpretations and implications of jokes, in particular sick ones, is the context in which the joke is told, that is, the cultural or social environment, who the joke tellers and their audience are, and factors such as tone of voice and introduction of the joke.

Ursula Beermann

See also Aggressive and Harmless Humor; Coping Mechanism; Doggerel; Gallows Humor; Insult and Invective; Jest, Jestbooks, and Jesters; Joke Cycles; Jokes; Obscenity; *Philogelos*; Play and Humor; Satire; Scatology; Targets of Humor; Travesty

Further Readings

Brock, A. (2008). Humor, jokes, and irony versus mocking, gossip, and black humor. In G. Antos & E. Ventola (Eds.), *Handbook of interpersonal communication* (pp. 541–565). Berlin, Germany: Mouton de Gruyter.

Craik, K. H., Lampert, M. D., & Nelson, A. (1996). Sense of humor and styles of everyday humorous conduct. *HUMOR: International Journal of Humor Research, 9*, 273–302.

Davies, C. E. (2011). Jokes about disasters: A response to tales told on television full of hype and fury. In C. Hoffstadt & S. Höltgen, *Sick humor* (pp. 11–40). Bochum, Germany: Projektverlag.

Dundes, A. (1979). The dead baby joke cycle. *Western Folklore, 38*, 145–157.

Dundes, A. (1987). *Cracking jokes: Studies of sick humor cycles and stereotypes.* Berkeley, CA: Ten Speed Press.

Herzog, T. R., & Anderson, M. R. (2000). Joke cruelty, emotional responsiveness, and joke appreciation. *HUMOR: International Journal of Humor Research, 13*, 333–352.

Hierocles. (1983). *The Philogelos, or, laughter-lover* (B. Baldwin, Ed. & Trans.). Amsterdam, Netherlands: J. C. Gieben.

Graham, J. H. C. (2009). *When Grandmama fell off the boat: The best of Harry Graham.* London, UK: Sheldrake Press.

Mindess, H., Miller, C., Turek, J., Bender, A., & Corbin, S. (1985). *The Antioch Humor Test: Making sense of humor.* New York, NY: Avon Books.

Narvaez, P. (2003). *Of corpse: Death and humor in folklore and popular culture.* Logan: Utah State University Press.

Oring, E. (1987). Jokes and the discourse on disaster. *Journal of American Folklore, 100*, 276–286.

Saroglou, V., & Anciaux, L. (2004). Liking sick humor: Coping styles and religion as predictors. *HUMOR: International Journal of Humor Research, 17*, 257–277.

Sutton-Smith, B. (1960). "Shut up and keep digging": The cruel joke series. *Midwest Folklore, 10*, 11–22.

Simple Form

Simple forms (SFs) refers to a concept of folk literature as the expression of elementary cognitive attitudes (mental dispositions, modes of thought) and provides a theoretical umbrella term to systematically cover various verbal folklore genres. As a term, *SF* is the English translation of *Einfache Formen* (EF), a book published in 1930 by art historian and literary scholar André Jolles, which has continued to give theoretical impulses as well as reason for confusion and critique. This book was never translated into English, but it continues to be published in German and remains influential.

Jolles was born in 1874 in the Netherlands. After school, as a poet and promoter of the symbolist movement, he founded and contributed to various literary and cultural journals. Studying in Italy, France, the Netherlands, and Germany, he finished archeology and history at Freiburg University. In 1907, Jolles became a university teacher, moving to Berlin in 1908. After receiving German citizenship (1914), Jolles volunteered in World War I until 1916, then becoming professor of archeology and art history in German-occupied Ghent (Belgium). In 1918, he was appointed professor of Flemish and Dutch at Leipzig University, becoming professor of comparative literature in 1923. From 1933 on, Jolles was a supporter of Nazi ideology and a party member, who after the war admitted only academic consultation with the regime concerning the history and symbolism of 18th-century Freemasonry. Jolles became an emeritus professor in 1941 but remained at the university until the end of the war, where he taught seminars on the psychology of races and cultures. He was one of the last honorees to receive the renowned Goethe-Medaille für Kunst und Wissenschaft (Goethe Medal for Art and Science) in 1944. Jolles died in 1946, before making a decision about whether to return to the Netherlands.

Based on various prestudies from the 1920s, Jolles attempted to define specifically and systematically what had before been termed *Naturpoesie* (natural poetry) by Jacob Grimm in the early 19th century. Grimm characterized natural poetry as divinely inspired and spontaneous, as opposed to *Kunstpoesie* (artistic poetry), the result of individual acts of creation. In contrast to literary scholarship focusing the individual genius (*Genieästhetik*), Jolles postulated the "determination of form" (*Formbestimmung)* and the "interpretation of pattern" (*Gestaltdeutung*) as central morphological tasks. Referring to Johann Wolfgang von Goethe, he defined this task with regard to poetry as a whole, asking if the various patterns form a common, internally coherent and ordered whole, a *system*.

With special focus on folk literature, Jolles anticipated German morphological literary approaches of the 1940s (Emil Staiger, Gunther Mueller, Horst Oppel); he did not, however, concentrate on individual texts: His rather phenomenological approach is far from being structuralist in orientation, and his interests in morphology must by no means be confounded with early structuralist ideas as, for example, Vladimir Propp's *Morphology of the Russian Folk-Tale* (1928). Jolles's approach, though similar in inclination, also differs from ideas simultaneously propagated by Roman Jakobson and Pëtr Bogatyrëv. In their 1929 seminal essay "Folklore as a Special Form of Artistic Creation," these authors attempted to determine similarities and differences of folklore and literature, favoring a *functional* view, introducing the notion of "preventive censorship of the community," and assuming that only the forms operating in a given community will survive in folklore.

Thus, at a time when in Russia formalist approaches to literature were already converting into structuralism, Jolles adhered to a Romantic concept of language as an "anthropomorphic deity" and "Goddess language," as early reviews phrased it.

In order to identify the patterns of this allegedly closed system of simple forms, Jolles referred to so-called mental occupations (*Geistesbeschäftigungen*) underlying them. A summary of these simple forms and their corresponding mental occupations follows: legend (*Legende*)—imitation; saga (*Sage*)—family, or tribe; myth (*Mythe*)—knowledge; riddle (*Rätsel*)—knowledge; saying (*Spruch*)—experience; case (*Kasus*)—norm; memorabilia (*Memorabile*)—real/actual; folk-tale (*Märchen*)—marvelous; joke (*Witz*)—comic.

Jolles excluded transitions between SFs or derivations from one SF to another. Although, for example, both myth and riddle are related to "knowledge," emphasizing question and answer, the riddle for him is a question asked in the present to be answered in the future, whereas the myth is a question from the past answered in the present. Jolles refused to identify SFs with concrete genres (and even less with specific texts). Rather, in analogy to the Saussurean opposition of *langue* (language) and *parole* (speech) in linguistics, Jolles saw an SF to exist only potentially (*potentialiter*); only when (re-)produced in oral or written form does it come into being actually (*actualiter*). When Jolles therefore juxtaposed a "pure" SF (*Reine* EF) to an "actual(ized)" SF (*Aktuelle, Vergegenwärtigte* EF), he had in mind some kind of archetypes; referring to the modern genotext–phenotext concept (based on the well-known genotype-phenotype distinction in genetics), one might adequately use the terms *genogenre* versus *phenogenre* to refer to Jolles's idea. Jolles could thus interpret Ancient Greek victory odes (*epinikia*) as well as modern sport reports to be actualizations of the legend. For the joke, Jolles considered relief or discharge as characteristic, when something bound is released or (dis)solved—what allows for a comparison with other concepts of humor. Depending on historical, geographical, and other factors, the pure SF joke may thus be actualized in concrete genres such as the pun; Jolles here even referred to the schwank, seeing its essence in the derision of individual characters or typical figures. Pure and actual(ized) SFs must not be confounded with what Jolles called an analogical, related, or derived SF, that is, individually authored texts, literary creations, based on or even pretending to be SFs, as for example, literary tales, riddles, or even novels.

Modern concepts have elaborated the concept of SF and (re-)interpreted it from different theoretical perspectives, including structuralist approaches (e.g., those of Elli Köngäs-Maranda and Pierre Maranda, and of Grigorij L. Permjakov), concentrating on analogies between SFs and processes of elaboration or condensation, and semiotic attempts considering SFs as prototypes of more elaborated ("higher") literary genres and cultural prototypes. Historical-diachronical studies have demonstrated interrelations between SFs, for example, myth and riddle, originally being related by specific rituals. Conceptually integrating cultural processes of stepwise profanation (desecularization) and ridiculization, or the process of making something ridiculous, might well help explain the evolution of individual SFs (*sacred riddle → everyday riddle → joke riddle → meta-linguistic riddle*) and evolutionary transitions between SFs (e.g., *myth → folktale → schwank → joke*).

Peter Grzybek

See also Folklore; Jokes; Puns; Riddle; Schwank; *Witz*

Further Readings

Eismann, W., & Grzybek, P. (1987). *Semiotische Studien zum Rätsel* [Semiotic studies about the riddle]. In W. Eismann & P. Grzybek (Eds.), *Simple forms reconsidered II*. Bochum, Germany: Brockmeyer.

Grzybek, P. (1984). *Semiotische Studien zum Sprichwort* [Semiotic studies about the proverb]. In P. Grzybek (Ed.), Simple forms reconsidered I. Tübingen, Germany: Narr. [Special issue of *Kodikas Code · Ars Semeiotica. An International Journal of Semiotics*, 3/4]

Jolles, A. (1930). *Einfache Formen: Legende, Sage, Mythe, Rätsel, Spruch, Kasus, Memorabile, Märchen, Witz* [Simple forms: Legend, saga, myth, riddle, saying, case, report of memorable events, tale, joke]. Tübingen, Germany: Niemeyer.

Koch, W. A. (1994). *Simple forms: An encyclopaedia of simple text-types in lore and literature*. Bochum, Germany: Brockmeyer.

Köngäs-Maranda, E., & Maranda, P. (1971). *Structural models in folklore and transformational essays*. The Hague, Netherlands: Mouton de Gruyter.

Permyakov, G. L. (1970/1979). *From proverb to folk-tale: Notes on the general theory of cliché*. Moscow, Russia: Nauka.

Sitcoms

Sitcoms, or situational comedies, are one of the dominant forms of television and radio comedy in the world, with a history aligned with that of global broadcasting and a wealth of programming from multiple nations. This entry outlines the key characteristics of the majority of sitcoms, and examines how the humor within sitcoms commonly functions.

Defining Sitcoms

The most fruitful way to think of sitcoms is as a television and radio genre. Genres are forms of culture that have characteristics in common but can never be concretely defined to the point that what belongs in such a category is beyond discussion; therefore, deciding what is and is not a sitcom is always up for debate. That said, there are characteristics that can be seen to recur often across the genre and that are commonly understood to be indicative of sitcoms.

Sitcoms are a serial form of television and radio, made up of many episodes (sometimes into the hundreds) often across many years. This serial format is common in broadcasting, where the regular nature of the schedule encourages program making that is episodic. This distinguishes sitcoms from comedy in other media because, unlike the theater, film, or the novel, sitcoms are not predicated on getting to the end of the narrative. While individual episodes may have self-contained stories, the ongoing, episodic nature of sitcoms means that the overall ending is repeatedly delayed, and, therefore, only the middle portion of the story is presented to the audience. This fact has caused many problems for the use of traditional comedy analysis when one studies sitcoms because most of those frameworks argue that comedy can be defined by its happy ending. Analysis of sitcoms has, therefore, had to develop new models that acknowledge the genre's episodic structure.

This episodic structure accounts for the kinds of settings that recur in sitcoms, as a program needs to have a setup that can facilitate multiple characters and many episodes. Many sitcoms are set in the home, where the main characters are a family and the comedy centers on familial relationships and misunderstandings. Similarly, sitcoms are often set in workplaces, where multiple characters repeatedly interact in a restricted setting. The idea of place is key to sitcoms, and it is common for them to have very few sets. Location shooting has traditionally been rare in sitcoms; sitcoms are usually considered a studio-bound genre.

Most sitcoms are 30 minutes long in broadcast time and, in commercial broadcasting systems, must include narrative breaks in order to accommodate advertising. For many decades, the dominant way in which sitcoms were filmed was in front of a live studio audience, whose laughter was recorded and broadcast alongside the program. This laugh track remains one of the most obvious defining characteristics of the genre, even though there have been programs that have not used it. Although the lack of a laugh track has become more prevalent in recent years, the laugh track remains an interesting characteristic of the genre: It means that sitcoms are a form of culture that acknowledges the audience it is performed for and invites audiences at home to align themselves with those who were at the recording, which can be seen as being indicative of comedy's communal nature and the social aspects of humor and laughter.

The narrative structure of sitcoms is one that has conventionally been examined as working within an equilibrium-disequilibrium-equilibrium schema. That is, an episode of a sitcom depicts a set of social norms, which are then problematized via characters' actions, external forces, or other events. The comedy in the sitcom therefore arises from characters' attempting to reassert their equilibrium and the mismatch between their characteristics and the situations they are placed in. Sitcoms can be seen to rely heavily on incongruity for their humor. Because many analyses argue that sitcom episodes end when the initial equilibrium has been restored, the genre has often been criticized for being conservative and for suggesting that a happy ending is one in which changes are rejected. While such analyses may be appropriate for individual episodes, the episodic nature of broadcasting means that how narratives function in episodes might be quite different from that for series, and the potential progressive nature of sitcoms is one of the key debates that arises from analyses of it.

Origins

The origins of sitcoms reveal why the laugh track came into being. The genre evolved out of the movement of comedians who had been working in theatrical traditions such as vaudeville and the music hall into radio and television broadcasting. While the theater allowed comedians to repeatedly perform the same routine to different audiences, broadcasting required large amounts of new material to fill multiple episodes for a mass audience. To fill such space, extra characters were added to the series and plot lines were introduced. Radio comedy, therefore, slowly evolved into a form in which comedy was centered on multiple characters in a defined setting. When television began, this format moved to the new medium. Sitcoms can be seen as a logical solution to the problem of how to do comedy in broadcasting. The characteristics of sitcoms belie their theatrical origins, whereas the serial nature of sitcoms takes advantage of the particularities of broadcasting. In that sense, sitcoms are a useful genre for the specificities of radio and television broadcasting.

Sitcoms' theatrical origins can also be seen in performance style, which is often quite different from that of other radio and television genres. Performance in sitcoms is often less naturalist than that in straight drama and instead highlights comedic moments through its excess. Such performance also draws on the relationship between actors and the audience in the studio to whom they are performing, and actors' pauses and responses often take audience reactions into account. In that sense, performance in sitcoms often captures the theatrical nature of the moment of recording and, unlike much television fiction, acknowledges it is a piece of fiction explicitly created for entertainment purposes. While sitcoms without laugh tracks might be assumed to move away from such a performance style because of the lack of a relationship between performer and audience, such programs often similarly employ acting that is excessive compared to the norms for drama. Performance, therefore, is a vital element in sitcoms' makeup and also routinely marks distinctions between serious and comedic fiction.

Performance differences also depend on national and cultural contexts. For example, analyses of U.S. sitcoms argue that the genre must be understood relative to its Jewish origins, as many writers and performers of early sitcoms were Jewish and Jewish culture has had an influence on American culture as a whole. It has been argued that since the 1990s, sitcoms have become much more open about their Jewish aspects, when, in earlier times, production teams on programs like *The Dick Van Dyke Show* (1961–1966) were encouraged to make programs more WASPish. A preponderance in American sitcoms of self-aware characters whose comedy results from their analysis of their own situation is seen to be a result of sitcoms' Jewish origins and thus, their Jewish nature. By comparison, the United Kingdom repeatedly depicts resolutely un-self-aware characters instead, and the comedy arises from those characters' failings, social inadequacies, and ignorance of how others see them.

Representation and Culture

Analyses of sitcoms have often focused on issues of representation, in a manner similar to debates about comedy as a whole. For example, much work has explored how women have been portrayed in comedy, especially as many sitcoms have male characters in the lead roles. Women have, therefore, often served as the butt of comedy, and sitcoms have been criticized for offering the male point of view as the norm that audiences must identify with. Some critics have argued that sitcoms have offered a powerful place for funny women to appear and reach mass audiences and that the comedy they offer critiques patriarchal norms. For example, many feminist critiques cite *Roseanne* (ABC, 1988–1997) as offering a portrayal of women and femininity quite at odds with the majority of such representations and note that the humor used by the female characters empowers them.

Representational debates similarly focus on issues of race and ethnicity. For example, some sitcoms have been criticized for their depictions of Black and African American characters, which are seen as comparable to racist uses of humor in a variety of comedy. Multiple studies have been carried out on the sitcom *The Cosby Show* (NBC, 1984–1992), which was a highly successful program depicting the routine events in an upper middle-class African American family in the United States. In its depiction of such lives in an everyday manner, with characters who are knowingly funny and intelligent, the program has been lauded as a breakthrough in such representations; however, the series has also been criticized for failing to acknowledge the political and social problems that individuals encounter and for conforming to racial stereotypes in some of its performances. While it is impossible to come to definitive conclusions in such debates, they show the social significance often applied to sitcoms, whereby the comedic content and representational strategies of series are seen as indicative of wider social perceptions and norms. Thus, sitcoms have often been employed in studies of race, gender, and social power as being powerfully emblematic of wider social concerns, and the genre's strategies are repeatedly placed in the spotlight.

The majority of sitcoms have been produced in the United States and the United Kingdom, and the genre can claim to primarily be an English-speaking one. Programs made in both countries have been exported all over the world, and so have become one of the key ways in which representations of those nations move across countries. Many countries also make their own versions of sitcoms that originated elsewhere; indeed, UK series have been remade into series in the United States. Such programs are useful for analyzing the cultural specificities of humor and the national norms of broadcasting. For example, comparisons of versions of *The Office* (BBC, 2001–2003)—which originated in the United Kingdom but has been remade in the United States, France, Germany, Canada, Chile, Sweden, and Israel—can be used to explore the kinds of jokes that people in each of those countries find funny, and the ways in which comedy functions in relationship with national broadcasting. Sitcom's transnational movement across the globe suggests that it functions as a powerful cultural and economic force.

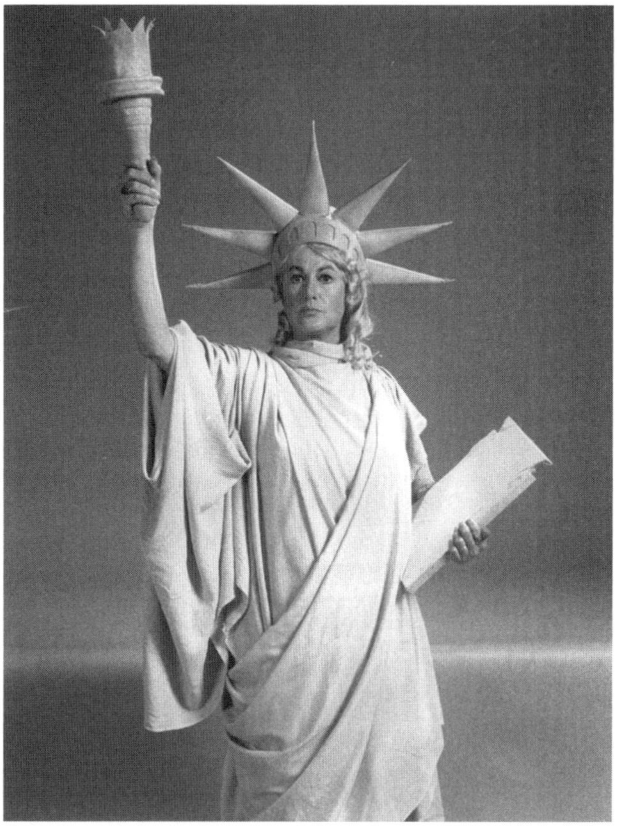

Bea Arthur in a publicity photo for the TV series *Maude*, in which she starred. The sitcom, directed by Norman Lear, ran from 1972 to 1978.

Source: Wikimedia Commons.

The Future of Sitcoms

Although this entry has focused on television and radio sitcoms, newer technologies have resulted in new media where sitcoms can exist. There has been a growth of sitcoms on the Internet due to online broadcasting, and a number of writers and performers have used the Internet to bypass traditional broadcasting systems to disseminate comedy. This opens up the potential for sitcoms to become a genre made by a wider range of people than was previously the case, which may not only ensure the genre's future as a core element in worldwide comedy but also broaden the kinds of sitcoms available to audiences. So, how the genre will develop in the future is up for debate.

Brett Mills

See also Comedy; Gender Roles in Humor; Incongruity and Resolution; Jewish Humor; Music Hall; National and Ethnic Differences; Race, Representations of

Further Readings

Brook, V. (2003). *Something ain't kosher here: The rise of the "Jewish" sitcom.* New Brunswick, NJ: Rutgers University Press.

Cook, J. (Ed.). (1982). *B.F.I. Dossier 17: Television sitcom.* London, UK: British Film Institute.

Grote, D. (1983). *The end of comedy: The sit-com and the comedic tradition.* Hamden, CT: Archon.

Mills, B. (2005). *Television sitcom.* London, UK: British Film Institute.

Mills, B. (2009). *The sitcom.* Edinburgh, Scotland: Edinburgh University Press.

Morreale, J. (Ed.). (2003). *Critiquing the sitcom: A reader.* Syracuse, NY: Syracuse University Press.

Sketch Comedy Shows

Sketch comedy shows, also called sketch shows, are a common form of television and radio comedy produced throughout the history of broadcasting and evident in a number of nations. This entry outlines the key characteristics of the majority of sketch comedy shows, and examines how the humor within them commonly functions.

Defining Sketch Comedy Shows

Sketch shows are considered a radio and television comedy genre, that is, a certain kind of comedy that has a set of characteristics and is assumed to have enough in common to constitute a set of norms or traditions. While all genres encompass flexibility and genre definitions can never be concrete or fixed, defining sketch shows is perhaps more difficult than doing so for other comedy genres, such as sitcoms. Indeed, perhaps one of the key characteristics of sketch shows is their flexibility, thereby ensuring problems in definition.

Sketch shows are characterized by individual episodes that are made up of many shorter, typically stand-alone, comedic pieces. There are as many sketches as are necessary to fill the length of the episode, which is commonly 30 minutes. Individual sketches may vary in length from a couple of seconds to many minutes, and there are few restrictions on subject matter or form, other than those imposed by the practical and economic factors within which any particular program works. Sketch shows are therefore a highly flexible format, which places few boundaries upon its makers and can encompass a multitude of performance styles, comedic intentions, and varieties of humor.

Because sketch shows are made up of many individual elements, and one episode is likely to be part of a much longer series containing many episodes, it is difficult to analyze in terms of narrative. This has caused problems for the academic study of sketch shows because many such frameworks define comedy by its happy ending and it is not feasible to delineate the narrative end of a sketch show. Indeed, while many forms of media comedy have been explored within academic study, sketch shows have remained visibly absent from such analyses. There is a real lack of work in this area, perhaps because it is assumed that sketch shows are of less significance than other comedic forms; however, it may also be a consequence of the difficulty in transferring existing analytical frameworks to the genre.

While sketch shows can be made up of many entirely unrelated comic moments; in practice most series use recurring characters, settings, and situations. Series can often come to be defined by the key characters that recur in multiple sketches, and later episodes of a particular series may foreground such characters more, showing how series respond to audience feedback and the comedic success of particular elements. Sketch shows—like sitcoms—also often employ catchphrases, which are sayings or responses associated with a particular character whose use of them commonly becomes the point of a particular sketch. It is not uncommon for popular and successful catchphrases to catch on outside the program and to be used by fans and viewers in everyday speech. Catchphrases offer an interesting counterpoint to many frameworks for the analysis of comedy that assume surprise is a key element in a successful joking moment because catchphrases are pleasurable precisely because they are expected and hoped for. The success of catchphrases points to the communal pleasures that exist in comedy, whereby audiences are invited to enjoy predicting the appearance of a catchphrase as part of a community that enjoys a particular sketch show or character.

Although the flexible nature of sketch shows can encourage a wide array of settings and situations, series often focus on locations and characters intended to be recognizable to the audience. Sketch shows, therefore, frequently focus on families, workplaces, schools, and other everyday institutions. Indeed, because segments in sketch shows are often so short, commonplace settings are foregrounded because there is not much time available to ensure the audience knows what is going on; therefore, recognizable locations become a shorthand way of quickly setting up a sketch. Furthermore, recognizable and recurring settings can be a way of cutting costs in production, which can be more expensive for sketch shows than for other forms of media comedy because of the multiple sets and costumes needed being significantly more than for, say, sitcoms. Most sketch shows are filmed in studios rather than on location although—as will be discussed later—newer forms of technology are affecting this convention.

The majority of sketch shows are filmed in front of live studio audiences, and therefore, they approximate a kind of live theater. The responses made by audiences at such recordings are included in the broadcast as a laugh track. As with sitcoms, a laugh track is a key defining characteristic of sketch shows, even though some series may not use it. The use of a laugh track is an interesting feature of these genres, as it means these programs acknowledge and aurally include the audience for whom the program is made. In that sense, the response to the comedy is seen to be as important to the final broadcast as the comedic content itself. It is quite common in sketch shows to see the ways in which performers are responding to the audience whose laughter is being recorded, and therefore the "live" experience of such recording becomes an element in the program. This is perhaps most evident when sketch shows use catchphrases and performers sometimes leave long pauses before the expected phrase is uttered, inviting the audience to enjoy the anticipation of its arrival. That genres such as this retain the live audience as part of the program must be emphasized, as this is quite at odds with the majority of broadcast material, which, in a realist mode, refuses to acknowledge its production processes.

Comedy is often examined for what it says about the culture that produces it, and debates about humor's progressive or regressive nature abound. Exploring sketch shows in this way is problematic because of the lack of coherent and linear narrative and because the "meaning" of one particular sketch might be quite at odds with that which precedes or follows it. Recurring characters in sketch shows tend to have little progression, and their comedic value is predicated on their stability. Can we read this as the genre therefore relying on regressive and simplistically stable representations? Or does the complex panoply of characters and sketches rubbing up against one another instead construct a collage of meanings, none of which can be definitively tied down? The format of multiple elements common to sketch shows remains difficult to grasp analytically.

Origins

Like much television and radio comedy, the origins of sketch shows lie in the theater, in the traditions of music hall in the United Kingdom and vaudeville in the United States. Sketch shows' format of multiple unrelated elements making up a sequence of comedic entertainment approximates neatly with theatrical comedic traditions in which a series of performers (comedians, singers, novelty acts) made up an evening's bill. Early radio transplanted such acts wholesale into broadcasting, in essence acting merely to disseminate to a wider listening audience material that had been circulating onstage for many years. Sitcoms have similar origins, though in that genre the disparate elements came to coalesce around a particular character and setting, and narrative became foregrounded with the idea of story being central. Sketch shows, however, retain a clearer link with the theatrical antecedents that begat both sitcoms and the sketch shows, rejecting the idea of narrative being central as in sitcoms.

For some time variety was a key element in radio and television broadcasting in the United Kingdom and the United States, with many series explicitly adopting theatrical conventions, such as performers standing in front of a curtain. While elements of variety remain in much of broadcasting (such as in chat shows and talent competitions), it is rather rare now to see variety shows of the format that was once popular on television. It can, then, be argued that sketch shows are the closest we have now to that variety heritage, and it is not uncommon for sketch shows to signal that history again through tropes such as performers standing in front of a theater-like curtain. It is interesting to note that these conventions persist, particularly as it is probable that younger audience members are unlikely to have ever experienced the theatrical traditions that are being referenced. In that sense, it can be argued that such conventions are now more accurately those of sketch shows, with the link to a theatrical past little more than a historical curiosity.

That said, it is not uncommon for performers and writers in sketch shows to come out of a theatrical context, though this is more likely to be via stand-up comedy routes. In the United Kingdom, for example, many broadcasting executives scour the comedy circuit at the annual Edinburgh Festival to find writers and performers to whom they can offer broadcasting contracts, and such performers are usually offered a sketch show as their first commission. Presumably this is because of the assumption that the format of sketch shows is the most straightforward evolution of stand-up and on-stage material. In that sense, sketch shows remain an important training ground for new talent, and it can be argued that in this genre the future direction of broadcast comedy can be most consistently discerned.

Furthermore, one of the key characteristics of sketch shows is that it is extremely common for a program's performers to also be its writers; while this sometimes occurs in other genres, it is not as apparent to the extent it is in sketch shows. The concept of the writer-performer correlates with ideas about the authorship of comedy and suggests that comedy relies on certain comic "voices" that are particular to individuals and groups. Sketch shows can therefore be examined in terms of the range of voices offered, as well as those that are less common; for example, representations of different races, genders, and ethnicities can—as with all comedy—be explored.

The Future of Sketch Comedy Shows

New technologies offer a wide range of opportunities for sketch shows, especially because, as noted above, the genre is one often employed by people new to broadcast comedy. Many comedians and comedy groups wanting to break into television and radio comedy now post material online, often setting up YouTube channels. This material is typically quite short, with individual sketches lasting no longer than one minute or so, and aim to show individuals' skills in writing and performing jokes. In that sense, the sketch is the calling card of the aspiring comedy star, not least because such short material is more easily produced on a limited budget. While online material demonstrates that sketch material can now be found in a wider range of places than before, it also raises questions about how sketch shows are defined: What is it that turns many sketches into a sketch *show*? Is there any worthwhile difference between many sketches on a YouTube channel and those sketches collected into a half-hour format and broadcast on a traditional television channel? Thinking this through highlights the particularities of sketch shows, and that making sense of the genre requires exploring the relationships between individual sketches and the text as a whole. To be sure, the growth of online material suggests that sketches and sketch shows have an ensured future, and they remain a key format for highlighting the future of comedy and the work of the next generation of comedians.

Brett Mills

See also Comedy; Comedy Ensembles; Comic Opera; Humor Content Versus Structure; Music Hall; Musical Comedy; Punch Line; Sketch Comedy Shows; Travesty; Variety Shows

Further Readings

Creeber, G. (Ed.). (2009). *The television genre book*. London, UK: British Film Institute.

Landy, M. (2005). *Monty Python's* Flying Circus. Detroit, MI: Wayne State University Press.

Lockyer, S. (Ed.). (2012). *Reading* Little Britain*: Comedy matters on contemporary television*. London, UK: I. B. Tauris.

Tueth, M. V. (2005). *Laughter in the living room: Television comedy and the American home audience*. New York, NY: Peter Lang.

Wilmut, R. (1980). *From fringe to* Flying Circus*: Celebrating a unique generation of comedy, 1960–1980*. London, UK: Methuen.

Slapstick

Slapstick is a form of physical comedy generally involving broad humor, horseplay, absurd situations, or violent actions. Other familiar examples are pies in the face, pratfalls (landing on one's backside), walking into walls, slipping on banana peels, goofy faces, and "wedgies" (pulling up someone's underwear at the waistband so as to wedge it between the buttocks). The term comes from a slapstick, a theatrical prop consisting of two sticks that slap on each other so that they produce a loud clap when applied with little force, thus simulating a hard blow with no risk to the actors.

Film examples of slapstick include works by or starring The Three Stooges, Laurel and Hardy, Lucille Ball, Jerry Lewis, Dick Van Dyke, Mel Brooks, Rowan Atkinson, Chris Farley, Michael Richards, Sacha Baron Cohen, and Jim Carrey, which feature cartoonish physical (and verbal) abuse, tit-for-tat fights, near-elastic facial expressions, over-the-top gesticulating, and general physical clowning. In fact, some of these stars are so recognized for their slapstick talents that they've had difficulty succeeding in serious roles.

Slapstick comedy also serves as a convention of some of Hollywood's earliest feature-length comedy subgenres. For example, the Marx Brothers' anarchic comedies such as *Horse Feathers* (Norman Z. McLeod, 1932) and *Duck Soup* (Leo McCarey, 1933) incorporated broad physical humor alongside complex double entendres, sight gags, and stream-of-consciousness plots (Monty Python and the aforementioned Mel Brooks almost singlehandedly revived this declining subgenre in the 1970s). As well, screwball comedies such as *Bringing Up Baby* (Howard Hawks, 1938) and *His Girl Friday* (Howard Hawks, 1940) featured pratfalls and roughhousing alongside rapid-fire verbal gymnastics, farce, and heterosexual romantic plotlines. Today's audiences will recognize the same in screwball descendants such as *Bridget Jones's Diary* (Sharon Maguire, 2001) and *Something's Gotta Give* (Nancy Meyers, 2003). Finally, many of Hollywood's animated shorts were constructed almost entirely of slapstick situations. Warner Bros.'s Wile E. Coyote, Elmer Fudd, and Daffy Duck, for instance, frequently fall down holes, fly off cliffs, shoot themselves in the face, find their heads stuck in rocks, or crash into painted images of caves. More recently, animated television shows such as *Spongebob Squarepants* (1999–), *Family Guy* (1999–), and *Phineas and Ferb* (2007–) carry on this tradition in some of their episodes.

But Hollywood "talkies" and television shows are not the only media to embrace slapstick. In fact, since slapstick humor can also be understood and appreciated without words, screen clowns such as Charlie Chaplin, Buster Keaton, Harold Lloyd, Mabel Normand, and Mack Sennett's Keystone Cops relied heavily on the form in their silent films. For instance, to escape a skirmish and gunfire in *The Gold Rush* (Charlie Chaplin, 1925), Chaplin's Little Tramp climbs up and down walls, ducks under tables, and leaps dexterously from one piece of furniture to the next. In a later scene, to avoid plummeting to his death over a cliff, the character seesaws across the floor in a teetering cabin as well as shimmies up a gold-prospector's body, ultimately standing atop his companion's head. Most famous perhaps are the scenes from *The Gold Rush* in which Chaplin's Tramp, virtually dying of hunger, attempts to eats his own shoe and in which the prospector, also famished, hallucinates the Tramp as a giant chicken. While silent, the comedy here is broad, the situations absurd.

Still, silent cinema is not the first to employ slapstick. In fact, slapstick comedy originated in the 16th century from a style of Italian theater known as *commedia dell'arte*. In brief, *commedia dell'arte* features stock character types, masks with exaggerated features, copious props, women performers (for a time at least), outdoor locations, satire, improvisation, jokes, and themes of jealousy, love, and adultery. Significantly, one of the stock characters, Arlecchino—a clever and acrobatic but somewhat simpleminded servant—carries a prop called a *batocchino*, which in English translates to "slapstick." Arlecchino's slapstick is made of two flat paddles of wood separated at the handle, so when an unsuspecting character is whacked with it, often on the backside, the audience hears a surprisingly loud sound. And then they laugh. Heartily. This appeal to our baser selves is one reason slapstick is often delineated as a form of lowbrow comedy. Indeed, slapstick differs from puns or wit or satire, for example, which usually targets a more sophisticated audience.

Nonetheless, this slapstick style spread quickly across 16th-century Europe and ultimately found its way into the works of William Shakespeare, among others. Theatergoers experience this most notably in one of Shakespeare's earliest plays, *The Comedy of Errors* (ca. 1590). Based on the confusion over two sets of identical twins, *The Comedy of Errors* includes farce, madcap chase sequences, and wrongful beatings, the latter of which would have highlighted the slapstick for comedic effect. Slapstick elements are also found in Shakespeare's *The Merry Wives of Windsor* (ca. 1600) in which Falstaff (he of the red nose and large belly) is tricked into hiding in a dirty laundry basket that is eventually tossed into the Thames River. In the play, Falstaff also dresses in drag, is pinched by "fairies" (local school children), and beaten by a woman. Scholars have not always been kind to *The Comedy of Errors* and *The Merry Wives of Windsor* because of their inclusions of slapstick, but modern audiences of London's National Theatre for instance, continue to find them "a comic delight" and "magnificently funny."

The same may be said of the form in general. After all, audiences are still flocking to media that feature this broad, violent, and often silly physical humor. Some recent testaments to this notion, most of which are wildly popular and financially successful: the gross-out (or animal) comedies of Judd Apatow; spoof or parody movies such as *Scary Movie* (Keenan Ivory Wayans, 2000) and Austin Powers: *Goldmember* (Jay Roach, 2002); sketch shows such as *Saturday Night Live* (1975–), *Chappelle's Show* (2003–2006), and *Key & Peele* (2012–); reality programs such as *Jackass* (2000–2002) and *America's Funniest Home Videos* (1989–); and videos uploaded onto YouTube by people who record their own slapstick experiences, hoping someone out there will watch. From the 16th-century Italian stage, to silent and sound cinema, to television, and now to the Internet, slapstick comedy is still going strong.

Kelli Marshall

See also *Commedia Dell'Arte*; Farce; Gag; *Lazzi*; Movies; Parody; Puns

Further Readings

Crafton, D. (1955). Pie and chase: Gag, spectacle, and narrative in slapstick comedy. In K. B. Karnick & H. Jenkins (Eds.), *Classical Hollywood comedy* (pp. 106–119). New York, NY: Routledge.

Dale, A. S. (2000). *Comedy is a man in trouble: Slapstick in American movies*. Minneapolis: University of Minnesota Press.

King, R. (2011). The spice of the program: Educational pictures, early sound slapstick, and the small-town audience. *Film History: An International Journal, 23*(3), 313–330.

Nashawaty, C. (2012, April 6). The Three Stooges collection, Vol. One [Review of DVD]. *Entertainment Weekly*, pp. 70–71.

Parker, J. (2010, October). The *Jackass* effect. *The Atlantic*, pp. 56–59.

Wagner, K. A. (2011). Have women a sense of humor? Comedy and femininity in early twentieth-century film. *The Velvet Light Trap*, *68*, 35–46.

Websites

National Theatre Live (*The Comedy of Errors*): http://www.nationaltheatre.org.uk/shows/the-comedy-of-errors

Smiling and Laughter: Expressive Patterns

Although smiling and laughter are universal, studying these phenomena is a highly complex process. Unpacking the expressive patterns involved in smiling and laughter helps researchers understand and measure the meaning of the expression being conveyed. For example, when Fredrick Redlich, Jacob Levine, and Theodore Sohler (1951) presented patients with cartoons, they were also interested in the nonverbal responses, which they coded while interacting or from video. Six responses (N = negative response, O = no response, s = half-smile, S = full smile, C = chuckle, and L = laughter) were identified as important and constituted the "mirth spectrum." Ordering them according to intensity of response, Edward Zigler, Jacob Levine, and Laurence Gould (1966) created the mirth-response index. Occasionally, chuckle and negative responses were not included, and often the index ranges from no response (0 points) to half-smile (1 point), smile (2 points), and laughter (3 points), which was assumed by some research as being prototypical and exhaustive.

What was revolutionary 50 years ago is no longer tenable. Negative and positive responses are not on a same dimension and might even blend into one single expression (e.g., disgust jokes). Researchers now doubt that laughter should be scored higher than smiling as they propose that smiling and laughing signify different things and thus should not be included in the same index. Importantly, types of smiles, laughter, and negative responses do matter for a comprehensive understanding, but researchers do not believe that words carry the information. Rather, researchers believe it is important to provide accurate morphological observation, that is, how the laughter or smile is created. Moreover, current assessment tools are used for all body movement or all facial actions and are not restricted to smiling and laughter. This entry discusses how researchers measure and classify smiles and laughter as well as the emotions expressed through smiles and laughter and other nonverbal gestures.

Measurement of Smiles and Laughter

Facial measurement is typically based on facial electromyography (or facial EMG) or coding systems. The former is economic but may be less valid. Surface (or needle) electrodes gather signals generated when muscles contract. A reference electrode is also needed. Advantages include continuous measurement and saving time. While fine-grained intensity may vary, the amplitude is not standardized and not comparable across people, as the strength of the signal is affected not only by degree of muscle contraction but also by factors such as muscle thickness, exact muscle placement, skin thickness, and fat layers. Furthermore, muscles may "cross-talk," especially when using surface electrodes (e.g., one electrode placed on one muscle may actually pick up the electric activity from the muscle below or next to it).

Coding systems differ in level of sophistication, usually trading how much information they offer for how time consuming they are. The leading tool, the Facial Action Coding System (FACS) significantly updated by Paul Ekman, Wallace V. Friesen, and Joseph C. Hager in 2002, is an anatomically based, comprehensive, objective technique for measuring all observable facial movement, distinguishing 44 action units (AUs). These are the minimal units that are anatomically separate and visually distinguishable. Each AU can be measured in terms of occurrence, intensity (5 steps), symmetry/asymmetry, and duration. To become a certified coder of FACS, 100 hours of instruction and a final test are required. Different variants (baby FACS, chimpanzee FACS) exist. Although automated coding procedures that identify many AUs exist, they do not catch all AUs and are often inaccurate regarding intensity scores. Hence, they are not yet able to replace manual coding.

Important AUs for the study of smiling and laughter are AU12, AU6, AU7, AU25, AU26, and AU27. AU12 ("lip corner puller") refers to the contraction of the zygomatic major muscle, which pulls the lip corner up diagonally toward the cheekbone. AU6 ("cheek raiser and lid compresser") and AU7 ("lid tightener") describe the actions of the outer and inner part of the orbicularis oculi muscle. The action of the former raises the cheek and causes crow's feet and bulging of the skin below the eye; the latter raises and tightens the lower eyelid. AU25 ("lips part") refers to parting lips, AU26 ("jaw drop") to lowering the jaw, and AU27 ("mouth stretch") to stretching the lower jaw.

The Duchenne Display

Defining smiling as an upward turn of the lip corners is not sufficient for adequate measurement because it does not allow distinguishing among movements by the five facial muscles inserting into the lip corners: the zygomatic major (AU12), zygomatic minor (AU11, "nasolabial furrow deepener"), levator anguli oris (or caninus; AU13, "sharp lip puller"), buccinator (AU14, "dimpler"), and risorius (AU20, "lip stretcher"). It is only the zygomatic major muscle that creates the changes that are typical for a happy smile, the pulling of the lip corners upward and backward. French anatomist Duchenne du Bologne in 1872 discovered that the mere contraction of the zygomatic major muscle gave the impression of a fake smile; a happy expression additionally required contraction of the orbicularis oculi (AU6). Rediscovering this observation, Paul Ekman, Richard Davidson, and Wallace Friesen (1990) named this facial configuration the *Duchenne display*. The Duchenne smile display may include parting of the lips (AU25) and/or lowering (AU26) or stretching (AU27) of the jaw, but other facial action casts doubt that the individual is experiencing joy or a variant of pleasurable emotion. The Duchenne smile is expected to be within two-thirds of a second and 4 seconds, be symmetrical, with both muscles reaching apex at the same time and both onset and offset being smooth.

Willibald Ruch showed that the Duchenne smile is the one elicited by humor stimuli. Studies with jokes and cartoons, funny clips, and interactions between experimenter and participants also elicited laughter, and it became clear that the laughter in response to humor is also based on the Duchenne display, albeit a literature review showed that laughter in general may involve more muscles.

Smiling Is Less Than, Different From, or Equal to Laughter?

The mirth-response index assigns lower numbers to smiling than to laughter, assuming it is qualitatively comparable to but less than laughter. This idea was pioneered by Charles Darwin (1872/1998) who proposed that a graduated series can be followed from "violent to moderate laughter, to a broad smile, to a gentle smile, and to the expression of mere cheerfulness" (p. 206). A second tradition is based on ethological proposed results that smiling and laughter have evolved independently from each other across species. Hence, smiling and laughter should be treated separately in experiments. A third approach treats smiling and laughter equally, and the intensity estimate is based on the intensity of the facial expression (whether or not laughter syllables are uttered).

There is evidence that laughter is indeed more than smiling when occurring in response to humor; it occurs at higher AU12 intensities and when people rate jokes as funnier. The idea of a graduated series cannot be applied when the emotions differ; that is, a contempt smile is not just less than a happy laughter. While Darwin's work on smiling was based on the findings of Duchenne du Bologne, for laughter he added intensified contractions; but for "strongest" or "violent" laughter, he postulated that "frowning" occurs at the apex (i.e., a contraction of the corrugator muscle, AU4 in FACS) as well.

Expressions of Emotions

Positive Emotions

For Darwin, laughter and smiling are expressions of joy. Traditionally, humor research rarely included joy but used more specific emotions. Meanwhile, emotion research distinguishes among different facets of joy. It is evident that in these models the responses to humor are captured by the term *amusement* (i.e., awareness of incongruity in a situation and feeling playful with others in the environment). Michelle N. Shiota, Dacher Keltner, and Oliver P. John (2006) list eight positive emotions: amusement, awe, contentment, gratitude, interest, joy, love, and pride. Ekman (2003) posits that there are 16 universal enjoyable emotions. In addition to five sensory pleasures (tactile, olfactory, auditory, visual, and gustatory), there is amusement, contentment, excitement, relief, wonder, ecstasy (self-transcendent rapture), *fiero* (pride in one's own achievements), *naches* (pride in the achievements of others with whom you have a relationship), elevation, gratitude, and *Schadenfreude* (the joy of a rival's misfortune). Furthermore, he speculates that while the 16 enjoyable emotions differ in their parameters (onset/offset, duration of apex and/or emotion event, and intensity), they will be based on the Duchenne display smile (enjoyment smile).

Other terms or concepts were proposed. Some researchers prefer the term *mirth*; however, no explicit concept of what this emotion entails exactly has been proposed. One concept that was fleshed out in detail was exhilaration (understood as a quick raise and decline in cheerful state or state of hilarity). Exhilaration is the literal translation from the German term *Erheiterung*, which is similar to amusement.

Darwin claims laughter is expressing joy, yet it may occur during other positive emotional states too. In the list of enjoyable emotions by Ekman, it remains unclear which go along with laughter, but amusement, *Schadenfreude*, relief, and tactile are likely candidates.

Negative Emotions

Smiles also go along with negative emotions and are created differently. The unilateral contraction of the buccinator (AU14) muscle is indicative of contempt. There is also a fear smile that involves a symmetric AU20. Also, AU12 is involved in (among other AUs) smiles during negative states, such as sadistic and embarrassment smiles. Furthermore, the AU12 is involved in blends of joy and negative emotions, and in smiles masking negative emotion. Laughter also goes along with negative states—scorn, embarrassment, and hysteria being prominent. It is not clear how these variants of laughter are different from the prototype: for example, whether they are also based on the Duchenne display smile or whether their facial expression involves elements of negative emotions.

Other Types of Smiling and Laughter

One important distinction is whether a smile (or laugh) is emotional (spontaneous) or false (faked). The latter are based on voluntary contractions of the facial muscles (controlled by the motor strip of the neocortex), which happens when wanting to appear joyful when no joy is felt. In a *phony smile* a person does not feel any emotion while smiling (i.e., sole AU12). In *masking smiles*, negative emotions are felt (and partly expressed) that are insufficiently covered by AU12 smiles. Markers of faked expressions have been identified. In humor studies, AU13 has been observed, which still has unknown meaning but occurs when there was some slight resentment to jokes. Further smile types include flirtatious, "grin and bear it," and listener coordination smiles. Various authors distinguish up to 20 different types of smiles. No such classification exists for laughter, but it is clear that contrived laughter exists as well.

Body Movements, Posture, and Gestures

Smiling is purely facial, but laughter (higher intensity) involves the whole body. Darwin states that during excessive laughter, the whole body is often thrown backward and shakes, almost convulsing. Some actions are associated with respiratory movements; for example, backward tilting of the head facilitates forced exhalations, and forced inhalation interrupting two laughter cycles will raise and straighten the trunk. Massive respiratory movements underlying laughter pulses may cause the observed shaking of the shoulders and vibrations detectable on the trunk and extremities. However, changes in posture and body movements have received least attention in the study of laughter.

Tracey Platt and Willibald Ruch

See also Laugh, Laughter, Laughing; Laughter, Psychology of; Laughter and Smiling, Physiology of

Further Readings

Darwin, C. (1998). *The expression of the emotions in man and animals.* New York, NY: Oxford University Press. (Original work published 1872)

Ekman, P. (2003). *Emotions revealed: Recognizing faces and feelings to improve communication and emotional life.* New York, NY: Time Books.

Ekman, P., Davidson, R. J., & Friesen, W. V. (1990). The Duchenne smile: Emotional expression and brain physiology II. *Journal of Personality and Social Psychology, 58*, 342–353.

Ekman, P., Friesen, W. V., & Hager, J. C. (2002). *Facial Action Coding System: A technique for the measurement of facial movement.* Palo Alto, CA: Consulting Psychologists Press.

Redlich, F. C., Levine, J., & Sohler, T. P. (1951). A mirth response test: Preliminary report on a psychodiagnostic technique utilizing dynamics of humor. *American Journal of Orthopsychiatry, 21*(4), 717–734.

Ruch, W. (1993). Exhilaration and humor. In M. Lewis & J. M. Haviland (Eds.), *The handbook of emotions* (pp. 605–616). New York, NY: Guilford Press.

Ruch, W., & Ekman, P. (2001). The expressive pattern of laughter. In A. W. Kaszniak (Ed.), *Emotion, qualia, and consciousness* (pp. 426–443). Tokyo, Japan: Word Scientific.

Shiota, M. N., Keltner, D., & John, O. P. (2006). Positive emotion dispositions differentially associated with Big Five personality and attachment style. *The Journal of Positive Psychology, 1*(2), 61–71.

Zigler, E., Levine, J., & Gould, L. (1966). Cognitive processes in the development of children's appreciation of humor. *Child Development, 37*(3), 507–518.

Social Interaction

Humor plays a major role in interaction between people—in conversation and other forms of spoken discourse and in interactive writing such as online communication and letter writing. The role of humor in such contexts has been studied in various forms of discourse analysis that examine both the formal properties of humor and, importantly, the interactional functions it fulfills. Humor may be an explicit focus of such research, but studies of language play, or creativity in language, often address similar phenomena, and examples of these are included herein.

Formal Properties of Humor

Researchers have identified certain formal categories of humor that occur in interaction between people. For instance, Neal Norrick identifies four categories of conversational humor: jokes, personal anecdotes, wordplay, and irony. Norrick's purpose is theoretical: to distinguish relatively clear examples of these categories and identify differences among them in terms of their humor mechanisms, internal structure, and integration into discourse. A limitation of such categories, however, is that they do not uniquely distinguish particular humorous utterances. In practice, the situation is more complex than these prototypical "clear examples" might suggest. Norrick himself notes that categories blend in conversation, with joke punch lines becoming wisecracks, witty repartees growing into anecdotes, and so on.

Other work has focused on the internal structure of certain types of humor. In important early research, conversation analyst Harvey Sacks analyzes a dirty joke in narrative form, told by a teenage boy to friends, and presented as having been told to the boy by his 12-year-old sister. Sacks identifies a three-part sequential organization in the narrative joke: a "preface," a "telling," and a "response" sequence, and focuses in detail on how each sequence is developed. He discusses further how the sequential organization of the joke packages information in a way that is relevant to the interests of its original teller and intended recipients (i.e., circulating among a 12-year-old girl and her friends).

Many more recent studies have focused on how humor is structured—produced and responded to—within a particular interaction. The following dialogue is from Ronald Carter's study of a 5-million-word corpus of spoken interaction in which several examples of language play were identified:

Members of a family are preparing food for a party:
C: Foreign body in here. What is it?
B: It's raisins and [inaudible]
C: Er oh it's rice with raisins is it?
D: No no no. It's not supposed to be [laughter] erm
C: There must be a raisin for it being
in there. [laughter]
(Adapted from Carter, 2004, p. 93; B, C, and D
refer to speakers)

The pun here ("there must be a raisin ...") emerges during the course of a conversation while preparing food. It plays on a previous mention of the word *raisin*. It is a fleeting performance, responded to by laughter from the audience. Such playful talk is sometimes identified as "conversational joking" or "situational humor," in contrast to the more conventional joke format evident in "joke telling." How such humorous talk is structured collaboratively has been analyzed by various scholars, such as Diana Boxer and Florencia Cortés-Conde, Jennifer Coates, and Norrick, sometimes adopting Gregory Bateson's notion of play frame, the idea that conversationalists can frame and signal their talk as playful and hence not serious. Because such conversational humor is usually spontaneous, its production requires on-the-spot coordination between speakers. Coates adopts a musical metaphor to explain this, comparing the way conversationalists collaborate in a play frame to the coordination required by jazz players.

Humor may exploit the potential of particular modes and media. Angela Goddard's 2011 research on online play includes an instance where a new arrival to a chat room is welcomed with a prolonged and humorously exaggerated greetings routine. The humor is enhanced, she argues, by the postings popping up, in rapid succession, on the screen. Janet Maybin (2011) discusses creativity and play in letter writing, for example, where two penfriends use metaphor playfully in repeated references to postal delays, producing dialogic riffs that extend over several letters. In these examples, as in the spoken dialogue above, humor is collaboratively produced by participants, and the forms it takes relate to the affordances and constraints of the modes and media in which it is produced (face-to-face talk, online chat, letter writing).

In bilingual humor, interactants may exploit the resources of different languages. This is easiest to see in bilingual wordplay, such as, in an example from the south of India, a joking reference to a cow eating a door marked "Pull." The joke plays on the similarity in sound between the English word *pull* and the Tamil word for grass (this and other examples have been collected by R. Amritavalli and S. Upendran, 2011). In a 2012 study of play in digital media interactions between bilingual (English and isiXhosa) speakers in South Africa, Ana Deumert comments that some types of humorous play (e.g., playful flirting) have been associated more with English than with isiXhosa, but that other types (e.g., the playful use of text message abbreviations) have spread from English to isiXhosa. It is likely that what are considered to be appropriate forms of humor across languages will change over time.

A prolific strand of research employs conversation analytical methods to scrutinize how laughter is used in conversation. In key early work, Gail Jefferson (1979) demonstrates how speakers may invite laughter by laughing at the end of what they say. However, while laughter is often thought of as a response to humor, the stimuli of laughter have been widely acknowledged to be complex. Jefferson has examined laughter in nonhumorous contexts; and Phillip Glenn (2003) emphasizes the many other stimuli of laughter including socializing, nervousness, and embarrassment.

Functions of Humor

Researchers interested in humor in social interaction tend to focus on its interactional functions as much as the particular forms it takes. This is prefigured in Sacks's study of a narrative joke, where sequential organization was related to the interests of speakers and listeners. It may seem self-evident that humor is often ludic: designed to amuse or entertain (as discussed by Cook, 2000). However, it also fulfills a wider range of interactional functions.

Importantly, humor is associated with interpersonal functions and with the expression and negotiation of identities between speakers and writers. Humor is often thought of as "oiling the wheels" of communication and with inclusivity and the expression of friendly relations. Maybin's research on letter writing suggests the playful dialogue evident in some letters contributes to mutual alignment, strengthening correspondents' experience of friendship. But (as argued by Cook) humor may also serve as a form of critique or to exclude others.

Various empirical studies reveal that humor may be used to carry out potentially aggressive acts and, simultaneously, to perform in-group rapport building (evident in research by, e.g., Boxer & Cortés-Conde, Holmes, & Norrick). The use of forms such as irony and (self-) teasing may create interpersonal ambiguity or mitigate a potential face threat. In a discussion of such phenomena in higher education discourse, Yu Wang (2012) cites an example of playful critique by a lecturer of his students. Referring to the homework previously assigned to his students, the lecturer comments, "You are going to tell me all the things you've discovered, aren't you?"

The lecturer's critique of his students is ironically implied, and their (joint) understanding of this implied meaning indicates a shared perception of the students' lack of commitment to homework. This, in turn, indicates commonality between the lecturer and students, and potentially enhances their rapport.

A number of studies have focused on humor and identity construction. Mary Crawford (2003) provides a review of work on humor and gender. In a major study of workplace discourse, Janet Holmes shows how humor is used by female and male workers to construct or, at times, challenge and undermine stereotypical gender identities. She also demonstrates that humor in the workplace is associated with institutional power relations. Used by someone in authority, humor may serve to bolster power relations between speakers, but in other contexts (e.g., when used by subordinates) it may alternatively subvert or destabilize power relations.

Goddard's study of online discourse suggests that the lack of visibility in online spaces allows participants to play with different social and institutional roles. In the following example, a UK student playfully adopts the voice of an authority figure (a teacher) in addressing his fellow students:

Andrew: Come on children let's talk about work.

Bilingual humor, such as the Tamil-English pun discussed previously, expresses a bilingual and bicultural identity: both telling a joke and showing appreciation in laughter display familiarity with two linguistic and cultural realms, allowing participants to identify, in this case, as English educated and Indian Tamil-speaking.

Quantitative analyses of large corpora of spoken interaction, such as research by Jennifer Hay (2001) and Hilary Nesi (2012), have also explored sociocultural-identity aspects of humor. Hay, for example, in a quantitative analysis of a corpus of conversations between friends in New Zealand, noted that women are much more likely to share funny personal anecdotes than men.

Studies of humor in institutional contexts (e.g., Holmes's workplace study and Wang's study of humor in higher education discourse) have provided evidence of how humor facilitates both interpersonal and institutional tasks in these contexts: For Holmes, the boundaries between the two are permeable. Holmes focuses on the contention that humor may stimulate workplace creativity. She finds that, while instances are comparatively rare, and associated more with some workplace groups than others, humor may indeed help generate constructive ideas. Play and humor in classroom contexts are also argued to facilitate learning, including language learning (see Cook, 2000; Pomerantz & Bell, 2007).

Such studies tend to focus on the role of particular humorous episodes in particular settings and demonstrate, among other things, the variability of humor and the diverse functions with which it may be associated, suggesting that a relatively contextualized analytical approach is needed for its study. On the other hand, these studies are not always informed by theoretical work on humor, such as the general theory of verbal humor, though this does receive discussion by Norrick. In a critical account of various discourse approaches, Salvatore Attardo suggests that these do not go beyond the general primary functions of humor identified in earlier theoretical work, and there may indeed be a tension between contextualized approaches and the needs of general theory.

A value of the study of humor in social interaction is that this has implications across several academic fields (e.g., pragmatics, conversation analysis, sociolinguistics, applied linguistics) and may have practical implications in areas such as workplace communication or language in education.

Joan Swann and Yu Wang

See also Conversation; Cross-Cultural Humor; Education, Humor in; Linguistic Theories of Humor; Social Network; Workplace Humor

Further Readings

Amritavalli, R., & Upendran, S. (2011). Wordplay across languages and cultures: Interview with G. D. Jayalakshmi. In J. Swann, R. Pope, & R. Carter (Eds.), *Creativity in language and literature: The state of the art* (pp. 103–105). Basingstoke, UK: Palgrave Macmillan.

Attardo, S. (1994). *Linguistic theories of humour.* Berlin, Germany: Mouton de Gruyter.
Attardo, S. (2008). A primer for the linguistics of humour. In V. Raskin (Ed.), *The primer of humour research* (pp. 101–155). Berlin, Germany: Mouton de Gruyter.
Bateson, G. (1953). The position of humour in human communication. In H. von Foerster (Ed.) *Cybernetics, Ninth Conference* (pp. 1–47). New York, NY: Josiah Macey Jr. Foundation.
Boxer, D., & Cortés-Conde, F. (1997). From bonding to biting: Conversational joking and identity display. *Journal of Pragmatics, 27*(3), 275–294.
Carter, R. (2004). *Language and creativity: The art of common talk*. London, UK: Routledge.
Coates, J. (2007). Talk in a play frame: More on laughter and intimacy. *Journal of Pragmatics, 39*(1), 29–49.
Cook, G. (2000). *Language play, language learning.* Oxford, UK: Oxford University Press.
Crawford, M. (2003). Gender and humor in social context. *Journal of Pragmatics, 35*(9), 1413–1430.
Deumert, A. (2012). Txtpl@y: Creativity in South African digital writing. In D. Allington & B. Mayor (Eds.), *Communicating in English: Talk, text, technology* (pp. 216–223). New York, NY: Routledge.
Glenn, P. J. (2003). *Laughter in interaction.* Cambridge, UK: Cambridge University Press.
Goddard, A. (2011). look im over here: Creativity, materiality and representation in new communication technologies. In J. Swann, R. Pope, & R. Carter (Eds.), *Creativity in language and literature: The state of the art* (pp. 141–155). Basingstoke, UK: Palgrave Macmillan.
Hay, J. (2001). The pragmatics of humour support. *HUMOR: International Journal of Humour Research, 14*(1), 55.
Holmes, J. (2000). Politeness, power and provocation: How humour functions in the workplace. *Discourse Studies, 2*(2), 159–185.
Holmes, J. (2007). Making humour work: Creativity on the job. *Applied Linguistics, 28*(4), 518–537.
Jefferson, G. (1979). A technique for inviting laughter and its subsequent acceptance declination. In G. Psathas (Ed.), *Everyday language: Studies in ethnomethodology* (pp. 79–96). New York, NY: Irvington.
Jefferson, G. (1984). On the organisation of laughter in talk about troubles. In J. M. Atkinson & J. Heritage (Eds.), *Studies in emotion and social interaction* (pp. 346–369). Cambridge, UK: Cambridge University Press.
Maybin, J. (2011). Intimate strangers: Dialogue and creativity in penfriend correspondence. In J. Swann, R. Pope, & R. Carter (Eds.), *Creativity in language and literature: The state of the art* (pp. 129–140). Basingstoke, UK: Palgrave Macmillan.
Nesi, H. (2012). Laughter in university lectures. *Journal of English for Academic Purposes, 11*(2), 79–89.
Norrick, N. R. (1993). *Conversational joking: Humor in everyday talk.* Bloomington: Indiana University Press.
Norrick, N. R. (2003). Issues in conversational joking. *Journal of Pragmatics, 35*(9), 1333–1359.
Pomerantz, A., & Bell, N. D. (2007). Learning to play, playing to learn: FL learners as multicompetent language users. *Applied Linguistics, 28*(4), 556–578.
Sacks, H. (1974). An analysis of the course of a joke's telling in conversation. In R. Bauman & J. Sherzer (Eds.), *Explorations in the ethnography of speaking* (pp. 337–353). London, UK: Cambridge University Press.
Sacks, H. (1978). Some technical considerations of a dirty joke. In J. Schenkein (Ed.), *Studies in the organization of conversational interaction* (pp. 249–269). New York, NY: Academic.
Schnurr, S., & Holmes, J. (2009). Using humour to do masculinity at work. In N. R. Norrick & D. Chiaro (Eds.), *Humour in interaction* (pp. 101–123). Amsterdam, Netherlands: John Benjamins.
Wang, Y. (2012). *Chinese students' perceptions of humour in British academic lectures.* Unpublished doctoral thesis, The Open University, Centre for Research in Education and Educational Technology, UK.

Social Network

A social network is a system of interrelationships between actors within a social system. Most typically, the actors of interest are individuals within some defined social group, such as members of a family, students within a classroom, employees within an organization, or residents within a town. Researchers in disciplines such as anthropology, sociology, psychology, epidemiology, and communications use social networks to define characteristics of groups or individuals within the network. For example, "dense" networks are those with many interconnections between individuals. At the individual level, individuals can be described as being "central" (or popular) if they are connected to many others, or as representing "structural holes" if the individual helps bridge a relationship between two otherwise unconnected people.

Social networks can be described using both qualitative and quantitative methods. Qualitatively, social networks can be defined or portrayed through techniques such as participant observation or interviews with members of social groups. Quantitatively, social networks can be established through sociometric methods, in which researchers typically ask individuals to provide numerical responses to questions about some aspects of their relationships with other group members. Social networks are often represented graphically in a sociogram, which depicts who each individual or "node" is connected to, and sometimes the strength of those connections (i.e., strong or weak ties), or their valence (i.e., positive or negative ties).

Social networks are relevant to the discussion of humor because humor is thought to play an important role in creating and maintaining the social relationships that define a social network, and social networks provide the social context in which humor behavior happens. In other words, humor is both a cause and an effect of social networks, as it influences both whether and how people affiliate with one another. This entry discusses the role of humor in the formation, maintenance, and perpetuation of social networks and as a consequence of social network structure.

Humor and the Formation of Social Networks

Ties form within social networks for many reasons, including proximity, similarity, social sharing of knowledge, expertise, or kinship. However, humor might also play an important role in forming social relationships and shaping social networks insofar as it facilitates liking and interpersonal attraction. There is also considerable evidence to suggest that humor appreciation and positive emotions are closely related, even at a neurological level. When we associate another person with positive emotions (i.e., it "feels good" to be around him or her), we want to be around that person more. In addition, there is some evidence that the sound of another person's laughter tends to attract people to that individual, and even more so over time. That is, over time, we associate the pleasurable experience of positive emotions with individuals with whom we share humor and laughter, and the very sound of our laughter tends to reinforce others' bonds to us.

Cecily Cooper (2008), in her relational process model of humor, expanded upon the impact of positive affect on relationships by noting that humor can be used to facilitate self-disclosure and perceptions of similarity and can decrease perceptions of hierarchy or status differences. For example, people can use humor to reveal things about themselves, which tends to heighten a sense of closeness and intimacy. Similarly, the types of things people joke about tend to reveal something about them, and if one's humor makes that person seem more similar to us, we like the person even more. Finally, humor has the potential to reduce perceptions of formal status differences between people, which might otherwise represent barriers to the development of relationships. In particular, self-deprecating humor on the part of a higher status person might alleviate concerns that a lower status person might have about developing a relationship with a high-status individual. However, it is important to note that humor can also be used to reinforce status differences and limit the formation of relationships. For example, use of strongly aggressive or sarcastic humor by high-status individuals, or humor that belittles or disparages others, tends to make the high-status person less accessible by others. In social network terms, positive affect, liking, similarity, and hierarchical salience can influence whether a given interpersonal bond exists at all, and if it exists, whether it is strong or weak, or positive or negative.

Humor and the Maintenance and Perpetuation of Social Networks

Once a social network is formed, as in a work group or group of friends, humor can play an important role in its maintenance and perpetuation. Within social groups, humor allows individuals to voice concerns or anxieties about the group, or to relieve stress experienced by the group's members. In addition, humor helps people communicate about serious matters in a less confrontational manner. Conflict within social groups is inevitable, but if it is not handled effectively, it can lead to member withdrawal, or even complete dissolution of the group. Humor is thought to be valuable in this regard because serious issues can be raised under the guise of "joking around." For example, humor can be used by a group member to communicate mild rebukes or criticism of a group member in a way that reduces defensiveness and helps the individual save face.

Another finding regarding humor and social network maintenance is that social groups tend to develop unique "joking cultures." Joking cultures involve a shared understanding of topics that are appropriate or forbidden for the purposes of humor and often involve a significant learning component whereby subtle "inside" jokes are strongly shared only by members of the in-group. Indeed, joking cultures can determine the boundaries of the social network, and the strength of ties within it.

Some researchers, most notably Avner Ziv (1979), have used sociometric techniques for examining characteristics of humor within social groups. Typically, these techniques ask group members to indicate something about the humor of other group members, such as who has a good or bad sense of humor or how frequently other individuals within the social network use humor. These techniques explicitly recognize the important social character of humor and have the benefit of relying on an accumulation of experience that social network members have as both humorist and audience over a longer period of time. Such measures also avoid problems associated with self-report and can be used to examine the relationships between humor behavior within a group, and characteristics of social networks such as density, centrality (popularity), structural holes, and strong and weak ties. Indeed, sociometric measures of humor tend to be related to social network characteristics, such as number of friendships, liking by others, network centrality, and leadership.

Humor as a Consequence of Social Network Structure

There is some evidence that the nature of social relationships within a social network can influence the type of humor that individuals use and can dictate who is socially permitted to use various types of humor. One interesting set of findings about humor use within social networks concerns teasing behavior. Researchers have generally found that individuals who are teased by others in the group tend to be those with numerous and strong ties to others, rather than newcomers or peripheral members of the group. In addition, individuals who do a lot of teasing also tend to be the target of teasing. These findings suggest that good-natured teasing humor (as opposed to ridicule or humiliation) is an indicator of in-group status within social networks, as indicated by a high number of strong ties to others.

Some of the more complicated findings regarding humor and networks concern the role of hierarchical status in driving humor behavior, and there has been some debate surrounding this issue. Some scholars have maintained that humor tends to occur much more frequently in a downward direction in social groups where individuals differ in terms of formal hierarchical status. That is, humor by people such as managers in organizations is more acceptable than humor by low-status individuals, and that humor tends to be more aggressive and aimed at maintaining status differences and social control. In a similar vein, lower status individuals often push back against perceived status discrepancies by engaging in subversive humor such as mocking and ridicule outside of the presence of high-status individuals.

However, other researchers have found that high-status individuals can become part of the normal pattern of humor interactions within groups, particularly if they are first accepted by others as friends within the core social network. Also, as mentioned, humor can be used to reduce the impact of formal hierarchical differences between individuals. In social network terms, this line of research suggests that people with formal hierarchical status often use aggressive humor to maintain social distance and weak ties with others within the social network, and similarly, lower status individuals can use subversive types of humor to maintain that distance and to strengthen ties with other low-status individuals. However, it is also possible for high-status individuals to become more accepted and to forge strong ties by avoiding aggressive humor and perhaps using self-deprecating humor to reduce apparent status differences.

Christopher Robert

See also Joking Relationship; Relationships, Nonromantic; Subversive Humor; Teasing; Workplace Control; Workplace Humor

Further Readings

Burt, R. S. (1992). *Structural holes: The structure of competition*. Cambridge, MA: Harvard University Press.

Cooper, C. (2008). Elucidating the bonds of workplace humor: A relational process model. *Human Relations, 61*(8), 1087–1115.

Duncan, W. J. (1984). Perceived humor and social network patterns in a sample of task-oriented groups: A reexamination of prior research. *Human Relations, 37*(11), 895–907.

Fine, G. A., & De Soucey, M. (2005). Joking cultures: Humor themes as social regulation in group life. *HUMOR: International Journal of Humor Research, 18*(1), 1–22.

Gest, S. D., Graham-Bermann, S. A., & Hartup, W. W. (2001). Peer experience: Common and unique features of number of friendships, social network centrality, and sociometric status. *Social Development, 10*, 23–40.

Scogin, F. R., & Pollio, H. R. (1980). Targeting and the humorous episode in group process. *Human Relations, 33*(11), 831–852.

Ziv, A. (1979). Sociometry of humor: Objectifying the subjective. *Perceptual and Motor Skills, 49*, 97–98.

SOCIOLOGY

Sociology is the scientific study of social relations and human societies. It is an empirical social science that employs a range of data and research methodologies. Sociology is characterized by theoretical pluralism: There is no one overarching theoretical perspective to which all sociologists adhere. Sociology shares research methodologies and theoretical perspectives with related social sciences like anthropology, folklore, cultural studies, communication, or social history. It differs from these disciplines by its traditional focus on complex contemporary societies and its insistence on including all aspects of social life from microinteractions to long-term macrodevelopments.

Although humor and laughter are social phenomena, sociologists have paid scant attention to humor. The majority of sociological research deals with "serious" topics: social problems and policy-related issues. Hence, insofar as sociologists have researched humor, it has been overwhelmingly concerned with forms of humor considered problematic or dangerous like ethnic, sexist, or political humor, and to the relation between humor and social control, conflict, and exclusion. Systematic attempts to develop a more wide-ranging sociological theory of humor are scarce, and have remained marginal within the field.

This entry first gives an overview of theoretical perspectives on humor. Then, it discusses important current (and recurring) debates in the sociology of humor and gives an overview of research methodologies and strategies in humor sociology.

Theoretical Perspectives

Sociological perspectives on humor can be divided into five broad categories: functionalism, conflict theory, symbolic interactionism, phenomenology, and comparative-historical sociology. These five perspectives are not necessarily mutually exclusive: They highlight different aspects of humor and vary greatly in scope. They are associated with specific research methodologies and types of data, and sometimes with wider societal or political views.

Functionalism

Functionalist sociology interprets humor in terms of the social functions it fulfills for a society or social group. Three general functions of humor are highlighted: relief, control, and social cohesion. Functionalist analyses have argued that humor maintains and supports the social order, first, by acting as a safety valve and allowing people to blow off tensions inherent in social relations. Moreover, humor serves as a means for social control, by reflecting and reinforcing social hierarchies. In particular, jokes and laughter ridicule and mock what does not fit the social order, thus excluding and sanctioning deviant behavior. Finally, humor upholds the social order through maintaining social cohesion: It brings people closer and cements social bonds. Humor is quite unique in its capacity to perform all these functions at once, combining the seemingly contradictory functions of hierarchy building and tension management with bringing about solidarity. Rose Coser's 1959 studies of humor in a hospital setting are important examples of functionalist analysis. Functionalist explanations of humor and laughter are associated with various research methodologies, ranging from small ethnographic studies to macroanalyses of relations between humor and wider social relations.

Functionalism was the dominant perspective in sociology in the mid-20th century. Its insistence that all social phenomena serve to maintain the social order has been widely criticized. This assumption makes functionalist explanations circular and basically untestable. Moreover, functionalism tends to ignore that humor can also be detrimental for the social order, failing to note or explain social change or conflict. Since the 1970s, sociologists rarely employ functionalism as a complete theory or comprehensive framework. However, most social analyses of humor cannot escape paying attention to the functions humor fulfills. Today, sociologists take care not to make a priori assumptions about the functions of humor or its positive contributions to the social order. Instead, context and content are taken into account when establishing which productive or disruptive functions humor may fulfill for whom and at which moment.

Conflict Theory

Conflict theories (also known as critical theories) see humor as an expression of conflict, struggle, or antagonism. In contrast with functionalist theories, humor is interpreted not as venting off—and hence as an avoidance or reduction—but as an expression or correlate of social conflict: humor as a weapon, a form of attack, a means of defense. The edited volume *Humor in Society: Resistance and Control* by Chris Powell and George Paton (1988) offers several examples of conflict approaches to humor. Conflict theories of humor have been used especially in the analysis of ethnic and political humor: In both forms, humor has a clear target, and tends to be correlated with conflict and group antagonism. Conflict analyses highlight the double-edged nature of humor. Those in control can use humor to exercise power; but people in less powerful positions may use it to express resistance. For instance, political or ethnic humor supports existing power relations when the powerful mock the weak, but the weak can also muster it to satirize or ridicule dominant groups or persons. However, most analyses conclude that "upward" humor is less common and less effective than "downward" humor supporting existing power relations.

Conflict theory like functionalism is a broad perspective that claims to capture all forms of humor. It is therefore associated with a wide range of methods, from ethnography to cross-national comparative research. Like functionalism, it has been critiqued for its claim to explain all instances of humor using a single framework and the danger of circularity inherent in encompassing frameworks. Conflict analyses of humor usually are embedded in wider theoretical frameworks explaining culture and society from social conflict, for example, (neo-)Marxism or post-structuralism. They also have affinity with superiority theories of humor.

The conflict approach is used most often to explain and analyze potentially offensive forms of humor, and thus is directly connected with societal controversies about ethnic, sexist, or political humor. This approach to humor (like all aggression or superiority theories of humor) suffers somewhat from conceptual unclarity: Hostility, aggression, superiority, and ethnic or political rivalry are not clearly distinguished or delineated. An important criticism leveled at the conflict approach is that it takes humor too literally, ignoring humor's basic ambiguity: Even if a joke mirrors societal antagonisms, this does not mean that every telling of this joke expresses hostility or conflict. Also, conflict theories generally fail to explain why and when people in situations of conflict decide to use humor rather than more serious expressions of antagonism.

Symbolic Interactionism

Symbolic interactionism here is used to describe a range of microsociological approaches to humor (ethnomethodology, conversation analysis, etc.) that focus on the role of humor in the construction of meanings and social relations in social interaction. What all these approaches have in common is that social relations and social reality are not seen as fixed and given, but as constructed and negotiated in the course of social interaction. A key figure in the microsociology of humor is Erving Goffman, who in 1974 analyzed the role of humor in "the performance of self," and coined the term *framing* to describe the separation of serious interactions from playful and nonserious modes of communication like humor. Symbolic interactionism also is a common approach in sociolinguistic studies of humor.

Humor, while not central to big social structures and processes, plays an important role in everyday interaction. Its ambiguity makes it well suited to negotiations and manipulations of selves and relationships. Symbolic interactionists have analyzed this through detailed studies of social interactions, using ethnographic data or transcripts of conversations. An important theme in this body of research is the relation between gender and the use of humor in interactions. Within humor studies, the microinteractionist approach gave a strong impetus to small-scale studies of spontaneously occurring humor, as an alternative to the analysis of standardized forms of humor (joke cycles, comedy performances) and joke ratings from questionnaires. Moreover, this perspective has made laughter a central theme in sociological humor studies, not only as an automatic response to a humorous stimulus, but as a form of communication on its own.

Symbolic interactionist approaches to humor are usually modest in their theoretical and explanatory ambitions. In the analysis of humor, symbolic interactionism has been combined with functionalist, conflict, or phenomenological theoretical approaches. It is also quite compatible with the classical incongruity, superiority, and relief theories. Critics of this approach have pointed out that symbolic interactionist studies tend to be overly descriptive and particular, and hence, hard to generalize. Moreover, the relation between microsituations and larger institutional and societal structures often remains underanalyzed and undertheorized.

Phenomenology

The phenomenological approach to humor conceptualizes humor as a specific worldview or mode of perceiving and constructing the social world. This humorous outlook is one option among several in the social construction of reality, which phenomenological sociologists see as an ongoing social process. Humor stands out from other worldviews—for instance, the serious outlook dominant in everyday life, or spiritual or religious modes of perception—because of its nonserious, playful outlook. This nonseriousness enables social experimentation and negotiation and allows people to become aware of the constructedness of social life itself. The playful distantiation provided by humor is interwoven with other modes of perception and happens throughout everyday interactions. However, it can also become a more sustained outlook that is embedded in institutionalized roles (the comedian, the satirist), humorous domains like comedy, and rituals like carnival, which can function as an alternative sphere of freedom and resistance. The most complete and sophisticated analysis of the social functions and consequences of the humorous worldview is presented in Michael Mulkay's 1988 *On Humour: Its Nature and Its Place in Modern Society*. Most phenomenologists do not collect their own data, but instead rely on findings from other studies, including a wide range of historical, ethnographic, or textual data, to develop an integrated perspective on humor.

Critics have pointed out that phenomenological approaches to humor tend to essentialize humor. By focusing on humor as worldview, they neglect other meanings and functions of humor, including negative or dysfunctional effects. Moreover, phenomenological approaches overstate the importance of humor by giving it a unique and central function in social life—a claim that is hard to test or substantiate. Finally, phenomenological sociology often borders on philosophy and is hard to operationalize: It provides inspiring insights but it is unclear how these are to be used in actual empirical research. However, unlike other approaches, the ambiguity and nonseriousness of humor are central to this perspective. Hence, phenomenological sociology takes into account the peculiarities of humor that are ignored or downplayed in especially the functionalist and conflict frameworks.

Comparative-Historical Approach

Comparative-historical sociology attempts to understand and explain the social role of humor through comparisons in time and place. Strictly speaking, it is a method rather than a theory: Comparative-historical studies of humor draw on different theoretical traditions and may include insights from functionalist, conflict, or phenomenological approaches as well as general sociological theories. Most sociological work on humor since the 1990s is probably best captured by this broad umbrella term. Christie Davies's work on jokes and targets around the world is the prime example of this comparative-historical approach. Comparing joke cycles around the world, Davies found that specific humorous scripts (e.g., stupidity, dirtiness) are found in many places around the world and are associated with specific relations between jokers and their targets. Thus, comparison both unveils humorous universals (people all over the world tell stupidity jokes), and it uncovers the factors determining systematic variations in joking patterns across cultures (social relations determine who calls whom stupid). In other words, whom people joke about reveals something about the relationship between the jokers and the butts of their jokes; and what people joke about reflects what they find important and what is a source of concern to them. Other comparative studies have used a similar approach to analyze differences across social groups and historical periods in topics of humor, humorous styles and genres, as well as the status of humor.

Comparative-historical studies require research materials that allow systematic comparison over time and place. Archival research, for instance of folklore or historical archives, as well as secondary data analysis is common in this type of research. Occasionally, comparative-historical studies are based on original data collection, for instance data comparing sense of or use of humor by men and women, different ethnic groups, or different nations. The main critique leveled against this type of research is that it may reveal more about the societies or periods it compares than about humor per se. Indeed, comparative-historical studies may pay very little attention to the specificity of humor, treating it as yet another cultural expression. Consequently, comparative-historical studies work best when complemented with more specific theoretical insights from theories about humor and laughter.

Recent Developments and Debates in the Sociology of Humor

The main debate in the sociology of humor (and in humor studies generally) has to do with the potential serious implications of humor. This debate has focused on "dangerous" or "contested" forms of humor like political, ethnic, and sexist humor. Conflict theorists (and some symbolic interactionists) typically stress the serious potential of humor in social conflict. For instance, they argue that anti-hierarchical humor—for example, feminist humor, political satire in totalitarian regimes—functions as resistance, and that "top-down" humor supports power structures and oppresses the powerless. Their opponents in the debate typically counter that such theorists overstate the import of humor: Its fundamental ambiguity makes its "real" meaning impossible to establish, and its impact negligible compared with real exercise of force.

This debate has been rekindled in the 21st century with a broader scope. After many centuries in which humor and laughter had a bad reputation, modern humor studies have stressed the beneficial character of humor, both for society and for the psyche. Phenomenological humor sociologists also stress the positive aspect of humor. This has sparked a counter-reaction: the emergence of the "critique of humor." Scholars like Michael Billig, Sharon Lockyer, and Paul Lewis have pointed to the "dark side of humor": its capacity to hurt, shame, exclude, and exercise social control. This debate repeated many arguments of earlier debates about the seriousness or harmfulness of ethnic and political humor. However, it differed in its greater nuance in discussing various types of humor and in its inclusion of claims from psychological studies, distinguishing clearly between positive and negative forms of humor.

Another important recent development in the sociology of humor has been the growing attention to mediated forms of humor. People increasingly consume and share humor via (electronic) media. This leads to new questions, as well as the rephrasing and reframing of old questions. First, the question arises whether the functions and social mechanisms associated with humor in interactions are the same in mediated interactions. For instance, in mediated interactions jokers cannot always foresee or adapt to their audience responses. Second, the rise of mediated humor leads to the increasing globalization, or cross-national diffusion, of humor. As a consequence, humor audiences are increasingly culturally diverse. This may lead to a greater diversity in responses, sometimes with unexpected consequences. However, the globalization of humor also provides researchers with fascinating new arenas to explore cross-national differences in sense of humor: What jokes travel where? How are jokes adapted as they move across cultural or linguistic boundaries? Finally, the growing attention to mediated forms of humor has brought to the fore the issue of genre. Most sociological humor scholarship has been concerned with a limited number of humorous forms. People increasingly enjoy humor not in face-to-face interaction but through a variety of media: print, television, the Internet. This mediatization of humor and the rise of the Internet have resulted in the emergence of new, mediated, humorous forms, and to the reinvention of older humorous genres, many of which are derived from earlier folk genres. Sociologists, as well as communication scholars and folklorists, are currently debating the meanings and functions of these new humorous genres and forms.

Research Methodologies

Sociology is a predominantly empirical discipline: Attempts to theorize humor as a social phenomenon are usually combined with empirical inquiry, and theories are tested on the basis of empirical evidence. Early sociological studies of humor typically draw on rather impressionistic armchair analysis; recent theoretical explorations of humor have also drawn on a wide variety of sources and personal impressions to substantiate theories. However, most studies today rely on systematically collected data.

An important research method for studying humor, in particular nonscripted or conversational humor, is (ethnographic) observation of small-scale interactions. Observations and ethnography of humor have become increasingly systematic, using sound or video recordings of humorous interactions, and coding schemes to analyze data. Sociologists of humor also have relied on surveys and questionnaires, especially to map and compare use and evaluation of types of humor in different social groups. Many researchers have asked respondents to rate jokes, and then compared responses of, for instance, people with different ethnic backgrounds, genders, political affiliations, or degrees of hostility against the groups targeted in jokes. A third common method for sociologists is to rely on recorded instances of humor, such as comic texts and registration of performances, archival materials, jokes, historical writings, cartoons, literary sources, or historical accounts by others. In this type of research, various mediated forms of communication (e.g., Internet humor, television programs) are also increasingly analyzed—although this is more common in the adjacent field of communication studies. In humor research, such materials are especially important because it is difficult to "catch" humor in the everyday interactions where it is most common. These materials can then be analyzed further, for instance through qualitative or quantitative content analysis. Moreover, sociologists have studied the reception of such secondary materials, using other sources (e.g., newspaper reviews, commentaries). The rise of the Internet has enabled researchers to trace the spread and reception of humorous materials with increasing ease and sophistication.

Other sociological research methods have been less commonly employed in humor studies. Experimental research is common in humor psychology but rarely used in sociology. Interviews and focus groups (group interviews) are used occasionally to elicit humor tastes and opinions on humor. A recurring problem in this method is the problematic relation between people's statements and their actual behavior. Finally, mixed-methods studies, which combine different research methodologies to answer a research question, are increasingly common in humor sociology.

Giselinde Kuipers

See also Culture; Ethnicity and Humor; Gender and Humor, Psychological Aspects of; Political Humor; Social Interaction

Further Readings

Billig, M. (2005). *Laughter and ridicule: Towards a social critique of humor.* London, UK: Sage.

Coser, R. (1959). Some social functions of laughter. *Human Relations*, *12*, 171–182.

Davies, C. E. (1990). *Ethnic humor around the world: A comparative analysis*. Bloomington: Indiana University Press.

Davies, C. E. (2011). *Jokes and targets*. Bloomington: Indiana University Press.

Kuipers, G. (2006). *Good humor, bad taste: A sociology of the joke*. Berlin, Germany: Mouton de Gruyter.

Kuipers, G. (2008). The sociology of humor. In V. Raskin (Ed.), *The primer of humor research* (pp. 365–402). Berlin, Germany: Mouton de Gruyter.

Lewis, P. (2006). *Cracking up: American humor in a time of conflict*. Chicago, IL: University of Chicago Press.

Lockyer, S., & Pickering, M. (Eds.). (2005). *Beyond the joke: The limits of humour*. Basingstoke, UK: Palgrave.

Mulkay, M. (1988). *On humour: Its nature and its place in modern society.* Oxford, UK: Polity.

Powell, C., & Paton, G. (Eds.). (1988). *Humour in society: Resistance and control.* New York, NY: St. Martin's Press.

Robinson, D., & Smith-Lovin, L. (2001). Getting a laugh: Gender, status, and humor in task discussions. *Social Forces, 80,* 123–158.

Shiffman, L. (2007). Humor in the age of digital reproduction: Continuity and change in Internet-based comic texts. *International Journal of Communication, 1,* 187–209.

South African Humor

There is a very small body of historical writing on humor specific to South Africa, within a growing corpus of literature on humor in the broader African context. Much of this research is functionalist, asking, for example, as Ebenezer Obadare (2010) does: "What can humor accomplish when faced with unbending state power in a continent ravaged by the most horrendous fatalities? If comics cannot remove sit-tight despots, of what use are they?" (p. 92). Humor certainly can operate as a subversive force, exposing the incongruities both in the prominent structures of power and in its quotidian exercise of dominance, rendering the familiar unfamiliar and thereby challenging the status quo and producing opportunities for critique. So, humor can operate as a weapon of resistance but, as this entry shows, it can also act as an instrument of state control in which an autocratic leader or regime uses satire to undermine its challengers. Focusing largely on the postapartheid transition from 1994 onward, this entry discusses humor in South Africa's fractured history and fractious society.

Both models of humor appear in Sandra Swart's (2009) research into the laughter of the conquered Boers (later Afrikaners) after the South African War (1899–1902). Reading through diaries and war chronicles, one observes how the Boers managed to "keep joking" even during the worst of the conflict. Humor could act as a way of passing on morality tales and codes of behavior, thereby maintaining social cohesion, defining the boundaries of the community, and fostering solidarity. Thus "the fraternal laughter of insiders also posted a *no trespassing* sign to outsiders." Laughter could operate as a social instrument, deployed to neutralize tension, to police behavior, to reinforce group identity, and to lift morale. In the aftermath of war, in the first "New South Africa," the defeated Boers smuggled in political protest in comic camouflage, through satirical poems. The Boer republics became part of the British imperial dominion and English was made the sole official language. This lead to the kind of humor embedded in the very mechanics of social power: A familiar story told by Afrikaners was that their children who dared speak more than the three hours of "Dutch-Afrikaans" permitted at school had to bear a board that read, "I'm a donkey, I spoke Dutch." Arguably, this was the humor of the powerful, but not the *all*-powerful. The new regime still needed to disparage those who did not conform in order to protect the dignity of the new order.

As the century progressed, the apartheid state enacted the Suppression of Communism Act (1950) and the Publications and Entertainments Act (1963) to crack down on dissent. In response, *Drum* magazine—the most widely read among Black South Africans at the time—used humor to evade the censors and allowed artists to "accommodate to oppression without going mad" (Dodson, 1974, p. 318). Don Dodson has argued that much of the humor was actually socially conservative—it posed little threat to authority so it was permitted to exist, it eased the troubled soul of the artist, and it diverted, however briefly, an unhappy readership—thus it really served "the interests of everyone in an oppressive system" except "those who dare to change it" (p. 328). This leads historians to challenge the idea of the joke as a minirevolution: Sometimes humor offers not insurgence but only its illusion. As Khalid Kishtainy (1985) contended, "people joke about their oppressors, not to overthrow them but to endure them" (pp. 7, 179). Indeed, even overtly political jokes may sometimes be accommodations with authoritarianism: They permit the joke tellers to feel as though they are exercising agency, but without taking action. Thus, as Swart (2009) argued of some of the post-South African War humor, some "jokes are not an instrument of revolution but, quite the reverse, an index of resignation."

Nevertheless *Drum* reporters demonstrated courage by investigating labor exploitation scandals and prison conditions—its staff were under security police surveillance and it was banned between 1965 and 1968. Many pieces in *Drum* simultaneously deployed irony to subtly sabotage the social order. Likewise, many South African musicians adopted satire to escape censorship. Other case studies have shown how oppressed groups used humor to critique apartheid. Thomas Blom Hansen (2005) has demonstrated, for example, how South African Indians, marginalized under apartheid, employed spontaneous jokes, wordplay, and everyday mockery of the stereotypes about themselves, all of which offered a way to reflect on a painful past and present. Mohamed Adhikari has considered the nuances of a racist joke told against Coloureds under apartheid, and noted how humor could be rallied for retribution, observing the popularity of the "Van der Merwe" joke in Coloured communities (which made fun of a stock Afrikaner character who figured in the jokes as uncouth, boorish, and stupid). Similarly, homosexual men, another group oppressed by the conservative social order and discriminatory laws, developed a gay argot with roots in the witty, barbed *moffietaal* (homosexual language) of Coloured drag culture, which filtered into the White gay community. Many words in Gayle, an English- and Afrikaans-based gay argot, are playful alliterative formations using women's names, such as *Priscilla* for "police" and *Jennifer Justice* for "the Law," used with parody and self-irony. Their self-deprecating humor posed a gallant resistance to the dour conservatism of apartheid South Africa.

Humor may also be used for overt social engineering. For example, after the first fully democratic election in 1994, the South African Broadcasting Corporation commissioned the situation comedy *Suburban Bliss* at a cost of 11 million rand, to promote what Dorothy Roome called "nation-building and cultural reconciliation" using humor as a way to address sensitive issues for a racially diverse audience.

Another body of comedic work appeals to a multicultural audience, which is still rare even in democratic South Africa, but makes no claims to such social engineering. Instead, historians of the recent past can use it as a complex lens into the historiographical model: Afrikaans comedian Leon Schuster (1951–) started as a "candid-camera" prankster for White South African audiences of the state broadcaster in the 1970s, but converted to mainstream movie making. He captured a considerable and diverse audience for his earthy, slapstick films. Indeed, his *Mr. Bones* became the highest grossing South African movie. In it, a fictitious "tribe" needs the help of a White *sangoma* ("witch doctor" or, more properly, a practitioner of herbal medicine, divination, and counseling), the eponymous Mr. Bones (played by Schuster). Schuster has been critiqued for his lowbrow brand of populism and his refusal to offer serious political satire. Yet, other critics have argued that Schuster uses comedy to “conceal his motives”—to “negatively define black people through laughter” (Mamatu, 2006, p. 6). Indeed, Tsepo Mamatu accuses him of “cinemythologising” the “Dark Continent” and infantilizing Africans. Yet, Schuster’s movies have a broad Black following in South Africa.

Political Satire

Interestingly, in postapartheid South Africa some of the bravest political satire has come from a fast-food chicken chain. The Nando’s chain, which specializes in fiery flame-grilled chicken marinated in peri-peri sauce (using the chili pepper also known as piri piri), also provides equally blistering political commentary. Their advertisements deal with contemporary and quintessentially South African issues—such as racism, neighboring Zimbabwe’s despotic Robert Mugabe, and racial stereotyping. An advertisement satirizing xenophobia was banned by the state-funded public broadcaster. Nando’s responds rapidly to sociopolitical events—frequently through advertisements that “go viral,” through electronic mail and social networking sites. Interestingly, members of the public have also started to create amateur versions in the same vein—which reflects the exercise of agency by ordinary people who participate in politics amid widespread alienation. In one example, as a critique of the premier’s profligacy and promiscuity, a local artist depicted South African President Jacob Zuma in a painting called *The Spear of the Nation.* In it Zuma adopts a pose reminiscent of Soviet posters of Lenin, but with his genitals exposed. The image triggered a defamation lawsuit by Zuma’s ruling African National Congress and outrage from both pro-state culture-brokers and pro-freedom of expression groups. Cyberspace saw the rapid dissemination of these two playful advertisements, with or without official Nando’s endorsement, with the tagline added (unofficially), “we are not scared to show our cocks.”

This cartoon depicts President Jacob Zuma about to engage in a rape of Lady Justice. Published in the South African *Sunday Times* on September 7, 2008, it shows Zuma being egged on by his political allies, who are pinning Lady Justice to the ground.

Source: Zapiro.

The company itself claims that the South African public has come to view Nando’s as a plucky vox populi challenging the establishment’s pecking order, and has compared itself to satirical cartoonist Jonathan Shapiro. Like Nando’s, Shapiro (known as Zapiro) has also focused a good deal of his satirical attention on the president’s sexual mores. Born in 1958, in the 1980s Shapiro became active in the newly formed anti-apartheid movement, the United Democratic Front, and participated in the End Conscription Campaign. He was arrested under the Illegal Gatherings Act and scrutinized by government intelligence agents.

Zapiro also caricatured the *Spear of the Nation,* replacing the genitals with a showerhead. In 2005, Zuma faced allegations of having raped a family friend who was HIV-positive. He denied the rape allegations and was later acquitted of rape charges, but he acknowledged having unprotected sex with the woman and testified that he took a shower afterward in the misapprehension this would minimize the risk of contracting the virus. Thereafter Zapiro depicted him with a shower permanently attached to his head (see cartoon). In another cartoon, Zapiro drew an erect penis with a face and legs and a showerhead on its head looking at itself in a mirror. The cartoon was condemned by the ruling party and its allies.

Zapiro is part of a tradition of cartoonists dating to the mid-19th century. In South Africa’s earlier political history, cartoonists played a significant political role. Political cartoons (a perennial primary source for historians) first drew heavily on British satirical style, as in *Sam Sly’s African Journal,* which appeared from 1843 to 1851, and upheld the conservative social mores of White settlers at the Cape. Christopher Holdridge has shown how the “collective tittering” of colonists affords historians a window into the fissures within bourgeois culture and the distinctive discourse of racism developing at the Cape of Good Hope. The first prominent local cartoonist, D. C. Boonzaier (1865–1950), satirized socioeconomic developments, creating a stock figure of Hoggenheimer, a corpulent cigar-smoking capitalist. He also critiqued high politics, and was widely regarded as (at least partly) responsible for the fall of General Louis Botha, the first premier of the Union of South Africa after emancipation from British rule.

Ken Vernon has discussed the "penpricks" to the state's conscience by political cartoons under apartheid, despite the shield provided by the often draconian censorship laws. An example is Donald Kenyon's cartoon in the *Daily Dispatch* in 1977, which referenced the murder of Black activist Steve Biko in police custody. The minister of justice casually peruses a newspaper report of the death, while Lady Justice helplessly gestures in the background, seemingly to question "Why?"

Similarly, in the postapartheid milieu, Zapiro and others have targeted high-ranking government officials. In 2008, in the run-up to Zuma's corruption trial, Zapiro portrayed Zuma undoing his belt to rape Lady Justice, while she lay pinned down by his political henchmen. This triggered a public debate around issues of freedom of speech, gender violence, and racial stereotyping. The cartoon showed an ANC cabal abusing the judiciary, theoretically a shield against the abuse of power by the combined executive and legislative authorities. It also prompted the public to remember Zuma's previous trial in 2006, in which he was acquitted of rape charges. In 2006, Zapiro was sued by Zuma in a multimillion rand defamation lawsuit for the cartoonist's depictions of the ANC leader around the time of his rape trial. After the publication of the "Rape of Justice," Zuma sued both the *Sunday Times* and Zapiro—for 5 million rand. But just before the case was supposed to start, Zuma's legal team dropped the "dignity" claim of 1 million rand and reduced the defamation damages amount from 4 million rand to 100,000 rand and an unconditional apology. Zapiro rejected this offer. Days before the trial, Zuma withdrew his case altogether. Zuma had to pay a portion of the newspaper's legal fees.

Stand-up comedy has taken off astonishingly in South Africa in the last 2 decades. As noted by Zoe Parker, women remain scarce in post-1994 comedy circuits, though: Perhaps while the racial order has changed, with multicultural audiences and performers, the gender order has been slower to shift. Stand-up has become very politically thematic, challenging the shifting ontology of democracy in postapartheid South Africa. As Julia Katherine Seirlis (2011) argues, this "before-and-after story" narrates the transition between the "puritanical strictures and censorship of the National Party's apartheid" and the "new possibilities for freedom . . . in a democracy riddled with profound social and political problems of extreme violence and poverty—and run by the ANC, a ruling party with a strong sense of entitlement to State power."

Humor destabilizes the dignity of those in power, rupturing hegemonic narratives. As Obadare has shown, in 2002, a diplomatic rift was only just avoided between South Africa and Nigeria when Nigerian president Olusegun Obasanjo objected to his ample belly being mocked by a pair of South African radio DJs. Jokes do cross borders. As Roome has argued, for example, there is a strong overlap among multiple variations of trickster figures in Africa that crosses national borders—and there are powerful thematic similarities in the humor of the Hausa people and South African situation comedies. The idiographic should not be confused with the exceptional.

Tellingly, in the run-up to the ruling party's elective conference at the end of 2012 and in the wake of new accusations of corruption against Zuma, members of the South African Communist Party, which is allied with the ANC, militated for legislation to prevent the parody of the office of the president and render illegal the impugning of the president's "dignity." Perhaps this is the strongest indication of the power of joking. Moreover, this move has a precedent: Two generations before, the Nationalist Party leader General James Barry Munnik Hertzog tried to introduce legislation in 1937 to "protect" leaders and foreign heads of state and diplomats from "insults"—after the German ambassador grumbled about the South African press' mockery of the Nazis. One of the ideas behind the proposed new legislation was to cleanse such "anti-" and "un-national" elements from the press. The attempt was scuppered by General Jan Smuts's replacing Hertzog and declaring war on the Third Reich. But when the Nationalists returned to power, they promulgated the 1961 Republic of South Africa Constitution Act criminalizing any act calculated to violate the dignity of a state president.

Free of the censorship and media restrictions of the apartheid era, South Africans now engage in vigorous and often humorous criticism of society's powerful. It remains to be seen whether those in power will hem in the freewheeling culture of humor in South Africa.

Sandra Swart

See also Cartoons; Journalism; Political Humor; Satire; Stand-Up Comedy

Further Readings

Adhikari, M. (2006). God made the White man, God made the Black man . . .: Popular racial stereotyping of coloured people in apartheid South Africa. *South African Historical Journal, 55*(1), 142–164.

Cage, K., with Evans, M. (2003). *Gayle—the language of kinks and queens: A history and dictionary of gay language in South Africa.* Houghton, South Africa: Jacana Media.

Dodson, D. (1974). The four modes of *Drum*: Popular fiction and social control in South Africa. *African Studies Review, 17*(2), 317–343.

Hansen, T. B. (2005). Melancholia of freedom: Humour and nostalgia among Indians in South Africa. *Modern Drama, 48*(2), 297–315.

Holdridge, C. (2010). Laughing with Sam Sly: The cultural politics of satire and colonial British identity in the Cape Colony. *Kronos, 36*(1), 28–53.

Kishtainy, K. (1985). *Arab political humour.* London, UK: Quartet Books.

Mamatu, T. (2006). *The colonising laughter in* Mr. Bones *and* Sweet and Short. Johannesburg, South Africa: University of the Witwatersrand.

Mantzaris, E. A. (1985). Jokes, humour, and society: The South African case. *South African Journal of Sociology, 16*(3), 111–116.

Mason, A. (2003). Black and White in ink: Discourses of resistance in South African cartooning. In A. Zegeye & R. L. Harris (Eds.), *Media, identity and the public sphere in post-apartheid South Africa* (pp. 147–168). Boston, MA: Brill.

Merrett, C. (1994). *A culture of censorship: Secrecy and intellectual repression in South Africa.* Cape Town, South Africa: David Philip.

Obadare, E. (2009). The uses of ridicule: Humour, "infrapolitics" and civil society in Nigeria. *African Affairs, 108*(431), 241–261.

Obadare, E. (2010). State of travesty: Jokes and the logic of socio-cultural improvisation in Africa. *Critical African Studies, 2*(4), 92–112.

Page, M. E. (1981). "With Jannie in the jungle": European humor in an East African campaign, 1914–1918. *The International Journal of African Historical Studies, 14*(3), 466–481.

Parker, Z. (2002). Standing up for the nation: An investigation of stand-up comedy in South Africa post-1994 with specific reference to women's power and the body. *South African Theatre Journal, 16*(1), 8–29.

Roome, D. (1999–2000). Humor as "cultural reconciliation" in South African situation comedy: Suburban bliss and multicultural female viewers. *Journal of Film and Video, 51*(3–4), 61–87.

Roome, D. (2002). The serious "consequences" of comedy: Negotiating cultural change and difference through humour. *South African Theatre Journal, 16*(1), 44–62.

Seirlis, J. (2011). Laughing all the way to freedom? Contemporary stand-up comedy and democracy in South Africa. *HUMOR: International Journal of Humor Research, 24*(4), 513–530.

Swart, S. (2009). "The terrible laughter of the Afrikaner"—Towards a social history of humour. *Journal of Social History, 42*(4), 889–917. Retrieved from http://sun025.sun.ac.za/portal/page/portal/Arts/Departemente1/geskiedenis/docs/The%20laughter%20of%20the%20Afrikaner.pdf

Vernon, K. (2000). *Penpricks: The drawing South Africa's political battlelines.* Cape Town, South Africa: Spearhead Press.

South American Literature, Humor in

Addressing humor in South America, specifically in Latin American literature, involves a web of possibilities and three major considerations: (1) infiltration in all literary genres, including some resurrected from ancient times and those created by their authors; (2) unpredictable apparitions, be they in works that handle humor as an incidental aesthetical resource mingled with other resources, or in works that are preeminently humorous; and (3) manifestation in different kinds, be it as function of satirizing vices, defects, and abuse of power and the neocolonial attitudes in societies of Latin American nations; or as what Ramón Gómez de la Serna called *humorismo*, namely, a humor that is not strictly ideological but ludic, whether in an intellectual or a popular vein. This entry discusses humor in Latin American literature, focusing on its development and trends and highlighting several exemplary literary works.

Development

Humor has in fact been present in Hispanic American literature from the onset. During the colonial period (1492–1820), two major satirists emerged. The first, Sor (Sister) Juana Inés de la Cruz (1651–1695), lived in Mexico. A self-taught child prodigy and proto-feminist, she wrote satires, among other works. A woman, argues Sor Juana, in the *Sátira filosófica* (Philosophical Satire, Poem 92), cannot win because, in the game of seduction: "If not willing, she offends / but willing, she infuriates" (translation by Margaret Sayers Peden). The second colonial author, Juan del Valle y Caviedes (1645–1697), lived in Peru. He wrote social and political satires, targeting colonialist administrators and the medical profession.

El Periquillo Sarniento (The Mangy Parrot), written in 1816 by José Joaquín Fernández de Lizardi—the first Hispanic American novel—exposed readers to a satirical outlook that swings between moral didacticism and the mischievous mishaps of its main character, Pedro Sarmiento. Throughout the 19th century, other works with humorous segments emerged in the new nations, such as *Tradiciones peruanas* (Peruvian Traditions, 1872–1875) by Ricardo Palma and *Martín Fierro* (1872–1879) by José Hernández. Yet, among the modernists, humor did not find a place of privilege. An exception to this is the poetry of Colombian postmodernist Luis Carlos López. Avant-garde fiction writers and poets of the early 20th century brought about a humor boom. As a consequence of literary trends that presumed rejection of a strictly sentimental and pure conception of beauty rooted in romanticism, symbolism, and modernism, avant-garde poets featured a critical, liberating attitude and a high sense of ludic experimentalism, where irreverence for traditional life styles and aesthetic notions led to irony and humor.

An author who considerably contributed to promote this new spirit was Spaniard Ramón Gómez de la Serna, inventor of *greguerías*, a concise genre defined as metaphor + humor De la Serna's surreal wit has been widely praised. Cutting-edge poets, such as Argentinian Oliverio Girondo and Uruguayan Alfredo Mario Ferreiro, were inspired by de la Serna in *Veinte poemas para leer en el tranvía* (Twenty Poems to Be Read on the Tram, 1922) and *El hombre que se comió un autobus* (The Man Who Ate a Bus, 1927), respectively. In addition to the *greguería,* two other techniques are manifest and become of essence for humor in avant-gardism: (1) *collage* as an experimental principle of unpredictable juxtaposition and combination of words or fragments from socially disconnected languages; and (2) free or analogical fantasy in the creation of poetic imagery, understood as transcending the narrow boundaries of the *greguería.*

Macunaíma (1928) by Brazilian Mario de Andrade is an avant-garde novel with multiple funny situations. This novel shows the survival of the carnival tradition, as in the theory of Mikhail M. Bakhtin, both for free fantasy nurtured by the wonderful folklore flavor and the polyphonic arrangement of voices. *Macunaíma* has been called an epic-comic poem, but its fictional conception resembles the style of *La vie de Gargantua et Pantagruel* (Gargantua and Pantagruel, ca. 1532–ca. 1564) by François Rabelais, and therefore provides a connection with Menippean satire.

Trends

Anti-Poetry

In 1952, Nicanor Parra and a group of his creative friends, among them Enrique Lihn and Alejandro Jodorowsky, as if following instructions from Tristan Tzara to write a Dada poem with randomly pasted clippings from the daily news, exhibited in Ahumada Street at Santiago de Chile different humorous collages extracted from newspapers. The humorous effect on passersby was evident. It was the soundest foundation for the emergence of anti-poetry, which may be traced back to 1954, when Parra's book *Poemas y antipoemas* (Poems and Anti-poems) was published.

The essential strategy of anti-poetry stems firstly from critical denial of the bourgeoisie's worldview, social alienation, and stupidity, and secondly from rejection of poetry based on an emotional or subjective concept of beauty. Anti-poetry is a revolt against the narcissist poetic self. The lyric poet with a modernist background is replaced by the anti-poet, or by anti-poets invented by Parra as the characters *energúmeno* (madman) and the *Cristo de Elqui.* Among the techniques that cause humorous effects are the collage, the manipulation of dialogue, and other traditional humorous techniques. While not all poems included in anti-poetry may be classified as humorous, as there is an existential and pathetic streak that runs through them, it can be said that Parra's anti-poetic humor takes four major directions: *satirical,* against social and political order; *festive,* by incorporation to the *La cueca larga* (a type of dance) of humor in popular Chilean poetry; *dark,* which spins around his obsession with death; and a more *intellectual* humor maintained within the boundaries of verbal wit, as in *Artefactos* (Artifacts, 1972).

Intellectual Humor

Among the writers who use intellectual humor, we find Argentinians Macedonio Fernández and

Jorge Luis Borges, as well as Uruguayan Felisberto Hernández. Although his style is quite different from Parra's, it may be said that Macedonio Fernández designed an aesthetic negation proposal that he called *belarte*, as it contemplated destruction of realistic effect in the novel. With this, according to Emir Rodríguez Monegal (1972), Fernández created the first Hispanic American anti-novel. As opposed to realism, *belarte* prose occurs in two genres: the novel and *belarte* of the illogical. The latter one is nurtured by the conceptual joke, a type of intellectual humor based on the absurd. Thus, "I have so little to say, gentlemen, that I'm afraid it will take me too long to find in a brief toast a tiny place to insert the end" (Fernandez, 1974, *Papeles de Recienvenido* [Newcomer Papers], 122, translated by Leticia Damm).

Concerning the humor of Borges, one should consider the parody in his joint work with Adolfo Bioy Casares. While humor cannot be considered a predominant feature in Borges's poems and short stories, in some of the latter intellectual humor emerges. In "El Aleph" (The Aleph), for instance, the verses of character Carlos Argentino Danieri are a parody of affected poetry, and repetition of the Z in the last names Zunino, Zungri, and Zunni in a single sentence also creates a humorous effect. *"El informe de Brodie"* (The Brodie Report) partially parodies *Gulliver's Travels* by Jonathan Swift, where one of the absurd habits of the Yahoos is veneration of a single god they call *Estiércol* (Manure). Through fantastic fabulation, another short story writer who created certain humorous effects was Felisberto Hernández. Motifs such as the ladies hosiery salesman who uses tears as bait to sell *"El cocodrilo"* (The crocodile) or the repetitive effect of a publicity slogan injected on a pedestrian, in *"Muebles 'El Canario'"* (Furniture "The Canary") are conceptually humorous.

Popular Humor

Next to intellectual humor, another extensive trend is popular humor. Excluding manifestations of oral poetry from *cantores populares* (street singers), there are authors who forged their work in a popular vein, generally associated with a wider critical perspective against social order and oppression. Two poets who fully respond to humor in this popular vein are Cuban Nicolás Guillén and Venezuelan Aquiles Nazoa. With *Motivos del son* (Motifs of Son, 1930), Guillén reproduced in poems distinctive voices of Cuban Blacks and mulattos. To the extent that poems such as "Negro bembón" (Boastful Black Man), "Mulata" (Mulattress), or "Mi chiquita" (My Little Girl), for instance, capture critical facets of Black people's conflicts, his expression concurrently entails some tenderness and humor. Something that also attracts a lot of attention in Guillén's poetry is humor expressed openly: "I already heard, *mulata, mulata*, I know you've been sayin' / my nose resembles / the knot of a necktie" (83–84, translated by Leticia Damm). In general terms, Guillén's ambivalent and satirical popular humor entails a liberating purpose against racial discrimination, neocolonialism, and ethnocentrism.

Aquiles Nazoa, in turn, is one of the funniest poets of the 20th century, and almost all the poems in *Poesía de amor y humor* (Poem of Love and Humor, 1976) are seasoned with a fair dosage of humor. Nazoa keeps within poetic genres' boundaries and skillfully exploits rhyme to create humorous effect. As compared to Parra and Guillén, Nazoa stands out as most closely linked to circumstances that occur around him. This means his poems challenge the daily news, anecdotes, and situations in everyday life. His attitude is frank, similar to that of both Parra and Guillén. Nazoa's work also highlights free humorous fantasy and social critique. Besides his poems, Nazoa also cultivated the literary genre known as *astracanada*; namely, versified farce adaptations from classics such as the book of Genesis in the Bible, Johann Wolfgang von Goethe's *Faust*, or William Shakespeare's *Romeo and Juliet*.

La vida inútil de Pito Pérez (The Useless Life of Pito Pérez, 1938) by José Rubén Romero is a Mexican picaresque novel in line with *El Periquillo Sarniento*. It is about a boozer rogue who for a bottle a day tells his follies and adventures to a poet. Although the novel does not maintain humorous intensity throughout, it has some funny passages and parodies critical of the Mexican society of its time. *En babia, el manuscrito de un braquicéfalo* (Daydreaming, The Manuscript of a Brachycephalic), a 1940 novel by Puerto Rican author José Isaac De Diego Padró, relates the carousing environment where two playboys living in New York spend their time. In this novel, humor occurs in a grotesque vein, in outlandish situations, and, mainly, in the mocking depiction of the characters. Both Padrò's novel and Arturo Cancela's 1944 *Historia funambulesca del profesor Landormy* (The Grotesque Story of Professor Landormy) have been scarcely studied in spite of their humor contents. Cancela's novel, as in his earlier *Palabras socráticas a los estudiantes* (Socratic Words for Students) in

1928, displays satirical irony and humor. In *Historia funambulesca del profesor Landormy* we find the ridicule of MODIVE (*Monopolio Oficial de Ilustres Visitantes Extranjeros*; Official Monopoly of Distinguished Foreign Visitors), an elite of snobs who are highly servile with a French archeologist who is not precisely a dazzling intellectual but, simply for being French, is overwhelmed with undeserved and exhausting attentions.

Satirical and Ironic Humor

In the second half of the 20th century, many authors wrote satirical humor. Two unmistakably humorous authors are Mexican Jorge Ibargüengoitia and Guatemalan Augusto Monterroso, a nationalized Mexican. Ibargüengoitia started out as a playwright, but was also a journalist, essayist, and author of both short stories and novels. The satirical vein of his plays depicted either the sleazy, low-expectations environment of Mexico in the 1950s and 1960s or historical events and scenarios. Among his humorous plays are *Llegó Margó* (Margot Arrived, 1951), *Susana y los jóvenes* (Susan and the Young People, 1954), and chiefly the comedy of errors *El viaje superficial* (The Superficial Travel, 1960). Ibargüengoitia's humor is considered to be most intense and ingenious in his short stories, mainly *La ley de Herodes* (Herod's Law) in 1967.

Augusto Monterroso was a polygraphist but mainly gained fame in the short literary genres. His 1978 novel *Lo demás es silencio* (The Rest Is Silence) is best known, but short stories, fables, aphorisms, and essays constitute most of his work. Beginning with his first book in 1959, *Obras completas* (Complete Works), readers may find a predilection for ironic style. In this book, his famous one-sentence story resembling a joke—"When he awoke, the dinosaur was still there" (p. 77, translated by Leticia Damm)—is found.

Juan José Arreola and Rosario Castellanos also contributed to Mexican literary humor. These two authors' work was not conceived under a humorous standpoint, but they wrote two masterpieces in which humor and satire blend: *La feria* (The Fair) in 1963 by Arreola and *El eterno femenino* (The Eternal Feminine) in 1975 by Castellanos. *La feria* is a novel that, by means of a polyphonic construction, recreates the voices of the inhabitants of a village called Zapotlán el Grande in the state of Jalisco, who are about to have their annual fair to honor Saint Joseph, the city's patron. With the farce titled *El eterno femenino*, Castellanos—who had gained fame as a poet, short story writer, and novelist—produced one of the funniest works of the 1970s. A complex and difficult to enact farce, it pivots around Lupita, a young girl who goes to the beauty shop to have her hair done on her wedding day and, as a result of an electronic device in the drier, takes a trip to her past and future that makes her cancel her marriage plans. This farce constitutes a feminist critique against machismo and certain feminine attitudes.

Around 1967, a number of novels with manifest satirical humor were published. With *Tres tristes tigres* (Three Sad Tigers) in 1967, Cuban Guillermo Cabrera Infante manages, by means of highly different stylizations of Havana speech, a novel overflowing with ingenuity and humor about the nightlife in Havana of three young bohemians before the revolution. Cabrera Infante depicts in his novel the Cuban *choteo* (puns) or *relajo* (messing around). One of the most memorable and controversial passages is the chapter "The death of Trotsky as told by different Cuban writers, years after—or before" where he intertwines a variety of parodies of Cuban writers.

Although as a whole Mario Vargas Llosa is known for his neorealistic novels, he also expanded into humor and satire with *Pantaleón y las visitadoras* (Pantaleón and the Visitors, 1973) and *La tía Julia y el escribidor* (Aunt Julia and the Scriptwriter, 1977). The former one satirizes a real-life event: the organization of a business to provide brothel services to soldiers stationed in a jungle zone of northern Peru. Pantaleón is the soldier who has been commissioned to undertake the project, which is conceived to prevent soldiers from raping local females. This satire of machismo and the military is written in diverse genres, a differentiation that renders it a polyphonic novel, as it ends up in irony and humor. Regarding *La tía Julia y el escribidor*, Vargas Llosa uses the technique of confronting two vastly dissimilar stories, the first one re-creating his experience when he fell in love and secretly married his aunt-in-law Julia and the second one a series of outlandish stories told by a Bolivian typist named Pedro Camacho who goes crazy and turns things around, thus generating the humorous effect.

Popular Speech, Grotesque Realism, and Carnivalization

The publication of *Cien años de soledad* (One Hundred Years of Solitude) by Colombian Gabriel

García Márquez in 1967 constituted a turning point for humor for the Hispanic American novel. However, García Márquez's humor is not restricted to this book; as found in *El otoño del patriarca* (The Autumn of the Patriarch, 1975), *Crónica de una muerte anunciada* (Chronicle of a Death Foretold, 1981), *El amor en los tiempos del cólera* (Love in the Time of Cholera, 1985), and some of his short stories, humor is a component of the author's style. Literary critic Mario Vargas Llosa recognized in *Cien años de soledad* the common people's viewpoint as an element of his humor. Consequently, it may be said that García Márquez is a cultured author who writes in a common vein. Even more so, critics such as Vargas Llosa and Óscar Collazos also found in *Cien años de soledad* some images that recall *La vie de Gargantúa et Pantagruel* by François Rabelais. This is a paradigmatic work of grotesque realism and carnivalism. Definitely, the humor in *Cien años de soledad* degrades serious issues through the physical-corporal principle and neutralizes the tragic side of predestination in Macondo, the setting of the novel.

With *El mundo alucinante* (Hallucinations) in 1969, Reinaldo Arenas used the biography of Fray Servando Teresa de Mier, patriot of Mexican Independence, to write a novel of adventures in which he combines skepticism with humor. While his skepticism addresses his social unconformity with the Cuban revolutionary regime, his humor ranges from irony to sarcasm. An evident feature throughout this novel is the use of grotesque realism, which not only mixes the hyperbolic with degradation, but also the scatological and free fantasy. With *Macunaíma* and *Cien años de soledad, El mundo alucinante* is one of the novels that is pervaded with carnivalization, that is, the liberating influence of popular humor.

Other Caribbean authors who created narrative humor are Puerto Ricans Emilio Díaz Valcárcel, Luis Rafael Sánchez, and Ana Lydia Vega. In some way, these authors subscribe a trend initiated by Cabrera Infante, who claimed he wrote in Cuban. Both Díaz Valcárcel and Sánchez decided to do likewise for their country. With *Figuraciones en el mes de marzo* (Schemes in the Month of March, 1972), writing in Puerto Rican gains significance in a number of letters received by character Eduardo Leiseca and his wife Yolanda, both living in Madrid. Four years after *Figuraciones en el mes de marzo*, the novel *La guaracha del macho Camacho* (Macho Camacho's Beat) by Luis Rafael Sánchez was published in 1976, which likewise includes humorous elements supported by stylization of popular speech, grotesque realism, and carnivalization, although to a lower extent than in Díaz Válcarcel's work. Also in this narrative tradition that depicts common speech and people's ways and manners is the book *Encancaranublado y otros cuentos de naufragio* (Encancaranublado and other Shipwreck Tales) by Ana Lydia Vega (1982).

There have been other humorous writers, who cannot be discussed for lack of space. Among them are Peruvian Alfredo Bryce Echenique and Mexican Sergio Pitol. The humor of Bryce Echenique stands out, for instance, in the short story "Muerte de Sevilla en Madrid" (Death of Seville in Madrid) and the novel *La vida exagerada de Martín Romaña* (The Exaggerated Life of Martín Romaña, 1981). Pitol has deliberately written carnivalesque work as in *Trilogía del Carnaval* (Trilogy of Carnival), as clearly shown in *Domar a la divina garza* (Divine Tame Heron, 1988), the first book of the trilogy.

Eduardo E. Parrilla Sotomayor

See also Literature; Poetry

Further Readings

Bakhtin, M. M. (1984). *Rabelais and his world* (H. Iswolsky, Trans.). Bloomington: Indiana University Press.

Collazos, Ó. (1986). *García Márquez: La soledad y la gloria; su vida y su obra* [Garcia Márquez: Solitude and glory, his life and work]. Barcelona, Spain: Plaza y Janés.

Cruz, J. I. de la. (1997). *Poems, protest, and a dream: Selected writings* (M. S. Peden, Trans.). New York, NY: Penguin.

Cruz, J. I. de la. (n.d.). *Sátira filosófica* [Philosophical satire, poem 92]. Retrieved from http://www-personal.umich.edu/~dfrye/SORJUANA.html

Costa, R. de. (1999). *El humor en Borges* [Humor in Borges]. Madrid, Spain: Catedra.

Cueto, S. (1999). *Versiones del humor* [Versions of humor]. Rosario, Argentina: Beatriz Vitervo Editora.

Díaz Bild, A. (2000). *Humor y literatura: Entre la liberación y la subversión* [Humor and literature: Between liberation and subversion]. La Laguna, Santa Cruz de Tenerife: Universidad de la Laguna, Servicio de Publicaciones.

Fernandez, M. (1974). *Obras completas* [Complete works]. Buenos Aires, Argentina: Corregidor.

Gómez de la Serna, R. (1943). *Ismos* [Isms]. Buenos Aires, Argentina: Poseidón.

Guillén, N. (2002). *Obra poética* (tomo 1) [Poetic works (Vol. 1)]. La Habana, Cuba: Letras Cubanas.

Monterroso, A. (1971). *Obras completas y otros cuentos* [Complete works and other stories]. México: Editorial Joaquín Mortiz.

Rodríguez Monegal, E. (1972). *El boom de la novela latinoamericana* [The Latin American novel's boom]. Caracas, Venezuela: Editorial Tiempo Nuevo.

Sotomayor, E. E. P. (2012). *Vertientes imaginativas en cien años de soledad* [Imaginative aspects in One Hundred Years of Solitude]. Germany: Editorial Académica Española.

Vargas Llosa, M. (1971). *García Márquez: Historia de un deicidio* [García Márquez: The story of a deicide]. Barcelona/Caracas: Barral.

Southeast Asia, Cartooning in

Humor has played a key role in the cartooning traditions of Southeast Asia, where it has appeared in political cartoons, newspaper strips, and comic books, or cartoon and humor magazines. These comics are invariably meant to spark laughter, poke fun at the foibles of society, or uncover the mysteries of politics and politicians. This entry discusses how cartoons in Southeast Asia have dealt with politics and other topics and describes some of the region's most popular cartoonists and their works.

Political Cartoons

As they do elsewhere, political cartoons in Southeast Asia employ humor through exaggerated portrayals of personalities, the ridiculousness of current events made more ridiculous, and funny allusions to various metaphors. Frequently, political cartooning has been dwarfed during the region's many periods of oppression; nevertheless, it has managed to survive (sometimes barely) since colonial and dynastic times. In fact, in three countries—the Philippines, Indonesia, and Vietnam—the first political cartoons were attributed to the independence fighters José Rizal (1861–1896), Sukarno (Kusno Sosrodihardjo, 1901–1970), and Ho Chi Minh (1890–1969), respectively. In Thailand, King Rama VI (ruled 1910–1925) supposedly drew that country's first cartoons so as to embarrass corrupt government officials. Rama VI also designated the words *paap lor* (parodic image) to identify cartoons.

Because all of Southeast Asia (except Thailand) had been colonized by one power or another, it was natural that the earliest cartoons should lampoon the foreign occupiers. Cartoons in Philippine newspapers and satirical magazines made the Spanish, and then the Americans, look foolish from the 1890s until the1940s; in Myanmar, pioneering cartoonists Ba Gale from the 1910s and Ba Gyan shortly afterward made fun of the British; and the same treatment was given to the British in Malaysia, the Dutch in Indonesia, and the French in Indochina. The first Singaporean cartoons in 1907, published in Chinese reformist leader Sun Yat-sen's political organ, *Chong Shing Yit Pao,* satirized Qing Dynasty officials of the time.

Political cartoonists have trod very cautiously in each country at times because of intolerance of criticism by authoritarian governments, both during colonial periods and postindependence. In Singapore, political cartoons were dropped from the major newspaper chain, *The Straits Times,* from 1961 to 1979, and those that now exist deal with universal or foreign issues. With the sole exception of the works of Zunar (Zulkiflee Anwar Haque, b. 1962), Malaysian cartoons are also tepid. For his political cartoons, Zunar was arrested and jailed for two days in September 2010 under Malaysia's Sedition Act. In the Philippines, conglomerate-owned newspapers often stymie the efforts of political cartoonists. To get around the censorship, much subtlety is used in Southeast Asian cartoons, through metaphors, hints, symbolism, innuendo, historical allusions, and intentional mistakes. An example of the last was a cartoon in an issue of Myanmar's government newspaper that showed a steadfast Myanmar soldier with "Defecto (rather than De facto) Government" emblazoned on his chest.

Comic Strips and Comic Books

The humor found in Southeast Asian newspaper strips and comic books differs little from that elsewhere, probably because of influences brought in by colonizers. Usually, themes revolve around wacky family adventures, husband-wife relationships, country bumpkins trying to be city slickers, well-intentioned idiots, young men's misadventures while trying to impress women, funny antics of humanized animals, clashes of traditional and modern lifestyles, and politics and society satirized.

The region's earliest comics played on these themes. Indonesia's first newspaper strip Kho Wang Gie's *Put On,* in 1931, displayed the daily life of a young, single, middle-class man and the never-ending hassles and entanglements he faced both in the big city and with his nagging mother, teasing brothers, and difficult boss. In the Philippines, the first comic strip, *Kenkoy*, drawn by Tony Velasquez in 1929 for *Liwayway Magazine,* was a ludicrous portrait of a Filipino trying to be an American; some others that followed in the 1930s carried plots and characters imitative of U.S. strips. The earliest comic strip characters in Vietnam, Ly Toet drawn by Nhat Linh and Xa Xe drawn by Nguyen Gia Tri, played on the bodily physique of Western comedy teams—one character thin (Ly Toet), the other short and stout (Xa Xe). At the beginning, Ly Toet was depicted as muddling through Vietnamese colonialism, and from 1936–1941, the pair epitomized the lower classes while at the same time they criticized backward lifestyles, the wickedness of the colonialist government, authoritarianism, and corruption.

Comic strips in Malaysia started with *Wak Ketok* (Uncle Knock, named for his penchant for attacking), created in 1939 by Rahim Kajai and Ali Sanat. Like other pioneering strips, it used long captions, often with proverbs and *pantuns* (folk ditties) and elaborate rhyming sentences. Postindependence (in 1957), the cartoonists Raja Hamzah, Rejabhad, and Mishar followed the well-worn social commentary patterns of family life and husband-wife intrigues. Prominent, beginning with his work in the 1960s, has been Lat (Mohammad Nor Khalid), who created *Si Mamat* (1968–1994) and then *The Kampung Boy*. The latter was a cartoon book, published in 1979, which became a phenomenal success and has been translated into many foreign languages. It is a nostalgic account of Lat growing up in a village in the 1950s and 1960s. Through its warm and sympathetic depictions of people and places, the book did much to promote interethnic harmony.

The history of the comic strip in Singapore reflects the seesaw existence this form has had in the region. Responsible for early strips was high school teacher Qiu Gao Peng, who created Wang Er in 1950, a character similar to the popular street urchin character Sanmao in Mainland China. Three years later, Qiu produced the weekly *Mr. Nonsense*, which lasted only 2 years until it was stopped for portraying Singaporean political leaders as pigs and as Adolf Hitler. Strips were rare, short-lived, and poorly executed in the 1960s and 1970s but were invigorated in the following decade when the *Straits Times* publishing group emphasized domestic cartoons. Sprouting during that time were Victor Teh's Crocko, an environment-friendly cockroach; *Life's Like That*, a gag strip by Lee Chee Chew; the pioneering strip by Cheah Sin Ann for *The Straits Times*, *House of Lim*, about a Chinese family called Lim, with each episode based on a weekly theme; *Orchid Road* by 18-year-old Colin Goh; and *Mr. Kiasu* by Johnny Lau and James Suresh. The topics of strips that followed in the late 1980s and early 1990s featured quirky characters, bickering married couples, a family headed by a rock fan–guitarist father, impossible teenage buddies, and, in the case of the very popular *Mr. Kiasu*, Singaporeans' self-perceptions, so much on the mark that *kiasuism* as a word came to represent the people's obsession with being number one and their fear of losing out. *Mr. Kiasu* originated as a comic book issued once yearly, and spun off into a strip, other media forms, licenses, and products, including a McDonald's "Kiasuburger."

This very intimate cartoon shows Malaysian cartoonist Lat (Mohammad Nor Khalid) handling family life and professional challenges in the mid-1980s.

Source: Lat.

The Straits Times group's interest in publishing domestic comic strips fizzled quickly, attributable to the high costs of production and the cartoonists' lack of new ideas, a number of which were based on a very American-based type of humor and worn-out slapstick jokes. Some recent strips include Hup's (Lee Hup Kheng) *What's Hup*, an account of a boy's summer with his grandparents; Cheah's popular *Billy and Saltie*, tropical adventures of an Australian aboriginal boy and a crocodile; and Lau's *Skipping Class*, the tale of a primary school student who can travel between parallel school worlds on alternate days—one day, the school is like a pressure-cooker, the next, wacky and more creative.

For years, humorous strips have found audiences among newspaper and magazine readers in Indonesia. Some have been collected into anthologies, while G. M. Sudarto's funny political strip *Oom Pasikom* became the country's first to be made into a movie (in 1990, directed by Chaerul Umam). Two popular cartoons that began in the 1970s are *Djon Domino* by Johnny Hidajat and *Panji Koming* by Dwi Koendoro. Hidajat drew for 10 to 15 periodicals, producing a prodigious amount of work daily. His modus operandi was to take an event or issue and bring out five versions of *Djon Domino* daily, each with its own title and joke. One version was *Djon Taremolneok* (conglomerate spelled backwards in Indonesian), about big firms and their executives. The jokes and warm style of *Djon Domino* made it a favorite in the 1970s through the 1990s. It helped that the strip contained a daily number that readers could use to play in the national lottery, as well as occasional tinges of obscenity and sexuality mixed with politics. Koendoro's *Panji Koming* usually acted as a commentary on the matching of elite positions with ignorance.

Newer Indonesian comic strips include *Mr. Bei*, featuring a character who gets things wrong despite good intentions; the politically oriented *I Brewok*; *Lotif*, whose leading character often fouls up while trying to attract women; *Doyok*, about a shrewd thinker, sarcastic but realistic, who comments on sociopolitical matters; and *Benny & Mice*, by Benny Rachmadi and Muhammad Misrad, a blockbuster comic about adults acting like teens and avoiding societal norms.

In the later 20th century, Philippine daily newspapers had an array of very popular stock character strips, and some are still running. Among them were Larry Alcala's *Siopawman*, a slapstick parody of Superman; *Slice of Life*, a one-panel cartoon with Alcala's caricature carefully hidden in its midst; Nonoy Marcelo's *Tisoy*, about the dilemma of urbanized youth; *Ikabod*, a comic with double-coded dialogue characters that, during martial law (1972–1981), managed to deflect while still acknowledging then President Ferdinand Marcos; Roni Santiago's *Baltic and Co.*, about the goings-on in a typical business office; and Jess Abrera's *A. Lipin*, a current affairs-oriented strip. Cambodian and Myanmar newspapers rarely carry any domestic strips, while in Malaysia they more often appear in Bahasa Malaysia language dailies. Strips in Vietnamese newspapers dwindled significantly after the early 1990s, with major dailies now devoid of them. In Thailand, a few survive, the major one for many years being Chai Rachawat's village-based *Poo Yai Ma Kap Tung Ma Muen* (*Headman Poo Yai Ma and the Village of Tung Ma Muen*).

In most Southeast Asian comic books, humor takes a backseat to other genres. This is evident in the Philippines where the rich *komiks* tradition began in 1946 with *Halakhak* (a word that sounds like and denotes laughter) but that favored love, romance, and fantasy over humor. For many years, funny comics were reserved for children (e.g., *Filipino Funny Komiks for Children*), and often were spin-offs of television shows or imitations of the American *MAD* magazine. Yet comedy or romance-comedy comic books proved more likely to be turned into feature films than other genres, demonstrating their marketability.

In Thailand, a single company, Banlue Sarn, has dominated the humor comics field, starting with its first children's comic book, *Nuja* (Little Children), created by Jamnoon Leksomtic in 1957. Two years later, the company added *Baby* by Wattana Petchuwan and both can still be found. The company focuses on the advantages of funny comics being easy to read and understand and their universal appeal. Their anchor comic is *Kai Hua Roh* (Selling Laughter), made up of one- and three-panel gags. Many series in *Kai Hua Roh* have been converted into comic books. While Banlue Sarn dominates, other companies also publish children's humor and gag comic books.

Though now invisible in Cambodia, humorous comic books had a brief life during the 1980s. Comics about legends and romance, and educational comics sponsored by nongovernmental organizations, make up the country's sparse offerings. Both historically and in the present, Vietnamese comic books tend to be poor quality reprints of Disney and other foreign titles, pirated and recredited to Vietnamese authors, as well as funny accounts of fairy tales and historical events. A recently spoofed fairy tale is *Banh Chung Banh Day* (Square and Round Glutinous Rice Cakes), which mixed traditional folk wisdom with contemporary culture. The story revolves around the fabled origin of these traditional New Year foods where a young prince dreamt that a god told him how to prepare a special rice dish to offer his father the king. In the funny comic book, the prince dreams he has entered a popular television cooking contest.

Malaysian humorous comic books originated in the early 1970s with *Bambino* and *Bujol*; but in 1998, when Art Square Group brought out *Gempak*, humor comics began to thrive. *Gempak*, one of Malaysia's top magazines, was different—heavier on plot and lighter on cheap laughs. In Myanmar, humor has been the mainstay of comic strips and comic books. Some famous comic books are Tin Aung Ni's *Ko Pyar Leung* (Mischievous One), which became the subject of at least five films; Than Htun's *Maung Ti Htwin* (Mr. Inventor); and others by Ngwe Kyi, based on humorous Myanmar folklore.

Cartoon and Humor Magazines

The country with the earliest dedicated cartoon and humor magazines is undoubtedly the Philippines, which spawned satirical periodicals such as *Te Con Leche, Biro-Biro,* and others between 1898 and 1901 in order to lampoon both Spaniards and Americans as colonial powers. Sporting the most sustained history of such magazines is Malaysia, which in 1973 already had *Ha Hu Hum* and had developed at least 50 others since *Gila-Gila* (Mad About Mad) started its own long life in 1978. *Gila-Gila,* at one time Malaysia's largest circulation magazine, succeeds with an assortment of funny cartoons based on traditional Malaysian literature, folktales, animal fables, history, and film parodies. By 2000, with a glut of Malaysian cartoon and humor magazines, special audiences were being targeted—teens (*Ujang*), religion (*Lanun*), and women (*Cabai*).

Other cartoon and humor magazines were published in Vietnam, such as *Tuoi Tre Cuoi* (Youth Laugh), conceived in 1984 by then Prime Minister Vo Van Kiet and still appearing, and in Myanmar, beginning with Aung Shein's *Popular* in 1953, which was succeeded by others, including the governmental *Shwe Thway,* issued regularly since 1969. Indonesia had *Stop* and *Astaga* (Good Lord) in the 1970s, followed in the 1980s and 1990s by *Idola* (Ideal) and by two different cartoon magazines both called *HumOr.*

Overall, the role of humor in Southeast Asian cartooning has proved less than stable, varying widely over time and from country to country because of disruptions in culture caused by war, political and economic turmoil, the prevalence of different sociocultural and political backgrounds that define and limit what is accepted as funny in each country, and influence by foreign comics for both good or bad.

John A. Lent

See also Art and Visual Humor; Cartoons; Comic Books; Comic Strips

Further Readings

Lent, J. A. (Ed.). (1997). Cartooning & comic art in Southeast Asia. *Southeast Asian Journal of Social Science, 25*(1), 1–166.

Lent, J. A. (1998). Comics in The Philippines, Singapore, and Indonesia. *HUMOR: International Journal of Humor Research, 11*(1), 65–77.

Lent, J. A. (2009). *The first one hundred years of Philippine komiks and cartoons.* Tagaytay, Philippines: Yonzon Associates.

Lent, J. A. (Ed.). (2014). *Southeast Asian cartoon art: History, trends and problems.* Jefferson, NC: McFarland.

Lent, J. A. (in press). *Asian comics.* Jackson: University Press of Mississippi.

Mahamood, M. (2004). *The history of Malay editorial cartoons (1930s–1993).* Kuala Lumpur, Malaysia: Utusan Publications & Distributors.

Speech Play

Speech play is the playful manipulation of elements and components of language, in relation to one another, in relation to the social and cultural contexts of language use, and against the backdrop of other verbal possibilities in which speech play is not foregrounded. The elements manipulated can be at any level of language, from sound patterns to syntax, semantics, and discourse; they can include the various languages used in multilingual situations, and relations between verbal and nonverbal communication. Speech play can be conscious or unconscious, noticed or not noticed, purposeful or nonpurposeful, and humorous or serious. Nonetheless, given the focus on manipulation, speech play typically involves a degree of selection and consciousness beyond that of ordinary language use.

While speech play is present to some degree in all speech—informal, formal, conversational, or artistic—it is most evident in certain conventional forms that are found in many societies. These include play languages, puns, jokes, verbal dueling, proverbs, and riddles. There is a close connection between speech play and verbal art (verbal art is a focus on the aesthetic use of language, both oral and written). Speech play provides the means and resources, such as metaphor, parallelism, and narrative manipulations, out of which verbal art is created. At the same time, there are various and overlapping ends served by speech play, comic or humorous, religious, rhetorical, mnemonic, competitive, rehearsal, and artistic. After discussing the academic study of speech play, this entry examines the concepts and functions of play and its relation to culture.

Academic Study

The study of speech play is relevant to various disciplines and scholarly concerns. For linguists, speech play provides insight into linguistic structure by revealing the ways in which various elements of language can be manipulated in different contexts. Speech play is relevant to both linguistic theory and linguistic methodology. It provides insight into the nature of language in general, as play is an important component of language structure and language use; play is inherent in grammar and grammar provides potential for play actualized in discourse. The study of speech play also reveals information about particular languages, indicating what parts are available for play, how, and why. Methodologically, speech play provides a tool for the investigation of both language structure and language use. From the perspective of sociolinguistics, because speech play often emerges from language, styles, and varieties in contact, its study provides insights into the use and the attitudes toward the sociolinguistic repertoire of a community.

For anthropologists, speech play can be seen as being at the heart of intersections among language, culture, and society—testing, experimenting with, and sometimes creating the boundaries of appropriate behavior. While there is always some play for play's sake, play often involves culture exploring and working out both its essence and the limits of its possibilities. It can be a cultural theme, and as such is at the heart of the intersection of language, culture, thought, and individual expression. Play occurs as people—not just children—work out, experiment, exercise, and define the properties of their languages, cultures, and societies, and especially the intersections and relations among them. In this view, language and culture and their interaction and intersection are viewed as dynamic, not static, and in flux, not fixed. Methodologically, the study of people's speech play gives researchers a tool for analyzing how natives express and live their own language and culture. For literary critics, attention to speech play focuses on the texture of language use and helps define the nature of verbal art.

The study of speech play has a history that relates to several disciplines, including anthropology, linguistics, sociology, psychology, philosophy, literary criticism, and folklore. Anthropologists have treated play and humor as marginal to concerns traditionally considered more basic, such as social organization and kinship, or more recently, political economy and the world system. Recent writing in both literary criticism and anthropology considers the concept of play to be central to their enterprise but rarely provides extended and detailed linguistic analysis of specific forms.

The discipline of linguistics has also marginalized the study of speech play, with some significant, mainly methodological exceptions. And yet, speech play is critically relevant to linguistics. It enables one to deal with not only standard topics in the study of the grammars of languages, but also and especially with topics that are salient for the speakers of particular languages, for example, an orientation to and focus on form, shape, texture, movement, and direction, found in many languages, or sound symbolism and onomatopoeia also common in the languages of the world. An orientation to speech play also leads one to recognize, indeed insist on, alternative rather than unitary solutions to analytical problems. Paying attention to speech play argues for a plurality of theories and methods, an openness to different ways of conceiving of language and to different ways of collecting and analyzing data.

Speech play, while sometimes humorous, is often deeply serious and significant. It is precisely because play is so important that it is so widespread in the world. A focus on speech play contributes to and is indeed a logical continuation of a tradition in anthropology and linguistics with regard to the relationship between language and culture, linguistic structures on the one hand and worldview or perception on the other. There are aspects of linguistic form and linguistic structure that only emerge through the study of language use in verbally playful and verbally artistic discourse. In fact, speech play and verbal art involve language in its essence, on display. Potentials inherent in language are packed and pushed to their highest limits. Playfully imaginative and artistically creative language constitute the richest point of intersection of the relationship among language, culture, society, and individual expression and therefore, the place in which language, cognition, perception, and worldview come together in their most distilled form.

Heteroglossia (languages, dialects, and speech styles in contact and competition within communities) and intertextuality (combinations of forms of discourse) can be both sources of play and results of play.

Concepts and Functions of Play

The various meanings of the word *play*, in English as well as other languages, are all relevant to an understanding of speech play. One meaning is "manipulation" and along with it freedom, but always within a set of rules. In language, the different ways of pronouncing the same word or expressing the same idea are quite analogous to this sense of play. So is the lack of perfect fit between and among the various levels and components of language, Another meaning of *play* is that of "performance," as in the playing of a musical instrument. Still another meaning of *play* is that of playing a "game," which raises the significant relation between play and games. Not all play takes the form of games, with opponents and winners and losers, but some forms, such as verbal dueling, quite clearly do. Finally there is the idea of play as the opposite of serious or literal, for which the Latin-derived term *ludic* has been used.

Different languages and cultures combine these concepts of play in different ways. In French as in English, *play* (*jouer*) is used for manipulation, musical performance, games, and nonserious behavior such as joking and jesting. In Spanish, the word *jugar* is used for manipulation and games as well as nonseriousness, while *tocar* (literally, "touch") is used for musical performance. In Kuna, an indigenous language of Colombia and Panama, *totoe* is used for playing and joking in the sense of tricking and fooling as well as playing games and dancing. The Indonesian word *main* signifies playing games as well as nonseriousness. In English, as in French, the word *play*, as both a verb and a noun, is used for theatrical performance. One of the functions of reduplication in Indonesian languages is to indicate that an object or activity is nonserious or for play. A similar function is achieved in Kuna by means of the use of a verbal prefix *pinsa* which has the meaning "for the hell of" or "just for play."

These different meanings of *play* lead us to the very useful notions of frame and metacommunication, as developed by such scholars as Gregory Bateson and Erving Goffman. Frame is the definition/conception/organization of an activity as real or literal, rehearsed or practiced, talked about or lied about, or dreamt or fantasized. Play then is a type of frame. Related to frame is the concept of function of language and of communication more generally. In addition to functioning referentially, naming things and providing information about them, language functions socially, expressively, metacommunicatively, and poetically. Speech play combines several of these functions. In turn, speech play, as a form of language use, has various functions: psychological, cultural, humorous, and poetic.

These functions of language in general and speech play in particular overlap with one another and can be played down or foregrounded in particular instances. At one level, there is no language use without speech play and verbal art being involved to some degree. At the same time, there are verbal forms in which speech play, verbal art, or both are the central and total focus. The notion of consciousness and purpose is notable here. There are forms of play that are totally unconscious and unintended, certain sound or word associations for example. Others are conscious, intended, and performed, such as jokes or stories. And there are various possibilities in between, as when an unintended pun gets laughed at and becomes the focus of commentary. This provides us with an insight into the nature of humor, clearly intimately related to play. Many scholars, including Sigmund Freud and Henri Bergson, have noticed that humor results from surprise juxtapositions. The sudden coming into consciousness and public awareness and commentary of an unintended speech play is a good example. Add to this the backdrop of entangled cultural and personal presuppositions and assumptions and one can begin to understand particular instances of humor, which can be quite complex.

It is useful to ask where exactly play is located. Play is located in language structure and grammar and is an inherent aspect of the formal properties of language. The inherent play aspects of language are exploited in rhetorical and poetic forms, as well as in discourse more generally. Play is located, again both actually and potentially, in sociolinguistic situations, in the juxtaposition of languages, dialects, and styles in use. Play is also located in everyday speech in the form of puns, word associations, repetitions and parallelisms, and clever responses and comebacks which feel creatively poetic. And play is located in well-defined and developed discourse forms such as play languages, jokes, put-ons, stories, riddles, proverbs, and verbal dueling.

Relation to Culture

This focus on play fits well within current conceptions of discourse and culture, including language, as constructed, imagined, negotiated, and (re-) invented. Instead of viewing language and culture as systems where everything holds together nicely and neatly, they can be seen as open systems with fuzziness, leaks, inventions, constructions, negotiations, imaginations, and constantly emergent. Discourse is crucial to the language and culture intersection, the locus of the actualization of potentials provided by language and culture as well as personal experience. In this intersection, creativity, imagination, and play are essential. Another way to view this is that there is a lack of fit between words and world so that while at times language reflects the world, it often is the creator of experience and perception. Again, speech play and verbal art are at the heart of this process and help us to understand not only relationships among language, culture, and thought, but also the creative spirit that leads to constantly new forms of expression and aesthetic creation.

Joel Sherzer

See also Culture; Jokes; Play and Humor; Puns; Puppets; Riddle; Verbal Dueling

Further Readings

Bateson, G. (1972). *Steps to an ecology of mind.* New York, NY: Ballantine Books.

Bergson, H. (1911). *Laughter: An essay on the meaning of the comic.* New York, NY: Macmillan. (Original work published 1900)

Crystal, D. (1998). *Language play.* London, UK: Penguin.

Freud, S. (1905). *Jokes and their relation to the unconscious.* London, UK: Hogarth.

Goffman, E. (1974). *Frame analysis: An essay on the organization of experience.* New York, NY: Harper & Row.

Huizinga, J. (1955). *Homo ludens: A study of the play-element in culture.* Boston, MA: Beacon Press.

Nachmanovitch, S. (1990). *Free play: Improvisation in life and art.* Los Angeles, CA: Jeremy P. Tarcher.

Sherzer, J. (2002). *Speech play and verbal art.* Austin: University of Texas Press.

Yaguello, M. (1998). *Language through the looking glass: Exploring language and linguistics.* Oxford, UK: Oxford University Press.

Spoofing

English music hall entertainer Arthur Roberts (1852–1933) introduced the word *spoof* into the English language via a card game of his own invention. The first mention of the game *Spoof* dates to 1884, and within 5 years the term *spoof* entered into regular usage distinct from Roberts's parlor-room pastime. Signifying trickery and nonsense, *spoof* was originally synonymous with "hoax," while the verb *to spoof* meant to engage in deception or bluffing, particularly in jest. By the mid-20th century, however, the concept shifted toward its contemporary meaning, that is, lighthearted satire or good-natured parody.

At the root of any act of spoofing is the use of misrepresentation to make light of or ridicule a person or thing. Like many forms of humor, spoofing relies on the gap between reality and representation (or more often, misrepresentation) to produce mirth. Similar to parody, spoofing reproduces stylistic peculiarities of an external subject to achieve humor; however, spoofs typically target a distinct work or genre for mockery, thus requiring a higher level of parasitism than is necessary for parody.

While sharing a focus on the visual with burlesque, spoofing rarely transgresses societal norms, although poking fun at traditional mores is common. Distinct from satire and harsher forms of lampooning, spoofing eschews polemics, generally avoids overt political content, and rarely aims at normative outcomes. In order to mitigate the inherent tension between playful misrepresentation and actual deception, a spoof must be understood by its audience as a hoax, otherwise its author runs the risk of confusing the spectator and thus being "unfunny."

Today, spoofing is most associated with genre-busting cinema wherein a specific film or a well-defined genre is parodied through the application of deliberate anachronisms, breaking with character, double entendre, intertextuality, and the purposeful subversion of established conventions of the style. The spoof film, despite its low level of respect within the movie industry, enjoys a long history.

One of the earliest spoofs, *Hellzapoppin'* (1941), made fun of *Citizen Kane*—considered by many critics to be the best film ever made—and included the following disclaimer: "Any resemblance between

Hellzapoppin' and a motion picture are coincidental." In the postwar era, the comedic duo of William "Bud" Abbott and Lou Costello starred in a series of horror send-ups including *Abbott and Costello Meet Frankenstein* (1948) and *Abbott and Meet the Mummy* (1955).

Following the cultural upheaval of the late 1960s, the spoof film emerged as a genre in its own right, owing to a generational shift in audience tastes and the rise of a cadre of daring comedians-turned-filmmakers. With *Blazing Saddles* (1974), Mel Brooks established himself as the auteur of the spoof. Playing a number of the characters including a Yiddish-speaking Indian chief, Brooks appeared alongside his standard comedic lineup of Harvey Korman, Dom DeLuise, and Madeline Kahn in a full-length jape of the Western. Not totally devoid of satiric content, Brooks's film tilted at the genre's failure to deal honestly with issues of racial intolerance in the American West. Following his parody of the cowboy movie, Brooks took aim at silent films, psychological thrillers, horror flicks, historical epics, and sci-fi operas over the next two decades. In his final spoof, *Dracula: Dead and Loving It* (1995), Brooks directed actor Leslie Nielsen, whom film critic Roger Ebert once labeled the "Laurence Olivier of spoofs."

With his supporting role in *Airplane!* (1980), Nielsen established himself as the master of deadpan comedy within the spoof genre. He later won starring roles in *The Naked Gun* series by directors Jim Abrahams, David Zucker, and Jerry Zucker, the comedic trio behind *The Kentucky Fried Movie* (1977), a film-length series of sketch comedies mocking blaxploitation, kung fu, and other 1970s genres. Abrahams also worked on the *Godfather* spoof *Mafia!* (1988) and the *Hot Shots!* (1991 and 1993) parodies of the testosterone-driven action films of the late Cold War. David Zucker continued his work in the genre by taking over the successful *Scary Movie* franchise (2000–2006) in 2003 following the departure of its original creators, the Wayans Brothers.

In the last decade, spoof cinema has become a reliable commodity in Hollywood, with nearly every summer blockbuster triggering a parody or—at the very least—deserving of a segment within a mashup spoof. Representative examples include the prosaically named films *Epic Movie* (2007) and *Superhero Movie* (2008).

British humorists have greatly contributed to spoofing. The surreal comedy troupe Monty Python parlayed its successful TV show into two spoof films: *The Holy Grail* (1974), a goof on the Arthurian legend, and *Life of Brian* (1979), a jaundiced religious epic focused on Jesus's neighbor, Brian Cohen. Around the new millennium, British comedians Chris Morris and Sacha Baron Cohen generated controversy with their respective spoof documentary programs, *Brass Eye* (1997–2001) and *Da Ali G Show* (2000–2004). More recently, English actor Simon Pegg has made a career of intelligently spoofing zombie films (*Shaun of the Dead*), cop buddy flicks (*Hot Fuzz*), and alien encounter movies (*Paul*).

Spoofing is common in other humorous media as well. Since it began publication in 1952, *MAD* magazine has spoofed nearly every major motion picture from *The Caine Mutiny* (1954) to the final installment of the Harry Potter series in 2011, while also going after television shows, comic books, and other media. *National Lampoon* (1970–1978), a competing magazine, also made spoofing a regular part of its editorial repertoire, including a full-length parody of *MAD,* which appeared in 1971. *The Onion* has created a mini-empire of spoof, from its national newspaper and website to a television show and series of books on topics ranging from professional sports to world history. The Grammy Award-winning artist "Weird Al" Yankovic even made a career of spoofing pop hits, most famously Michael Jackson's "Beat It" ("Eat It") in 1983.

Sketch comedy programs such as *Saturday Night Live* (1975–present), *In Living Color* (1990–1994), and *MADtv* (1995–2009) are famous for their use of spoofing and have spawned a number of entertainers who would go on to become masters of the style, including the Wayans Brothers (*Scary Movie*) and Mike Myers (*Austin Powers*). Late night talk shows often include brief spoof segments between the introductory monologue and the celebrity interviews. Conan O'Brien, a former writer for the spoof-laden cartoon series *The Simpsons* (1989–present), is particularly known for his parodies of television commercials, awards shows, and other forms of popular culture, while *Saturday Night Live* veteran Jimmy Fallon has garnered kudos for his good-natured spoofs of singer Neil Young and the reality TV show *The Jersey Shore.*

Occasionally traversing the border between spoof and satire, Comedy Central's highly successful series *The Daily Show With Jon Stewart* and *The Colbert Report* undertake episode-length spoofs of contemporary cable news programming, frequently making news in their own right.

In recent years, the conceptual reach of spoofing has expanded beyond the boundaries of humor, most notably with the use of the term to refer to the employment of forged Internet Protocol (IP) addresses for purposes of hiding the identity of the sending computer. IP spoofing is most commonly used as a tactic for conducting denial-of-service attacks intended to crash a website or to test for weaknesses in a computer network.

Robert A. Saunders

See also Burlesque; Hoax and Prank; Lampoon; Parody; Satire

Further Readings

Bonnstetter, B. E. (2011). Mel Brooks meets Kenneth Burke (and Mikhail Bakhtin): Comedy and burlesque in satiric film. *Journal of Film & Video, 63*(1), 18–31.

Colletta, L. (2009). Political satire and postmodern irony in the age of Stephen Colbert and Jon Stewart. *Journal of Popular Culture, 42*(5), 856–874.

Day, A., & Thompson, E. (2012). Live from New York, it's the fake news! Saturday Night Live and the (non)politics of parody. *Popular Communication, 10*(1–2), 170–182.

Gilbey, R. (2009, August 6). *Spoofs: The films that ate Hollywood.* Retrieved from http://www.theguardian.com/film/2009/aug/06/spoof-airplane-scary-movie

Miller, J. S. (2004). *The horror spoofs of Abbott and Costello: A critical assessment of the comedy team's monster films.* Jefferson, NC: McFarland.

Roberts, A. (1927). *Fifty years of spoof.* London, UK: John Lane.

Saunders, R. A. (2008). *The many faces of Sacha Baron Cohen: Politics, parody, and the battle over Borat.* Lanham, MD: Lexington Books.

Turner, M. R. (2003). Cowboys and comedy: The simultaneous deconstruction and reinforcement of generic conventions in the western parody. *Film & History, 3*(2), 48–54.

Spoonerism

See Inversion, Topsy-Turvy; Puns

Sports

Sport may be defined as physical activity that is governed by a set of rules or customs and often engaged in competitively. As a social activity, it is akin to drinking alcohol: It's apt to reveal aspects of the personality of both participants and onlookers that would otherwise not be apparent. This is because sport necessarily entails stress and this, in turn, is because sport is inherently competitive. Without a winner and a loser, the French tennis player Suzanne Lenglen once wrote, no game could exist. Neither was it a dishonor to lose nor to desire ardently to win. The tension that derives from trying to win, or to avoid defeat, or to watch, empathetically, as others engage in this struggle, is often a source of humor. Humor has variously expressed, mitigated, and even celebrated that tension. There are various familiar manifestations of this.

Participants

Most males who have played contact sports have at some stage received a painful blow to the genitalia. While they were doubled up in agony, it's likely that another player loudly advised "Don't rub them. Count them." This joke long since became a male rite, its main function being to remind men of their masculinity, counseling them not to show that they have been hurt (a male expectation across a variety of cultures) and simultaneously to divert attention, in a manly and heterosexual way, to the sexual role of this appendage.

Humor can also be used either to mock or undermine opponents. The boxer Muhammad Ali (previously Cassius Clay) continually taunted his opponents before their fights, using humorous jibes and rhymes. Prior to fighting Sonny Liston for the World Heavyweight title in 1964, he teased Liston with a poem that contained the lines: "When Cassius says a mouse can outrun a horse / Don't ask how; put your money where your mouse is!" This playfulness doubtless helped Clay deal with any fears he may have had about the coming bout, while making the other fighter a figure of fun. The poem was incongruous behavior—childish levity in a serious masculine social world.

Humor also expresses the at-all-costs competitiveness that high-level sport now demands. Take this exchange between two NFL players of the 1980s. On hearing Joe Jacoby of the Washington Redskins make the familiar proclamation that "I'd run over my own mother to win the Super Bowl," Matt Millen of the Oakland Raiders said: "To win, I'd run over Joe's mom, too."

This underlines the fact that there is a strong gender dimension to much sport humor. Examples of the expression of humor in relation to women's sport are less evident in accounts of sport. This is because, historically, by social convention, females have not been expected either to play sport or to be amusing. Despite important social changes in this regard, less attention is therefore paid to women on these two counts. Two developments can, however, be observed here. One is the discomfiture that can still be manifested, via humor, over the fact that women have entered previously male sporting domains. Consider this obviously sexist joke: "Question: Why don't women know how to ski? Answer: Because it doesn't snow between the kitchen and the bedroom." Like a lot of contemporary humor, this can be read on at least two levels: It could be thought to express genuine distaste for sporting females and, equally, it could be using postmodern irony to satirize those same (largely male) attitudes. The humor of the passage is in the eyes of the beholder.

Secondly, though, humor is prominent in the resistance to male expectation that women are increasingly mounting. Take for instance these T-shirt slogans aimed at women: "I run like a girl, so try to keep up!" and "See Dick Run. See Jane Run Faster."

Onlookers

Fans, like families, often decry their own, usually to protect themselves from disappointment. The comedian Bernard Manning once praised a new stand recently built at Maine Road, home ground of his club, Manchester City, adding, "The only trouble was it was facing the fucking pitch." Lately these jokes have begun to play with contemporary sexual diversity (and fears). Take this joke told about Australian rugby:

> Little Bruce was in his junior school class when the teacher asked the children what their fathers did for a living. All the typical answers came up; fireman, policeman, salesman, politician. Bruce was being uncharacteristically quiet and so the teacher asked him about his father. "My father's an exotic dancer in a gay club and takes off all his clothes in front of other men. Sometimes, if the offer's really good, he'll go out with a man, rent a cheap room and let them sleep with him." The teacher hurriedly set the other children to work on some colouring and then took Little Bruce aside to ask him, "Is that really true about your father?" "No," said Bruce, "My father plays rugby for Australia, but I was just too embarrassed to say."

When not playfully disparaging their own, fans will use humor to disparage (usually superior) opposition—when a team has beaten an ostensibly superior and far wealthier club, its supporters will raise a chorus of "Can we play you every week?" and, with the growing gap between major football (soccer) clubs and the others, a refracted class resentment is expressed through the burgeoning fund of jokes at the expense of big clubs such as Manchester United, for example: "Q: Did you hear that the British Post Office has just recalled their latest stamps? A: Well, they had photos of Manchester United players on them—folk couldn't figure out which side to spit on."

Humor, then, has a fundamental part to play in sport and exercise culture; it helps both players and fans deal the fundamentals of that culture—winning and losing and the relationship of that culture to ever-fluctuating gender identities.

Stephen Wagg

See also Gender and Humor, Psychological Aspects of; Humorous Names; Identity; Play and Humor

Further References

Snyder, E. E. (1991). Sociology of sport and humor. *International Review for the Sociology of Sport, 26*(2), 119–131.

Young, C. (2007). Two world wars and one World Cup: Humor, trauma and the asymmetric relationship in Anglo-German football. *Sport in History, 27*(1), 1–23.

SSTH

See Linguistic Theories of Humor

Stand-Up Comedy

Stand-up comedy is a conversational form of professional humorous talk that occurs on a stage in front of and directed toward a responsive audience. Although there is a clear demarcation between the performer and the audience, the two are in dialogue, and the audience collectively, albeit not uniformly, contributes to the performance through their reactions. Applause, booing, answers to questions, pregnant pauses, and—above all—laughter are key elements within the overall comedic performance, without which the text is fundamentally different. Key to the success of stand-up is the creation of a persona and a performed autobiography that helps situate the performer in relation to the audience and thus establish rapport despite sociocultural distances. With its growth since the 1960s and its pervasiveness through television, cable, and recordings, stand-up comedy is one of the most conspicuous forms of humor in the contemporary public sphere. This entry discusses the style and aesthetics of stand-up comedy, its antecedents, its use of amplification, and the methods performers use to create intimacy and build an audience.

Style and Aesthetics

Informality and a lack of contrivance are hallmarks of its contemporary style. The stand-up comedian performs for the most part without conspicuous staging, props, or costuming. Effective use is made of the diegetic space of the (deliberately) bare stage, namely a microphone stand and a stool or a table; the performer wears a costume that is a deliberate "non-costume" of what he or she would typically wear as an audience member. This informality extends to the form of talk itself: It is in prose and without musical accompaniment. Patterning of the speech—rhythm, cadence, repetition—might emerge out of this more prosaic talk, only to return again to a less-stylized performance. Characterizations are achieved through mimicry, gesture, and facial expression, and not through costume or makeup: Moreover, although gifted impressionists will create opportunities for characterization by constructing routines around particular voices, characterization is a means within the more general flow of talk and not an end in and of itself. The overall appearance of spontaneity, even if and when the audience is aware that what is being performed is not extemporaneous, is integral to the aesthetics of stand-up comedy. Props, costumes, and music break that illusion, and comedic performances where they are in use are typically reframed as different from, or a subtype of, stand-up comedy proper.

American stand-up comedian, actress, and writer Amy Schumer, performing in 2006.

Source: Maryanne Ventrice/Wikimedia Commons.

Antecedents

While it is tempting to locate stand-up comedians along an axis that includes both court jesters and early American humorists such as Mark Twain and Will Rogers, doing so frames stand-up comedy either by function or by content. Rather, if one begins with identifying what the stand-up comedian actually does, one sees that the more direct antecedents are small-scale artistic verbal performances in small groups, whether variously labeled *stylin' and profilin,' talking shit*, or *shit talk*, or unnamed traditions of a recognized verbal artist momentarily taking focus (and granted license to do so by those present) on engaging in conversational play. This differs from the jester tradition, in which the person is irrevocably "othered" as opposed to emerging from the group as a peer, and is different from the monologist who performs a fixed text that works independent of audience participation.

The Role of the Microphone and Amplification

Much as the microphone allowed for the intimate singing voice of the crooner to take over from the belter, use of the microphone allowed for the professionalization of this type of casual yet stylized talk by making it feasible to occur on a stage. Prior to amplification, the one voice of the comedian was in dynamic competition with that of the crowd: To cease control of the back and forth was to be overwhelmed by it. To maintain control delivery tended to be loud, rapid-fire, and direct, suitable for the telling of jokes. With a microphone, the stand-up comedian's voice is equal to that of the crowd. Speaking in a natural register allows for greater use of tone and inflection; furthermore, tangents, false starts, muttering, and other verbal transgressions can occur and yet control can still be maintained. Amplification not only allows for traditional verbal art performances on a larger scale, it allows for that unpatterned, unstylized talk that often precedes it: In short, the microphone brought the intimate voice to the stage, investing it with power. The microphone is so central to the art of stand-up comedy that it is the most frequent symbol used to represent it.

Creating Intimacy

If one of the requirements for intimate talk among peers is a common reference frame—a storehouse of shared experiences, beliefs, and opinions that can be drawn from as subject matter for the performed text—then for a comedian to move outside of the peer group and engage with strangers requires strategies of quick intimacy creation. Moreover, professionalism brings with it the idea that, in exchange for money, the comedian will deliver a laughter-inducing performance that meets the expectations of the audience in a novel way. As older joke-telling comedians had been part of already established entertainment circuits (e.g., the African American Chitlin' Circuit, the Jewish Borscht Belt theaters in the Catskills), comedians could experiment with this newer form of talking comedy to an audience that was ostensibly suitable, at least according to the booking agents who ran the circuits.

Meanwhile, comedians appeared alongside folk musicians in the burgeoning coffee house scenes in urban centers and university towns, each invested in performances marked by intimacy and, howsoever defined, "authenticity." The trope of the comedian performing in front of a bare brick wall relates in part to these stripped-down performances, and the casual dress of Mort Sahl and Lenny Bruce contrasts with the tuxedos of the Las Vegas comedians of the era. Mutual participation in the same cultural scene, marked by both cosmopolitanism and a disenfranchisement from the dominant culture, served to frame the comedian as a potential intimate. Subject matter would be rooted in the same concerns as the audience's: politics, popular culture, and the negotiation of the quotidian urban landscape. The focus on the everyday and speaking to the seemingly mundane yet shared experiences provided a technique to establish a common reference frame that could transcend additional barriers to intimacy such as race, gender, or region. These scenes caught the attention of broadcasting tastemakers (such as Steve Allen, Johnny Carson, and Ed Sullivan) and the comedians began to appear on network television, further cultivating an audience for the form. The sheer economics of stand-up comedy as an entertainment—a solitary performer on a bare stage with a fixed set-up—meshed with growing demand and encouraged a comedy club circuit. This club style emerged as the dominant form in what was deemed mainstream broadcasting, although niche programming such as country variety shows and, later, specialty cable allowed regional and ethnic forms to stake and maintain a claim to the media landscape.

Building an Audience

Amplification changed the potential audience size for intimate verbal art, but for stand-up comedy to become viable as a profession the individual comedian needs to cultivate larger markets. Audiences may be fluent with the idea of what a stand-up comedian is—what they could expect from a stand-up comedy performance—yet not know the specific comedian at a particular performance. As one would do with any nonintimate, the comedian is located by the audience within certain social categories defined by visual cues: In addition to a host's introduction, comedians initially employ their appearance and their costume to locate themselves within an easily identifiable frame of reference for the audience's interpretation. Expectations established by this frame of reference may be immediately met or thwarted once talk begins: Korean American Henry Cho speaks with an undeniably Tennessee accent, which early in his career was part of his introductory repertoire, whereas on his first appearance on the *Tonight Show*, Bill Cosby began talking about karate rather than speaking from an obviously African American perspective. The comedian locates him or herself in relation to the audience, and difference is addressed to create points of similarity.

Strategies of intimacy creation are more conspicuous the more the performer is not socioculturally similar to the audience, but the same processes of quickly establishing a perspective and relating that perspective to that of the audience are present in all performances, whether that be through the subject matter of mediated and popular culture, through observations on mundane commonplaces, or through establishing a solidarity of marginalization by referencing an absent, dominating other. This performance of resistance and the creation of a marginalized self is irrespective of the off-stage privileges accorded to the performer either by the sociocultural categorization or celebrity: The "oppressions" of everyday life—contemptuous politicians, market forces, family dynamics—are arranged to create an empathetic character, with empathy decided at the discretion of the audience. As the performance is always framed as play, the audience tends to allow this display of marginalization to occur despite its often obvious conceit.

Further intimacy can be created through esoteric references, referring to tacit insider knowledge that can forge further connections to the audience. These connections can be made by making references to the local cultural landscape and intercommunity rivalries, either through digressionary observations at the beginning of a performance or as part of established routines that can be tagged with an appropriate piece of inside understanding. Additionally, on occasion the comedian will build solidarity through making specific statements about faith positions or politics or other sensitive issues that are affirmed through applause or cheers rather than laughter.

An autobiography and a persona are composed on stage, if initially only in the broadest of strokes. Through repeated performances, through recordings, and through media exposure, the comedian might develop a reputation and a known cumulative repertoire: Audiences are not coming to performances to see "a" comedian but this specific one. The strategies for establishing rapport with an audience are increasingly unnecessary, and the comedian anticipating this familiarity can bring shading and texture to that initially sketchy autobiography and more fully flesh out the persona into one increasingly contiguous with the one lived offstage. If the comedian moves to a different or a larger market (whether that means performing in more venues or receiving wider dissemination through broadcast), the processes of establishing intimacy occur anew, and the comedian must negotiate the expectations of this new venue, market, or medium.

Mediation

Proof of the requirement of a reactive audience for stand-up comedy performances is how, on broadcasts and recordings, the audience immediately present to the performer at the recording venue is always captured and forms an integral part of the what is presented to and interpreted by the nonpresent audience. However, two audiences inform the performance: the finite reactive one that shapes the text, and the indeterminate, nonpresent audience at the receiving end of the performance's mediation, distant whether in space (as is the case with live or as-live broadcasts) or in space and time (as in the case of syndicated broadcasts and recordings). The laughter and other reactions on the mediation provide an entry point for the media's "at home" audience, but those captured reactions need to build upon material that is not so esoteric as to be alienating for those not present. Material needs to be relatable to the nonpresent audience that the comedian wishes to cultivate. Again, with time, the comedian might begin to develop a reputation with an audience and material can build on the extant goodwill. A comedian's individual broadcast and recording history tends to demonstrate a shift toward the personal and idiosyncratic.

Although access to the broadest forms of distribution has often been controlled by programmers and bookers making decisions based on notions of either the widest possible audiences or the most desirable markets (generally middle-class Whites), the ostensibly countercultural nature of stand-up comedy has allowed for a surprising amount of mainstream commercial success for comedians from marginalized groups. Moreover, the economics of stand-up have allowed for the development of large markets independent of a broad media presence, and newer forms of media (such as specialty cable television and digital distribution) have allowed for narrowcasting, or the widespread distribution of cultural products that do not intend or presume universal appeal.

Conclusion

Although manifested in a variety of specific styles, stand-up comedy at its most general is a professional humorous verbal art performance directed toward a responsive audience with whom the performer attempts to establish a form of intimacy and solidarity that is ultimately validated through laughter. It allows for a broad swath of topics and messages, from attempts at psychological or political profundity to exaggerated excursions into silliness and the absurd. Although it is markedly different from traditional storytelling it is rooted in the same basic impetuses of meaning making and community building through narrative and verbal play.

Ian Brodie

See also Anecdote, Comic; Folklore; Genres and Styles of Comedy; History of Humor: U.S. Modern and Contemporary

Further Readings

Brodie, I. (2008). Stand-up comedy as a genre of intimacy. *Ethnologies, 30*(2), 153–180.

Georges, R. A. (1969). Toward an understanding of storytelling events. *Journal of American Folklore, 82*(326), 313–328.

Koziski, S. (1984). The standup comedian as anthropologist: Intentional culture critic. *Journal of Popular Culture, 18*(2), 57–76.

Mintz, L. E. (1998). Stand-up comedy as social and cultural mediation. In N. A. Walker (Ed.), *What's so funny? Humor in American culture* (pp. 193–204). Wilmington, DE: Scholarly Resources.

Misje, A.-K. (2002). Stand-up comedy as negotiation and subversion. In S.-E. Klinkmann (Ed.), *On the study of imagination and popular imagination: Essays on fantasy and cultural practice* (pp. 87–112). Turku, Finland: Nordic Network of Folklore.

Stereotypes

Stereotypes are forms of representation that evaluate particular categories of people in homogenized, unyielding terms. They implicitly claim that those belonging to such categories have certain traits or characteristics that are absolute and unchanging. Those assigned to them are reduced to these traits or characteristics without qualification. When stereotypes are aligned with jokes or other comic modes, the stock features associated with them are the source and object of the humor, and the humor functions primarily as a way of ridiculing, demeaning, and belittling people outside of the social group that enjoys the humor. This entry examines what is involved in the relationship of stereotyping and humor; how their combination operates and has a determining effect on the humor; and how, at least to a degree, reverse humor can be used to challenge stereotypes.

When stereotypes are given expression in comic frames, a particular perspective is being signaled. This does not necessarily belong to any broader outlook or worldview, but it does register the discourse of expression as apparently nonserious, though of course that may not be recognized or accepted, and the comic expression may have serious implications, such as making the stereotypes of those "joked about" gain hold despite—or rather, because of—the laughter thus generated. In any event, stereotypes within comic frames cannot be regarded as straightforwardly equivalent to stereotypes in general because their use in humor modifies the status of their meaning and how the stereotypes are understood. The general import of a stereotype within a comic frame may be more or less identical to the same stereotype outside that frame, but where in another context, such as a war film or a spy novel, the stereotypical representation acquires a moral or political value relevant to the outcome of the narrative, with comic stereotyping what is represented acquires a different value—that of being a warranted object of amusement and hilarity in and of itself. The humor is legitimated by the stereotype, and vice versa. The shift has various implications for the operation, circulation, and reception of a stereotype, and so we need to look into the relationship between humor and stereotyping, and see what happens when they are brought into combination.

The Nexus of Comicality and Stereotyping

An idealized conception of joking and engaging in humor holds that they subvert our habitual ways of seeing, make the familiar seem strange, or allow us to accept the absurd in what we take seriously. If we adhere to this conception we might suppose that comic forms will work to undermine common stereotypes in everyday circulation and the seriousness with which they are understood, that they will compromise the conjunction between prejudicial expectation and perceived reality that stereotyping causes and confirms. In the main, this does not happen. Humor may of course have the effect that this idealized conception of it claims, but in the nexus of comicality and stereotyping humor's transformative capabilities are usually diffused or nullified. Humor is then used to reinforce and perpetuate existing stereotypes, not only because the stereotype is seen as the source of the humor, but also because the comic dimension is unevenly weighted in favor

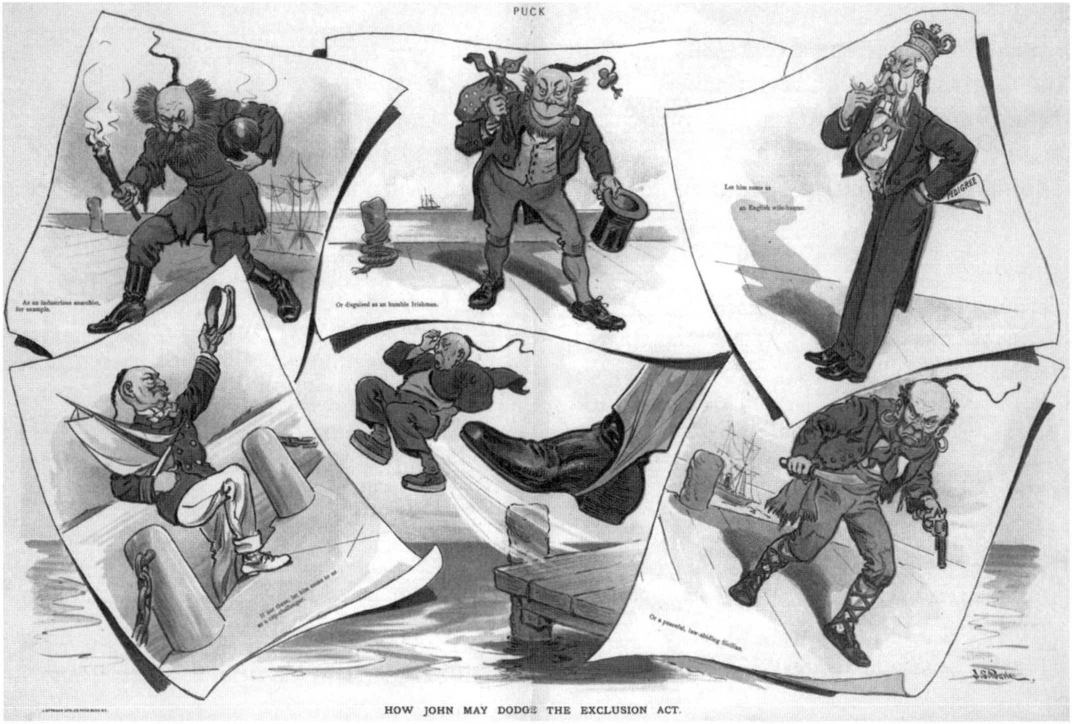

The Chinese Exclusion Act was the subject of a 1905 cartoon by J. S. Pughe titled "How John may dodge the exclusion act." Vignettes show how the Chinese could emigrate to the United States—by coming "as an industrious anarchist," "disguised as an humble Irishman," "as an English wife-hunter" with "pedigree" in his pocket, "as a cup-challenger" in yacht races, or wielding knife and handgun, as a mean-looking "peaceful, law-abiding Sicilian." The cartoon played on stereotypes not only about Chinese but other ethnic groups as well.

Source: Library of Congress Prints and Photographs Division, Washington, DC, Reproduction Number LC-DIG-ppmsca-25972.

of the stereotype. The stereotype also carries greater rhetorical power and force than the humor so that it becomes difficult for humor to acquire the capacity to expose a stereotype as baseless and render it discursively harmless. The more usual consequence is for a stereotypical trait or characteristic to transform the quality of humor into a form of abuse, regardless of whether this occurs in mundane conversation or in the routines of professional comedians.

Although comic stereotyping is not equivalent to stereotyping in general, it has by definition to operate by focusing on a singular aspect of behavior or attitude, as for instance in the way it may isolate an alleged inability or disinclination. This is then used to define certain social groups since it is this inability or disinclination, above all else, that is held to be essential to who they are and what they do. The definition is highly reductive because all individuality in a person's character or disposition is cast aside and rendered peripheral in favor of this aspect, whether it be the laziness of Mexicans, the stupidity of the Irish, or the sexual promiscuity of the Essex girl that is involved. Each of these stereotypes has been regarded as comic, as for example with the joke that Mexicans are short because when they were children their parents told them that, upon growing up, they would have to get a job.

While one particular feature may be identified as the object of the humor, comic stereotyping is generally more complicated than this in that the identified feature usually implies or depends upon another. So, with the Q & A format of Essex girl jokes, asking why young women from this targeted English county wear hoop earrings leads to the retort: They have to have somewhere to rest their ankles. The explicit claim that they are sexually promiscuous is supported by the implicit claim that they are stupid, and vice versa. The two claims mutually reinforce each other even though in such jokes it is usually only one or the other stereotype that is in the comic frame at any one time. This process can be extended so that a broader regime of stereotyping, such as sexism or Orientalism—stereotyping Arabs and Muslims based on romanticized images of Asia and the Middle East—is implicated in any one comic example. Regardless of the definite focus or more general range that may in some sense be drawn in, what is nevertheless always clear is that those who are stereotyped are regarded as deserving of comic ridicule or derogation.

This is where comic stereotyping performs a neat trick. The serious import of stereotypes is disguised by the comic frame in such a way that the comicality appears to be the primary point, and not the stereotype. This does not always happen of course. Bernard Manning's joke that the Irish have invented a new type of parachute, one that opens on impact, does not try to hide the imputation that the Irish are innately stupid; indeed, it revels in this comically framed insult. But in everyday interaction, where such a joke causes offense and objections are voiced, the comic frame easily becomes a disclaimer—as if the joke is a joke and nothing more, and as if jokes do not have any relation to, or interaction with, other forms of social discourse. The disclaimer that "it's just a joke" means that it is not meant to be taken seriously, and where it is, this is evidence that the person or group to whom offence is caused cannot take or appreciate the joke. That is the trick: to turn culpability onto the object of comic abuse, and not on its perpetrator. The object of comic stereotyping is then doubly hit, first by the stereotype, and then by the accusation. The perpetrator is exonerated, almost invisibly.

Stereotypes and Comic Ambiguity

It is in such ways that comic stereotyping both supports and conceals relations of power and domination, or inequalities of resource and opportunity. Yet those with relatively little power or privilege may also use stereotypes of other social categories in joking relationships, maybe as a way of salvaging status or esteem, or perhaps by resorting to scapegoats by giving expression to feelings of anger, frustration, or disaffection deriving from their own lack of power or advantage. Here again, the comic frame can obscure the displaced aggression that is involved in these situations, but there are also cases where stereotypes are—or appear to be—internalized, as for example when Black people have adopted a comic persona associated with stereotypes of them. Historically there are well-known examples of this in the context of blackface minstrelsy, but these always need careful analysis because all may not be as it seems. Billy Kersands is an interesting case in point.

Kersands was the most famous Black comedian of the late 19th century, in both Britain and North America. He adopted the White-produced stereotype of the slow, dim-witted Black man, and played up to racist physical grotesquerie by dancing with a cup and saucer in his mouth. In one of his comic songs, he even reiterated White-centered stereotypical fears by singing of "a big Black coon" running away with his daughter. However, the fact of his being Black altered the comicality of the song, possibly even mocking White fears, and his utilization of African American vernacular culture in ways new to minstrelsy not only helps to explain his appeal to Black people but also initiated the process of undermining the racist Sambo stereotype even as he openly acted it out on stage. Analytically, then, Kersands's comedic persona and act cannot be simply dismissed as rubber-stamping the demeaning caricature of Black stereotyping as portrayed by Whites in minstrelsy and elsewhere. As he once said, without a smile: "Son, if they hate me, I'm still whipping them, because I'm making them laugh." Kersands faced a difficult dilemma and walked a perilous line: Laughter has multiple causes and consequences. Making White audiences laugh was nevertheless a small but significant step toward regaining control over how he—and African American people generally—were represented in public culture.

This example shows comic stereotyping is often accompanied by considerable ambiguity, especially as its performance can involve saying one thing while doing another. Added to this, the intention in a joke or comic act is not necessarily realized in how it is received. This is particularly the case with comic impersonation. It may be that it is taken as affirming the stereotypical inferiority of the group represented in the impersonation, and then by implication a culturally sanctioned social hierarchy. When Whites put on the blackface mask, for example, this invariably affirmed the racialized demarcations between "them" and "us," yet at the same time it allowed Whites a certain interval of license to indulge in clownish buffoonery or enjoy a taste of what their own social realities repressed. Alternative interpretative possibilities are intrinsic to comic impersonation. It may, for instance, be intended to satirize the type of person impersonated, as was the case with the central character of Alf Garnett, the working-class racist in the television situation comedy, *Till Death Us Do Part* (BBC, 1965–1975), but contrary to this, some audience members celebrated Alf Garnett's stereotypical attitudes. The bigoted comic butt became a role model for racists. The same happened with Garnett's North American counterpart, Archie Bunker. Such transmutation was possible because of the inherent ambiguities of comic impersonation.

Comic impersonation plays upon the polysemous qualities of humor and the interpretative possibilities—or, in a different take, the interpretative difficulties—that can accompany such impersonation. The TV and film character Ali G is an obvious case of this. The impersonation was composed of elusive layers of identity: a wannabe English suburban homeboy adopting the stereotypical persona of a young inner-city Black American who is unashamedly misogynistic, homophobic, and affiliated with drug culture and gangsta rap, being played by a Jewish middle-class graduate of Cambridge University, Sacha Baron Cohen. Who was impersonating whom here? Was Ali G a *wigger*—a White person who wants to be Black—and how was the wigger stereotype being satirized? Was Ali G White or Asian, was he a White pretending to be Black, a White pretending to be Asian pretending to be Black, or a Jewish man pretending to be an Asian pretending to be a White man pretending to be Black? The difficulties increased as the possibilities spread, and both critics and audience members were drawn into a guessing game with no guaranteed outcome. Yet despite the manifold ambivalences, the young Black male stereotype was neither subverted by the comic act nor amenable to being adopted by Blacks themselves for their own satirical or comedic projects. Even if we don't see the persona of Ali G as an attenuated and less fixed latter day version of blackface entertainments, acting out the streetwise Black male stereotype is a White privilege with no equivalent reverse impersonation of a middle-class White graduate by a young ghetto-bound Black.

Comically Reversing the Stereotype

The case of Kersands, outlined earlier, raised the possibility of using humor to undermine or defuse existing stereotypes. The scope for this was quite limited in White-controlled minstrel entertainment during the period of Kersands's career, but beyond such racially determined theatrical constraints, the incongruity and ambivalence of much humor and comedy can be more assertively employed to resist stereotypes and challenge the views and values stemming from and supporting them. This is sometimes referred to as reverse humor, with stereotypes being used in such a way as to subvert their dominant meaning. A nice illustration of this is Lenny Henry, a Black British comedian, explaining why he felt it beneficial that his White friends kept him company: "They'd be out stealing hubcaps otherwise, you know what they're like . . ." This joke counters the stereotype of Black criminality and highlights the prejudicial assumptions upon which it rests. Its reverse semantic effect is that of turning the Black racist stereotype on its head and attributing its alleged trait to White people.

Another example of reverse humor is provided by the light bulb formula. This involves asking how many people associated with a particular social group are needed to change a light bulb. The answer usually revolves around the group behaving or responding in a stereotypical manner. When the question is asked of how many feminists it takes to change a light bulb, the response is: "That's not funny!" Here the joke relies on the stereotypical assumption that feminists are overserious and far too earnest. They are lacking in a sense of humor and unable to laugh at themselves; they are suspicious that any question might lead to the reproduction of a sexist stereotype, and so liable to take offence where none is intended. The joke perpetuates the stereotype, but even with this standard joke genre, reverse humor can occur. Here is an example. Q: How many electricians does it take to change a light bulb? A: One. The joke in this instance is at the expectation of a stereotype being comically affirmed in the answer. Its humor achieves the reversal of this expectation, with the straight-faced response confirming that electricians are competent in doing what they have been trained to do.

The strategy with reverse humor is to play with the stereotype, as for instance by exaggerating it to the point where it becomes clear it is a stereotype and not a developed characterization, then using the realization of this to divert the expected validation of a stereotype and so undermine the perceived risible "otherness" that the stereotype contains and sustains. In deploying this strategy, there is always the risk of confirming the stereotype rather than dispelling it, for while a stereotype can be comically played with, the ambiguity of humor always underwrites the possibility of responses being made in quite alternative directions. It is in any case easy to exaggerate the extent to which reverse humor may be successful, for it is unlikely that racists would accept the Lenny Henry example if their belief in the stereotype of Black criminality is sufficiently entrenched. Anti-racism cannot be guaranteed when reverse humor depends upon, and amplifies, comic ambiguities and the divergent interpretative possibilities upon which humor pivots.

Knots of Symbolic Configuration

The strength and resilience of stereotypes should not be underestimated. Once established, they can prove highly resistant to challenge and critique, not least because of the at-hand boundary-making devices they offer in complex modern societies, and because of their success in achieving representational fixity in public discourse. When they are taken up and allied with various forms of humor and comedy, their relation to the groups they target acquires not only the added force of comic ridicule but also a convenient alibi when offense is taken—the "only joking!" exclamation of mock surprise, or some other variant on this. Comic stereotyping is in this respect even more difficult to counter than stereotyping in general, with the hurt and damage it can cause having no means of redress because of seeming confined to the joking relationship.

Public awareness and disapproval of this hurt and damage has nevertheless grown in recent times. It is now regarded as unacceptable to transmit negative stereotypes of minorities or socially marginalized groups, at least in the mainstream media. This advance is not without its detractors, and pernicious forms of comic stereotyping have not disappeared. They have continued to circulate in everyday interaction among certain groups, resurfaced in various websites, and gained textual presence in new forms of social media. Comic stereotypes are tenacious and persistent.

They are so because of their paradoxical quality. Humor encourages us to embrace ambivalence and think in more fluid, less hidebound ways. Even with a simple joke structure, there is a combination of conventional description in the lead-up and unexpected outcome in the punch line, and where this is expanded into more complex comedic forms, humor can be used to counter settled assumptions and static perceptions of others. Stereotypes operate with an opposite descriptive logic in their legitimation of such assumptions and perceptions; they aid and abet rigid and hostile ways of seeing and thinking. When they operate within comic frames, they are harder to contest, not least because they are then associated with the pleasurable qualities of laughing and being amused. The humor both supports and exonerates their tight knots of symbolic figuration. That is why comic stereotypes need to be understood as having psychological and sociological dimensions, for they raise questions not only about how others are to be regarded as we strive personally to make sense of the world around us, but also about how others are to be represented in public forms of discourse and communication. These questions together are central to what constitutes a positive sense of identity.

Michael Pickering

See also Ambiguity; Ethnic Jokes; Ethnicity and Humor; Insult and Invective; National and Ethnic Differences

Further Readings

Billig, M. (2005) *Laughter and ridicule.* London, UK: Sage.

Lockyer, S., & Pickering, M. (Eds.). (2009). *Beyond a joke: The limits of humor.* Basingstoke, UK: Palgrave Macmillan.

Lockyer, S., & Pickering, M. (2010). You must be joking: The sociological critique of humor and comic media. In M. Pickering (Ed.), *Popular culture* (pp. 247–258). London, UK: Sage.

Pickering, M. (2001) *Stereotyping: The politics of representation.* Basingstoke, UK: Palgrave Macmillan.

Pickering, M. (2008). *Blackface minstrelsy in Britain.* Surrey, UK: Ashgate.

Wagg, S. (Ed.). (1998). *Because I tell a joke or two.* London, UK: Routledge.

Weaver, S. (2011). *The rhetoric of racist humor.* Surrey, UK: Ashgate.

Stress

Stress is a concept originally described by Richard Lazarus in 1984 as a process of an individual perceiving and responding to environmental stimuli requiring adaptation. As such, stress seems to come from the realm of "negative psychology." Humor, which is described as a psychological phenomenon that increases positive arousal and decreases negative arousal, is considered part of "positive psychology" as introduced by Martin Seligman and Mihaly Csikszentmihalyi in 2000. However, as discussed in this entry, there are more relationships between the two than one may think at first sight.

Stress

In the case of stress, environmental stimuli seem to challenge the personal resources of an individual who encounters them, which is why they are usually called *stressors*. One of the most obvious demonstrations of the relationship between stress and humor is nervous laughter. When nervous or distressed, a person may laugh in a typical way. Although at first sight, the person may seem to be having fun, that individual is in fact experiencing an internal state of anxiety or stress but expressing it through laughter.

Stress and Humor

In the 1960s and 1970s, researchers became interested in the physical manifestations of stress and its relationship to humor. An important concept in their work is *arousal*, referring to the response of the autonomic nervous system to stressors. These bodily responses are typically called fight-or-flight responses because they prepare the body for physical action (e.g., confronting an enemy or running away). They include an increase in heart and respiration rates and an extra delivery of blood sugars to the muscles to enable them to perform fast actions. The question for humor researchers in the 1960s and 1970s was how arousal was related to humorous responses.

Berlynes's Arousal Boost-Arousal Jag Hypothesis

Daniel Berlyne (1972) proposed that humor increases pleasurable arousal and decreases unpleasant arousal, the so-called arousal boost–arousal jag hypothesis. The arousal boost part of this hypothesis states that certain combinations of new or unexpected stimuli (as in humor) raise pleasurable arousal. The arousal jag part of the hypothesis states that humor reduces very high levels of negative arousal, making humor pleasurable. Investigating the arousal boost part of the hypothesis, Michael Godkewitsch's work in the 1970s showed that high levels of sexual arousal in jokes were related to a higher perceived funniness and a higher heart rate. In 2008, Nicole Giuliani, Kateri McRae, and James Gross confirmed this finding by showing that people were more aroused (had faster respirations and stronger heart activity) when watching amusing films than when watching neutral films. Thus, it has been shown that humorous material contributes to higher levels of (pleasurable) arousal.

The arousal jag part of Berlyne's hypothesis shows quite another way in which humor may be pleasurable to a person: by reducing negative arousal. Usually this has been investigated using the concept of humorous coping, the active use of humorous behaviors or thoughts to adapt to stressors. These humorous coping responses are aimed at avoiding or reducing the unpleasant states or emotions that accompany stressors. Although not many studies have been done on the effects humorous coping may have on negative arousal, an experimental study conducted by Michelle Newman and Arthur Stone in 1996 showed that it is possible to influence one's own arousal with humorous coping.

Sibe Doosje

See also Anxiety; Arousal Theory (Berlyne); Coping Mechanism; Laugh, Laughter, Laughing; Mirth; Positive Psychology; Release Theories of Humor

Further Readings

Berlyne, D. E. (1972). Humor and its kin. In J. H. Goldstein & P. E. McGhee (Eds.), *The psychology of humor: Theoretical perspectives and empirical issues* (pp. 43–60). New York, NY: Academic Press.

Giuliani, N. R., McRae, K., & Gross, J. J. (2008). The up- and down-regulation of amusement: Experiential, behavioral, and autonomic consequences. *Emotion, 8*(5), 714–719.

Godkewitsch, M. (1972). The relationship between arousal potential and funniness of jokes. In J. H. Goldstein & P. E. McGhee (Eds.), *The psychology of humor: Theoretical perspectives and empirical issues* (pp. 143–158). New York, NY: Academic Press.

Godkewitsch, M. (1976). Physiological and verbal indices of arousal in rated humour. In A. J. Chapman & H. C. Foot (Eds.), *Humour and laughter: Theory, research and applications* (pp. 117–138). London, UK: Wiley.

Lazarus, R. S. (1984). *Stress, appraisal, and coping.* New York, NY: Springer.

Newman, M. G., & Stone, A. A. (1996). Does humor moderate the effects of experimentally-induced stress? *Annals of Behavioral Medicine, 18*(2), 101–109.

Seligman, M. E., & Csikszentmihalyi, M. (2000). Positive psychology: An introduction. *The American Psychologist, 55*(1), 5–14.

Subversive Humor

While its most overt and recognized function is to amuse and entertain, humor is duplicitous and has the ability to serve other less positive functions. *Subversive humor* is the label for humor that aims to resist and challenge while implying that any critical content is intended in jest. This often neglected subversive function has received attention in the fields of organizational communication and workplace discourse where researchers investigate the ways in which humor can be used to unsettle power asymmetries at work. Political resistance is another area in which subversive humor is highly relevant due to its ability to create a safe space for dissenters. Here subversive humor (e.g., cartoons critiquing a regime or jokes targeting entrenched gender discrimination) operates as a challenge to the status quo. These two distinct research areas are outlined below to demonstrate the so-called dark side of humor.

Humor and Power

The inherent hierarchy in organizations has provided a fruitful context in which to examine humor as an acceptable strategy for conveying critical or negative intent. While powerful managers and leaders may use humor to maintain control and repress subordinates, it is also available to those in less powerful positions as a socially acceptable means to subvert authority. The ambiguity of humor offers the opportunity to express dissatisfaction and undermine existing power relationships in a form that is indirect and less likely to result in rebuke. As an example, consider this teasing comment: "Callum has to ask!" It refers to a pedantic manager who questions every move his team makes and it was contributed by a more junior staff member. On the one hand, the quip amused the team (including Callum), but it simultaneously criticized the heavy-handed control that the manager was taking, a complaint that was unlikely to be expressed directly, especially with Callum present. Similarly, in a longer extract, Barry and Eric challenge the motivation of an organizational leader (Josh) who is only interested in sales figures rather than the important and necessary technical details on which their team focuses. Barry's challenge is implicit; it relies on shared understandings within the group about their senior and is signaled only by his laughter. Eric's response is more explicit as he provides the answer they expect to receive from Josh. It is uttered in a derisive tone and adds support to the humor created by Barry.

Barry: I've sent an e-mail to Josh as well so it'll be interesting to see what I get back from Josh [laughs]
Eric: Josh'll look at it going "uh I can't sell anything"

In both utterances, the humor challenges the authority of the leader who, in the view of the team, has a questionable approach to business. The example provides evidence of how subversive humor can be used to draw a dividing line between an "us" and a "them" by emphasizing the social boundaries between the speaker and the target of the humor. Humor may isolate the powerful person or group, identifying ways in which the person or group does not conform to the shared norms and ideals of those who are subject to the domination.

Humor as Resistance

While the workplace is a context in which contesting authority is not without consequences, the stakes in political environments are often much higher. In some extreme contexts, contentious statements can even be considered dangerous to the speaker. Here again humor creates the opportunity for protests and criticisms to be made in a form that reduces the risk of recrimination.

A particularly well -ecognized form is the political cartoon, and some communities have long traditions of making use of this form of subversive humor to resist oppression and extreme political regimes (e.g., the Arab world, notably Egypt, and former communist countries such as East Germany). The comic veil of a cartoon that uses a caricature of a tyrannical leader or regime to reveal cruel and unjust behavior makes use of a safe space created by humor in the public domain. This form of confrontation again uses the distancing effect of humor to provide a socially acceptable and recognized means of encoding critical intent. Subversive humor becomes a political tactic or tool for expressing dissidence and a culturally licensed way to reject repression.

The use of humor as social protest has the potential to mobilize a community against oppression in many forms. Historically, for example, the U.S. suffragette movement of the late-19th century and early-20th century made use of humorous slogans, retorts, and parodies of popular songs to demonstrate its anger and refusal to accept the gender discrimination that underlay a woman's inability to vote. The modern equivalent is the feminist joke, whether repeated in water cooler conversations among colleagues or as viral humor distributed by e-mail. These jokes typically aim to subvert gender stereotypes and sexist behavior, contrasting roles, behaviors, and attributes of men and women. Making ironic comments about a woman's subjugated role in the public arena, or in society more generally, aims to expose this representation of women as unacceptable. By highlighting gender ideologies, the jokes address a goal of promoting social change.

Subversive humor is thus a potent tool for challenging social inequalities, whether hierarchical differences at work, an unjust political status quo, or powerful societal stereotypes. It can be seen in many different forms from cartoons and slogans resisting political regimes, to song parodies and canned jokes that challenge dominant societal ideologies, or even simple throwaway quips against the senior members of a business team. In these contexts, subversive humor affords the opportunity to express dissatisfaction with power imbalances and prevailing attitudes and ideologies by making use of its distancing effect. Because humor inherently carries a sense of entertainment, the ambiguity protects the speaker from the need to accept full responsibility for the critical content of his or her actions.

Meredith Marra

See also Gender and Humor, Psychological Aspects of; Political Humor; Workplace Humor; Workplace Resistance

Further Readings

Ackroyd, S., & Thompson, P. (1999). Only joking? From subculture to counter-culture in organizational relations. In S. Ackroyd & P. Thompson (Eds.), *Organizational misbehaviour* (pp. 99–120). Thousand Oaks, CA: Sage.

Holmes, J., & Marra, M. (2002). Over the edge? Subversive humor between colleagues and friends. *HUMOR: International Journal of Humor Research, 15*(1), 1–23.

Rodrigues, S. B., & Collinson, D. L. (1995). "Having fun"? Humor as resistance in Brazil. *Organization Studies, 16*(5), 739–768.

't Hart, M., & Bos, D. (Eds.). (2007). *Humour and social protest.* Cambridge, UK: Cambridge University Press.

Supreme Court

As a term, *Supreme Court humor* may seem paradoxical to readers. However, in a place where gods, goddesses, angels, and statues of historical figures suggest the solemn nature of the Court's task, visitors would hardly expect a U.S. Supreme Court justice to discuss his underwear. And yet, during *Safford Unified School District v. Redding* (2009), Justice Stephen G. Breyer openly revealed an intimate detail of his personal childhood, which will likely be forever remembered for its supremely embarrassing nature and the resulting howls of laughter that followed.

Justice Breyer: In my experience when I was 8 or 10 or 12 years old, you know, we did take our clothes off once a day, we changed for gym, okay? And in my experience, too, people did sometimes stick things in my underwear—

(Laughter.)

Justice Breyer: Or not my underwear. Whatever. Whatever.

Justice Breyer's description of the teasing he received as a boy drew raucous laughter and howls at the justice's indecorous comment. But Justice Breyer is not the only justice who has embarrassed himself. Recently, during the Affordable Care Act Cases (*Florida v. Department of Health and Human Services,* Docket No. 11-400), Justice Antonin Scalia offered a Freudian slip:

Justice Scalia: You know the old Jack Benny thing, "Your money or your life?" and he says, "I'm thinking. I'm thinking." It's funny because it's no choice.... Now whereas if the choice were "Your life or your wife's?" that's a lot harder.... You can't refuse "your money or your life?" but "your life or your wife's?" I could refuse that one. (laughter).

Laughter overran the courtroom and forced Chief Justice John Roberts to calm the Court, remarking, "That's enough frivolity for a while." The Chief Justice's chiding sounded more appropriate for a group of high school students than for members of the Supreme Court. But these two examples suggest that humor is alive and well at the Supreme Court, offering scholars a rich area of study.

Despite the rich landscape of Supreme Court humor, advocates generally avoid humor, perhaps because the Court's *Guide for Counsel* cautions advocates by warning "attempts at humor usually fall flat." This suggestion may have arisen because of advocates' past uses of inappropriate humor. In *Roe v. Wade* (1973), Jay Floyd, arguing for the State of Texas, infamously set the tone for his argument with a failed joke in his opening statement. Floyd began, "Mr. Chief Justice and may it please the Court. It's an old joke, but when a man argues against two beautiful ladies like this, they are going to have the last word." Waiting for laughter and hearing only silence, Floyd struggled through the rest of his argument. Despite the Court's warnings and prior advocates' blunders, humor occurs regularly in the courtroom; however, few scholars consider the topic, making it an underdeveloped and richly dynamic area of study.

Justice Breyer's earlier comment likely caught audience members by surprise due to its personal and indecorous nature; rarely do people—much less Supreme Court justices—openly share their personal experience with objects in their underwear. There is little doubt Justice Breyer's comment resulted from an unfortunate incident of logorrhea, but he shares this affliction with others on the Court, as readers saw in Justice Scalia's willingness to sacrifice his wife for his money. However, most humorous situations at the Court lack embarrassing qualities and tend to be good-natured in spirit. On Halloween day in Chief Justice Robert's first term, a light bulb exploded during the oral arguments for *Central Virginia Community College v. Katz* (2006). The gunshot-like sound frightened the Court and rattled the nerves of justices and advocates. Easing the tension, Chief Justice Roberts joked, "I think we're . . . I think it's safe. It's a trick they play on new Chief Justices all the time." Drawing laughter, his comment prompted Justice Scalia's welcoming reply of "Happy Halloween," which brought about even more laughter from the audience and the Court. Not to be outdone, Chief Justice Roberts responded, "We're even more in the dark now than before."

Like her other colleagues, Justice Elena Kagan brings a humorous wit to the Court. During her time as Solicitor General, she often invoked humor. In *United States v. Comstock* (2010), Kagan called Justice Scalia "Mr. Chief," by mistake, but wryly corrected herself, stating, "excuse me, Justice Scalia—I didn't mean to promote you quite so quickly." Laughter rang through the courtroom, and Chief Justice Roberts responded, "Thanks for thinking it was a promotion"; Justice Scalia continued the joking by turning to Chief Justice Roberts and sarcastically remarking, "And I'm sure you didn't." From these examples readers can recognize a lighter side to the Court's serious task.

As noted, few scholars conduct research on the topic of humor in the Supreme Court, even though it occurs regularly. This area may lack attention because transcript laughter notations and the identification of individual justices in transcripts only began in the 2004–2005 term. In 2005, Jay Wexler published the first study that considered Supreme Court humor. The three-page article, "Laugh Tracks," tabulated the number of "(laughter)" notations in the Court's 2004–2005 oral argument transcripts, crowning Justice Scalia "funniest justice" because he garnered the most laughs. Wexler's subsequent studies focused on the changes from the 2004–2005 to the 2006–2007 Court term. Wexler's research prompted significant attention from media outlets and his studies have spawned further research from other scholars.

Functionally, Supreme Court humor takes place in a communication environment where significant institutional, social, and intellectual barriers influence communication between humans. These barriers or social norms and explicit rules grant justices significant authority to control humor in the courtroom. However, instead of limiting humor, the justices occasionally invite it by jesting with the advocates, regularly teasing other justices, or laughing at their own misstatements. Although not to the extent of the justices, advocates also prove humorous, deriving humor most frequently by gently teasing the justices or the Court as a whole and also laughing at their own personal mistakes. The Court's willingness to engage in and tolerate humor from advocates dissolves normative barriers and promotes a sense of equality among participants.

In an adversarial environment, surprisingly, humor reveals the justices' willingness to reduce their power and control by diminishing significant institutional, social, and intellectual barriers, in turn allowing and inviting others to laugh at them and with them. Humor's ability to equalize members of differing hierarchical positions is a testament to its power. Instead of reinforcing or upholding positions of superiority, the justices treat advocates as near equals and enhance the communication environment in the judicial process by reducing barriers and offering a more effective and egalitarian environment for communication.

Mark Twain has been quoted as saying, "[laughter] is the great thing, the saving thing. The minute it crops up, all our irritations and resentments slip away and a sunny spirit takes their place." While humor is neither a panacea for a justice's grouchiness nor is likely to spur a justice into loquaciousness, it exerts a powerful moment of temporary unity. Ineffable in its impact, when a justice or lawyer makes a humorous remark, particularly during a dull argument, a significant shift can occur in the room: Tension or boredom may briefly dissipate, the audience may become more attentive, and the arguing advocate may relax and become more composed. As a result of a humorous moment, every person in the room shares the same insight, takes part in the collective laughter, and may feel a sense of equality that only humor can generate.

Ryan A. Malphurs

See also Legal Education; Legal Restriction and Protection of Humor

Further Readings

Affordable Care Act Cases, 567 U.S. __ (2012).

Barnes, R. (2011, January 17). Supremely funny: Study covers court's penchant for laughter. *The Washington Post*. Retrieved from http://www.washingtonpost.com/wp-dyn/content/article/2011/01/16/AR2011011604004.html

Cassens Weiss, D. (2011, January 18). Scalia teases Breyer the most, and gets the most laughs, new study concludes. *American Bar Association Journal*. Retrieved from http://www.abajournal.com/news/article/scalia_is_funniest_and_grouchiest_justice_laughter_study_concludes

Central Virginia Community College v. Katz, 546 U.S. __ (2006).

Liptak, A. (2005, December 31). So, guy walks up to a bar and Scalia says . . . . *The New York Times*. Retrieved from http://www.nytimes.com/2005/12/31/politics/31mirth.html

Liptak, A. (2011, January 24). A taxonomy of Supreme Court humor. *The New York Times*. Retrieved from http://www.nytimes.com/2011/01/25/us/25bar.html?_r=0

Lithwick, D. (2011, March 1). He'll be here all week. The verdict is in: Chief Justice John Roberts is hilarious. *Slate Magazine*. Retrieved from http://www.slate.com/articles/news_and_politics/supreme_court_dispatches/2011/03/hell_be_here_all_week.html

Malphurs, R. A. (2010). People did sometimes stick things down my underwear. *Communication Law Review*, *10*(2), 48–75.

Mears, B. (2011, June 16). Justice Kagan stays alert with a little bench humor. *CNN U.S.* Retrieved from http://www.cnn.com/2011/US/06/16/scotus.kagan.humor/index.html

Peppers, T. C. (2011). Did you hear the one about Chief Justice Burger and the itinerant litigant? *The Green Bag*, *15*(1), 25–40.

Richey, W. (2010, June 30). Elena Kagan shows off sense of humor in confirmation hearings. *The Christian Science Monitor*. Retrieved from http://www.csmonitor.com/USA/Politics/2010/0630/Elena-Kagan-shows-off-sense-of-humor-in-confirmation-hearings

Roe v. Wade, 410 U.S. 113 (1973).

Safford Unified School District v. Redding, 557 U.S. __ (2009).

United States v. Comstock, 560 U.S. __ (2010).

Wexler, J. D. (2005). Laugh track. *The Green Bag, 9*(1), 59–61.

Wexler, J. D. (2007). Laugh Track II—Still laughin'! *The Yale Law Journal, 117,* 130–132. Retrieved from http://www.yalelawjournal.org/the-yale-law-journal-pocket-part/supreme-court/laugh-track-ii-%E2%80%93-still-laughin%E2%80%99!

Surprise

See Incongruity and Resolution

T

Tall Tale

The tall tale is a fictional, exaggerated, humorous folk narrative, often told in the first person or as an account of the experiences of a relative or friend. It contains an increasingly implausible series of events, usually related to the weather, rural life, or traditional male occupations. Other names for the tall tale include *lie*, *tall story*, *windy*, *whopper*, *long bow*, and *yarn*. The act of telling a tall tale may be called *tall-talking*, *lying*, or *leg-pulling*. These terms suggest that the tall tale is a deliberately dishonest narrative, which it is; yet its primary purpose is entertainment. It thrives in oral performance, especially with a skillful teller and an appreciative audience. As an example of traditional folk humor, it has significant artistic value and can be appreciated for its method of presentation as well as for the tale itself.

Tall tales evoke the improbable. "The Wonderful Hunt" is a well-known example that recalls the adventures of a hunter who has such remarkable luck that a single shot from his rifle kills both birds in the air and animals on the ground. When he wades into the water to get his game, even his boots fill up with fish. "The Split Dog" describes a dog that was cut in half and stitched back together with its back legs upside down. In another tale, the weather is so cold that people who speak to each other have to wait until spring for their words to thaw out and be heard. This entry discusses how tall tales are constructed, how they flourished on the American frontier in the 1800s, and how tall-tale images became popular as postcards in the 1900s.

An Artistic Construction

The tall tale progresses deliberately, with each new plot detail building on the statement that preceded it. The teller may begin his narrative in a serious manner, setting the scene with a description of an ordinary activity, such as fishing. For example, a man is fishing with several friends in a small boat. He throws out his line and feels a tug of tremendous force. After

An 18-foot-tall statue of Paul Bunyan, the giant lumberjack, and his gigantic companion, Babe the Blue Ox, in Bemidji, Minnesota. Tall tales about Paul and Babe circulated around lumberjack camps in the 1860s and were later popularized by American newspapers. The tales were used in promotional brochures by the Red River Lumber Company during the early 20th century. According to one tale, Paul excavated the Grand Canyon when he accidentally dragged his pickax behind him.

Source: Bobak Ha'Eri/Wikimedia Commons.

a struggle of several days, he reels in a fish so big that there is no room for anyone else in the boat. The tale concludes by stating the fish is so big that its scales are used to make shingles for a four-room house. This final description signals the climax of the narrative. Increasingly outrageous exaggerations have been piled on top of each other in a perpendicular fashion until the "tall" tale, a perilous structure, cannot support them. At this point the narrative's credibility collapses, and the audience responds with laughter, even if they had been fooled, briefly, when it began.

The tall tale typically concludes with one final, hilarious lie, as when the narrator describes the split dog as being even better after its reconstruction, for it could run on two legs until it was tired, and flip over to the other two legs for added stamina. Other tales end with understatement, such as the narrator who remarked that it was indeed "fairly cold" on the day that people's words froze, or that the man who killed so much game with one rifle shot was "a pretty good hunter."

A conclusion also can occur in response to a question from the audience. For example, in the midst of a story about a fisherman encountering an impossibly thick bed of flounder, the narrator says that the bed was made of rubber. When someone asks how a bed of fish could be made of rubber, the narrator answers, "So I can stretch it to any size I want." He finishes the story with a humorous acknowledgment of its falsehood (and his power to bend the truth), moving the audience out of the realm of artful deception and back to reality. If there is lively audience involvement with the narrator, the give-and-take rapport between them adds to the success of the performance. Inherent in this success is a willingness to tell a lie and to be lied to, knowing that the end result will be shared amusement.

The American Frontier

Although the tall tale flourished in Europe in the hands of master liars like German Baron Münchhausen (1720–1797), in the 1800s, the American frontier proved to be fertile for lying stories. In a vast untamed continent, truthful accounts of extreme weather, abundant crops or game, and men of phenomenal strength lent themselves to exaggerated, fictional narratives, especially if they were being told to newcomers. These greenhorns might find themselves listening to tales about a catfish that could be saddled and ridden like a horse or a bear so big that even its track weighed 11 pounds.

The protagonists of these tales, usually male, enjoy remarkable success. They accomplish

Tall-tale postcard, "Showing Off the Corn," created by William H. Martin, 1908.

Source: Reprinted with permission from the Wisconsin Historical Society (Image no. WHi-44614).

impossible tasks, kill numerous animals, or display overwhelming strength, especially during moments of adversity. In one tale, a hunter bends the barrel of his gun to shoot a deer that is disappearing around the side of a hill. In another, a man defends himself from a vicious dog by putting his hand into the dog's mouth, grabbing the dog by the tail, and turning the dog inside out.

The Tall-Tale Postcard

The tall-tale postcard, a visual manifestation of the verbal tall tale, enjoyed great popularity in America in the early 1900s when the commercial postcard was making its debut as an inexpensive way for travelers to send home enticing images from faraway places. Tall-tale postcards depicted a world that was exaggerated beyond belief, where fruits and vegetables were larger than the people who harvested them (see postcard image).

The pictorial juxtaposition of everyday settings with ridiculously large objects created the same balance between absurdity and real life that tall-tale narratives achieved verbally.

Nancy Cassell McEntire

See also Folklore; Jokes; Schwank

Further Readings

Brown, C. S. (1987). *The tall tale in American folklore and literature.* Knoxville: University of Tennessee Press.

Henningsen, G. (1965). The art of perpendicular lying: Concerning a commercial collecting of Norwegian sailors' tall tales (W. E. Roberts, Trans.). *Journal of the Folklore Institute, 2,* 180–219.

McEntire, N. C. (2009). Tall tales and the art of exaggeration. *Acta Ethnographica Hungarica, 54,* 125–134.

Randolph, V. (1951). *We always lie to strangers.* New York, NY: Columbia University Press.

Welsch, R. L. (1976). *Tall-tale postcards: A pictorial history.* New York, NY: A. S. Barnes.

Taoism

Taoism arose in China about five centuries before the Common Era. The word *Taoism* is now applied to many things in Chinese culture, including religious rituals, divination, alchemy, and a worldview. This entry focuses on the Taoist worldview and its connections with humor.

Chinese Worldviews

Several scholars have argued that the religions and worldviews of China, including Taoism, are more hospitable to humor than the monotheistic religions of the West. The God of the Bible and the Qur'an is the all-powerful, all-knowing creator, lawgiver, and judge. He has the single correct understanding of things, he dictates what is right and wrong, and he determines everyone's eternal fate. The gods of China, by contrast, lack this perfection and power. They are more like fallible human beings—indeed, many of them used to be humans and became divine only after death. They do not establish moral codes and do not consign people to heaven or hell. More like the gods of ancient Greece and Rome, they show the kind of mental flexibility and tolerance for disorder needed to laugh about human shortcomings.

Besides Taoism, the other great religious traditions of China are Confucianism and Buddhism. Confucianism, which arose about the same time as Taoism, shares with it features such as optimism that might have inclined it toward a comic vision of life. But in Confucianism there is an emphasis on law, order, tradition, obedience, and propriety that works against the anti-authoritarianism and spontaneity valorized in the comic vision. Taoism questions all of these and therefore is much more inclined toward humor and the comic vision of life. When Buddhism was brought to China in the 1st century CE, it gradually combined with Taoism to produce the tradition called *Chan*, which in Japan became *Zen*. Like Taoism, Zen Buddhism has comic tendencies.

Lao Tzu and Chuang Tzu

There are two great writers in Taoism: Lao Tzu and Chuang Tzu. The first is the purported author of the *Tao Te Ching*. This text describes the Tao as the ultimate reality, but it is not, as in Western religions, a personal being. The Tao has no desires, issues no commandments, requires and answers no prayers, and does not interfere with the natural order of events. *Tao* is sometimes translated "the Way." Another word that comes close is *Nature*, understood not as the plants, animals, mountains, stars, and other things in the universe, but as the force that regulates all of them. One feature of Taoism that makes it receptive to humor is its overall optimism about this force: Like the writer of a comedy, the Tao make events turn out for the best.

According to the *Tao Te Ching*,

1. The Tao underlies everything. All events occur within it.
2. The Tao does not exert itself. It includes everything and so there is nothing for it to act upon.
3. What happens in accordance with the Tao—whatever is natural—is good.
4. Human beings are part of the Tao; they are not above it. They will be happy to the extent that they go along with the Tao.
5. Things and qualities exist as *yin* and *yang*—opposites such as hot and cold, light and dark, male and female. Yin and yang are not in conflict; rather they complement each other and work together. Opposition is the source of all growth.

Because the world naturally unfolds in a good way, the *Tao Te Ching* says, it is foolish to try to manipulate things or people. Being discontented with one's lot in life and wanting to change oneself is unrealistic and self-defeating. Similarly, the desire to change other people is a mistake. The best way to deal with people is to let them develop in their own way without imposing our ideas or standards on them. This live-and-let-live attitude shows the comic virtues of tolerance for diversity and tolerance for people's shortcomings.

While the *Tao Te Ching* is addressed to rulers and maintains an air of dignity, the writing of Chuang Tzu shows considerable playfulness and humor, and makes generous use of irony, paradox, and hyperbole. It does not just tolerate human limitations and shortcomings but celebrates them and makes fun of human desires for self-improvement. Like Zen Buddhism, which it influenced, the writing of Chang Tzu also challenges standard rationality and logic in a way that is often funny. As in comedies, nothing in life need be what it seems, and our surprise can be a source of delight and amusement. A famous example is Chuang Tzu's story in which he dreamed he was a butterfly. On waking up, he was unsure whether he was Chuang Tzu who had dreamed he was a butterfly, or instead was a butterfly who dreamed he was Chuang Tzu. Enriching the humor here is Chuang Tzu's humble self-critical stance: In poking fun at his confusion after the dream, he drops all pretense of being a sage dispensing wisdom to the rest of us. Like a stand-up comedian, his best jokes are on himself.

There is another way in which Chuang Tzu's writing is like stand-up comedy. Treated as a religious document, it has not always been interpreted in the playful, imaginative way he intended. When he wrote, for example, about flying "supermen" who dined on air, sipped dew, were immune to heat and cold, and lived forever, he was not serious. But taking these passages literally, some readers took them to be literal descriptions of "The Immortals" and set out to develop magical techniques to become immortal themselves. Chuang Tzu would have laughed at their misinterpretations and at their desire to outmaneuver death, which for him was something natural and not to be feared. Playful and comic writing, then, like serious and tragic writing, requires a certain attitude on the part of readers.

Taoism and the Comic Vision of Life

Western culture has two great dramatic traditions, comedy and tragedy, with tragedy ranked superior by virtually all authorities. Many literary critics have written of the "tragic vision of life" in Western literature and religion. In Taoism, as in Chinese culture generally, the tragic vision has never taken hold. The Chinese do not celebrate the individual hero needed for tragedy nor do they valorize struggle or protest as responses to suffering. Instead they celebrate the social group and cooperation rather than conflict. Those emphases make Chinese culture, and especially Taoism, amenable to humor and to the comic vision of life.

Part of having a sense of humor is the ability to enjoy experiences in which something violates our ordinary understanding of the world and our expectations. A standard way to say that is that humorous amusement is a way of enjoying incongruity. Not all violations of our expectations are enjoyable, of course. Instead of laughing, we may respond to surprising events with fear, anger, disgust, or sadness. Such responses are common when we make mistakes or experience failure. To have a sense of humor about life as a whole, we need a basic trust in the universe. We have to believe that when things do not go as we expected, there is probably something to be enjoyed in that experience, something that calls for laughter rather than fear, anger, disgust, or sadness. Those who lack that trust tend to be suspicious when their conceptual patterns and expectations are violated. Paranoid people, for example, who tend to see all surprises as threatening, seldom find anything to laugh about in naturally occurring experiences of incongruity.

Like some other religions and worldviews that lean toward the comic, Taoism teaches the basic trust in the universe required for having a sense of humor about life as a whole. It says that everything will work out for the best in the end, even if that happy ending is not clear right now. The way events naturally unfold, the *Tao Te Ching* teaches, cannot be improved upon; someone who tries to redesign a natural process is bound to spoil it.

This cosmic optimism allows Taoists to relax and enjoy the surprises in their lives, especially the small violations of their expectations that would otherwise elicit negative emotions. With trust in the Tao, the mistakes, failures, and disappointments of daily life are not matters for great concern and often are something to laugh about. This is not to say that Taoists are always happy-go-lucky and carefree, but their worldview fosters the development of a sense of humor about life in general.

Here the *yin/yang* way of seeing opposites is conducive to humor. Heroic visions of life, as found in epic and tragedy, typically treat opposing things and forces as enemies combating each other, and that understanding suppresses our ability to enjoy things that do not go our way. Understanding opposition as the source of growth, as the *Tao Te Ching* does, by contrast, allows us to appreciate and be amused by what opposes us.

The fundamentally nonpractical stance of Taoism also fosters a comic vision of life. Many analyses of humor have discussed the opposition between laughing about something and having a practical attitude toward it. Most humor is about a thing, situation, or event not being as good as we expected it to be. This is obvious in fictional humor such as stage comedy, where for millennia stock characters have been the drunk, the fool, the liar, the klutz, the pedant, the coward, and others making mistakes and failing. As Aristotle pointed out, while tragic characters tend to be better than average people, comic characters tend to be worse.

It is usually easy to suspend ordinary practical concerns in comedy because we know that what is happening is not real. But laughing about similar events in real life is often harder. Here Taoism is supportive of humor because it advocates a nonpractical attitude. The leading virtue in Taoism is *wu wei*—effortlessness, letting things happen naturally. That fits nicely with the comic theme that the best thing to do or say may be nothing, and that we may accomplish the most by not trying. While humor often involves things going wrong, many comedies are built on the theme of serendipity, happy accidents, and good things falling into people's laps.

With its valorization of *wu wei,* Taoism runs counter to heroic ideologies based on force and struggle. Since military action is the strongest form of such action, Taoism rejects militarism. The person who follows the Tao avoids weapons and conflict and sees fighting as a last resort. Rejecting the heroic ethos, too, Taoism rejects the militarist virtues of pride, honor, and unquestioning loyalty. All of this fits well with the pacifism of traditional Western comedy that began with Aristophanes's feminist anti-war play *Lysistrata* and continues to today.

Because it rejects the use of force, Taoism is also opposed to governments, especially those with burdensome laws and taxes. According to the *Tao Te Ching,* the more laws that are passed and the more taxes assessed, the greater the number of lawbreakers and tax evaders. From this attitude comes a general suspicion of city life and a preference for agrarian village life.

Beyond its opposition to militarism and governments, Taoism questions hierarchical social systems in general. Wherever there is someone exerting authority over others, the proper attitude is at least suspicion, and perhaps protest. Like its opposition to the military, Taoism's general opposition to authority is similar to the mocking of authority in Western comedy.

Perhaps the most general link between Taoism and humor lies in Taoism's celebration of freedom and spontaneity. In each situation, the best way to act is not mechanically, according to personal habits and cultural habits, but flexibly and creatively, the way heroes in comedy typically do. The person who lives that way is not only more in tune with nature, but happier and more successful.

John Morreall

See also Biblical Humor; Buddhism; Christianity; Comic Versus Tragic Worldviews; Confucianism

Further Readings

Morreall, J. (1999). *Comedy, tragedy, and religion.* Albany: State University of New York Press.

Simpkins, C., & Simpkins, A. (1999). *Simple Taoism: A guide to living in balance.* Tokyo, Japan: Tuttle.

Tzu, C. (1996). *Chuang Tzu: The basic writings.* New York, NY: Columbia University Press.

Tzu, L. (2006). *Tao Te Ching: A new English version* (S. Mitchell, Trans.). New York, NY: HarperCollins.

Targets of Humor

Any subject can be a target of humor, and indeed, a Google search for "targets of humor" brings up more than six million websites. Humor is an irrepressible force that, from time immemorial, has skewered people, places, institutions, and anything else one might think of. This entry discusses targets of humor and how they are chosen, as well as how they are related to various theories of humor and techniques of humor.

Targets of Humor and Theories of Humor

One way to deal with a subject of this size is to consider the targets of humor in terms of how humor is understood in the most important theories of humor, which are themselves targets of humor when proponents of one theory make fun of those who hold other views about the nature of humor. The most commonly accepted theories of humor—that is, theories that explain why we find something funny—are the incongruity theory, the superiority theory, the release theory, and various cognitive theories about humor as communication and metacommuncation. The most common form of humor is the *joke*, which can be defined as a short narrative with a punch line that is meant to amuse and cause mirthful laughter. But there are countless other forms of humor, such as witticisms, puns, comic verse, parodies, and so on. There is often an element of surprise in humorous texts, as, for example, in the punch lines in jokes.

Incongruity Theory

Incongruity theory is based on the notion that there is often a difference between what we expect and what we get. In many cases, there is a comic dimension to these chance events, accidents, or what you will; thus, for an incongruity theorist, anyone and anything can be a target of humor.

Superiority Theory

To a superiority theorist, humor expresses feelings of superiority over others or even over a former state of oneself—oneself "formerly," as Thomas Hobbes put it. For superiority theorists, a legitimate object of humor is anyone who is not our equal. We laugh at the characters in the comic strip *Dilbert* because we recognize them as being like many people we know, all of whom are inferior to us and thus are acceptable targets.

Release Theory

According to the release (relief) theory, humor is, in essence, a form of masked aggression that releases built-up tensions. Because people have many hostile and aggressive feelings, there are countless targets for humor—generally tied to personal relationships, sex, marriage, the family, politics, and so on, that present themselves every day. One of the classic examples of release theory occurred when someone on a Groucho Marx radio program said "Sometimes, I think I'm my worst enemy." "Not as long as I'm alive," replied Groucho, not missing a beat in reflecting his comic persona.

Communication and Metacommunication

The notion that humor is tied to communication and metacommunication processes in our brains that we do not completely understand, such as paradox, suggests that any topic relating to human communication and functioning in society is a legitimate target of humor, though those who perpetrate the humor may not fully understand what they are doing and why their humor works. An example is the definition of capitalism in a comment often attributed to John Kenneth Galbraith: "Under capitalism, man exploits man. Under communism, it's just the opposite."

Spatiality and Targets of Humor

We can also look at targets of humor in terms of spatiality or distance from the self. From this perspective, there is a continuum starting with oneself, one's spouse or partner, one's children, one's family, one's parents, one's in-laws (especially mothers-in-law in the United States), one's gender, other genders, that spreads outward to one's boss, one's colleagues at work, one's religion, other people's religions, friends, political figures, sports heroes, politicians, ethnic groups and racial groups in one's country, attitudes toward money and sex, and various other preoccupations of the common man and woman, and then people in other countries and their national characteristics.

Much of this humor involves certain figures who are the most common targets of humor. Phyllis Diller joked about "Fang," her inept husband. The situation comedy *Frasier* had two contrasting brothers: one effete and snobbish, the other slightly more down to earth but never able to have a decent relationship with women, and both very different from their blue-collar father. Jack Benny made a career of being cheap. His joke writers put in a gag about him being cheap once; it got such a terrific response that they added other gags, and eventually he developed a brilliant comic persona that he exploited for 40 years. Perhaps Benny's most famous gag on his radio show was when somebody held him up and said "Your money or your life!" There was silence for around 10 or 15 seconds, and the robber repeated, "Your money or your life!" Benny replied "I'm thinking it over." Much of Benny's humor was victim humor directed toward himself, which means he didn't alienate others. Other comedians make fun, ridicule, and insult everyone and everything; for example, the comedian and rabbi Jackie Mason makes fun of Jewish people, Italians, Puerto Ricans, politicians, and countless others.

Classification of Techniques Used in Humor

Research by Arthur Asa Berger (1997) on the techniques found in humorous texts of all kinds resulted in a list of about 45 techniques that can be found in everything from Roman comedies to the theater of the absurd, as well as in the routines of comedians and in jokes that are told informally or shared on the Internet. All these techniques could be classified as humor involving identity, humor involving language, humor involving logic and reasoning, or humor that involves action or visual phenomena. The classification of techniques is shown in Table 1.

These techniques are explained in detail in Berger's 1993 *An Anatomy of Humor* and 1997 *The Art of Comedy Writing*. The repertoire of techniques used by comedians shapes the targets they select as the objects of their humor. For example, parody is an important technique of humor, but for parody to work, audiences must recognize the text being parodied. Currently, comedians who parody television news programs are very popular; many young and not-so-young Americans get most of their news from *The Daily Show With Jon Stewart* and Stephen Colbert's *The Colbert Report*. Much of their satire is political in nature.

Stereotyping

Stereotypes are a very common form of humor that rely on notions people have about what members of some ethnic, racial, or religious group are like or what people from foreign countries are like (i.e.,

Table 1 Techniques Used in Humor

Logic	*Language*	*Identity*	*Visual*
Absurdity	Allusion	Before/After	Chase
Accident	Bombast	Burlesque	Speed
Analogy	Definition	Caricature	Slapstick
Catalogue	Exaggeration	Eccentricity	
Coincidence	Facetiousness	Embarrassment	
Comparison	Insults	Exposure	
Disappointment	Infantilism	Grotesque	
Ignorance	Irony	Imitation	
Repetition	Misunderstanding	Impersonation	
Reversal	Overliteralness	Mimicry	
Rigidity	Puns/Wordplay	Parody	
Theme and Variation	Repartee	Scale	
Sarcasm	Ridicule	Stereotypes	
	Unmasking	Satire	

Source: Berger, A. A. (1997). *The Art of Comedy Writing*. New Brunswick, NJ: Transaction, p. 3.

their national character). Following is an example of a joke targeting national characteristics:

> The United Nations asks a group of scholars to write a book on elephants. The following books are contributed: The French write *The Love Life of the Elephant*. The English write *The Elephant and English Social Classes*. The Germans write *A Short Introduction to the Elephant in Five Volumes*. The Italians write *Elephants and the Renaissance in Italy*. The Americans write *How to Grow Bigger and Better Elephants*. The Jews write *Elephants and The Jewish Question*.

At various times in the United States, there were popular joke cycles about Polish Americans (Polish jokes), Jewish American "princesses" (JAP jokes), and blondes. Some examples are "How many Poles does it take to change a light bulb? Five. One to hold the bulb and four to move the table on which the first one is standing." "How does a Jewish American Princess commit suicide? She piles all her clothes on her bed, gets on top of them, and jumps off."

Other jokes may target specific demographic groups, as in the following:

> A man goes to Miami for a vacation. After four days he notices he has a tan all over his body, except for his penis. So the next day he goes to a deserted area of the beach early in the morning, takes his clothes off and lies down. He sprinkles sand over himself until all that remains in the sun is his penis. Two little old ladies walk by on the boardwalk and one notices the penis. "When I was 20," she says, "I was scared to death of them. When I was 40, I couldn't get enough of them. When I was 60, I couldn't get one to come near me . . . and now they're growing wild on the beach."

When much of Eastern Europe was controlled by the Soviet Union, there were countless jokes about socialism, the Russian character, and related matters. (An example: Someone calls Radio Erevan in Russian Armenia and asked "Would it be possible to bring socialism to the Sahara?" "Yes," replied the Radio Erevan host, "But after five years we would have to start importing sand.") The targets of our jokes often reflect matters of great concern to people. For example, the Eastern European jokes and others like them target governments that oppressed people. In some cases, the targets are obvious—those who oppress others—but in other cases, they may reflect unconscious concerns that manifest themselves in humor that does not seem immediately related to the cause of the humor.

There are countless targets of humor, from ourselves and our inadequacies to our friends and their inadequacies, radiating out to other people, other nationalities, and anyone who is, in any way, different from us, as well as people who are like us. Certain targets for humor seem preeminent. These include sexuality, politics, ethnic and racial groups, and various personality types one encounters as particularly important targets for our humor—that is, the humor we make (puns, wordplay, etc.)—and the humor of professional comedians. But anyone and anything is grist for our personal comic militancy, which is limited only by our imaginations and by the techniques of humor with which we feel most comfortable.

Targeting Political and Religious Leaders: Positive and Negative Impacts

In recent years, humor targeting religious and political leaders has generated controversy and even violence. Attempts to make Islam and the Muslim prophet Muhammad a target of humor have sometimes resulted in threats and bloody protests. Extremists responded violently in 2005 and 2006 after the Danish newspaper *Jyllands-Posten* published cartoons lampooning Muhammad. The protests ignited a worldwide controversy over freedom of the press and fundamentalist censorship. The U.S. Department of State condemned the publication of the cartoons, while defending the right of the newspapers to publish them. Similar issues arose in 2012 when a French newspaper published caricatures of Muhammad and an anti-Islam video appeared on YouTube. Elsewhere, political satire has been attacked. For example, in South Africa, President Jacob Zuma sued a cartoonist and a media company after the publication of an anti-Zuma cartoon.

In much of the world, however, people relish humorous portrayals of politicians, religious leaders, celebrities and just about everyone else, for they permit us to laugh and obtain another measure of pleasure from life. Humor is vitally connected to human sociability; thus, everything that can serve as a foil or a target for comedians and humorists is valued the world over.

Arthur Asa Berger

See also Aggressive and Harmless Humor; Ethnic Jokes; Insult and Invective; Joke Cycles; Jokes; National and Ethnic Differences; Prejudice, Humor and; Satire

Further Readings

Apte, M. L. (1985). *Humor and laughter: An anthropological approach*. Ithaca, NY: Cornell University Press.

Berger, A. A. (1997). *The art of comedy writing*. New Brunswick, NJ: Transaction.

Boskin, J. (1979). *Humor and social change in twentieth century America*. Boston, MA: Trustees of the Public Library.

Davies, C. (1990). *Ethnic humor around the world*. Bloomington: Indiana University Press.

Davies, C. (2011). *Jokes and targets*. Bloomington: Indiana University Press.

Dundes, A. (1987). *Cracking jokes: Studies of sick humor cycles and stereotypes*. Berkeley, CA: Ten Speed Press.

Mindness, H. (1971). *Laughter and liberation*. Los Angeles, CA: Nash.

Ziv, A. (1988). *Personality and sense of humor*. New York, NY: Springer.

Teachers' Evaluations, Effect of Humor Use in Classroom on

When teachers enact a variety of verbal and nonverbal messages to elicit laughter and smiling from students, they employ a teaching strategy labeled *instructional humor*. Much of the research on this topic has explored how teachers' use of instructional humor affects students either positively or negatively. Extant scholarship indicates that teachers' use of instructional humor increases students' cognitive and affective learning, creates a comfortable learning environment, improves relationships between students and teachers by reducing tension and anxiety, and increases students' willingness to engage in outside-of-class communication. Poorly executed or inappropriate instructional humor can negatively impact student motivation and learning and erode student-teacher relationships. This entry looks at how the use of humor can affect students' evaluations of teachers and how the effect may vary depending on the type of humor used and the characteristics of the teachers and students.

Teachers also reap a number of benefits from using instructional humor. Use of instructional humor is often associated with being labeled a "popular" or well-liked teacher. Instructors' strategic use of humor in the classroom can increase student attendance, participation, and likelihood of forming professional student-teacher relationships based on trust. Not surprisingly, award-winning teachers use moderate amounts of instructional humor. Research also indicates that teachers' use of humor is linked to more favorable student evaluations.

Several studies have explored the connection between instructional humor and student evaluations of teachers. For example, in 1980, Jennings Bryant, Jon S. Crane, Paul W. Comisky, and Dolf Zillmann conducted seminal work in this area that explored how teachers' use of humor affected how students evaluate their teaching. Their research investigated the relationship between instructors' use of different types of humor and student evaluations of teaching effectiveness as well as individual differences that confound this relationship. The researchers asked 70 students to unobtrusively tape record instructors' lectures, transcribe the lectures, and complete questionnaires on the instructors' teaching effectiveness. Next, two coders independently analyzed all of the humorous content and identified the type of humor enacted (i.e., joke, riddle, funny story, humorous comment), whether the humor was prepared or spontaneous, whether the humor involved the instructor or student, who the target or butt of the humor was, and whether the humor was related or unrelated to the lecture content.

Bryant et al. found that humor was seamlessly integrated into the instructors' lectures; that humorous enactments occurred an average of 3.34 times during a 50-minute lecture; and that male instructors used more humor than female instructors. Instructional humor was correlated with student-reported teaching effectiveness. From their study findings, the researchers argued that only male instructors should use humor in the classroom because female instructors' use of the same humorous behaviors seemed to diminish their classroom effectiveness.

Katherine Van Giffen also investigated the relationship between instructional humor and student ratings of teaching effectiveness in 1990 using a different approach. A total of 849 students evaluated the teaching effectiveness of 24 (12 male and 12 female) faculty members from different academic departments who were selected because they used humor in their lectures. Students indicated whether the instructor was an effective teacher and the extent to which the instructor used humor to maintain student interest. Use of instructor humor was correlated positively with students' overall perceptions of teacher effectiveness. Unlike previous work from

Bryant et al., Van Giffen noted that female instructors benefited more from humor use than male instructors did. Van Giffen also noted that students' perceptions of instructor humor use were not associated with perceived warmth and friendliness. These findings are not particularly surprising because certain types of humor such as disparaging or tendentious forms are often construed as aggressive and hurtful by receivers.

Findings from this research indicate that there is a positive relationship between instructional humor and students' evaluations of teacher effectiveness. However, it is important to note the substantial differences in how these two studies were conducted to understand how to approach similar research in the future. While Bryant and his colleagues' work examined the type of humor used during actual lectures, Van Giffen assessed students' global perceptions of instructional humor. In the Bryant et al. study, which looked at the specific types of humor used, the findings indicated that female teachers could only use hostile and aggressive humor to enhance student perceptions of teaching effectiveness, while males could use any type of humor. While these findings are certainly perplexing, they illustrate the need to further explore the type of instructional humor enacted, the appropriateness of the humor, and source and receiver characteristics that influence how humor is perceived (i.e., sex, culture, age, personality differences, etc.). In order for instructors to learn how to use humor effectively and appropriately, researchers must not only study the effects of different types of humor on teacher evaluations but also source and receiver characteristics that influence how humorous content is perceived.

Students who enact humor more often and perceive themselves as effective at producing humor, known as humor-oriented individuals, evaluate humorous professors more favorably than students who do not regularly enact humor. Research by Melissa B. Wanzer and Ann B. Frymier (1999) on the relationship between student and teacher humor orientation and learning indicated that humor-oriented students reported learning the most from those instructors perceived as humor oriented. Steve Booth-Butterfield and Melanie Booth-Butterfield (1991) show that in order to truly understand the relationship between teachers' use of humor and students' evaluations of teaching effectiveness, it is important to measure the impact of individual differences such as humor orientation.

The relationship between instructional humor and student evaluations is a complex one that can only be understood by studying all elements of the interaction. Future research on this topic should explore communication-based personality differences (i.e., humor orientation) or source characteristics (i.e., sex, culture, age) that impact how humor is enacted in the classroom. Similarly, receiver characteristics should also be examined to determine the role that individual differences play in how humorous messages are interpreted.

Research indicates that the amount and type of humor used by the instructor affects learning outcomes. In 1990, Joan Gorham and Diane M. Christophel found that students are cognizant of instructors' use of tendentious humor and that a reliance on this type of humor negatively impacts affect toward content area. More recent research, such as that by Wanzer, Frymier, and Jeffrey Irwin in 2010, indicates that appropriate types of instructor humor like "related humor" affects student learning and motivation positively, while inappropriate types such as "other disparaging and offensive" humor do not increase learning; thus, it is also important to examine how competent use of humor in the classroom affects students' assessments of their teachers.

Melissa Bekelja Wanzer

See also Education, Humor in; Pedagogy; Testing and Evaluation

Further Readings

Booth-Butterfield, S., & Booth-Butterfield, M. (1991). The communication of humor in everyday life. *Southern Communication Journal, 56,* 205–218.

Bryant, J., Crane, J. S., Comisky, P. W., & Zillmann, D. (1980). Relationship between college teachers' use of humor in the classroom and students' evaluations of their teachers. *Journal of Educational Psychology, 72,* 511–519.

Gorham, J., & Christophel, D. M. (1990). The relationship of teachers' use of humor in the classroom to immediacy and student learning. *Communication Education, 39,* 46–62.

Van Giffen, K. (1990). Influence of professor gender and perceived use of humor on course evaluations. *HUMOR: International Journal of Humor Research, 3,* 65–73.

Wanzer, M. B. (2002). Use of humor in the classroom: The good, the bad, and the not-so-funny things that teachers say and do. In J. L. Chesebro & J. C. McCroskey (Eds.), *Communication for teachers* (pp. 116–125). Boston, MA: Allyn and Bacon.

Wanzer, M. B., & Frymier, A. B. (1999). The relationship between student perceptions of instructor humor and student's reports of learning. *Communication Education, 48,* 48–62.

Wanzer, M. B., Frymier, A. B., & Irwin, J. (2010). An explanation of the relationship between humor and student learning: Instructional humor processing theory. *Communication Education, 59,* 1–18.

Wanzer, M. B., Frymier, A. B., Wojtaszczyk, A., & Smith, T. (2006). Appropriate and inappropriate uses of humor by teachers. *Communication Education, 55,* 178–196.

Ziv, A. (1979). *L'humor en education: Approche psychologique* [Humor in education: A psychological approach]. Paris, France: Editions Social Francaises.

Ziv, A. (1988). Teaching and learning with humor: Experiment and replication. *Journal of Experimental Education, 57,* 5–15.

Teasing

Teasing has been of primary importance in research on socialization because of its ambiguity both as a means to strengthen solidarity through the creation of intimacy, or through enforcement of conformity to in-group behavior, whether it be within the family, the classroom, or other social categories. Among the important features of a tease is that the target be a present participant in the conversation; thus, teasing is a phenomenon that emerges in interaction, playing with the meaning and using the context and the interpersonal knowledge participants have of each other to create a double-edged sword that can both bond and bite. Teasing has been seen as a continuum that goes from bullying to banter. There is, however, a debate in the literature on the biting and bonding qualities of teasing. On one side, it is stated that teasing excludes aggressiveness by definition, as it is mock disrespect. On the other side, it is seen as covertly aggressive behavior. Research on the perception of teasing suggests that one's role as teaser or tease recipient determines which view is held. In addition, the power relationship between teaser and tease recipient might also be a determining factor in these perceptions. In the end, ambiguity is at the center of research in conversational joking and humorous interaction in both its dangerous edge and its bonding potential. The need to signal the play frame with disclaimers, such as "just kidding," reveals that as far as the target goes, teasing can indeed bite despite the intentions of the teaser. This entry discusses how teasing works and the purpose it serves.

Teasing is structured around the relationship between the teaser and the teased, since teasing must be directed to a participant in the interaction; this includes self-directed teasing. Teasing occurs primarily among intimates (friends, family, partners) since teasing among strangers is more likely to be misunderstood. Studies of teasing in the classroom and work context—where the power differential is a major concern—center around differentiating this behavior from bullying and harassment. The difficulty in making the distinction is not only due to the lack of cues or disclaimers but in ascertaining the intentionality of the exchange. While jokes involve incongruity resolution, sarcasm, and irony, teasing relies on incongruity of meaning. In other words, what is said is not what is meant, but what is meant is actually never said. The content of a tease is assumed to be always negative; nonetheless, cases have been registered where the tease is meant to challenge fixed roles and create new positive ones. That can be seen in the following examples from Florencia Cortés-Conde and Diana Boxer (2010).

Female 1: I told her [to Female 3] she *needs a little action*
Female 2: yeah, a *little action*
Female 3: He called . . .

In the context of challenging female identities as less sexually aggressive, the first two women tease the third one about needing "a little action" (meaning a sexual encounter). The content might seem negative, but there is no bite in this tease. In general, however, teasing can function as underestimation or permissible disrespect that reinforce hierarchical roles (mother, father, older sibling, etc.) or peer relationships (friends, colleagues, etc.). It can be a way to correct errors or behavior, while at the same time permitting the interlocutor to save face, a way to release aggression in a play format. A tease can lead to a retort from the target and other playful turns and this multiturn tease is considered banter:

Female 1: My husband's been walking the dog for a year.
Female 2: He went to get cigarettes.
Female 1: He went to get alcohol and cigarettes.
Female 3: What can I say, I'm waiting for him to come back.

Teasing as Socialization

Unlike irony and sarcasm, the point of the tease is not the ambiguity itself, but the relationship it establishes between the teaser and the teased. In family settings, teasing is a frequent occurrence allowing for a parental correction of behavior or a sibling's release of tension. In this sense, teasing is a nip that creates a play frame allowing one to learn a behavior in a certain context; this can be the family context, the workplace, the classroom, or the playground where one can learn to stand up for oneself. Misuse of the tease, even when the intention was just to play, can constitute for the target of the tease a perception of aggressive behavior, a put-down, and bullying. Put-downs and bullying create distance and establish hierarchy; teasing, on the other hand, builds rapport between interlocutors by signaling a shared schema. Among intimates and peers, teasing is a display of a relationship that is strong enough to play with the limits between bonding and biting.

Teasing as Mitigation

The ambiguity of teasing can be the result of a tension in the encounter between teaser and teased. There is, however, no resolution of the emergent incongruity as is the case with the joke. The incongruity creates a playful frame that mitigates the tension and acts as a face-saving act. In the following exchange, we find a tease that turns into banter as intimate friends talk about divorce (Cortés-Conde & Boxer, 2010):

Female 1: And then there is C*** here *who engages in slap therapy.*
Female 2: How does that work?
Female 3: I kept thinking that if I slapped you verbally you'd snap out of it.
Female 1: Please let up, let up. [*playing at begging*]
Female 3: [You should] get a *B.A. in slap therapy*

The multiturn tease alleviates the tension of the self-disclosure and reveals the intimate bond between friends: the one who engages in "slap therapy" as a means to make her friend come to her senses, and the one who is slapped and is grateful for it. There is no bite in this exchange, but the tension is mitigated by the humor of the interaction.

Self-Teasing

The self-tease is a remark that can be construed as disparaging to the one that utters it. Here is an example from Cortés-Conde and Boxer (2010):

Female 1: I get up off the couch. I walk with him [her son] to the cabinet, I open up the bottle, and I put it [aspirins] in his hand. [Laughter] I'm cringing at what I'm doing, but I love him to death. [high-pitched sound] I just want to take care of him.
Female 2: But you love her [your daughter] just as much?
Female 1: I do, but to her [her daughter] I just say "they're in the cabinet." (Laughter) *Mama's boy, mama's boy! Of course he is a mama's boy, whatta I care? I'm his mama!* [Laughter]

The self-tease in this case is self-deprecating. There is no avoiding the self-criticism in this statement, but the tease relieves the tension of the self-disclosure and the self-deprecation.

Florencia Cortés-Conde

See also Conversation; Incongruity and Resolution

Further Readings

Ahmed Al-Jabali, M. (2011). Same-sex and cross-sex teasing categories and reactions among Jadara University students. *International Journal of Linguistics, 3*(1), 23.

Boxer, D., & Cortés-Conde, F. (1997). From bonding to biting: Conversational joking and identity display. *Journal of Pragmatics, 27*, 275–294.

Cortés-Conde, F., & Boxer, D. (2010, November). Humorous self disclosures as resistance to socially imposed gender roles. *Gender and Language, 4*(1).

Dynel, M. (2008). No aggression, only teasing: The pragmatics of teasing and banter. *Lodz Papers in Pragmatics, 4*(2), 241–261.

Dynel, M. (2009). Beyond a joke: Types of conversational humour. *Language and Linguistics Compass, 3*(5), 1284–1299.

Ervin-Tripp, S. M., & Lampert, M. D. (2009). The occasioning of self-disclosure humor. In N. R. Norrick & D. Chiaro (Eds.), *Humor in interaction* (chap. 1). Amsterdam, Netherlands: John Benjamins.

Keltner, D., Capps, L., Kring, A. M., Young, R. C., & Heerey, E. A. (2001). Just teasing: A conceptual analysis and empirical review. *Psychological Bulletin, 127*(2), 229–248.

Keltner, D., Young, R. C., Heerey, E. A., Oeming, C., & Monarch, N. D. (1998). Teasing in hierarchical and intimate relations. *Journal of Personality and Social Psychology, 75*(5), 1231–1247.

Schieffelin, B. B., & Ochs, E. (Eds.). (1986). *Language and socialization across cultures*. Cambridge, UK: Cambridge University Press.

Test Measurements of Humor

Humor researchers use instruments to assess individual differences in humor, to display a person's humor profile, to relate these differences to other phenomena (like personality or health), and to document changes in humor due to interventions. The question of what instrument to use arises. Is it one for all research questions? Is it the one with the highest number of subscales or the most recent one, the one with the most sophisticated name? Several formal- and content-related factors determine the choice of which instrument to use for what purposes. This entry first discusses the criteria used to determine if a test is psychometrically sound. Second, currently used humor instruments (joke/cartoon tests and questionnaires) are presented.

Formal Criteria

Formal criteria refer to the construction and documentation of a test and to the psychometric properties. A well-documented test will contain information on the nature of the concepts to be measured (e.g., how spare vs. elaborated the variable definition is and if it is based on a theory), the type of construction procedure employed (e.g., factor analytic, empirical, rational), how elaborate the construction stage was (e.g., how were the items generated, how many samples were used, was there an item analysis), and the psychometric properties.

Psychometric properties—mainly objectivity, reliability, and validity—allow an evaluation of the quality of the test measurement. According to Gustav A. Lienert and Ulrich Raatz (1998), objectivity is standardization in procedure, scoring, and interpretation. Reliability is the degree to which the measurement is free from error variance, that is, how accurately the test measures. Validity of a test is the extent to which it measures or predicts some criterion of interest. Sufficient objectivity is the necessary precondition for high reliability; and high reliability, in turn, is required to achieve satisfying validity.

Reliability varies between 0 (unreliability) and 1 (perfect reliability), and should exceed .60 for group assessment and .80 for individual assessment. Reliability can be estimated through *internal consistency* (i.e., the intercorrelations of all scale items; a frequently reported measure for continuous measures is Cronbach's Alpha), the *parallel-test method* (correlation of two parallel tests), and the *retest method* (stability; correlation of the same test across two points in time).

Validity entails several aspects, of which construct and content validity will be discussed in more detail. Frederic Lord and Melvin R. Novick (2008) distinguish between empirical and theoretical validity, that is, relations of a measurement with observable variables versus latent variables (e.g., hypothetical, nonobservable constructs). Construct validity belongs to theoretical validity and indicates the efficiency of a test in terms of measuring what it was designed to measure. It comprises convergent (high correlations with scales that measure the same or a similar construct) and discriminant validity (low correlations with scales that measure a dissimilar construct). Construct validity can be tested in a multitrait-multimethod (MTMM) analysis, which traditionally involves comparing correlation matrices of at least two measures and traits. Modern statistical approaches to conduct MTMM analyses include structural equation modeling (SEM) and multilevel modeling.

Content validity has been described as the degree to which a test represents the criterion or construct to be measured. Content validity can be ensured by (a) defining the scope of the criterion or construct of interest and (b) obtaining expert ratings of the representativeness of the test items according to the definition. In humor research, tests employing jokes and cartoons to assess humor appreciation or production are inherently content valid, as they obtain direct ratings of the criterion at hand (like the funniness of a joke or writing a humorous cartoon caption).

The Measurements

The different kinds of humor assessment tools can be grouped into eight categories:

1. Informal surveys, joke-telling techniques, or diary methods;
2. Joke and cartoon tests;
3. Questionnaires, self-report scales;
4. Peer reports;
5. State measures;
6. Children's humor tests;
7. Humor scales in general instruments; and
8. Miscellaneous and unclassified.

More than 60 instruments have been developed that fall into one of these categories. Meanwhile, more than two dozen new measures were constructed. A survey of the various instruments allowed some conclusions about them, most of which are still valid today. One was that over the entire span covered, the instruments often purported to measure "sense of humor" even when the methods used or the contents diverged largely (questionnaires, joke/cartoon tests) and zero correlations can be expected between the instruments.

Until the 1980s, joke and cartoon tests were most frequent and more recently questionnaires have been more frequent. Little effort has been invested in peer-evaluation techniques or experimental assessments. Also, most instruments are for adults and few are applicable to children. Many instruments are trait oriented and thus not well suited for measuring change (e.g., as needed in intervention studies). Another observation was that the same labels do not necessarily imply the same concepts (as in *nonsense*, which may stand for harmless jokes or ones that do not resolve incongruity), and scales with different labels might still measure the same construct. Also, there has been little interest in multiple operationalizations of the same construct to determine convergent validity. This would allow determining how much method variance and how much content variance are in the measures. Another observation is that very often an instrument was designed for one study only, and only a couple of tests were published with a company (e.g., the IPAT Humor Test of Personality). While work was devoted to constructing scales, comparatively little effort was spent on working on the concepts.

Humor Assessment Tests Currently in Use

The selection of current instruments for the assessment of humor traits and states in children and adults that follows is not comprehensive, but it contains measurements of humor with adequate psychometric properties.

Joke and Cartoon Tests

- The *3 WD Test of Humor Appreciation* obtains ratings of funniness and aversiveness (each on unipolar 7-point scales) of incongruity-resolution, nonsense, and sexual humor. In addition, scores for the total funniness and total aversiveness of humor, structure preference (incongruity-resolution vs. nonsense), and appreciation of sexual content (with removed variance of structure) can be assessed. There are different versions of the 3 WD, including a short version (30 items, plus 5 "warming up" items). Many studies across several nations showed its construct validity.

- The *Escala de Apreciación del Humor* (EAHU; Humor Appreciation Scale) measures six dimensions of humor appreciation, of which two are structure-related (incongruity-resolution and nonsense), and four are content-related (sexual, black, woman disparagement, and man disparagement). The test comprises 32 items, which are rated on funniness and aversiveness on unipolar 5-point scales.

- The *Cartoon Punch Line Production Test* (CPPT) is a measure of quantity or fluency (i.e., number of produced punch lines) and quality or origence (i.e., peer-rated funniness and originality) of humor production. As many funny captions as possible are written in response to 15 caption-removed cartoons of incongruity-resolution, nonsense, and sexual humor in a 30-minute time limit (the short form, or CPPT-k, features six cartoons and a 15-minute time limit). Besides quality and quantity of humor production, wit and imagination of the participant are assessed as well. The instrument was tested for construct validity.

Questionnaires

- Humorous Behavior Q-Sort Deck (HBQD) assesses 10 humor styles located on five bipolar dimensions, namely socially warm versus cold, reflective versus boorish, competent versus inept, earthy versus repressed, and benign versus mean-spirited. It consists of 100 humorous behaviors, which are ranked on bipolar 7-point scales according to their typicality using a Q-sort technique. In contrast to Likert-type scales, which allow the comparison of results across individuals, this technique forces a normal distribution of answers and thus results in ipsative scoring (i.e., an intraindividual ranking of the items).

- The *Humor Styles Questionnaire* (HSQ) measures four everyday functions of humor (affiliative, self-enhancing, aggressive, and self-defeating). The HSQ has 32 items with a unipolar 7-point answer format. There is initial evidence for its construct validity and a large body of studies showing predictive validity. Recently, a children's version of the HSQ has been developed.

- The *Sense of Humor Scale* (SHS) measures playful versus serious attitude, positive versus negative mood, and six facets of sense of humor (enjoyment of humor, laughter, verbal humor, finding humor in everyday life, laughing at yourself, and humor under stress), which can be combined into one "humor quotient." The instrument has 40 items with a bipolar 7-point answer format.

- The *State-Trait-Cheerfulness-Inventory* (STCI) measures cheerfulness, seriousness, and bad mood as traits and states using a 4-point answer format. The trait version (STCI-T) assesses the temperamental basis of humor and comes in different versions (a short, standard, and long form with 30, 60, and 106 items, respectively). The STCI-T has a well-studied content and construct validity. The state version (STCI-S) has 30 items and instructions for different time spans (now, last week, last month, in general) and is suited for pre- and post- comparisons. In addition, a peer-report version and a version for children and adolescents of the STCI-T exist.

- The *Values in Action Inventory of Strengths* (VIA-IS) measures 24 character strengths with a total of 240 items in a bipolar 5-point answer format. Humor (playfulness) forms one of these strengths (assessed with 10 items), and is related to the virtues of temperance, humanity, and wisdom.

Willibald Ruch and Sonja Heintz

See also Appreciation of Humor; Cheerfulness, Seriousness, and Humor; Children's Humor Research; Factor Analysis of Humor Scales; 3 WD Humor Test

Further Readings

Campbell, D. T., & Fiske, D. W. (1959). Convergent and discriminant validation by the multitrait-multimethod matrix. *Psychological Bulletin, 56,* 81–105.

Carretero-Dios, H., Pérez, C., & Buela-Casal, B. (2010). Assessing the appreciation of the content and structure of humor: Construction of a new scale. *HUMOR: International Journal of Humor Research, 23,* 307–325. doi:10.1515/humr.2010.014

Casu, G., & Gremigni, P. (2012). Humor measurement. In P. Gremigni (Ed.), *Humor and health promotion* (pp. 253–274). Hauppauge, NY: Nova Science.

Cattell, R. B., & Tollefson, D. L. (1966). *The IPAT Humor Test of Personality.* Champaign, IL: Institute for Personality and Ability Testing.

Craik, K. H., Lampert, M. D., & Nelson, A. J. (1996). Sense of humor and styles of everyday humorous conduct. *HUMOR: International Journal of Humor Research, 9,* 273–302. doi:10.1515/humr.1996.9.3-4.273

Köhler, G., & Ruch, W. (1995). On the assessment of "wit": The Cartoon Punch Line Production Test. *European Journal of Psychological Assessment, 11*(Suppl. 1), 7–8.

Köhler, G., & Ruch, W. (1996). Sources of variance in current sense of humor inventories: How much substance, how much method variance? *HUMOR: International Journal of Humor Research, 9,* 363–397. doi:10.1515/humr.1996.9.3-4.363

Lienert, G. A., & Raatz, U. (1998). *Testaufbau und Testanalyse* [Test construction and test analysis]. Weinheim, Germany: Psychologie Verlagsunion.

Lord, F. M., & Novick, M. R. (2008). *Statistical theories of mental test scores.* Reading, MA: Addison-Wesley.

Martin, R. A., Puhlik-Doris, P., Larsen, G., Gray, J., & Weir, K. (2003). Individual differences in uses of humor and their relation to psychological well-being: Development of the Humor Styles Questionnaire. *Journal of Research in Personality, 37,* 48–75.

McGhee, P. E. (1999). *Health, healing, and the amuse system: Humor as survival training.* Dubuque, IA: Kendall/Hunt.

Peterson, C., & Seligman, M. E. P. (2004). *Character strengths and virtues: A handbook and classification.* Washington, DC: American Psychological Association.

Ruch, W. (1992). Assessment of appreciation of humor: Studies with the 3 WD humor test. In C. D. Spielberger & J. N. Butcher (Eds.), *Advances in personality assessment* (Vol. 9, pp. 27–75). Hillsdale, NJ: Lawrence Erlbaum Associates.

Ruch, W. (1998). *The sense of humor: Explorations of a personality characteristic.* Berlin, Germany: Mouton de Gruyter.

Ruch, W., & Köhler, G. (1999). The measurement of state and trait cheerfulness. In I. Mervielde, I. Deary, F. De Fruyt, & F. Ostendorf (Eds.), *Personality psychology in Europe* (Vol. 7, pp. 67–83). Tilburg, Netherlands: Tilburg University Press.

Sireci, S. G. (1998). Gathering and analyzing content validity data. *Educational Assessment, 5*(4), 299–321. doi:10.1207/s15326977ea0504_2

Testing and Evaluation

The title of this entry has multiple interpretations, each carrying some truth. Indeed, using *testing* and *humor* in the same sentence sounds to many people like an oxymoron. Some might argue that the use of humor on a test can contaminate, or interfere with, what the test is intended to measure because some test takers won't understand the humor. Yet humor can reduce anxiety, thereby reducing another testing contaminant. Claims made for humor used in testing and evaluation include that humor encourages the participants to appreciate and extend the content on which they are being tested, and that it improves test performance by raising self-esteem and reducing anxiety, stress, depression, and loneliness. It also is said to improve the test takers' perception of the person giving the test.

This entry examines the impact of using humor in testing and evaluation, first looking at test-takers' self-report responses about such uses of humor and then briefly considering what the test scores do or don't say about the use of humor in the testing context. It then discusses types of humor and their appropriateness, concluding with guidelines for using humor with tests.

Research on Humor in Tests and Evaluations

Test-Takers' Judgments

Several researchers have investigated test-takers' opinions regarding humor in testing. Most of the test takers were undergraduate students, some were graduate students, and some were high school students. The results were positive and consistent; for example, students rated the humor as humorous and helpful to learning, the instructor and the lesson were rated highly, and anxiety was reduced. Some students found the humor confusing or distracting, but students more often found it amusing, comforting, supportive, and reassuring. In one study, students who had taken an exam that contained humor requested that subsequent exams include humor.

Effect on Test Scores

Despite extremely supportive data on test-taker preferences for and judgments about the use of humor in testing, the research does not provide strong evidence for test score gains as a result of humor. This is not surprising given the limitations of these studies. For example, the use of humor may be decidedly not funny to the participants, leaving the humor treatment impotent for this sample of people. Still, more generally, there is support for using humor in testing as long as guidelines, including those discussed below, are reviewed and carefully considered.

Types of Humor

If all the classifications used to conceptualize humor were joined end-to-end, the collection of conceptualizations would never end. In their 1979 study of humor in the college classroom, Jennings Bryant, Paul Comisky, and Dolf Zillmann identified the types of humor used in lectures as jokes, riddles, puns, funny stories, humorous comments, and other humorous items. Funny stories, funny comments, cartoons, and puns can all be used in a positive way in the classroom or on tests. Sarcasm, ethnic humor, aggressive or hostile humor, and sexual humor are negative forms of humor and are inappropriate for the classroom.

> An illustration of an item and variations that use humor: A Speed Bump cartoon by Dave Coverly shows a speech writer advising a man seated at a desk to keep "The only thing we have to fear is fear itself" in his speech but to remove "and clowns." This lead could be supported as a test item with questions such as "Whose speech is being edited?" or "Who used this line about 'fear itself' and why?" or as a multiple-choice item with options such as (a) Winston Churchill, (b) Franklin Delano Roosevelt, (c) Herbert Hoover, (d) Bill Cosby, and (e) Big Bird.

Guidelines for Using Humor in Testing and Evaluation

The following guidelines can help ensure that the use of humor will be helpful, or at least not inadvertently destructive, in the evaluation process. These guidelines should be refined and extended to meet the goals and challenges faced by the developer of the assessment or evaluation.

Avoid negative humor. Test developers and professionals more generally should consider their preferences for and comfort with humor topics and types, but in any case, should not use negative humor. Put-downs of people, for example, can have terrible consequences, and attacking one student can sour all the students. Negative humor is improper, inappropriate, and counterproductive in class and in testing. The 2002 work of methodologist and humor specialist Ronald Berk is especially helpful in developing test items (multiple-choice, essay, performance items, etc.) that use positive humor. He also elaborates on why negativity should be avoided in instruction and in testing.

Don't wait until the test to use humor. An instructor should set the stage with humor before the test or evaluation (if appropriate). The instructor could use humor in class and perhaps even give practice examinations that review the content and acclimate students to the inclusion of humor. Further, in general, the instructor could consider engaging in occasional actions that help rule out any view of him or her as lifeless, rigid, and humorless.

Be relevant. Test developers should use humor relevant to the topic (if available). Some humor even helps extend understanding of the topic as well as providing a smile break. An example of a test item used in a course on test development:

> "Murphy can run faster than any other dog in the neighborhood in his weight class." This interpretation is essentially
>
> A. Domain referenced
> B. Expectancy-table referenced
> C. Norm-referenced
> D. Lab-based

Test developers should consider where to incorporate humor in the test. Possibilities include in the directions, headings for subsets of items, item stems (the beginning of the item, or problem to be solved), item options (answers), context-dependent material, even reports for presenting test and evaluation results. Some humor can be content relevant, some content irrelevant. Humorous distractors may be used to add interest to existing items.

Get feedback. Test developers should solicit reactions to humor. The developers can select and refine their humor creations and should seek oral or written evaluations. No comedian would open on Broadway relying on untested material.

Watch for misunderstandings. Test developers should watch for humor that is too foreign for some test takers. Groups that might not understand specific applications of humor include international or second language students, and those who are intellectually delayed. At a minimum, the developer could acknowledge the limitation for such test takers, explain enough to ease anxiety, encourage questions about misunderstandings, and note the extra learning being provided at no extra charge.

Don't make the test harder. Humor should not interfere with a test taker's ability to answer the item correctly. Test developers should ensure that a student who doesn't understand the humor but does have a good grasp of the content can still respond correctly to the test item. One goal of using humor is to increase the likelihood of answering items correctly for the right reasons, perhaps by lowering excessive anxiety, for example.

Humor can be a tricky variable to deal with in research. If a test taker sees humor in a test but doesn't think it funny, did he or she receive the humor treatment?

Be compatible. A review of item-writing guides by Thomas M. Haladyna, Steven M. Downing, and Michael C. Rodriguez advises only using humor on tests if it is compatible with the teacher and learning environment.

Robert F. McMorris and Zachary B. Warner

See also Aggressive and Harmless Humor; Appreciation of Humor; Education, Humor in; Pedagogy; Teachers' Evaluations, Effect of Humor Use in Classroom on

Further Readings

Berk, R. A. (2002). *Humor as an instructional defibrillator: Evidence-based techniques in teaching and assessment.* Sterling, VA: Stylus.

Bryant, J., Comisky, P., & Zillmann, D. (1979). Teachers' humor in the college classroom. *Communication Education, 28,* 110–118.

Haladyna, T. M., Downing, S. M., & Rodriguez, M. C. (2002). A review of multiple-choice item-writing guidelines for classroom assessment. *Applied Measurement in Education, 15*(3), 309–334.

McMorris, R. F., Boothroyd, R. A., & Pietrangelo, D. J. (1997). Humor in educational testing: A review and discussion. *Applied Measurement in Education, 10,* 269–297.

McMorris, R. F., & Kim, Y. (2003). Humor for international students and their classmates: An empirical study and guidelines. *Journal on Excellence in College Teaching, 14*(1), 129–149.

Torok, S. E., McMorris, R. F., & Lin, W. C. (2004). Is humor an appreciated teaching tool? Perceptions of professors' teaching styles and use of humor. *College Teaching, 52,* 14–20.

3 WD Humor Test

The 3 WD (3 *Witz-Dimensionen*) Test of Humor Appreciation is a performance test measuring both funniness and aversiveness of jokes and cartoons for the three humor categories, incongruity-resolution humor, nonsense humor, and sexual humor. Several stages in the taxonomic development of the 3 WD test were necessary as a comprehensive assessment of humor should cover a classification of humor stimuli, responses to humor, and a typology of the receiver. Four samples of adults from Austria and Germany provided results for factor and item analytic studies of 120 jokes and cartoons. Stable factor patterns across all four samples were selected and matched in pairs for content, mean funniness, loading patterns, and style, namely verbal or pictorial, with or without captions.

From an individual difference perspective regarding the perception of humor, two different sources of pleasure have to be distinguished. Humor theorists have long acknowledged two sources, content and structure (e.g., joke work vs. tendency, thematic vs. schematic, cognitive vs. orectic factors). Factor analytic studies confirm that both sources are potent variance-producing factors. Two structural factors consistently appear: incongruity-resolution (INC-RES) humor and nonsense (NON) humor. The jokes and cartoons relating to these factors have different contents (e.g., themes, targets) but share structural properties and the way they are processed. The jokes and cartoons pertaining to INC-RES humor are characterized by punch lines where a surprising incongruity can be completely resolved. The common facet in this type of humor is that the recipient first discovers an incongruity, which is then fully resolvable upon consideration of information in the joke or cartoon. The surprising or incongruous punch line was also found for nonsense humor; however, the punch line may provide no resolution or only a partial resolution (leaving an essential part of the incongruity unresolved), or create new absurdities or incongruities. In nonsense humor, the resolution information gives the appearance of making sense out of incongruities without doing so. Evidence in fMRI research suggests that different neural networks apply to INC-RES and NON humor. The third factor, sexual (SEX) humor, may have either structure but is homogeneous with respect to the sexual content.

Factor analysis was used to uncover the dimensions of appreciation. Results show that the response mode is defined by two nearly orthogonal components of positive and negative responses represented by ratings of funniness and aversiveness. Maximal appreciation of jokes and cartoons consists of high funniness and low aversiveness, while minimal appreciation occurs if the joke is not considered funny but aversive. However, a joke can also be considered not funny but be far from being aversive; or it can make one laugh although there are annoying aspects (e.g., considering the punch line original or clever but disliking the content).

Characteristics of the Scale

Initially, three versions of the test (short form: 3 WD-K, parallel versions: 3 WD-A, and 3 WD-B) were constructed, and then the best items were combined in the final 3 WD. The 3 WD contains 35 (forms A and B) jokes and cartoons, which are rated on "funniness" and "aversiveness" using two 7-point scales. The funniness rating ranges from not at all funny = 0 to very funny = 6. The aversiveness scale ranges between not at all aversive = 0 to very aversive = –6. The first five items are to "warm up" and therefore are not scored. The test booklet contains two or three jokes or cartoons per page. The instructions are typed on separate answer sheets containing the two sets of rating scales. Six scores can be derived from each form of the test: three for funniness of incongruity-resolution, nonsense, and sexual humor (i.e., INC-RESf, NONf, and SEXf) and three for their aversiveness (i.e., INC-RESa, NONa, and SEXa). The six scores generated indicate an individual's humor preference at a general level. Structure preference index or SPI (obtained by subtracting INC-RES from NON, indicating the relative preference for one type over the other) and an index of liking of sexual content (built by removing the variance due to liking of structure) have been derived and validated. Funniness and aversiveness of a humor type may be combined to form a general appreciation score.

Reviewing studies of the psychometric properties shows that the reliability estimates are satisfactory to very good for the scales of all forms of the 3 WD. Internal consistency varies between .68 and .95, mostly exceeding .80. Parallel test reliability of the six scales ranges between .67 and .93 with a median of .86 when both scales are completed on the same day. With a time lag of between 2 and 4 weeks, the results had coefficients of between .54 and .85, with a median of .73.

Validity

The 3 WD humor test has been extensively validated in, for example, aesthetics, personality, attitudes, needs, and intelligence. Appreciation of humor structure reflects a generalized need to be in contact with either structured and redundant stimulus configurations (INC-RES) or ones high in stimulus uncertainty (NON). Appreciation of sexual content is positively related to sexual experience and libido, and more generally to toughmindedness and extraversion.

Tracey Platt and Willibald Ruch

See also Appreciation of Humor; Factor Analysis of Humor Scales; Humor Content Versus Structure

Further Readings

Ruch, W. (1981). Humor and personality: A three-mode analysis. *Zeitschrift für Differentielle und Diagnostische Psychologie, 2,* 253–273.

Ruch, W. (1992). Assessment of appreciation of humor: Studies with the 3 WD humor test. In C. D. Spielberger & J. N. Butcher (Eds.), *Advances in personality assessment* (pp. 27–75). Hillsdale, NJ: Lawrence Erlbaum Associates.

Ruch, W., & Malcherek, J. (2009). Sensation seeking, general aesthetic preferences, and humor appreciation as predictors of liking of the grotesque. *Journal of Literary Theory, 3,* 333–351.

Ruch, W., & Platt, T. (2012). Separating content and structure in humor appreciation: The need for a bimodal model and support from research into aesthetics. In A. Nijhold (Ed.), *Computational humor 2012: Extended abstracts of the 3rd International Workshop on Computational Humor* (pp. 23–27). Amsterdam, Netherlands: University of Amsterdam.

Samson, A. C., Zysset, S., & Huber, O. (2008). Cognitive humor processing: Different logical mechanisms in nonverbal cartoons–an fMRI study. *Social Neuroscience, 3,* 125–140.

Tickling

The word *tickle* refers to at least two somewhat distinct phenomena—labeled as *knismesis* and *gargalesis* by the prominent late 19th-century psychologist G. Stanley Hall. Knismesis refers to the peculiar sensation, akin to a moving itch, that is produced by something moving lightly across the skin. One can readily produce knismesis in oneself by lightly dragging one's fingernails across virtually any body area. The annoying sensation can outlast the stimulation by seconds and produces a desire to rub or scratch the stimulated area (doing so tends to obliterate the sensation). This type of tickle usually does not make people laugh. The type of tickle that produces laughter, gargalesis, usually requires a heavier pressure repeatedly applied to specific "ticklish" areas of the body such as the ribcage or armpits. One of the most intriguing aspects of gargalesis is that people cannot produce it in themselves or at least cannot do so to the point of laughter. The rest of this entry focuses on laughter-inducing tickling.

Humor and Tickle

One of the most mysterious aspects of tickling is that a physical stimulus can produce a response that looks so much like that which occurs during amusement and humor. The fact that smiling and laughter appear during both tickling and humor has led many to assume that the two reflect the same positive emotional state. Charles Darwin (1872/1965), the father of evolution, was one of the most notable advocates of this view. He thought that tickling was essentially a physical joke. In arguing for this, Darwin suggested that both humor and tickling require similar preconditions in order for laughter to emerge, including an element of surprise, a pleasurable mental state, and a "light" elicitor (a light touch for tickling and a nonserious topic for humor).

While this view has intuitive appeal, several research findings suggest that tickle and humor are not simply two forms of the same internal state. For one, with humor there is a warm-up effect such that jokes that occur later in a series are found to be funnier than those that occur earlier in the series. However, listening to jokes does not make people laugh and smile more in response to tickling, and being tickled right before listening to jokes does not make the jokes seem funnier. Thus, there does not seem to be a warm-up effect that transfers from humor to tickling or vice versa, as would be expected if the two states were really tapping into the same internal experience.

Detailed analyses of facial expression also suggest differences between tickle and humor. The smile that accompanies positive emotional states such as humor usually includes two facial actions: the upturning of the lips (contraction of the zygomatic major), and a crinkling around the eyes (contraction of the orbicularis occuli), called a *Duchenne smile*. This type of smiling occurs less frequently during tickling than during comedy, and when it does occur seems different. For example, in one study, some people displayed Duchenne smiles even when they were not feeling positive emotions (i.e., did not report being particularly happy or amused). Duchenne smiles also were correlated with finding the tickle sensation unpleasant for some people. Furthermore, when tickled, people who report generally not enjoying being tickled smiled just as much as people who reported generally enjoying it. The dissociation between smiling and self-reported positive affect during tickling provides some support for the hypothesis that tickle-induced laughter and smiling are not dependent on positive affect. This suggests that these expressions need not reflect merriment and mirth any more than crying when cutting onions need reflect sorrow and sadness.

Low-Level Physiological Response

Another prominent view of tickle is that rather than being an emotional response, it is a low-level physiological response that is akin to a complex reflex, fixed action pattern, or some other type of species-typical stereotypical response. This raises the question of why we can't elicit tickle-induced laughter in ourselves. After all, we are perfectly able to elicit our own knee-jerk reflex. It may be that tickle is more similar to the startle reflex, which also cannot be produced readily in oneself without the use of some external aid such as a gunshot. Of note, both startle and tickle seem to require some element of surprise and both produce facial expressions that resemble the types of expressions that usually occur during emotion, but are arguably not in and of themselves emotional states. This does not imply that the tickle response is unmodifiable. In fact, some reflexes such as startle can be influenced by mood or other psychological states and so may be the case with tickle.

Sociality of Tickling

The fact that one cannot tickle oneself has led some to suggest that ticklish laughter requires the belief that another person is performing the tickling. However, the one study that has directly examined this possibility suggests that although ticklish laughter requires that some external source perform the tickling stimulation, the emergence of laughter does not require that one believe that source is human. Experimenters found that people readily laughed and smiled when they thought they were being tickled by what appeared to be a fully automated machine, and did so even when they thought they were alone with the machine. (In fact, the tickling was actually done by a carefully hidden research assistant).

Ontogeny of Tickle

A newborn infant does not laugh. It is not until somewhere around the fourth month of life that laughter emerges in humans. Laughter in response to being tickled appears to be even more delayed—usually not appearing until approximately 6 months.

Tickling in Nonhumans

While many mammals appear to experience knismesis (e.g., think of a dog scratching at a flea or a horse swatting a fly), gargalesis seems less common in the animal world. Primatologists, however, have observed gargalesis in some primates such as chimpanzees and gorillas during the course of rough-and-tumble play. During such play bouts, chimpanzees produce what appears to be a nonhuman primate version of laughter—a breathy panting sound that is accompanied by a relaxed open mouth and quivering lower jaw.

Christine R. Harris

See also Laugh, Laughter, Laughing; Laughter, Psychology of; Laughter and Smiling, Physiology of; Smiling and Laughter: Expressive Patterns

Further Readings

Darwin, C. (1965). *The expressions of the emotions in man and animals*. London, UK: John Murray. (Originally published 1872)

Davila-Ross, M., Owren, M. J., & Zimmermann, E. (2010). The evolution of laughter in great apes and humans. *Communicative and Integrative Biology, 3*, 191–194.

Hall, G. S., & Allin, A. (1897). The psychology of tickling, laughter, and the comic. *American Journal of Psychology, 9*, 1–42.

Harris, C. R. (1999). The mystery of ticklish laughter. *American Scientist, 87*, 344–351.

Harris, C. R., & Alvarado, N. (2005). Facial expressions, smile types, and self-report during humor, tickle, and pain. *Cognition & Emotion, 19*, 655–669.

Harris, C. R., & Christenfeld, N. (1997). Humour, tickle and the Darwin-Hecker hypothesis. *Cognition & Emotion, 11*, 103–110.

Harris, C. R., & Christenfeld, N. (1999). Can a machine tickle? *Psychonomic Bulletin & Review, 6*, 504–510.

Tom Swifty

Tom Swifty might be considered the 20th-century development of the form of folklore called *wellerism.* Wellerisms, named for Charles Dickens's character Samuel Weller, are normally made up of three parts: (1) a statement, (2) a speaker who makes this remark, and (3) a phrase that places the utterance into an unexpected, contrived situation ("Everyone to his own taste," as the farmer said when he kissed the cow). What is typical for Tom Swifty? It is a wellerism conventionally based on the punning relationship between the way an adverb describes a speaker and simultaneously refers to the meaning of the speaker's statement. The speaker is traditionally Tom, his statement is usually placed at the beginning of the Tom Swifty, and the adverb at the end of it, for example, *"I see," said Tom icily* (icily vs. I see). Since a number of adverbs end with an *-ly*, originally this form of folklore was called *Tom Swiftly*, but nowadays Tom Swifty or Tom Swiftie are more frequently used. This entry gives a definition and historical background of the Tom Swifty, addresses different types of punning employed in Tom Swifties, and discusses topics emerging in them.

Tom Swifty is supposedly named after the fictional character of Tom Swift or rather, two fictional characters, Tom Swift Sr. and Tom Swift Jr., of adventure books that began in the early 20th century and now total more than 100 volumes. The original books were written by the prolific American writer Edward Stratemeyer (1862–1930), who under the pseudonym Victor Appleton, after having published a number of books in the first Tom Swift series, founded the Stratemeyer Syndicate and later hired ghost writers to write Tom Swift novels. The first novel of the first series, titled *Tom Swift and His Motor-cycle; or Fun and Adventure on the Road,* was published in 1910. While the first series (1910–1941) portray Tom Swift Sr., the books after that have depicted his son, Tom Swift Jr. In his various incarnations, Tom Swift, usually in his teens, is inventive, science minded, and adventurous.

In a true Tom Swifty, the pun is in the adverb: *"Is your name Frank Lee?" Tom asked frankly* (frankly vs. Frank Lee). However, not only adverbs can produce puns in Tom Swifties, but also verbs, nouns, and even adjectives, for example, *"I telephoned John twice," Tom recalled.* Strictly speaking, such puns were conventionally not called Tom Swifties, but as the existence of numerous examples posted on various websites under the term *Tom Swifties* has proven, nowadays they are also generally classified as Tom Swifties. In a number of Tom Swifties, the statement Tom says might consist of a proverb or proverbial phrase: *"Time flies," said Tom entomochronometrically* (combining the scientific words for insect and time).

Sometimes, in cases when the pun of a Tom Swifty lies in the name of the speaker, the conventional Tom is substituted by either a fictitious or real person: *"My extreme emotional instability arises from a psychoneurosis," hissed Eric* (hissed Eric vs. hysteric); *"I wonder why uranium is fluorescent," said Mary curiously* (Mary curiously vs. Marie Curie). Characters, or even titles of well-known poems, novels, tales, or paintings might occasionally replace the name of Tom: *"I'm tired of smiling," moaned Lisa* (moaned Lisa vs. Mona Lisa); *"Do you call this a musical?" asked Les miserably* (Les miserably vs. "Les Misérables," the title of a novel by French writer Victor Hugo and subsequent musical). The first names or surnames of famous poets and writers, composers and singers, politicians and scholars, and other famous personalities (hidden or referred to in adverbs or statements) might also constitute the base of puns: *"I collect fairy tales," said Tom grimly* (grimly vs. German folklorists the Brothers Grimm); *"Carmen is my favorite opera," said Tom busily* (busily vs. the composer George Bizet). Puns in Tom Swifties might also play upon or allude to geographical names and places: *"South Korea has a lovely capital city," said Tom soulfully* (soulfully vs. Seoul); *"Don't let me drown in Paris!" pleaded Tom insanely* (insanely vs. in the Seine).

The following Tom Swifty, based on phonetic and graphemic similarity of words from two languages (English and German), is a good example of a bilingual pun: *"Mama is German," Tom muttered* (muttered vs. Mutter). Certain puns in Tom Swifties involve not simply single words but groups of words: *"This is the real male goose," said Tom producing the propaganda* (propaganda vs. proper gander); *"I am wearing a ring" said Tom with abandon* (abandon vs. a band on).

Paronomastic puns—puns involving two similar but not identical strings of sounds and graphemes—constitute by far the largest class of puns in Tom Swifties: *"Would you like to buy some cod?" asked Tom selfishly* (selfishly vs. shellfish); *"I've an urgent appointment," said Tom in Russian* (in Russian vs. in rush). Numerous additional Tom Swifties have provided good models for exploiting ambiguity through the use of a single word that is polysemous (i.e., having two meanings) or two words that are homonymous (i.e., having identical graphemic and phonemic representation): *"I do not have a multiple personality disorder," said Tom, trying to be frank* (frank vs. Frank); *"I'm here—with a gift!" said Tom presently* (presently vs. with a present). Homophones (words pronounced the same but spelled differently) are relatively rare: *"I've only enough carpet for the hall and landing," said Tom with a blank stare* (stare vs. stair); *"I visit my parents every Sunday," said Tom weakly* (weakly vs. weekly).

Also in vein with the scope and emphasis of the Tom Swift novels promoting the role of science, invention, and technology, conventional Tom Swifties also touch upon technical and academic achievements, adventures, and inventions: *"I haven't developed my photographs yet," said Tom negatively; "Eating uranium makes me feel funny," said Tom radiantly.* Numerous texts of Tom Swifties are sexually oriented: *"I don't believe in mixed marriages," said Tom gaily.* There is hardly a topic Tom Swifties do not address. Among the themes treated in Tom Swifties are women and men, money and love, marriage and divorce, alcohol and drugs, children and parents, and God and religion.

Anna T. Litovkina

See also Anti-Proverb; Puns; Wellerism

Further Readings

Lippman, L. G., Bennington, K., & Sucharski, I. L. (2002). Contextual connections to puns in Tom Swifties. *The Journal of General Psychology, 129*(2), 202–208.

Mieder, W., & Kingsbury, S. A. (Eds.). (1994). *A dictionary of wellerisms.* New York, NY: Oxford University Press.

Tragicomedy

Properly speaking, a tragicomedy is either a dramatic work that combines elements associated with both tragic and comic forms, or one that sustains a consistently tragic or heroic tone but avoids a catastrophic ending. The adjective *tragicomic* may be more loosely applied to nondramatic literary forms or to real-life situations in which humorous and tragic aspects coexist, usually with the implication that the combination is somehow disconcerting, that an impulse to laugh at the comic element is inhibited by a sense of disquiet or disgust.

Origins and Development

The term was first applied to drama, rather whimsically, by Plautus (b. 254 BCE). Ancient drama was strictly divided into tragedy, which dealt with gods, and comedy, which dealt with mortals; but the story of Alcmene, a woman so virtuous that Jupiter could seduce her only by adopting the form of her husband Amphitryon, involved a crossover between gods and mortals, so in dealing with it, Plautus was almost required to invent a hybrid genre and called it *tragicomoedia.* After Jupiter, assisted by Mercury who also takes on the form of a low-born mortal, Sosia, has seduced Alcmene, the real Amphitryon returns home to a welcome that does not seem to him commensurate with his long absence on a noble military expedition. This focus on sexual infidelity and mistaken identity ensures that almost all treatments of the story, including Plautus's, remain essentially comic, but the presence of Jupiter, the exploration of serious themes (jealousy, exploitation, outraged innocence, and distress), and the fact that the play foreshadows the birth of Hercules, all contribute a heroic and philosophical tone as counterpoint to the silliness, innuendo, and imbroglio of the humorous episodes. The genre of tragicomedy came to be typified by the combination of the heroic with the trivial, the intense with the domestic, and the philosophical with the burlesque that characterized subsequent dramatizations of the same story, notably those by Molière (1668), Heinrich von Kleist (1807), and Jean Giraudoux (1929).

In the post-Renaissance world, tragicomedy was first defined and illustrated in Italy: Giovanni-Battista Guarini's 1590 pastoral tragicomedy, *Il Pastor Fido* (*The Faithful Shepherd*), exemplified the genre. From defenses of that play emerged a theoretical position (summarized in Guarini's *Compendium of Tragicomic Poetry* in 1601) that underscored debates on drama for over a century in Italy, France, and England. Tragicomedy depicted persons of high birth (often but not necessarily in an Arcadian pastoral context), engaged in private rather than state affairs. It explored passion and desire but avoided their more destructive aspects; it could depict danger but ended with resolution and celebration. Its humor should not be unruly or raunchy and should always be modest. A typical tragicomedy thus sounds and feels like a tragedy for most of its length, but its ending, like that of a comedy, achieves a feel-good resolution that should be neither artificial nor contrived.

This purist definition excludes some related but different phenomena. The moments of ribald comic relief that punctuate Shakespearean tragedies—Macbeth's porter, Hamlet's interaction with gravediggers—do not turn those works into tragicomedies. *The Winter's Tale* is tragic during most of its first half, exploring destructive passion and depicting brutal death, while most of the action in Bohemia is clearly comic, involving romance, innuendo, and wit: Only the final sequence brings the play potentially into the area of tragicomedy, and even here, the convenient coupling of lower class characters (Paulina and Camillo) allows an intrusion from a baser comic world of coincidence and bawdry. This and similar plays are usually referred to as *romances*.

English tragicomedies of the period include those by John Fletcher and Philip Massinger, such as Fletcher's adaptation of *Il Pastor Fido* as *The Faithful Shepherdess* (1608). Sir Philip Sidney (1554–1586), champion of classical purity in poetry and drama, did not spare "mongrel tragicomedy" from his contempt, although what he called the incongruous juxtaposition of "hornpipes and funerals" was for him but a symptom of a wider ignorance of proper Aristotelian principles. As the term *tragicomedy* came into use in Jacobean England, it pointed more to plot devices than to tone: The genre was likely to be characterized by exoticism, grandiloquence, and extreme examples of classical peripeteia (reversal of fortunes).

French Classicism and Dramatic Genres

In France, too, tragicomedy was caught up in the battle between those who sought to impose a classical aesthetic on theater and those who resisted it. The most intense controversy surrounded Pierre Corneille's *Le Cid* (1637), initially described by him as a *tragicomédie*, but later—with some textual changes but no fundamental reworking—as a tragedy. Previously, Robert Garnier (*Bradamante,* 1582), Jean de Schelandre (*Tyr et Sidon* [Tyre and Sidon], 1608), Jean de Rotrou (*L'Hypocondriaque* [The Hypochondriac], 1628), Georges de Scudéry (*Ligdamon et Lidias,* 1630), and the prolific Alexandre Hardy (d. 1632) had ensured that tragicomedy—alongside coarser farces—dominated the Paris stage, characterized above all by irregularity, rhetorical excess, and roughness. Even Jean Mairet, one of the strictest defenders of classical regularity, tolerated the label *tragicomedy*, provided that it referred not so much to a mixture of tones as to a serious literary play in which a disaster threatens but is ultimately averted. In his preface to his tragicomedy *La Silvanire* (1630), he expounded the case for the classical Aristotelian unities (of time, place, and action on stage), in response to spirited defenses of irregularity by the priest and literary theorist François Ogier (1597–1670) and others.

Since neither version of *Le Cid* can easily be taken as representing the tragicomic genre, Corneille's use of the label deserves further investigation. Throughout the play, its star-crossed lovers, Rodrigue and Chimène, are in despair after a petty dispute between their families obliges Rodrigue—under a code of honor endorsed by Chimène—to challenge his beloved's father to a duel in which the older man is killed. Although never wavering in her adoration of Rodrigue, Chimène refuses to marry the killer of her father, and after further military and legal ordeals (which he passes with flying colors), even Rodrigue finally accepts with dignity the king's decree that he must wait a further year in the hope that Chimène will come to accept him. Although the only death in the play is that of Chimène's father, the threat of death is imminent throughout and a happy ending, while possible, lies far off in the future. Earlier, the king, seeking to establish Chimène's true feelings, bids the court pretend that Rodrigue, although victorious in battle, has been mortally wounded. Corneille's critics saw this deceit as a lapse of tone and taste—the king laying aside his crown for a jester's cap. Few directors, however, would play this scene for comic effect, and there is nothing else approaching humor in the play.

In adapting the play to suit the label tragedy, Corneille shifted the emphasis of the denouement very slightly: In the original, tragicomic version, Chimène demands to know how she can be expected to marry her father's killer "so soon," and so the king's suggestion of a year's grace on both sides is logical, but by no stretch of the imagination can a genuinely happy ending be considered a sure outcome. In the later version of the play, Corneille removes the emphasis on time, and Chimène's last words are a firm refusal to accept her fate as the price of national security, thus generating tragic intensity from the heroine's desolate isolation in a scene of militaristic rejoicing. The definition of tragicomedy as a play serious in tone and subject matter but where catastrophe is ultimately averted needs to be pressed to its extreme to include either version of *Le Cid,* and the fact that Corneille changed the generic label with so small a shift in the content shows how hesitant he was in handling the genre at this turning point in the development of classical French drama. His previous play, *L'Illusion comique* (The Comic Illusion, performed in March 1636), was defined as a comedy. It opens with a pastoral scene outside a magician's grotto, portrays three deaths and an imprisonment, discusses love and jealousy, gives a thoughtful defense of infidelity, and includes a generous act of forgiveness and self-abnegation. This serious material is, however, combined with one of the most hilarious caricatures in all French theater, the *miles gloriosus* or boastful soldier Matamore; along with a highly contrived happy ending, this gives the play more in common with Shakespeare's problem plays than any other French play from this period. Even so, Corneille appears not to have considered the label tragicomedy in this case.

Don Juan: From Tirso to Molière and Mozart

The character of Don Juan/Don Giovanni was another dramatic subject that flourished across Europe in this period and sheds particular light on the tragicomic genre. Juan is essentially a comic figure who ends up dead. His dramatic life began in the highly moralistic and melodramatic comedy *El Burlador de Sevilla* (*The Trickster of Seville*) by Tirso de Molina (d. 1648). He then featured in several buffoonish versions in the *commedia dell'arte* tradition, before entering France in two tragicomedies, titled *Le Festin de Pierre* (*The Stone Banquet*) and performed in 1659 by actor-dramatists Dorimond (1628–1664) and Jean de Villiers (1600 or 1601–1681). Juan attained world literature status with Molière's prose comedy *Dom Juan* (1665) and Wolfgang Amadeus Mozart's opera *Don Giovanni* (1787), referred to by the librettist as a *dramma giocoso* and by the composer as an *opera buffa.* In all these works, the central character has the energy, wit, and creativity of an inspired comic genius, who wins the sympathy (grudging or otherwise) of most audiences for his suppleness of mind, but who causes death, dishonor, and heartache—for which his own death and damnation are presented as a fitting and just reward.

Molière's comedy combines the literary and moralizing qualities of his Spanish and French models with the vulgar and physical comic style of the *commedia dell'arte*; as a result, it lacks the classical coherence that was expected by theatrical purists by the mid-1660s. The play traces Dom Juan's moral development in an episodic structure—the calculating seducer, having already married and abandoned Done Elvire, attempts to capture two young peasant girls, before turning into a defiant freethinker and then a blatant hypocrite. In the course of his exploits, he finds the statue of a commander whom he has earlier killed (this episode occurs on stage in the works of Tirso and Mozart but is referred to only indirectly by Molière, perhaps because its serious nature, acceptable in a tragicomedy, would be out of place in a comedy). He playfully invites the statue to dine with him, and the play ends spectacularly when the statue drags Dom Juan down to a flaming underworld. Serious themes, debates, and actions are here set alongside comic episodes, mostly generated by Dom Juan's cowardly and incompetent valet Sganarelle (the role played by Molière himself) whose practical response to the dramatic ending is concern for his own wages.

Mozart's librettist, Lorenzo da Ponte (1749–1838), took from Tirso the melodramatic elements surrounding the murder of the commander and from Molière the witty verbal and mental dexterity of the seducer. His servant Leporello combines the moralizing earnestness of Tirso's Catalinón with the comic gluttony and cowardice of Sganarelle; but Mozart—probably going beyond what his librettist expected—could not resist enduing his female victims with a tender and ethereal quality that they attain in scarcely any other dramatization of the Don Juan story. Indeed, the transforming power of music makes opera less uncomfortable than spoken drama with the juxtaposition of opposing tonalities: Giacomo Puccini's *La Bohème* (1896), Richard Strauss's *Ariadne auf Naxos* (1912), even Benjamin Britten's *Peter Grimes* (1945), and many others, allow scenes and characters of almost grotesque comedy to rub shoulders with the pathos and heroic endurance of essentially tragic structures. Don Juan himself reappears with tragicomic status in George Bernard Shaw's *Man and Superman* (1903), although this is more a comedy of manners containing a philosophical interlude than a real fusion. Shaw's Juan, John Tanner, is the quarry rather than the hunter, in what the author described as "the tragicomic love chase of the man by the woman."

French Romanticism and Its Legacy

Provocative attempts were made to fuse together the passion of tragedy with the intellectual challenge of comedy during the brief flourishing of the French Romantic theater, anticipated in theory by Denis Diderot (1713–1784) and by Stendhal (1783–1842), and exemplified in practice by the works of Victor Hugo (*Hernani,* 1830, and *Ruy Blas,* 1838) and Alfred de Musset (*Lorenzaccio,* 1834). Although they did not use the label *tragicomedy* to define their plays, Hugo did explicitly wish to combine what he called "the grotesque and the sublime"—light and shade, comic and tragic—taking, as he said in the Préface to *Ruy Blas,* the depiction of passions from tragedy and the exploration of characters from comedy. Stendhal's 1823–1825 essay, *Racine et Shakespeare,* made it clear that the playwrights he supported were rejecting classicism in favor of a dramatic system derived from Shakespeare. The humor of the works listed is in fact often closer to Shakespeare's use of comic relief to make an ultimately tragic denouement even more poignant than it is to the traditional pattern of a serious play in which danger is ultimately averted.

Although Giuseppe Verdi (1813–1901) turned to French Romantic dramatists as well as to Shakespeare for many of his plots, he retained, unlike some other operatic composers, a clear distinction between comic and tragic modes—*Falstaff* (1893) is a fizzing comedy and *La Traviata* (1853) a heart-stopping tragedy. Even *Rigoletto* (1851), although it contains some elements of grotesque humor, is consistently tragic in its tone as well as in its ending. The most vibrant legacy of the Romantic *drame* was not to opera or high culture but rather to the French Boulevard Theater that flourished in the late-18th and 19th centuries. Named for the great Parisian boulevards where many of the theaters were to be found, this style of theater embraced a varied dramatic bill of fare that included *mélodrames* (plays dramatizing real-life contemporary crimes such as murders), acrobatic shows, and later *comédies d'intrigue* and *vaudevilles.* Marcel Carné's 1944 film, *Les Enfants du Paradis* (Children of the Gods), memorably celebrates that world. The French *vaudeville* is distinguished from the later, raunchy American vaudeville show presently undergoing something of a feminist revival in some English-speaking countries. *Mélodrames* were dramas, usually romantic or tragicomic, in which orchestral music accompanied spoken dialogue. The shorter *vaudeville* form had plots that turned upon a simple short song called a *vaudeville,* and was perfected by Eugène Scribe (1791–1861, master of the so-called well-made play). Musical comedy inherited these traditions, and popular works such as Andrew Lloyd Webber's French-inspired *Phantom of the Opera* (1986) and *Les Misérables* (1987, loosely based on Hugo's 1862 novel) continue today the spirit of heroic tragicomedy.

In both Victorian England and the United States, melodrama flourished, borrowing heavily from the French form and characterized by tragicomic plots influenced by Gothic horror literature. This tends to reduce characters to stereotypes and plots to sensationalism: In a context where high emotion and comedy rub shoulders, the serious is apt to seem histrionic. At the other end of the cultural spectrum, Henrik Ibsen's *A Doll's House* (1879) and Anton Chekhov's *The Cherry Orchard* (1904) show that with sensitive handling and understated language, tragicomic drama, far from trivializing the serious, can bring out the significance of the trivial without sentimentality.

Contemporary Tragicomedy

In the 20th century, conventional generic divisions were so widely blurred that almost all theatrical activity drew on resources from both comic and tragic traditions. Absurd Theater explored fundamentally serious themes through extremes of hilarity and comic inventiveness. Death and destruction can be very real and very violent in plays such as Eugène Ionesco's *La Leçon* (The Lesson, 1951) and *Rhinocéros* (1959); but the distancing effects used ensure that the abiding impression of these works is of a mad world in which nothing is trustworthy. An overwhelmingly bleak sense of pointlessness is generated, confirming the cliché that comedy conveys hopelessness more powerfully than tragedy does. In Samuel Beckett's *Waiting for Godot* (performed in 1953), despair is tangible alongside the virtuoso wit that permeates the text. Tom Stoppard's *Rosencrantz and Guildenstern Are Dead* (1966) shares with *Waiting for Godot* a focus on two marginalized characters who appear to lead a pointless existence in a context where significance—if there is any—is relegated to an undefined and unattainable elsewhere. As with the Theater of the Absurd, Stoppard's play indulges in wit and in comedy arising from confusion of identity and from the breakdown of logic; but its playfulness does not prevent it from exploring themes of philosophical significance, such as chance and the relationship between cause and effect. Edward Albee's 1962 play, *Who's Afraid of Virginia Woolf?* brings a tragicomic perspective to domestic drama. It starts out as a dark comedy about marital strife and sexual inadequacy, but as the jokes and games-playing become increasingly bitter, the play becomes ever darker, the comedy ever more grotesque, and the implications ever more tragic.

Tragicomedy has proved itself a powerful structure, allowing full play to a wide range of dramatic emotions, once the fundamental break with strict classical theory was achieved by the French dramatists and theoreticians. It is, however, by no means limited to the European theater, nor indeed to the drama. Modern and postmodern tragicomic novels, operas, films, and TV soap operas abound. Worldwide, traditions such as the Sanskrit drama, Japanese *kabuki* theater, Peking opera, even Javanese *wayang* shadow drama, developed independently their own forms of this inclusive and powerful model, bequeathing different combinations of the comic and the tragic—even the philosophic—to their own dramatists and to audiences of today.

Edward Forman

See also Absurdist Humor; Ancient Roman Comedy; Aristotelian Theory of Humor; Comic Relief; Comic Versus Tragic Worldviews; Genres and Styles of Comedy; History of Humor: Classical and Traditional China; History of Humor: Modern and Contemporary Europe; History of Humor: 19th-Century Europe; History of Humor: Premodern Japan; Musical Comedy; Plautus; Sanskrit Humor; Science, Science Fiction, and Humor; Shakespearean Comedy; Stereotypes

Further Readings

Dutton, R. (1986). *Modern tragicomedy and the British tradition: Beckett, Pinter, Stoppard, Albee and Storey.* Brighton, UK: Harvester Press.

Forman, E. (1981). Don Juan before Da Ponte. In J. Rushton (Ed.), *W. A. Mozart: Don Giovanni.* Cambridge, UK: Cambridge University Press.

Foster, V. A. (2004). *The name and nature of tragicomedy.* Aldershot, UK: Ashgate.

Gassner, J. (1977). The duality of Chekhov. In E. K. Bristow (Ed.), *Anton Chekhov's plays.* New York, NY: Norton.

Hirst, D. L. (1984). *Tragicomedy.* London, UK: Methuen.

Howarth, W. D. (1988). *Corneille: Le Cid.* London, UK: Grant & Cutler.

Translation

Translation is an extremely broad and far-reaching notion that first and foremost refers to what Roman Jakobson famously labeled *interlingual translation,* namely the transfer of a message from one language to another (e.g., English into Arabic, Spanish into Russian, Chinese into Italian, etc.). Translating humor between languages is notoriously considered to be a particularly difficult task.

The role of script opposition, an aspect of the general theory of verbal humor (GTVH) proposed by Salvatore Attardo and Victor Raskin (1991), is an essential element of verbal humor. According to this theory, instances of verbal humor such as jokes, gags, and witticisms are composed of two overlapping scripts, one of which is concealed while simultaneously overlapping another more hidden script in a watertight manner. Concurrently, however, these two coinciding scripts also oppose each other in such a way as to create a humorous incongruity. A basic canned joke such as

Q: "What invention made it possible for humans to walk through walls?"
A: "The door."

contains two scripts, one that leads the recipient to imagine an invention that would allow people to *literally* walk through solid walls and a second, more straightforward, albeit "hidden" script that refers to the everyday object that allows us to move between the different parts of a building separated by walls, namely doors. Such a joke presents no particular problems in terms of translation because, while playing upon the indistinctness of the preposition "through" collocated with the concept of "crossing walls" and thus conjuring up a literal as well as a more commonsensical script, most modern languages possess similar notions regarding walls and how to overcome them through the use of doors, as can be seen by the Spanish and German translations:

P: "*¿Cuál fue el invento que permitió a los seres humanos atravesar las paredes?*"
R: "*La puerta.*"
F: "*Dank welcher Erfindung können Menschen durch Wände laufen?*"
A: "*Türen.*"

While Spanish and German are very different languages in formal terms, both translations closely mirror the original English witticism in both form and content. Furthermore, the script opposition remains identical in both languages. Translational problems arise when verbal humor is either extremely language specific, extremely culture specific, or, as is often the case, a combination of lingua-cultural specificity.

Equivalence and (Un)translatability

The translation of humor challenges two major principles of translation theory that have been greatly debated over the centuries, namely those of *equivalence* and *translatability.* Due to the very nature of languages, which are all different from one another in terms of, for example, diverse words, unlike syntactic structures, grammatical systems, and so on, *formal equivalence* in translation is virtually impossible to achieve. Similarly, the notion of *translatability,* which refers to the transfer of meaning from one language to another without suffering major changes with respect to the source text, is especially hard to sustain in the case of humor, owing to factors pertaining to lingua-cultural divergence. Yet verbal humor *is* translated—suffice it to think of the verbal dexterity of writers such as William Shakespeare, Giovanni Boccaccio, and James Joyce and comedians like the Marx Brothers and Woody Allen, all of whom have been successfully translated into dozens of languages. However, many such translations are quite different from the original texts. In fact, what is actually meant by (un)translatability in the case of humor are the radical changes that a text has to undergo from one language to another, changes that often involve the forgoing of formal equivalence in exchange for *dynamic* equivalence. Dynamic equivalence refers to a type of correspondence that sets out to produce an effect on the target reader that is similar to the effect caused by the source text on the source reader even if this means forgoing formal likeness. Thus, in the case of humorous texts, dynamic equivalence is the means by which a humorous effect can be achieved even though the translation may involve drastic departures from the source text in order to justify a positive humor response in the recipient.

Language and Culture

Hilaire Belloc's well-known epigram: "When I am dead, I hope it may be said / 'His sins were scarlet but his books were read'" exemplifies how verbal humor can exploit linguistic ambiguity to extremes. In this case, the lingua-specificity of the homophone *red/read,* which is counterpointed with the term *scarlet* creates two perfectly overlapping scripts in which hidden oppositions pleasantly surprise and amuse the reader. It is unlikely that there are other languages in which the words *red* and *read* will contain the same identical duplicity and this creates a translational challenge that will inevitably lead translators to employ a series of strategies that will overcome the linguistic hurdles involved.

One of the most radical strategies adopted in the translation of verbal humor is omission. It is not at all unusual to find instances of verbal humor in a book, play, or film that are absent in its translated versions. Another common strategy is that of substitution of the humorous quip with a totally different instance of verbal humor, although ideally, the choice of substitution will involve retaining something of the source text, its essence, or what Anton Popovič labeled the *invariant core.*

Q: "What do you call a man who forgets to put on his underpants?"
A: "Nicholas."

Theoretically the canned joke above can only be translated into a language that has a man's name that sounds like a word meaning "without pants." (In the version above, *Nicholas* rhymes with *knickerless.*) However, an adequate Italian translation could be

D: "*Come chiameresti uno che si dimentica di indossare le mutande?*"
R: "*Libero Lassotto*"

The male name *Libero* literally means "free" while the surname *Lasotto* can be deconstructed into "*Là*" + "*sotto*" (literally "down there"—back translation "free down below"). Thus formal equivalence has been retained in the question half of the joke, while the concept of "lack of underwear" has been embraced as the invariant code between source and target while opting for dynamic equivalence.

The issue becomes more complex when verbal humor involves culture specificity. Once more, the British playground offers us the following riddle:

Q: "How do you make a sausage roll?"
A: "Easy, push it down a hill."

This canned joke contains a pun on the word *roll* combined with a highly culture-specific reference to the "sausage roll"—a typically British delicacy consisting of a pork sausage wrapped in puff pastry. The GTVH states that in order for verbal humor to be understood, the recipient needs to possess a number of "Knowledge Resources" that include recognition of language and script oppositions. However, the oppositions working in this riddle are cultural as well as linguistic, so a functional solution could be to replace the sausage roll with a foodstuff in the target language that alludes to some kind of movement. In Italian, *saltimbocca* (a veal cutlet) provides a suitable replacement as the term *saltimbocca* literally means "jump in your mouth."

D: *"Come si fa un saltimbocca?"* (How do you make a saltimbocca?)
R: *"Prendendo bene la rincorsa"* (By taking a running jump)

Translational matters are further complicated when jokes are based on popular culture:

Patient: "Doctor, Doctor, I keep thinking I'm Cliff Richard."
Doctor: "Well, I must say, you've become a shadow of yourself!"

The Knowledge Resources required to get this joke involve recognizing (a) Cliff Richard, an elderly pop singer from the 1950s who had a backup group called The Shadows and (b) the idiomatic expression "to be a shadow of oneself." A translation needs not only to come to terms with a personality who is probably unknown beyond the British Isles, but also to tie his name to a linguistic element within the text. A feasible Italian translation could exploit an aging Italian pop star, Little Tony, who like Cliff Richard was popular in the 1950s and 1960s. Little Tony was especially famous for the song "*Un cuore matto*" (literally, "a crazy heart") and as hearts can be responsible for sickness, an invariant core has been localized for an adequate Italian translation:

Paziente: "*Dottore, Dottore, continuo a pensare di essere Little Tony*"
Dottore: "*Ma lei e matto! e il suo cuore non e da meno*"
(Back translation: "Doctor, Doctor, I think I'm Little Tony!"
"You must be crazy, and so is your heart.")

Given that absolute translation of verbal humor is unmanageable, it would appear that faithfulness to the original text may best be relegated to second place behind attempts at a re-created text recognizable as humorous to target recipients.

Delia Chiaro

See also Audiovisual Translation; Linguistic Theories of Humor

Further Readings

Attardo, S. (1994). *Linguistic theories of humor.* Berlin, Germany: Mouton de Gruyter.

Attardo, S., & Raskin, V. (1991). Script theory revis(it)ed: Joke similarity and joke representational model. *HUMOR: International Journal of Humor Research, 4*(3–4), 293–347.

Chiaro, D. (Ed.). (2005). Humor and translation [Special issue]. *HUMOR: International Journal of Humor Research, 18*(2).

Chiaro, D. (2008). Verbally expressed humor and translation. In V. Raskin (Ed.), *The primer of humor research* (pp. 569–608). Berlin, Germany: Mouton de Gruyter.

Chiaro, D. (Ed.). (2010). *Translation, humor and literature.* London, UK: Continuum.

Delabastita, D. (Ed.). (1996). *Wordplay and translation* [Special Issue]. *The Translator: Studies in Intercultural Communication, 2*(2). Manchester, UK: St. Jerome.

Delabastita, D. (Ed.). (1997). *Traductio: Essays on punning and translation.* Manchester, UK: St. Jerome.

Jakobson, R. (1959). On linguistic aspects of translation. In R. A. Bower (Ed.), *On translation* (pp. 232–239). Cambridge, MA: Harvard University Press.

Newmark, P. (1981). *Approaches to translation.* Oxford, UK: Pergamon Press.

Nida, E. A. (1964). *Toward a science of translation.* Leiden, Netherlands: E. J. Brill.

Popovi , A. (1976). *A dictionary for the analysis of literary translation.* Edmonton, Canada: Department of Comparative Literature, University of Alberta.

Raskin, V. (1985). *Semantic mechanisms of humor.* Dordecht, Netherlands: D. Reidel.

Vandaele, J. (Ed.). (2002). Translating humor [Special issue]. *The Translator, 8*(2). Retrieved from https://www.stjerome.co.uk/tsa/issue/16

Travesty

In literary contexts, a *travesty* is a type of parody or humorous distortion, in particular one that treats a serious subject comically. In theatrical contexts, travesty denotes the practice of performers playing roles of the opposite sex, a tradition that often lends itself to exaggeration and comedy. In popular parlance, the term is also used to describe a deplorable version of something, most commonly found in the phrase *a travesty of justice,* or in a shorthand version, as in "The election process was a travesty"; in this last sense, the term does not denote something intentionally comic.

The term in English is originally derived from the French past participle *travesti,* descended from Italian *trans* ("across, to the opposite") and *vesti,* the past participle of *vestire* ("to dress"). Accordingly, in its earliest incarnations, the word denoted a disguise or cross-dressing, sometimes designating a person disguised in clothes of the same sex, at other times a person wearing clothes of the opposite sex, particularly a man in women's clothes, and by extension dressed ridiculously or for the sake of parody. This meaning of disguise or impersonation has been expanded in various contexts. In modern France, a *travesti* is a transvestite; in Latin America, a *travesti* is a genetically born male who assumes the gender identity of a woman.

In theatrical contexts, *travesti* or travesty has come to denote the practice of actors playing the roles of the opposite sex, often described by the pseudo-French phrase *en travesti.* These roles have not invariably been comic, although the possibilities of comedy have been exploited in appropriate situations, such as the tradition of men playing comic older women in ballet and pantomime. These roles are traditionally performed in extravagant fashion so that the difference between the gender of the performer and that of the role is ludicrously exaggerated.

In literature, the travesty form was inaugurated by the Italian writer Giovanni Battista Lalli, whose *L'Eneide travestita* (1633) parodied Virgil's *Aeneid.* Lalli inspired the French man of letters Paul Scarron, who published his own Virgilian burlesque, *Virgile travesti,* between 1648 and 1653. Scarron in turn influenced the English writer Charles Cotton, who penned the immensely popular *Scarronides; or, Virgile Travestie, A Mock Poem on the First and Fourth Books of Virgil's Aeneis in English Burlesque* (1664–1665). Cotton's poem began "I sing the Man (read it who list, / A Trojan true as ever pist) . . ." and continued in the same vein for hundreds of couplets, with the earthy lampoon made sweeter by the fact that the *Aeneid* was still a foundation of every learned person's education. Cotton's burlesque ignited a fashion for Virgilian travesties in English, and *Scarronides* was followed by *Maronides, or Virgil Travesty* (1672) by John Phillips, nephew and sometime collaborator of Milton, and by a host of other examples. The texts utilized a familiarity with Virgil as part of their humor, but that humor was typically also directed at contemporary mores; the texts were thus half mockery of Virgil and half social satire. The apogee of the mock-heroic genre was Alexander Pope's *Dunciad,* published in three versions beginning in 1728. The *Dunciad* was a full-length parody of the *Aeneid,* a cultural and political satire about the crowning of the king of Dulness [sic]. By Pope's time, the mock-heroic was a self-explanatory and well-established genre, and the term travesty had dropped out of titles. The *Dunciad,* like Pope's other mock-epic masterpiece *The Rape of the Lock,* had outgrown its generic beginnings and is more self-sufficient as a text than its progenitors, though it still employs the contrast between the lofty subject matter of its model and its own preposterous narrative for comic effect.

This juxtaposition between the register and genre of the original and that of the imitation characterizes travesty and distinguishes it from similar genres such as pastiche, the latter often defined as a genre in which the elements are intermingled to a greater degree. It is true, however, that critics have struggled to differentiate the terms *travesty, parody, caricature, pastiche,* and *burlesque,* with no critical consensus as to exactly where the demarcations lie. Recent examples of the use of the literary term *travesty* have tended to embrace the aspect of distortion or debasement inherent in the phrase a travesty of justice. Perhaps the most prominent example is Tom Stoppard's 1974 play *Travesties,* which brings together Vladimir Lenin, James Joyce, and Tristan Tzara, the founder of the absurdist cultural movement Dada, against a backdrop and reenactment of Oscar Wilde's play *The Importance of Being Earnest.* Wilde's play intrudes into or is distorted into Stoppard's play so that the melding of movements, absurdity, and history becomes a comic commentary on meaning. The whole is a tour de force that revives and extends the reach of literary travesty. Other instances of the form do not employ the word *travesty* as such but encompass the juxtaposition of serious original and absurdist distortion. An early landmark of modern travesty is Alfred Jarry's (1903) short piece "La Passion considérée comme course de côte" ("The Crucifixion Considered as an Uphill Bicycle Race"), which inspired J. G. Ballard's "The Assassination of John Fitzgerald Kennedy

Considered as a Downhill Motor Race" (1973). The two races are then portrayed as happening concurrently in the *Trilogy, Illuminatus!* by Robert Shea and Robert Anton Wilson (1975), a purposeful travesty of all orthodoxies. Thus, the practice of travesty lives on in many forms, both deliberate and accidental.

Martha Bayless

See also Absurdist Humor; Burlesque; Caricature; Comedy; Comic Opera; Genres and Styles of Comedy; Insult and Invective; Inversion, Topsy-Turvy; Irony; Lampoon; Mock Epic; Music Hall; Nonsense; Parody; Satire; Sketch Comedy Shows; Subversive Humor; Travesty; Variety Shows

Further Readings

Genette, G. (1997). *Palimpsests: Literature in the second degree* (C. Newman & C. Doubinsky, Trans.). Lincoln: University of Nebraska Press. (Originally published 1982)

Hoesterey, I. (2001). *Pastiche: Cultural memory in art, film, literature.* Bloomington: Indiana University Press.

Karrer, W. (1997). Cross-dressing between travesty and parody. In B. Müller (Ed.), *Parody: Dimensions and perspectives* (pp. 91–112). Amsterdam, Netherlands: Rodopi.

Senelick, L. (2000). *The changing room: Sex, drag, and theatre.* London, UK: Routledge.

THE PUNISHMENT OF LOKI.

The Norse trickster Loki, as portrayed in "The Punishment of Loki" by 19th-century French artist Louis Huard

Source: Keary, A., & Keary, E. (1893). *The heroes of Asgard: Tales from Scandinavian mythology.* London, UK: Macmillan; Wikimedia Commons.

Trickster

The trickster is a type of character found in myths and folk tales around the world, who throws cultural boundaries into relief by crossing them in sly and audacious ways. Tricksters often display primal and unbridled desire as well as clever thinking, pursuing gratification in an almost infantile manner even as their cravings remain decidedly adult. Ever on the move, they illuminate the centers of culture by carrying out their exploits from the margins. This entry discusses different types of tricksters, issues surrounding tricksters, and the appearance of tricksters in literature.

Trickster incarnations around the world include Eshu (Nigerian), Hermes (Ancient Greek), Loki (Norse), Till Eulenspiegel (German), Susa-No-o (Japanese), Bricriu (Irish), Maui (Maori), and Agu Tompa (Tibetan). Tricksters sometimes take animal form, such as Monkey (Chinese), the spiders Anansi (West African) and Ture (Central African), Bre'r Rabbit (African American), and various Native American manifestations, including Coyote, Hare, Raven, and Mink. The medieval tale of Marcolf, which gained particular popularity in Germany, pits the physically deformed peasant in competitive dialogue with the biblical paragon of wisdom, King Solomon, during which the trickster trumps his opponent's every pronouncement with a base and witty riposte. Lists of tricksters see a certain amount of overlap with those of fools and clowns.

Paul Radin's *The Trickster: A Study in American Indian Mythology,* published in 1956, is considered a breakthrough attempt to collect and theorize

Statue of the German trickster Till Eulenspiegel in Mölln, Germany

Source: Hans Weingartz/Wikimedia Commons.

indigenous trickster cycles, although his critical stance is problematized by contributors to *Troubling Tricksters: Revisioning Critical Conversations* (2010). Radin's study includes an essay by psychoanalyst Carl G. Jung, who theorizes a trickster archetype that embodies an undifferentiated consciousness with divine aspirations. In the social sciences, anthropologists like Claude Lévi-Strauss, Victor Turner, and Mary Douglas have in their own ways called attention to tricksters' engagements with categories of social thought and framing.

Trickster Qualities

William J. Hynes (1997) notes six characteristic trickster-like traits, not all of which may appear in any given manifestation: (1) ambiguity, anomaly, or interplay of opposites; (2) deception and trickery; (3) disguise and shape-shifting; (4) inversion of situation or position; (5) uncertain or mixed birth, somewhere between the godly and earthly; and (6) a "sacred and lewd *bricoleur*" in Claude Lévi-Strauss's sense of someone who resourcefully transforms whatever objects are at hand, including the body's coarsest products. In many cases, trickster machinations connect to narratives about origins or transformations of the world and its inhabitants. This last feature leads sometimes to their characterizations as culture heroes and spiritual guides.

Trickster figures and their mischievous exploits are often humorous. They routinely engage in disapproved behaviors like lying and cheating, putting the spectator in the ambivalent position of joining in the ridicule while, perhaps, deriving vicarious pleasure from it. Their best laid plans often reverse laughably upon themselves to humiliating effect, which in common comic custom never prevents them from returning to scheme another day.

Political and Ethical Issues

The dangers of attributing universal qualities or effect to mythic and folk characters has been emphasized in recent years by storytellers and scholars in whose cultures the trickster figure remains alive and present. They warn against the imperialist impulse in which Western scholars presume to analyze trickster-related meanings without full and nuanced awareness of cultural thought and practice. It should be noted that the term *trickster* derives from 19th-century anthropology and not the oral literatures themselves.

Tricksters are almost always male and their exploits are almost always justified within heterosexual norms. Lewis Hyde (1998) mentions a few female incarnations, including the pre-Christian Sheela-na-gig and the ancient Greek Baubo. Franchot Ballinger (2004) suggests that the gender imbalance derives from the disinterest of male researchers in recording instances of female tricksters in the field or in seeking out female storytellers, who were more likely to tell such tales, since female tricksters are likely to be found in matrilineal cultures.

Trickster Tales as Oral Literature

Trickster exploits are often transmitted through oral literatures, sometimes, as in Native American contexts, either ritually or with culturally mandated guidelines as to who can tell the stories and under what circumstances. In other cases, trickster tales circulate as stories told to children or otherwise embedded in cultural custom. These embodied practices have an added level of interest from a humor-studies perspective. Astute uses of voice, gesture, facial expression, characterization, and manipulation of narrative tone can always court laughter over and above the words being spoken.

It should also be emphasized that oral literatures deny the possibility of a single fixed or authorized text. A trickster tale may differ from teller to teller and even telling to telling, undergoing change over time as social and historical developments are reflected in character shadings. A Native American trickster like Coyote, who may once have served as the frequent victim of his own misbehavior, turns his machinations in some latter-day tales upon mercenary White traders, exposing their arrogance and gullibility.

Trickster tales are generally officially sponsored narratives in which antisocial or unapproved behaviors, however clever and entertaining, end in some degree of comeuppance for the perpetrator. At the same time, tricksters appear designed to expose the fault lines in social frameworks by crossing them with abandon, expressing the undeniable straining of bodied drives against social mandates. Often unconstrained by earthly and biological realities, they encourage playful thinking and alternative problem solving. The Native American writer Gerald Vizenor has coined the phrase *trickster discourse*, as an avowedly comic impulse to disrupt, counter, and subvert dominant and dominating cultural narratives.

Tricksters in Other Literatures

The African trickster, Ananse, can be seen in Efua Sutherland's 1975 play *The Marriage of Anansewa*, which draws directly upon local storytelling tradition. Derek Walcott's *Ti-Jean and His Brothers* (1958) employs a trickster figure in dramatizing a Caribbean folk tale. The indigenous Canadian playwright Tomson Highway has used the trickster Nanabush as a shape-shifting embodiment for theatrically inventive effect as well as political intervention in his 1986 *The Rez Sisters*. Puck from William Shakespeare's *A Midsummer Night's Dream* (1595–1596) may be seen as a trickster figure, as can, more recently, the title character in Caryl Churchill's play, *The Skriker* in 1994. Trickster protagonists have featured in contemporary novels by the likes of Vizenor in *Griever: An American Monkey King in China* (1986) and Chinese American author Maxine Hong Kingston's *Tripmaster Monkey: His Fake Book* (1989).

Eric Weitz

See also Anthropology; Clowns; Folklore; Fools

Further Readings

Apte, M. (1985). The trickster in folklore. In *Humor and laughter: An anthropological approach*. Ithaca, NY: Cornell University.

Ballinger, F. (2004). *Living sideways: Tricksters in American Indian oral traditions*. Norman: University of Oklahoma.

Hyde, L. (1998). *Trickster makes this world: Mischief, myth, and art*. New York, NY: North Point.

Hynes, W. J., & Doty, W. G. (Eds.). (1997). *Mythical trickster figures: Contours, contexts, and criticisms*. Tuscaloosa: University of Alabama Press.

Radin, P. (1956). *The trickster: A study in American Indian mythology: With commentaries by Karl Kerényi and C. G. Jung*. London, UK: Routledge & Kegan Paul.

Reder, D., & Morra, L. M. (Eds.). (2010). *Troubling trickster: Revisioning critical conversations*. Waterloo, IA: Wilfred Laurier University.

U

Urban Legends

An urban legend, in general, is an account of a bizarre occurrence that is purported to have taken place in the informant's community, often happening to a friend of the narrator's friend. Some such stories are based on true events, though the details are typically exaggerated and the events streamlined through multiple tellings. But in practice, most urban legends turn out to be well-traveled apocryphal stories that have been told in a variety of locations with variant details. So the term *urban legend* is often used in popular speech to refer to a "hoax" or untrue story. While many such stories relate horrifying or threatening events, such as encounters with ghosts or sinister criminals, a large number are intended to be humorous or satirical in nature. Daniel Barnes has noted that the structure of many urban legends is similar to that of pranks or practical jokes, in that the story leaves a significant detail of the narrative untold, until it is presented at the very end. Thus the narrator of a good urban legend misleads the audience and then cleverly reveals the trick in a device much like the punch line of a typical joke. And while some commentators imply that urban legends are a new form of folklore, in fact some such stories can be traced back to similar stories told in classical or medieval times as exempla or fabliaux, satirizing common human failings and reinforcing social mores.

Many such humorous legends involve sexual misadventures. In one of the oldest, a couple engaged in illicit fornication becomes stuck together in the act of lovemaking. Medical help is required to separate them, resulting in their exposure and mutual embarrassment. The story, preserved in medieval collections of sermon illustrations, survives in a modern version in which a wife breaks in on the sinning couple and uses Superglue to cement them together. Another common "exposure" legend describes a group who arrange a surprise birthday party for a young woman. They wait in a darkened room for her to enter, and then are surprised to find her naked and often involved in some indiscreet act: preparing to make love with her boyfriend, or enticing the family dog, or simply shouting "come and get it while it's clean!" The story, generally related as "absolutely true" and set in the narrator's home town, continues to emerge in new forms as sexual mores continue to evolve. Yet another, current in various forms since the 1800s, describes an unfaithful husband who arranges to meet a prostitute in a hotel room. When they meet face to face, the call girl turns out to be his own wife, or in some versions, his daughter.

Many such legends have a strong "revenge" theme in which the errant partner is detected and given a comic punishment. A legend popular in the previous century describes a businessman traveling by sleeper car who accepts the invitation of a pretty woman to join her in her compartment. In the morning, he finds that she has absconded with his wallet, and worse still, the car he is in has been switched to a different destination than the car with his luggage and clothes. In a less sexually charged version, a wife traveling in the back of the family's travel trailer hears her husband stop for gas. Sleepily, she goes to the station's restroom, and the husband, not knowing she had gotten out, drives off, leaving her there in her pajamas. In one common story, the person responding to an advertisement purchases a fancy car at an absurdly low price. The woman selling it admits that it belonged to her husband, who had run away with another woman, leaving instructions to "sell my car and send me the money."

Other stories involve embarrassing accidents, often portraying the participants as naive or simply the innocent victims of a misunderstanding. In one such, a husband starts to work underneath the family car (or climbs under the sink to do some plumbing). Sometime later, the wife walks past and, seeing the man's legs dangling out, reaches in and fondles his genitals. Shortly after, she is surprised to find the husband inside, who explains that he had asked a more experienced neighbor to take over the job. Another widespread story involves the unwise use of a flammable chemical to cleanse a toilet. When the person using it soon afterward drops a cigarette butt into the bowl, an explosion results. In many variants, the victim is further injured when a member of the rescue squad cannot stop laughing at the story and drops him off the stretcher. In such cases, the absurdity of the situation is the source of humor, rather than the failings of the participants.

Such narratives are obviously intended to be funny and now are often circulated through the Internet as joke texts (though still with the assertion that they are "true stories"). However, even legends that can be narrated as scary or cautionary stories are often parodied or told "for laughs" in oral performance. Gillian Bennett (1993) has indicated a number of metanarrative markers to indicate this intention in narrative texts, and Bill Ellis (1987) has described a carnivalesque narration of "The Hook in the Door," usually a scare story, with overtly comic and sexually suggestive innuendoes included. Clearly one common function of all such legends is to show one's mastery of social situations, especially dealing with sexuality, that are potentially dangerous if handled unwisely. To that extent, urban legends continue the function of older moral stories, in that they illustrate what could happen if social rules of decorum are violated. Yet by allowing audiences to imagine violating social rules, the stories, like other forms of humor, allow them to flout conversational rules in a lawful way. Hence the conservative lessons underscored by the legends' conclusions allow the stories themselves to include content that would not be allowed in most polite conversation. One of the advantages of urban legends is that they both acknowledge the attraction of rebellious behavior, and at the same time, present a conservative moral in a ribald and outrageous way.

Bill Ellis

See also Fabliau; Folklore; Hoax and Prank; Punch Line; Spoofing

Further Readings

Barnes, D. R. (1984). Interpreting urban legends. *ARV: Nordic Yearbook of Folklore, 40*, 67–78.

Bennett, G. (1993). The color of saying: Modern legend and folktale. *Southern Folklore, 50*, 19–32.

Brunvand, J. H. (2002). *Encyclopedia of urban legends.* New York, NY: Norton.

Ellis, B. (1987). Why are verbatim texts of legends necessary? In G. Bennett, P. Smith, & J. D. A. Widdowson (Eds.), *Perspectives on contemporary legend II* (pp. 31–60). Sheffield, UK: Sheffield Academic Press.

Uses and Gratifications Theory

Uses and gratifications theory is a theory within the field of communication focusing on the individual. The premise states that people look for and select media content, including humorous content, hoping that it will satisfy a specific necessity. These media uses will then have different consequences for different individuals. The theory attempts to answer questions such as why people choose to access humorous content from a vast array of media content available, and what are some of the intended consequences of such media consumption. This entry provides a definition for the theory of uses and gratifications as it relates to humor, contextualizes it within the field of communication, examines the specific motivations and consequences for the use of humorous content, and explains how recent technological advancements have made this an especially valuable approach.

Among the assumptions that make uses and gratifications such a unique perspective is the understanding that audiences are active consumers as opposed to passive recipients of media messages.

Audiences look for and select media messages that can satisfy their needs. Another assumption is that audience members anticipate the gratifications they will get from their media use when deciding their media consumption. Media competes then not only with other media for that audience member's attention but also with other communication forms that could satisfy the specific need of the individual. In the case of humorous entertainment media, for instance, media companies not only compete with each other to provide humorous content but also compete with nonmediated humor entertainment providers, such as stand-up comedy acts.

Although the extent to which an audience member plays an active role in the media selection can vary, uses and gratifications theory states that individual differences will lead to different consumption of media content and, therefore, constrain the effects of media. Social and psychological factors influence the individual's selection of media content.

Uses and gratifications theory is rooted in a functional analysis of mass media. In 1948, Harold Lasswell, one of the most influential communication theorists, identified the main functions played by mass media within a societal level; in other words, he identified why societies use media. These functions included the surveillance of the environment, correlation of social parts, and transmission of social norms. Entertainment and anxiety reduction, which are intrinsically related to humor, are among other societal functions of media added by other scholars to this list later on. A shift of focus from the societal level of functional analysis to an individual level of functional analysis of mass media marked the beginning of the conceptualization of uses and gratifications theory.

What started in the 1940s as descriptive research had, by the 1970s, grown into a deeper search for reasons individuals seek media messages and a typology for how these messages satisfy specific needs. Uses and gratifications theorists, such as Elihu Katz, Michael Gurevitch, and Hadassah Haas, have indentified five basic needs sought by audience members. Among those needs are cognitive needs, affective needs, personal integrative needs, social integrative needs, and tension release needs. It is within the affective needs (e.g., pleasurable experience) and tension release needs (e.g., escape and diversion) that humorous messages have been sought.

In an attempt to synthesize the empirical study of uses and gratifications theory, which by the 1970s had been extensively replicated and explored internationally, Katz, Jay Blumler (1974), and Gurevitch created an operational definition of uses and gratifications theory as being concerned with

> (1) the social and psychological origins of (2) needs, which generate (3) expectations of (4) the mass media or other sources, which lead to (5) differential patterns of media exposure (or engagement in other activities), resulting in (6) needs gratifications and (7) other consequences, perhaps mostly unintended ones. (p. 20)

Some critics of the theory state that it is too individualistic, too narrowly focused on the individual. Although one could argue that there is lack of generalization, the focus on the individual and the social and psychological factors influencing individual choices of media selection have brought about new perspectives in the analysis of media effects. Scholars in the field of communication have addressed some of this criticism by creating models providing synthesis to the uses and gratifications approach. The use of self-reporting as the main research methodology for uses and gratifications theory was also highly criticized. Early studies of uses and gratifications relied on individuals identifying for themselves why it is that they choose the media that they choose. Although some audience members are conscious of the gratification sought in their media choices, not all media decisions come at a conscious level. More recent studies have utilized experiments and other methodologies to understand audiences' unconscious decision-making processes.

Dolf Zillmann, a prolific scholar in the area of entertainment communication, has conducted experimental research to understand the reasons behind message selection. His 1988 research focuses on the connection between media choices and mood regulation. His mood management theory asserts that individuals select stimuli (such as media content) to minimize bad moods and maximize good moods. In other words, individuals choose, consciously or unconsciously, to regulate their moods and try to put themselves in a positive mood. Messages containing humor are especially powerful tools to enhance moods, which helps explain the popularity of humor in mediated messages. Scholars tackling the issue of mood management have found, for example, that women's choices for media messages correlate to their menstrual cycle, and that media messages containing humor are more likely selected by women in their premenstrual phase. The idea being that these women unconsciously select media messages containing humor as a way to counterbalance the depressive mood associated with that menstrual cycle phase. The individual, in this case, is still active in the selection of the media message. It is not, however, a selection done at the conscious level. Mood management theory focuses on the affective needs of the individual and is an application of uses and gratifications theory to communication messages containing humor.

The affective need, or the emotional need, is considered an important motivation in the media message selection. This is especially true with entertainment types of media messages. It is no coincidence that we have seen an increase in the offering of entertainment programs in media, as well as the hybridization of media genres, such as infotainment and the inclusion of humor in news programs. Gratifications sought in such programs include wanting to be in a better mood but also feeling morally good and competent. Anne Bartsch, Roland Mangold, Reinhold Viehoff, and Peter Vorderer (2006) developed the concept of metaemotions to account for the different aspects of emotional gratifications that can come into play simultaneously as individuals attempt to make a media selection. These authors also emphasized the fact that many of such selections are not done consciously.

There is a rise of entertainment-type media messages offered, with a plethora of programming containing humor as its main component. Humor has also become an important component of media genres that did not traditionally incorporate humor in their messages, such as journalism. It is common now to have large segments of the news dedicated either to humorous topics or framed with a humorous topic line. A whole new genre of media message has been created to indicate this mesh of entertainment and information, called *infotainment*. Not only have these types of contents been offered more often, but there are also more individuals choosing to accesses these messages to fulfill certain needs.

Recent technological advancements in communications have increased the potential offerings of media messages to individuals. These advancements include the proliferation of media channels with the development of cable and satellite television, the Internet and its sites offering content from media companies and from regular citizens, and the vast number of software applications for mobile devices. With this increase in media channels, there has also been increased offering of mediated humorous messages. This scenario has increased competition for audience attention among media providers, but it has also offered new ways audiences can express their individual choices and satisfy their particular needs. It has provided new ways that audiences can practice their active role, a basic assumption to use and gratifications theory.

In this newer environment, with so many media message choices available and competing with each other and with nonmediated communications, understanding what people do with media and the consequences of this use has become more pertinent than ever. One popular choice of media type is entertainment, particularly humorous messages. Mood management theory, an offshoot of uses and gratifications theory, has offered some explanations as to why people choose media messages containing humor and with what consequences. Other studies focusing on affective needs have also advanced the understanding of why we choose to access messages containing humor and what are some of the effects, on the individual level, of this particular type of media message use.

Vanessa de Macedo Higgins Joyce

See also Audience; Comedy; Framing Theory; Journalism; Psychology; Satire News; Sociology; Stand-Up Comedy

Further Readings

Bartsch, A., Mangold, R., Viehoff, R., & Vorderer, P. (2006). Emotional gratifications during media use—An integrative approach. *Communications, 31*, 261–278.

Katz, E., Blumler, J. G., & Gurevitch, M. (1973). Uses and gratifications research. *The Public Opinion Quarterly, 37*(4), 509–523.

Katz, E., Blumler, J. G., & Gurevitch, M. (1974). Utilization of mass communication by the individual. In J. G. Blumler & E. Katz (Eds.), *The uses of mass communications: Current perspectives on gratifications research* (Vol. 3, SAGE Series in Communication Research, pp. 19–32). Beverly Hills, CA: Sage.

Lasswell, H. D. (1948). The structure and functions of communication in society. In L. Bryson (Ed.), *The communication of ideas* (pp. 37–51). New York, NY: Harper.

Rubin, A. (2009). Uses-and-gratifications perspective on media effects. In J. Bryant & M. B. Oliver (Eds.), *Media effects: Advances in theory and research* (pp. 165–184). New York, NY: Routledge.

Zillmann, D. (1988). Mood management through communication choices. *The American Behavioral Sciences, 31*(3), 327–341.

V

Variety Shows

Variety shows were composed of a series of performances, unconnected by a narrative structure or unifying theme. Variety was part of theater in the United States from at least the 18th century and emerged as an independent theatrical form in the mid-19th century. The second half of the 19th century saw the development of a support infrastructure for variety, and the division of the genre into respectable and disreputable strands, which developed respectively into vaudeville and burlesque in the early 20th century. Vaudeville was severely affected by the Great Depression in the 1930s and further undermined by competition from radio, film, and television. By the mid-20th century, vaudeville was in severe decline, but many of the performers who had once worked in that genre moved into the newer forms of entertainment, especially film and television. Influence from vaudeville can be seen in the fractured narratives of early musical comedies, both film and staged works, and through the interpolation of novelty acts from vaudeville into these works. Television further adapted vaudeville into the televised variety show, which featured singers, dancers, and comedians as well as interviews, and also into the talent show in which amateurs competed in songs, dances, and comedy for prizes and to launch careers as professional entertainers. This entry discusses the evolution of variety shows out of the variety acts presented during theater performances, the spread of variety shows and development of circuits of variety show theaters, and the different types of acts featured in variety shows.

Variety Acts Lead to Variety Shows

The earliest presentations of variety acts occurred in the context of spoken theater. They were known as *olios* because performers appeared at the front of the stage in front of the oiled drop cloth that was lowered between acts during set changes. These performers distracted the audience, especially the rowdy men who were seated in the pit and gallery of the theater. Given that alcohol was freely available in the auditorium, and men in the audience expected theater to be an interactive experience, olio acts functioned to prevent fights and other disturbances in these areas of the theater. By the 1840s, variety shows began to be staged independently of drama in concert rooms attached to saloons in New York. During the 1850s, variety spread to Philadelphia, Washington, D.C., and other large cities on the East Coast of the United States. The spread of variety as an independent form did not end the practice of staging olio performances, and as new popular forms emerged, they also included olios. Before the Civil War, variety olios had become a standard part of both melodrama and minstrelsy, and independent variety shows had increased in scale, offering two acts of individual performances, followed by a comic one-act play, a reenactment of sensational topical events such as train crashes, or, sometimes, staged circus displays.

The grand scale of variety shows in New York was brought to a halt by the passage of a law, popularly

An 1877 wood engraving showing "The Western Drama—A Variety Show Entertainment" in Cheyenne, Wyoming.

Source: Frank Leslie's Illustrated Newspaper, Vol. 45, No. 1150, October 13, 1877. Library of Congress Prints and Photographs Division, Washington, DC, Reproduction Number LC-USZ62-2109.

known as the Anti-Concert Saloon Law, in 1862. The costs of staging shows had been underwritten by income from alcohol sales, and this law forbade any variety manager from holding both a liquor license and a theatrical license. This law shut many New York theaters, and those that survived did so by cutting back on the lavish displays and introducing a higher admission charge. They reduced the number of acts from three to two: a variety first act followed by a one-act comic play or burlesque. In order to please their now more sober but no less volatile audience, managers began to rely more heavily on both male and female performers who used comedy and song to engage the sympathies of their male audience. Other more sensational acrobatic, dance, and novelty acts continued to be staged but on a smaller scale than earlier, and the most valued variety performers were those who could assist in the acts of other performers and in the comic afterpiece as well as appearing in their own act. Away from New York City, variety managers appear to have staged a much more simple show, and the changes to the licensing laws in New York brought that city in line with variety elsewhere.

During and after the Civil War, variety shows expanded into the Midwest and then into Southern cities following trading routes, including the Mississippi River route as well as rail routes. In order to provide a regular supply of performers to these theaters, a variety support infrastructure emerged in the same period that included agents, specialist press that catered to variety performers, and a structure for advertising and reviewing performances. By 1872, the most sought-after variety performers could command salaries of $150 or more per week, although most performers earned $75 or less. Even so, these wages were significantly higher than the wages earned by the working-class audiences who patronized variety shows, and they reflect the great demand for skilled variety performers. In 1873, the United States was plunged into a deep and long-lasting depression, largely due to overspeculation on railroads, which had been rapidly expanding since the 1860s. The financial crash caused theaters all over the nation to close, and for the first time in a decade or more, variety was no longer expanding.

As had been the case in 1862, the managers who survived this crash did so by quickly adapting to the circumstances. The touring variety troupe was the most important development that emerged from this depression, and it further encouraged the development of infrastructure that could support troupes that spent the best part of the season on the road. It also encouraged the formation of circuits of theaters in which regional managers worked cooperatively to be able to attract the best performers to their theaters by guaranteeing a minimum number of weeks' bookings. Managers with interests in more than one theater became increasingly common by the 1880s; probably the best-known variety circuit was the Keith-Albee circuit, but this was just one of many circuits that emerged in the 1880s. The 1880s and 1890s saw the further consolidation of variety into circuits dominated by individual managers, and variety performers found themselves unable to negotiate for improvements in wages or performing conditions. Indeed, the growing infrastructure associated with the Keith-Albee circuit, which included a booking agency and a system of manager reports to inform the booking process, left performers at a distinct disadvantage. Several attempts to organize a union during the 1880s were unsuccessful, as was a strike in the early 20th century. But during this period, vaudeville, as variety was now known, had competition, both from low-class variety staged in dime museums and other disreputable theaters, as well as from radio and then film. By the 1940s, vaudeville was clearly in decline, although it never really disappeared completely; rather it was absorbed into radio and television in the 1950s.

Types of Variety Acts

The kinds of acts that appeared in variety differed greatly depending on the century in which variety shows were staged. In the early 19th century, classically trained female ballet dancers and male jig and clog dancers were particularly popular as olio acts. Singers sometimes appeared in this context too. The earliest saloon shows relied heavily on male and female singers, who entertained their audiences and also led them in communal sing-alongs. Because of limited performance space, dancers were less common in this context. During the 1850s, as concert saloons staged more and more elaborate shows on larger raised stages, circus acrobatic and trapeze acts were in great demand, as were classical ballet dancers, who held great appeal for their male audience. Singers were at a great disadvantage in the noisy auditorium, but the anti-concert saloon law benefited them by removing alcohol and serving girls from the auditorium. The 1870s saw an increase in the number of singers active on the variety stage, and they continued to dominate variety into the 20th century, although dancers and acrobatic novelty acts continued to be popular. Troupes of ballet dancers appeared in variety until the 1873 depression, but these women were among the first performers to be eliminated from the program after the crash, primarily because they had only a single skill. After 1880, only the lowest-class variety shows that offered a sexually suggestive show to an all-male audience featured corps of dancers in the can-can. Respectable variety increasingly came to rely on performers who could sing and dance, had comic skills, and the ability to improvise. While vaudeville resulted in increased standardization of acts, the all-around performer continued to be highly valued into the 20th century.

Most of the singers active in variety shows were comedians, but rather than offering spoken routines of jokes, they presented a small number of character types through song. Variety songs relied on a standardized structure and comic singers interpolated lines of spoken commentary on the text or some local topic, most often between the verse and the chorus. While there is little discussion of audiences singing along with choruses in variety in the 1870s, the insertion of a spoken monologue at that point in the song would have allowed the performer to retain control of the performance, preventing the audience from jumping into the chorus early. Singers also frequently inserted longer spoken monologues that relied heavily on puns and wordplay as well as topical references into the middle of songs. During those sections, the accompanying theater orchestra most likely stopped playing, leaving the pianist, who often led the ensemble, to vamp until the sung material resumed. Comic skills and the ability to improvise comedy were the most valued skills possessed by these performers, and songs were often delivered in heightened speech. In many ways, these comic character singers can be seen as the precursors to stand-up comedians.

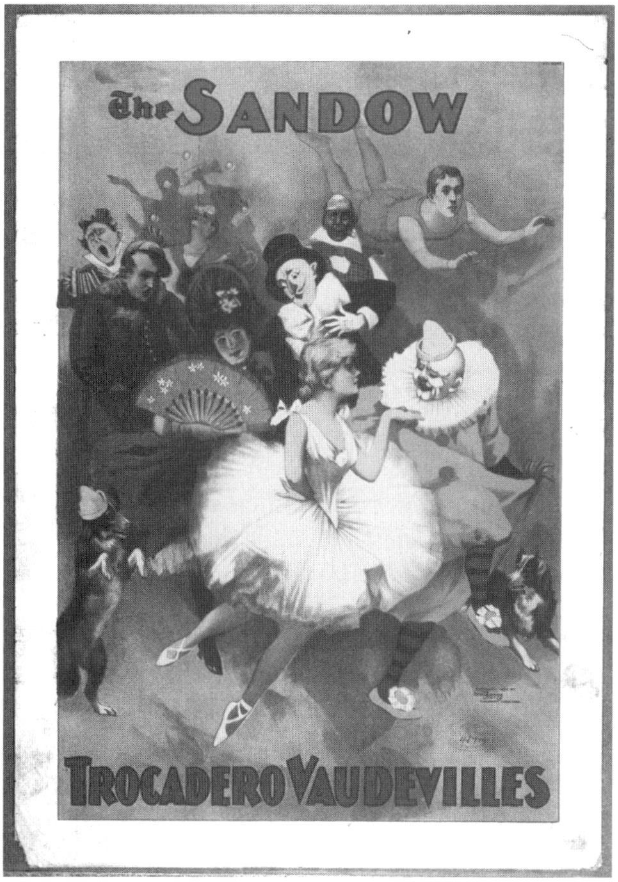

An 1894 promotional poster for the Sandow Trocadero Vaudevilles (1894), showing dancers, clowns, trapeze artists, and costumed dogs.

Source: Strobridge Lithographing Co., Cincinnati, Ohio, and New York. Library of Congress Prints and Photographs Division, Washington, DC, Reproduction Number LC-USZC4-12307.

The characters represented by comic singers were most often based on an ethnic or racial identity. The blackface minstrel character came to variety from minstrelsy and functioned in a fairly similar way in both contexts, although in variety the blackface character was always the butt of the joke. The Irish character also came from minstrelsy, and other ethnic characters, including the "Dutch" (German) and the "Hebrew" (Jewish), were added during the 1870s and 1880s. During the 1870s, there was only one comic role available for female performers—that of the male impersonator. These women depicted high-class men offering both the fantasy of leisure and class critique to the men in their audiences. Other female comic roles, such as the Irish tough girl depicted by Maggie Kline, appeared toward the end of the 19th century and were soon joined by Jewish female characters, but female comics were always vastly outnumbered by men.

In the 20th century, this tendency continued, although women sometimes acted as the straight partner to a comic. This was particularly true for husband and wife acts. Both the audience and variety, and later vaudeville, managers seem to have found the idea of women in comedy disturbing. The overwhelming role for women was to be pretty and tuneful. While women could perform novelty acts that involved nontraditional roles, such as acrobats or multi-instrumentalists, these women were always exceptions, and there is no indication that women ever took part in the kind of knockabout comedy performed by acrobats. There seems to have been a great reluctance for women to appear grotesque or unattractive, on the part of performers, managers, and the audience. This tendency continued well into the 20th century, although by mid-century there were certainly female performers in ethnic roles who were willing to rely on physical comedy for humor.

Gillian M. Rodger

See also Comedy; Dialect Humor; Low Comedy; Sketch Comedy Shows; Travesty

Further Readings

Jenkins, H. (1992). *What made pistachio nuts? Early sound comedy and the vaudeville aesthetic.* New York, NY: Columbia University Press.

Rodger, G. M. (2010). *Champagne Charlie and Pretty Jemima: Variety theater in the nineteenth century.* Urbana: University of Illinois Press.

Slide, A. (Ed.). (1994). *The encyclopedia of vaudeville.* Westport, CT: Greenwood Press.

Snyder, R. W. (1989). *The voice of the city: Vaudeville and popular culture in New York.* New York, NY: Oxford University Press.

Staples, S. (1984). *Male-female comedy teams in American vaudeville, 1865–1932.* Ann Arbor: UMI Research Press.

Vaudeville

See Comic Opera; Music Hall; Musical Comedy; Sketch Comedy Shows; Travesty; Variety Shows

Verbal Dueling

Among the array of verbal practices that count as speech play, *verbal dueling* is a practice in which the talk that frequently characterizes everyday humor interactions is formalized and ritualized to produce a competitive display of wit and dexterity. Verbal dueling requires at least two participants who know and understand the performance conventions that govern the language game for their social group. In a verbal duel, a participant produces an utterance; a second participant must then surpass the utterance of the first with a repartee that listeners consider to be cleverer than the contribution of the first participant. The participant manipulates linguistic features at any level, in relation to each other and in relation to the sociocultural contexts in which they occur, to produce an unexpected redirection or reinterpretation of a previously introduced idea. The result is language that is innovative, humorous, and creative. Within the category of verbal dueling lie games of ritual insult, where participants vie in publicly hurling insults and invectives at each other. The African American game of ritual insult known variously as *dozens, sounding, ranking, snapping, capping,* and *scoring* has had a global impact on popular culture.

Researchers have observed verbal dueling cross-culturally and diachronically. It generally has specific conventions that vary with the sociocultural context of a group. Joel Sherzer (2002), who has studied speech play across cultures, observes that rhyme and rhythm, as well as phonological, syntactic, and semantic play, may be involved in verbal dueling. In some cultures, it is poetic or combines with musical dueling. Shakespearean literature is a rich source of verbal dueling. In a scene from *Romeo and Juliet,* for example, Mercutio and Romeo engage in dialogue in which Mercutio conceptualizes Romeo's wit as cheverel and a "most sharp sauce." The two then compete in creatively redirecting focus and meaning through metaphoric extension.

In contemporary United States, verbal dueling often occurs in public venues, as an icebreaker at business and social gatherings and among friends. Joel Sherzer relates an exchange where an unexpected pragmatic juxtaposition of meaning leads to a verbal duel based on a proverb. Researchers associate verbal dueling in some cultures exclusively with men, but in this exchange in the United States, the exchange takes place between two female participants. In complaining about finding dates, the first participant quotes the first clause of the familiar proverb: "You can lead a horse to water . . . ." While commiserating with the first participant, the second participant has the last word in creativity; she provides a clever and innovative alternative to the standard follow-up clause "but you can't make it drink," pointing out instead that "you can't make it ask you for a date."

While the broad category of verbal dueling involves competition in displaying wit and cleverness, there is not necessarily an intent to attack the other participant. In the subcategory of ritual insult, on the other hand, the goal is to outdo an opponent in uttering insults. Despite the apparent aggressiveness of ritual insult, the practice is often a form of friendly teasing, done without animus. Ritual insult often follows a standard structure that includes a linguistic or not linguistic form that serves as a marker that the material is in the spirit of a game. Certain topics are acceptable in ritual insult, while others can lead to interpretation of a playful jibe as a serious insult. One cue that an insult is not meant as a serious affront is the sheer implausibility of a claim made by a participant; if a participant makes a claim that the targeted participant could take as true, it might be seen as a serious affront.

The nature of the social relationship that holds between the participants and the audience witnessing a game of insult is a central criterion in determining the potential for an insult to receive a humorous interpretation. Performance before other members of a social group tends to mediate interpretation of an insult as part of a game, rather than as a serious insult. Listeners who are part of the social group share background knowledge, conventions, assumptions, and cultural understandings that color their interpretations. They presumably also share goodwill and solidarity with members of the group.

Researchers have observed joking practices involving insult among groups from diverse regions of the world, including Australia, Turkey, Africa, the Aleutian Islands, and Greenland. In some cultures, games of ritual insult serve the function of a safety valve, relieving tension or settling disputes without seriously antagonistic confrontation; even in these instances, there is often an element of play. In Israel, for example, both boys and girls are encouraged to engage in a game of formalized ritual insult called *brogez,* in order to regulate conflict. Greenland Eskimos use ritual insult as a way of settling an argument between two men. The tribe assembles to watch the men engage in sessions where they accompany themselves on drums as they hurl invectives and satirical abuse at each other. They may, during the course of the event, make aggressive, threatening gestures toward each other. The bashing sessions sometimes continue, at intervals, for many months or even years. The game of insult ends when either one of the participants runs out of witty insults or the audience shows through its reactions that one participant has clearly outdone the other. The winner of the verbal matches is then determined to be the winner of the dispute that triggered the competition. The victor gains or maintains prestige within the group, while the loser may experience loss of face or even disgrace that sends him into voluntary exile.

In the European tradition, a form of ritual insult known as *flyting* existed in early Anglo-Saxon and Germanic cultures. Flyting derives from an Old English word that means "to contend" or "to strive," generally in a sense of scolding or wrangling. The genre of flyting flourished during Viking times; its popularity in England declined and the genre disappeared in the 15th century, though the tradition held an important place in Scots literature during the Renaissance. Originally, episodes of flyting occurred before street crowds that spontaneously formed to hear the competition. Opponents in flyting used sexual and scatological reference to bait and tease each other, as if attempting to instigate a physical confrontation. The insulting and egging on of opponents, largely through accusations of cowardice and perceived sexual perversion, allowed a public outlet for venting, without participants actually engaging in violence. The verbal rivalry between Beowulf and

Unferth in the epic *Beowulf* provides an example where flyting is a prelude to battle and a form of combat itself. Stefan Einarsson (1957) cites instances of flyting in Icelandic literature. One such story has two missionaries to Iceland accused of homosexuality: The bishop is said to have given birth to nine children, with his assistant being the father.

Outrageously implausible insults occur in the African American tradition of playing the dozens. A game of dozens begins when a speaker, usually a male adolescent, delivers a humorously insulting statement to another person, who is generally a member of his social group. He speaks in a loud voice, for the benefit of other members of his social group who are usually present and able to witness the game of dozens. To save face, the speaker receiving the insult is then obligated to enter the game by responding with an insult meant to surpass the insult of the first speaker in cleverness and wit. The responding insult may be unrelated to the first or it may build on an idea expressed in the previous insult.

In the dozens, the focus is typically on topics that are taboo, such as incest, personal flaws, sexual topics, and relatives. Topics such as dead relatives and menstruation are disallowed. "Mother" is the primary target; a participant may make ridiculous mother claims regarding weight, style of dress, smell, poverty, and ugliness. The following examples of dozens are from the 1972 work of William Labov, who conducted extensive research on the linguistic practices of African American male adolescents. The insults are framed in the syntax and phonology of African American Vernacular English, as in the following insult targeting ugliness in a mother: "Your mama sent her picture to the lonely hearts club. They wrote her back and said, 'We ain't that lonely.'"

"At least my . . ." is one of several conventional markers that may launch a response to an insult. The example below illustrates an initial insult that attacks mother, followed by an insult beginning with "at least" that builds on the first by making a comparison meant to surpass the first insult in a display of verbal acumen and wit.

Participant 1: Your mother live in a garbage can.
Participant 2: Least I don't live on 1122 Boogie Woogie Avenue, two garbage cans to the right.

In the sequence above, the second participant expands and elaborates on the idea of a garbage can as a home by creating a community of garbage can homes located at a dubious site named for an element of earlier African American culture. The insult does not specifically mention mother, but an indirect message is that she also lives there. Because of the sacred position that *mother* holds, joking about mother may have implications of smashing an icon, in the African American community, as well as in other groups in which mother insults occur.

Researchers identify "mother rhymes," similar to those that occur in the contemporary African American tradition of the dozens, among Yoruba, Efik, Dogon, and Bantu groups. In West African societies, community members sang "songs of derision," where they engaged in satirical public commentary to express complaints and criticisms of others. Songs of derision allowed speakers to avoid face-to-face confrontation, providing a safer, more effective way of criticizing and dealing with conflict; the target of a song was forced to accept the public criticism, similar to the way Americans must "be a good sport." Scholars believe that slaves brought West African songs of derision with them to America. In the fields, slaves in America publicly used coded satirical commentary to air complaints against other slaves and against the master. Researchers believe the contemporary game of dozens evolved from West African mother rhymes and songs of derision; dozens, particularly those of past generations, are often characterized by rhymes and distinctive rhythms

The practice of *battling* in hip-hop culture has roots in the African American community that connect it closely with the tradition of playing the dozens. Battling, also known as *freestyling,* is a rap competition in which two rival hip-hop artists compete in extemporaneously boasting and insulting each other in rhyme. A difference between playing the dozens and battling is that while the dozens requires making claims that are absurd or impossible, artists engaged in battling produce insults that they may intend for an audience and opponent to perceive as true. As in other forms of ritual insult, what can count as an insult is dependent on the values of the culture in which the battle takes place. As a counterculture grounded in the African American urban environment, the hip-hop movement rejects establishment values. This plays out in battling results that privilege the difficulties associated with urban street life, while disparaging the comforts of suburban life. A battling scene from the movie *8 Mile* (2002), featuring the White artist Eminem, highlights the markedness of establishment values.

In the movie, Eminem battles an African American artist. White hip-hop artists have experienced difficulty gaining acceptance in hip-hop culture because of perceptions of affluent background and lack of cultural authenticity. Eminem turns the tables by producing an insult that casts his African American opponent as an imposter who comes from a suburban home where he has an intact nuclear family.

Through battling, ritual insult has expanded from the African American community to become a part of international hip-hop. In the United States, it has become a part of popular culture; youth of all ethnicities engage in playing the dozens, and the Internet is rife with examples of "yo mama" jokes. In 2006 and 2007, MTV aired a game show called *Yo Momma* in which contestants vied against one another in playing the dozens. Speech play having elements of ritual insult occurs in relation to more serious issues, as well. Jerome Neu (2007), who has studied the nature and effects of insults, observes that in the longstanding feud between Gore Vidal and Norman Mailer, at a social event, Vidal made a cleverly phrased criticism of Mailer's most recent book. Mailer responded with his fist, knocking Vidal to the floor. Maintaining composure while rising from the floor, Vidal continued to insult with the quick repartee, "Once again, words have failed Norman." Neu acknowledges that this story is "perhaps apocryphal." We do not know with certainty that Vidal delivered the quote or, if delivered, what the exact phrasing was. Still, versions of the story appear in various locations.

Politicians engage in a type of public insult that is to some extent ritualized when they regularly hurl insults and criticisms at each other. Since opponents in an election are not often in each other's presence, they typically refer to each other in the third person in describing what they portray as failed policies and flawed vision. When an election is over, they shake hands and often share a joke or engage in other non-insulting forms of speech play.

Jacquelyn Rahman

See also Play and Humor; Verbal Humor

Further Readings

Einarsson, S. (1957). *A history of Icelandic literature.* New York, NY: Johns Hopkins University Press.

Hughes, G. (1998). *Swearing: A social history of foul language, oaths and profanity in English.* New York, NY: Penguin.

Katriel, T. (1985). Brogez: Ritual and strategy in Israeli children's conflicts. *Language in Society, 14,* 467–490.

Labov, W. (1972). *Language in the inner city: Studies in the Black English vernacular.* Philadelphia: University of Pennsylvania Press.

Morgan, M. (2002). *Language, discourse and power in African American culture.* New York, NY: Cambridge University Press.

Neu, J. (2007). *Sticks and stones: The philosophy of insult.* New York, NY: Oxford University Press.

Rahman, J. (2012, June). The N word: Its history and use in the African American community. *Journal of English Linguistics, 40,* 137–171.

Sherzer, J. (2002). *Speech play and verbal art.* Austin: University of Texas Press.

van Dam, T. (1954). The influence of West African songs of derision in the New World. *African Music, 1*(1), 53–56.

Wajnryb, R. (2005). *Expletive deleted: A good look at bad language.* New York, NY: Free Press.

Verbal Humor

The term *verbal humor* has been used in two different and incompatible ways. This entry discusses both uses separately.

Verbal Humor as Opposed to Referential Humor

Verbal humor can be used to distinguish humor that is expressed verbally but is not "referential humor." Verbal humor is humor that involves, crucially and besides the normal semantic and pragmatic mechanisms of any form of humor, a reference to the linguistic form of the signifier of the utterance or parts of it. The signifier is the physical medium of the linguistic expression (sounds, written letters, etc.). This includes all "formal" levels: the phonetic, phonological, morphological, and syntactic levels. Referential humor, on the contrary, is based only on semantic and pragmatic factors, or the meaning of words and their context.

The distinction between referential and verbal humor is meant to parallel the distinction, already introduced by Cicero, between humor *de re* (of the subject matter) and *de dicto* (of the expression). Cicero's exact wording in *De oratore LIX* (sections 240, 248) is as follows: jokes (*facetiae*) can be "about what is said" (*dicto*) or about "the thing" (*re*). This opposition has been used by many scholars often with a different terminology and without acknowledging the original source, including Violette Morin (*referential vs. semantic*) Umberto Eco (*situational play vs. play on words*), Pierre Guiraud (*bon mots [quips] vs. puns*), Charles Hockett (*prosaic vs. poetic*), Sigmund Freud (*verbal vs. conceptual*), and many others.

Neurolinguistic research suggests that there is a neurological basis for the distinction. MRIs have shown that different areas of the brain are involved in the processing of verbal and referential jokes (phonological and semantic jokes, respectively, in Vinod Goel and Raymond Dolan's terminology). Verbal/phonological jokes activate Broca's area, which is used in language processing, while referential ones do not.

Cicero went so far as to propose a test for the determination of whether an instance of humor is verbal or referential. The test consists of translating the text into a different language or paraphrasing it. If the change in wording results in the loss of the humor, then the humor is verbal, otherwise it is referential. This test is not without its flaws, as systematic and unsystematic parallelisms may exist between languages that would allow one, albeit infrequently, to translate a given pun from one language to another while preserving the humor. So one would need to refine the test, stipulating that it needs to work if the text is translated into any language, thus making the test impractical. Furthermore, skilled translators can often find equivalent situations or wordings that allow the construction of an equivalent joke in the target language and it thus becomes difficult to assess whether the translation is literal enough to warrant being considered as valid in the test. Therefore, while both interlinguistic translation and paraphrasing can serve as good heuristics to decide whether a given instance of humor is verbal or referential, they cannot be used for scientific purposes.

The decision as to whether an instance of humor is verbal or referential must therefore include a full linguistic analysis. The criterion will be whether reference must be made in the analysis to a formal level of language or whether only reference to semantics and pragmatics is necessary. In the former case, the humor is verbal, in the latter referential. For example, in the pun "Why did the cookie cry?" "Its mother had been away for so long," the string of phonemes underlying "away for" can be interpreted as ambiguous with the string "a wafer." Clearly, if the pun is translated in another language, the humor is lost (since the overlap between "a wafer" and "away for" will no longer be present). Any description of the semantic mechanisms underlying the joke will likewise have to reference the phonological/phonetic level.

It is important to stress that verbal humor is not limited to puns, although puns can be considered the prototypical example of the category. Verbal humor includes morphological and syntactic ambiguity and any situation in which one linguistic form may be subject to two (or more) analyses.

However, there exist some phenomena such as alliterative humor in which the repetition of phonemes or morphemes has a humorous effect, which also fall under the category of verbal humor. These phenomena are not tied to ambiguity in any significant way, thus showing that ambiguity need not be a defining characteristic of verbal humor.

Finally, there exist ambiguous cases, such as pragmatic ambiguity (i.e., cases in which there is an ambiguity in the text, but it does not depend on the form of the signifier of the text) that could be classified as either verbal or referential, depending on one's definition of *linguistic form*.

Verbal Humor as Opposed to Nonverbally Expressed Humor

Verbal humor has also been used to indicate all linguistically expressed humor, as opposed to visual or gestural humor, for example. In this second sense, verbally expressed humor is the larger class, which includes "verbal humor" in the sense discussed in the first part of the entry (i.e., nonreferential humor). *Verbally expressed humor* seems to exclude from its scope all paralinguistic markers, such as smiling, eye movements, and so forth that have been recently linked to the production of humor and are not expressed verbally.

It should be noted that the general theory of verbal humor, uses the term *verbal humor* in the broader sense, in its name, but that it makes full use of the narrower distinction, specifying particular requirements for nonreferential verbal humor.

Salvatore Attardo

See also Ambiguity; Humor Markers; Linguistic Theories of Humor; Translation

Further Readings

Attardo, S. (1994). *Linguistic theories of humor.* Berlin, Germany: Mouton de Gruyter.

Chiaro, D. (2004). Investigating the perception of translated verbally expressed humour on Italian TV. *ESP Across Cultures, 1*, 35–52.

Eco, U. (1983). Introduzione [Introduction]. In R. Queneau, *Esercizi di stile* [Exercises in style] (V–XIX). Turin, Italy: Einaudi.

Freud, S. (1905). *Der Witz und seine Beziehung zum Unbewussten* [Jokes and their relation to the unconscious]. Leipzig, Germany: Deuticke.

Freud, S. (1960). *Jokes and their relation to the unconscious* (J. Strachey, Trans.). New York, NY: Norton.

Goel, V., & Dolan, R. J. (2001). The functional anatomy of humor: Segregating cognitive and affective components. *Nature Neuroscience, 4*(3), 237–238.

Guiraud, P. (1979). *Les jeux de mots* [Puns] (2nd ed.). Paris: Presses Universitaires de France.

Hockett, C. F. (1977). Jokes. In C. F. Hockett, *The view from language: Selected essays, 1948–1974* (pp. 257–289). Athens: University of Georgia. (Reprinted from M. E. Smith, Ed., *Studies in linguistics in honor of George L. Trager* [1973, pp. 153–178]. The Hague, Netherlands: Mouton de Gruyter.)

Morin, V. (1966). L'histoire drôle [The funny story]. *Communications, 8*, 102–119.

Ritchie, G. (2000). *Describing verbally expressed humour* (Informatics Report Series EDI-INF-RR-0012). University of Edinburgh. Retrieved from http://www.era.lib.ed.ac.uk/handle/1842/3403

Ritchie, G. (2001). Current directions in computational humour. *Artificial Intelligence Review, 16*(2), 119–135.

W

Wellerism

The term *wellerism* is the international designation for a unique subgroup of proverbs. A wellerism usually consists of three parts: a short statement that is often a proverb or a proverbial expression, a speaker uttering it, and an unexpected situation in which the discourse takes place. Typical wellerisms from folk speech are "'There's no fool like an old fool,' as the old man said when he married his fourth wife"; "'Let there be light,' murmured the raven-haired beauty, as she drew forth the peroxide bottle"; and "'Keep your mouth shut,' said Daniel, as he entered the lion's den." While such triadic formulations have also been called quotation proverbs, Yankeeisms, perverted proverbs, or anti-proverbs, the 19th-century word *wellerism* has been adopted as the general term. It was coined from the character Samuel Weller, who in Charles Dickens's novel *The Pickwick Papers* (1836) makes ample use of such verbal twists that add considerable humor to his pregnant observations, among them "'I only assisted natur,' ma'm,' as the doctor said to the boy's mother, arter he'd bled him to death" and "'If I do see your drift, it's my 'pinion that you're a comin' it a great deal too strong,' as the mail-coachman said to the snowstorm, ven it overtook him."

To be sure, wellerisms did not originate with Dickens. They have been traced back to the Sumerian cuneiform tablets of about 2500 BCE; they have been found in writings of the ancient Egyptians; and they were certainly popular already in classical antiquity, with Plato citing "'The water will tell you,' said the guide when the travelers asked him how deep the river was." Wellerisms have also been found in the oral tradition of Africa, but they gained particular popularity in northern Europe, with Martin Luther in Germany using their biting humor as an expressive form of satire. Following the success of Dickens's *Pickwick Papers* in the United States, wellerisms became incredibly popular in magazines and newspapers as short statements full of puns, wit, humor, irony, and satire. The media experienced a literal welleristic craze with pages full of invented wellerisms based on this formerly orally transmitted genre of folk speech. The new literary creations exploited the triadic structure of the traditional wellerism to express various kinds of criticism by way of joking indirection. Some of these texts contained serious satirical comments regarding 19th-century American society and politics, while others were created for the sheer fun of verbal play that could also include sexual humor by way of a sanctioned folkloric structure. An example of frontier humor might be "'Put on the steam! I am in haste,' cried the snail that had crept into a railroad car"; having a bit of fun with the Bible comes through in "'Eaves dropping again,' said Adam, as his wife fell out of a tree"; and a wellerism like "'Business before pleasure,' as the man said when he kissed his wife before he went out to make love to his neighbor's," enabled witty people to express some sexual humor in a rather puritanical environment.

Many of these wellerisms were one-day printed wonders and did not gain any currency among the folk. There are, however, some wellerisms that are known nationally or even internationally, such as "'Much noise and little wool,' said the devil and sheared a pig"; "'Everyone to his taste,' said the farmer and kissed the cow"; and "'I see,' said the blind man, as he picked up his hammer and saw." The last example also exists in the truncated form of "'I see,' said the blind man" with its obvious grotesque humor. Wellerisms based on the blind man seeing abound in many variants in numerous languages, with the third part verbalizing such gallows humor as "to his deaf dog as they stepped off a cliff," "as he fell in the well," "as he threw away his glasses," "as he walked into the wall," "to his deaf wife," and so on. Such cruel wellerisms would be considered politically incorrect today, but they indicate changing social norms of acceptable folk humor, in this case at the expense of a disadvantaged person. But people to this day are well aware that wellerisms are perfectly suited for humorous relief, as can be seen from more modern texts as "'All's well that ends well,' said the monkey as the lawnmower ran over his tail" and "'I won't have guts enough to do that again,' as the bug said as he hit the windshield."

Besides Dickens, such modern writers as the dramatist Bertolt Brecht and the detective fiction writer Leslie Charteris also cited or coined wellerisms, with the latter being known for a series of suggestive texts as "'This is my idea of a night out,' as the bishop said to the actress" and "'But I'm not nearly satisfied yet,' as the actress said to the bishop." Some of these actress-bishop wellerisms have taken hold of the folk imagination, and new texts with sexual or obscene messages, albeit by way of welleristic indirection, can be found in oral and written communication. Wellerisms as a folk speech genre continue to compete with jokes, one-liners, puns, and other short forms of humor, and while they often exaggerate or enter the obscene or scatological sphere, they represent a common well-structured form of verbal humor that extends from the nonsensical to the sublime by way of parody, punning, joking, or more generally stated, the delight of speech play.

Wolfgang Mieder

See also Anti-Proverb; Folklore; Gallows Humor; Obscenity; Parody; Puns; Speech Play

Further Readings

Baer, F. (1983). Wellerisms in The Pickwick Papers. *Folklore*, *94*, 173–183.

Carson Williams, F. (2002). *Wellerisms in Ireland.* Burlington: University of Vermont.

Mieder, W. (1982). Sexual content of German wellerisms. *Maledicta*, 6, 215–223.

Mieder, W. (Ed.). (1985). *The proverb*. Cambridge, MA: Harvard University Press. (Reprinted from A. Taylor, *The proverb*. Cambridge, MA: Harvard University Press, 1931.)

Mieder, W. (1989). *American proverbs. A study of texts and contexts*. Bern, Switzerland: Peter Lang.

Mieder, W., & Kingsbury, S. (1994). *A dictionary of wellerisms*. New York, NY: Oxford University Press.

Speroni, C. (1953). *The Italian wellerism to the end of the seventeenth century.* Berkeley: University of California Press.

Witz

The German concept *Witz* (pl. *Witze*) is relevant to humor research in two ways. In contemporary German *Witz* refers to the text type joke. Etymologically the word *Witz* is related to English "wit": originally it denoted knowledge or wisdom, however over time it came to be associated with the important poetic terms *wit* and *esprit*, as discussed below.

Contemporary *Witz*

In contemporary German, *Witz* is a short, humorous, and fictional prose narrative that ends with a laughter-triggering punch line (in German, *Pointe*). Sometimes a stricter definition, which includes additional features such as orality, anonymity of the author, or the use of present tense, is used to narrow down the genre. In addition, the way in which it is differentiated from other humorous short forms such as anecdote, aphorism, fabliau, farce, riddle, or sketch may also be defined differently.

It is difficult to determine the role of *Witz* in relation to the general historical development of jokes. German jokes tend to be differentiated either in terms of the particular ethnic or social group that produced them (e.g., *jüdische Witz*, or Jewish joke), or the ethnic groups that have been the butt of them (e.g., jokes about people from East Friesland [*Ost-Friesenwitz*] or jokes about Jewish people [*Judenwitz*]). It is also difficult to say anything about *Witz* in the context of the totalitarian political system of the Third Reich or the socialist regime of the former German Democratic Republic as relatively few serious studies have been conducted in this area.

In Germany, the study of *jokes*, respectively *Witze*, began in disciplines such as philosophy and psychology, but since the 1970s, other disciplines such as linguistics and literary studies have found this an area of interest (although research in literary studies is strongly influenced by older concepts of *Witz*). Initially, the German tradition of joke studies was marked by an interest in ordering jokes according to their diverse typologies. The most prominent joke typology was proposed by Sigmund Freud's 1905 *Der Witz und seine Beziehung zum Unbewußten* (*The Joke and Its Relation to the Unconscious*). Freud's identification of joke techniques (e.g., *verdichtung* [condensation], *doppelsinn* [double meaning]) was partly derived from linguistic observation, partly from his psychoanalytic *Interpretation of Dreams* (1899). Besides typological issues, there has also been a continuous interest in the internal structure of jokes. For instance, the Dutch-German scholar André Jolles hypothesized in his 1929 study *Einfache Formen* (*Simple Form*) that a particular spirit or mental attitude will manifest in a particular literary form, and that the process of "untying" conventional mental connections will ultimately materialize in jokes.

History of the Word and Concept

The contemporary meaning of *Witz* as the German name for the text type joke came to the fore during the 19th century. However, due to the word's complex etymological history, *Witz* also represents an important aesthetic concept.

In Old German, *wizzi* referred to the domain of knowledge, reason, and wisdom. This ancient meaning of *Witz* has—with the exception of a few derivations such as *Mutterwitz* ("mother wit")—disappeared from contemporary German usage.

During the 17th century, the concept of *Witz* was influenced by a philosophical and poetical debate sparked by the French essayist Dominique Bouhours's (1962/1671) assertion that a German *bel esprit* was a rare thing (p. 223). In the ensuing prominent (and frequently nationalistic) debate, *esprit* was frequently translated as *Witz*, as a particular talent for producing witty expressions. The debate, in which German scholars drew on the British concept of wit, respectively "true wit" and "false wit" to support their arguments, and during which the meaning of *Witz* came to be increasingly associated with French *esprit* and English *wit*, also touched on aesthetic issues such as what constituted the best kind of *Witz* and how it could be appropriately employed in literature.

As a consequence of this philosophical and poetical debate, *Witz* came to be associated with the human faculty of discovering similarities between dissimilar things (cf. e.g., Christian Wolff: *Vernünfftige Gedancken von der Menschen Thun und Lassen* [Reasonable Thoughts About the Human Being's Dos and Don'ts], 1733, §308f.), a faculty that had previously been regarded as a key talent in rhetorical invention, for instance in Aristotle's third book of *Rhetoric* (chap. 10) on the invention of metaphor, or in Renaissance treatises on conceits. As a consequence, *Witz* became an important aesthetic term. Toward the end of the 18th century, it was reinterpreted to mean a general combinatorial force beyond objective similarities.

The last phase in the terminological development of *Witz* resulted from the difficulty in differentiating between the mental disposition when using *Witz* and the actual products of *Witz*. It was during the 19th century that *Witz* began to refer mostly to jokes. A very early example of this can be found in Johann Wolfgang von Goethe's conversations with Johann Peter Eckermann on "Berlin jokes" at the beginning of the 19th century. In contemporary German usage, this has now become the typical meaning of *Witz*.

Ralph Müller

See also Joke; *Pointe*; Punch Line; Simple Form

Further Readings

Bouhours, D., & Brunot, F. (1962). *Les entretiens d'Ariste et d'Eugène* [Conversations of Ariste and Eugène]. Paris, France: A. Colin. (Original work published 1671)

Freud, S. (1960): Jokes and their relation to the unconscious. In J. Strachey, A. Freud, A. Strachey, & A. Tyson (Eds.), *The standard edition of the complete psychological works of Sigmund Freud* (Vol. 8). London, UK: Hogarth Press. (Original work published 1905)

Gabriel, G. (1997): *Logik und Rhetorik der Erkenntnis: Zum Verhältnis von wissenschaftlicher und ästhetischer Weltauffassung* [Logic and rhetoric of knowledge: On the relationship between scientific and aesthetic perception of the world]. Paderborn, Germany: Mentis Verlag.

Hill, C. (1993). *The soul of wit: Joke theory from Grimm to Freud.* Lincoln: University of Nebraska Press.

Jolles, A. (1958): *Einfache Formen: Legende, Sage, Mythe, Rätsel, Spruch, Kasus, Memorabile, Märchen, Witz* [Simple forms: Saints' legends, saga, myth, riddle, proverb, example, report of memorable events, fairy tale, joke] (2nd ed.). Tübingen, Germany: Niemeyer.

Preisendanz, W. (1970). *Über den Witz* [On the joke]. Konstanz, Germany: Universitätsverlag.

Röhrich, L. (1977). *Der Witz: Figuren, Formen, Funktionen* [Joke: Characters, forms, functions]. Stuttgart, Germany: Metzler.

Schmidt-Hidding, W. (1963). *Humor und Witz* [Humor and wit]. München, Germany: Hueber.

Wenzel, P. (1989). *Von der Struktur des Witzes zum Witz der Struktur: Untersuchungen zur Pointierung in Witz und Kurzgeschichte* [From the structure of the joke to the joke of the structure: Studies on the pointedness in jokes and short stories]. Heidelberg, Germany: Winter.

Winkler, M., & Goulding, C. (2000). *Witz*. In K. Brack & M. Fontius (Eds.), *Ästhetische Grundbegriffe* [Basic aesthetic concepts] (Vol. 6, pp. 694–729). Duisburg, Germany: Metzler Verlag.

Workplace Control

The term *workplace control* refers to attempts by managers to get workers to do what is required to meet the organization's goals. This entry discusses some direct and indirect uses of humor that have been documented over the years to control workers.

A workplace, unlike most other places, has both a common purpose and an authority structure to keep the energy focused on that purpose. For this reason, workplace humor could be classified into three broad categories: (1) humor that tends to support the purpose; (2) humor that tends to thwart that purpose; and (3) humor, usually silly, that has nothing to do with that purpose.

Humor that resists the purpose of the organization or that resists attempts by management to push for the organization's purpose is usually characterized as resistance, while silly humor, which is irrelevant to the purpose of the organization, is usually characterized as comic relief. Humor that supports the purpose of the organization, either directly or indirectly, has received less attention.

Direct Worker Control

The idea of using humor for any kind of control is usually traced to the early superiority theories of Aristotle and Thomas Hobbes. For example, Richard Stephenson argues that sarcasm, caricature, or parody can be used to ridicule deviant behavior and thus discourage people from repeating it. Humor can be used to tease people who violate social or other norms and encourage them to get back in line. Using humor this way in the workplace might be called direct workplace control. This is different from the more indirect method of using humor to vent resistance so that it does not become dangerous.

In an article based on her 1957 doctoral thesis in cultural anthropology, Pamela Bradney described the efforts of clerks in a London department store to tease trainees who demonstrated deviant behaviors. In this way, they brought new employees in line with the norms and expectations of the workplace. Since then, similar work has shown that humor can be used to gently correct the behaviors of those in machine shops and restaurant kitchens.

Another way that humor is used to control people is by the cultural rules about who is authorized to joke with whom. Anthropologist Alfred Radcliffe-Brown (1881–1955) has written that we can learn about levels of authority and respect by noting who jokes with whom. In a recent era, it was de rigueur for male comedians to make fun of their mothers-in-law, for example. Studies of this phenomenon have shown how mental health workers show deference to psychiatrists and similar power relationships. For a managers, though, this presents an opportunity to demonstrate respect (or lack thereof) through their willingness to joke with or about others.

Of course, this sort of chiding humor can be a diversionary tactic to hide aggressive messages that would be unacceptable if expressed directly. When this happens, the attempt at worker control often backfires. The manager who is seen as backbiting gains neither power nor respect. Also, there is a very different way to use humor in support of the organization and its goals.

Indirect Worker Control

More common than direct ridicule of deviant behavior is an indirect form of workplace control. Workers are allowed or encouraged to vent resistance harmlessly through humor, much as a pressure release valve in a machine might prevent an explosion. For example, Scott Adams's comic strip *Dilbert* is rightly seen as cynical commentary on vacuous management theories. However, unlike the subversive humor that led to the unionization of some call centers in India, or the effective resistance to management documented in Brazil by Suzana B. Rodrigues and David L. Collinson (1995), Adams's humor expresses a grudging acceptance of the situation as absurd, but survivable. After giving vent to the alienation and dehumanization of the office cubicle, employees return to work refreshed and invigorated.

There is even a certain joy in having the work to complain about. This is evident in a workplace when an equipment breakdown stops the work and employees notice that they miss joking about the working conditions. Humor has been shown to deflect workers' awareness of the dehumanizing aspects of the job. Those who would prefer to see the workers experience the pain and rise up against it characterize such humor as an "anesthetic."

Other examples include the "banana time" documented by Donald Roy (1960), during which workers put down their tasks as one worker routinely stole and enjoyed another's banana. This "clowning" behavior was not initiated or officially sanctioned by management but was wisely tolerated by supervisors who recognized the value of letting the workers have a moment to vent their feelings of helplessness and dependence with this entirely harmless show of force.

Co-Opting Worker Humor

Anna Pollert documented the joking in a Bristol tobacco factory and how supervisors appropriated it to soften discipline. Although the joking routines were initiated by the workers, company leadership was "allowed" to tap into them and use them for pro-organization purposes. Whether the involvement of supervisory staff is welcomed or not is an important indicator of the health of the relationship between supervisors and their employees.

Some writers, such as Simon Critchley, have tried to decode, from the humor in use at an organization, the incongruity that drives it. For example, much humor is based on the incongruity between the way things are, from the perspective of the jokers, and the way they think things ought to be. Thus, a thoughtful analysis of employee humor might unearth suggestions for how to build a workplace that workers would find rational, reasonable, and not funny.

Meta-analysis supports the idea that workplace humor in general is correlated with positive outcomes such as satisfaction and workplace cohesion, but it is not clear which is causing what. It seems likely that any factors leading to satisfaction and cohesion would also lead to happy relationships among workers. Humor can be used as a positive factor in controlling workers and their work, but its effects are not entirely predictable and any attempt by management to co-opt the fun might backfire severely.

Jim Lyttle

See also Management; Workplace Humor; Workplace Resistance

Further Readings

Boland, R. J., & Hoffman, R. (1983). Humor in a machine shop: An interpretation of symbolic interaction. In L. R. Pondy (Ed.), *Organizational symbolism* (pp. 187–198). Greenwich, CT: JAI Press.

Bradney, P. (1957). The joking relationship in industry. *Human Relations, 10* (2), 179–187. doi:10.1177/001872675701000207

Burawoy, M. (1979). *Manufacturing consent: Changes in the labor process under monopoly capitalism.* Chicago, IL: University of Chicago Press.

Collinson, D. L. (1988). Engineering humor: Masculinity, joking and conflict in shop-floor relations. *Organizational Studies, 9*(2), 181–199.

Coser, R. L. (1960). Laughter among colleagues. *Psychiatry, 23*, 81–95.

Critchley, S. (2013). Humour as practically enacted theory, or, why critics should tell more jokes. In R. Westwood & C. Rhodes (Eds.), *Humour work and organization* (pp. 17–32). London, UK: Routledge.

Fleming, P., & Sturdy, A. (2009). Just be yourself! Towards neo-normative control in organisations? *Employee Relations, 31*(6), 569–583. doi:10.1108/01425450910991730

Mak, B. C. N., Liu, Y., & Deneen, C. C. (2012). Humor in the workplace: A regulating and coping mechanism in socialization. *Discourse & Communication, 6*(2), 163–179. doi:10.1177/1750481312437445

Mesmer-Magnus, J., Glew, D. J., & Viswesvaran, C. (2012). A meta-analysis of positive humor in the workplace. *Journal of Managerial Psychology, 27*(2), 155–190. doi:10.1108/02683941211199554

Noon, M., & Blyton, P. (2007). *The realities of work: Experiencing work and employment in contemporary society* (3rd ed.). New York, NY: Palgrave.

Rodrigues, S. B., & Collinson, D. L. (1995). Having fun? Humour as resistance in Brazil. *Organization Studies, 16*(5), 739–768. doi:10.1177/017084069501600501

Roy, D. F. (1960). Banana time: Job satisfaction and informal interaction. *Human Organization, 18*, 158–168.

Stephenson, R. M. (1951). Conflict and control functions of humor. *American Journal of Sociology, 56*(6), 569–574.

Taylor, P., & Bain, P. (2003). "Subterranean worksick blues": Humour as subversion in two call centres. *Organization Studies, 24*(9), 1487–1509. doi:10.1177/0170840603249008

Workplace Humor

The international success of the television show *The Office* and the lasting and far-reaching success of the cartoon strip *Dilbert* both demonstrate that though the workplace is often a serious and formal place, it can also be a productive site for humor. When we chuckle at the lampooning of modern "office speak" in *The Office,* or when we cut out a Dilbert cartoon on the absurdity of office bureaucracy and post it on our cubicle wall, we are acknowledging the humor on some level fits our own organizational experiences. Scholarship of organizational humor often looks beyond humor made about the modern workplace and focuses more on jokes and humor made within the workplaces. Humor scholarship focuses on the everyday use of humor in organizational settings and reveals humor at work is more than trivial banter. It is an essential part of organizational life.

In the last 10 years, there has been a significant amount of research on humor's use at work. Using a broad brush, these studies focus on how humor facilitates the formation and maintenance of organizational culture, managerial effectiveness, and how employees use humor to make sense of and perform their complex roles in organizations. Why this focus on workplace humor? Humor is a pervasive and meaningful aspect of organizational life. Focusing on *what* (or *who*) organizational members joke about, *how* they joke (e.g., the language they use), *where* they joke (the location they choose or are allowed to tell jokes in), or with *whom* they share humor (the audience they share a workplace joke with) reveals and offers a unique and often unfiltered glimpse into an organization's culture.

Researchers focus on humor to better understand everyday experiences in organizational life. Specifically, researchers have focused on how workplace humor is used at work to do the following: form and maintain workgroup cohesion and group boundaries (who is in the in-group and who is an outsider); manage emotional stress at work; make the monotony of work bearable; make sense of contradictory aspects of organizational life and policy; negotiate power, both formal hierarchical power and social power; and structure everyday tasks and workplace relations. Humor is found in almost every workplace and clearly it does much more than make work life bearable. Many organizational scholars argue humor makes work "work," or function. Humor many not be an essential cog but it is the grease that keeps the engine running.

Humor is seldom without a power dimension; there is after all often a butt to a joke, but due to the hierarchical and formal nature of work, workplace humor is often revealing about the power dynamics in a particular workplace. As a result, there is a rich history of critical organizational scholarship that examines how workplace power is actualized via legitimate power (legal basis for power), dispositional power (traits or a sense of power), and situational power (position of power within an environment or task). With each of these forms of power, there are discursive power practices, or the social and political strategies that shape the identity of actors and the capacity to act (agency) within their social contexts.

Organizational humor scholars provide richly detailed workplace examples of humor as an essential part of discursive power practices. Humor is part of the power play used to exert control over others, but it is also used to resist attempts by to others trying to exert control. Managers use humor to directly and indirectly control their employees. Humor is also used by employees to control and influence their workplace peers and the labor process. Humor is used to form and maintain labor-related identities (e.g., the gendered identity of work, professional identity of work, and/or the prestigious nature of work and the workers themselves). Critical scholars not only focus on humor as a means of control but also as a form of resistance, where employees use humor to criticize and challenge managerial authority, organizational policy, or both.

Functional Use of Humor

The functional use of humor on an interpersonal level is the tactical use of humor by organizational members to achieve an end goal. The functional use of humor on an interpersonal level is often determined through discourse analysis of conversations at work. The analysis is based on a sender-focused transmission model of interpersonal communication. This model is often termed S.M.C.R, for sender, message, channel, and receiver. A large work discourse data set could include audio or video recordings of weekly team meetings over a period of 6 months to show humorous messages in organizational context. The researcher observes the humor message within conversation and notes: who the sender of the message was, the humor message itself, and the humor effectiveness. A humor message is noted as effective on two levels. The first is on the humor's level—that the humor message elicited a positive verbal or nonverbal response from the receiver, such as a smile or a laugh. The second level is determining effectiveness, that is, whether the humor successfully communicated the sender's intentions. This is more complicated because the researcher has to determine the intended meaning or purpose of the sender. This can be determined by questioning the sender on the form of humor used, the sender's intention, and whether the sender felt the humor was successful for the intended purpose. This sender-focused transmission model has revealed a wide range of interpersonal functions for humor at work. This use of workplace humor includes but is not limited to the following: to transmit verbally aggressive messages; to demean others; to control others; to defend the ego against possible attack; to put others in place; to disarm potentially aggressive others; to decrease aggression; to minimize others' anxiety; to disclose difficult information; to allow others to cope with difficult situations; to allow insight into another's state of mind; to adjust to a new role; to ease tensions around new information and situations; to express feelings; and to avoid revealing important or sensitive information.

Functional humor on an organizational level is humor used to increase managerial and organizational effectiveness and has gained increased academic and business interest in recent years. Popular instructional books detail how humor can be used by managers to increase organizational goals, increase profit, increase worker compliance, and reduce employee stress. Humor is held as an important component of a successful business culture. The research on organizational level humor and its function over time is not typically based on the sender-message model but rather on qualitative case study research (e.g., organizational ethnography, organizational narrative research). It considers more than the sender's intention or message effectiveness. It focuses instead on the receiver's interpretation of the joke and the broader influence the humor had within the workplace relationship and the work processes. Many organizational ethnographers report that they discovered or realized the importance of humor unintentionally. The researcher often went into a workplace to observe an organizational process over time and recognized the continued use of humor. As a result, humor is typically "uncovered" as a consistent aspect of workplace dialogue and often recognized as a part of completing a successful relational task. An example from recent research is the importance of humor's use by both employees and managers during an employee's job performance review to reduce tension but also to underscore strengths and weaknesses during the evaluation process. Another example is the routine humor used by pediatricians during patient exams and by obstetricians and other medical staff early in the child birthing process to reduce tension. In both of these examples, the researchers, like many who are engaged in the study of a workplace over time, recognize and regard humor as an important part of performing a certain task but also as part of maintaining the organization's unique culture.

However, just because humor can be used to improve organizational culture and processes does not mean it can easily be deployed or always have the intended effect. Organizational researchers often warn that humor is a double-edged sword and attempts to manage humor may actually suppress it. Attempts to control humor may lead to a resurgence of undesired (unproductive) forms of workplace humor.

Managerial Use of Humor at Work

Humor has been linked with effective transformative and transactional leadership alike. Leaders who use humor find innovative solutions to problems. Managers and those of high hierarchical status can use humor effectively to gain compliance without emphasis on the power differentials between themselves and their subordinates. The managerial use of humor to reduce the sting of authoritative intent has been well documented in humor studies of the workplace. Recent research demonstrates that the use of humor to soften authoritative intent is especially significant for female managers as they use humor daily to reduce distance but also help negotiate the paradoxes and pitfalls of being both a woman and a middle manager in gendered organizations.

Workplace Humor as Uniting and Dividing

Workplace humor functions to strengthen workplace collegiality and team fidelity. It helps facilitate relationship initiation as well as reduce tensions. It can defuse anger as well as soften criticism; however, humor can "bite"—be used to tease and hurt. Case study research shows that subtle quips and overt jocular abuse are used by workers to point out flaws or distance others at work. Within friendship groups at work, humor can be both bonding and cruel, particularly in blue-collar work environments. This inclusion (bonding) and exclusion (distancing) role of relational humor at work engenders in-group and out-group conflicts. At work these in- and out-group boundaries are (re)produced by excluding individuals (or groups) who do not have the stock knowledge of the in-group's references, skills, language, and sense-making process.

Workplace Humor and Identity

Professional and organizational identity is not constructed in isolation but in relation to organizational processes, structures, and the group we interact with and see ourselves as part of in our everyday work, from a relational perspective. This area of organizational humor research focuses on how workers use humor to react to and manage their personal identity in response to their stressful work. Humor is used to elect meanings that affirm one's sense of self, as well as to demonstrate how this humor conforms and constrains the group's identity and sense-making process at work. Employees depend on humor to clarify and affirm their sense of self. Humor is used in the process of organizing work itself to retain, protect, and reify the values and agency of workers within their actual work process. Humor is revealed to be more than a coping device in order to do one's job. It is a means through which the workers maintain identity as they make sense of and perform their organizing role.

Employee Use of Humor at Work

The most documented form of employee-specific humor in case studies is humor used by employees to safely criticize a higher member or an organizational process. It has long been argued that subordinate humor (directed at a superior) functioned *as sanctioned disrespect,* especially if the humor had clear support from the audience—that is, generated immediate laughter in the workplace. It is "sanctioned" or allowed simply because jokes are very difficult to object to by the target of the humor, especially if the target has hierarchical power. If a subordinate's joke is told in a meeting and is laughed at by some of the people present, the superior must challenge the response of the audience to the humor, as well as the underlying meaning of the message. What can be equally difficult is when the superior must separate the humor completely from the message before objecting to it and possibly sanctioning the teller. To do this the superior must first acknowledge the humor (the basis of laughter), excuse the audience for laughing, and finally, separate the objectionable message from the joke. The manager would have to say something like this: "It is OK to laugh at the perceived lack of planning (the meaning) on my part, and I too think it is funny, but in this context, the joke does not fit or is even inappropriate because. . . ." Clearly for a superior to sanction subordinate humor is difficult because by objecting to a joke, the superior risks the appearance of being viewed as oversensitive, not being able to take a joke, or having no sense of humor. As a result, doing so exposes one to the risk of appearing weak on traits associated with strong leadership.

However, this does not mean that a workplace joke's content is always beyond contestation or is unsanctionable at work. If the joke is targeted at someone without authority (e.g., an intern), a manager with little risk to his or her own standing can object to its use. The leadership trait of concern for employees' well-being trumps the need to be seen as being thick-skinned or having a sense of humor. If the joke could be considered offensive (e.g., sexist or racist), a superior can easily object to it and, in many workplaces, peers can object as well, especially if the joke did not elicit a humorous response from others. Even though humor is difficult to sanction, the humor defense "I was only joking" is rarely an effective defense for offensive humor at work, especially if the target of the humor or fellow coworkers communicate that they did not find the humor to be "funny" on the grounds of its content. Indeed, if an organizational member formally communicated objection to a joke's content as *offensive* or *hostile,* the employer must make reasonable steps to avoid future humor of this kind or risk being held legally responsible for harassment.

Though subordinate humor is used to resist the hierarchy, it does not change the hierarchical power structure. Workers use humor to make fun of a manager, policy, or practice in the workplace and, in so doing, temporarily resolve organizational incongruity and paradox. However, humor does not seem to subvert or have a transformational effect on the target of the joke. With incongruity or relief as its basis, without removing the cause for the tension itself, the brief respite gained from resistance humor is akin to blowing off steam and is thus called *safety valve resistance*. Discourse analysis of recorded workplace meetings over time demonstrates that employees in these situations use subordinate humor frequently to challenge the status quo on three levels: individual—to take down a superior member of a group; organizational—to challenge the values of the larger organization; and societal—to challenge the values of the broader society.

With the focus on humor as a release of tension there are two developing areas of organizational humor research: (1) how employees use humor to control each other, or *concertive control* humor, and (2) the use of humor by employees as actual resistance to managerial control or change organizational process. Concertive control asserts that workers develop the means for their own control as self-managed teams. Their communication norms become the basis for rules that replace the centralized and hierarchical system of control. Concertive control humor occurs when in-group members use humor discourse to ensure all members of an organizational activity conform to the members' standards and norms. Resistance humor has been observed as an effective medium for preserving self- and in-group identity by resisting external control of the labor process. Perhaps nothing reflects the duality of humor more than the difference between concertive control humor and subversive humor.

Owen Hanley Lynch

See also Workplace Control; Workplace Productivity; Workplace Resistance

Further Readings

Collinson, D. L. (1988). Engineering humor: Masculinity, joking and conflict in shop floor relations. *Organization Studies, 9*(2), 181–199.

Collinson, D. L. (2002). Managing humor. *Journal of Management Studies, 39*(3), 269–288.

Holmes, J., & Marra, M. (2002). Having a laugh at work: How humor contributes to workplace culture. *Journal of Pragmatics, 34*, 1683–1710.

Holmes, J., & Marra, M. (2006). Humor and leadership style. *HUMOR: International Journal of Humor Research, 19*(2), 119–138.

Lynch, O. H. (2009). Kitchen antics: The importance of humor and maintaining professionalism at work. *Journal of Applied Communication Research, 37*, 444–464.

Lynch, O. H. (2010). Kitchen talk: Cooking with humor: In-group humor as social organization. *HUMOR: International Journal of Humor Research, 23*, 127–160.

Workplace Productivity

Although some people perceive humor to be a distraction from serious work, abundant research has identified multiple ways in which humor actually contributes to enhancing people's workplace productivity. This entry discusses the ways in which humor can increase workplace productivity.

Although it is often assumed among employers that humor is a distraction that diverts their employees' attention from achieving their serious work objectives, research has identified and described various benefits of humor at work—especially in regard to increasing workplace productivity. Empirical studies conducted in a range of different workplaces, including a hotel kitchen, police briefing rooms, health care settings, white-collar workplaces, factory floors, and many more, have found that rather than being a waste of time and resources, humor may actually perform a wide array of positive functions in a workplace context. One of these positive functions is the ability of humor to contribute to people's workplace productivity. The impact of humor on workplace productivity can be observed in several activities. Among the diverse positive functions of humor that have been identified by research studies in workplace contexts are constructing and maintaining collegial relationships, facilitating teamwork, relieving tensions and dealing with stress (e.g., between staff and management but also among colleagues), stimulating people's intellectual activity and preventing boredom and fatigue, sparking up discussions, and encouraging lateral thinking, or solving problems through an indirect approach. These functions are briefly discussed below.

Constructing and Maintaining Collegial Relationships

In its most basic function, humor facilitates the construction and maintenance of positive and collegial relationships among colleagues and contributes to creating a positive workplace atmosphere. These functions, in turn, may have positive effects on people's productivity at work. More specifically, friendly collegial relationships and a positive workplace atmosphere contribute to creating a place where people are more likely to enjoy their work, and as a consequence, they may be more satisfied with their jobs, are more likely to deal well with stress and change, and are less likely to be sick. In short, people who enjoy their work are generally reported to perform better.

Relieving Tensions and Dealing With Stress

Humor may also function as a valve to release stress and express anxiety or dissatisfaction with the management or any other aspect of workplace reality. In this context, humor may provide a relatively safe channel through which the status quo and "the way things are done around here" may be challenged and criticized. In other words, it may enable employees to voice their resistance toward institutional practices in acceptable ways. And wrapping a negative message (such as a complaint or criticism) in humor—especially when it is directed upward—makes it not only more acceptable but makes it also safer for those who have uttered it as they can always say that they were "just joking."

Stimulating Intellectual Activity and Preventing Boredom and Fatigue

Another positive function of humor and the laughter (or other responses) that it often triggers lies in its ability to spice up boring routines and make people more alert. This function is particularly useful in lengthy meetings or heated discussions. When used in these contexts, humor may encourage people's participation and involvement; it may also build bridges between opposing viewpoints, and it may facilitate the communication of potentially threatening messages (such as disagreements). Moreover, humor in the form of apparently nonsense suggestions (e.g., during a brainstorming activity) may encourage thinking from a new perspective, which may result in participants coming up with creative ideas and solutions.

Exploiting the Positive Functions of Humor

Given these various positive functions of humor, it is perhaps not surprising that this close link between humor, creativity, and ultimately productivity is also increasingly recognized by companies, which are developing ways of encouraging their employees to have fun and to use humor to shake up their everyday workplace routines. Often quoted examples of such concrete implementations include the establishment of "humor rooms" that provide employees with a dedicated space in the company where they can take some time out to play and enjoy themselves. The underlying motivation for these rooms is that after some fun and playtime, employees will be more creative and productive in performing their work-related tasks.

As the examples and discussion above have shown, humor at work is far from being superfluous. It performs a wide variety of positive functions in a workplace context and should thus be taken seriously. In particular, the various positive functions humor may perform to increase people's creativity and productivity illustrate why humor is a valuable asset in a workplace context.

Stephanie Schnurr

See also Humor and Relational Maintenance; Management

Further Readings

Brown, R. B., & Keegan, D. (1999). Humor in the hotel kitchen. *HUMOR: International Journal of Humor Research, 12*(1), 47–70.

Caudron, S. (1992). Humor is healthy in the workplace. *Personnel Journal, 71*, 63–68.

Clouse, R. W. (1995). Corporate analysis of humor. *Psychology, 32*(3–4), 1–24.

Holmes, J. (2007). Making humor work: Creativity on the job. *Applied Linguistics, 28*(4), 518–537.

Huang, K.-P., & Kuo, W.-C. (2011). Does humor matter? From organization management perspective. *Journal of Social Sciences, 7*(2), 141–145.

Mesmer-Magnus, J., Glew, D. J., & Viswesvaran, C. (2012). A meta-analysis of positive humor in the workplace. *Journal of Managerial Psychology, 27*(2), 155–190.

Morreall, J. (2009). Applications of humor: Health, the workplace, and education. In V. Raskin (Ed.), *The primer of humor research* (pp. 449–478). Berlin, Germany: Mouton de Gruyter.

Plester, B., & Sayers, J. (2007). Taking the piss: Functions of banter in the IT industry. *HUMOR: International Journal of Humor Research, 20*(2), 157–187.

Vinton, K. L. (1989). Humor in the workplace: It is more than telling jokes. *Small Group Research, 20*, 151–166.

Workplace Resistance

In the last 30 years, organizational scholars have systematically studied workplace humor to understand its role within organizational settings. Workplace humor has been studied from a variety of practical and theoretical perspectives, and it is clearly documented that humor functions as a form of workplace resistance. Workers use jokes and other forms of humorous interaction to resist managerial power and control and to create and maintain some amount of dignity in the workplace, whereas managers in a variety of white- and blue-collar industries use humor to resist unwanted stereotypes of particular occupations. Understanding how and why humor functions as workplace resistance is an essential element in any comprehensive work on humor, especially since most people will work for an organization at some point in their lives. Humor provides one communicative avenue for workers to resist managerial attempts to further control their work lives. This entry first provides a brief discussion of the theoretical underpinnings behind workplace humor in general and then highlights two types of humorous workplace resistance: illusory and substantive resistance.

Workplace Humor

The earliest forms of humor research explored the psychological reasons behind why people use humor rather than analyzing humorous interactions and comments. The consensus in the psychological literature was that people use humor for three main reasons: to relieve tension, to create a feeling of superiority over others, and to highlight incongruous events. Humor studies have explored the relationship between these three theories and have demonstrated the processes through which people use workplace humor to simultaneously achieve all three functions.

The type of workplace humor that is enacted is an outcome of the work environment. Scholars have analyzed how workers use humor to create, sustain, and transform the meanings of masculinity in industrial settings. In blue-collar workplaces, workers socially construct their identities in response to the power imbalance between themselves and management. Masculine forms of vulgar, offensive, and aggressive humor are common to this context, which is much different than the forms of humor occurring in corporate or white-collar contexts. Since white-collar workers are expected to use professional language, workers in corporate settings often use nonderogatory humorous statements to publicly disagree with authority figures and to engage in practical jokes with other coworkers. Although workplace bullying is found in many white-collar environments, many of these offenses are malicious personal attacks rather than attempts at nonmalicious workplace humor.

For example, many white-collar workers will use humor to disguise a disagreement with a boss during a meeting. Cloaking a disagreement with the boss in a humorous manner allows any coworkers who hear the statement to interpret it in a number of socially acceptable ways. Corporate workers also engage in a variety of practical jokes, pranks, or spoofs. These actions are to point out the silliness of many corporate policies and settings. Practical jokes can range from covering a coworker's desk with aluminum foil to sending a phony "You're Fired" e-mail. In short, workers can use humor as a form of workplace resistance without using racist, sexist, or other derogatory comments. Although nonderogatory humor does take place in blue-collar workplaces as well, the majority of blue-collar humor studies have looked at the negative, dysfunctional humor in these settings. The key component of workplace humor, however, is that other workers understand and share the meanings that emerge from the humorous actions.

Humor scholars analyze how individuals create shared meanings and how these meanings develop during interactions. Meanings are not simply static entities but rather are dynamic and fleeting ideas that people try to manage. Humor is viewed as one way to try and manage shared or ambiguous workplace meanings. Workplace humor, as a form of resistance, is also directly tied to context. Contexts include workplace relationships, the physical setting of the workplace, relevant economic, political, and cultural factors, and other unique characteristics of the workplace such as hierarchical ordering, promotion norms, and conflict management procedures. Studies have shown that the more ambiguous the workplace context, the more workers and managers will use humor to resist ambiguous policies, procedures, and rules. For example, workers sanction individuals and cause and diffuse conflict caused by coworker competition through humorous comments. Workplace humor can also enforce worker created norms, can call attention to differences between management and workers, and can differentiate groups of workers and their associated job duties.

In addition to highlighting differences, humor gives organizational employees the opportunity to express disagreement in a socially acceptable manner, which is a form of relieving tension. For example, expressing a potentially taboo topic in a humorous manner allows employees to discuss uncomfortable topics in front of management. This process can build cohesion and trust between the two groups, but it can also increase tension, anxiety, and blame shifting. Humor allows employees to probe the attitudes, perceptions, and feelings of coworkers and management in a nonthreatening manner. In defining boundaries, humor directed toward organizational outsiders can clarify both social and moral boundaries. As a coping device, humor helps individuals reduce anxiety over failure, frustration, and stress.

Within an organizational setting, humor has the ability to help people cope with problems, act as a tension release valve, offer a new perspective, and provide provisional relief from restrictive regulations. Although humor can be used to reduce tension, build relationships, socialize new members, save face, and manage conflict, it can also function to dissolve relationships, increase anxiety, demean others, and differentiate in-group from out-group. These contradictory processes often occur simultaneously and the outcomes are dependent on whose perspective is being presented. This dysfunctional humor is what scholars are referring to when they study subversive humor, gallows humor, or negative humor. Workers and managers who use humor for antisocial purposes often produce negative workplace outcomes. Negative humor can contribute to a divided work force, create conflict, and generate bitter feelings between coworkers and between workers and management. This humor can be used by both sides to strategically reinforce power relationships and lead to a wider hierarchical gap.

Humorous Workplace Resistance

Illusory Resistance

When workers think they are resisting managerial dictates with humorous actions they can actually be reinforcing them. Unless the status quo is changed due to a humorous action, the resistance that is achieved from it is illusory rather than substantive. For example, giving a boss a "World's Worst Boss" coffee mug, questioning a managerial policy in a joking manner, and even vandalizing company property to get a laugh from coworkers all leave the organizational power structure intact. These humorous actions do nothing to make substantive change in the workplace. Rather, when management allows, acknowledges, or even takes part in humorous acts initiated by workers, these actions reinforce the managerial norms that are already in place. Workers are bolstering their subordination through the very acts that they believe are resisting authority. An extended example will better explain this process.

Blue-collar workers can simultaneously resist managerially authorized forms of identity expression and reinforce negative public stereotypes associated with their workplace identities. Humor norms that include sexist, racist, or otherwise crude humor lead to the reification of negative stereotypes, and the resulting pattern of dirty humor reinforces media stereotypes regarding working-class values and behaviors. The humorous process objectifies the negative stigma associated with their work. The employees do not realize how dirty humor confirms negative public stereotypes of their work, nor do they recognize how dealing with insecurities through dirty humor only strengthens such stereotypes. To resist the threat of being labeled incompetent, these workers make crude jokes and vandalize company property. Superiority humor may relieve tension and resist stigma during immediate situations, but it objectifies the stigma of the employees and industry longitudinally.

Researchers have described how workers and managers in certain occupations actively search for ways to reframe the negative views attributed to their jobs. In these settings, humor is less a form of resistance against authority and more of an identity management mechanism that helps workers deal with an occupation with low societal prestige. In many cases, the acts deemed humorous by the in-group workers not only reinforce managerial norms of identity expression but they also strengthen society's negative stereotype associated with manual labor. For example, if a petroleum industry worker places an "Oil Field Trash: Make My Day" sticker on his truck, he may be attempting to be humorous, as explained by incongruity theory, but this action strengthens society's view of manual laborers as uneducated and aggressive, even if this is not the case. Although he is trying to resist negative societal attributions associated with his occupational identity, he is in fact supporting them. In short, when workplace humor maintains rather than challenges the status quo advocated by management or societal expectations, it may be argued that these humorous actions are actually in line with authoritative objectives and are not resisting anything.

Substantive Resistance

Substantive humorous resistance can be defined as any humorous action that leads to real change in the workplace. This change can include but is not limited to modifications in organizational policy; union organizing; direct and unambiguous challenges to organizational mission, vision, and values; and modification to organizational processes. Substantive changes can occur in both white- and blue-collar organizational settings, and the change can be a result of a humorous interaction initiated by management or workers.

The following subversive humorous functions and outcomes occur in the work environment. Workers use humor to socialize new organizational members to unsanctioned work norms like "working to the rule." This means that workers will play pranks on employees who are working too quickly because they feel if management notices the new employee's efficiency all other workers will be forced to pick up their work pace. This type of resistance, resistance to productivity, hits organizations in their most vulnerable spot: profit margins. Workers can also humorously disagree with organizational policies, and if they are persistent, they can get those policies altered. For instance, a corporate worker could say, "Another round of riveting performance evaluations will brighten my day." This strategic comment can start an employee-management dialogue that could end with a change in performance evaluation policy. Workers in manual labor and industrial settings have also used humor to remove restrictive break-time policies, to alter employee surveillance, and to increase their pay.

Workplace humor as resistance can function as a form of misbehavior, cynicism, deviance, and distance creation, but unless real organizational changes emerge in response to these behaviors, the individual who engages in workplace humor is achieving more of a psychological release rather than a substantive form of resistance. When organizations respond with policy-based or procedural changes that emanate from a humorous interaction, however, it can be argued that workplace humor is serving as a substantive form of resistance. Overall, employees and management both use humor to accomplish personal and organizational functions. They use humor to resist each other, to resist unfair organizational policies, and to resist negative societal stereotypes in real and illusory ways.

Zachary A. Schaefer

See also Hoax and Prank; Subversive Humor; Workplace Control; Workplace Humor; Workplace Productivity

Further Readings

Ackroyd, S., & Thompson, P. (1999). Only joking? From subculture to counter-culture in organizational relations. In S. Ackroyd & P. Thompson (Eds.), *Organizational misbehavior* (pp. 99–120). London: Sage.

Collinson, D. L. (1988). Engineering humor: Masculinity, joking and conflict in shop-floor relations. *Organization Studies, 9,* 181–199.

Lynch, O. H. (2007). *Humorous organizing: Revealing the organization as a social process.* Saarbrücken, Germany: VDM.

Lynch, O. H. (2009). Kitchen antics: The importance of humor and maintaining professionalism at work. *Journal of Applied Communication Research, 37,* 444–464.

Lynch, O. H. (2011). Cooking with humor: In-group humor as social organization. *HUMOR: International Journal of Humor Research, 23*(2), 127–159.

Schaefer, Z. A. (2013). Getting dirty with humor: Co-constructing workplace identities through performative scripts. *HUMOR: International Journal of Humor Research, 26*(4), 511–530. doi: 10.1515/humor-2013-0035

Tracy, S. J., Myers, K. M., & Scott, C. W. (2006). Cracking jokes and crafting selves: Sensemaking and identity management among human service workers. *Communication Monographs, 73,* 283–308.

X

Xeroxlore

Xeroxlore and *photocopylore* are two terms folklorists apply to a corpus of humorous traditional materials that circulate in physical form and are reproduced through mechanical means, such as photocopiers, scanners, mimeographs, typing, and printing. Much of this corpus has been shown to circulate in the United States, Great Britain, South America, and European nations. Like jokes, legends, and other folklore speech genres, xeroxlore texts have no known creator, are updated to remain current, and evolve into variants. Within the field of folklore, xeroxlore has been assumed to be an offshoot of the joke tradition. This entry discusses the content of xeroxlore, the major analytical approaches to it, its transmission and use in social life, and the role of graphics.

In form, xeroxlore is very heterogeneous and probably cannot be defined as a genre or subgenre based on structure. Some of the documented stories and jokes are not specific to xeroxlore but also circulate orally. In addition to narratives, there are parodies of official forms, lists of one-liners, and drawings. Graphics are often roughly drawn, crass, and obscene in their content. Sexual and scatological acts are portrayed explicitly, and no personage—political, religious, sports, management, or worker—escapes a scathing portrayal.

The introduction and improvement of printers, computers, faxes, and other technological means of replication enabled the mass dissemination of xeroxlore texts. Partly because these innovations were expensive when introduced and were located in businesses, workplaces became one of the primary sites of xeroxlore transmission. Drawings accompany or comprise a large percentage of xeroxlore texts, and disseminating graphics requires an easy means of mechanical reproduction. Since reproductive technologies, including the Internet, have become common in homes and small offices, the transmission of xeroxlore has become much more widespread. The content of xeroxlore may be affected by technology in a profound manner: narratives and jokes that are shared in xeroxlore are often longer than in oral tradition. Brevity has been a hallmark of American humor but this appears less true in xeroxlore.

Analysis of xeroxlore has been hampered by the reluctance of academic presses to publish the coarser materials. Consequently, the more "literary" examples (parodies of memos, letters, regulations, etc.) are probably overrepresented in publications while drawings are probably still underrepresented.

Alan Dundes described xeroxlore as work related, urban, and concerned with contemporary ills. Since xeroxlore contains sarcasm, irony, and even vitriol in jokes about incompetent bosses and malfunctioning bureaucracy, folklorists have tended to read it as subversive of corporate cultures. These two ideas—that xeroxlore expresses protest or subversion and that xeroxlore is particularly associated with the modern corporate work environment—have informed the scholarly discourse since then.

Arguments purporting that xeroxlore is subversive rest on several observations. The first is that the content of the texts often violates social rules and decorum, emphasizing the body and bodily functions

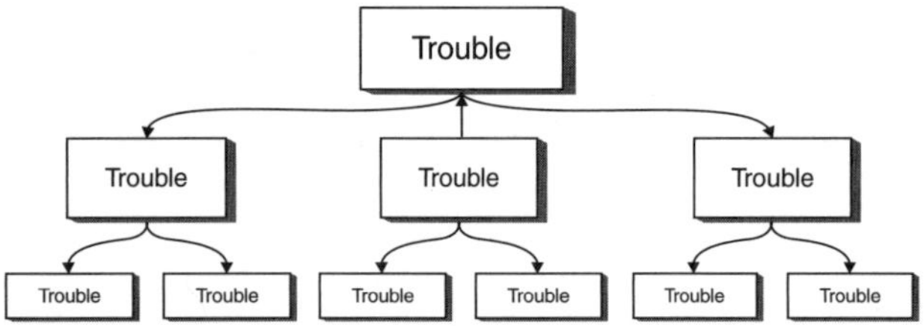

Figure 1 Xeroxlore Parodies Often Depend on the Reader's Familiarity With Corporate Forms

and reasserting earthiness and the carnivalesque. The second sign of subversion, according to folklorists, is that xeroxlore involves the personal use of regulated (company) property. Xeroxlore also represents misspent time (from the corporate viewpoint). It is the production of noninstrumental goods for individual and small group—not corporate—use.

Xeroxlore is transmitted in several ways. Like most folklore, it is shared within networks of friends and family. Coworkers and colleagues share xeroxlore at work but also take it home and share it with acquaintances outside work settings. In some business organizations, limited display of texts is possible in areas out of the public eye; people may post xeroxlore texts on bulletin boards, tape them to the sides of file cabinets, or hang them on cubicle walls.

A xeroxlore text is not re-created in performance in the same way as an urban legend or oral joke. Nonetheless, when people choose to pass on xeroxlore texts or display them, they and their audiences negotiate and enact rules of social interaction within the frames of humor. Because face-to-face interaction is not required in transmission of xeroxlore in the workplace, a joker may choose to give a text to an employee anonymously. Like humor generally, the initiator or joker may be motivated by anything from sharing laughter to a malicious desire to ridicule. A text can be placed on a desk quietly or inserted into an interoffice mail package and the joker may, like a practical joker, assume credit and responsibility retroactively or choose to remain hidden, depending on his or her motive and the reader's reaction.

Some people collect and maintain files of xeroxlore to select and share at opportune moments. Others take the trouble to retype or redraw texts that have become too faint or too unclear due to extraneous marks; they may alter or update the texts at that time.

The frequent use of graphics in xeroxlore texts offers some new areas for research. The interrelation of drawings, forms, and words in conveying the meanings of the texts bears study. Office parodies, for example, are dependent on the reader's familiarity with corporate forms, language style, and information conduits to create the joke. Additionally, many xeroxlore texts incorporate drawings to carry the message. At a gross level, the relation of the drawing to the text might be summarized in one of three ways. In one type, the drawing is "mere decoration" or extraneous (e.g., a caption that reads "I must be a mushroom, they keep me in the dark and feed me bullshit" below a picture of a mushroom). A second type requires both drawing and text in juxtaposition to create the meaning (e.g., a caption that reads "Before Work / After Work" below two cartoons of Garfield—the first looking sleek and happy, the second frazzled and upset). A third type consists of a drawing alone or accompanied by an extraneous caption (e.g., a mouse gives "the finger" to a large bird of prey swooping down to devour him).

Nancy P. Michael

See also Carnivalesque; Folklore; Internet Humor; Jokes; Scatology; Workplace Humor

Further Readings

Bell, L. M., Orr, C., & Preston, M. J. (1976). *Urban folklore from Colorado: Photocopy cartoons.* Ann Arbor, MI: University Microfilms International.

Dundes, A., & Pagter, C. R. (Eds.). (1978). *Work hard and you shall be rewarded: Urban folklore from the paperwork empire.* Bloomington: Indiana University Press.

Hatch, M. J., & Jones, M. O. (1997). Photocopylore at work: Aesthetics and collective creativity and the social construction of organizations. *Studies in Cultures, Organizations and Societies, 3,* 263–287.

Michael, N. (1995). Censure of a photocopylore display. *Journal of Folklore Research, 32,* 247–259.

Preston, M. J. (1994). Traditional humor from the fax machine. *Western Folklore, 53,* 147–170.

Roemer, D. M. (1994). Photocopylore and the naturalization of the corporate body. *Journal of American Folklore, 107,* 121–138.

Smith, P. (1984). *The complete book of office mis-practice.* London, UK: Routledge & Kegan Paul.

XIANGSHENG

Xiangsheng is a staged comic performance genre popular throughout China, with regional variations.

It is usually performed by two male actors but sometimes as a monologue (*dankou xiangsheng*), or with three or more actors. A few women have also recently taken up the performance form, initially in Taiwan but also on the mainland. The performance is scripted, with minimal action, costuming, or scenery, and the humor is derived from the dialogue and not from clowning. There are frequent references to Peking and local operas, or, in traditional scripts, to local street color such as vendor calls. Because of its reliance on puns, slang, references to current affairs, and historical allusions, it is often difficult to translate.

Xiangsheng is sometimes called "crosstalk" or "comic dialogue" in English, because it refers to two performers talking to each other in a comic way. Unlike much Western stand-up comedy, it is formally structured, with introduction, development, and conclusion, but still as a form it bears remarkable resemblance to Japanese *Manzai* or Western comic dialogues such as those of William "Bud" Abbott and Lou Costello. Perhaps each in its own way fulfills the basic social need for humor to help cope with the difficulties of life.

In the Republican period (1911–1949), *xiangsheng* flourished in Beijing and Tianjin, the two main cities of North China, where living standards were higher and the entertainment sector flourished. *Xiangsheng* actors came mainly from poor families, and the plots that they developed reflected working-class black humor, attacked the foibles of the rich and powerful, and mocked foreign colonials. However, they were not pointedly political as the performers aimed to amuse and retain loyal audiences on whom they depended for their livelihood.

After the Chinese Communist Party came to power in 1949, all actors were enrolled in collectives and educated in Marxism and Mao Zedong thought. "*Xiangsheng* modernization groups" were formed, to weed out unseemly language and subject matter from old scripts and to compile new ones in keeping with party objectives of building social cohesion and loyalty and modernizing the economy. Only a narrow range of subject matter was permitted. Artists struggled to survive under successive political campaigns. These culminated in the Cultural Revolution of 1966–1976 when no *xiangsheng* or other theatrical performances were allowed (apart from the eight model operas sanctioned by Mao Zedong's wife, Jiang Qing). At this time, many old scripts and recordings were destroyed and some performers were persecuted to death.

As Zhang Letian (2012) has pointed out, after 1949 the key problem for *xiangsheng* artists was how to use the weapon of sarcasm in a constructive way, as approved by the party, that is, directing it at "enemy" elements that the party targeted. Sometimes the actors ironically turned their weapon against themselves, making themselves out to be politically naive or backward. Unfortunately this laid them open to accusations of disloyalty to the party.

Notable *xiangsheng* writers and performers include Hou Baolin (1911–1993). He had trained to sing Peking Opera and was admired for his vocal technique. His work adhered to party policies but he was still able to extract humor from everyday situations, as can be seen in the following excerpt from his script titled "Getting Drunk" (*Zui jiu*). The second actor in this routine, which can be viewed on YouTube, was Guo Qiru (1900–1969):

Hou:	The more drunk someone is, the more he boasts. . . .
Hou [slurring speech and unsteady on feet]*:*	"Look at me, it wouldn't matter if I drank another half pint."
Guo:	It wouldn't matter at all. The other one wouldn't concede, what did he say?
Hou:	"Hey, half pint—still not drunk. Hey, when you talk, your tongue's shorter."
Guo:	His tongue wasn't working properly either.
Hou:	"Look, let's drink another bottle—drink another bottle."
Guo:	Oh, drinking from the bottle.
Hou:	"Let's drink from the bottle."
Guo:	If that's not boasting, what is?
Hou:	As soon as he hears that, this one goes, "Get this."
Guo:	What is he doing?
Hou:	He gets a torch out, slaps it on the table and switches it on. When he switches it on, a beam of light comes out.
Guo:	Oh! A column of light shines up.
Hou:	Ah, listen to what he says—is he drunk or not?
Guo:	What does he say?
Hou:	"Come on, climb up this column."
Guo:	That's a column for climbing up?
Hou:	How can you climb up it?
Guo:	What does he do?

Hou:	When he hears that. [looks up and down without speaking.]
Guo:	Just look at him.
Hou [makes dismissive gesture]*:*	"Don't try it on. I know [what you're up to]. If I climb up—if I climb up, you'll switch it off and I'll fall down."

(Translation by Jocelyn Chey.)

Economic reforms in the 1980s brought liberalization of thought and artistic expression. After a period when *xiangsheng* seemed on the decline, there has been a resurgence of the genre, not unconnected with the fact that it is eminently suited to dissemination on Youku and other video-sharing applications. Because of the updating of subject matter and stage conventions, many commentators now categorize *xiangsheng* as either traditional or contemporary. Contemporary works are generally sharper, more sarcastic, and more political than older ones, while retaining lightness of touch and popular appeal.

Some performers today have achieved rock-star eminence, such as Zhou Libo (b. 1967), who is based in Shanghai. Zhou's work, influenced by Western stand-up comedy, is largely unscripted monologues in Shanghai dialect, as well as Mandarin Chinese and even English, concerning contemporary issues and national and international affairs. Other immensely popular performers include Guo Degang (b. 1973) in Beijing. His stage performances were censored and studio closed in 2010 because his mockery of political leaders was too close to the bone. Another star performer in Northeast China is Xiao Shenyang (b. 1981), who uses local dialect for humorous effect and assumes a disconcerting androgynous persona to confuse the audience. Here is an excerpt from one of his monologues:

> Sometimes I was lucky in love. The other day, with my little bag, *dear friends* . . . As you know, I come from Northeastern China, somewhere near Shenyang . . . with my little bag, I was walking on the street. *Piapiade.* I was walking. *Piapiade.* As I was walking, a girl came up to me, who looked quite outstanding, and quite pretty. She was about 17 or 18 and excitedly asks me, "Bro, are you the guy who performs in the 'two-person act'? The guy named Xiao Shenyang?" I responded: "Yeah. So?" "Bro, every time I look at you, I think that I see the sea." How sweet she was, *dear friends!* That was the first time I was praised as "the sea"! I was so happy! I asked, "Do you like me? Are you falling in love with me?" This girl's answer was so irritating. "Bro, please don't misunderstand me," she said, "I get seasick. When I see the sea, I just throw up."

Translation by Steven Lin, with some adaptation by the author; see Alice Xin Liu (2009).

Jocelyn Chey

See also Comedy Ensembles; Dialect Humor; History of Humor: Modern and Contemporary China; History of Humor: Modern Japan; Improv Comedy; Social Interaction; Stand-Up Comedy; Verbal Humor; *Xiangsheng*, History of

Further Readings

Chuantong xiangsheng ji [Traditional *xiangsheng* collection]. (1981). Shanghai, China: Shanghai wenyi chubanshe.

Du, W. (1998, June). *Xiaopin*: Chinese theatrical skits as both creatures and critics of commercialisation. *The China Quarterly, 151,* 382–399.

Goldkorn, J. (2004). *Stifled laughter: How the communist party killed Chinese humour.* Retrieved March 27, 2012, from http://www.danwei.org/tv/stifled_laughter_how_the_commu.php

Hou, B. (1980). *Xiangsheng* and me—An interview with Hou Baolin. In M. Dun (Ed.), *Chinese literature* (p. 101). Beijing, China: Foreign Language Press.

Link, P. (1984). The genie and the lamp: Revolutionary *xiangsheng.* In B. McDougall (Ed.), *Popular Chinese literature and performing arts in the People's Republic of China, 1949–1979* (pp. 83–111). Berkeley: University of California Press.

Link, P. (2007). The crocodile bird: *Xiangsheng* in the early 1950s. In J. Brown & P. G. Pickowicz (Eds.), *Dilemmas of victory: The early years of the People's Republic of China* (pp. 207–231). Cambridge, MA: Harvard University Press.

Liu, A. X. (2009). *Who the hell is Xiao Shenyang?* Retrieved March 27, 2012, from http://www.danwei.org/video/post_37.php

Zhang, L. (2012). Satire and humour in contemporary Chinese art. In C. Roberts (Ed.), *Go figure: Contemporary Chinese portraiture* (pp. 58–72). Canberra, Australia: National Portrait Gallery.

Websites

The complete performance of the Xiangsheng routine "Getting Drunk" (*Zui jiu*): http://www.youtube.com/watch?v=2IGTExwACYA

Xiangsheng, History of

One of the most popular humor forms in China throughout the last century and up to the present time is the verbal art of "crosstalk," the name being the conventional (flawed) translation of the Chinese term *xiangsheng*, literally "face and voice," indicating that the art form primarily emphasizes facial expression and vocal skills. Crosstalk is one of a large number of Chinese folk oral performance literature forms in the category of *quyi* ("vocal arts," or sometimes translated as "minor performing arts"). Westerners seeing the form for the first time are usually strongly reminded of American stand-up comedy, particularly the classic American comedy duos such as Dean Martin and Jerry Lewis, or 1960s TV acts like Rowan and Martin and the Smothers Brothers. Indeed, the surface similarity is striking: two performers stand up on a stage in front of a live audience and engage in rapid-fire humorous repartee, with their interaction following the tried-and-true formula of a straight man acting as an exasperated foil to the muddle-headedness of an illogical clowner. However, whereas much American standup is structured as a series of jokes on different topics, a crosstalk performance consists of a set routine with a general theme that sets up a context for comedic interplay. The closest parallel would be Abbott and Costello's famous "Who's on First?" routine, which is very similar in style and structure to a crosstalk piece.

The content of crosstalk concentrates on language and wordplay. Puns, homonyms, dialects, idioms, and double entendre abound. Performers are expected to have mastered four basic aspects of performance: *shuo* (speaking ability), *xue* (imitation skills), *dou* (joking ability), and *chang* (singing). A typical performance might involve parodies of Peking Opera, verbal jousting with word games, reciting of outlandish tongue-twisters, Chinese character puzzles, twisted versions of pop songs, or an astounding verbal memory feat called *guankou*—"talk strings" or "word fountains," in which the performer recites lists of hundreds of geographic place names or regional dishes with dizzying rapid-fire delivery.

The origins of crosstalk date from the late Qing Dynasty, following the death of the Xianfeng emperor in 1861, when a ban on entertainment during the mourning period forced out-of-work opera performers out into the street to earn their livelihood. The result was a kind of ad hoc street theater involving lively dialogues and slapstick humor to attract the crowds. In the early part of the 20th century, the art form gradually moved into the teahouses and theaters as a new vocal performing art in and of itself.

The political upheavals and social disruptions of the 1930s and 1940s made it difficult for the art form to develop in a mature fashion, and crosstalk humor became increasingly earthy, bawdy, and politically incorrect, lampooning corrupt officials, country bumpkins, prostitutes, and various aspects of polite society. It is said that if a woman with children inadvertently wandered into a crowd of male spectators watching a performance, the performers would stop the performance, bow to the woman and politely suggest that she leave the area.

When Mao Zedong took power in 1949, crosstalk found itself at a crisis point. The traditional pieces that developed in the turbulent previous decades were considered too unhealthy and politically out of step with the new proletarian communist ideology. A group of writers and performers was assembled to revise and clean up the crosstalk repertoire to provide humor performances for the new society. The task force was spearheaded by popular performer Hou Baolin, who would go on to become the most beloved crosstalk performer of all time, producing a body of classic recordings that are still listened to by Beijing cab drivers.

During the Cultural Revolution, crosstalk became a sterile propaganda tool, with performers instructed to write pieces that emphasized *gesong*, "praise" for the new society, rather than *fengci*, "satire." The result was a decade of decidedly unfunny pieces with titles like "Emulate [Proletarian Model Citizen] Lei Feng," and "Chairman Mao's Policies Are Correct." Mao Zedong himself was a fan of crosstalk, and for a time invited crosstalk performers to perform at private parties every Saturday evening at his residence in Zhongnanhai. Ironically, however, Mao had no interest in the new, sanitized, and politically correct pieces, requesting that the actors perform the traditional, down-to-earth repertoire.

After the fall of the Gang of Four after the death of Mao, crosstalk regained its former vitality. With new acceptable targets for satire—the "White-boned Demon" (Mao's wife), and the Gang of Four, and the excesses of the era's political movements—crosstalk performers now could offer audiences genuinely cathartic laughter. Crosstalk flourished, and a new crop of young performers sprang up who were able to address new social topics and experiment with new styles of performance.

As television became part of Chinese life in the 1980s, crosstalk evolved from its theatrical roots into a form more suited for the new electronic medium. Many of the traditional pieces were quite long, up to an hour in length, and in order to meet stringent time demands of television, long introductions and digressions had to be pruned. Though many aficionados found the resulting pieces lacking in the subtlety and complexity of the traditional performances, a single crosstalk show could now be watched and enjoyed by hundreds of millions of viewers, and is now a ritual part of the annual CCTV Spring Festival Gala.

David Moser

See also History of Humor: Classical and Traditional China; History of Humor: Modern and Contemporary China; *Xiangsheng*

Further Readings

Link, P. (1984). The genie and the lamp: Revolutionary Xiangsheng. In B. McDougall (Ed.), *Popular Chinese literature and performing arts in the People's Republic of China, 1949–1979*. Berkeley: University of California Press.

Link, P. (2007). The crocodile bird: Xiangsheng in the early 1950s. In J. Brown & P. G. Pickowicz (Eds.), *Dilemmas of victory: The early years of the People's Republic of China*. Cambridge, MA: Harvard University Press.

Moser, D. (1989). Lao She and Xiangsheng. *Spring and Autumn Papers, Graduate Journal of the Center for Chinese Studies*, University of Michigan, Vol. V, No. 1.

Moser, D. (2004). *Stifled laughter: How the communist party killed Chinese humor: A history of Chinese crosstalk*. Retrieved from http://www.danwei.org/tv/stifled_laughter_how_the_commu.php

XIEHOUYU

The *xiehouyu* is a common figure of speech in standard Chinese and many dialects. The term is often translated into English as "a proverb with the second part suspended" but is better left in Chinese as it is a unique linguistic form. Herbert Giles, an early China scholar and dictionary compiler, defined *xiehouyu* as "set phrases of which only the protasis is uttered, and the apodosis is understood by the speaker, not literally but in a punning sense" (Giles, 1912/1967, entry for character no. 4361, quoted in Sun, 1981, p. 521). Many *xiehouyu* contain no puns, but certainly contain humor. This arises from the incongruity of the protasis or second part being understood from an unexpected angle. Adding to the trangressive quality of the humor, many *xiehouyu* are very colloquial or even vulgar.

The form has been compared to Cockney rhyming slang (in which, for instance, "my old China" stands for "plate/mate"), but the latter depends entirely on rhyme, whereas *xiehouyu* draw their humor from double entendre. However, the two figures of speech are both ways of sharing humor with an in-group. Cockney rhyming slang arose from street gang code words. *Xiehouyu* draw on shared common references and historical and literary allusions not immediately comprehensible to outsiders. When used in conversation, the hearers are expected to recognize the allusion and acknowledge complicity in understanding with smiles or laughter ("Wink, wink, nudge, nudge, know what I mean?").

In December 1970, American journalist Edgar Snow interviewed Mao Zedong, chairman of the Chinese Communist Party. In an article published in *Life* on April 30, 1971, Snow wrote, "As he courteously escorted me to the door, he said he was not a complicated man, but really very simple. He was, he said, only a lone monk walking in the world with a leaky umbrella." Mao was in fact using a common *xiehouyu* that revealed he was by no means the uncomplicated, simple man that he told Snow he was.

Mao used only the first part of the *xiehouyu*, leaving Snow to intuit the second, but it seems he failed to grasp the reference or the full meaning. The complete saying is: *Lao heshang da san: wu fa wu tian* 老和尚打傘：無髮無天 (literally, when the old monk opens his umbrella: there is no hair and no sky). A Chinese Buddhist monk is tonsured so that he has no hair, and when he opens his umbrella he obscures the sky. The deeper meaning is understood by a hearer who knows that *fa* 髮 (hair) is a homonym for *fa* 法 (law) and that *tian* 天 can refer to the sky or to Heaven or God. The real meaning is therefore that neither law nor moral principle apply to the situation or person under discussion.

Xiehouyu are common in everyday usage. For instance, one might tell another person not to interfere by saying, "Stop acting like a dog catching mice," using the first part of the *xiehouyu: Gou na haozi: duo guan xianshi* (literally, Dog catches mice: excessive meddling in irrelevant matters). Since catching mice is the proper business of cats, if a dog took up this practice, it would be meddling in the cat's affairs. The second part is not expressed but its meaning is understood by the listener.

The wit of some *xiehouyu* may be appreciated only by those with a modicum of education in Chinese history and literature because they involve cultural references. These need more explanation for non-Chinese. One such equates roughly to the English expression, "to kill two birds with one stone": *Zhang Fei tai Cao Cao: yi ju liang de* 張飛抬曹操：一舉兩得 (literally, Zhang Fei carries Cao Cao: there is one lift for two De's). Most Chinese are familiar with the classical historical novel *San guo yanyi* (Romance of the Three Kingdoms), a 14th-century work still popular today and immortalized in drama and opera. General Zhang Fei and the warlord Cao Cao are two of the main characters in this novel. Their second, unofficial names were respectively Yi-de 翼德 and Meng-de 孟德. If Zhang Fei carried Cao Cao, there would be two (people named) De involved in one lift. The listener would know this without it being stated and would also understand that the character used in both personal names De 德 was a homonym for *de* 得, which means to gain or achieve something. From this he or she would derive the meaning as one action achieving two results.

Xiehouyu are found in many dialects as well as in Standard or Mandarin Chinese. These are not usually intelligible to people from other dialect groups. Cantonese dialect provides many examples, including, for instance, *A tsai yam sha shi: yau hei kong m cheut* (literally, a dumb man drinks sarsaparilla [carbonated soft drink]: there is gas but he cannot speak of it). In Cantonese the word *hei* 氣 (Standard Chinese *qi*) has two meanings, referring both to gas or air and also to anger, so the intuited meaning of the second part of this xiehouyu is "to swallow one's anger."

Jocelyn Chey

See also Anti-Proverb; Aphorism; Epigram; Irony; Maxim; Puns

Further Readings

Chengyu xiehouyu daquan [Encyclopedia of proverbs and *xiehouyu*]. Retrieved March 15, 2012, from http://cy.5156edu.com/cyxhy.html

Chey, J., & Milner Davis, J. (Eds.). (2011). *Humour in Chinese life and letters: Classical and traditional approaches.* Hong Kong, China: Hong Kong University Press.

Giles, H. A. (1967). *A Chinese-English dictionary* (2nd rev. ed.). Taipei, Taiwan: Ch'eng-wen. (Original work published 1912)

Ma, J.-H. S. (2009). *Chinese* xiehouyu*: Classical and contemporary folk expressions and allegories.* Hong Kong, China: Commercial Press.

Sun, C. C. (1981). *As the saying goes: An annotated anthology of Chinese and equivalent English sayings and expressions, and an introduction to* Xiehouyu *(Chinese wit).* St. Lucia, Australia: Queensland University Press.

Appendix A

CHRONOLOGY

Date(s)	***Event(s)/Publication***
2600 BCE	First recorded political joke in Egypt about how to entertain a pharaoh.
2055–1650 BCE	*The Tale of the Shipwrecked Sailor* and *The Mouse as Vizier* are written in ancient Egypt's Middle Kingdom.
ca. 2000 BCE	Inscription of *The Epic of Gilgamesh*, probably the oldest written narrative, found in Sumer. It includes comic scenes.
1999–1001 BCE	The story of "The Poor Man of Nippur" is documented from this millennium. It is the clearest example of humorous literature in Babylon.
1887–1064 BCE	(20th dynasty) *The Contendings of Horus and Seth* is written in Egypt.
1499–1401 BCE	Queen Hatshepsut of Egypt has the Deir el-Bahri temple complex built, in which a bas-relief depicts the Queen of Punt as obese.
1298–1187 BCE	(19th dynasty) *The Instructions of Dua-Khety*, also known as *The Satire of the Trades*, is written in ancient Egypt. This work makes fun of various jobs performed by common workers.
1292–1069 BCE	(Ramessid period) The Turin Erotic Papyrus is created. This ancient Egyptian work displays crude and sexual humor. It gets its name from the Museum of Egyptology in Torino, Italy.
999–699 BCE	The Chinese *Book of Poetry* is compiled, containing the earliest comic poems in Chinese literature.
999–1 BCE	*The Illiterate Doctor of Isin*, a text that uses humor for didactical purposes, is composed in Babylon.
750 BCE	Founding of Rome.
620 BCE	Presumed date of birth of Aesop, an ancient Greek author of fables.
599–501 BCE	In this century, material from the stories of the wise Assyrian Ahiqar are discovered on an Aramaic papyrus. These stories become much of the base work for the later written *The Aesop Romance*.
551–479 BCE	Lifetime of Chinese philosopher Confucius.
550–375 BCE	Time span during which comic images are painted on vases in Athens.
540–450 BCE	Period of Doric Comedy. Epicharmus writes numerous comedies in ancient Greece.
501 BCE	First drama competition that included satyr plays in the Festival of Dionysus in Athens.

Date(s)	*Event(s)/Publication*
500–422 BCE	First works in Old Comedy in ancient Greece; comedic works by Susarion, Chionides, Magnes, Crates, Cratinus, and Eupolis are written. None of these has been preserved.
499–401 BCE	Satyr plays featuring a chorus of satyrs and based in Greek mythology start to be written. They contain themes of, among other things, drinking, overt sexuality (often including large phallic props), pranks, and general merriment.
487–486 BCE	First known comedies are performed at Festival of Dionysus in Athens, marking the beginning of the traditional Old Comedy period.
440–437 BCE	The leading Greek politician Cleon attempts to prosecute Aristophanes for his plays' political statements.
430 BCE	Mimes become popular. The most famous are by Sophron, of Syracuse, Italy, the author of prose dialogues in the Doric dialect.
427–287 BCE	First theories of humor are written: Plato's (427–347 BCE) *Filebus,* Aristotle's (384–322 BCE) *Poetics,* Theophrastus's (372–287 BCE) *Moral Characters.*
411 BCE	Aristophanes (ca. 447–ca. 385 BCE) writes *Lysistrata,* one of the earliest examples of political humor.
404 BCE	Traditional end of Old Comedy period in ancient Greece.
403–ca. 321 BCE	Middle Comedy period in ancient Greece.
400–300 BCE	Phlyax plays (phlyakes or hilarotragedy) are common. These are plays of a burlesque dramatic form featuring heavy use of masks that developed in the Greek colonies of Magna Graecia.
399–301 BCE	*The Longer Rules*, which contains probably the first attempt at classifying laughter as good or bad, is written by Basil the Great in Byzantium.
342/341–291/290 BCE	Menander, a pupil of Theophrastus, writes more than 100 plays in ancient Greece. Only one (known as *Dyskolos*, *The Misanthrope*, or *The Bad-Tempered Man*) is preserved nearly complete.
ca. 335 BCE	Aristotle writes *Poetics*, the first known book to examine systematically laughter and the comic.
321 BCE	New Comedy begins in ancient Greece. It is traditionally believed to have begun after the death of Alexander the Great. Love is a central subject of this period's works.
300 BCE	Fabula Atellana, a tradition of farces, parodies, and satires influenced by late Greek models, becomes common in Rome.
285 BCE	First Alexandrine commentary on Aristophanes is written in Greece, by Lycophron.
ca. 250 BCE	Menippus, a Greek cynic philosopher, writes satires mixing prose and verse.
250–240 BCE	Mimeiambics, realistic mimes in choliambic verse often depicting bawdy situations, are common. A papyrus containing some 700 readable lines of mimeiambics by Herodas (or Herondas) is extant from this time.
240 BCE	Native Italian dramas, such as Atellan farces, phlyakes, and Fescennine verses, dominate the Roman stage.
ca. 210–160 BCE	Roman Comic Theater period.
193–160 BCE	Lifetime of Dongfang Shuo, one of the most famous court jesters in Chinese history.

Date(s)	*Event(s)/Publication*
184 BCE	Death of Roman playwright Plautus.
159 BCE	Death of Roman playwright Terence.
146 BCE	Roman conquest of Greece.
143 BCE	Traditional date of the end of New Comedy.
100 BCE	Marcus Tullius Cicero writes *De oratore,* which contains a discussion of humor.
18 BCE	Roman lyric poet and satirist Horace writes *Ars poetica.*
0 CE	Traditional date of the birth of Christ.
ca. 75	Petronius writes *Satyricon,* possibly the first surviving Western novel with sophisticated satirical humor in it.
95	Roman orator Quintilian writes *Insitutio oratoria* (The Institutes of Oratory).
101–199	During this century, *The Aesop Romance* is written. It is a highly fictional biography of the wily and cunning Aesop.
120–180	Greek writer Lucian writes *Dialogues of the Gods, Dialogues of the Dead, Lucius or The Ass* (source of Apuleius's *Golden Ass*), and *The True Story* (ancestor of modern science fiction).
ca. 160	Roman writer Apuleius writes *The Golden Ass.*
165	Lucian writes the satire *The Passing of Peregrinus.*
ca. 220	*Xiaolin* (Forest of Laughter), the first collection of jokes in Chinese literature, is written. It is usually ascribed to Handan Chun.
329–379	Life of Basil of Caesarea, a Greek bishop who writes over 300 *Letters,* condemning laughter under any circumstance.
347–420	Life of Saint Jerome. He writes the *Letters* in which he condemns laughter.
387	John Chrysostom writes *The Homilies on the Statues to the People of Antioch,* regarding the citizens of Antioch ridiculing statues. Claims that laughter is diabolical.
401–599	*Philogelos* (The Laughter-Lover) is written. It is a collection of about 265 jokes written in Greek.
410	Sack of Rome by the Visigoths.
425	Eastern Roman Emperor Theodosius and Western Roman Emperor Valentinian forbid comedies and circus games on Sundays and on religious holidays.
480–547	Life of Saint Benedict from Norcia (founder of the Benedictine order), who forbade laughter and humor in his Holy Rule for the Benedictine order.
491–518	Choricius, of Gaza, Greek sophist and rhetorician, writes an apology of laughter, against its Christian detractors. First recorded mention of the healing properties of laughter.
ca. 500	Approximate beginning of the Middle Ages in Europe. Humor has a small place in society and is not widely recorded. It is often seen in gargoyles, margins of manuscripts, feasts, and carnivals.
501–599	During this century, the *Ioca monachorum* is written, in a question-and-answer format with "funny" questions.
501–599	The text of the *Shishuo xinyu* (New Account of Tales of the World), which records the deeds of famous people from the 3rd to 5th centuries, emerges in China. The content is similar to that of the *Forest of Laughter.*

Date(s)	*Event(s)/Publication*
501–599	Buddhism arises in China.
524	Boethius, in his commentary of Porphiry, defines laughter as the "proprium" of man, an Aristotelian definition meaning a property common to all the members of a class.
540–604	Pope Gregory I the Great claims that only two types of laughter are acceptable: that against evil and that in praise of good.
542	First outbreak of the plague.
570	Birth of the Islamic prophet Mohammed, who records incidents of prophetic humor in the hadith.
581–618	The reign of the Sui dynasty in China, during which an official called Hou Bai is ascribed to have written the next collection of humorous anecdotes after the *Forest of Laughter.*
601–699	King Mahendravarmana writes *Mattavilasa* (Drunken Sports), a short one-act Sanskrit play, in India.
601–699	In China, the text of the *Forest of Laughter* is first recorded in the bibliography chapter of the Sui dynasty's history.
712	Japan's oldest chronicle, the *Kojiki* (Record of Ancient Matters), is presented to the empress. It contains Japan's first recorded comedy performance, a myth surrounding the sun goddess, Amaterasu Ōmikami.
712	Death of the Arabic poet Umayyad 'Umar Ibn Abī Rabī'a, who used humor and satire in love verses.
723	The earliest possible date that the extant version of Chinese *Qiyan lu* (Record of Bright Smiles) found in the caves of Dunhuang can be from.
742–814	Lifetime of Charlemagne, who gathered the best of literati from around the world. Their humor survives today in various records from the time.
801–899	Bhatta Jayanta writes *Agamadambara* (Much Ado About Religion) in India.
814	Death of Abu Nuwas, who is considered the most prominent figure of humorous Arab poetry.
868	Death of al-Jāhiz, the Arabic author of the famous *Kitāb al-Bukhalā'* (Book of Misers), which consists of social critiques in the form of funny stories.
891	Liu Hsieh's Chinese text *The Literary Mind and the Carving of Dragons* is known to have been read in Japan. This represents the first text in Japan to have discussed a theory of humor.
892	Japan's oldest dictionary, the *Shinsen Jikyo,* defines the Japanese word for funny as "an ugly appearance, so funny that one cries aloud."
935–1002	The Benedictine canoness Hroswitha of Gandersheim lives and writes a religious set of plays to create an alternative to Terence's licentious works.
ca. 1000	Old English riddles are collected in the *Exeter Book.*
ca. 1000	The first record of personal humor in Japan in Sei Shōnagon's *Makura no Sōshi* (Pillow Book).
ca. 1052	Sketches that include obvious farce appear in *Sarugaku,* a form of theater that is the origin of the Japanese comic theater *Kyōgen.*
1053–1140	Lifetime of Abbot Toba in Japan. A Buddhist priest known for his whimsical cartoon scrolls that heavily influenced contemporary Japanese comic art.

Date(s)	Event(s)/Publication
1096–1141	Hugh of St. Victor, a German theologian, distinguishes between *gaudium* (Latin, joy) and *risus* (Latin, laughter). He considered *gaudium* good, *risus* bad.
1101–1199	Vatsaraja's *Hasyacudamani* (The Crest-Jewel of Laughter) is written in India.
1101–1199	*The Executioner or the Doctor,* a Byzantine satire targeting medical practitioners, is written by Theodore Prodromos.
1115–1180	John of Salisbury (theologian, scholar, student of Abelard) accepts modest cheerfulness while decrying excessive jesters.
1117–1200	Ibn al-Jawzī's *Akhbār al-ḥamqā wa al-mughaffalīn* (Stories of Fools and Madmen), an Arabic collection of jokes and anecdotes, is written.
1138	*Baucis et Traso,* a 12th-century renaissance Latin comedy, is written anonymously in France.
1148	The Flemish *Ysengrimus,* an early Latin fabliau and mock epic, is written. This is also an early medieval form of humor, the beast fable.
1150–1200	Latin comedies are prevalent in the Renaissance of the 12th century.
1170	*Roman de Renart* is written, with anthropomorphic animal tales and satire. This is another example of a beast fable.
1180	*Speculum stultorum* is written. It is a satire of monks that involves a donkey (Brunellus) that thinks its tail is too short and travels to several universities (Salerno, Paris) seeking remedies. It is also considered to be a beast fable.
1199	First annual *Warai-Ko* laughter ritual is held in Hofu City, Yamaguchi Prefecture, Japan. It still takes place today.
ca. 1200	The fabliaux, short comic verse tales composed for listening audiences, begin to appear anonymously. They are common in France during the 12th, 13th, and early 14th centuries.
1201–1499	*Renga*, a Japanese game of linking short witty verses, is played and later develops into the poetic genre of *Haiku* and then into the comic genre of *Senryū.*
1226–1240	Jacques de Vitry, French cardinal and theologian, writes his sermons, which contain the first collection of *exempla*, or brief, often funny moral anecdotes used in sermons.
1230	The *Carmina Burana,* a Goliardic collection of poems dating back to the late 11th and 12th centuries, is written down. It is a Bavarian text, parts of which are humorous and/or licentious.
1248	Rutebeuf, a French poet, writes *Poèmes de l'infortune* (Poems of Misfortune), with the themes of poverty, cold, gambling, women, and debauchery.
1260	Rutebeuf's *Le dit de l'herberie* (The Tale of the Herb Market) is written.
1265–1321	Lifetime of Dante Alighieri, author of the *Divine Comedy.*
1271–1368	The reign of the Yuan dynasty in China, during which a collection of humorous texts called the *Shuofu* (Outskirts of Texts) is compiled, where Lü Benzhong's *Xuanqu lu* (Records of Laughing) and Tian Hezi's *Shanxue ji* (Collection of Good Jokes) are both preserved.
1281	*Il novellino* (The Hundred Old Tales), an anonymous collection of 100 stories, some humorous, is written.
1300s	Luo Guanzong writes *Romance of the Three Kingdoms* in China.

Date(s)	*Event(s)/Publication*
1320	Robert de Basevorn, the author of *The Form of Preaching,* a treaty on preaching published in Paris, says that humor is acceptable in a sermon at most three times.
1320	Watriquet de Couvins writes *The Three Ladies of Paris,* marking the approximate end of the genre of fabliaux.
1330	Franco Sacchetti writes *Il trecentonovelle* (The Three Hundred Short Stories).
1349–1351	Giovanni Boccaccio writes *The Decameron,* which consists of a hundred mostly comic/satirical tales.
ca. mid-1300s	The term *kyōgen* ("mad words") is first used to describe stage art in Japan.
1368–1644	The Ming period in China; collecting humorous stories becomes popular among educated people.
ca. 1400	*The Bunbuku Chagama* (The Badger That Turned Into a Tea Kettle), one of the most amusing Japanese folktales featuring a trickster, emerges.
1400–1500	The Renaissance begins in Italy.
1401–1453	The *Comedy of Katablattas* is written in Byzantium; it is ascribed to John Argyropoulos.
1431–1445	Council of Basel, which bans in 1435 the Feast of Fools and Feast of Asses.
1453	Fall of Constantinople, the capital of the Eastern Roman Empire, to the Ottomans.
ca. 1470	Lodovico Carbone writes *Cento trenta novelle o facetie* (One Hundred Thirty Short Stories or Jokes), a jestbook in the Italian vernacular.
1478	William Caxton publishes Geoffrey Chaucer's *The Canterbury Tales,* one of the earliest texts printed in English.
1492	"Discovery" of America by Christopher Columbus.
1492–1549	Lifetime of Marguerite de Navarre, Francis I's sister, who wrote (but died before completing) a spin-off of *The Decameron* called *The Heptameron.*
1501–1599	The term *clown* comes into use.
1508	Aldus Manuntius prints the first modern edition of the Greek text of Aristotle's *Poetics.*
1509	Desiderius Erasmus (Erasmus of Rotterdam), a major humanist, publishes *Praise of Folly,* a satire.
1511	Vettore Fausto publishes *De comoedia libellus* (Booklet Concerning Comedy).
1516	Thomas More, English Renaissance humanist, publishes *Utopia.*
1518	Niccolò Machiavelli writes *La mandragola* (The Mandrake Root), one of the earliest plays with *commedia dell'arte*–like characters and plot.
1526	*A Hundred Mery Talys* (Anonymous), the first of the "Shakespeare jestbooks," is published.
1528	Baldesar Castiglione publishes *The Book of the Courtier.*
1528	The Council of Sens forbids the use of stories for laughter in preaching.
1532	*The Prince* by Machiavelli is published.
ca. 1532	*Tales and Quicke Answeres,* one of the earliest known English jestbooks, is published.

Date(s)	***Event(s)/Publication***
1532–1564	François Rabelais's five-volume mock epic *The Life of Gargantua and of Pantagruel* is published in France.
1545	First record of the formation of an Italian professional acting troupe, at Padua.
1548	Italian literary theorist Francesco Robortello publishes his *Treatises on Humor.*
1550	Vincenzo Maggi publishes *De ridiculis* (Concerning the Ridiculous).
1550–1627	Lifetime of Zhao Nanxing, who compiles a collection of humorous Chinese texts called *Xiaozan* (Appraisal of Jokes).
1551	Italian poet and author Girolamo Muzio publishes his *Dell'arte poetica* (On Poetics).
1555–1605	Lifetime of Chinese Jiang Yingke, who compiles a collection of hitherto forgotten humorous texts called *Xue Tao xiaoshuo* (Xue Tao's Stories).
1558	Queen Elizabeth I begins her reign. The Elizabethan era begins in England.
1561	Italian scholar Giulio Cesare Scaligero publishes *Poetices libri VII* (Seven Books on Poetics), which deals with humor.
1562	Italian poet and scholar Giangiorgio Trissino's *Poetica* is published in full, posthumously. It articulates an Aristotelian theory of literature, including comedy.
1565	First references to *commedia dell'arte* characters (e.g., Zanni and Pantalone) in connection with acting companies of *commedia dell'arte.*
1568	First mention of the Gelosi Company of *commedia dell'arte* in Milan, Italy.
1570	Italian literary critic Lodovico Castelvetro publishes *On the Art of Poetry.*
1570	Paintings depicting *commedia dell'arte* appear.
1571	Gelosi Company of *commedia dell'arte* makes its first visit to Paris, where it acts at the house of the Duke of Nevers before Charles IV. Company of Zan Ganassa (Alberto Naseli) also in Paris this year. This marks the beginning of foreign touring by *commedia* troupes and first illustration of the character Arlecchino.
1572	Bernardo Pino da Cagli publishes *Breve considerazione intorno al componimento de la comedia de' nostri tempi* (A Short Consideration Concerning the Composition of Comedy in Our Times) in Italy.
1573	English playwright Ben Jonson is born. His comedy of humors is the first forum in which humor and the comic are systematically linked.
1574–1646	Lifetime of Feng Menglong, who produced the most famous humorous texts collection of the Ming period in China: *Xiaofu* (Treasury of Laughs).
1575	Gelosi Company is invited to Venice, Italy, to play for French King Henri III (the third son of Catherine de Medici).
1576	Henry III of France requests the Italian company of *commedia dell'arte* he had seen in Venice to perform in Paris.
1579	Laurent Joubert publishes his *Traité du ris* (Treatise on Laughter), the earliest substantial work on laughter in the vernacular.
1587	Confidenti Company of *commedia dell'arte* performs in Spain.
1591	English playwright John Lyly publishes *Endymion.*
1594	Robert Greene, an Elizabethan playwright, publishes *Friar Bacon.*

Date(s)	*Event(s)/Publication*
1594	Sforza Oddi, a lawyer from Perugia, Italy, publishes *Erofilomachia,* a comedy that was widely successful in the Renaissance and the Baroque periods.
1595	English author Philip Sidney publishes *An Apology for Poetry.*
1595	Around this time, William Shakespeare's *A Midsummer Night's Dream* is first performed, as well as *Romeo and Juliet.*
1598	Ben Jonson publishes *Every Man out of His Humor*, in which he defines a metaphorical application of the theory of humors to comedy.
1599	Thomas Dekker, an Elizabethan playwright, publishes *The Shoemaker's Holiday.*
1603	Death of Queen Elizabeth I. End of the Elizabethan era in England.
1605	The first part of Spanish writer Miguel de Cervantes's *Don Quijote* is published.
1605	*Philogelos* is translated into Latin.
1607	English playwright Francis Beaumont publishes *The Knight of the Burning Pestle,* which influences the latter parts of Don Quijote.
1615	The second part of Miguel de Cervantes's *Don Quijote* is published.
1618	*Philogelos* is translated into German for the first time.
1621	Robert Burton publishes *The Anatomy of Melancholy* in Britain.
1623	William Shakespeare's (1564–1616) *First Folio* is published.
1633	Philip Massinger, English playwright, publishes *A New Way to Pay Old Debts.*
1637	*Chi soffre speri* (Who Suffers May Hope), which is known as the first true comic opera and composed by Virgilio Mazzocchi and Marco Marazzoli, is performed in Rome.
1644–1912	The reign of the Qing dynasty in China, when the original material of Feng Menglong's *Treasury of Laughs* is adapted and merged in the *Xiaolin guangji* (Extensive Records of the Forest of Laughter), a joke collection that is still published today.
1649	French philosopher René Descartes completes *The Passions of the Soul,* which includes a description of laughter.
1650	English philosopher Thomas Hobbes publishes *Human Nature,* which contains a definition of laughter as superiority.
1651	Thomas Hobbes publishes *Leviathan,* proposing arguably one of the most influential theories of humor, the "sudden glory" or "superiority" theory.
1658	Comédie Italienne shares the Petit Bourbon in Paris with Molière's company of *commedia dell'arte*, the Compagnie de Monsieur.
1659–1673	French playwright Molière (Jean-Baptiste Poquelin) writes 31 comedies for the court of Louis XIV.
1660	*Kyōgen-ki,* the first known collection of written scripts for *Kyōgen* plays, is published.
1678	Isaac Barrow, an English bishop, publishes *Several Sermons on Evil Speaking,* which condemns laughter, but only when "foolish and impertinent."
1678	In Japan, Fujimoto Kizan publishes *Ōkagami* (The Great Mirror) in which he discusses the proper way for a courtesan to laugh.
1680	The Hôtel de Bourgogne in Paris is given to Comédie Italienne.

Date(s)	*Event(s)/Publication*
1684	*Narukami* (The Thunder God), a Japanese *Kabuki* play, is staged. It features a comical seduction scene notable for its trappings of high comedy.
1687	Ihara Saikaku, one of Japan's most famous comic authors, publishes *Nanshoku Ōkagami* (The Great Mirror of Male Love), an example of Japan's common sexual humor.
1688–1704	The *Yakusha Rongo* (The Actors' Analects) is compiled by *Kabuki* actors in Japan and outlines three general styles of comic roles and advises on acting in them.
1695	English dramatist William Congreve publishes *Concerning Humour in Comedy.*
1697	Comédie Italienne is expelled from Paris for satirizing the royal mistress, Madame de Maintenon.
1700s	Hasidic rabbis in Poland-Russia create the philosophical *vertl,* a paradoxical quip or snap anecdote.
1708–1709	Anthony A. Cooper, Earl of Shaftesbury, publishes "A Letter Concerning Enthusiasm to My Lord Sommers" and "An Essay on the Freedom of Wit and Humour."
1711	English writer Joseph Addison publishes humorous essays in *The Spectator,* Nos. 35, 62, and 249.
1712	English poet Alexander Pope publishes the first version of *The Rape of the Lock.*
1725	Francis Hutcheson publishes *Reflections Upon Laughter* in Scotland.
1726	Jonathan Swift publishes *Gulliver's Travels,* one of the best known examples of prose satire.
1728	Alexander Pope publishes anonymously the first version of *The Dunciad.*
1729	Jonathan Swift publishes his *A Modest Proposal for Preventing the Children of Poor People in Ireland From Being a Burden to Their Parents or Country, and for Making Them Beneficial to the Publick*, possibly one of the great satirical works of all time.
1733	*La serva padrona* (The Maid as Mistress) is composed by Giovanni Battista Pergolesi and helps spread Italian comic opera throughout Europe.
1736–1825	Lifetime of German author Johann Paul Friedrich Richter, who, in an influential essay in his *Vorschule der Aesthetik* (School of Aesthetics), defines humor as "inverted sublime."
1739	Carlo Goldoni becomes dramatist for Medebach's company of *commedia dell'arte* in Venice.
1741	Twenty-eight jokes from *Philogelos* appear in English in an anonymous article (believed to have been authored by Samuel Johnson) published in *The Gentleman's Magazine* under the title "The Pedants, or Jests of Hierocles."
1742	Antonio Sacchi, the great Arlecchino, forms his own company of *commedia dell'arte.*
1743	Carlo Goldoni writes *Servant of Two Masters* for Sacchi.
1744	Corbyn Morris publishes *An Essay Towards Fixing the True Standards of Wit, Humour, Raillery, Satire, and Ridicule* in England.
1747	In colonial America, Benjamin Franklin draws "The Waggoner and Hercules," which is believed to be the first political cartoon.

Date(s)	*Event(s)/Publication*
1748–1752	Lord Chesterfield writes most of his letters, published as *Letters to His Son*, by his son's widow in 1774. He approves of smiling but not of laughter.
1749	English novelist and dramatist Henry Fielding publishes *Tom Jones.*
1752	French writer Voltaire (François-Marie Arouet) publishes *Micromégas.*
1752	English author and poet Charlotte Lennox publishes *The Female Quixote.*
1759	Voltaire publishes *Candide.*
1759–1768	Irish-born English novelist Laurence Sterne publishes *The Life and Opinions of Tristram Shandy, Gentleman.*
1762	Goldoni leaves Venice to work with the Comedie Italienne in Paris.
1762	England's first caricature book, *A Book of Caricaturas,* is published by Mary Darly.
1771	Japanese author Hiraga Gennai's *Gesaku* (meaning "playful works") is translated as *On Farting.*
1773	Irish-born dramatist Oliver Goldsmith publishes *An Essay on the Theatre; or, A Comparison Between Laughing and Sentimental Comedy.*
1773–1853	Lifetime of Ludwig Tieck, one of the German founders of romanticism, who wrote the novel *Des Lebens Überfluß* (Life's Luxuries).
1775–1821	Lifetime of Italian political satirist Carlo Porta.
1775–1850	Traditional span of the romantic movement in Europe.
1785–1859	Lifetime of English essayist Thomas de Quincey, writer of *On Murder Considered as One of the Fine Arts.*
1788	Antonio Sacchi, the last great Arlecchino/Harlequin player of *commedia dell'arte*, dies.
1790	German philosopher Immanuel Kant publishes *Critique of Judgment.*
1790	*Rakugo* begins to move from large households onto the stage in Japan.
1791–1863	Lifetime of Italian poet Giuseppe Gioachino Belli, writer of humorous sonnets.
1797–1856	Lifetime of German poet Heinrich Heine who wrote satirical political poetry.
1798–1874	Lifetime of German political satirist August Heinrich Hoffmann von Fallersleben.
1799–1837	Lifetime of Russian author Aleksandr Sergeyevich Pushkin.
1801–1862	Lifetime of Austrian actor and writer Johann Nepomuk Nestroy.
1803	Leandro Fernández de Moratín (1760–1828) publishes *El baron* (The Baron).
1803?–1856	Lifetime of Yiddish- and Hebrew-language poet Solomon Ettinger, who created epigrams and the comedy *Serkele.*
1804–1806	English writer Sydney Smith publishes *Elementary Sketches of Moral Philosophy,* which contains a section "On Wit and Humour."
1806	Spanish dramatist and poet Leandro Fernández de Moratín publishes *El sí de las niñas* (The Maidens' Consent).
1808	German writer Heinrich von Kleist (1777–1811) publishes his successful play *Der zerbrochne Krug* (The Broken Jug).
1810–1899	Lifetime of Avrom-Ber Gotlober, who created satirical and parodic poetry and wrote the comedy *Der dektukh* (The Bridal Veil).

Date(s)	***Event(s)/Publication***
1811	English writer Jane Austen (1775–1817) publishes *Sense and Sensibility.*
1812	Adamantios Korais translates *Philogelos* into French and Modern Greek.
1812–1888	Lifetime of English nonsense writer Edward Lear.
1812–1891	Lifetime of Russian novelist Ivan Aleksandrovich Goncharov.
1813	Jane Austen publishes *Pride and Prejudice.*
1813–1880	Lifetime of Antonio García Guttiérrez, whose play *Simón Bocanegra* turned into Giuseppe Verdi's opera *Simon Boccanegra.*
1814	Jane Austen's *Mansfield Park* is published.
1815	Jane Austen's *Emma* is published.
1815–1888	Lifetime of Eugène Labiche, the foremost French author of comic theater of his time.
1816	English writer Thomas Love Peacock (1785–1866) publishes *Headlong Hall.*
1817	Thomas Love Peacock publishes *Melincourt.*
1818	English writer Samuel Taylor Coleridge publishes *Lecture IX: Wit and Humour.*
1818	Manuel Eduardo de Gorostiza (1789–1851) publishes *Indulgencia para todos* (Indulgence for All).
1818	Jane Austen's *Northanger Abbey* is published posthumously.
1818–1824	English poet Lord Byron (1788–1824) writes the epic satire *Don Juan.*
1819	German philosopher Arthur Schopenhauer publishes *The World as Will and Idea.*
1819	William Hazlitt publishes *Lectures on the English Comic Writers.*
1820	Aleksandr Sergeyevich Pushkin publishes *Ruslan i Liudmila* (Ruslan and Liudmila).
1821	German writer Johann Wolfgang von Goethe (1749–1832) publishes his satirical novel *Wilhem Meisters Wanderjahre* (Wilhelm Meister's Apprenticeship).
1822	German author Ernst Theodor Wilhelm Hoffmann (1776–1822) publishes *Lebensansichten des Katers Murr* (The Life and Opinions of the Tomcat Murr).
1827	Chinese author Li Ruzhen finishes *Flowers in the Mirror.*
1832–1837	French writer Honoré de Balzac (1799–1850) publishes *Cent contes drôlatiques* (The Hundred Comical Tales).
1833	French writer Alfred de Musset (1810–1857) publishes his most famous play *On ne badine pas avec l'amour* (One Does Not Take Love Lightly).
1833	Manuel Eduardo de Gorostiza publishes *Contigo Pan y Cebolla* (With You, Bread And Onion).
1835	Augustus Baldwin Longstreet publishes *Georgia Scenes: Characters, Incidents, &c., in the First Half Century of the Republic,* one of the foundational texts of the U.S. frontier humor.
1835–1836	Nikolai Gogol (1809–1852) publishes *The Nose.*
1837	English writer Charles Dickens (1812–1870) publishes *The Pickwick Papers.*
1837–1901	Victorian era (Queen Victoria's reign).
1839	Charles Dickens publishes *Oliver Twist.*

Date(s)	*Event(s)/Publication*
1840	Spanish dramatist Manuel Bretón de los Herreros (1796–1873) publishes *El pelo de la dehesa* (The Countryside).
1841	English novelist William Makepeace Thackeray's (1811–1863) *Catherine* is published.
1841–2002	The British humor magazine *Punch* is published (with interruptions).
1842	Nikolai Gogol publishes *The Overcoat.*
1848	William Makepeace Thackeray publishes *The Book of Snobs.*
1850	Ivan Aleksandrovich Goncharov publishes his novel *Oblomov.*
1851	Ivan Sergeyevich Turgenev (1818–1883) publishes *Mesiats v derevne* (A Month in the Country), his Chekhovian comedy.
1852	William Makepeace Thackeray publishes *Charity and Humour.*
1853–1925	Lifetime of Eduardo Scarpetta, who is commonly regarded as the creator of dialectal theater in Italy.
1855	French writer Charles Baudelaire publishes *On the Essence of Laughter.*
1855–1905	Lifetime of French writer and humorist Alphonse Allais.
1856	English writer George Eliot publishes *German Wit: Heinrich Heine.*
1856	Russian satirist Mikhail Evrgrafovich Saltykov-Shchedrin (1826–1889) publishes *Provincial Sketches.*
1857	Charles Dickens publishes *Little Dorrit.*
1858–1929	Lifetime of French novelist Georges Courteline.
1859	Scottish philosopher Alexander Bain publishes *The Emotions and the Will.*
1859	French folklorist Alfred Canel uses the term *blason populaire* for the first time in *Blason populaire de la Normandie* (*Blason populaire* of Normandy).
1859–1916	Lifetime of Yiddish author and playwright Sholem Aleichem (Sholem Naumovich Rabinovich), who created the characters that later appear in *Fiddler on the Roof.*
1860	English philosopher Herbert Spencer publishes *The Physiology of Laughter.*
1860–1904	Lifetime of Russian writer Anton Pavlovich Chekhov, the prolific writer of short stories, many of which are comic.
1860–1937	Lifetime of Scottish author James Matthew Barrie, who wrote humorous works of fiction for adults and children and is best known for *Peter Pan.*
1862–1921	Lifetime of great French vaudeville author Georges Feydeau.
1863	French writer Théophile Gautier (1811–1872) publishes *Le Capitaine Fracasse* (Captain Fracasse).
1864–1918	Lifetime of German satirist and expressionist Frank Wedekind.
1865	English writer Lewis Carroll's (1832–1898) *Alice's Adventures in Wonderland* is published.
1867–1916	Lifetime of Natsume Sōseki, the first modern Japanese writer to successfully use humor in the novel.
1868	Restoration of the emperor to power and beginning of Meiji era in Japan.
1869	French writer Alphonse Daudet (1840–1897) publishes *Lettres de mon moulin* (Letters From My Mill).

Date(s)	***Event(s)/Publication***
1870	English dramatist and librettist William S. Gilbert (1836–1911) writes the operetta *The Palace of Truth.*
1870–1916	Lifetime of remarkable Edwardian humorist Saki.
1871	William S. Gilbert writes his operetta *Pygmalion and Galatea.*
1871	Lewis Carroll's *Through the Looking Glass and What Alice Found There* is published.
1871–1950	Lifetime of Carlo Alberto Salustri (a.k.a. Trilussa), the best known Italian dialectal writer of his time.
1872	Charles Darwin publishes *The Expression of the Emotions in Man and Animals.*
1872	The first policy statement is issued in Japan encouraging the use of humor in theater.
1872	English author Samuel Butler (1835–1902) publishes his scathing satire *Erewhon.*
1872	Alphonse Daudet publishes *Tartarin de Tarascon.*
1872–1956	Lifetime of English writer Max Beerbohm.
1873–1907	Lifetime of French author Alfred Jarry, who is best known for the character of Père Ubu.
1874–1936	Lifetime of Austrian writer Karl Kraus, editor of *Die Fackel* (The Torch).
1876	The *Harvard Lampoon,* the longest continually published humor magazine to date, starts publishing.
1877	English writer George Meredith (1828–1909) publishes *The Idea of Comedy and the Uses of the Comic Spirit,* an essay notable for its contribution to the theory of humor.
1877	James Sully publishes *Ridicule and Truth.*
1880	French writer Guy de Maupassant (1850–1893) publishes his best known work, *Boule de suif* (Ball of Fat).
1881	The first cabaret, Le Chat Noir (The Black Cat), is opened by Radolphe Salis, in Paris.
1881	French writer Gustave Flaubert's (1821–1880) unfinished comic novel *Bouvard et Pécuchet* is published posthumously.
1881–1936	Lifetime of Lu Xun, who compiles the most complete collection of humorous anecdotes from premodern China.
1883	Italian writer Carlo Collodi (1826–1890) publishes *The Adventures of Pinocchio.*
1885	A Shakespearean play (a *Kabuki* version of the *Merchant of Venice*) is staged for the first time in Japan, in Osaka.
1885	English dramatist Arthur Wing Pinero (1855–1934) publishes his farce *The Magistrate.*
1886	Arthur Wing Pinero publishes *The Schoolmistress.*
1887	Irish writer Oscar Wilde (1854–1900) publishes *The Canterville Ghost.*
1889	The Moulin Rouge is built in Paris.
1889	English writer Jerome K. Jerome (1859–1921) publishes *Three Men in a Boat.*

Date(s)	*Event(s)/Publication*
1892	Oscar Wilde publishes *Lady Windermere's Fan.*
1892–1901	*The Idler,* the British humor magazine started by Jerome K. Jerome, is published.
1893	Irish writer George Bernard Shaw (1856–1950) publishes *Mrs. Warren's Profession.*
1893	Georges Courteline publishes *Messieurs les ronds-de-cuir* (The Employees).
1894	George Bernard Shaw publishes *Arms and the Man* and *Candida.*
1895	Oscar Wilde writes the plays *The Importance of Being Earnest* and *An Ideal Husband.*
1895	George Bernard Shaw publishes *The Man of Destiny.*
1895	Richard Felton Outcault's *The Yellow Kid,* one of the earliest comic strips, begins publishing in the *New York World.*
1897	*The Happy Hypocrite,* by Max Beerbohm, appears in *The Yellow Book.*
1897	French poet and dramatist Edmond Rostand (**1868–1918**) publishes his verse comedy *Cyrano de Bergerac.*
1899	The satirical magazine *Die Fackel* (The Torch) begins publication in Austria.
1899–1900	French philosopher Henri Bergson publishes *Le rire* (Laughter), proposing his theory of the comic.
ca. **1900**	Nonsense humor appears in China and becomes increasingly popular starting in the 1980s.
1900–1999	The Japanese terms *Manga* for "cartoon" and *Anime* for "animation" become English words, marking Japan's worldwide contribution to humor.
1901–1910	Edwardian era (reign of King Edward VII) in England.
1903	English literary critic Edmund Kerchever Chambers publishes *The Mediaeval Stage*, in the first volume of which he presents more than 150 pages of records on fools' festivals.
1904	A comedy genre called *Shinkigeki* (New Comedy), which produces plays and extended comedy skits, begins in Japan.
1905	George Bernard Shaw publishes *Major Barbara.*
1905	Sigmund Freud publishes *Der Witz und seine Beziehung zum Unbewußten* (The Joke and Its Relation to the Unconscious).
1908	Italian writer Luigi Pirandello publishes *L'umorismo* (On Humor).
1911–1913	Gustave Flaubert's *Dictionary of Accepted Ideas* is published posthumously using his notes.
1914	German-language writer Franz Kafka publishes *The Metamorphosis.*
1914–1918	World War I.
1916	Dadaism, centering on a nonsensical theme and pop culture, begins in neutral Zürich, Switzerland, during World War I and peaks.
1919	The Marx Brothers rise to fame.
1920	Dadaism begins to die out. Surrealism begins; it is best known for the visual artworks and writings of the group members. The works feature the element of surprise, unexpected juxtapositions, and non sequiturs.

Date(s)	Event(s)/Publication
1920–1929	Radio program *Amos 'n' Andy* is first broadcast; notable for having Black characters who were not servants or wholly based on stereotypes.
1921	Jacques Copeau founds L'École du Vieux-Colombier, which rejuvenates French acting. Copeau's use of masks influences the practice of mimes.
1921–2000	Life of Israeli cartoonist Kariel Gardosh.
1929–1941	Russian scholar Mikhail Bakhtin (1895–1975) formulates the concept of the "carnivalesque."
1929–1946	The radio program *The Goldbergs* runs, presenting Jewish life in an accessible way. Later became a television series that ran from 1949 to 1956.
1932	The *Tankō bushi* (Coal Mine Song), a song exemplifying early modern folk humor in Japan, is released on gramophone record.
1934	Italian writer Luigi Pirandello wins the Nobel Prize in Literature.
1938	Orson Welles broadcasts on radio a series of news bulletins reporting Martian attacks (based on H. G. Wells's short novel *The War of the Worlds,* 1898) sending many people into a frenzy and thus making hoax history.
1947	Kitano Takeshi, Japan's most influential TV comedy performer, known for his taboo-breaking humor, is born.
1949	Samuel Beckett publishes his absurdist play *Waiting for Godot.*
1951	CBS first airs the *Amos 'n' Andy* television series, the first TV series to feature an all-Black cast. The show was canceled in 1953 following protests by the National Association for the Advancement of Colored People.
1960	Daniel Berlyne proposes the arousal theory of humor.
1961	Lenny Bruce (1925–1966) first faces obscenity charges but is acquitted.
1961–1969	Richard Pryor introduces a new style of stand-up comedy that still influences stand-up comedians today.
1964	Arthur Koestler publishes *The Act of Creation,* which introduces the influential bisociation theory of humor.
1964	*Fiddler on the Roof* is first performed.
1964	Lenny Bruce is convicted on obscenity charges.
1965	Mikhail Bakhtin's *Rabelais and His World* is published.
1969–1974	*Monty Python's Flying Circus,* one of the most famous sketch comedy TV programs, is on the air. The show quickly gained cult status.
1970	Cold humor appears in Taiwan for the first time and spreads in China in the next decade.
1973	Yaakov Kirschen's series *Dry Bones* is first published in the *Jerusalem Post.*
1975	*Saturday Night Live* airs for the first time.
1975–1979	Oneida American Indian comedian Charlie Hill begins performing.
1976	First humor conference, held in Cardiff, Wales.
1978	Gerald Vizenor, an Anishinaabe American Indian who is believed to be the first to include the trickster tradition in his novels, publishes *Darkness in Saint Louis Bearheart.*

Date(s)	*Event(s)/Publication*
1979–1992	English writer Douglas Adams writes *Hitchhiker's Guide to the Galaxy* series.
1980	Italian writer Umberto Eco publishes *The Name of the Rose.*
1980–1989	Jerk humor appears as one of the three distinguishable forms of modern humor in China.
1980–1999	*Xiangsheng* (Chinese crosstalk) becomes popular and reaches its climax.
1982	Don and Alleen Nilsen found World Humor and Irony Membership (WHIM) at the University of Arizona.
1985	Mahadev Apte publishes *Humor and Laughter: An Anthropological Approach.*
1985	Victor Raskin proposes the first formal linguistic theory of humor: the semantic script theory of humor (SSTH).
1987	International Society of Humor Studies is founded.
1987–1992	*The Cosby Show* airs on NBC.
1988	Last WHIM conference is held at Purdue University.
1988	*HUMOR: International Journal of Humor Research* begins publication.
1988	*Humoresques* begins publication in France.
1988–1997	*Roseanne* airs on ABC.
1989–1998	*Seinfeld* airs on NBC.
1990	Christie Davies publishes *Ethnic Humor Around the World.*
1990–1999	Internet humor emerges as a dominant medium of communication.
1993	American Indian writer Sherman Alexie publishes *The Lone Ranger and Tonto Fistfight in Heaven.*
1998	Jon Stewart takes over hosting Comedy Central's *The Daily Show.*
2000	*E'gao* Internet spoofs first appear in China.
2001	The first fMRI study on humor, carried out by Vinod Goel and Raymond J. Dolan, appears in *Nature Neuroscience.*
2001–2003	The British workplace comedy *The Office* is on the air.
2003–2006	*Chappelle's Show* airs on Comedy Central.
2005	Chinese film director Chen Kaige's blockbuster *The Promise* is released and subsequently spoofed by Hu Ge in *A Bloody Case Caused by a Steamed Bun.*
ca. 2007	LOLcats, advice animals, and rage comics start becoming popular forms of Internet humor.
2007	Rod Martin publishes *The Psychology of Humor.*
2008	*The Primer of Humor Research,* edited by Victor Raskin, is published.
2010	Memes start emerging as a prominent medium of Internet humor.
2011	A Japanese minister resigns after making an inappropriate comment regarding the 2011 tsunami and resultant nuclear crisis in his country.
2012	Stephen Colbert forms his own "super PAC" during the 2012 presidential election on his show *The Colbert Report,* a spin-off of *The Daily Show With Jon Stewart.*
2014	The *Encyclopedia of Humor Studies* is published.

Appendix B

HUMOR ASSOCIATIONS AND PUBLICATIONS

The following is a nonexhaustive listing of associations and programs, as well as stand-alone journals that deal primarily or completely with humor research. Whereas some of these associations and publications have existed for more than 25 years, many associations and sometimes journals appear suddenly and disappear almost as quickly. Therefore, the main criterion for inclusion in this listing is a certain stability and continuity in operation. Whenever possible, Internet contact information has been provided. Because Internet addresses change often, these should be taken as merely orientational.

American Humor Studies Association

This society promotes research and criticism of American humor. The American Humor Studies Association (AHSA) sponsors a scholarly journal, *Studies in American Humor*, as well as a biannual newsletter, *To Wit*. For more information, see http://americanhumorstudiesassociation.wordpress.com.

American School of Laughter Yoga

Although the center is located in Los Angeles, California, the online resource provides information on the underlying theories and practice of laughter yoga, tips on how laughter can improve the overall quality of life, as well as online training sessions. For more information, see http://www.laughteryogaamerica.com.

Association for Applied and Therapeutic Humor

The Association for Applied and Therapeutic Humor (AATH) is a nonprofit association that seeks to promote the most up-to-date research on the connection between humor, laughter, and well-being, as well as provide resources, education, and support for its members who come from various interdisciplinary health care professions. The AATH sponsors two publications: *E-zine* and *Humor Connection*. For more information, see http://www.aath.org.

Association for the Study of Play, The

This academic organization promotes interdisciplinary research surrounding the concept of play. The Association for the Study of Play's (TASP) multidisciplinary scope includes play research from fields such as anthropology, biology, communication, culture studies, education, history, kinesiology, philosophy, psychology, sociology, and more. TASP publishes *Play Review*, a quarterly newsletter, as well as *Play & Culture Studies*, an annual volume. TASP also holds an annual conference. For more information, see http://www.tasplay.org.

Australasian Humor Studies Network

The Australasian Humor Studies Network (AHSN) was developed to create and maintain a network between humor scholars across Australia and New Zealand. One of the AHSN's priorities is to provide resources and support to students dealing with humor-related topics in various fields. The AHSN holds annual colloquia and offers an e-newsletter. For more information, see http://sydney.edu.au/humourstudies/about.shtml.

Big Apple Circus—Clown Care

This community outreach program performs circus acts for hospitalized children in more than 16 facilities nationwide. For more information, see http://www.bigapplecircus.org.

Bumper "T" Caring Clowns

This nonprofit volunteer-based organization provides humorous performances for hospital patients and their families in Pennsylvania, New Jersey, and Maryland. For more information, see http://www.bumpertcaringclowns.org.

Caring Clowns International

This charity-based organization consists of more than 40 clowns around the world whose primary aim is to bring laughter to those who need it most. The members perform in a variety of venues, from prisons to orphanages. For more information, see http://www.caringclownsinternational.org.

Carolina Health and Humor Association

Carolina Health and Humor Association (Carolina HaHa), a nonprofit organization, provides art therapy programs as well as humor training, health care, and other stress relief methods to promote and support healthy living. For more information, see http://www.carolinahealthandhumor.org.

Centro Ricerca Umorismo

Centro Ricerca Umorismo (CRU) is an Italian resource for humor researchers. The website offers discussions on research in the field and provides information regarding other humor-related organizations. For more information, see http://www.ricercaumorismo.it.

Clowns Without Borders

The members of this organization devote their time to bringing laughter to children in areas of crisis around the world, such as conflict or famine zones, refugee camps, places receiving relief following natural disasters, and other crises. For more information, see http://www.clownswithoutborders.org.

Comedy Cures Foundation

This nonprofit organization provides both live and digital forms of therapeutic comedy programs for children and adults who face difficulties in life such as illness, disabilities, or abuse. For more information, see http://www.comedycures.org.

Comedy Studies

Based in the United Kingdom, this journal offers insight on various interdisciplinary aspects of comedy and comedians. Contributors include writers, academics, comedians, and more. For more information, see http://www.intellectbooks.co.uk.

CORHUM, Association française pour le développement des recherches sur le comique

This organization promotes interdisciplinary research surrounding humor and laughter, including but not limited to the historical, sociological, anthropological, linguistic, and psychological aspects. CORHUM has a biannual publication, *Humoresques*, which is distributed by the House of Human Sciences. For more information, see http://www.humoresques.fr.

Fools for Health

Based in Canada, members of this group role-play as clown-doctors in hospital settings in order to bring laughter to patients and their families.

Gliner Center on Humor Communication and Health

This center is a branch of the University of Maryland's Department of Health Services Administration. The purpose of this center is to explore the ways in which humor and laughter can facilitate good health. While maintaining a relationship with the academic research of humor and health, this organization also provides various outreach programs to educate the community on the benefits of humor in relation to good health. For more information, see http://www.sph.umd.edu/hlsa/Gliner/index.cfm.

Ha-P

This organization is geared toward providing information and opportunities to discover the importance of optimism, laughter, and happiness on life. Ha-P offers workshops, from professionals and motivational speakers, and programs such as the Joy Care Leadership. For more information, see http://www.ha-p.com.

Humor Gráfico

Humor Gráfico is an international organization based out of the Universidad de Alcalá, Madrid, Spain, that aims to promote the recognition of the cartoonist profession, as well as a cartoonist's role in culture. For more information, see http://www.humorgrafico.org.

Humor in America

This blog covers American humor and humor studies. The blog invites authors to submit articles on a variety of topics, such as humor theory, the pedagogy of humor, interviews with humor scholars or comedians, humorous literature, and many more. For more information, see http://humorinamerica.wordpress.com.

Humor Project, Inc., The

This online resource focuses on the positive power of humor by offering up-to-date information regarding humor-related conferences, publications (both academic and nonacademic), life-coaching tips, and discussion boards. For more information, see http://www.humorproject.com.

International Society for Humor Studies

This scholarly organization supports the advancement of humor studies and research. The majority of the society's members are academics from a wide variety of disciplines. The International Society for Humor Studies (ISHS) publishes the quarterly journal, *HUMOR: International Journal of Humor Research,* and holds annual conferences and workshops. The society is a hub for connections in the field of humor research; it offers information and resources about other organizations, as well as connections with the researchers themselves. For more information, see http://www.hnu.edu/ishs.

International Society for Luso-Hispanic Humor Studies, The

The International Society for Luso-Hispanic Humor Studies (I.S.L.H.H.S.) promotes the study of humor in the Spanish and Portuguese languages to encourage the expansion of communication and research in the field of humor. For more information, see http://ilhhumorsoc.org.

International Studies in Humour

International Studies in Humour (ISH) accepts interdisciplinary research in the field of humor for its biannual publication. For more information, see http://www.doc.gold.ac.uk/ephraim/Humor-E-Journals/IntStudiesHumour/Global/links-webpage.htm.

International Summer School and Symposium on Humour and Laughter

Also known as the Humour Summer School, this organization focuses on providing students and established researchers with the fundamental theories and methods in humor-related research, as well as past and present approaches used in the field. The annual course is held at various international locations. For more information, see http://www.humoursummerschool.org.

Israeli Journal of Humor Research

This international e-journal is the publication of the Israeli Society for Humor Studies, with an interdisciplinary academic focus in the field of humor. For more information, see http://www.israeli-humor-studies.org/site/index.asp?depart_id=122789.

Israeli Society for Humor Studies, The

This society, based in Israel, supports international interdisciplinary research in the field of humor. The society publishes two e-journals: *Israeli Journal of Humor Research* and *Humor Mekuvvan: A Research Journal in Humor Studies*. For more information, see http://www.israeli-humor-studies.org/122789/The-Israeli-Society-for-Humor-Studies.

Japan Humor and Laughter Society

This society's primary goal is to minimize professional and academic barriers of humor researchers and increase understanding of the relationship between humor and laughter. Members of the society include academic professors, as well as nonacademic professionals.

Laughter Heals Foundation

The primary purpose of this nonprofit organization is to promote physical and mental healing through laughter. For more information, see http://laughterheals.org.

Lawhaha.com

This online news source was started by law professor Andrew McClerg. The website touches on topics of legal education, legal oddities, and humorous law-related stories. For more information, see http://lawhaha.com.

Le Rire Médicin

Le Rire Médicin is a French association of medical professionals dedicated to bringing humor to hospital patients. Founded in 1988, this association organizes training workshops for hospital clowns. For more information, see http://www.leriremedecin.asso.fr.

Museum House of Humour and Satire

Located in Gabrovo, Bulgaria, this museum exhibits cultural artifacts and historical records revolving around the local carnivals and humor folklore of Gabrovo. The exhibits not only portray the history of Gabrovo but also showcase the hardships that led to the distinct Gabrovo humor so ingrained in that culture. Artwork, antique wagons, masks and other carnival attire, and instruments are among the many pieces one can find at the Museum House of Humour and Satire. For more information, see http://www.humorhouse.bg/enindex.html.

North East Texas Humor Research Conference

The North East Texas Humor Research Conference (NETHRC) is a regional organization that holds annual conferences focusing on multidisciplinary areas of humor research. The conferences are held in the North East Texas area and typically include plenary, roundtable, paper, and poster sessions, as well as workshops.

Popular Culture Association/American Culture Association

The Popular Culture Association/American Culture Association (PCA/ACA) consists of scholars and nonscholars who share common ideas and interests about a specific topic in the field of popular culture. Such topics may include film, advertising, politics, literature, gender studies, and many more. The PCA/ACA publish two journals: the *Journal of Popular Culture*, which is a peer-reviewed journal with a broad interdisciplinary focus published six times a year, and the *Journal of American Culture*, which focuses mainly on the arts. The PCA/ACA also offers regional, national, and international annual conferences. For more information, see http://pcaaca.org.

Rx Laughter

This nonprofit group seeks to aid individuals dealing with life's greatest challenges, such as trauma, addiction, grief, illness, or pain, by means of laughter and comedy entertainment. For more information, see http://www.rxlaughter.org.

Umorismo Formazione

This Italian organization offers educational activities surrounding humor and humor theory, such as workshops, laughter therapy, comedy lessons, and training models aimed toward improving the social and cultural quality of life. For more information, see http://www.lescuoledirecitazione.it/piemonte/torino/umorismo-formazione.

Audrey C. Adams

Index

Entry titles and their page numbers are in **bold**.

MATHEMATICS

Grade 3 • Student Edition

Second Edition

purposeful design®
publications

Colorado Springs, Colorado

Second edition 2016

Printed in the United States of America
22 21 20 19 18 17 16 1 2 3 4 5 6 7

Mathematics, Grade 3 – Student Edition
Purposeful Design Mathematics series
ISBN 978-1-58331-581-1, Catalog #40031

Purposeful Design Publications is the publishing division of the Association of Christian Schools International (ACSI) and is committed to the ministry of Christian school education, to enable Christian educators and schools worldwide to effectively prepare students for life. As the publisher of textbooks, trade books, and other educational resources within ACSI, Purposeful Design Publications strives to produce biblically sound materials that reflect Christian scholarship and stewardship and that address the identified needs of Christian schools around the world.

References to books, computer software, and other ancillary resources in this series are not endorsements by ACSI. These materials were selected to provide teachers with additional resources appropriate to the concepts being taught and to promote student understanding and enjoyment.

Purposeful Design Publications
A Division of ACSI
PO Box 65130 • Colorado Springs, CO • 80962-5130
Customer Service Department: 800/367-0798 • Website: www.purposefuldesign.com

Table of Contents

Chapter 11 Decimals

Chapter 12 Time and Money

Chapter 13 Equations and Cumulative Review

Problem-Solving Path

1. Understand the question.

? ? ? ? ?

- Underline the <u>QUESTION</u>.

2. Analyze the data.

- Circle the key information.

3. Plan the strategy.

- Write an equation.
- Draw a picture.
- Make a table.
- Make an estimate.

$2 + 2 = 4$

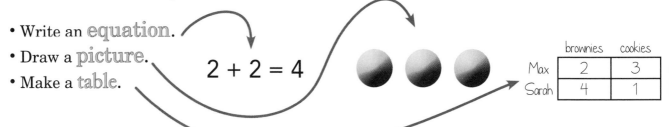

	brownies	cookies
Max	2	3
Sarah	4	1

4. Solve the problem.

- Show your **work**.
- Label the **answer**.

5. Evaluate the result.

$$\begin{array}{r} \boxed{1} \\ 9 \\ +\ 1 \\ \hline 10 \end{array}$$ **balls**

$10 + 5 = 15$ **elbows**

- Compare **the answer with the estimated answer.**
- Does the answer **make sense**?

Chapter 1
Place Value

"Suppose one of you has a hundred sheep and loses one of them. Doesn't he leave the ninety-nine in the open country and go after the lost sheep until he finds it?"
Luke 15:4

Key Ideas:

Patterns: skip counting, odd and even numbers

Place Value: identifying whole numbers to hundred thousands, comparing and ordering whole numbers, using place value

Number Theory: reading and writing numerals through 999,999 and ordinal numbers through 100th

Probability and Statistics: collecting and recording data

Name ______________________________

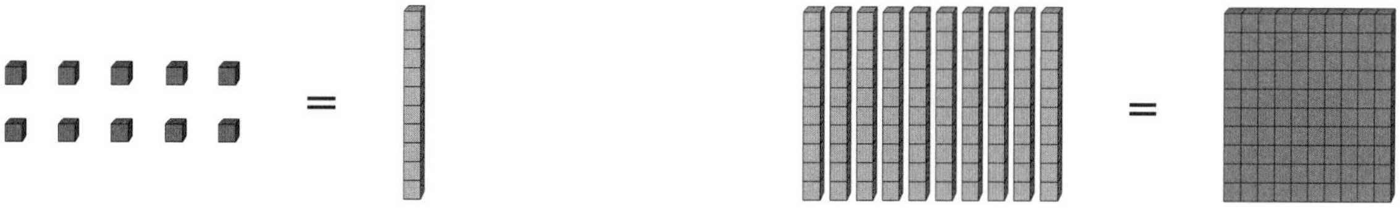

10 ones = 1 ten 10 tens = 1 hundred

All numbers are made up of digits.
0, 1, 2, 3, 4, 5, 6, 7, 8, 9
Place value is the placement of individual digits that tells what a number is worth.

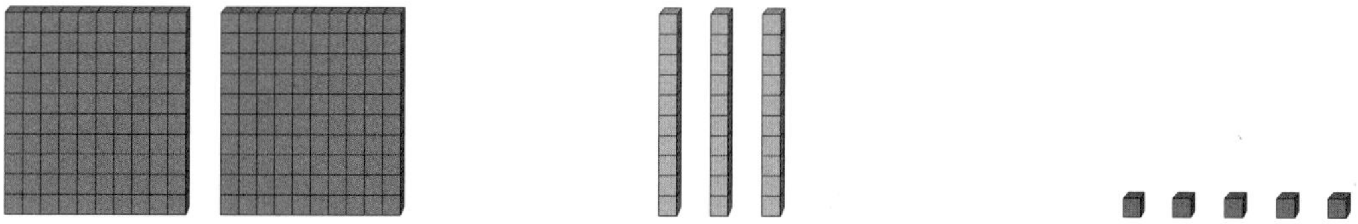

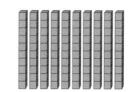

hundreds	tens	ones
2	3	5

The number is 235.

Fill in the chart. Write the number.

1.

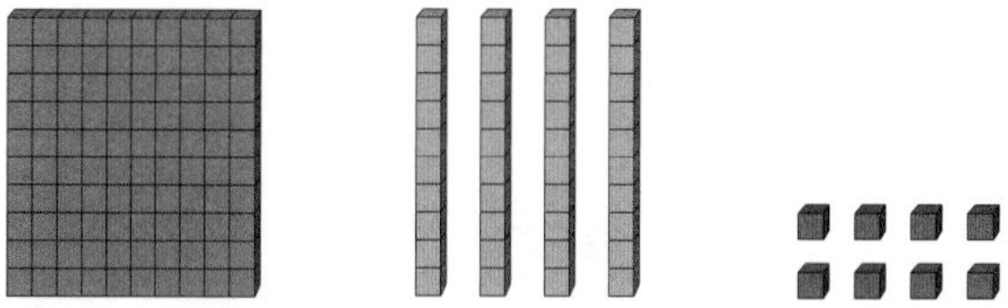

hundreds	tens	ones

The number is ______.

2.

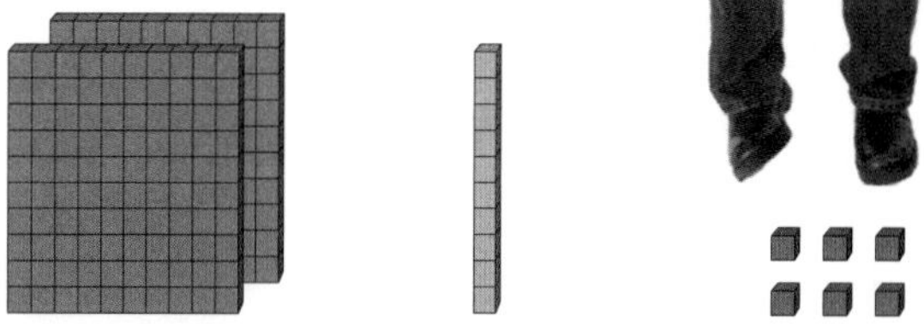

hundreds	tens	ones

The number is ______.

Numbers can be written in expanded form or standard form.

hundreds	tens	ones
4	8	3

Expanded form: 400 + 80 + 3

Standard form: 483

Write the expanded form for each number.

3. 921 = ____________________

4. 278 = ____________________

5. 604 = ____________________

Write the standard form of the number your teacher reads.

6. ____________________

7. ____________________

8. ____________________

9. ____________________

Write the value of the underlined digit.

10. $7\underline{2}4$ ______

11. $\underline{4}95$ ______

12. $90\underline{2}$ ______

13. $4\underline{1}1$ ______

14. $5\underline{8}$ ______

15. $4\underline{3}0$ ______

16. $\underline{8}06$ ______

17. $9\underline{9}0$ ______

Solve.

18. The total pounds of wool that the rancher sheared were 1 hundred, 3 tens, and 5 ones. How many pounds of wool did he shear?

_______ pounds of wool

19. The rancher separated his sheep into groups of 10. If he made 8 groups, how many sheep does he have?

_______ sheep

20. Order the numbers 215, 152, and 521 from least to greatest.

______ ______ ______

Name ______________________________

Use Counting Patterns 1.2

Even numbers end in 0, 2, 4, 6, or 8.
Odd numbers end in 1, 3, 5, 7, or 9.

Numbers can also be counted by 1s, 5s, 10s, and 100s. Look for a pattern.

… 63, 64, 65, 66, 67 …	… 20, 30, 40, 50, 60 …
… 75, 80, 85, 90, 95 …	… 400, 500, 600, 700, 800 …

Number lines can help too.

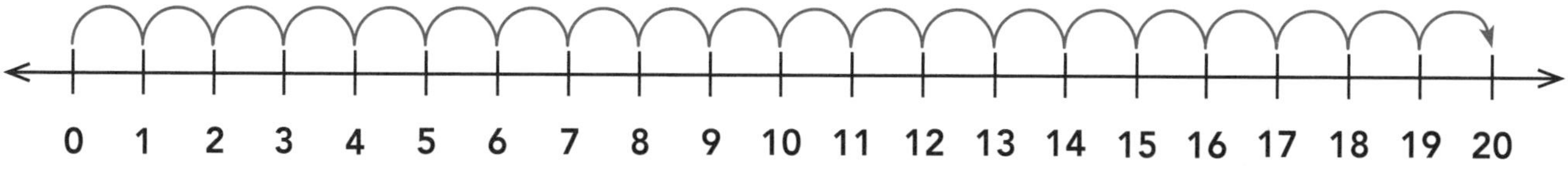

Fill in the blanks with the missing numbers.

1\.

1 ___ 3 ___ 5 ___ 7 ___ 9

The numbers you have written are ____________.
odd, even

2\.

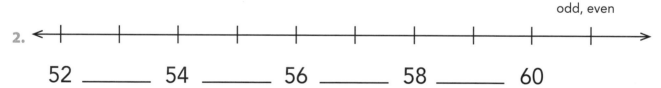

52 ______ 54 ______ 56 ______ 58 ______ 60

The numbers you have written are ____________.
odd, even

Write the next three numbers of each pattern.

3\. 15 20 25 30 ____ ____ ____

4\. 8 10 12 14 ____ ____ ____

5\. 13 15 17 19 ____ ____ ____

6\. 40 50 60 70 ____ ____ ____

7\. 250 350 450 ____ ____ ____

8\. 308 408 508 ____ ____ ____

Write the next three numbers of each pattern.

9. 21 23 25 ____ ____ ____

10. 72 74 76 ____ ____ ____

11. 43 45 47 ____ ____ ____

12. 159 160 161 ____ ____ ____

13. 220 230 240 ____ ____ ____

14. 336 346 356 ____ ____ ____

Write each number under the correct heading.

15.

19 120 710 456 967

63 381 185 880 228

Even ____ ____ ____ ____ ____

Odd ____ ____ ____ ____ ____

Write the next four even numbers.

16. 68 ____ ____ ____ ____

Write the next four odd numbers.

17. 71 ____ ____ ____ ____

Count to solve these problems.

18. Seven pairs of shoes were donated to the homeless shelter. How many shoes are there in all?

____ shoes

19. A volunteer sorted the church's puppets into stacks of 10. She counted 60 puppets in all. How many stacks of puppets did she make?

____ stacks

Review

Write these numbers in standard and expanded form.

	hundreds	tens	ones			
20.	3	0	2	=	____	____
21.	5	1	8	=	____	____
22.		2	5	=	____	____

Name ______________________________

Compare Hundreds 1.3

The old windmill measures 80 feet tall. The solar windmill measures 328 feet tall. Which windmill is taller?

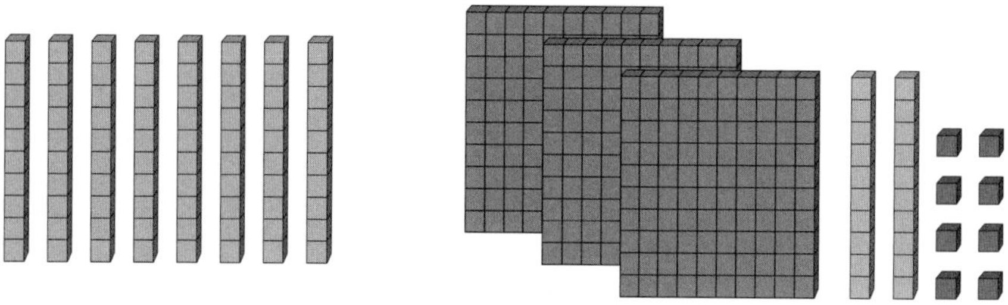

80 is less than 328.
80 feet < 328 feet

The sign > means greater than.
The sign < means less than.
The sign = means equal value.

Hint: The point of the sign, < or >, always points to the smaller number.

Always start comparing numbers at the left.
Begin with hundreds. Both are 3.
Go to tens. 2 is less than 6.
So, 325 is less than 369.

325 ____ 369
325 (<) 369
325 < 369

Write the numbers on the lines. Then, write > or <.

1.

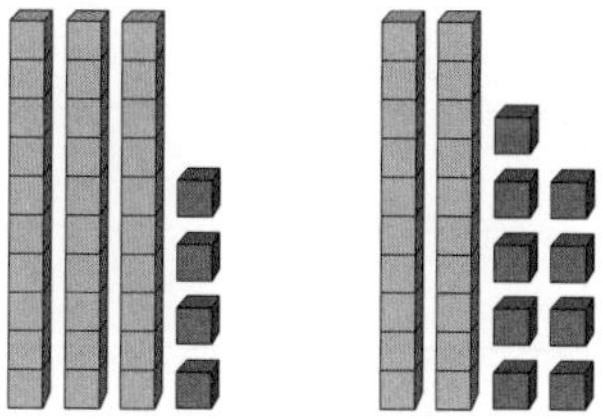

____ ◯ ____

2.

____ ◯ ____

3.

____ ◯ ____

Use the chart to compare. Write the number on the blanks. Write < or >.

4.

tens	ones
8	7
6	5

_____ ◯ _____

5.

hundreds	tens	ones
4	6	2
4	7	1

_____ ◯ _____

6.

tens	ones
5	9
8	2

_____ ◯ _____

7. 623 ◯ 69
9. 432 ◯ 482
11. 861 ◯ 288
13. 942 ◯ 934

8. 102 ◯ 182
10. 511 ◯ 412
12. 392 ◯ 396
14. 114 ◯ 302

Order the numbers from greatest to least.

15. 394 _____
611 _____
402 _____
561 _____

16. 783 _____
729 _____
746 _____
772 _____

Fill in the blanks. Write a comparison sentence using >, <, or =. Circle the answer to the question.

17. Micah has 12 posters. Tess had 15 but gave 5 to her cousin. Who has more posters, Micah or Tess?

Micah _____ ◯ Tess _____

18. Will had 8 posters. He received 3 more for his birthday. Who has more posters, Will or Tess?

Will _____ ◯ Tess _____

Review

Write the next three numbers of each pattern.

19. 311 321 331 _____ _____ _____

20. 486 488 490 _____ _____ _____

Fill in the chart.

	hundreds	tens	ones
21. 805			
22. 641			
23. 711			
24. 930			

Name ______________________________

Ordinal Numbers 1.4

Everyone in the family helps out at McMinn's ranch. The children enjoy watching the horse trainers.

Who is second? Who is fifth?

-st	1st	21st	31st
-nd	2nd	22nd	32nd
-rd	3rd	23rd	33rd
-th	4th	24th	34th

First, second, third, fourth, and fifth are **ordinal numbers**. Ordinal numbers describe the order or position of things in a line or list.

Ordinal numbers can be written like this.

25th

It is read "twenty-fifth." Most ordinal numbers end with –th, but some have other endings.

Answer these questions about the months of the year.

1. In what position is December? ____________
2. What is the fifth month of the year? ____________
3. What is the tenth? ____________
4. In what position is February? ____________
5. In what position is August? ____________
6. In what position is March? ____________

Write the ordinal number.

7. sixty-first ______ 8. thirteenth ______ 9. ninth ______

Write the ordinal number and ordinal number word.

10. 5 ______ ______________ 11. 92 ______ ______________

Answer the questions. Label the answers.

12. By noon Pedro's father had fixed the tenth section of fence around the ranch. How many sections of fence did he fix earlier that morning?

____

13. During the past week 5 foals were born. Pedro found another foal had been born overnight. What ordinal word describes the newest foal?

____

Mark the picture. Start at the left.

14. Circle the fourteenth person.
15. Draw a star above the ninth person.
16. Underline the twelfth person.
17. Draw a smiley face above the nineteenth person.
18. Write the ordinals on the lines above the young people.

Name ________________________________

Round to Tens and Hundreds 1.5

You have learned how to use place value to compare numbers. Place value is also used to round numbers. Rounding is increasing or decreasing a number to a specific place value.

Garrett's rope is 18 feet long.
Is its length closer to 10 feet or to 20 feet?

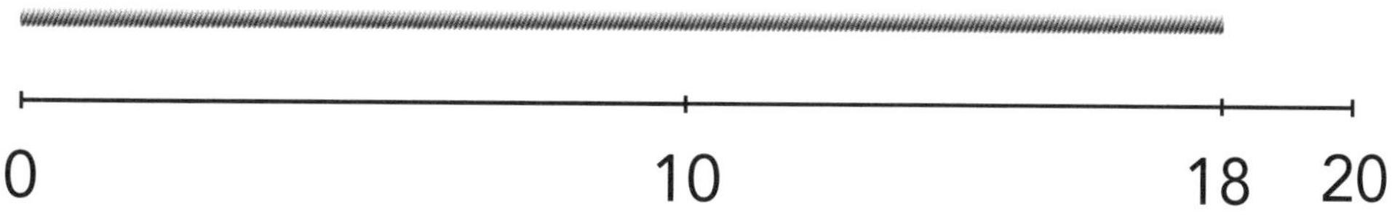

To round numbers to the closest 10, think about which two tens the number falls between. Then, look at the digit in the ones place. Digits 1, 2, 3, and 4 round to the smaller ten. Digits 5, 6, 7, 8, and 9 round up to the next ten.

53 is between 50 and 60. It has 3 ones, so it is closer to 50 than to 60.

59 is between 50 and 60. It has 9 ones, so it is closer to 60 than to 50.

55 is exactly halfway between 50 and 60. It is rounded to 60.

Round 67 to the nearest ten. Answer the questions.

1. Between which two tens is 67? _____ and _____

2. Which digit is in the ones place? _____
   Is this digit 1, 2, 3, or 4? If so, round down.
   Is this digit 5, 6, 7, 8, or 9? If so, round up.

3. So, 67 is rounded to _____.

Round to the nearest ten.

4. 17 _____	7. 48 _____	10. 32 _____	13. 28 _____
5. 65 _____	8. 59 _____	11. 43 _____	14. 89 _____
6. 71 _____	9. 24 _____	12. 75 _____	15. 21 _____

It is roundup time on the Circle W Ranch. There are **242** head of cattle in the barn. There are **281** head of cattle out on the open range. Which group of cattle is closer to 200 head of cattle? Which group is closer to 300 head of cattle?

To round to the closest hundred, look at the digit in the tens place.

The number 242 is between 200 and 300. It has 4 tens. That makes the numeral closer to 200. If the digits in the tens place are 0 to 4, you round down.	The number 281 is also between 200 and 300, but it has 8 tens. The number can be rounded to 300 because the digit in the tens place is between 5 and 9.

16. Between which two hundreds is 872? ______ and ______

17. What digit is in the tens place? ______

18. So, 872 is rounded to ______.

Round to the nearest ten.

19. 483 ______

20. 115 ______

21. 963 ______

22. 437 ______

23. 45 ______

24. 706 ______

Write a numeral to fit each description by using the digits in the ropes.

25. 1, 7, 9 rounds to 700 ______

26. 8, 1, 0 rounds to 100 ______

27. 6, 2, 8 rounds to 900 ______

28. 7, 5, 3 rounds to 600 ______

Name ____________________

Thousands 1.6

A Brahma bull can weigh between 1,600 and 2,200 pounds.

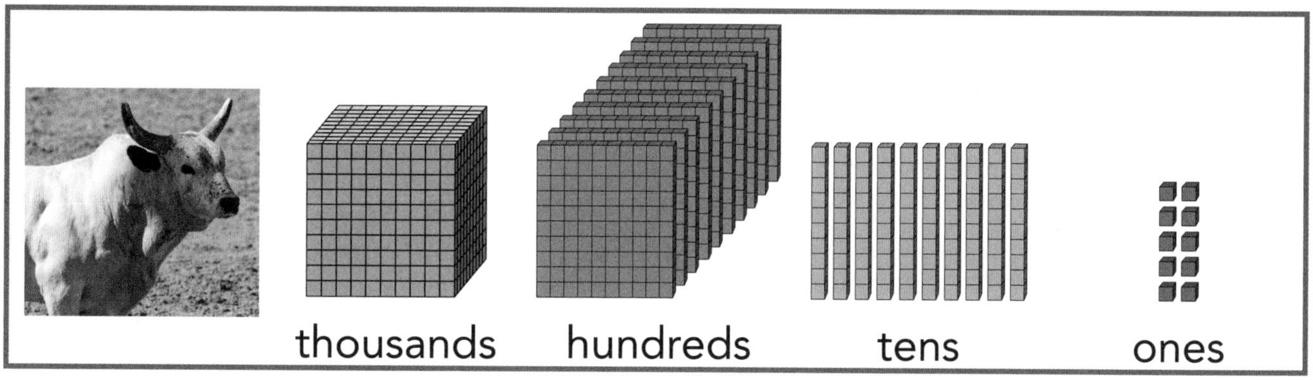

There are 10 tens in 100.

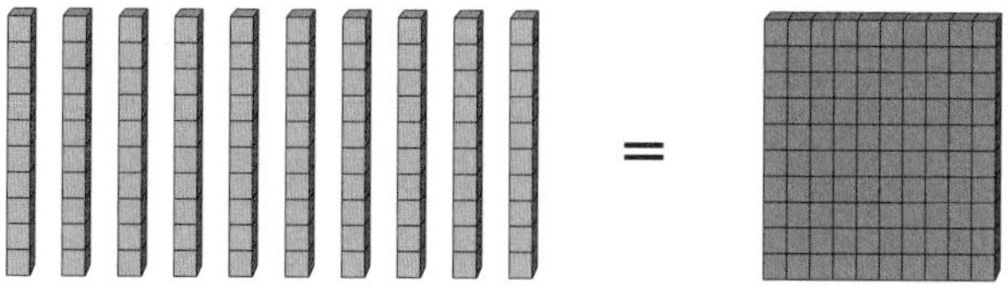

There are 10 hundreds in 1,000.

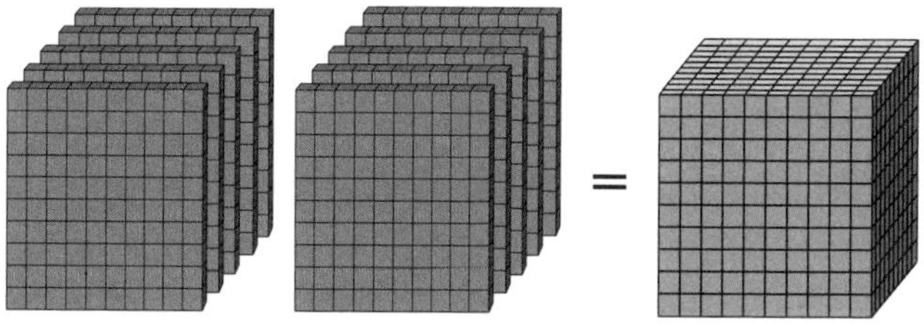

The thousands place is to the left of the hundreds place.

thousands ,	hundreds	tens	ones
,			

Notice that there is a comma between the thousands and hundreds place.

Look at the Base 10 blocks. Write the numerals. Remember to write a 0 if needed.

1. 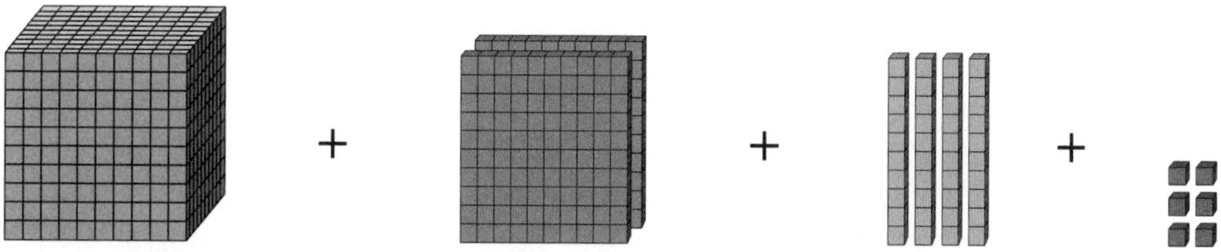 ________

2. 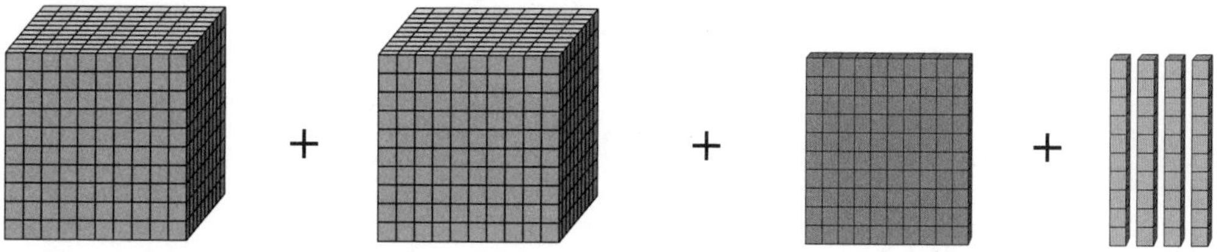 ________

Expanded form shows a numeral as the sum of the value of its digits. The expanded form for 3,756 is 3,000 + 700 + 50 + 6.

The place value table shows the digits in the numeral. Write each numeral in expanded form on the line.

	thousands ,	hundreds	tens	ones	
3.	8 ,	0	2	9	= ______________
4.	6 ,	4	0	0	= ______________
5.	5 ,	2	8	1	= ______________

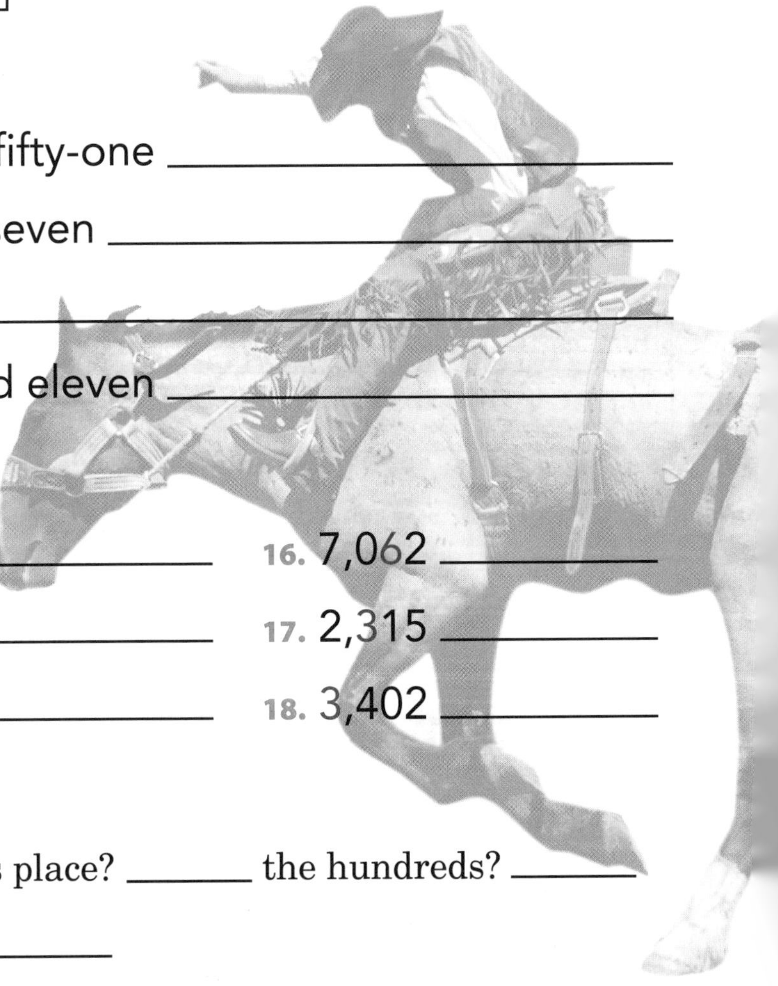

Write the standard form.

6. two thousand, four hundred fifty-one ______________
7. one thousand, five hundred seven ______________
8. five thousand, forty-five ______________
9. seven thousand, one hundred eleven ______________

Write the value of the red digit.

10. 9,741 __________
11. 8,032 __________
12. 6,539 __________
13. 4,110 __________
14. 8,874 __________
15. 2,865 __________
16. 7,062 __________
17. 2,315 __________
18. 3,402 __________

Answer the questions about 6,578.

19. What numeral is in the thousands place? ______ the hundreds? ______

the tens? ______ the ones place? ______

20. What number is 1,000 more than 6,578? ______________

21. What number is 1,000 less than 6,578? ______________

Name ________________________________

Compare Thousands 1.7

Two Clydesdale horses are pulling a plow. The horse on the left weighs 1,845 pounds. The one on the right weighs 1,956 pounds.

Compare their weights.

1. Write the horses' weights in the place value chart. Circle the name of the horse that weighs more.

	thousands ,	hundreds	tens	ones
left horse	,			
right horse	,			

Write the numerals in the place value chart.

	thousands ,	hundreds	tens	ones
2. 4,862	,			
3. 2,643	,			
4. 8,729	,			
5. 5,925	,			
6. 2,063	,			
7. 6,488	,			

Now use the chart to compare. Write > or <.

8. 4,862 ◯ 5,925

9. 2,643 ◯ 2,063

10. 8,729 ◯ 6,488

Compare. Write >, <, or =.

11. 1,645 ○ 1,712	14. 3,478 ○ 1,288	17. 6,045 ○ 3,839
12. 2,391 ○ 2,391	15. 2,453 ○ 2,470	18. 4,901 ○ 4,800
13. 1,263 ○ 1,577	16. 2,983 ○ 2,873	19. 5,027 ○ 5,071

Use the animals' weights to answer these questions.

Arabian	1,000 pounds
Chincoteague pony	850 pounds
Clydesdale	2,200 pounds
Lipizzaner	1,150 pounds

20. Which horse weighs the most?

____

21. Which horse weighs the least?

____

22. Write the animals' weights from least to greatest.

________ ________ ________ ________

Write the numerals in order from least to greatest.

23. 4,568 8,627 3,125 ________ ________ ________

24. 7,021 7,892 7,483 ________ ________ ________

25. 3,498 3,475 3,487 ________ ________ ________

Review

Add or subtract.

26.

8	15	3	4	18	14	5	9
+ 9	− 7	+ 9	+ 8	− 9	− 6	+ 8	+ 7

Name ______________________________

Ten and Hundred Thousands 1.8

Goats have been domesticated since Bible times. They are raised all over the world, especially in Asian countries such as Nepal. In Kathmandu, a city in Nepal, 260,000 goats are sold each year.

Periods make large numerals easier to read. A period is a group of three digits separated by commas in a multidigit number.

thousands period			ones period		
hundred thousands	ten thousands	thousands ,	hundreds	tens	ones
2	6	3 ,	3	5	1

To read a large numeral, say the numeral, and then the period name. Do not say, "ones." To write a large numeral, separate the periods with a comma.

263,351 means 200,000 + 60,000 + 3,000 + 300 + 50 + 1
263,351 is read as
"two hundred sixty-three thousand, three hundred fifty-one."

Write the expanded form of each numeral.

1. 824,625 = ______________________________

2. 361,754 = ______________________________

3. 608,426 = ______________________________

Write the standard form of each numeral.

4. eight hundred seventy-three thousand, four hundred fifty ______________

5. six hundred five thousand, three hundred twenty-one ______________

6. two hundred forty thousand, sixty-five ______________

Write the standard form.

7. 400,000 + 50,000 + 8,000 + 500 + 10 + 6 ________

8. 900,000 + 80,000 + 2,000 + 100 + 7 ________

9. 500,000 + 50,000 + 1,000 + 300 + 50 + 9 ________

10. 200,000 + 10,000 + 100 + 60 + 2 ________

11. 800,000 + 60,000 + 2 ________

12. two hundred forty-six thousand, seven hundred eighty-nine ________

13. thirty-two thousand, ninety-six ________

14. ninety-four thousand, three hundred sixteen ________

15. seven hundred two thousand, thirteen ________

Write the value of the underlined digit in words.

16. $\underline{5}2,365$ ________

17. $\underline{5}84,951$ ________

18. $612,02\underline{6}$ ________

Use the table to answer the questions.

type of goat	country of origin	city	distance to Washington, DC
Kiko	New Zealand	Auckland	8,603 miles
Nigerian Dwarf	Nigeria	Abuja	5,529 miles
Anglo-Nubian	United Kingdom	London	3,674 miles
Saanen	Switzerland	Zurich	4,143 miles

19. Which city is farthest from Washington, DC? ________

20. Which city is closest to Washington, DC? ________

21. Which city is about 4,000 miles from Washington, DC? ________

Name ______________________________

Graph: Conduct a Survey 1.9

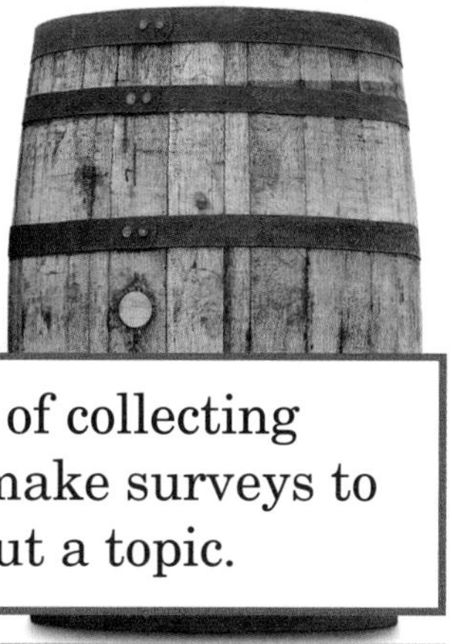

A survey is a way of collecting information. People make surveys to learn more about a topic.

Daniel and his family live on a ranch. They raise quarter horses. Daniel wanted to know what kinds of horses other ranchers raised.

He decided to use his computer to make a survey. Then, he e-mailed the survey to his neighbors. When Daniel received all the surveys back from his neighbors, he made the table below.

Types of Ranch Horses

quarter horses	Tennessee walkers	Appaloosas	ponies	others
200	100	150	50	250

1. Use the information from Daniel's table to make a pictograph. Let each symbol stand for 50 horses.

quarter horses					
Tennessee walkers					
Appaloosas					
ponies					
others					

2. Make a bar graph from the pictograph. Write a title for the graph on the line.

____

quarter horses											
Tennessee walkers											
Appaloosas											
ponies											
others											
	0	25	50	75	100	125	150	175	200	225	250 275

Make a tally chart with the information below.

3. Blue Canyon Ranch has 5 stallions, 25 mares, 23 geldings, 7 fillies, and 5 colts.

____

Name ______________________________

Chapter 1 Review 1.10

1. **Match each word to its definition.**

_____ expanded form

_____ digit

_____ period

_____ ordinal number

_____ standard form

_____ rounding

a. a number that describes the order or position of something in a line or list

b. a way to write a number as the sum of the value of its digits

c. a way to write a number using the digits 0–9 and place value

d. each group of three digits separated by commas in a multidigit number

e. increasing or decreasing a number to a specific place value

f. any of the numerals 0–9

Write the number.

2. 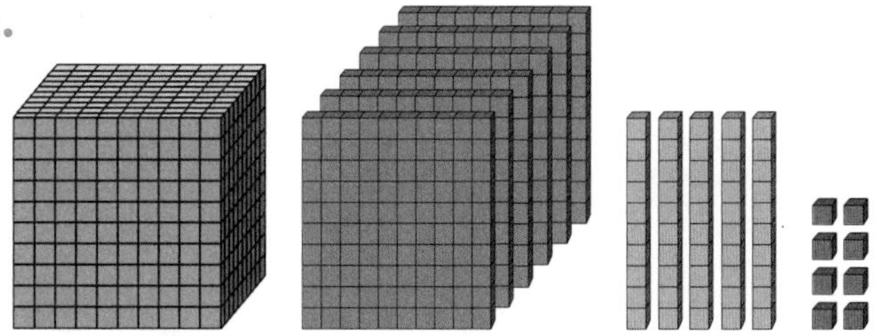

____

3.

thousands ,	hundreds	tens	ones
3 ,	9	6	2

____

4.

hundred thousands	ten thousands	thousands ,	hundreds	tens	ones
2	4	8 ,	0	1	6

____

5. Show 20,507 in the chart.

ten thousands	thousands ,	hundreds	tens	ones
	,			

Label odd or even.

6. 612 ______ 7. 745 ______ 8. 9,314 ______

Compare. Write <, >, or =.

9. 469 ◯ 483 10. 3,040 ◯ 2,865 11. 7,212 ◯ 7,221

Write the number.

12. 6,000 + 100 + 5 ______

13. fifty-two thousand, sixty ______

14. 40,000 + 8,000 + 300 + 90 + 6 ______

15. three thousand, seven hundred thirteen ______

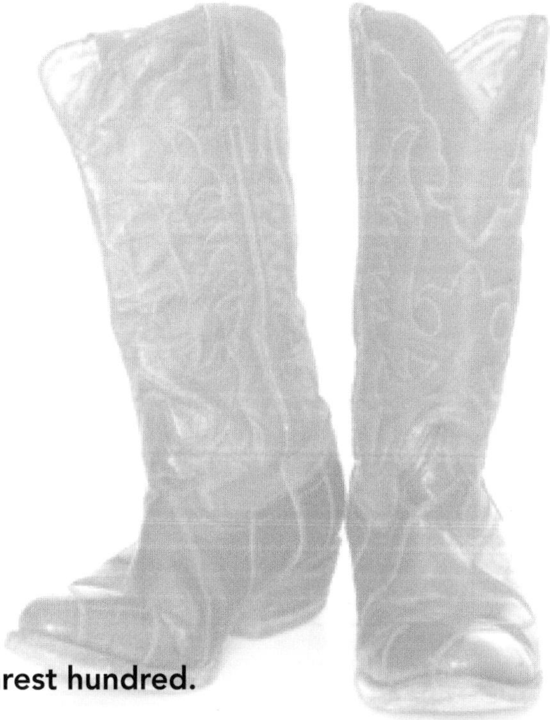

Write the next three numbers in each pattern.

16. 648 650 652 ______ ______ ______

17. 360 370 380 ______ ______ ______

Write the ordinal number.

18. fourteenth ______

19. ninety-third ______

20. fifty-second ______

21. forty-first ______

Round to the nearest ten.

22. 36 ______

23. 75 ______

Round to the nearest hundred.

24. 486 ______

25. 221 ______

Chapter 2
Addition

But seek first His kingdom and His righteousness, and all these things will be given to you as well.
Matthew 6:33

Key Ideas:

Addition: using the counting on, doubles, doubles plus one, and making a ten strategies

Addition: using the Order Property of Addition, the Zero Property of Addition, and the Grouping Property of Addition

Addition: adding three- and four-digit numbers with and without regrouping

Addition: estimating sums

Name ______________________________

Addition Facts to 18

part	part	whole
4 horses	3 horses	7 horses
or		
3 horses	4 horses	7 horses

There are 7 horses. The whole is 7. It is the **sum**. The parts are 3 and 4. They are the **addends**. A number sentence written with an equals sign is an equation.

3	+	4	=	7
addend		addend		sum

$$\begin{array}{rl} 4 & \text{addend} \\ +\,3 & \text{addend} \\ \hline 7 & \text{sum} \end{array}$$

The Order Property of Addition Changing the order of addends does not change the sum.

A fact family is a group of related facts. The two equations above are part of a fact family.

Draw a picture. Write the sum.

1. 2 + 8 = ____

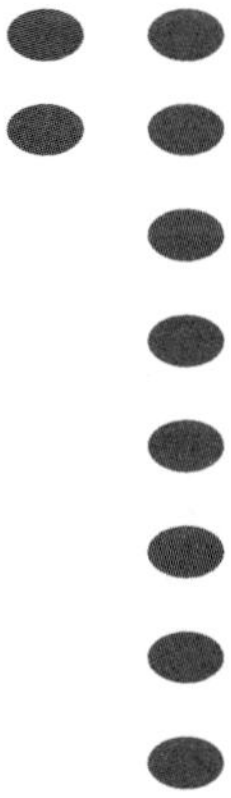

2. 8 + 2 = ____

3. 9 + 3 = ____

4. 7 + 0 = ____

The Zero Property of Addition The sum of 0 and any other number is that number.

How many sheep are there? __________ sheep

If zero more are added, how many sheep will there be? __________ sheep

Write the equation. ______ + ______ = ______

Solve and label using **addend** and **sum**.

5. 7 addend
+ 7 addend
14 sum

6. 5 ________
+ 8 ________
____

7. 9 ________
+ 9 ________
____

8. 6 ________
+ 9 ________
____

Write each sum.

9. 9 + 8

10. 4 + 7

11. 3 + 8

12. 9 + 5

13. 8 + 0

14. 7 + 6

15. 8 + 8

16. 9 + 7 = ____

17. 7 + 9 = ____

18. 4 + 8 = ____

19. 8 + 4 = ____

20. 6 + 5 = ____

21. 5 + 6 = ____

22. 5 + 7 = ____

23. 7 + 5 = ____

Review

Write > or <.

24. 1,359 ◯ 1,395

25. 4,408 ◯ 4,048

26. 13,124 ◯ 8,960

27. 7,987 ◯ 6,199

28. 608,741 ◯ 680,04

29. 127,643 ◯ 127,49

Name ______________________________

Addition Strategies 2.2

Begin to **count on** with the greater addend. To add 3 + 8, remember that the sum is the same as the sum of 8 + 3.

Start at 8 and
count on 3 numbers.
8 + 3 = 11

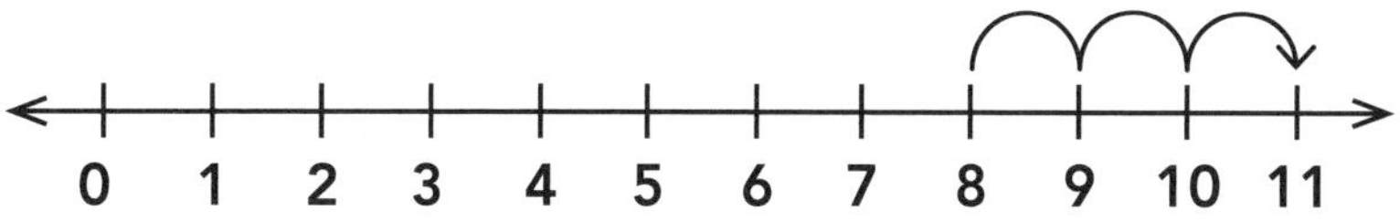

Circle the greater addend. Count on and write the sum.

1.	2.	3.	4.	5.	6.	7.
8	1	2	12	6	14	2
+ 3	+ 9	+ 7	+ 3	+ 3	+ 1	+ 9

To add 8 + 4, first make a ten. Then, add the extras.

8 + 2 + 2 = 12
(8 + 2 → 10)

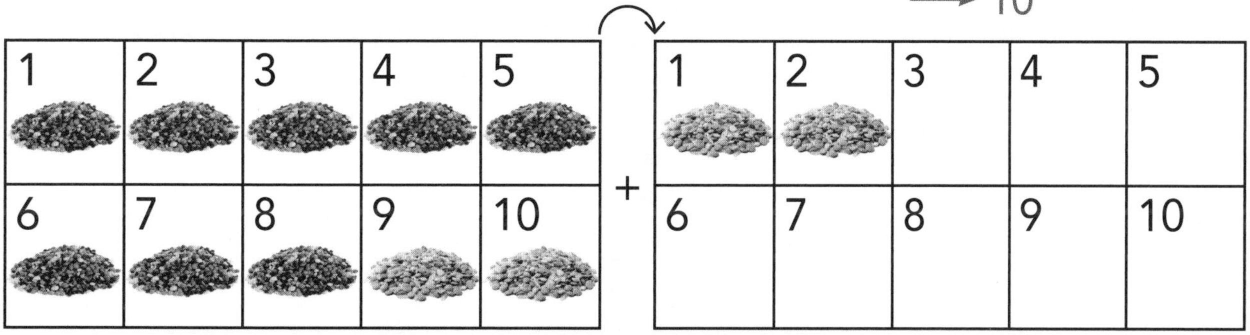

= 12

8 + 2 = 10

Add 2 more.

8 + 4 = ______

Make a ten and add. Write the sum.

8. 7 + 8 = ______

(10 + ___) = ______

9. 9 + 6 = ______

(10 + ___) = ______

10. 8 + 9 = ______

(10 + ___) = ______

Two hens each laid 5 eggs. How many eggs did they lay altogether?

$$5 + 5 = \underline{\qquad} \text{ eggs}$$

One of the hens laid an extra egg. Now how many eggs are there?

$$5 + 6 = \underline{\qquad} \text{ eggs}$$

Since $5 + 5 = 10$, count on one.

$$5 + 5 + 1 = \underline{\qquad} \text{ eggs}$$

Write a double and then add 1 to find the sum.

11.
$$\begin{array}{r} 3 \\ + 3 \\ \hline 6 \end{array} \qquad \begin{array}{r} 3 \\ + 4 \\ \hline \end{array}$$

12.
$$\begin{array}{r} \underline{\qquad} \\ + \underline{\qquad} \\ \hline \end{array} \qquad \begin{array}{r} 8 \\ + 9 \\ \hline \end{array}$$

13.
$$\begin{array}{r} \underline{\qquad} \\ + \underline{\qquad} \\ \hline \end{array} \qquad \begin{array}{r} 6 \\ + 5 \\ \hline \end{array}$$

14.
$$\begin{array}{r} \underline{\qquad} \\ + \underline{\qquad} \\ \hline \end{array} \qquad \begin{array}{r} 5 \\ + 4 \\ \hline \end{array}$$

Use an addition strategy and solve.

15. $9 + 5 = \underline{\qquad}$

16. $7 + 7 = \underline{\qquad}$

17. $8 + 3 = \underline{\qquad}$

18. $7 + 8 = \underline{\qquad}$

19. $8 + 7 = \underline{\qquad}$

20. $7 + 9 = \underline{\qquad}$

21. $3 + 9 = \underline{\qquad}$

22. $6 + 7 = \underline{\qquad}$

23. $8 + 9 = \underline{\qquad}$

24. $7 + 6 = \underline{\qquad}$

Name ____

Word Problems 2.3

A word problem can be solved several ways.

Write an equation. Rosa's family of 6 are picking apples. Her friend's family of 8 will join them. How many people will pick apples?

$$6 + 8 = 14$$

Draw a diagram. Rosa's family picked 7 bushels of apples the first hour and 9 bushels the next hour. How many bushels of apples did they pick?

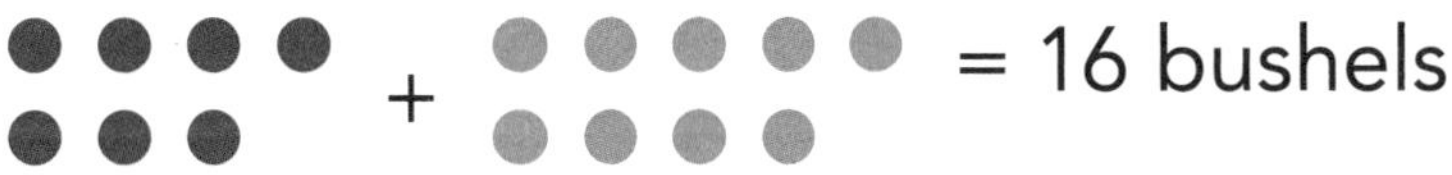

Make a table. If each of Rosa's family members wears work gloves, how many gloves will they need?

workers	1	2	3	4	5	6
gloves	2	4	6	8	10	12

Circle the strategies that you could use to solve each word problem.

1. Six farm workers gathered by the front gate. They all wore work boots. How many work boots could you count?

   equation   picture   table

2. Nine goats were born on Monday. Five more were born on Tuesday. How many goats were born on these two days?

   equation   picture   table

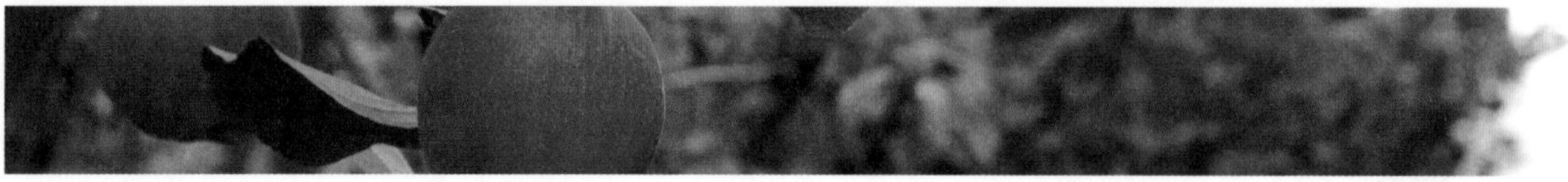

Solve each problem. Label each answer.

3. Ryan's teacher gave each student a bandanna. The class received 6 blue, 3 red, and 4 green bandannas. How many students were there? Draw a picture.

____

4. Olivia rode her horse 8 miles. Madison also rode her horse 8 miles. How many miles did the girls ride? Write an equation.

____

5. Sam drove the tractor to plow 5 rows. Later, he plowed 6 rows. How many rows did Sam plow? Write an equation.

____

6. At a school fund-raiser, people paid $5 to have a photo taken with newborn lambs. How much money was raised if 4 people had their pictures taken? Make a table.

____

7. The 9 pinto horses and 8 draft horses will appear in a parade. How many horses will be in the parade? Write an equation.

____

8. Tori has 7 seed packets. Her brother has 8. How many seed packets in all? Draw a picture.

____

Review

Add. Draw a straight line to match each sum to an egg.

9. $\begin{array}{r} 4 \\ +9 \\ \hline \end{array}$

10. $\begin{array}{r} 8 \\ +3 \\ \hline \end{array}$

11. $\begin{array}{r} 7 \\ +2 \\ \hline \end{array}$

12. $\begin{array}{r} 2 \\ +9 \\ \hline \end{array}$

13. $\begin{array}{r} 6 \\ +4 \\ \hline \end{array}$

14. $\begin{array}{r} 3 \\ +6 \\ \hline \end{array}$

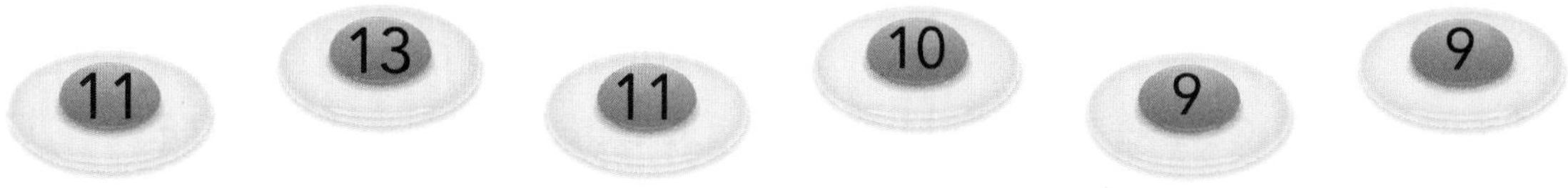

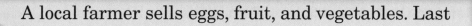

Name ____________________

A local farmer sells eggs, fruit, and vegetables. Last week the farmer sold 15 baskets of green peppers. The red peppers were sold on 2 days last week. Seven baskets of them sold on Wednesday and 6 baskets sold on Friday. How many red-pepper baskets were sold last week?

Problem-Solving Path

1. Understand the question.
   - Underline the question.

2. Analyze the data.
   - Circle the key information.

3. Plan the strategy.
   - Write an equation.
   - Draw a picture.
   - Make a table.

4. Solve the problem.
   - Show your work.
   - Label the answer.

5. Evaluate the result.
   - Compare the answer with the estimated answer.
   - Does the answer make sense?

1. Draw a line under the question in the word problem.

2. Circle the key information in the word problem.

3. Plan the strategy you will use to solve the word problem.

   Estimate the answer.

   I estimate ____ red-pepper baskets.

4. Solve and label the answer.

5. Compare the answer with the estimated answer. Does the answer make sense? Circle your answer.

   yes no

Refer to the Problem-Solving Path. Underline the question. Circle the key information. Draw a picture or write an equation. Label the answer.

6. Shu and Amy picked sweet potatoes. Shu picked 6 baskets and Amy picked 8. How many baskets of sweet potatoes did the girls pick?

____

7. Shu's mother bought 2 baskets of strawberries, 2 baskets of raspberries, 1 basket of beans, and 3 baskets of peas. How many baskets did Shu's mother buy?

____

8. Roberto and his mom bought peaches. They each picked out 9. How many peaches did they buy?

____

9. Roberto's family has 6 people, including Roberto. He bought 2 ears of corn for each person. How many ears of corn did he buy?

____

Review

Round to the nearest ten.

10. 42 ______ 11. 75 ______ 12. 29 ______ 13. 83 ______ 14. 98 ______

Round to the nearest hundred.

15. 566 ______ 16. 216 ______ 17. 495 ______ 18. 722 ______

Group any two addends.
Then, add the third addend.

$$
\begin{array}{l}
3 \\
5 \\
+\,7 \\
\hline
1\,5
\end{array}
\;\Big\rangle\, 8
\qquad
\begin{array}{l}
3 \\
5 \\
+\,7 \\
\hline
1\,5
\end{array}
\;\Big\rangle\, 12
\qquad
\begin{array}{l}
3 \\
5 \\
+\,7 \\
\hline
1\,5
\end{array}
\;\Big\rangle\, 10
$$

The sum is still the same!

The Grouping Property of Addition) Changing the grouping of the addends does not change the sum.

● ● ● ● ● ● ● ● ● ● ●

Circle two addends and write that sum on the side. Add the third addend.

1.
$$
\begin{array}{l}
⑦ \\
2 \\
+⑤ \\
\hline
1\,4
\end{array}
\;\Big\rangle\, 12
$$

2.
$$
\begin{array}{l}
6 \\
2 \\
+\,3 \\
\hline
\end{array}
$$

3.
$$
\begin{array}{l}
7 \\
3 \\
+\,5 \\
\hline
\end{array}
$$

4.
$$
\begin{array}{l}
5 \\
2 \\
+\,5 \\
\hline
\end{array}
$$

Rewrite these equations to change the grouping. Add.

5. (2 + 3) + 5 = _____

 __2__ + (__3__ + __5__) = _____

6. (4 + 4) + 7 = _____

 ___ + (___ + ___) = _____

7. (4 + 2) + 5 = _____

 ___ + (___ + ___) = _____

8. (2 + 5) + 8 = _____

 ___ + (___ + ___) = _____

9. 3 + (4 + 9) = _____

 (___ + ___) + ___ = _____

10. (2 + 6) + 8 = _____

 ___ + (___ + ___) = _____

Add.

11. $\begin{array}{r} 7 \\ 2 \\ +\ 3 \\ \hline \end{array}$ 12. $\begin{array}{r} 4 \\ 5 \\ +\ 3 \\ \hline \end{array}$ 14. $\begin{array}{r} 4 \\ 5 \\ +\ 4 \\ \hline \end{array}$ 16. $\begin{array}{r} 6 \\ 3 \\ +\ 3 \\ \hline \end{array}$ 18. $\begin{array}{r} 8 \\ 1 \\ +\ 3 \\ \hline \end{array}$ 20. $\begin{array}{r} 9 \\ 2 \\ +\ 3 \\ \hline \end{array}$

13. $\begin{array}{r} 3 \\ 4 \\ +\ 5 \\ \hline \end{array}$ 15. $\begin{array}{r} 6 \\ 1 \\ +\ 7 \\ \hline \end{array}$ 17. $\begin{array}{r} 7 \\ 3 \\ +\ 6 \\ \hline \end{array}$ 19. $\begin{array}{r} 8 \\ 2 \\ +\ 5 \\ \hline \end{array}$ 21. $\begin{array}{r} 5 \\ 4 \\ +\ 6 \\ \hline \end{array}$

Write an equation, solve, and label.

22. Shen noticed the cows had colored tags on their ears. There were 4 yellow tags, 5 red tags, and 4 green tags. How many colored tags were there in all?

____

23. Shen counted 6 cows with black faces, 4 cows with white faces, and 8 cows with black-and-white faces. How many cows did Shen count?

____

Review

Add.

24. $\begin{array}{r} 5 \\ +\ 5 \\ \hline \end{array}$ $\begin{array}{r} 5 \\ +\ 6 \\ \hline \end{array}$ 25. $\begin{array}{r} 6 \\ +\ 6 \\ \hline \end{array}$ $\begin{array}{r} 6 \\ +\ 7 \\ \hline \end{array}$ 26. $\begin{array}{r} 7 \\ +\ 7 \\ \hline \end{array}$ $\begin{array}{r} 7 \\ +\ 8 \\ \hline \end{array}$ 27. $\begin{array}{r} 8 \\ +\ 8 \\ \hline \end{array}$ $\begin{array}{r} 8 \\ +\ 9 \\ \hline \end{array}$

28. $5 + 7 =$ ______ 30. $7 + 8 =$ ______ 32. $8 + 9 =$ ______

29. $4 + 9 =$ ______ 31. $9 + 2 =$ ______ 33. $5 + 9 =$ ______

Name ______________________________

Add Without Regrouping

One beehive has produced 42 pounds of honey. Another has produced 36 pounds. How much honey have the two hives produced?

42
4 tens and 2 ones

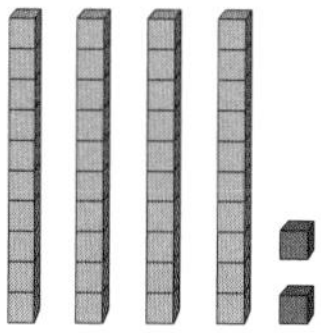

+

36
3 tens and 6 ones

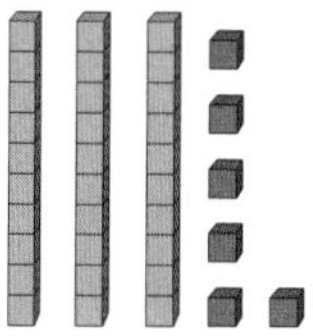

=

78
7 tens and 8 ones

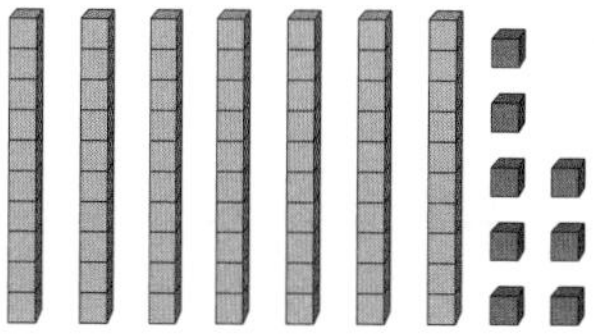

They produced 78 pounds of honey.

	t	o
	4	2
+	3	6
	7	8

Add the ones.
Add the tens.

Add.

1.

	t	o
	2	3
+	1	5

2.

	t	o
	8	1
+	1	6

3.

	t	o
	1	2
+	1	7

4.

	t	o
	6	4
+		5

5.

	t	o
	2	4
+	1	4

6.

	t	o
	4	5
+	5	2

Circle the ones column to mark your starting point. Add.

7. $63 + 21$	9. $55 + 32$	11. $47 + 51$	13. $93 + 6$	15. $45 + 52$
8. $18 + 61$	10. $92 + 7$	12. $33 + 34$	14. $84 + 14$	16. $71 + 26$

17. Add 15 to each of these numbers.

20 ______ 30 ______ 40 ______ 50 ______ 60 ______

Add. Label the answer.

18. The Webbers keep honeybees at their farm. They have just added 42 beehives to the 45 hives they already had. How many hives do the Webbers have now?

____

19. On Saturday, Mrs. Webber sold 32 pints of honey at the farmers' market. The next week, she sold the same amount. How much honey did Mrs. Webber sell?

____

Review

Write the digit in the ones place.

20. 26 ______ 21. 34 ______

Write the digit in the tens place.

22. 157 ______ 23. 83 ______

Write the digit in the hundreds place.

24. 521 ______ 25. 4,928 ______

Write the digit in the thousands place.

26. 13,289 ______ 27. 2,814 ______

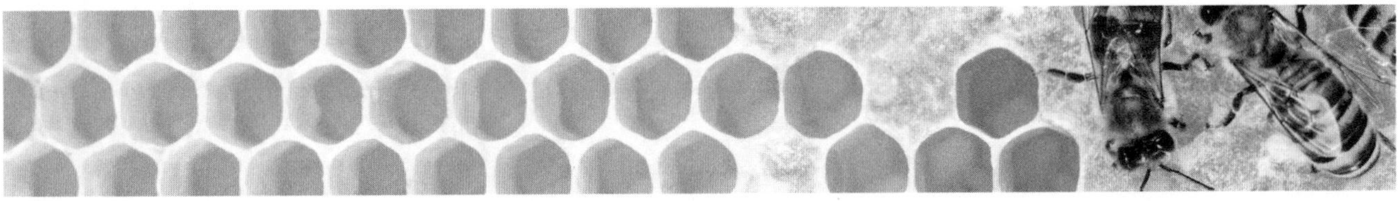

Name ______________________________

Regrouping Ones

On Monday, the Riveras family sheared 48 of their sheep. On Tuesday, they sheared another 47 sheep. How many did they shear in all?

48 + 47 = 95 sheep

4 tens and 8 ones + 4 tens and 7 ones = 9 tens and 5 ones

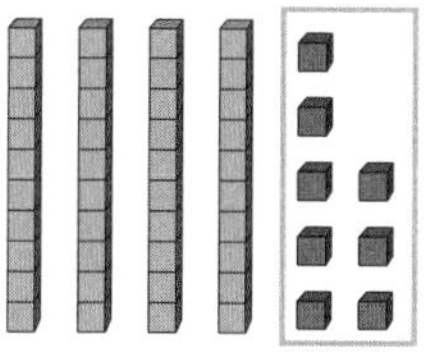

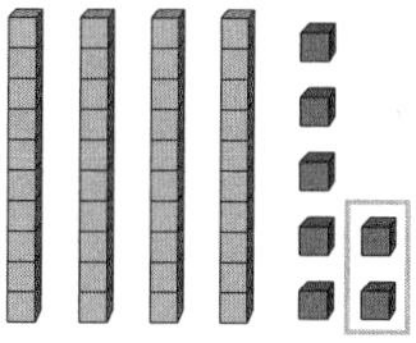

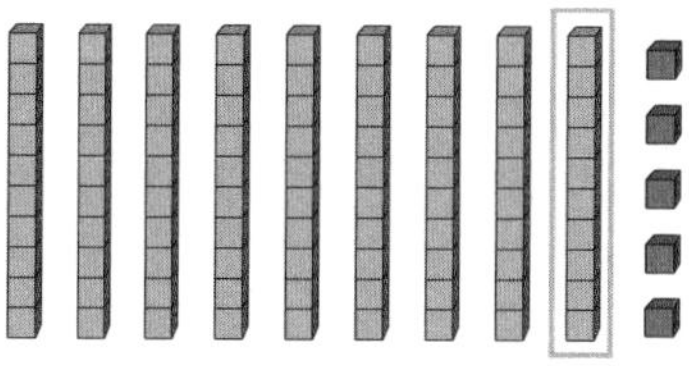

Regroup 10 ones as 1 ten. → 9 tens and 5 ones

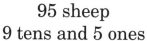

	t	o
	1	
	4	8
+	4	7
	9	5

Add the ones. 15 ones
Write **5** in the ones column.
Write **1** above the tens column.
Add the tens. 9 tens

When the sum of a column is 10 or more, trade or regroup.

Add.

1.

	t	o
	4	6
+	2	5

2.

	t	o
	4	9
+	3	4

3.

	t	o
	4	2
+	1	8

4.

	t	o
	2	8
+	6	4

Circle the ones column. Add.

5. $39 + 56$
7. $24 + 26$
9. $19 + 38$
11. $27 + 37$
13. $79 + 16$
15. $52 + 29$

6. $46 + 25$
8. $28 + 37$
10. $42 + 38$
12. $34 + 56$
14. $68 + 14$
16. $27 + 33$

Solve and label each answer.

17. The ram's wool weighed 23 pounds. The ewe's wool weighed 18 pounds. How many pounds of wool did both sheep produce?

____

18. How many pounds of wool would 2 ewes produce?

____

Add. Write each problem's letter in the box that matches the sum.

19.

$29 + 53$	$47 + 14$	$28 + 15$	$57 + 23$	$19 + 19$	$45 + 17$
E	W	S	O	G	B
$43 + 39$	$51 + 39$	$49 + 11$	$18 + 25$	$36 + 46$	
E	L	D	S	E	

___	___	___	___	___	___	___	___	___	___	___
38	80	60	62	90	82	43	43	82	61	82

Name ______________________________

Farmer Medina's red hens produced 52 eggs last summer. His white hens laid 64 eggs during the same period. How many eggs were produced in all?

Last year, Farmer Medina sold 162 brown eggs and 174 white eggs to the local market. How many eggs did he sell?

[1]

$$\begin{array}{r} 52 \\ +\,64 \\ \hline 116 \end{array}$$ eggs

Add the ones.
Add the tens.
Regroup tens as hundreds.

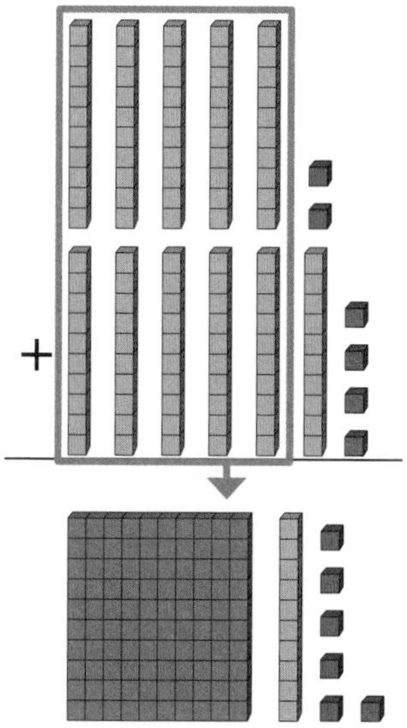

[1]

$$\begin{array}{r} 162 \\ +\,174 \\ \hline 336 \end{array}$$ eggs

Add the ones. Add the tens.
Regroup tens as hundreds.
Add the hundreds.

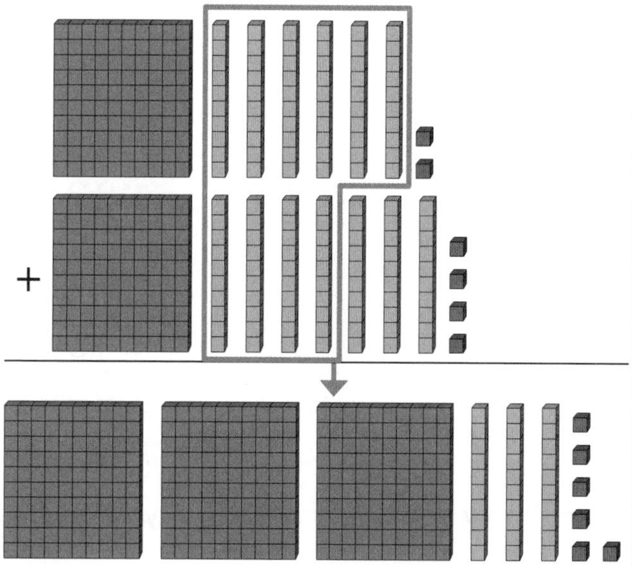

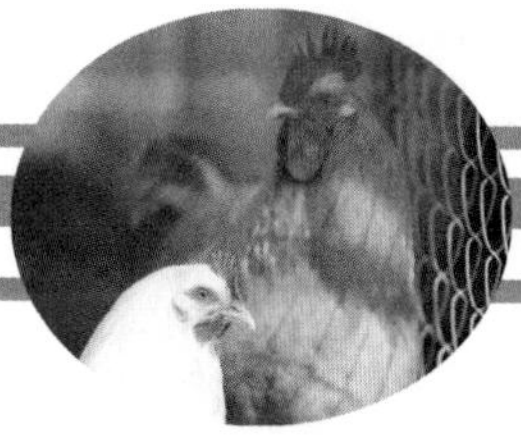

Add. Regroup the tens.

1. [ ] $\begin{array}{r} 64 \\ +\,53 \\ \hline \end{array}$

2. [ ] $\begin{array}{r} 349 \\ +\,480 \\ \hline \end{array}$

3. [ ] $\begin{array}{r} 187 \\ +\,452 \\ \hline \end{array}$

4. [ ] $\begin{array}{r} 98 \\ +\,31 \\ \hline \end{array}$

Add. Regroup the tens.

5. 57 + 51	6. 63 + 54	7. 81 + 37	8. 56 + 70	9. 35 + 82	10. 73 + 62

Add. Regroup the tens.

11. 267 + 362	12. 142 + 575	13. 573 + 286	14. 339 + 380	15. 425 + 191	16. 756 + 182

Add. Regroup as needed.

17. 63 + 55	20. 48 + 61	23. 681 + 243	26. 26 + 83	29. 452 + 263	32. 43 + 16
18. 394 + 112	21. 283 + 426	24. 86 + 82	27. 75 + 52	30. 636 + 82	33. 83 + 64
19. 45 + 91	22. 372 + 261	25. 483 + 356	28. 124 + 194	31. 292 + 253	34. 553 + 294

Solve. Show your work and label your answer.

35. Farmer Medina sold 53 eggs at a roadside stand. He sold twice as many to the market. How many eggs did he sell to the market?

Review

Round to the nearest ten.

36. 64 ______ 27 ______ 33 ______ 55 ______ 89 ______

Round to the nearest hundred.

37. 631 ______ 487 ______ 708 ______ 921 ______

Name ____

Practice: Regrouping 2.9

Celia's family sells piglets. Her family sold 67 piglets last week and 45 this week. How many piglets were sold?

1 67 +45 2	Add the ones. 12 ones Write **2** in the ones column. Write **1** above the tens column.
11 67 +45 112	Add the tens. 11 tens Write **1** in the tens column. Write **1** above the hundreds column.

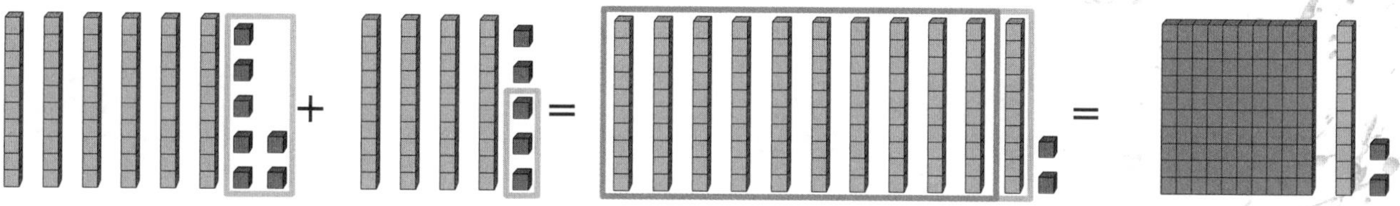

67 + 45 = 112 piglets

6 tens and 7 ones; 4 tens and 5 ones; 1 hundred, 1 ten, 2 ones

Add. Fill in the circles to show where you had to regroup.

1. $36 + 25$
   ○ ones ○ tens ○ neither
2. $49 + 50$
   ○ ones ○ tens ○ neither
3. $246 + 391$
   ○ ones ○ tens ○ neither
4. $385 + 465$
   ○ ones ○ tens ○ neither
5. $253 + 168$
   ○ ones ○ tens ○ neither

Add. Regroup the ones and tens as needed.

6. $74 + 69$
7. $77 + 46$
8. $156 + 488$
9. $59 + 48$
10. $29 + 73$
11. $694 + 228$
12. $87 + 33$
13. $56 + 46$
14. $378 + 475$
15. $72 + 98$
16. $83 + 79$
17. $249 + 375$
18. $86 + 35$
19. $39 + 87$
20. $756 + 176$
21. $94 + 96$
22. $63 + 67$
23. $614 + 189$

Add. Regroup as needed.

24. $78 + 23$
25. $138 + 630$
26. $70 + 37$
27. $472 + 138$
28. $39 + 63$
29. $147 + 359$
30. $55 + 82$
31. $75 + 60$
32. $11 + 48$
33. $23 + 94$
34. $727 + 194$
35. $128 + 109$

Solve. Label your answer.

36. Celia's piglet is 1 month old and weighs 11 pounds. When it turns 6 weeks old, it will double its current weight. How much will the piglet weigh at 6 weeks?

____

37. These two piglets weigh 25 and 35 pounds. What is their combined weight?

____

Name ______________________________

4-Digit Numbers 2.10

Bessie weighs 2,465 pounds.
She produces 2,090 gallons
of milk each year.

Bea weighs 1,876 pounds.
She produces 988 gallons
of milk each year.

What do the two cows weigh altogether?
How much milk do the cows produce in a year?

$$\begin{array}{r} {\scriptstyle 1\ \ 11} \\ 2,465 \\ +\,1,876 \\ \hline 4,341 \end{array}$$ pounds

- Add the ones and regroup if needed.
- Add the tens and regroup if needed.
- Add the hundreds and regroup if needed.
- Add the thousands.

	2,	0	9	0
+		9	8	8
	3,	0	7	8

gallons per year

When adding a four-digit numeral to a two- or three-digit numeral, you must align the digits carefully!

Add.

1. $\begin{array}{r} 6,583 \\ +\,1,619 \\ \hline \end{array}$

2. $\begin{array}{r} 4,075 \\ +\,3,398 \\ \hline \end{array}$

3. $\begin{array}{r} 5,594 \\ +\,2,759 \\ \hline \end{array}$

4. $\begin{array}{r} 3,284 \\ +\,4,876 \\ \hline \end{array}$

Rewrite each problem. Add.

5. 7,089 + 650

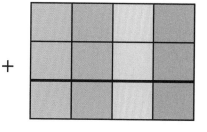

6. 8,026 + 92

7. 5,673 + 253

Add.

8. 2,778 + 3,041
12. 4,395 + 4,243
16. 7,281 + 1,464
20. 1,433 + 3,379
24. 3,596 + 6,278

9. 5,362 + 3,879
13. 8,081 + 1,589
17. 2,988 + 2,346
21. 4,681 + 3,499
25. 7,165 + 1,978

10. 1,824 + 193
14. 2,660 + 89
18. 3,725 + 83
22. 5,691 + 155
26. 8,952 + 83

11. 2,677 + 192
15. 888 + 21
19. 679 + 83
23. 491 + 348
27. 6,791 + 2,157

Solve. Show your work. Label your answer.

28. Andrew counted 1,563 Holstein cows.
He counted 44 Guernsey cows.
How many cows did Andrew count?

Review

29. **Subtract.**

15 − 6	17 − 8	10 − 4	16 − 8	14 − 7	12 − 9	18 − 9	9 − 3
11 − 5	8 − 6	15 − 7	17 − 9	10 − 6	16 − 7	14 − 5	13 − 6

Name ________________________________

Mental Addition 2.11

The Graf family owns a goat dairy. The dairy has 35 adult goats and 7 kids. How many goats are there in all?

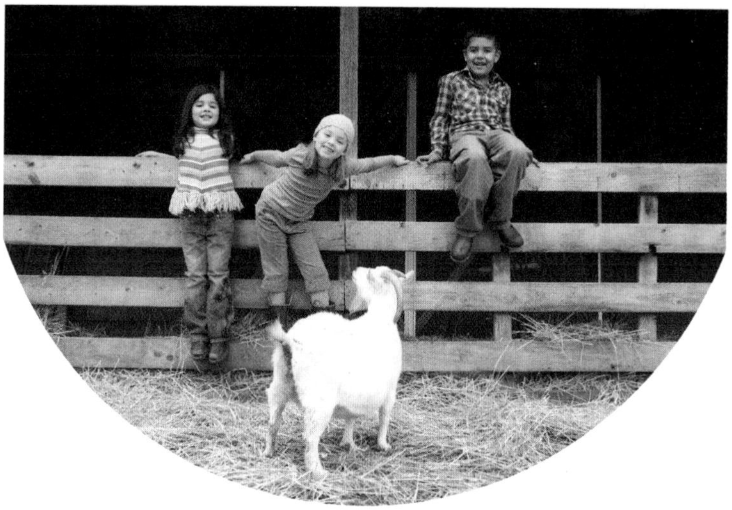

To add a one-digit number to a two-digit number, you must first know the basic addition fact for the ones. If the sum is 10 or more, add 1 to the tens.

Can you use mental addition to find the total number of goats?

$$\begin{array}{r} 35 \\ +\ \ 7 \\ \hline \end{array}$$

Add the ones in your mind.
$5 + 7 = 12$

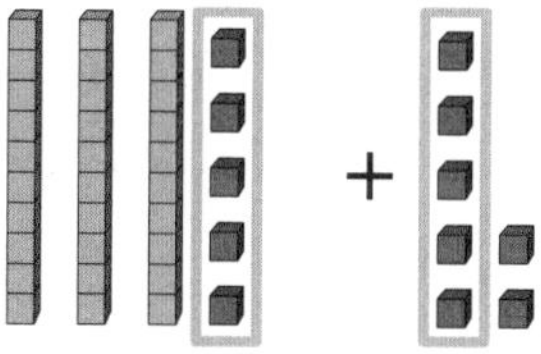

$12 = 1$ ten, 2 ones
The sum will have 2 ones.
Add 1 to the tens.

$35 + 7 = 42$ goats

Write the addition fact that will help you solve the problem. Add.

1. $\begin{array}{r} 76 \\ +\ 8 \\ \hline \end{array}$ ______ + ______

2. $\begin{array}{r} 35 \\ +\ 9 \\ \hline \end{array}$ ______ + ______

3. $\begin{array}{r} 18 \\ +\ 5 \\ \hline \end{array}$ ______ + ______

4. $\begin{array}{r} 66 \\ +\ 7 \\ \hline \end{array}$ ______ + ______

5. $\begin{array}{r} 84 \\ +\ 9 \\ \hline \end{array}$ ______ + ______

6. $\begin{array}{r} 43 \\ +\ 8 \\ \hline \end{array}$ ______ + ______

7. $\begin{array}{r} 26 \\ +\ 5 \\ \hline \end{array}$ ______ + ______

8. $\begin{array}{r} 52 \\ +\ 9 \\ \hline \end{array}$ ______ + ______

9. Will the sum of 29 + 8 be a number in the twenties or in the thirties? Explain your answer.

____

Use mental addition to find each sum.

10. $78 + 7$

12. $35 + 5$

14. $40 + 8$

16. $63 + 6$

18. $59 + 9$

20. $17 + 7$

11. $37 + 5$

13. $25 + 8$

15. $47 + 6$

17. $65 + 9$

19. $79 + 3$

21. $86 + 6$

22. 18 + 2 = ______

23. 67 + 5 = ______

24. 45 + 7 = ______

25. 28 + 9 = ______

26. 48 + 8 = ______

27. 85 + 3 = ______

28. 73 + 9 = ______

29. 55 + 8 = ______

30. 36 + 6 = ______

Use mental addition to solve each word problem. Label the answers.

31. A goat has 24 molars and 8 sharp teeth. How many teeth does a goat have?

____

32. The Grafs' goats produced 64 quarts of milk today. There are 53 quart bottles inside the milk house and 8 more in a box outside. Are there enough bottles to hold all of today's milk?

____

33. Abbie helps her parents milk the goats. Today, Abbie milked 4 goats. Her dad milked 27 goats. How many goats did they milk in all?

____

Many Native Americans used deer hide for clothing and shelter. They used antlers for tools and weapons. Deer meat, or venison, was a regular part of their diet.

One member of the Ojibwe tribe collected 16 hides. His brother collected 27. About how many hides did the men have?

$$
\begin{array}{r} 16 \\ +27 \\ \hline \end{array}
\quad \circ\!\!-\!\!\circ \quad
\begin{array}{r} 20 \\ +30 \\ \hline 50 \ \text{hides} \end{array}
$$

To **estimate** is to figure a close answer. You can estimate the sum by rounding each addend to the nearest ten. Then, add the rounded numbers.

$$
\begin{array}{r} 516 \\ +283 \\ \hline \end{array}
\quad \circ\!\!-\!\!\circ \quad
\begin{array}{r} 500 \\ +300 \\ \hline 800 \end{array}
$$

You can also use estimation to check your addition.
- You can estimate the sum by rounding each addend to the nearest hundred.
- Add to find the estimated sum.
- If you added correctly, the exact sum should be close to the estimate.

The exact sum is 799. It is very close to the estimate.

● ● ● ● ● ● ● ● ● ●

Round the addends to the nearest ten. Estimate the sum. Solve.

1. $\begin{array}{r} 39 \\ +47 \\ \hline \end{array}$ _____
 $+$ _____

2. $\begin{array}{r} 89 \\ +26 \\ \hline \end{array}$ _____
 $+$ _____

3. $\begin{array}{r} 64 \\ +92 \\ \hline \end{array}$ _____
 $+$ _____

Round the addends to the nearest hundred. Estimate the sum. Solve.

4. 942 + 589 = ____ + ____ = ____

6. 129 + 284 = ____ + ____ = ____

8. 342 + 438 = ____ + ____ = ____

5. 711 + 583 = ____ + ____ = ____

7. 140 + 321 = ____ + ____ = ____

9. 678 + 204 = ____ + ____ = ____

Number Bank
400
800
500
900
600
700

Choose an estimated sum from the Number Bank to match each addition problem.

10. 368 + 220

12. 185 + 214

14. 408 + 88

11. 803 + 98

13. 387 + 273

15. 481 + 312

Round to estimate.

16. Doli's mother is teaching her to spin yarn from wool for weaving. Doli's mother has woven 38 blankets and 42 rugs. Estimate the number of woven items she has made.

____

Review

Write the next three numerals in each pattern.

17. 25 35 45 ____ ____ ____

18. 118 128 138 ____ ____ ____

19. 497 498 499 ____ ____ ____

20. 235 335 435 ____ ____ ____

Name ______________________________

Column Addition 2.13

Jeremy's family raises rabbits. The family has 16 white rabbits, 22 gray rabbits, and 14 black rabbits. How many rabbits are there in all?

$$\begin{array}{r} 16 \\ 22 \\ +14 \\ \hline \end{array}$$

Column addition is used for adding addends vertically. You can use mental math to add columns.

- Add mentally to **make a ten**.

$$\begin{array}{r} ^{1} \\ 16 \\ 22 \\ +14 \\ \hline 52 \end{array} \text{ rabbits} \qquad 6 + 4 = 10, \quad 10 + 2 = 12$$

In this problem, you can make a 10 in the ones column.

Sometimes you can also make a 10 in the tens or hundreds columns.

- Add mentally using another strategy, such as **doubles**.

$$\begin{array}{r} ^{2} \\ 59 \\ 68 \\ +37 \\ \hline 164 \end{array} \qquad 9 + 8 = 17, \quad 17 + 7 = 24$$

In this problem, use a doubles fact to add the ones column.

Other strategies include **doubles plus one** and **counting on**.

Check the box that shows the strategy you would use to add the ones column. Add.

1. $\begin{array}{r} 84 \\ 69 \\ +56 \\ \hline \end{array}$ ☐ make a 10 ☐ use another strategy

2. $\begin{array}{r} 16 \\ 25 \\ +18 \\ \hline \end{array}$ ☐ make a 10 ☐ use another strategy

3. $\begin{array}{r} 26 \\ 32 \\ +88 \\ \hline \end{array}$ ☐ make a 10 ☐ use another strategy

4. $\begin{array}{r} 49 \\ 69 \\ +78 \\ \hline \end{array}$ ☐ make a 10 ☐ use another strategy

Add.

5.	7.	9.	11.	13.	15.
18	97	88	362	208	621
64	22	75	428	459	283
+ 52	+ 59	+ 43	+ 195	+ 512	+ 207

6.	8.	10.	12.	14.	16.
403	612	105	803	213	729
711	805	275	214	537	306
+ 336	+ 303	+ 688	+ 52	+ 628	+ 511

Solve. Show your work and label your answers.

17. Jeremy has 57 pictures of Dutch rabbits, 16 pictures of Angora rabbits, and 13 pictures of wild rabbits in his scrapbook. What is the total number of rabbit pictures?

____

18. Jeremy did research online to find the number of kits, or baby rabbits, in each litter. He discovered that a mother rabbit can have 14 kits in one litter! If a mother rabbit has 3 litters, how many kits would she have in all?

____

19. The rabbits that Jeremy raises are sold to pet shops. Last year, Jeremy sold 43 rabbits to Friendly Pets, 21 rabbits to Happy Pet Shop, and 18 rabbits to Gentle Pets. How many rabbits did Jeremy sell last year?

____

Name ______________________________

Graph: Pictograph 2.14

A **pictograph** is a graph that uses pictures or symbols to stand for a number of real objects.

Each pictograph has a title that tells what the graph represents. Labels are organized on one side of the graph. A key tells how many real objects are represented by each picture or symbol.

Animals Counted at Matsui's Farm in July

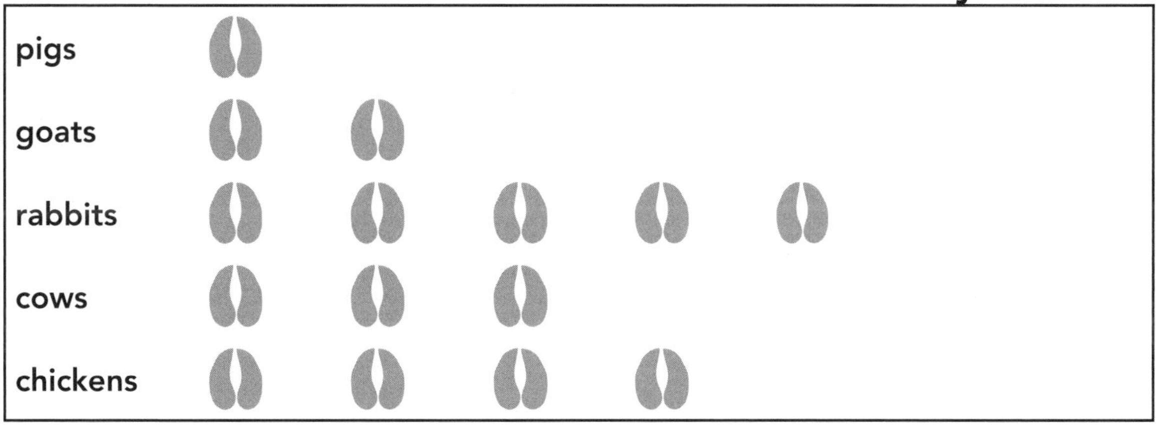

key [symbol] = 2 animals

Read the pictograph above. Answer the questions.

1. Where were the animals counted? ______________________________

2. When were the animals counted? ______________________________

3. How many cows were counted? __________

4. How many chickens? __________ How many goats? __________

5. How many more chickens were counted than cows? __________

6. How many animals were counted altogether? __________

Many American Indian tribes live in the Southwest. Read the pictograph. Answer the questions.

Performers in a Regional Powwow

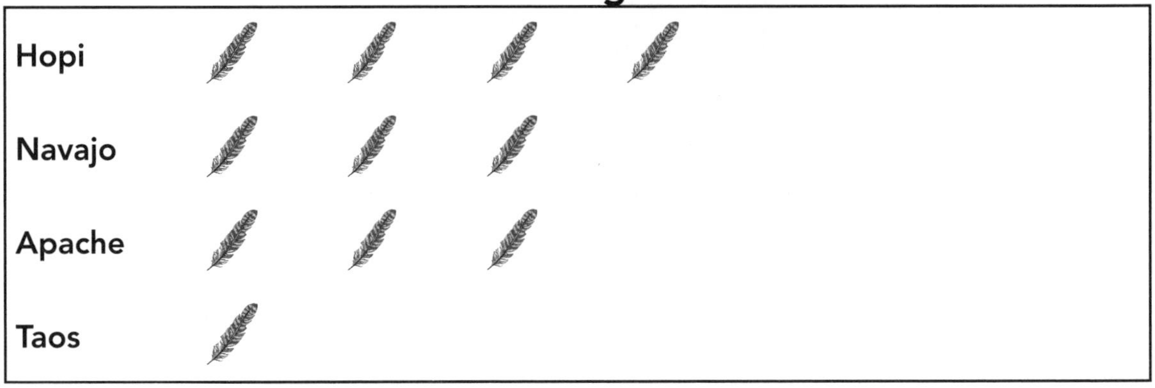

key = 4 performers

7. How many of the Hopi tribe performed at the powwow? ____________

8. Which tribes had exactly 12 performers? ____________

9. Which tribe had more performers than the Apaches? ____________

10. Which tribe had the fewest performers? ____________

---

11. Use the information from the tally chart to design a pictograph.

Performers	
boys	卌
girls	卌 |

____

key =

Name ______________________________

Write the letter of the correct word or property.

1. ______ a number sentence with an equals sign
2. ______ Changing the grouping of the addends does not change the sum.
3. ______ a graph that uses pictures or symbols
4. ______ to figure a close answer
5. ______ related addition and subtraction facts
6. ______ The sum of zero and any number is that number.

a. estimate

b. fact family

c. pictograph

d. equation

e. Zero Property of Addition

f. Grouping Property of Addition

Add mentally. Write the sum.

7. $75 + 8$ = ___

8. $89 + 6$ = ___

9. $34 + 8$ = ___

10. $45 + 6$ = ___

11. $88 + 8$ = ___

12. $97 + 9$ = ___

Round to the nearest ten or hundred. Estimate the sum.

13. $23 + 67$ → ___ + ___ = ___

14. $491 + 624$ → ___ + ___ = ___

15. $345 + 178$ → ___ + ___ = ___

Use column addition to find the sum.

16. $38 + 51 + 72$

17. $96 + 12 + 74$

18. $24 + 78 + 45$

19. $39 + 68 + 37$

Add.

20. $480 + 185$

21. $217 + 636$

22. $364 + 259$

23. $2,698 + 6,051$

24. $5,249 + 893$

Use the Problem-Solving Path to solve. Label the answer.

25. Rew and his dad are flying a UAV (unmanned aerial vehicle) over their farm. Its camera recorded 16 cows, 22 calves, and 18 horses. How many animals were there altogether?

____

Chapter 3
Subtraction

Do not add to what I command you and do not subtract from it, but keep the commands of the Lord your God that I give you.
Deuteronomy 4:2

Key Ideas:

Subtraction: using the counting back or counting on strategies

Subtraction: subtracting three- and four-digit numerals with and without regrouping

Subtraction: subtracting across zeros

Subtraction: estimating differences

Name ______________________________

Subtraction Facts to 18 3.1

There are 10 Asian monkeys on the log. Three monkeys run off to play. How many monkeys are left?

whole	
part	part

When you know a whole and one part, you subtract to find the other part.

10 monkeys	
3 monkeys	? monkeys

When you take one part away from the whole, the other part is the difference.

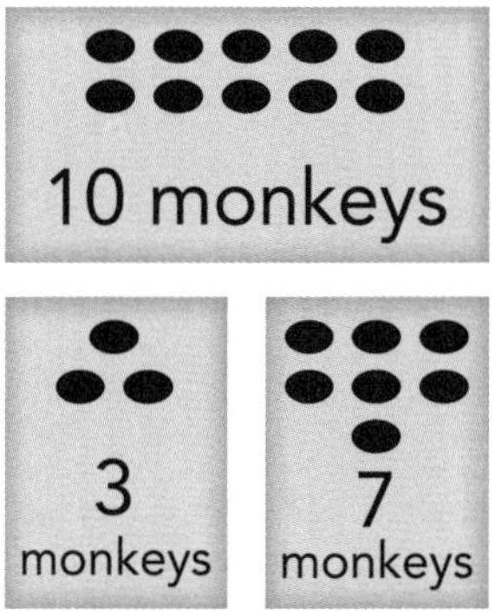

10 is the whole. Take away 3 and the difference is 7.

10 – 3 = 7 monkeys

Subtraction can also show the difference between two sets of objects. There are 8 adult monkeys and 2 babies. How many more adults are there than babies? The difference between the adults and babies is 6.

8 – 2 = 6 adults

Color the part being taken away. Circle the part that is left. Write the difference.

1. 10 – 6 = ______

3. 17 – 8 = ______

2. ______ = 12 – 9

4. ______ = 15 – 9

Label the whole, part, and difference. Solve.

5. 13 − 8 ________ ________ ________

6. 15 − 9 ________ ________ ________

7. 10 − 8 ________ ________ ________

Subtract.

8. 12 − 5

9. 16 − 7

10. 14 − 9

11. 17 − 8

12. 18 − 9

13. 13 − 7 = ____

14. 11 − 9 = ____

15. 12 − 6 = ____

Write an equation.

16. India has many snakes. Seventeen snakes were basking in the sun. Nine were king cobras and the rest were vipers. How many snakes were vipers?

____

17. How many more king cobras were there than vipers?

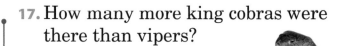

____

Review

Make a ten to add.

18. 9 + 4   10 + ____

19. 9 + 8   10 + ____

20. 7 + 4   10 + ____

21. 8 + 4   10 + ____

Add.

22. 7 + 3 + 3

23. 3 + 4 + 5

24. 1 + 6 + 4

25. 1 + 7 + 2

26. 2 + 4 + 4

Name ____

The boys collected 9 bugs for their science project. Two bugs escaped. How many bugs are left?

Of the 7 bugs, only 4 were used for the project. How many bugs were not used?

9 – 2 = ______ bugs   7 – 4 = ______ bugs

To subtract 1, 2, or 3, count back from the whole.

count back 2 numbers

9 – 2

9 8 7

9 – 2 = 7

To subtract larger numbers, count on to the whole.

7 – 4

4 5 6 7

7 – 4 = 3

count on 3 numbers

Should you count back or count on? Circle one.

1. 10 – 8
count back
count on

2. 11 – 2
count back
count on

3. 11 – 8
count back
count on

4. 8 – 6
count back
count on

Count back to solve and circle the difference.

5. 12 – 3
12 ___ ___ ___

6. 10 – 1
10 ___

7. 9 – 3
9 ___ ___ ___

8. 10 – 2
10 ___ ___

Count on to solve and circle the difference.

9. 11 – 8
8 ___ ___ ___

10. 8 – 6
6 ___ ___

11. 10 – 9
9 ___

12. 11 – 9
9 ___ ___

The third-grade class had 14 plants. They took 8 of them out for an experiment. How many plants were left in the classroom?

14 – 8 = ______ plants

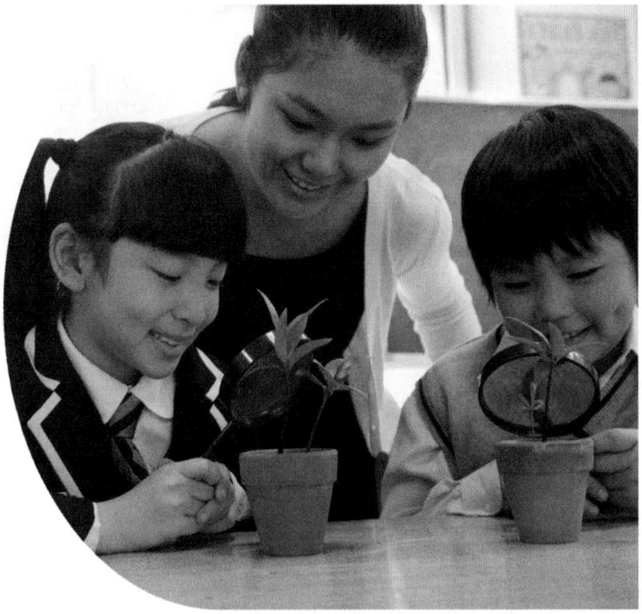

Eight plants were taken away. Put 8 in the ten-frame. Then, make a 10 by filling in the frame and counting up to 14.

14 – 8 = 6 plants

2 + 4 = 6
6 plants were left in the classroom.

Subtract by making a 10.

13. 13 − 9 = ______ To make 10; ______ To make 13

14. 17 − 8 = ______ To make 10; ______ To make 17

15. 16 − 7 = ______ To make 10; ______ To make 16

16. 15 − 9

17. 11 − 9

18. 12 − 8

19. 18 − 9

20. 14 − 8

21. 17 − 9

22. 11 − 8

23. 15 − 8

24. 14 − 9

Name ______________________________

Fact Families 3.3

The Asian area of the zoo has 2 giant pandas and 3 Bactrian camels.

A fact family rearranges the three numbers.

$3 + 2 = 5$ $\quad$ $5 - 3 = 2$

$2 + 3 = 5$ $\quad$ $5 - 2 = 3$

whole	
part	part

5 animals	
3 camels	2 pandas

●●●●● 5 animals	
●●● 3 camels	●● 2 pandas

Complete each fact family.

1. $6 + 5 = 11$

   ____ + ____ = ____

   $11 - 6 =$ ____

   ____ − ____ = ____

2. $7 + 8 = 15$

   ____ + ____ = ____

   ____ − ____ = ____

   ____ − ____ = ____

3. $8 + 5 =$ ____

   ____ + ____ = ____

   ____ − ____ = ____

   ____ − ____ = ____

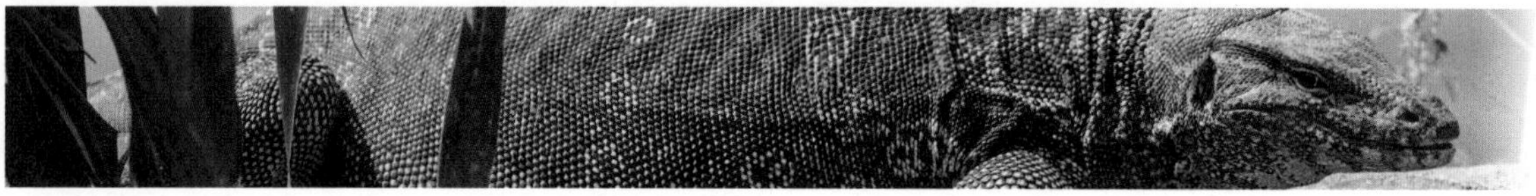

Use these numbers to write fact families.

4. 5 12 7

______
______
______
______

5. 8 14 6

______
______
______
______

6. 9 16 7

______
______
______
______

Find the difference. Write a related addition problem.

7. $13 - 7 =$ ______ ; + ______

8. $12 - 3 =$ ______ ; + ______

9. $14 - 9 =$ ______ ; + ______

Review

Add.

10. $6 + 1 + 7$

12. $3 + 1 + 7$

14. $6 + 2 + 2$

16. $2 + 2 + 8$

18. $4 + 1 + 9$

11. $4 + 5$

13. $6 + 6$

15. $6 + 7$

17. $8 + 8$

19. $8 + 9$

Subtract by making a ten. Fill in the blanks.

20. $13 - 8$ ______ to make 10; ______ to make 13

21. $15 - 9$ ______ to make 10; ______ to make 15

Name ____

Choose an Operation 3.4

Mr. Zhang's third-grade class went on a hike. The girls saw 8 squirrels and the boys saw 5 squirrels. How many squirrels did the class see? **Think:** Do I need to find the whole (add) or a part (subtract)?

+ or − ?

Addition and subtraction are inverse operations. You can use inverse, or opposite, operations to check your work.

Does 8 + 5 = 13?

Yes, because 13 − 8 = 5.

Solve. Check each answer.

1. Sara took 34 pictures of flowers and 62 pictures of butterflies. How many pictures did she take? **Think:** Whole or part? **+** or **−**?

solve	check

2. Philip saw 16 deer. When he looked again, he saw only 13. How many deer had run away? **Think:** Whole or part? **+** or **−**?

solve	check

Solve. Check each answer.

3. The class brought 29 bags of snacks. Now there are only 7 bags left. How many bags of snacks have been eaten?

4. By the waterfall, the class counted 78 goldfish and 21 red fish. How many fish did they see?

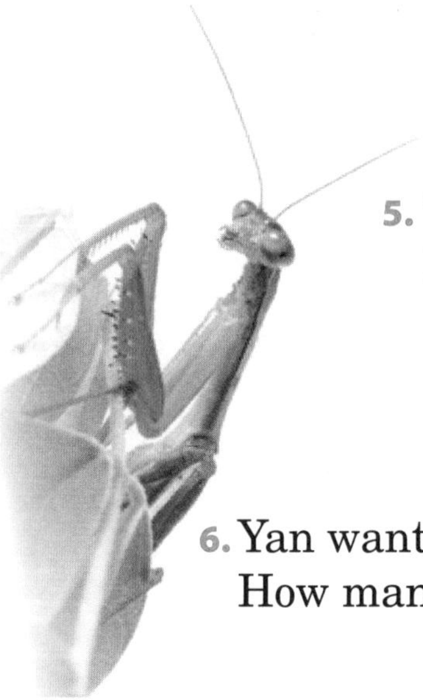

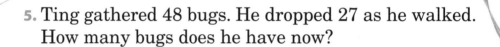

5. Ting gathered 48 bugs. He dropped 27 as he walked. How many bugs does he have now?

6. Yan wants to take 24 photos of animals. She has only taken 3. How many pictures does she still need to take?

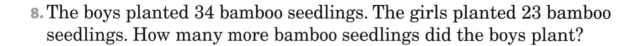

7. A map of the park costs 55¢. Ron only has 25¢. How much more money does he need to buy a map?

8. The boys planted 34 bamboo seedlings. The girls planted 23 bamboo seedlings. How many more bamboo seedlings did the boys plant?

Name ____

Subtract Without Regrouping 3.5

A group of 34 Asian short-clawed otters live near the rice field. Twelve of them live together in the same lodge. How many otters do not live in the lodge?

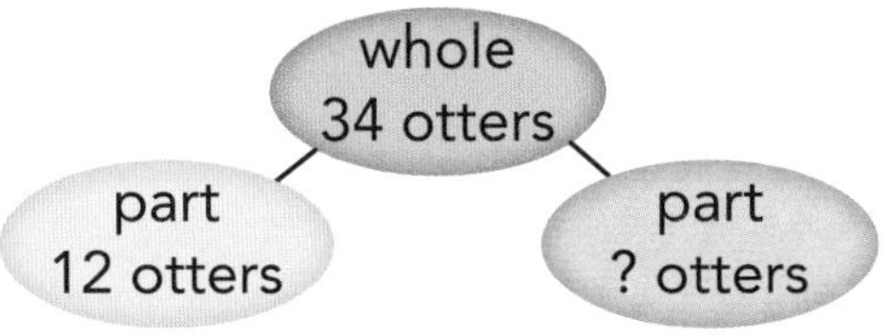

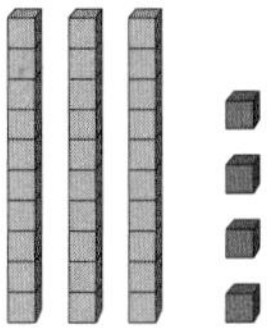

Show 34.

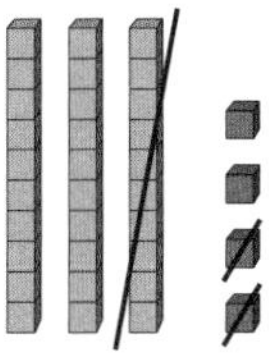

Take away 12.

34 – 12 = 22

	t	o
	3	4
–	1	2
	2	2

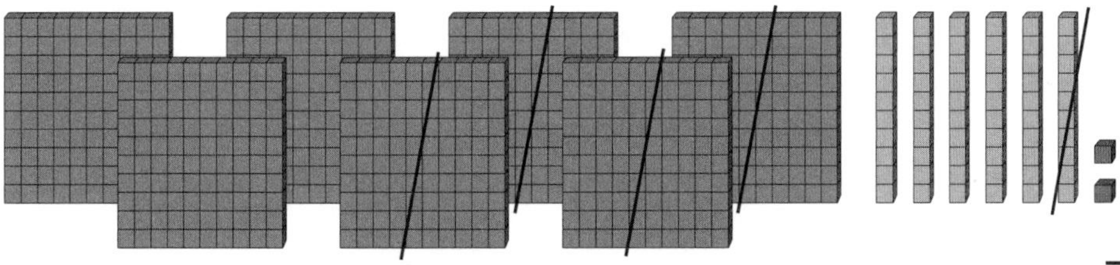

Subtract 410 from 762.

762 – 410 = 352

	h	t	o
	7	6	2
–	4	1	0
	3	5	2

Subtract.

1.

	t	o
	4	8
–	1	6

2.

	h	t	o
	4	9	1
–		6	1

3.

	h	t	o
	8	4	9
–	5	3	7

Subtract.

4. $\begin{array}{r} 65 \\ -14 \\ \hline \end{array}$

7. $\begin{array}{r} 52 \\ -31 \\ \hline \end{array}$

10. $\begin{array}{r} 49 \\ -27 \\ \hline \end{array}$

13. $\begin{array}{r} 37 \\ -13 \\ \hline \end{array}$

5. $\begin{array}{r} 367 \\ -244 \\ \hline \end{array}$

8. $\begin{array}{r} 841 \\ -530 \\ \hline \end{array}$

11. $\begin{array}{r} 670 \\ -560 \\ \hline \end{array}$

14. $\begin{array}{r} 573 \\ -152 \\ \hline \end{array}$

6. $\begin{array}{r} 765 \\ -123 \\ \hline \end{array}$

9. $\begin{array}{r} 642 \\ -210 \\ \hline \end{array}$

12. $\begin{array}{r} 432 \\ -101 \\ \hline \end{array}$

15. $\begin{array}{r} 331 \\ -220 \\ \hline \end{array}$

Solve and label the answer.

16. One otter caught 57 crabs yesterday. Today it caught only 34 crabs. How many more crabs did it catch yesterday?

____

17. The library has 42 books about Asian animals. Twelve of them are checked out. How many books about Asian animals are available at the library?

____

Review

Round to the greatest place value and give the estimated answer. Solve the problem and compare the answers.

18. $\begin{array}{r} 64 \\ +39 \\ \hline \end{array}$ ______ + ______

19. $\begin{array}{r} 395 \\ +616 \\ \hline \end{array}$ ______ + ______

20. $\begin{array}{r} 719 \\ +288 \\ \hline \end{array}$ ______ + ______

Add.

21. $\begin{array}{r} 62 \\ 91 \\ +58 \\ \hline \end{array}$

22. $\begin{array}{r} 44 \\ 26 \\ +92 \\ \hline \end{array}$

23. $\begin{array}{r} 363 \\ 404 \\ +125 \\ \hline \end{array}$

24. $\begin{array}{r} 205 \\ 418 \\ +126 \\ \hline \end{array}$

Name ______________________________

Regrouping Tens 3.6

The loris eats an assortment of insects and berries. Yesterday it ate 74 insects and 58 berries. How many more insects than berries did it eat?

Since 8 cannot be taken from 4, regroup 1 ten as 10 ones. Write the new amounts.

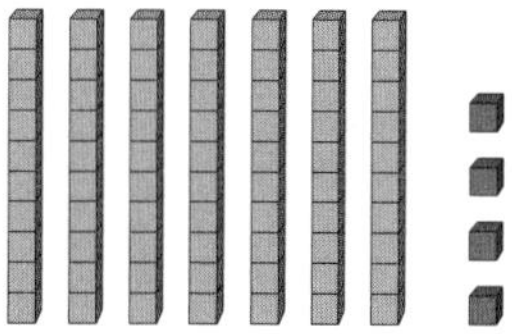

$$\begin{array}{r} \square\square \\ 74 \\ -\,58 \\ \hline \end{array}$$

Subtract the ones. Then subtract the tens.

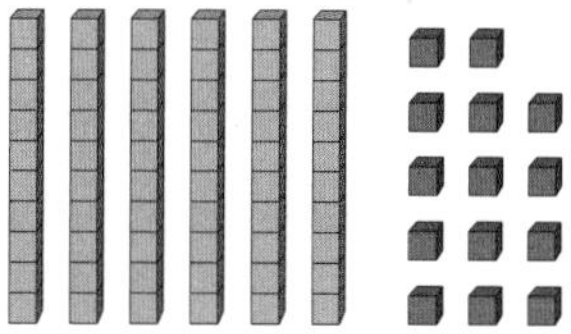

$$\begin{array}{r} \boxed{6}\,\boxed{14} \\ \not{7}\not{4} \\ -\,58 \\ \hline \end{array}$$

There are 16 more insects than berries.

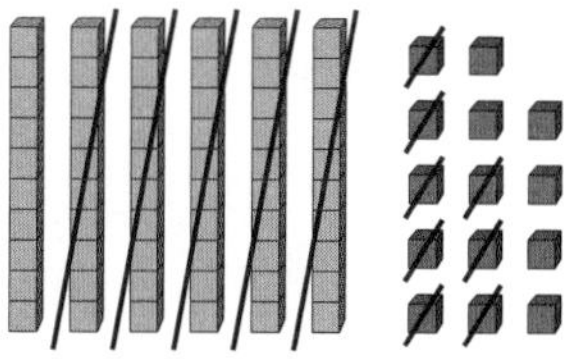

$$\begin{array}{r} \boxed{6}\,\boxed{14} \\ \not{7}\not{4} \\ -\,58 \\ \hline 16 \end{array}$$

Subtract. Regroup by crossing out a ten and drawing ones.

1. 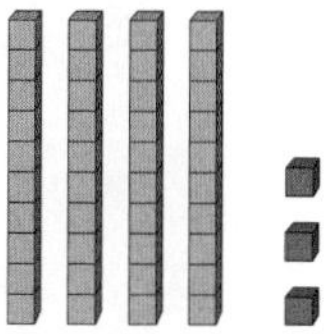

$$\begin{array}{r} 43 \\ -\,17 \\ \hline \end{array}$$

2. 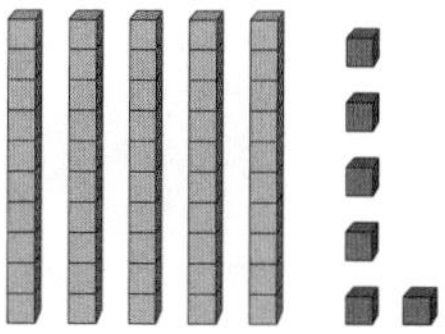

$$\begin{array}{r} 56 \\ -\,28 \\ \hline \end{array}$$

3. $\begin{array}{r} 62 \\ -\,44 \\ \hline \end{array}$

4. $\begin{array}{r} 81 \\ -\,29 \\ \hline \end{array}$

5. $\begin{array}{r} 73 \\ -\,48 \\ \hline \end{array}$

6. $\begin{array}{r} 623 \\ -\,214 \\ \hline \end{array}$

7. $\begin{array}{r} 531 \\ -\,306 \\ \hline \end{array}$

Subtract.

8. $\begin{array}{r} 36 \\ -\,28 \\ \hline \end{array}$

11. $\begin{array}{r} 61 \\ -\,34 \\ \hline \end{array}$

14. $\begin{array}{r} 79 \\ -\,49 \\ \hline \end{array}$

17. $\begin{array}{r} 92 \\ -\,76 \\ \hline \end{array}$

9. $\begin{array}{r} 32 \\ -\,25 \\ \hline \end{array}$

12. $\begin{array}{r} 53 \\ -\,38 \\ \hline \end{array}$

15. $\begin{array}{r} 24 \\ -\,16 \\ \hline \end{array}$

18. $\begin{array}{r} 382 \\ -\,159 \\ \hline \end{array}$

10. $\begin{array}{r} 582 \\ -\,237 \\ \hline \end{array}$

13. $\begin{array}{r} 964 \\ -\,425 \\ \hline \end{array}$

16. $\begin{array}{r} 331 \\ -\,118 \\ \hline \end{array}$

19. $\begin{array}{r} 746 \\ -\,439 \\ \hline \end{array}$

Solve and label the answer. Then, check each answer.

20. Lorises live in Southeast Asia and India. The animal rescue center cared for 32 lorises last month. This month 15 were reintroduced to the wild. How many lorises are still at the rescue center?

____

21. People donated \$180 to the rescue center. The center spent \$77 on medicines for the lorises. How much of the donated money is left?

____

Find the sum or difference. Write that answer at the top of the next equation. Solve.

22.

$\begin{array}{r} 683 \\ -\,216 \\ \hline \square \end{array}$ → $\begin{array}{r} \square \\ +\,254 \\ \hline \square \end{array}$ → $\begin{array}{r} \square \\ -\,313 \\ \hline \square \end{array}$ → $\begin{array}{r} \square \\ +\,552 \\ \hline \square \end{array}$

Name ____________________

Scientists think that there are only 40 Amur leopards left in their native habitat of southern Russia and northern China. There are only 310 Amur leopards in zoos around the world. They are in danger of becoming extinct. What is the difference in number between the Amur leopards in zoos and those in the wild?

Since you cannot take 4 tens from 1 ten, regroup 1 hundred as 10 tens. Write the new amounts.

```
 □□
 310
-  40
-----
```

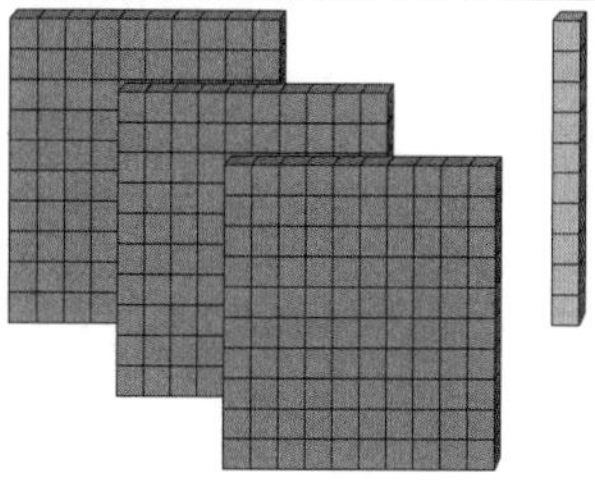

```
 2 11
 3̸1̸0
-  40
-----
```

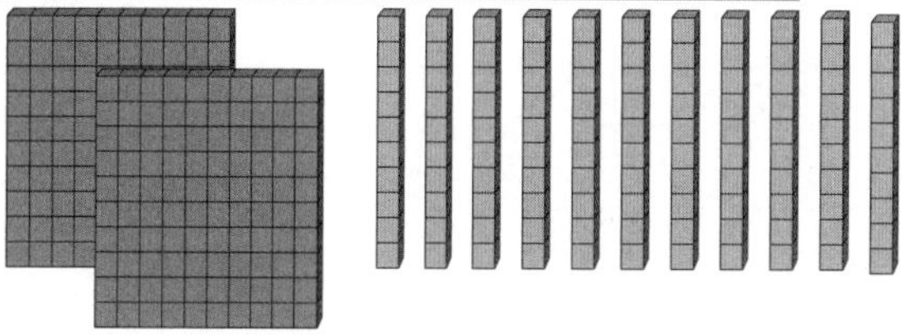

Subtract the ones. Subtract the tens. Subtract the hundreds.

```
 2 11
 3̸1̸0
-  40
-----
 270
```

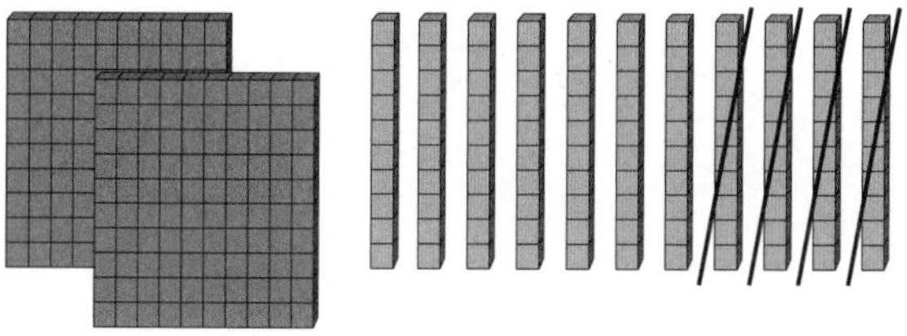

Remember: An open space means subtracting zero.

There are 270 more Amur leopards in zoos than those in the wild.

Subtract.

1. 325 − 182

2. 637 − 297

3. 429 − 167

4. 273 − 92

Subtract.

5. 628 − 485

6. 325 − 185

7. 645 − 352

8. 983 − 91

9. 715 − 482

10. 941 − 770

11. 285 − 93

12. 841 − 571

13. 237 − 84

14. 462 − 270

15. 526 − 264

16. 418 − 155

17. 844 − 392

18. 123 − 72

19. 863 − 480

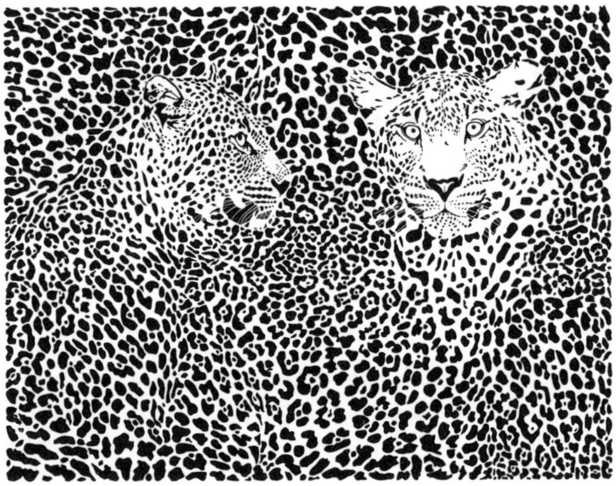

20. Write this problem in vertical format on scrap paper. Solve. Check your addition and subtraction with a calculator.

347 – 135 + 265 – 475 = ________

Review

Add.

21. 181 + 529

22. 84 + 13

23. 167 + 383

24. 215 + 648

25. 37 + 18

26. 468 + 124

27. 524 + 346

28. 45 + 28

29. 6,578 + 1,133

30. 4,046 + 2,631

Name ______________________________

Regrouping Tens and Hundreds 3.8

Male giant pandas can weigh 250 pounds or more, but female pandas rarely reach 220 pounds. What is the difference in weight between a male panda that weighs 253 pounds and a female panda that weighs 199 pounds?

```
 □□
 253
-199
----
```

Write the subtraction problem.

Since 9 > 3, regroup 1 ten as 10 ones. Subtract.

```
  4 13
 2 5̸ 3̸
- 1 9 9
-------
      4
```

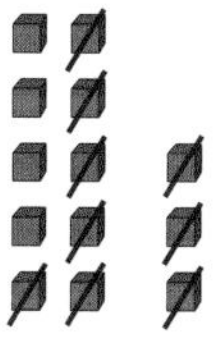

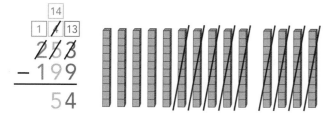

Since 9 > 4, regroup 1 hundred as 10 tens. Subtract.

```
   14
 1 4̸ 13
 2̸ 5̸ 3̸
- 1 9 9
-------
    5 4
```

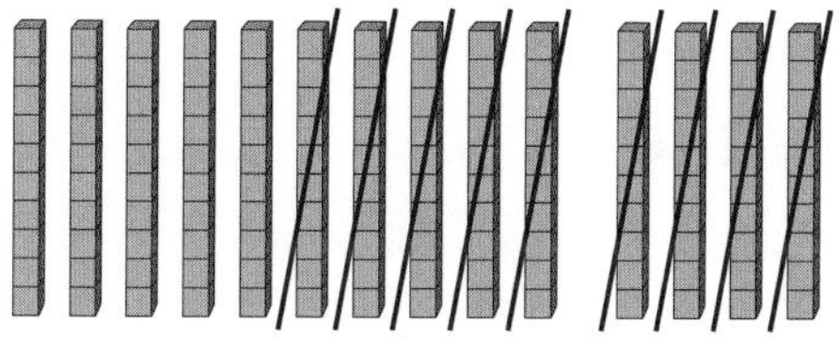

Subtract the hundreds.

```
   14
 1 4̸ 13
 2̸ 5̸ 3̸
- 1 9 9
-------
    5 4
```

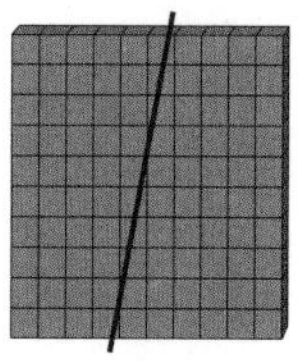

The difference is 54 pounds.

Subtract.

1.

	h	t	o
	3	2	1
–	1	8	5

2.

	h	t	o
	6	3	2
–	4	5	3

3.

	h	t	o
	5	5	6
–	1	6	8

Subtract.

4. 312 − 134	7. 414 − 356	10. 481 − 277	13. 842 − 659	16. 615 − 349
5. 631 − 574	8. 732 − 343	11. 546 − 378	14. 851 − 686	17. 523 − 257
6. 927 − 348	9. 427 − 179	12. 251 − 193	15. 554 − 83	18. 164 − 87

Subtract. Fill in the circle to show which place value was regrouped.

19. 945 − 328
O tens
O hundreds
O both
O neither

21. 572 − 197
O tens
O hundreds
O both
O neither

23. 267 − 183
O tens
O hundreds
O both
O neither

20. 419 − 312
O tens
O hundreds
O both
O neither

22. 236 − 129
O tens
O hundreds
O both
O neither

24. 985 − 491
O tens
O hundreds
O both
O neither

Find the difference.

25. There are 365 days in a year that is not a leap year. By July 7, 186 days have passed. How many days are left in the year?

____

Review

Compare. Write > or <.

26. 18 − 9 ◯ 17 − 9   27. 16 − 8 ◯ 15 − 6   28. 13 − 7 ◯ 14 − 5

Name ______________________________

Subtract Across Zeros 3.9

The Elephant Listening Project uses high-tech audio tracking of Asian elephants in the wild. There were 200 elephants in one herd. This technology was used on 127 of the elephants. How many elephants in the herd were not tracked?

Step 1

$$\begin{array}{r} 200 \\ -\,127 \\ \hline \end{array}$$

Regroup 200 as 1 hundred and 10 tens. Regroup 10 tens as 9 tens and 10 ones.

Step 2

$$\begin{array}{r} \,\,9 \\ 1\ \cancel{10}\ 10 \\ \cancel{2}\cancel{0}\cancel{0} \\ -\,127 \\ \hline 73 \end{array}$$

Subtract the ones. Subtract the tens.

Step 3

$$\begin{array}{r} \,\,9 \\ 1\ \cancel{10}\ 10 \\ \cancel{2}\cancel{0}\cancel{0} \\ -\,127 \\ \hline 73 \end{array}$$

Subtract the hundreds.

Practice regrouping so all columns have digits greater than zero. First, regroup 1 hundred as 10 tens. Next, regroup 1 ten as 10 ones.

1.

	h	t	o
Next		9	10
First	4	10	
	5	0	0

2.

h	t	o
3	0	0

3.

h	t	o
7	0	0

Subtract.

4. $\begin{array}{r} 500 \\ -\,263 \\ \hline \end{array}$

5. $\begin{array}{r} 300 \\ -\,125 \\ \hline \end{array}$

6. $\begin{array}{r} 700 \\ -\,548 \\ \hline \end{array}$

7. $\begin{array}{r} 600 \\ -\,416 \\ \hline \end{array}$

Subtract.

8. $\begin{array}{r} 250 \\ -\ 113 \\ \hline \end{array}$

10. $\begin{array}{r} 603 \\ -\ 418 \\ \hline \end{array}$

12. $\begin{array}{r} 400 \\ -\ 134 \\ \hline \end{array}$

14. $\begin{array}{r} 640 \\ -\ 225 \\ \hline \end{array}$

16. $\begin{array}{r} 308 \\ -\ 176 \\ \hline \end{array}$

9. $\begin{array}{r} 800 \\ -\ 529 \\ \hline \end{array}$

11. $\begin{array}{r} 570 \\ -\ 48 \\ \hline \end{array}$

13. $\begin{array}{r} 740 \\ -\ 563 \\ \hline \end{array}$

15. $\begin{array}{r} 901 \\ -\ 557 \\ \hline \end{array}$

17. $\begin{array}{r} 100 \\ -\ 13 \\ \hline \end{array}$

Draw a line to show how each top numeral should be regrouped. Subtract.

18. $\begin{array}{r} 304 \\ -\ 115 \\ \hline \end{array}$ •

h	t	o
2	9	14

19. $\begin{array}{r} 300 \\ -\ 54 \\ \hline \end{array}$ •

h	t	o
3	2	10

20. $\begin{array}{r} 330 \\ -\ 114 \\ \hline \end{array}$ •

h	t	o
2	9	10

Review

Write the value of each underlined digit.

21. 2,$\underline{8}$45 ______

22. 43,8$\underline{7}$1 ______

23. $\underline{2}$1,178 ______

24. 10$\underline{5}$,864 ______

25. $\underline{2}$32,605 ______

Write the numeral.

26. thirty-eight ______

27. twelve thousand, three hundred forty-one ______

28. two thousand, eight hundred nine ______

29. ninety-seven thousand, seven hundred fifty ______

Name ______________________________

4-Digit Numbers 3.10

Blackbuck antelope are native to Asia where they once thrived. Today, the blackbuck live mostly in India and its neighbor, Nepal. In 1975, there were only 19 blackbuck antelope left in Nepal. Thanks to conservation, by 2014 their numbers increased to 300. How many years passed from 1975 to 2014?

Practice subtraction from numerals in the thousands. Subtract 1,975 from 2,014.

$$\begin{array}{r} {\scriptstyle 9\ 10} \\ {\scriptstyle 1\ \ 10\ 0\ 14} \\ 2{,}014 \\ -\ 1{,}975 \\ \hline 9 \end{array}$$

Regroup the tens, hundreds, and thousands. Subtract the ones.

$$\begin{array}{r} {\scriptstyle 9\ 10} \\ {\scriptstyle 1\ \ 10\ 0\ 14} \\ 2{,}014 \\ -\ 1{,}975 \\ \hline 39 \end{array}$$

Subtract the tens.

$$\begin{array}{r} {\scriptstyle 9\ 10} \\ {\scriptstyle 1\ \ 10\ 0\ 14} \\ 2{,}014 \\ -\ 1{,}975 \\ \hline 39 \end{array}$$ years

Subtract the hundreds and thousands.

Subtract

1. $\begin{array}{r} 7{,}543 \\ -\ 4{,}237 \\ \hline \end{array}$

2. $\begin{array}{r} 8{,}466 \\ -\ 2{,}143 \\ \hline \end{array}$

3. $\begin{array}{r} 5{,}726 \\ -\ 1{,}248 \\ \hline \end{array}$

4. $\begin{array}{r} 2{,}957 \\ -\ 1{,}846 \\ \hline \end{array}$

5. $\begin{array}{r} 6{,}052 \\ -\ 3{,}873 \\ \hline \end{array}$

6. $\begin{array}{r} 6{,}370 \\ -\ 252 \\ \hline \end{array}$

7. $\begin{array}{r} 2{,}000 \\ -\ 721 \\ \hline \end{array}$

8. $\begin{array}{r} 9{,}895 \\ -\ 2{,}729 \\ \hline \end{array}$

Subtract.

9. $\begin{array}{r} 6,421 \\ -\quad 78 \\ \hline \end{array}$

10. $\begin{array}{r} 7,000 \\ -\quad 98 \\ \hline \end{array}$

11. $\begin{array}{r} 3,806 \\ -\quad 418 \\ \hline \end{array}$

12. $\begin{array}{r} 8,503 \\ -2,645 \\ \hline \end{array}$

13. $\begin{array}{r} 4,032 \\ -\quad 695 \\ \hline \end{array}$

14. $\begin{array}{r} 2,325 \\ -1,088 \\ \hline \end{array}$

15. $\begin{array}{r} 1,200 \\ -\quad 575 \\ \hline \end{array}$

16. $\begin{array}{r} 6,000 \\ -3,524 \\ \hline \end{array}$

Endangered Species Weight (in pounds)		
	Grevy's zebra	950
	black rhinoceros	3,080
	giant panda	250
	red wolf	80
	gray wolf	110

Use information from the table to answer the questions. Label your answers. Use the space beside the table to show your work.

17. How much more does the Grevy's zebra weigh than the giant panda?

____

18. How much more does the gray wolf weigh than the red wolf?

____

19. Record the difference in weight between the heaviest and lightest animals.

____

Name ______________________________

Estimate Differences 3.11

Mandarin ducks are native to China. Recently, their numbers have declined because of a loss of habitat. They are protected in zoos.

Estimate the total number of ducks that would be left if a zoo donated 26 of its 42 Mandarin ducks to another zoo. Begin by rounding to the nearest ten.

$$\begin{array}{r} 42 \\ -26 \\ \hline \end{array} \longleftrightarrow \begin{array}{r} 40 \\ -30 \\ \hline 10 \end{array} \text{ ducks}$$

The zoo would have about 10 ducks to display.

Estimation gives a close answer.

$$\begin{array}{r} 4{,}285 \\ -1{,}819 \\ \hline \end{array} \longleftrightarrow \begin{array}{r} 4{,}000 \\ -2{,}000 \\ \hline 2{,}000 \end{array}$$

Round to the nearest ten, hundred, or thousand. Subtract.

An estimated difference allows you to check your subtraction. If the estimated difference is 2,000, the exact difference should be close.

$$\begin{array}{r} \scriptstyle 3\ \ 12\ 7\ 15 \\ \not{4},\not{2}\not{8}\not{5} \\ -1{,}819 \\ \hline 2{,}466 \end{array}$$

Estimated difference: 2,000

Exact difference: 2,466

The exact difference rounds to the estimated difference.

Round both numbers of each problem to the highest place value and find the estimated difference. Solve.

1. $\begin{array}{r} 68 \\ -21 \\ \hline \end{array}$ ______ − ______ ______

2. $\begin{array}{r} 416 \\ -188 \\ \hline \end{array}$ ______ − ______ ______

3. $\begin{array}{r} 7{,}982 \\ -3{,}014 \\ \hline \end{array}$ ______ − ______ ______

Round both numbers to the highest place value. Write the estimated difference. Solve.

4. 525 − 283 = ______ − ______ = ______

6. 821 − 692 = ______ − ______ = ______

8. 68 − 29 = ______ − ______ = ______

5. 1,200 − 676 = ______ − ______ = ______

7. 483 − 202 = ______ − ______ = ______

9. 2,899 − 716 = ______ − ______ = ______

Subtract.

10. 912 − 199

12. 467 − 218

14. 579 − 114

16. 690 − 513

18. 885 − 608

11. 300 − 79

13. 565 − 389

15. 6,421 − 2,986

17. 9,029 − 4,297

19. 6,400 − 4,003

Write the estimated difference. Then, subtract to find the exact difference. Show your work. Label your answer. Compare the estimated difference to the exact difference.

20. Peafowl are birds that are native to India and Sri Lanka. The male bird is called a peacock. The longest can measure 51 inches from head to tail, but the shortest only measure 27 inches. Estimate the difference between the longest and shortest peacocks.

______

21. Bahar learned that the female bird is called a peahen. Babies are called peachicks. Peacocks can weigh up to 13 pounds. Bahar weighs 59 pounds. What is the difference in weight between Bahar and a peacock?

______

Name ______________________________

Problem-Solving Path

1. Understand the question.
2. Analyze the data.
3. Plan the strategy.
4. Solve the problem.
5. Evaluate the result.

Mr. Lee's third graders worked to clean up a pond in the park near their school. One afternoon, they picked up newspapers, empty bottles, and aluminum cans. Use the Problem-Solving Path to solve the word problems about the cleanup.

Choose the right operation. Then, write an equation.

1. The students collected 40 cans and bottles. They collected 26 newspapers. How many more cans and bottles did they collect than newspapers?

_______________ more cans and bottles

Make a graph or table to organize information.

If you need to compare amounts, make a graph.

2. The students collected 10 bottles, 30 cans, and 26 newspapers. How many more newspapers did they find than bottles?

_______________ more newspapers

If you need to know the amounts for more than one item, make a table or tally chart.

3. Mr. Lee's students received a 5¢ deposit for each bottle that they recycled. How much money did they collect?

_______________ ¢

Estimate the answer.

4. Mr. Lee's class returned to the park one week later. They picked up 18 cans, 12 newspapers, and 8 bottles. How many items did they collect that day in all?

_______________ items

18	→	20
12	→	10
+ 8	→	+ 10
		40

Expect your answer to be about 40.

Solve each problem. Show your work, including tables, graphs, estimation, and computation. Label your answers.

5. Mrs. Scott's class joined Mr. Lee's class for a second cleanup effort. Mrs. Scott's class picked up 21 cans, 19 newspapers, and 14 bottles. Mr. Lee's class picked up a total of 38 items. How many more items did Mrs. Scott's class collect than Mr. Lee's class?

____

6. How much money did Mrs. Scott's students receive for recycling the 14 bottles at 5¢ per bottle?

____

7. The cleanup was a success. The two classes picked up a combined total of 51 newspapers that would have ended up in a landfill. If Mrs. Scott's students picked up 19 of the newspapers, how many did Mr. Lee's class pick up?

____

Name ______________________________

Draw lines to match the same value.

1. 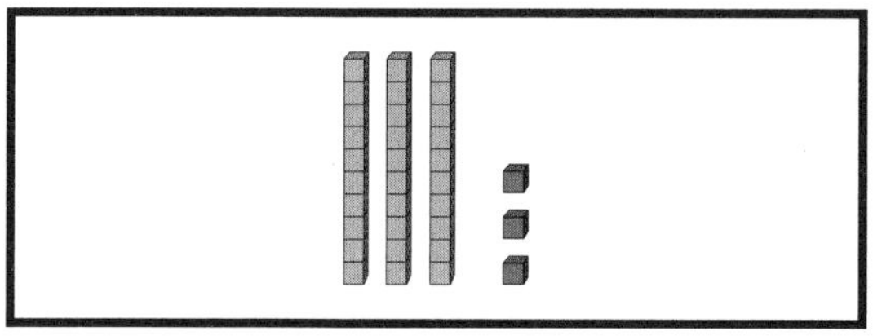 • • 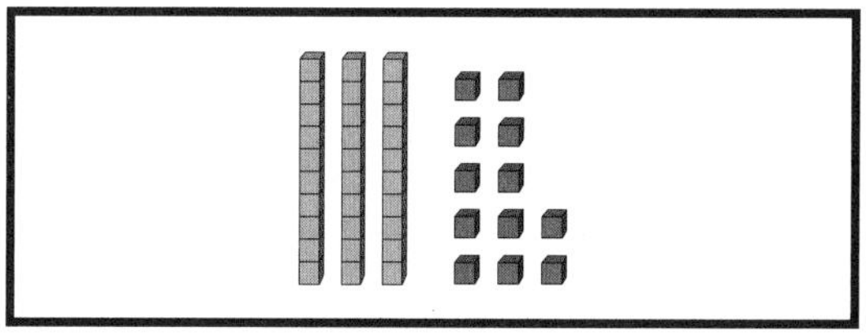

2. 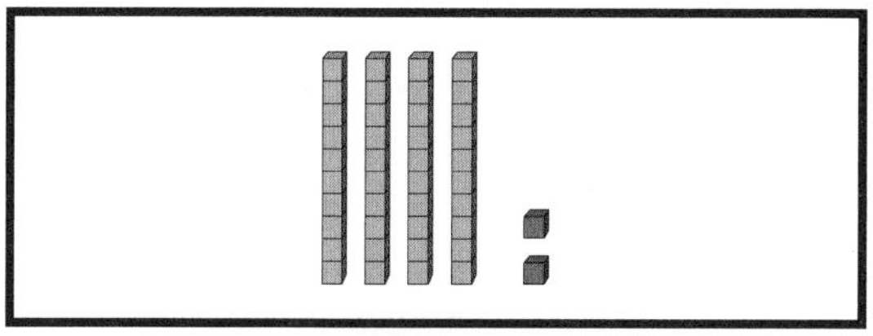 • • 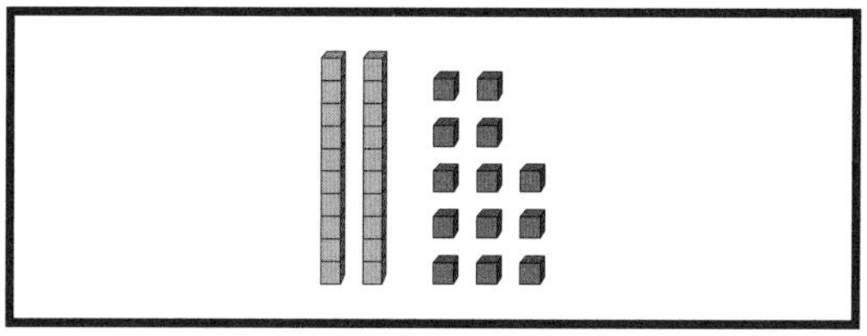

3. 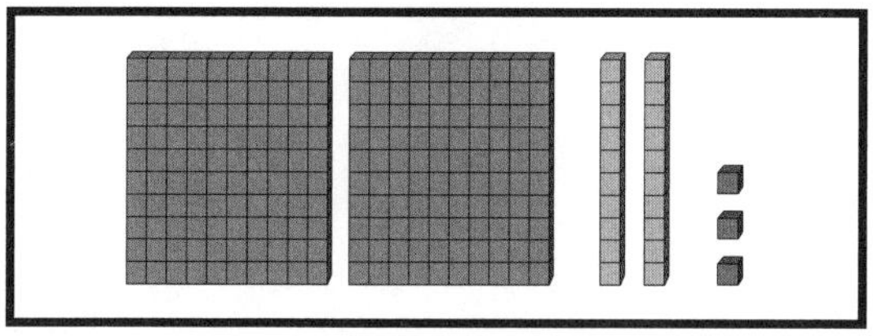 • • 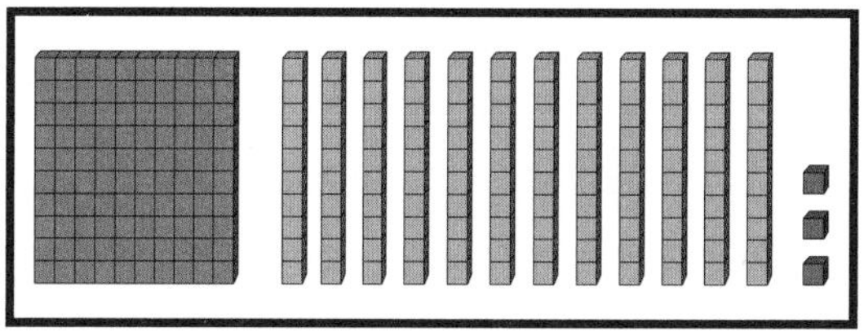

Should you count back or count on? Circle one.

4. $9 - 7$
count back
count on

5. $12 - 2$
count back
count on

6. $14 - 3$
count back
count on

Subtract.

7. $628 - 452$

8. $784 - 396$

9. $900 - 626$

10. $420 - 215$

11. $226 - 183$

12. $6{,}000 - 5{,}099$

13. $345 - 124$

14. $520 - 184$

15. $415 - 261$

16. $600 - 87$

17. $839 - 625$

18. $7{,}250 - 5{,}183$

19. $245 - 21$

20. $2{,}045 - 1{,}004$

21. $414 - 103$

Round both numbers to the nearest hundred. Write the estimated difference. Solve.

22. $\begin{array}{r} 379 \\ -\ 122 \\ \hline \end{array}$ $\begin{array}{r} \underline{\hspace{2cm}} \\ -\ \underline{\hspace{2cm}} \\ \underline{\hspace{2cm}} \end{array}$

23. $\begin{array}{r} 559 \\ -\ 101 \\ \hline \end{array}$ $\begin{array}{r} \underline{\hspace{2cm}} \\ -\ \underline{\hspace{2cm}} \\ \underline{\hspace{2cm}} \end{array}$

24. $\begin{array}{r} 267 \\ -\ 118 \\ \hline \end{array}$ $\begin{array}{r} \underline{\hspace{2cm}} \\ -\ \underline{\hspace{2cm}} \\ \underline{\hspace{2cm}} \end{array}$

Solve each word problem. Use the inverse operation to check each answer.

25. The third-grade class project collected money to send to an orphanage in Thailand. The boys collected $210 and the girls collected $195.

Who collected more money? ______________
How much more did they collect?

____

26. Skyla visited the zoo and counted 83 animals from Asia. She discovered that 38 of those animals were from China. How many Asian animals were not from China?

____

27. Wes studied the giant pandas. He discovered that one older survey counted 3,000 pandas in the wild, but that number is now lower by 1,136. How many pandas are in the wild now?

____

Name ____

Chapters 1–3 Review 3.14

Write the numerals in expanded form.

1. 23,749 = ________________________________

2. 281,067 = ________________________________

Write the next three numbers in each pattern.

3. 707 709 711 ______ ______ ______

4. 6,225 6,230 6,235 ______ ______ ______

Write > or <.

5. 65 ◯ 70

6. 2,049 ◯ 2,047

7. 191 ◯ 119

8. 4,605 ◯ 4,608

9. 818 ◯ 188

10. 8,126 ◯ 8,136

Write the numbers from least to greatest.

11. 206 232 217

______ ______ ______

12. 4,093 4,027 4,054

______ ______ ______

Add or subtract.

13. $\begin{array}{r} 48 \\ +39 \\ \hline \end{array}$

14. $\begin{array}{r} 83 \\ -47 \\ \hline \end{array}$

15. $\begin{array}{r} 388 \\ +525 \\ \hline \end{array}$

16. $\begin{array}{r} 732 \\ -177 \\ \hline \end{array}$

17. $\begin{array}{r} 1,182 \\ +1,057 \\ \hline \end{array}$

18. $\begin{array}{r} 5,634 \\ -2,879 \\ \hline \end{array}$

19. $\begin{array}{r} 6,000 \\ -1,842 \\ \hline \end{array}$

20. $\begin{array}{r} 8,120 \\ -2,865 \\ \hline \end{array}$

21. $\begin{array}{r} 714 \\ 526 \\ +321 \\ \hline \end{array}$

Solve.

22. Kalitha's family drove 236 miles to her aunt's house. From there, they drove another 185 miles. How many miles did Kalitha's family travel?

____

23. Vincent's family drove 423 miles on their vacation. They made their first stop after driving 75 miles. How many more miles did Vincent's family drive after the first stop?

____

The Brookview Christian School students earned an ice cream party. Each class voted on their favorite flavors.

Find the total for each flavor.

kindergarten	10 chocolate	4 mint chip	10 vanilla	5 bubble gum	
first grade	10 chocolate	11 mint chip	4 vanilla		13 rocky road
second grade	7 chocolate	13 mint chip		8 bubble gum	10 rocky road
third grade	12 chocolate	6 mint chip	6 vanilla		12 rocky road
fourth grade	6 chocolate	12 mint chip	5 vanilla	7 bubble gum	5 rocky road

24. Total _______ _______ _______ _______ _______

Mark the information into the graph.

25.

flavors	favorite ice-cream flavors										
chocolate											
mint chip											
vanilla											
bubble gum											
rocky road											

10 20 30 40 50 60 70 80 90 100

Fill in the blanks.

26. Which flavor received the most votes? ____________________

Which received the least? ____________________

What is the difference between the two numbers? ____________________

27. How many more students voted for chocolate than rocky road?

____

28. How many more students voted for vanilla than bubble gum?

____

Chapter 4 Multiplication Facts

Bring out every kind of living creature that is with you—the birds, the animals, and all the creatures … so they can multiply on the earth and be fruitful and increase in number on it.
Genesis 8:17

Key Ideas:

Multiplication: facts 0–9

Multiplication: using multiplication strategies

Algebra: using zero, order, and grouping properties

Patterns: skip counting in multiplication

Name ______________________

Multiplication Strategies 4.1

Rabbits are woodland animals. Each rabbit has 2 long ears. How can you find the total number of ears on 6 rabbits?

6 sets of 2 ears

$2 + 2 + 2 + 2 + 2 + 2 = 12$

6 twos = 12

Multiplication is the repeated addition of the same number. A multiplication sentence uses the multiplication sign (×). You read the multiplication sign as "times."

2 sets of five

$5 + 5 = 10$
$2 \times 5 = 10$

5 sets of two

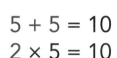

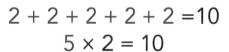

$2 + 2 + 2 + 2 + 2 = 10$
$5 \times 2 = 10$

Circle equal sets. Add, then multiply.

1. 3 sets of 2

$2 + 2 + 2 =$ ______

3 twos = ______

$3 \times 2 =$ ______

2. 4 sets of 3

$3 + 3 + 3 + 3 =$ ______

4 threes = ______

$4 \times 3 =$ ______

3. 3 sets of 4

$4 + 4 + 4 =$ ______

3 fours = ______

$3 \times 4 =$ ______

Write an addition equation and a multiplication equation for each number line.

4.
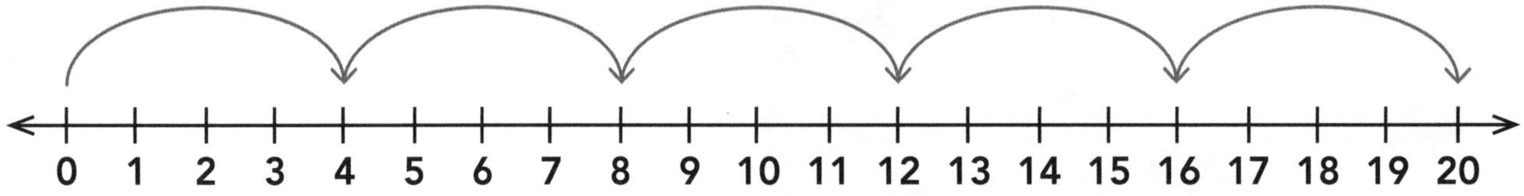

+ ____________________ × ____________________

5.
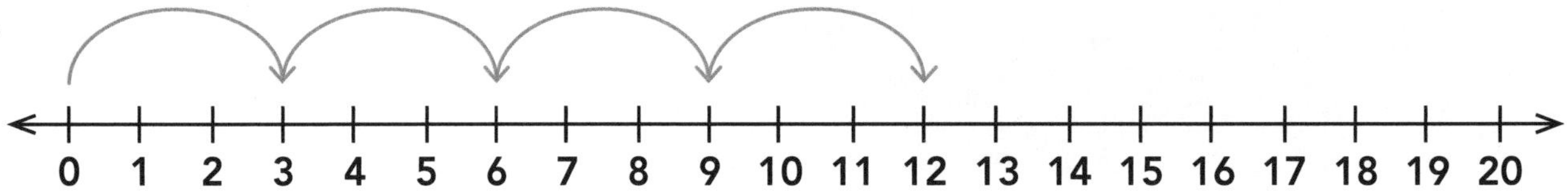

+ ____________________ × ____________________

6.
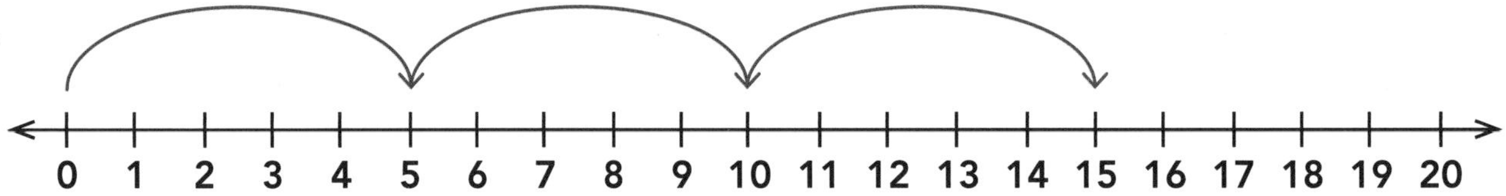

+ ____________________ × ____________________

Write a multiplication equation for each exercise.

7. 4 + 4 + 4 + 4 = 16 ____________________

8. 2 + 2 + 2 = 6 ____________________

9. 7 + 7 + 7 = 21 ____________________

10. two 4s ____________________

11. five 2s ____________________

12. three 4s ____________________

Draw skips on the number line for each multiplication equation.

13. 4 × 2 = 8
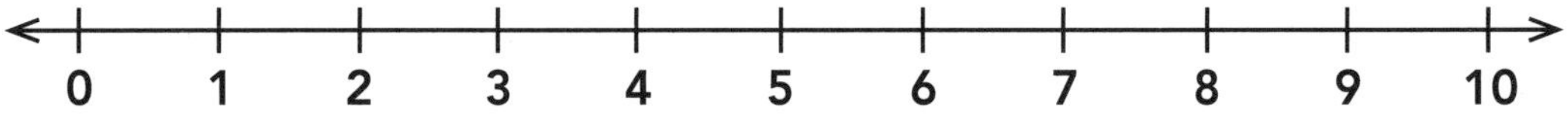

14. 3 × 3 = 9
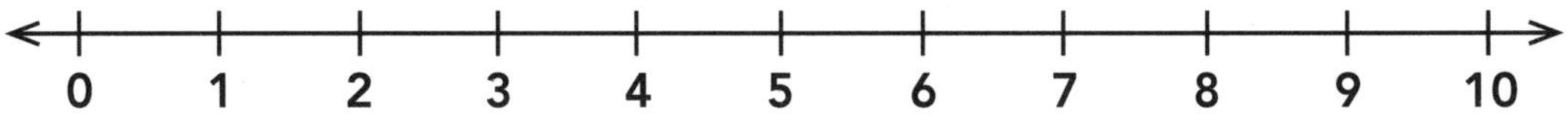

Name ____

Multiply by 2 4.2

Each woodland owl has 2 eyes. You can find the total number of eyes by multiplying.

2 + 2 + 2 + 2 = 8
4 twos equal 8

A **factor** is one of the two numbers that are multiplied. The **product** is the result of multiplication. Multiplying by a factor of 2 is the same as adding doubles.

The Order Property of Multiplication Changing the order of the factors does not change the product.

Memorize these facts.

1 × 2 = 2	4 × 2 = 8	7 × 2 = 14
2 × 2 = 4	5 × 2 = 10	8 × 2 = 16
3 × 2 = 6	6 × 2 = 12	9 × 2 = 18

Match the addition double with the correct multiplication equation.

1.  • • 2 × 2 = 4

2.  • • 2 × 6 = 12

3.  • • 2 × 3 = 6

4.  • • 2 × 5 = 10

Write a multiplication sentence for each addition double.

5. 7 + 7 ________

6. 1 + 1 ________

7. 3 + 3 ________

8. 5 + 5 ________

9. 9 + 9 ________

10. 6 + 6 ________

11. 4 + 4 ________

12. 8 + 8 ________

Write a multiplication equation for each picture. Label the parts of your equation.

13. 

____ ________
× ____ ________
____

14. 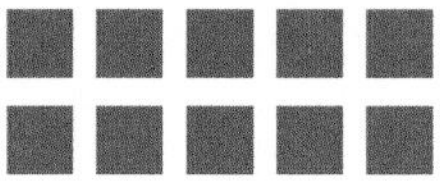

____ ________
× ____ ________
____

Multiply. Then, write the related multiplication fact.

15. $\begin{array}{r} 2 \\ \times\ 6 \\ \hline \end{array}$ ____ × ____

16. $\begin{array}{r} 2 \\ \times\ 4 \\ \hline \end{array}$ ____ × ____

17. $\begin{array}{r} 2 \\ \times\ 9 \\ \hline \end{array}$ ____ × ____

18. $\begin{array}{r} 2 \\ \times\ 8 \\ \hline \end{array}$ ____ × ____

19. Draw a picture to show 2 x 6.

20. Draw skips to show 2 x 4.

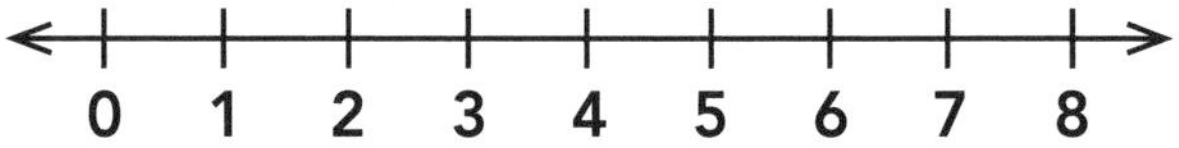

Review

Write the standard form.

21. 2,000 + 500 + 70 + 4 ________

22. 6,000 + 30 + 2 ________

23. 10,000 + 5,000 + 800 + 70 + 9 ________

24. 50,000 + 6,000 + 900 + 30 + 1 ________

25. 80,000 + 200 + 10 + 1 ________

26. 1,000 + 300 + 80 + 5 ________

Name ____

Multiply by 3 4.3

Three young raccoons are hiding in this log. How many raccoons would there be if there were 3 raccoons in each of 4 logs?

3	×	4	=	12
raccoons		logs		raccoons

Counting on is a helpful way to multiply factors of 3.

You know that 2 x 4 = 8.

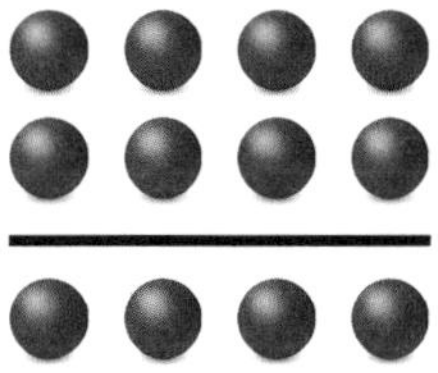

Memorize these facts.

1 × 3 = 3	4 × 3 = 12	7 × 3 = 21
2 × 3 = 6	5 × 3 = 15	8 × 3 = 24
3 × 3 = 9	6 × 3 = 18	9 × 3 = 27

3 x 4 means 3 fours, so count on one more set of 4.

Complete the multiplication sentence for each picture.

1.

3 × 3 = ______

2.

3 × ______ = ______

3.

3 spiders × 8 legs

= ______ legs

Use counting on to complete each exercise.

4. $2 \times 5 =$ ______

$3 \times 5 =$ ______

5. $2 \times 7 =$ ______

$3 \times 7 =$ ______

6. $2 \times 8 =$ ______

$3 \times 8 =$ ______

7. $2 \times 2 =$ ______

$3 \times 2 =$ ______

8. $2 \times 3 =$ ______

$3 \times 3 =$ ______

9. $2 \times 9 =$ ______

$3 \times 9 =$ ______

Skip count to solve.

10. $\begin{array}{r} 3 \\ \times\ 6 \\ \hline \end{array}$

0 1 2 3 4 5 6 7 8 9 10 11 12 13 14 15 16 17 18

11. $\begin{array}{r} 3 \\ \times\ 4 \\ \hline \end{array}$

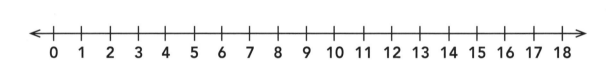

0 1 2 3 4 5 6 7 8 9 10 11 12 13 14 15 16 17 18

12. Multiply.

$\begin{array}{r} 3 \\ \times\ 5 \\ \hline \end{array}$ $\begin{array}{r} 2 \\ \times\ 8 \\ \hline \end{array}$ $\begin{array}{r} 6 \\ \times\ 3 \\ \hline \end{array}$ $\begin{array}{r} 4 \\ \times\ 2 \\ \hline \end{array}$ $\begin{array}{r} 9 \\ \times\ 2 \\ \hline \end{array}$ $\begin{array}{r} 3 \\ \times\ 8 \\ \hline \end{array}$ $\begin{array}{r} 2 \\ \times\ 5 \\ \hline \end{array}$ $\begin{array}{r} 3 \\ \times\ 2 \\ \hline \end{array}$

$\begin{array}{r} 2 \\ \times\ 6 \\ \hline \end{array}$ $\begin{array}{r} 1 \\ \times\ 3 \\ \hline \end{array}$ $\begin{array}{r} 3 \\ \times\ 3 \\ \hline \end{array}$ $\begin{array}{r} 7 \\ \times\ 2 \\ \hline \end{array}$ $\begin{array}{r} 2 \\ \times\ 1 \\ \hline \end{array}$ $\begin{array}{r} 4 \\ \times\ 3 \\ \hline \end{array}$ $\begin{array}{r} 2 \\ \times\ 2 \\ \hline \end{array}$ $\begin{array}{r} 3 \\ \times\ 7 \\ \hline \end{array}$

Write a multiplication equation. Label the product.

13. Amara made 3 trips to the zoo last summer. Each time, she took 8 pictures with the camera on her phone. How many pictures did she take at the zoo?

____

Name ________________________________

Multiply by 4 4.4

Timber wolves live in packs that are led by one male and one female wolf. A female wolf usually has 4 to 7 pups per year. The entire pack helps raise the young wolves. If a female wolf has 4 pups per year, how many pups would she have in 3 years?

An array is a set of rows and columns that are used to represent a multiplication sentence. You can make an array to solve for the number of pups.

year 1

year 2

year 3

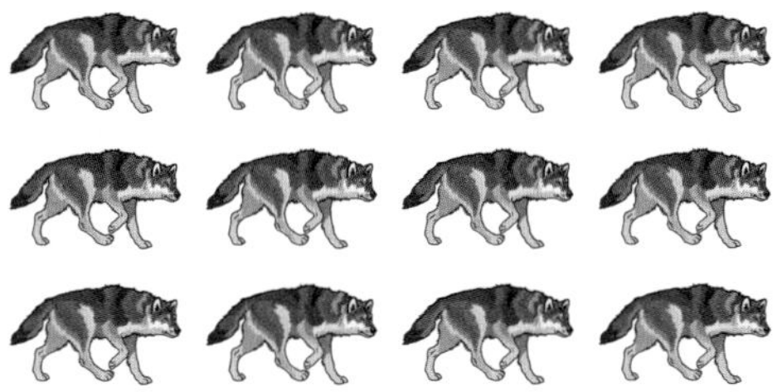

3 years × 4 pups = 12 pups

Making an array helps you see the factors. You can count the dots to solve for the product.

Make 4 rows of 6 or 6 rows of 4.

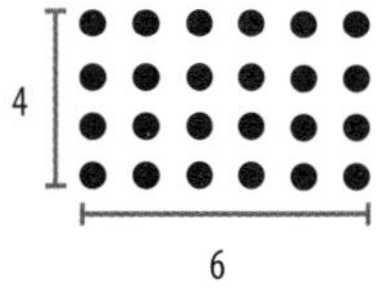

4 × 6 = 24

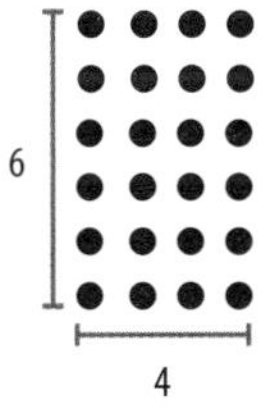

6 × 4 = 24

Memorize these facts.

1 × 4 = 4	6 × 4 = 24
2 × 4 = 8	7 × 4 = 28
3 × 4 = 12	8 × 4 = 32
4 × 4 = 16	9 × 4 = 36
5 × 4 = 20	

Make an array for each multiplication fact. Multiply. Write the products.

1. 2 × 4 = _____
2. 4 × 5 = _____
3. 1 × 4 = _____
4. 4 × 4 = _____

Write a multiplication equation for each rectangle.

5. 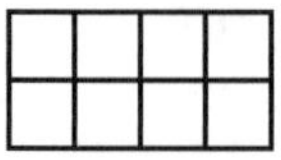

rows x squares in a row

_____ × _____ = _____

6. 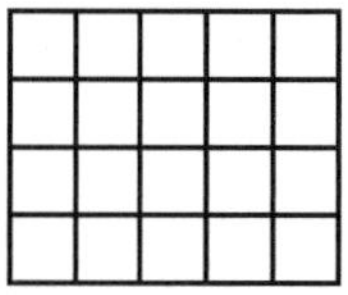

_____ × _____ = _____

7. 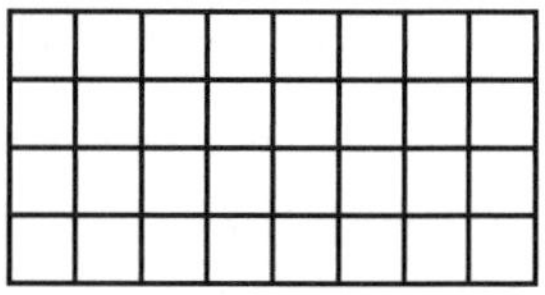

_____ × _____ = _____

Count on to solve.

8. $2 \times 3 =$ _____	9. $7 \times 3 =$ _____	10. $6 \times 3 =$ _____	11. $5 \times 3 =$ _____
$2 \times 4 =$ _____	$7 \times 4 =$ _____	$6 \times 4 =$ _____	$5 \times 4 =$ _____

12. Multiply.

2×4	3×6	4×3	2×2	1×3	4×7	2×9	3×8
5×2	3×2	6×4	4×1	4×4	5×3	8×2	4×9

Write a multiplication equation for the number of wolf tracks you see.

13. 

_____ × _____ = _____

Review

Add or subtract.

14. $6{,}321 + 1{,}489$	16. $821 - 275$	18. $850 + 366$	20. $4{,}002 - 1{,}587$
15. $2{,}369 - 983$	17. $726 + 214$	19. $2{,}199 + 3{,}825$	21. $2{,}500 - 821$

Name ______________________________

Practice: Multiply by 3 and 4 4.5

Squirrels are common forest animals. They store the nuts and seeds that they will need to survive during the snowy winter months.

If 3 squirrels each find 9 acorns, how many acorns will they find in all?

9 + 9 + 9 = 27
3 nines equal 27

If 4 squirrels each store 8 walnuts, how many walnuts will they have for the winter?

8 + 8 + 8 + 8 = 32
4 eights equal 32

If 6 squirrels each hide 4 sunflower seeds, how many seeds will the squirrels store in all?

4 + 4 + 4 + 4 + 4 + 4 = 24
6 fours equal 24
6 x 4 = 24

Skip count by threes.

1. ____ ____ ____ ____ ____ ____ ____ ____ ____

Skip count by fours.

2. ____ ____ ____ ____ ____ ____ ____ ____ ____

3. Complete the table.

×	1	2	3	4	5	6	7	8	9
3									
4									

4. **Multiply.**

4×4	4×6	4×5	4×9	3×3	4×8	3×9	3×7
4×2	6×3	7×4	5×3	9×4	3×5	8×3	9×3

The products below have factors of 3 or 4. Write the products under the correct heading.

27 28 21 36 18 20 32 9

5. Has a factor of

______ ______

______ ______

6. Has a factor of

______ ______

______ ______

Draw an array to solve.

7. Nine squirrels each hid 4 nuts for the winter. How many nuts did they hide in all?

______________ nuts

Review

Round to the thousands place.

8. 2,674 ________ 9. 7,012 ________ 10. 5,941 ________

Name ____

Memorize these facts.

1 × 5 = 5	6 × 5 = 30
2 × 5 = 10	7 × 5 = 35
3 × 5 = 15	8 × 5 = 40
4 × 5 = 20	9 × 5 = 45
5 × 5 = 25	

Wood thrushes are known for their beautiful songs. They build their nests in trees or bushes. The nests are made of dead grass, leaves, or stems. They are lined with mud. The female lays eggs in mid-May and again in July. If 8 female wood thrushes each laid 5 eggs, how many eggs would they lay in all?

5 + 5 + 5 + 5 + 5 + 5 + 5 + 5 = 40

8 fives equal 40

8 x 5 = 40 eggs

A multiplication table can help you locate and learn the facts.

×	1	2	3	4	5	6	7	8	9
1	1	2	3	4	5	6	7	8	9
2	2	4	6	8	10	12	14	16	18
3	3	6	9	12	15	18	21	24	27
4	4	8	12	16	20	24	28	32	36
5	5	10	15	20	25	30	35	40	45

Circle sets of five. Multiply. Complete each multiplication equation.

1. 

_____ × _____ = _____

2. 

_____ × _____ = _____

3. 

_____ × _____ = _____

Correct this math paper by writing a C next to every correct product and an X next to every error.

4. $5 \times 2 = 10$

5. $5 \times 7 = 32$

6. $5 \times 6 = 30$

7. $5 \times 3 = 15$

8. $3 \times 5 = 15$

9. $5 \times 1 = 5$

10. $5 \times 9 = 48$

11. $8 \times 5 = 43$

12. $7 \times 5 = 35$

13. $6 \times 5 = 30$

14. $1 \times 5 = 5$

15. $2 \times 5 = 10$

16. Complete the multiplication table. Circle the products that have factors of 5.

×	1	2	3	4	5	6	7	8	9
1		2			5			8	
2		4	6				14		
3	3								27
4					20				
5		10					35		

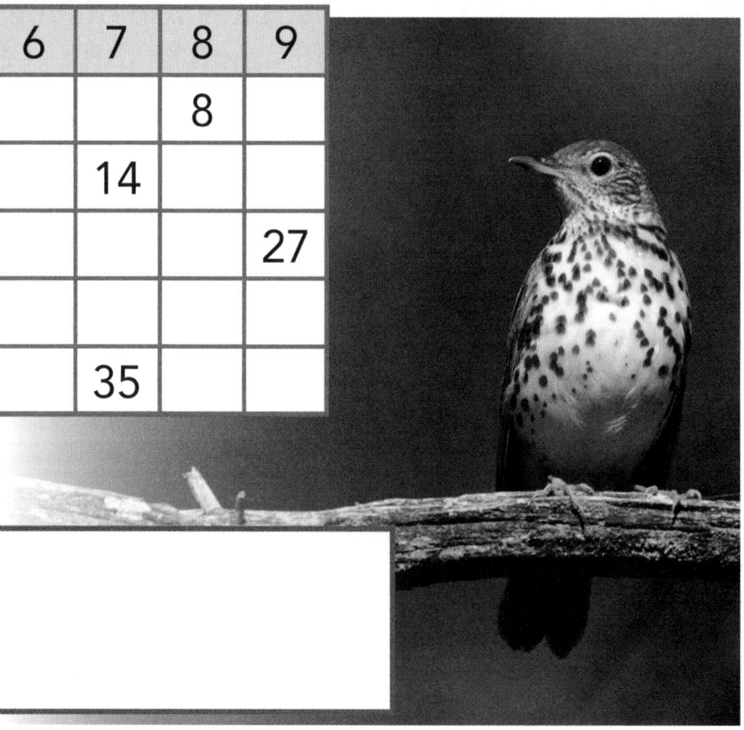

17. Draw an array.

$15 = 5 \times 3$

18. Solve.

2×8 3×6 5×5 4×7 7×2 8×3

4×9 5×6 4×8 9×2 3×7 5×9

Name ____

Multiply by 0 and 1 4.7

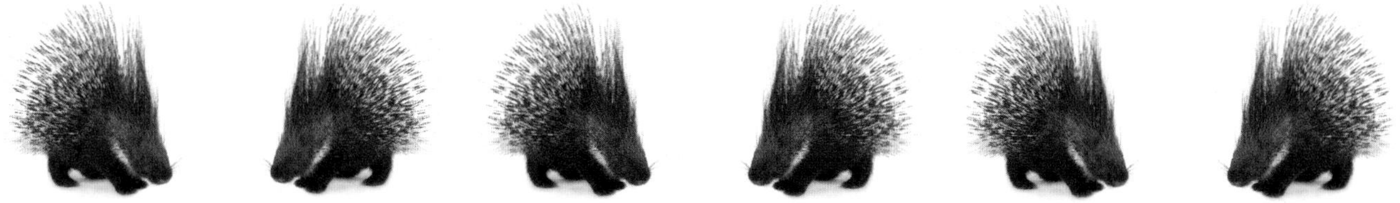

The Property of Zero The product of 0 and any other number is 0.

Porcupines are covered with sharp quills. If predators touch the quills they get hurt. If 2 predators come near a porcupine but do not touch it, how many quills will hurt them?

Porcupines live about 7 years. Females may have 1 or more babies each year. If a porcupine has 1 baby each year for 7 years, how many babies will be born?

$0 + 0 = 0$
2 zeros equal 0
$2 \times 0 = 0$

$1 + 1 + 1 + 1 + 1 + 1 + 1 = 7$
7 ones equal 7
$7 \times 1 = 7$

The Property of One The product of any number and 1 is the number itself.

Write a multiplication equation for each picture.

1. 

_____ × _____ = _____

2. 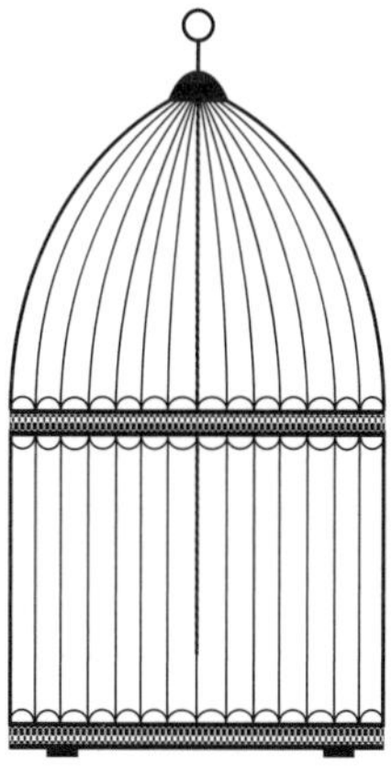

_____ × _____ = _____

3. 

_____ × _____ = _____

4. **Multiply.**

3×2	5×3	4×1	2×8	0×7	1×6	4×5	2×9
1×4	3×3	5×7	0×8	2×4	1×5	5×5	3×6
0×9	4×6	2×6	5×8	3×9	1×2	0×1	5×9

Solve.

5. A forest is home to 6 porcupines. There are 4 forests in the area and each has 6 porcupines. How many live in the area?

_______________ porcupines

6. Many porcupines sleep during the day. They are active for about 8 hours each night. In 4 nights, how many hours might a porcupine be awake?

_______________ hours

7. A forest ranger saw the paw prints of 5 young porcupines. Each one has 4 paws. How many paw prints did the ranger see?

_______________ paw prints

Review

Add or subtract.

8. $4{,}000 + 1{,}245$

9. $7{,}325 - 1{,}065$

10. $208 - 79$

11. $582 + 277$

12. $34 + 56 + 25$

Name ____________________

Problem Solving: Multiply 4.8

Because multiplication is repeated addition, read word problems carefully to choose multiplication or addition. Ask yourself, "Are there equal sets or groups in the problem? Is the same number repeated?" Once you know the operation, choose the best way to solve the problem.

Problem–Solving Path

1. Understand the question.
2. Analyze the data.
3. Plan the strategy.
4. Solve the problem.
5. Evaluate the result.

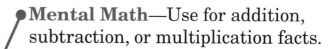

- **Mental Math**—Use for addition, subtraction, or multiplication facts.
- **Paper and Pencil**—Use for numbers that are too large to solve mentally. Use for numerals that have between two and four digits.
- **Calculator**—Use for numbers that are too large to compute easily on paper.

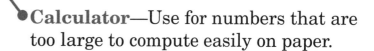

Moose are the largest members of the deer family. You can recognize bull moose by their huge, pointed antlers. This bull moose has 13 points on his antlers. Moose can move quickly. They can run 35 miles per hour and trot at 20 miles per hour.

Read the word problems. Choose a strategy to solve the problem. Solve.

1. If 3 young moose each had antlers with a total of 7 points, how many points would there be?

   ○ mental math ○ paper and pencil ○ calculator

   __________ points

2. A moose trots at 20 miles per hour for 5 hours. How far does it travel?

   ○ mental math ○ paper and pencil ○ calculator

   __________ miles

Solve. Use mental math, pencil and paper, or a calculator.

3. Park rangers needed to move 2 male moose to other locations. They weighed each moose. The total weight of the 2 moose was 3,000 pounds! One moose weighed 1,323 pounds. What was the weight of the second moose?

____

4. The height of a moose from hoof to shoulder is about 6 feet. About how much taller is a 350-foot tall redwood tree than a moose?

____

5. Twin moose calves each weigh 30 pounds. How much do the 2 calves weigh altogether?

____

6. Each moose has 4 hooves. How many hooves would you count if 7 moose passed by?

____

7. A mother moose and her 2 calves were joined by another mother with 2 calves. How many moose were there in all?

____

8. Moose are good swimmers. Park rangers noticed that one moose stayed underwater for a period of 30 seconds, then for 25 seconds, and finally for 29 seconds. How long did the moose stay under the water?

____

Name ____

If each of these 6 ducks had 8 ducklings, how many ducklings would there be?

$8 + 8 + 8 + 8 + 8 + 8 = 48$
$6 \times 8 = 48$ ducklings

A **multiple** is the product of a factor and any other number.

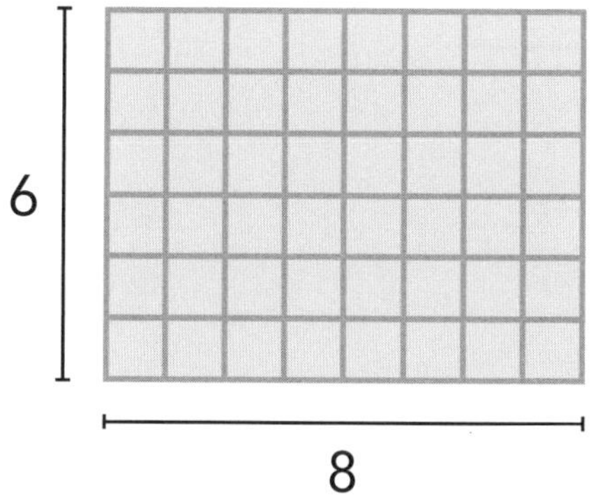

$6 \times 8 = 48$

Memorize these facts.

$1 \times 6 = 6$	$4 \times 6 = 24$	$7 \times 6 = 42$
$2 \times 6 = 12$	$5 \times 6 = 30$	$8 \times 6 = 48$
$3 \times 6 = 18$	$6 \times 6 = 36$	$9 \times 6 = 54$

6, 12, 18, 24, 30, 36, 42, 48, and 54 are multiples of 6.

Circle all multiples of 2. Shade all multiples of 6.

1	2	3	4	5	6	7	8	9	10
11	12	13	14	15	16	17	18	19	20
21	22	23	24	25	26	27	28	29	30
31	32	33	34	35	36	37	38	39	40
41	42	43	44	45	46	47	48	49	50
51	52	53	54	55	56	57	58	59	60

1. What do you notice about these two groups of multiples?

____

Write a multiplication sentence for each array.

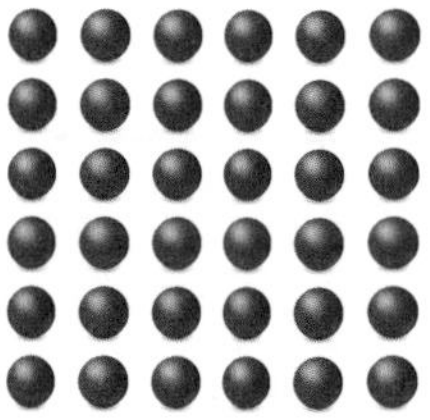

2. ______ × ______ = ______

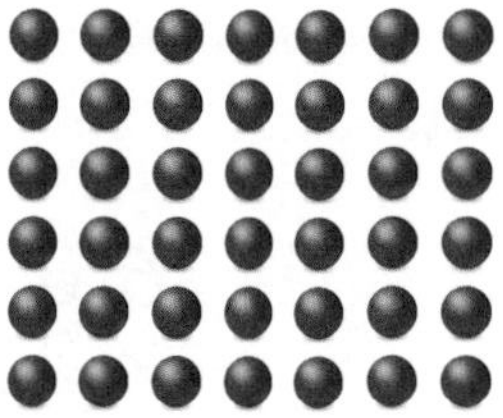

3. ______ × ______ = ______

Write a multiplication sentence for each array.

4. 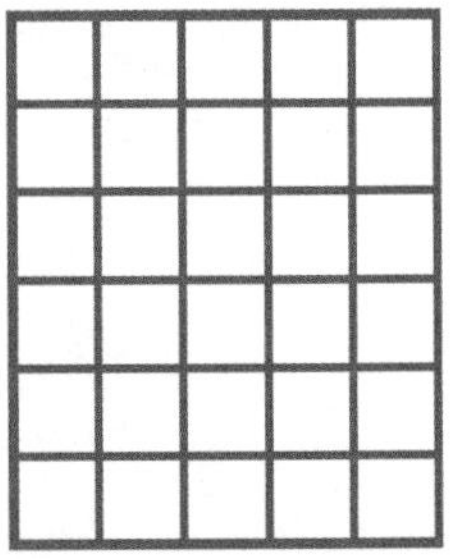

5. 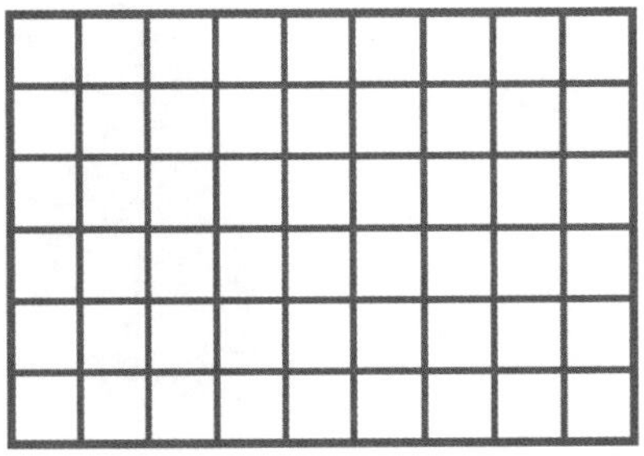

6. 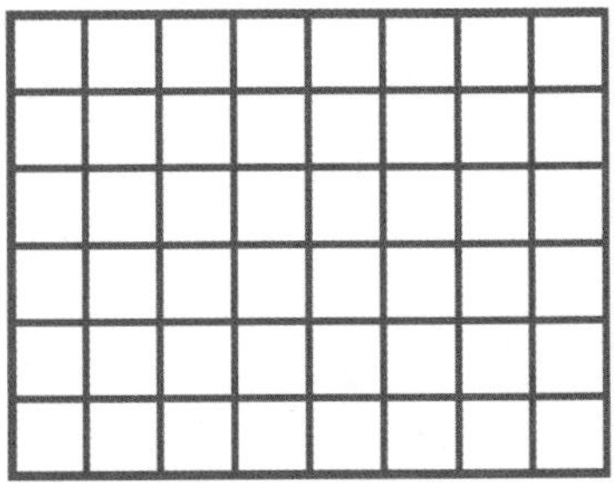

_____ × _____ = _____   _____ × _____ = _____   _____ × _____ = _____

Draw an array for each multiplication sentence. Solve.

7. 6 x 3 = ______   8. 6 x 2 = ______

9. Multiply.

5	4	9	3	6	8	7	6
× 6	× 6	× 5	× 5	× 7	× 4	× 6	× 2

Write any three multiples of each number.

10. ______ ______ ______

12. ______ ______ ______

11. ______ ______ ______

13. ______ ______ ______

Review

Add or subtract.

14.	15.	16.	17.	18.
2,436	6,019	5,037	8,315	7,999
+ 1,875	− 2,220	+ 2,498	− 4,056	+ 1,384

Name ____________________

Multiply by 7

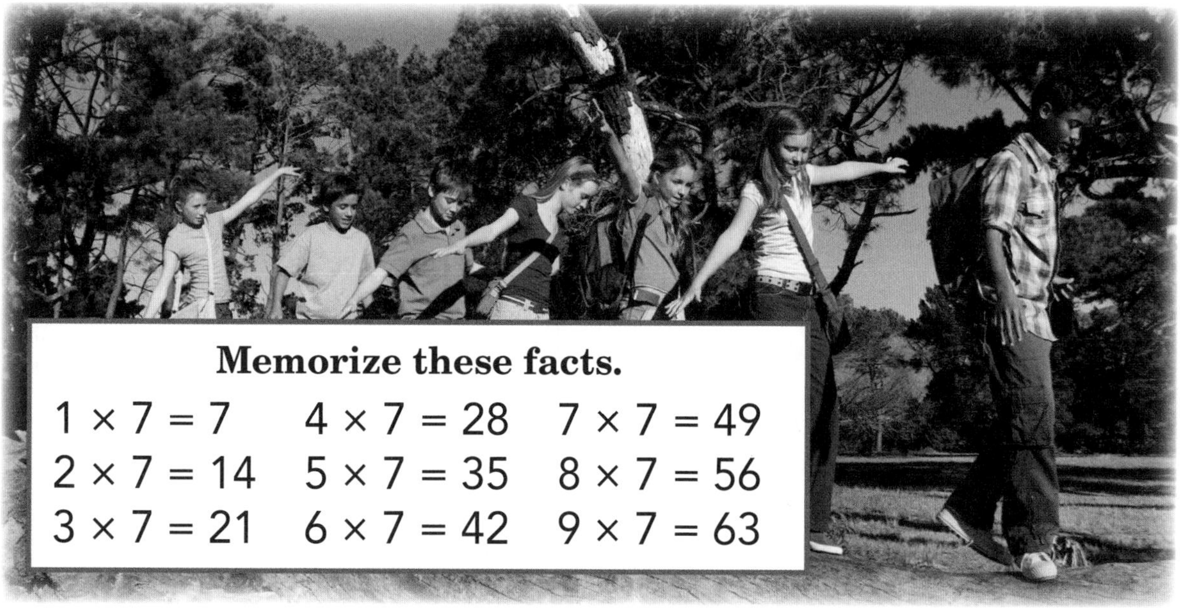

Memorize these facts.

1 × 7 = 7	4 × 7 = 28	7 × 7 = 49
2 × 7 = 14	5 × 7 = 35	8 × 7 = 56
3 × 7 = 21	6 × 7 = 42	9 × 7 = 63

These students exercise 3 times every day. How many exercise sessions do they complete each week?

3	×	7	=	21
exercise sessions per day		days per week		exercise sessions per week

morning

afternoon

evening

Circle sets of 7. Write a multiplication fact for each picture.

1. 

____ × ____ = ____

2. 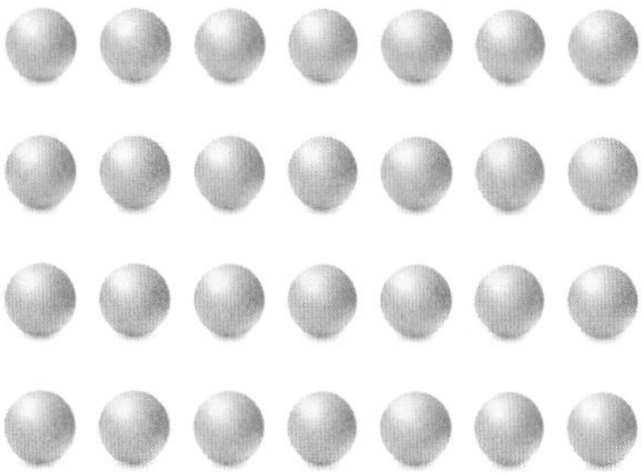

____ × ____ = ____

3. 

____ × ____ = ____

4. **Color only multiples of 7.**

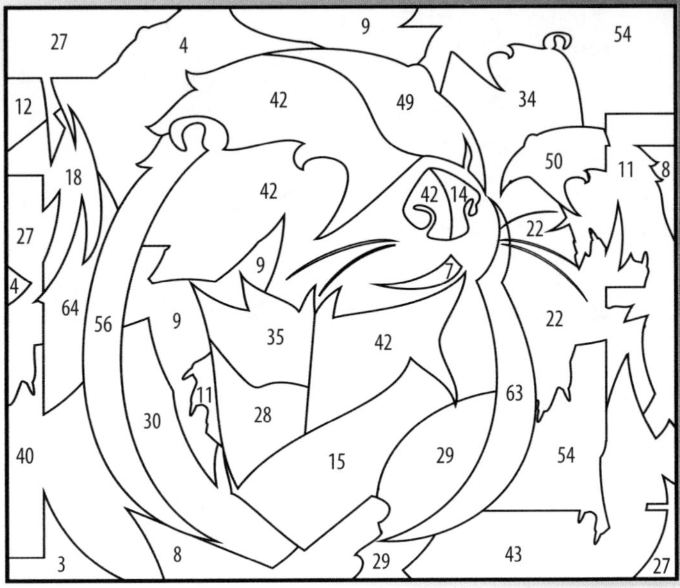

5. **Multiply.**

3×2	5×3	4×1	2×8	0×7	1×6	4×5	2×9
1×4	3×3	5×7	0×8	2×4	1×5	5×5	3×6
0×9	4×6	2×6	5×8	3×9	1×2	0×1	5×9

Use the Order Property of Multiplication to write the related fact.

6. $7 \times 4 =$ _____

_____ × _____ = _____

7. $8 \times 7 =$ _____

_____ × _____ = _____

8. $7 \times 6 =$ _____

_____ × _____ = _____

Solve.

9. The 7 Norton sisters ate fruit at each meal yesterday. How many fruits did they eat yesterday?

____

10. An otter ate 7 fish every day for a week. How many fish did it eat in a week?

____

Name ______________________________

Practice: Multiply by 6 and 7 4.11

1. Write the multiples of 6.

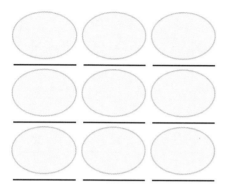

2. Write the multiples of 7.

3. Which multiple do 6 and 7 have in common? ______________

Write a multiplication fact with a factor of 6 or 7 on the line. Then, draw a picture or write a sentence describing how you would use each strategy to find the product.

4. skip counting

____

5. making an array

____

6. knowing doubles

____

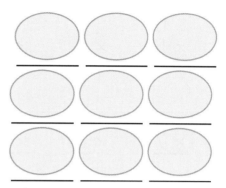

7. **Multiply.**

6 × 8	0 × 5	6 × 9	5 × 8	6 × 6	4 × 7	1 × 3	2 × 9
0 × 8	5 × 7	9 × 6	8 × 6	6 × 4	6 × 3	7 × 5	4 × 1

Solve.

8. Every day for a week, Talia saw a herd of 9 deer. How many deer did she see during the week?

____

9. Skyler found 6 nests with 8 eggs in each nest. How many eggs did he find?

____

Review

Write > or <.

10. 6,049 ◯ 3,919

11. 1,432 ◯ 1,441

12. 5,607 ◯ 5,670

13. 2,895 ◯ 2,985

14. 4,738 ◯ 4,387

15. 9,864 ◯ 9,846

Name ______________________________

Multiply by 8 4.12

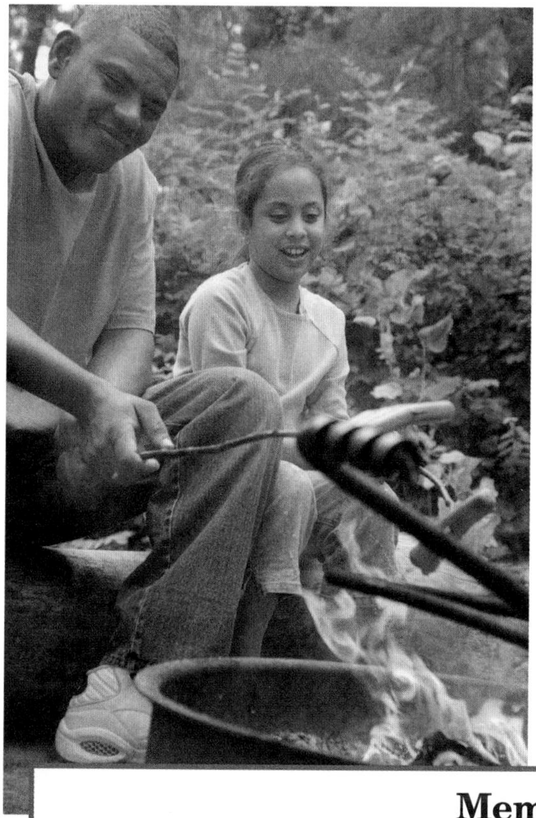

The third graders took a field trip to the forest. They brought 9 packages of hot dogs to roast. Each package had 8 hot dogs. How many hot dogs did they have?

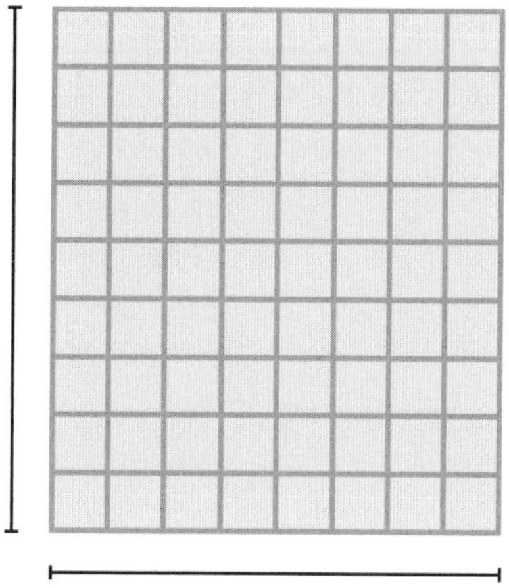

$9 \times 8 = 72$

They had 72 hot dogs.

Memorize these facts.

$1 \times 8 = 8$ $3 \times 8 = 24$ $5 \times 8 = 40$ $7 \times 8 = 56$ $9 \times 8 = 72$

$2 \times 8 = 16$ $4 \times 8 = 32$ $6 \times 8 = 48$ $8 \times 8 = 64$

Circle each group of 8. Write a multiplication fact. Then, use the Order Property of Multiplication to write the related fact.

1.

_____ × _____ = _____

_____ × _____ = _____

2.

_____ × _____ = _____

_____ × _____ = _____

3.

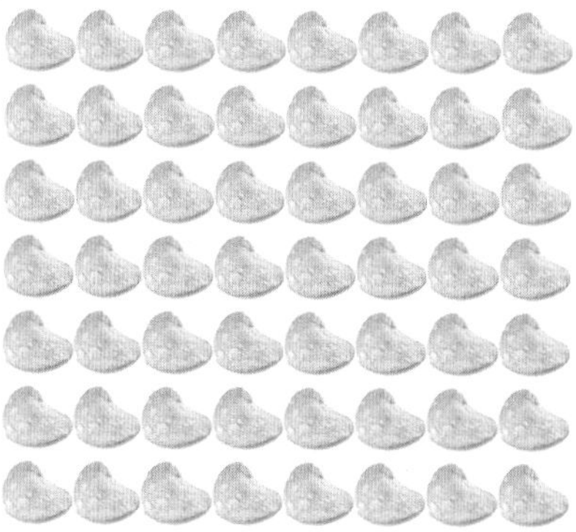

_____ × _____ = _____

_____ × _____ = _____

4. Trace the path of multiples of 8 from start to finish.

start

8	12	15	18	12	24	30	54	48
19	16	24	22	21	18	35	42	49
61	9	12	32	40	48	56	64	10
20	16	24	52	14	28	45	36	72

finish

5. Multiply.

8×3	5×7	2×9	5×8	2×8	8×9	6×3
4×7	8×8	6×7	3×4	6×4	9×5	5×4

6.

×	0	1	2	3	4	5	6	7	8	9
8										

Solve.

7. Tevin invited his Bible-study friends to a cookout. His mom bought 2 packages of hot dogs. There are 8 hot dogs in each package. How many hot dogs did she buy?

____

8. Tevin's mom found 1 package of hot dogs in the freezer. Now how many hot dogs do they have?

____

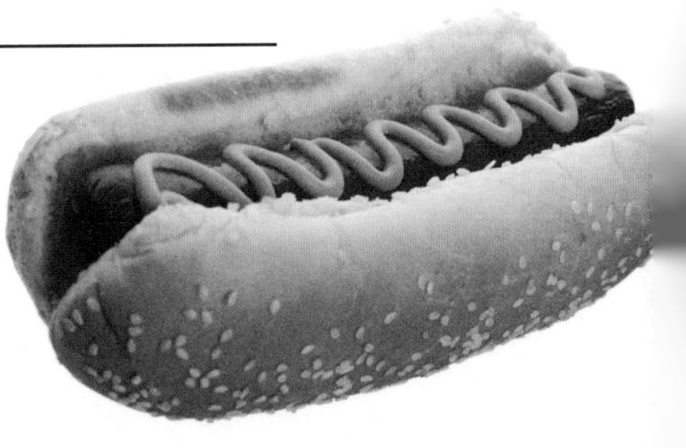

Name ______________________________

Multiply by 9 4.13

The chipmunk gathered 9 peanuts from the picnic area. It went back and found 9 more peanuts. How many peanuts did it gather?

$2 \times 9 = 18$

If you know $2 \times 9 = 18$,
you know $9 \times 2 = 18$.

Memorize these facts.

$1 \times 9 = 9$	$3 \times 9 = 27$	$5 \times 9 = 45$	$7 \times 9 = 63$	$9 \times 9 = 81$
$2 \times 9 = 18$	$4 \times 9 = 36$	$6 \times 9 = 54$	$8 \times 9 = 72$	

Use the Order Property of Multiplication to complete the multiplication sentences.

1. $8 \times 9 =$ ______
   $9 \times 8 =$ ______

2. $3 \times 9 =$ ______
   $9 \times 3 =$ ______

3. $4 \times 9 =$ ______
   $9 \times 4 =$ ______

4. $2 \times 9 =$ ______
   $9 \times 2 =$ ______

5. $7 \times 9 =$ ______
   $9 \times 7 =$ ______

6. $1 \times 9 =$ ______
   $9 \times 1 =$ ______

7. $6 \times 9 =$ ______
   $9 \times 6 =$ ______

8. $5 \times 9 =$ ______
   $9 \times 5 =$ ______

9. **Multiply.**

$\begin{array}{r} 8 \\ \times\ 8 \\ \hline \end{array}$	$\begin{array}{r} 9 \\ \times\ 3 \\ \hline \end{array}$	$\begin{array}{r} 6 \\ \times\ 2 \\ \hline \end{array}$	$\begin{array}{r} 4 \\ \times\ 6 \\ \hline \end{array}$	$\begin{array}{r} 5 \\ \times\ 7 \\ \hline \end{array}$	$\begin{array}{r} 6 \\ \times\ 3 \\ \hline \end{array}$	$\begin{array}{r} 9 \\ \times\ 4 \\ \hline \end{array}$
$\begin{array}{r} 7 \\ \times\ 8 \\ \hline \end{array}$	$\begin{array}{r} 5 \\ \times\ 9 \\ \hline \end{array}$	$\begin{array}{r} 2 \\ \times\ 4 \\ \hline \end{array}$	$\begin{array}{r} 7 \\ \times\ 9 \\ \hline \end{array}$	$\begin{array}{r} 2 \\ \times\ 8 \\ \hline \end{array}$	$\begin{array}{r} 4 \\ \times\ 8 \\ \hline \end{array}$	$\begin{array}{r} 6 \\ \times\ 5 \\ \hline \end{array}$

Multiply to find the product. Then, add.

10. $(2 \times 5) + 6 =$ ______

11. $(3 \times 5) + 3 =$ ______

12. $(9 \times 3) + 5 =$ ______

13. $(6 \times 8) + 3 =$ ______

14. $(4 \times 4) + 4 =$ ______

15. $(9 \times 8) + 5 =$ ______

Review

Round to the highest place value.

16. 87 ______
17. 22 ______
18. 349 ______
19. 53 ______
20. 92 ______
21. 216 ______
22. 45 ______
23. 114 ______
24. 469 ______
25. 68 ______
26. 621 ______
27. 772 ______

Name ______________________________

Practice: Multiply by 8 and 9 4.14

Write or draw an example of each property or strategy. Use different multiplication facts with factors of 8 or 9.

1. Order Property of Multiplication

____

2. Multiplication Property of Zero

____

3. Multiplication Property of One

____

4. array

5. skip counting on ______________

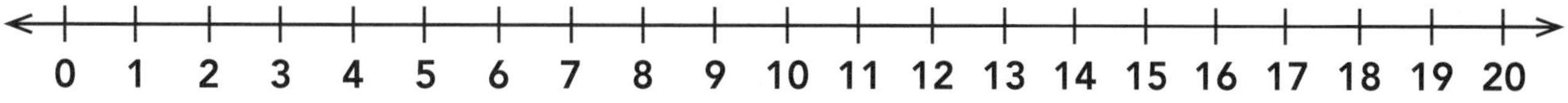

6. squares

____

Number the fingers. Write a multiplication fact. Mark an X over the finger that would be hidden. Write the product.

7. nines ______________

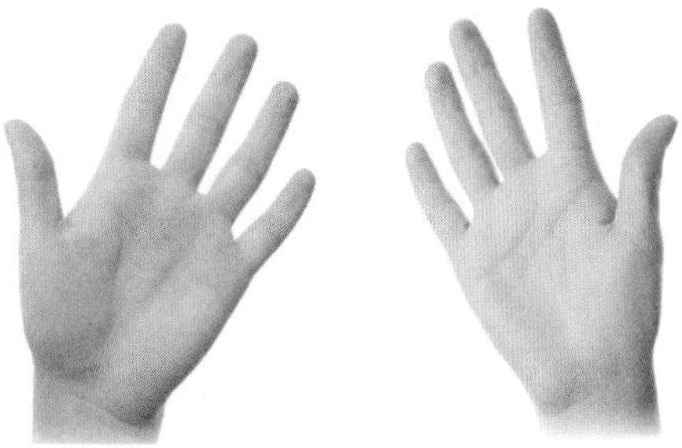

8. Complete the multiplication table.

×	1	2	3	4	5	6	7	8	9
1									
2									
3									
4									
5									
6									
7									
8									
9									

Write any four multiples for these numbers.

9. 7 ______ ______ ______ ______

10. 8 ______ ______ ______ ______

11. 6 ______ ______ ______ ______

12. 9 ______ ______ ______ ______

Multiply, and then add.

13. $(7 \times 8) + 6 =$ ______

14. $(4 \times 6) + 7 =$ ______

15. $(6 \times 2) + 9 =$ ______

16. $(7 \times 7) + 4 =$ ______

17. $(6 \times 3) + 4 =$ ______

18. $(4 \times 9) + 8 =$ ______

19. Six foxes each chased 9 rabbits. How many rabbits did they chase?

______

20. Yolanda saw 8 birds each day for a week. How many birds did she see in a week?

______

Name ______________________________

Graph: Bar Graphs 4.15

Bar graphs are used to show comparisons. The lengths of the bars help show the differences.

The **title** is descriptive and complete.

The **scale** shows the range of numbers starting at 0.

The **bars** extend as far as the number they represent.

Each bar has a **label**.

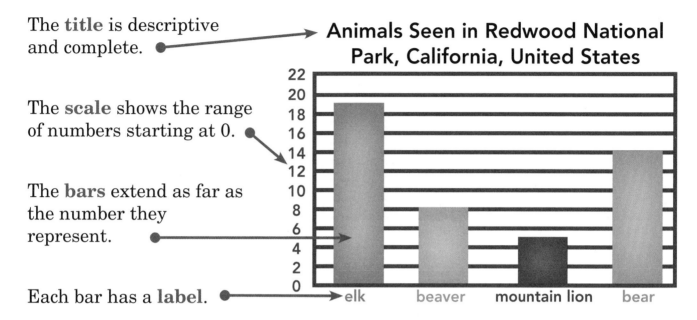

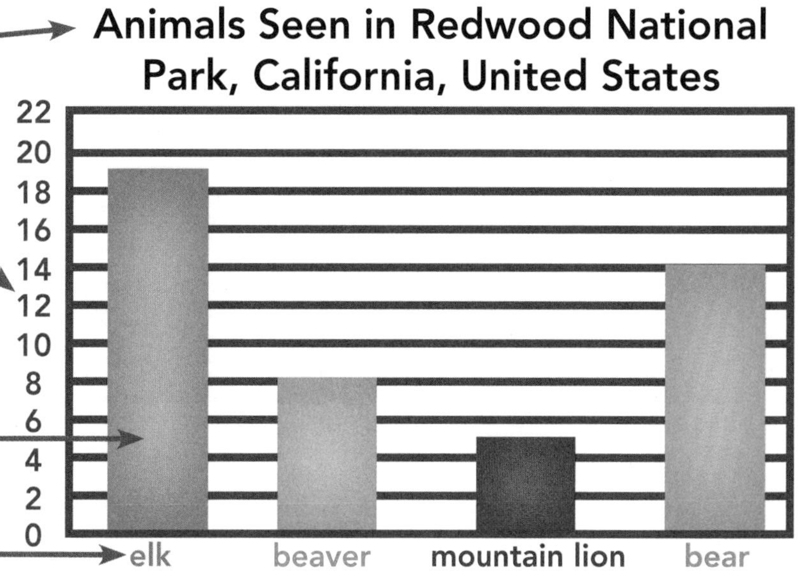

Forest rangers in Redwood National Park keep a record of animal populations. They spotted these animals at a lake.

Use the graph to answer the questions.

1. What are the highest and lowest numbers reported? ______________

2. Which animal was most often seen by the rangers? ______________

3. How many elk were seen in Redwood National Park? ______________

   How many mountain lions? ______________

4. What is the difference in number between the least and most seen animals?

   ____

5. What is the total number of bears, beavers, and mountain lions seen?

   ____

Use this graph to answer the questions.

Snacks Sold at Redwood National Park Visitor Center

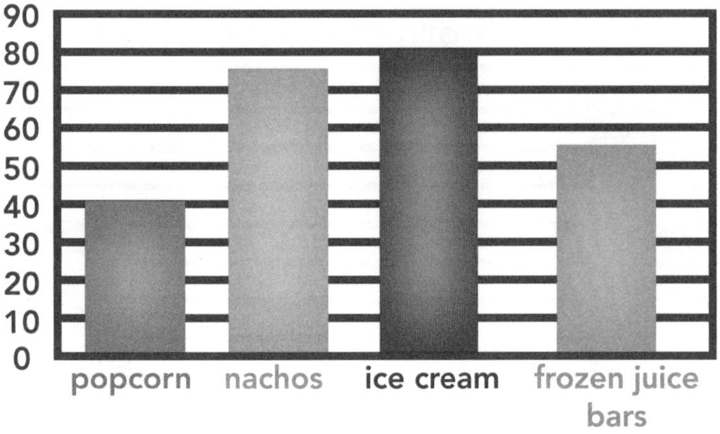

6. Which snack was sold the most?

____

7. Which snack was sold the least?

____

8. How many frozen juice bars were sold?

____

9. If you were the snack-bar manager, which two snacks would you want to have available?

____

10. Transfer all the information from this tally chart to the bar graph. Write the title.

Third-Grade Visitors June 2–6	
Monday	𝍸 𝍸 𝍸 ||
Tuesday	𝍸 𝍸 𝍸 𝍸 𝍸 𝍸
Wednesday	𝍸 𝍸 𝍸 𝍸 𝍸 𝍸 𝍸 𝍸
Thursday	𝍸 𝍸 𝍸 𝍸
Friday	𝍸 𝍸 𝍸 𝍸 𝍸 𝍸 ||

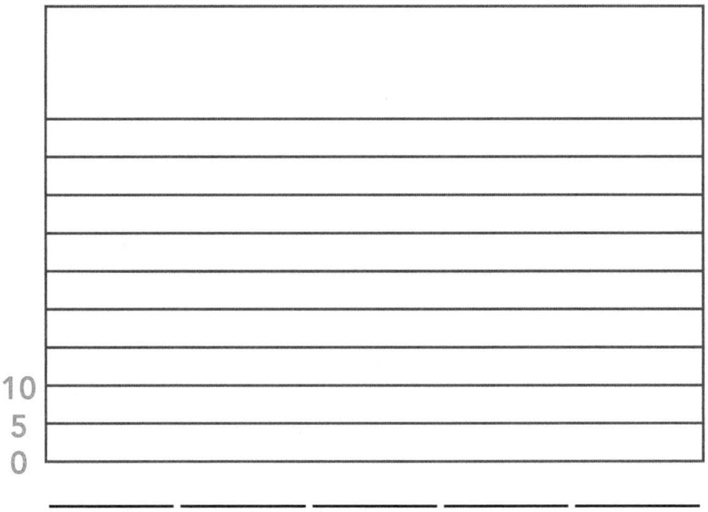

Review

Use the numbers to write addition and subtraction fact families.

11. 6, 5, 11 ________ ________ ________ ________

12. 9, 4, 13 ________ ________ ________ ________

13. 7, 8, 15 ________ ________ ________ ________

Name ____________________

Chapter 4 Review 4.16

1. Match each word to its definition.

_______ factor

_______ product

_______ multiplication

_______ multiplication sign (×)

_______ array

_______ multiple

a. the product of a given factor and any other number

b. the symbol for multiplication

c. repeated addition of the same number

d. rows and columns used to represent a multiplication sentence

e. the result of multiplication

f. one of two numbers that are multiplied

Write multiplication sentences for these arrays.

2.

_____ × _____ = _____

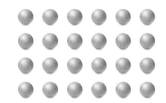

3.

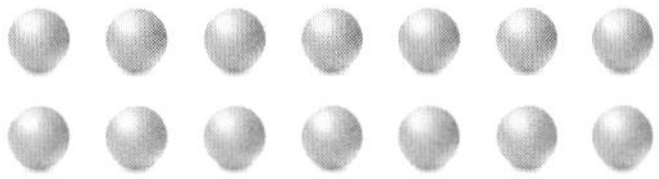

_____ × _____ = _____

4.

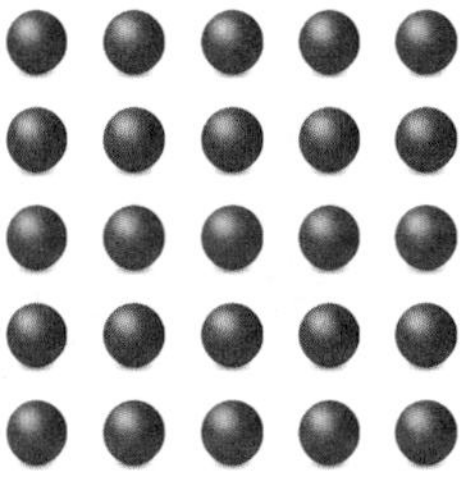

_____ × _____ = _____

Write multiplication sentences for these number lines.

5.

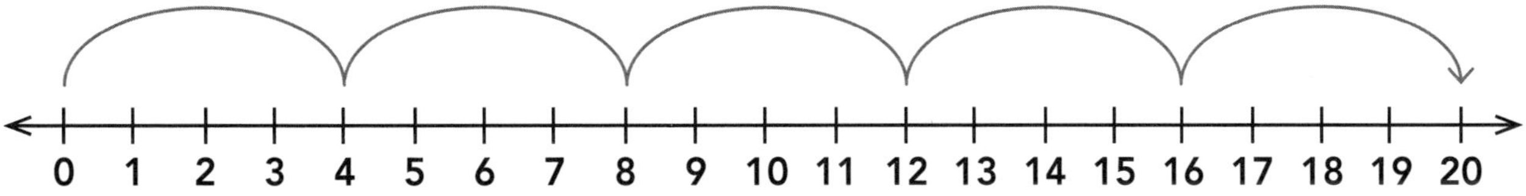

_____ × _____ = _____

6.

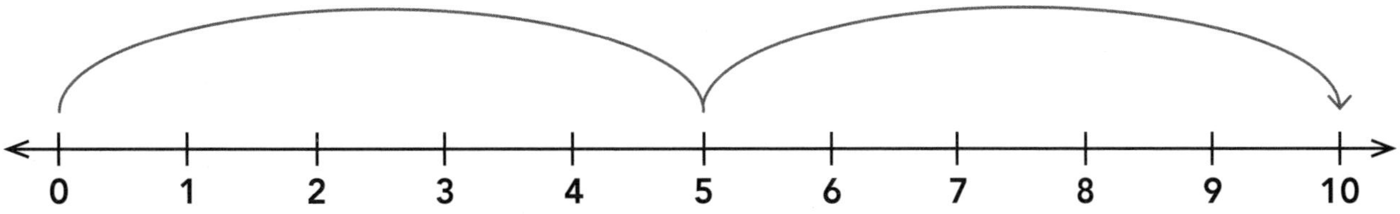

_____ × _____ = _____

Draw an array for each problem. Solve.

7. $2 \times 4 =$ ______

8. $4 \times 4 =$ ______

9. $5 \times 3 =$ ______

10. **Multiply.**

6	7	8	0	5	3	6
× 3	× 8	× 9	× 6	× 6	× 7	× 9
5	2	1	6	3	8	9
× 5	× 9	× 4	× 7	× 8	× 8	× 4

Multiply, and then add.

11. $(2 \times 6) + 3 =$ ______

12. $(9 \times 2) + 6 =$ ______

13. $(6 \times 7) + 5 =$ ______

14. $(7 \times 6) + 7 =$ ______

15. Solve the puzzle.

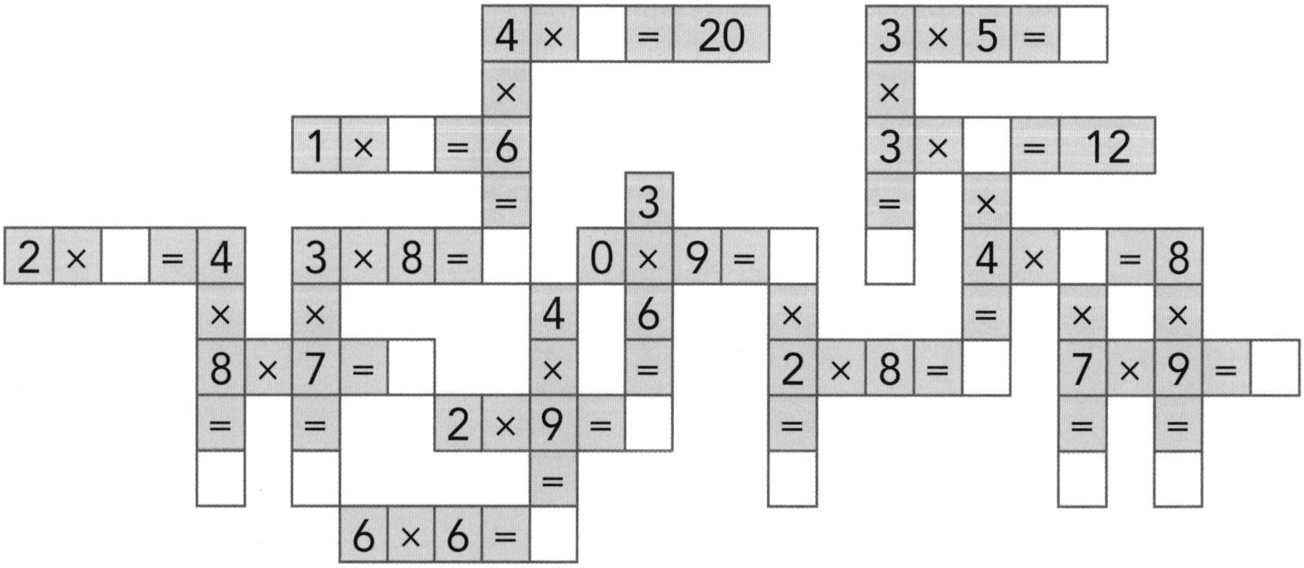

Chapter 5
Division Facts

I urge you, brothers and sisters, to watch out for those who cause divisions and put obstacles in your way that are contrary to the teaching you have learned.
Romans 16:17a

Key Ideas:

Division: relating division to repeated subtraction

Division: relating division to multiplication

Division: facts 0–9

Division: dividing one- and two-digit numbers without remainders

Name ______________________________

Division Strategies 5.1

This sand crab has 8 legs. It has 2 sides to its body. How many legs are on each side?

8 = 2 sets of 4

$8 \div 2 = 4$

Division is an operation that separates a number into equal sets.

The division sign (÷) is read as "divided by."

Multiplication: add sets	Division: subtract sets
$4 + 4 = 8$, so $2 \times 4 = 8$	$8 - 4 = 4$; $4 - 4 = 0$ so $8 \div 2 = 4$

There are 8 coconut milk drinks and 4 people.

How many drinks can each person have? Draw a tally mark in each circle to divide up the 8 drinks.

$8 \div 4 = 2$ ◯ ◯ ◯ ◯

Circle sets to solve. Fill in the answers.

××××××
××××××

×××××××
×××××××
×××××××

×××××××
×××××××
×××××××

1. 2 sets of ______
   $12 \div 2 =$ ______

2. 3 sets of ______
   $18 \div 3 =$ ______

3. 3 sets of ______
   $21 \div 3 =$ ______

Complete the related multiplication and division sentences for these arrays.

4.

X X X X X
X X X X X
X X X X X

$3 \times 5 =$ ______

______ $\div 3 = 5$

5.

O O O O O O
O O O O O O
O O O O O O
O O O O O O

$4 \times 6 =$ ______

______ $\div 4 = 6$

6.

□ □ □ □ □ □
□ □ □ □ □ □
□ □ □ □ □ □

$3 \times 6 =$ ______

______ $\div 3 =$ ______

Write the fact family for each set of numerals.

7. 4 5 20 ______ ______ ______ ______

8. 7 28 4 ______ ______ ______ ______

9. 30 6 5 ______ ______ ______ ______

Solve.

10. The third-grade class saw hermit crabs in the tide pools. They counted 32 crabs in 4 tide pools. If each pool had the same number of hermit crabs, how many were in each tide pool?

______

Review

Write the estimated sum in the box. Solve and check your estimate.

11. $\begin{array}{r} 38 \\ +67 \\ \hline \end{array}$ □

13. $\begin{array}{r} 41 \\ +88 \\ \hline \end{array}$ □

15. $\begin{array}{r} 55 \\ +69 \\ \hline \end{array}$ □

17. $\begin{array}{r} 682 \\ +114 \\ \hline \end{array}$ □

12. $\begin{array}{r} 523 \\ +685 \\ \hline \end{array}$ □

14. $\begin{array}{r} 288 \\ +706 \\ \hline \end{array}$ □

16. $\begin{array}{r} 919 \\ +275 \\ \hline \end{array}$ □

18. $\begin{array}{r} 621 \\ +909 \\ \hline \end{array}$ □

Name ______________________________

Divide by 2 5.2

Lemurs live on the island of Madagascar. Some lemurs have rings on their tails. Two lemurs have a total of 16 rings on their tails. Their tails both have the same number of rings. How many rings does each lemur have?

Each division sentence has three parts. The dividend is the number divided. The divisor is the number the dividend is divided by. The quotient is the result.

$2 \div 2 = 1$	2 = one 2	(1 + 1)
$4 \div 2 = 2$	4 = two 2s	(2 + 2)
$6 \div 2 = 3$	6 = two 3s	(3 + 3)
$8 \div 2 = 4$	8 = two 4s	(4 + 4)
$10 \div 2 = 5$	10 = two 5s	(5 + 5)
$12 \div 2 = 6$	12 = two 6s	(6 + 6)
$14 \div 2 = 7$	14 = two 7s	(7 + 7)
$16 \div 2 = 8$	16 = two 8s	(8 + 8)
$18 \div 2 = 9$	18 = two 9s	(9 + 9)

You can write a division sentence to find the number of rings.

dividend		divisor		quotient
16	÷	2	=	8
total rings		**lemurs**		**rings per lemur**

Sixteen rings, divided between 2 lemurs, equals 8 rings per lemur.

Divide the objects into two equal sets. Complete the division sentence.

1. 

$8 \div 2 =$ ______

2. 

$12 \div 2 =$ ______

3. 

$14 \div 2 =$ ______

Write **dividend, divisor,** or **quotient** for each red number.

4. 14 ÷ 2 = 7 ______
5. 10 ÷ 2 = 5 ______
6. 18 ÷ 2 = 9 ______
7. 14 ÷ 2 = 7 ______

Write an addition double. Complete the division sentence.

8. 12 = ____ + ____

12 ÷ 2 = ____

9. 8 = ____ + ____

8 ÷ 2 = ____

10. 16 = ____ + ____

16 ÷ 2 = ____

11. Write the quotient.

18 ÷ 2 = ____ 6 ÷ 2 = ____ 4 ÷ 2 = ____ 10 ÷ 2 = ____

8 ÷ 2 = ____ 16 ÷ 2 = ____ 12 ÷ 2 = ____ 14 ÷ 2 = ____

Write the fact family for each set of numerals.

12. 2, 16, 8

______
______
______
______

13. 10, 2, 5

______
______
______
______

14. 7, 14, 2

______
______
______
______

Solve.

15. The zookeeper was preparing fruit to feed the lemurs. She had 18 bananas to divide between 2 lemurs. How many bananas would each lemur receive?

______

Name ____

Cami saw 9 parrots. She took 3 photos of the birds. Each photo had the same number of birds. Each bird was in only 1 picture. How many birds were in each picture?

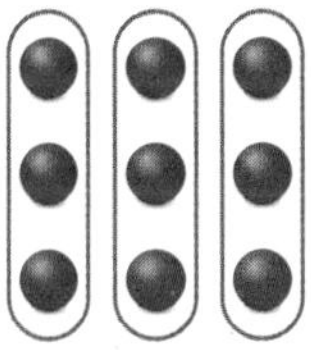

9 ÷ 3 = _____ birds

Cami took pictures of 12 Indonesian monkeys. Each picture showed 3 monkeys. Each monkey was in only 1 picture. How many photos did Cami take?

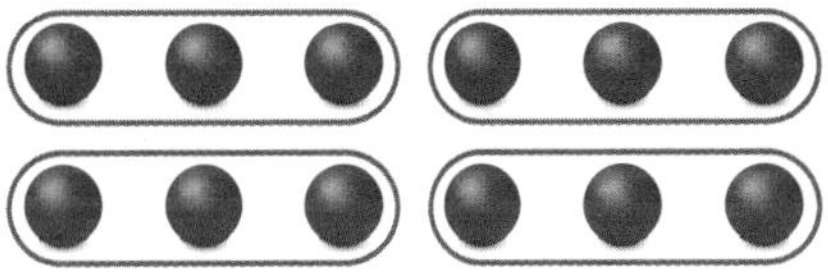

12 ÷ 3 = _____ photos

Memorize these facts.

3 ÷ 3 = 1	9 ÷ 3 = 3	15 ÷ 3 = 5	21 ÷ 3 = 7	27 ÷ 3 = 9
6 ÷ 3 = 2	12 ÷ 3 = 4	18 ÷ 3 = 6	24 ÷ 3 = 8	

Draw circles to divide the objects into sets of three. Write the division equation.

1. 

_____ ÷ _____ = _____

2. 

_____ ÷ _____ = _____

3. 

_____ ÷ _____ = _____

Write two related multiplication equations. Then, write the quotient for each division equation.

4. 21 ÷ 3 = _____

_____ × _____ = _____

_____ × _____ = _____

5. 15 ÷ 3 = _____

_____ × _____ = _____

_____ × _____ = _____

6. 18 ÷ 3 = _____

_____ × _____ = _____

_____ × _____ = _____

7. **Write the quotient.**

18 ÷ 3 = _____	15 ÷ 3 = _____	12 ÷ 2 = _____	6 ÷ 3 = _____
14 ÷ 2 = _____	6 ÷ 2 = _____	18 ÷ 2 = _____	12 ÷ 3 = _____
4 ÷ 2 = _____	24 ÷ 3 = _____	8 ÷ 2 = _____	27 ÷ 3 = _____
21 ÷ 3 = _____	16 ÷ 2 = _____	9 ÷ 3 = _____	10 ÷ 2 = _____

Write ÷ or × in the circle.

8. 3 ◯ 9 = 27
9. 8 ◯ 3 = 24
10. 12 ◯ 3 = 4
11. 6 ◯ 2 = 3
12. 18 ◯ 3 = 6
13. 9 ◯ 2 = 18
14. 14 ◯ 2 = 7
15. 2 ◯ 6 = 12
16. 16 ◯ 2 = 8
17. 3 ◯ 3 = 9
18. 10 ◯ 2 = 5
19. 21 ◯ 3 = 7

Solve.

20. There were 21 parrots on 3 acacia trees. If the trees held equal numbers of the birds, how many parrots would be on each tree?

____

21. A class of 27 students split into equal groups to share 3 Bibles. Each group had 1 Bible. How many students were in each group?

____

Name ___________________________________

Divide by 4 5.4

Geckos are found all over the world. They eat insects. If 9 geckos shared 36 insects equally, how many insects did each gecko receive?

36 ÷ 9 = 4 insects

What if there were ...

4 geckos?	36 ÷ 4 = 9 insects
6 geckos?	36 ÷ 6 = 6 insects
9 geckos?	36 ÷ 9 = 4 insects

Memorize these facts.

4 ÷ 4 = 1	24 ÷ 4 = 6
8 ÷ 4 = 2	28 ÷ 4 = 7
12 ÷ 4 = 3	32 ÷ 4 = 8
16 ÷ 4 = 4	36 ÷ 4 = 9
20 ÷ 4 = 5	

As the divisors increase in value, the quotients decrease in value.

Write a multiplication fact to complete these equations. Underline the correct word in the parentheses.

1. 

4 × _____ = 12

12 ÷ 4 = _____

The quotient would (increase, decrease) if the divisor were 6 instead of 4.

2. 

4 × _____ = 20

20 ÷ 4 = _____

The quotient would (increase, decrease) if the divisor were 2 instead of 4.

3. 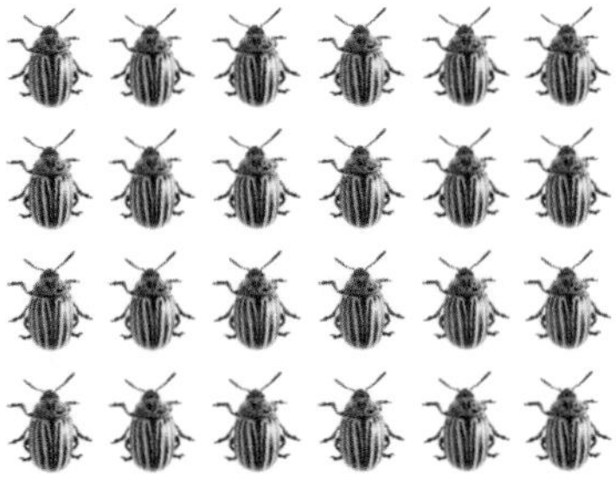

4 × _____ = 24

24 ÷ 4 = _____

The quotient would (increase, decrease) if the divisor were 8 instead of 4.

4. **Divide.**

8 ÷ 4 = ______ 28 ÷ 4 = ______ 12 ÷ 4 = ______

16 ÷ 4 = ______ 24 ÷ 4 = ______ 20 ÷ 4 = ______

36 ÷ 4 = ______ 8 ÷ 4 = ______ 32 ÷ 4 = ______

5. **Divide each number by 4. Write the quotient.**

32	20	8	12	36	16	24	28

6. **Divide.**

10 ÷ 2 = ______ 21 ÷ 3 = ______

16 ÷ 2 = ______ 8 ÷ 4 = ______

20 ÷ 4 = ______ 12 ÷ 2 = ______

9 ÷ 3 = ______ 28 ÷ 4 = ______

16 ÷ 4 = ______ 15 ÷ 3 = ______

4 ÷ 2 = ______ 18 ÷ 2 = ______

18 ÷ 3 = ______ 6 ÷ 2 = ______

12 ÷ 4 = ______ 24 ÷ 3 = ______

Write equations and solve.

7. Mr. López had 32 students work in equal small groups to study 8 types of geckos. Each group studied 1 type of gecko. How many students were in each group?

______

8. Bella used the Internet to find information on geckos. In 24 minutes, she visited 6 science websites. She spent the same amount of time looking at each website. How many minutes did Bella spend per website?

______

Name ______________________________

Divide by 5 5.5

Five rescued sea lions performed at a show. They each made the same number of leaps through a ring. They made 15 leaps total. How many leaps did each sea lion make?

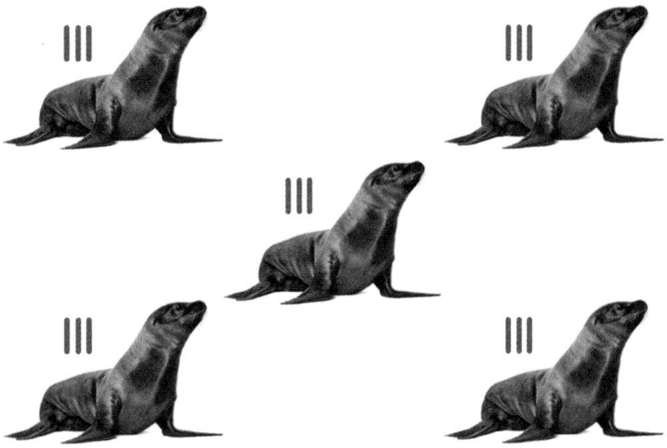

5 lions   15 total leaps

15 ÷ 5 = 3 leaps

To find the quotient, you can ...

use counters,  5 sets of 3

count back by 5s, or  15 10 5 0   3 skips

think of a multiplication fact.   5 × 3 = 15   15 ÷ 5 = 3

Memorize these facts.

5 ÷ 5 = 1	15 ÷ 5 = 3	25 ÷ 5 = 5	35 ÷ 5 = 7	45 ÷ 5 = 9
10 ÷5 = 2	20 ÷ 5 = 4	30 ÷ 5 = 6	40 ÷ 5 = 8	

Circle groups of 5 to divide. Fill in the quotient.

1. 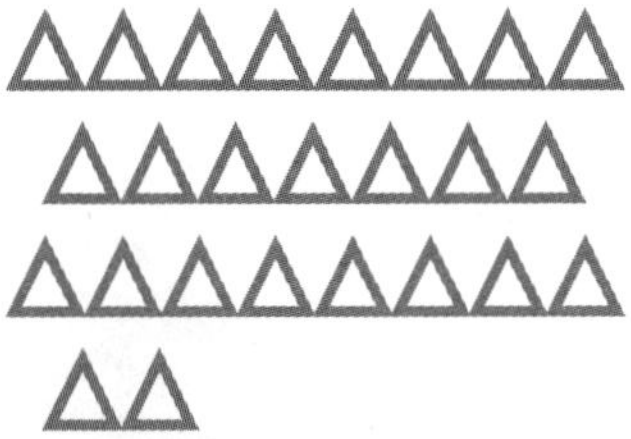

25 ÷ 5 = ______

2. 

20 ÷ 5 = ______

3. 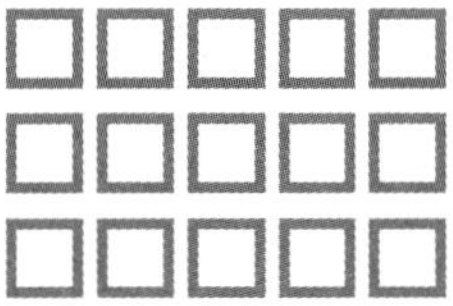

15 ÷ 5 = ______

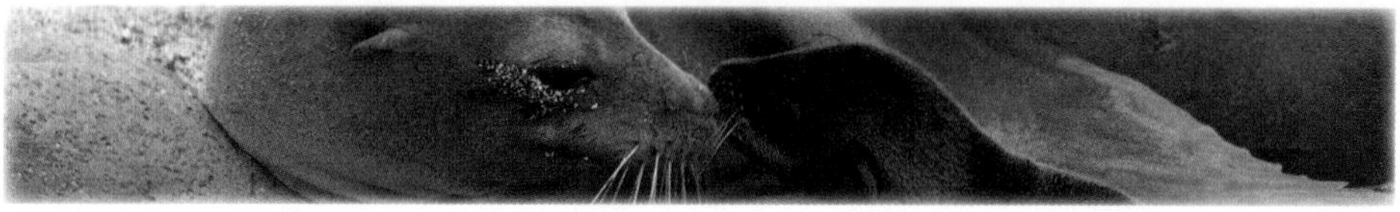

Count back to find the quotient.

4. 20 ÷ 5 = ______

(______ ______ ______ ______)

5. 10 ÷ 5 = ______

(______ ______)

Think of a multiplication fact to find the quotient.

6. 40 ÷ 5 = ______

5 × ______ = 40

7. 35 ÷ 5 = ______

5 × ______ = 35

8. 45 ÷ 5 = ______

5 × ______ = 45

Solve.

9. Make tally marks to show the number of tricks performed. For every 5 tricks, the sea lions received a treat. How many treats did each sea lion receive? Write the numbers.

sea lion	number of tricks	trick tally	number of treats
Zu Zu	12		
Sardine	10		
Rip Tide	16		
Pippa	11		
Oyster	15		

10. Divide.

45 ÷ 5 = ______

35 ÷ 5 = ______

18 ÷ 2 = ______

36 ÷ 4 = ______

30 ÷ 5 = ______

28 ÷ 4 = ______

10 ÷ 5 = ______

27 ÷ 3 = ______

12 ÷ 4 = ______

16 ÷ 4 = ______

15 ÷ 5 = ______

20 ÷ 5 = ______

25 ÷ 5 = ______

24 ÷ 3 = ______

40 ÷ 5 = ______

24 ÷ 4 = ______

Name ______________________________

Zero and One in Division 5.6

There are 4 surfboards and 4 surfers. How many surfboards will each surfer get?

4 surfboards divided by 4 surfers

$4 \div 4 = 1$

A number divided by itself equals 1.

The surf store did not sell goggles. How many goggles did the surfers buy?

0 goggles divided by 4 surfers

$0 \div 4 = 0$

Zero divided by any number is 0.

Val rode 4 waves today. How many waves did Val ride?

4 waves divided by 1 surfer

$4 \div 1 = 4$

A number divided by 1 equals itself.

Write two division facts for each picture.

1.

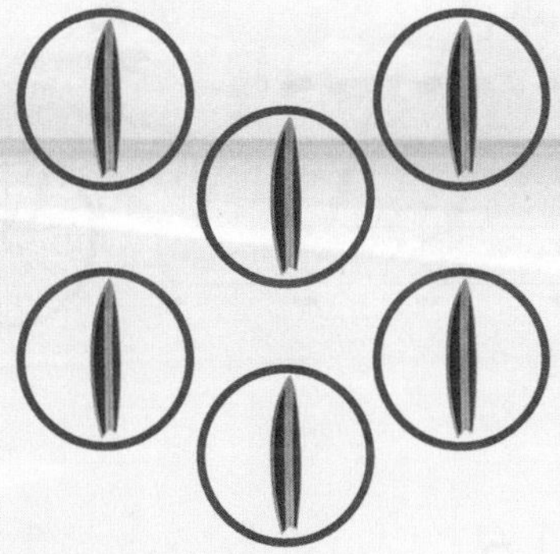

_____ ÷ _____ = _____

_____ ÷ _____ = _____

2.

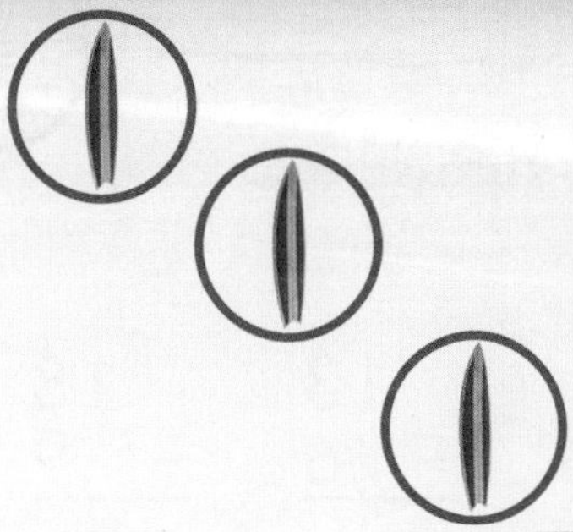

_____ ÷ _____ = _____

_____ ÷ _____ = _____

3.

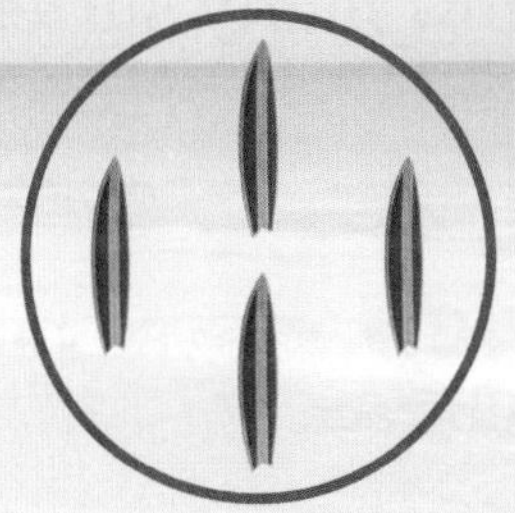

_____ ÷ _____ = _____

_____ ÷ _____ = _____

Draw a picture for each division fact.

4. $7 \div 1 = 7$	5. $6 \div 6 = 1$

Solve the division problem. Write a related multiplication sentence.

6. $8 \div 8 =$ ______   ______ × ______ = ______

7. $7 \div 1 =$ ______   ______ × ______ = ______

8. $57 \div 57 =$ ______   ______ × ______ = ______

9. Divide.

$7 \div 7 =$ ______	$6 \div 6 =$ ______	$8 \div 1 =$ ______
$9 \div 1 =$ ______	$24 \div 4 =$ ______	$3 \div 1 =$ ______
$12 \div 2 =$ ______	$5 \div 5 =$ ______	$4 \div 4 =$ ______
$0 \div 2 =$ ______	$0 \div 1 =$ ______	$9 \div 3 =$ ______

Solve.

10. This bike has 4 seats. Each of the surfers needs 1 seat. How many surfers can ride the bike?

____

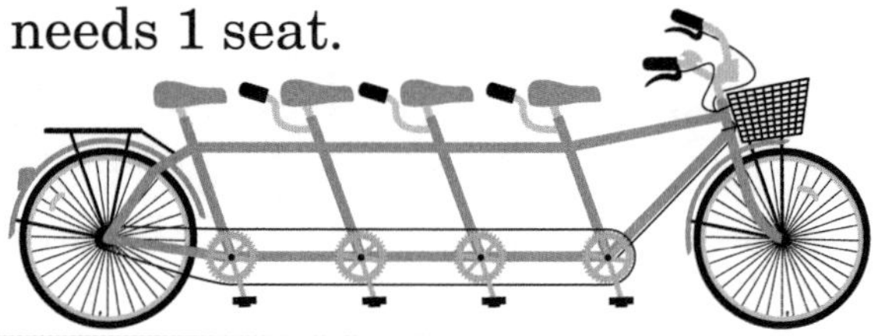

Review

11. Subtract.

$17 - 8$	$15 - 9$	$14 - 8$	$13 - 6$	$18 - 9$	$16 - 7$	$15 - 8$	$12 - 3$
$16 - 8$	$14 - 5$	$17 - 9$	$12 - 5$	$16 - 9$	$15 - 6$	$13 - 4$	$14 - 7$

Name ______________________

There are 6 turtles on the island. How many pairs of turtles are there?

6	÷	2	=	3
turtles		turtles in a pair		pairs

To divide you can ...

use repeated subtraction,

$6 - 2 = 4$ → $4 - 2 = 2$ → $2 - 2 = 0$

(1) (2) (3)

Subtracting 3 times means 6 ÷ 2 = 3.

count back, or

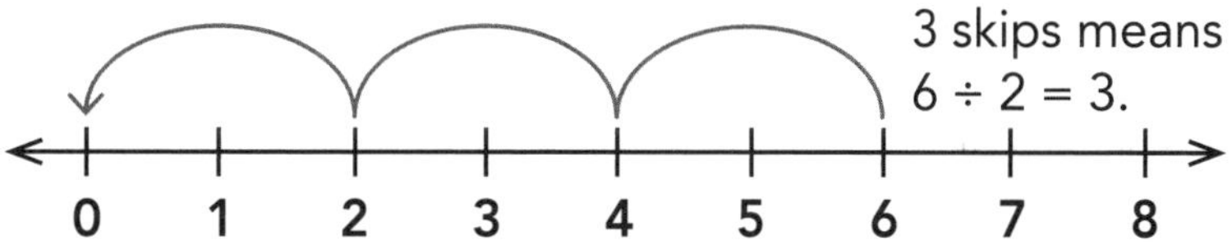

3 skips means 6 ÷ 2 = 3.

think of a multiplication fact. $2 \times 3 = 6$

Think of the 3s fact family.
2 × 3 = 6 means 6 ÷ 2 = 3.

Circle to match the divisor. Fill in the quotient.

1. 

12 ÷ 4 = ______

2. 

15 ÷ 3 = ______

3. 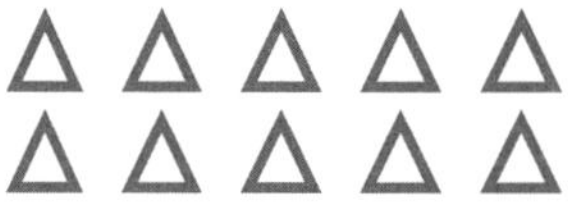

10 ÷ 2 = ______

Draw skips on the number line. Complete the division equation.

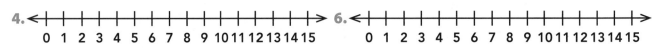

4. 0 1 2 3 4 5 6 7 8 9 10 11 12 13 14 15

$8 \div 4 =$ ______

6. 0 1 2 3 4 5 6 7 8 9 10 11 12 13 14 15

$14 \div 2 =$ ______

5. 0 1 2 3 4 5 6 7 8 9 10 11 12 13 14 15

$12 \div 3 =$ ______

7. 0 1 2 3 4 5 6 7 8 9 10 11 12 13 14 15

$15 \div 5 =$ ______

Write the fact family for each set of numbers.

8. 2, 9, 18 ______ ______ ______ ______

9. 6, 4, 24 ______ ______ ______ ______

10. 8, 4, 32 ______ ______ ______ ______

11. 9, 5, 45 ______ ______ ______ ______

12. Divide.

$40 \div 5 =$ ______ $25 \div 5 =$ ______ $9 \div 3 =$ ______

$20 \div 4 =$ ______ $24 \div 4 =$ ______ $18 \div 2 =$ ______

$12 \div 3 =$ ______ $4 \div 4 =$ ______ $21 \div 3 =$ ______

$45 \div 5 =$ ______ $0 \div 3 =$ ______ $24 \div 3 =$ ______

$8 \div 2 =$ ______ $8 \div 1 =$ ______ $28 \div 4 =$ ______

Solve.

13. David's parents are missionaries. They started an aquaponics farm on the island of Aruba. David helps with the fish and the plants. He planted 25 tomato seeds, 5 in each row. How many rows did he plant?

______

Name ______________________________

Problem Solving: Evaluate Results 5.8

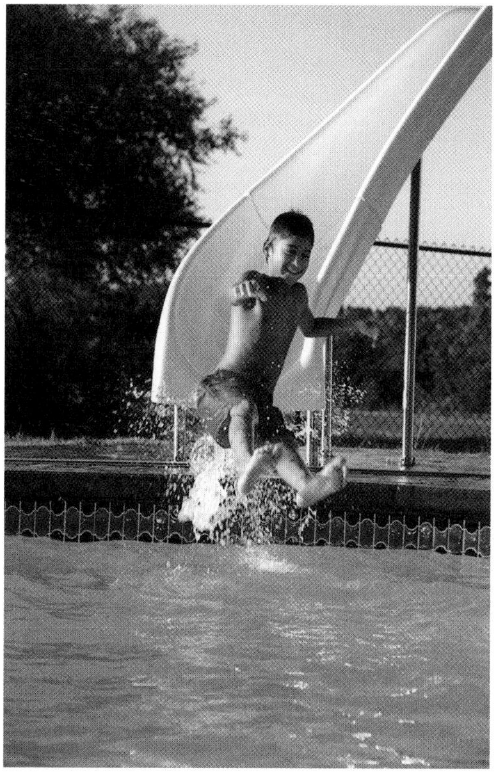

Help Jordan and his mother plan a pool party for his church class. Besides Jordan, there will be 11 people.

food

hot dogs	8 in a package
buns	10 in a package
juice boxes	3 in a package
chips	6 in a variety package

supplies

balloons	15 in a bag
water balloons	10 in a bag
squirt guns	4 in a package
noisemakers	6 in a package

Problem–Solving Path

1. Understand the question.
2. Analyze the data.
3. Plan the strategy.
4. Solve the problem.
5. Evaluate the result.

- Compare the answer with the estimate.
- Think: Does the answer make sense?

Answer the question.

1. How many packages of squirt guns should they buy?

____

Evaluate the result. Fill in the blanks.

2. Would 2 packages be enough? ______ because 2 x 4 = ______
3. Would 4 packages be too many? ______ because 4 x 4 = ______
4. Does it make sense to buy 3 packages? ______ because 3 x 4 = ______

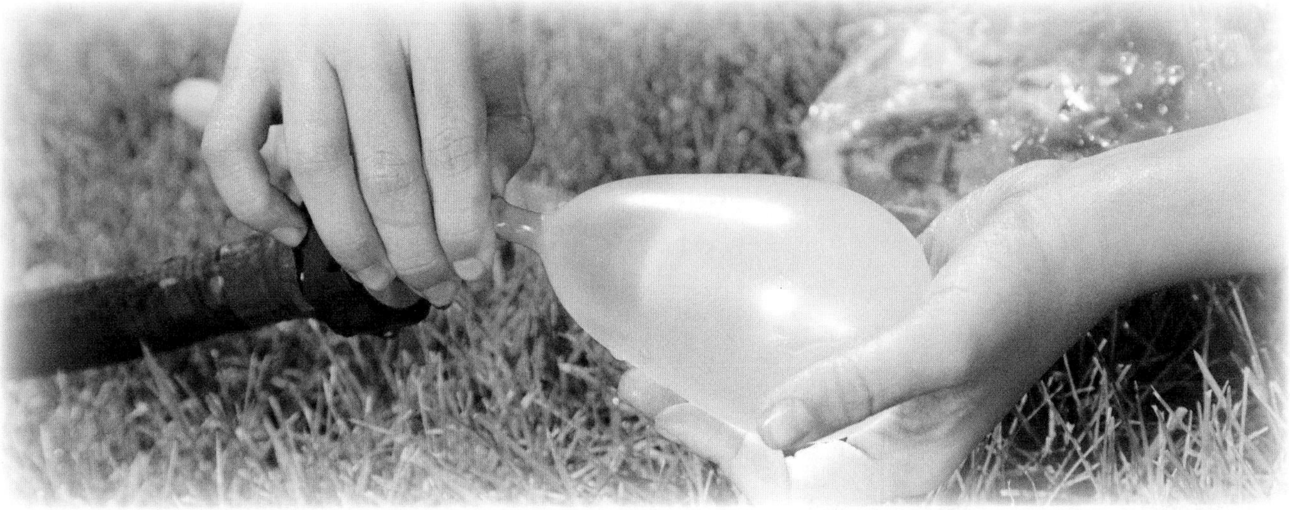

Use the party food and supplies list to solve each word problem.

5. How many packages of hot dogs should Jordan's mom buy to feed 12 people?

____

6. If everyone eats 2 hot dogs, how many hot dogs should Jordan's mom buy?

____

7. If everyone gets 1 juice box, how many packages of juice boxes should Jordan's mom buy?

____

8. Each person will toss 1 water balloon at a target. How many bags of water balloons should Jordan's mom buy?

____

9. How many packages of noisemakers should Jordan's mom buy?

____

10. Only half the noisemakers were used. How many extra noisemakers are left?

____

Name ______________________________

Divide by 6 5.9

Memorize these facts.

$6 \div 6 = 1$	$36 \div 6 = 6$
$12 \div 6 = 2$	$42 \div 6 = 7$
$18 \div 6 = 3$	$48 \div 6 = 8$
$24 \div 6 = 4$	$54 \div 6 = 9$
$30 \div 6 = 5$	

Iguanas gather on the rocks. Each rock has 6 iguanas. Webb took pictures of 30 iguanas. How many rocks did Webb photograph?

30 iguanas	÷	6 iguanas on a rock	=	5 rocks

$$\begin{array}{r}5\\6\overline{)30}\end{array}$$ is another way to write $30 \div 6 = 5$

The 5 is written above the zero in the ones place in the dividend. Both are read "thirty divided by six equals five."

Circle sets of 6. Complete each division equation.

1. 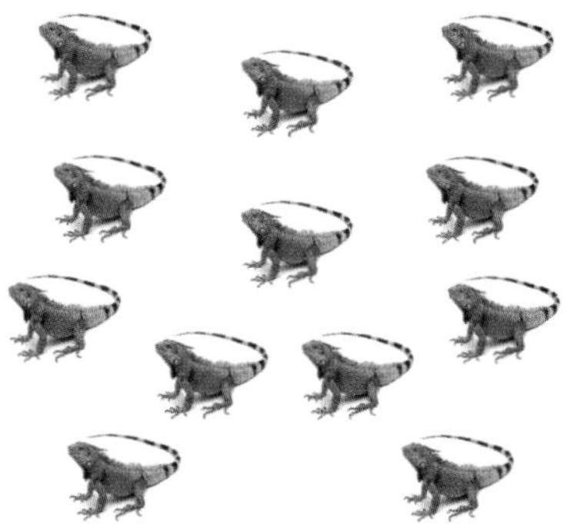

_______ ÷ 6 = _______

2. 

_______ ÷ 6 = _______

3. 

_______ ÷ 6 = _______

Write the answer. Label each part as **quotient, divisor,** or **dividend.**

4. ____________ $6\overline{)48}$ ____________ ____________

5. ____________ $6\overline{)18}$ ____________ ____________

6. Write the quotient above the ones place in the dividend.

$6\overline{)36}$	$9\overline{)9}$	$6\overline{)24}$	$6\overline{)0}$	$6\overline{)30}$
$6\overline{)54}$	$2\overline{)16}$	$4\overline{)32}$	$2\overline{)18}$	$6\overline{)42}$
$6\overline{)48}$	$3\overline{)15}$	$3\overline{)27}$	$3\overline{)21}$	$5\overline{)25}$
$6\overline{)12}$	$1\overline{)8}$	$5\overline{)40}$	$5\overline{)10}$	$6\overline{)30}$
$6\overline{)42}$	$3\overline{)24}$	$2\overline{)6}$	$6\overline{)18}$	
$4\overline{)28}$	$5\overline{)0}$	$6\overline{)54}$	$4\overline{)20}$	

Review

Add.

7. $\begin{array}{r} 478 \\ +344 \\ \hline \end{array}$
8. $\begin{array}{r} 255 \\ +296 \\ \hline \end{array}$
9. $\begin{array}{r} 583 \\ +337 \\ \hline \end{array}$
10. $\begin{array}{r} 681 \\ +162 \\ \hline \end{array}$
11. $\begin{array}{r} 577 \\ +367 \\ \hline \end{array}$

Subtract.

12. $\begin{array}{r} 743 \\ -255 \\ \hline \end{array}$
13. $\begin{array}{r} 500 \\ -275 \\ \hline \end{array}$
14. $\begin{array}{r} 384 \\ -199 \\ \hline \end{array}$
15. $\begin{array}{r} 841 \\ -418 \\ \hline \end{array}$
16. $\begin{array}{r} 262 \\ -177 \\ \hline \end{array}$

Name ______________________________

Divide by 7 5.10

This year the Olson family will vacation at the beach. They will leave in 35 days. How many weeks until their vacation?

35	÷	7	=	?
days		days in a week		weeks

Memorize these facts.

7 ÷ 7 = 1	42 ÷ 7 = 6
14 ÷ 7 = 2	49 ÷ 7 = 7
21 ÷ 7 = 3	56 ÷ 7 = 8
28 ÷ 7 = 4	63 ÷ 7 = 9
35 ÷ 7 = 5	

You can use a multiplication table to find the quotient.

Look down the left side to find the divisor, 7.
Look across to find the dividend, 35.
Look up to find the quotient, 5.
Since 7 × 5 = 35, then 35 ÷ 7 = 5.

×	1	2	3	4	5	6	7	8	9
1	1	2	3	4	5	6	7	8	9
2	2	4	6	8	10	12	14	16	18
3	3	6	9	12	15	18	21	24	27
4	4	8	12	16	20	24	28	32	36
5	5	10	15	20	25	30	35	40	45
6	6	12	18	24	30	36	42	48	54
7	7	14	21	28	35	42	49	56	63

There are 5 weeks until their vacation.

Use the multiplication table to find the quotient.

1. 42 ÷ 7 = ______
2. 21 ÷ 7 = ______
3. 49 ÷ 7 = ______
4. 63 ÷ 7 = ______

Write a division sentence.

5. 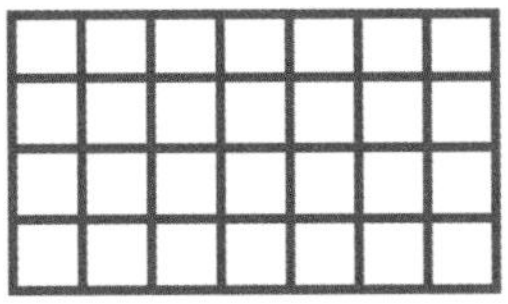

6. 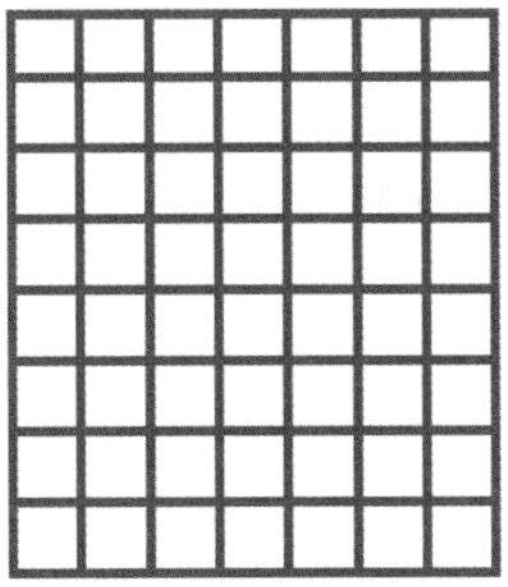

7. 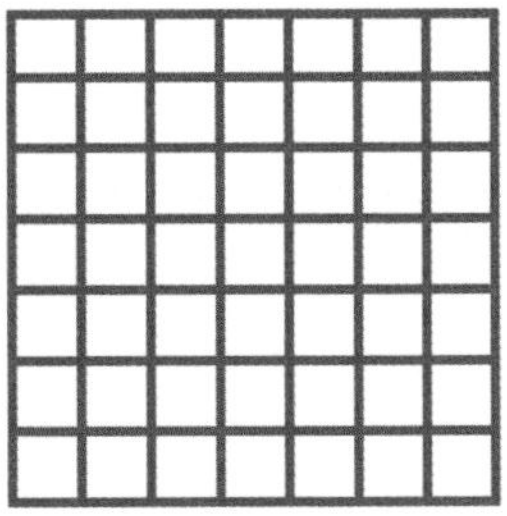

_____ ÷ 7 = _____   _____ ÷ 7 = _____   _____ ÷ 7 = _____

Fill in the missing part of each equation.

8. 7 × ______ = 14	9. 7 × ______ = 28	10. 7 × ______ = 63
14 ÷ 7 = ______	28 ÷ 7 = ______	63 ÷ 7 = ______

11. **Divide.**

$7\overline{)35}$	$6\overline{)54}$	$6\overline{)12}$	$5\overline{)35}$	$3\overline{)24}$
$4\overline{)16}$	$5\overline{)45}$	$7\overline{)21}$	$7\overline{)7}$	$4\overline{)32}$
$7\overline{)63}$	$6\overline{)48}$	$7\overline{)56}$	$7\overline{)0}$	$4\overline{)36}$
$2\overline{)16}$	$7\overline{)49}$	$5\overline{)30}$	$6\overline{)36}$	$5\overline{)40}$

Write × or ÷ in the circle.

12. 8 ◯ 7 = 56	15. 18 ◯ 3 = 6	18. 8 ◯ 4 = 2
13. 28 ◯ 7 = 4	16. 3 ◯ 4 = 12	19. 4 ◯ 6 = 24
14. 5 ◯ 5 = 25	17. 42 ◯ 7 = 6	20. 48 ◯ 6 = 8

Name ______________________________

Practice Dividing by 6 and 7 5.11

Circle sets of 6 or 7. Write division sentences for each.

1. 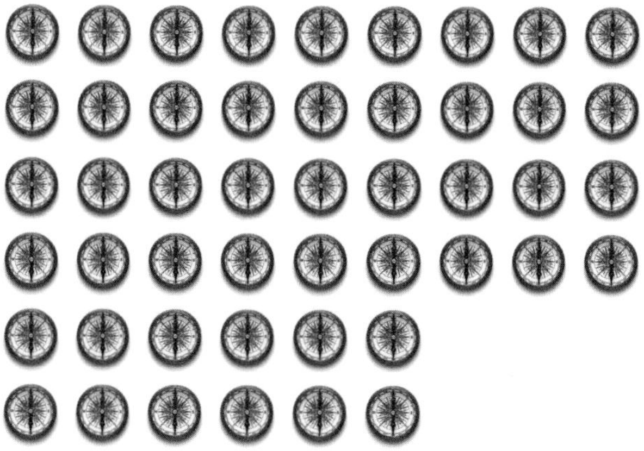

_____ ÷ 6 = _____

3. 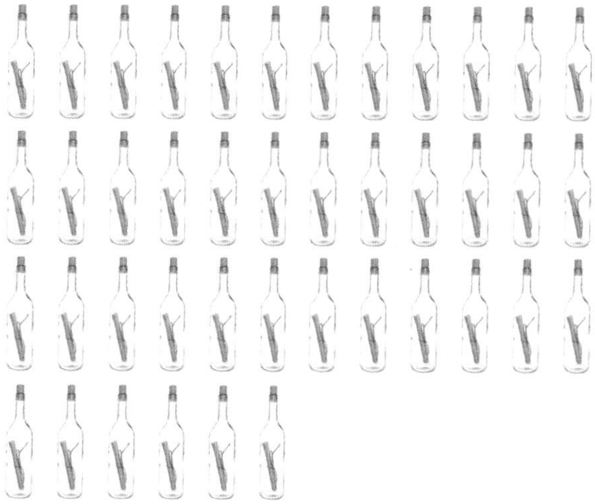

_____ ÷ 7 = _____

2. 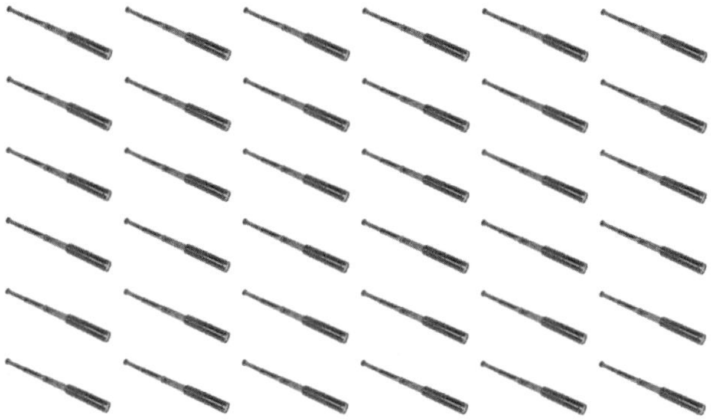

_____ ÷ 6 = _____

4. 

_____ ÷ 7 = _____

Write a 6s or 7s division fact on the blank as an example for each strategy.

5. Repeated subtraction

____

6. Fact families

____

7. Count back

______________ ______________ ______________ ______________

8. **Divide.**

0 ÷ 7 = ______ 36 ÷ 6 = ______ 18 ÷ 6 = ______ 35 ÷ 7 = ______

54 ÷ 6 = ______ 21 ÷ 7 = ______ 48 ÷ 6 = ______ 49 ÷ 7 = ______

$6\overline{)12}$ $6\overline{)24}$ $7\overline{)7}$ $7\overline{)28}$ $6\overline{)0}$

$6\overline{)30}$ $7\overline{)56}$ $6\overline{)54}$ $6\overline{)6}$ $7\overline{)63}$

Solve.

9. Maren collected 28 sand dollars. She sorted 7 in each pile. How many piles did she make?

____

Review

Write > or <.

10. 5,243 ◯ 4,911

11. 6,414 ◯ 6,441

12. 8,097 ◯ 9,078

13. 1,835 ◯ 1,925

14. 4,366 ◯ 4,633

15. 7,298 ◯ 7,289

Name ____________________

Divide by 8 5.12

There are 24 flamingos gathered in the bay. They stand in groups of 8. How many groups of 8 are there?

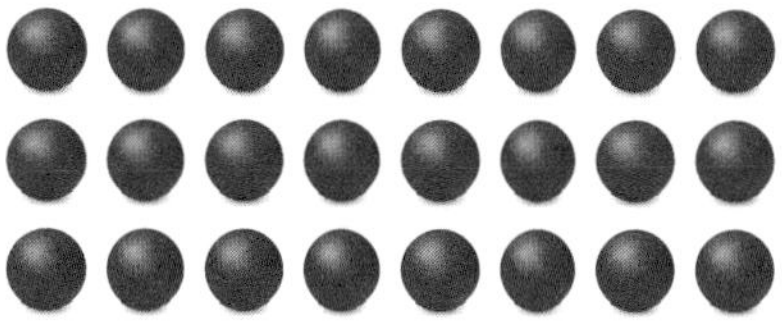

24	÷	8	=	?
flamingos		in a group		groups

Memorize these facts.

8 ÷ 8 = 1	32 ÷ 8 = 4	56 ÷ 8 = 7
16 ÷ 8 = 2	40 ÷ 8 = 5	64 ÷ 8 = 8
24 ÷ 8 = 3	48 ÷ 8 = 6	72 ÷ 8 = 9

There are 3 groups of flamingos.

Write a division equation for each picture.

1.

______ ÷ 8 = ______

2.

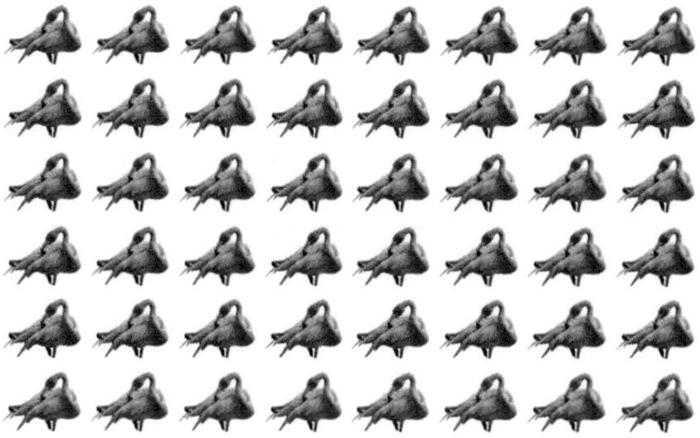

______ ÷ 8 = ______

3.

______ ÷ 8 = ______

Draw a picture to represent each division fact.

4. $16 \div 8 = 2$ 5. $8 \div 8 = 1$ 6. $24 \div 8 = 3$

7. Write the missing factor.

$8 \times$ ______ $= 40$ $8 \times$ ______ $= 64$ $8 \times$ ______ $= 0$ $8 \times$ ______ $= 56$

$8 \times$ ______ $= 32$ $8 \times$ ______ $= 48$ $8 \times$ ______ $= 72$ $8 \times$ ______ $= 8$

8. Divide.

$8\overline{)48}$ $4\overline{)28}$ $8\overline{)8}$ $4\overline{)36}$ $7\overline{)49}$

$8\overline{)16}$ $5\overline{)40}$ $7\overline{)56}$ $8\overline{)72}$ $5\overline{)0}$

Solve.

9. Forty-eight tourists watched the hula show. If they sat on 8 benches, how many tourists were on each bench?

____

Review

Follow the arrows to solve the problem.

10. 56 → ÷ 8 → + 7 → ÷ 2 = ☐

11. 72 → ÷ 8 → + 16 → ÷ 5 = ☐

12. 48 → ÷ 8 → + 15 → ÷ 3 = ☐

Name ______________________________

Divide by 9 5.13

The crocodiles in the lagoon laid 36 eggs. Each nest has 9 eggs hatching. How many nests are there?

Memorize these facts.

$9 \div 9 = 1$ $54 \div 9 = 6$
$18 \div 9 = 2$ $63 \div 9 = 7$
$27 \div 9 = 3$ $72 \div 9 = 8$
$36 \div 9 = 4$ $81 \div 9 = 9$
$45 \div 9 = 5$

36	÷	9	=	4
eggs		eggs in each nest		nests

Circle sets of 9. Complete each division equation.

1. 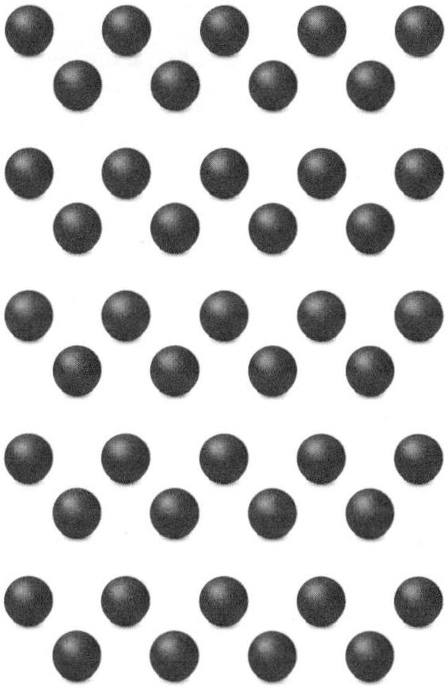

______ ÷ 9 = ______

2. 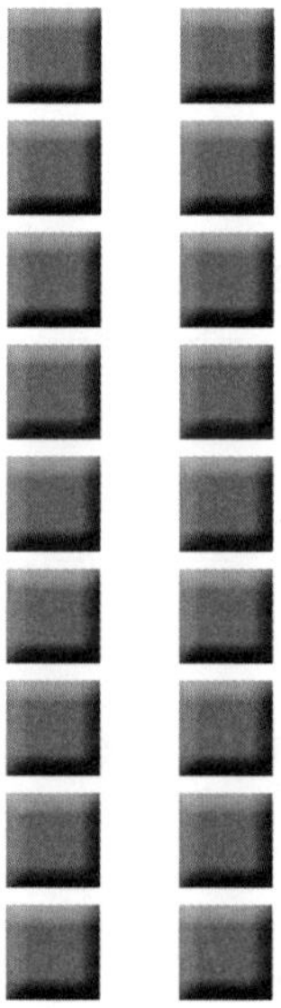

______ ÷ 9 = ______

3. 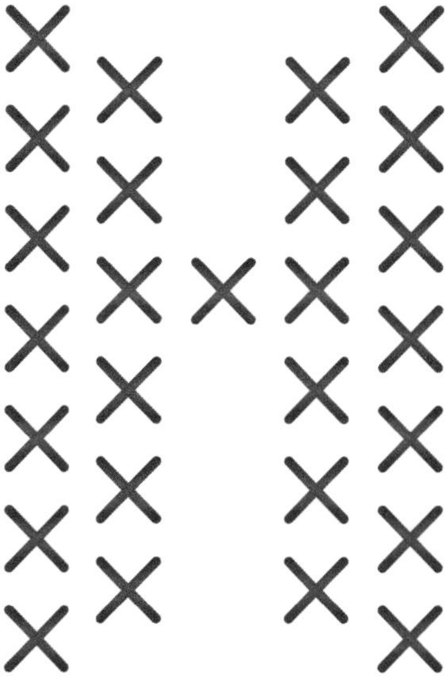

______ ÷ 9 = ______

Write the missing factor.

4. 54 = 9 × ______

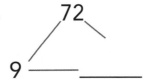

5. 72 = 9 × ______

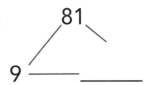

6. 81 = 9 × ______

Complete these multiplication and division sentences.

7. 9 × ______ = 0
0 ÷ 9 = ______

8. 9 × ______ = 45
45 ÷ 9 = ______

9. 9 × ______ = 18
18 ÷ 9 = ______

10. 9 × ______ = 27
27 ÷ 9 = ______

11. 9 × ______ = 36
36 ÷ 9 = ______

12. 9 × ______ = 9
9 ÷ 9 = ______

13. Divide.

9)81	6)48	7)42	5)45	8)64
8)72	9)63	4)28	3)27	9)36
2)14	5)40	8)56	9)54	7)0

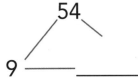

Solve.

14. Twenty-seven scientists built 9 robots to do underwater tasks. The scientists worked in equal groups. How many scientists worked on each robot?

______

Review

Add.

15.	16.	17.	18.	19.	20.
301	263	418	219	368	176
223	345	291	400	42	207
+ 114	+ 362	+ 306	+ 521	+ 485	+ 354

Name ______________________________

Practice Dividing by 8 and 9 5.14

Rachel used 27 tickets to ride the spinning tea cups at the island fair. Each ride is 9 tickets. How many tea cup rides did she have?

27	÷	9	=	?
tickets		tickets per ride		rides

Count back 9 skips.

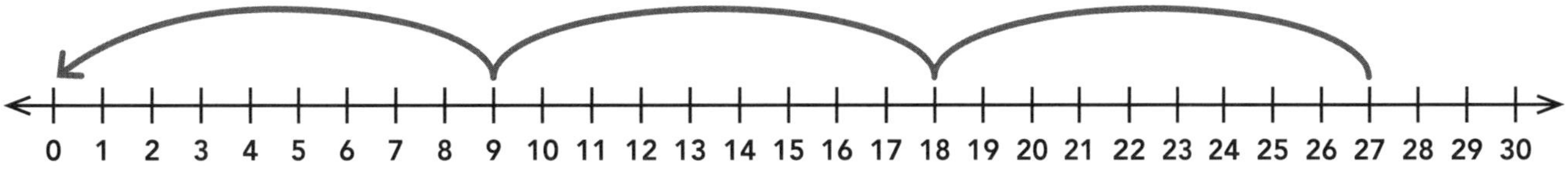

Fact families

$3 \times 9 = 27$
$9 \times 3 = 27$
$27 \div 3 = 9$
$27 \div 9 = 3$

Multiplication table

×	2	3	4	5	6
5	10	15	20	25	30
6	12	18	24	30	36
7	14	21	28	35	42
8	16	24	32	40	48
9	18	27	36	45	54

Rachel had 3 tea cup rides.

Write the number of rides you could take.

tea cups	5 tickets
Ferris wheel	6 tickets
tilt-a-whirl	8 tickets
roller coaster	9 tickets

	number of tickets used	rides	number of rides
1.	48	Ferris wheel	
2.	32	tilt-a-whirl	
3.	54	roller coaster	
4.	45	tea cups	

5. **Divide.**

6)18	5)25	8)32	6)36	9)27	7)21
7)49	9)72	5)35	8)48	6)0	9)63
5)40	6)42	5)45	4)36	8)56	3)24
6)48	2)2	9)54	7)35	4)32	6)6
5)0	9)81	8)72	6)54	9)0	8)64

Write × or ÷ in the circles.

6. 8 ◯ 7 = 56
7. 28 ◯ 7 = 4
8. 5 ◯ 5 = 25
9. 18 ◯ 3 = 6
10. 3 ◯ 4 = 12
11. 42 ◯ 7 = 6
12. 8 ◯ 4 = 2
13. 4 ◯ 6 = 24
14. 48 ◯ 6 = 8

Review

Write each number.

15. forty-six thousand, three hundred twenty-eight ______________________
16. seven hundred eight thousand, two hundred fourteen ______________________
17. three hundred eleven thousand, nine hundred sixty-three ______________________
18. 10,000 + 5,000 + 800 + 20 + 4 ______________________
19. 600,000 + 80,000 + 5,000 + 700 + 60 + 2 ______________________
20. 500,000 + 2,000 + 70 + 1 ______________________

Name ____________________

On Big Major Cay in the Bahamas, the "swimming pigs" lie on the beach in the sun. They swim out to visiting boats for treats.

Average Temperatures on Big Major Cay in the Bahamas

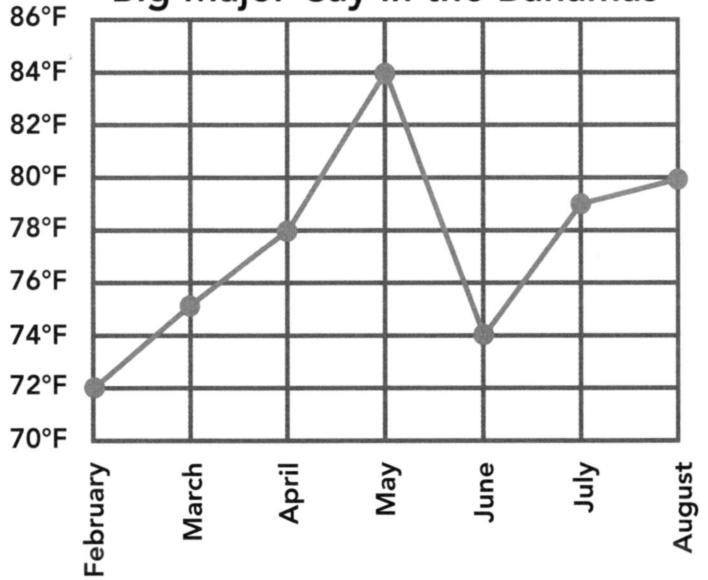

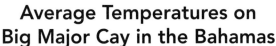

Read the graph. Answer the questions.

1. What is the subject of this graph? ____________________

2. What time span is covered? ____________________

3. Which month had the lowest temperature? ____________________

4. What is the highest temperature? ____________________

   When did it occur? ____________________

Number of Ferris-Wheel Riders During the Island Fair

Tuesday—256
Wednesday—269
Thursday—260
Friday—275
Saturday—305

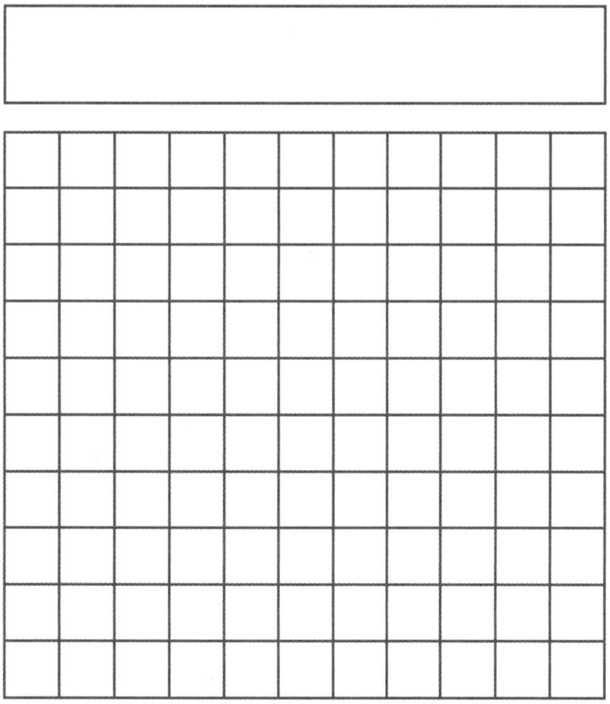

Use the information to design a line graph. Follow the directions.

5. Write a descriptive title.
6. Write the letters for the day of the week along the bottom. Use abbreviations. (Skip lines.)
7. Write a scale by 5s, from 255 to 305, along the left-hand side.
8. Draw the dot for each day.
9. Draw straight lines to connect the dots.

Use the line graph you designed to answer these questions.

10. What is the subject? ______________________
11. What changed each day? ______________________
12. What time span is covered? ______________________
13. Which day had the fewest riders? ______________________
14. Which day had the most riders? ______________________
15. Was there an increase or decrease from Friday to Saturday?

____

Name ______________________________

Write the letter of the definition that matches each term.

1. dividend ______

2. divisor ______

3. quotient ______

a. a number that is divided by another number

b. the result of dividing one number by another

c. the number by which the dividend is divided

Write a division sentence for each picture.

4. 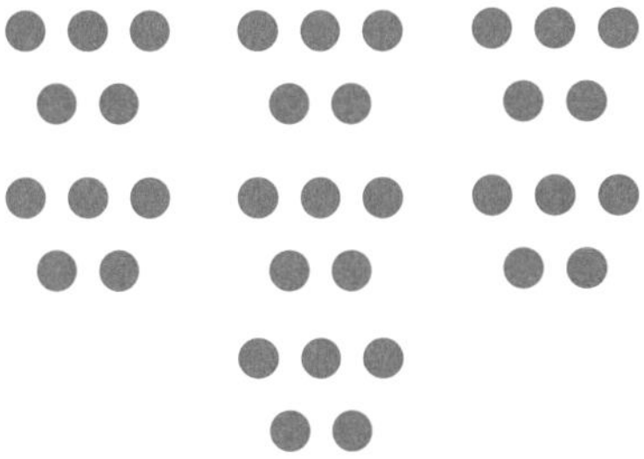

5. 

6. 

____ ÷ ____ = ____   ____ ÷ ____ = ____   ____ ÷ ____ = ____

Write a division equation for each number line.

7. 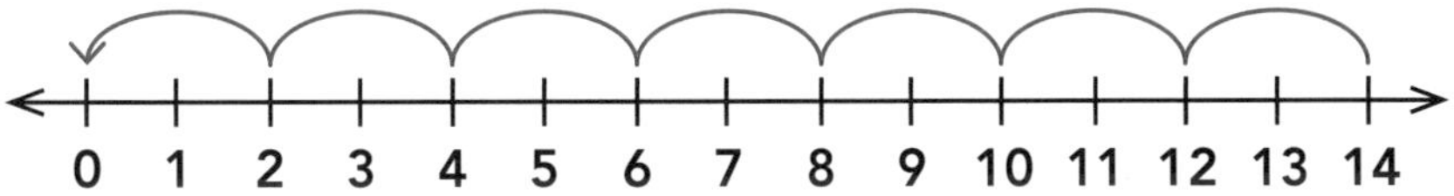

____ ÷ ____ = ____

8. 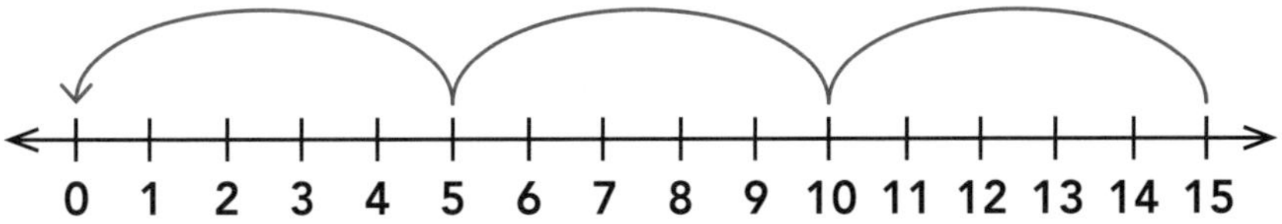

____ ÷ ____ = ____

9. 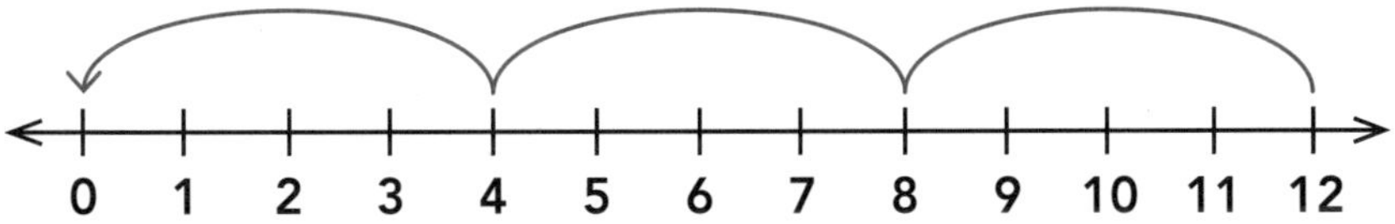

____ ÷ ____ = ____

Complete the sentence.

10. Any number divided by itself equals ______________________.

11. Any number divided by 1 equals ______________________.

12. Zero divided by any number equals ______________________.

Draw a picture for each division fact. Complete the division equation.

13. $12 \div 3 =$ ______ 14. $16 \div 2 =$ ______ 15. $8 \div 4 =$ ______

16. **Divide.**

$6\overline{)18}$	$7\overline{)56}$	$8\overline{)72}$	$6\overline{)0}$	$5\overline{)30}$	$7\overline{)21}$
$9\overline{)54}$	$5\overline{)25}$	$2\overline{)18}$	$4\overline{)4}$	$7\overline{)42}$	$3\overline{)24}$
$8\overline{)64}$	$4\overline{)36}$	$7\overline{)0}$	$8\overline{)32}$	$3\overline{)6}$	$7\overline{)28}$
$6\overline{)48}$	$9\overline{)45}$	$6\overline{)24}$	$3\overline{)9}$	$5\overline{)20}$	$9\overline{)27}$
$7\overline{)49}$	$9\overline{)63}$	$4\overline{)28}$	$2\overline{)4}$	$5\overline{)35}$	$6\overline{)12}$

Write the multiplication and division fact family for each set of numbers.

17. 

______ ______ ______ ______

18. 

______ ______ ______ ______

19. 

______ ______ ______ ______

20. 

______ ______ ______ ______

Chapter 6
Multiplication

And the word of God increased; and the number of the disciples multiplied in Jerusalem greatly.
Acts 6:7a (KJV)

Key Ideas:

Multiplication: multiplying two- and three-digit numbers by one-digit numbers

Multiplication: multiplying with and without regrouping

Multiplication: rounding a factor in order to estimate a product

Probability and Statistics: making and interpreting graphs

Name ___________________________

Write a multiplication equation to solve each word problem.

1. Multiplication Property of One — The pattern on each giraffe's coat is unique. None are alike. There are 9 giraffes in the group. How many patterns are there in the group?

   ____

2. Order Property of Multiplication — Giraffe babies are born with 2 horns. How many horns would 8 baby giraffes have in all?

   ______________ or ______________

3. Squares — A zoologist observes 7 giraffes. He makes a note about each giraffe every day for a week. At the end of the week, how many notes will he have made?

   ____

4. Nines — A giraffe's neck is about 6 feet long. What is the total length of 9 giraffes' necks?

   ____

Use the number line to solve.

5. Skip count — A sick baby giraffe is fed 3 bottles of milk 6 times a day. How many bottles are given to the giraffe?

   ____

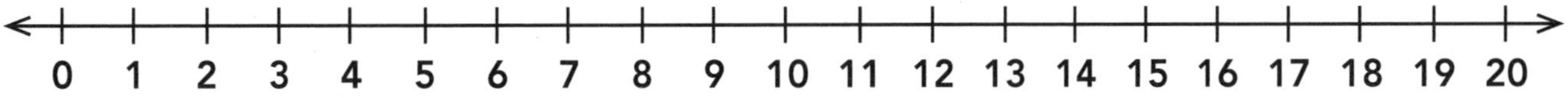

Draw an array. Complete each multiplication fact.

6. $4 \times 6 =$ ______ 7. $3 \times 5 =$ ______ 8. $9 \times 2 =$ ______

9. **Multiply.**

5×4	2×8	3×6	7×6	8×3	9×6
9×8	6×1	4×7	9×9	8×5	8×4
4×4	3×9	5×7	8×0	7×2	6×6

Solve.

10. There are 8 cell phone owners in each of 6 remote villages. They all came to the solar charging station to charge their phones. How many phones need to be charged?

______

Review

Multiply, and then add.

11. $(5 \times 6) + 3 =$ ______

12. $(6 \times 8) + 4 =$ ______

13. $(3 \times 4) + 6 =$ ______

14. $(8 \times 8) + 5 =$ ______

15. $(4 \times 7) + 2 =$ ______

16. $(3 \times 9) + 5 =$ ______

Name ______________________________________

Knowing the basic facts will help you multiply by multiples of 10. How many meerkats are in 2 rows if 40 meerkats are in each row?

2×40

2×4 tens

two 40s

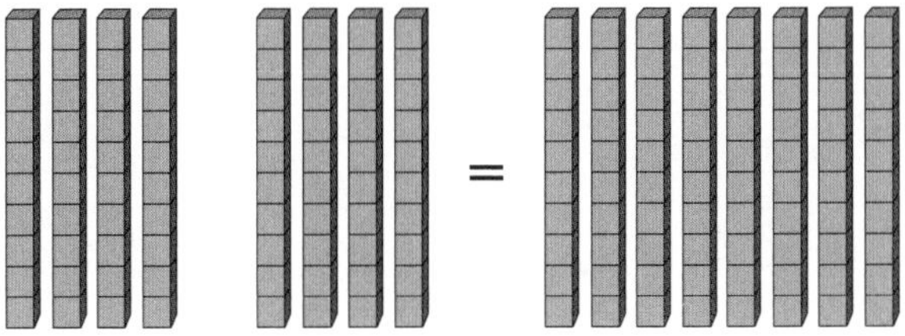

Think: $2 \times 4 = 8$ $2 \times 4\underline{0} = 8\underline{0}$

There are 80 meerkats.

Memorize these facts.

$1 \times 10 = 10$	$4 \times 10 = 40$	$7 \times 10 = 70$
$2 \times 10 = 20$	$5 \times 10 = 50$	$8 \times 10 = 80$
$3 \times 10 = 30$	$6 \times 10 = 60$	$9 \times 10 = 90$

Complete.

1. $3 \times 1 =$ ______

   3×1 ten = ______

   $3 \times 10 =$ ______

2. $2 \times 2 =$ ______

   2×2 tens = ______

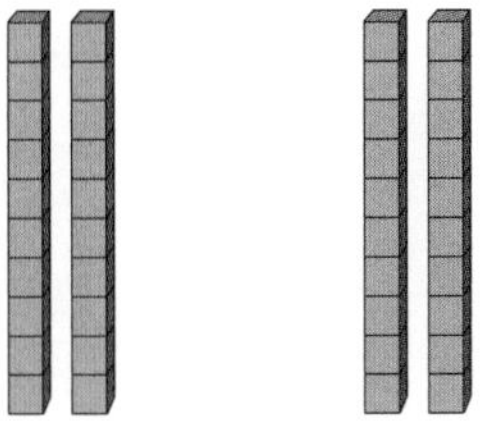

   $2 \times 20 =$ ______

3. $2 \times 3 =$ ______

   2×3 tens = ______

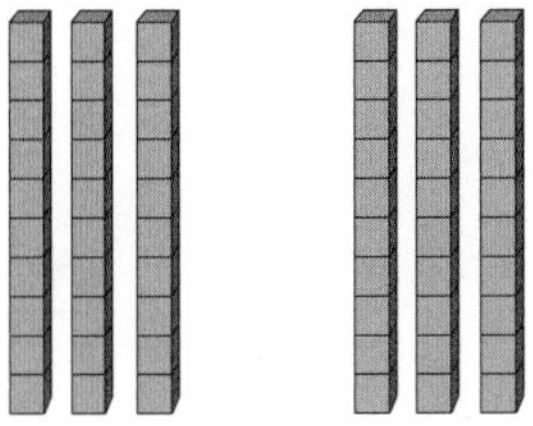

   $2 \times 30 =$ ______

Complete.

4. 3 × 4 ones = ______

3 × 4 tens = ______ tens

______ tens = ______

5. 6 × 8 ones = ______

6 × 8 tens = ______ tens

______ tens = ______

Multiply.

6. 4 × 4 = ______

4 × 40 = ______

7. 6 × 1 = ______

6 × 10 = ______

8. 7 × 3 = ______

7 × 30 = ______

9. 3 × 9 = ______

3 × 90 = ______

10. 8 × 4 = ______

8 × 40 = ______

11. 9 × 4 = ______

9 × 40 = ______

12. 5 × 2 = ______

5 × 20 = ______

13. 6 × 4 = ______

6 × 40 = ______

14. 4 × 7 = ______

4 × 70 = ______

Circle the basic multiplication fact. Multiply by multiples of 10.

15. 5 × 50 = ______

16. 5 × 10 = ______

17. 2 × 60 = ______

18. 4 × 70 = ______

19. 6 × 90 = ______

20. 3 × 60 = ______

21. 7 × 50 = ______

22. 3 × 80 = ______

23. 6 × 70 = ______

24. 8 × 20 = ______

25. 9 × 80 = ______

26. 5 × 90 = ______

Review

27. **Add or multiply.**

3 × 4	3 × 3	4 + 8	2 × 8	4 + 7	3 × 8	8 × 5	7 + 1
7 + 3	5 + 7	3 × 9	6 × 5	5 + 4	4 + 9	3 × 5	8 × 7

Name ____________________

How many zebras are in 3 herds of 200 zebras each?

3×200

3×2 hundreds

three 200s

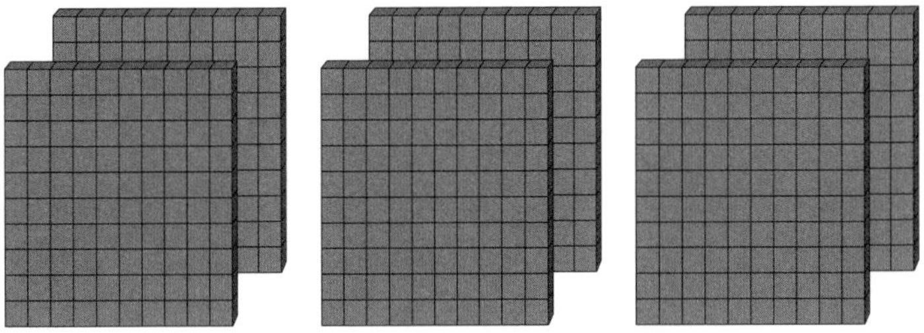

Think: $3 \times 2 = 6$ $\quad 3 \times 2\underline{00} = 6\underline{00}$

There are 600 zebras.

The basic facts will help you multiply by multiples of 100.

$2 \times 4 = 8$ $\quad 2 \times 40 = 80$ $\quad 2 \times 400 = 800$

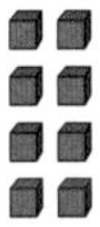

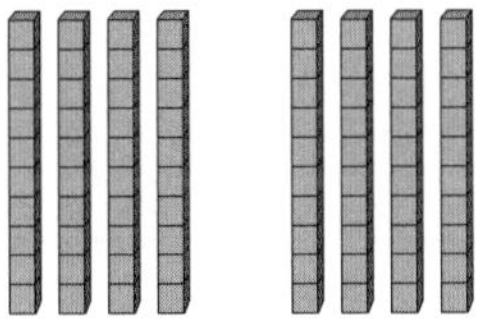

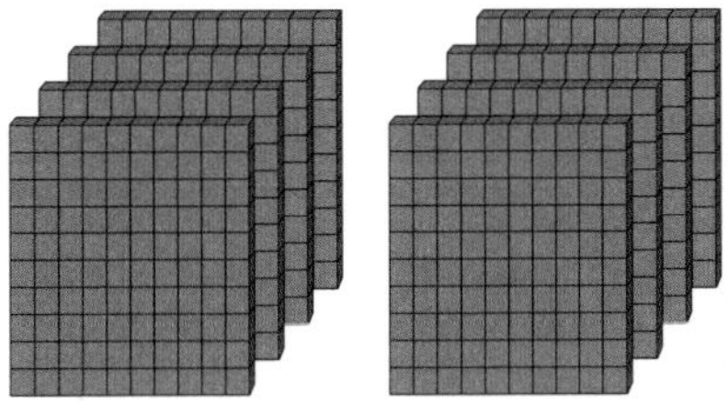

What do you notice about the number of zeros in the products?

$5 \times 3\underline{0} = 15\underline{0}$ $\quad 5 \times 3\underline{00} = 1{,}5\underline{00}$ $\quad 5 \times 6\underline{00} = 3{,}0\underline{00}$

Complete.

1. 2×3 ones = ____________

   2×3 tens = ____________

   2×3 hundreds = ____________

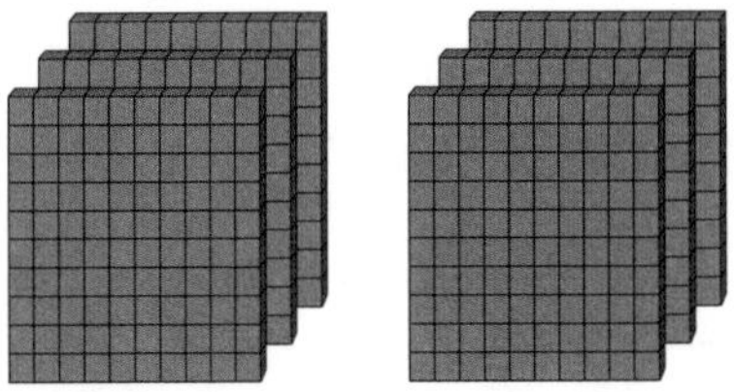

2. 3×4 ones = ____________

   3×4 tens = ____________

   3×4 hundreds = ____________

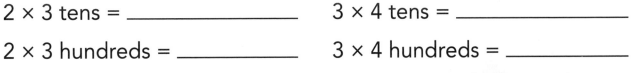

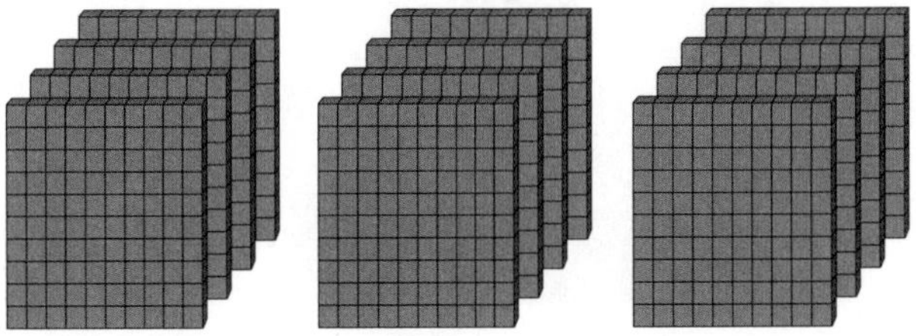

Complete.

3. 3×7 ones = ________

3×7 tens = ________

3×7 hundreds = ________

4. 4×9 ones = ________

4×9 tens = ________

4×9 hundreds = ________

Multiply.

5. $3 \times 6 =$ ____

$3 \times 60 =$ ____

$3 \times 600 =$ ____

6. $4 \times 8 =$ ____

$4 \times 80 =$ ____

$4 \times 800 =$ ____

7. $5 \times 7 =$ ____

$5 \times 70 =$ ____

$5 \times 700 =$ ____

8. **Multiply.**

$5 \times 100 =$ ____ $3 \times 100 =$ ____ $7 \times 100 =$ ____ $4 \times 100 =$ ____

$$\begin{array}{r} 100 \\ \times \quad 2 \\ \hline \end{array} \qquad \begin{array}{r} 100 \\ \times \quad 6 \\ \hline \end{array} \qquad \begin{array}{r} 100 \\ \times \quad 8 \\ \hline \end{array} \qquad \begin{array}{r} 100 \\ \times \quad 9 \\ \hline \end{array} \qquad \begin{array}{r} 100 \\ \times \quad 3 \\ \hline \end{array} \qquad \begin{array}{r} 100 \\ \times \quad 7 \\ \hline \end{array}$$

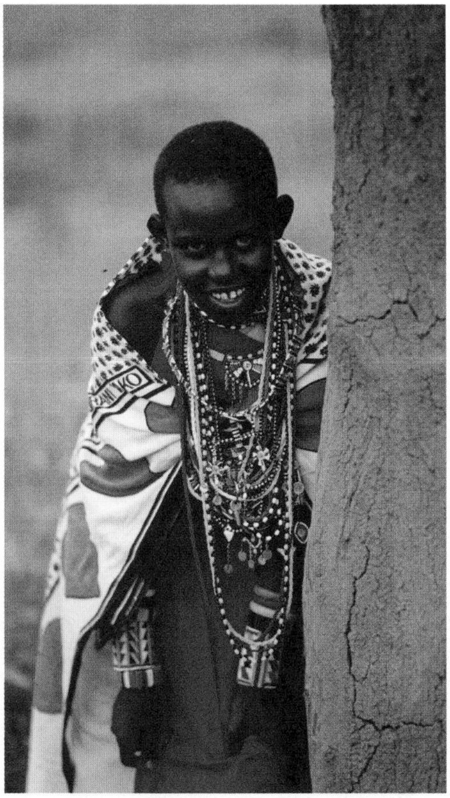

Solve.

9. The African Children's Choir sang at church. After the concert, the church served dessert. Zane's mother bought paper plates that were sold in packages of 500. She bought 4 packages. How many plates did she buy?

____

10. Many villages in Africa have no electric lights. But solar panels are becoming popular. A solar lighting company in Kenya sells 300 solar panels a day. How many panels would they sell Monday through Friday?

____

Name ______________________________

One antelope weighs 41 kilograms.

Two antelope weigh a total of _____ kilograms.

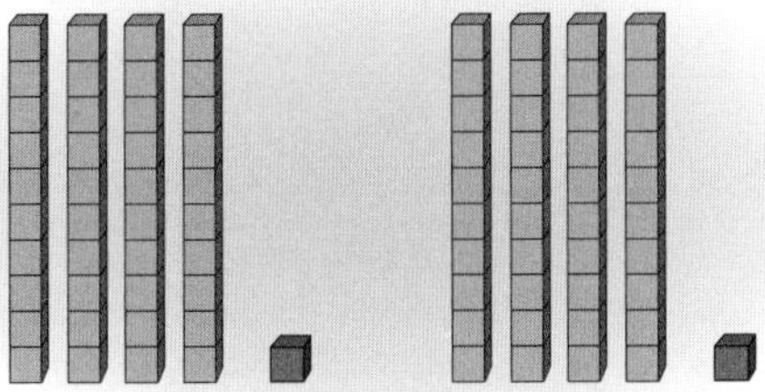

$41 \times 2 = 82$

Step 1

$$\begin{array}{r} 41 \\ \times\ 2 \\ \hline 2 \end{array}$$

Multiply the ones.

Step 2

$$\begin{array}{r} 41 \\ \times\ 2 \\ \hline 82 \end{array}$$

Multiply the tens.

Two antelope together weigh 82 kilograms.

Write a multiplication sentence to match each picture.

1.

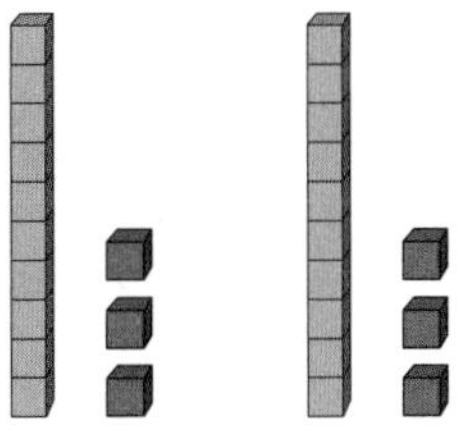

_____ × 2 = _____

2.

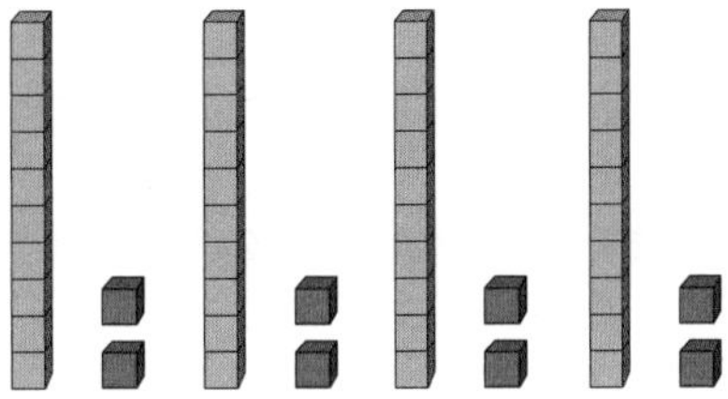

_____ × 4 = _____

3.

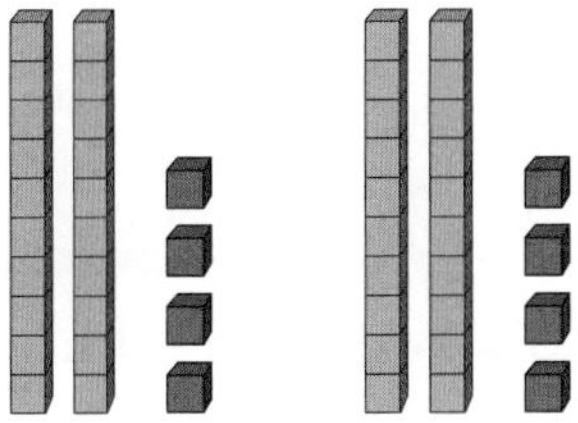

_____ × _____ = _____

4. **Multiply.**

14 × 2	23 × 3	11 × 5	31 × 2	32 × 3

13 × 3	41 × 2	12 × 4	11 × 8	12 × 3
44 × 2	24 × 2	21 × 4	23 × 2	11 × 7
11 × 2	20 × 3	32 × 2	42 × 2	43 × 2
22 × 3	31 × 3	40 × 2	33 × 3	30 × 2

Solve.

5. Sophie had a row of 12 antelope stickers on a page in her sticker album. How many stickers would she have in 3 rows of stickers?

____

6. Max took pictures of antelope for two days. Each day he took 24 pictures. How many pictures did Max take?

____

Review

Multiply and then add.

7. (7 × 5) + 3 = ______

8. (8 × 4) + 8 = ______

9. (6 × 8) + 5 = ______

10. (7 × 7) + 6 = ______

Name ______________________________

Regrouping Ones 6.5

Cheetahs hunt gazelles, impalas, and wildebeest calves. They stalk their prey to within 33 feet, and then begin their chase. One cheetah chased its prey for 18 seconds. Another cheetah chased its prey 3 times longer than the first. How long was the second cheetah's chase?

$$\begin{array}{r} 18 \\ \times\ \ 3 \\ \hline 54 \end{array}$$ seconds

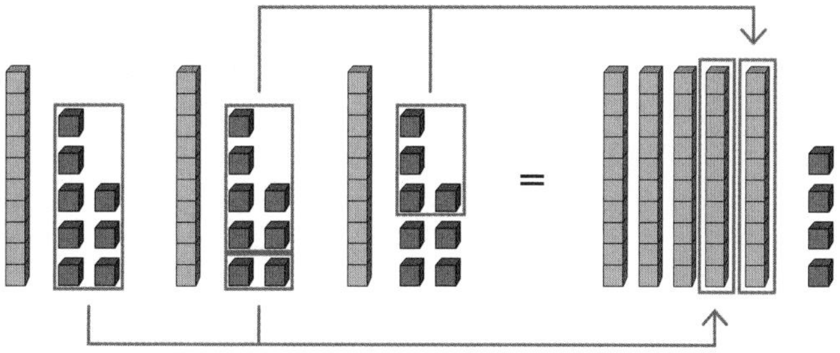

Three groups of 18 can be regrouped as 54.

Multiply the ones.

$$\begin{array}{r} {}^{2} \\ 18 \\ \times\ \ 3 \\ \hline 4 \end{array}$$

8 × 3 = 24

Regroup ones as tens.

Multiply the tens.

$$\begin{array}{r} {}^{2} \\ 18 \\ \times\ \ 3 \\ \hline 4 \end{array}$$

1 ten × 3 = 3 tens

Add the regrouped tens to the product of the tens.

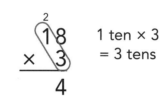

$$\begin{array}{r} {}^{2} \\ 18 \\ \times\ \ 3 \\ \hline 54 \end{array}$$

3 tens + 2 tens = 5 tens

Cross out ones and draw tens to regroup. Write the product.

1.

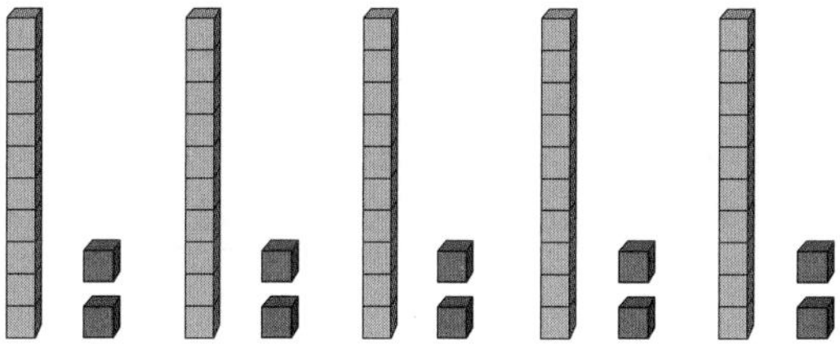

5 × 12 = ______

2.

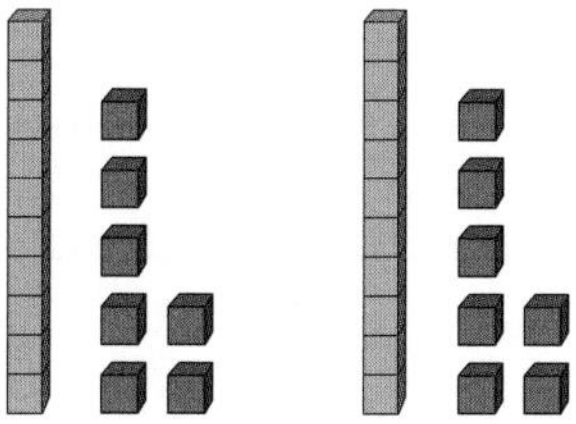

2 × 17 = ______

3. Multiply.

☐			☐			☐			☐			☐		
	1	6		2	3		1	9		2	6		1	7
×		2	×		4	×		3	×		3	×		5

$$\begin{array}{r} 12 \\ \times\ 7 \end{array} \quad \begin{array}{r} 24 \\ \times\ 3 \end{array} \quad \begin{array}{r} 21 \\ \times\ 3 \end{array} \quad \begin{array}{r} 23 \\ \times\ 2 \end{array} \quad \begin{array}{r} 16 \\ \times\ 5 \end{array} \quad \begin{array}{r} 17 \\ \times\ 4 \end{array} \quad \begin{array}{r} 18 \\ \times\ 2 \end{array}$$

$$\begin{array}{r} 15 \\ \times\ 6 \end{array} \quad \begin{array}{r} 13 \\ \times\ 7 \end{array} \quad \begin{array}{r} 12 \\ \times\ 8 \end{array} \quad \begin{array}{r} 25 \\ \times\ 2 \end{array} \quad \begin{array}{r} 30 \\ \times\ 3 \end{array} \quad \begin{array}{r} 14 \\ \times\ 7 \end{array} \quad \begin{array}{r} 23 \\ \times\ 3 \end{array}$$

$$\begin{array}{r} 20 \\ \times\ 2 \end{array} \quad \begin{array}{r} 16 \\ \times\ 6 \end{array} \quad \begin{array}{r} 19 \\ \times\ 4 \end{array} \quad \begin{array}{r} 12 \\ \times\ 3 \end{array} \quad \begin{array}{r} 14 \\ \times\ 5 \end{array} \quad \begin{array}{r} 22 \\ \times\ 2 \end{array} \quad \begin{array}{r} 18 \\ \times\ 6 \end{array}$$

Review

Write the next two numbers in each pattern.

4. 82 84 86 _____ _____

7. 42 48 54 _____ _____

5. 35 42 49 _____ _____

8. 126 136 146 _____ _____

6. 105 110 115 _____ _____

9. 515 518 521 _____ _____

Round to the nearest ten.

10. 63 _____ **11.** 95 _____ **12.** 21 _____ **13.** 17 _____ **14.** 54 _____

Round to the nearest hundred.

15. 816 _____ **17.** 638 _____ **19.** 454 _____

16. 703 _____ **18.** 921 _____

Name ____________________

Regrouping Tens 6.6

Impalas can make leaps that are 10 feet high and up to 30 feet long. Two impalas' leaps were measured. Which impala leaped the greater number of feet?

4 leaps × 26 feet **or** 3 leaps × 27 feet

4×26

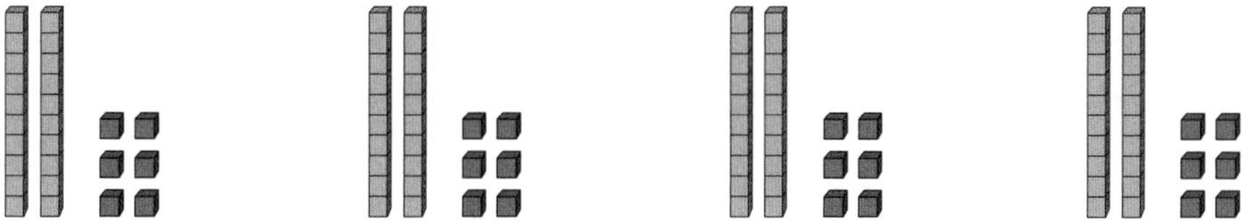

Separate the tens and ones. Multiply.

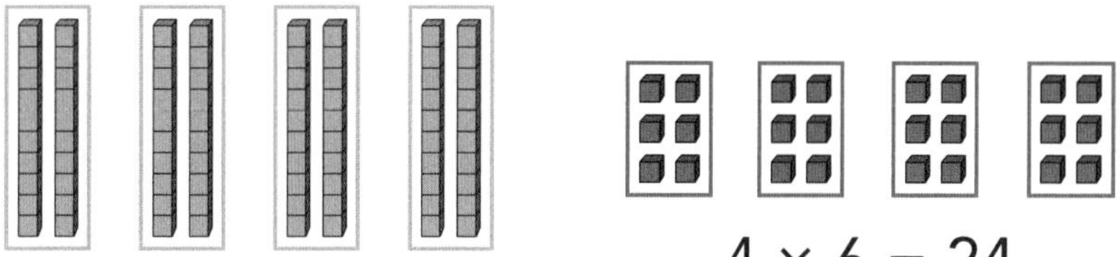

$4 \times 20 = 80$

$4 \times 6 = 24$

Regroup the ones and add.

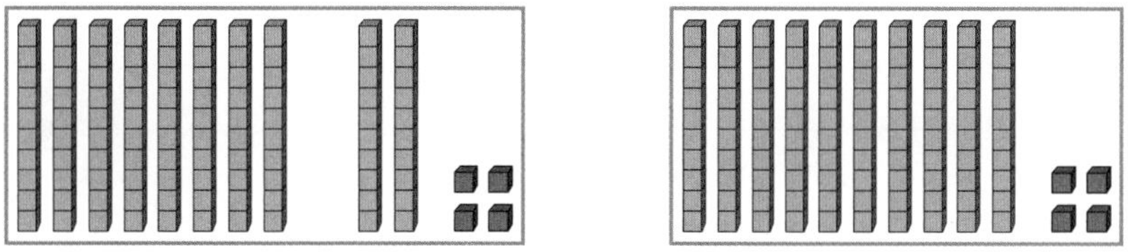

80 + 24 = 10 tens and 4 ones

Regroup the tens.

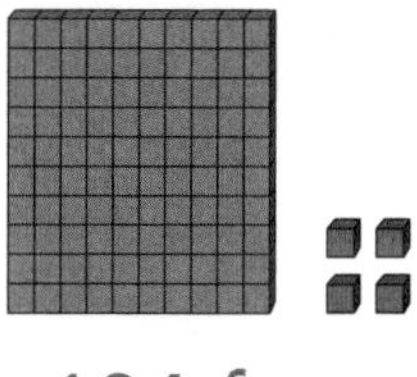

104 feet

$$\begin{array}{r} {\scriptstyle 2} \\ 26 \\ \times\ \ 4 \\ \hline 104 \end{array}$$

← Putting 2 here is a shortcut. It represents the 2 regrouped tens from the 24, the product of 6 × 4.

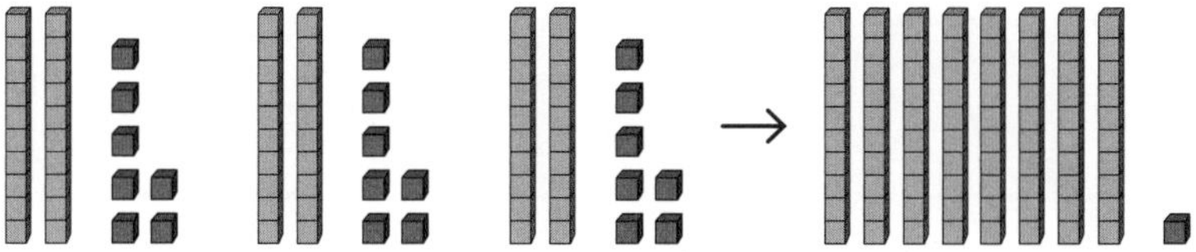

3×27 → 81 feet

$$\begin{array}{r} {\scriptstyle 2} \\ 27 \\ \times\ \ 3 \\ \hline 81 \end{array}$$

The impala that jumped four 26-foot jumps leaped the greater number of feet.

Multiply.

1. + ☐
$$\begin{array}{r} 63 \\ \times \ \ 5 \\ \hline \end{array}$$

2. + ☐
$$\begin{array}{r} 23 \\ \times \ \ 9 \\ \hline \end{array}$$

3. + ☐
$$\begin{array}{r} 87 \\ \times \ \ 3 \\ \hline \end{array}$$

4. + ☐
$$\begin{array}{r} 42 \\ \times \ \ 8 \\ \hline \end{array}$$

Use graph paper to write each multiplication problem vertically. Solve, and write the products on the lines. Write > or <.

5. 62 × 3 ◯ 25 × 8

_____ _____

6. 84 × 2 ◯ 39 × 4

_____ _____

7. 81 × 7 ◯ 92 × 8

_____ _____

Solve.

8. Computer class lasts 45 minutes. If the third graders have computer class 3 times a week, how many minutes do they spend using the computers?

____

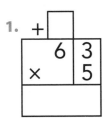

Multiply. Circle the letters in the boxes that match the products. Write the circled letters in order on the lines to complete the sentence.

9. $\begin{array}{r} 28 \\ \times \ 3 \\ \hline \end{array}$

10. $\begin{array}{r} 74 \\ \times \ 5 \\ \hline \end{array}$

11. $\begin{array}{r} 19 \\ \times \ 5 \\ \hline \end{array}$

12. $\begin{array}{r} 52 \\ \times \ 7 \\ \hline \end{array}$

13. $\begin{array}{r} 33 \\ \times \ 4 \\ \hline \end{array}$

14. $\begin{array}{r} 85 \\ \times \ 6 \\ \hline \end{array}$

15. $\begin{array}{r} 69 \\ \times \ 2 \\ \hline \end{array}$

84	281	370	95	228	364	413	132	510	318	138
S	T	A	V	M	A	L	N	N	B	A

16. Impalas live in the African

_____ _____ _____ _____ _____ _____ _____.

Name ____

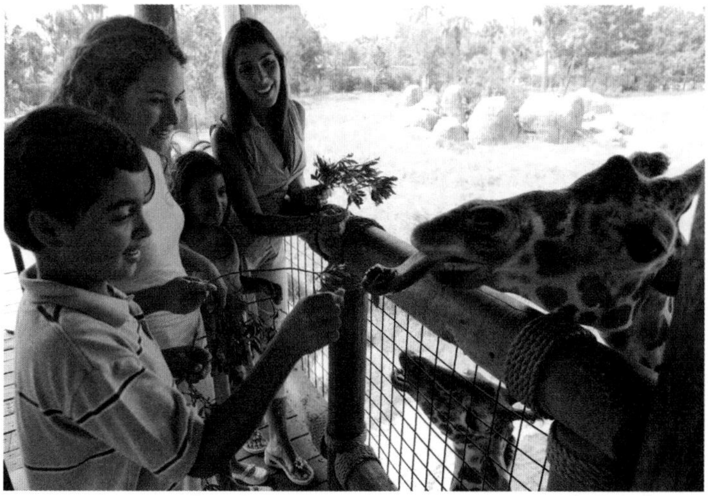

Zoofari Park Souvenirs

Puzzle	$10.95
Pop-up book	$12.85
Animal mask	$ 2.12
Stuffed animal	$ 6.95
Safari action figure set	$ 7.25

Cody and his family are at Zoofari Park. Cody wants to buy 2 masks and a puzzle. About how much money will he need to pay for the 3 items?

Use estimation when you need a close, but not exact, answer.

Problem-Solving Path

1. **Understand the question.**
   - Underline the question.
   - Does it call for an exact answer or an estimate?

   The question calls for an ______________.

2. **Analyze the data.**
   - Circle the key information in the word problem above.

   Cody wants 2 masks and 1 puzzle. A mask costs $2.12 and a puzzle is $10.95.

3. **Plan the strategy.**
   - Write an equation.

   This problem will take two operations. First, ______________, then ______________.

4. **Solve the problem.**
   - Show your work.
   - Label the answer.

   Round the prices to the nearest dollar. Round $2.12 to $2.00. Round $10.95 to $11.00. Cody wants to buy 2 masks, so multiply $2.00 by 2.

   $2.00 × $2 = ________

   $4.00 + $11.00 = ________

5. **Evaluate the result.**
   - Does the answer make sense?

   Does it make sense that Cody will pay about $15.00 for the 3 items? ______________

Estimate to solve each word problem. Use the price list on the previous page. Show your work on a separate piece of paper.

6. Arturo wants to buy 2 stuffed animals. About how much will they cost?

____

7. Isabella has $20.00. Will she have enough to buy 2 puzzles?

____

8. Gil wonders what the price will be for 2 pop-up books and a puzzle. Estimate the cost.

____

9. Braeden wants to buy a Safari action figure set for himself and 2 animal masks for his sisters. About how much will Braeden need to pay for the 3 items?

____

10. Jenna has $26.00 to buy pop-up books. How many pop-up books can she buy with her money?

____

11. Cassidy wants to purchase one of each souvenir. About how much money will she need?

____

Name ______________________________

3-Digits: Regrouping Ones 6.8

Cape buffalo form herds of hundreds. This herd includes 239 buffalo. If another herd of the same number exists, how many Cape buffalo would there be in the 2 herds combined?

$239 \times 2 =$ ______ Cape buffalo

The base 10 blocks show the factors and the product.

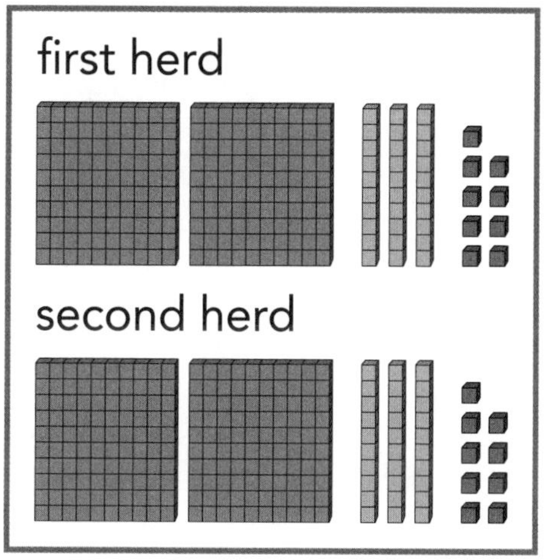

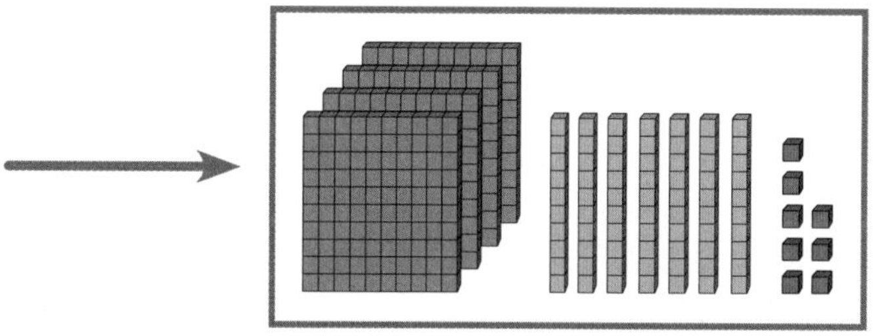

There are 478 Cape buffalo.

To multiply 239 by 2, follow the steps.

1. Multiply the ones.

$$\begin{array}{r} 9 \\ \times\ 2 \\ \hline 18 \end{array}$$

2. Multiply the tens.

$$\begin{array}{r} 30 \\ \times\ \ 2 \\ \hline 60 \end{array}$$

3. Multiply the hundreds.

$$\begin{array}{r} 200 \\ \times\ \ \ 2 \\ \hline 400 \end{array}$$

4. Add the products.

$$\begin{array}{r} 400 \\ 60 \\ +\ \ 18 \\ \hline 478 \end{array}$$

Multiply the ones in the red box first. Then multiply the tens in the yellow box. Last, multiply the hundreds in the blue box. Add the products.

1. $\begin{array}{r} 312 \\ \times\ \ \ 3 \\ \hline \end{array}$ ← $\begin{array}{r} 300 \\ \times\ \ \ 3 \\ \hline \end{array}$ ← $\begin{array}{r} 10 \\ \times\ \ 3 \\ \hline \end{array}$ ← $\begin{array}{r} 2 \\ \times 3 \\ \hline \end{array}$

______ + ______ + ______ = [ ]

Multiply. Start with the ones.

2. 143 × 2 → 100 × 2 ____ + 40 × 2 ____ + 3 × 2 ____ = [ ]

3. 428 × 2 → 400 × 2 ____ + 20 × 2 ____ + 8 × 2 ____ = [ ]

4. 328 × 2 → 300 × 2 ____ + 20 × 2 ____ + 8 × 2 ____ = [ ]

5. 206 × 4 → 200 × 4 ____ + 6 × 4 ____ = [ ]

6. 103 × 7 → 100 × 7 ____ + 3 × 7 ____ = [ ]

Review

Add.

7. 384 + 649

8. 8,264 + 1,126

9. 2,073 + 88

10. 962 + 562

11. 6,045 + 2,964

12. 639 + 59

13. 2,058 + 414

14. 6,884 + 2,631

15. 874 + 626

16. 449 + 204

Name ______________________________

During the dry season, herds of wildebeests travel hundreds of miles to find fresh grass. If a herd travels 387 miles one way, how many miles would the herd travel in a round-trip?

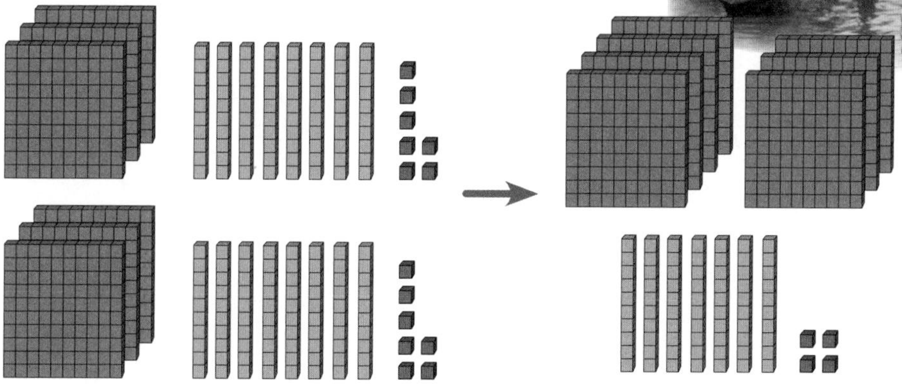

$$\begin{array}{r} 387 \\ \times \quad 2 \\ \hline \end{array}$$

miles

2 groups of 387 can be regrouped as 774.

Multiply the ones.	Multiply the tens. Add the regrouped tens.	Multiply the hundreds. Add the regrouped hundreds.
$\begin{array}{r} {}^{1}\quad \\ 387 \\ \times \quad 2 \\ \hline 4 \end{array}$ Regroup the ones as tens.	$\begin{array}{r} {}^{1\,1}\quad \\ 387 \\ \times \quad 2 \\ \hline 74 \end{array}$ This is 80 x 2, plus 1 more ten. Regroup the tens as hundreds.	$\begin{array}{r} {}^{1\,1}\quad \\ 387 \\ \times \quad 2 \\ \hline 774 \end{array}$ This is 300 x 2, plus 1 more hundred.

Multiply.

1. $\begin{array}{r} 379 \\ \times \quad 2 \\ \hline \end{array}$ $\begin{array}{r} 300 \\ \times \quad 2 \\ \hline \end{array}$ $\begin{array}{r} 70 \\ \times \; 2 \\ \hline \end{array}$ $\begin{array}{r} 9 \\ \times 2 \\ \hline \end{array}$

   ______ + ______ + ______ = ☐

2. $\begin{array}{r} 113 \\ \times \quad 5 \\ \hline \end{array}$ $\begin{array}{r} 100 \\ \times \quad 5 \\ \hline \end{array}$ $\begin{array}{r} 10 \\ \times \; 5 \\ \hline \end{array}$ $\begin{array}{r} 3 \\ \times 5 \\ \hline \end{array}$

   ______ + ______ + ______ = ☐

Multiply.

3. □□ 145 × 3

4. □□ 369 × 2

5. □□ 164 × 5

6. □□ 279 × 2

Multiply. Regroup when necessary.

7. 83 × 6

9. 134 × 2

11. 169 × 4

13. 245 × 2

15. 365 × 2

17. 237 × 3

8. 79 × 5

10. 304 × 3

12. 271 × 2

14. 95 × 5

16. 164 × 6

18. 259 × 2

Use your own paper to complete the subtotal. Then, total the receipt on your calculator.

	Thank you for shopping at Morning Glory Supermarket.			
	item	quantity	price	subtotal
19.	milk ($\frac{1}{2}$ gallon)	3	\$1.79	
20.	peanut butter	2	\$3.56	
21.	jelly	2	\$1.89	
22.	bread	3	\$2.35	
23.	chips	2	\$2.55	
24.			total	

Name ______________________________

3-Digits: Regrouping Hundreds 6.10

Kruger National Park in South Africa is home to a large number of mammal, reptile, bird, and insect species. Visitors have a close-up view of lions, elephants, leopards, and buffalo. Kruger National Park is 352 kilometers from north to south.

The García family will travel 278 kilometers through Kruger National Park. Three other families will make the same trip. What will be the total number of miles traveled by the 4 families?

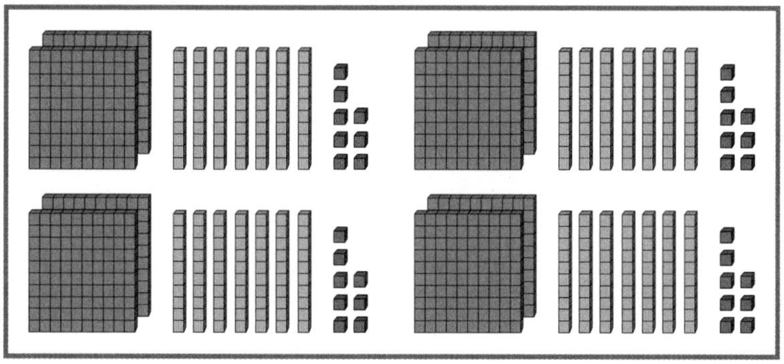

→

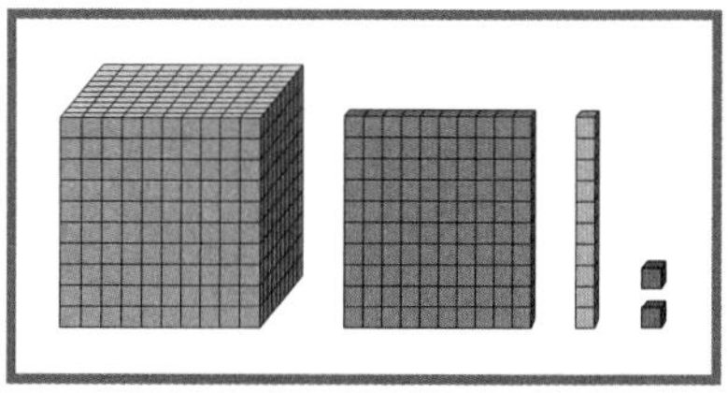

$$\begin{array}{r} 278 \\ \times \quad 4 \\ \hline 1{,}112 \end{array}$$ kilometers

Multiply the ones.

$$\begin{array}{r} {}^{3}\quad \\ 278 \\ \times \quad 4 \\ \hline 2 \end{array}$$

Regroup the ones as tens.

Multiply the tens. Add the regrouped tens.

$$\begin{array}{r} {}^{3\ 3}\quad \\ 278 \\ \times \quad 4 \\ \hline 12 \end{array}$$

This is 70 x 4, plus 3 more tens.

Regroup the tens as hundreds.

Multiply the hundreds. Add the regrouped hundreds.

$$\begin{array}{r} {}^{3\ 3}\quad \\ 278 \\ \times \quad 4 \\ \hline 1{,}112 \end{array}$$

This is 200 x 4, plus 3 more hundreds.

11 hundreds = 1,100.

Multiply.

1. $\begin{array}{r} 544 \\ \times \quad 6 \\ \hline \end{array}$

2. $\begin{array}{r} 695 \\ \times \quad 2 \\ \hline \end{array}$

3. $\begin{array}{r} 428 \\ \times \quad 7 \\ \hline \end{array}$

4. $\begin{array}{r} 763 \\ \times \quad 9 \\ \hline \end{array}$

5. Write C next to the correct answers. Write X next to the incorrect answers.

a. $\begin{array}{r} 549 \\ \times \quad 8 \\ \hline 4{,}392 \end{array}$

b. $\begin{array}{r} 816 \\ \times \quad 3 \\ \hline 2{,}439 \end{array}$

c. $\begin{array}{r} 280 \\ \times \quad 5 \\ \hline 1{,}415 \end{array}$

d. $\begin{array}{r} 637 \\ \times \quad 6 \\ \hline 3{,}822 \end{array}$

Multiply.

6. $\begin{array}{r} 342 \\ \times \quad 3 \\ \hline \end{array}$

9. $\begin{array}{r} 261 \\ \times \quad 5 \\ \hline \end{array}$

12. $\begin{array}{r} 712 \\ \times \quad 4 \\ \hline \end{array}$

15. $\begin{array}{r} 846 \\ \times \quad 2 \\ \hline \end{array}$

18. $\begin{array}{r} 457 \\ \times \quad 6 \\ \hline \end{array}$

7. $\begin{array}{r} 514 \\ \times \quad 9 \\ \hline \end{array}$

10. $\begin{array}{r} 623 \\ \times \quad 7 \\ \hline \end{array}$

13. $\begin{array}{r} 905 \\ \times \quad 5 \\ \hline \end{array}$

16. $\begin{array}{r} 392 \\ \times \quad 8 \\ \hline \end{array}$

19. $\begin{array}{r} 218 \\ \times \quad 7 \\ \hline \end{array}$

8. $\begin{array}{r} 784 \\ \times \quad 7 \\ \hline \end{array}$

11. $\begin{array}{r} 823 \\ \times \quad 9 \\ \hline \end{array}$

14. $\begin{array}{r} 436 \\ \times \quad 6 \\ \hline \end{array}$

17. $\begin{array}{r} 508 \\ \times \quad 2 \\ \hline \end{array}$

20. $\begin{array}{r} 677 \\ \times \quad 4 \\ \hline \end{array}$

21. Complete the table. Write the problems on your own paper.

×	421	88	212
3			
5			
6			
8			

Name ______________________________

Graph: Analyze Information

Cape buffalo are grazing animals. They migrate to find good pasture. Fully grown, a Cape buffalo can weigh over 900 kilograms. The graph shows the weight gain for one young Cape buffalo over a period of 5 weeks of grazing.

Cape Buffalo Weight

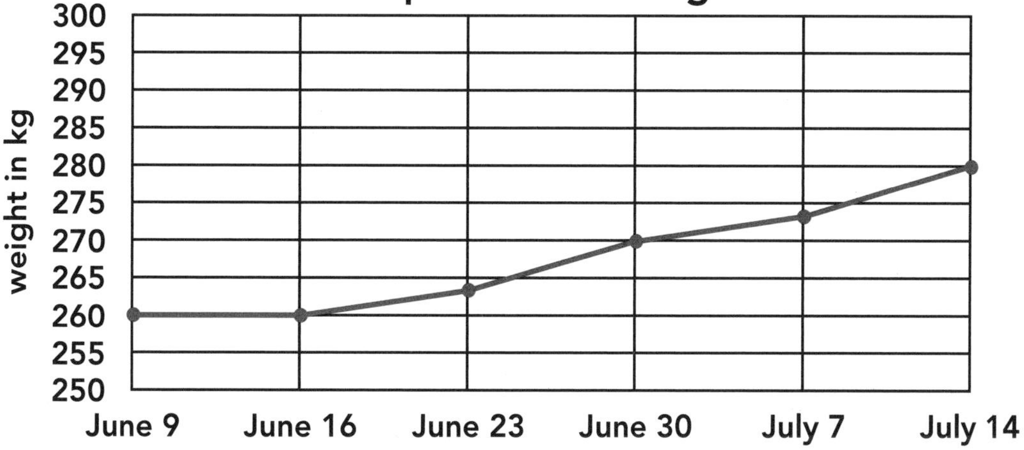

Line graphs differ from other graphs in that they compare changes in one subject over time. This Cape buffalo's weight has increased each week in July.

Read the graph. Answer the questions.

Daily High Temperatures in Kruger National Park

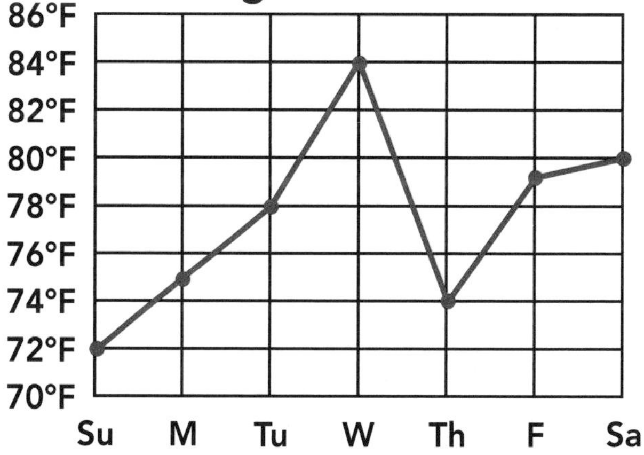

1. What is the subject of this graph?

____

2. What changes each day?

____

3. What time span is covered?

____

4. Which day had the highest temperature?

____

5. Follow the directions. Use the information given in the table to design a line graph.

- Write a title for the graph.
- Write the abbreviations for the days of the week along the bottom. Skip lines.
- Number the left-hand side by 5s from 255 to 305.
- Put a dot on the graph to match the number of visitors for the day.
- Connect the points with straight lines.

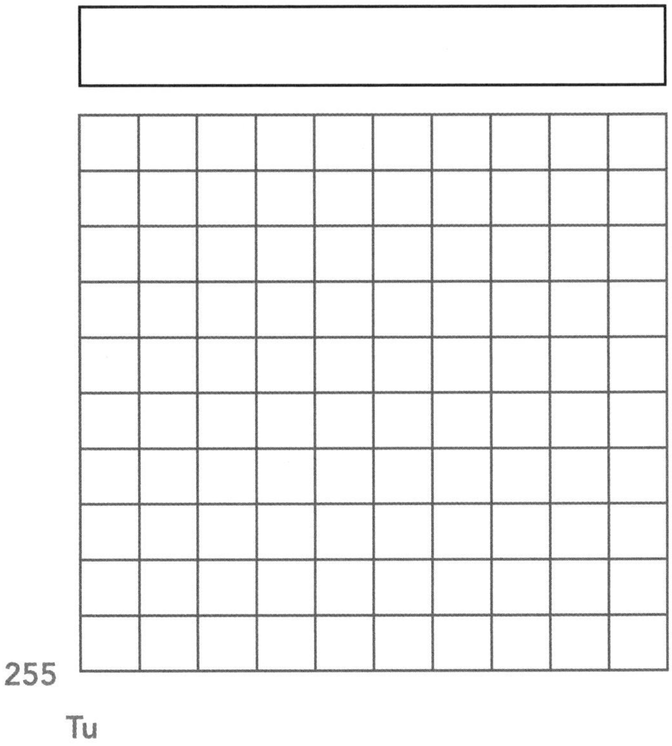

Visitors to Kruger National Park

Tuesday—255
Wednesday—270
Thursday—260
Friday—275
Saturday—305

Use the graph you designed to answer the questions.

6. What is the subject of the graph? ____________________

7. What changes from day to day? ____________________

8. What time span is covered? ____________________

9. Which day had the fewest number of visitors? ____________________

10. Which day had the most visitors? ____________________

11. Was there an increase or decrease from Friday to Saturday?

____

Name ____________________

Chapter 6 Review 6.12

Write a word to complete each sentence.

Word Bank
factors
product
regrouping
estimate

1. To ________________ is to figure a close answer.
2. The process of combining sets of ten and then trading to higher place values is called ________________.
3. The ________________ is the result of multiplication.
4. Numbers that are multiplied are ________________.

Write a multiplication equation for each picture.

5.

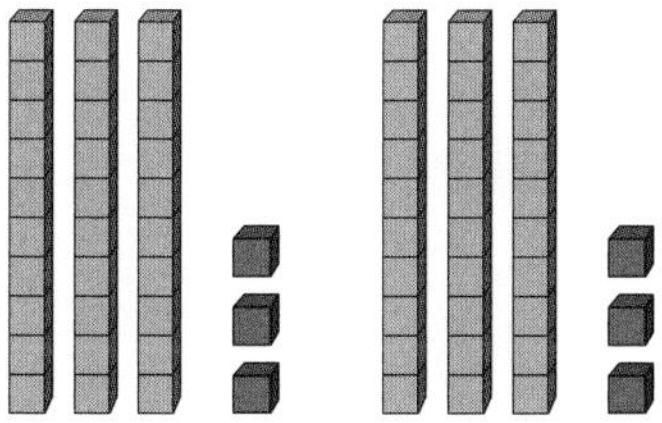

____

6.

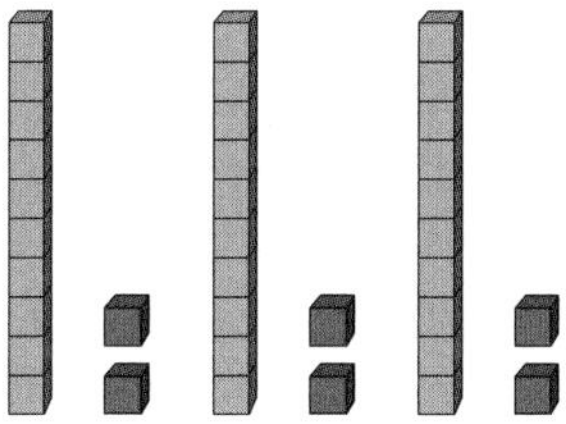

____

7.

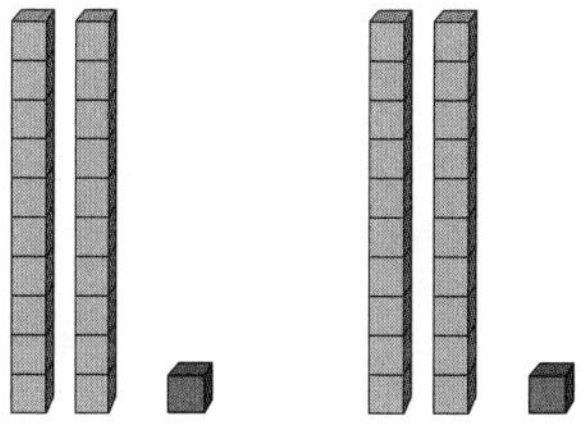

____

Match the model on the left that shows the same number regrouped on the right.

8.

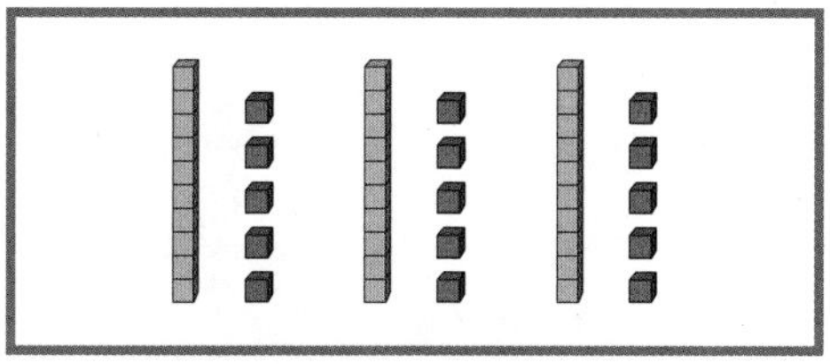

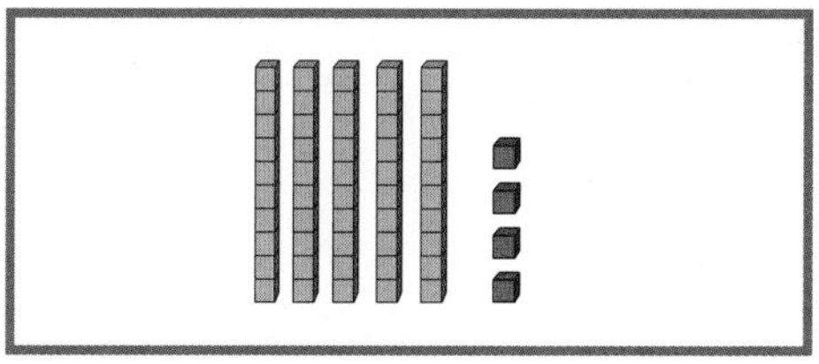

9.

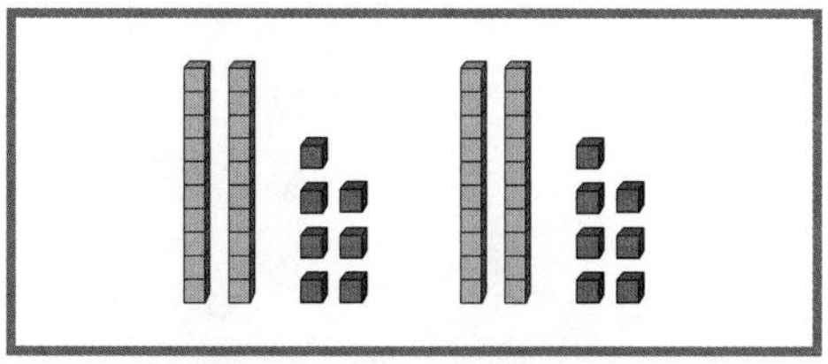

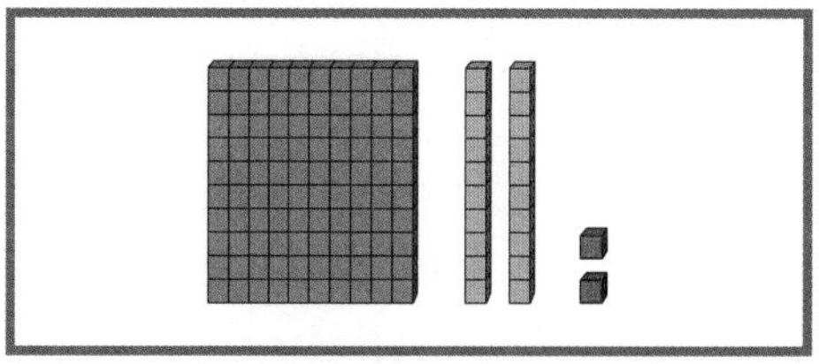

10.

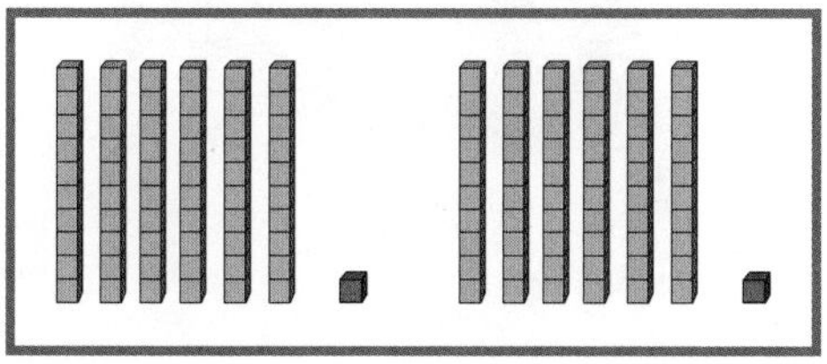

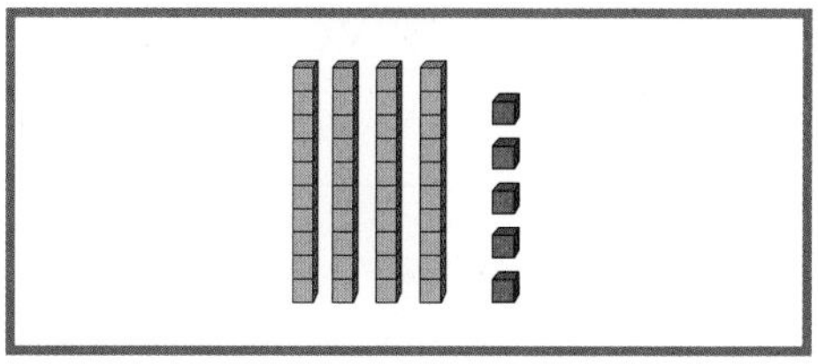

Multiply.

11. $\begin{array}{r} 58 \\ \times \ 2 \\ \hline \end{array}$

12. $\begin{array}{r} 24 \\ \times \ 2 \\ \hline \end{array}$

13. $\begin{array}{r} 408 \\ \times \ 2 \\ \hline \end{array}$

14. $\begin{array}{r} 24 \\ \times \ 4 \\ \hline \end{array}$

15. $\begin{array}{r} 43 \\ \times \ 4 \\ \hline \end{array}$

16. $\begin{array}{r} 121 \\ \times \ 5 \\ \hline \end{array}$

17. $\begin{array}{r} 72 \\ \times \ 5 \\ \hline \end{array}$

18. $\begin{array}{r} 65 \\ \times \ 3 \\ \hline \end{array}$

19. $\begin{array}{r} 261 \\ \times \ 6 \\ \hline \end{array}$

20. $\begin{array}{r} 49 \\ \times \ 2 \\ \hline \end{array}$

21. $\begin{array}{r} 27 \\ \times \ 3 \\ \hline \end{array}$

22. $\begin{array}{r} 135 \\ \times \ 2 \\ \hline \end{array}$

23. $\begin{array}{r} 37 \\ \times \ 4 \\ \hline \end{array}$

24. $\begin{array}{r} 48 \\ \times \ 4 \\ \hline \end{array}$

25. $\begin{array}{r} 283 \\ \times \ 2 \\ \hline \end{array}$

26. **Multiply mentally.**

4×60 _____ 3×20 _____ 8×80 _____ 9×30 _____

5×70 _____ 6×30 _____ 7×400 _____ 8×700 _____

Estimate the product.

27. Alaina gives weekly offerings to her church. She has given $14.89 each week for 3 weeks this month. Estimate her total gifts to her church.

____

Write the exact product.

28. Carson hopes to go on a mission trip to Africa. He and his parents save $417 each week for their trip. If they save for 9 weeks, how much will they have in all?

____

Chapter 7
Division

So the Israelites divided the land,
just as the Lord had commanded Moses.
Joshua 14:5

Key Ideas:

Division: dividing one-, two-, three-, and four-digit numbers, with and without remainders

Division: finding averages

Probability and Statistics: making predictions

Name _____

Review Division Strategies 7.1

Division is the operation that separates a number into equal sets. The number divided is the dividend. The number you divide by is the divisor. The quotient is the result of division.

This group of puffins can be divided into 2 equal groups. How many puffins will be in each group?

You can divide this problem with the division symbol or with the division bracket.

$$4 \div 2 = 2$$
dividend divisor quotient

$$\begin{array}{r} 2 \\ 2\overline{)4} \end{array}$$ quotient
dividend
divisor

You can use strategies to divide.
- Use Base 10 blocks or connecting cubes to model the problem.
- Think of a related multiplication fact.
- Use a multiplication table.
- Make an array.

Match the division problem to the correct model.

1. $22 \div 2$ •

•

2. $26 \div 2$ •

•

3. $2\overline{)24}$ •

•

© *Mathematics* Grade 3

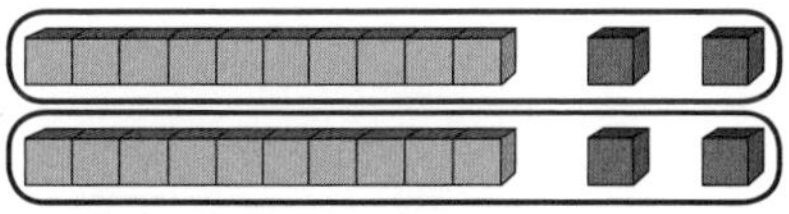

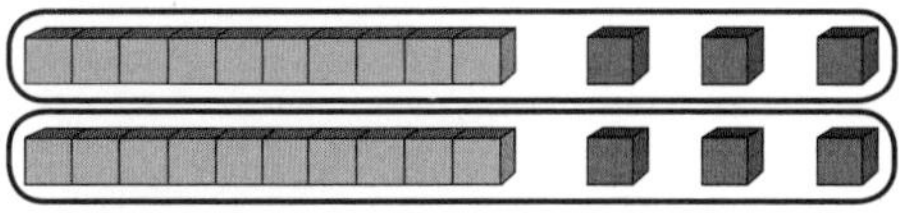

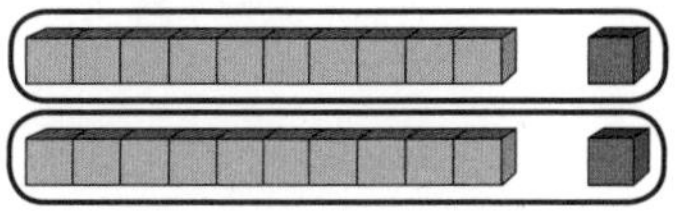

Write the related multiplication fact for each division problem.

4. 45 ÷ 9 = ______
   9 × ______ = 45

6. 27 ÷ 3 = ______
   3 × ______ = 27

8. 36 ÷ 6 = ______
   6 × ______ = 36

5. 54 ÷ 6 = ______
   6 × ______ = 54

7. 20 ÷ 4 = ______
   4 × ______ = 20

9. 36 ÷ 9 = ______
   9 × ______ =36

10. Complete the multiplication table.

×	3	4	5	6	7	8	9
3	9		15		21	24	
4	12		20	24			
5	15	20	25	30	35		45
6		24	30	36	42	48	
7	21		35		49		63
8	24	32				64	
9			45	54	63		

Divide. Use the multiplication table as needed.

11. $9\overline{)81}$

13. $6\overline{)48}$

15. $7\overline{)42}$

17. $5\overline{)45}$

19. $8\overline{)64}$

12. $8\overline{)72}$

14. $9\overline{)63}$

16. $4\overline{)28}$

18. $3\overline{)27}$

20. $9\overline{)36}$

Name ____________________

Divide by Multiples of 10 7.2

During the winter, musk oxen travel through the Arctic tundra in herds of 50 or more. In the summer, the herds roam the tundra in smaller numbers.

If a herd of 50 musk oxen were evenly divided into 5 groups, how many musk oxen would be in each group?

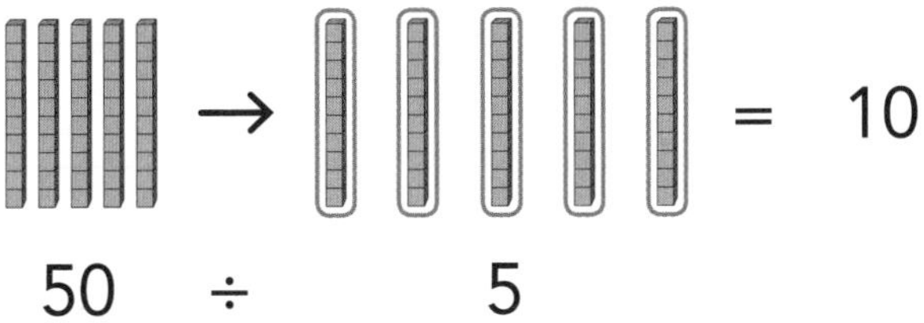

50 musk oxen ÷ 5 groups = 10 musk oxen in each group

Musk oxen were once nearly extinct. Now there are over 2,000 musk oxen in Alaska. If this number were evenly divided into 4 groups, how many musk oxen would be in each group?

2,000 ÷ 4 = 500 musk oxen

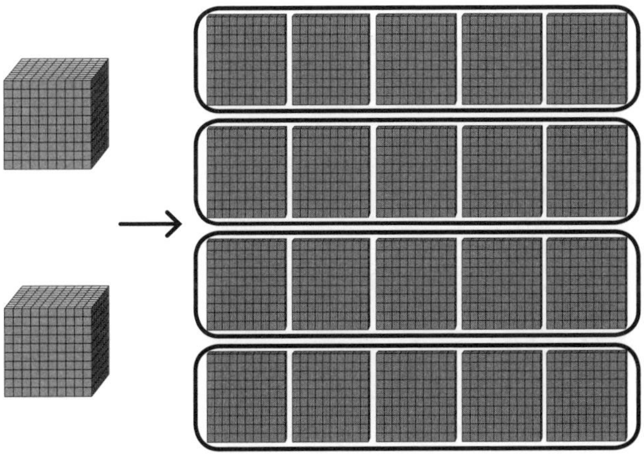

Regroup 2 thousands as 20 hundreds.

Complete the division sentences.

1. 6 ÷ 3 = ______

   6 tens ÷ 3 = ______

   6 hundreds ÷ 3 = ______

   6 thousands ÷ 3 = ______

2. 7 ÷ 7= ______

   7 tens ÷ 7 = ______

   7 hundreds ÷7 = ______

   7 thousands ÷ 7 = ______

Complete the division sentences.

3. $8 \div 4 =$ ______
$80 \div 4 =$ ______
$800 \div 4 =$ ______
$8{,}000 \div 4 =$ ______

4. $9 \div 3 =$ ______
$90 \div 3 =$ ______
$900 \div 3 =$ ______
$9{,}000 \div 3 =$ ______

5. $28 \div 4 =$ ______
$280 \div 4 =$ ______
$2{,}800 \div 4 =$ ______

Trace the example. Write the multiplication and division patterns for the given fact.

Example: 3×4		6. 6×8	
$3 \times 4 = 12$	$12 \div 3 = 4$	______	______
$3 \times 40 = 120$	$120 \div 3 = 40$	______	______
$3 \times 400 = 1{,}200$	$1{,}200 \div 3 = 400$	______	______

Use the division facts you know. Find the quotient.

7. $480 \div 8 =$ ______
8. $50 \div 5 =$ ______
9. $900 \div 3 =$ ______
10. $4{,}200 \div 7 =$ ______
11. $490 \div 7 =$ ______
12. $6{,}400 \div 8 =$ ______
13. $600 \div 2 =$ ______
14. $200 \div 2 =$ ______
15. $180 \div 6 =$ ______
16. $150 \div 5 =$ ______
17. $630 \div 9 =$ ______
18. $2{,}700 \div 9 =$ ______
19. $800 \div 4 =$ ______
20. $400 \div 2 =$ ______
21. $240 \div 4 =$ ______
22. $350 \div 7 =$ ______
23. $560 \div 7 =$ ______
24. $160 \div 4 =$ ______

Solve. Check by multiplying.

25. Eliana collects wildlife stickers. Her grandmother sent her 300 stickers of Arctic animals. She received 3 sheets of stickers. How many stickers were on each sheet?

______

26. Eliana gave 150 stickers to her brother. He placed 5 stickers on each page of his sticker book. If he put the same number of stickers on each page, how many pages did he use?

______

Name ____________________

Three hungry walruses watched a group of 22 squid swim toward them. If each of the walruses ate an equal number of squid, how many squid would each walrus eat?

$22 \div 3 \qquad 3\overline{)22}$

You cannot divide 22 evenly by 3. Estimate the number of 3s in 22. Which multiple of 3 is closest to 22 without going over?

$3 \times 6 = 18$

$3 \times 7 = 21 \longrightarrow 21 \div 3 = 7$

$3 \times 8 = 24$

The estimated quotient is 7. Each walrus will eat 7 squid. One squid is left over. A number left over in a division problem is called a remainder.

$$\begin{array}{r} 7 \text{ R1} \\ 3\overline{)22} \\ -21 \\ \hline 1 \end{array}$$

−21 ⟵ 3 groups of 7

1 ⟵ remainder

Write the remainder in the quotient, 7 R1.

Circle the fact that is closest to the dividend without going over.

1. $6\overline{)38}$

$6 \times 5 = 30$
$6 \times 6 = 36$
$6 \times 7 = 42$

2. $7\overline{)48}$

$7 \times 6 = 42$
$7 \times 7 = 49$
$7 \times 8 = 56$

3. $4\overline{)18}$

$4 \times 4 = 16$
$4 \times 5 = 20$
$4 \times 6 = 24$

4. $9\overline{)70}$

$9 \times 6 = 54$
$9 \times 7 = 63$
$9 \times 8 = 72$

Write two multiplication facts that have products closest to the dividend without going over. Write the estimated quotient above the ones place in the dividend.

Example:

5. $8\overline{)30}$ (quotient 3)
 8 × 3 = 24
 8 × 4 = 32

6. $2\overline{)9}$
 ____
 ____

7. $5\overline{)43}$
 ____
 ____

8. $3\overline{)19}$
 ____
 ____

Divide. Write the remainder.

9. $5\overline{)29}$ R

11. $8\overline{)62}$

13. $2\overline{)11}$

15. $9\overline{)19}$

17. $6\overline{)45}$

10. $3\overline{)25}$ R

12. $7\overline{)38}$

14. $4\overline{)18}$

16. $5\overline{)18}$

18. $8\overline{)27}$

Solve.

19. The zookeeper at the Center City Zoo had 25 fish to feed to 4 walruses. If each received an equal share, how many fish did each walrus eat? How many fish were left over?

____

20. Twenty-five students viewed the 6 Arctic exhibits at the zoo. About how many students were in each group if the students were placed into groups as equally as possible?

____

Review

Solve.

21. 56 ÷ ⑦ × [2] − 4 = ______

22. 28 ÷ ④ × [5] − 8 = ______

Name ______________________________

2-Digit Quotients 7.4

Each year, thousands of harp seals migrate from cold Arctic waters to the icy shores of Canada. If 74 seals are divided equally into 2 groups, how many seals would be in each group?

1. Divide.
Divide 7 tens by 2. There are 2 groups of three tens. Decide where to place the first digit.

$$2\overline{)74}\quad\text{quotient: }3$$

$2 \times 2 = 4$
$2 \times 3 = 6$ (circled)
$2 \times 4 = 8$

2. Multiply.
Multiply the divisor by the first digit of the quotient.

$$2\overline{)74}\quad\text{quotient: }3,\ \text{product: }6$$

How many tens were used?

$2 \times 3 = 6$ tens

3. Subtract.
Subtract the product from the first digit in the dividend.

$$\begin{array}{r} 3 \\ 2\overline{)74} \\ -6 \\ \hline 1 \end{array}$$

How many tens are left over?

7 tens − 6 tens = 1 ten

4. Compare.
The difference must be less than the divisor.

5. Bring down.
Bring down the next digit, 4, and repeat the steps.

$$\begin{array}{r} 37 \\ 2\overline{)74} \\ -6\downarrow \\ \hline 14 \\ -14 \\ \hline 0 \end{array}$$

Divide	$14 \div 2 = 7$
Multiply	$2 \times 7 = 14$
Subtract	$14 - 14 = 0$
Compare	$0 < 2$

Divide. Follow the steps and then repeat.

1. $2\overline{)48}$ Divide / Multiply / Subtract / Compare / Bring down

2. $3\overline{)54}$ Divide / Multiply / Subtract / Compare / Bring down

3. $5\overline{)65}$ Divide / Multiply / Subtract / Compare / Bring down

Divide.

4. $5\overline{)90}$
7. $3\overline{)78}$
10. $6\overline{)84}$
13. $2\overline{)62}$
16. $3\overline{)87}$

5. $5\overline{)70}$
8. $4\overline{)88}$
11. $7\overline{)91}$
14. $2\overline{)38}$
17. $6\overline{)78}$

6. $5\overline{)75}$
9. $4\overline{)96}$
12. $2\overline{)56}$
15. $3\overline{)69}$
18. $4\overline{)56}$

Circle only the problems with correct quotients.

19. $\begin{array}{r}18\\4\overline{)72}\end{array}$
20. $\begin{array}{r}15\\5\overline{)80}\end{array}$
21. $\begin{array}{r}38\\2\overline{)74}\end{array}$
22. $\begin{array}{r}32\\3\overline{)96}\end{array}$
23. $\begin{array}{r}15\\6\overline{)90}\end{array}$

Solve.

24. Biologists weighed 2 baby harp seals. The seals' total weight was 48 pounds. If the seals weighed the same, what did each seal weigh?

____

Name ______________________________

A polar bear's main source of food is seal blubber. Blubber is the layer of fat under a seal's skin.

Four polar bears have 75 kilograms of seal blubber to share among them. How many kilograms of blubber will each bear eat if it is divided evenly among them?

$$\begin{array}{r} 18 \\ 4\overline{)75} \\ -4\downarrow \\ 35 \\ -32 \\ \hline (3) \end{array}$$

1. Divide.	How much is 7 tens divided by 4?
2. Multiply.	4 × 1 = 4
3. Subtract.	7 − 4 = 3
4. Compare.	3 < 4
5. Bring down.	Bring down the 5 and repeat the steps.

Check.

$$\begin{array}{r} 18 \\ \times\ 4 \\ \hline 72 \\ +\ 3 \\ \hline 75 \end{array}$$

1. Multiply the quotient by the divisor.
2. Add the remainder.

After division, there is a remainder of 3. The quotient is 18 R3.

$$\begin{array}{r} 18 \text{ R3} \\ 4\overline{)75} \end{array}$$

Each polar bear gets 18 kilograms of seal blubber. There are 3 kilograms left.

Circle the remainder. Write the complete quotient.

1. $$\begin{array}{r} 8 \\ 5\overline{)43} \\ -40 \\ \hline (3) \end{array}$$

______

2. $$\begin{array}{r} 12 \\ 8\overline{)98} \\ -8\downarrow \\ 18 \\ -16 \\ \hline 2 \end{array}$$

______

3. $$\begin{array}{r} 13 \\ 6\overline{)82} \\ -6\downarrow \\ 22 \\ -18 \\ \hline 4 \end{array}$$

______

4. $$\begin{array}{r} 29 \\ 2\overline{)59} \\ -4\downarrow \\ 19 \\ -18 \\ \hline 1 \end{array}$$

______

Divide.

5. $3\overline{)38}$
6. $8\overline{)42}$
7. $4\overline{)65}$
8. $6\overline{)81}$
9. $2\overline{)31}$
10. $9\overline{)33}$
11. $5\overline{)62}$
12. $5\overline{)73}$
13. $7\overline{)55}$
14. $3\overline{)49}$

Estimate.

15. A biologist measured the growth of a polar bear cub. It gained 89 pounds in 8 months. About how many pounds had it gained per month?
Another polar bear cub gained 60 pounds in 5 months. About how many pounds had it gained per month?

________________ ________________

Review

Solve.

16. $\begin{array}{r} 365 \\ 240 \\ +149 \\ \hline \end{array}$

17. $\begin{array}{r} 4,802 \\ -1,958 \\ \hline \end{array}$

18. $\begin{array}{r} 28 \\ \times\ 8 \\ \hline \end{array}$

19. $\begin{array}{r} 367 \\ \times\ 5 \\ \hline \end{array}$

20. $\begin{array}{r} 6,002 \\ -5,103 \\ \hline \end{array}$

Name ______________________________

1. Divide.

The 3 in the hundreds place cannot be divided into sets of 8, so divide 36 tens by 8.

36 ÷ 8 =

$$8\overline{)364}\quad \text{quotient: } 4\_$$

2. Multiply.

How many tens were used?

8 × 4 tens = 32 tens

$$\begin{array}{r} 4 \\ 8\overline{)364} \\ 32 \end{array}$$

3. Subtract.

How many tens are left?

36 tens − 32 tens = 4 tens

$$\begin{array}{r} 4 \\ 8\overline{)364} \\ -32 \\ \hline 4 \end{array}$$

4. Compare.

4 < 8

5. Bring down.

4 < 8, so bring down 4 ones and continue.

$$\begin{array}{r} 4 \\ 8\overline{)364} \\ -32\downarrow \\ \hline 44 \end{array}$$

Repeat.

Divide.
44 ÷ 8 =
Multiply.
8 × 5 = 40
Subtract.
44 − 40 = 4
Compare.
4 < 8
Write the remainder.

$$\begin{array}{r} 45 \text{ R4} \\ 8\overline{)364} \\ -32\downarrow \\ \hline 44 \\ -40 \\ \hline 4 \end{array}$$

There would be about 45 caribou in each family group.

A herd of 364 caribou (reindeer) has 8 family groups of nearly equal size. About how many caribou would be in each family?

Circle the correct first step in division. Write the first digit of the quotient in the correct place value column.

1. $6\overline{)413}$ (quotient: 6)
   - 4 ÷ 6
   - (41 ÷ 6) (circled)

2. $2\overline{)855}$
   - 8 ÷ 2
   - 85 ÷ 2

3. $3\overline{)169}$
   - 1 ÷ 3
   - 16 ÷ 3

4. $8\overline{)364}$
   - 3 ÷ 8
   - 36 ÷ 8

Check.

Multiply the quotient by the divisor and add the remainder.

$$\begin{array}{r} 45 \\ \times\ 8 \\ \hline 360 \\ +\ 4 \\ \hline 364 \end{array}$$

5. **Divide and check.**

$2\overline{)341}$ Check.

$8\overline{)277}$ Check.

$6\overline{)329}$ Check.

Divide. Check on a separate piece of paper.

6. $5\overline{)204}$ 7. $6\overline{)204}$ 8. $7\overline{)204}$ 9. $8\overline{)204}$

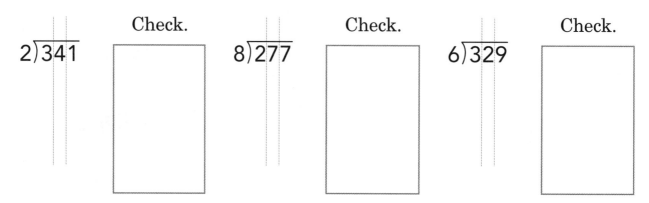

10. A population of 189 seals was tracked by 9 drones. How many seals did each drone track?

11. Riverside Christian school has 377 students in 8 grades. About how many students are in each grade?

Review

Write each numeral.

12. five thousand sixteen ____

13. twenty-nine thousand three hundred eleven ____

14. four hundred fourteen thousand ninety-one ____

15. one hundred thousand nine ____

Name ______________________________

The Arctic hare, the tundra hare, and the snowshoe hare are the 3 types of hares that live in Arctic tundra. Suppose a population of 1,278 hares is made up of an equal number of the 3 types. How many of each type of hare would there be?

```
    426
3)1,278
 −1 2↓
    07
   −6↓
    18
   −18
     0
```

Divide	Multiply	Subtract	Compare	Bring down
12 ÷ 3	3 × 4 = 12	12 − 12 = 0	0 < 3	7
7 ÷ 3	3 × 2 = 6	7 − 6 = 1	1 < 3	8
18 ÷ 3	3 × 6 = 18	18 − 18 = 0	0 < 3	

There would be 426 of each type of hare.

Circle the correct first step. Write the first digit of the quotient in the correct place.

1. 7)2,361 (quotient: _ 3 _ _)
   - 2 ÷ 7
   - (23 ÷ 7) — circled

2. 4)5,640
   - 5 ÷ 4
   - 56 ÷ 4

3. 2)1,075
   - 1 ÷ 2
   - 10 ÷ 2

4. 9)7,415
   - 7 ÷ 9
   - 74 ÷ 9

5. **Divide and check.**

```
   491
6)2,946
 -24↓ |
   54 |
  -54 ↓
    06
   - 6
     0
```

Check.

$3\overline{)5,403}$

Check.

$8\overline{)2,717}$

Check.

$7\overline{)8,211}$

Check.

$4\overline{)9,264}$

Check.

$9\overline{)1,049}$

Check.

Complete.

		animal	typical weight	typical height or length	pounds per foot
6.		walrus	2,208 pounds	9 feet	
7.		polar bear	1,208 pounds	8 feet	
8.		moose	1,785 pounds	7 feet	
9.		harp seal	324 pounds	6 feet	

Name ____

2-, 3-, and 4-Digit Dividends 7.8

God has given the Arctic fox a coat that can change color with the seasons. This ability to change color helps the fox to find food and to avoid predators. Arctic foxes can live in temperatures below –50°F. They have a range (area that they are found in) that is larger than any other land animal.

If 7 Arctic foxes share an area of 1,175 square kilometers, about how large an area would each fox have?

You cannot divide the thousands place by 7, so regroup the 1 thousand as 10 hundreds. Now you have 11 hundreds.

$$\begin{array}{r} 167 \\ 7\overline{)1{,}175} \\ -\ \ 7\downarrow \\ \hline 47 \\ -42\downarrow \\ \hline 55 \\ -49 \\ \hline 6 \end{array}$$

Divide	Multiply	Subtract	Compare	Bring down
11 ÷ 7	7 × 1 = 7	11 – 7 = 4	4 < 7	7
Divide	**Multiply**	**Subtract**	**Compare**	**Bring down**
47 ÷ 7	7 × 6 = 42	47 – 42 = 5	5 < 7	5
Divide	**Multiply**	**Subtract**	**Compare**	**Remainder**
55 ÷ 7	7 × 7 = 49	55 – 49 = 6	6 < 7	6

Each Arctic fox would have an area of about 167 square kilometers.

Check the example division problem by multiplying. If it is incorrect, rewrite it and solve.

1. Check. **2. Rewrite.**

$$\begin{array}{r} 846 \\ 9\overline{)7{,}425} \end{array}$$

Divide and check.

3. $5\overline{)525}$ Check.

6. $8\overline{)488}$ Check.

9. $3\overline{)693}$ Check.

4. $7\overline{)9{,}321}$ Check.

7. $8\overline{)8{,}432}$ Check.

10. $6\overline{)3{,}216}$ Check.

5. $3\overline{)38}$ Check.

8. $5\overline{)75}$ Check.

11. $6\overline{)46}$ Check.

Solve.

12. At one time, fur seals were almost extinct because of overhunting. Now, scientists keep track of the number of seals. They do this by putting tags on the seals' flippers. Nine scientists track a group of 459 fur seals. If each scientist oversees the same number of seals, how many seals does each scientist track?

____

Name ___________________________________

A biologist tracked the caribou she saw over a four-day period. Each day, she counted a slightly different number of animals. The numbers are shown in the chart below. About how many animals could she expect to see on the fifth day?

To estimate the number of caribou, you can find an average. The average is calculated by dividing the sum of a set of numbers by the number of addends. Find the average number of caribou that the biologist saw during the four days.

Monday	Tuesday	Wednesday	Thursday	Friday
54	48	40	35	______

Add the numbers.

Divide the sum by the number of addends.

$$\begin{array}{r} \overset{1}{5}4 \\ 48 \\ 40 \\ +35 \\ \hline 177 \end{array}$$

4 addends ⟶

$$\begin{array}{r} 44 \text{ R1} \\ 4\overline{)177} \\ -16\downarrow \\ 17 \\ -16 \\ \hline 1 \end{array}$$

The biologist can expect the number of caribou she will see on Friday to be about 44.

Arctic temperatures can be cold! Find the average temperature for each group of days.

1.

Monday	Tuesday	Wednesday	Thursday
37°F	40°F	42°F	45°F

$4\overline{)\quad\quad}$ °F

+ ______

2.

Friday	Saturday	Sunday
83°F	89°F	95°F

$\overline{)\quad\quad}$ °F

+ ______

Find the average for each set of numbers. Check on the calculator.

3.
67
112
139
+

4.
16
8
21
3
+

5.
275
308
114
91
+

6.
47
5
212
+

Use a calculator to solve.

7. Jun kept a record of his spelling scores. Last month, he scored 98, 89, 85, and 96 percent on his tests. What is his average score?

____

8. Last week's high temperatures included 1 day at 73°F, 2 days at 68°F, and 1 day at 63°F. What was the average temperature for those 4 days?

____

9. Church attendance for the 4 Sundays in May was 314, 352, 289, and 321 people. What was the average church attendance for May?

____

10. A meteorologist measured Arctic snowfall in inches for 3 months. He measured 16 inches in January, 19 in February, and 25 inches in March. What is the average number of inches of snowfall?

____

Review

Write the estimated difference in each rectangle. Solve the equations and compare.

11. $83 - 28$ ☐

12. $60 - 38$ ☐

13. $55 - 21$ ☐

14. $82 - 69$ ☐

Name ____

Problem Solving: Mixed Operations 7.10

Clayton and his parents donate food to help hungry people in their community. This week, they gave five 8-ounce cans of fruit and seven 16-ounce cans of fruit to the food bank. How many ounces of fruit did the family donate in all?

Use the Problem-Solving Path to help you solve the problem.

Problem-Solving Path

1. Understand the question.
   - Underline the question.
2. Analyze the data.
   - Circle the key information.
3. Plan the strategy.
   - How many operations are needed?
   - Which step should come first?
4. Solve the problem.
   - Show your work.
   - Label the answer.
5. Evaluate the result.
   - Does the answer make sense?

1. Understand the question.

The problem asks for the total number of ounces of fruit.

2. Analyze the data.

The key information tells you that the family donated 5 cans that were 8 ounces each and 7 cans that were 16 ounces each.

3. Plan the strategy.

To find the total number of ounces, two operations are needed. Multiply.

$$\begin{array}{r} 8 \\ \times 5 \\ \hline \underline{\qquad} \end{array} \qquad \begin{array}{r} 16 \\ \times \ 7 \\ \hline \underline{\qquad} \end{array}$$

4. Solve the problem.

Add the two products.

$$\begin{array}{r} 112 \\ + \ 40 \\ \hline \underline{\qquad} \end{array}$$ ounces of fruit

5. Evaluate the result.

Check your calculations.

Solve.

6. Pastor Martin stocks shelves at the church's food bank. Each shelf holds 9 cans of tomato sauce. He has 154 cans to place on the shelves. How many shelves will he fill? How many cans were extra and did not fill a shelf?

____

____

7. People donated boxes of cereal. By the end of the day, 5 boxes, 4 boxes, 13 boxes, and 6 boxes were donated. What was the average number of boxes of cereal?

____

8. Elsa and her sister put rice into plastic bags at the food bank. They had 241 pounds of rice to divide. Each plastic bag could hold 6 pounds of rice. About how many plastic bags could the girls fill?

____

9. The food bank gave out 379 loaves of white bread and wheat bread. Of those, 192 loaves were wheat bread. How many were white bread? How many fewer loaves of white bread were given than wheat bread?

____

____

10. Mr. Joseph checked the food pantry for juice pouches. There were 4 full boxes of 8 juice pouches in each box. There were also 3 loose juice pouches. How many juice pouches were there in all?

____

11. Mrs. Thompson's third-grade class went to volunteer at the food bank. Mrs. Thompson normally had 22 students, but on that day 2 students were absent. She arranged the rest of the students into groups of 4. How many students were in each group?

____

12. Jamar helped at the food bank on Mondays, Wednesdays, and Fridays after school. Last week, he gave out 432 pounds of food to hungry families. How many pounds of food is that per day that Jamar worked?

____

Name ______________________________

Understand Probability 7.11

Arctic terns travel over 25,000 miles from their Arctic breeding grounds to Antarctica. This migration is the longest of any bird! Arctic terns have their babies on offshore islands where there are few predators. This way, the terns increase the chance of having their eggs survive.

Probability is the chance that something might happen. Some events are more probable, or likely to occur, than others.

Read the statements. Write P if the event described is likely (probable) to happen.

1. Your class will study reading at some time this week. ______
2. You will go to recess on the next school day. ______
3. An Arctic tern will speak to you. ______
4. A friend will come to your home sometime in the next two weeks. ______
5. You will help a parent with household chores. ______
6. You will drive the car to the market. ______
7. Your class will recite a pledge sometime this week. ______
8. An Arctic tern will build its nest in your backyard. ______
9. You will visit Antarctica this year. ______
10. Your teacher will take you to Antarctica on a field trip. ______
11. You will see some of the Arctic animals that you have learned about in this chapter. ______

The greater the number of chances that something will happen, the greater the probability.

Look at the hat. Answer each question.

12. If you wrote your name on 5 pieces of paper and placed them into the hat, would your name be more or less likely to be drawn than if you only wrote your name once?

____

13. If there were only two names in the hat, and your name was one of them, would your name be more or less likely to be drawn than if the hat was full of names?

____

14. Is it likely or unlikely that your name would be drawn if there were 150 names in the hat? Why?

____

15. Write your name and the names of nine friends on slips of paper. Without looking, draw a name. Return the name to the group. Repeat this 9 more times. How many times did you draw your own name?

____

Review

Rewrite each group of numbers from least to greatest. Circle all even numbers you write. Box all odd numbers.

16. 346 ________	17. 288 ________	18. 592 ________
400 ________	213 ________	561 ________
364 ________	254 ________	534 ________
307 ________	267 ________	527 ________

Name ______________________________

Match the division problem to the correct model.

1. $3\overline{)63}$ •

• 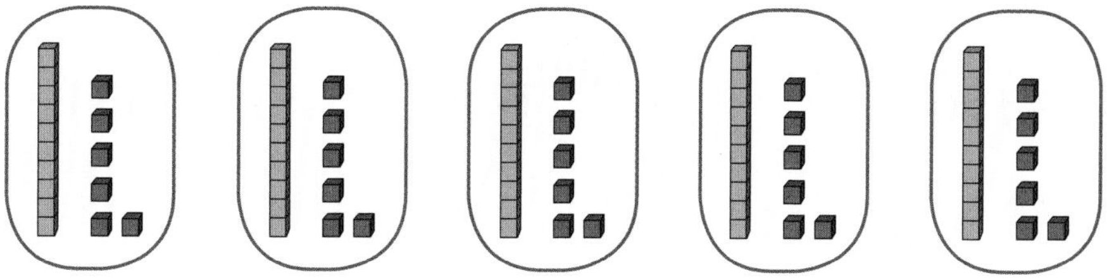

2. $5\overline{)80}$ •

• 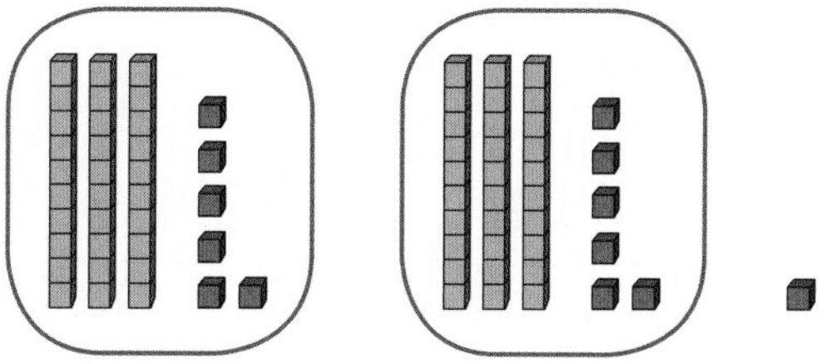

3. $2\overline{)73}$ •

• 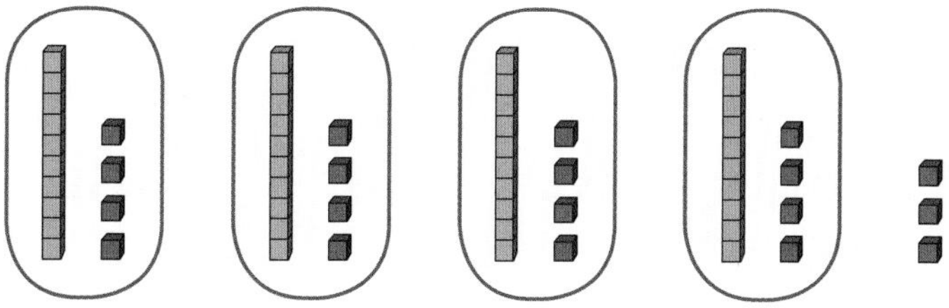

4. $4\overline{)59}$ •

• 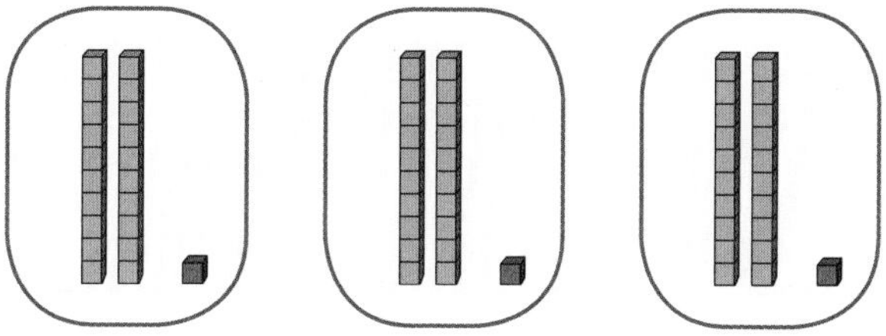

Complete the pattern.

5. 8 ÷ 4 = ______

80 ÷ 4 = ______

6. 9 ÷ 3 = ______

90 ÷ 3 = ______

7. 24 ÷ 6 = ______

240 ÷ 6 = ______

Estimate the quotient.

8. $6\overline{)16}$

9. $7\overline{)50}$

10. $3\overline{)29}$

11. $4\overline{)34}$

Solve.

12. Emily has 8 red, 2 blue, and 16 white socks in the clothes dryer. If she pulls out one sock witout looking, which color is she most likely to pick?

____

Divide.

13. $4\overline{)66}$

15. $2\overline{)71}$

17. $4\overline{)821}$

19. $3\overline{)645}$

14. $5\overline{)320}$

16. $2\overline{)3{,}710}$

18. $7\overline{)3{,}049}$

20. $9\overline{)1{,}456}$

Divide and check.

21. $3\overline{)405}$ Check.

22. $2\overline{)738}$ Check.

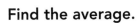

Find the average.

23. $\begin{array}{r} 17 \\ 39 \\ +61 \\ \hline \end{array}$ $\overline{)\quad}$

24. $\begin{array}{r} 2{,}072 \\ 496 \\ +1{,}503 \\ \hline \end{array}$ $\overline{)\quad}$

25. $\begin{array}{r} 213 \\ 87 \\ 93 \\ +199 \\ \hline \end{array}$ $\overline{)\quad}$

Name ______________________________

Chapters 4–7 Review 7.13

Fill in the missing words.

Word Bank
factor
product
inverse
quotient
remainder
divisor
dividend

1. The number by which another number is divided is the ______________________.
2. The result of multiplication is the ______________.
3. The answer to a division problem is the ______________________.
4. Multiplication and division are ______________ operations.
5. A number that is divided by another number is a ______________.
6. One of two numbers that are multiplied is a ______________.
7. A number that is left over when one number does not divide evenly into another number is a ______________________.

Multiply.

8. 7×8

9. 6×4

10. 3×2

11. 9×9

12. 8×4

13. 9×7

14. 6×8

15. 4×4

16. 32×2

17. 24×3

18. 18×9

19. 17×8

20. 24×7

21. 63×2

22. 21×5

23. 43×3

24. **Divide.**

$24 \div 6 =$ ____ $24 \div 3 =$ ____ $42 \div 6 =$ ____ $24 \div 8 =$ ____

$20 \div 5 =$ ____ $56 \div 7 =$ ____ $64 \div 8 =$ ____ $28 \div 7 =$ ____

$32 \div 8 =$ ____ $49 \div 7 =$ ____ $27 \div 9 =$ ____ $81 \div 9 =$ ____

Solve. Check.

25. $3\overline{)36}$

27. $5\overline{)74}$

29. $3\overline{)136}$

26. $4\overline{)282}$

28. $8\overline{)92}$

30. $2\overline{)246}$

Write the five steps of division.

31. ____________________

____

____

____

____

Chapter 8
Geometry

Where can I go from Your Spirit? Where can I flee from Your presence?
Psalm 139:7

Key Ideas:

Geometry: parallel and intersecting lines, plane and solid figures, congruent figures

Measurement: finding perimeter and area

Geometry: translation, rotation, reflection

Patterns: geometric patterns

Algebra: graphing ordered pairs

Name ______________________________

Lines and Line Segments 8.1

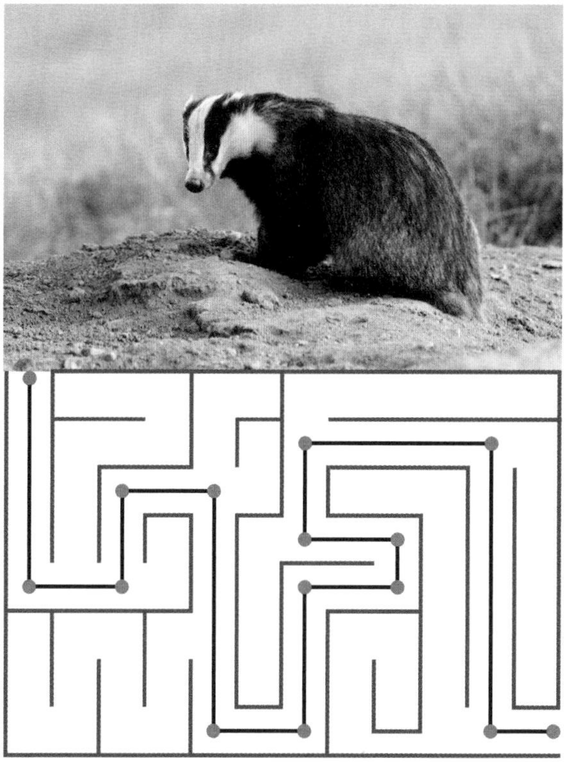

The study of lines, line segments, and shapes in mathematics is called geometry. A line is a straight path that continues in two directions without ending.

A line segment is a straight path that has two definite endpoints. It is part of a line.

You can draw a line segment by first making two endpoints. Then, use a ruler to connect the points.

The European badger builds large underground burrow systems. Count the 14 line segments that make a path through this badger home.

You can join line segments to make pictures.

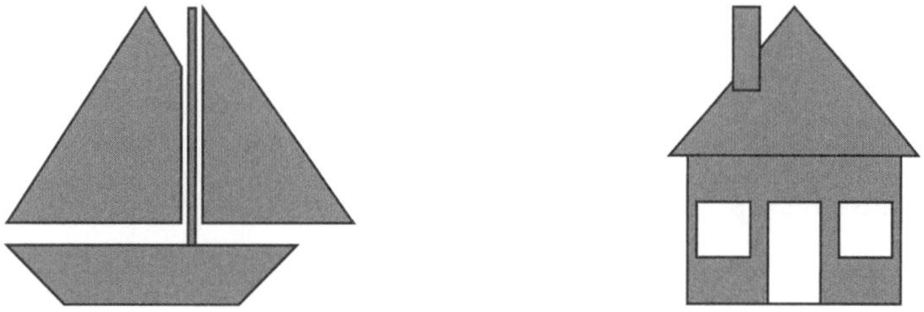

Count the number of line segments in each figure.

1. 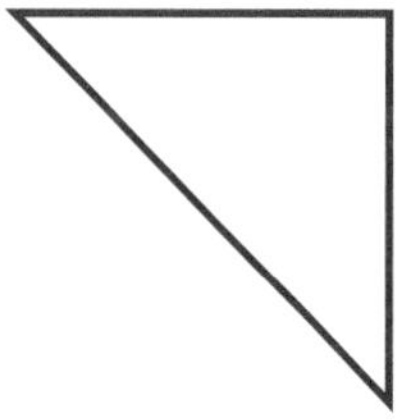

______

2. 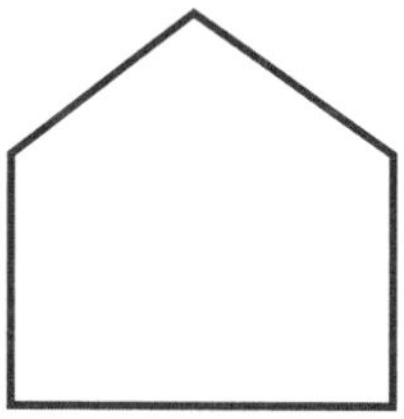

______

3. 

______

4. 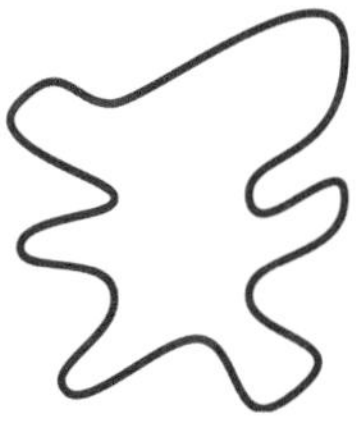

______

Count the number of line segments in each figure.

5. 

______

7. 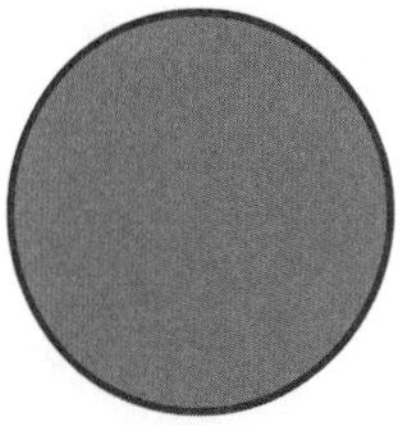

______

9. 

______

11. 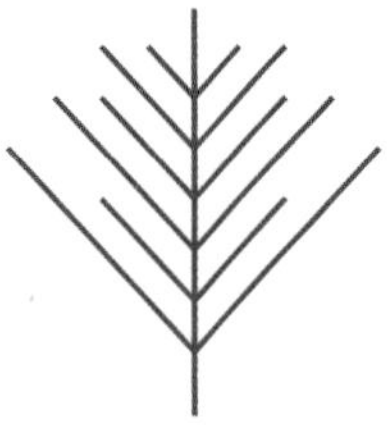

______

6. 

______

8. 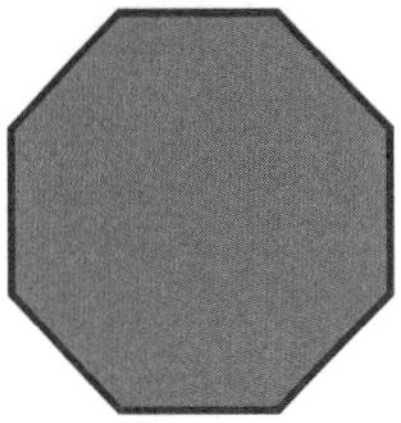

______

10. 

______

12. 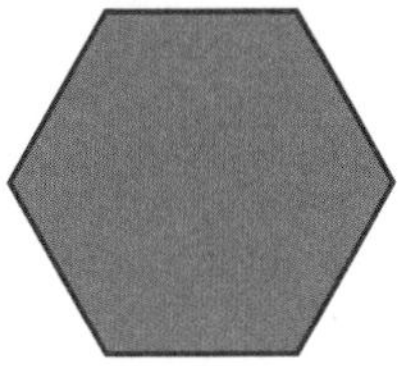

______

13. Use your ruler to draw a line segment between these two points.

14. Draw two points. Make a line connecting the points and continuing on. Add arrowheads to the line to show that it continues.

Draw as many line segments as possible between the points.

15. 

16. 

17. 

18. 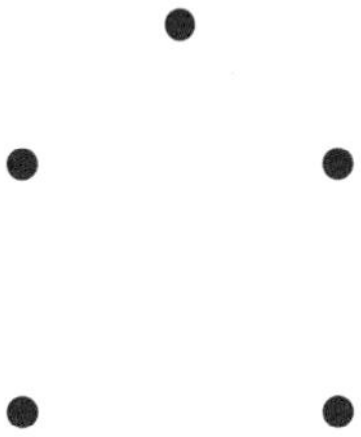

Review

Add or subtract.

19. $\begin{array}{r} 200 \\ -\,118 \\ \hline \end{array}$

20. $\begin{array}{r} 556 \\ +\ \ 84 \\ \hline \end{array}$

21. $\begin{array}{r} 4{,}184 \\ +\,3{,}129 \\ \hline \end{array}$

22. $\begin{array}{r} 555 \\ -\,372 \\ \hline \end{array}$

23. $\begin{array}{r} 583 \\ -\,137 \\ \hline \end{array}$

Name ____

There are many poisonous and non-poisonous snakes in Europe.

These snakes are traveling in exactly the same direction. They are examples of parallel lines.

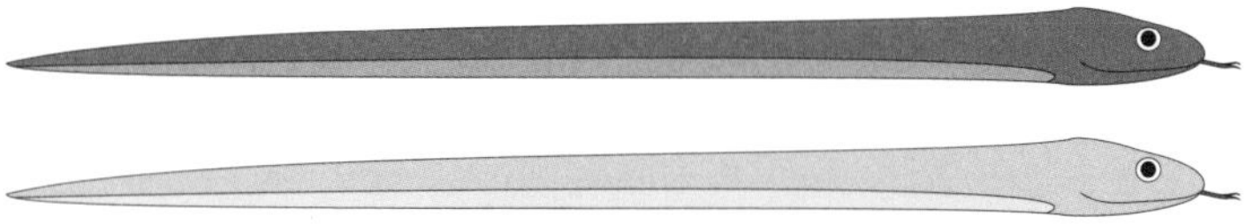

These snakes are crossing one another. They are examples of intersecting lines.

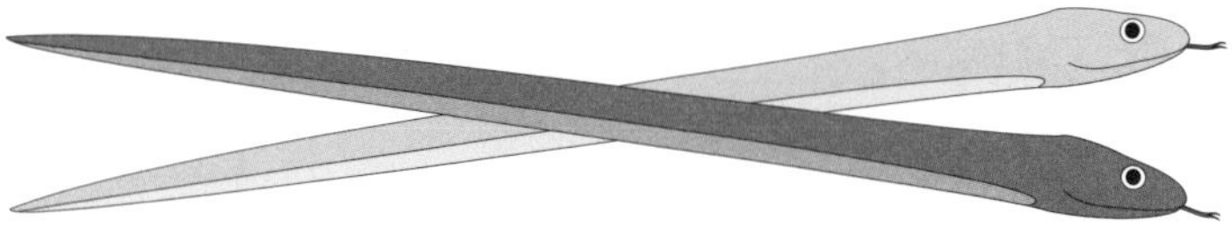

The space between parallel lines is always the same, so they will never intersect. Look at the parallel and intersecting lines below.

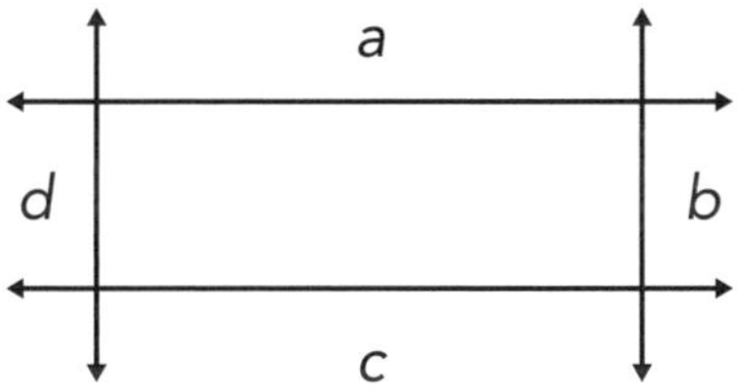

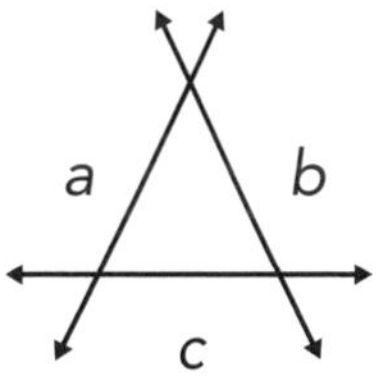

parallel lines	*a* and *c*
	b and *d*

intersecting lines	*a* and *b*
	b and *c*
	c and *a*

Label each pair of lines using P for parallel and I for intersecting.

1.

______

2.

______

3.

______

4.

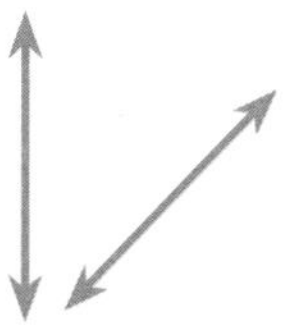

______

Label each pair of lines using P for parallel and I for intersecting.

5. 

______

6. 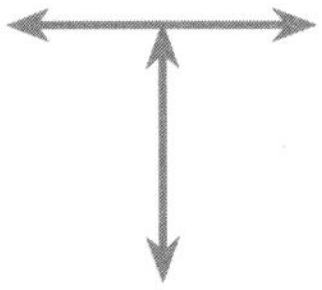

______

7. 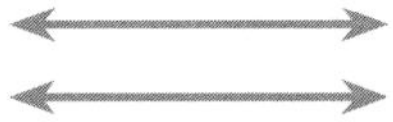

______

8. 

______

9. **Write three uppercase letters that have intersecting lines.**

______ ______ ______

10. **Fill in the chart with pairs of lines.**

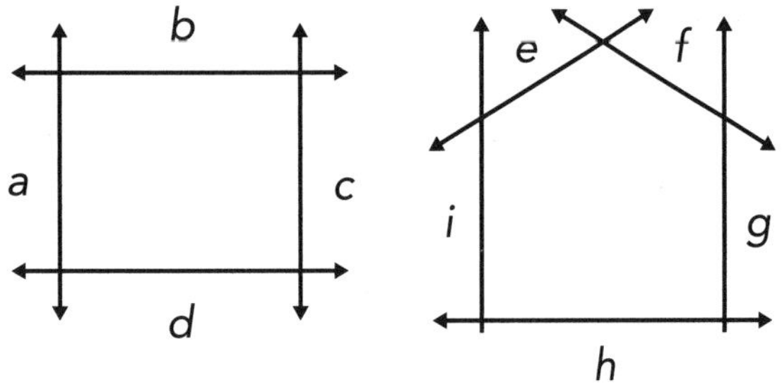

parallel lines
a, c

intersecting lines		
e, i		

Draw a snake to make a pair of lines as described. One snake is drawn for you.

11. parallel

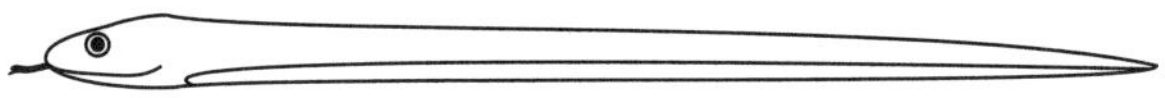

12. intersecting

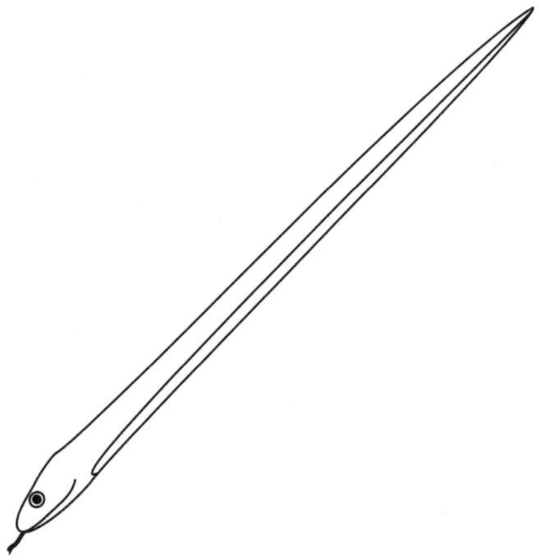

Name ____________________

Line segments on the ibex meet at points. They form angles.

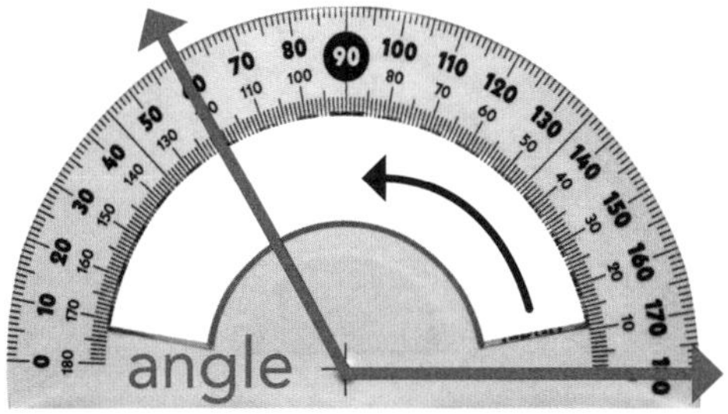

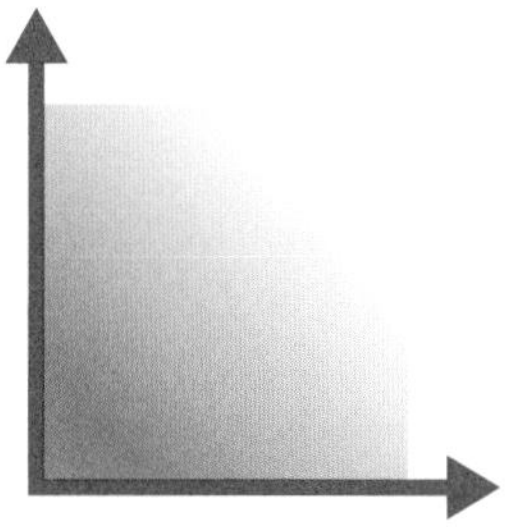

An angle that makes a square corner is a right angle. It measures 90°.

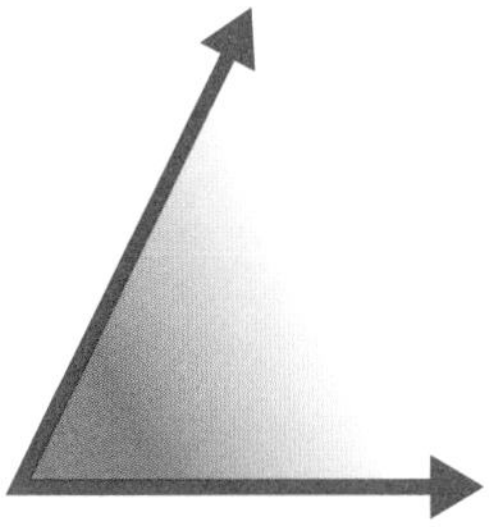

An angle that is narrower than a right angle is an acute angle. It measures less than 90°.

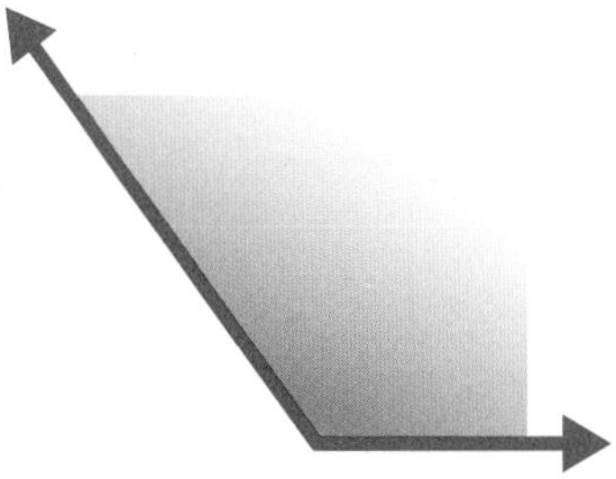

An angle that is wider than a right angle is an obtuse angle. It measures more than 90°.

Count the number of angles in each figure. Circle the right angles.

1. 

______

2. 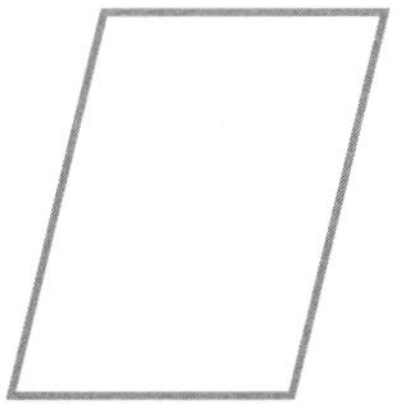

______

3. 

______

4. 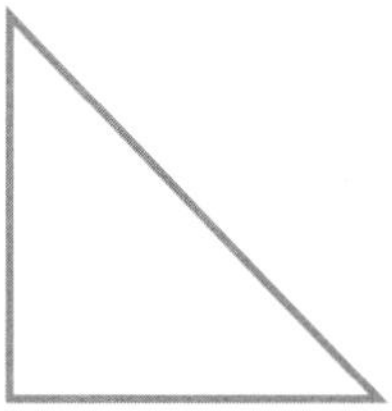

______

Identify the angles in each figure. Write **right**, **acute**, or **obtuse** on the line.

5. 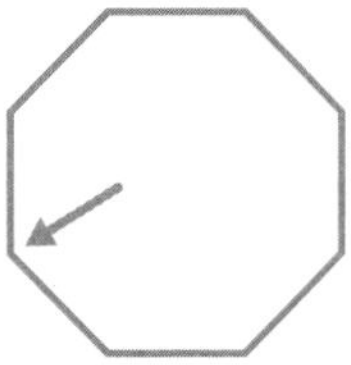

____

6. 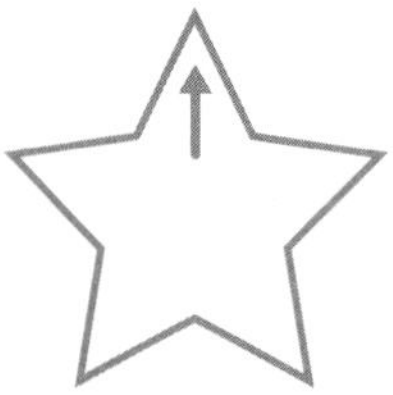

____

7. 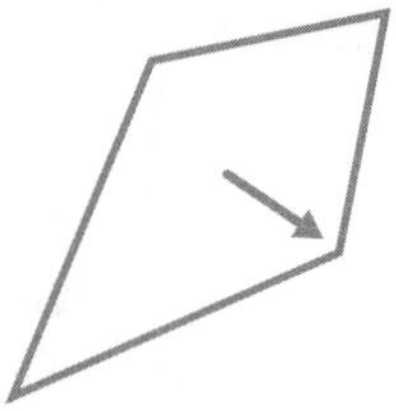

____

8. 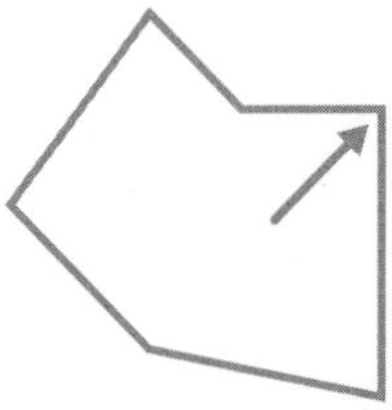

____

Circle the angles. Count the number of angles in each figure. You should find at least six in each figure.

9. 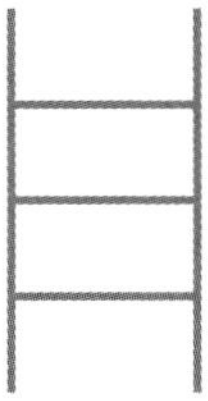

____

10. 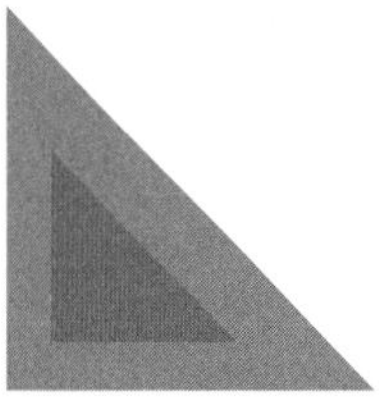

____

11. 

____

12. 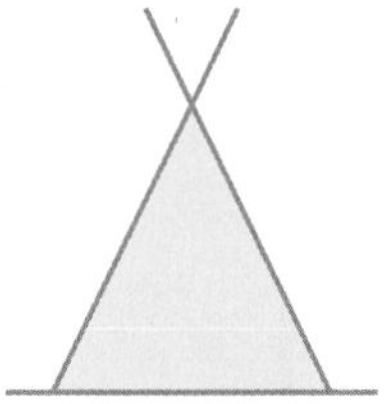

____

Connect the dots with your ruler to make two line segments that form an angle. Label the angle formed as **right**, **acute**, or **obtuse**.

13. 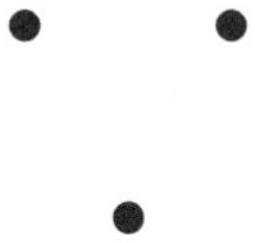

____

14. 

____

15. 

____

16. 

____

Review

Multiply or divide.

17. $\begin{array}{r} 238 \\ \times \quad 4 \\ \hline \end{array}$

18. $\begin{array}{r} 609 \\ \times \quad 8 \\ \hline \end{array}$

19. $8\overline{)296}$

20. $4\overline{)1,296}$

Name ______________________________

Plane Figures 8.4

square	rectangle	triangle	rhombus	circle
4 right angles 4 equal line segments	4 right angles 4 line segments	3 angles 3 line segments	4 angles 4 equal line segments	no angles no line segments

The shapes above are plane figures. They are flat, closed figures that begin and end at the same point. A closed figure with straight sides is a polygon. An open figure has both a starting and an ending point.

closed  open

Write the names of the plane figures you see in each picture. Put an X on each polygon.

1. ______________ 2. ______________ 3. ______________

Name two objects in your classroom that look like each figure.

4. square ______________ ______________

5. rectangle ______________ ______________

6. triangle ______________ ______________

7. circle ______________ ______________

8. **Count the shapes and write the numbers. Color according to the key.**

______ ■ red

______ ▬ black

______ ▲ blue

______ ● purple

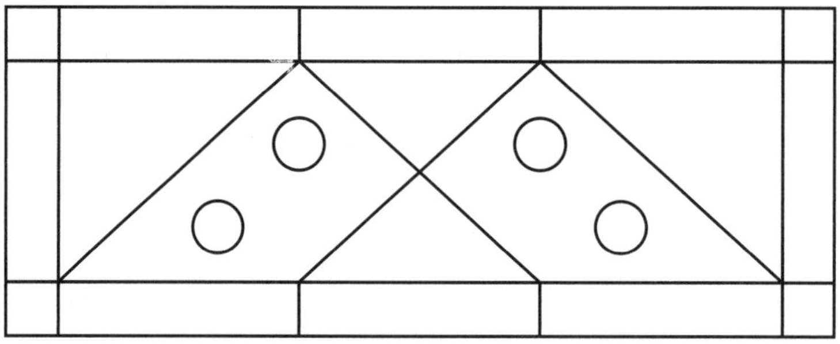

9. **Complete the table.**

figure	number of angles	number of line segments
square		
rectangle		
triangle		
circle		

10. **Use your ruler and these dots to draw the figures. Make two different sizes and shapes of each figure.**

triangle

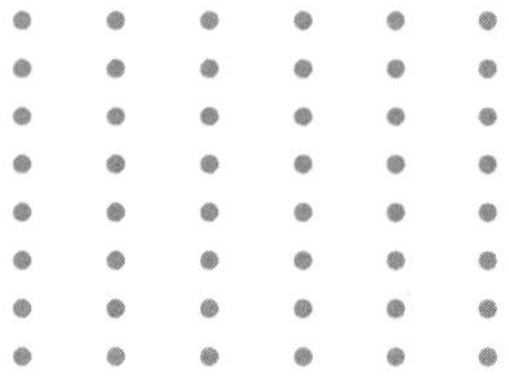

rectangle

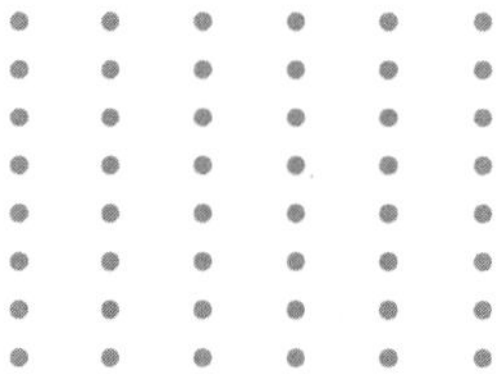

Review

Rewrite each group of numbers from least to greatest.

11. 642 981 723 249 ______ ______ ______ ______

12. 263 463 163 663 ______ ______ ______ ______

13. 584 583 586 585 ______ ______ ______ ______

14. 874 816 855 892 ______ ______ ______ ______

15. 461 429 416 492 ______ ______ ______ ______

Name ______________________________

Congruent Figures 8.5

These two triangles are the same shape and the same size. They are congruent.

The triangles can be turned in any direction. Turning will not change their size or shape.

Are these Lippizaner horses congruent?

______

Are these flags congruent?

______

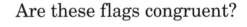

Write yes if the figures are congruent. Write no if they are not congruent.

1. 

______

2. 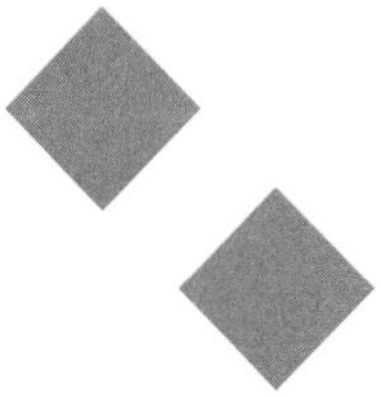

______

3. 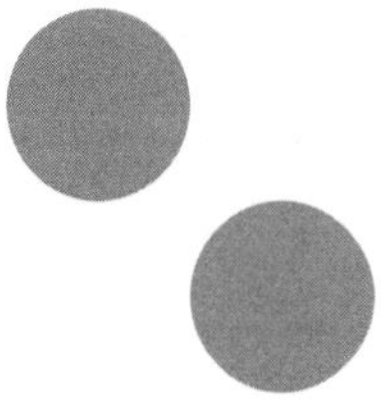

______

4. 

______

Write yes if the figures are always congruent. Write no if they are not.

5. two pine trees ______
6. two pages of this book ______
7. two mountain goats ______
8. two tulips ______
9. two third graders ______
10. two dimes ______

Write yes if the figures are congruent. Write no if they are not.

11.

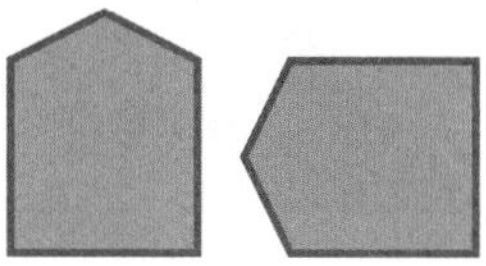

______

12.

______

13.

______

14.

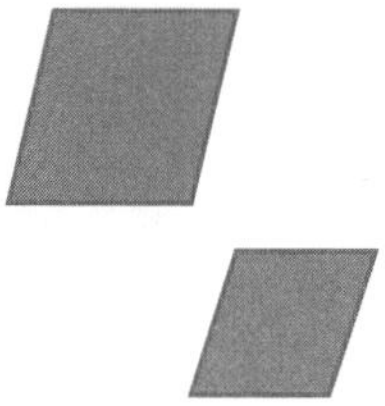

______

Circle the figure that is congruent to the example.

15.

16.

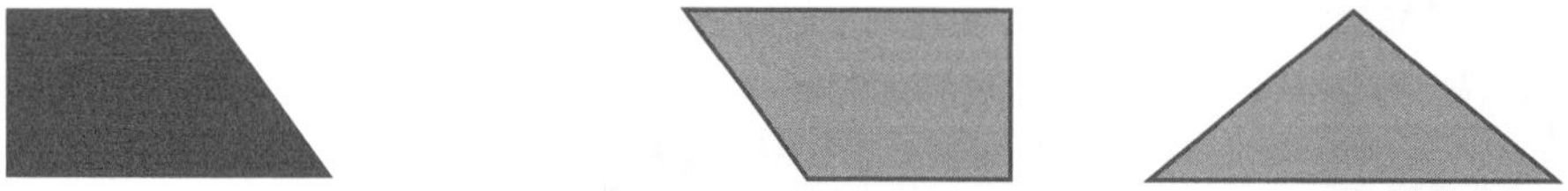

17.

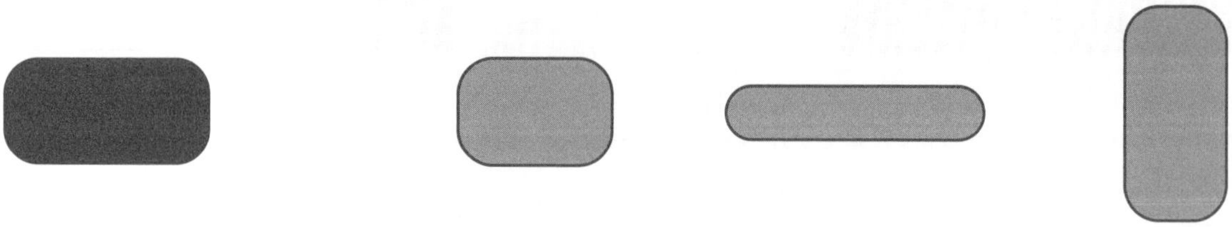

Draw a figure that is congruent to the example.

18.

19.

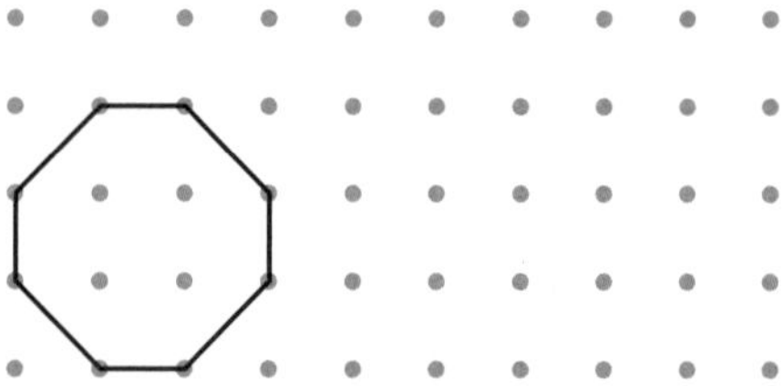

Name ____

A solid figure has height, length, and width. It takes up space.

A face is a flat surface of a solid figure.

An edge is a line segment where two faces meet.

A corner is the point where two edges meet.

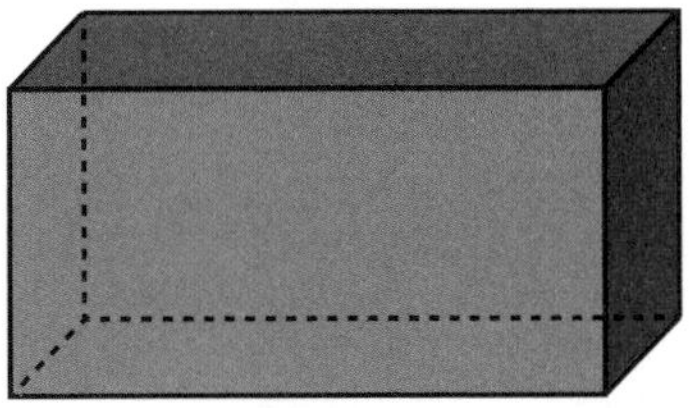
rectangular prism

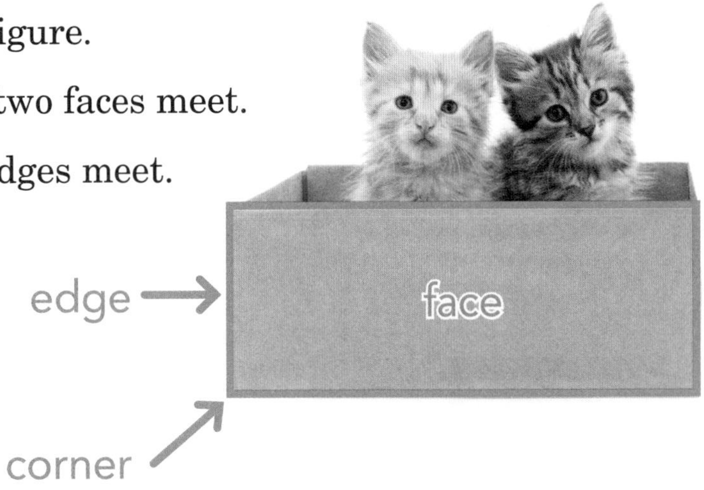

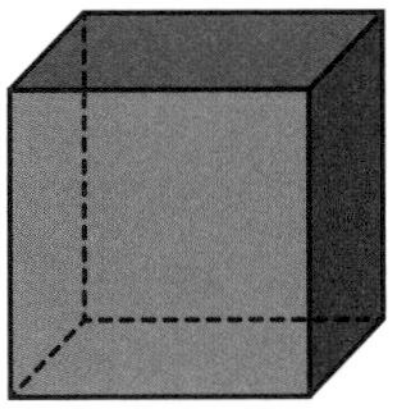
cube

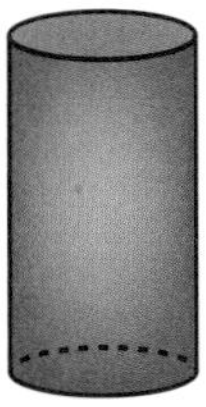
cylinder

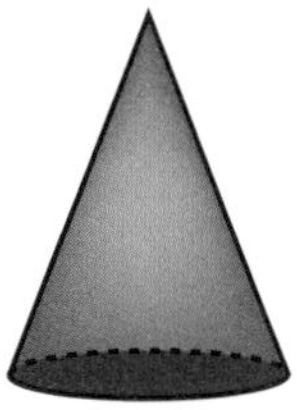
cone

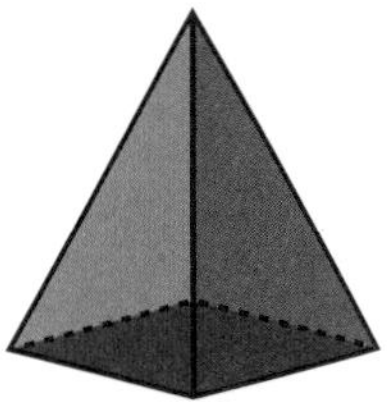
pyramid

sphere

Write the name of each solid figure below. Count and write the number of faces, edges, and corners for each figure.

		figure	faces	edges	corners
1.	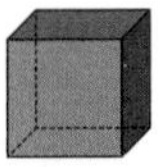				
2.	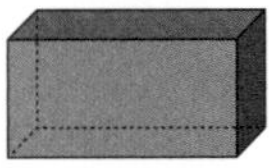				
3.					
4.					
5.	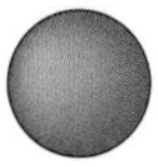				

Match each figure to the correct term.

6. ______ 

7. ______ 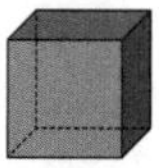

8. ______ 

9. ______ 

10. ______ 

a. cube

b. rectangular prism

c. cone

d. pyramid

e. sphere

Solve.

11. Sid twisted his puzzle cube until each side was a single color. He found that the cube had ______ faces. He multiplied to discover the number of color tiles on one face, ______ tiles. Then, he multiplied that number by the number of faces to discover how many color tiles were on his cube. He had ______ color tiles.

Review

Divide on a separate piece of paper. Check by multiplying.

12. $6\overline{)228}$

13. $8\overline{)652}$

14. $5\overline{)487}$

15. $9\overline{)783}$

16. $4\overline{)674}$

17. $2\overline{)975}$

Name ______________________________

Spatial Geometry 8.7

You can see geometric solids in many places.

pyramid

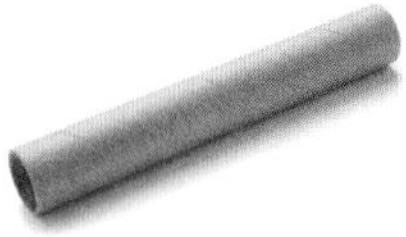

cylinder

rectangular prism

sphere

Write the letter of the correct name for each solid figure.

1. ______ 

2. ______ 

3. ______ 

4. ______ 

5. ______ 

6. ______ 

7. ______ 

8. ______ 

a. cube

b. rectangular prism

c. cone

d. pyramid

e. sphere

f. cylinder

Circle the two shapes that are combined to make the object.

9.

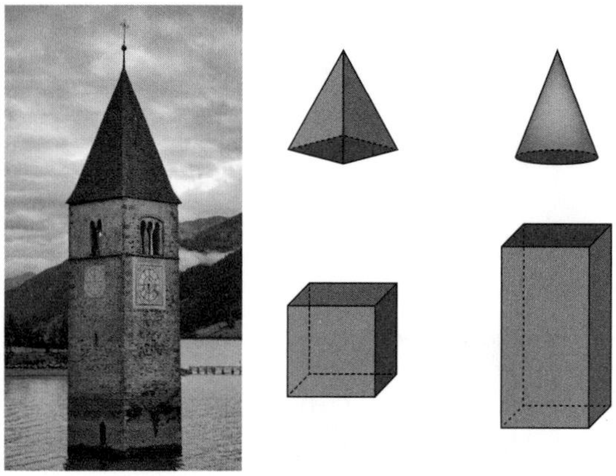

10.

Identify and label each shape.

Word Bank

cone	pyramid	square
sphere	rectangular prism	circle
cylinder	cube	rectangle

11.

12.

13.

Name ________________________________

Violet rode around the French marketplace. How far did she ride?

The distance around the sides of a figure is the perimeter.

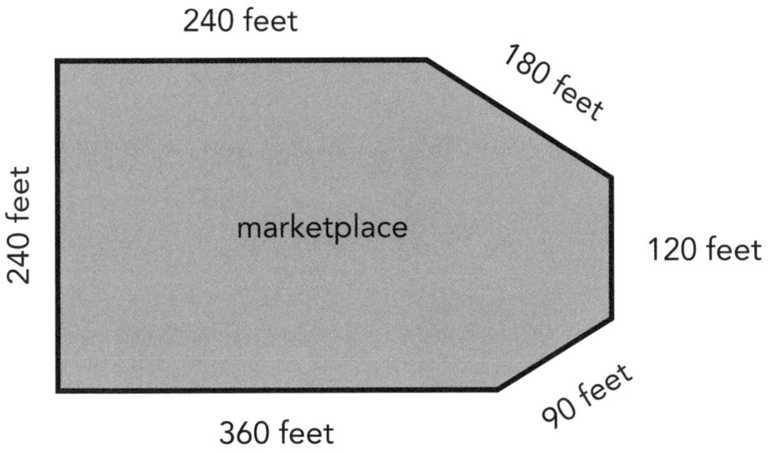

$$\begin{array}{r} 360 \text{ feet} \\ 90 \text{ feet} \\ 120 \text{ feet} \\ 180 \text{ feet} \\ 240 \text{ feet} \\ +\,240 \text{ feet} \\ \hline 1{,}230 \text{ feet} \end{array}$$

Violet rode 1,230 feet.

Shane rode a carriage around the town square. How far was that ride?

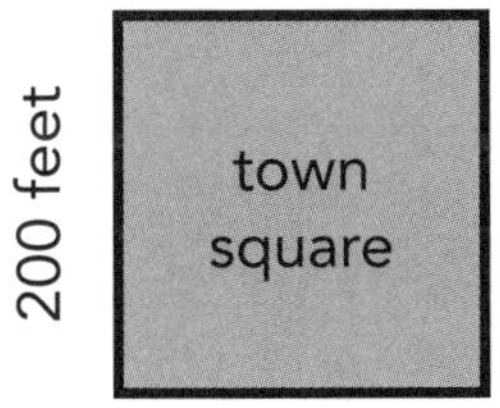

$$\begin{array}{r} 200 \text{ feet} \\ \times\quad 4 \text{ feet} \\ \hline 800 \text{ feet} \end{array}$$

Shane rode 800 feet.

Calculate the perimeter of each figure. All measurements are in inches.

1.
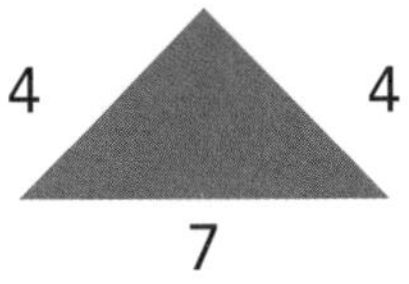

______ inches

2.

All sides are the same.

______ inches

3.

______ inches

4.
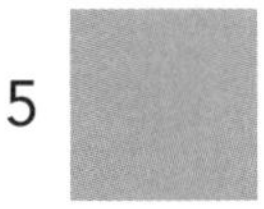

______ inches

Add to find the perimeter of each figure in inches.

5.
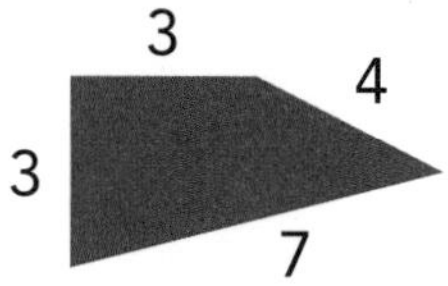

_____ inches

6.

All sides are the same.

_____ inches

7.
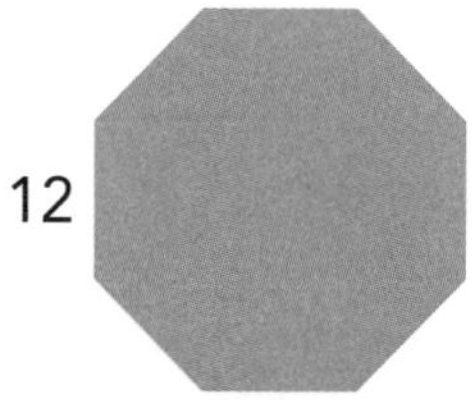

All sides are the same.

_____ inches

8.
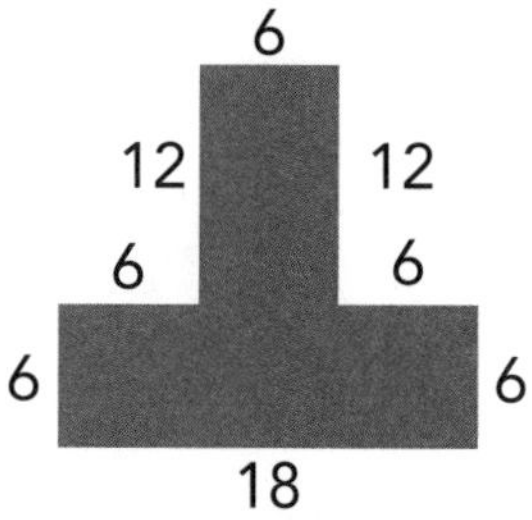

_____ inches

Find the perimeter of each square or rectangle in centimeters.

9.
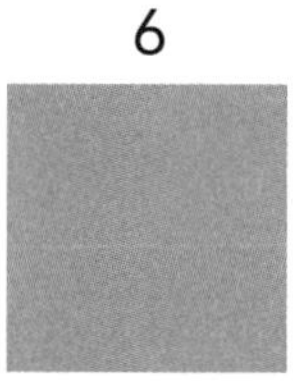

_____

11.
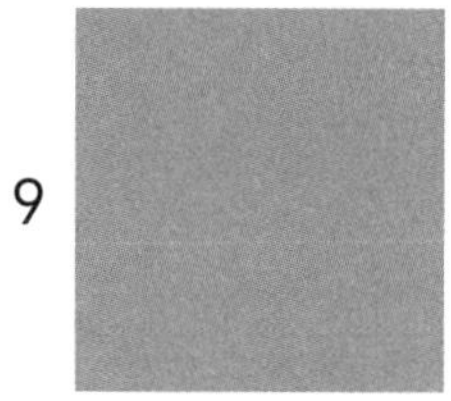

_____

13.
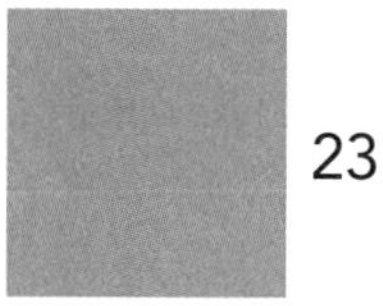

_____

15.

_____

10.
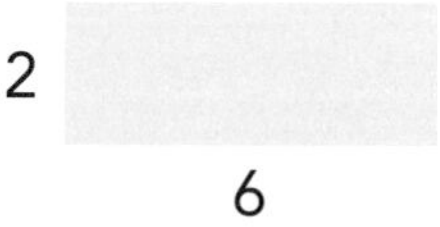

_____

12.
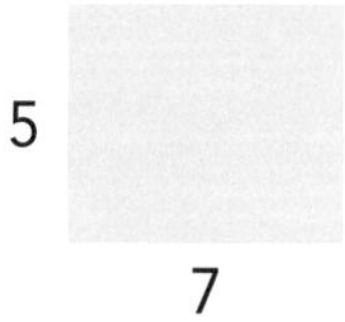

_____

14.

_____

16.

_____

Solve.

17. A hiker in the Swiss mountains was lost. A UAV (Unmanned Aerial Vehicle) was sent to find him. It flew around a square-shaped area with each side measuring 5 km and found the lost hiker. How many kilometers did the UAV fly?

_____

18. Draw a Bible with a perimeter of 20 units. Label the length of each side.

Name ______________________________

Area 8.9

Third graders learned about the animals of Europe. They made pictures of the animals.

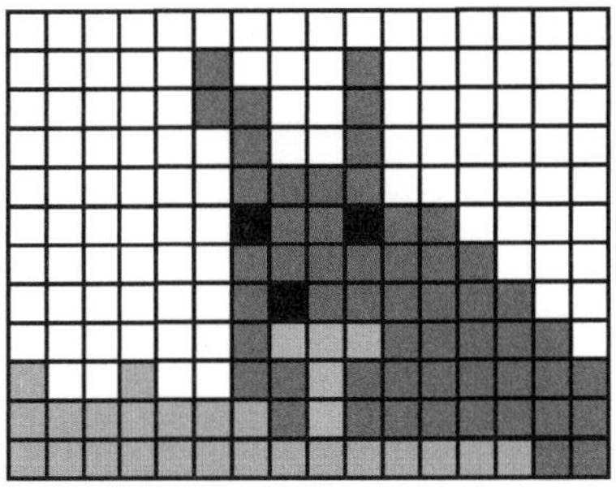

Area is the number of square units needed to cover the surface of a figure. What is the area of the squirrel's body in the picture? Count the squares.

The squirrel is 62 square units.

The area of this rectangle is 8 square units.

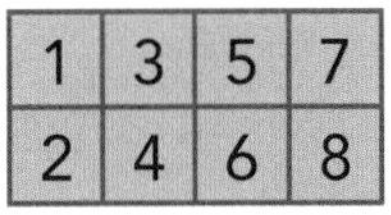

The area of this figure is also 8 square units.

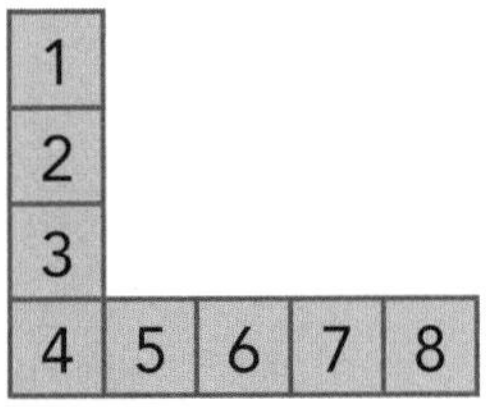

Count the full squares first. Count 2 triangles as one full square. The area is 7 square units.

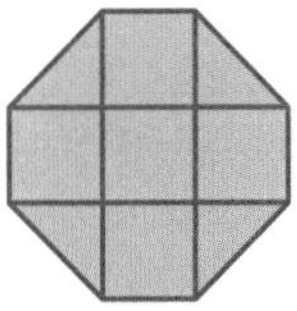

Write the area of each figure.

1. 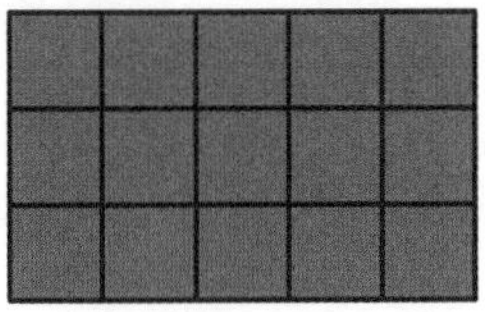

_____ square units

2. 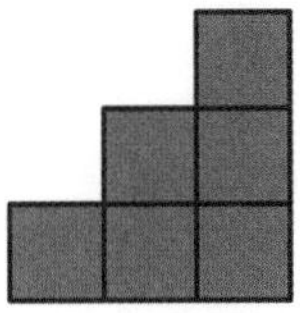

_____ square units

3. 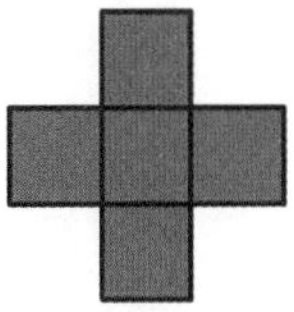

_____ square units

4. 

_____ square units

Use your ruler to draw the lines to make square units. Write the area.

5. 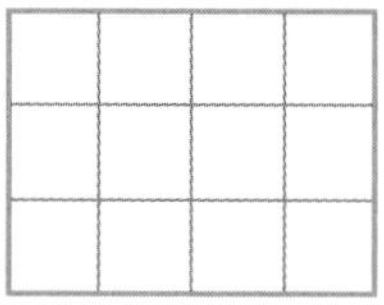
______

6. 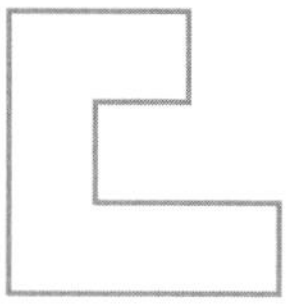
______

7. 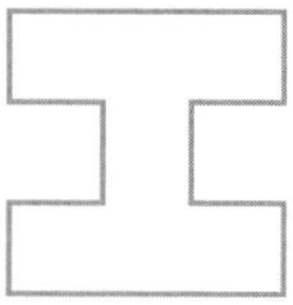
______

8. 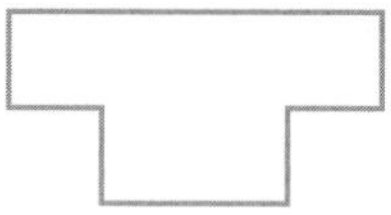
______

Use multiplication to find the area. Write the multiplication fact.

9. 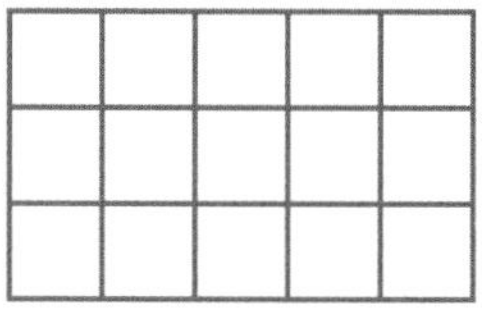
______
______

10. 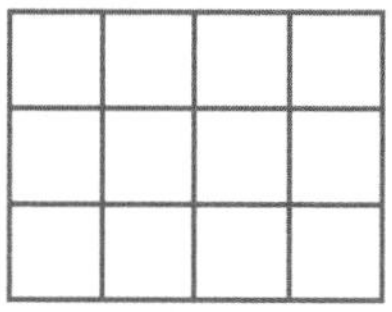
______
______

11. 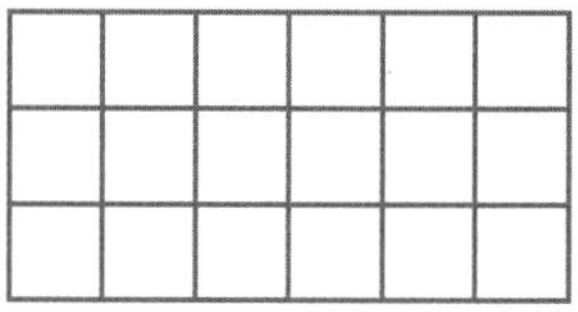
______
______

Outline the shape of each animal on the grid. Count the squares to find the area.

12. 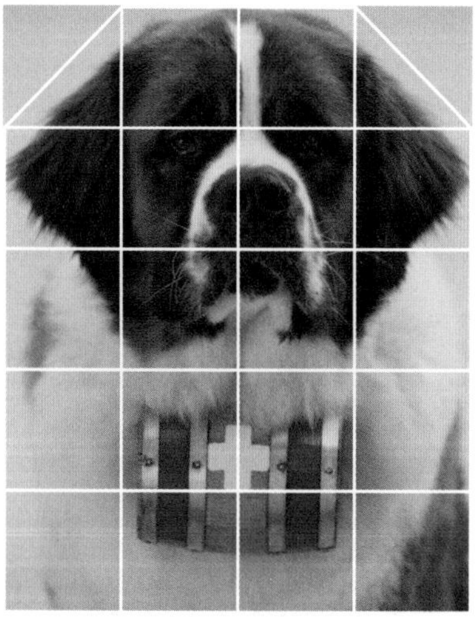
______

______

Review

Multiply, then add.

13. (6 × 7) + 3 = ______

14. (4 × 3) + 8 = ______

15. (2 x 4) + 9 = ______

16. (4 x 5) + 7 = ______

Name ______________________

Transformations 8.10

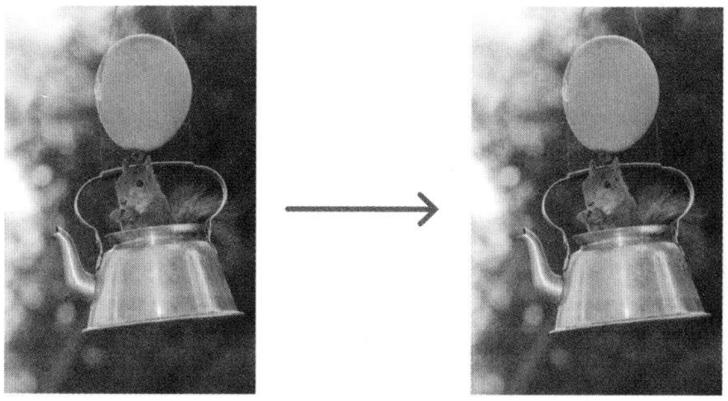

A slide (translation) occurs when a figure is moved in any direction in a straight line.

A flip (reflection) occurs when a figure is flipped or turned over.

A turn (rotation) occurs when a figure is rotated around a point.

Label each pattern slide, flip, or turn. Draw 1 figure in each box to complete the pattern.

1. ______________________

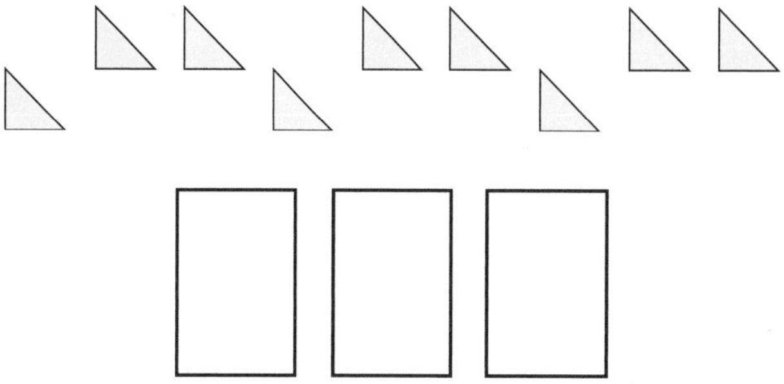

2. ______________________

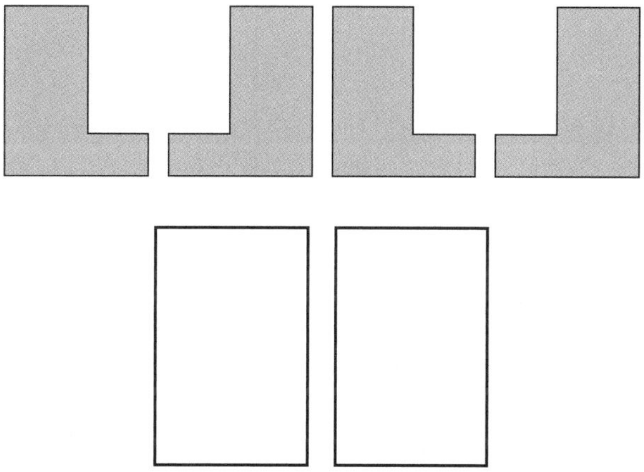

3. ______________________

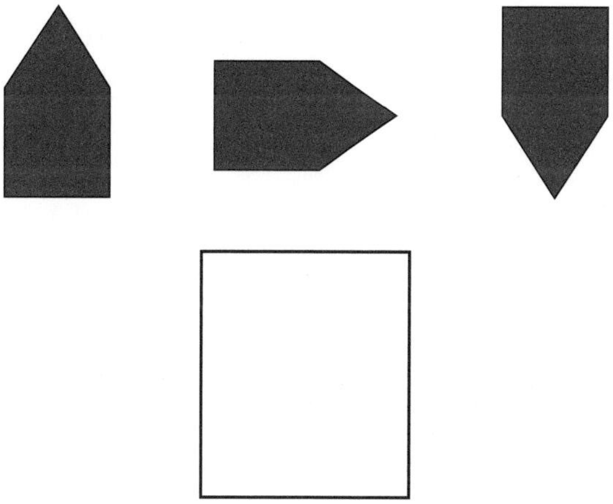

Color or draw to complete the pattern of each quilt square.

4. slide

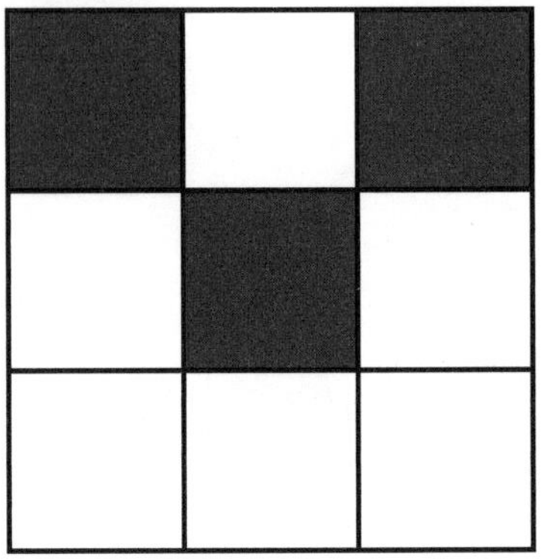

5. flip

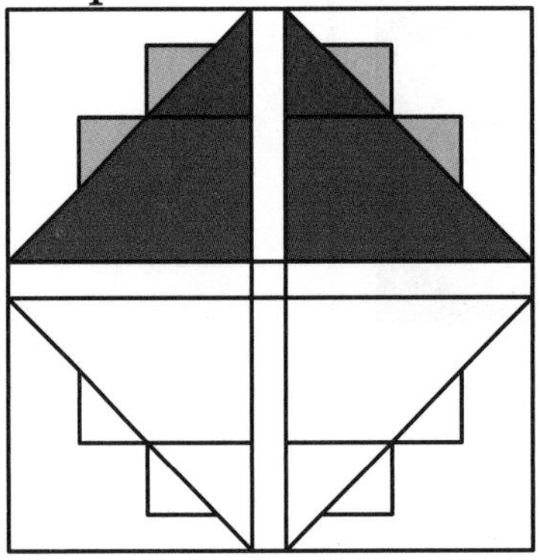

6. turn

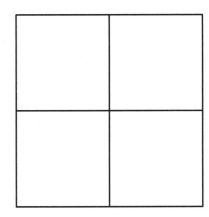

You will need a cozy quilt to stay warm in the Swiss Alps. Choose a shape you like, draw your shape on a piece of paper, and cut it out. Slide, flip, and turn the design to make three quilt squares.

7. slide

8. flip

9. turn

Review

Subtract to show the change given.

10. $\begin{array}{r} \$4.00 \\ -\ 1.65 \\ \hline \end{array}$

11. $\begin{array}{r} \$6.00 \\ -\ 1.87 \\ \hline \end{array}$

12. $\begin{array}{r} \$10.00 \\ -\ 3.99 \\ \hline \end{array}$

13. $\begin{array}{r} \$12.00 \\ -\ 8.55 \\ \hline \end{array}$

Mentally add eight to each number.

14. 26 ______

16. 62 ______

18. 58 ______

15. 45 ______

17. 19 ______

19. 73 ______

Name ______________________________

Lines of Symmetry 8.11

A line of symmetry divides a figure into two matching halves. If each hedgehog picture were folded in half, only one would be symmetrical.

symmetrical

not symmetrical

Some objects have more than one line of symmetry.

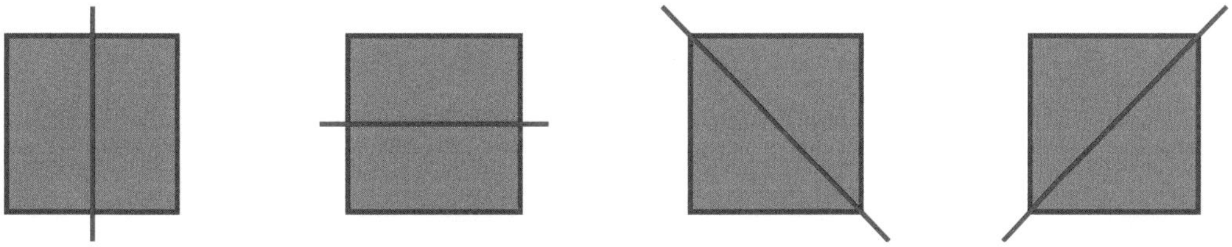

Write yes if the shape is symmetrical. Draw the line of symmetry. Write no if it is not.

1. 

____

3. 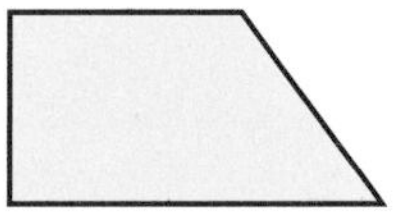

____

5. 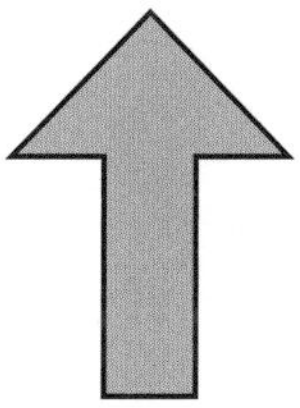

____

2. 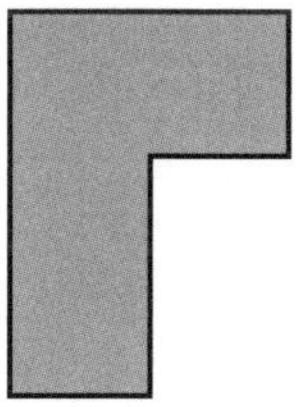

____

4. 

____

6. 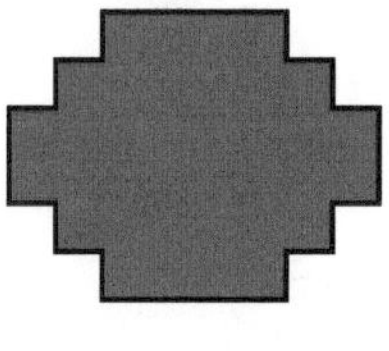

____

Write **yes** if the line is a line of symmetry. Write **no** if it is not symmetrical.

7.  __________

8. 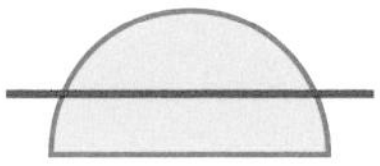 __________

9. 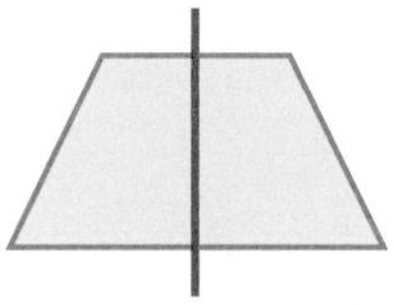 __________

10. 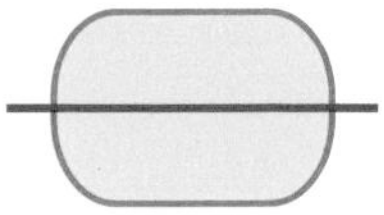 __________

Draw a line of symmetry for each of these pictures.

11. 

12. 

13. 

14. 

Draw the lines of symmetry in each figure. Write the number of lines of symmetry.

15.  __________

17. 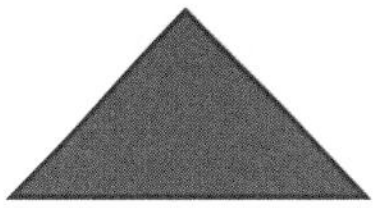 __________

19. 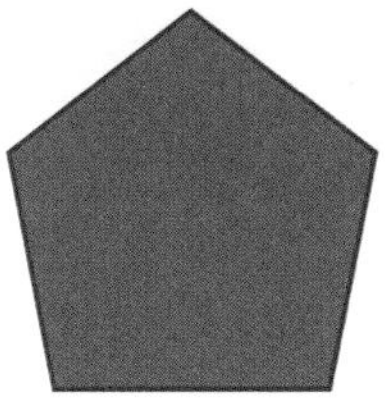 __________

21. 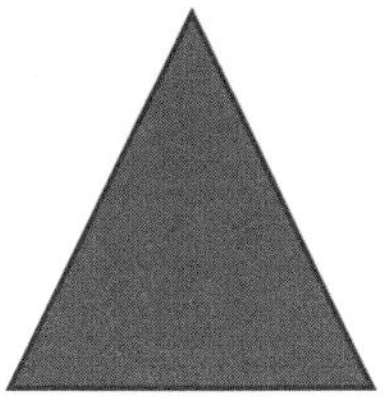 __________

16.  __________

18.  __________

20.  __________

22. 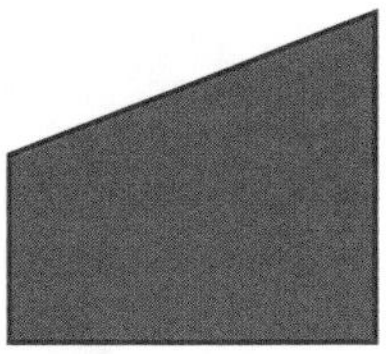 __________

Review

Copy the problems onto another piece of paper. Divide. Check by multiplying.

23. $6\overline{)453}$

24. $7\overline{)686}$

25. $8\overline{)304}$

26. $9\overline{)621}$

Name ____________________

Geometric shapes and concepts are everywhere!

Draw lines to match each picture with the geometric concepts. Some pictures match more than one concept.

1. 

2. 

3. 

4. 

intersecting lines

congruent shapes

acute angles

symmetry

5. Draw a line to an example of each geometric concept.

a. line segment

b. right angle

c. circle

d. symmetry

e. parallel lines

f. intersecting lines

g. congruent figures

h. rectangle

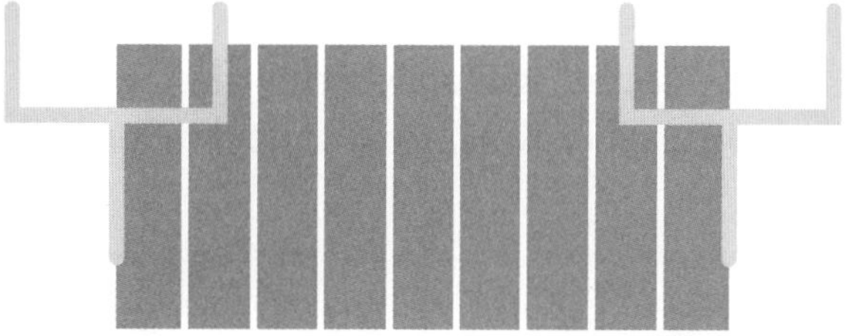

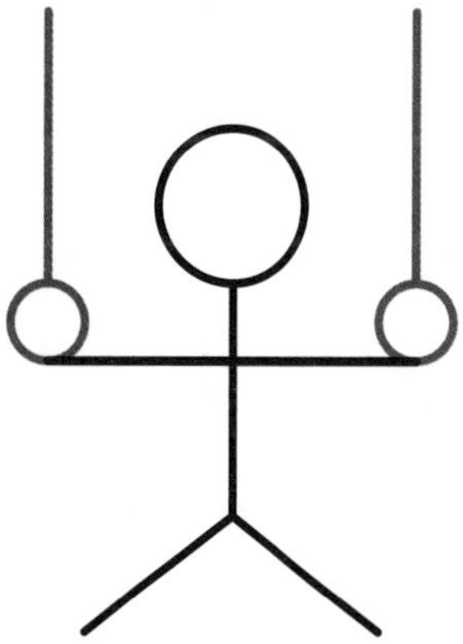

6. Design a picture using only line segments and basic plane figures, such as circles, squares, triangles, and rectangles. Write a sentence to describe your picture.

sample

____

____

7. Use a **red** crayon to circle five line segments. Use a **blue** crayon to circle five plane figures (circles, squares, triangles, or rectangles). Use a **green** crayon to outline five solid figures (cubes, prisms, cylinders, cones, pyramids, or spheres).

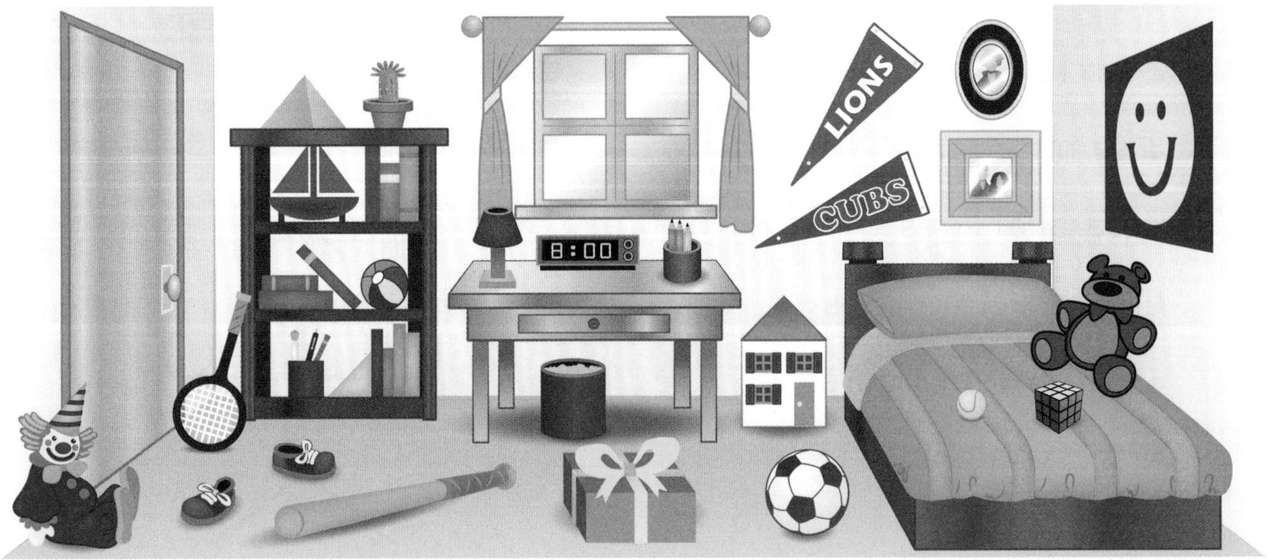

Name ______________________________

Locate Ordered Pairs 8.13

This grid contains colored shapes. Each shape has its own location. An ordered pair is a combination of two numbers that can be used to find a specific point on a grid or map. Ordered pairs are also called coordinates.

The first number tells how many spaces to go to the right. The second number tells how many spaces to go up.

The  is at (5, 1). Start at 0. Move 5 spaces to the right. Move up 1 space.

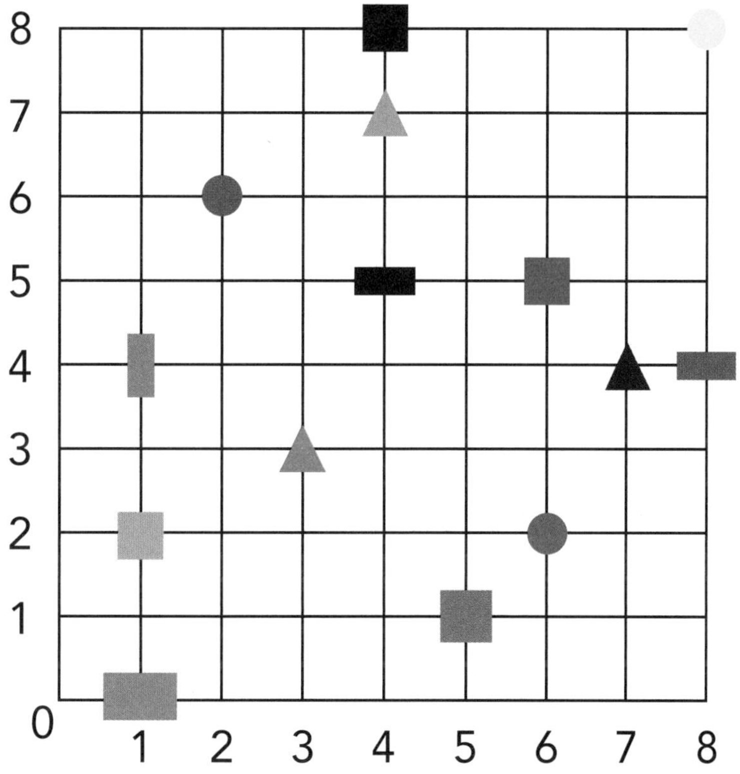

Draw and color the shape for each ordered pair.

1. (3, 3) ______ 3. (8, 8) ______ 5. (6, 5) ______ 7. (5, 1) ______

2. (8, 4) ______ 4. (4, 7) ______ 6. (1, 4) ______ 8. (1, 0) ______

Write the ordered pair for each shape.

9.  ______ 11.  ______ 13.  ______

10.  ______ 12.  ______ 14.  ______

Write a number from the grid to match each ordered pair. Solve.

15. _______ × _______ = _______
(7, 4) (3, 4)

16. _______ + _______ = _______
(1, 5) (6, 7)

17. _______ ÷ _______ = _______
(7, 1) (2, 1)

18. _______ − _______ = _______
(4, 2) (1, 3)

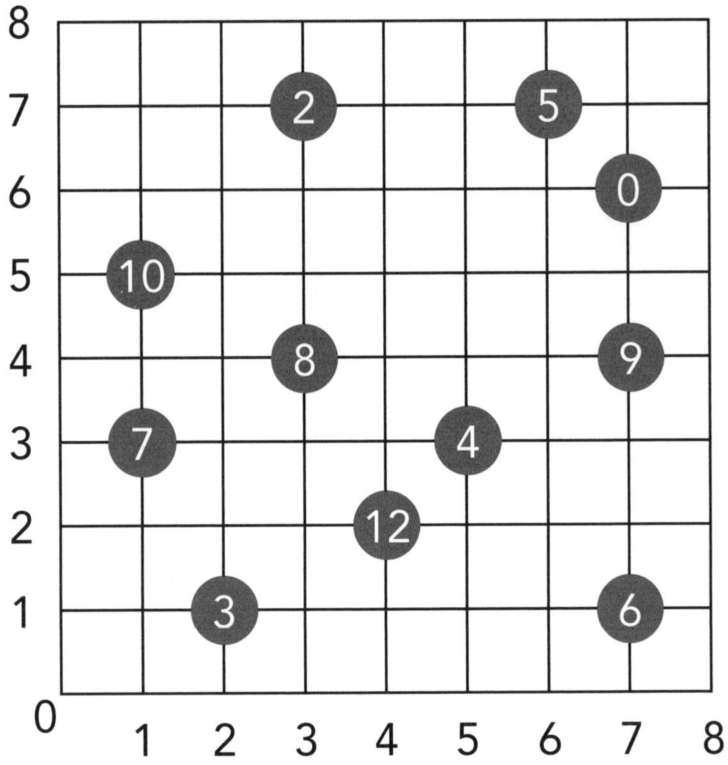

Make a point for each ordered pair. Connect the points using line segments.

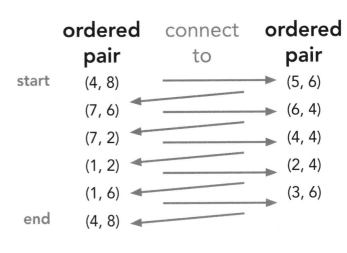

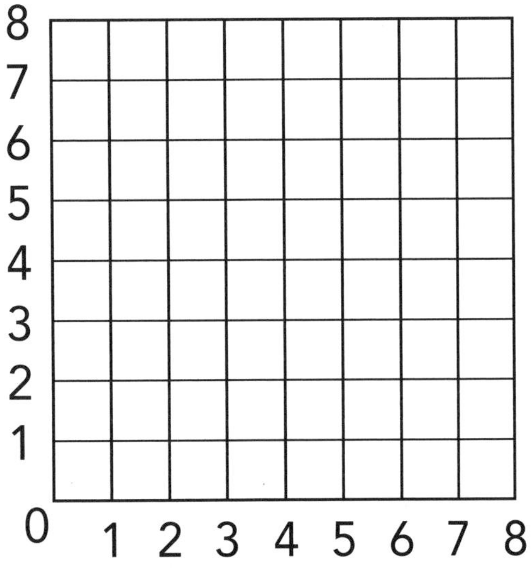

	ordered pair	connect to	ordered pair
start	(4, 8)	→	(5, 6)
	(7, 6)	← →	(6, 4)
	(7, 2)	← →	(4, 4)
	(1, 2)	← →	(2, 4)
	(1, 6)	← →	(3, 6)
end	(4, 8)	←	

19. What do you see? _______________

Review

Multiply.

20. 386 × 7

21. 813 × 5

22. 499 × 6

23. 702 × 9

24. 685 × 8

Name ____________________

Mapping Coordinates 8.14

Maps show locations. This map shows places and things in a village in Europe. Ordered pairs (coordinates) are used to locate things on a map. What is located at (3, 4)? Start at 0. Go 3 spaces to the right. Then, go up 4 spaces. The statue is at (3, 4).

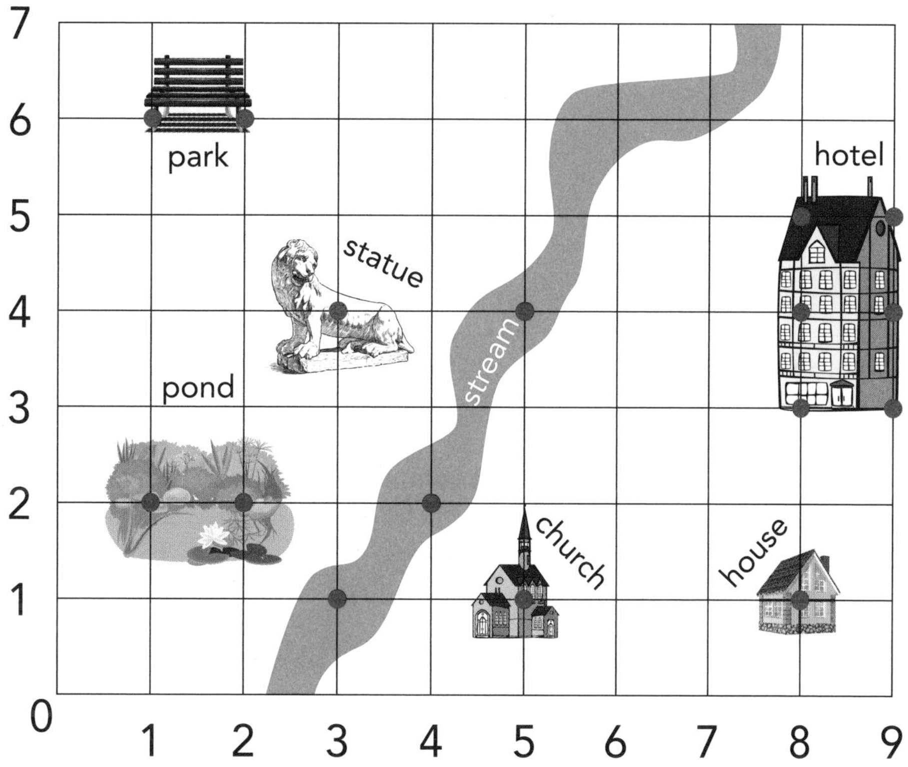

Use the map to answer.

1. What is at (5, 1)? ____________________

2. What is at (1, 2)? ____________________

3. Which two places have coordinates that begin (8, _)?

____

4. List two coordinates for points in the park. ____________ and ____________

5. List three ordered pairs for points in the stream.

____________, ____________, and ____________

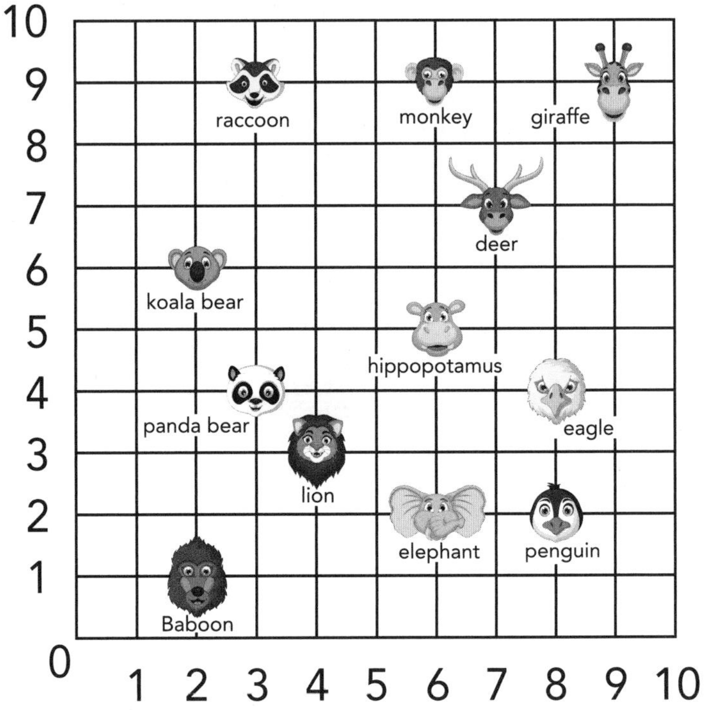

Name the animal found at each ordered pair on the zoo map.

6. (2, 6) ________________

7. (8, 4) ________________

8. (4, 3) ________________

9. (3, 9) ________________

10. (7, 7) ________________

11. (9, 9) ________________

Write the ordered pair for each animal.

12.  ____________

13.  ____________

14.  ____________

15.  ____________

16.  ____________

17.  ____________

Solve.

18. What is the perimeter of the zoo in units?

______ units

19. What is the area of the zoo in square units?

______ square units

Review

Write < or > to compare the numbers.

20. 1,065 ◯ 1,056

21. 4,989 ◯ 4,889

22. 7,234 ◯ 8,233

Name ______________________________

Make Predictions 8.15

A mountain lake has sturgeon, salmon, and trout. If Stefan catches a fish, predict which type it is most likely to be.

sturgeon salmon trout

You can use probability to predict an outcome.

The ______________ is most likely to be caught because there are more ______________ than ______________ or ______________.

Write the number of each type of fish out of the total number of fish.

1. The sturgeon are ______ out of ______.

2. The salmon are ______ out of ______.

3. The trout are ______ out of ______.

Pretend that you will spin this spinner. Answer the questions.

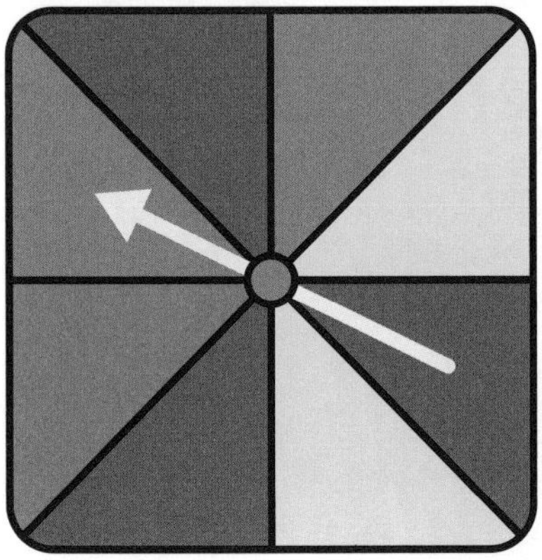

4. List the colors of each possible outcome.

____

____

____

____

5. Predict the most probable outcome. _______________

6. Which outcomes are equal in probability?

____

Write the answer about each color of fishing lure. Write the color of lure that you predict will be chosen.

7. white

_____ out of _____ _______________

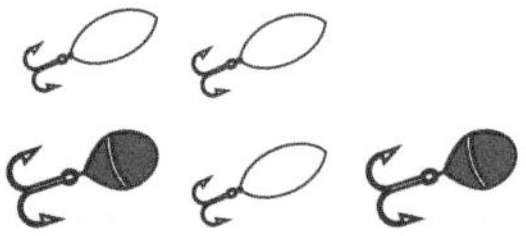

8. white

_____ out of _____ _______________

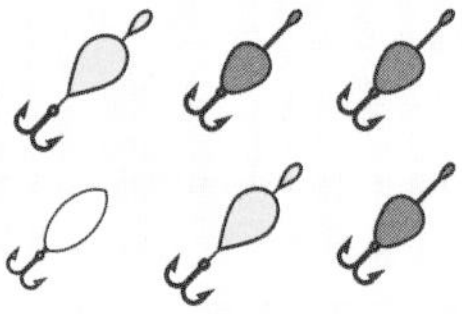

9. green

_____ out of _____ _______________

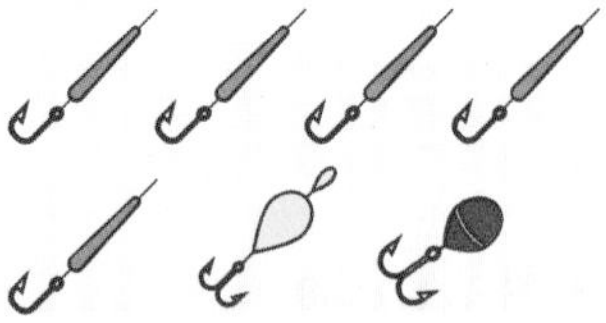

10. orange

_____ out of _____ _______________

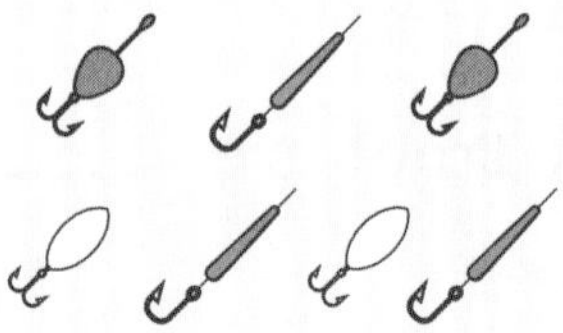

Name ______________________________

Circle the line. Make an **X** on the line segment.

1. 

2. 

Label each angle as **right, obtuse,** or **acute.**

3. 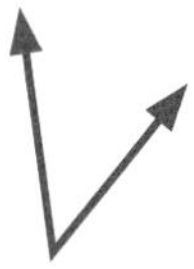
____

4. 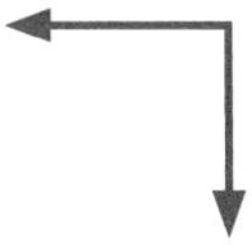
____

5. 
____

6. 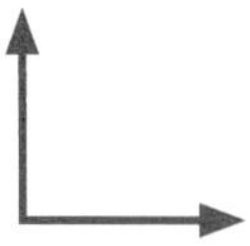
____

Count the number of line segments.

7. 
______

8. 
______

9. 
______

10. 
______

11. 
______

12. Complete the chart.

solid figure	faces	edges	corners
cone			
pyramid			
cube			
sphere			

Is the figure symmetrical? Write **yes** or **no.**
If you wrote yes, draw a line of symmetry.

13.  ______

14.  ______

15. 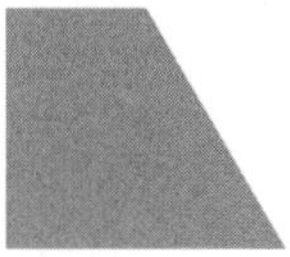 ______

16. ______

Solve.

17. perimeter

______ inches

18. area

______ square inches

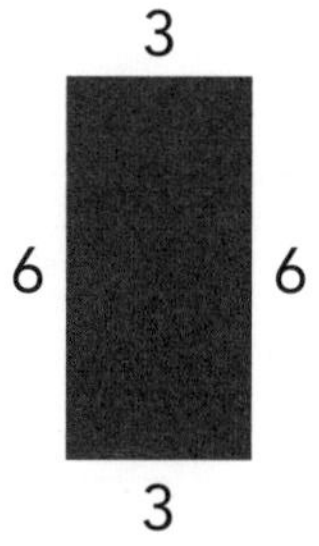

Circle the parallel lines. Make an X on the intersecting lines.

19. 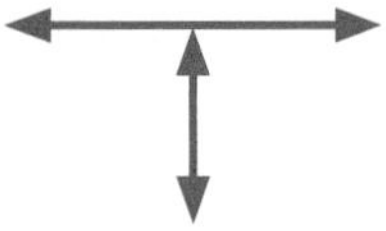

20. 

21. 

22. 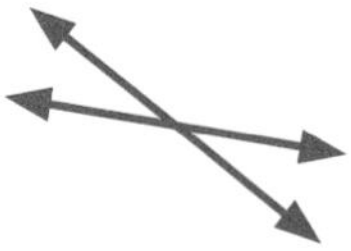

Predict the color most likely to be chosen. Write the answer. Circle the congruent figures.

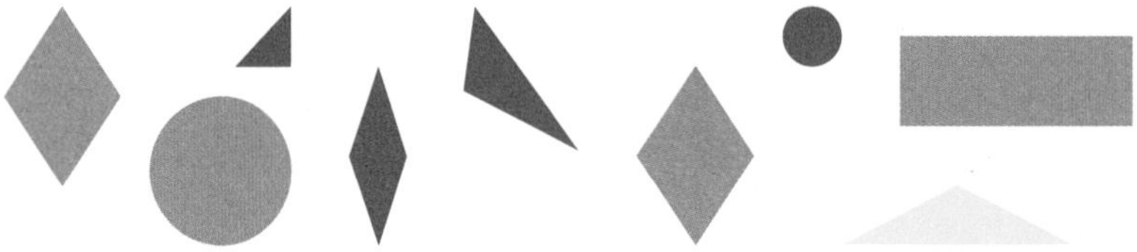

23. I predict ____________ because there are _______ out of _______ shapes.

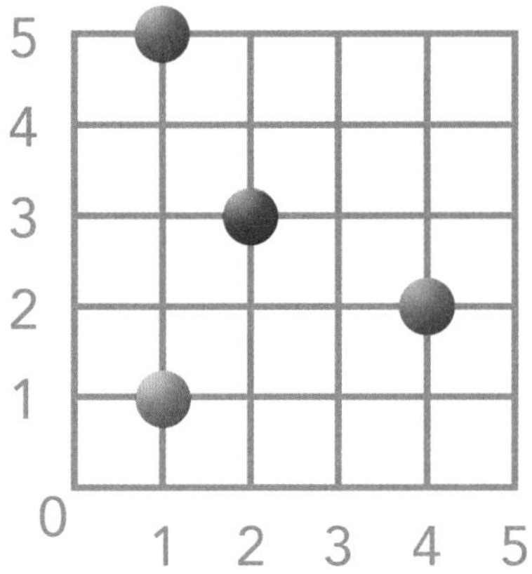

Write the color for each ordered pair.

24. (2, 3) _______

25. (1, 5) _______

Write the ordered pair.

26.  _______

27.  _______

Look at the transformation of the first shape. Label each as **slide**, **flip**, or **turn**.

28. 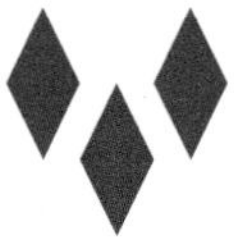
____

29. 
____

30. 
____

31. 
____

Label the cube **a**, the rectangular prism **b**, the sphere **c**, the cone **d**, and the pyramid **e**.

32. 
____

33. 
____

34. 
____

35. 
____

36. 
____

Chapter 9
Measurement

Christ … gave the apostles, the prophets, the evangelists, the pastors and teachers, to equip His people … until we all reach unity in the faith … and become mature, attaining to the whole measure of the fullness of Christ.

Ephesians 4:11–13

Key Ideas:

Measurement: customary length, capacity, and weight

Measurement: metric length, capacity, and weight

Measurement: customary and metric temperature

Name ____________________

Length: Nonstandard Units 9.1

Can you imagine measuring without measuring tools? How would you describe the distance from your home to school without mentioning miles or kilometers? How could anyone be sure that the length of one soccer field was the same as another? What might happen if the height of a basketball net on one side of the court was lower than the net on the other side?

Over the years, many people have worked to standardize the systems of measurements that you use today.

Use the objects listed to measure the feather. Then, answer the questions.

1. The feather is _____ paper clips long.
2. The feather is _____ crayons long.
3. The feather is _____ unit cubes long
4. The feather is _____ erasers long.
5. The feather is _____ pennies long.
6. Which object is the easiest to use?

   ____

7. Which object was closest to the actual size of the feather?

   ____

8. Why do people use standard units to measure things instead of using everyday objects?

   ____

Work with a partner. Measure each object using the width of your index finger. Estimate the length to the nearest number. Your partner will do the same. Complete the chart.

	object	my answer	________'s answer
9.	ladybug		
10.	worm		
11.	grasshopper		

Use a small paper clip to measure each ribbon.

12.  ______ paper clips long

13.  ______ paper clips long

14.  about ______ paper clips long

Review

15. Divide.

$7\overline{)56}$	$5\overline{)45}$	$9\overline{)27}$	$6\overline{)42}$	$4\overline{)32}$
$9\overline{)63}$	$3\overline{)12}$	$8\overline{)40}$	$7\overline{)49}$	$5\overline{)30}$
$4\overline{)36}$	$9\overline{)54}$	$6\overline{)48}$	$3\overline{)21}$	$2\overline{)18}$

Name ______________________________

Length: Inches and Feet 9.2

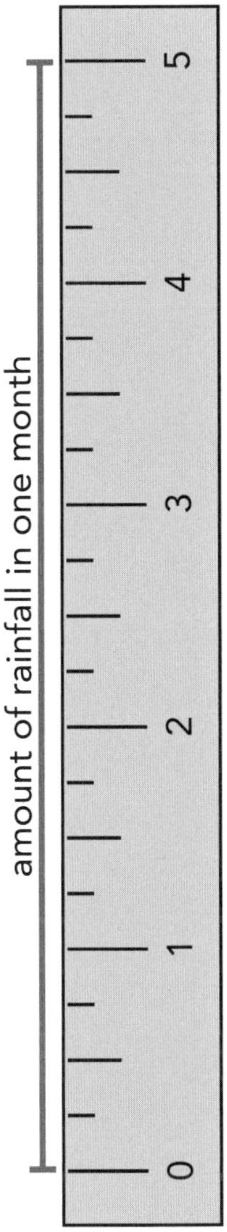

A South American rain forest can average 5 inches of rainfall every month of the year. Rainfall totals are often more than 60 inches, or 5 feet, of rain in just one year!

This ruler shows inches (in.). Inches are units of measurement in the customary system, which is used mostly in the United States. There are 12 inches in 1 foot (ft).

A paper clip is about an inch long.

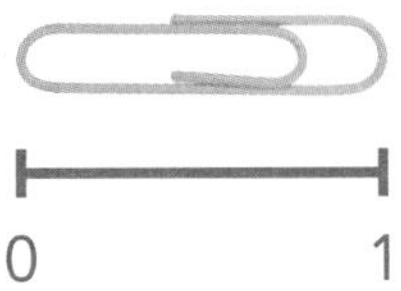

A football is about a foot long.

Which unit would you use to measure each of the following items? Write inch or foot.

1. the length of a dining table ______________________
2. the length of your toothbrush ______________________
3. the length of a piece of notebook paper ______________________
4. the length of a flashlight ______________________
5. the length of your bedroom ______________________
6. the length of your desk at school ______________________

Fill in the circle in front of the better estimate.

7. A teacher is ______ tall.
   ○ 5 feet ○ 45 inches

8. A hairbrush is ______ long.
   ○ 1 foot ○ 7 inches

9. A dictionary is ______ thick.
   ○ 1 foot ○ 4 inches

10. A computer mouse is ______ long.
    ○ 2 feet ○ 4 inches

11. A jump rope is ______ long.
    ○ 6 feet ○ 6 inches

12. A pine tree is ______ high.
    ○ 120 inches ○ 30 feet

Complete the chart. Look indoors and outdoors to find objects that fit each description.

		indoors	outdoors
13.	1–6 in. long		
14.	6–12 in. long		
15.	1–3 ft long		

Complete each conversion.

16. 2 ft = ______ in.
17. 8 ft = ______ in.
18. 7 ft = ______ in.
19. 5 ft = ______ in.
20. 3 ft = ______ in.
21. 9 ft = ______ in.

Solve.

22. A biologist used a rain gauge to measure rainfall in a habitat. In May, June, and July he reported a combined total of 15 in. of rain. How many feet and inches are there in 15 in.?

______

Review

23. **Multiply.**

$\begin{array}{r} 85 \\ \times\ 6 \\ \hline \end{array}$ $\begin{array}{r} 92 \\ \times\ 9 \\ \hline \end{array}$ $\begin{array}{r} 52 \\ \times\ 8 \\ \hline \end{array}$ $\begin{array}{r} 468 \\ \times\ 4 \\ \hline \end{array}$ $\begin{array}{r} 609 \\ \times\ 7 \\ \hline \end{array}$ $\begin{array}{r} 894 \\ \times\ 3 \\ \hline \end{array}$

Name ____________________

Length: Nearest Inch or Half Inch

Red-eyed tree frogs live in the rain forests of Central and South America. The damp air keeps the frogs' skin moist. Tree frogs eat flies, crickets, and moths.

The red-eyed tree frog is about 3 inches long.

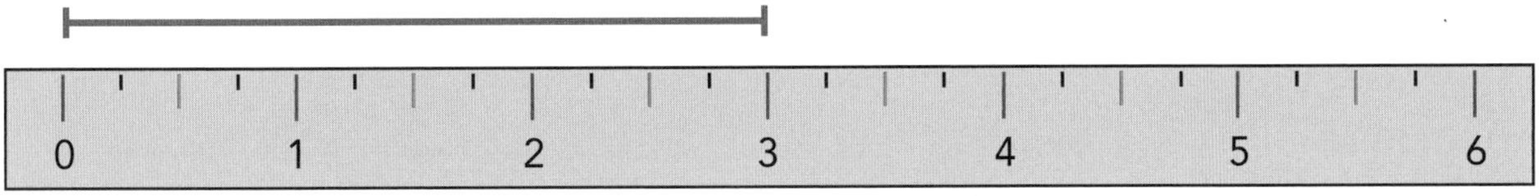

An inch is the distance from one numbered line to the next. One half inch is half this distance. Half inches are marked with lines that are almost as long as inch markings and are marked in blue on these rulers.

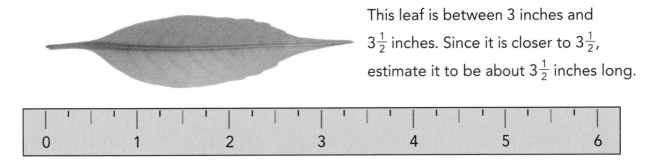

This leaf is between 3 inches and $3\frac{1}{2}$ inches. Since it is closer to $3\frac{1}{2}$, estimate it to be about $3\frac{1}{2}$ inches long.

Measure each pencil to the nearest half inch.

1. 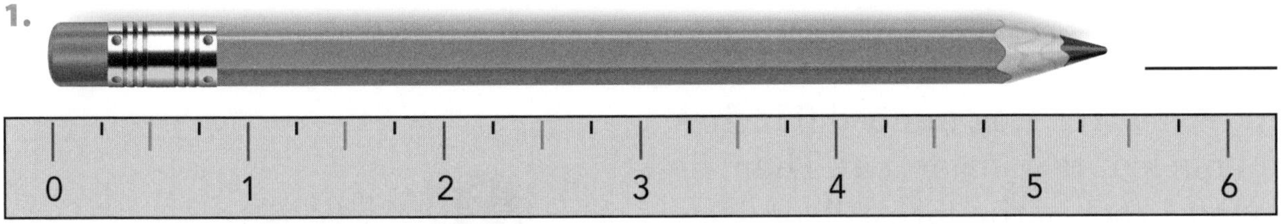

______ in.

2. 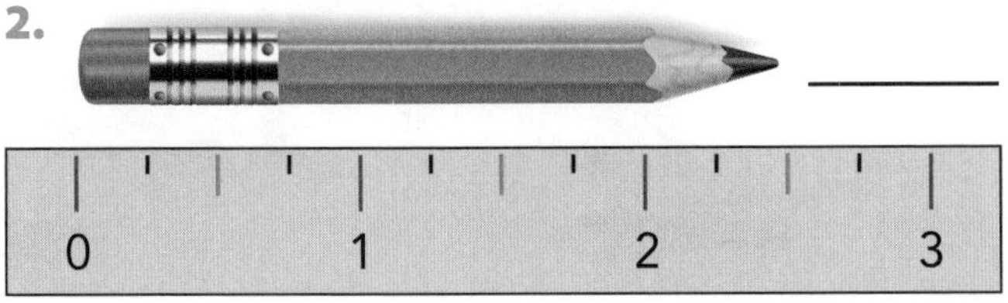

______ in.

3. 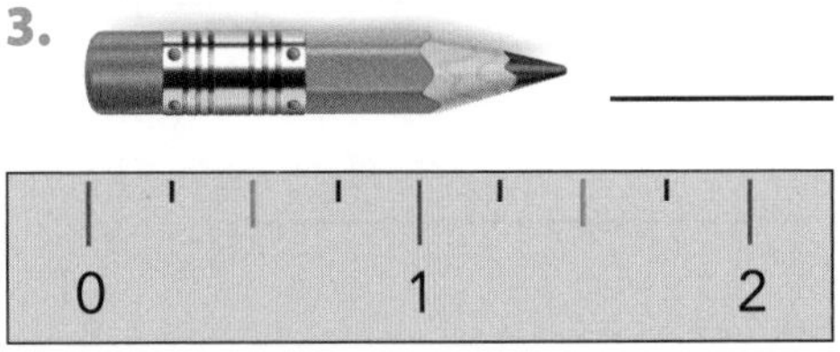

______ in.

Measure the computer cables to the nearest half inch.

4.  ______ in.

5.  ______ in.

6.  ______ in.

7.  ______ in.

Measure each classroom object to the nearest half inch.

8. the length of a chalkboard eraser ______________________________

9. the length of your math book ______________________________

10. the width of your math book ______________________________

11. the length of a bulletin board ______________________________

Draw a line segment of the length shown. Begin at the dot.

12. 4 inches •

13. $1\frac{1}{2}$ inches •

14. 5 inches •

15. $3\frac{1}{2}$ inches •

Solve.

16. A red-eyed tree frog jumped 6 inches from his leaf to a lower leaf. Then, he jumped 1 foot to the forest floor. How many inches did he jump? (Convert 1 foot to inches.)

____

Name ____

Length: Yards and Miles 9.4

Leafcutter ants live in the rain forest. Hundreds and thousands of ants march across the rain forest floor. Each ant carries a small piece of a leaf. Their moving trails often stretch over 100 feet across the ground and up and down the trunks of trees. The leafcutter ant's journey of 100 feet is about 33 yards.

inch

foot

12 inches (in.) = 1 foot (ft)
3 feet = 1 yard (yd)
36 inches = 1 yard
1,760 yards = 1 mile (mi)
5,280 feet = 1 mile

yard

Complete each sentence by writing more or less.

1. The height of your bedroom wall is __________ than one mile.
2. The length of your desk is __________ than one yard.
3. The length of a city block is __________ than one yard.
4. The length of the playground is __________ than one mile.
5. The distance from Earth to the moon is __________ than one mile.
6. The length of a pickup truck is __________ than one yard.

Which unit would you use to measure each length? Write inch, yard, or mile.

7. the length of a crayon

____

8. the height of a door

____

9. the length of a hallway

____

10. the distance between cities

____

11. the length of a grasshopper

____

12. the length of a car

____

Fill in the circle in front of the better estimate.

13. A sofa is about ______ long.

○ 2 yards ○ 2 feet

14. The store is ______ from the library.

○ 4 yards ○ 4 miles

15. The height of the classroom is ______ high.

○ 3 yards ○ 3 miles

16. The height of a pro basketball player is ______ high.

○ 2 feet ○ 2 yards

Complete the chart. Start with feet. Multiply by 12 to find the number of inches. Divide by 3 to find the number of yards.

	inches	× 12	feet	÷ 3	yards
	36	←	3	→	1
17.		←	6	→	
18.		←	9	→	

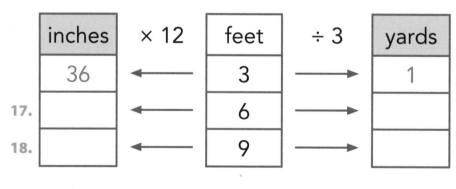

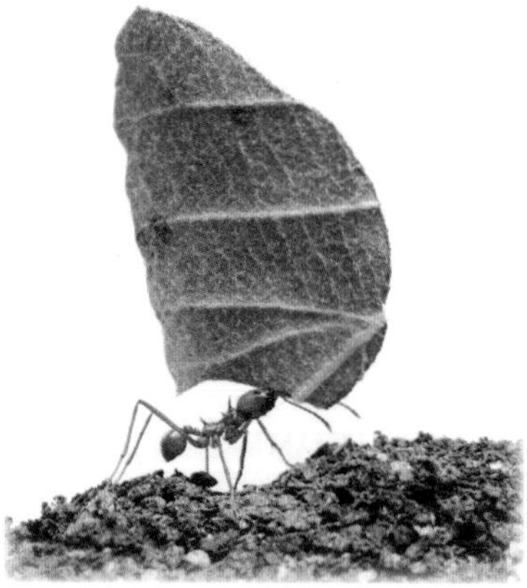

Review

19. **Multiply.**

$\begin{array}{r} 34 \\ \times\ 2 \\ \hline \end{array}$ $\begin{array}{r} 61 \\ \times\ 3 \\ \hline \end{array}$ $\begin{array}{r} 42 \\ \times\ 4 \\ \hline \end{array}$ $\begin{array}{r} 305 \\ \times\ 5 \\ \hline \end{array}$ $\begin{array}{r} 628 \\ \times\ 3 \\ \hline \end{array}$

Name ___________________________________

Length: Metric Units 9.5

The tiny poison dart frog is native to the South American rain forest. Its bright colors warn enemies that it is highly poisonous! The poison dart frog is only about $2\frac{1}{2}$ to 5 centimeters long.

Centimeters are units of measurement in the metric system, a measurement system that uses multiples of 10. A meter (m) is the basic unit of length in the metric system.

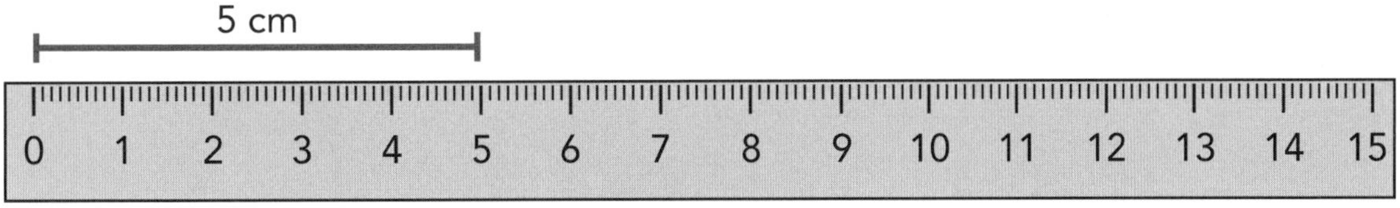

This is a centimeter ruler.

The numbered sections are called centimeters (cm). Each centimeter is divided into 10 smaller units. Each smaller unit is a millimeter (mm). The closely spaced lines on the ruler show millimeters.

10 millimeters (mm) = 1 centimeter (cm) 100 centimeters = 1 meter

Measure to the nearest centimeter.

1. 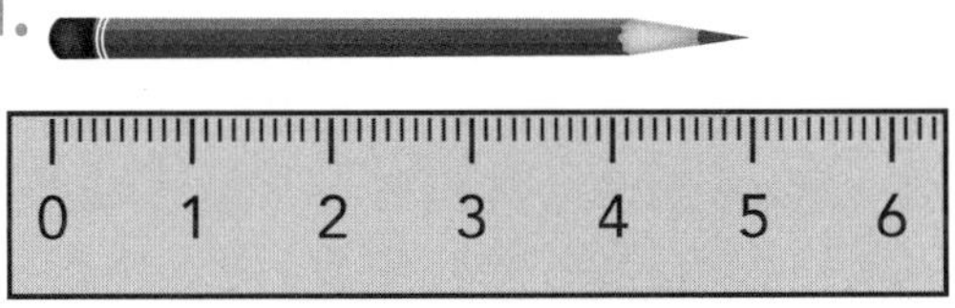

_______ cm

2. 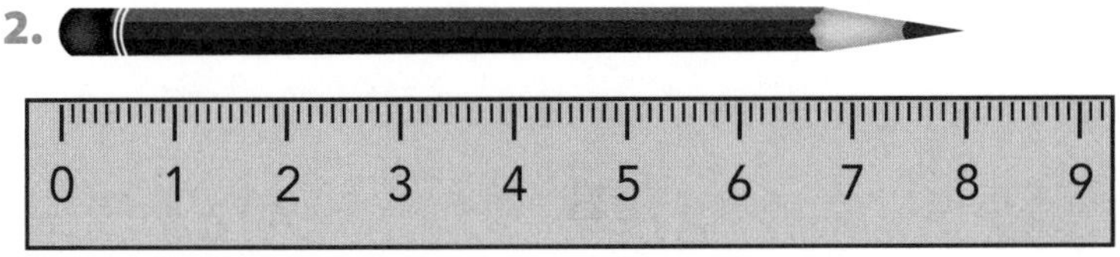

_______ cm

3. 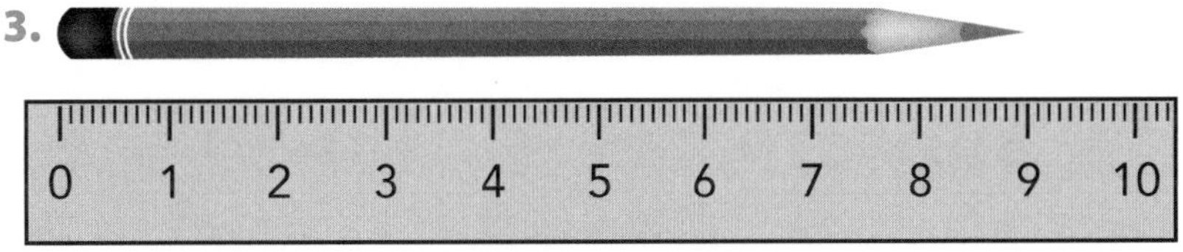

_______ cm

4. 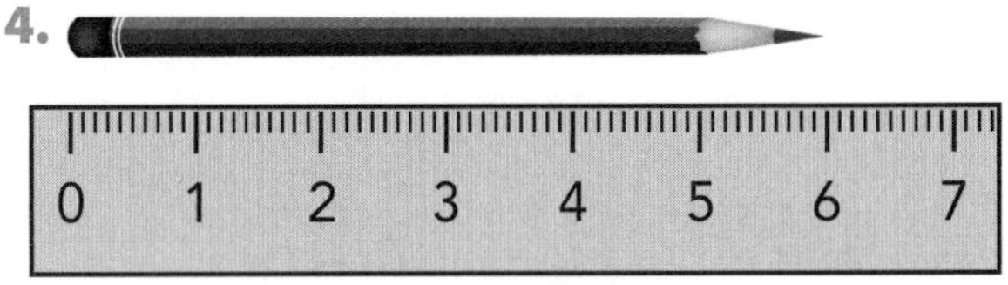

_______ cm

Measure to the nearest centimeter.

5.

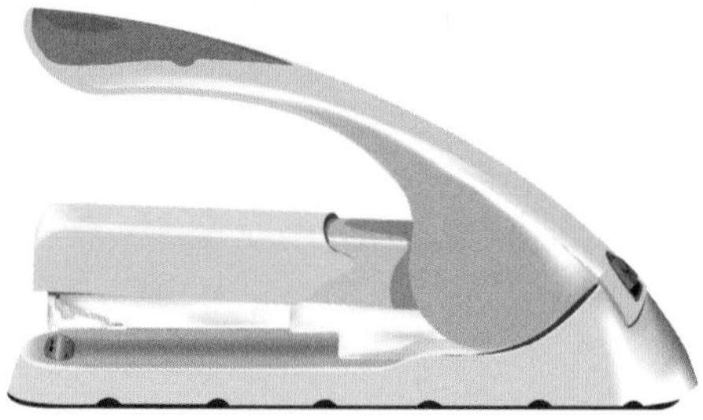

_____ cm

7.

_____ cm

6.

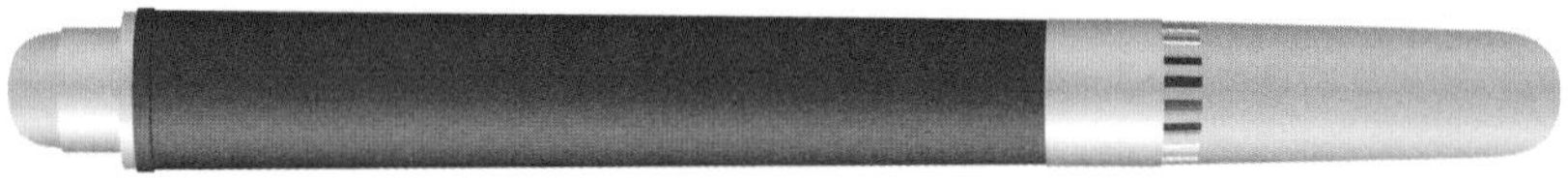

_____ cm

8.

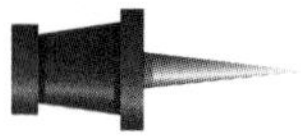

_____ cm

Write an object that is about the length given.

9. 4 cm __________
11. 2 cm __________
13. 20 cm __________
10. 13 cm __________
12. 5 cm __________
14. 8 cm __________

Draw a line segment of the length shown. Begin at the dot.

15. 8 cm •

16. 3 cm •

17. 1 cm •

18. 5 cm •

Review

19. **Divide.**

$9\overline{)22}$ $7\overline{)46}$ $5\overline{)32}$ $8\overline{)19}$ $6\overline{)44}$

Name ____________________

Length: Meters and Kilometers 9.6

Both a meter (m) and a kilometer (km) are measurements in the metric system. They are used to measure length and distance.

100 centimeters (cm) = 1 meter (m)
1,000 meters = 1 kilometer (km)

The Amazon River is home to many rain forest animals. It flows across South America and empties into the Atlantic Ocean. The Amazon is 6,400 kilometers long.

Write more or less to complete each sentence.

1. A page in a book is ____________ than a meter.
2. The height of a wall is ____________ than a meter.
3. The length of a school bus is ____________ than a meter.
4. The length of your foot is ____________ than a meter.
5. The height of the classroom door is ____________ than a kilometer.
6. The distance between two cities is ____________ than a kilometer.

Choose the unit of measurement that you would use to measure each object. Write **meter, kilometer,** or **centimeter.**

7. the height of a basketball net ____________

8. the width of a desk ____________

9. the length of a sailboat ____________

10. the distance from home to school ____________

11. the length of a butterfly in the Amazon ____________

Write two objects that you could measure with each unit of measurement.

centimeter	meter	kilometer
12. ____________	14. ____________	16. ____________
13. ____________	15. ____________	17. ____________

Circle the better estimate.

18.	the distance from New York to Boston	348 m	348 km
19.	the length of a pickup truck	6 m	60 m
20.	the length of a porch	12 m	120 m
21.	the length of a swimming pool	44 m	4 km

Solve.

22. The Amazon River is about 6,400 km long. If a boat is 4,337 km from one end of the river, how far is it from the other end?

____

23. A missionary in a canoe crossed the Amazon where it was 11 km wide. Then, he returned to the other side. How far did he travel on the round trip?

____

Name ______________________________

You will need to complete more than one operation to solve some word problems.

The students at Grace Christian School have a sister school in Brazil. To help their sister school raise money for new math books, Grace Christian School students decided to hold a skate-a-thon. Ten of the third graders skated 4 kilometers. Fifteen of the third graders completed 5 kilometers. How many kilometers did the students skate in all?

Problem-Solving Path

1. Understand the question.
   - Underline the question.
2. Analyze the data.
   - Circle the key information.
3. Plan the strategy.
   - Is there more than one operation needed to solve the problem?
   - If so, which operation should be done first?
4. Solve the problem.
   - Complete the operations in the correct order.
   - Label the answer.
5. Evaluate the result.
   - Does the result answer the question?
   - Is the answer reasonable?

Follow the directions to solve the word problem.

1. Draw a line under the question.
2. Circle the key information.
3. Plan the strategy to solve the problem. Circle the operations that are needed to solve the problem.

   addition multiplication

   subtraction division

4. Solve each part of the problem.

   $\begin{array}{r} 10 \\ \times\ 4 \\ \hline \end{array}$ $\begin{array}{r} 15 \\ \times\ 5 \\ \hline \end{array}$ $\begin{array}{r} 40 \\ +75 \\ \hline \end{array}$

5. Evaluate the result. Is your answer reasonable?

   ____

Refer to the Problem-Solving Path. Solve. Show your work on a separate piece of paper.

6. Christina skated 5 km. Each kilometer is equal to 1,000 meters. How many meters did she skate?

____

7. Devon skated for 1,250 m, took a break, and then skated for another 2,750 m. How many kilometers did Devon skate? (Convert meters to kilometers.)

____

8. Mrs. Baker bought 36 yd of rope to mark both the start and finish lines for the skate-a-thon. She cut the rope in half so each line would be the same length. How long was each piece of rope?

____

9. Caselle skated 4,500 m and Greyson skated 5,500 m. Evan skated 6 km. Who skated farther, Caselle and Greyson together or Evan?

____

10. Mrs. Baker brought a box of treats for the class. The box lid measured 10 in. long by 4 in. wide. What was the perimeter of the lid? (Perimeter is the total length of all 4 sides of a rectangle.)

____

11. Every time the third graders completed a lap, they handed their punch cards to Mrs. Baker so she could punch them. Chloe had 25 punches on her card. Brant had 4 rows of 5 punches each. Who completed more laps and how many more of them were there?

____

12. Josef and Ben wore roller blades. Each roller blade had 4 wheels. How many wheels did the boys have in all?

____

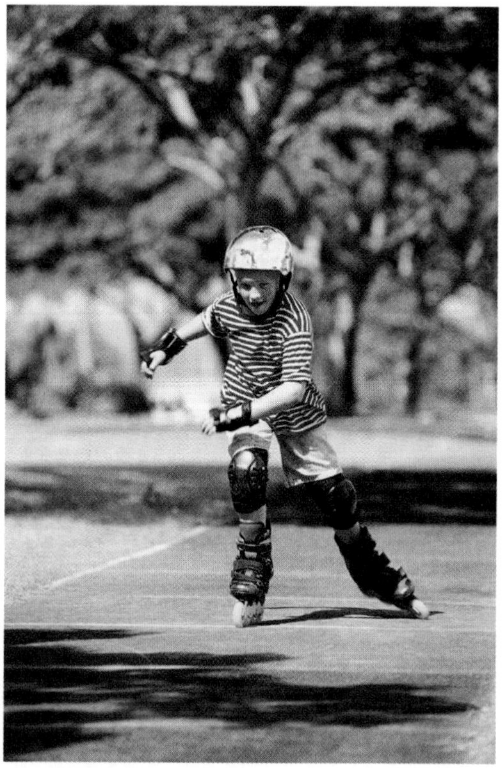

Name ______________________________

Weight: Customary 9.8

The tamandua is an anteater that tears apart anthills and termite nests with its claws. It pokes its long, sticky tongue inside and captures the insects.

The tamandua weighs 13 ounces at birth.
Adult tamanduas weigh 17 pounds.

An **ounce** (oz) and a **pound** (lb) are units of measurement in the customary system.

16 ounces = 1 pound

ounce

pound

Which unit would you use to weigh each object? Write ounce or pound.

1.

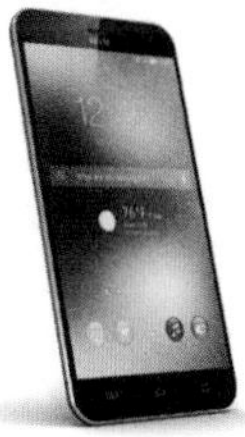

____

2.

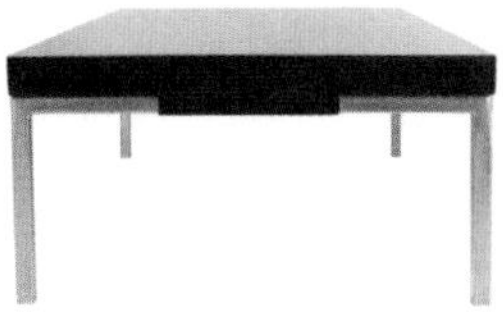

____

3.

____

4.

____

Which customary unit would you use to weigh each object? Write **ounce** or **pound**.

5. newborn kitten ____________
6. bunch of bananas ____________
7. toothbrush ____________
8. birthday card ____________
9. sticker ____________
10. bag of books ____________

11. This scale measures in pounds. Circle the items that would weigh about 1 pound.

2 large apples	a pencil	a coffee cup
a penny	3 jelly beans	a baseball mitt
2 softballs	a pineapple	a crayon

Multiply and add to change each mixed measurement to ounces.

12. 3 lb, 4 oz

13. 5 lb, 12 oz

14. 8 lb, 5 oz

15. 6 lb, 8 oz

16. Number these babies' weights 1 through 4 from lightest to heaviest. To make the weights easier to compare, change ounces and pounds to ounces.

7 lb, 5 oz ______

8 lb, 5 oz ______

116 oz ______

111 oz ______

Review

17. Add or subtract.

$149.58 + 85.12	$117.00 + 86.99	$204.78 + 8.12	$30.30 + 66.55
$16.03 − 0.48	$51.12 − 8.50	$238.67 − 129.45	$321.75 − 150.89

Name ________________________________

The marsupial frog and the green iguana both live in the rain forest. The marsupial frog is about 1 to 2 inches ($2\frac{1}{2}$ to 5 cm) long. The green iguana can grow up to 6 feet in length.

A **gram** (g) is the basic unit of weight in the metric system. A **kilogram** (kg) is 1,000 grams. A large paper clip, 2 raisins, or a button weigh about a gram. A brick, a pair of shoes, and a pineapple each weigh about a kilogram.

1,000 grams (g) = 1 kilogram (kg)

Which animal should be weighed in grams? Which should be weighed in kilograms?

1. **Which metric unit would you use to weigh each item? Write gram or kilogram.**

dog	bicycle	seashell	car
______	______	______	______
leaf	paper plate	table	bed
______	______	______	______
peanut	pencil	feather	envelope
______	______	______	______

Circle the better estimate.

2.	pencil	4 g or 4 kg	6.	push pin	1 g or 1 kg
3.	quarter	10 g or 10 kg	7.	eraser	8 g or 8 kg
4.	football	400 g or 400 kg	8.	nail	1 g or 1 kg
5.	box of books	16 g or 16 kg	9.	baseball	150 g or 150 kg

Convert kilograms to grams.

10. 1 kg = _____ g
11. 43 kg = _____ g
12. 116 kg = _____ g
13. 14 kg = _____ g
14. 68 kg = _____ g
15. 103 kg = _____ g
16. 8 kg = _____ g
17. 87 kg = _____ g
18. 155 kg = _____ g

Which metric unit would you use to measure each of the following? Write cm, m, km, g, or kg.

19. length of a sofa _____
20. length of a toy car _____
21. length of a train ride _____
22. weight of a dictionary _____
23. weight of a feather _____
24. length of a race _____
25. weight of a cracker _____
26. weight of a box of toys _____

Review

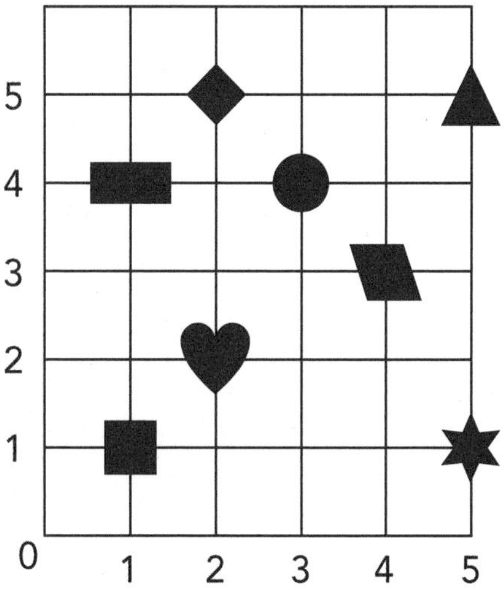

Draw the shape you find at each ordered pair.

27. (2,2) _____
28. (1,4) _____
29. (4,3) _____
30. (3,4) _____

Write the ordered pair for each shape.

31. ◆ _____
32. ■ _____
33. ▲ _____
34. ✶ _____

Name ______________________________

Capacity is the amount a container can hold. Customary units of capacity are a cup, **pint** (pt), **quart** (qt), and **gallon** (gal). These units are used to measure capacity.

4 quarts = 1 gallon
2 pints = 1 quart 8 pints = 1 gallon
2 cups = 1 pint 4 cups = 1 quart 16 cups = 1 gallon

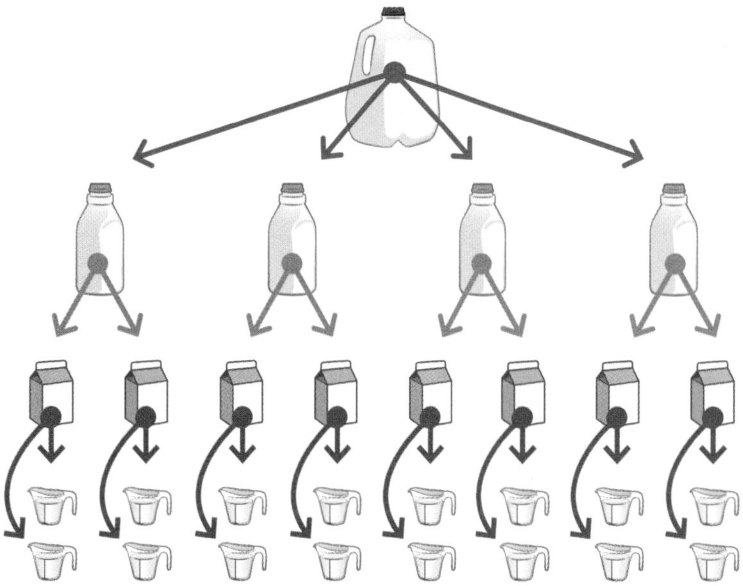

Mr. Chan bought 2 quarts of lowfat milk. Mrs. Lee bought 5 pints of chocolate milk. Who bought more milk? Look at the chart. Compare 2 quarts and 5 pints. Mrs. Lee bought more milk.

2 pints = 1 quart   5 pints = 2 quarts + 1 pint

Which unit would you use to measure the capacity of each item? Write cup or quart.

1. juice box ____________
2. pitcher of lemonade ____________
3. bowl of soup ____________
4. glass of water ____________

Which unit would you use to measure the capacity of each item? Write pint or gallon.

5. pool filled with water ____________
6. bottle of shampoo ____________
7. saucepan of soup ____________
8. personal water bottle ____________

Circle the better estimate.

9.

3 qt or 3 cup

11.

1 pt or 1 qt

13.

1 qt or 1 cup

10.

10 gal or 10 pt

12.

1 pt or 1 gal

14.

10 gal or 10 pt

Complete.

15.

cups	4	6	8	10	12	14
pints						

16.

quarts	8	12	16	20	24	28
gallons						

17.

cups	8	12	16	32	48
pints					
quarts					
gallons					

Write < or >.

18. 3 cup ◯ 3 pt

19. 5 cup ◯ 2 pt

20. 1 gal ◯ 5 qt

21. 6 pt ◯ 4 qt

22. 7 qt ◯ 2 gal

23. 12 cup ◯ 7 pt

24. 10 cup ◯ 4 pt

25. 18 pt ◯ 2 gal

26. 1 gal ◯ 15 cup

Name ______________________________

Capacity: Metric 9.11

Kitchen shops sell containers for cooking, storing, and serving liquids. Not all containers are the same. Some have a greater capacity than others.

A teakettle holds about 2 L of water.

A teacup holds about 250 mL of tea.

A liter (L) is a unit of capacity in the metric system. Another unit of capacity is a milliliter (mL). There are 1,000 milliliters in a liter.

These containers each hold about 1 liter.

Write more if the container holds more than a liter. Write less if it holds less.

1. a bathtub ____________
2. a swimming pool ____________
3. a jar lid ____________
4. a birdbath ____________
5. a spoon ____________
6. an aquarium ____________
7. a bucket ____________
8. a sink ____________
9. a coffee mug ____________
10. a pitcher of juice ____________

Fill in the circle that shows the correct estimate.

11. 

○ 10 mL ○ 10 L

12. 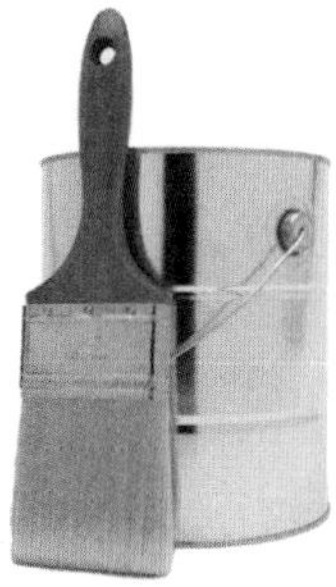

○ 4 L ○ 4 mL

13. 

○ 1 L ○ 1 mL

14. 

○ 500 mL ○ 50 L

15. 

○ 750 mL ○ 75 L

16. 

○ 2 L ○ 20 L

17. 

○ 600 mL ○ 6 L

18. 

○ 700 mL ○ 7 mL

19. 

○ 250 mL ○ 2 mL

Solve.

20. The Ramirez children drink 12 L of milk per week. About how many liters do they drink in one month?

____

21. Mr. Ramirez poured 375 mL of milk into his 1 L thermos. Then, he added coffee until the thermos was full. How much did he add?

____

Name ________________________________

Find Volume 9.12

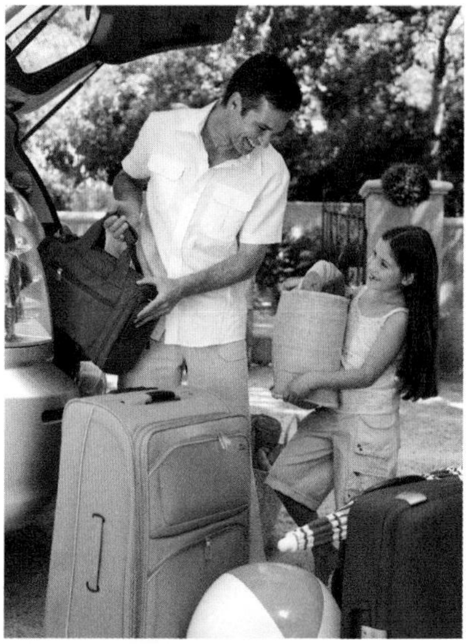

Claudia and her dad are packing for their trip to Brazil. They have several suitcases. How much can a suitcase hold? What is its volume?

Volume is the number of cubic units needed to fill a solid figure. The volume of a rectangular prism is determined by its length, width, and height.

This figure has a length of 5 units, a width of 2 units and a height of 2 units.

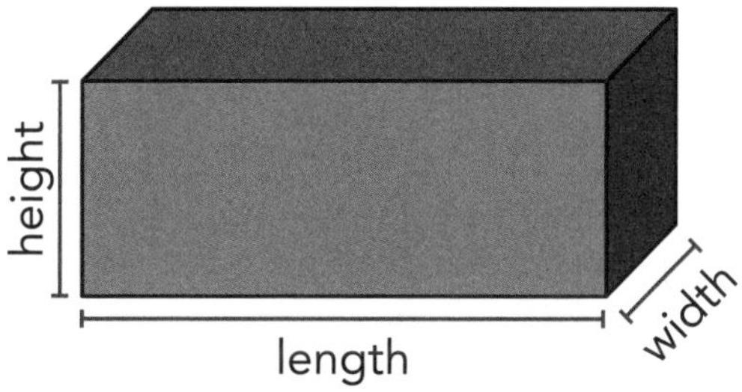

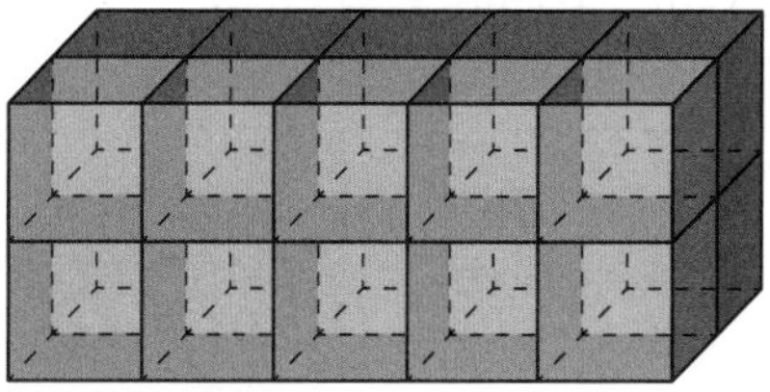

The volume is 20 cubic units.

What is the volume of this suitcase?

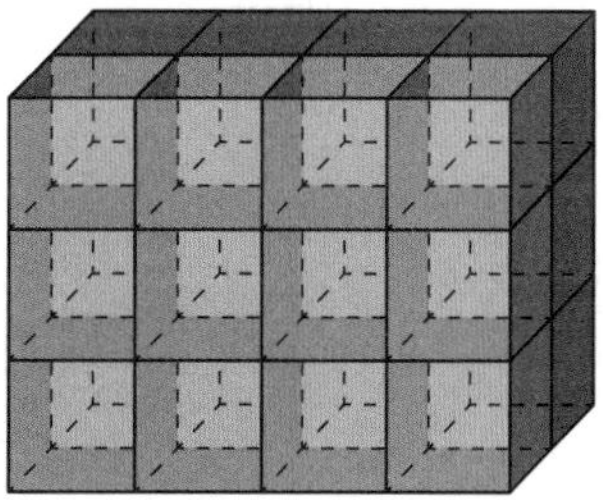

The volume of this suitcase is 24 cubic units.

Use connecting cubes to make a model of each rectangular prism. Write the volume of each prism.

1.

______ cubic units

2.

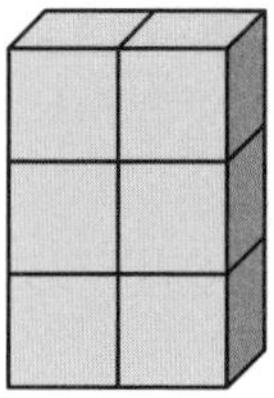

______ cubic units

3.

______ cubic units

Write the volume of each shape in cubic units. Use connecting cubes as needed.

4. 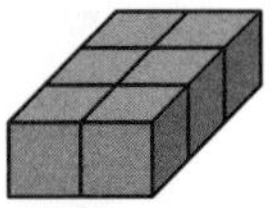 ______

5. 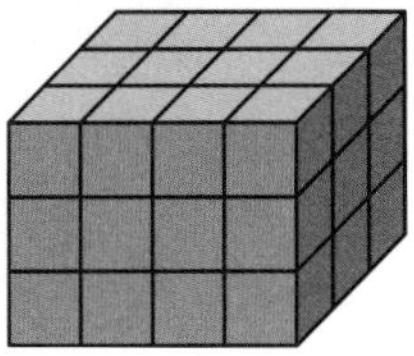 ______

6. 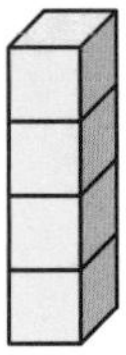 ______

7.  ______

8. 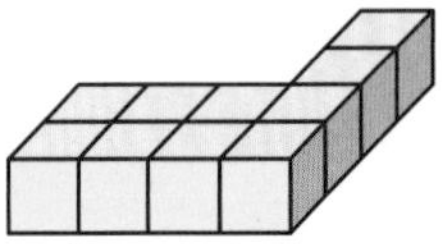 ______

9.  ______

10.  ______

11.  ______

12.  ______

13.  ______

14.  ______

15.  ______

16.  ______

17. 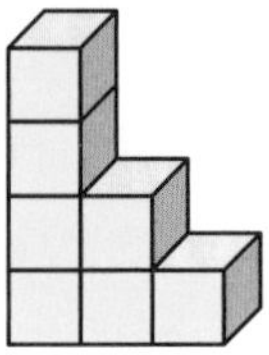 ______

18. 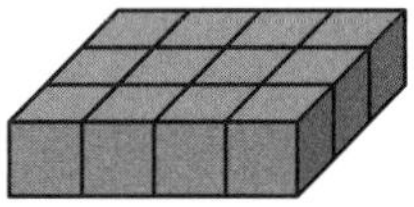 ______

19.  ______

Review

20. **Divide.**

$8\overline{)32}$ $2\overline{)10}$ $7\overline{)21}$ $5\overline{)45}$ $5\overline{)30}$ $7\overline{)35}$ $3\overline{)27}$

$6\overline{)24}$ $8\overline{)72}$ $9\overline{)9}$ $1\overline{)7}$ $8\overline{)64}$ $6\overline{)6}$ $4\overline{)36}$

Name ____________________

Temperature: Fahrenheit 9.13

The climate of the rain forest helps a wide variety of animals grow and thrive. Daily rainfall gives animals the water supply they need. A constant temperature of 75 to 80 degrees Fahrenheit is ideal for animals that live in the tropical rain forest.

Temperature is measured in degrees Fahrenheit (°F) in the customary system.

212°F is the boiling point of water.

98.6°F is normal body temperature.

32°F is the freezing point of water.

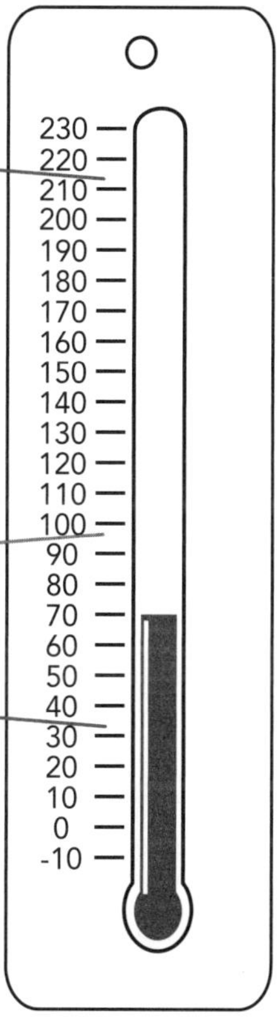

Reading a Thermometer

Some thermometers have small marks every 2 degrees. Begin at the bottom of the thermometer. Find the number that is below the level of the liquid, but close to it. Count up by 2s to the space at the level of the liquid.

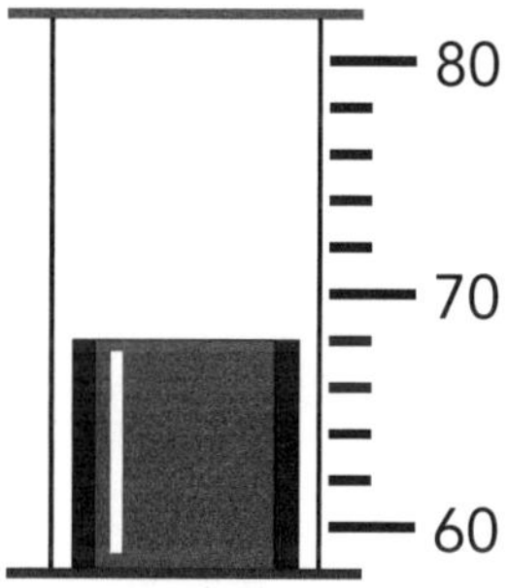

This thermometer shows 68°F.

1. Write the letter of the temperature that best matches each picture.

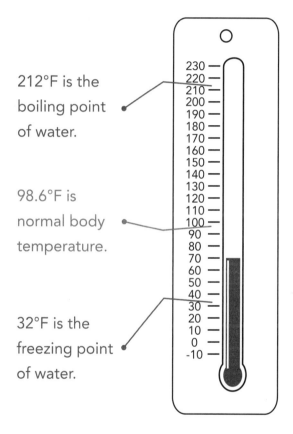

_______ _______ _______ _______

a. 95°F

b. 65°F

c. 32°F

d. 212°F

Write the temperature in degrees Fahrenheit.

2. 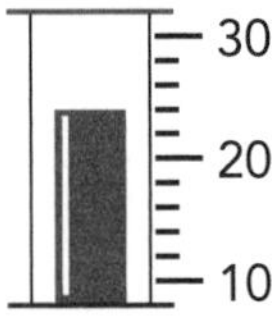

______

4. 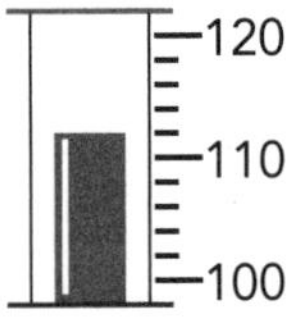

______

6. 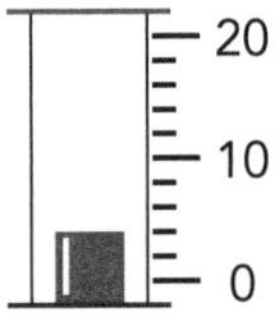

______

3. 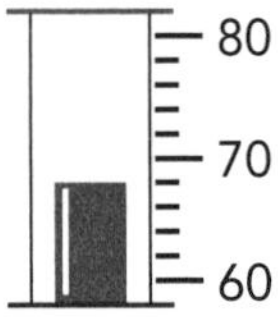

______

5. 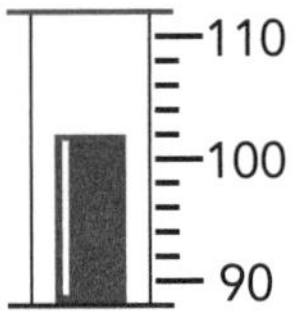

______

7. 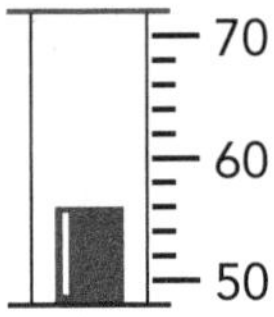

______

Use a red colored pencil to show the correct temperature.

8. 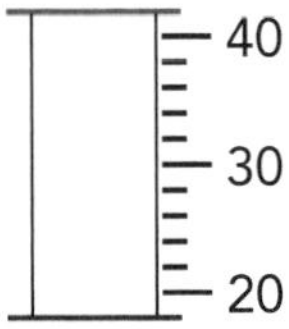

32°F

9. 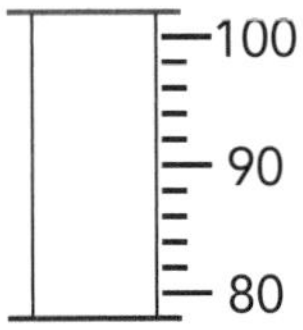

98°F

10. 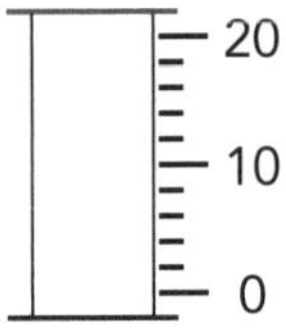

6°F

11. 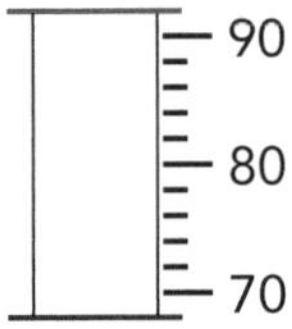

74°F

12. 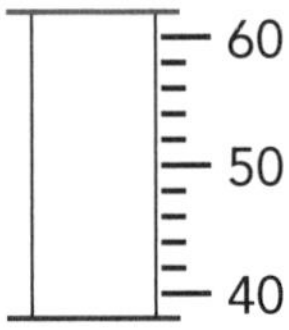

56°F

13. 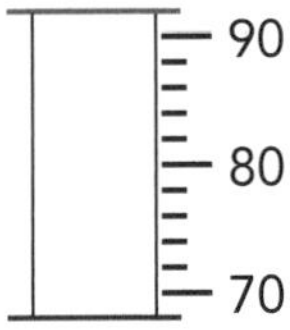

78°F

Complete the chart.

	Day	High Temperature	Low Temperature	Difference
	Sunday	68°F	54°F	14°
14.	Monday	62°F	50°F	
15.	Tuesday	56°F	46°F	
16.	Wednesday	61°F	53°F	
17.	Thursday	59°F	47°F	
18.	Friday	55°F	46°F	
19.	Saturday	50°F	37°F	

Name ____

In the metric system, temperature is measured in degrees Celsius (°C).

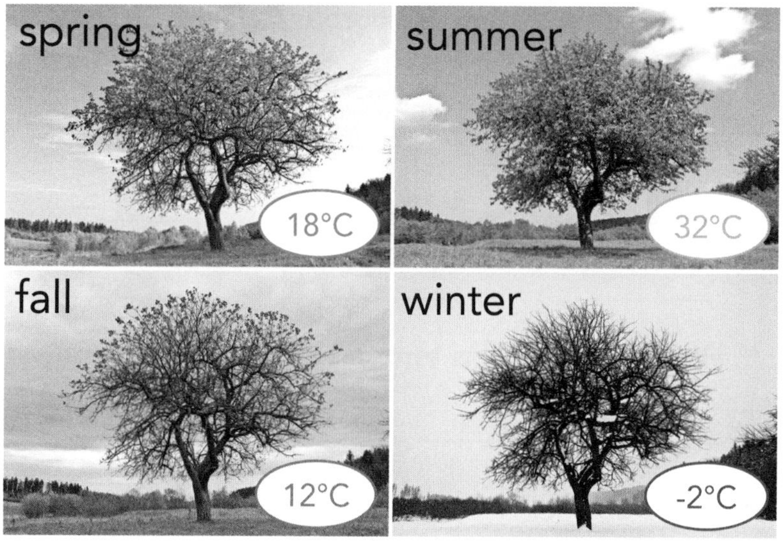

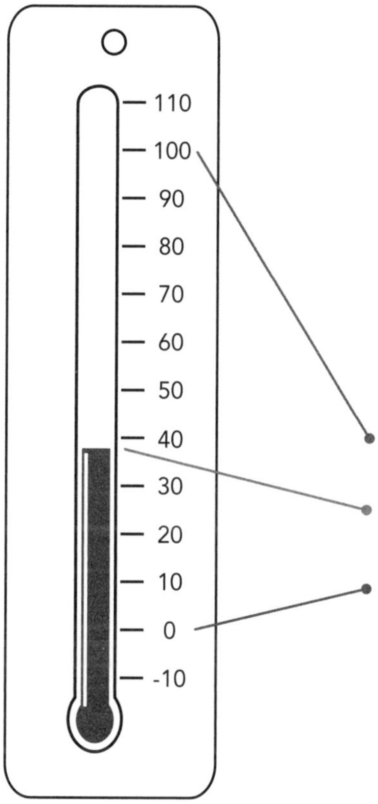

100°C is the boiling point of water.

37°C is normal body temperature.

0°C is the freezing point of water.

1. Write the letter that best matches the temperature of the season in which you would use each item.

_______ _______ _______ _______

a. −5°C

b. 17°C

c. 35°C

d. 10°C

Write the temperature in degrees Celsius.

2. 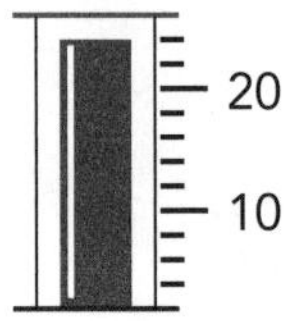

____

3. 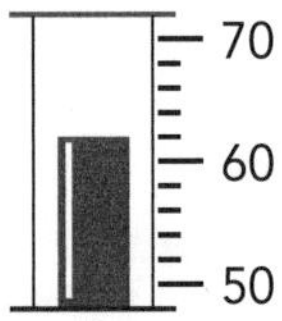

____

4. 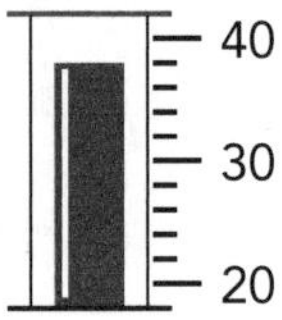

____

5. 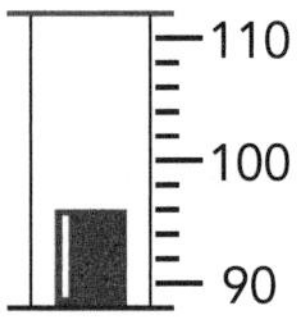

____

6. 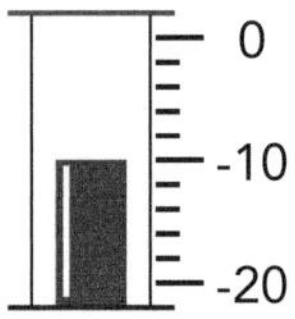

____

7. **Write the 5 Celsius temperatures in order from coolest to warmest.**

________ ________ ________ ________ ________

Color the correct temperature with a red colored pencil.

8. 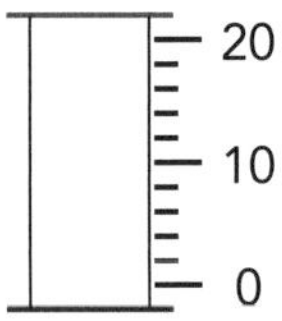

14°C

9. 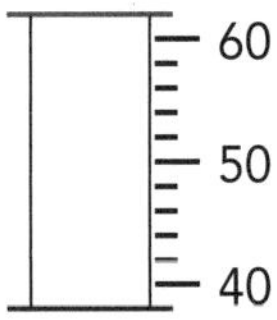

52°C

10. 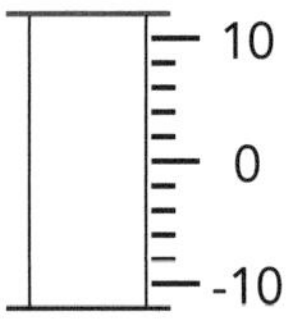

-4°C

11. 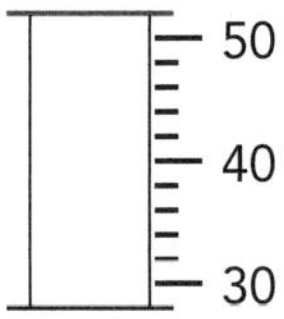

30°C

12. 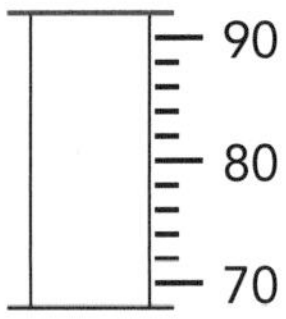

78°C

Solve.

13. Saturday's low temperature was 22°C and the high temperature was 35°C. Sunday's low temperature was 17°C and the high temperature was 33°C. Which day's temperature difference was greater?

____

14. Kinsley took a pan of cookies out of the oven at 175°C. She cooled the cookies to 56°C. What is the temperature difference?

____

Review

Find the average Celsius temperature. Add the temperatures and then divide by the number of temperatures. Check your calculations with a calculator.

15. 4°C, 12°C, 14°C, 19°C, 21°C = ______

16. 5°C, 6°C, 6°C, 7°C, 8°C, 10°C = ______

17. 0°C, 1°C, 1°C, 3°C, 5°C, 14°C = ______

Name ____________________

Biblical Units of Measurement 9.15

Neither customary nor metric units were used to measure things in Bible times, but the people did have standard units of measurement. Some biblical units are listed below.

Units of Length	Units of Weight	Units of Capacity
handbreadth = about 3 in.	shekel = about $\frac{2}{5}$ of an oz	log = about $\frac{1}{3}$ qt
span = about 9 in.	mina = about $1\frac{1}{4}$ lb	hin = about 1 gal
cubit = about 18 in.	talent = about 75 lb	bath = about 6 gal

Choose a biblical unit of measurement for each item. Write handbreadth, span, cubit, shekel, mina, talent, log, hin, or bath.

1. your height ____________________
2. the length of your desk ____________________
3. your weight ____________________
4. the amount of water in a lake ____________________
5. the weight of a gold necklace ____________________
6. the amount of lemonade in a large glass ____________________

7. **Match each word to its Bible reference.**

______ handbreadth	**a.** Psalm 39:5
______ cubit	**b.** Exodus 30:13
______ mina	**c.** 1 Kings 10:17
______ shekel	**d.** Genesis 6:16

Compare each biblical measurement. Write < or >.

8. handbreath ◯ span
9. cubit ◯ span
10. talent ◯ mina
11. shekel ◯ mina
12. hin ◯ bath
13. log ◯ hin

Compare each biblical measurement. Solve.

14. 4 spans = about ______ in.
15. 5 cubits = about ______ in.
16. 2 minas = about ______ lb
17. 4 talents = about ______ lb
18. $5\frac{1}{2}$ spans = about ______ in.
19. 10 baths = about ______ gal

Review

20. **Add.**

$$\begin{array}{r} 63 \\ +58 \\ \hline \end{array} \qquad \begin{array}{r} 24 \\ +79 \\ \hline \end{array} \qquad \begin{array}{r} 246 \\ +365 \\ \hline \end{array} \qquad \begin{array}{r} 63 \\ 32 \\ +19 \\ \hline \end{array} \qquad \begin{array}{r} 56 \\ 18 \\ +43 \\ \hline \end{array} \qquad \begin{array}{r} 6{,}028 \\ +2{,}562 \\ \hline \end{array}$$

$$\begin{array}{r} 62 \\ -49 \\ \hline \end{array} \qquad \begin{array}{r} 34 \\ -18 \\ \hline \end{array} \qquad \begin{array}{r} 445 \\ -176 \\ \hline \end{array} \qquad \begin{array}{r} 700 \\ -247 \\ \hline \end{array} \qquad \begin{array}{r} 1{,}088 \\ -\quad 592 \\ \hline \end{array} \qquad \begin{array}{r} 3{,}143 \\ -1{,}874 \\ \hline \end{array}$$

Name ____________________

Write the letter of the definition that matches each vocabulary word.

1. ______ meter
2. ______ metric system
3. ______ pint
4. ______ kilometer
5. ______ gram
6. ______ ounce
7. ______ liter
8. ______ volume
9. ______ Fahrenheit
10. ______ Celsius

a. temperature in the customary system

b. metric unit of weight

c. measurement system based on multiples of 10

d. temperature in the metric system

e. metric unit of length equal to 1,000 m

f. number of cubic units need to fill a solid figure

g. customary unit used to measure capacity

h. customary unit of weight

i. metric unit of capacity

j. basic unit of length in the metric system

11. Complete.

______ cm = 1 m	______ °F = boiling point of water	______ m = 1 km
______ oz = 1 lb	______ °C = freezing point of water	______ cups = 1 pt
______ ft = 1 yd	______ in. = 1 ft	______ °F = freezing point of water

Circle the best unit for measuring.

12. the length of this page	m	cup	in.
13. how much a drinking glass can hold	gal	cup	g
14. the weight of 5 peanuts	g	lb	ft
15. the temperature of an oven	°F	qt	cm
16. the distance between Maine and Iowa	ft	oz	km

Measure each line segment to the nearest centimeter.

17. ______ cm

18. ______ cm

19. ______ cm

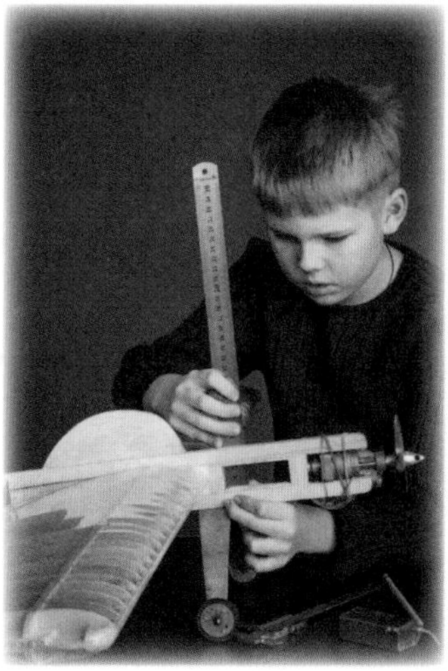

Measure to the nearest half inch.

20. ______ in.

21. ______ in.

22. ______ in.

Complete.

23. ______ in. = 3 ft 24. ______ qt = 4 gal 25. ______ oz = 2 lb

Write each temperature.

26.

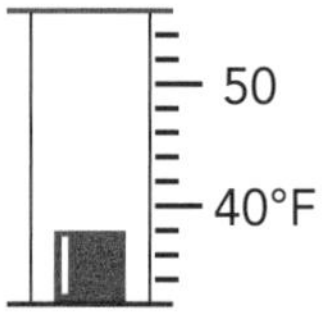

______

28.

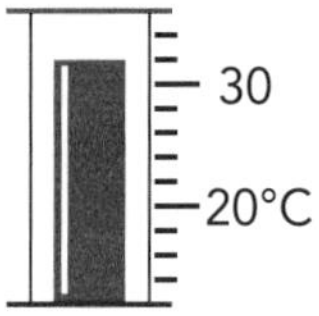

______

27.

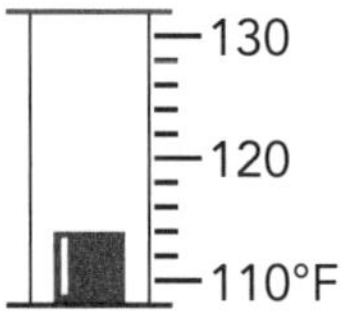

______

29.

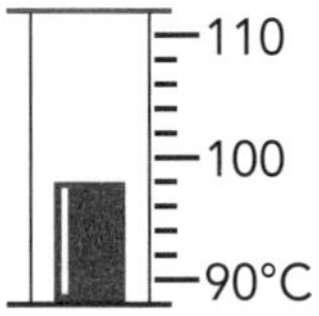

______

Circle the better estimate.

30. aquarium of water	5 gal	5 cup
31. height of a desk	1 cm	1 yd
32. soda bottle	2 gal	2 L
33. a bicycle	5 km	5 ft
34. a turkey	17 g	17 lb
35. a hot day	85°F	5°C

Solve.

36. Cari has 32 cm of ribbon for a craft project. She cuts 5 ribbons, each 6 cm long. What is the length of the ribbon left over?

______

37. **Find the volumes in cubic units.**

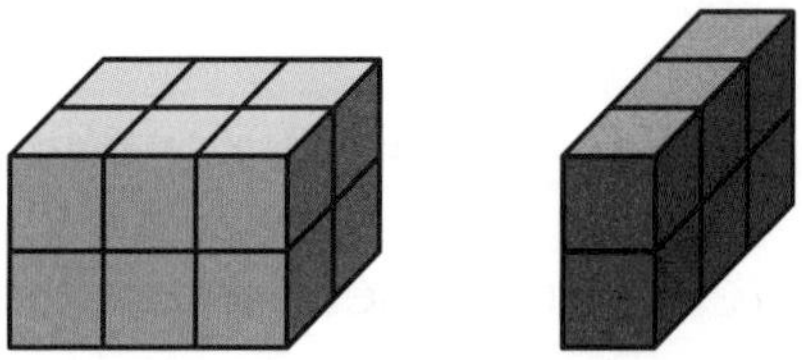

______ ______

Chapter 10
Fractions

A river watering the garden flowed from Eden; from there it was separated into four headwaters.
Genesis 2:10

Key Ideas:

Place Value: comparing fractions

Fractions: reading, writing, and drawing fractions and mixed numbers

Fractions: forming equivalent fractions

Addition: adding fractions

Subtraction: subtracting fractions

Name ________________________________

Fractions can be used to name numbers less than one. Fractions name equal parts of a whole.

1 whole

halves

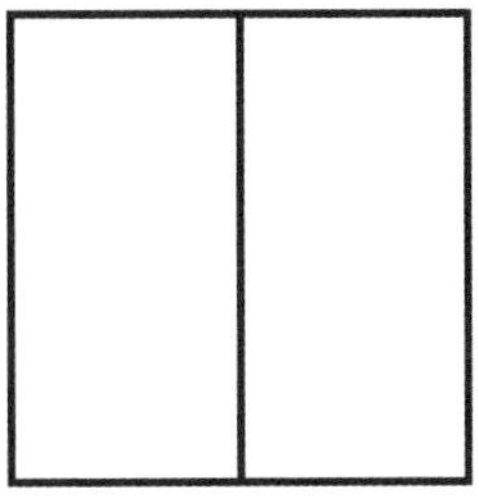

2 equal parts

thirds

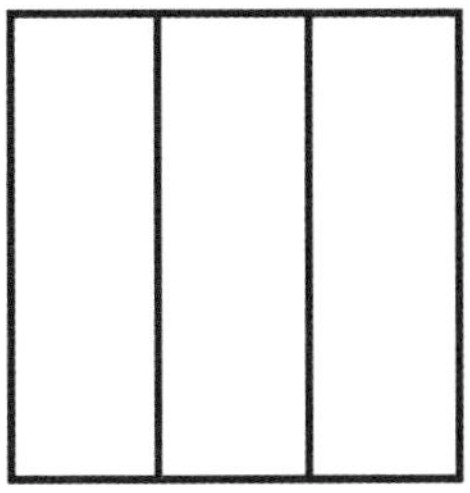

3 equal parts

fourths

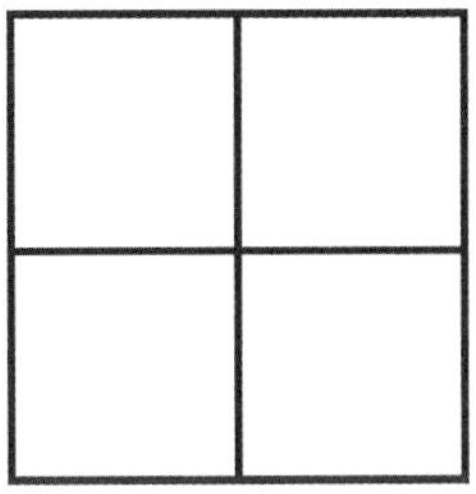

4 equal parts

sixths

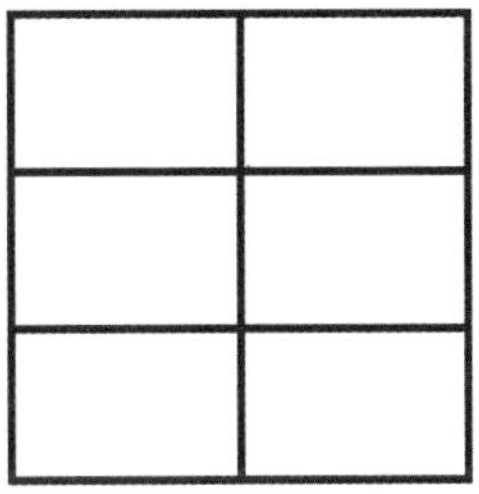

6 equal parts

eighths

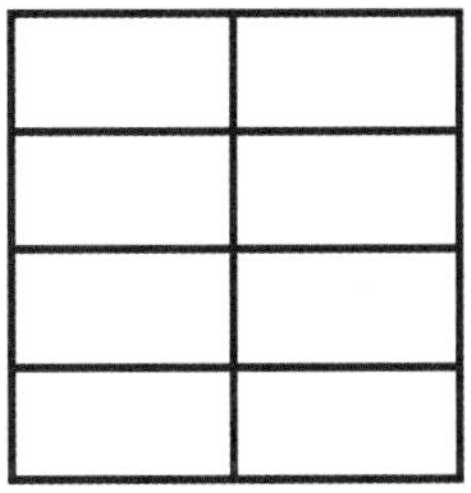

8 equal parts

The denominator is the number written below the line in a fraction.

The numerator is the number written above the line.

The denominator is the total number of equal parts in one whole. → $\frac{1}{2}$ ← The numerator is the number of equal parts being separated.

Fill in the missing numerator or denominator of the fraction for the colored parts.

1. 

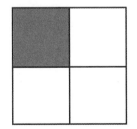

$\frac{1}{\square}$

2. 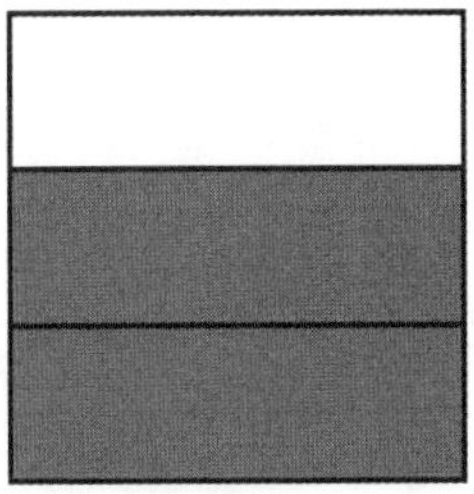

$\frac{\square}{3}$

3. 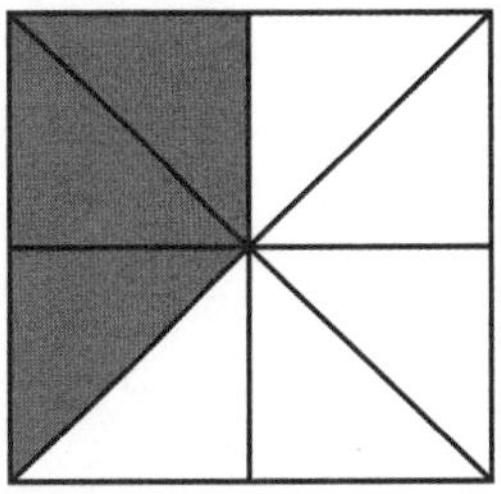

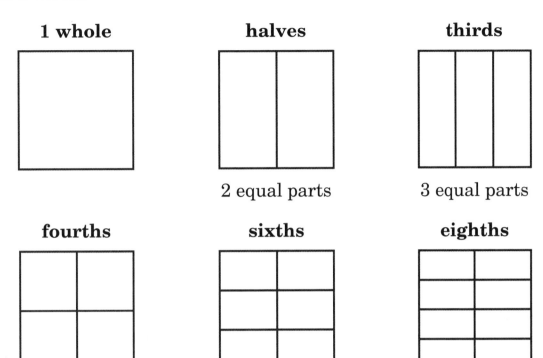

$\frac{\square}{8}$

Match the fraction name to the colored part of the model.

4. 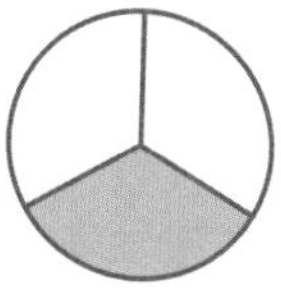 • • one-fourth

5. 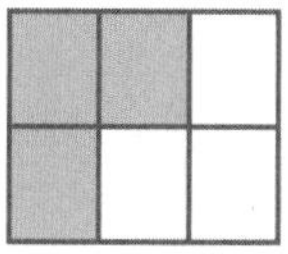 • • three-sixths

6. 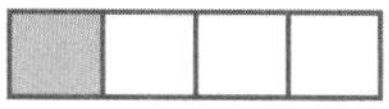 • • one-third

7. 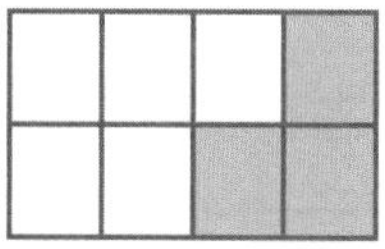 • • three-eighths

8.  • • $\frac{1}{2}$

9. 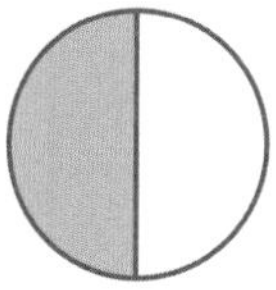 • • $\frac{3}{4}$

10. 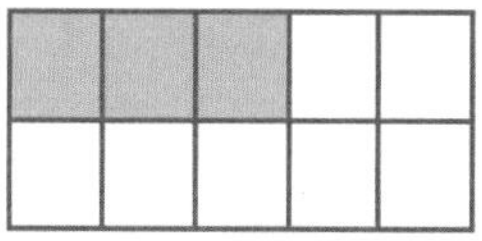 • • $\frac{1}{4}$

11.  • • $\frac{3}{10}$

Shade the model to show each fraction.

12.  $\frac{1}{3}$

13. 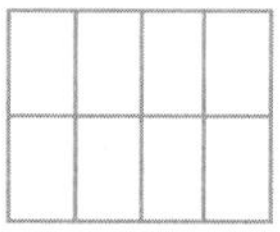 $\frac{5}{8}$

14. 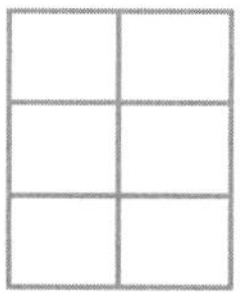 $\frac{2}{6}$

15. 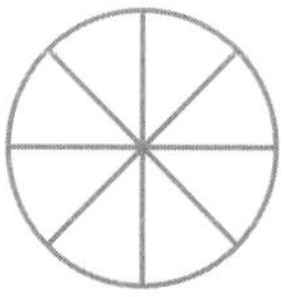 $\frac{3}{8}$

16.  $\frac{3}{4}$

Review

17. **Multiply.**

$\begin{array}{r} 24 \\ \times\ 2 \\ \hline \end{array}$ $\begin{array}{r} 36 \\ \times\ 4 \\ \hline \end{array}$ $\begin{array}{r} 45 \\ \times\ 5 \\ \hline \end{array}$ $\begin{array}{r} 205 \\ \times\ 8 \\ \hline \end{array}$ $\begin{array}{r} 314 \\ \times\ 7 \\ \hline \end{array}$ $\begin{array}{r} 600 \\ \times\ 9 \\ \hline \end{array}$

$\begin{array}{r} 2,314 \\ \times\ 2 \\ \hline \end{array}$ $\begin{array}{r} 1,823 \\ \times\ 3 \\ \hline \end{array}$ $\begin{array}{r} 4,078 \\ \times\ 6 \\ \hline \end{array}$ $\begin{array}{r} 2,879 \\ \times\ 4 \\ \hline \end{array}$ $\begin{array}{r} 7,821 \\ \times\ 2 \\ \hline \end{array}$ $\begin{array}{r} 5,736 \\ \times\ 5 \\ \hline \end{array}$

Name ______________________________

Fractions show equal parts of a whole.

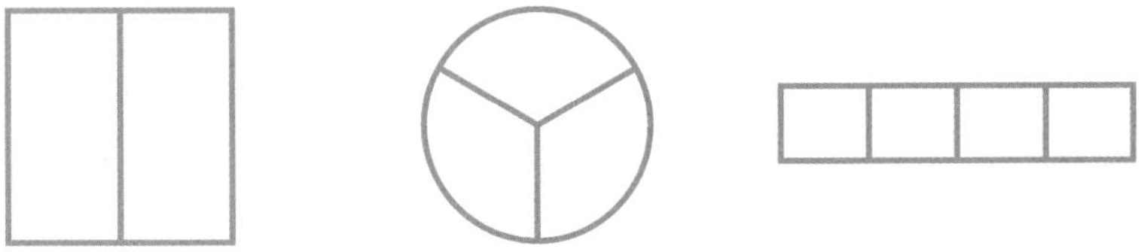

halves **thirds** **fourths**

Fractions also show the number of parts being separated.

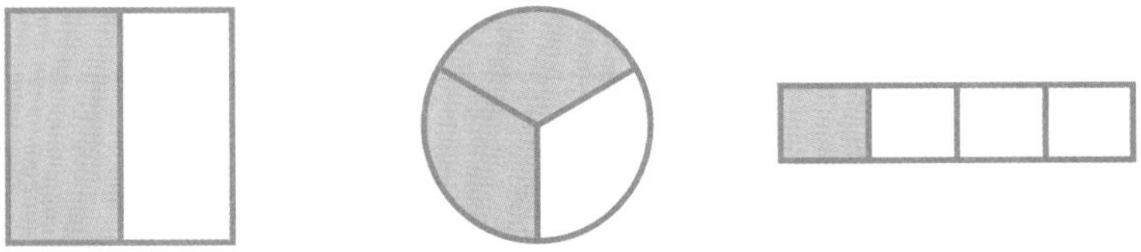

one-half **two-thirds** **one-fourth**

$\frac{1}{2}$ $\frac{2}{3}$ $\frac{1}{4}$

Is the green part $\frac{1}{3}$?

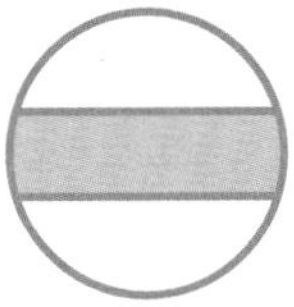

No, the 2 white parts are larger than the green part. Fractions must have equal parts.

$\frac{1}{3}$ is like saying "1 out of 3."

Each green section equals $\frac{1}{3}$.

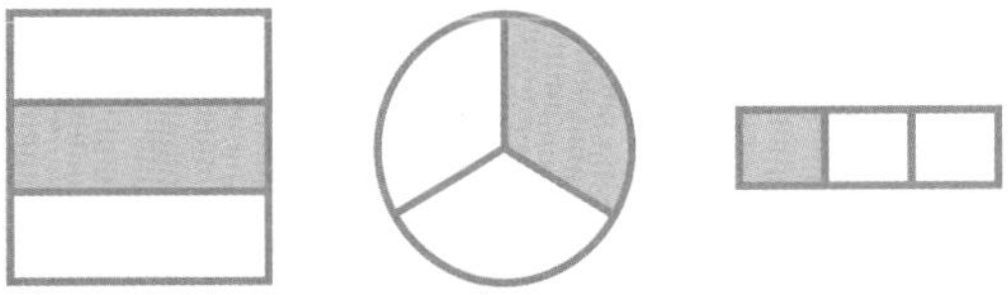

Write the fraction for the shaded part.

1.

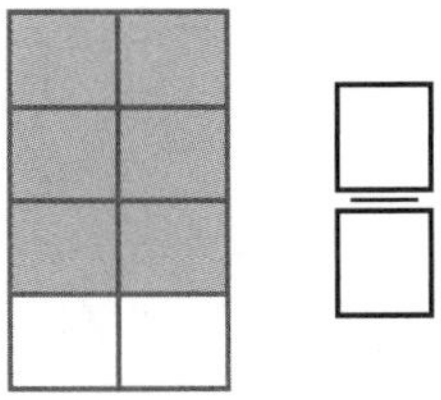

2.

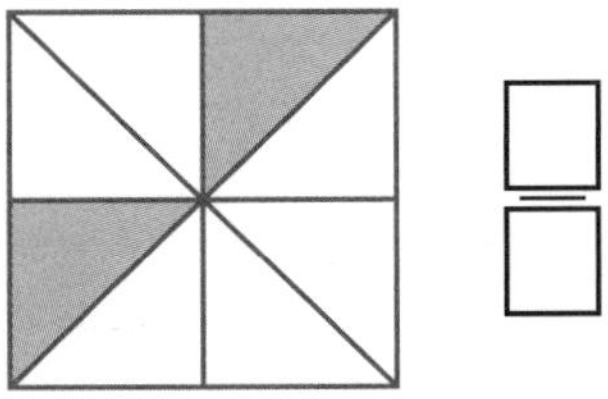

3.

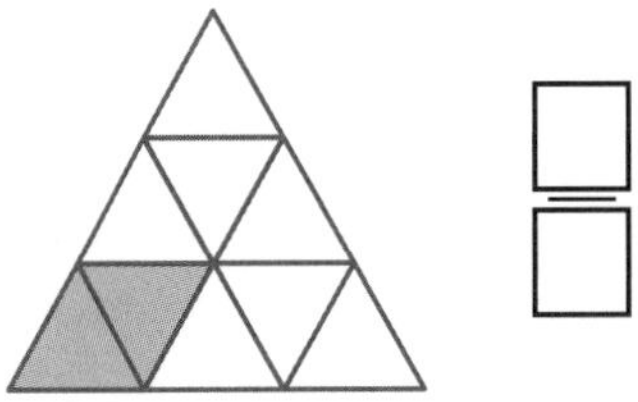

Write the fraction for the shaded part.

4. 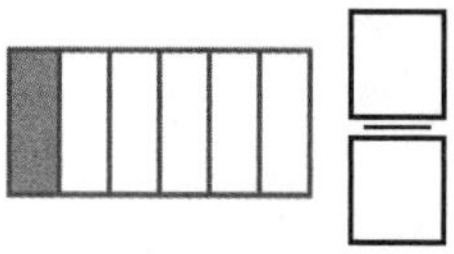

5. 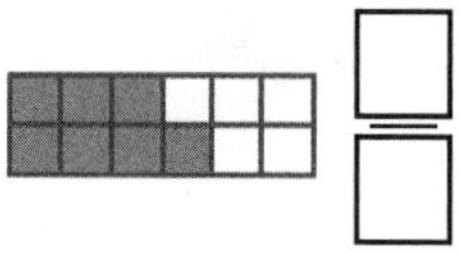

6. 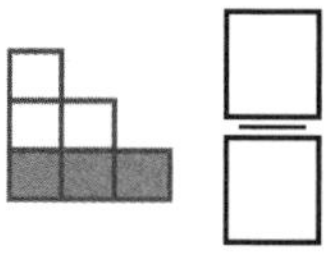

7. 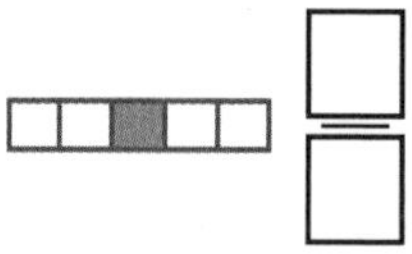

8. 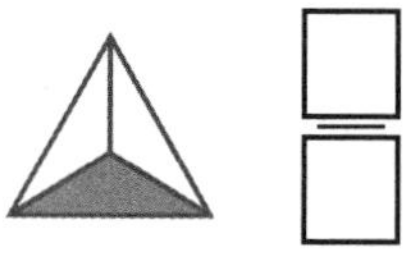

9. 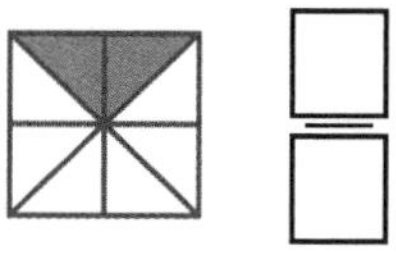

10. 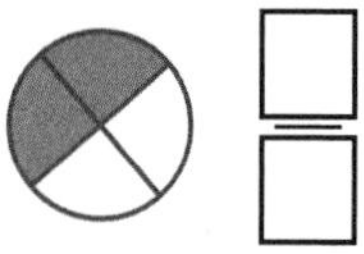

11. 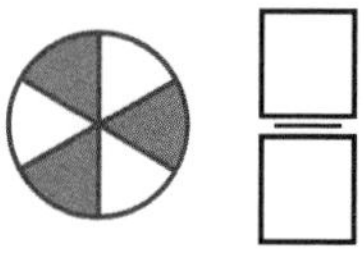

Circle the picture that shows equal parts of the fraction.

12. $\frac{1}{3}$ 

13. $\frac{1}{4}$ 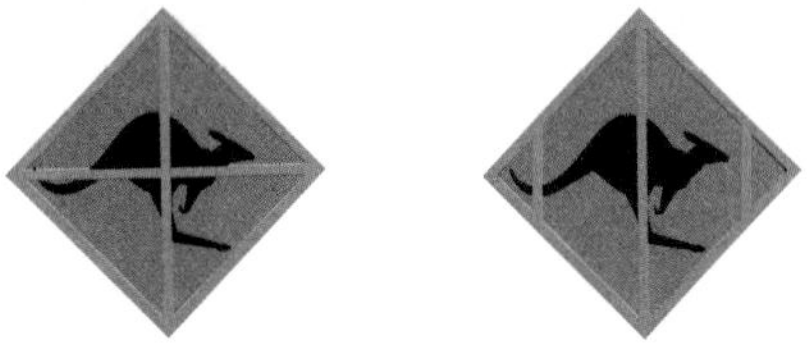

14. $\frac{1}{6}$ 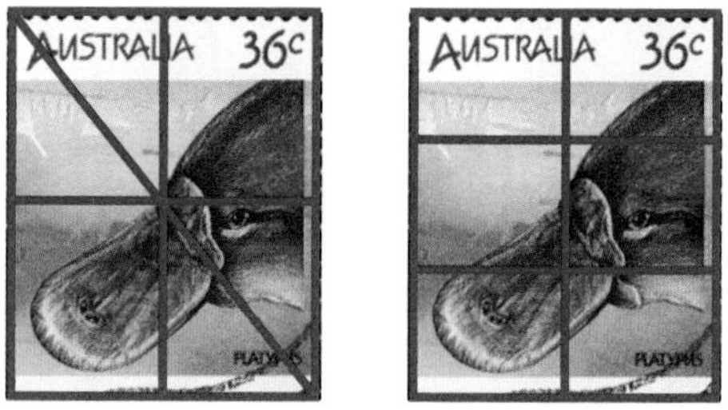

Draw a figure for each fraction below.

15. $\frac{1}{5}$ 16. $\frac{2}{3}$ 17. $\frac{2}{6}$ 18. $\frac{7}{8}$

Review

Complete the chart.

	inches	feet	yards
19.	36		
20.			4
21.		6	

22. Solve. Follow the path. Keep a running total.

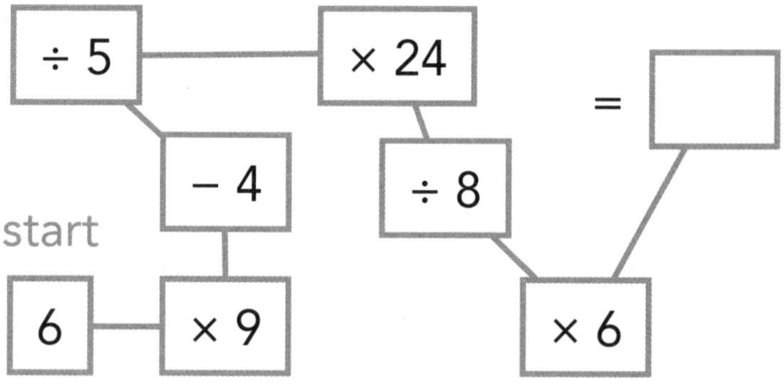

Name ______________________________

There are 9 koalas in the eucalyptus forest. Four of them are in trees. What fraction of these koalas are in the trees?

number of equal parts being separated → 4
total number of equal parts in one set → 9

$\frac{4}{9}$ of the koalas are in the trees.

You have already written fractions for parts of a whole.

$\frac{1}{4}$ is broken off.

You can also write fractions for parts of a set.

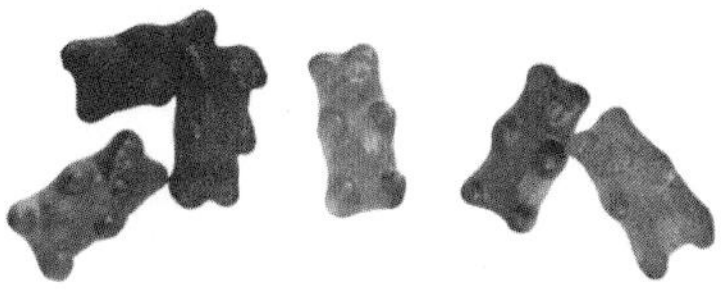

$\frac{3}{6}$ are green.

Write the letter of the fraction of the set that is red.

a. $\frac{3}{5}$ **b.** $\frac{4}{5}$ **c.** $\frac{2}{6}$ **d.** $\frac{1}{8}$

1.

______

2.

______

3.

______

4.

______

Write the fraction.

5. What fraction shows the red apples?

6. What fraction shows the girls?

7. What fraction of the gifts have dots?

Read the chart.

student	age	favorite color	favorite sport
Lindsey	8	purple	soccer
Isaac	9	black	football
Adam	9	green	football
Brittany	8	yellow	ice skating
Jared	8	red	football
Patrick	8	red	basketball
Jessica	9	purple	ice skating
Jillian	8	blue	soccer

8. Write the fraction of the students who are girls. ______

9. Write the fraction of the boys who are 8 years old. ______

10. Write the fraction of the girls whose favorite color is yellow. ______

11. Write the fraction of the students whose favorite sport is football. ______

12. Write the fraction of the boys whose favorite sport is basketball. ______

13. Write the fraction of the students who are 9 years old. ______

Name ______________________________

Identify Equivalent Fractions

There are other fractions that name the same amounts as one half.

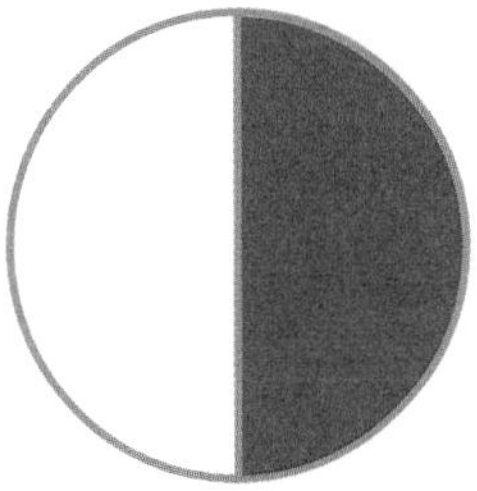

$\frac{1}{2}$

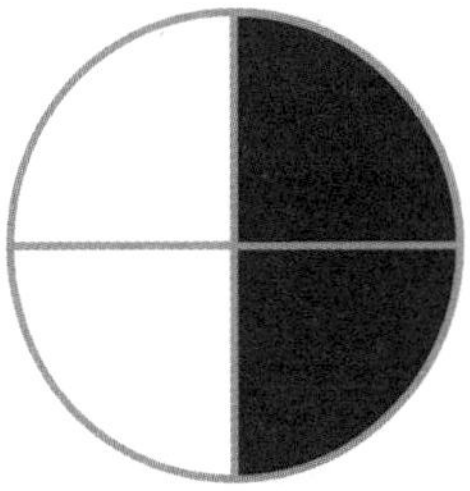

$\frac{2}{4}$

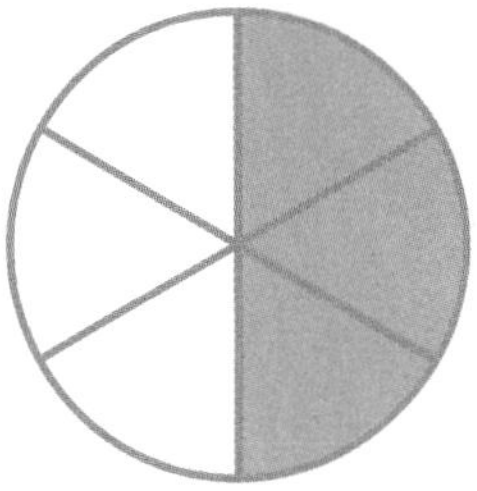

$\frac{3}{6}$

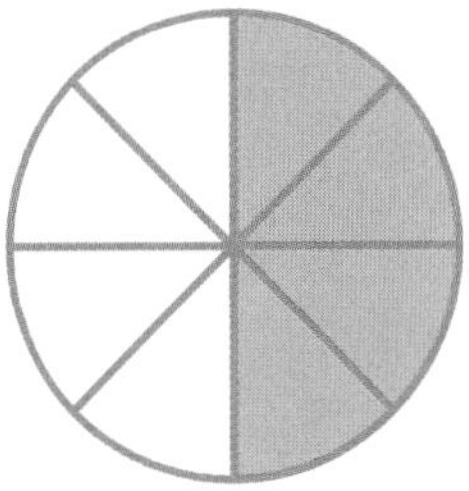

$\frac{4}{8}$

Equivalent fractions are fractions that name the same amount.

How many fourths are in $\frac{1}{2}$?

How many sixths are in $\frac{1}{2}$?

How many eighths are in $\frac{1}{2}$?

Color the lower bar to show an equivalent fraction. Complete the fraction.

1. 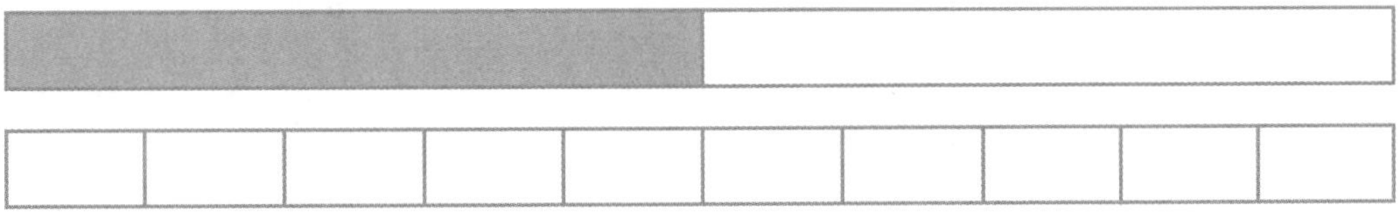

$\frac{1}{2} = \frac{\square}{10}$

2. 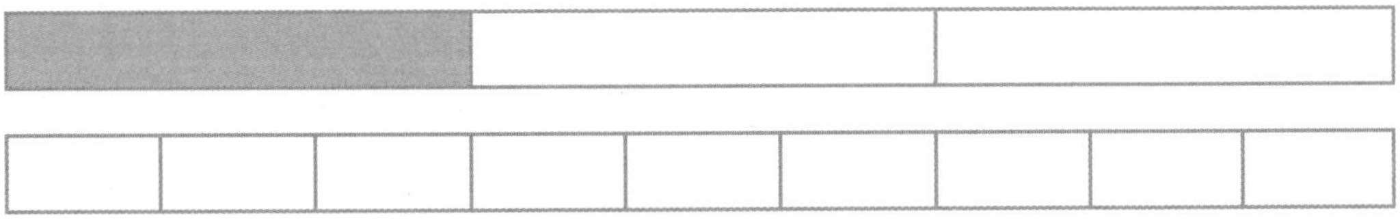

$\frac{1}{3} = \frac{\square}{9}$

3. 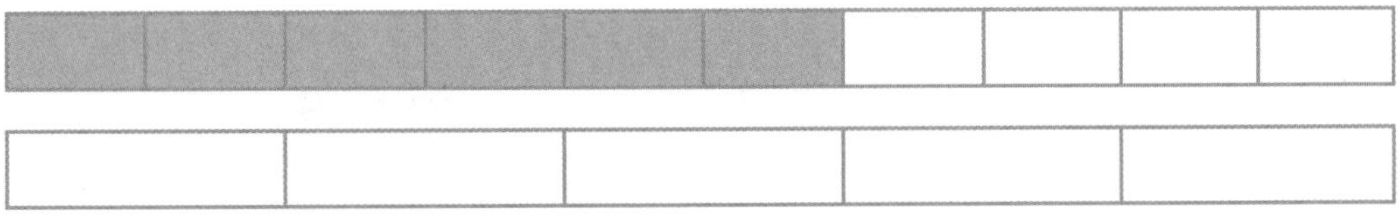

$\frac{6}{10} = \frac{\square}{5}$

Complete the fraction.

4. 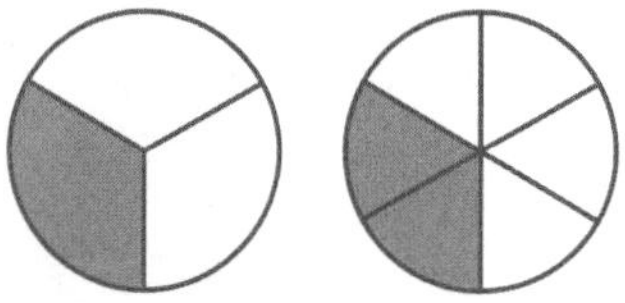

$\frac{1}{3} = \frac{\square}{6}$

6. 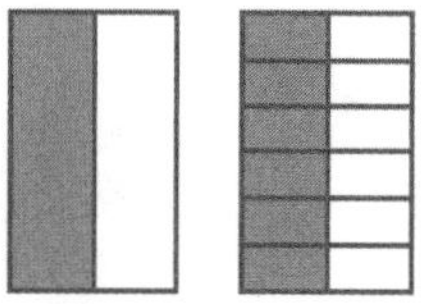

$\frac{1}{2} = \frac{\square}{12}$

8. 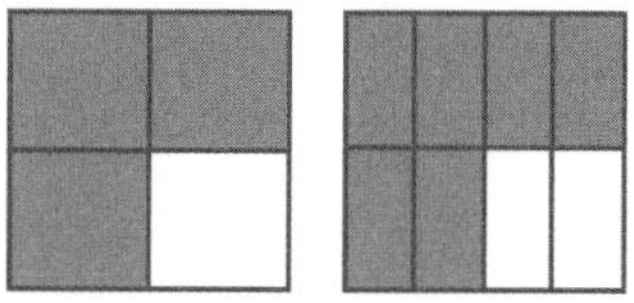

$\frac{3}{4} = \frac{\square}{8}$

5. 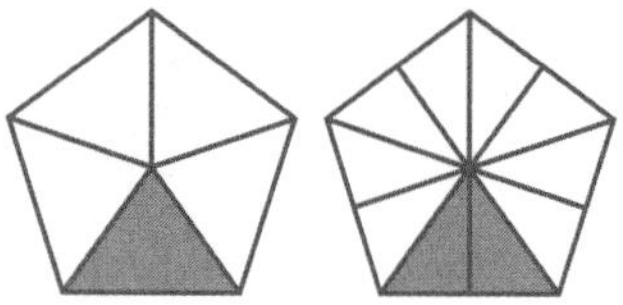

$\frac{1}{5} = \frac{\square}{10}$

7. 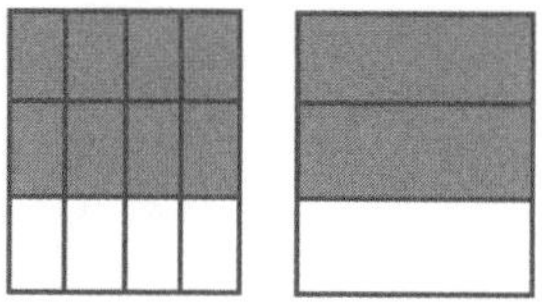

$\frac{8}{12} = \frac{\square}{3}$

9. 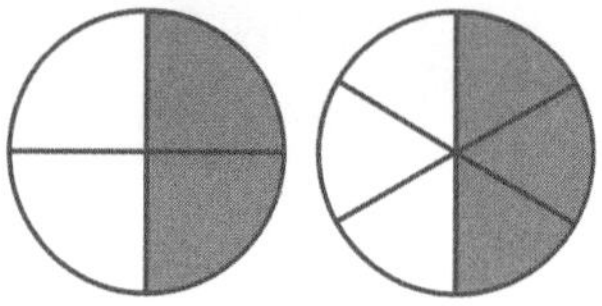

$\frac{2}{4} = \frac{\square}{6}$

Write the equivalent fraction.

10. 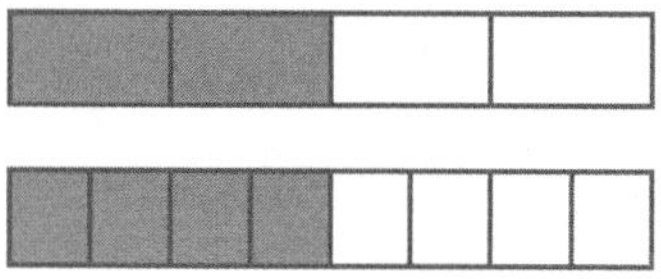

$\frac{2}{4} = \frac{\square}{\square}$

12. 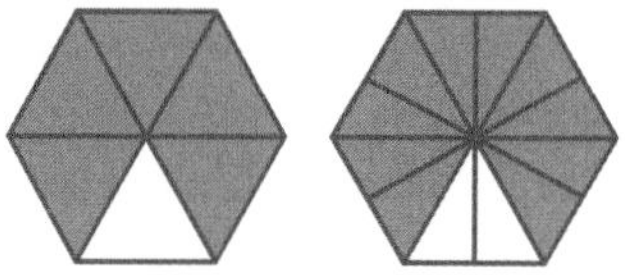

$\frac{5}{6} = \frac{\square}{\square}$

11. 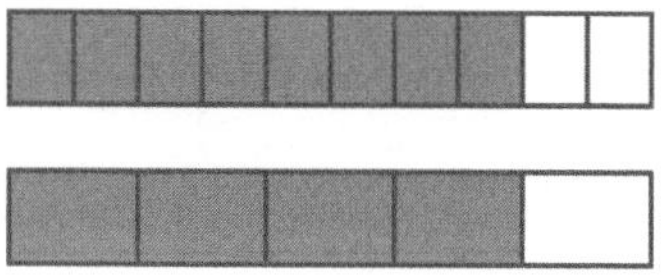

$\frac{8}{10} = \frac{\square}{\square}$

13. 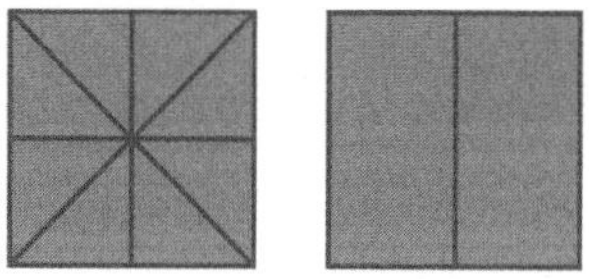

$\frac{8}{8} = \frac{\square}{\square}$

14. 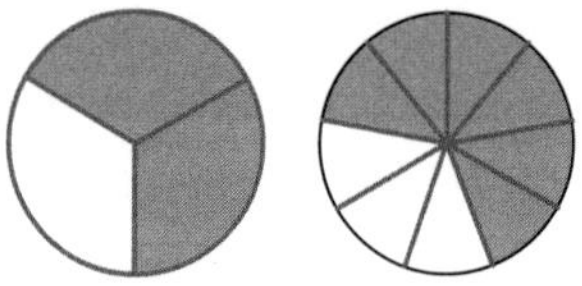

$\frac{2}{3} = \frac{\square}{\square}$

Review

15. **Solve.**

$\begin{array}{r} 468 \\ +293 \\ \hline \end{array}$ $\quad$ $\begin{array}{r} 1,047 \\ -\ \ 829 \\ \hline \end{array}$ $\quad$ $\begin{array}{r} 562 \\ \times\ \ \ 7 \\ \hline \end{array}$ $\quad$ $6\overline{)704}$ $\quad$ $6\overline{)1,704}$

Name ______________________________

Compare Fractions 10.5

Miss Watkins' class earned a pizza party for learning Bible verses. Their two pizzas were the same size. Five-eighths of the sausage slices and $\frac{1}{4}$ of the pepperoni slices were left uneaten. Were more sausage slices left or more pepperoni?

More sausage slices were left.

$\frac{5}{8} > \frac{1}{4}$

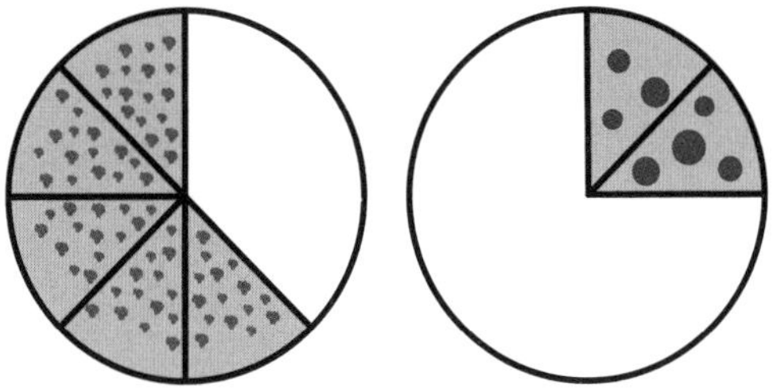

To compare fractions with the same denominator, look at the numerators. The larger the numerator, the larger the fraction.

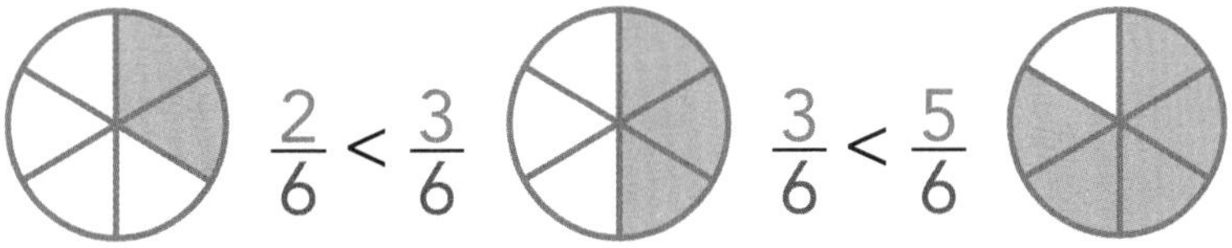

$\frac{2}{6} < \frac{3}{6}$ $\frac{3}{6} < \frac{5}{6}$

To compare fractions with the same numerator but different denominators, remember that the larger the denominator, the smaller the parts.

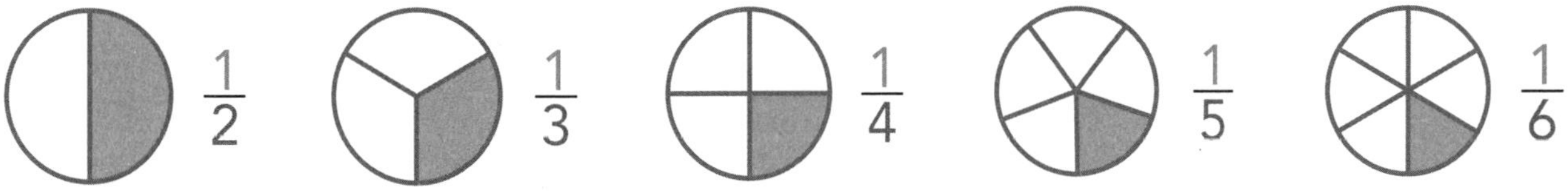

$\frac{1}{2}$ 2 parts | $\frac{1}{3}$ 3 parts | $\frac{1}{4}$ 4 parts | $\frac{1}{5}$ 5 parts | $\frac{1}{6}$ 6 parts

Circle the larger fraction.

1. $\frac{1}{3}$ 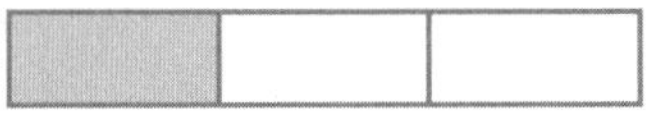

   $\frac{2}{3}$ 

2. $\frac{7}{8}$ 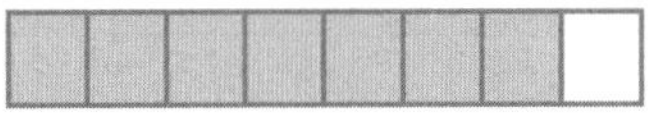

   $\frac{2}{8}$ 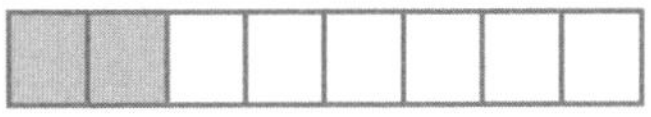

3. $\frac{3}{5}$ 

   $\frac{1}{2}$ 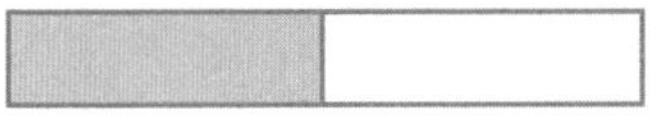

Write >, <, or =.

4. 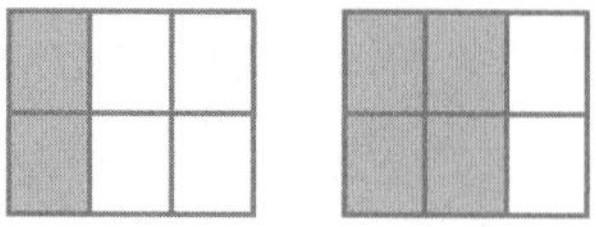

$\frac{2}{6} \bigcirc \frac{4}{6}$

6. 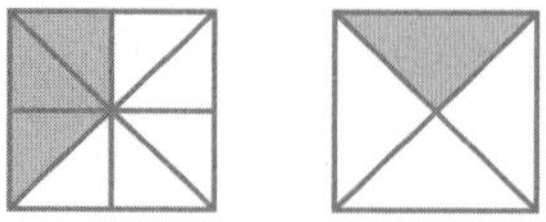

$\frac{3}{8} \bigcirc \frac{1}{4}$

8. 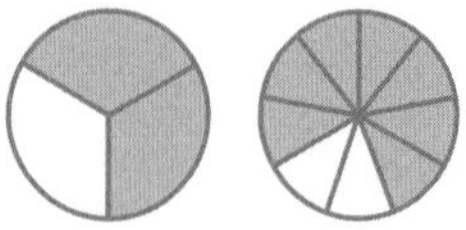

$\frac{2}{3} \bigcirc \frac{7}{9}$

5. 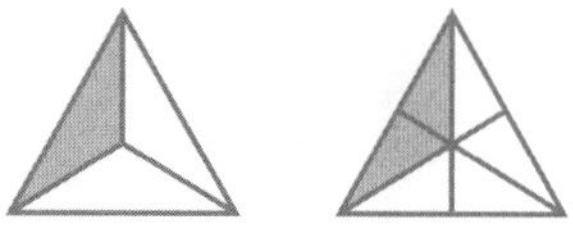

$\frac{1}{3} \bigcirc \frac{2}{6}$

7. 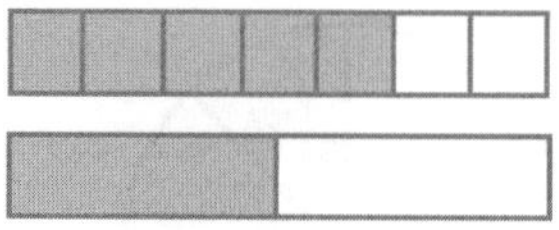

$\frac{5}{7} \bigcirc \frac{1}{2}$

9. 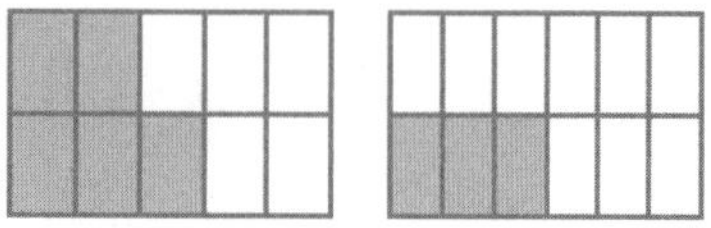

$\frac{5}{10} \bigcirc \frac{3}{12}$

Shade the models to show each fraction. Write >, <, or =.

10. 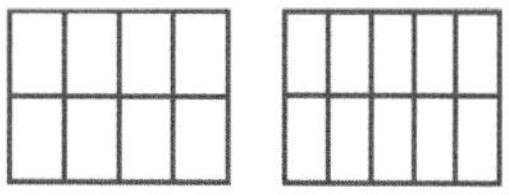

$\frac{1}{8} \bigcirc \frac{1}{10}$

11. 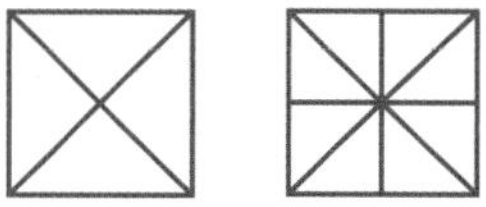

$\frac{2}{4} \bigcirc \frac{3}{8}$

12. 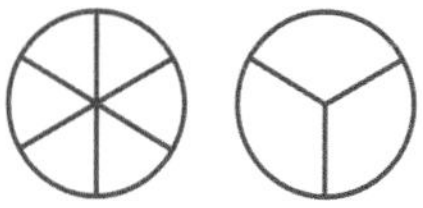

$\frac{4}{6} \bigcirc \frac{1}{3}$

13. 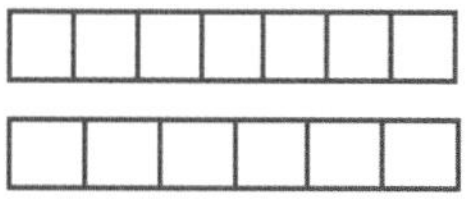

$\frac{3}{7} \bigcirc \frac{3}{6}$

Use pencil to lightly shade the fraction strips to help you compare the fractions.
Write >, <, or =.

14. $\frac{1}{3} \bigcirc \frac{4}{6}$

15. $\frac{1}{4} \bigcirc \frac{2}{6}$

16. $\frac{5}{8} \bigcirc \frac{2}{5}$

17. $\frac{2}{7} \bigcirc \frac{3}{4}$

18. $\frac{5}{6} \bigcirc \frac{4}{8}$

19. $\frac{2}{4} \bigcirc \frac{3}{6}$

a. 

b. 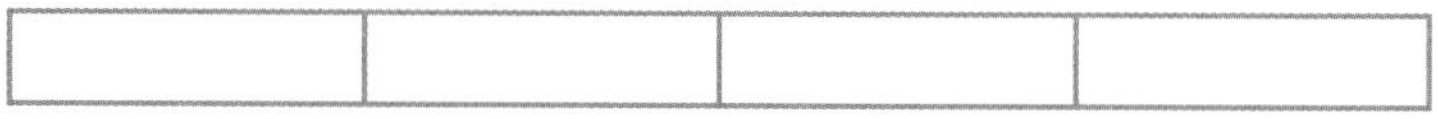

c. 

d. 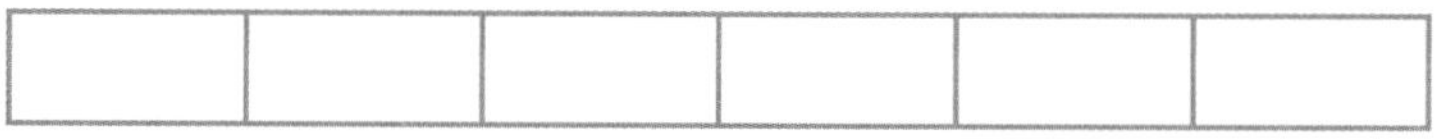

e. 

f. 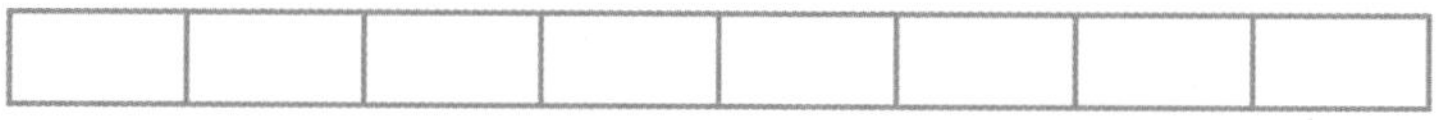

Name ____________________

Equivalent Fractions 10.6

A scientist recorded that one-half the wallabies in an Australian animal park had joeys, which are baby wallabies. If there were 12 wallabies, how many of them had joeys?

$$\frac{1}{2} = \frac{?}{12}$$

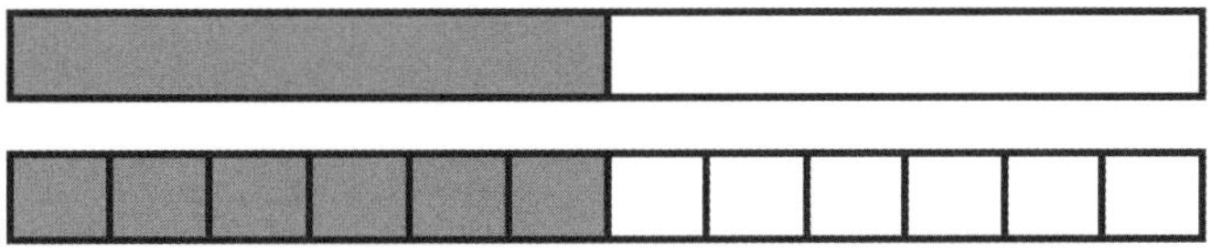

$$\frac{1}{2} = \frac{6}{12}$$

Six of the wallabies have joeys.

Since $\frac{1}{2}$ and $\frac{6}{12}$ are the same amount, then $\frac{1}{2} = \frac{6}{12}$. They are equivalent fractions.

Use models to identify equivalent fractions.

$\frac{1}{3}$

$\frac{2}{6}$

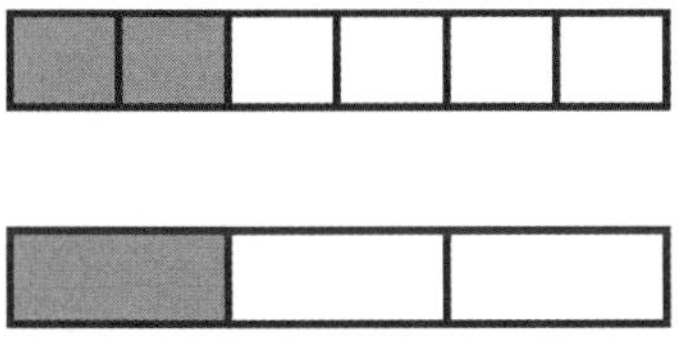

$$\frac{1}{3} = \frac{2}{6}$$

$\frac{1}{4}$ $\frac{2}{8}$

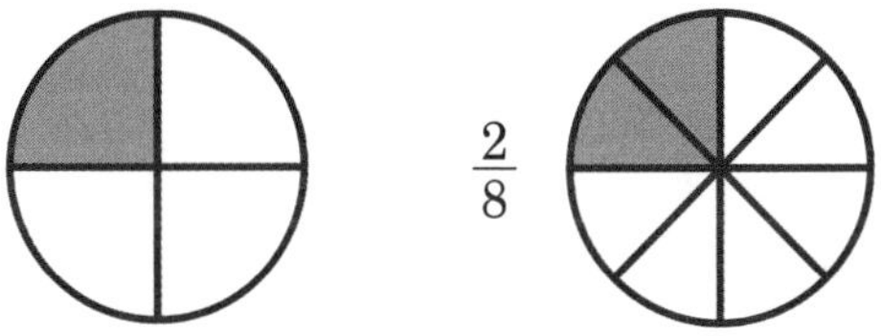

$$\frac{1}{4} = \frac{2}{8}$$

1. Use multiplication and division to find equivalent fractions. Shade in the fraction strips to check the answer.

Step 1—Divide.

$$\frac{2}{5} = \frac{?}{10}$$

÷

$10 \div 5 =$ ________

Step 2—Multiply. Multiply that quotient by the numerator.

×

$$\frac{2}{5} = \frac{?}{10}$$

$2 \times 2 =$ ________

$$\frac{2}{5} = \frac{?}{10}$$

$$\frac{2}{5} = \frac{\square}{10}$$

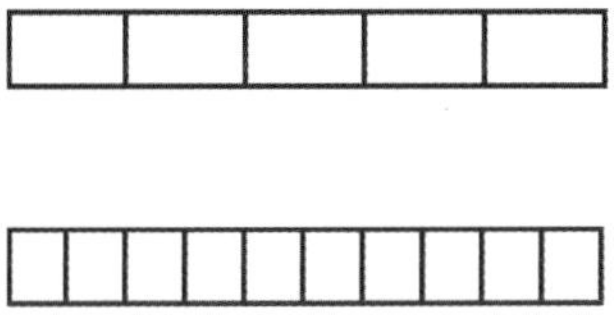

2. **Divide the ninths into 3 equal groups. Shade 2 of those groups. Fill in the blanks.**

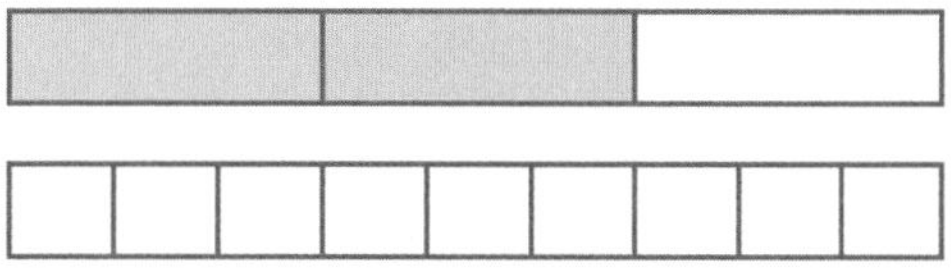

$\frac{2}{3} = \frac{?}{9}$

$\frac{2}{3} = \frac{\square}{9}$

$9 \div 3 = \_\_\_\_$

$2 \times \_\_\_\_ = \_\_\_\_$

3. **Divide the tenths into 5 equal groups. Shade 3 of those groups. Fill in the blanks.**

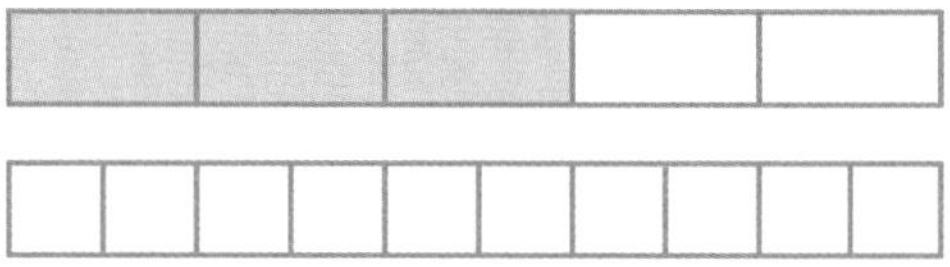

$\frac{3}{5} = \frac{?}{10}$

$\frac{3}{5} = \frac{\square}{10}$

$10 \div 5 = \_\_\_\_$

$3 \times \_\_\_\_ = \_\_\_\_$

Find the equivalent fraction.

4. $1 \times 3 = 3$
$\frac{1}{3} = \frac{3}{9}$
$9 \div 3 = 3$

6. $\frac{3}{8} = \frac{\square}{16}$

8. $\frac{6}{10} = \frac{\square}{20}$

10. $\frac{4}{5} = \frac{\square}{10}$

11. $\frac{2}{6} = \frac{\square}{12}$

5. $1 \times 4 = 4$
$\frac{1}{2} = \frac{\square}{8}$
$8 \div 2 = 4$

7. $\frac{2}{7} = \frac{\square}{21}$

9. $\frac{1}{9} = \frac{\square}{18}$

Complete the fractions. Solve.

12. One-third of the third graders wear glasses. If there are 15 students in the class, how many of them wear glasses?

$\frac{\_\_}{\_\_} = \frac{\_\_}{\_\_}$

____

Name ______________________________

By noon, $\frac{3}{8}$ of a pack of dingoes found a stream of water to drink from. By evening, another $\frac{4}{8}$ of the pack found water. Altogether, what part of the pack found water to drink?

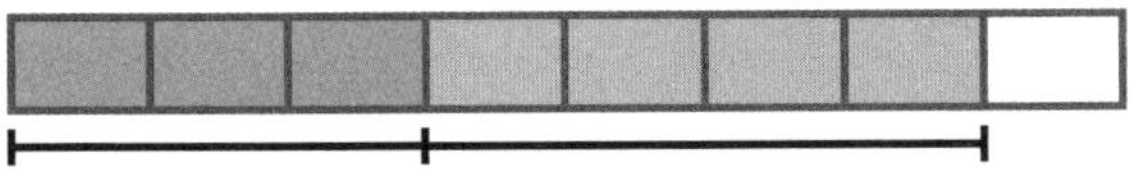

$\frac{3}{8}$ $\frac{4}{8}$

$$\frac{3}{8} + \frac{4}{8} = \frac{7}{8}$$

$\frac{7}{8}$ of the dingo pack found water.

To add fractions with the same denominators, just add the numerators. The denominator stays the same.

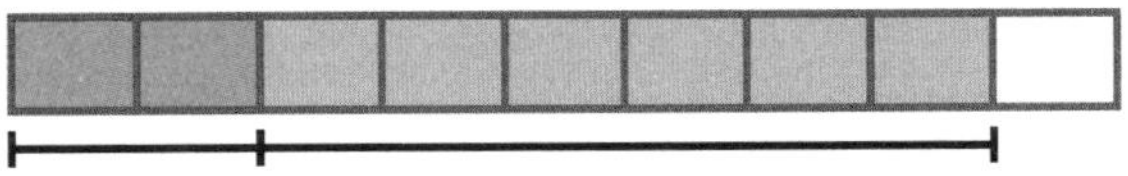

$\frac{2}{9}$ $\frac{6}{9}$

$$\frac{2}{9} + \frac{6}{9} = \frac{8}{9}$$

Add the numerators. Write the denominator. Shade the model to show the answer.

1. $\frac{3}{12} + \frac{4}{12} = \_\_\_$

2. $\frac{2}{18} + \frac{7}{18} = \_\_\_$

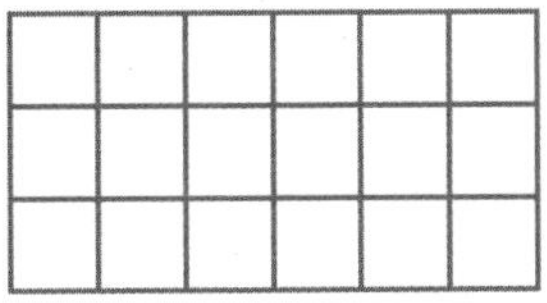

3. $\frac{5}{10} + \frac{2}{10} = \_\_\_$

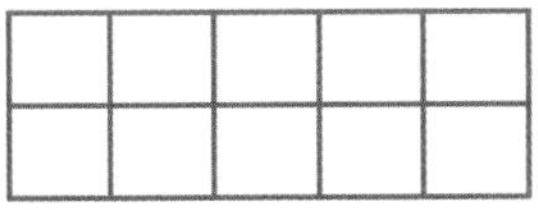

Add.

4. $\frac{3}{8} + \frac{4}{8} = $ ___

5. $\frac{5}{9} + \frac{1}{9} = $ ___

6. $\frac{8}{12} + \frac{3}{12} = $ ___

7. $\frac{2}{18} + \frac{8}{18} = $ ___

8. $\frac{6}{10} + \frac{2}{10} = $ ___

9. $\frac{7}{11} + \frac{2}{11} = $ ___

10. $\frac{10}{15} + \frac{3}{15} = $ ___

11. $\frac{11}{20} + \frac{3}{20} = $ ___

12. $\frac{3}{14} + \frac{9}{14} = $ ___

13. $\frac{4}{15} + \frac{10}{15} = $ ___

14. $\frac{14}{30} + \frac{11}{30} = $ ___

15. $\frac{7}{19} + \frac{8}{19} = $ ___

16. $\frac{7}{12} + \frac{3}{12} = $ ___

17. $\frac{4}{6} + \frac{1}{6} = $ ___

18. $\frac{7}{25} + \frac{14}{25} = $ ___

Solve.

19. There were 50 solar cars in a race across the Australian Outback. Fifteen cars were red, 27 were yellow, and the rest were blue. What fraction of the cars were red or yellow?

____

Review

Circle the figure congruent to the figure on the left.

20.

21.

22.

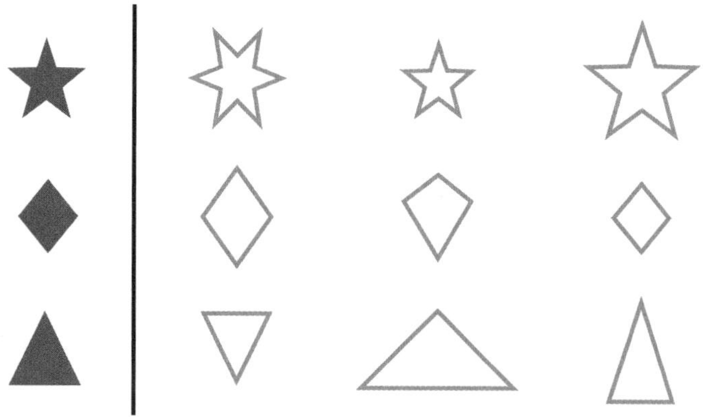

Name ______________________

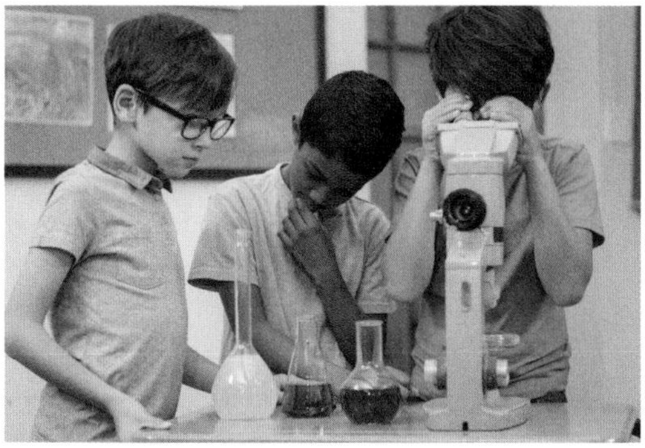

For an experiment, the boys filled a set of 3 flasks. If $\frac{1}{3}$ of the flasks were used, what fraction were not used?

To subtract fractions with the same denominators, subtract the numerators. The denominator stays the same.

$$\frac{2}{3} + \frac{1}{3} = \frac{3}{3}$$

$$\frac{3}{3} - \frac{1}{3} = \frac{2}{3}$$

Subtract the numerators. Write the difference.

$$\frac{3}{3} - \frac{1}{3} = \frac{2}{3}$$

The denominator stays the same. Write the denominator.

Compare the two problems above. What is different? What is the same?

Subtract. Mark the fraction you take away.

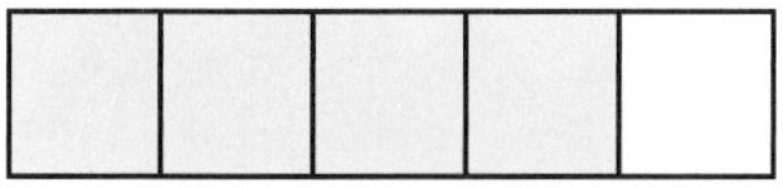

$$\frac{4}{5} - \frac{3}{5} = \frac{1}{5}$$

1. How much of the whole is shaded to start? ________

How much of the shaded part will you take away?

____

How much of the shaded part is left? ________

2.

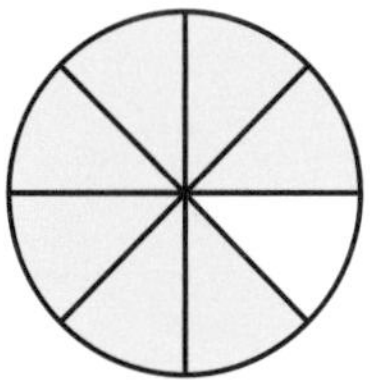

$$\frac{7}{8} - \frac{3}{8} = \_\_$$

3.

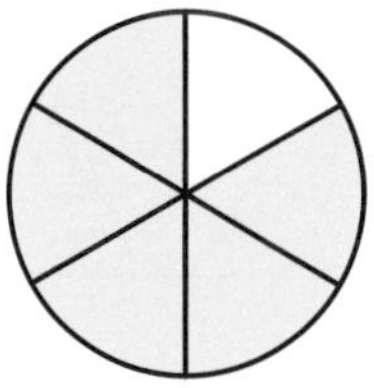

$$\frac{5}{6} - \frac{1}{6} = \_\_$$

4.

$$\frac{4}{4} - \frac{2}{4} = \_\_$$

Subtract.

5. $\dfrac{8}{12} - \dfrac{3}{12} = $ ———

6. $\dfrac{9}{12} - \dfrac{5}{12} = $ ———

7. $\dfrac{6}{7} - \dfrac{2}{7} = $ ———

8. $\dfrac{5}{9} - \dfrac{2}{9} = $ ———

9. $\dfrac{7}{10} - \dfrac{4}{10} = $ ———

10. $\dfrac{13}{16} - \dfrac{5}{16} = $ ———

11. $\dfrac{10}{15} - \dfrac{8}{15} = $ ———

12. $\dfrac{14}{30} - \dfrac{11}{30} = $ ———

13. $\dfrac{11}{12} - \dfrac{1}{12} = $ ———

14. $\dfrac{9}{10} - \dfrac{3}{10} = $ ———

15. $\dfrac{7}{9} - \dfrac{4}{9} = $ ———

16. $\dfrac{9}{10} - \dfrac{6}{10} = $ ———

Add or subtract.

17. $\dfrac{5}{8} + \dfrac{2}{8} = $ ———

18. $\dfrac{4}{5} - \dfrac{1}{5} = $ ———

19. $\dfrac{3}{4} - \dfrac{2}{4} = $ ———

Solve.

20. Tabor cut a watermelon into 12 slices. He ate 2 slices and then served the remaining $\dfrac{10}{12}$ of the watermelon slices to his family's Bible study group. They ate $\dfrac{7}{12}$ of the slices. How much of the watermelon was left over?

Review
Multiply.

21. $\begin{array}{r} 56 \\ \times\ 6 \\ \hline \end{array}$

22. $\begin{array}{r} 42 \\ \times\ 5 \\ \hline \end{array}$

23. $\begin{array}{r} 777 \\ \times\ \ 7 \\ \hline \end{array}$

24. $\begin{array}{r} 536 \\ \times\ \ 9 \\ \hline \end{array}$

25. $\begin{array}{r} 609 \\ \times\ \ 8 \\ \hline \end{array}$

Name ____________________

This sandwich is cut into fourths. Since all 4 of the fourths are here, there are $\frac{4}{4}$ or 1 whole. No matter how you slice it, each is one whole sandwich.

$\frac{2}{2}$  $\frac{4}{4}$  $\frac{8}{8}$ 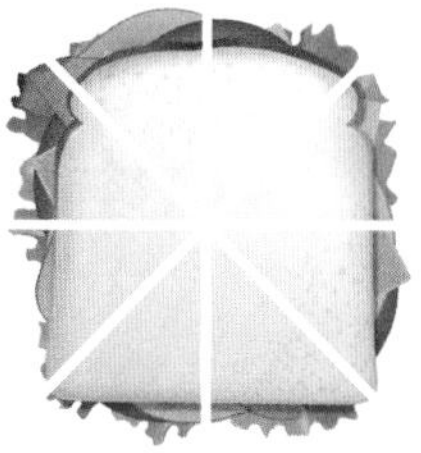

$1\frac{1}{4}$ 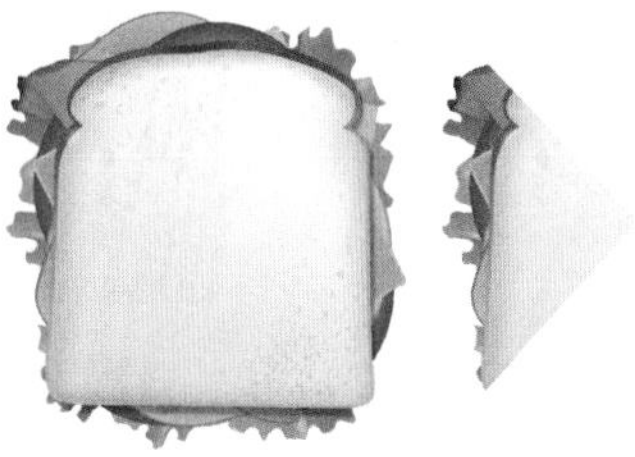

What if you were hungry enough to eat more than one sandwich? If you ate this much, you would have eaten one and one-fourth. Write it as $1\frac{1}{4}$. Say, "One and one-fourth."

> A mixed number is a whole number and a fraction, such as $1\frac{1}{4}$.

Write the mixed number.

1.  ____________

2. 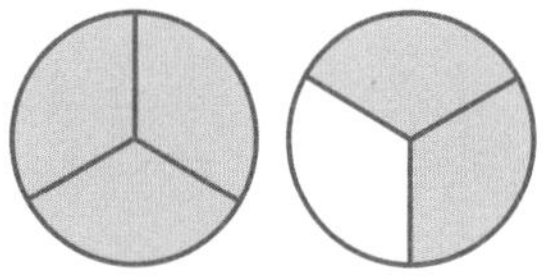 ____________

3. 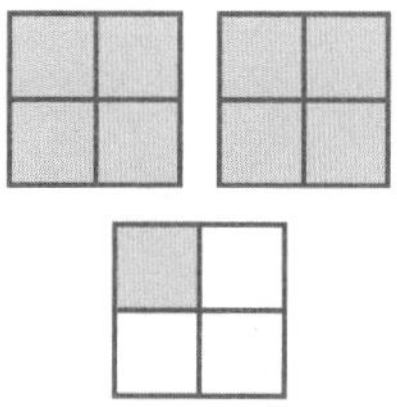 ____________

4. 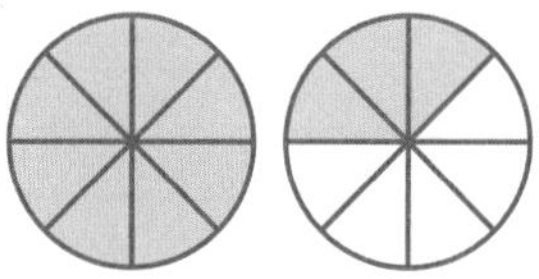 ____________

Write the mixed number.

5. 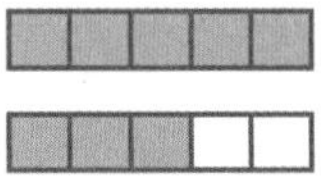

6. 

7. 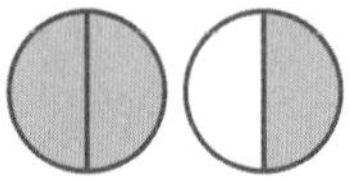

8. 

______ ______ ______ ______

Write the letter of the model that matches the object.

a. 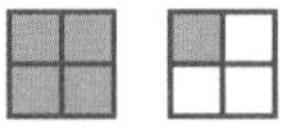

b. 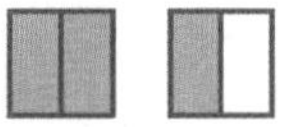

c. 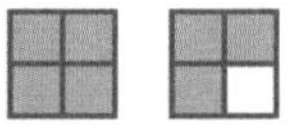

d. 

9. 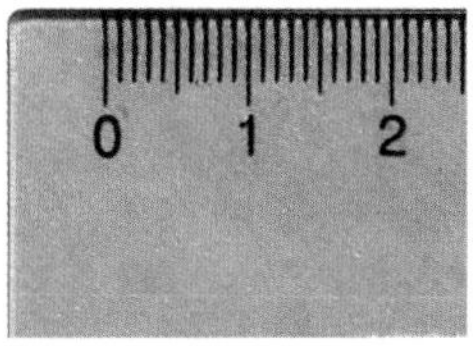

10. 

11. 

12. 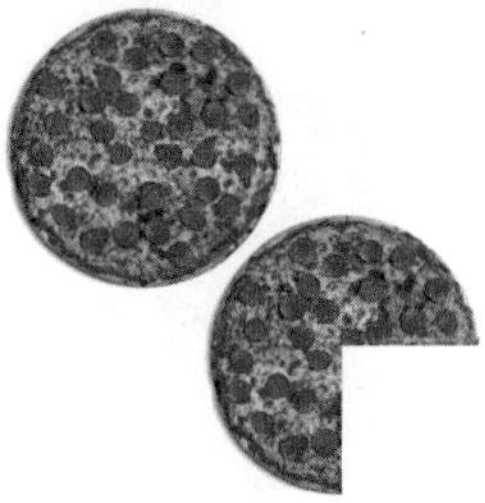

______ ______ ______ ______

Draw a model and divide it to show each fraction.

13. $\frac{5}{5}$

14. $1\frac{1}{5}$

15. $2\frac{2}{6}$

Review

Measure each line to the nearest centimeter and nearest inch.

16. ______________________________

17. __________________________________

18. __________________

19. ____

	cm	in.
16.		
17.		
18.		
19.		

Name ______________________________

Fractions on Number Lines 10.10

Number lines can help you understand the order of numbers, fractions, and mixed numbers.

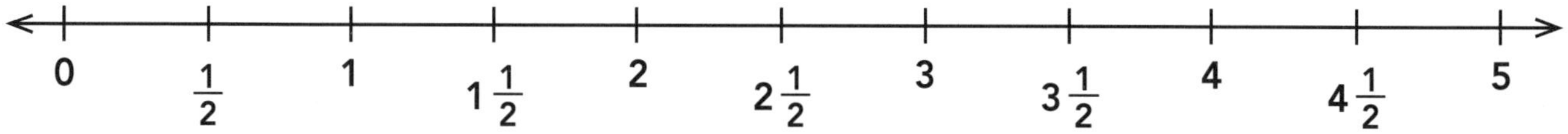

Which platypus is longer?

This platypus is $\frac{1}{2}$ meter long.

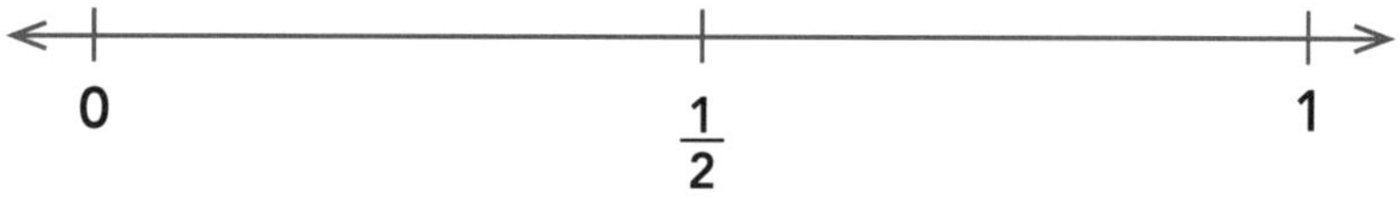

This platypus is $\frac{2}{5}$ meter long.

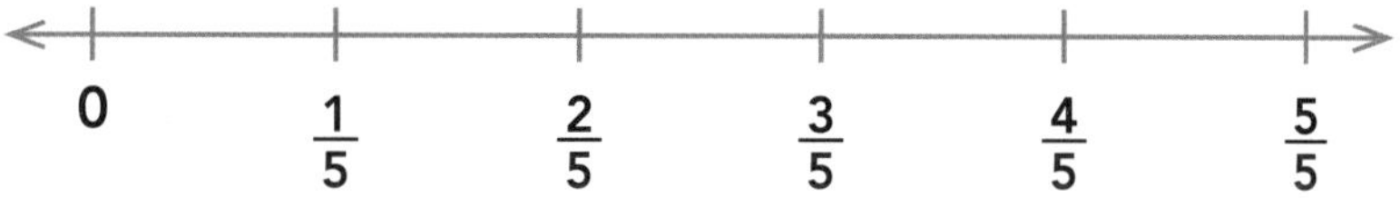

Since $\frac{1}{2}$ m is longer than $\frac{2}{5}$ m, the first platypus is longer.

Fill in the missing numbers on the number line.

1.

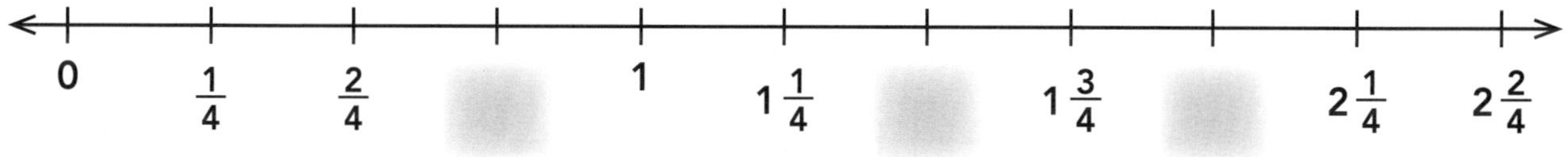

2.

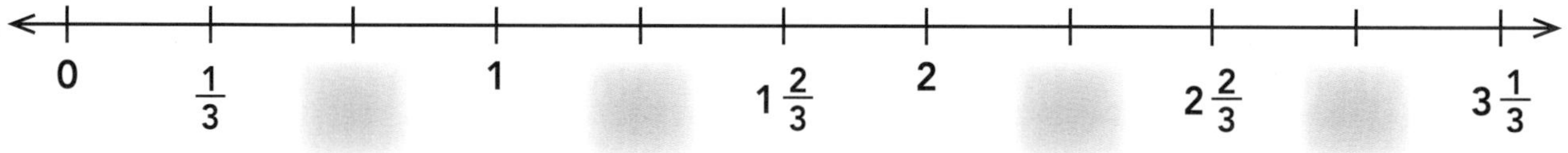

3.

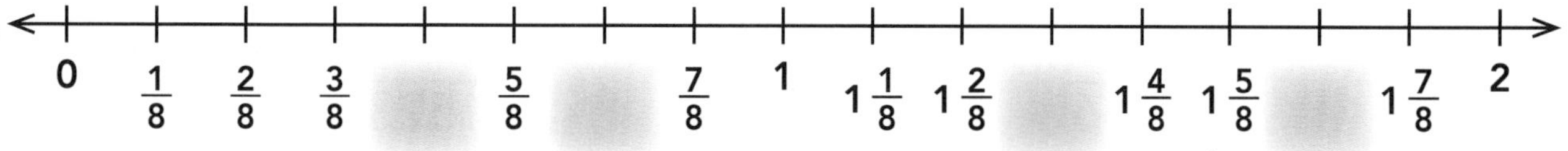

4. Write the length of the skip shown on each number line.

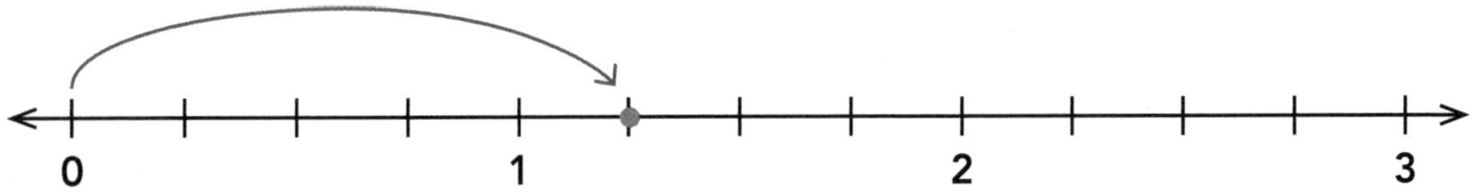

______

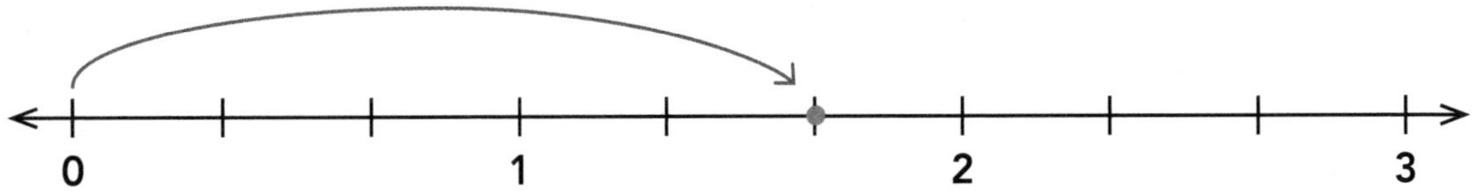

______

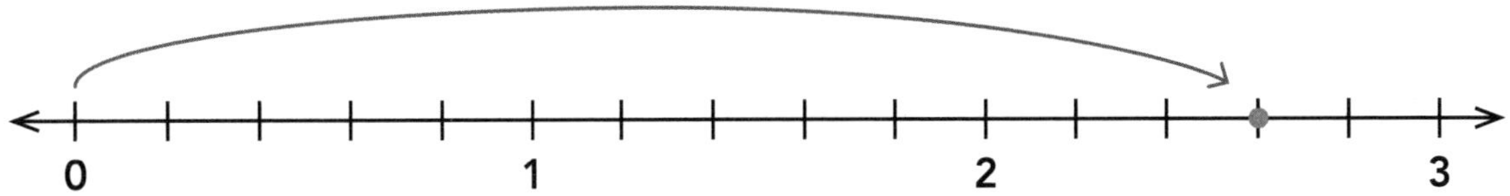

______

5. Draw a skip to the correct place on each number line.

$1\frac{5}{8}$ 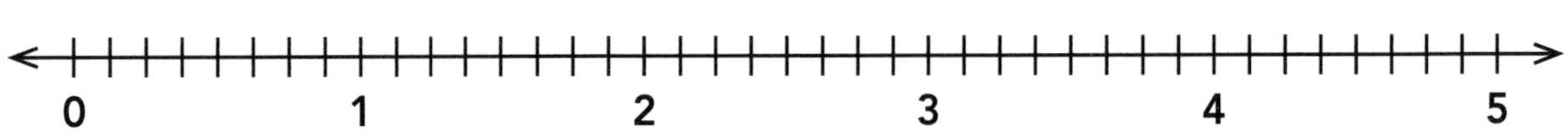

$2\frac{1}{3}$ 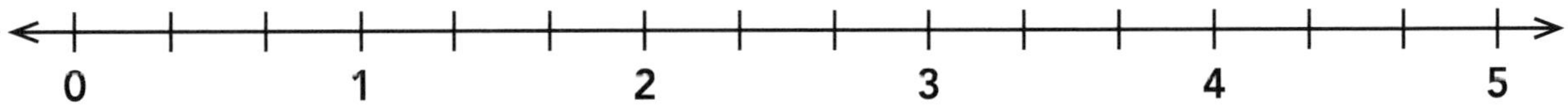

6. Draw skips to show how fractions can be added. Write the sum.

$\frac{2}{6} + \frac{3}{6} =$ 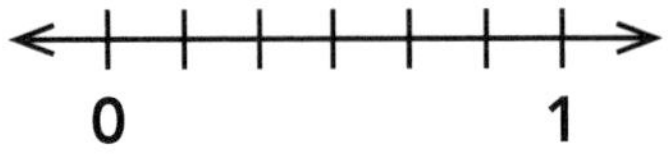

$\frac{3}{4} + \frac{1}{4} =$ 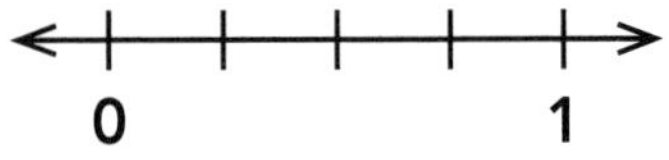

$\frac{3}{8} + \frac{3}{8} =$ 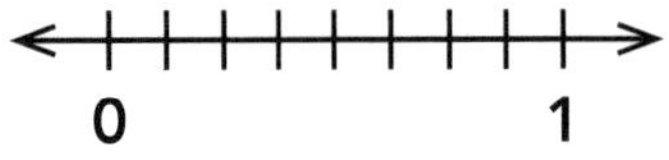

$\frac{1}{6} + \frac{3}{6} =$ 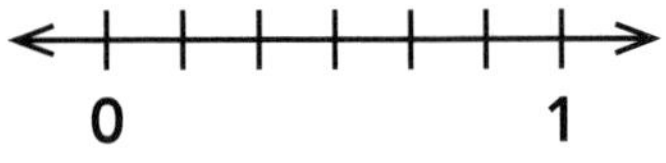

Review

Divide.

7. $3\overline{)69}$ 8. $2\overline{)46}$ 9. $7\overline{)123}$ 10. $4\overline{)523}$ 11. $2\overline{)650}$

Name ______________________________

A cook can halve a recipe to make less. The cook will use exactly half of all the listed ingredients.

To halve fractions, make an equal fraction that can be halved.

$1\frac{1}{2}$ cups brown sugar = $1\frac{2}{4}$ ⟶ half of $1\frac{2}{4}$ = $\frac{3}{4}$ cup brown sugar

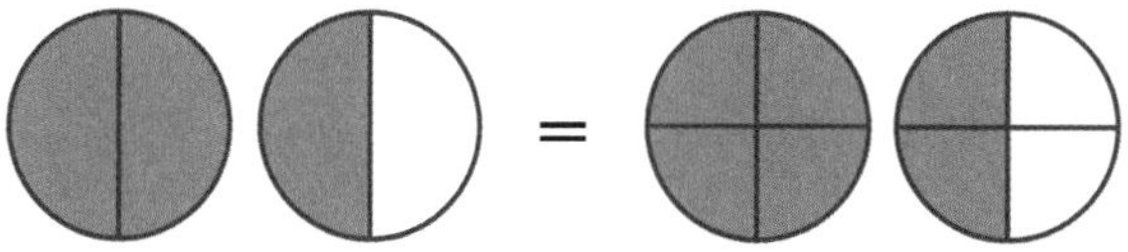

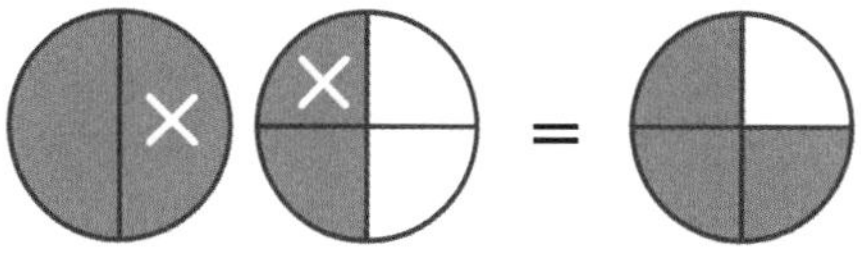

$\frac{3}{4}$ cup chopped walnuts = $\frac{6}{8}$ cup chopped walnuts ⟶ half of $\frac{6}{8}$ = $\frac{3}{8}$ cup chopped walnuts

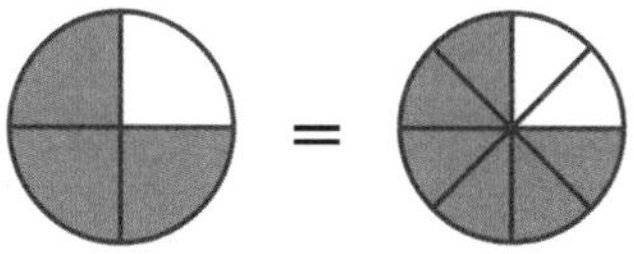

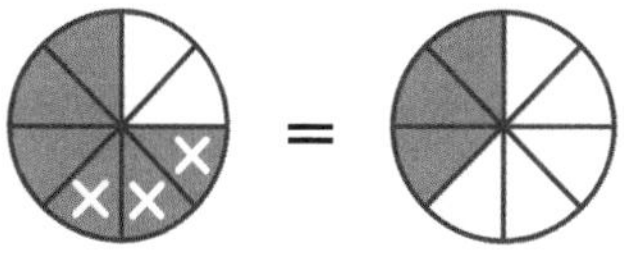

Use models to halve the recipe. Rewrite each quantity of an ingredient.

Australian Anzac Biscuits

1. $1\frac{1}{2}$ cups oats
2. $1\frac{1}{2}$ cups shredded coconut
3. $1\frac{1}{2}$ cups flour
4. $\frac{3}{4}$ cup sugar
5. $\frac{1}{2}$ cup butter
6. $1\frac{1}{2}$ tablespoons light corn syrup
7. $1\frac{1}{2}$ teaspoons baking soda
8. $4\frac{1}{2}$ tablespoons water

Mark an X to halve each amount. Write the new amount.

9. half of $\frac{3}{4}$ cup = ______ cup

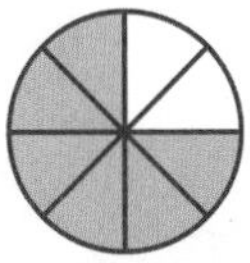

10. half of $\frac{2}{3}$ cup = ______ cup

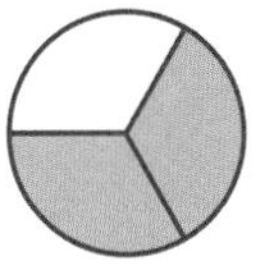

11. half of $1\frac{1}{4}$ cups = ______ cups

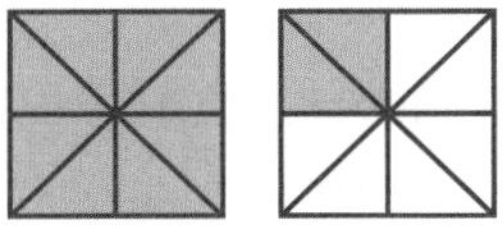

12. half of $1\frac{1}{2}$ lb = ______ lb

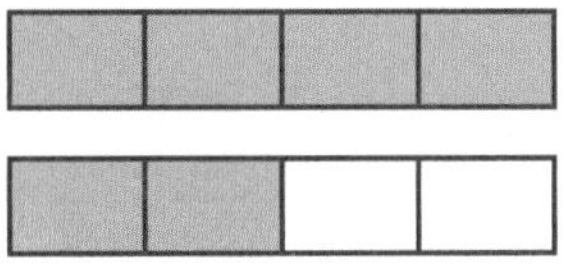

Solve.

13. Maria's mom told her to buy 2 packages of chopped nuts. One package had $\frac{3}{4}$ cup and the other had 1 cup. Which amount is larger?

____

14. Sydney poured $\frac{2}{3}$ cup of milk into the batter. After mixing, he added $\frac{1}{3}$ cup more. How much milk did Sydney use in the recipe?

____

15. Niko will make a half recipe of brownies. The full recipe requires $2\frac{1}{2}$ cups flour. How much flour will he use?

____

16. There was $\frac{3}{4}$ cup of flour in a container. D'Ette used $\frac{1}{4}$ cup in a recipe. How much flour is left?

____

17. Grandpa's caramel corn recipe uses $\frac{2}{3}$ cup of corn syrup. To make half the recipe, how much corn syrup is needed?

____

18. Violeta poured $\frac{1}{2}$ cup of tomato sauce into her chili. Later, she added $\frac{1}{2}$ cup more. How much tomato sauce did she use?

____

Name ______________________________

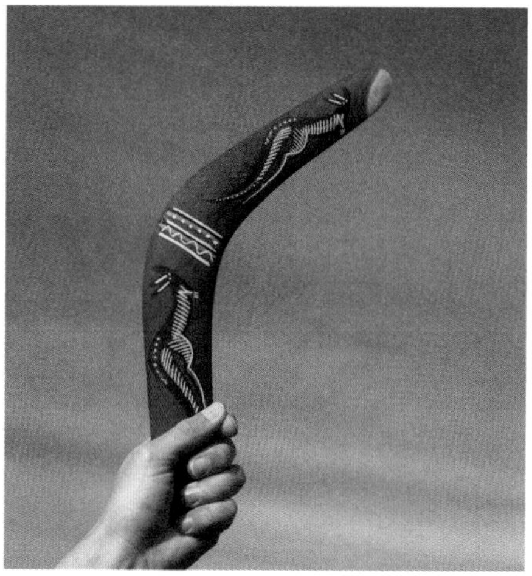

Australians enjoy throwing boomerangs. Stores sell many styles and colors of boomerangs. So far today, one store has sold 6 boomerangs. Three of them had painted patterns, 1 was red, and 2 were green. If the store sold another 6, for a total of 12, predict how many of each style would be sold.

If 3 out of 6 have a pattern,
then 6 out of 12 will have a pattern.

$$\frac{\text{pattern}}{\text{boomerangs}} \quad \frac{3}{6} \overset{\times}{=} \frac{6}{12} \quad (\div)$$

If 1 out of 6 is red,
then 2 out of 12 will be red.

$$\frac{\text{red}}{\text{boomerangs}} \quad \frac{1}{6} \overset{\times}{=} \frac{2}{12} \quad (\div)$$

If 2 out of 6 are green,
then 4 out of 12 will be green.

$$\frac{\text{green}}{\text{boomerangs}} \quad \frac{2}{6} \overset{\times}{=} \frac{4}{12} \quad (\div)$$

A boomerang store sold a total of 18 boomerangs. How many of each style did they probably sell?

1.

$$\frac{3}{6} = \frac{\quad}{18}$$

2.

$$\frac{1}{6} = \frac{\quad}{18}$$

3.

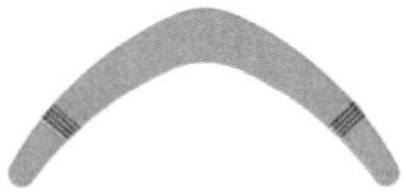

$$\frac{2}{6} = \frac{\quad}{18}$$

Answer the questions about the tennis balls.

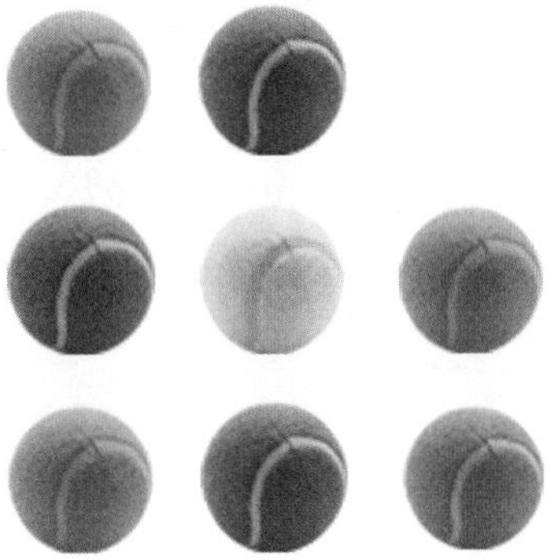

4. Are you more likely to pick a yellow or a purple ball?

____

5. Which two colors are you equally likely to pick?

____

6. How many orange balls are you likely to get in

8 picks? ____________ in 16 picks? ____________

Complete the following probabilities.

7. 2 out of 5, what would you predict for 10 picks? ____________

8. 2 out of 8, what would you predict for 24 picks? ____________

9. 4 out of 9, what would you predict for 18 picks? ____________

10. 1 out of 4, what would you predict for 12 picks? ____________

11. 5 out of 6, what would you predict for 18 picks? ____________

12. 5 out of 8, what would you predict for 16 picks? ____________

These Australian animal stickers are in a bag. You pick one without looking. Answer the questions.

13. Name an impossible outcome. ____________

14. Name a certain outcome. ____________

15. Name all possible outcomes. ____________

Write the probability for each outcome.

16. koala	17. kangaroo	18. cockatoo
____________	____________	____________

Name ____________________

Chapter 10 Review 10.13

Write the letter of the definition on the line.

1. ____ fraction
2. ____ numerator
3. ____ denominator
4. ____ equivalent fractions
5. ____ mixed number

a. a whole number and a fraction

b. the bottom number in a fraction that shows the total number of parts in one whole

c. a number that names part of a whole or part of a set

d. the top number in a fraction that shows the number of equal parts being separated

e. fractions that are the same amount

Draw a line to match the fraction with the model.

6. 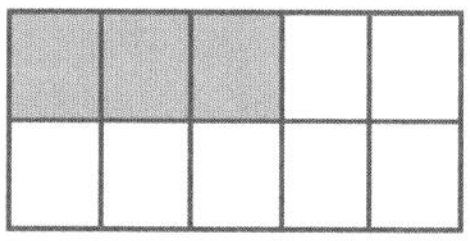 •

7. 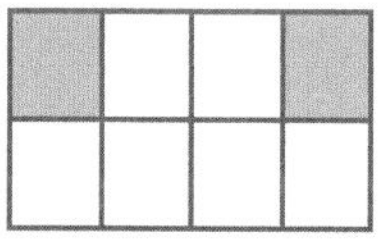 •

8. 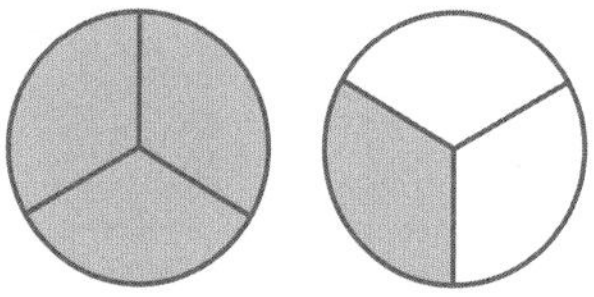 •

9. 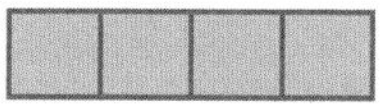 •

• two-eighths

• $\frac{4}{4}$

• $\frac{3}{10}$

• one and one-third

Write >, <, or =.

10. 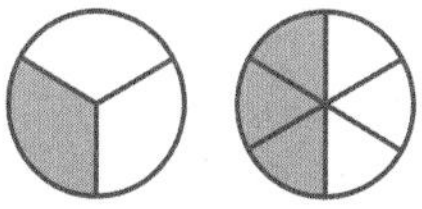

$\frac{1}{3} \bigcirc \frac{3}{6}$

11. 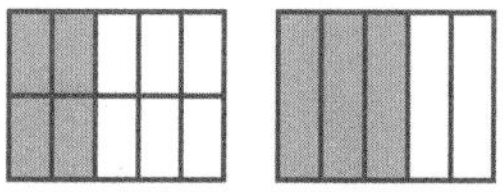

$\frac{4}{10} \bigcirc \frac{3}{5}$

12. 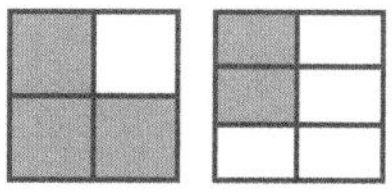

$\frac{3}{4} \bigcirc \frac{2}{6}$

Write the fraction or mixed number.

13.  ______

14. 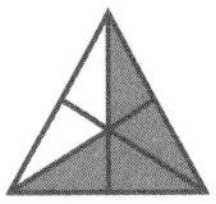 ______

15. 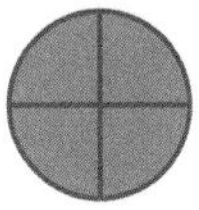 ______

16. 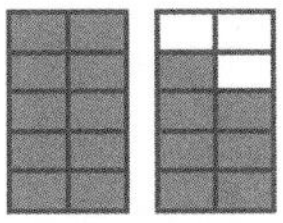 ______

Write the equivalent fraction.

17. 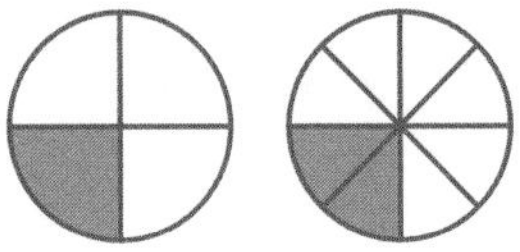

$\frac{1}{4} = $ —

18. 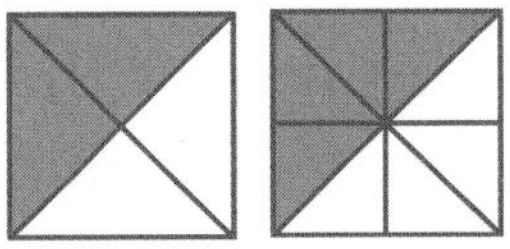

$\frac{2}{4} = $ —

19. 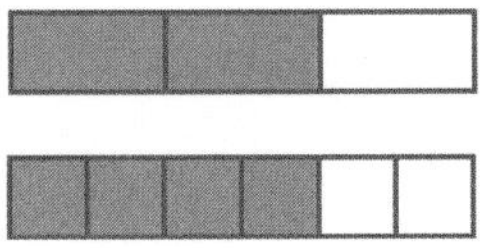

$\frac{2}{3} = $ —

20. 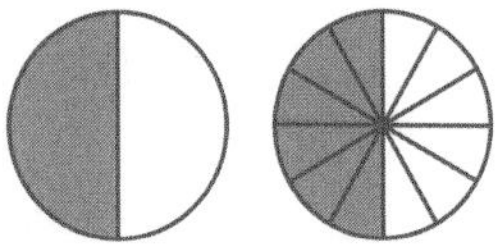

$\frac{1}{2} = $ —

Write the equivalent fraction.

21. $\frac{3}{4} = \frac{\square}{16}$ (× ÷)

22. $\frac{2}{9} = \frac{\square}{18}$ (× ÷)

23. $\frac{2}{8} = \frac{\square}{24}$ (× ÷)

24. $\frac{1}{2} = \frac{\square}{10}$ (× ÷)

25. $\frac{3}{7} = \frac{\square}{28}$ (× ÷)

Add or subtract.

26. $\frac{3}{8} + \frac{2}{8} = $ —

28. $\frac{1}{6} + \frac{4}{6} = $ —

30. $\frac{9}{10} - \frac{5}{10} = $ —

27. $\frac{7}{9} - \frac{1}{9} = $ —

29. $\frac{7}{12} - \frac{4}{12} = $ —

31. $\frac{8}{8} - \frac{1}{8} = $ —

Draw a skip to the correct place on each number line.

32. $1\frac{3}{8}$ 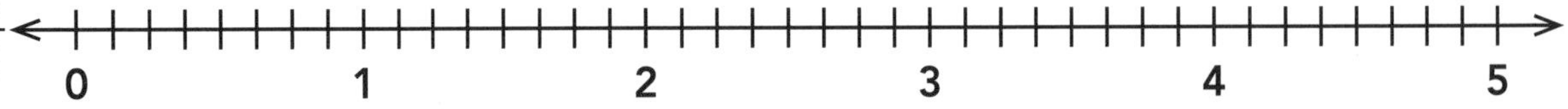

33. $2\frac{2}{3}$ 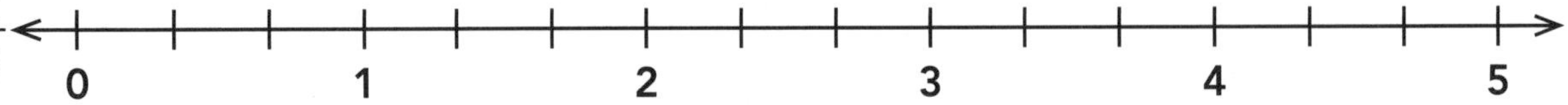

Name ______________________________

Label each angle as **right**, **obtuse**, or **acute**.

1. 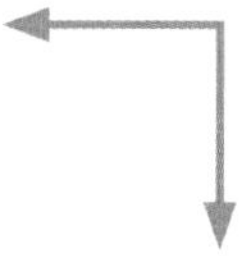 ______________

2.  ______________

3.  ______________

4. 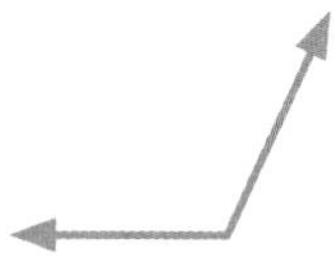 ______________

Complete the chart.

	plane figure	number of line segments	number of angles
5.	circle		
6.	triangle		
7.	rectangle		

Label each pattern **slide**, **flip**, or **turn**. Complete the pattern.

8. ______________ S S S ______________

9. ______________ E Ǝ E ______________

10. ______________ ⊢ T ______________

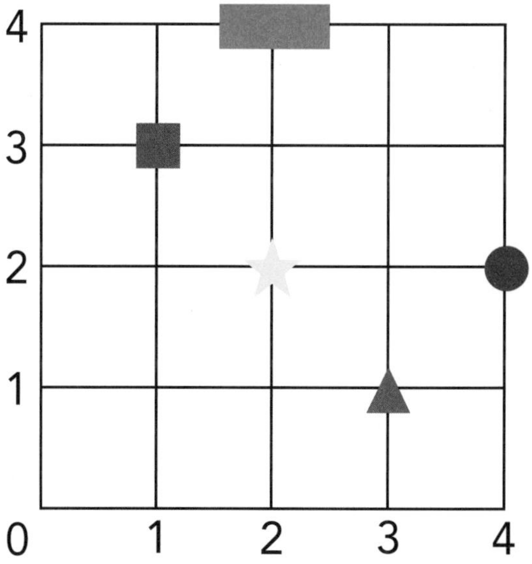

Draw the shape for each ordered pair.

11. (3, 1) ________ 12. (4, 2) ________

Write the ordered pair for each shape.

13.  ________ 14.  ________

Measure each line segment to the nearest half inch and centimeter.

15. ______ in. ______ cm

16. ______ in. ______ cm

Write the temperature.

17. 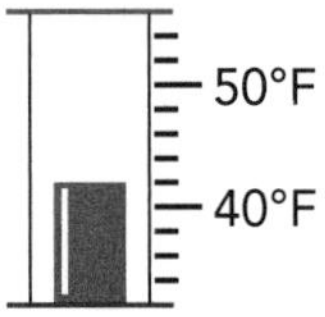

______

18. 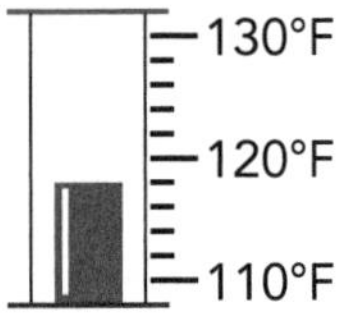

______

19. 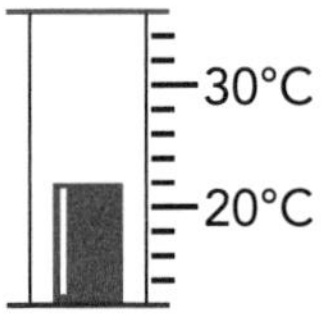

______

20. 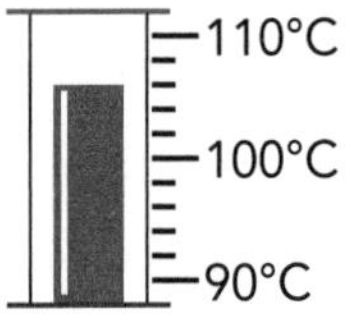

______

Circle the better estimate.

21. kangaroo tail 30 in. or 30 ft

22. boomerang 3 oz or 3 lb

23. soda bottle 2 gal or 2 L

24. kangaroo hop 10 ft or 10 km

Write the fraction or mixed number.

25. 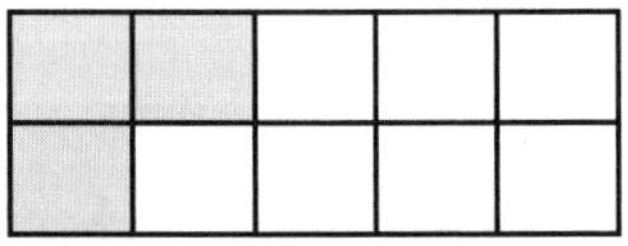
______

26. 
______

27. 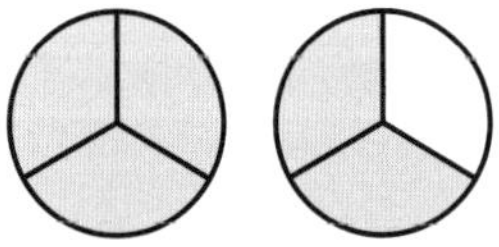
______

Write >, <, or =.

28. $\frac{3}{6} \bigcirc \frac{1}{6}$

29. $\frac{4}{5} \bigcirc \frac{5}{5}$

30. $\frac{6}{8} \bigcirc \frac{5}{8}$

31. $\frac{8}{8} \bigcirc 1$

Make equivalent fractions.

32. $\frac{3}{7} = \frac{\square}{14}$ (× above, ÷ below)

33. $\frac{9}{10} = \frac{\square}{40}$ (× above, ÷ below)

34. $\frac{3}{3} = \frac{\square}{9}$ (× above, ÷ below)

35. $\frac{5}{8} = \frac{\square}{24}$ (× above, ÷ below)

Chapter 11
Decimals

Every tithe of the herd and flock—every tenth animal that passes under the shepherd's rod—will be holy to the Lord.
Leviticus 27:32

Key Ideas:

Place Value: identifying decimals to hundredths

Decimals: relating fractions to decimals and reading, writing, comparing, and ordering decimals

Addition: adding decimals

Subtraction: subtracting decimals

Money: relating money to decimals

Name ____________________

Many desert animals live in the Sonoran desert in Arizona. A scorpion is a desert insect that has large front claws and a stinger on its tail.

Phoenix, Arizona is a desert city. It is 107.8 miles from Tucson, Arizona. The decimal number 107.8 means $107\frac{8}{10}$. The same distance in kilometers is 173.48 km, or $173\frac{48}{100}$ km.

A decimal number uses place value to show a part of a whole. Decimal numbers use a decimal point, a small dot, to separate the whole numbers from the decimal numbers. One place to the right of the decimal point is the tenths place.

107.8 =

hundreds	tens	ones .	tenths
		.	

Two places to the right of the decimal point is the hundredths place.

173.48 =

hundreds	tens	ones .	tenths	hundredths
		.		

Write the numbers in the correct places on each chart.

1. 1.6

ones .	tenths
.	

2. 3.8

ones .	tenths
.	

3. 1.62

ones .	tenths	hundredths
.		

4. 3.85

ones .	tenths	hundredths
.		

Fill in the chart. If there are no ones, write a zero in the ones place on the chart.

5. 0.03 7. 0.63 10. 4.04

6. 0.41 8. 1.75 11. 3.78

9. 2.12

	ones .	tenths	hundredths
5.	.		
6.	.		
7.	.		
8.	.		
9.	.		
10.	.		
11.	.		

Circle the digit in the ones place.

12. 1.62 13. 0.91 14. 1.08 15. 1.5 16. 1.74

Circle the digit in the tenths place.

17. 1.18 18. 1.26 19. 0.85 20. 0.04 21. 1.93

Circle the digit in the hundredths place.

22. 2.34 23. 4.59 24. 0.38 25. 6.78 26. 1.24

Review

Solve.

27. $\begin{array}{r} 365 \\ 240 \\ +149 \\ \hline \end{array}$

28. $\begin{array}{r} 4{,}802 \\ -1{,}958 \\ \hline \end{array}$

29. $\begin{array}{r} 28 \\ \times\ 8 \\ \hline \end{array}$

30. $\begin{array}{r} 367 \\ \times\ 5 \\ \hline \end{array}$

31. $\begin{array}{r} 6{,}002 \\ -5{,}103 \\ \hline \end{array}$

Name ______________________________

A jackrabbit jumped 6 feet. It is able to leap 10 feet. The jackrabbit leaped $\frac{6}{10}$ of its longest leap.

Each bar is one tenth.

$\frac{6}{10}$ 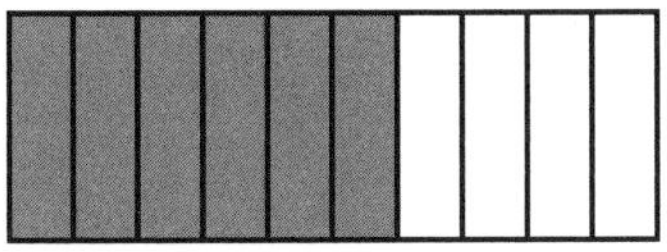

The shaded bars are $\frac{6}{10}$ of the total.

You can write $\frac{6}{10}$ as a decimal. The decimal number 0.6 is read "six-tenths."
A tenth is 1 part out of 10.

Color.

1. 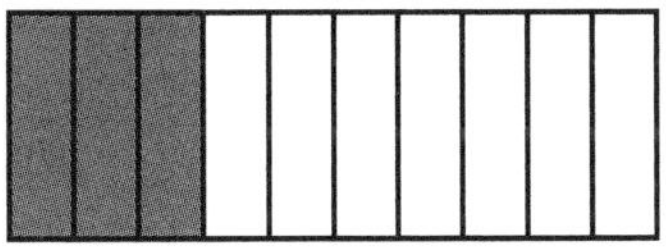

3 out of 10,

$\frac{3}{10}$ = 0.3,

three-tenths

2. 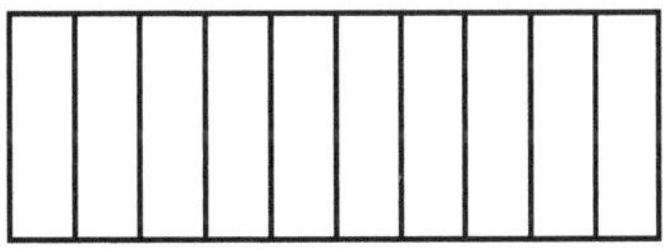

7 out of ______,

$\frac{7}{\square}$ = 0. ______,

______ -tenths

3. 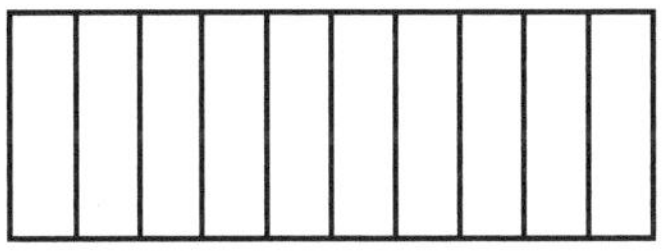

9 out of ______,

$\frac{\square}{10}$ = 0.______,

______ -tenths

Write the fraction and the decimal for each picture.

4. 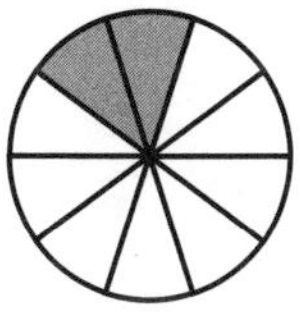

$\frac{\square}{\square}$ ______

5. 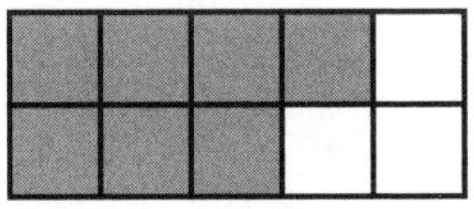

$\frac{\square}{\square}$ ______

6. 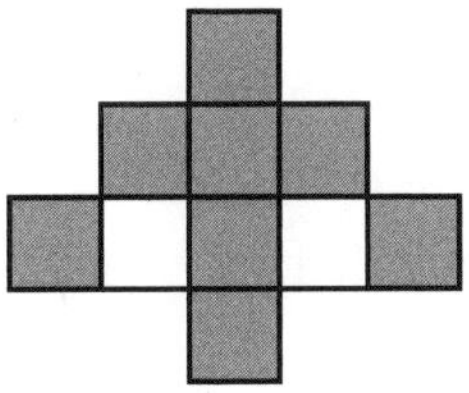

$\frac{\square}{\square}$ ______

7. 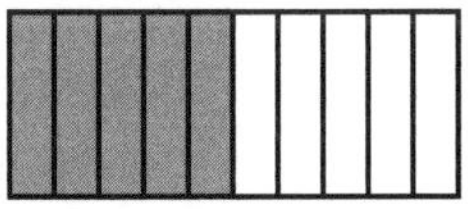

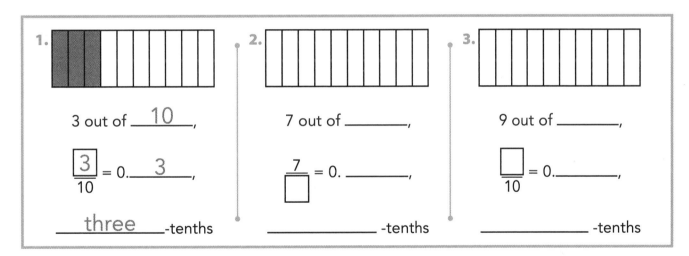

$\frac{\square}{\square}$ ______

Write the decimal number.

8. 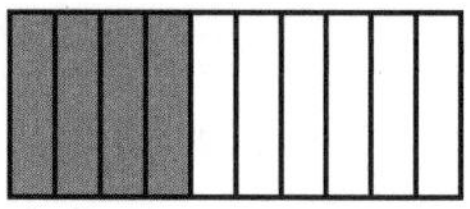

______

9. 

______

10. 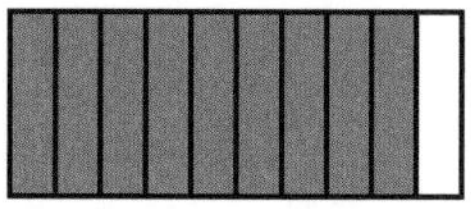

______

11. **Write the decimal for each fraction.**

$\frac{2}{10}$ = ______ $\frac{8}{10}$ = ______ $\frac{3}{10}$ = ______ $\frac{6}{10}$ = ______

12. **Write the fraction for each decimal.**

$0.9 = \frac{\square}{\square}$ $0.6 = \frac{\square}{\square}$ $0.1 = \frac{\square}{\square}$ $0.4 = \frac{\square}{\square}$ $0.5 = \frac{\square}{\square}$

13. **Write the decimal.**

five-tenths ______ eight-tenths ______ two-tenths ______

Solve. Write the answer in decimal form.

14. The Very Large Array radio telescope is located in the desert near Socorro, New Mexico in the United States. Visitors can take a 45-minute tour. Nine out of 10 visitors enjoy the tour. What part of the visitors enjoy the tour?

____

15. Seven out of 10 students who visit the Very Large Array want to return the next year. What part of the students want to return?

____

Name ______________________________

Desert tortoises once thrived in the Sonoran Desert. The number of wild tortoises is now quite small. It is against the law to pick up and to keep wild desert tortoises. However, people can join a program to take care of a tortoise. Marcus' family spent $189.95 to build a safe area to take care of a desert tortoise.

In this price, the 189 stands for whole dollars. The .95 stands for a part of another dollar, or 95 cents. Read this decimal number as "ninety-five hundredths" of a dollar. A hundredth is 1 part out of 100.

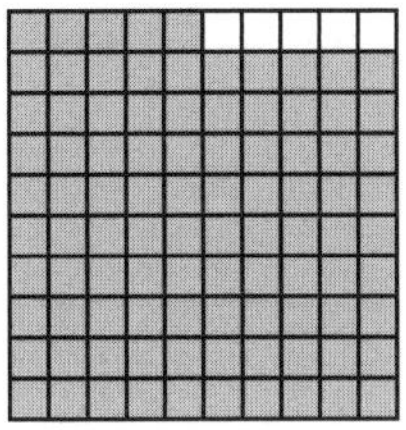

$\frac{95 \text{ cents}}{100 \text{ cents}}$ or $0.95

How much change would you receive from $190.00?

$\frac{5 \text{ cents}}{100 \text{ cents}}$ or $0.05

This zero shows that there are no tenths.

Write the decimal and the fraction for the shaded part of each picture.

1.

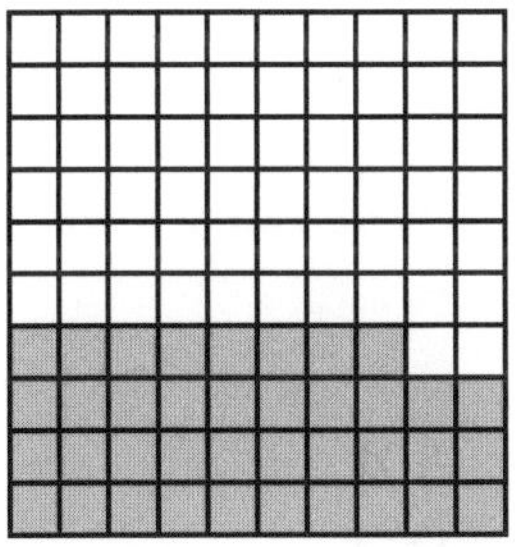

______ $\frac{\square}{\square}$

2.

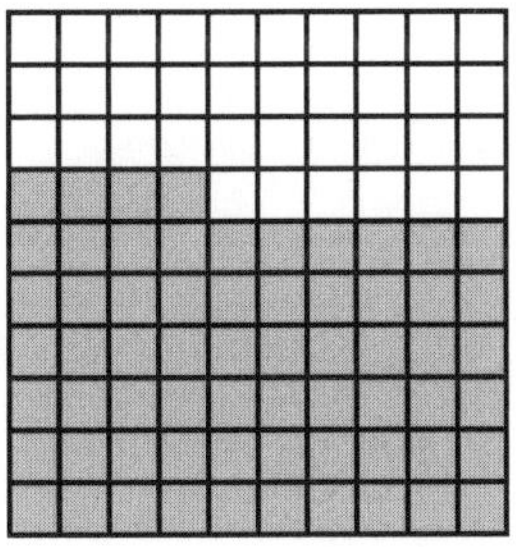

______ $\frac{\square}{\square}$

3.

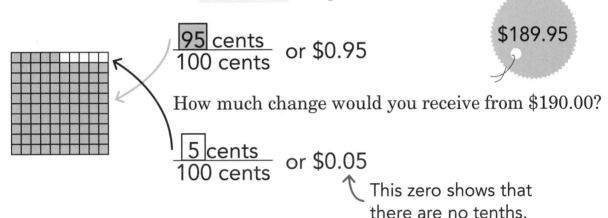

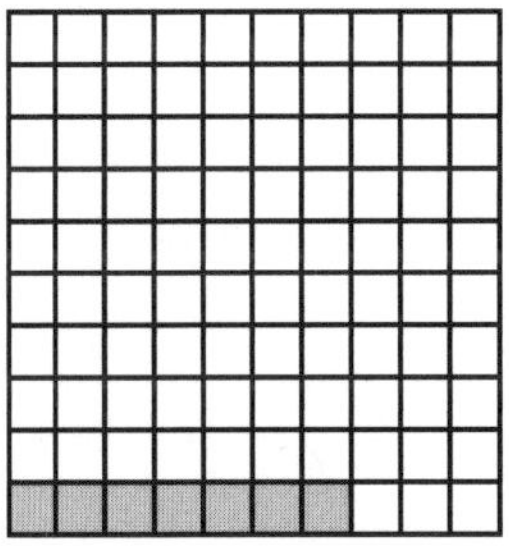

______ $\frac{\square}{\square}$

Write the decimal for each shaded fraction shown.

4. 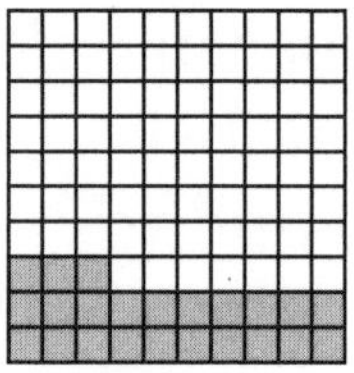 ______

5. 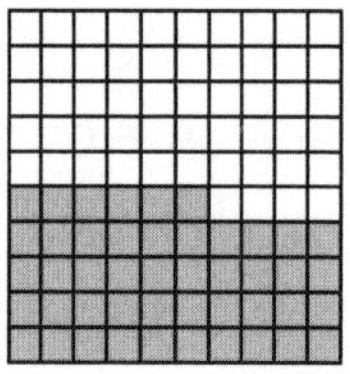 ______

6. 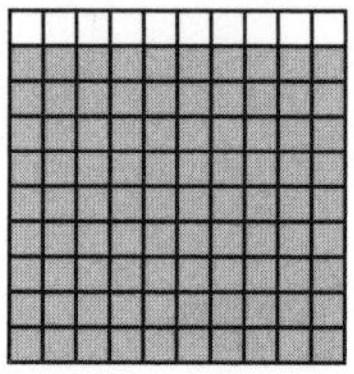 ______

7. 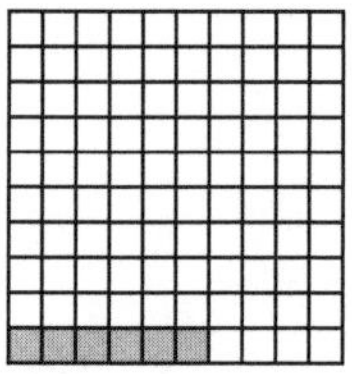 ______

8. Write the decimal for each fraction.

$\frac{29}{100}$ = ______ $\frac{32}{100}$ = ______ $\frac{9}{100}$ = ______ $\frac{17}{100}$ = ______

9. Write the fraction for each decimal.

0.79 = $\frac{\square}{\square}$ 0.14 = $\frac{\square}{\square}$ 0.02 = $\frac{\square}{\square}$ 0.64 = $\frac{\square}{\square}$

10. Explain the difference between 0.07 and 0.7. ______________________________

____

Solve. Write the answer in decimal form.

11. Out of 100 people who live in the same desert neighborhood, 63 said that they would like to adopt a desert tortoise. What part of this group might become caretakers of a desert tortoise?

____

Review

Find the average.

12. 124
136
202 ______

13. 403
369
321 ______
199

14. 14
82
37 ______
51

Name ____________________

Relate Fractions and Decimals 11.4

Both reptiles and amphibians live in the desert. Tiger salamanders need to lay their eggs in water, so they live near ponds or springs in the desert. One salamander laid ten eggs that hatched.

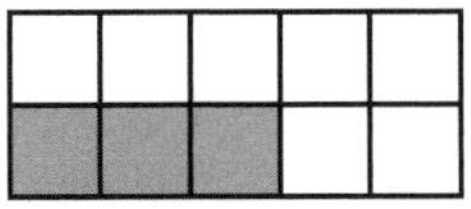

$\frac{3}{10}$ of these baby salamanders are female.

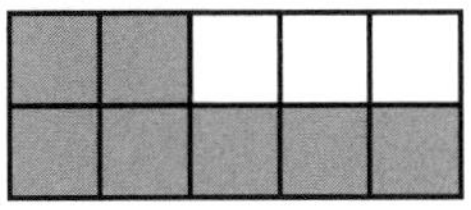

$\frac{7}{10}$ of these baby salamanders are male.

Decimals express parts of a whole without using numerators and denominators. Decimals use place value to show the relationship between the parts and the whole.

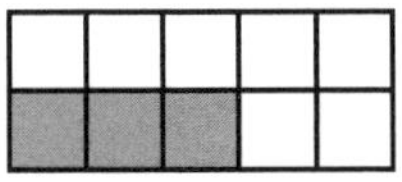

$\frac{3}{10}$ $\frac{\text{part}}{\text{whole}}$ = 0.3

3 is the part.

One digit to the right of the decimal point is the tenths place. The parts are tenths of a whole.

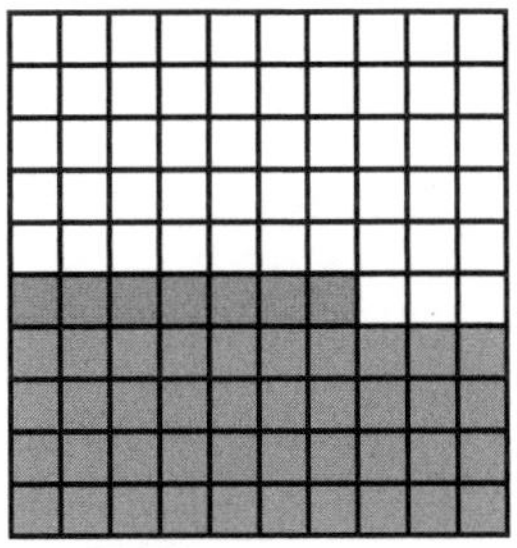

$\frac{47}{100}$ $\frac{\text{part}}{\text{whole}}$ = 0.47

47 is the part.

Two digits to the right of the decimal point is the hundredths place. The parts are hundredths of a whole.

Write a fraction for each picture. Then, write the decimal that has the same value as the fraction.

1.

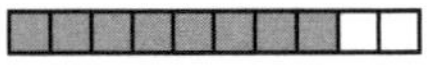

$\frac{\square}{\square}$ = ______

2.

$\frac{\square}{\square}$ = ______

3.

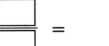

$\frac{\square}{\square}$ = ______

4.

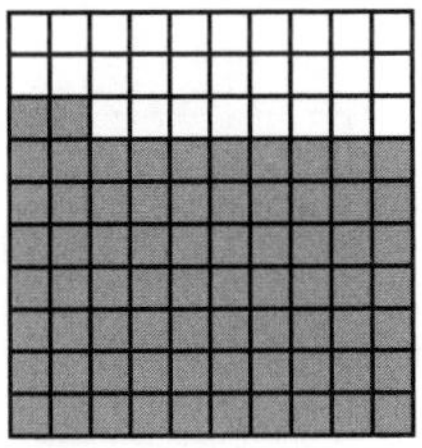

$\frac{\square}{\square}$ = ______

Color the squares to represent each fraction. Write the decimal. Place a zero in the ones place to show that there are no ones.

5. $\frac{2}{10}$ | | | | | | | | | | ______

6. $\frac{9}{10}$ | | | | | | | | | | ______

7. $\frac{7}{10}$ | | | | | | | | | | ______

8. $\frac{4}{10}$ | | | | | | | | | | ______

9. $\frac{6}{10}$ | | | | | | | | | | ______

Match the decimal with the equivalent fraction.

10. $\frac{30}{100}$ • • 0.20

11. $\frac{46}{100}$ • • 0.46

12. $\frac{20}{100}$ • • 0.30

Write the fraction for each decimal.

13. $0.5 = \frac{\square}{\square}$

14. $0.8 = \frac{\square}{\square}$

15. $0.14 = \frac{\square}{\square}$

16. $0.23 = \frac{\square}{\square}$

Review

Complete each row using the operations in the order given.

		+	−	×	÷	
17.	6	2	3	4	2	= 10
18.	8	5	6	5	7	= ______
19.	2	12	6	3	4	= ______
20.	7	9	6	3	5	= ______

Name ______________________________

Compare and Order Decimals 11.5

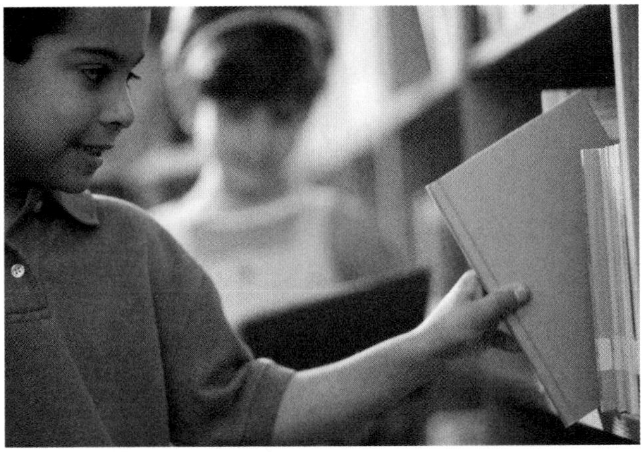

- 0–99 General Information
- 100s Philosophy
- 200s Religion
- 300s Social Science
- 400s Language
- 500s Natural Science
- 600s Technology and Applied Science
- 700s Fine Arts and Decorating
- 800s Literature
- 900s Geography and History

Eduardo found a book on desert reptiles in the library's online catalog. Now, he is looking for the book on the shelf. The book is numbered 598.2. Will it come before or after the book numbered 598.5?

ones .	tenths	hundredths
0 .	2	

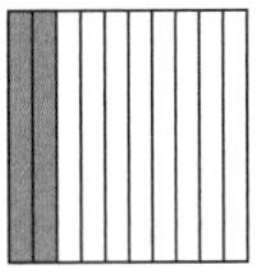

<

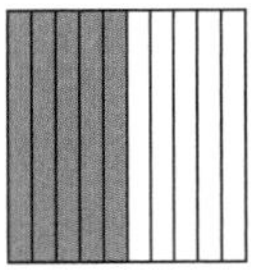

ones .	tenths	hundredths
0 .	5	

Since 0.2 is less than 0.5, Eduardo's book will come first.

Write both decimals in the place value chart. Add a zero in the hundredths place if there are no hundredths. Circle the greater decimal.

1. 0.5 0.8

ones .	tenths	hundredths
.		
.		

2. 0.64 0.46

ones .	tenths	hundredths
.		
.		

3. 0.01 0.1

ones .	tenths	hundredths
.		
.		

4. 0.3 0.93

ones .	tenths	hundredths
.		
.		

Write > or < to compare.

5. 0.4 (>) 0.2

6. 0.6 ◯ 0.9

7. 0.17 ◯ 0.28

8. 0.04 ◯ 0.56

9. 0.2 ◯ 0.19

10. 0.5 ◯ 0.61

11. 0.1 ◯ 0.2

12. 0.4 ◯ 0.3

13. 0.64 ◯ 0.32

14. 0.67 ◯ 0.77

15. 0.38 ◯ 0.8

16. 0.11 ◯ 0.1

17. 0.7 ◯ 0.8

18. 0.1 ◯ 0.3

19. 0.11 ◯ 0.01

20. 0.22 ◯ 0.44

21. 0.98 ◯ 0.7

22. 0.29 ◯ 0.1

Write the numbers of each set of library books in order from least to greatest.

23.

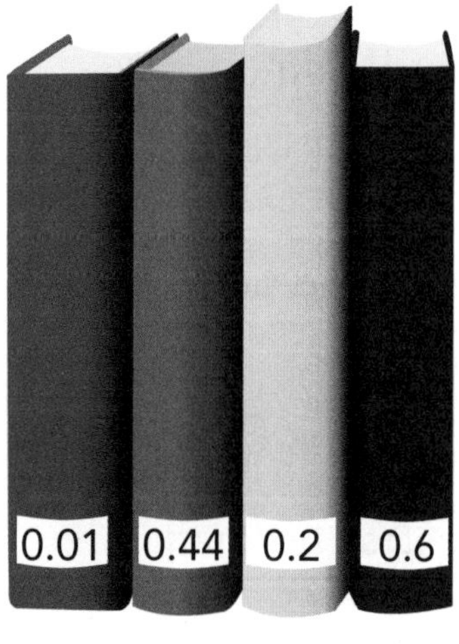

______
______
______
______

24.

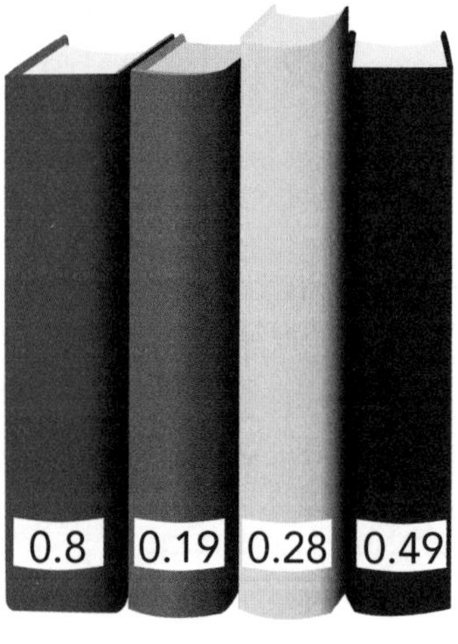

______
______
______
______

Review

25. Complete each table.

×	2	3	4	5
2				
3				
4				
5				

×	6	7	8	9
6				
7				
8				
9				

Name ______________________________

A biologist places electronic tags on two groups of javelina, desert mammals that look like wild boar. She has already tagged one group of 10 and has placed tags on 3 animals in a second group. The groups are 1.67 km apart. The tags will allow the biologist to know when and where they move.

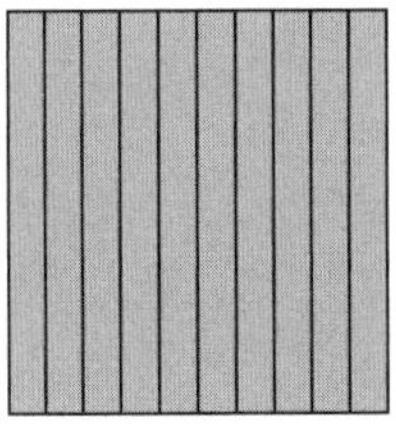 1 + 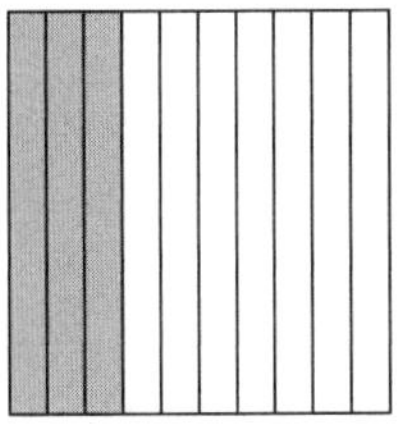 $\frac{3}{10}$ =

ones .	tenths	hundredths
1 .	3	

one and three-tenths

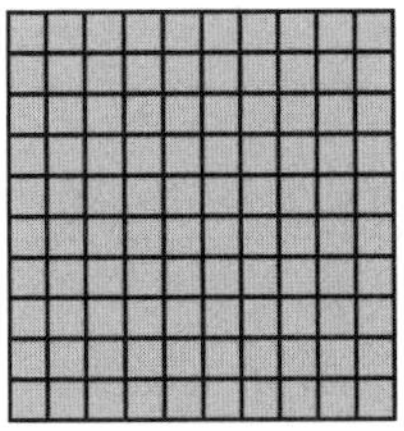 1 + 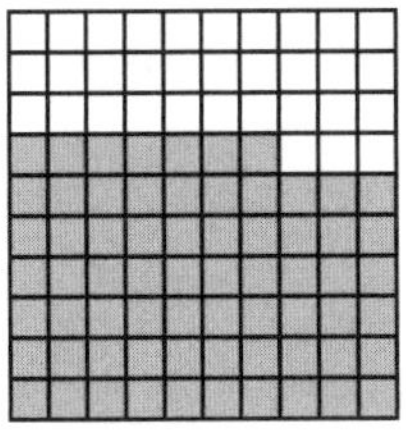 $\frac{67}{100}$ =

ones .	tenths	hundredths
1 .	6	7

one and sixty-seven hundredths

Write the mixed number and the decimal for each picture.

1. 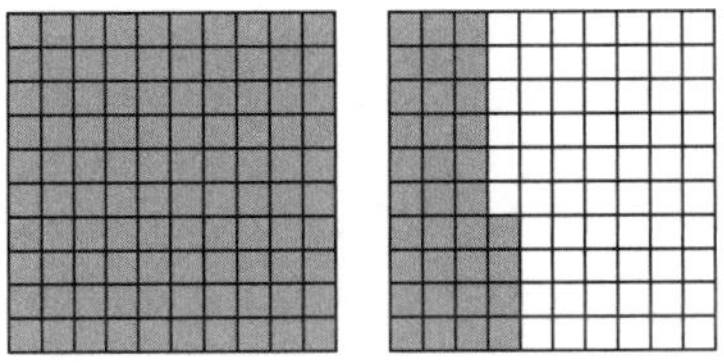 ________ ________

2. 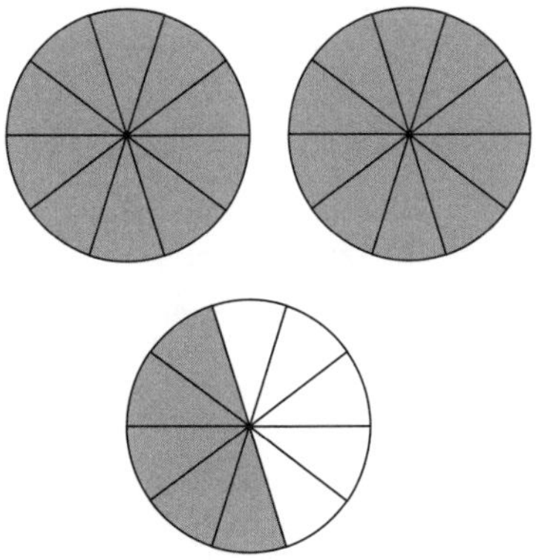 ________ ________

3. 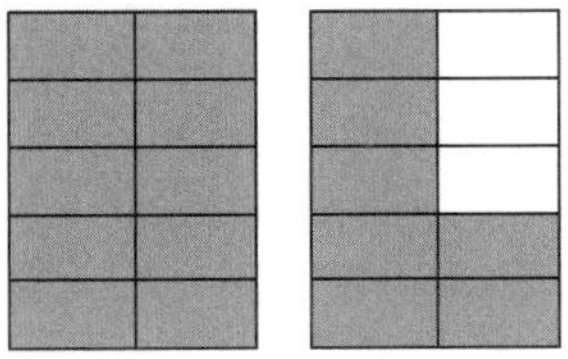 ________ ________

4. 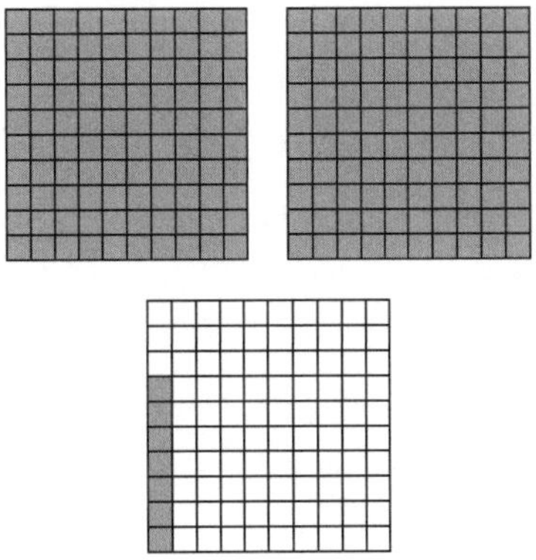 ________ ________

Write the decimal for each mixed number.

5. $1\frac{28}{100} =$ _____

6. $18\frac{1}{10} =$ _____

7. $12\frac{15}{100} =$ _____

8. $3\frac{2}{100} =$ _____

9. $4\frac{81}{100} =$ _____

10. $2\frac{7}{10} =$ _____

11. $524\frac{9}{10} =$ _____

12. $104\frac{4}{100} =$ _____

13. $82\frac{56}{100} =$ _____

Write the decimal. Remember, the word and represents the decimal point.

14. one and eight-tenths _____

15. sixty-one and fourteen-hundredths _____

16. ninety-three and two-hundredths _____

17. two hundred forty-seven and five-tenths _____

18. five hundred nine and eighty-eight hundredths

19. one hundred thirty-four and seventy-nine hundredths _____

Write the mixed number for each decimal.

20. $38.1 =$ _____

21. $1.01 =$ _____

22. $2.36 =$ _____

23. $216.47 =$ _____

24. $25.3 =$ _____

25. $612.5 =$ _____

26. $15.09 =$ _____

27. $58.22 =$ _____

28. $108.02 =$ _____

Name ____________________

Ariana's body temperature is 98°F. The temperature inside her pet iguana's terrarium is 89°F. Which temperature is warmer?

Since 98 > 89, 98°F is the warmer temperature.

Which is greater, 1.5 or 1.7?

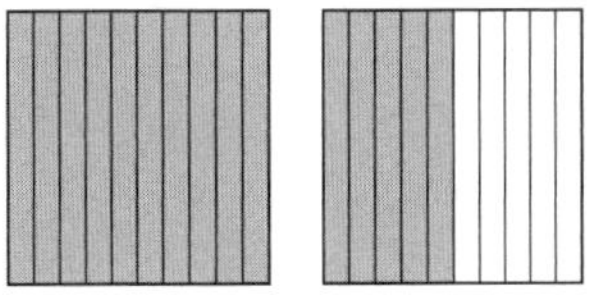

1.5

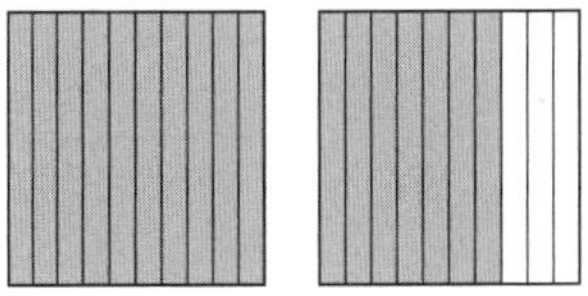

1.7

Both have 1 in the ones place,
but since 0.7 > 0.5,
1.7 > 1.5.

Which is greater, 2.34 or 2.3?

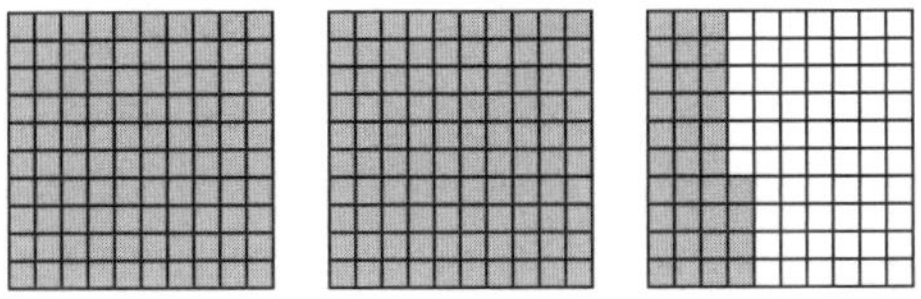

2.34

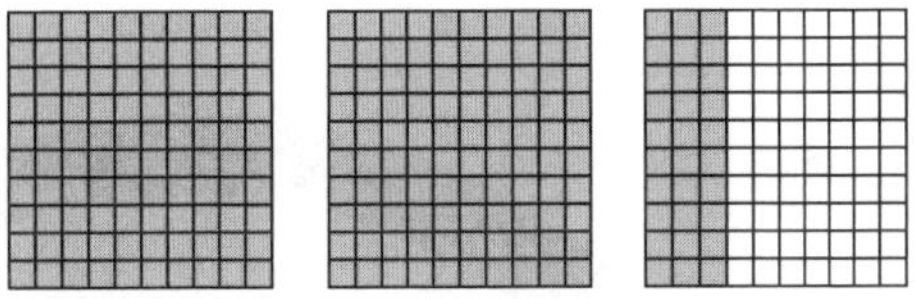

2.3

2.3 = 2.30
2.34 > 2.30
2.34 > 2.3

Circle the greatest number in each set.

1.	2.	3.	4.
4.89	6.2	13.02	64.9
5.89	3.87	13.12	64.83
		13.1	64.99
			64.89

Write > or <.

5. 16.3 ◯ 16.6
6. 11.6 ◯ 11.7
7. 58.9 ◯ 58.8
8. 1.89 ◯ 1.87
9. 3.17 ◯ 2.17
10. 2.45 ◯ 2.5
11. 21.5 ◯ 21.3
12. 58.9 ◯ 58.8
13. 76.23 ◯ 76.27
14. 36.42 ◯ 36.4
15. 87.26 ◯ 87.62
16. 91.06 ◯ 91.6
17. 345.1 ◯ 345.7
18. 812.4 ◯ 812.2
19. 594.53 ◯ 594.58
20. 102.1 ◯ 102.01
21. 423.01 ◯ 423.12
22. 674.12 ◯ 674.22

23. **Write the number for each space on the gauge.**

Name ______________________________

Estimate Sums and Differences 11.8

The Great Plains skink is found throughout most of Texas. These skinks can range from 6.5 to 13.75 inches in length. About how much difference (in inches) is there between the longest and shortest skinks?

To estimate the difference, you can round the decimal numbers to the nearest whole number and then subtract.

Is 13.75 closer to 13 or 14?

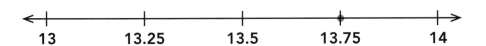

13 — 13.25 — 13.5 — 13.75 — 14

13.75 is closer to 14. Round to 14.

Is 6.5 closer to 6 or 7?

6 — 6.25 — 6.5 — 6.75 — 7

6.5 is halfway between 6 and 7. Round 6.5 to the next highest whole number, 7.

Subtract the rounded numbers, 14 − 7 = 7. The difference in the skinks' lengths is about 7 inches.

Place a dot on the number line where the decimal would be. Round to the nearest whole number.

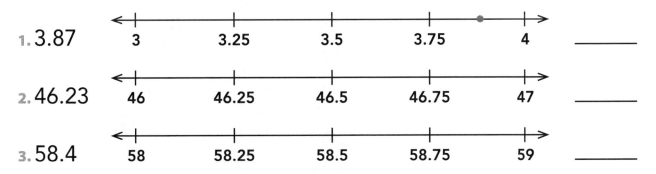

1. 3.87 — 3 — 3.25 — 3.5 — 3.75 — 4 ______

2. 46.23 — 46 — 46.25 — 46.5 — 46.75 — 47 ______

3. 58.4 — 58 — 58.25 — 58.5 — 58.75 — 59 ______

Round to the nearest whole number. Add the estimates. Add the problem.

4. $\begin{array}{r} 9.22 \\ +5.00 \\ \hline \end{array}$ $\begin{array}{r} \_\_\_\_ \\ +\_\_\_\_ \\ \hline \end{array}$

5. $\begin{array}{r} 25.88 \\ +14.14 \\ \hline \end{array}$ $\begin{array}{r} \_\_\_\_ \\ +\_\_\_\_ \\ \hline \end{array}$

6. $\begin{array}{r} 85.69 \\ +38.40 \\ \hline \end{array}$ $\begin{array}{r} \_\_\_\_ \\ +\_\_\_\_ \\ \hline \end{array}$

Round to the nearest whole number. Subtract the estimates. Subtract the problem.

7. $\begin{array}{r} 8.02 \\ -3.67 \\ \hline \end{array}$ $\begin{array}{r} \_\_\_\_ \\ -\_\_\_\_ \\ \hline \end{array}$

8. $\begin{array}{r} 15.31 \\ -\ 9.95 \\ \hline \end{array}$ $\begin{array}{r} \_\_\_\_ \\ -\_\_\_\_ \\ \hline \end{array}$

9. $\begin{array}{r} 68.71 \\ -11.5 \\ \hline \end{array}$ $\begin{array}{r} \_\_\_\_ \\ -\_\_\_\_ \\ \hline \end{array}$

Write the estimated sum or difference.

10. $\begin{array}{r} 5.17 \\ +3.6 \\ \hline \end{array}$

12. $\begin{array}{r} 9.82 \\ +8.43 \\ \hline \end{array}$

14. $\begin{array}{r} 11.55 \\ -\ 2.98 \\ \hline \end{array}$

16. $\begin{array}{r} 6.86 \\ +3.2 \\ \hline \end{array}$

18. $\begin{array}{r} 15.69 \\ -\ 8.04 \\ \hline \end{array}$

11. $\begin{array}{r} 20.14 \\ -\ 5.83 \\ \hline \end{array}$

13. $\begin{array}{r} 16.85 \\ -\ 9.2 \\ \hline \end{array}$

15. $\begin{array}{r} 7.72 \\ +3.72 \\ \hline \end{array}$

17. $\begin{array}{r} 13.2 \\ -\ 5.89 \\ \hline \end{array}$

19. $\begin{array}{r} 3.87 \\ +4.18 \\ \hline \end{array}$

Round to the nearest whole number to estimate.

20. The desert is a great place for pilots to test new jets. They can fly faster than the speed of sound, which is 343.2 meters per second. If a jet flies 345.9 meters per second, how much faster is it flying than the speed of sound?

____

21. The temperature before the test flight was 102.1°F. It rose 3.9°F by the time the pilots completed their flights. About how hot was the temperature after the flight?

____

Name ______________________________

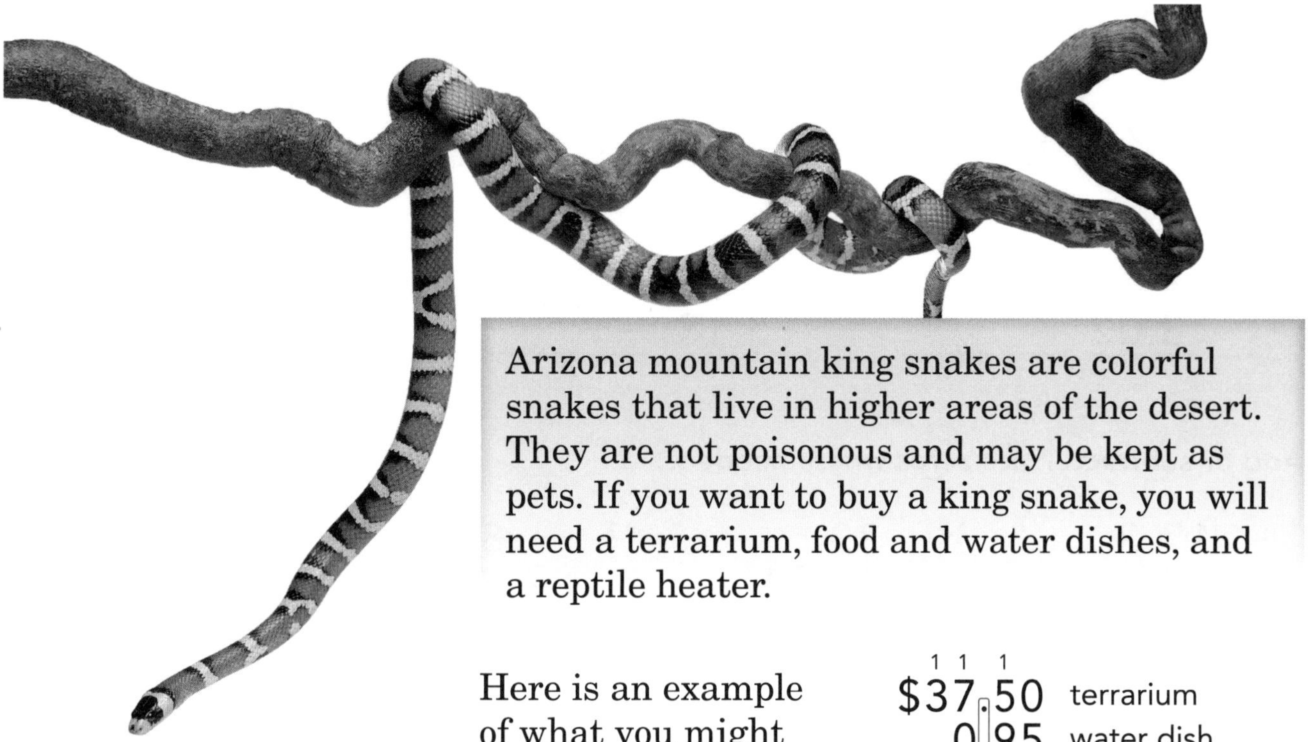

Arizona mountain king snakes are colorful snakes that live in higher areas of the desert. They are not poisonous and may be kept as pets. If you want to buy a king snake, you will need a terrarium, food and water dishes, and a reptile heater.

Here is an example of what you might pay for the supplies for your snake.

	$37.50	terrarium
	0.95	water dish
+	9.36	reptile heater
	$47.81	

If you purchase your snake's supplies with a $50 bill, how much change will you receive?

	$50.00
−	47.81
	$ 2.19

When adding or subtracting decimals, be sure to line up the decimal point. Add zeros to the place values if needed. You will receive $2.19 in change.

Rewrite each problem in vertical form. Line up the decimal points. Add zeros as needed to fill in the place values. Solve.

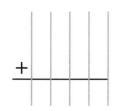

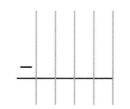

1. 1.67 + 0.81
2. 12.4 − 6.35
3. 15.21 + 3.7 + 4.16
4. 8.4 − 2.75

Round to the nearest whole number. Estimate. Find the real sum or difference.

5. $\begin{array}{r} 13.8 \\ +\ 5.67 \\ \hline \end{array}$ $\quad \begin{array}{r} \underline{\qquad} \\ +\ \underline{\qquad} \end{array}$

7. $\begin{array}{r} 14.02 \\ +\ 9.11 \\ \hline \end{array}$ $\quad \begin{array}{r} \underline{\qquad} \\ +\ \underline{\qquad} \end{array}$

9. $\begin{array}{r} 18.60 \\ +\ 2.49 \\ \hline \end{array}$ $\quad \begin{array}{r} \underline{\qquad} \\ +\ \underline{\qquad} \end{array}$

6. $\begin{array}{r} 26.55 \\ -\ 3.02 \\ \hline \end{array}$ $\quad \begin{array}{r} \underline{\qquad} \\ -\ \underline{\qquad} \end{array}$

8. $\begin{array}{r} 8.9 \\ -5.13 \\ \hline \end{array}$ $\quad \begin{array}{r} \underline{\qquad} \\ -\ \underline{\qquad} \end{array}$

10. $\begin{array}{r} 17.3 \\ -\ 2.86 \\ \hline \end{array}$ $\quad \begin{array}{r} \underline{\qquad} \\ -\ \underline{\qquad} \end{array}$

Add or subtract. Place zeros where needed.

11. $\begin{array}{r} 17.30 \\ -\ 9.86 \\ \hline \end{array}$

14. $\begin{array}{r} 32. \\ -18.31 \\ \hline \end{array}$

17. $\begin{array}{r} .87 \\ +7.23 \\ \hline \end{array}$

20. $\begin{array}{r} 99.99 \\ -48.36 \\ \hline \end{array}$

12. $\begin{array}{r} 68.02 \\ +\ 9.86 \\ \hline \end{array}$

15. $\begin{array}{r} 71.5 \\ -49.63 \\ \hline \end{array}$

18. $\begin{array}{r} 11.02 \\ +\ 7.8 \\ \hline \end{array}$

21. $\begin{array}{r} 42.9 \\ -28.45 \\ \hline \end{array}$

13. $\begin{array}{r} 28.3 \\ -14.55 \\ \hline \end{array}$

16. $\begin{array}{r} 16.30 \\ +47.21 \\ \hline \end{array}$

19. $\begin{array}{r} 9.8 \\ +19.73 \\ \hline \end{array}$

22. $\begin{array}{r} 56. \\ -26.34 \\ \hline \end{array}$

Solve.

23. NASA's Desert RATS (Research and Technology Studies) test space equipment in the desert. Even on cool days desert temperature can reach 104°F. Sometimes the Desert RATS work in temperatures up to 115.5°F. What is the difference between the two temperatures?

____

Review

Write the next three numbers in each pattern.

24. $3 \quad 3\frac{1}{4} \quad 3\frac{2}{4}$ ____ ____ ____

25. $6\frac{1}{2} \quad 7 \quad 7\frac{1}{2}$ ____ ____ ____

Name ______________________________

Problem Solving: Decimals 11.10

You can use estimation to solve problems. To estimate a total cost, round to the nearest whole number of dollars.

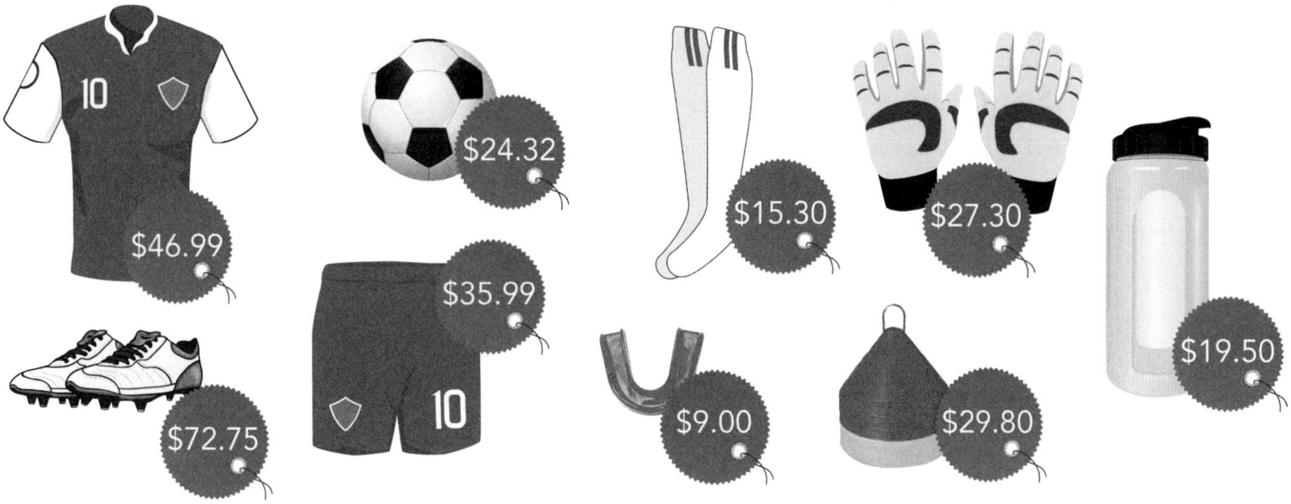

Complete the chart by rounding the prices to the nearest dollar.

	money on hand	desired items	estimated total	actual total	Do you have enough money? yes or no
1.	$30	soccer ball			
2.	$50	mouth guard and shorts			
3.	$45	cones and water bottle			
4.	$85	soccer jersey and shorts			
5.	$100	cleats and goalie's gloves			
6.	$100	soccer jersey, shorts, and socks			

Use your own paper to write each problem. Estimate an answer and then compute the actual answer.

7. Helena's mother kept track of the attendance for Vacation Bible School (VBS) for the last 3 years. The first year, the church had 34 children, the second year 44 children, and last year, they had 51 children. What is the average number of children per year?

____

8. Because Helena's church is located in the desert, the outdoor temperature was 104.4°F. The church sets the indoor temperature to 70°F. What is the difference between the outdoor and indoor temperatures?

____

9. Helena has been saving her money to give an offering to help with VBS. So far, she has saved $45.60. How much more does she need to reach $50?

____

10. Many of the children who attend VBS buy T-shirts for $5.30. Helena is buying a T-shirt. She is paying with a $10 bill. What is her change?

____

Write the estimated change for the Vacation Bible School craft supplies.

	total cost	payment	change
11.	$16.23	$20	
12.	$5.88	$10	
13.	$2.45	$5	
14.	$12.33	$20	
15.	$8.05	$10	
16.	$9.89	$10	

Name ______________________________

Dr. Bomar, a biologist, took a group of third graders to the desert for a field trip. Many desert animals are nocturnal—active at night. The third graders did not see the animals, but they saw the animals' footprints on the sandy desert floor in the morning. They made a pictograph and a bar graph from their observations.

Footprints We Saw in the Desert

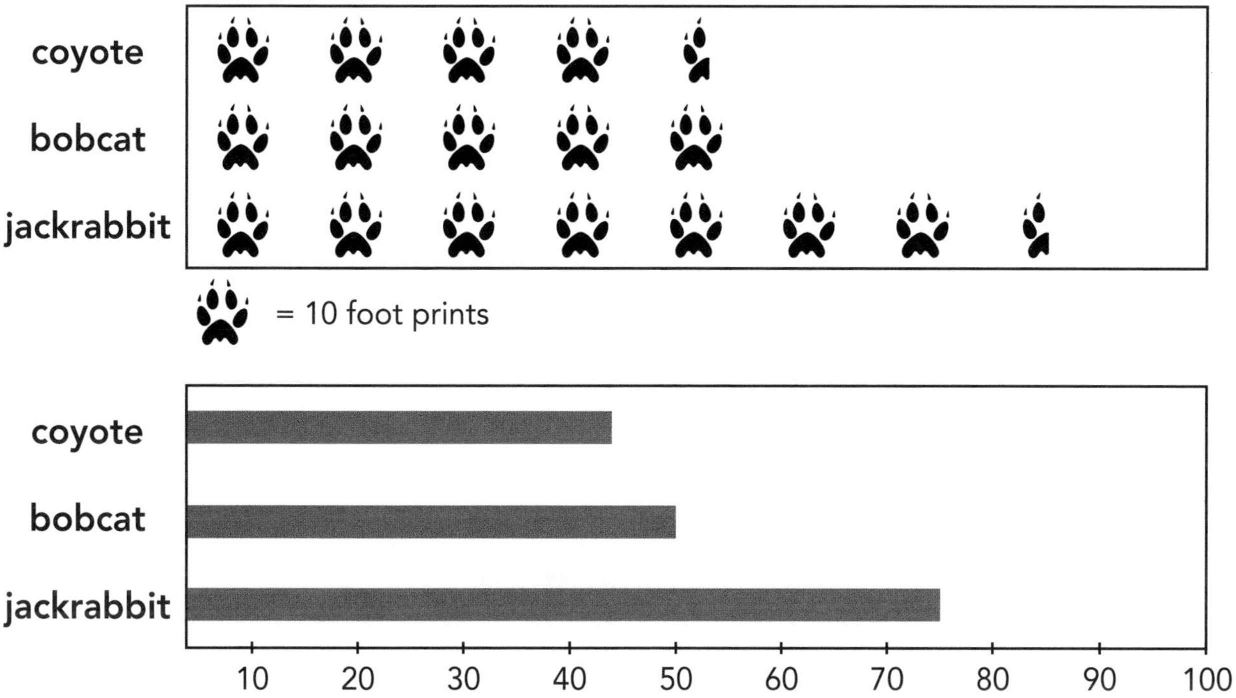

Use the pictograph and the bar graph to answer the questions.

1. Do the graphs show the same or different numbers of footprints?

____

2. How many coyote footprints were seen? ______________________________

3. Which animal had the fewest footprints? ____________ The most? ____________

4. The bar graph could show up to 100 footprints. Write a decimal number for each animals' footprints out of 100.

coyote ____________ bobcat ____________ jackrabbit ____________

Ethan took this picture of his dog with a special camera. The camera shows temperature as different colors. Look at the warmer and cooler areas on the dog's body. Read the scale to see the color values.

90.5 °F 100° 102.5 °F

time	temperature
9:00 AM	102.5 °F
10:00 AM	103 °F
11:00 AM	103.5 °F
noon	104 °F

Ethan lives in the desert. The temperature was 102.5°F when he took the picture. As the day went on, the temperature rose.

5. **Use the time and temperature table to plot the temperatures on the line graph. Connect the points with your ruler.**

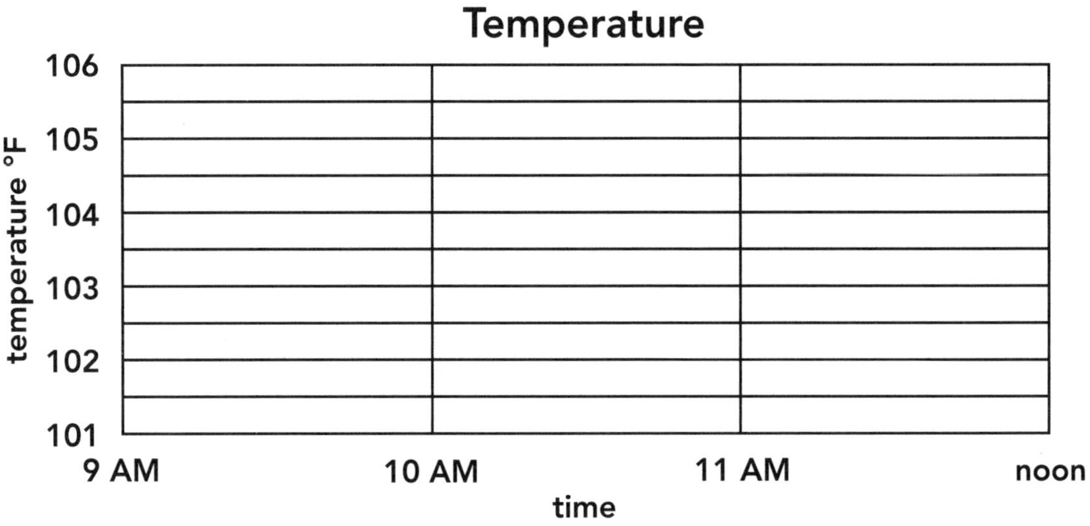

Review

Measure each line to the nearest half inch and nearest centimeter.

6. ______ in. ______ cm

7. ______ in. ______ cm

8. ______ in. ______ cm

Name ______________________________

Write the fraction and decimal for each picture.

1. 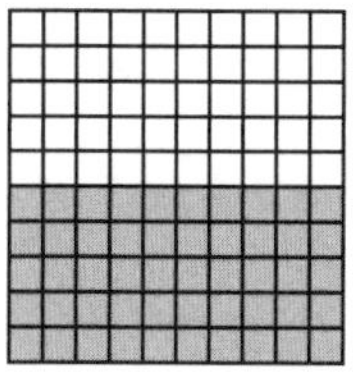

$\frac{\square}{\square}$ ______

2. 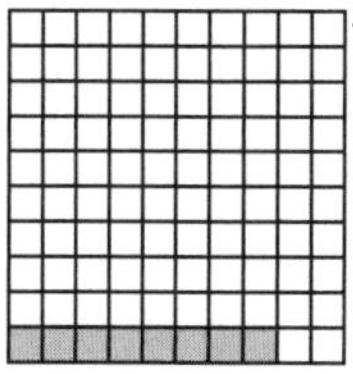

$\frac{\square}{\square}$ ______

3. 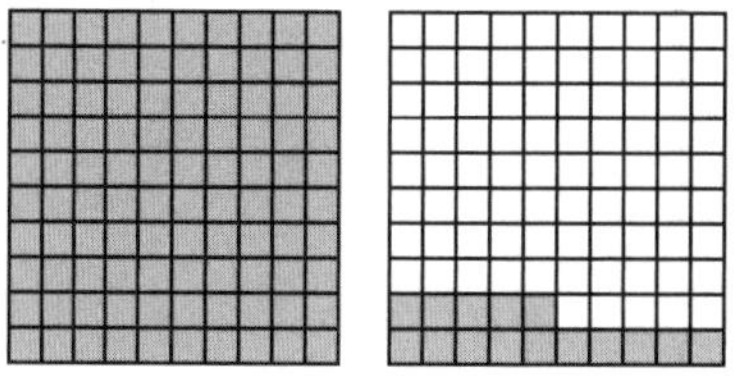

$\frac{\square}{\square}$ ______

Write each number on the chart in decimal form. Make sure each digit is in the correct place value.

	hundreds	tens	ones	tenths	hundredths
4. $46\frac{2}{100}$			.		
5. $70\frac{8}{10}$			.		
6. $\frac{65}{100}$			.		
7. 15.32			.		
8. 912.5			.		
9. 1.39			.		
10. 607.07			.		

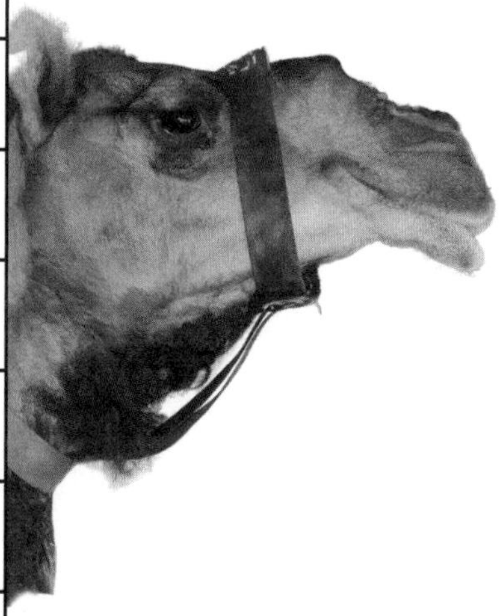

11. Write the decimal for each fraction or mixed number.

$\frac{2}{100}$ = ______ $1\frac{32}{100}$ = ______ $\frac{43}{100}$ = ______

12. Write the fraction or mixed number for each decimal.

0.5 = $\frac{\square}{\square}$ 0.01 = $\frac{\square}{\square}$ 1.62 = $\frac{\square}{\square}$ 0.89 = $\frac{\square}{\square}$

13. Write > or < to compare.

0.43 ○ 0.64   0.02 ○ 0.20   0.48 ○ 0.38   1.82 ○ 1.84

0.31 ○ 0.11   0.6 ○ 0.5   0.9 ○ 0.89   2.87 ○ 5.13

Round to the nearest whole number. Estimate. Find the real sum or difference.

14. 4.12 + 3.94 = ____   + ____

16. 55.91 − 16.14 = ____   − ____

18. 64.08 + 21.79 = ____   + ____

15. 9.88 − 3.14 = ____   − ____

17. 31.02 − 17.96 = ____   − ____

19. 45.55 + 25.10 = ____   + ____

Add or subtract. Add zeros where needed.

20. 2.23 + 3.1

22. 8.41 − 3.5

24. 16.3 + 7.45

26. 52.08 − 34.7

21. 97. − 26.25

23. 67.21 − 18.5

25. 13.84 + 9.2

27. 49.02 − 11.8

Fill in the circle to answer the questions.

28. Which kind of graph uses pictures or symbols to show information?

○ bar graph   ○ pictograph   ○ line graph

29. Which kind of graph is the best to show how something changes over time?

○ bar graph   ○ pictograph   ○ line graph

Chapter 12
Time and Money

Teach us to number our days,
that we may gain a heart of wisdom.
Psalm 90:12

Key Ideas:

Time: telling AM and PM to the nearest minute

Time: computing elapsed time and reading a schedule

Money: identifying coins and bills

Money: adding and subtracting money and making change

Patterns: Venn diagrams

Name ______________________________

Hour, Half Hour, and Quarter Hour

Pete walks his dog every morning at 7:00.

The hour hand tells what hour it is.

The minute hand tells what minute it is.

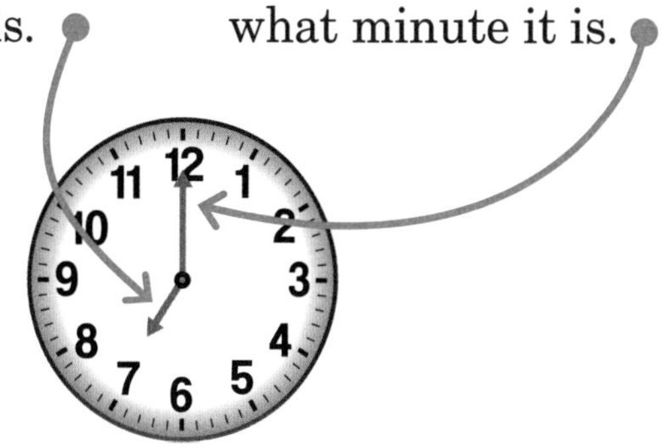

It takes one hour, or 60 minutes, for the hour hand to move from one number to the next.

It takes one minute for the minute hand to move from one minute mark to the next.

7:00
seven o'clock

7:30
seven thirty
or
half past seven

7:15
seven fifteen
or
quarter after seven

7:45
seven forty-five,
quarter to eight,
or
quarter of eight

Write the letter of the correct time in each box.

1.  ______

2.  ______

3.  ______

4.  ______

a. five thirty

b. quarter to ten

c. eleven fifteen

d. three o'clock

5. Match each clock to the correct time.

• quarter to two •

• 9:15 •

• 12:00 •

• half past four •

6. Write the numeric times for each clock.

 ______

 ______

 ______

Draw an hour hand and a minute hand to show each time.

7. 

6:15

8. 

1:00

9. 

11:30

10. 

12:45

Review

Write the ordinal number.

11. 2 ______

12. 17______

13. 4 ______

14. 21 ______

15. 23 ______

16. 99 ______

17. 62 ______

18. 85 ______

Name ______________________________

Sonia and her class are going on a field trip to the robotics expo. The bus will leave at noon.

What time is it now? ______

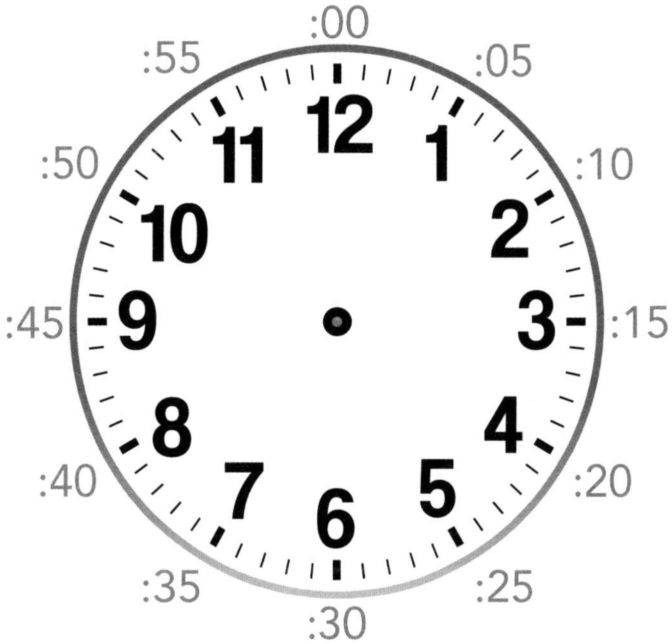

Each number on the clock shows that 5 minutes have passed.

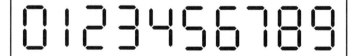

Write the time on the digital clock.

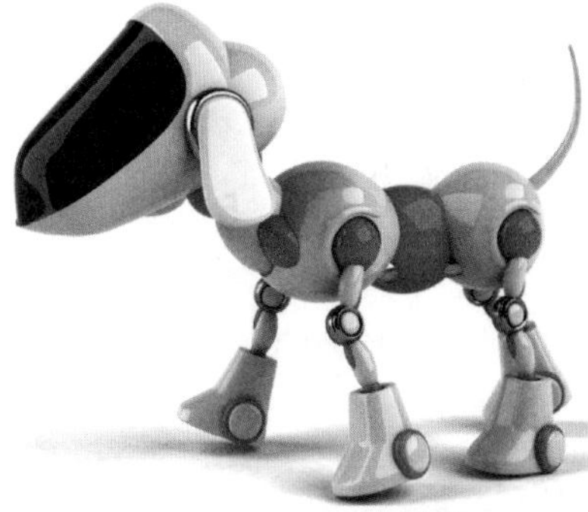

Digital Numbers Bank

0 1 2 3 4 5 6 7 8 9

1.

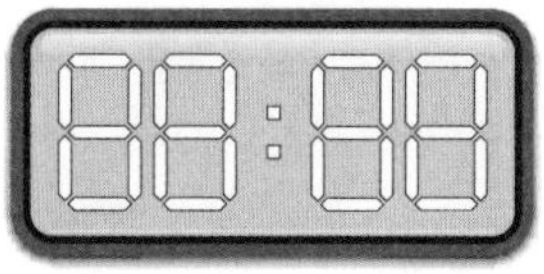

2.

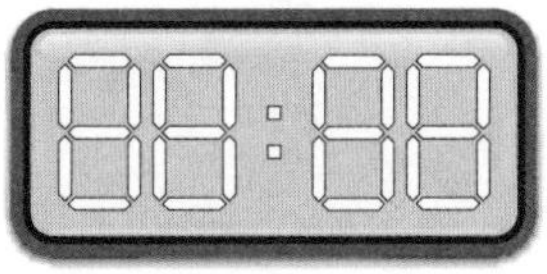

3.

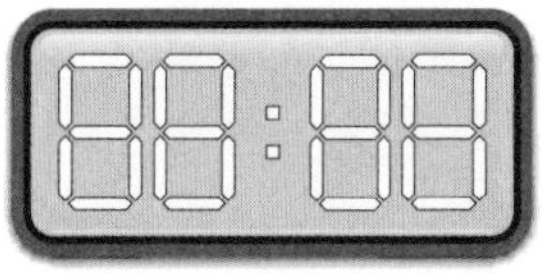

4.

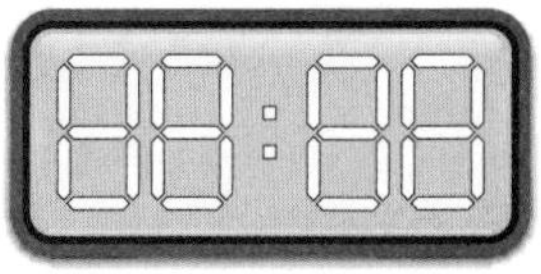

Write the letter of the correct time by each time word.

5. ______ o'clock
6. ______ quarter after
7. ______ five minutes after
8. ______ quarter to
9. ______ half past

a. :30
b. :05
c. :15
d. :00
e. :45

Read each time. Draw in the hands to show each time.

10. 
eight twenty-five

11. 
two fifty

12. 
eleven fifteen

13. 
five ten

14. 
four forty

15. 
seven thirty-five

Review

16. **Divide.**

$5\overline{)206}$ $4\overline{)187}$ $6\overline{)3,240}$ $8\overline{)4,409}$ $9\overline{)2,825}$

Name ____

City Cat's Diary

6:55 Woke up.
6:56 Ate breakfast and drank milk.
7:08 Played with catnip mouse toy.
7:11 Sat in the windowsill.
7:26 Played with the fish.
7:38 Jumped on Ravi to wake him up.

The minute hand will show 26 minutes after 7. Start at a familiar point like 7:15 and count on.

7:15 

7:20 

7:26 

To tell time to the nearest minute, count on or count back from the nearest five-minute point.

7:40 

7:39 

7:38 

Write the time on the line.

1. 

____

2. 

____

3. 

____

4. **Write the correct time.**

_______ _______ _______

_______ _______ _______

Draw hands to show each time.

5.

7:09

7.

2:50

9.

9:24

6.

4:14

8.

10:21

10.

3:42

Review

Write the number of line segments and angles for each plane figure.

11.

line segments _______

angles _______

12.

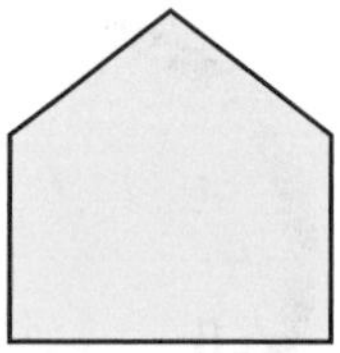

line segments _______

angles _______

13.

line segments _______

angles _______

Whitney has two new guinea pigs, Topsy and Turvy. Topsy woke up at 6:45. Turvy woke up at 15 minutes before 7. Which pet woke up earlier?

6:45
45 minutes after 6

15 minutes before 7
quarter to 7

Both guinea pigs woke at the same time, 6:45 AM or 15 minutes before 7 AM.

The time from midnight to noon is AM.	The time from noon to midnight is PM.

Write the time on the line. Fill in the missing numbers.

1.

____

minutes
________ after ________

minutes
________ before ________

2.

____

minutes
________ after ________

minutes
________ before ________

3.

____

minutes
________ after ________

minutes
________ before ________

Fill in the missing numbers.

4. 

_______ minutes after _______

5. 

_______ minutes before _______

6. 

_______ minutes before _______

7. 

_______ minutes after _______

8. 

_______ minutes after _______

9. 

_______ minutes before _______

Circle the earlier time in each box.

10. 10 minutes to 5 / five ten

11. 2:40 / thirteen minutes before three

12. quarter to 7 / 6:35

Answer each question.

13. What is an activity you might do at 10:30 AM?

____

14. What is an activity you might do at 7:00 PM?

____

Name ________________________________

Tong began cleaning his pet lizard's cage at 9:15. He finished cleaning at 9:30. How long did it take him to clean the cage?

You can count back to find the elapsed time.

9:30 — 9:25 — 9:20 — 9:15

5 5 5

5 minutes + 5 minutes + 5 minutes =
15 minutes

Elapsed time is time that has passed. For longer periods of elapsed time, count from the beginning time to the ending time.

begin

end

7:20 to 8:20 is 1 hour.

8:20 — 8:25 — 8:30 — 8:35 — 8:40

5 + 5 + 5 + 5 = 20 minutes

elapsed time = 1 hour and 20 minutes

Write the elapsed time.

1. begin

end

____

2. begin

end

____

Draw hands to show the finished time.

3. begin 8:00
end 50 minutes

4. begin 9:30
end 45 minutes

5. begin 3:45
end 1 hour, 15 minutes

Fill in the chart for Tong's pet lizard named Izzy.

	pet care	time began	time finished	time elapsed
6.	took Izzy for check-up	11:45 AM	12:00 PM	
7.	let Izzy sleep	12:15 PM		2 hours and 15 minutes
8.	went to the store to buy Izzy's food	12:00 PM	2:00 PM	
9.	played with Izzy	9:10 AM	9:35 AM	
10.	cleaned Izzy's cage	3:50 PM		20 minutes

Solve.

11. The science club designed and built a ramp for wheelchairs. They started at 10:10 AM. They finished 3 hours and 20 minutes later. What time did they finish?

____

12. At 7:30 AM, Ruby started testing her design for a new pet toy. She finished at 9:15 AM. How long did she test the toy?

____

13. At 6:05 PM, Quinton started to build a flashlight from a kit. It took him 1 hour and 15 minutes. What time was the flashlight finished?

____

14. You arrived at the video-game design fair at 2:35 PM. You spent 45 minutes in line and tested a game for another 15 minutes. What time did you finish?

____

Name ______________________________

1	JANUARY
2	FEBRUARY
3	MARCH
4	APRIL
5	MAY
6	JUNE
7	JULY
8	AUGUST
9	SEPTEMBER
10	OCTOBER
11	NOVEMBER
12	DECEMBER

There are 12 months in a year.

There are 365 days in a year.

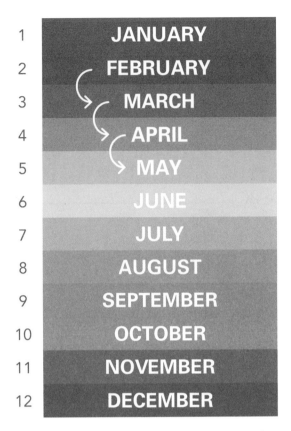

Wyatt's puppy is 3 months old today. If it was born on February 10, what is today's date?

Today is May 10. Dates are read as ordinal numbers, so today's date is read "May tenth."

August

S	M	T	W	Th	F	Sat
		1	2	3	4	5
6	7	8	9	10	11	12
13	14	15	16	17	18	19
20	21	22	23	24	25	26
27	28	29	30	31		

1. Color the first Wednesday red.
2. Color the third Sunday yellow.
3. Color the fourth Saturday blue.
4. Color the fifth Tuesday green.
5. Write the day of the week for August 11.

   ____

6. Write the date of the last Monday in August.

   ____

June

S	M	T	W	Th	F	Sat
			1	2	3	4
5	6	7	8	9	10	11
12	13	14	15	16	17	18
19	20	21	22	23	24	25
26	27	28	29	30		

Write the day of the week for each date.

7. June 2 ____________________

8. June 6 ____________________

9. June 18 ____________________

10. June 26 ____________________

Write the dates one week before and one week after each date.

11. June 8 ________ ________

12. June 12 ________ ________

13. June 16 ________ ________

14. June 24 ________ ________

Use the calendar at the top of the page. Solve.

15. Wyatt's puppy has a vet visit on June 28. Today is June 12. How many days until the vet visit?

____

16. You are going to Bible camp in 18 days. If today is June 3, what date do you go to camp?

____

17. Elliot's cousin arrives on the second Tuesday of June and leaves on the fourth Tuesday. What date does his cousin leave?

____

18. You will care for your neighbors' dog for 10 days. If they return on the last day of June, when do you start caring for the dog?

____

19. You put all of the June dates in a bag and pick one out. Which two days of the week have a higher chance of being selected?

____

Name ______________________________

Yanna and her third-grade friends are beginning to take gymnastics classes. What time is the girls' introductory class? How long is the class?

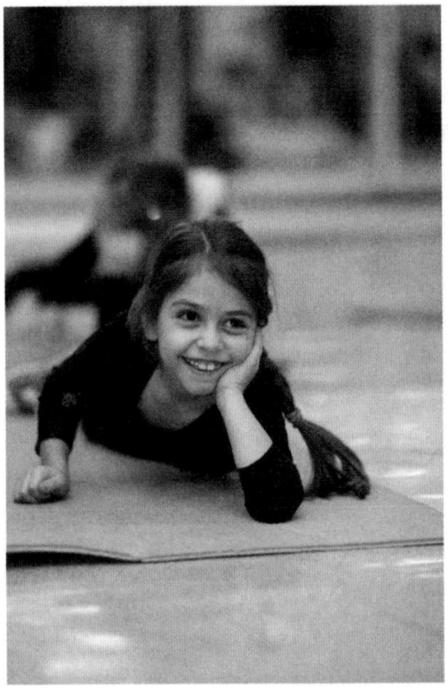

City Gym Saturday Schedule

time	session	group
9:00–9:50	Tumbler Tots	preschool class
10:00–10:50	Intro Girls	ages 6–10
11:00–11:50	Intro Boys	ages 6–10
12:00–1:00	Open Gym Kids	ages 2–5
1:00–2:00	Open Gym Kids	ages 6–10
2:00–2:50	Competitive	boys and girls

Yanna's class begins at 10:00. It lasts for 50 minutes.

Use the schedule to answer the questions.

1. Which is the first class of the day? ______________________

   What time does it begin? ______________________

2. Which lasts longer, Open Gym or Competitive? ______________________

3. What time does Competitive begin? ______________________

4. Yanna arrives at 12:30. How long must she wait for her age's Open Gym?

   ____

On Tuesday mornings, Mrs. White's third graders study Bible from 8:45 to 9:30, read from 9:30 to 10:30, do math from 10:45 to 11:30, and study spelling from 11:30 to noon.

Organize Mrs. White's class information on the Tuesday morning schedule.

Mrs. White's Tuesday Schedule

	time	class
5.		
6.		
7.		
8.		

Answer these questions about the Tuesday morning schedule.

9. Which class lasts the longest? ____________________

10. Which class lasts the shortest? ____________________

11. How many minutes long is Bible class? ____________________

12. When would you schedule in recess time? ____________________

13. When would lunch begin? ____________________

Review

14. **Add or subtract.**

$$\begin{array}{r} 3,269 \\ +1,158 \\ \hline \end{array} \quad \begin{array}{r} 6,000 \\ -2,891 \\ \hline \end{array} \quad \begin{array}{r} 9,863 \\ -745 \\ \hline \end{array} \quad \begin{array}{r} 1,099 \\ 2,654 \\ +6,024 \\ \hline \end{array} \quad \begin{array}{r} 2,457 \\ 4,623 \\ +759 \\ \hline \end{array}$$

Name ________________________________

When counting money, begin with bills or coins of greatest value and count to the coins of least value.

5 dollar bill	1 dollar bill	half-dollar	quarter	dime	nickel	penny
\$5.00	\$1.00	50¢	25¢	10¢	5¢	1¢

Use \$ for dollars and cents or use ¢ if you have only cents. A decimal point separates the dollar amount from the cents.

Teagan wants to buy a pet for \$6.95. Does he have enough money?

Teagan has \$7.21. This is more than enough to buy the pet.

Count. \$5.00 \$6.00 \$6.50 \$6.75 \$7.00 \$7.10 \$7.15 \$7.20 **\$7.21**

Write the money amount for each group of bills and coins.

1.

____

2.

____

3.

____

4. **Write the amount for each set of money.**

______ ______ ______

Read each list and write the amount.

5.
1 dollar bill
3 quarters
1 dime
2 pennies

6.
6 dollar bills
2 half-dollars
1 dime
11 pennies

7.
8 quarters
5 dimes
2 nickels
1 penny

8.
1 dollar bill
2 half-dollars
1 quarter
4 nickels

Draw the bills and coins for each amount.

9. $4.72

10. $1.98

11. $3.46

Fill in the chart by showing the fewest coins needed for each amount.

	half-dollar	quarter	dime	nickel	penny
Example 40¢	0	1	1	1	0
12. 55¢					
13. 68¢					
14. 76¢					
15. 82¢					

Name ______________________________

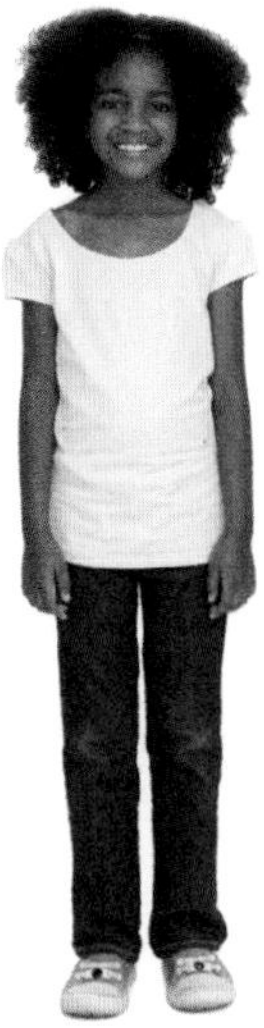

Troy and Dena each have saved $2.88 to spend at their church's yard sale for missions. Dena has more coins, but both amounts are equivalent.

=

Dena

Troy

An amount of money may be represented several ways.

25¢

25¢

25¢

25¢

Match the equivalent amounts of money.

1.  •

• 

2.  •

• 

3.  •

• 

4.  •

• 

Write the amount of the coins in each box. Then, write the letter of the money amount that matches the equivalent set of coins. Letters may be used more than once.

a.  ______

b.  ______

c.  ______

d.  ______

5. ______ 3 quarters, 5 pennies

6. ______ 2 quarters, 2 dimes, 1 nickel

7. ______ 1 half-dollar, 1 dime, 5 pennies

8. ______ 4 dimes

9. ______ 1 half-dollar, 1 dime, 1 nickel

10. ______ 4 dimes, 4 nickels, 20 pennies

Draw a combination of coins that equals each amount.

11. 1 half-dollar
1 quarter
2 dimes

12. 1 half-dollar
2 dimes
1 nickel
2 pennies

13. 1 half-dollar
1 dimes

14. 3 dimes
5 pennies

Review

Draw a line of symmetry for each shape.

15. 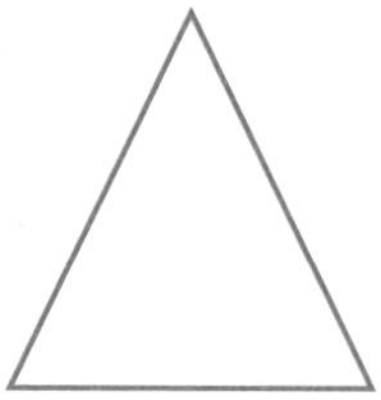

16. 

17. 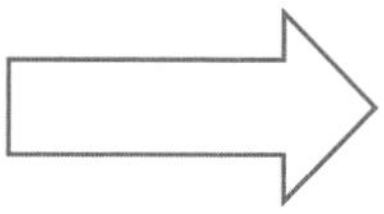

18. 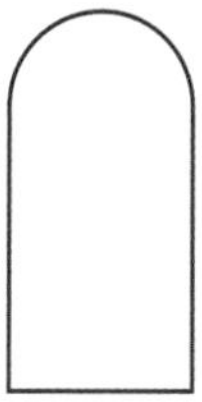

19. 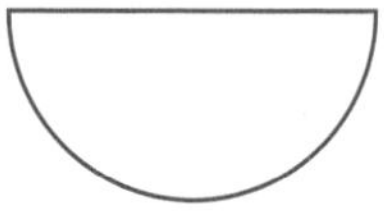

Name ______________________________

Raoul loves to play math games. The game he wants to buy costs \$9.25. By last week, he had saved up \$7.63. This week, he earned \$1.88. Does he have enough money to buy the new math game?

$$\begin{array}{r} {\scriptstyle 1\ \ 1} \\ \$7.63 \\ +\ \ 1.88 \\ \hline \$9.51 \end{array}$$

Yes! Raoul can buy the game.

> When adding or subtracting money,
> → line up the decimal points and
> → add or subtract.

How much money will he have left over after buying the computer game?

$$\begin{array}{r} {\scriptstyle 4\ 11} \\ \$9.\not{5}\not{1} \\ -\ \ 9.25 \\ \hline \$0.26 \end{array}$$

He will have 26¢ left over.

Add these money amounts. Remember to add the dollar sign to the sum.

1. $\begin{array}{r} \$4.75 \\ +\ \ 2.39 \\ \hline \end{array}$

2. $\begin{array}{r} \$7.21 \\ +\ \ 0.84 \\ \hline \end{array}$

3. $\begin{array}{r} \$3.89 \\ +\ \ 1.99 \\ \hline \end{array}$

4. $\begin{array}{r} \$5.86 \\ +\ \ 3.34 \\ \hline \end{array}$

Subtract these money amounts.

5. $\begin{array}{r} \$4.71 \\ -\ \ 0.69 \\ \hline \end{array}$

6. $\begin{array}{r} \$6.24 \\ -\ \ 2.11 \\ \hline \end{array}$

7. $\begin{array}{r} \$8.25 \\ -\ \ 5.13 \\ \hline \end{array}$

8. $\begin{array}{r} \$7.46 \\ -\ \ 2.55 \\ \hline \end{array}$

Estimate your answer in whole dollars. Then, solve each problem.

9. $\begin{array}{r} \$6.85 \\ -\ 3.44 \\ \hline \end{array}$ $\begin{array}{r} \underline{\qquad} \\ -\ \underline{\qquad} \end{array}$

11. $\begin{array}{r} \$5.37 \\ +\ 4.21 \\ \hline \end{array}$ $\begin{array}{r} \underline{\qquad} \\ +\ \underline{\qquad} \end{array}$

13. $\begin{array}{r} \$3.62 \\ +\ 5.10 \\ \hline \end{array}$ $\begin{array}{r} \underline{\qquad} \\ +\ \underline{\qquad} \end{array}$

10. $\begin{array}{r} \$6.41 \\ +\ 2.72 \\ \hline \end{array}$ $\begin{array}{r} \underline{\qquad} \\ +\ \underline{\qquad} \end{array}$

12. $\begin{array}{r} \$8.64 \\ -\ 3.87 \\ \hline \end{array}$ $\begin{array}{r} \underline{\qquad} \\ -\ \underline{\qquad} \end{array}$

14. $\begin{array}{r} \$4.45 \\ -\ 0.97 \\ \hline \end{array}$ $\begin{array}{r} \underline{\qquad} \\ -\ \underline{\qquad} \end{array}$

15. Add or subtract.

$\begin{array}{r} \$3.05 \\ -\ 0.79 \\ \hline \end{array}$ $\begin{array}{r} \$7.26 \\ -\ 0.97 \\ \hline \end{array}$ $\begin{array}{r} \$0.42 \\ +\ 0.82 \\ \hline \end{array}$ $\begin{array}{r} \$6.12 \\ +\ 0.88 \\ \hline \end{array}$

$\begin{array}{r} \$5.13 \\ +\ 1.82 \\ \hline \end{array}$ $\begin{array}{r} \$7.89 \\ +\ 0.49 \\ \hline \end{array}$ $\begin{array}{r} \$6.00 \\ -\ 2.34 \\ \hline \end{array}$ $\begin{array}{r} \$5.18 \\ +\ 0.34 \\ \hline \end{array}$

$\begin{array}{r} \$4.25 \\ -\ 1.63 \\ \hline \end{array}$ $\begin{array}{r} \$5.24 \\ -\ 1.73 \\ \hline \end{array}$ $\begin{array}{r} \$3.35 \\ -\ 2.18 \\ \hline \end{array}$ $\begin{array}{r} \$0.77 \\ +\ 0.13 \\ \hline \end{array}$

Solve.

16. Raymond buys crackers priced at \$2.63. He uses a coupon for 25¢ off. How much does he pay for the crackers?

____

17. One brand of juice costs \$1.69 per can, and the other costs \$1.14. If Stella buys the juice for \$1.14, how much money will she save?

____

Review

18. Circle the triangles that contain right angles.

Name ____________________

Takeshi bought a snack for $2.50. He paid with 3 one-dollar bills. What was his change?

paid	count on			change
	item's price			
$3.00	$2.50	$2.75	$3.00	$0.50

When making change,
→ start with the price of the item and
→ then count on to the amount that was paid.

Count on from the price to the amount paid. Write the amount of change.

	price	paid	count on	change
1.	$0.65	$1.00	 $0.65 ____ ____	
2.	$0.45	$1.00	 ____ ____ ____	
3.	$1.35	$1.00	 ____ ____ ____ ____ ____	
4.	$1.59	$1.00	 ____ ____ ____ ____ ____	

Subtract to find the amount of change. List the bills and coins you could receive as change.

	price	amount paid	bills and coins	change
5.	$0.45	$1.00	____________	________
6.	$0.70	$1.00	____________	________
7.	$1.77	$2.00	____________	________

8. Write the change. Use the fewest bills or coins possible.

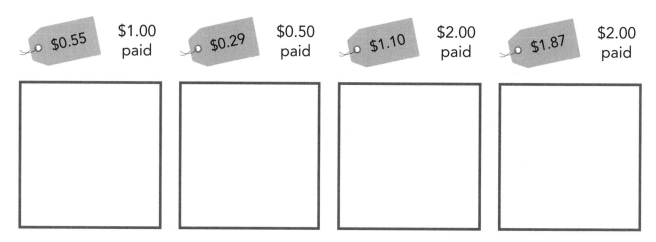

$0.55	$0.29	$1.10	$1.87
$1.00 paid	$0.50 paid	$2.00 paid	$2.00 paid

Complete the chart. Draw coins and then count on to the amount paid. Write the change.

		amount paid	count on	change
9.	$0.16	$0.25	coins count	
10.	$1.60	$2.00	coins count	
11.	$1.84	$2.00	coins count	

Name ____

Use a Venn diagram to help you organize information and compare information.

The items listed inside a circle have the characteristics of that circle's label.

The items listed inside an overlapped area of circles have characteristics of every circle in which they appear.

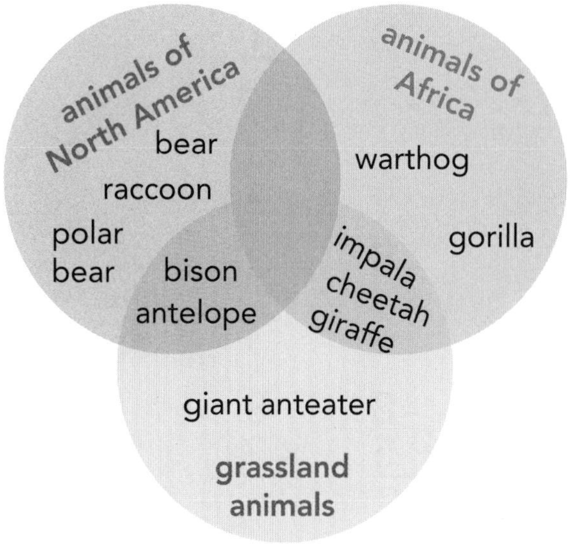

Write each name on the Venn diagram.

1. cat owners

Jack
Gracie
Liz
Scott

2. dog owners

Lisa
Scott
Savannah
Asher

3. fish owners

Laura
Jack
Kristi
Scott

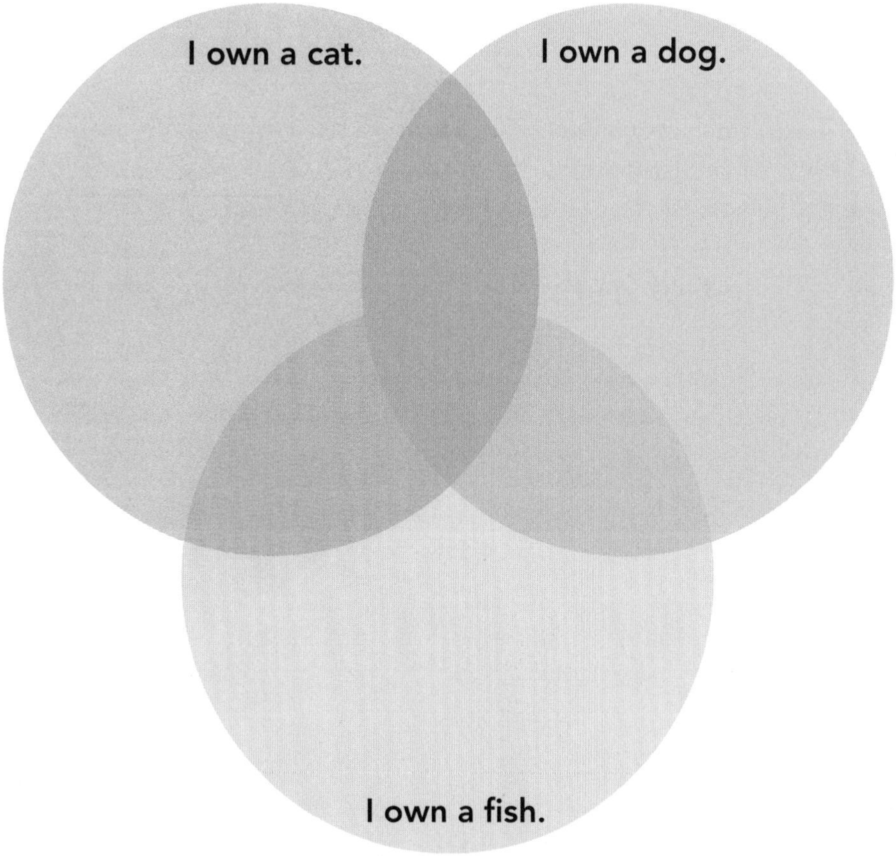

4. Write each product.

$$\begin{array}{r} 2 \\ \times 6 \\ \hline \end{array} \qquad \begin{array}{r} 5 \\ \times 2 \\ \hline \end{array} \qquad \begin{array}{r} 9 \\ \times 1 \\ \hline \end{array}$$

$$\begin{array}{r} 3 \\ \times 7 \\ \hline \end{array} \qquad \begin{array}{r} 9 \\ \times 6 \\ \hline \end{array} \qquad \begin{array}{r} 5 \\ \times 5 \\ \hline \end{array}$$

$$\begin{array}{r} 4 \\ \times 5 \\ \hline \end{array} \qquad \begin{array}{r} 8 \\ \times 5 \\ \hline \end{array} \qquad \begin{array}{r} 8 \\ \times 9 \\ \hline \end{array}$$

$$\begin{array}{r} 6 \\ \times 3 \\ \hline \end{array} \qquad \begin{array}{r} 3 \\ \times 5 \\ \hline \end{array} \qquad \begin{array}{r} 6 \\ \times 5 \\ \hline \end{array}$$

5. Write the products from Exercise 4 in the Venn diagram.

under 30 over 30

multiples of 10

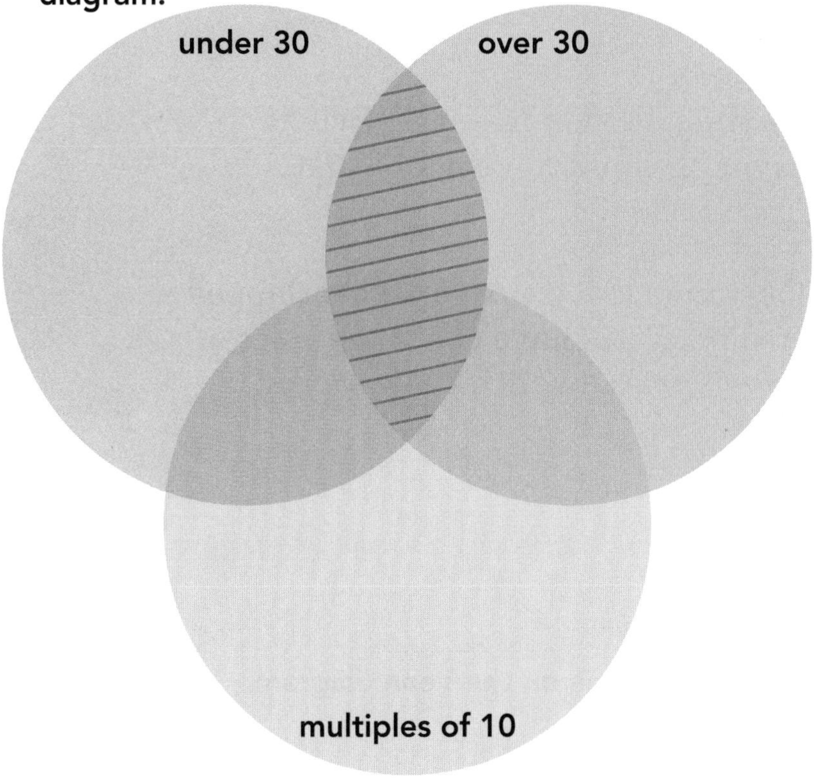

6. Design your own Venn diagram.
Think of 3 categories.
Label each circle.

list of items

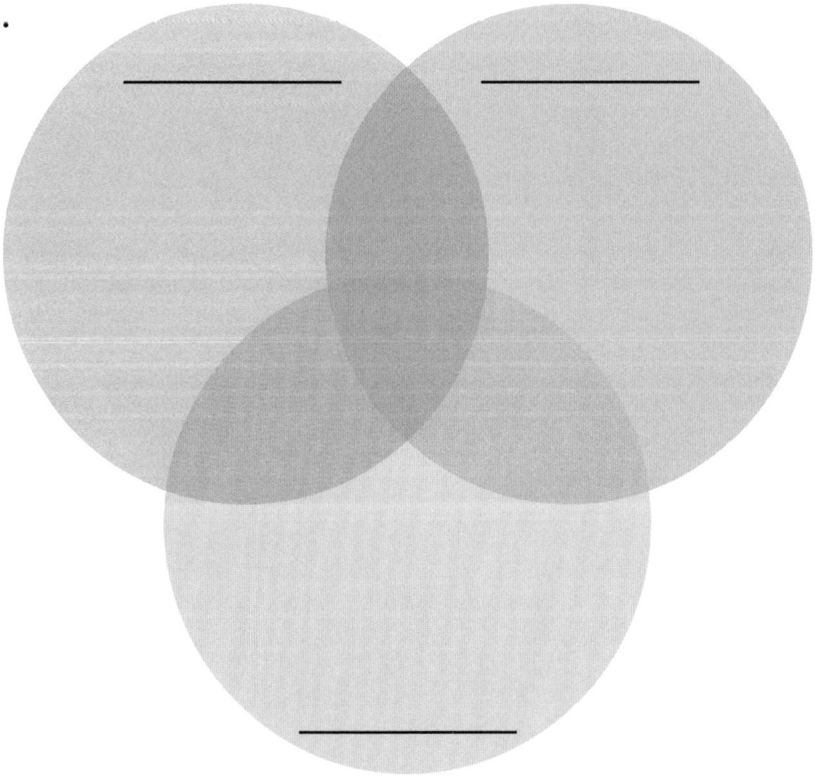

Name ______________________________

Write the letter of the definition that matches each term.

1. AM _______
2. PM _______
3. elapsed time _______
4. Venn diagram _______

a. a visual way to organize and compare information

b. the 12 hours from midnight until noon

c. the 12 hours from noon until midnight

d. the time that has passed

Fill in the missing numbers.

5. It takes _______ minutes for the hour hand to move from number one to number two on the clock.

6. It takes _______ minutes for the minute hand to move from one number to the next.

Draw 3 different coin combinations to represent 26¢.

7.

8.

9.

Write the time.

10. 

____

11. 

____

12. 

____

13. 

____

Draw clock hands for each time.

14. 10 minutes to 8

15. 25 minutes to 4

16. Begin at 6:00. Finish 1 hour and a half later.

Use the calendar and schedule to answer each question.

March

S	M	T	W	Th	F	Sat
	1	2	3	4	5	6
7	8	9	10	11	12	13
14	15	16	17	18	19	20
21	22	23	24	25	26	27
28	29	30	31			

Talent Show Auditions

8:00–9:00	Musicians (ages 6–9)
9:00–10:00	Musicians (ages 10–12)
10:00–10:15	Break
10:15–10:45	Vocalists
10:45–11:15	Actors
11:15–12:00	Jugglers, Magicians

17. What date is one week before March 14?

____

18. What day of the week was the last day of February?

____

19. When should Mindy, age 7, audition as a musician?

____

20. How long is the audition time for actors?

____

Write the money amount.

21. 

____

22. 

____

Solve.

23. $\begin{array}{r} \$2.87 \\ +\ 1.05 \\ \hline \end{array}$

24. $\begin{array}{r} \$8.05 \\ -\ 1.66 \\ \hline \end{array}$

Draw coins to show the change.

25. paid $1.00

price $0.67

change $______

Name ______________________________

Decimals use place value to show numbers that are less than one.

Write the fraction for each decimal.

1. 0.23 ______
2. 0.41 ______
3. 0.2 ______
4. 0.15 ______
5. 0.99 ______
6. 0.7 ______
7. 0.1 ______
8. 0.33 ______
9. 0.78 ______
10. 0.6 ______

Write the decimal numbers in order from least to greatest.

11. 1.23 5.32 0.32 1.32 1.2 ______ ______ ______ ______ ______

12. 4.06 4.6 6.4 6.44 0.64 ______ ______ ______ ______ ______

13. 3.2 3.23 3.32 0.23 0.3 ______ ______ ______ ______ ______

14. 0.5 0.05 0.55 1.05 0.1 ______ ______ ______ ______ ______

Solve. Place extra zeros where needed.

15. $2.5 + 3.64$

16. $3.02 - 1.6$

17. $3.8 - 2.21$

18. $7.4 + 1.88$

19. $6.7 + 4.29$

20. $2.3 - 1.99$

Write the correct time.

21.  ____________

22.  ____________

23.  ____________

24.  ____________

Draw hands for each time.

25. 20 minutes to 9

26. 10 minutes after 11

27. Begin at half past 5.
End 45 minutes later.

Write the money amount.

28. 

____

29. 

____

Draw bills and coins to show each amount in the fewest bills and coins.

30. $0.65

31. $6.37

Fill in the chart.

	price	paid	change
32.	$0.72	$1.00	
33.	$1.11	$2.00	
34.	$1.84	$5.00	
35.	$5.49	$10.00	

Chapter 13
Equations and Cumulative Review

In their hearts humans plan their course,
but the Lord establishes their steps.
Proverbs 16:9

Key Ideas:

Algebra: using the order of operations to solve problems

Algebra: solving problems that have missing numbers

Algebra: writing equations

Review and reinforcement of skills and concepts taught in Grade 3

Name ________________________________

Elias and his family traveled around Jesus' homeland, Israel. The first day, they traveled 80 km. The next day they went another 80 km. The third day, they drove 270 km. How far did Elias travel in Israel?

Follow the order of operations.

- **Step 1:** Complete the operation in parentheses.
- **Step 2:** Multiply or divide.
- **Step 3:** Add or subtract.

Multiply 2 × 80. Rewrite the problem. Add.

$(2 \times 80) + 270 =$ ______ km

$160 + 270 =$ ______ km

$$\begin{array}{r} \scriptstyle 1 \\ 160 \\ +270 \\ \hline 430 \text{ km} \end{array}$$

Elias traveled 430 km.

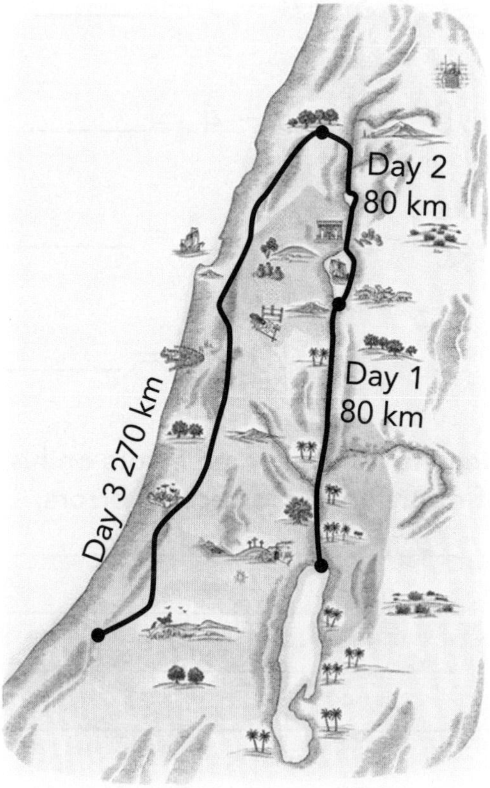

If there are no parentheses in an equation, go to Step 2. You can write () to help see the problem. Multiply or divide.

$64 \div 8 + 2 =$ ______

$(64 \div 8) + 2 =$ ______

$8 + 2 = 10$

Solve each problem. Follow the order of operations.

1. $6 \times 7 + 4 =$ ______
2. $6 + (4 \times 4) =$ ______
3. $(9 \times 7) - 3 =$ ______
4. $24 \div 6 + 4 =$ ______
5. $2 + (4 \times 5) =$ ______
6. $30 \div (5 + 1) =$ ______

Solve. Use the order of operations.

7. $6 + 8 \times 2 - 2 =$ ______

8. $7 \times 3 + 4 - 5 =$ ______

9. $8 + 2 \times 3 - 4 =$ ______

10. $54 - 9 \times 6 + 1 =$ ______

11. $2 \times 9 - 10 + 3 =$ ______

12. $5 + 3 \times 5 + 10 =$ ______

13. $6 - 3 \times 1 + 7 =$ ______

14. $(1 + 2) \times 7 =$ ______

15. $1 + 2 + (17 - 9) =$ ______

16. $(12 \div 2) \times 7 - 10 =$ ______

Devantre made some errors on his math worksheet because he did not follow the order of operations. Correct his errors.

17. $4 + 4 \times 9 = 17$

19. $6 + 2 \times 6 = 48$

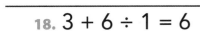

18. $3 + 6 \div 1 = 6$

Name ____

Sand cats live in the deserts in Israel. They look like house cats but are wild. One sand cat traveled 9 km during the night. A second sand cat roamed at night also. Both cats traveled a total of 17 km. How many kilometers did the second cat travel?

The first step is to write down the information from the word problem.

9 km + ______ = 17 km

part – part = whole

Because an addend is missing, subtract the known addend from the sum.

17 – 9 = ______

whole – part = part

The distance traveled by the second sand cat was 8 km.

To solve for a missing number in a subtraction problem, analyze the problem.

______ – 25 = 12

whole – part = part

If the missing number is the whole, add the difference to the part you know.

25 + 12 = 37

If the missing number is a part, subtract the part you know from the difference.

37 – ______ = 12

whole – part = part

37 – 12 = 25

Write the missing numbers.

1. 24 – ______ = 12
2. 5 + ______ = 13
3. 15 – ______ = 5
4. 28 – ______ = 8
5. 7 + ______ = 13
6. ______ – 7 = 14

Solve for the missing numbers. Show your work below each problem. The first one is done for you.

7. 20 – ______ = 12

20 – 12 = 8

8. 5 + ______ = 8

9. 4 + ______ = 13

10. 14 – ______ = 9

11. 18 – ______ = 8

12. 20 – ______ = 8

13. 7 + ______ = 15

14. ______ – 6 = 14

15. ______ – 16 = 14

16. The perimeter of each shape is 62 cm. Find the length of the missing side.

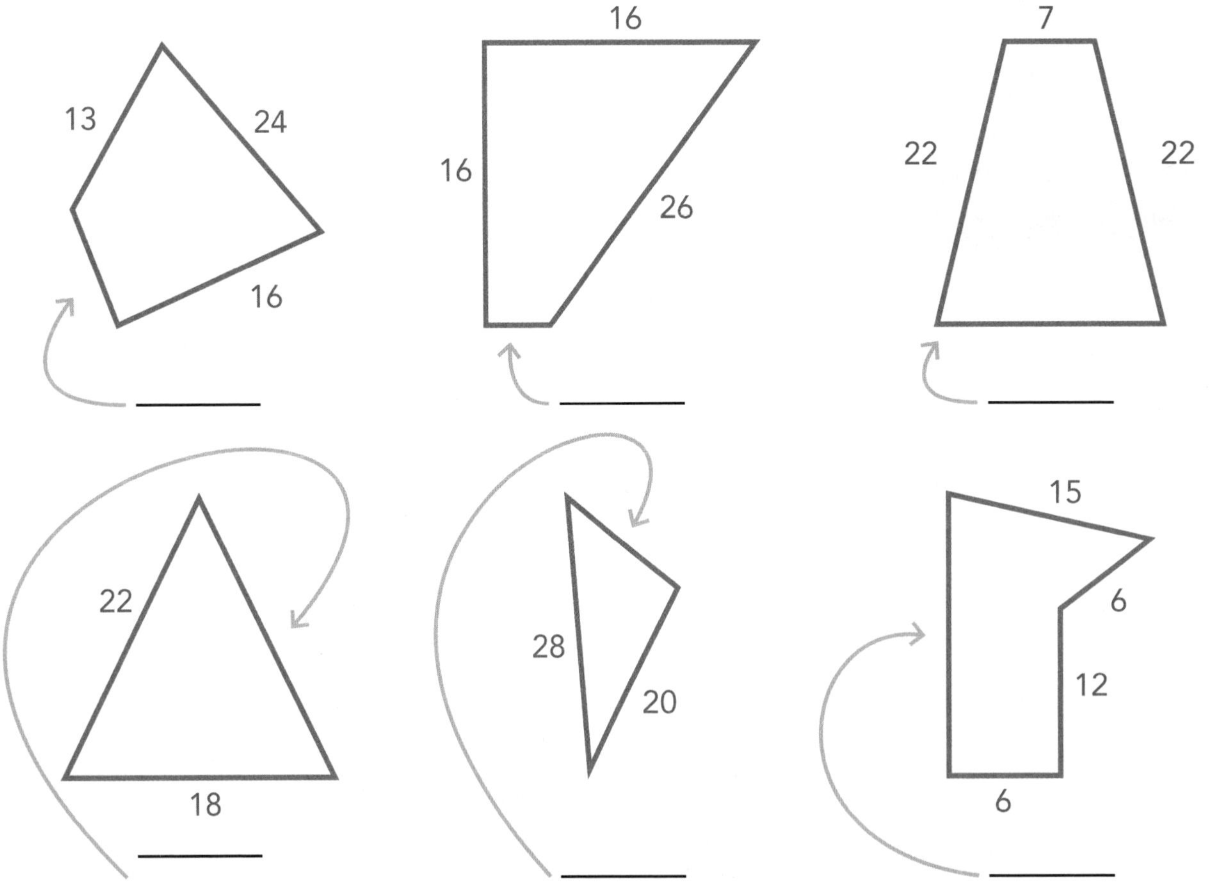

Name ______________________________

The Dead Sea, the lowest place on Earth, is an enormous salt lake. The Jordan River flows into it but no water flows out. Because the Dead Sea has no outlet, the water evaporates but the salt remains. This makes the Dead Sea more than 10 times saltier than the ocean.

If a cup of water from the Dead Sea contains 80 grams of salt, how many grams of salt would the same amount of ocean water contain?

$$\_\_\_\_\_ \text{ g salt} \times 10 = 80 \text{ g salt}$$

Look at the number sentence. What is missing, a part or the whole? To find a missing number in a multiplication sentence, choose division.

$$80 \text{ g salt} \div 10 = 8 \text{ g salt}$$

The ocean water would contain 8 grams of salt.

If a dividend is missing from an equation, you can multiply the divisor by the quotient to find it.

$\_\_\_\_\_ \div 9 = 6$

dividend ÷ divisor = quotient

$9 \times 6 = 54$

Find the missing factor or dividend.

1. $\_\_\_\_\_ \times 4 = 32$
2. $\_\_\_\_\_ \div 7 = 4$
3. $6 \times \_\_\_\_\_ = 48$
4. $\_\_\_\_\_ \times 7 = 49$
5. $\_\_\_\_\_ \div 8 = 8$
6. $\_\_\_\_\_ \times 9 = 72$
7. $\_\_\_\_\_ \div 7 = 8$
8. $\_\_\_\_\_ \div 6 = 6$
9. $\_\_\_\_\_ \div 9 = 9$
10. $3 \times \_\_\_\_\_ = 24$
11. $\_\_\_\_\_ \div 7 = 5$
12. $\_\_\_\_\_ \div 2 = 5$

Solve for the missing numbers.

13. ______ × 8 = 40
14. ______ ÷ 4 = 6
15. 8 × ______ = 80
16. ______ × 7 = 42
17. ______ ÷ 9 = 7
18. ______ × 9 = 45
19. ______ ÷ 6 = 9
20. ______ ÷ 5 = 6
21. ______ ÷ 9 = 1
22. 3 × ______ = 18
23. ______ ÷ 7 = 2
24. ______ ÷ 2 = 8

25. **Complete the chart. Find the missing factors or products.**

×	2		4	7	9
3		9			
	8	12	16	28	36
5	10		20		
8		24		56	
10	20	30			90

Find the missing measurements.

26.

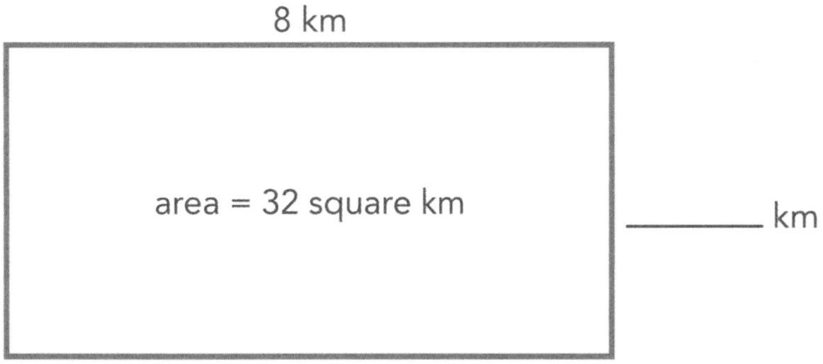

27.

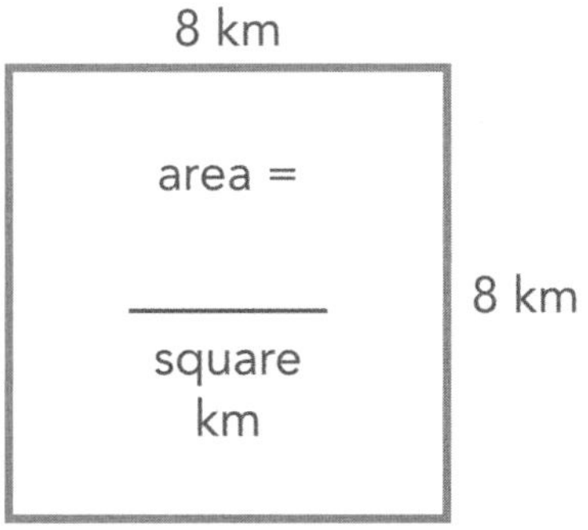

Name ______________________________

Dates, figs, olives, and pomegranates are all grown in Israel. Bekah and her mother purchased dried figs and dates at the market. They bought 1 kg of dried figs. They bought twice as many kilograms of dates. How many kilograms of dried fruit did they buy in all?

First, understand the question. The clue words **in all** tell you to add. Then, analyze the data. The word **twice** tells you to multiply by 2.

The word problem can be stated in this way.

1 kg figs + twice as many kg of dates = total

You can change the words into an equation to help you solve the problem.

$$1 \text{ kg} + (2 \times 1 \text{ kg}) = \_\_\_\_ \text{ kg}$$

Remember to follow the order of operations to solve the problem.

$$1 \text{ kg} + (2 \text{ kg}) = 3 \text{ kg}$$

Bekah and her mother bought 3 kg of fruit.

Write an equation to match the words. Use a blank for a missing number. Solve each equation.

1. The sum of 6 and 2. ______________________________
2. The product of 3 and 4. ______________________________
3. A number plus 5 equals 13. ______________________________
4. Thirty divided by a number equals 6. ______________________________
5. Fourteen minus a number equals 8. ______________________________

Solve each number sentence. Write the letter of the number sentence that matches the word problem.

a. 38 + 2 = ______	**c.** 2 × 40 = ______	**e.** 16 + ______ = 38
b. 2 × 12 = ______	**d.** 2 × 7 = ______	

6. ______ Church camp begins in two weeks. How many days is that?

7. ______ Twice as many children are going to camp this year than last year. Forty children went to camp last year. How many are going this year?

8. ______ Sixteen children ride on the left side of the church bus. Others ride on the right side. The church bus holds 38 children. How many children ride on the right side?

9. ______ Barney, the bus driver, loaded 38 sleeping bags into the church bus. The storage space will hold 2 more sleeping bags. How many sleeping bags will fit in all?

10. ______ The children sang 2 dozen songs on their way to camp. How many songs is that?

Fill in the circle to choose the equation that matches the word problem. Solve.

11. The camp dining hall served watermelon for lunch. The camp purchased 24 watermelons. Each of the four cabins received the same number of watermelons. How many did each cabin receive?

○ 4 × ______ = 24 ○ 24 × 4 = ______

12. Addie made a cross necklace at camp last year. She used red and blue beads. Some of the beads were red and 16 were blue. There were 30 beads in all. How many were red?

○ 30 + ______ = 16 ○ ______ + 16 = 30

Name ______________________________

Jerusalem is a city of contrasts. Buildings and streets that are centuries old are alongside modern homes, shops, and roads.

Write the next three numbers in each pattern.

1. 718 728 738 ______ ______ ______

2. 524 526 528 ______ ______ ______

Write the numbers from least to greatest.

3. 621 302 481

______ ______ ______

Write > or <.

4. 2,175 ◯ 2,172

5. 6,402 ◯ 6,420

6. 2,112 ◯ 2,121

Write each number in standard form.

7. sixty-three thousand, one hundred twenty-nine ______________

8. two hundred eleven thousand, five hundred sixty-eight ______________

Add or subtract.

9. $\begin{array}{r} 48 \\ +\,39 \\ \hline \end{array}$

11. $\begin{array}{r} 388 \\ +\,525 \\ \hline \end{array}$

13. $\begin{array}{r} 1{,}182 \\ +\,1{,}057 \\ \hline \end{array}$

15. $\begin{array}{r} 714 \\ 526 \\ +\,321 \\ \hline \end{array}$

10. $\begin{array}{r} 83 \\ -\,47 \\ \hline \end{array}$

12. $\begin{array}{r} 732 \\ -\,177 \\ \hline \end{array}$

14. $\begin{array}{r} 5{,}634 \\ -\,2{,}879 \\ \hline \end{array}$

16. $\begin{array}{r} 6{,}000 \\ -\,1{,}842 \\ \hline \end{array}$

Solve.

17. A cafe near the Via Dolorosa in Jerusalem served 1,200 meals last week. On Monday, the owners served 389 meals. How many meals did they serve during the rest of the week?

____

Add or subtract.

18. $52 - 19$	21. $61 + 24$	24. $45 - 29$	27. $82 + 67$	30. $47 - 39$
19. $35 + 17$	22. $33 - 15$	25. $75 + 48$	28. $43 - 37$	31. $51 + 24$
20. $94 - 36$	23. $73 + 44$	26. $61 - 49$	29. $84 + 55$	32. $42 - 37$

Write the letter of the correct term.

33. _______ a number sentence with an equals sign

34. _______ the grouping of the addends does not change the sum

35. _______ the order of the addends does not change the sum

36. _______ to figure a close answer

37. _______ related addition and subtraction facts

38. _______ the sum of zero and any number is that number

a. estimate

b. fact family

c. Order Property of Addition

d. equation

e. Zero Property of Addition

f. Grouping Property of Addition

Name ______________________________

Bethlehem is about 8 miles from Jerusalem. It is a busy, modern city. There you can visit the Church of the Nativity, which is thought to be near the stable where Jesus was born.

Multiply. Fill in the circle of the correct product.

1. 8 × 7 = ____
   ○ 55
   ○ 59
   ○ 56

3. 6 × 8 = ____
   ○ 64
   ○ 36
   ○ 48

5. 3 × 5 = ____
   ○ 21
   ○ 15
   ○ 18

7. 7 × 4 = ____
   ○ 21
   ○ 28
   ○ 11

2. 9 × 8 = ____
   ○ 71
   ○ 72
   ○ 78

4. 3 × 9 = ____
   ○ 27
   ○ 26
   ○ 31

6. 6 × 4 = ____
   ○ 24
   ○ 10
   ○ 20

8. 9 × 6 = ____
   ○ 45
   ○ 54
   ○ 63

Solve.

9. Archer and his family traveled from Bethlehem to Jerusalem and back again. The distance one way was 8 miles. How far was the round trip?

   ____

Multiply. Fill in the circle of the correct product.

10. 29×5
    ○ 145
    ○ 120
    ○ 195

12. 44×6
    ○ 264
    ○ 260
    ○ 244

14. 45×3
    ○ 135
    ○ 165
    ○ 128

11. 63×2
    ○ 126
    ○ 125
    ○ 1,206

13. 132×6
    ○ 790
    ○ 792
    ○ 798

15. 85×2
    ○ 280
    ○ 167
    ○ 170

Divide. Fill in the circle of the correct quotient.

16. 48 ÷ 6 = _____

○ 4
○ 8
○ 12

17. 72 ÷ 9 = _____

○ 8
○ 6
○ 9

18. 15 ÷ 3 = _____

○ 8
○ 5
○ 12

19. 40 ÷ 8 = _____

○ 16
○ 2
○ 5

20. 24 ÷ 8 = _____

○ 3
○ 6
○ 9

21. 27 ÷ 9 = _____

○ 5
○ 3
○ 4

Solve.

22. Carmen divided a bag of 56 Bethlehem almonds among herself and 7 friends. How many almonds did each receive?

____

Divide. Fill in the circle of the correct quotient.

23. $6\overline{)94}$

○ 17
○ 15 R4
○ 16 R1

24. $8\overline{)94}$

○ 8 R3
○ 11 R6
○ 12

25. $5\overline{)22}$

○ 4 R2
○ 4
○ 40

26. $3\overline{)6,421}$

○ 2,140 R1
○ 2,149
○ 2,250 R2

27. $7\overline{)62}$

○ 9
○ 80 R6
○ 8 R6

28. $4\overline{)2,980}$

○ 645 R10
○ 745
○ 3,940

29. $3\overline{)41}$

○ 13 R2
○ 14
○ 13 R1

30. $8\overline{)2,571}$

○ 321 R3
○ 320
○ 3,021 R3

Name ______________________________

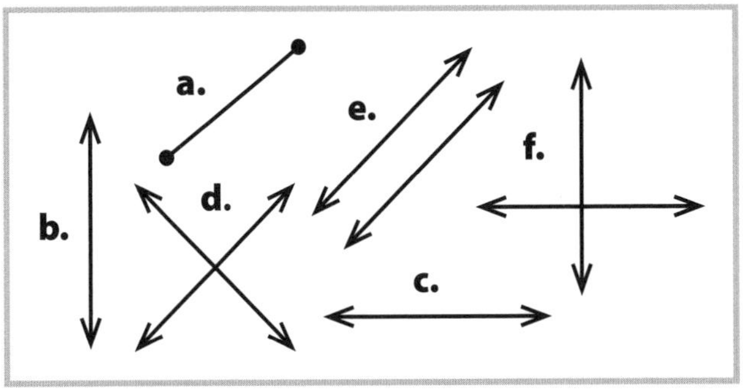

Write the letter of the lines, line segments, parallel lines, and intersecting lines.

1. ______ lines

2. ______ line segments

3. ______ parallel lines

4. ______ intersecting lines

During the time of King Solomon, the port city of Jaffa was a gateway for the cedar trees used to build the temple.

Write the letter of the correct term.

5. ______ meter

6. ______ foot

7. ______ perimeter

8. ______ area

9. ______ gram

a. metric unit of length

b. distance around a figure

c. the number of square units needed to cover the surface of a figure

d. customary unit of length

e. metric unit of weight

10. ______ pound

11. ______ liter

12. ______ volume

13. ______ Fahrenheit

14. ______ Celsius

a. customary unit of weight

b. temperature in the metric system

c. metric unit used to measure liquids

d. number of cubic units needed to fill a space

e. temperature in the customary system

Color the lower fraction bar to show an equivalent fraction. Write the fractions.

15. 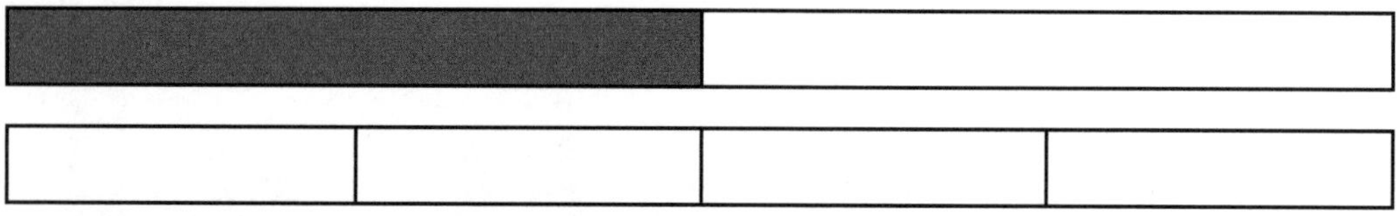

$\frac{\_\_}{2} = \frac{\_\_}{\_\_}$

16. 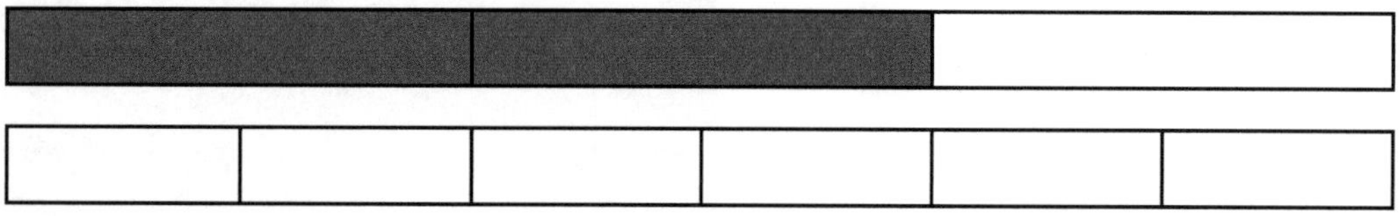

$\frac{\_\_}{3} = \frac{\_\_}{\_\_}$

17. 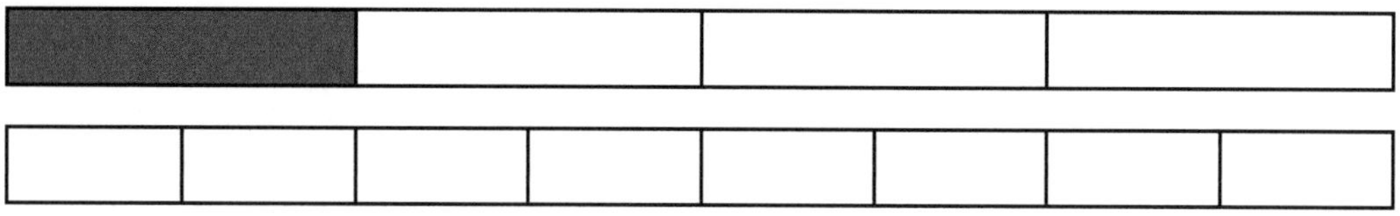

$\frac{\_\_}{4} = \frac{\_\_}{\_\_}$

18. 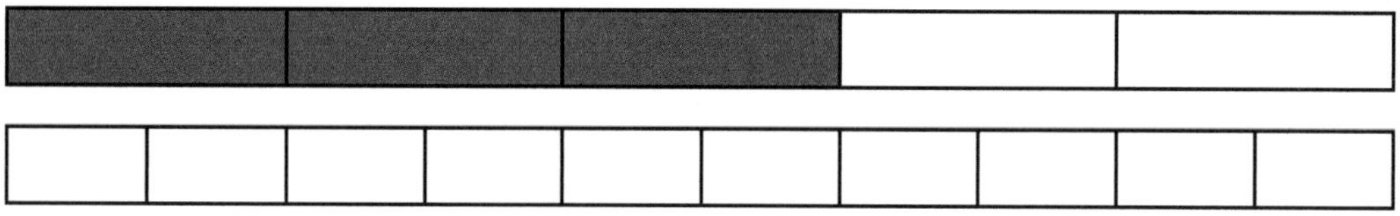

$\frac{\_\_}{5} = \frac{\_\_}{\_\_}$

Look at the fraction bars above. Compare the fractions. Write <, >, or =.

19. $\frac{1}{2} \bigcirc \frac{1}{4}$

20. $\frac{2}{3} \bigcirc \frac{3}{6}$

21. $\frac{1}{4} \bigcirc \frac{2}{8}$

22. $\frac{2}{3} \bigcirc \frac{1}{4}$

23. $\frac{3}{5} \bigcirc \frac{5}{10}$

24. $\frac{3}{5} \bigcirc \frac{7}{10}$

Solve.

25. Angelica's class was four-sixths girls and one-third boys. Were there more boys or more girls in her class? Draw and color fraction circles to show your answer.

____

Name ____________________

Word Bank
a. ones **b.** tens **c.** hundreds **d.** thousands **e.** ten thousands **f.** hundred thousands **g.** tenths **h.** hundredths

Write the letter that shows the value of the digit 7 in each number.

1. 47,839 ______
2. 3.07 ______
3. 703,521 ______
4. 171.04 ______
5. 65.7 ______
6. 497.3 ______
7. 276,405 ______
8. 720.4 ______

Write each number on the chart. Each digit must be in the correct place value. Write the decimal point. Remember to write a zero if needed.

		hundreds	tens	ones	tenths	hundredths
9.	74.08					
10.	117.23					
11.	362.1					
12.	474.05					

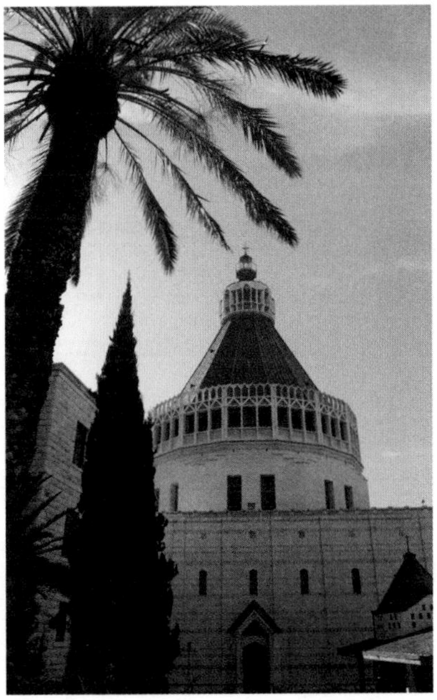

Write the decimal for each fraction or mixed number.

13. $1\frac{2}{10}$ ______
14. $\frac{7}{100}$ ______
15. $\frac{3}{10}$ ______
16. $4\frac{1}{10}$ ______

Write the fraction or mixed number for each decimal.

17. 3.08 ______
18. 2.1 ______
19. 98.6 ______
20. 5.99 ______

Write each time.

21. 

______

22. 

______

23. 

______

24. 

______

Draw hands for each time.

25. 

8:15

26. 

1:30

27. 

10:08

28. 

3:46

Write the money amount.

29. 

______

Draw bills and coins to show each amount. Use the fewest coins necessary.

30. $2.38

Solve.

31. Natalie started dance class at noon. Her mother picked her up at a quarter to one, just as class ended. How long was her dance class?

______

32. Rex earned $11.05 last week. He used his money to buy a book for $8.50. How much change did he get back?

______

Table of Measures

Customary Units

Length

1 foot (ft) = 12 inches (in.)
1 yard (yd) = 3 feet
1 yard = 36 inches
1 mile (mi) = 1,760 yards
1 mile = 5,280 feet

Weight

1 pound (lb) = 16 ounces (oz)

Capacity

1 cup (c) = 8 fluid ounces
1 pint (pt) = 2 cups
1 quart (qt) = 2 pints
1 quart = 4 cups
1 gallon (gal) = 4 quarts

Metric Units

Length

1 centimeter (cm) = 10 millimeters (mm)
1 decimeter (dm) = 10 centimeters
1 meter = 100 centimeters
1 kilometer (km) = 1,000 meters

Weight

1 kilogram (kg) = 1,000 grams

Capacity

1 liter (L) = 1,000 milliliters (mL)

Temperature

32°Fahrenheit (F)—water freezes
212°Fahrenheit—water boils
98.6°F—normal body temperature
0°Celsius (C)—water freezes
100°Celsius—water boils
37°C—normal body temperature

Units of Time

1 minute (min) = 60 seconds (sec)
1 hour (hr) = 60 minutes
1 day = 24 hours
1 week (wk) = 7 days
1 year = 12 months
1 year = 52 weeks
1 year = 365 days
1 decade = 10 years
1 century = 100 years

Signs and Symbols

<	is less than	$	dollars
>	is greater than	¢	cents
=	is equal to	:	separates hours from minutes
×	multiply	.	separates whole from part in decimals
÷	divide	°	degree
$\overline{)}$	divide		

Properties of Addition

Grouping Property: Changing the grouping of the addends does not change the sum.

Order Property: Changing the order of the addends does not change the sum.

Zero Property: The sum of zero and any other number is that number.

Properties of Multiplication

Multiplication Property of One: The product of any number and 1 is the number itself.

Multiplication Property of Zero: The product of 0 and any other number is 0.

Order Property: Changing the order of the factors does not change the product.

acute angle page 213

an angle that is narrower than a right angle

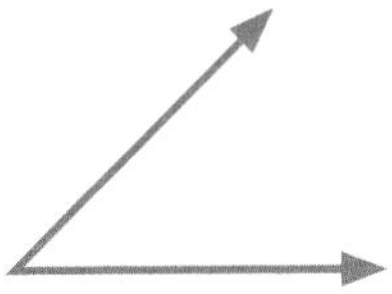

AM page 339

the 12 hours from midnight until noon

angle page 213

a figure formed when two lines or line segments meet

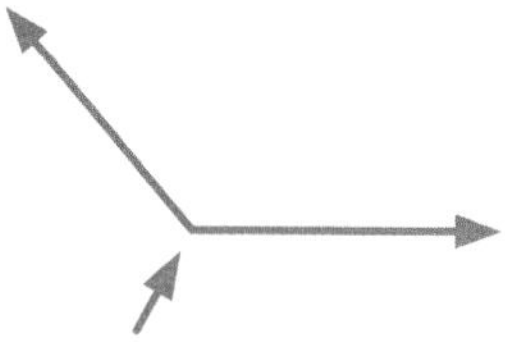

area page 225

the number of square units that cover the surface of an object

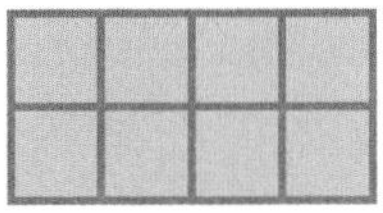

Area = 8 square units

array page 93

rows and columns used to represent a multiplication sentence

average page 197

the number calculated by dividing a sum by the number of addends

capacity page 261

the amount a container can hold

Celsius page 269

the temperature scale used in the metric system

congruent page 217

the same shape and the same size

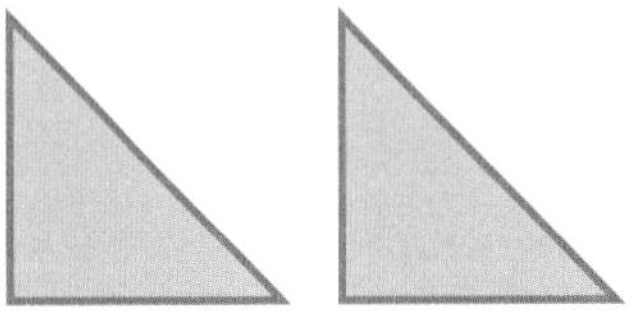

decimal page 307

a number that uses a decimal point and place value to separate the whole from the part

1.27

decimal point (.) page 307

the symbol that separates whole numbers from decimal numbers

denominator page 277

the bottom number in a fraction that shows the total number of parts in a whole

$$\frac{1}{5} \leftarrow$$

digit page 3

any of the numerals 0–9

dividend page 123

a number that is divided by another number

$$4\overline{)28} \leftarrow \quad (\text{quotient } 7)$$

division page 121

the operation that separates a number into equal sets

divisor page 123

the number by which the dividend is divided

$$\rightarrow 3\overline{)15} \quad (\text{quotient } 5)$$

edge page 219

a line segment where two faces meet

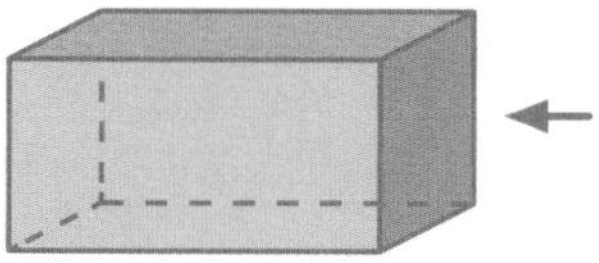

elapsed time page 341

the time that has passed

equation page 25

a number sentence written with an equals sign

$$8 + 3 = 11$$

equivalent fractions page 283

fractions that are the same amount

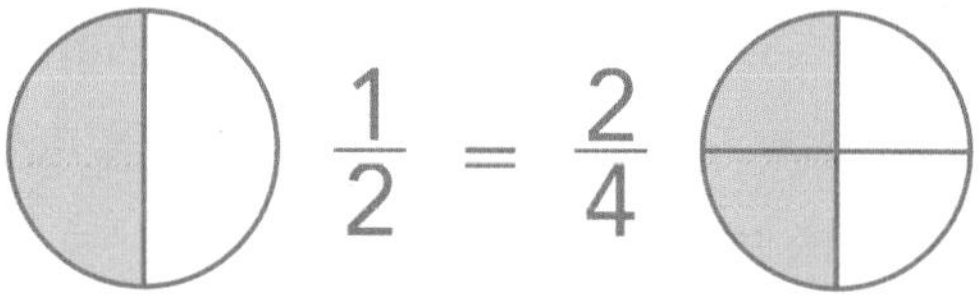

estimate page 47

to figure a close answer

expanded form page 4

a way to write a number as the sum of the value of its digits

$$276 = 200 + 70 + 6$$

face page 219

the flat surface of a solid figure

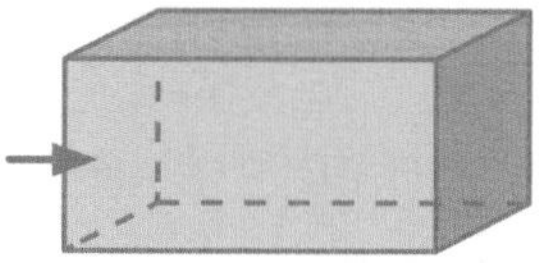

fact family page 25

a set of related addition and subtraction or multiplication and division sentences

factor page 89

one of two numbers that are multiplied

$$4 \times 5 = 20$$

Fahrenheit page 267

the temperature scale used in the customary system

fraction page 277

a number that names part of a whole or part of a set

$\frac{1}{4}$ 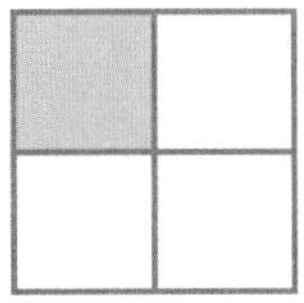 or 

gallon (gal) page 261

4 quarts

geometry page 209

the part of mathematics that includes points, lines, angles, surfaces, and solids

gram (g) page 259

the basic unit of weight in the metric system

hundredth page 311

one part out of 100

1.27

intersecting lines page 211

lines that cross one another

inverse operation page 63

the opposite operation

kilogram (kg) page 259

1,000 grams

kilometer (km) page 253

1,000 meters

line page 209

a straight path, through two points, that continues without an end

line of symmetry page 229

a line that divides a figure into two matching halves

liter (L) page 263

the basic unit of capacity in the metric system

meter (m) page 251

the basic unit of length in the metric system, equal to 100 centimeters

metric system page 251

a system of measurement that is based on multiples of 10

milliliter (mL) page 263

a metric unit of capacity; 1,000 milliliters equal 1 L

millimeter (mm) page 251

a metric unit of length; 10 millimeters equal 1 centimeter

mixed number page 293

a whole number and a fraction

$2\frac{3}{4}$

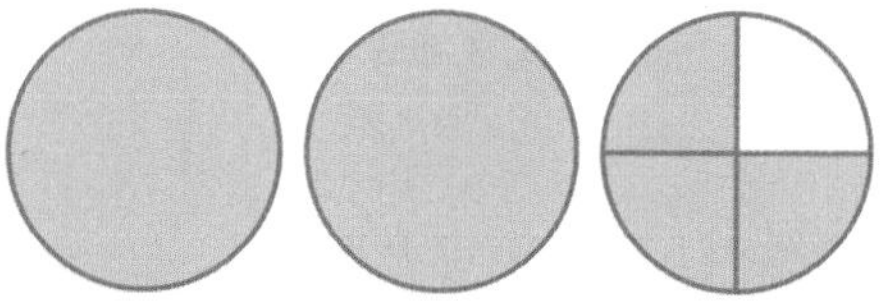

multiple page 103

the product of a given factor and any other number

multiplication page 87

repeated addition of the same number

numerator page 277

the top number in a fraction that shows the number of equal parts being separated

$$\frac{2}{4} \leftarrow$$

obtuse angle page 213

an angle that is wider than a right angle

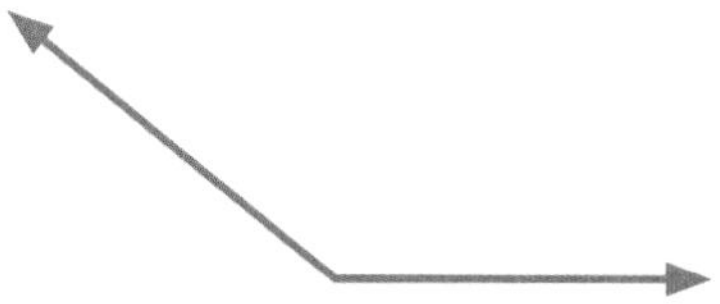

ordered pair page 233

two numbers that locate a specific point on a grid or map

ordinal number page 9

a number that describes the order or position of something in a line or list

ounce (oz) page 257

the basic unit of weight in the customary system

parallel lines page 211

lines that go in exactly the same direction

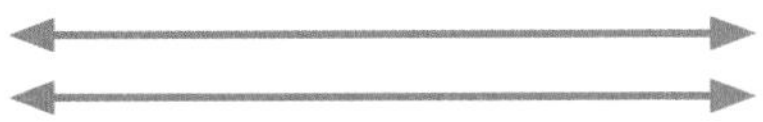

perimeter page 223

the distance around the sides of a figure

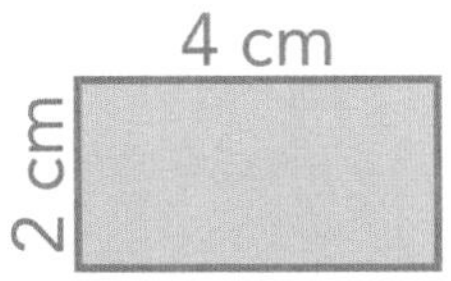

Perimeter = 12 cm

period page 17

each group of three digits separated by commas in a multidigit number

pictograph page 51

a graph that uses pictures or symbols to show values

pint (pt) page 261

2 cups

plane figure page 215

a two-dimensional shape that is flat

PM page 339

the 12 hours from noon until midnight

polygon page 215

a closed figure with straight sides

pound (lb) page 257

16 ounces

probability page 201

the chance that something might happen

product page 89

the result of multiplication

$$6 \times 8 = 48$$

↑

quart (qt) page 261

2 pints

quotient page 123

the result of dividing one number by another

$$7\overline{)21}$$ with quotient 3 ←

remainder page 185

the number that is left over when one number does not divide evenly into another number

```
    3 R3 ←
7)24
 −21
    3
```

right angle page 213

an angle that makes a square corner and measures 90°

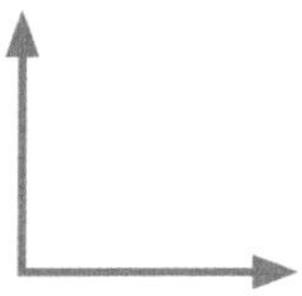

rounding page 11

increasing or decreasing a number to a specific place value

solid figure page 219

a figure with height, length, and width

standard form page 4

a way to write a number using the digits 0–9 and place value

subtraction page 57

finding the difference between the whole and one part

tenth page 309

one part out of 10

1.27
↑

Venn diagram page 355

a visual way to organize and compare information

volume page 265

the number of cubic units needed to fill a solid figure

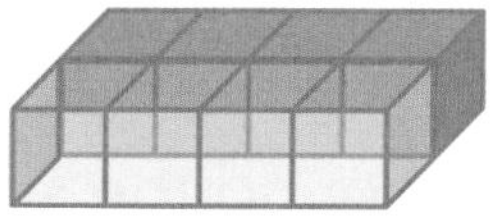

Volume = 8 cubic units